THE OXFORD H

HUME

THE OXFORD HANDBOOK OF

HUME

Edited by

PAUL RUSSELL

OXFORD

UNIVERSITY PRESS

OXFORD
UNIVERSITY PRESS

Oxford University Press is a department of the University of Oxford. It furthers
the University's objective of excellence in research, scholarship, and education
by publishing worldwide. Oxford is a registered trade mark of Oxford University
Press in the UK and certain other countries.

Published in the United States of America by Oxford University Press
198 Madison Avenue, New York, NY 10016, United States of America.

Library of Congress Cataloging-in-Publication Data
The Oxford handbook of Hume / Edited by Paul Russell.
pages cm
Includes bibliographical references and index.
ISBN 978–0–19–974284–4 (hardcover : alk. paper) | ISBN 978–0–19–009539–0 (paperback : alk. paper)
1. Hume, David, 1711–1776. I. Russell, Paul, 1955– editor.
B1498.O94 2015
192—dc23
2015016482

In memory of Annette Baier (1929–2012)

CONTENTS

PART III PASSION, MORALITY, AND POLITICS

PART IV AESTHETICS, HISTORY, AND ECONOMICS

PART V RELIGION

PART VI   HUME AND THE ENLIGHTENMENT

PART VII   AFTER HUME . . .

Acknowledgments

My research assistant, Jamie Hellewell, has been a remarkably reliable and congenial person to work with. Throughout the process of preparing this work for publication I have relied on his careful and diligent editing of the contributions that we have received. My good friend and esteemed colleague Peter Millican, with whom I have discussed all aspects of Hume's philosophy over many years, also provided helpful advice and comment concerning this project, particularly in its early stages. I would also like to thank Peter Ohlin at OUP for his early enthusiasm and support for this project. I consider myself unusually fortunate to have a publisher of his quality and sound judgment. I am similarly grateful to his colleagues at OUP who have worked in such a professional and efficient way to bring this volume into print.

Finally, this collection is dedicated to the memory of Annette Baier, a distinguished and much admired colleague, as well as a friend and mentor to many in the community of Hume scholarship. Her death, shortly after completing and submitting her contribution to this volume, is a great loss for us all.

Paul Russell,
Gothenburg,
Sweden
25 August, 2015

Abbreviations of References to Hume's Writings

T   *A Treatise of Human Nature.* Edited by D. F. Norton and M. J. Norton. Oxford: Clarendon, 2007.

Note: Following the convention given in the Nortons' *Treatise* (and Beauchamp's *Enquiries*), citations are to Book.Part.Section.Paragraph, followed by *page* references to the Selby-Bigge/Nidditch editions. Thus T, 1.2.3.4/34: will indicate *Treatise* Bk. 1, Pt. 2, Sec. 3, Para. 4/Selby-Bigge/Nidditch p. 34.

* For the Introduction to the *Treatise* citations are to T, Intro, para./pages.

TA   *An Abstract of a Treatise of Human Nature.* Reprinted in T.

Note : Citations follow the format provided for the *Treatise* above: e.g., TA, 1/645 refers to *Abstract* Para. 1 in Nortons' edition and p. 645 in Selby-Bigge.

LG   *A Letter from a Gentleman to His friend in Edinburgh.* Edited by E. C. Mossner and J. V. Price. Edinburgh: Edinburgh University Press, 1967.

MEM   *Hume's Early Memoranda, 1729–40: The Complete Text,* edited with a foreword by E. C. Mossner, *Journal of the History of Ideas* 9 (1948), 492–518.

EU   *An Enquiry Concerning Human Understanding.* Edited by T. L. Beauchamp. Oxford: Clarendon, 2000.

EM   *Enquiry Concerning the Principles of Morals.* Edited by Tom L. Beauchamp. Oxford: Clarendon, 1998.

Note: References are also provided to the Selby-Bigge/Nidditch editions of the *Enquiries.* See remarks under the *Treatise* above.

ESY   *Essays: Moral, Political, and Literary.* Revised edition by E. F. Miller. Indianapolis: Liberty Classics, 1985.

EF   "An early fragment on evil." In M. A. Stewart, "An early fragment on evil." In M. A. Stewart and J. P. Wright, eds. *Hume and Hume's Connexions.* University Park, PA: Pennsylvania State University Press, 1995.

HE   *The History of England,* 6 Vols. Foreword by W. B. Todd. Indianapolis: Liberty Classics, 1983.

DP   *A Dissertation on the Passions.* In T. Beauchamp, ed. *A Dissertation on the Passions; The Natural History of Religion.* Oxford: Clarendon Press, 2008.

NHR *The Natural History of Religion.* In T. Beauchamp, ed. *A Dissertation on the Passions; The Natural History of Religion.* Oxford: Clarendon Press, 2008.

MOL *My Own Life.* Reprinted in *Essays: Moral, Political, and Literary.* Revised edition by E. F. Miller. Indianapolis: Liberty Classics, 1985.

Ad "Advertisement." An advertisement originally appearing in the front matter of the second volume of the 1777 edition of ESY, at the time entitled *Essays and Treatises on Several Subjects.* London: T. Cadell. Reprinted in EU front matter.

D *Dialogues Concerning Natural Religion.* In D. Coleman, ed. *Dialogues Concerning Natural Religion and Other Writings.* Cambridge: Cambridge University Press, 2007.

Note: Citations are to paragraph numbers.

LET *The Letters of David Hume,* 2 Vols. Edited by J. Y. T. Greig. Oxford: Clarendon Press, 1932.

NHL *New Letters of David Hume.* Edited by R. Klibansky and E. C. Mossner. Oxford: Clarendon, 1954.

List of Contributors

Henry E. Allison is Professor Emeritus at the University of California, San Diego and Boston University.

Annette Baier was Distinguished Service Professor of Philosophy at the University of Pittsburgh.

Donald L. M. Baxter is Professor of Philosophy and Department Head at the University of Connecticut.

Helen Beebee is Samuel Hall Professor of Philosophy at the University of Manchester.

Martin Bell is Professor Emeritus at the University of York.

Simon Blackburn is Distinguished Research Professor of Philosophy at the University of North Carolina at Chapel Hill. He was formerly The Bertrand Russell Professor of Philosophy at the University of Cambridge.

Georges Dicker is Distinguished Professor of Philosophy at the College at Brockport, State University of New York.

Lorne Falkenstein is Professor of Philosophy at the University of Western Ontario.

Don Garrett is Silver Professor of Philosophy at New York University.

Paul Guyer is Jonathan Nelson Professor of Humanities and Philosophy at Brown University.

Ryan Patrick Hanley holds the Mellon Distinguished Professorship in Political Science at Marquette University.

James A. Harris is Reader in the History of Philosophy at the University of St. Andrews, Scotland.

Yoram Hazony is President and Senior Fellow at the Herzl Institute in Jerusalem.

Peter Kail is a Fellow of St. Peter's College and University Lecturer in the History of Modern Philosophy at Oxford University.

Peter Kivy is Board of Governors Professor Emeritus of Philosophy at Rutgers University.

Eugenio Lecaldano is Emeritus Professor of Philosophy at the University of Rome, Sapienza.

Michael Levine is Professor of Philosophy at the University of Western Australia.

Neil McArthur is Associate Professor of Philosophy at the University of Manitoba.

Peter Millican is Gilbert Ryle Fellow and Professor of Philosophy at Hertford College, Oxford University.

Samuel Newlands is William J. and Dorothy K. O'Neill Collegiate Associate Professor in Philosophy at the University of Notre Dame.

David Owen is Associate Professor of Philosophy at the University of Arizona.

Charles Pigden is Associate Professor of Philosophy at the University of Otago.

Tony Pitson is Honorary Research Fellow at the University of Stirling.

Jesse Prinz is Distinguished Professor of Philosophy at the City University of New York, Graduate Center.

Paul Russell is Professor of Philosophy at the University of British Columbia and the University of Gothenburg, where he is also Director of the Gothenburg Responsibility Project.

Tatsuya Sakamoto is Professor of History of Social and Economic Thought in the Faculty of Economics at Keio University, Tokyo.

Geoffrey Sayre-McCord is Morehead-Cain Alumni Distinguished Professor of Philosophy at the University of North Carolina at Chapel Hill.

Eric Schliesser is Professor of Political Theory at the University of Amsterdam and prior to that he was BOF Research Professor in Philosophy and Moral Sciences at the University of Ghent.

Karl Shafer is Professor of Philosophy at the University of California, Irvine.

Donald T. Siebert is Distinguished Professor Emeritus of English Language and Literature at the University of South Carolina.

Galen Strawson holds the President's Chair in Philosophy at the University of Texas at Austin.

Barry Stroud is Willis S. and Marion Slusser Professor of Philosophy at the University of California, Berkeley.

Christine Swanton is an Honorary Research Fellow at the Department of Philosophy at the University of Auckland.

Jacqueline Taylor is Professor of Philosophy at the University of San Francisco.

Rico Vitz is Professor and Chair of Philosophy at Azusa Pacific University.

Wayne Waxman has taught philosophy at the New School for Social Research and the University of Colorado at Boulder. He currently lives and writes in New Zealand.

Kenneth P. Winkler is Professor of Philosophy at Yale University.

John P. Wright is Professor Emeritus of Philosophy at Central Michigan University.

Keith E. Yandell is Professor Emeritus of Philosophy at the University of Wisconsin.

INTRODUCTION

The wise in every age conclude,
What Pyrrho taught and Hume renewed,
That dogmatists are fools.

– Thomas Blacklock

IN April 1776 David Hume, who had been in declining health for some time, added a short codicil to his last will and testament. The codicil gave instructions concerning a monument that was to be built where he was to be buried on Edinburgh's Calton Hill.[1] Hume died, aged sixty-five, the following August. According to Hume's instructions his monument should have "an Inscription containing only my Name with the Year of my Birth and Death, leaving it to Posterity to add the Rest." The fact that Hume could assume that posterity would take an interest in him indicates that by the end of his life he had already acquired a reputation among his own contemporaries as one of the most significant thinkers of his age. Hume was well aware, however, that the fate of an author's reputation is both fragile and volatile and depends, in the end, on those who come after and what they are or are not able to make of the work that has been left to them. From our own perspective, further down the track of posterity, it is evident that Hume has secured an enduring reputation as one of the greatest thinkers of all time and, in particular, as having a strong claim to be the greatest of the English-speaking philosophers. It is the burden of this *Handbook* and the various contributions that it contains to explain the basis of Hume's achievement and how posterity has understood it and responded to it over the years that have followed his death, up to the present time.

With regard to Hume's reputation, reception, and legacy, ironies abound. One of the most obvious of these ironies is that Hume, who was unusually frank about the extent to which he was ruled by his passion for "literary fame" (MOL, xl), was, nevertheless, from his youth until his final years, constantly frustrated by and disappointed in the reception that his work had received. Hume's ambitions as well as his intellectual standards were very high, but in consequence of this he always remained vulnerable to the assessments of his audience—which were not uniformly favorable or even interested. In his brief account of his own life, which was published after his death, Hume makes very clear that his high expectations were routinely disappointed in one way or another. With respect to the audience for his works Hume's attitude much of the time is that it is a case of casting pearls before swine (see, for example, his sardonic remarks at the end of the opening paragraph of the third book of his *Treatise*: T, 3.1.1.1).

It is ironic, from our own contemporary perspective, that Hume's reputation while he was alive depended very largely on the success of works that are no longer considered to belong to his greatest contributions. The works that proved most successful within his own lifetime—the most popular and best selling—were his *Essays*, which came out in numerous editions beginning in 1741, and his *History of England*, which appeared in six volumes between 1754 and 1761. After a long period of relative neglect, there is a revived interest in these works—but they remain secondary in terms of Hume's contemporary standing and fame. Without any doubt, it is Hume's major philosophical works, especially his *Treatise*, that now serve as the basis of his standing as one of the greatest thinkers of all time. It is no small irony, therefore, that even in his final days Hume would look back at the reception of his *Treatise* and pronounce that it "fell dead-born from the press" (MOL, xxxiv). The failure of this work was such that in late 1775, when Hume was near the end of his life, he prepared an "Advertisement" that was to be placed on all future editions of his *Essays and Treatises*, declaring that his later works alone were to be "regarded as containing his philosophical sentiments and principles" (EU, 83). Although Hume's assessment of the reception that the *Treatise* received may be exaggerated, it is also true that this work was never reissued in his lifetime and further editions did not appear until well into the nineteenth century. Whatever responses it did secure in print were, for the most part, dismissive, if not plainly derogatory. The works that followed generally fared better than the *Treatise*, although they too often received a mixed reception that disappointed and troubled their author. Much of the *Treatise* was "cast anew" in the form of the two *Enquiries*, the first concerning human understanding (1748) and the second concerning morals (1751). It is these three works, the *Treatise* and the two *Enquiries*, that provide much of the core of Hume's philosophical achievement and they were all completed and in print by the time he was 40 years of age. There are two other particularly important later works that also need to be mentioned, both of which have been widely regarded as containing Hume's principal statements of his views on religion. In 1757 Hume published *Four Dissertations*, the most significant and controversial of which was "The Natural History of Religion." At this time Hume decided not to publish two other pieces, which were his essays on suicide and immortality, both of which were published posthumously. During this period (i.e., the 1750s) Hume had mostly completed his *Dialogues Concerning Natural Religion*, which also had to wait for posthumous publication in 1779. It is these works, taken together, that constitute the essential core of Hume's philosophy and along with his *Essays* and *History* provide the material from which the various contributions to this *Handbook* will draw.

The organization and structure of this *Handbook* reflect, to a considerable extent, Hume's own divisions and distinctions within and among his various works. The range of Hume's contribution and achievement is evident from a casual glance over the contents. Topics covered include metaphysics and epistemology, mind and emotion, morals and politics, aesthetics, economics, history, and religion. It is no exaggeration to say that almost every major field within contemporary philosophy has felt the force of Hume's thought in one way or another. In many, if not all, of these fields Hume's contributions continue to exercise influence, providing real options or suggesting avenues for further investigation and research. After an account of Hume's life and works, the first group of contributions examines and explores some of the major themes and interpretations currently on offer concerning his philosophy. This is followed by a group devoted to metaphysics and epistemology, covering many of the most celebrated and well-known topics of Hume's philosophy. These include the theory of ideas, causation and necessity, induction and probable reasoning, the external world, and the self and personal identity. Following this, the next group of contributions takes up a set of issues that is broadly concerned with Hume's views on morals, politics, and society and how these issues may be understood in terms of the operations of human nature. Topics covered here include the role of reason and emotion in moral motivation and evaluation, the question of free will, the nature and extent of sympathy and benevolence, and questions concerning society, politics, and the foundations of government. These are followed by contributions on Hume's aesthetics, history, and economics and, then, another group concerned with problems of religion. The last two groupings are divided between a set of contributions discussing Hume's philosophy in relation to several other significant thinkers, who in one way or another help to shed light on important aspects of Hume's thought. This includes Isaac Newton, whose towering achievements in science and mathematics profoundly influenced Hume's contemporaries, and two of Hume's great Scottish contemporaries, his friend Adam Smith and his most distinguished critic Thomas Reid. The collection concludes with a pair of contributions, one that considers Hume's philosophy in light of a later thinker, Nietzsche, and the other, in relation to recent developments in cognitive science and contemporary philosophy. The overall aim of this format is to ensure, as far as possible, that readers are provided with both general and specific analyses of Hume's most significant contributions as found throughout his writings.

When it comes to selecting contributors, like most other editors of volumes of this kind, I have had to choose among many able scholars and philosophers, any number of whom have already made valuable and worthwhile contributions to the study of Hume. Having said this, three qualities carried particular weight with me: accuracy (truth), interest, and influence. Ideally, of course, the contributions in this collection would possess all three of these qualities. Unfortunately it is equally clear that this cannot be the case, since apart from anything else, many of the contributors disagree with each other in their various interpretations and assessments of Hume's work. (This includes my own relations with any number of the contributions contained in this volume.) My aim has not been to select contributions that I, as editor, can endorse as in some way correct or reliable. This would exclude several contributions that I believe still belong in this collection. What I do hope is that all the contributions satisfy at least one, preferably two, and, perhaps, on occasion, all three of the qualities that I have mentioned. It is fair to say, I believe, that in a collection of this kind the aim is not only to obtain as accurate an account and assessment of Hume's work as we can but also to provide, as far as possible, an accurate and comprehensive picture of the state of contemporary *thinking about Hume*. It is here, most obviously, that the views of a contributor may be judged important and worthy of inclusion primarily because of their influence and impact, as much as any considerations relating to accuracy or intrinsic interest (either of which critics may still entertain doubts about).

NOTE

1. This was something of a late concession on Hume's part. Just a few years earlier, late in his life, Hume complained to his close friend Gilbert Elliot of Minto that he had "been accustom'd to meet with nothing but Insults & Indignities from [his] native country: But if it continue so, *ingrate patria, ne ossa quidem habebis*." The quotation is from Scipio's tomb and translates: "ungrateful fatherland, you will not even have my bones." See also Hume's later remarks, continuing this exchange with Elliot, in which he makes clear that he does not consider himself an Englishman [contrary to Elliot's insinuation, LET, II, 469n], as he is plainly a Scotsman [LET, II, 470]. He then continues: "I am a Citizen of the World; but if I were to adopt any Country, it would be that in which I live at present [i.e. France]...." Suffice it to say that Hume's general disappointment with the reception of his work, which is described further below, was keenly felt in relation to his own country [i.e., Scotland]—an attitude that was not entirely without foundation.

CHAPTER 1

....

HUME'S LIFE AND WORKS

....

JAMES A. HARRIS

THE key to understanding Hume's intellectual biography is the connection between his three principal interests: philosophy, politics, and religion. In the eighteenth century, "philosophy" was sometimes a style of reasoning that could be applied to chemistry and geology, as well as to speculative questions concerning the fundamental concepts of human cognition and conation. For present purposes, though, "philosophy" is to be taken in a more familiar and narrower sense, as a distinct subject of inquiry, a subject comprising, among other things, logic, epistemology, metaphysics, and ethics: that is, as a subject to which *A Treatise of Human Nature* and the two *Enquiries* were notable contributions. "Politics" is to be understood broadly as including the study of party or faction in the *Essays, Moral and Political*; the political economy in the *Political Discourses*; and the political history that is the *History of England*. "Religion" is to be understood to include Hume's skeptical inquiry into the rational basis of theism, both natural and Christian, in the first *Enquiry* and the *Dialogues*, his examination of the historical and psychological origins of theism in the *Natural History of Religion*, and also his various discussions, scattered throughout all of his books, of the effect of religious belief on morals and politics.

On the usual way of telling the story of Hume's career, philosophy comes first, both in order of time and in order of importance, and politics is taken to be a derivative and less significant part of the Humean oeuvre. The most extreme version of this approach is the one, popular in the later nineteenth century, according to which Hume took up writing about politics as a result of his failure to achieve success in philosophy, in order to make himself famous, and perhaps also to make himself rich. Hume's writings on politics are taken more seriously now, but it is still generally believed that what Hume most wanted to be was a philosopher, in fact a professor of philosophy, and that Hume turned to politics because that desire was frustrated, principally by the reputation for atheism he had acquired as a result of his writings on religion. It is at least equally likely, however, that from the beginning Hume was as interested in politics as he was in philosophy; that a career as an independent man of letters and not as a professional philosopher was what he most wanted; and that that career was a success, with the *History of England* its triumphant culmination. Hume's religious skepticism, this would be to say, was no obstacle to his living the life that he most wanted to live, the life of a sophisticated and widely respected citizen of the European republic of letters.

I 1711–1741

We know virtually nothing about the first 30 years of Hume's life.[1] What we do know includes that he was born in Edinburgh on April 26, 1711 (Old Style), that his father died when he was very young, and that he grew up with his mother and elder brother and sister on the family estate in Chirnside, about 10 miles from Berwick upon Tweed, while also spending time in Edinburgh at the family apartment there. He went to study at the College of Edinburgh in 1721. He stayed there for 4 years, but, as was common at the time, did not graduate. He followed the arts syllabus, which at Edinburgh meant Latin language and literature in the first year, Greek in the second, logic and metaphysics in the third, and natural philosophy in the fourth. There is little evidence this course of study made much of an impression on him. "There is nothing to be learnt from a Professor, which is not to be met with in Books," he would later declare: "I see no reason why we shou'd either go to an University, much more than to any place, or ever trouble ourselves about the Learning or Capacity of Professors" (Mossner 1958: 32).

As a second son, Hume needed a profession, and it was decided that he would be a lawyer. He attended law lectures at Edinburgh,[2] but legal study proved not to be to Hume's taste. It appears that fairly soon after leaving college he decided instead to devote his life to literature, understood broadly to include speculative philosophy, essay writing, and history. For the moment at least, Hume was young enough to be indulged by his mother and brother, and he spent his time reading omnivorously, in both modern literature and ancient. His earliest surviving letters show him discussing this reading and exchanging "papers" with an Edinburgh friend, possibly a former tutor, named Michael Ramsay. Closer to home, in the Borders villages close to Chirnside, there were others with whom Hume would have swapped ideas, including the philosophical lawyer Henry Home of Kames.[3] A copy of Shaftesbury's *Characteristicks* survives with Hume's autograph, dated 1726, and it is possible that, like many of his contemporaries, Hume found a mirror for his ambitions in the process of self-cultivation that Shaftesbury both described and sought to encourage in his reader. Shaftesbury conceived of himself as a latter-day Stoic, devoted to the union of beauty, virtue, and philosophic truth, and a letter Hume would later write to an anonymous physician (probably George Cheyne) suggests that in this period he may well have done the same.[4]

That same letter makes it clear that, if this was what Hume was experimenting with in the 1720s, the experiment was not a success. Having glimpsed "a new Scene of Thought" and felt an access of ardor and "boldness of temper," in September 1729 Hume seems to have suffered a kind of breakdown, one that left him both physically and mentally exhausted. Recovery was accompanied with a sense of the intellectual bankruptcy of the project he been pursuing up until now. He had taken his sense of how to live, and of what to write about and how to write about it, from a system of philosophy that lacked a proper foundation. This was the system of antiquity. It took human nature as its point of departure, as its guide in matters of both morality and taste. That was as it should be. The problem, as Hume came to see it, was that the picture of human nature involved was "entirely Hypothetical" and depended "more upon Invention than Experience" (LET i.16). In the early 1730s, Hume reconceived his task as being that of laying out a theory of human nature that was true to experience. It is natural to suppose that he found inspiration in the writings of near contemporaries such as Hutcheson and Butler, both of whom had rejected the ethical rationalism of Samuel Clarke in favor of the idea of deriving the content and obligatory nature of morality from inductive study of the powers of the human mind. But there was a crucial difference between their versions of this project and Hume's. For, at around the same time that he had had his breakdown, Hume had lost the religious faith in which he had been brought up. Once he began moving away from the beliefs of his childhood, he found no stopping point either in Clarke's a priori demonstrations of religious principles or in what experimental science was revealing about the natural world. He was left with no religious belief at all. It was not surprising, then, that his study of the mind would fail to reveal human beings as, in the last resort, dependent on religion for their sense of how to manage their passions and conduct their dealings with others. One of the things that sharply differentiated Hume from his contemporaries was that he appears not to have *needed* to believe in God and a life to come. There is no sign that he ever missed what he had lost. Indeed, he seems henceforth to have been unable to take religion at all seriously. He had come to find it absurd and could not restrain a good joke about it whenever one occurred to him. This would infuriate his enemies and perplex his friends.

In the early 1730s, Hume also seems to have developed an interest in the writings of Bernard Mandeville. Letters of the period, including the letter to the physician, contain apparent allusions to Mandeville, and so does the earliest surviving piece of philosophical writing from Hume's pen, a fragmentary manuscript entitled "Historical Essay on Chivalry and Modern Honour."[5] This, however, is not to say that Hume made himself a disciple of Mandeville's. The "Essay on Chivalry" suggests that Hume was developing a philosophical cum historical style of his own by working out a middle-way between Mandeville's insistence on the artificiality of moral and social distinctions, on the one hand, and Hutcheson's insistence on their naturalness, on the other. Also evident in this early text is Hume's characteristic willingness to hazard a bold explanatory psychological hypothesis as a means of bridging the gap between the purely artificial and the purely innate. It is possible, moreover, that there is a hint of rueful autobiography in the remark that philosophy, "tho' it cannot produce a different World in which we may wander, makes us act in this as if we were different Beings from the rest of Mankind; at least makes us frame to ourselves, tho' we cannot execute them, Rules of Conduct different from these which are set to us by Nature" (Wright 2012: 205).

Mandeville would have led Hume naturally to Pierre Bayle—if Hume had not found his way there already. In a letter of 1732, Hume thanks Ramsay for his "trouble about

Baile" (LET i.12). Possibly, Ramsay had bought or borrowed something by Bayle for Hume, who was still in relative seclusion in Chirnside, slowly regaining his health and his ability to concentrate on reading and writing. Bayle would have made compelling reading for a young man in the process of losing his religion. And it may have been Bayle who turned Hume's thoughts from morals to "logic," to the study of the capacities and limits of human understanding.

By 1734, the date of the letter to the physician, Hume's recovery was not yet complete. A more active life appeared to promise a cure for his physical and psychological ills, and he left Scotland to work in the office of a merchant in Bristol. This life did not suit him either. Later in 1734, he decided that France would be the best place to go to test his literary vocation. After time in Paris and Rheims, he settled in La Flèche in Anjou. We do not know why he went there. It is possible that among the fairly large Scottish expatriate community in France, there was a friend or distant relative willing to make him welcome in the town in which Descartes had gone to college. In "My Own Life," the brief autobiography that Hume composed shortly before he died, Hume wrote that, in France, he "laid that plan of life, which I have steadily and successfully pursued. I resolved to make a very rigid frugality supply my deficiency of fortune, to maintain unimpaired my independency, and to regard every object as contemptible, except the improvement of my talents in literature" (MOL xxxiv).

Hume worked hard at La Flèche, and he seems also to have worked, intellectually speaking, more or less completely alone. The result was a draft of Books 1 and 2 of *A Treatise of Human Nature*, a work that does not read as if it were conceived in the midst of dialogue and discussion. In it, Hume pushed unsettling arguments to extreme conclusions, developed theories all of his own, elaborated them to their fullest extent, and made a bid to accommodate recalcitrant mental phenomena of every kind. He did all this in an idiosyncratic prose style, a style that had little of the polished urbanity of his later writings. The English of polite letters was, of course, not the English that Hume spoke, and it was perhaps not yet a language that he was fully at home in. An additional problem for the style of the *Treatise* will have been the fact that Hume was working in a Francophone environment. It is likely that he made good use of the library of the Jesuit college in La Flèche. Certainly, the *Treatise* bears the mark of an engagement on Hume's part with the dominant French philosophy of the time, Malebranche's version of Cartesianism, as well as with Bayle, and also with more obscure figures, such as the mathematician Nicolas de Malézieu, drawn on for one of the arguments for the finite divisibility of space in Part 2 of Book 1.

Hume returned to Britain in the autumn of 1737 to find a publisher for his book. He was fully aware of its unusual nature. From London, he wrote to Kames that his philosophical principles were "so remote from all the vulgar Sentiments on this Subject, that were they to take place, they wou'd produce almost a total Alteration in Philosophy" (NHL 3). Hume came to think that, in fact, what he had written was probably too remote from vulgar sentiment, and, as he told Home, he "castrated" it in order to improve its chances of a favorable reception (NHL 2–3). It is not clear what the character was of the "noble Parts" which Hume removed, but it is possible that they were sections that drew out the implications of Humean skepticism for the rationality of religious belief.

Fairly soon, the bookseller John Noon signed with Hume, and Books 1 and 2 of the *Treatise* appeared in early 1739. Hume's plan was that three additional volumes would be added to the *Treatise*'s account of the understanding and the passions, on morals, "criticism", and politics. By September 1739, Hume had a draft of the volume on morals and had sent it to Hutcheson for comments. Hutcheson's response does not seem to have been very favorable, even though he had expressed admiration, in a letter to Home, of Books 1 and 2.[6] Hume seems to have made substantial alterations to his manuscript in light of Hutcheson's response, as a means of preemptively warding off the charge that he had come too close to the uncomfortable doctrines of Mandeville, Hobbes, and the Epicureans. A conclusion was added at this stage and so may have been the entirety of Part 1 and the first section of Part 2. Hutcheson was not so hostile to the finished product as to refuse to recommend it to his own publisher, Thomas Longman, who brought it out by the late autumn of 1740.

II 1741–1751

Hume now waited for reviews to come in and betrayed a first-time author's anxiety that he be properly understood by putting out an "abstract" of the first two volumes of the *Treatise* less than a year after they were published, in early 1740. But, at the same time, he had another project in hand, possibly in partnership with Home. This would be a journal of polite literature and political commentary, a sort of combination of Addison's *Spectator* and Bolingbroke's *Craftsman*, intended, presumably, to show that Edinburgh might rival London in refinement of taste and moderation of politics. There is no reason to think that Hume regarded his future as a man of letters as resting entirely on the fortunes of the *Treatise*. So-called "early memoranda" that survive from this period make it plain that Hume's intellectual interests were very wide indeed and suggest that he was already as engaged as any of his contemporaries by issues to do with government, manufacturing, trade, and military expenditure.[7] They suggest also that Hume thought through these issues in the same way that his contemporaries did, in terms of comparison and contrasts between the situations of the different countries of Europe and between the modern world and the ancient.

Whatever plans there were of an Edinburgh-based journal came to nothing. The pieces that he had been working on came out instead in two volumes of *Essays, Moral and Political*, published in 1741 and 1742. These were miscellaneous collections, designed to appeal to several different kinds of reader, but prominent was a new variation on the familiar English theme of criticism of factional party politics from a self-proclaimed "impartial" and "moderate" point of view. Despite the fact that Bolingbroke's *Craftsman* was named by Hume as one of his models, the general political perspective of the *Essays* was distinctly Walpolean, or "Court Whig," in the sense that there was no affinity expressed with the fear that British liberty might be under threat from "corruption." Hume went further than the Court Whigs, however, in refusing to see party politics as such as a danger to the constitution. Party politics needed to be better understood, and Hume would deepen his analysis considerably in *The History of England*, but it was not in itself a problem. Hume's political thinking was from the first closely engaged with current affairs, and it developed in response to the course of events later in the decade. This can be seen in works written in the wake of the Jacobite rebellion of 1745–6: a pamphlet defending the conduct of the Lord Provost of Edinburgh at the time of the rebellion, Hume's friend Archibald Stewart,[8] and three essays reflecting on the issues at the rebellion's heart, "Of the Original Contract," "Of Passive Obedience," and "Of the Protestant Succession."[9]

During the '45, Hume was in England, working as tutor and companion to the young and mentally unstable Marquess of Annandale. Immediately before taking up this position, he had been involved in a controversy concerning who would replace John Pringle as Professor of Moral Philosophy at Edinburgh.[10] Hume's name had been put forward in May 1744 by the Lord Provost, John Coutts, when Hutcheson had turned the job down. It took a year for the matter to be finally settled, and in the end, the successful candidate was not Hume, but rather William Cleghorn, who had been fulfilling all the duties of the professor while Pringle had been on an extended leave of absence in Europe. That Hume failed to be appointed is explicable in more than one way. He was on the wrong side of the Scottish politics that determined how this kind of decision was made. He would have been seen as a candidate sponsored by the "Argathelian" party owing allegiance to the third duke of Argyll and led by Argyll's brother the Earl of Ilay. The rival "Squadrone" faction backed Cleghorn. Also, his candidacy was opposed within the Argathelian party itself by influential men such as William Wishart, the Principal of the University, William Leechman, Professor of Divinity at Glasgow, and Hutcheson. Wishart proposed himself as a rival Argathelian candidate and published a pamphlet attacking Hume's philosophical views as part of his campaign. Hume's supporters responded by publishing *A Letter from a Gentleman to His Friend in Edinburgh*, a point-by-point reply to Wishart's charges worked up by Henry Home from a text hastily put together by Hume. Wishart, Leechman, and Hutcheson were all modernizers as regards the issues that divided the Church of Scotland at the time. All had suffered at the hands of the more rigidly Calvinist "Popular" party. Moreover, Leechman and Hutcheson, at least, were personal friends of Hume's. Hume's reputation for, as he put it, "Heresy, Deism, Scepticism, Atheism &c &c &c" (LET i.57) did not worry them in their private dealings with him. But it made Hume a less than ideal choice for a position that was crucial in terms of the increasingly bitter fight between modernizers and traditionalists over the role that religion should now play in Scottish public life. They would have known that Hume could not be relied on to take this issue as seriously as it needed to be taken if the Popular party were to be defeated. In fact, it is doubtful whether he really wanted the job in the first place. "I never was very fond of this Office of which I have been disappointed," he wrote afterward, "on account of the Restraint, which I foresaw it wou'd have imposed on me" (NHL 17).

What really mattered to Hume, in any case, was not so much an academic position as financial independence. This came closer as a result of the patronage of General James St. Clair. Hume was Secretary to St. Clair in the summer of 1746 on what was supposed to have been an invasion of Quebec but turned into a disastrous assault on the French town of Lorient. In 1748, again as St. Clair's secretary, he went on an embassy to the courts of Vienna and Turin. In between these two expeditions, Hume wrote the three new political essays mentioned earlier and also prepared for publication a recasting of some of the principal arguments of Book 1 of the *Treatise*, to be published in 1748 with the title *Philosophical Essays Concerning Human Understanding*.[11] Although the *Treatise* had not been ignored by the reviewers and had by some been praised for its originality and ambition,[12] it had failed to effect a philosophical revolution. Part of the reason for this, Hume had come to believe, was the way it was written. In the *Abstract* of Books 1 and 2, he had noted that the *Treatise* "has been complained of as obscure and difficult to be comprehended."[13] The brevity and clarity of the essay form had the potential to win Hume's ideas a wider readership. This new version of Hume's account of the understanding omitted a great deal of what had been included in *Treatise* Book 1, and focused the reader's attention on some of the conclusions reached in the analysis of causal reasoning. In this respect, there was a similarity between the *Philosophical Essays* and the *Abstract*. Hume also wanted to clarify the nature of his skepticism, and, in this respect, there was a similarity to the *Letter from a Gentleman*. In no sense did this reformulation of his ideas amount to a compromise on Hume's part.[14] Indeed, he now had the confidence to make plain the consequences of his skepticism for the possibility of giving religious belief a foundation in reason. Neither natural nor revealed religion could be said to have a rational basis, Hume argued, and it was impossible to give a plausible philosophical explanation of the prevalence of evil in the world. If Hume believed that drawing out these implications of his views would make his philosophy better known, he would be proved right. In "My Own Life," he lamented that the controversy generated by Conyers Middleton's *Free Enquiry into Miraculous Powers* prevented notice being taken of the *Philosophical Essays*, but this did not stop him sharpening his treatment of miracles in the second edition of 1750 by borrowing a crucial argument from Middleton. And responses to Hume's views, especially as regards miracles, duly began to appear with increasing frequency.[15]

By April 1749, Hume was at home again in Chirnside. He would remain based there until he finally left the family home and moved to Edinburgh in the summer of 1751.[16] Nothing new was published during this period, but Hume was far from idle. He took stock of his achievements thus far and planned for the future. Having recovered his command of ancient Greek, he read very widely in the classics with the intention, it would seem, of gaining himself the reputation of a scholar. The essay "Of the Populousness of Ancient Nations" and the dissertation "The Natural History of Religion" were among the most notable results of this self-consciously acquired erudition. Hume's work on the former piece engaged him in friendly disagreement with the Edinburgh clergyman Robert Wallace, whose view that the population of the ancient world was greater than that of the modern was diametrically opposed to Hume's. The debate with Wallace was for Hume a paradigm of how intellectual relations should be conducted. "Why cannot all the World," Hume asked Wallace in a letter, "entertain different Opinions about any Subject, as amicably as we do?" (NHL 30).

Wallace's friendliness to Hume was to his credit, given that he had been offended by Hume's characterization of priests in a note to the essay "Of National Characters." This essay had been written in Turin and has sometimes been read as, in its main argument, a reply to claims made in Montesquieu's *De l'Esprit des Lois* concerning the influence of physical causes, such as climate and soil, on a people's manners and customs. The date of the publication of Montesquieu's book makes this very unlikely,[17] but it is certainly true that *De l'Esprit des Lois* made a deep impression on Hume. He read it carefully and, in a long letter of April 1749, offered Montesquieu some critical comments (LET i.133–38). He was subsequently involved in the publication in Edinburgh of two of the book's chapters on the English constitution.[18] Hume's time at Chirnside must have been to a significant extent spent reflecting on the implications of Montesquieu's achievement. Hume disagreed with many of the French author's views—for example, Montesquieu was another one of those who believed that the world's population was in decline—but he was sure that *De l'Esprit des Lois* had shown the manner in which political, economic, and historical questions needed henceforth to be treated.

The influence of Montesquieu is apparent in the two works that Hume brought out next, *An Enquiry Concerning the Principles of Morals*, published in London in 1751, and *Political Discourses*, published in Edinburgh in 1752. The *Enquiry* was another recasting into essay form of arguments from the *Treatise*. As with the *Philosophical Essays*, elegance and clarity were Hume's goals here, in place of the dense and complex argumentative strategies of his first work. A single line of argument, concerning the determination of moral distinctions by considerations of utility and agreeableness, was carefully and comprehensively elaborated. Issues that had been prominent in Book 3 of the *Treatise* and that had diverted attention away from this line of argument—whether moral distinctions were the work of reason or sentiment, whether or not justice could be said to be a "natural" virtue—were relegated to appendices. Hume's immersion in the classics altered the tone of his moral philosophy, providing it with a comparative historical dimension and supplementing it with numerous examples from the ancient world. In the section on justice, Montesquieu, "[a] late Author of great Genius, as well as extensive Learning," was described as having demonstrated in *De l'Esprit des Lois* the importance of "the Constitution of Government, the Manners, the Climate, the Religion, the Commerce, the Situation of each Society" to the understanding of laws (EM 3.34 n.12/197). The concluding part, "A Dialogue," brought to the fore the question of the historical and geographical variability of moral standards and explored them in a manner reminiscent of another of Montesquieu's works, the *Lettres Persanes*.

From the first, Hume was pleased with the *Enquiry*'s combination of abstract philosophical argument and polished literary style. In 1753, he told his friend David Dalrymple, to whom he often wrote for advice about style and language, that he had "a partiality for that Work, & esteem it the most tolerable of anything I have published"

(LET i.175). Twenty years later, Hume felt the same way. In "My Own Life," he called it "of all my writings, historical, philosophical, or literary, incomparably the best" (MOL xxxvi).

In the *Enquiry*, Hume chose to highlight his disagreements with Mandeville rather than the affinities between them but, even so, no more than was the case with the *Philosophical Essays* did the *Enquiry* involve a watering down of the philosophical radicalism of the *Treatise*. A focus on utility and agreeableness in the formation of moral principles was an implicit rejection of the very idea of absolute moral value, of something's being good in itself, and morally obligatory regardless of the consequences. By the same token, it was a self-identification on Hume's part with the morality of Epicureanism and a rejection of the neo-Stoicism prevalent in the moral philosophy of many of his contemporaries.

In *De l'Esprit des Lois*, Montesquieu had argued that, far from inevitably corrupting the martial spirit and general morals of a country, commerce was a civilizing influence whose natural effect was to lead to political liberty and to peace among nations. In the opening two essays of *Political Discourses*, Hume took up this theme, denying that there was a need to choose between the manufacturing and trading success of a state and its military and naval greatness, and then arguing that there were tight connections between the spread of luxury, improvements in scientific knowledge, and refinements in manners and morals. By this time, this was a well-established perspective on the consequences of an increase in manufacture and trade, familiar to Hume, not just from Mandeville, but from the wider reading he had been doing in the literature on commerce since the 1730s. Nor was there anything especially original to the more particular arguments made in the essays that followed. Others before Hume had made the case against the acquisition of money as being a political end in itself and for the importance of keeping money circulating; the case for the activity of the economy (rather than the quantity of money in it) being the key determinant of interest rates; and the case in favor of replacing an obsession with a "positive balance of trade" with legislation to free up trade and reduce tariffs and duties.

What was significant about the *Political Discourses* was not so much what it argued as how the arguments were prosecuted. Again, it was Hume's deployment of the essay form that was crucial. This was a means whereby issues that had hitherto been the preserve of manufacturers, merchants, and politicians were brought into the realm of polite discourse. Hume made intelligible to everyone what the central questions were when it came to the political management of trade and how those questions might be further explored. Furthermore, he did so in a way designed to moderate the characteristically chauvinist and belligerent nature of British public opinion. One of the more important messages of the *Political Discourses* concerned the practical contradictions inherent in a narrowly patriotic, beggar-thy-neighbor approach to trading success. Hume wrote from a European perspective, and this surely helped his book become a success abroad. Soon after publication, there were two separate translations into French. According to the maker of one of these translations, the Abbé le Blanc, Hume's work in political economy sold "*comme un roman*" (Burton, 1846: i.458).

At the same time as he was writing the *Enquiry* and the *Political Discourses*, Hume completed a first draft of what would be published, posthumously, as *Dialogues Concerning Natural Religion*. In 1751, he sent the manuscript to Gilbert Elliot of Minto, imagining that, did they only live nearer each other, he and Elliot might have brought the dialogue to life, with Hume taking on the character of the skeptic Philo and Elliot that of the moderate proponent of inductive natural religion Cleanthes. "I believe, too, we could both of us have kept our Temper very well," he wrote to Elliot, even if Elliot "had not yet reach'd an absolute philosophical Indifference on these points" (LET i.154). Inspired by his friendships with men such as Elliot and Wallace, and also Hutcheson and Leechman and Adam Smith, Hume had developed by this time a vivid sense of what intellectual community could be in the Scotland of his day. The relationship in the *Dialogues* between Philo and Cleanthes, who live in the same house despite their dis-agreements, was, surely, in part an idealized representation of Hume's relations with his less skeptical friends. When he moved to Edinburgh in 1751, it would have been in the hope that he would find his ideal realized in the everyday life of Scotland's capital city. To a great extent, this hope was not disappointed. It is true that, soon after he arrived in Edinburgh Hume's name was put forward by his friends for the logic chair at Glasgow, and that, again, Hume's reputation as a skeptic played a part in ensuring that he did not get the job.[19] But this was done, as Hume wrote to John Clephane, "contrary to my opin-ion and advice" (LET i.164), and the outcome did not much upset him.

III 1751–1762

In Edinburgh, Hume was made a Secretary to the newly revived Philosophical Society, and in February 1752 was elected librarian to the Faculty of Advocates. The librarian-ship provided a small income of £40 per annum, but was more significant in so far as it provided Hume with a position in society. Also, he was now, as he told Clephane, "mas-ter of 30,000 volumes"(LET i.167), and this prompted him to begin writing a history of England that would build on his long-term interest in history both ancient and modern. At the same time, he put together a new and, for the moment at least, definitive presenta-tion of his literary achievements thus far. *Essays and Treatises on Several Subjects*, pub-lished in four duodecimo volumes in 1753, was a major event in Hume's career.[20]

In 1753, Hume wrote to Clephane that "there is no post of honour in the English Parnassus more vacant than that of History": "Style, judgement, impartiality, care, everything is wanting to our historians" (LET i.170). The skeptical character of his phi-losophy and the perspective he had developed on English party politics combined to provide Hume with a sense of being able to write a new kind of English history, one that would achieve the impartiality that all previous writers on the subject had, by common consent, failed to achieve. Hume would write history as a Whig for whom the Revolution of 1688 had inaugurated a new era of peace and prosperity and who had no sympathy at all for Tory conceptions of divine right and passive obedience. But his Whiggism had no basis in the political radicalism of men like Algernon Sidney and John Locke, nor, crucially for the purposes of the writing of history, in the myth of an ancient English constitution. Hume was unable to take seriously the idea of a set of timeless liberties that provided a means of deciding for or against the conduct of English monarchs from William I to George II. Liberty as Englishmen—or, rather, Britons—enjoyed it in the mid-eighteenth century was an entirely modern phenomenon and was also, as Montesquieu had emphasized in *De l'Esprit des Lois*, a quite unique one when regarded in a European context. It needed a new kind of history to make sense of it.

Hume's first decision was where such a history should begin. He accepted the idea, first formulated in the seventeenth century by Francis Bacon and James Harrington, that the decisive event in modern English history was the property legislation of Henry VII, legislation that was intended merely to limit the power of the feudal barons but which eventually caused a transfer of power from the nobility to those whom Bacon had called the "middle people." This process of change was slow, though, and for a long time invisible, and a history would have more interest and drama that began when its effects had begun unmistakably to shape English politics. This would begin with the accession of the House of Stuart in 1603. As Hume told the story of the Stuarts, they were not evil despots determined to rob the English of their liberties but rather men struggling and failing to reconcile a traditional conception of kingship with novel political, social, and economic conditions. Conflict between the crown and the newly wealthy House of Commons was inevitable and could only be intensified and made more intractable by the consequences of an incomplete and still divisive Protestant Reformation. *The History of Great Britain*, published in two volumes in 1754 and 1757, presented neither side as entirely right or wrong and no major protagonist as wholly good or bad. The Revolution brought the story to an end, but the settlement of 1689 was a messy compromise that left many key issues unresolved. A "most entire system of liberty" had been introduced, but, so Hume made sure to add, an entire system of liberty was not the same thing as "the best system of government" (1754–7: ii.443).

Hume's first thought had been of a three-volume *History of Great Britain* that ended with the Hanoverian succession in 1714. But he changed his mind and decided to go backward to the Tudors, mostly, at least so he said in letters, because he was worried that he would not be given access to the collections of papers held by the great families of the English nobility. Hume resolved to remain in Scotland despite the fact that during the time he worked on the second volume of the *History*, he was again drawn into the ongoing struggle between traditionalist and modernizing factions within the Church of Scotland. In meetings of the General Assembly in the summers of 1755 and 1756, moves were made by the traditionalists toward having Hume prosecuted for blasphemy and excommunicated from the Church. Henry Home, now Lord Kames, was also under attack for his *Essays on the Principles of Morality and Natural Religion* (published in 1751) and, had the prosecution been successful in his case, his legal career might have come to a premature end. By contrast, it is not obvious what the consequences of such a prosecution would have been for Hume, although it would certainly have made his social life more difficult. The real object of the traditionalists, though, was not so much to make life awkward for Hume and Kames as to discredit the modernizers through their close association with the authors of infidel writings. This was the time when William Robertson, Hugh Blair, Adam Ferguson, Alexander Carlyle, John Home, and others were in the process of forming an organized party in the Church, the "Moderates," in the first instance to ensure victory in the vexed question of patronage, but more generally to propagate a form of religion in Scotland more suited to the age of Union, commerce, and politeness in both learning and manners.

Hume's decision to publish at this juncture a small collection of essays or "dissertations" that had been written some time previously is perhaps to be understood in terms of a desire to do what he could for the Moderate cause. The collection comprised a new version of the *Treatise*'s analysis of the passions, what sounds like a recasting of the *Treatise*'s treatment of space and time, a discussion of tragedy that might have borne some relation to the planned volume of the *Treatise* on "criticism," and the "Natural History of Religion." In the circumstances, the account given in the "Natural History" of the corruptions of "popular" religion was bound to be read as applying to the kind of Protestantism espoused by the traditionalists. Having been persuaded that the dissertation on the metaphysics of geometry was fatally flawed, Hume for a time thought of including essays on suicide and on the immortality of the soul. He then came to see that these would cause more trouble than they were worth and replaced them with a hastily written essay on the standard of taste. When the volume was ready for publication, events had taken a turn that made its contents, and especially the essay on tragedy, seem even more pertinent to events in Scotland. Hume's friend John Home, Minister of Athelstaneford in East Lothian, had written and had had performed a tragedy called *Douglas*, and legal action was being taken against him (and against other ministers who had attended performances) by the traditionalists. Hume's response was to dedicate the *Four Dissertations* to his friend.[21]

None of the moves made by the traditionalists against Hume and his friends was successful, and henceforth the Moderates usually held sway in the Church of Scotland. This permitted the full flowering of the Scottish Enlightenment, one of the greatest achievements of which was at the time generally taken to be the six-volume *History of England* that Hume had completed by 1762. The decision to take the story backward from 1603 rather than forward from 1688 had made a change of title necessary. Hume's account of the Tudors had been published in 1759, in two volumes, one of which was wholly given over to Elizabeth and to examination of the myths both Whig and Tory that surrounded her reign. Hume debunked the usual contrast between the freedom of Englishmen under Elizabeth and their unfreedom under the Stuarts. He was also unsparing in his portrait of Mary Queen of Scots and self-consciously objective in his account of how "her egregious indiscretions, shall I say, or atrocious crimes, threw her from the height of her prosperity, and involved her in infamy and ruin" (1759: 472). Another important element of the Tudor volumes was, of course, the Reformation, according to Hume "one of the greatest events in history" (1759: 116), and Hume was much occupied by the destabilizing political consequences it had, in England and Scotland as in Europe more generally, throughout the sixteenth century.

Three years later, after a year in London in 1758-9 during which Hume made use of the library of the newly opened British Museum, the *History of England* was completed by two volumes dealing with the period from the first Roman invasion in 55 BC to 1485. Here, the major historiographical issue was the significance of the Norman invasion of 1066. Whigs were reluctant to see it as a conquest and liked to trace ways in which an ancient Saxon or "Gothic" constitution survived it, discernible, for example, in the clauses of the *Magna Carta* of 1215 and in Henry III's recognition of the place of the Commons in the English Parliament. Hume took the Tory historian Robert Brady as his guide and insisted on the reality of the Norman conquest of the English and on the completeness with which a feudal constitution replaced the Anglo-Saxon one. The facts, Hume claimed, "are so apparent from the whole tenor of the English history, that none would have been tempted to deny or elude them, were they not heated by the controversies of faction" (1762: i.201). His account of English history taken as whole was thus structured by the notion of a succession of different constitutional arrangements. This had the effect of intensifying the sense in which the Revolution of 1688 demanded to be understood as having inaugurated a wholly new political era. As he revised the Stuart volumes for inclusion in the complete *History* of 1762, Hume sought to remove residual bias toward vulgar Whig doctrines, but his sense of the irrelevance of the past to modern political conditions ensured that his historical vision remained fundamentally anti-Tory.[22]

IV 1762–1776

The completion of the *History of England* was the completion of Hume's bid to take a place among Britain's leading men of letters. Writing the *History* had not involved the abandonment of his commitment to philosophy, broadly understood. On the contrary, it was praised as highly and widely as it was precisely because of what was judged to be Hume's success in combining history with the precision and impartiality of the philosopher. In Hume's *History*, Voltaire wrote, "we find a mind superior to his materials: he speaks of weaknesses, blunders, cruelties as a physician speaks of epidemic diseases" (Mossner 1980: 318). The *History* built on the reputation of the *Political Discourses* and gave Hume a fame that was European in scope. It also made him reasonably wealthy. Hume was left unsure what to do next. It seems that in the early 1760s he did further work on the *Dialogues Concerning Natural Religion*. Letters suggest that he may have wanted to publish it at this time and that his friends refused to let him, presumably on account of the trouble it would cause even under the newly established Moderate ascendancy in Scotland.

In 1763, Hume rushed at the chance to leave the world of letters behind for a while and took up the offer of a post in the British embassy to Paris under Lord Hertford. Hugh Blair had joked in a letter that, were Hume to show the *philosophes* of Paris "the MSS of certain Dialogues," they might go so far as to erect a statue of him in the French capital (Mossner 1980: 320). Certainly, Hume established friendly relations with men like D'Alembert, Helvétius, Buffon, Holbach, and Turgot and wrote sometimes in his letters of the possibility of staying in Paris for the rest of his life. We know nothing, though, of the intellectual dimensions of his Parisian friendships. Anecdotal evidence suggests that he found the French literati too dogmatic, and they found him too skeptical. Nor was the relationship Hume formed with Jean-Jacques Rousseau a matter of the meeting of minds. Hume respected Rousseau's commitment to independence as a man of letters but thought that the most notable features of his writings were their eloquence and "extravagance." From the outset, Hume suspected that Rousseau "chooses his topics less from persuasion, than from the pleasure of showing his invention, and surprizing the reader by his paradoxes" (LET i.373).[23] But also Hume sympathized with Rousseau's plight after the burning of *Émile* by the Parliament of Paris, and when Hume returned to Britain in early 1766, he did so in Rousseau's company, intending to help find him a home across the Channel and also a pension. What followed was a disaster that became the talk of all Europe. Rousseau became convinced that Hume meant only to mock and dishonor him, and he spread stories intended to expose Hume as having formed a conspiracy with Voltaire and d'Alembert to ruin him forever. Hume was persuaded by his Parisian friends to publish an account of his quarrel with Rousseau, including their correspondence, and had an English translation made soon after.[24]

January 1767 saw Hume leave Scotland again, this time for London and a position as Under Secretary of State in the Northern Department under Hertford's brother General Henry Conway. "I am now, from a Philosopher, degenerated into a petty Statesman, and am entirely occupied in Politics," he wrote to a friend in Paris (LET ii.128). Yet, he told Turgot, "[u]pon Trial, my Situation appears far from disgreable, and I find, that to a Man of a literary turn, who has no great undertaking in view, Business, especially public Business, is the best Ressource of his declining years" (LET ii.137). He returned to Scotland for good in the summer of 1769 to devote himself to correcting the *Essays and Treatises* and the *History*. Politics remained at the front of his mind.[25] The many letters that survive from this period are filled with detailed commentary on the policies and personalities of the day. He condemned utterly the disorderly behavior of the supporters of the populist radical John Wilkes and condemned also what he saw as the feebleness of the measures taken against them. "Our Government has become an absolute Chimera," he wrote in October 1769: "So much liberty is incompatible with human Society: And it will be happy, if we can escape from it, without falling into a military Government, such as Algiers and Tunis" (LET ii.210).[26] On the other hand, he despaired of attempts to repress a growing movement in the American colonies in favor of independence from British control. Here, Hume was in agreement with the agitators for liberty, but his reasons for supporting the Americans were not their reasons. He did not believe in anything like Tom Paine's natural right to a government of one's own. His case for letting the colonies go was pragmatic and economic. Had he been party to Cabinet discussions, he wrote in 1775, he would have argued "that a forced and every day more precarious Monopoly of about 6 or 700,000 Pounds a year of Manufactures, was not worth contending for; that we shoud preserve the greater part of this Trade even if the Ports of America were open to all Nations; that it was very likely, in our method of proceeding, that we shoud be disappointed in our Scheme of conquering the Colonies; and that we ought to think beforehand how we were to govern them, after they were conquer'd" (LET ii.300).

In 1774, Hume began to be seriously troubled by what appears to have been a form of intestinal cancer, and by early 1776, he knew he did not have long to live. In April, he wrote a short autobiography, which he intended to be prefixed to the next edition of his works but which was first published separately, in 1777.[27] "My Own Life" is, as Hume says, really only a "History of My Writings" (1777: 1), but even in this respect it is highly selective. No mention is made, for example, of any of the several editions of *Essays and Treatises on Several Subjects*, nor of the account of the Rousseau affair, nor of the *Dialogues*, which Hume was working on again at the time when "My Own Life" was composed and which he was eager to see published after his death. By charting Hume's progress from having only a "very slender fortune" to being "very opulent," it underlines the importance he attached to the achievement of financial independence. But, at the same time, it leaves somewhat underexplained Hume's success in the satisfaction of the "passion for literature, which has been the ruling passion of my life, and the great source of my enjoyments" (1777: 4). The essays of 1741–2 were well received, we are told, and so was *Political Discourses*, but everything else, the *Treatise*, the *Philosophical Essays*, the *Enquiry*, and most of the *History*, was on publication either completely ignored or subject to unthinking condemnation by zealots both political and religious. "My Own Life" confirms what many of Hume's letters suggest, that he was much more sensitive to criticism than to praise, that he had very high expectations for all of his works, and that he found it hard to understand why the world did not from the first respond as he believed it should. He was disposed to construe criticism on the part of the religious as the manifestation only of prejudice and bigotry and to see in reservations about his politics only the crudest and most intolerant kind of Whiggery. It is unfortunate that Hume's biographers have had a tendency to take "My Own Life" as a reliable guide in its characterization of the reception of his writings.[28] The truth is that Hume was astonishingly successful in his realization of the dreams he had as a very young man of a career as a man of letters. Neither religious nor political controversy got in his way. He died a painful yet calm death on August 25, 1776.

ACKNOWLEDGMENTS

For comments and advice on this chapter, I am grateful to John Robertson, Mikko Tolonen, and, especially, Roger Emerson. I have benefited also from discussions at Middlebury College, the University of Richmond, and the Institute for Advanced Study in Princeton.

NOTES

1. The best account of what we do know is to be found in Stewart (2005); but see also Brandt (1977). Stewart's essay takes the story up until, roughly, the publication of the *Enquiry Concerning the Principles of Morals*; it is profitably read in conjunction with Emerson (2009). The most reliable summary account of Hume's life as a whole is Robertson (2004).
2. See Zachs (2011: 59). For a full development of the narrative sketched here, see Harris (2015).
3. Paul Russell has suggested that Hume may also have known of and been intellectually stimulated by debates between two other writers who lived in the Borders region, Andrew Baxter and William Dudgeon: see Russell (2008: chapter 4).
4. For a detailed analysis of this letter, see Wright (2003) and also Brandt (1977).
5. See Wright (2012), which includes a transcription of the "Essay on Chivalry" (NLS MS 23159/4).
6. See Ross (1966).
7. NLS MS 23159/14. A reasonably reliable transcription is provided in Mossner (1948). For the dating of the memoranda, see Stewart (2000): 276–288.
8. See Box et al. (2003).
9. On the advice of Charles Erskine, Hume withheld "Of the Protestant Succession" and replaced it with "Of National Characters." *Three Essays, Moral and Political* was published in late 1748, to be bound with the same year's third edition of *Essays, Moral and Political*. "Of the Protestant Succession" was published in *Political Discourses* in 1752.
10. See Stewart (1995); Emerson (1994); and Emerson (2008: 340–341).
11. The *Philosophical Essays* was retitled *An Enquiry Concerning Human Understanding* for the 1758 edition of *Essays and Treatises on Several Subjects*.
12. See the early reviews collected in Fieser (ed.), *Early Responses to Hume*, vol. iii, pp. 1–92.
13. Hume, *Abstract*, p. i.
14. As is emphasized in Stewart (2002).
15. See Fieser (2005), vol. v, 1–252.
16. The importance of this period for Hume's intellectual development is the theme of Baumstark (2007).
17. *De l'Esprit des Lois* was published in Geneva in October 1748. Hume's *Three Essays* appeared at the end of the following month. An ingenious argument that, even so, Hume might have written "Of National Characters" in response to Montesquieu is made in Chamley (1975).
18. *Two Chapters of a Celebrated French Work, Intitled, De L'Esprit des Loix, Translated into English*, Edinburgh, 1750.
19. See Emerson (1994: 14–16).
20. See Sher (2006: 45–46).
21. The best account of this episode and of the rise of the Moderates in general is Sher (1985).
22. There is detail about Hume's revisions, as well as a searching analysis of the politics of Hume's *History*, in Forbes (1975: chapter 8 and appendix). See also van Holthoon (1997).
23. Hume thought that *La Nouvelle Héloise* was Rousseau's masterpiece, and he thought that Rousseau's own view that his best book was *Du Contrat Social* "is as preposterous a Judgement as that of Milton, who preferd the Paradise regaind to all his other Performances" (LET ii.28).
24. *Exposé Succinct de la Contestation qui s'est Élevée entre M. Hume et M. Rousseau, Avec les Pièces Justificatives*, London [i.e., Paris], 1766; *A Concise and Genuine Account of the Dispute between Mr. Hume and Mr. Rousseau; With the Letters that Passed between them during their Controversy*, London, 1766.

25. See Pocock (1985); Baumstark (2012).

26. In a letter of March 1774, Hume makes mention for the first time of a new essay, "Of the Origin of Government," which can be understood as his response to the political controversies that Wilkes gave rise to. The essay was first published in the 1777 edition of *Essays and Treatises*.

27. Shortly before he died, Hume gave Smith permission to add to "My Own Life" an account, in the form of a letter to William Strahan, of how he had conducted himself during his final illness. It was included in the 1777 edition of *The Life of David Hume, Esq.*, and was also printed along with "My Own Life" at the beginning of the 1778 edition of *The History of England*. It occasioned considerable controversy: see Mossner (1980: 621–622).

28. The most obvious and influential example is Mossner (1980), which uses quotations from "My Own Life" as epigrams for many of its chapters. Baier (2011) is a commentary on "My Own Life."

BIBLIOGRAPHY

Baier, Annette C. (2011). *The Pursuits of Philosophy: An Introduction to the Life and Thought of David Hume*. Cambridge, Mass.: Harvard University Press.

Baumstark, Moritz. (2007). "David Hume: The Making of a Philosophical Historian." Edinburgh University, PhD dissertation.

Baumstark, Moritz. (2012). "The End of Empire and the Death of Religion: A Reconsideration of Hume's Later Political Thought," in *Philosophy and Religion in Enlightenment Britain: New Case Studies*, edited by Ruth Savage. Oxford: Oxford University Press, 231–257.

Box, M. A., David Harvey, and Michael Silverthorne. (2003). "A Diplomatic Transcription of Hume's "Volunteer Pamphlet" for Archibald Stewart: Political Whigs, Religious Whigs, and Jacobites." *Hume Studies* 29, 223–266.

Brandt, Reinhard. (1977). "The Beginnings of Hume's Philosophy'" in *David Hume: Bicentenary Papers*, edited by George Morice. Edinburgh: Edinburgh University Press, 117–127.

Burton, John Hill. (1846). *Life and Correspondence of David Hume*. 2 vols. Edinburgh: William Tait.

Chamley, Paul E. (1975). "The Conflict Between Montesquieu and Hume: A Study of the Origins of Adam Smith's Universalism," in *Essays on Adam Smith*, edited by Andrew S. Skinner and Thomas Wilson. Oxford: Oxford University Press, 274–305.

Emerson, Roger L. (1994). "The 'Affair' at Edinburgh and the 'Project' at Glasgow: The Politics of Hume's Attempts to Become a Professor," in *Hume and Hume's Connexions*, edited by M. A. Stewart and J. P. Wright. Edinburgh: Edinburgh University Press, 1–22.

Emerson, Roger L. (2008). *Academic Patronage in the Scottish Enlightenment: Glasgow, Edinburgh and St. Andrews Universities*. Edinburgh: Edinburgh University Press.

Emerson, Roger L. (2009). "Hume's Intellectual Development: Part II," in *Essays on David Hume, Medical Men and the Scottish Enlightenment*. Farnham: Ashgate.

Fieser, James. (2005). *Early Responses to Hume*. 2nd edn., 10 vols. Bristol: Thoemmes Continuum.

Forbes, Duncan. (1975). *Hume's Philosophical Politics*. Cambridge: Cambridge University Press.

Greig, J. Y. T. (ed.). (1932). *The Letters of David Hume*. 2 vols. Oxford: Clarendon Press.

Harris, James A. (2015). *Hume: An Intellectual Biography*. Cambridge: Cambridge University Press.

Hume, David. (1740). *An Abstract of a Book lately Published; Entituled, A Treatise of Human Nature, &c. Wherein the Chief Argument of that Book is farther Illustrated and Explained*. London.

Hume, David. (1751). *An Enquiry concerning the Principles of Morals*. London.

Hume, David. (1754–7). *The History of Great Britain*. 2 vols. London.

Hume, David. (1759). *The History England, under the House of Tudor*. London.

Hume, David. (1762). *The History of England, from the Invasion of Julius Caesar to the Accession of Henry VIII*. 2 vols. London.

Hume, David. (1777). *The Life of David Hume, Esq. Written by Himself*. London.

Klibansky, Raymond, and Ernest C. Mossner (eds.). (1954). *New Letters of David Hume*. Oxford: Clarendon Press.

Mossner, Ernest Campbell. (1948). "Hume's Early Memoranda, 1729–1740: The Complete Text." *Journal of the History of Ideas* 9, 492–518.

Mossner, Ernest Campbell. (1958). "Hume at La Flèche, 1735: An Unpublished Letter." *University of Texas Studies in English* 37, 30–33.

Mossner, Ernest Campbell. (1980). *The Life of David Hume*. 2nd edn. Oxford: Clarendon Press.

Pocock, J. G. A. (1985). "Hume and the American Revolution: The Dying Thoughts of a North Briton," in *Virtue, Commerce, and History: Essays on Political Thought and History, Chiefly in the Eighteenth Century*. Cambridge: Cambridge University Press, 125–141.

Robertson, John. (2004). "Hume, David (1711–1776)," in *Oxford Dictionary of National Biography*, edited by H. C. G. Matthew and Brian Harrison. 60 vols. Oxford: Oxford University Press. Vol. 28, 740–758.

Ross, Ian. (1966). "Hutcheson on Hume's *Treatise*: An Unnoticed Letter," *Journal of the History of Philosophy* 4, 69–72.

Russell, Paul. (2008). *The Riddle of Hume's Treatise: Skepticism, Naturalism, and Irreligion*. New York: Oxford University Press.

Sher, Richard B. (1985). *Church and University in the Scottish Enlightenment: The Moderate Literati of Edinburgh*. Princeton, N.J.: Princeton University Press.

Sher, Richard B. (2006). *The Enlightenment and the Book: Scottish Authors and Their Publishers in Eighteenth-Century Britain, Ireland and America*. Chicago: University of Chicago Press.

Stewart, M. A. (1995). *The Kirk and the Infidel*. Lancaster: Lancaster University Publications Office.

Stewart, M. A. (2000). "The Dating of Hume's Manuscripts," in *The Scottish Enlightenment: Essays in Reinterpretation*, edited by Paul Wood. Rochester, N.Y.: University of Rochester Press, 267–314.

Stewart, M. A. (2002). "Two Species of Philosophy: The Historical Significance of the First *Enquiry*," in *Reading Hume on Human Understanding*, edited by Peter Millican. Oxford: Oxford University Press, 67–95.

Stewart, M. A. (2005). "Hume's Intellectual Development, 1711–1752," in *Impressions of Hume*, edited by M. Frasca-Spada and P. J. E. Kail. Oxford: Clarendon Press, 11–58.

Van Holthoon, Frederic L. (1997). "Hume and the 1763 Edition of His *History of England*: His Frame of Mind as a Revisionist." *Hume Studies* 23, 133–152.

Wright, John P. (2003). "Dr. George Cheyne, Chevalier Ramsay, and Hume's Letter to a Physician." *Hume Studies* 29, 125–141.

Wright, John P. (2012). "Hume on the Origin of 'Modern Honour': A Study in Hume's Intellectual Development," in *Philosophy and Religion in Enlightenment Britain: New Case Studies*, edited by Ruth Savage. Oxford: Oxford University Press, 187–209.

Zachs, William (2011). *David Hume 1711–1776: Man of Letters, Scientist of Man*. Lady Stair's Close: Edinburgh.

PART I

CENTRAL THEMES

CHAPTER 2

NATURALISM AND SKEPTICISM IN THE PHILOSOPHY OF HUME

BARRY STROUD

HUME's *Treatise of Human Nature* was "An Attempt to introduce the experimental Method of Reasoning into MORAL SUBJECTS" (T subtitle/xi). The goal was a comprehensive "science of man" or "of human nature" that would reveal "the extent and force of human understanding, and . . . explain the nature of the ideas we employ, and of the operations we perform in our reasonings" (T Intro. 4/xv). A full development of that "science" would encompass human understanding not only in its "theoretical" employment, but also in morals, politics, religion, and social life, as well as in human desires, passions, and emotions.

Hume wanted to "introduce". . . "the experimental method of reasoning" into the study of human nature because he thought that method had not always been followed in the past. He found that:

> the moral Philosophy transmitted to us by Antiquity, labor'd under the same Inconvenience that has been found in their natural Philosophy, of being entirely Hypothetical, & depending more upon Invention than Experience. Every one consulted his Fancy in erecting schemes of Virtue & of Happiness, without regarding human Nature, upon which every moral Conclusion must depend. (LET i 16)

In comparing "moral philosophy" unfavorably with "natural philosophy," in this respect Hume apparently attributed much of the impressive success of the new science of physical nature to its "experimental" observational character. He accordingly envisaged a new "science of human nature" to be pursued by a similarly "experimental" method of investigation:

For to me it seems evident, that the essence of the mind being equally unknown to us with that of external bodies, it must be equally impossible to form any notion of its powers and qualities otherwise than from careful and exact experiments, and the observation of those particular effects, which result from its different circumstances and situations. (T Intro. 8/xvii)

But whatever general principles we might establish by such a study, and however firmly they might appear to be supported by the "experiments," "we cannot go beyond experience; and any hypothesis, that pretends to discover the ultimate, original qualities of human nature, ought at first to be rejected as presumptuous and chimerical" (T Intro./xxi).

Thus, when we have carried the investigation as far as we can, we must be willing to "sit down contented" and admit that "we can give no reason for our most general and most refined principles, beside our experience of their reality" (T Intro. 8/xvii). A "free confession" of our ignorance in this respect is the surest guarantee against "that error, into which so many have fallen, of imposing their conjectures and hypotheses on the world for the most certain principles" (T Intro. 9/xviii).

Hume is clear and emphatic about the purely observational "experimental" character of his project and about its corresponding limitations. But it is limited only by our limited human capacities and our own ingenuity. Hume notes one significant difference between the study of human nature and the procedures of experimentation in natural philosophy. It is possible to intervene directly in the processes of inanimate nature and observe the result, but intervening "experimentally" in human social life would so disturb the operation of natural principles that no just conclusions could be drawn:

We must therefore glean up our experiments in this science from a cautious observation of human life, and take them as they appear in the common course of the world, by men's behaviour in company, in affairs, and in their pleasures. (T Intro. 10/xix)

This conception of the proper study of human nature treats human beings and every aspect of their lives as natural phenomena to be studied like other parts of nature. They are to be understood solely in terms of what can be found out about them through the use of those capacities human beings are naturally endowed with for finding out anything. All this might now seem to go without saying. It is expressed for us in the familiar idea of the social or "human" sciences. It is perhaps difficult to realize that those ways of understanding human life have not always been with us. The very idea of such a study started only in Hume's day and gained momentum at least in part from the conception of a "science of human nature" as he understood it.

That comprehensive project could be called a form of "naturalism" as that term came to be used by certain self-styled "naturalist" philosophers of the twentieth and twenty-first centuries. It involves taking nothing for granted that cannot be found in nature, relying only on procedures whose reliability can be tested by their observable results, and explaining as much as possible of human life by appeal only to what can be discovered to be true of human beings and their relations to the world around them. No one would suppose anything more than that is needed for an understanding of animals and animal life, for instance. Hume had the parallel explicitly in mind; both the *Treatise* and *An Enquiry Concerning Human Understanding* contain a section "Of the Reason of Animals." But to insist that human beings and the other animals are to be studied and understood in the same generally "experimental" way is not to deny or to minimize the great differences between them. It is precisely those differences that make the "science of human nature" of distinctive interest and importance for us.

One way human beings are distinctive is in possessing and deploying an elaborate body of knowledge about the world they live in. In the middle of the twentieth century, the philosophical theory of knowledge was largely devoted to developing a schematic abstract structure of propositions or propositional forms in logical and confirmatory relations to one another that could serve as a model or "rational reconstruction" of all of human knowledge of the world. W. V. Quine reacted against that largely a priori enterprise by calling for a "naturalized epistemology" instead. "Why all this creative reconstruction, all this make believe?," Quine asked. "Why not just see how this construction really proceeds? Why not settle for psychology?" (Quine 1969: 75). The idea was to use the best means we have for understanding how human beings actually come to know the things they do, even if it involves making use of knowledge of the very kind we are trying to account for. Other recent forms of philosophical "naturalism" would look not only to the social sciences or to the study of animal life but to evolutionary biology and ecology more generally.[1]

And not only knowledge but all aspects of human thought and experience, even the presence of any meaning or intentionality in the world at all, are to be understood by, in effect, "naturalizing the mind" (Dretske 1995). These forms of "naturalism" are continuous with Hume's conception of his "science of human nature" and were at least indirectly influenced by it. This gives sense to a kind of "naturalism" in Hume even if he never used the word in that way.

Although his general project can be called "naturalistic," Hume's conception of what the project requires, and his particular way of carrying it out, led him in a very different direction from these more recent "naturalists." For Hume, the idea was to explain, among other things, how human beings get any thoughts or beliefs or knowledge of the world at all. And, apparently for that reason, he did not simply take for granted most of the very knowledge of the world that the project was meant to account for. Of course, he had to start somewhere. He started with what he thought human beings start with as knowers: what they perceive in sense-experience. And Hume thought perceivers never, strictly speaking, perceive how things are in the world they live in. The most they get from the world are fleeting and momentary impressions in which what they are aware of implies nothing about how things are in the world beyond. It is from these materials alone, Hume thought, that human beings construct their elaborate conception of the world and their place in it. "Nature" is at work in this process in the form of certain general "principles of association" or "principles of the imagination" according to which perceptions and their effects naturally come and go in human minds. That is simply part of the way things are in nature and not further explained. The task of the "science of human nature" was therefore to discover what those natural "principles" are and to see how they work. That would be to explain how the relatively meager materials human beings receive in perception lead them to form the rich body of thoughts, beliefs, and other responses they have to a world of objects, events, and other people.

There is a question of how Hume knew that human beings' perceptual access to the world is restricted in that way. That is what sets the whole problem for his version of the "science of human nature." But why did he start there? Is it something he found to be true of human beings by following "the experimental method of reasoning" in studying them? He says:

> 'tis universally allow'd by philosophers, and is besides pretty obvious of itself, that nothing is ever really present with the mind but its perceptions or impressions and ideas, and that external objects become known to us only by those perceptions they occasion. (T 1.2.6.7/67)

Was it by "the cautious observation of human life" that Hume discovered that "obvious" fact about perceptions? Or did he and many other philosophers simply "consult their Fancy" or depend "more upon Invention than Experience" and so impose "their conjectures and hypotheses on the world"? Hume does mention a few "experiments" he thinks reveal the fleeting and dependent character of our perceptions; for instance, if you press your eye with your finger in a certain way, you see double. And, he says, "a very little reflection and philosophy" is sufficient to convince you that the kind of thing you see in that case is all that anyone ever sees (T 1.4.2.45/210). But he does not explain the "reflection and philosophy" he thinks leads so easily to that conclusion.

It seems clear that Hume drew his conclusions from "experiments" and observations in his own mind. That is where he looked to explain the difference between perceiving something and merely thinking about it, between simple and complex impressions, between impressions of sensation and impressions of reflection, and all the rest of the structure he thought was present in every human mind.

Whatever it was that convinced Hume that human beings all start with nothing more than fleeting, momentary impressions, his attempt to explain all of human thought and experience on that basis led to disaster. It left him, and so appeared to leave all the rest of us, in a deeply unsatisfactory position. Part of the disaster was that we could never understand ourselves as having any reason to believe any of the things we believe about the world around us. Hume himself could therefore not even find reason to believe the very "results" he thought he had arrived at in the "science of human nature." The unfortunate position that would leave us in is often called "skepticism," and Hume himself sometimes calls it that.

But having argued at length and with great force that we are all in that "skeptical" position, Hume came to see and to feel the hopelessness of understanding ourselves in that way. He despaired of ever escaping from that plight. He eventually did manage to escape the despair, but not by showing that we are not really in the position he had proved we are in. Relief came only by continuing to accept those earlier skeptical conclusions while overcoming the hopelessness that discovering them had cast him into. That agreeable outcome is also a form of what Hume calls skepticism. It is deeper and more consequential than the earlier skepticism. It is a condition or state of mind Hume endorses. But he thinks that state becomes available to us only by our first passing through the earlier skeptical disaster that his "science of man" inevitably led him into.

The first step on the path into that disaster is the idea that, in perception, we never receive anything more than momentary, fleeting sense-impressions of this or that sensory quality, never objects or states of affairs in the "outer" world. This means, as Hume points out in many different ways, that we cannot find in our experience any reason to believe anything beyond our current perceptions. When we have found perceptions of a certain kind always followed by perceptions of another kind, for instance, we inevitably come to expect a perception of the second kind given one of the first. But the transition from what we have observed in the past to what we expect to find next is "*not* founded on reasoning, or any process of the understanding" (EU 4.15/32). Any attempt to support such an inference from past to future by appeal to past experience, Hume argues, "must be evidently going in a circle, and taking that for granted, which is the very point in question" (EU 4.19/36). But nothing other than past experience could ever support such an inference. Hume thinks there is no question that we do inevitably get such expectations in the circumstances he describes, but what we have experienced up to any point does not give us any reason to expect what we do.

Repeated experience of things of one kind regularly followed by things of another kind leads not only to a belief that the correlation will continue, but also to a belief that things of the first kind *cause* things of the second kind. That belief also goes beyond all past experience, and past experience gives us no reason to believe it. But the very idea of "cause" itself goes beyond anything to be found in experience, and so, Hume argues, it is not an idea of anything that is so in the world we come to think about. Causation as we think of it involves some kind of necessary connection between cause and effect, but necessity, Hume says, "is something, that exists in the mind, not in objects; nor is it possible for us ever to form the most distant idea of it, consider'd as a quality in bodies" (T 1.3.14.21/165–6). The scientist of human nature arrives at this verdict about causation by investigating the operation of those "principles of the imagination" that lead human beings to get the idea of cause or necessity from sense-impressions that never present any instances of causation. The operation of those principles alone is enough to ensure that perceivers will come to get the idea of causation, given the appropriate sensory experiences. But there is nothing in the "outer" or even in the "inner" world that answers to that idea of necessity or causation.

The same is true of the idea of an object's continuing to exist when it is not perceived. That is another fundamental idea we have and need, and Hume's account of perception also implies that we are never presented with any such thing in experience. He explains how we get the idea only by indulging in a certain kind of "fiction." In attending both to the similarities and to the differences between resembling but different series of perceptions, for instance, our thoughts can be pulled in opposite, incompatible directions. The mind "will naturally seek relief from the uneasiness" (T 1.4.2.39/206) by constructing a new idea that resolves the otherwise unavoidable conflict. We accordingly "suppose" or "feign" the identity and the continued existence of an object that remains one and the same while the perceptions change. That idea is a "fiction" in the sense that no such things are ever found in our perceptual experience, and they do not even have to exist in the world at all in order to explain how we come to get the idea of them.

This pattern of explanation runs throughout Hume's whole "science of human nature." The "science" is "naturalistic" in the sense of an empirical investigation and explanation of what actually goes on with human beings. But the only aspects of the "natural" world that are drawn on to explain the facts in question are the fleeting perceptions human beings receive and the "principles of the mind" that govern the comings and goings of the thoughts, beliefs, and other reactions that result from those perceptions. That restriction is what leads to the disaster. A more open-minded "naturalism" would make free use of *anything* we know about the world to help explain the thoughts, beliefs, and reactions it is interested in, even beliefs about how human beings come to believe and respond to the world as they do. There is no paradox in a psychological or developmental explanation of how human beings come to believe what they do about human psychology or human development. That conception of the "naturalistic" project as a form of social science leads to no "sceptical" quandary and so to no disaster.

Hume was left with a skeptical disaster despite what can be called his "naturalism," and he eventually faced the fact that that is what his "science of human nature" leads to. He came close to recognizing the source of deep trouble when he applied the explanatory treatment he had used elsewhere to the idea of personal identity—the idea each of us has of ourselves as a single person or mind continuing to exist through the whole course of our lives. In one of the most-cited sentences in all of Hume's works, he famously declared:

> when I enter most intimately into what I call *myself*, I always stumble on some particular perception or other . . . I never can catch *myself* at any time without a perception, and never can observe any thing but the perception. (T 1.4.6.3/253)

No being who "has" or undergoes those perceptions is present in any person's experience. If we think and speak of such "subjects" or persons, as we do, the idea we have of them cannot be an idea of anything we find in experience. The idea must be produced only by something that happens in our minds when we experience or contemplate the perceptions we find there.

That is the general pattern of explanation; the idea of the individual mind is a "fiction" in the sense that our having the idea is explained without supposing that there is any such thing. "The identity, which we ascribe to the mind of man," Hume says, "is only a fictitious one" (T 1.4.6.15/259). "There is properly no *simplicity* in [the mind] at one time, nor *identity* in different; whatever natural propension we may have to imagine that simplicity and identity" (T 1.4.6.4/253). We "imagine" or "suppose" there is "something that really binds our several perceptions together" (T 1.4.6.16/259), but "identity is nothing really belonging to these different perceptions, and uniting them together; but is merely a quality, which we attribute to them, because of the union of their ideas in the imagination, when we reflect upon them" (T 1.4.6.16/260).

Hume quickly became dissatisfied with this explanation of the origin of the idea of the "we" or "I" or "mind" that he says has a "propension" to "ascribe" or "attribute" a "fictitious" identity to a bundle of perceptions it "reflects" on. In an Appendix to the *Treatise,* he confessed "that this difficulty is too hard for my understanding," although perhaps not "absolutely insuperable" (T App. 28/636). But right after the section "Of Personal Identity" in the *Treatise* itself he added a poignant concluding section expressing his deep dissatisfaction with his whole treatment of "the understanding." At the end of Book 1 of the *Treatise* Hume found himself in a "forelorn solitude" (T 1.4.7.2/264), he clearly saw and felt the effects of the disaster his conception of the "science of human nature" leads to.

Hume had to acknowledge that, according to his theory of human nature, he has no reason to assent to anything beyond what is immediately present to his senses at a given moment. Even to regard some of his current perceptions as memories of perceptions he enjoyed earlier would require a step in thought from those present perceptions to a belief in the past perceptions they are believed to represent (T 1.4.7.3/265). And nothing in his current experience gives him any reason to make that step, just as nothing gives him reason to believe anything about the future. When generalized, this is an extremely skeptical conclusion to reach about human beings: that they have no reason to believe in anything beyond their current perceptual experience and that they would possess their most fundamental and apparently indispensable ideas even if those ideas were not true of anything in the world. Even the idea human beings have of "the world" they believe in is just one more of their "fictions."

But Hume's lament in his Conclusion of Book 1 of the *Treatise* is not simply that he has arrived at an outrageous view of human nature that no one will agree with. However unacceptable the view appears to be, if the best evidence from the study of human beings supported it above all others, we would have to accept it. If human scientists studying animals found that every aspect of animal behavior can be explained in terms only of what they receive in perception and how their internal constitution operates on that input to make them behave in all the ways they do, it would not be outrageous to conclude that animals have no reasonable beliefs and no accurate ideas of the world.

Hume's complaint about his own position has a different source. He is disturbed in a way that is unique to the study of human nature. Human beings who study animals can accept any theory that best accounts for everything animals do. But in the science of human nature, human beings are both the objects of the study and the agents who carry it out. They seek to understand themselves, so they must be able to accept the results they arrive at as true of themselves. I think what Hume sees, and feels, and expresses despair about is that, on his view, he can never achieve that kind of satisfaction in his own efforts at self-understanding. He complains that the position he has reached seems "to turn into ridicule all our past pains and industry, and to discourage us from future enquiries" (T 1.4.7.4/266). We take up the science of human nature to search for the causes of every phenomenon concerning the mind of man. But "how must we be disappointed" to find through our researches that this very idea of cause, for instance, is nothing more than the offspring of a determination of the mind, acquired by custom, to pass from one idea to that of its usual attendant (T 1.4.7.4/266). This "cuts off all hope of ever attaining satisfaction" (T 1.4.7.5/267), he says. It is here, in his talk of "satisfaction" and "disappointment," that I think Hume puts his finger on the real source of the disaster and the despair he finds himself in.

When he tries to apply to himself the conclusions he has reached about human beings in general, Hume cannot see himself as having any reason to believe anything.

> After the most accurate and exact of my reasonings, I can give no reason why I should assent to it; and feel nothing but a *strong* propensity to consider objects *strongly* in that view, under which they appear to me. (T 1.4.7.3/265)

As a scientist, he has discovered that to believe something is simply to have a "stronger" or "more lively" idea of it. But he has also found that what "enlivens some ideas beyond others" is nothing more than certain principles of the imagination operating on whatever perceptions happen to be present in the mind.

The memory, senses, and understanding are, therefore, all of them founded on the imagination or the vivacity of our ideas (T 1.4.7.3/265). This is the real source of the difficulty. By assigning the central role in the mind to "the imagination" as he does, Hume is left feeling the loss of what might be called "his own" role in what goes on in his mind. Because it is only "the imagination" that "makes" him consider certain objects "more strongly" or with "greater vivacity" than others, Hume sees that he would believe what he believes whether he could give any reason for assenting to it or not. This appears to be what he means in complaining that the imagination "seemingly is so trivial, and so little founded on reason" (T 1.4.7.3/265). It is not that the imagination is "trivial" in its effects; its influence is pervasive. The point is that the operations of the imagination seem only "trivially" or "accidentally" related to the truth or reasonableness of any of the beliefs they produce. They alone are what determine the effects of whatever impressions and ideas we happen to receive. That is why explaining the source even of apparently fundamental ideas by the operation of the imagination alone reveals them as "fictions": there need be nothing in the world to which those ideas are meant to apply in order for the imagination to produce them from the materials available to it.

This means not only that Hume is "discouraged from future enquiries" into human nature; he also cannot see that he has any reason to believe the conclusions he has reached or thinks he has reached in that "science" so far. Even the skeptical verdict that no human beings have any reason to believe anything beyond their current experience is something he sees he has no reason to believe. Even the "discovery" that the human imagination somehow "enlivens" some ideas rather than others is something he simply finds himself with a strong propensity to accept. In the state he is in at this pause in his reflections, he cannot see that he has any reason to believe in the very subject matter he has been investigating. What he calls the "science of human nature" appears to have vanished for him as a project he can find reason to pursue. He is completely at sea; despair seems total. What would otherwise perhaps have sounded like histrionic self-dramatization becomes more intelligible as a way of expressing his troubled frame of mind:

> I begin to fancy myself in the most deplorable condition imaginable, inviron'd with the deepest darkness, and utterly depriv'd of the use of every member and faculty. (T 1.4.7.8/268–269)

> I fancy myself some strange uncouth monster, who not being able to mingle and unite in society, has been expell'd all human commerce, and left utterly abandon'd and disconsolate. (T 1.4.7.2/264)

Hume's science of human nature has left him feeling scarcely like a human being at all. It is the dominance of what Hume calls "the imagination" that leads to all the trouble. We cannot deny its influence, but we cannot determine in advance how far we ought to yield to it. There is no reasoning oneself out of the dilemma of how far, if at all, we should go along with the imagination. Whatever we happened to decide would have no effect if things had been settled otherwise by the imagination.

> For my part, I know not what ought to be done in the present case. I can only observe what is commonly done; which is that this difficulty is seldom or never thought of; and even when it has once been present to the mind, is quickly forgot, and leaves but a small impression behind it. (T 1.4.7.7/268)

Hume here draws attention to the important fact that we simply cannot continue to believe the philosophical conclusions that we admit we cannot avoid reaching. This is put forward as a fact of the human condition, presumably discoverable by "the cautious observation of human life."

> Most fortunately it happens, that since reason is incapable of dispelling these clouds, nature herself suffices to that purpose, and cures me of this philosophical melancholy and delirium . . . (T 1.4.7.9/269)

This is an appeal to the force of "nature" over "reason," with its attendant skepticism: "Nature breaks the force of all sceptical arguments in time, and keeps them from having any considerable influence on the understanding" (T 1.4.2.12/187). As a result, "I find myself absolutely and necessarily determin'd to live, and talk, and act like other people in the common affairs of life" (T 1.4.7.10/269).

In "this blind submission" to the forces of nature, Hume says, "I shew most perfectly my sceptical disposition and principles" (T 1.4.7.10/269). The skepticism he has in mind at this point is brought about not by reflection but by the forces of nature operating on what had been the disastrous results of earlier philosophical reflections. It is skepticism in the sense of those skeptics of antiquity who were said to have achieved a contented, tranquil way of life by having overcome an obsession with reason and truth and simply gone along with their natural inclinations. But Hume thinks "nature" can have this kind of liberating effect only on those who have first engaged in philosophical reflections about human nature and found themselves in the disastrous skeptical plight he first reached. The "excessive," paralyzing effects of those earlier skeptical reflections are "mitigated" by the superior force of nature in the form of certain natural human instincts. That agreeable "natural" outcome cannot be achieved by reasoning and reflection alone. We can see and fully appreciate the superior force of nature over reason only by finding ourselves inevitably believing and acting in the very ways that our skeptical philosophical reflections had convinced us we have no good reason to do.

An Enquiry Concerning Human Understanding can be seen as a sustained defense of this conception of skepticism and so as a recommendation of the agreeable human condition Hume thinks it can lead to. The "Sceptical Doubts Concerning the Operations of the Understanding," explained and defended in Section 4 of that book, show that our beliefs in matters of fact beyond the present testimony of our senses and memory "are *not* founded on reasoning or any process of the understanding" (EU 4.15/32). If we believed only what we can see we have reason to believe, we would believe nothing. This would mean:

> All discourse, all action, would immediately cease; and men remain in total lethargy, till the necessities of nature, unsatisfied, put an end to their miserable existence. (EU 12.23/160)

The "Sceptical Solution of These Doubts" offered in the next section lies in the fact that "the great subverter of *Pyrrhonism* or the excessive principles of scepticism is action, and employment, and the occupations of common life" (EU 12.21/158–9). We inevitably get the beliefs we do as a result of the customary conjunctions we perceive in our experience. That we do in fact make such transitions is the "solution": "All these operations are a species of natural instincts, which no reasoning or process of the thought and understanding is able either to produce or to prevent" (EU 5.8/46–7). The "excessive," apparently paralyzing results of those earlier reflections will have no lasting effects on us. But that fact can have the most desirable liberating consequences only for someone who has followed the abstract reflections and is "once thoroughly convinced of the force of the Pyrrhonian doubt, and of the impossibility, that anything, but the strong power of natural instinct, could free us from it" (EU 12.25/162). Finding the negative skeptical conclusions about reason unanswerable is a necessary step to the desired outcome. "We must submit to this fatigue, in order to live at ease ever after" (EU 1.12/12).

The liberation this leads to is therefore not simply the acceptance of a certain attitude or the adoption of a correct abstract theoretical position. It is a state of mind or a condition of life that is "consequent to science and enquiry" (EU 12.5/150). It is the "natural result" (EU 12.25/162) of the profound skeptical doubts arrived at in philosophical reflection, together with the irrepressible forces of nature, that leads us to draw the everyday conclusions we do from whatever our experience presents us with. Living in full acknowledgment of both these aspects of human nature is the "more *mitigated* scepticism or *academical* philosophy" explained and defended in the last section of Hume's first *Enquiry*.

One of the benefits of reaching that state, Hume thinks, is that we will tend to be less "affirmative and dogmatical" in our opinions and will approach that "degree of doubt, and caution, and modesty, which, in all kinds of scrutiny and decision, ought for ever to accompany a just reasoner" (EU 12.24/162). We will also tend to be less "delighted with whatever is remote and extraordinary," and so to resist "distant and high enquiries" by restricting our attention "to such subjects as are best adapted to the narrow capacity of human understanding" (EU 12.25/162). With greater appreciation of the imperfections and limitations of the faculties available to human beings as we know them:

> While we cannot give a satisfactory reason, why we believe, after a thousand experiments, that a stone will fall, or fire burn; can we ever satisfy ourselves concerning any determination, which we may form, with regard to the origin of worlds, and the situation of nature, from, and to eternity? (EU 12.25/162)

The "mitigated scepticism" Hume recommends is a condition or state of mind that he regards not only as the most satisfactory outcome of philosophical reflection but also as the best way to live. It can be called a skeptical state or stance, but it is a purely natural result of intense philosophical reflections that lead inevitably to the "excessive" or "Pyrrhonist" skeptical quandary. The inevitability with which the curious human thinker is first driven into that disaster comes from the acceptance of reason as the distinctive foundation of human nature. The inevitability with which that same human being is eventually freed from that skeptical quandary comes from nature alone. Both movements of thought are essential for achieving the best human outcome. So there is a way in which both skepticism and naturalism are central to Hume's understanding of human nature and his conception of a full and distinctively human life. Pursuing the "science of man" in the way he proposes is what he thinks will bring this most agreeable human condition home to us.

Note

1. Penelope's Maddy's broad-minded "naturalism" encourages the use of anything at all that we happen to know that will help explain whatever aspects of the human world in which we are interested (Maddy 1997).

Bibliography

Dretske, Fred. (1995). *Naturalizing the Mind*. Cambridge, Mass.: MIT Press.

Maddy, Penelope. (1997). *Second Philosophy*. Oxford: Oxford University Press.

Quine, W. V. (1969). "Epistemology Naturalized," in *Ontological Relativity and Other Essays*, New York: Columbia University Press.

CHAPTER 3

REASON, NORMATIVITY, AND HUME'S "TITLE PRINCIPLE"

DON GARRETT

HUME describes himself in his philosophical writings as relying on something that he calls "reason," even though he reaches striking conclusions about its limitations—arguing, for example, that it cannot "found" the supposition of the uniformity of nature or the belief in an external world of bodies and that it cannot alone be the source of motivation to act or of moral distinctions. Thus far, there is no paradox: one can continue to use something for many purposes without supposing that it can be used for every purpose. More starkly and worryingly, however, Hume seems, on the one hand, not only to employ reason but to acknowledge from the very outset its normative role as a "tribunal" (T Intro. 1/xiii), and yet on the other he claims to discover not only limits to what it can do but also its liability to "doubt," "contradictions and imperfections," and "objections" that it seemingly cannot "defend against," "dispel," or "remove":

[Passage A] This sceptical doubt, both with respect to reason and the senses, is a malady which can never be radically cur'd, but must return upon us every moment, however we may chace it away, and sometimes may seem entirely free from it. 'Tis impossible, upon any system, to defend either our understanding or senses; and we but expose them further when we endeavour to justify them in that manner. As the sceptical doubt arises naturally from a profound and intense reflection on those subjects, it always encreases the further we carry our reflections, whether in opposition or conformity to it. (T 1.4.2.57/218)

[Passage B] The intense view of these manifold contradictions and imperfections in human reason has so wrought upon me, and heated my brain, that I am ready to reject all belief and reasoning, and can look upon no opinion even as more probable or likely than another. . . . [R]eason is incapable of dispelling these clouds. . . . (T 1.4.7.8-9/268–9)

[Passage C] [Pyrrhonian] objections . . . can have no other tendency than to shew the whimsical condition of mankind, who must act and reason and believe; though they are not able, by their most diligent enquiry, to satisfy themselves concerning the foundation of these operations, or to remove the objections, which may be raised against them. (EU 12.23/160; see also EU 12.15n/156)

The question of the normative role of reason in Hume's philosophy comes to a head in the concluding section of Book 1 of *A Treatise of Human Nature*, where he formulates and appears to adopt a principle requiring "assent to" reason in some instances but not in others:

> [Title Principle] Where reason is lively, and mixes itself with some propensity, it ought to be assented to. Where it does not, it never can have any title to operate on us. (T 1.4.7.11/270)

Several distinct but closely related questions have been posed in recent years about this "Title Principle," as I have called it (Garrett 1997). First, what does Hume mean by "reason" in it? Second, what exactly is the scope of its mandate? Third, what kind of normativity is expressed by the "ought" contained in it? Fourth, can it allow him properly to overcome—if only to some extent—the doubt, contradictions and imperfections, and objections concerning reason that he mentions? These are the central questions I seek to answer. I conclude this chapter with brief reflections on the significance for contemporary epistemology of Hume's treatment of the normativity of reason in relation to the Title Principle.

I THE MEANING OF "REASON"

The term "reason" has been used in many different senses—and this is so even apart from the several count-noun senses that allow such locutions as "the reason why" and "some reasons for and against." In an inclusive normative sense that is particularly close to the count-noun use and particularly common in contemporary philosophy, it signifies a general responsiveness to *good reasons* of any kind, whether for belief or action. The term can also be used, however, in a still quite extensive but more specifically epistemic sense to designate the faculty, power, or capacity of knowing or apprehending truths, regardless of the particular means employed. James Beattie (1770), a contemporary critic of Hume, lists this as one of several senses of the term "reason" used by philosophers, and Peter Millican (Garrett and Millican 2011) has recently noted its use by such eighteenth-century British philosophers as Francis Hutcheson and Richard Price. In addition, there is a narrower epistemic sense in which the term designates a faculty, power, or capacity of knowing with *certainty*; in this sense, arguably employed by Descartes among others, the term may be thought to encompass at most the intuition of self-evident truths plus demonstrations from them.

Finally, the term can be used in a logico-psychological sense to designate the power or faculty of *reasoning* or *inferring*—terms that Hume uses interchangeably. It is in this sense, Beattie remarks, that the term "is used by those who are most accurate in distinguishing." Because this includes the creation of arguments as well as the making of inferences, it is also the sense explicitly adopted and elaborated by John Locke—almost certainly the greatest single influence on Hume's philosophical terminology—in the chapter "On Reason" of *An Essay concerning Human Understanding* (1975; original edition 1689).[1] Like Locke, Hume distinguishes two species of reasoning: "demonstrative" and "probable." For Hume, demonstrative reasoning (1) depends on intuitions of relations among ideas; (2) yields certain conclusions, the denials of which are inconceivable; and (3) cannot establish the real existence of anything. It is most commonly useful, he thinks, in mathematics. Probable reasoning, in contrast, (1) depends on experience; (2) yields conclusions the denials of which are conceivable; and (3) concerns "matters of fact and real existence." All reasoning that is not demonstrative is "probable" in this broad Lockean sense, even when the experience on which it is based is judged to be conclusive.

Despite allowing that reason can serve as a tribunal, Hume does not use the term "reason" in the first and broadest normative sense. Although he frequently invokes *reasons to act* as well as *reasons to believe*, he reserves the separate terms "reasonable" and "reasonableness" to describe a general responsiveness to good reasons.[2] Instead, he argues that actions, whatever reasons we may have for them, cannot be "contrary or conformable to reason" on the grounds that "reason is the discovery of truth and falshood," whereas actions themselves are neither true nor false (T 3.1.1.9/458). Nor, although commentators have sometimes suggested otherwise, does he ever use the term "reason" in the narrow epistemic sense that would exclude probable reasoning from its scope. The few passages in which he may seem to do so are (1) clearly restricted by context to the discussion of demonstrative reasoning; (2) concern only what reason specifically *without benefit of experience* can do; or (3) exclude from the scope of reason not probable reasoning itself, but rather a key mental transition (namely, the "presumption of the uniformity of nature") that occurs within probable reasoning but is produced by "custom or habit."

In passages contrasting reason with the passions, Hume alludes to reason as "the same faculty, with that, which judges of truth and falshood" (T 2.3.3.8/417), and he writes of "reason, in a strict sense, as meaning the judgment of truth and falsehood" (DP 1.5). It is therefore not without some plausibility to propose, as Millican does, that Hume uses "reason" in the extensive epistemic sense, according to which it designates the overarching cognitive capacity to apprehend truths, whether by inference, intuition, memory, the senses, or some other means. Upon investigation, however, the passages just cited are less conclusive in this regard than they might appear.

Consider first the latter two passages, which characterize reason as the "judgment" of truth and falsehood. For Hume, memories and sense perceptions each carry with them their own immediate assent to their contents, without the need for any additional faculty to provide it. Something very similar is true of the immediate awareness of relations among ideas that Hume (following Descartes and Locke) calls "intuitions" and regards as essential starting points and components of demonstrative reasoning. Although he uses the term "assurance" rather than "assent" in this case, the assurance is again immediate and requires no additional faculty to provide it. It would be quite unnatural to speak of any of these kinds of immediate assent or assurance as exercises of "judgment" or species of "judging," and, in fact, Hume never uses those terms to describe any of them. On the contrary, he explicitly distinguishes both memory and the senses from "judgment" (T 1.3.9.3/108; T 1.3.10.10/632; T 3.3.4.13/612).

Hume recognizes, of course, that memory, sense perception, and intuition can, in virtue of the immediate assent or assurance they bestow on their contents, also provide *inputs* to processes of judging. He writes, for example, that animals (like humans) have need for "memory or sense" to "be the foundation of their judgment" concerning matters of fact (T 1.3.16.6/177–8). These inputs can also be weighed against each other in making a final judgment. Indeed, there can even be judgments concerning whether one or more of these inputs is itself correct or accurate. Yet memory, the senses, and intuition cannot *directly* confirm or contradict one another because they have different objects. Crucially, the only psychological process he ever describes by which any judgments depending on, integrating, or evaluating these inputs can occur is precisely the process of reasoning or inference itself (for example, T 1.3.9.11/112; T 1.3.10.9/122; T 1.3.13.17–19/152–4)—that is, the application to these inputs of reason in the logico-psychological sense. However, Hume never characterizes any of these inputs to judgment-by-reasoning as *themselves* due to reason; nor does he identify their sources as *parts* of reason.

Returning now to the first passage, concerning the "discovery" of truth and falsehood, it should be observed that Hume's argument about reason and action requires only that reason be a discovery of properties—namely, truth and falsehood—that voluntary actions lack; despite his incidental use of the definite article, he need not be characterizing reason as *any* discovery of truth and falsehood. Even if he is doing so, however, he also declares that reasoning is always a "discovery of . . . relations" (T 1.3.3.2/73), and he explicitly contrasts what is thus "discovered" by reasoning with what was instead already "immediately present to the memory and senses" (EU 7.27/59). To be sure, he does refer once to intuition as concerned specifically with those relations "discoverable at first sight" (T 1.3.1.2/70) rather than by reasoning and several times to "objects discovering themselves to the senses." When characterizing reason as "the discovery of truth and falshood," however, it is reasonable to suppose that Hume is thinking of the term "discovery" as implying some further investigative activity on the part of the mind itself—an "action of uncovering," in the common eighteenth-century sense noted in the *Oxford English Dictionary*—such as judging through reasoning, rather than mere receptivity of the kind involved in the "immediate" awareness of memory, the senses (bodies "discovering themselves to us"), and intuition.

As Millican rightly observes, Hume often freely interchanges the terms "reason" and "the understanding," doing so seemingly just for the sake of elegant verbal variation— even though in general usage "the understanding" often encompasses a wider scope of cognitive and conceptual activities than simply reasoning. One example of this interchange is Passage A. Another example (one highlighted by Millican) is Hume's treatment of a footnote—originally placed in Book 2 of the *Treatise*—intended to distinguish two senses of the term "imagination":

> To prevent all ambiguity, I must observe that where I oppose the imagination to the memory, I mean in general the faculty that presents our fainter ideas. In all other places, and particularly when it is oppos'd to the understanding, I understand the same faculty, excluding only our demonstrative and probable reasonings. (T 2.2.7.7n/371n)

He arranged for the removal of this version of the footnote from copies of the *Treatise*, however, in order to add an enlarged and modified version of it to Book 1, which reads in part:

> When I oppose the imagination to the memory, I mean the faculty, by which we form our fainter ideas. When I oppose it to reason, I mean the same faculty, excluding only our demonstrative and probable reasonings. (T 1.3.9.19n/118)

Far from showing that "reason" and "understanding" both have an *extensive* scope for Hume, however, this substitution suggests rather that both terms are alike *limited* to "our demonstrative and probable reasonings"—because all other cognitive and conceptual functions having to do with "fainter" (i.e., nonmemory) ideas are left with the imagination, even in the second and narrower sense of "imagination" that he here distinguishes. The replacement of "the understanding" by "reason" also suggests that, if Hume prefers one of the two terms as being more accurate in this context, it is "reason." Such a preference would make sense for him because he often implicitly treats the scope of "the understanding" as consisting in reasoning plus intuition, as when he writes:

> As the operations of human understanding divide themselves into two kinds, the comparing of ideas, and the inferring of matter of fact; were virtue discover'd by the understanding; it must be an object of one of these operations, nor is there any third operation of the understanding, which can discover it. (T 3.1.1.18/463)

The "comparing of ideas" is always by intuition or demonstrative reasoning, in his view, whereas the "inferring of matter of fact" is always by probable reasoning. If we assume that whatever can be immediately intuited could also be demonstrated, at least in principle, then the scope of what reason can do is the same as the scope of what the understanding can do, despite the latter's possible inclusion of intuition; and it is in remarks about what these faculties can do that Hume tends to interchange the two terms.[3]

While the case that Hume uses the term "reason" in an extensive epistemic sense is thus less powerful than it might appear, there are at least five reasons to conclude that he uses it specifically in the logico-psychological sense—the sense recognized by Beattie as that employed by those "most accurate in distinguishing." First, and most importantly, we have already seen that Hume consistently distinguishes demonstrative and probable reasoning as the two jointly exhaustive kinds of reasoning, and he argues in several crucial instances that *reason* cannot produce something simply on the grounds that neither of these two species of *reasoning* can produce it. This is his primary strategy for arguing that inferences from experience (what we would now call inductive inferences) are not "determin'd by reason" (T 1.3.6); it is one of his two strategies for arguing that "reason alone can never be a motive to any action of the will" (T 2.3.3); and it is one of his three strategies for establishing that moral distinctions are not "deriv'd from reason" (T 3.1.1). In this third case, in fact, he explicitly identifies what can be "*discover'd* by the understanding" with what can be "*inferred* by reason" (T 3.1.1.26/468; emphasis added).

Second, Hume evidently treats "reason" and "reasoning faculty" as equivalent terms. For example, the sections of the *Treatise* and of *An Enquiry concerning Human Understanding* entitled "Of the Reason of Animals" (T 1.3.16 and EU 9) are both devoted entirely to the topic of animal reasoning or inference, and the *Treatise* section is introduced as "examin[ing] the reasoning faculty of brutes" (T 1.3.15.12/176).

Third, not only does Hume never explicitly include the senses, memory, or even intuition within the scope of "reason," he regularly *contrasts* reason with the senses—as for example, when he examines whether an opinion is due to "the *senses, reason,* or the *imagination*" (T 1.4.2.1/187; italics in original) or alludes to qualities of which we are informed by "neither sense nor reason" (EU 4.16/33). Indeed, Passage A itself explicitly distinguishes a "sceptical doubt with respect to reason" (the topic of T 1.4.1, "Of scepticism with regard to reason") from one "with respect to the senses" (the topic of T 1.4.2, "Of scepticism with regard to the senses"). Hume is equally consistent in contrasting "the understanding" to the senses (for example, EU 7.1/60) and to both the senses and memory (T 1.4.7.3/264; quoted again by Hume at LG 4). Immediately after distinguishing the skeptical doubt about reason from that about the senses, Passage A continues: " 'Tis impossible upon any system to defend either our understanding or senses."

Fourth, the logico-psychological sense of "reason" lends itself more readily and naturally than does the epistemic sense to Hume's posing of the question of the "veracity" of reason (T 1.4.2.1/187) and of whether it "ought to be assented to." Millican proposes that Hume can intelligibly raise such questions even if "reason" is understood as a term for "the capacity for apprehending truths," in much the same way that it is intelligible to ask whether a physician's (proffered) cures do in fact really cure. Nevertheless, a "cure" that does not in fact cure deserves ultimately to lose the designation "cure," whereas Hume shows no inclination to consider withdrawing the title "reason" from the reasoning faculty regardless of the conclusions that might or might not be reached about its apprehension of truth.

Finally, as we shall see in the next section, each of the discoveries that Hume cites as motivating the Title Principle specifically concerns the faculty of "reasoning." In contrast, what he identifies as the most disturbing aspects of the "sceptical doubt . . . with respect to . . . the senses" to which he alludes in Passage A—namely, the essential role of confusions and conflations in generating the belief in an external world—are not even mentioned in the immediate lead-up to the Title Principle.

II Reason and the Scope of the Title Principle

In its reference to reason, the Title Principle thus approves assent to some but not all outcomes specifically of *the faculty of reasoning or inference*. To understand precisely what beliefs the principle endorses, however, it is necessary first to understand something of the dialectic by which it arises.

It is a central part of Hume's project to investigate, by means of "the experimental method," the nature and operations of the reasoning faculty. He claims to discover, for example, that all instances of demonstrative reasoning (like the intuitions from which they begin) depend on at least one of four particular relations (resemblance, contrariety, degrees in any quality, and proportions in quantity of number) that cannot be altered without altering the intrinsic character of the ideas so related. He claims to discover that all probable reasoning, in contrast, (1) constitutes a kind of "discovery" of causal relations; (2) requires experience of past "constant conjunctions," in which objects of one kind have always or usually followed objects of another; (3) proceeds from an impression or memory of something of one of these two kinds; and (4) results in a "lively" idea that is the belief in the existence (past, present, or future) of something of the other kind. He further claims to discover (5) that the inference to this belief depends on a "presumption" of the uniformity of nature; (6) that the making of this instrumental presumption is accomplished not by any mediating reasoning to a conclusion about the uniformity of nature but rather by the psychological mechanism of "custom or habit"; and (7) that the "belief or assent" (terms he uses interchangeably) that results from probable reasoning consists in a quantity of felt "liveliness" (also called "force and vivacity") that "enlivens" the idea as a result of the liveliness of the original impression or memory. The particular degree of "liveliness" varies with the degree of constancy of the experienced conjunction, the degree of similarity of the present impression or memory to elements of that conjunction, and other factors as well. The highest level of liveliness, resulting from a pervasive and completely uniform constant conjunction, he calls "proof"; lower levels he calls "probability" in a sense narrower (and more in accordance with everyday usage) than the broad sense employed in his adopted Lockean term "probable reasoning."

In the final section of the *Enquiry*, Hume explicitly distinguishes two species of skepticism. "Antecedent scepticism," identified with Descartes, requires that one doubt both one's own previous opinions and the veracity of one's own faculties until one has been positively assured of their veracity by "a chain of reasoning, deduced from some original principle, which cannot possibly be fallacious or deceitful" (EU 12.3–5/149–50). This kind of skepticism, Hume argues, (1) is psychologically unattainable and (2) would be incurable if it could be attained because its requirement for acceptable belief cannot be met. That this requirement cannot be met is not cause for alarm, however, since the requirement itself is not "reasonable." "Consequent scepticism," in contrast, occurs after inquiry and only as the result of specific discoveries about the infirmities of human cognitive faculties. Hume's own skepticism is consequent, and he proceeds to support it by considering a number of further specific discoveries.

Like the concluding section of the *Enquiry*, the concluding section of *Treatise* Book 1 (T 1.4.7, "Conclusion of this book") examines a number of specific discoveries about the workings of human cognitive faculties that are capable of inducing doubt about their veracity. The discoveries cited in the two works are partly overlapping. The discoveries cited in the *Enquiry* are the primary "objections" to which Passage C refers and are classified by subject matter: those concerning the senses, those concerning demonstrative ("abstract") reasoning, and those concerning probable reasoning. In contrast, each of the five discoveries cited in the *Treatise* is treated as primarily, if not always exclusively, implicating "reasoning" in some way. Four of these discoveries were made earlier in the *Treatise*; the fifth and final discovery, although dependent on an earlier one, is new. Because they lead directly to the formulation of the Title Principle, I focus on the discoveries cited in the *Treatise*.

The first doubt-inducing discovery cited in the *Treatise* is that assent to the conclusions of probable reasonings consists in liveliness (i.e., force and vivacity), produced by "experience" and "habit" through a process the veracity of which cannot be established by any non-question-begging reasoning. This incapacity results from the fact that all probable reasoning, via the operation of habit, presupposes the uniformity of nature, which is itself something that could not be established without probable reasoning; hence, Hume writes, "after the most accurate and exact of my reasonings, I can give no reason why I shou'd assent to it" (T 1.4.7.3 265, alluding to T 1.3.5–7). This "quality, by which the mind enlivens some ideas beyond others" is "seemingly . . . so trivial," he continues, and yet the understanding is "founded on" it. Indeed, Hume adds, the assent we give to the existence of external objects of sense perception and even the assent we give to the past existence of objects of memory—both of which are, of course, often also inputs to reasoning—consists in this liveliness as well. Presumably, these circumstances are disturbing for Hume because (1) the mind cannot directly observe that liveliness is constantly conjoined with truth and (2) the prospect of liveliness having nonveridical causes generates an argument in what he calls "the probability of chances" (T 1.3.11) for the conclusion that the truth of lively ideas is relatively improbable. (See Garrett, 2015, for a detailed account of this argument.)

The second doubt-inducing discovery is that there is a conflict between reason and the senses—"or more properly speaking, betwixt those conclusions we form from cause and effect, and those that perswade us of the continu'd and distinct existence of body" (T 1.4.3.15/231). This conflict, which he calls "the contradiction of the modern philosophy," arises from a "satisfactory" piece of probable reasoning for the conclusion that bodies lack qualities resembling the color perceptions and/or tactile perceptions that the mind must nevertheless employ to conceive specifically of how bodies occupy space. Because belief is itself a lively idea, however, conception is a prerequisite for it; hence, he concludes, it is not "possible for us to reason justly and regularly from causes and effects, and at the same time believe the continu'd existence of matter" (T 1.4.7.4/266; citing T 1.4.4).

Accordingly, we must either resist this particular piece of probable reasoning or find ourselves unable to specify the qualities by which we suppose bodies to occupy space.

The third doubt-inducing discovery is a defect in our "reasoning" concerning the relation of cause and effect itself. This defect, which lies in a natural illusion about causal necessity that results in part from conflating demonstrative and probable reasoning, leads us either to "contradict ourselves, or talk without a meaning" when we speak of a "tie" or "ultimate and operating principle" between causes and effects themselves (T 1.4.7.5/266–7; citing T 1.3.14).

The fourth discovery is the topic of the section "Of scepticism with regard to reason" (T 1.4.1) mentioned previously and affects both demonstrative and probable reasoning. First, although genuine demonstrations are infallible, reflection on the fallibility of our faculties in trying to perform them shows that "our reason must be consider'd as a kind of cause, of which truth is the natural effect; but such-a-one as by the irruption of other causes, and by the inconstancy of our mental powers, may frequently be prevented" (T 1.4.1.1/180). Accordingly, the certainty that a demonstration initially provides for its conclusion is naturally replaced by a degree of assent, lower than "proof," that is produced by probable reasoning from the less than completely uniform conjunction between attempted demonstration and truth. Thus "knowledge degenerates into probability" (T 1.4.7.3/181).

Second, however, the degree of assent that any probable reasoning provides for its conclusion is subject to a similar reflective review in light of experienced past successes and failures of probable reasoning. This review will serve to diminish to some extent the felt degree of assent to the original conclusion of probable reasoning; and the probable reasoning that constitutes this review is itself subject to a similar review. By applying an ordinary variety of probable reasoning—namely, "the probability of causes" (T 1.3.12), which applies to mixed experiences—each iterated probable reasoning would further diminish the felt assent to the conclusions of each of the previous reasonings, Hume argues, leading eventually, after a finite number of steps, to the loss of all assent or assurance whatever for any conclusion. This dire outcome does not actually occur, he explains, only because the unnatural posture of the mind in performing such iterated reflections turns out to prevent the repeated parallel reasonings from having the amount of reverberating destructive force they would otherwise have. Thus, he concludes:

> The understanding, when it acts alone, and according to its most general principles, entirely subverts itself, and leaves not the lowest degree of evidence in any proposition, either of philosophy or common life. We save ourselves from this total scepticism only by means of that singular and seemingly trivial property of the fancy, by which we enter with difficulty into remote views of things. (T 1.4.7.7/267–8; citing T 1.4.1)

By "degree of evidence in any proposition," as his use of the term elsewhere in the *Treatise* confirms, he means psychological "evidentness"—that is, degree of belief or assent. "The fancy" is a synonym for "the imagination."

Interpreting the details of this argument about reason's own (blocked) self-annihilation is a matter of controversy,[4] and critics have proposed a number of objections to it. What matters for present purposes, however, is that Hume accepts it in the *Treatise* and derives his fifth and final discovery primarily from it (although he also mentions the third discovery in this connection). This fifth discovery he calls "a very dangerous dilemma" concerning the question of when we ought to yield to trivial features of the imagination that affect reasoning and belief. To approve all such features would lead to the endorsement of the most extravagant and inconsistent opinions—a "false reason." To disapprove all of them, however—which might have seemed the safer and more obvious course—would be to reject the only feature of the mind that prevents reason's annihilation of its own initial assent and would leave us with "none [i.e., no reason] at all." The reasoning that would lead to reason's self-annihilation is "refin'd and elaborate," but we cannot make it a principle simply to reject all refined and elaborate reasoning. For this would cut off all science and philosophy; it would demand, by parity of reasoning, that we accept after all the other trivial features of the imagination as well; and it could not be justified by any reasoning that was not itself refined and elaborate and thus to be disapproved (T 1.4.7.7/267–8). Accordingly, Hume concludes, reason alone cannot resolve the Dangerous Dilemma concerning the appropriate standard for the epistemic endorsement of principles of the imagination as they affect reasoning and belief.

Having reached this new and disturbing discovery, Hume proceeds to narrate in the first person a succession of three moods or frames of mind initiated by his consideration of all of his five doubt-inducing discoveries, but most especially by the last. The first mood is one of "philosophical melancholy and delirium," and it is only in describing the psychology of this state that he writes in Passage B of "the *intense* view of these manifold contradictions and imperfections" as leaving him "ready to reject all belief and reasoning, and . . . look upon no opinion even as more probable or likely than another." He soon discovers that although reason itself is "incapable of dispelling these clouds," nature is capable of doing so, for the mood is not psychologically sustainable. With relaxation, activity, or "lively impressions of the senses," it is soon replaced by "indolence and spleen," a mood in which he (1) rejects skeptical speculations as "cold, and strain'd, and ridiculous"; (2) "submits" to his "senses and understanding" (thus reiterating the distinction between them) and, in doing so, returns to "belief in the general maxims of the world"; and (3) proposes to forswear "torturing" his brain with philosophy for the future.

Importantly, the Title Principle arises initially *not* through renewed reasoning about the veracity of reason in its various applications but rather as a natural expression of indolence and spleen. Soon, however, the return of the two passions of "curiosity" and "ambition"—along with more general reflection on the unavoidability of speculation about philosophical topics and the practical need to choose a guide to them less dangerous than religion—leads naturally from indolence and spleen to the third mood, an active return to philosophizing. As Hume now realizes, philosophical inquiry itself is "lively"—that is, it enlivens ideas, producing assent—*and* it "mixes with some propensity"—that is, it stimulates and satisfies desires or inclinations, such as curiosity and ambition. Philosophizing is therefore fully in accordance with the Title Principle. For this reason, endorsement of the Title Principle offers Hume the prospect of a resolution to his Dangerous Dilemma by providing a satisfactory principle after all for determining which reasoning to accept and which to reject. To see just how it does so, however, it is helpful to appreciate the default acceptance principle that it serves in effect to replace.

Because reason typically carries assent to its own conclusions with it, reasoners will naturally find themselves accepting the default principle: "Reason ought to be assented to." This default principle need not be understood to mean that *every* conclusion of reasoning should be accepted without further question, reflection, or revision, of course; further reasoning either about the facts or about the circumstances of success and failure in various kinds of past reasonings, or both, may often lead reason itself to give an ultimate verdict different from its initial or provisional one. Well before the final section of *Treatise* Book 1, Hume has already provided a set of "rules by which to judge of causes and effects" (T 1.3.15) that are themselves "founded on" reasoning concerning previous operations of reason and on (what we thereby come to regard as) the distorting factors to which it is often subject. The default principle should therefore be understood as stating that the final verdict of *reason, as developed by its own self-reflection,* ought to be assented to.

For Hume, however, the surprising moral of his fourth doubt-inducing discovery, giving rise to the Dangerous Dilemma, is that this natural default principle is unacceptable. For the toxic iterated reasoning that would lead to the loss of all assurance and assent is a set of reflective applications of reason to itself in accordance with the standard operations of probability. By granting normative approval *only* to the final outcomes of reflective reasoning that is "lively and mixes with some propensity," the Title Principle happily removes from the scope of approval the iterated destructive reasoning that leads to the Dangerous Dilemma. Indeed, that potentially toxic reasoning fails the Title Principle test on both counts. First, as a result of a feature of the imagination, it fails to be "lively" enough for the applications of its higher order conclusions to diminish assent to lower level conclusions. Second, unlike mundane and even philosophical reasoning of other kinds, it fails to mix with any propensity, even curiosity or ambition. Nor is that all. Although reasonings from the other doubt-inducing discoveries generate some lively assent to the proposition that our reason is so "infirm" as to be highly unreliable, the liveliness of those reasonings proves to be very limited beyond an initial shock; and they, too, mix little with any propensity. Accordingly, the Title Principle recommends retention of some considerable level of belief in the lively results of other, more ordinary reasoning even in the face of these disturbing discoveries. This recommendation is aided, Hume remarks, by the recognition that the reasonings to those doubt-inducing discoveries are themselves products of the very faculty whose veracity they then call into question (T 1.4.7.17/273).

III Normativity in the Title Principle

Thus far then, the Title Principle has (in a phrase Hume uses elsewhere) a "promising aspect," because its scope is precisely such as to mandate a return to philosophy in the face of the doubt-inducing discoveries. But what kind of normativity is expressed by its "ought"?

Hume acknowledges and discusses several kinds of normativity, encompassing both reasons to act and reasons to believe. For example, aesthetic normativity, as he explains it, is derived from the value of beauty and the disvalue of deformity in (a) perceptible natural objects, both animate and inanimate; and (b) productions of artifice including but not limited to visual, dramatic, and literary productions. Moral normativity, he argues, is derived from the value of virtue and the disvalue of vice in human characters. Epistemic normativity, he makes clear in a variety of contexts,[5] is derived from the value of truth and probable truth and the disvalue of falsehood and probable falsehood in beliefs. Probable truth and probable falsehood are relative to a body of experience, for Hume; truth and falsehood themselves are not (see Garrett 2015).

In narrating his progress from indolence and spleen to a renewed pursuit of philosophy through the return of curiosity and ambition, he writes:

> These sentiments spring up naturally in my present disposition; and shou'd I endeavor to banish them, by attaching myself to any other business or diversion, I *feel* I shou'd be a loser in point of pleasure; and this is the origin of my philosophy. (T 1.4.7.12/271)

This remark has suggested to some commentators that Hume denies any epistemic value to his beliefs and justifies his continuing to philosophize solely on the basis of his pleasure in doing so. However, the passage says nothing about the ultimate value or merit of his beliefs, pro or con; it reports only the cause of his not attempting to suppress his curiosity and ambition, and it thereby states an initial necessary causal condition of his return to philosophizing.

In fact, it is hardly possible for Hume to sustain a complete denial of epistemic value to his beliefs, because there is a very close connection for him between holding a given belief and holding the belief that that belief is true. To express this relation more easily, let us use braces —the symbol "{}"—to create names for ideas, so that "{p}" designates an idea of the possible matter of fact, p. According to his theory of belief, then, a basic *belief-that-p* is simply a *lively idea-of-p*. According to his theory of truth, truth consists "in the discovery of the proportions of ideas, consider'd as such, or in the conformity of our ideas of objects to their real existence" (T 2.3.10.2/448). For matters of fact, then, a basic *belief-that-{p}-is-true* consists simply of a lively idea that represents the conjunction of the *idea of p* with the possible matter of fact *p itself*—that is, a lively idea: {{p} & p}. Assuming that lively ideas of complexes are complexes of lively ideas for him, it follows that a *belief-that-{p}-is-true* already contains, as its second element, a *belief-that-p*. Moreover, simple reflection on the fact that one has a *belief-that-p* is sufficient to generate the complex lively idea that constitutes a *belief-that-{p}-is-true*. It is therefore psychologically untenable, in Hume's psychology, to continue to hold beliefs with a given degree of strength without, upon reflection, also holding with a similar degree of strength that those beliefs are true—thereby attributing to them a primary epistemic value. Similar considerations apply to the untenability of holding a belief while denying that it is probable that that belief is true.

This connection notwithstanding, Hume's admissions that reason is subject to doubts, contradictions and imperfections, or to objections that it cannot itself entirely defend against, dispel, or remove have led some commentators to propose that the "ought" of the Title Principle must ultimately be not epistemic but entirely moral. This proposal has some appeal, for, as David Owen (1999) has well observed, Hume does characterize "wisdom"—that is, the use of reason in accordance with the standards of judgment achievable by reflection—as a moral virtue.

However, Hume makes this remark about wisdom only in *Treatise* Book 3 ("Of Morals"), which was published separately from Books 1 and 2 and more than a year later, so it seems unlikely that he intended it to provide a key to interpreting the Title Principle at the conclusion of Book 1. In the passage in question, moreover, Hume writes that "wisdom and good-sense are valu'd because they are *useful* to the person possess'd of them" (T 3.3.4.8/611; emphasis original), in explicit contrast to other character traits that are virtues primarily because they are immediately agreeable to the possessor of the trait, immediately agreeable to others, or useful to others. Yet the appreciation of a character trait for its usefulness depends essentially for Hume on stable beliefs about the causal consequences of actions and characters. As we have seen, however, to reject the truth or probable truth of one's beliefs or even to remain agnostic about their truth or probable truth would, for Hume, inevitably undermine the stability of one's own beliefs about the causal consequences of actions and characters, and it would thereby undermine the moral approval of wisdom as well. Thus, although the disposition to reason in accordance with the Title Principle does indeed garner his moral approval as a trait that is useful to its possessor, that approval depends for its force on an independent epistemic approval of the results of such reasoning. It seems, in short, that being morally serious depends, for Hume, on being epistemically serious.

Partly because of this problem about causal reasoning, a different version of the moral interpretation of the "ought" in the Title Principle has been proposed by Michael Ridge (2003). According to this proposal, Hume's initial moral approval of the disposition to believe in accordance with the Title Principle is based on the disposition's immediate agreeableness to himself as a possessor of it, whereas moral approval based on other features or effects on other individuals arises only later. Because it is plausible to suggest that the immediate agreeableness of something to oneself might be known without causal reasoning, Ridge suggests, Hume can morally approve the disposition without any prior reliance on such reasoning.

There are several objections to this proposed interpretation, however. First, as we have already observed, Hume's own description of the moral approval of wisdom appeals exclusively to its usefulness to its possessor, rendering it unlikely that he regarded another basis for approval as prior. Second, the recognition of even immediate pleasure as *having been produced by* a feature of one's own character—especially one involving a relation to a rather unexpected principle such as the Title Principle—requires some causal reasoning. Third, as Ridge himself astutely notes and we shall soon have further occasion to observe, stable moral judgment requires, for Hume, that one's immediate moral sentiments be confirmed or corrected by reference to a standard of judgment consisting in what an idealized observer *would* feel from "steady and general points of view." Finally, and most importantly, the two passions that Hume describes as motivating his return to philosophy are (1) curiosity, which he also calls "love of truth"; and (2) ambition to "contribute to the instruction of mankind" by his "discoveries and inventions." Both of these passions require for their satisfaction that he achieve results that (he regards as) true or probably true. The Title Principle can be adopted and properly applied only if the beliefs that are in accordance with it are first judged to be beliefs that one ought *epistemically* to hold.

IV THE NORMATIVE ROLE OF REASON

The "ought" of the Title Principle must express epistemic normativity. But can Hume properly continue to grant epistemic value as he understands it—in particular, truth or the probability of truth—to the beliefs supposedly mandated by the Title Principle even in the face of the doubts, contradictions and imperfections, and objections that reason cannot defend against, dispel, or remove? To answer this question, we must examine more closely in the context of his philosophy (1) what exactly the doubts, contradictions and imperfections, and objections do and do not show about reason; (2) the precise character of reason's inability to defend against, dispel, or remove them; and (3) probability itself as a basis of epistemic normativity.

Hume does not treat any of the doubts, contradictions and imperfections, or objections as indicating a failure of reason or its products to meet a requirement for antecedent justification that a cognitive faculty or its results must meet before it can legitimately be employed; as we have seen, he rejects as unreasonable the suggestion that there are such antecedent standards. Instead, the difficulties arise consequently, from particular discoveries about reason made by reason itself. Nor does he treat these consequent discoveries as combining with substantive a priori epistemic normative principles to entail that no beliefs produced by reason have any epistemic value. He states no such principles, and there is no room within his naturalistic philosophy of mind and epistemology for an explanation of how any substantive normative epistemic principles could be known a priori. Indeed, he does not even treat the discoveries as showing that most beliefs produced by reasoning are not, all things considered, *probably true*. Although he describes himself in Passage B as temporarily attracted to an epistemic stance in which no belief is regarded as probably true, he does not endorse this stance; on the contrary, in *A Letter from a Gentleman to His Friend in Edinburgh*, he emphasizes that this stance is "positively renounced in a few Pages afterwards, and called the Effects of *Philosophical Melancholy* and *Delusion*" (LG 20).

Instead, each of the five discoveries constitutes a consideration that carries some negative weight in judging how probable or improbable it is that exercises of reason lead to truth. The first discovery, as we have observed, supports an argument from "the probability of chances" for assigning a fairly low probability to the veracity of probable reason. The second discovery supports a lowering of the probability of reason's veracity by showing that one important piece of methodologically satisfactory probable reasoning is false if another important and difficult-to-renounce belief—itself partly the result of an "irregular" kind of probable reasoning (T 1.4.2.20/241)—is true. The third discovery weighs against the probable veracity of reason by showing that the mind is subject to a pervasive illusion in the course of much or all of its most important probable reasoning. The fourth discovery shows that one application of regular probable reasoning would result in the loss of assurance and assent to any truth derived from either demonstrative or probable reasoning. The fifth discovery shows that reason alone cannot even reach a conclusion about *which* instances of reasoning will lead to truth or probable truth and which will not. Because one can reflectively sustain belief in a proposition, for Hume, only to the extent that one believes it to be probably true, lowering one's assessment of the probable veracity of reason must bring with it a lowering of one's first-order degree of assent to all of one's beliefs.

We may distinguish several different respects in which reason is unable to defend itself against, dispel, or remove the doubts, contradictions and imperfections, and objections constituted by these discoveries. First, reason cannot discover any irregularity in the reasoning that leads to any of the discoveries about the operations of reason themselves. Each discovery is made by regular reasoning that is in accordance with established reflective methodological standards reached by reason itself, and each discovery remains as an established thesis of Hume's philosophy when his confrontation with skepticism is concluded. Second, reason cannot completely destroy the capacity of any of the discoveries to function *as* a consideration weighing against the probability that reason leads to truth. On the contrary, as Hume points out in each of Passages A–C, intense focus on the discoveries themselves only serves to enhance their doubt-inducing capacity. Furthermore, he holds, appreciation of the discoveries tends to produce a standing diminution is one's overall level of assent. Third, as we have already noted, reason cannot provide a countervailing general argument for the veracity of probable reason that does not already presuppose that veracity. Finally, reason must be supplemented by passion in order both to discover the Title Principle that resolves the Dangerous Dilemma and to bring philosophical reasoning within the scope of that principle by allowing such reasoning to "mix with some propensity." These are all serious incapacities. They leave open, however, the question of whether the difficulties about reason's probable veracity can be at least partially outweighed by epistemic considerations in another way. The key to answering this question lies in Hume's concept—what he would call the "abstract idea"—of probability itself.

For Hume, the fundamental aesthetic and moral normative concepts are what we may call "sense-based" concepts.[6] That is, just as concepts of colors, sounds, tastes, and smells are derived from external senses, so, too, the concepts BEAUTY and DEFORMITY, VIRTUE and VICE[7] are derived from internal senses—which he calls the "sense of beauty" and the "moral sense," respectively. In the development of any Humean sense-based concept, the mind begins with a basic sensibility, consisting in a capacity to have certain felt responses—in these cases, aesthetic pleasure or displeasure, moral approbation or disapprobation—to particular stimuli. Ideas of things that resemble each other in producing the mental response characteristic of such a sense naturally become associated with each other and with a shared linguistic "general term," with the result that one idea, serving as a kind of exemplar, is reliably elicited by the general term while the mind is also disposed to call up or "revive" ideas of resembling objects and to use any of these ideas in discourse and reasoning (T 1.1.7; "Of abstract ideas"). Where the felt response itself admits of degrees, concepts of various degrees will arise as well.

In the development of any sense-based concept, natural divergences in response—both for one person at different times and between different persons even at the same time—are felt to be disturbing and so lead naturally to social convergence on a convenient "standard of judgment" by which we "correct our sentiments" (T 3.3.1 and ESY 23.3). This standard consists in an idealized perspective and an idealized set of sensitive endowments. Users of the concept come naturally to defer, in their application of the concept to particular instances, to the response that *would* be felt from this perspective with these endowments. In many cases, "rules" of judgment also arise as methods for anticipating what will or will not accord with the standard. When a lively idea of something is placed within the set of ideas associated with the exemplar for a concept, the result is a predicative judgment applying that concept. When the lively idea is of something that *would in fact* elicit the felt response from the idealized perspective and endowments constituting the standard of judgment, the predicative judgment is true.[8] Crucially, for Hume, the concept PROBABILITY—in the broad sense of "probability" that includes what he calls "proof"—is *also* a sense-based concept: the capacity to feel liveliness when conceiving a possible state of affairs may properly be called a "sense of probability." It is for this reason that he writes:

> All probable reasoning is nothing but a species of sensation. 'Tis not solely in poetry and music, we must follow our taste and sentiment, but likewise in philosophy. When I am convinc'd of any principle, 'tis only an idea, which strikes more strongly upon me. When I give the preference to one set of arguments above another, I do nothing but decide from my feeling concerning the superiority of their influence. (T 1.3.8.12/103)

The concept PROBABILITY develops from this sensibility through the correction of sentiments provided by a standard of judgment consisting simply of "experience"

(T 1.3.9.12/112) for an observer who "proportions his belief" to it (EU 10.4/110). Rules of probability serve to facilitate and precisify that standard. As previously noted, probability is always relative to a particular body of "experience."

Not all sense-based concepts are normative for Hume: the concepts of particular colors, sounds, tastes, and smells, for example, although equally derived from their own distinctive sensibilities through the development of standards of judgment, have no normative character. Nor is the sense-based concept PROBABILITY itself a normative concept, for to say that afternoon rain is probable is neither to praise nor to condemn that possible matter of fact. Furthermore, just as some concepts are sense-based without being normative, so, too, some concepts are normative without being sense-based. In particular, the concepts TRUTH and FALSEHOOD are not sense-based concepts for Hume; rather, he remarks, "truth is discerned merely by ideas, and by their juxtaposition and comparison" (T 3.1.1.4/456).

Because Hume is a naturalist about value, however, he will not allow that a concept's possession of normative character be explanatorily basic; rather, its acquisition of this character must be explained naturally, in virtue of its role in human life. We may distinguish at least two elements in his view of the acquisition of normative character by a concept. First, the quality conceived through that concept must be socially valued (either positively or negatively) by others as well as oneself and in its relation to others as well as to oneself.[9] Second, this shared approval or disapproval must become incorporated into the very meaning of the general term associated with the concept; the term must, as Hume himself puts it, come to be "taken in a good [or bad] sense."[10] In utilizing a term for a normative concept with a practical linguistic role of this kind, one thereby also expresses one's own commitment to the value of the quality it designates.

Indications of the process by which TRUTH and FALSEHOOD come to acquire the status of normative concepts for Hume can be found in the concluding section of *Treatise* Book 2, "Of curiosity, or the love of truth" (T 2.3.10; see Garrett 2015). (Curiosity is itself, of course, one of the two crucial passions that motivate Hume's return to philosophy and final adoption of the Title Principle.) The same psychological mechanisms that can explain the social appreciation of truth, however, serve equally to explain the valuing and social appreciation of *probable truth*—that is, the feature of beliefs that consists in their being *probably true*. It is thus that the probable truth of beliefs, as a special case of the probability of matters of fact more generally, comes to be an epistemic value.

The sense-based character of the concept of PROBABILITY has important consequences for its normative use in relation to the epistemically normative concept of PROBABLE TRUTH. The ultimate arbiters of moral and aesthetic value for Hume are sensibilities that have been corrected and refined through natural convergence on a standard to yield final (or at least provisionally final) moral and aesthetic verdicts. Although he of course endorses and employs morally and aesthetically normative principles or "rules for judging," these are themselves generalizations from the a posteriori deliverances of the aesthetic and moral senses. When general rules conflict with the sentiments that result from the idealization of perspective and endowments on which human beings stably converge as a standard, it is the rules, not the sentiments, that must yield.

The same relation between rules and refined sensibility applies to the case of the "probability" of truth as well. Hume's doubts about reason are the result of empirical discoveries about the various "infirmities" of human cognitive faculties, but the particular amount of belief-diminishing force that they *properly* have is to be determined ultimately precisely by their considered impact on the corrected and refined sense of probability itself, which establishes its own standard of judgment. It is not ruled out in advance that the corrected and refined sense of probability should approve as *probably true* the results of reason in spite of some doubt-inducing discoveries about that faculty, nor that that sense should ultimately disapprove the results of some otherwise quite regular probable reasoning that fails to have its expected effect on liveliness. In fact, assessments of both of these kinds occur at the conclusion of *Treatise* Book 1, in the adoption of the Title Principle.

For Hume, a certain *resistance to global error* is characteristic of sense-based concepts in general. He writes concerning morals:

> It must be observed, that the opinions of men, in this case, carry with them a peculiar authority, and are, in a great measure, infallible. The distinction of moral good and evil is founded on the pleasure or pain which results from the view of any sentiment or character; and, as that pleasure or pain cannot be unknown to the person who feels it, it follows, that there is just so much vice or virtue in any character as every one places in it, and that it is impossible in this particular we can ever be mistaken. (T 3.2.8.8/546–7)

Similarly in the *Enquiry*, when he rejects the proposal that human actions could not be morally blamable if they were necessary consequences of the design of a perfect Deity, he does so specifically on the grounds that such considerations are too distant to affect the morally authoritative moral sense (EU 8.33/103).

Just as Hume holds that the ultimate judge of morality is the ideally corrected and refined moral sense of all humankind, so he regards the ideally corrected and refined sense of probability as the ultimate judge of the probability of truth. Thus, for example, he dismisses the question of whether a possible matter of fact for which there is "a superior number of equal chances" is really more probable to occur on the grounds that it is a question about an "an identical proposition" (T 1.3.11.8/127), to which the answer is, trivially, "yes." For he has just delineated the probability of chances as that particular *species* of probability that lies in "a superior number of equal chances." To ask, therefore, whether a possible future matter of fact having this feature is really more probable to occur is to suggest a prospect of error where none is readily available. In just the same way that is it difficult to conceive how all humankind could always be wrong about what colors things are, what things are beautiful, or what characters are virtuous, so it will be difficult to conceive, on Hume's view, how all humankind could always be wrong about what is probable relative to a given body of experience.

Nevertheless, Hume is right to characterize the "peculiar authority" of the corrected and refined moral sense as "infallible" only "in a great measure." Sense-based concepts are only resistant, not immune, to global error. Not only can standards of judgment prove extremely difficult to apply properly in a particular case, but the process of developing a sense-based concept, investigating its applications, and reflecting on the results may ultimately undermine the application of that very concept. On one prominent view—although not on Hume's—this actually occurs in the case of color concepts derived from the sense of color, so that inquiry convinces us that no qualities corresponding to the requirements of color concepts can actually exist. It is unquestionably in serious danger of occurring for Hume with respect to probability in Passage B. Fortunately, however, this is a report of a transitory episode; ultimately, the deliverances of many (although not all) exercises of reason are approved as probably true, although with a diminished *degree* of probability resulting from the remaining "mitigated" force of the doubt-inducing discoveries, in accordance with the Title Principle. Accordingly, reason—which is at the heart of the sense of probability—retains a chastened status as a tribunal whose dictates carry normative weight in the determination of probable truth.

V CONTEMPORARY SIGNIFICANCE

Central to Hume's philosophical project is a two-part aim: (1) to investigate through "the experimental method" the operations of the cognitive faculty of reasoning or inference, and then (2) to apply the results of that investigation to the normative assessment of that very faculty. Although he shares the first part of that aim with Locke and others, the second part is largely his own innovation. This two-part aim remains of the greatest importance in contemporary cognitive psychology and epistemology. On the other hand, of the five particular doubt-inducing discoveries he proposes, perhaps none would be fully endorsed by contemporary cognitive psychologists, at least in their Humean forms. In particular, the argument concerning reason's potential annihilation of belief is no longer on the philosophical agenda, and without the need to disapprove the toxic iterated reasonings that it invokes, the urgency of the Title Principle is at least diminished. Nevertheless, the approach to epistemic normativity embodied in Hume's adoption of that principle has important connections with the most promising and influential approaches in contemporary epistemology for avoiding what Hume calls "excessive scepticism." I briefly mention only two: (1) Crispin Wright's conception of "entitlement" and (2) James Pryor's conception of "dogmatism."

For Wright, entitlement is a warrant to place trust in certain propositions without first having evidence for them. Thus, he offers the proposal that

> in all circumstance where there is no specific reason to think otherwise, we are each of us entitled to take it, without special investigative work, that our basic cognitive faculties are functioning properly in circumstances broadly conducive to their successful operation. If so, that immediately empowers us to dismiss the various scenarios of cognitive dislocation and disablement—dreams, sustained hallucination,

envatment and so on—which are the stock-in-trade of Cartesian scepticism. (2004: 194–195)

This is directly reminiscent of Hume's rejection of Cartesian antecedent skepticism; for Hume as for Wright, one may be entitled to employ one's faculties without having first vindicated their veracity. Prominent among the potential objects of entitlement for Wright is the uniformity of nature that underwrites what Hume calls "probable reasoning." Like Wright, Hume characterizes the uniformity of nature as something we "put trust in" without having an available argument (EU 4.19/35). Like Wright, too, Hume notes the importance of such trust to our epistemic and practical projects.

Whereas it has sometimes been objected that Wright's defense of entitlement ultimately offers only a practical rather than an epistemic source of approval, Hume's sense-based conception of probability allows him to go one step further. Dogmatism, as Pryor explains it, is the view that "whenever you have an experience as of p, you thereby have immediate prima facie justification for believing p," even in the absence of (1) anything that could ordinarily be called "evidence" for p or (2) any non–question-begging argument for p (Pryor 2002: 536). Pryor focuses initially on dogmatism about perceptual beliefs. If, however, the general capacity to feel degrees of assent is the basic "sense of probability" from which the concept PROBABILITY is derived, then there is a basis for extending dogmatism more broadly. Just as moral sentiments are prima facie (although highly defeasible) sources of information about virtue, the fundamental moral value, so, too, sentiments of belief are prima facie (although highly defeasible) sources of information about probable truth, a fundamental epistemic value.

Much more could be said, of course, about Hume's relation to entitlement, dogmatism, and contemporary epistemology more generally, and many qualifications, objections, and defenses would be in order in a more detailed examination. I hope it is clear, however, that his treatment of the normativity of reason in the face of skeptical discoveries still has much to offer.

Notes

1. Beattie does not list the broad normative sense or the narrow epistemic sense, but he adds two senses for which he cites Locke as providing a precedent: "that quality of human nature that distinguishes man from the inferior animals" and "the power of invention" in discovering and arranging proofs.
2. In one passage, however (T 3.1.1.10/458), Hume uses the terms "reasonable" and "unreasonable" more restrictedly, as synonyms for "conformity to reason" and "contrariety to reason," respectively, as the context of the argument clearly indicates.
3. Hume's rough identification of the scope of the understanding with that of reason is explicable in terms of Locke's own definition of "the understanding" as encompassing just three perceptive acts:

The Power of Perception is that which we call the Understanding. Perception, which we make the act of the Understanding, is of three sorts: 1. The Perception of Ideas in our Minds. 2. The Perception of the signification of signs. 3. The Perception of the Connexion or Repugnancy, Agreement or Disagreement, that there is between any of our Ideas. All these are attributed to the Understanding, or Perceptive Power, though it be the two latter only that use allows us to say we understand.

(*An Essay concerning Human Understanding* II.xxi.5)

With respect to the first element, Hume differs from Locke in not recognizing a separate mental act of perceiving ideas—what we call the perception of an idea by a mind is for Hume just the occurrence of that idea in the bundle that constitutes that mind. (And, in any case, Locke notes, the mere perceiving of ideas does not generally allow us to say, "we understand.") With respect to the second, Hume argues that grasping the meaning of signs is itself a species of association dependent on causal inference (T 1.3.6.14–15/93), so it need not be considered as an operation of the understanding distinct from reasoning or inference. (See also his mention of a dog "inferring" that by the use of "an arbitrary sound" its master "mean[s] him" [EU 9.3/105].) The third and remaining element, however, is just the kind of perception that Locke regards as always the result of either intuition or reasoning. Properly construed, therefore, the Lockean understanding comes for Hume to differ from reason at most by including also the immediate intuitions on which demonstrative reasoning depends for input.

4. I have presented a more detailed version of what I take to be the correct interpretation of it in Garrett (1997, chapter 10) and Garrett (2015, chapter 7).

5. Among these contexts are the Introduction to the *Treatise*, with its emphasis on acquiring "truth" and "knowledge"; the concluding section of *Treatise* Book 1, with its emphasis on contributing to "knowledge" and "the instruction of mankind"; the concluding section of *Treatise* Book 2 (T 2.3.10; "Of Curiosity, or Love of Truth"), which serves in part to explain why truth and probable truth are subject to "approbation"; and the *Abstract* of the *Treatise*, with its emphasis on "probability" as "the guide of life." At the outset of the first *Enquiry*, Hume describes it as a central task of philosophy to "fix the foundation of morals, reasoning, and criticism" and to "determine the source" of the distinctions between "truth and falsehood, vice and virtue, beauty and deformity" (EU, 1.2/6). He also characterizes "opinions" as subject not only to "assent" but also to "approbation" when they are judged to be true (T 3.3.2.2/592).

6. A more contemporary term would be "response-dependent." I will use the term "sense-based" to avoid unnecessary disputes about the precise meaning of "response-dependent."

7. I follow the common convention of using small capital letters to spell the names of concepts.

8. For a more detailed account of sense-based concepts, predicative judgments, and truth, see Garrett (2015).

9. Thus, Hume writes in *Treatise* Book 2 that the inciting of pride and humility, love and hatred "is, perhaps, the most considerable effect that virtue and vice have upon the human mind" (THN 3.1.2.5/473). Love, in turn, inspires benevolence and the doing of good offices, with all their complex social ramifications, whereas hatred inspires anger and the doing of harm. It is fair to say that Book 2 of the *Treatise* contains most of that work's naturalistic explanation of how and why VIRTUE and VICE are such importantly normative concepts.

10. In his essay "Of the Standard of Taste," Hume writes of this further "part" of the full meaning or "idiom" of the fundamental normative moral terms as follows:

> The word *virtue*, with its equivalent in every tongue, implies praise; as that of *vice* does
> blame: And no one, without the most obvious and grossest impropriety, could affix
> reproach to a term, which in general acceptation is understood in a good sense; or bestow
> applause, where the idiom requires disapprobation. (ESY 23.3/228)

REFERENCES

Beattie, James. (1770). *An Essay on the Nature and Immutability of Truth*. London: Edward and
Charles Dilly.

Garrett, Don. (2015). *Hume*. London and New York: Routledge.

Garrett, Don and Peter Millican. (2011). "Reason, Induction, and Causation," *Occasional Papers
of the Institute for Advanced Studies in the Humanities*. Edinburgh: University of Edinburgh
Institute for Advanced Studies in the Humanities.

Garrett, Don. (1997). *Cognition and Commitment in Hume's Philosophy*. New York: Oxford
University Press.

Locke, John. (1975). [original edition 1689]. *An Essay concerning Human Understanding*. P. H.
Nidditch, ed. Oxford: Oxford University Press.

Owen, David. (1999). *Hume's Reason*. New York: Oxford University Press.

Pryor, James. (2002). "The Skeptic and the Dogmatist," *Noûs* 34.4, 517–549.

Ridge, Michael. (2003). "Epistemology Moralized: David Hume's Practical Epistemology,"
Hume Studies 29.2, 165–204.

Wright, Crispin. (2004). *Aristotelian Society Supplementary Volume* 78, 167–212.

CHAPTER 4

··

REFLEXIVITY AND SENTIMENT IN HUME'S PHILOSOPHY

··

ANNETTE BAIER

HUME, in his unsent letter to a physician, told how, early in his life, he had some sort of revelation, an entry into a "whole new scene of thought" (LET I.13). Some, such as John Passmore (1952), thought that this was the revelation that "belief is more properly felt than judg'd of." But does "felt" here mean "sensed" or felt in the way passions and sentiments are felt? Or is it felt as pleasure and pain are felt, since although Hume classes them as impressions of sense, they surely differ from other sense impressions? In the conclusion of *Treatise* Book 1, Hume at one point resolved to let increase in pleasure, or at least not being a loser in point of pleasure, be the origin of his subsequent philosophy. Some find it to have been that from the start, since he had endorsed as normal thinking the associative transitions that Locke had found to be a bad mental habit, and he thought we do get a "sensible pleasure" from associative slides of the mind from one vivacious perception to a related and enlivened perception. But surely he did not equate thinking with pleasure seeking, even if he did think that belief is more properly the province of the sensitive than of the cogitative parts of our nature. When he said this, I think he meant that sense impressions, and the repetition found in them, play a major role in our belief formation, not that sentiment or desire for pleasure does. Pleasure is classed by him as a sensation, but usually when he speaks of sensation's role in belief formation it is not pleasure and pain, but rather what we see, hear, touch, smell, and taste that he is referring to. In any case, neither pleasure nor passion is quite what he meant by "sentiment," and it is sentiment, along with reflection, which is my topic. I delay saying just what sentiment covers.

Hume did say, in *Treatise* Book 2 when he looked at the way sympathy transforms our ideas of what others are feeling into fellow-feeling with them, that this mental move is confirmation of what he had said in Book 1 about the enlivening power of association. In that context, Hume argues that when belief is formed, it raises an idea by way of its relation with a sense impression (in the special case where there has been a constant conjunction between the objects of these) into a belief. In the same way, a belief about what passion another is feeling, can, by the relation between that person and oneself, whose passions are more than mere beliefs about passions, be raised into felt passions. But this claim is as troublesome for the thesis that belief and its formation is "affective" as it is confirmation of it. Whatever affectivity there is to belief, it is not the same as that in a felt passion. Otherwise, merely associating another's passion with one's own would be enough for fellow feeling, so that the second stage of the sympathy mechanism, as Hume describes it, would be unnecessary.

I think that Hume's new scene of thought more likely concerned the possibility of turning mental states on themselves, a project his *Treatise* is devoted to. This includes beliefs about belief, as well as passions concerning passions, and sentiments regarding sentiment.

What is a sentiment? Hume's first reference to sentiment is to the sentiment of metaphysicians concerning the infinite divisibility of space (T 1.2.2.3/30), and there are many references to sentiment in the rest of Book 1. At T 1.3.8.12/103, we have "taste and sentiment," whereas at T 1.3.13.14/151 we have "sentiment or opinion." These two combinations give us the two aspects of sentiment: belief and passionate reaction to it. Later, we have the contrasting sentiments Hume feels at the start and the finish of his section "Of Scepticism with Regard to the Senses" (T 1.4.2.56/217). It was the gloomy later sentiments he looks back to in the conclusion of Book 1, where he refers to "my sentiments in that splenetic humour" (T 1.4.7.10/269), which governed him after his intense view of the manifold contradictions and imperfections in human reason. He then refers to his "sentiments" of "spleen and indolence" (T 1.4.7.11/270). He had earlier termed them "philosophical melancholy and delirium" (T 1.4.7.9/269). These are followed by "a serious good humour'd disposition," and then by renewed but chastened ambition. "These sentiments spring up naturally in my present disposition" (T 1.4.7.12/271). Skeptical philosophical sentiments are "mild and moderate" (T 1.4.7.13/272) compared with religious superstition. The book ends with the wish that his occasional use of "'tis certain" be taken to show neither dogmatism nor conceit, "which are sentiments that I am sensible can become no body" (T 1.4.7.15/274).

Book 2 is about passions, and there we find reference to "sentiment or passion" (T 2.1.11.7/319), so it is also about sentiments. At its end, it expresses the sentiment of amusement at the absurdity of some of our passions, such as our love of truth that makes us pretend that the truths we discover are always useful. This is also a case of *reflexion*, of curiosity turned on curiosity. It is more successful than the attempt in Book 1 to turn intellect on intellect. But the prime case of reflexivity, as indeed of sentiment, is that of the moral sentiment, the topic of Book 3. It is a pleasure taken in pleasures, a sentiment directed on other sentiments, such as spleen and indolence, and on mental traits, including desires and other passions, as well as in natural abilities, such as wit. To feel such a thing, one must turn one's mental view onto human passions and abilities and see if, once surveyed, they give pleasures or pains. So reflection, in the sense of "reflexion," turning some mental act back on mental acts, is needed for the moral sentiment. Among the things the moral sentiment will take pleasure or pain in are tastes in other simpler pleasures. The moral judge will not feel approbation for the greedy one who takes too much pleasure in eating or drinking, nor for the licentious one who seeks sexual pleasure wherever it can be had. So a sentiment, for Hume, if the moral sentiment is typical, is a pleasure at a higher level, a pleasure in pleasures, or in desires for pleasure, or in passions which involve pleasure, or in abilities that give pleasure. All sentiments involve some previous thought—reflection in the broad sense. The many sentiments that succeeded one another in the conclusion of Book 1 were all thought-provoked.

In *An Enquiry Concerning the Principles of Morals*, Hume seems to be using the term "sentiment" in a broader way to include ordinary passions, not simply especially thoughtful ones, since he there contrasts the work of reason or judgment in its fact-finding that results in a "speculative proposition" with "an active feeling or sentiment" (EM App.1.11/290) needed to move us to action. This statement occurs, however, in the course of the First Appendix examination of the moral sentiment, and most of the occurrences of "sentiment" there are for this especially reflexive reaction to passions, other sentiments, desires, and acted-on abilities. The moral sentiment has to be active enough to dictate our moral approbations and, occasionally, to enable us to resist the temptation to act in ways that would display a vice, although Hume does not repeat, in EM, his "practicality argument" against the rationalists. Sentiments need not be very active in their results. Hume did liken the moral sentiment to aesthetic taste; "taste" in good human traits and good art works will show in the company we choose to keep and in the art works we put in our homes, but many art-lovers cannot afford to buy the works they admire and have to content themselves with going to art galleries. Nor can we always absent ourselves from those for whose characters we feel moral distaste. If they are our relatives, we may be stuck with them, and we may feel distaste for our own character without thereby having the means to change it. Hume is gloomy about the chances of success of self-reformation campaigns. Social institutions can redirect troublesome passions, like the love of gain, into more generally beneficial directions, and schools, the theater, and the pulpit can make some difference to human passions and sentiments, but simply resolving to be a better person rarely does much good if not helped by a change in circumstances. Hume himself failed to get his *Treatise* written at home in Scotland; it took a change of scene for him really to get down to writing it. He later expressed regrets that he had not taken more time to revise it and thought he had shown too much eagerness for the public's reception of it. The reception the book received disappointed him enormously, and he did take more care with later books. Still, it is mainly in that first book that he spoke of the human mind's wish to bear its own survey, and the book as a whole was an attempt to survey the human mind and the range of forms it takes.

Hume's attempt in Book 1 to understand our understanding, which is a special case of reflexion, led to rather negative results, especially when it came to understanding how we attribute lasting identity to things not continually under our eye. His attempt to understand our causal inferences was more successful and, indeed, ended in the formulation of rules for sounder such inferences. In the Conclusion of Book 1, he deplores the fact that his reflections on our habits of thought failed to make much impression on those habits when he had hoped that reflection would either endorse or reform them. Carelessness and inattention is the only remedy he finds for the despair that his uncovering of the "manifold contradictions and imperfections of human reason" (T 1.4.7.8/268) has led him to. Even with causal reasoning, he had, by a much criticized reduction of the meta-probabilities of error to one, expressed skepticism about them, too. Moreover, most of Hume's reasonings employ the "fiction" of lasting bodies since the events we predict are mostly seen as changes in lasting bodies. He does not say these predictions have a zero chance of coming true, so his skepticism about reason was half-hearted and rested on an argument about meta-probabilities that Quine and others rightly took to be fallacious. Such understanding of our understanding as he achieved did not lead him to admire it, and some aspects of it, such as our belief in our own identities over time, he thought he had failed even to understand. At first, he attributed this belief to our discerning of the natural relations between moments of our conscious lives, which, when looked back on, lead the surveying mind to associate such resembling and causally connected perceptions with one another, so giving some structure to the "bundle." But in the Appendix, such relations seemed too weak to explain the persistent belief each of us has in her own identity over a lifetime, so there, too, reflection not merely failed to endorse the belief as well based, but even failed to explain how it could arise.

Book 2 is devoted to cataloguing our passions, not primarily to expressing reflective passions or sentiments concerning them. Although, as noted earlier, it does twice contain the phrase "sentiment or passion," and since one passion is curiosity, Book 2 could be read as curiosity about our passions and so a case of reflexion, at least when curiosity is turned on itself, in the final section of Book 2. There, some amusement is felt at the parallel between truth seeking and hunting, in the way we like to feel that the results of the efforts we enjoy are useful. Such meta-feelings, feelings about feelings, are mainly the domain of the moral sentiment, the topic of Book 3. Hume takes this to be a pleasure or a pain taken in human passions, habits of thought, and in the actions they lead to. In Book 3, he sees himself as providing the anatomy of our moral reactions or indulging in curiosity concerning them, and he does not, until the last few paragraphs, judge them.

EM is in this respect rather different from the *Treatise* since Hume does, more or less from the start, there give a favorable judgment of the morals he is describing, expanding on the remark in the Conclusion of Book 3 of the *Treatise* that there was nothing but what is great and good in the rise and origin of our sense of morals (T 3.3.6.3/619). It was its origin in sympathy that was the "noble source" there mentioned, but sympathy's role is not gone into in EM, and it is more the agreeability and utility of the virtues and our recognition of them that is emphasized, whatever their ultimate source. But the goal of reflexive endorsement of what is found to be our nature and our moral nature remains the same as it had been in the *Treatise*. We do not, however, get any explicit expression of that goal. The test of bearing its own survey, which the understanding failed but which our moral sentiment passed, still seems to dictate the project of EM but is not avowed there. He does say his work is speculative, not practical (EM Appen.2.5/297–8), but he does do a little preaching in favor of virtue when he gives the honest man's attempted answer to the sensible knave at the end of the Conclusion. He has found our sense of morals to select for praise those qualities of character that are indeed ones conducive to a good life, provided religious moralists are banned and the "monkish virtues" transferred to the column of vices.

So the moral sentiment that he has described is not really that of his contemporaries, most of whom were religious believers. It is a fanciful secular version of the moral sentiment that survives its own survey. Hume had spoken of men of bright fancies as like angels who cover their eyes with their wings (T 1.4.7.6/267), and his portrayal of a secular society, recognizing only truly companionable and useful virtues, is one that blocks from its gaze the actual moral sentiments of his contemporaries, at least in Calvinist Scotland.

The end of all moral speculations, as Hume said from the start, was to teach us our duty and to get us to "embrace" the virtues, to let "what is honorable, what is fair, what is becoming, what is noble, take possession of the heart" (EM 1.7/172). He does set out to give us an attractive version of our moral sentiments rather than a true description of those of his fellows. He gives us an inspirational version of them, and he does admit that some of gloomy temperaments will reject it and that "men still dispute concerning the foundation of their moral duties." He knows the Calvinists will dispute his Epicurean foundation for them and see them as the commands of a jealous god, with power to punish infringements. He appends "A Dialogue" to EM, exploring cultural variations in toleration of homosexuality, adultery, suicide, and assassination of tyrants, and admitting that he has not described the moral sentiments of either a Diogenes or a Pascal, but of a rather imaginary reasonable person, a Cleanthes who is without delirious religious sentiments and without self-serving lack of consideration for those around him. He has engineered things so that the moral sentiment does come out great and good, rather than as a source of quarrel and opposed customs.

Being able to bear our own reflexion was indeed the goal that Hume set for us, having habits of belief formation and passions that survive their own survey. But he did not find all of our beliefs to pass this test, and he found only the sentiments of secular fellow-thinkers to pass it. He had trouble articulating the beliefs that should accompany enlightened sentiments, so his attempt to give us a version of the fully enlightened mind was only partial. In EU, he gave us his version of those beliefs that could pass the test of reflection, but they did not include any beliefs in the lasting identity of either bodies or minds. This is tantamount to an admission of failure. When he says it is by "instinct" not reflective reason that we take what we sense to be lasting bodies, he is admitting this failure. Instinct is a totally unreflective affair, not at all dependent on thought and understanding.

The test of bearing one's own survey, which the moral sentiment passes—as understanding did not, and which only some passions did—was all along a moral test, that of fulfilling one's duties to mankind and society. "A mind will never be able to bear its own survey, that has been wanting in its part to mankind and society" (T 3.3.6.6/620). Such a test seems inappropriate for the attempt to understand one's understanding, where one's moral uprightness would not seem to make any difference to the success of that enterprise unless cooperation with others is necessary to that enterprise, as it may well be.

It might be thought that seeing reason to be the slave of the passions, and in particular servant to a morally good will, might make it more comprehensible while examining it alone, out of relation to what it serves, will fail. And, indeed, this is the moral of the story about successful reflection: that only rich states of mind involving sentiments served by beliefs, such as the moral sentiment and to some extent the love of truth, when taken as a passion, can successfully bear their own survey. That was why I called my first book about Hume *A Progress of Sentiments* since there is in the *Treatise* a progress from Book to Book, from reason's frustration at its failure to understand itself in Book 1, to passion's partial success in satisfying curiosity about curiosity in Book 2 (and maybe pride in some forms of pride, such as pride in virtue), to the full success of the moral sentiment served by reason and regulating the passions in Book 3, when it finds itself great and good in the final pages. For the whole task of the moral sentiment is to get us to fulfill our part to mankind and society, and in EM the "sentiments which arise from humanity" (EM 9.7/273) are the noble source of morality itself.

ABBREVIATIONS OF WORKS CITED

EM   *Enquiry Concerning the Principles of Morals.* Edited by Tom L. Beauchamp. Oxford: Clarendon, 1998.

EU   *An Enquiry Concerning Human Understanding.* Edited by T. L. Beauchamp. Oxford: Clarendon, 2000.

LET   *The Letters of David Hume*, 2 Vols. Edited by J. Y. T. Greig. Oxford: Clarendon Press, 1932.

T   *A Treatise of Human Nature.* Edited by D. F. Norton & M. J. Norton. Oxford: Clarendon, 2007.

BIBLIOGRAPHY

Ardal, Pall S. (1966 and 1989). *Passion and Value in Hume's Treatise.* Edinburgh: Edinburgh University Press.

Baier, Annette C. (1991). *A Progress of Sentiments, Reflections on Hume's Treatise.* Cambridge, MA: Harvard University Press.

Brown, Charlotte R. (2008). "Hume on Moral Rationalism, Sentimentalism, and Sympathy," in E. Radcliffe, ed. *A Companion to Hume.* Oxford: Blackwell Publishing, 219–239.

Jones, Peter. (1982). *Hume's Sentiments.* Edinburgh: Edinburgh University Press.

Passmore, John. (1952). *Hume's Intentions.* Cambridge: Cambridge University Press.

Russell, Paul. (1995). *Freedom and Moral Sentiment, Hume's Way of Naturalizing Responsibility.* Oxford: Oxford University Press.

CHAPTER 5

·····································

HUME'S SKEPTICAL REALISM

·····································

JOHN P. WRIGHT

AT the beginning of his book *The Philosophy of David Hume*—a book that revolution-ized Hume scholarship in the mid-twentieth century—Norman Kemp Smith wrote of having discovered "the key to the *non-sceptical realist* teaching which Hume has expounded in Part iv, Book I, of the *Treatise*, and which he . . . carefully re-stated in the concluding section of the *Enquiry Concerning Human Understanding*" (1941: v; empha-sis added).[1] For Kemp Smith, the key to Hume's realism lay in the claim that our sense impressions are outwardly directed—that is, intentional—and that the passion or feeling that constitutes *belief* takes us beyond our subjective perceptions to a world of indepen-dent objects. He wrote that "as manifested in sense-perception . . . [belief] is . . . more than, and other than, any mere enlivening. It is a quite distinctive *attitude* of mind. It carries the mind beyond its immediately experienced, perishing states—in sense-perception to independent existing bodies" (1941: 444; cf. 169–170). The "two ultimate forms" of what Kemp Smith called Hume's "*natural* belief"—that is, "belief in continued and indepen-dent existence and . . . belief in causal connexion"—have the sanction of human nature and only lack that of reason (486). They are ' "natural', 'inevitable', 'indispensable', and are thus removed beyond the reach of our sceptical doubts" (1941: 87).

In my book *The Sceptical Realism of David Hume* (1983) and subsequent articles, I argued that although Kemp Smith was correct that Hume was a realist, he was wrong in arguing that what he (Kemp Smith) called *natural beliefs* lie beyond the reach of Hume's skepticism. I argued that Hume's natural beliefs or natural judgments remain cognitively opaque and so never lose their sceptical character. Throughout Hume's writings on human understanding there remains a Pyrrhonian opposition between our impression-derived ideas based on his *Copy Principle*[2] and the natural judgments formed by the imagination through the association of ideas. These latter are given their legitimacy through the fact that they are "permanent, irresistible, and univer-sal" and that, without them, "human nature must immediately perish and go to ruin" (T 1.4.4.1/225). But they never lose their incoherence, and they are based on "fictions"[3] or "illusions"[4] of the imagination. Hume's Academic or mitigated skepticism as formu-lated at the end of his *Enquiry Concerning Human Understanding* should be understood as being based on the recognition that our impression-derived ideas, including those that represent external objects as well as causes and effects, give us imperfect or inadequate representations of reality.

My aim in this chapter is to trace the development of Hume's skepticism through three topics: his discussion of the nature of space, the independent and continuous existence of the objects of our senses, and causal power. In each case, there is a direct opposition between the belief based on our impression-derived idea and the natural judgment of the imagination. On the first of these topics, Hume adopts Pyrrhonian skepticism in the classical sense: he balances the belief in a plenum (based on the impression-derived idea) against the belief in absolute space (based on a "fiction" generated by the imagination), and he withholds judgment on the real nature of space. In the case of the second topic, he focuses his discussion largely on explaining the origin of the natural judgment of the independent and continuous existence of body while at the same time making clear that this judgment, like the belief in absolute space, is based on a fiction or illusion of the imagination. Nevertheless, he holds that the strength and necessity for our survival of the latter judgment provides a justification for our belief. Finally, in the most controversial case, causal power, Hume's discussion focuses on tracing the origin of our impression-derived idea. He argues that this idea is purely subjective and cannot represent objective powers. Nevertheless, there is good reason to hold that our natural judgment of the existence of objective power is the basis for what he calls "a legitimate ground of Assent."[5] Hume's application of the Copy Principle leads to Pyrrhonian doubt, which can only be overcome by succumbing to the "strong power of natural instinct," which makes us judge that there are objective causal powers (EU 12.25/162). Hume adopts a mitigated or Academic skepticism in which "philosophical decisions are nothing but the reflections of common life, methodized and corrected."

I Pyrrhonian Skepticism in Hume's Philosophy: The Nature of Space

Pyrrhonian skepticism was described by Sextus Empiricus (fl. c. 200 C.E.) as "an ability to set out oppositions among things which appear and are thought of in any way at all, an ability by which, because of the equipollence in the opposed objects and accounts, we first come to suspension of judgment and afterwards to tranquillity" (1994: I.iv/4). There are three elements involved in this description of Pyrrhonism: (1) the opposition between what appears and the way things are thought about, (2) the suspension of judgment, and (3) the resulting state of tranquility. Sextus goes on to distinguish the appearance of the thing from the external object itself, noting that skeptics affirm the way things appear and only suspend their judgment concerning the external object: they "say what is apparent to themselves and report their own feelings without holding opinions, affirming nothing about external objects" (1994: I.vii/ 7; cf. II.vii.72/85).[6] The most important Pyrrhonian skeptic of the eighteenth century, Pierre Bayle, describes Pyrrhonism in a similar way as "the art of disputing about all things and always suspending one's judgment" and "the Pyrrhonian principle" as the principle "that the absolute and internal nature of objects is hidden from us and that we can only be sure of how they appear to us in various respects" (1965: 194–195).

As is well recognized by Hume scholars, the third element of the practice of Pyrrhonian skepticism does not apply to Hume's philosophy. Rather than leading to a state of tranquillity, Pyrrhonian or excessive doubt leads Hume, in the conclusion to Book 1 of the *Treatise,* to a state of "philosophical melancholy and delirium" (T 1.4.7.9/269). Likewise, he denies the possibility of adopting the second element of Pyrrhonism, namely, the "suspension of judgment" concerning the nature of external objects. He writes that he "must yield to the current of nature, in submitting to [his] senses and understanding" (T 1.4.7.10/269). In his *Abstract,* he writes that "philosophy wou'd render us entirely *Pyrrhonian,* were not nature too strong for it" (TA 27/657).[7] Finally, in the most definitive statement of skepticism in his philosophy, in Section 12 of his *Enquiry Concerning Human Understanding,* he writes that although "a PYRRHONIAN may throw himself or others into a momentary amazement and confusion by his profound reasonings; the first and most trivial event in life will put to flight to all his doubts and scruples, and leave him the same, in every point of action and speculation, with the philosophers of every other sect, or with those who never concerned themselves with any philosophical researches" (EU 12.23/160).[8]

However, in his discussion of space in Part 2 of Book I of the *Treatise,* Hume is very far from such a resolution. Indeed, the first half of his discussion supports a dogmatic resolution of the philosophical puzzle concerning the infinite divisibility of the parts of space based on the analysis of our impression-derived ideas according to his Copy Principle. He argues that we have minimal ideas of the parts of space and time and that such ideas are "adequate representations of objects" (T 1.2.2.1/29). He rejects the proofs of the infinite divisibility of space put forward by mathematicians and logicians in favor of his own argument that we have an idea of minimal parts of space based on an examination of our impressions (T 1.2.4.17/44–5; cf. T 1.2.1.4/27–8). It is only when he considers the question of the existence of a vacuum or empty space in Section 5, and particularly in his comments on that subject in the Appendix added to Book 3, that he allows that our clear and distinct impression-derived ideas of space may not give us adequate representations of external objects. Here, he suspends judgment on the question of whether it is our impression-derived idea of space or the association-produced belief in the vacuum that adequately represent space as it exists in reality. In other words, he here adopts the second element of Pyrrhonism—suspension of judgment—which he later argues (most explicitly, in the case of belief in an external world) cannot be maintained.[9]

To understand Hume's discussion of the vacuum, it is useful to consider the historical background. In Hume's day, there was still an ongoing dispute between British natural philosophers who generally maintained the existence of a vacuum or empty space, and French natural philosophers who held that all space or extension was filled with matter and that there could be no action at a distance. In 1733, the year before Hume set off to France, Voltaire published his *Letters Concerning the English Nation* where, in contrasting the philosophies of Descartes and Newton, he wrote that "a *Frenchman* who arrives in *London*, will find Philosophy, like every Thing else, very much chang'd there. He has left the World a *plenum*, and now he finds it a *vacuum*" (1733: 109). Clearly, the same was true in reverse for Hume when he traveled from England to France, where he spent three years writing his *Treatise of Human Nature*. He traveled from England, where most natural philosophers believed space was a container filled with a tiny amount of matter, to France, where the Cartesians still held that there was no space without matter.

Of particular relevance for understanding Hume's discussion of the vacuum is Bayle's article on "Zeno of Elea" in his *Historical and Critical Dictionary*, which Hume himself identified (among five other sources) as background to understand the "metaphysical Parts" of his reasoning.[10] In note I of this article, Bayle had, in Pyrrhonian fashion, opposed arguments for and against the vacuum. On the one hand, he argued that "the clear and distinct idea" of space favors the view that there is no distinction between space and matter and that all space is full (i.e., a plenum). "We have," he wrote, "a clear and distinct idea of [space] that makes us know that the essence of extension consists in the three dimensions and that the inseparable properties or attributes are divisibility, mobility, and impenetrability"—that is, the attributes of matter (1965: 379). On the other hand, Bayle noted that Newton and others had claimed to have "mathematically demonstrated" that without the existence of a vacuum—that is, a space that is "immobile, indivisible, and penetrable"—it would be impossible to explain the motion of the planets. Bayle wrote that "it is no small difficulty to be forced to admit the existence of a nature of which we have no idea and which is repugnant to our clearest ideas." After explaining the difficulties that result from considering each hypothesis, he concludes that "the simplest thing is to say that it [space or extension] can exist only in our minds" (1965: 385).

Like Bayle, Hume maintained that a vacuum or absolute space is inconceivable. He wrote that it is "impossible to conceive. . . a vacuum and extension without matter" (T 1.2.4.2/40). Hume based his argument against the conceivability of a vacuum on his Copy Principle—which, in this context, he expresses as the claim "that every idea, with which the imagination is furnish'd, first makes its appearance in a correspondent impression" (T 1.2.3.1/33).[11] He first appeals to the *impression* we have of space through sight and touch to argue that, as it appears to the senses, space is merely the "manner or order" in which co-existent objects appear to us (T 1.2.4.2/40). There is no separate impression of space beyond the way objects are presented to us in space either visually or tactually.[12] Hume stresses that space or extension (words he uses interchangeably) is a "compound impression" composed of minimal visual (or tactual) parts (T 1.2.3.15/38). He writes that "my senses convey to me only the impressions of colour'd points, dispos'd in a certain manner" (T 1.2.3.4/34). Applying his Copy Principle, he argues that the *idea* of space, which copies this impression, is itself a "compound idea" consisting of discrete parts (T 1.2.3.15/38; cf. T 1.4.4.8/228). This precludes our having an idea of a vacuum or extension without matter because such an idea, if we had it, would be of something completely simple, not consisting of parts. Hume concludes "that we can form no idea of a vacuum, or space, where there is nothing visible or tangible" (T 1.2.5.1/54).

At the same time, like Bayle (1965: 378), Hume recognizes that people naturally believe that there are spaces between objects and that these spaces are not filled with physical bodies. Hume seeks to explain this belief through the psychological principles of the imagination. To understand his explanation, one must recognize that he makes a distinction between "distance" and "space." In what he calls "our natural and most familiar way of thinking" (T 1.2.5.11/57), we tend to confuse "two kinds of distance" and, taking the one for the other, come to believe that there is space without matter (T 1.2.5.19/60). The one kind of distance he calls a "fictitious distance" (T 1.2.5.23/62) and illustrates it through a situation where we look at two objects (e.g., two stars in the night sky) separated by utter darkness—that is, by "the negation of light, or more properly of speaking, of colour'd and visible objects" (T 1.2.5.5/55). The perception of distance in this case is absolutely "simple and indivisible" and hence "can never give us the idea of extension" that, as we have seen, requires multiple parts between the two distant objects (T 1.2.5.12/58). But the movement of our eyes as we look from one of distant object to the other is the same as it would be if they were separated by a genuine extension filled with visible bodies. Likewise, there will be the same motion of the hand between two objects separated by nothing tangible as between the same two objects similarly placed with tangible objects between them (T 1.2.5.13/58). It is this and other resemblances between these "two kinds of distance" that makes us confuse the first with the second and think that we have an idea of space without matter.

Hume attributes this confusion of ideas to a principle of the imagination, which becomes key in his later discussions of our judgments of external existence, material substance, and personal identity. He writes that "we may establish it as a general maxim in this science of human nature, that wherever there is a close relation betwixt two ideas, the mind is very apt to mistake them, and in all its discourses and reasonings to use the one for the other" (T 1.2.5.19/60). It is association of ideas by way of *resemblance* that is the main cause of the confusion in the case of the idea of extension: "we may in general observe, that whenever the actions of the mind in forming any two ideas are the same or resembling, we are very apt to confound these ideas, and take the one for the other" (T 1.2.5.21/61). In mistaking the empty distance, which is absolutely simple, for a genuine extension (which consists of parts) we come to believe in the existence of space that is not filled with matter. This substitution of the one idea for the other takes place unconsciously, and Hume ascribes it to the physiology of the brain. He speculates that, all things being equal, when we intend to recover any idea from the imagination, the "animal spirits" or nervous fluids flow to the trace in the brain in which the idea is stored (T 1.2.5.20/60-1). However, when the ideas are closely related, the motion of the nervous fluid "naturally turns a little to one side or the other . . . [and so] . . . falling into the contiguous traces, present[s] other related ideas in lieu of that, which the mind desir'd at first to survey." We don't notice the substitution of the related idea that is stored in a contiguous part of the brain and "employ it in our reasoning, as if it were the same" with the original idea we intended to recover. The systematic and unconscious replacement of the idea of a genuine extension composed of parts with the idea of the "fictitious distance" is the source of our belief in the existence of absolute space.

The result is an opposition between the belief based on our clear and distinct impression-derived idea of space, on the one hand, and the natural common-sense belief in space generated by the substitution of ideas, on the other. It is important to note that Hume does not deny that people genuinely believe in space without body, even though he explains that belief by ascribing it to a confusion of ideas. He knew perfectly well that the belief that the universe consists of both the void and of atoms was a serious philosophical view maintained by ancient philosophers such as Epicurus, Democritus, and Leucippus—and revived by modern natural philosophers including Gassendi, Boyle, and Newton. While admitting that any attempt to answer the question concerning the real nature of things "will be full of scepticism and uncertainty," he asserts in the Appendix that he added to Book 3 that he himself is inclined to believe that there really is space without matter "as being more suitable to vulgar and popular notions" (T 1.2.5.26.n12/639). But this concession is quickly retracted, and he ends up by adopting "a fair confession of ignorance in subjects, that exceed all human capacity."

At the end of his discussion of space in his original text, Hume clearly adopts the stance of the Pyrrhonian skeptic: "My intention never was to penetrate into the nature of bodies, or explain the secret causes of their operation. For besides that this belongs not to my present purpose, I am afraid, that such an enterprise is beyond the reach of human understanding" (T 1.2.5.26/64). Like Sextus Empiricus and Bayle, Hume denies that he is making any claims about external objects. He is only describing the way objects appear and are thought about from different points of view. He is non-committal on the question of whether an improvement in our senses would reveal something between two objects where we presently detect nothing. Moreover, he admits that the invisible or intangible distance between the objects can be filled with visible or tangible objects without our being able to detect that any objects originally filling the space have been displaced. But these facts of experience only reveal "the manner in which objects affect the senses" and say nothing about the way space exists in itself apart from the way our senses are affected (T 1.2.5.25/63).

Still, it is important to recognize that, like Bayle, Hume makes an unequivocal claim concerning the nature of our *idea* of space: "we have no idea of any real extension without filling it with sensible objects, and conceiving its parts as visible or tangible" (T 1.2.5.27/64). Indeed, the main thrust of Hume's whole argument, including his application of the Copy Principle, was to prove that space without body is inconceivable. It might seem surprising that after taking so much trouble to establish the nature of our idea of space, Hume withholds judgment on whether it accurately represents space itself—and even states in his Appendix that he is inclined to accept the opposite view. But our surprise should disappear when we consider that a major aim of classical skeptics—at least of Academic skeptics—was to counter the claim of the Stoics that their clear and distinct "cataleptic impressions" provided a basis for knowledge.[13] In first establishing the nature of our clear and distinct idea of space—an idea that accords with that of the Cartesians[14]—and then acknowledging that it opposes our common-sense belief, Hume was stressing the limits of our human comprehension of reality.

II BELIEF IN BODY: RESOLVING THE PYRRHONIAN DOUBT IN FAVOR OF NATURAL JUDGMENT

Hume begins his discussion of our second topic, the nature of the objects of our senses, by denying that one can withhold belief in their independent existence. In the first paragraph of the *Treatise* section entitled "Of Scepticism Concerning the Senses," he writes that one "must assent to the principle concerning the existence of body," that "nature has not left this to . . . [our] choice," and that "we must take it for granted in all our reasonings" (T 1.4.2.1/187). It is true that, by the end of the section, after presenting two explanations of how the judgment arises through a "fiction" of the imagination, he admits that he is "*at present,* of a quite contrary sentiment" and is briefly inclined "to repose no faith at all in . . . [his] senses," but these doubts are quickly resolved when he reflects that as soon as he leaves his philosophical study and ceases his philosophical reflections, his doubts will vanish and he will "be persuaded that there is both an external and internal world" (T 1.4.2.56–7/217–18). He returns to the central project of Book 1 of the *Treatise,* that of discovering the principles of the imagination that account for our basic beliefs and inferences.

As noted at the beginning of this chapter, Kemp Smith claimed that sense perception in Hume's philosophy carries the mind beyond its immediate states to independently existing external bodies. In fact, Hume's account of "the SENSES" in "Of Scepticism with Regard to the Senses" leads to the opposite conclusion (T 1.4.2.3–13/188–93). Hume argues that our sense impressions are entirely subjective and mind-dependent and, hence, that we can have no impression-derived idea of objects that are independent of us. Although he does not explicitly appeal to the Copy Principle in this discussion, it is clear that its application leads to the conclusion that we have no legitimate impression-derived idea of an independent reality.

Hume presents an argument for the subjectivity of our sense impressions that has always seemed to me quite remarkable. He argues that since our sense impressions *really are* subjective and mind-dependent, they cannot *appear* otherwise. He writes that

> Every impression, external and internal, passions, affections, sensations, pains and pleasures, are originally on the same footing; . . . they appear, all of them, in their true colours, as impressions or perceptions. . . . Every thing that enters the mind, being in *reality* a perception, 'tis impossible any thing shou'd to *feeling* appear different. This were to suppose, that even where we are most intimately conscious, we might be mistaken. (T 1.4.2.7/190).

Hume does not appeal to a phenomenal account of the way objects appear to us—as independent and external—in order to determine their real nature. Rather, he argues from the real nature of sense impressions to a conclusion about the way they appear. As he states three paragraphs later, any conclusion about the independence of the objects of our senses "can never be an object of the senses; but any opinion we form concerning it, must be deriv'd from experience and observation" (T 1.4.2.10/191). Experience and observation lead us to the recognition that the objects of our senses are *really* mind-dependent.

It is sometimes said that Hume's conviction that our sense impressions are purely subjective is based on a "theory of ideas" that he merely accepts from his predecessors.[15] But there is good reason to think that his predecessors, including Locke, had a much richer notion of an *idea* than he did. Unlike Hume, they held that sense perceptions and their ideas *are* intrinsically intentional.[16] Hume bases his skepticism concerning the senses on "a few . . . experiments" that he anticipates in the discussion of the senses at the beginning of the section, but which he only presents later on (T 1.4.2.45/210–11). He describes an experiment in which one presses one's eyeball with one's finger and discovers that there are two images where there was one before. He argues that this double vision experiment shows that the immediate objects of sight "are dependent on our organs, and the disposition of our nerves and animal spirits." In contemporary parlance, the experiment shows that the impressions of our senses are mind- or brain-dependent. (In this context, Hume makes no distinction between mental and physical dependence.) He further remarks that "this experiment is confirm'd by the seeming encrease and diminution of objects, according to their distance"; by their changes of shape as they are viewed from different angles; by the changes of their qualities when we are ill; "and by an infinite number of other experiments of the same kind."[17] In short, Hume believes that these experiments show that our sensory impressions are neither spatially external to us, nor do they exist and operate independently of us.

Just like the belief in absolute space, the belief in the independent existence of body cannot be conceived through a clear and distinct idea. Although his argument is based on experience, unlike the key arguments of Berkeley,[18] Hume reaches the same conclusion concerning the inconceivability of external existence.

Hume's central goal in T 1.4.2 is to explain how the belief in independent existence of the objects of our senses arises through a "fiction" of the imagination. He begins his positive account by considering the features that distinguish the impressions to which we ascribe an independent existence from those, like pains, pleasures, passions, and affections, to which we do not. He calls these features "constancy" and "coherence" (T 1.4.2.18–19/194–5). Because he ends up relying mainly on *constancy* as the basis for our belief in independent existence, I focus here on that account.[19] Hume uses the term *constancy* to identify two different features of our sensory impressions.

First, Hume calls impressions *constant* when they repeat themselves in similar patterns after an interruption in observation. He reports that when he looks at the "mountains, and houses, and trees" outside the window of his study, then looks away, and then looks back again they return to him "without the least alteration" (T 1.4.2.18/194).

Or rather, to be more precise, *another* sensory impression appears to him that exactly resembles the earlier one. The first impression of the scene outside his window ceases to exist as soon as he looks away, and then, when he looks back, a new one appears that exactly resembles it.

The second feature of what Hume calls "constant" impressions becomes apparent as his exposition proceeds—namely, that during continuous observation these impressions do not change. Hume can observe those mountains, houses, and trees for some time without interruption, and the impression itself will remain unchanging. Such an observation becomes the source of the *fiction* of unchanging duration, or what in this section he calls "perfect identity" (T 1.4.2.24/199).

The core of Hume's explanation of our belief in the externality and independence of the objects of our senses lies in a principle of the imagination whereby we unconsciously substitute the second kind of constancy for the first. This principle, which I call the *identity substitution principle*,[20] is a corollary of the principle that he used to explain the belief in the vacuum, and Hume refers directly back to that principle in this discussion (T 1.4.2.32 n38/202 n1). In this case, the substitution occurs because of the resemblance between the two kinds of constancy—as well as the resemblance between the acts of mind by which we conceive of them. Hume judges that he is looking at the numerically identical mountain every time he looks out his window even if there is a long gap between his observations of these resembling perceptions. "This resemblance is observ'd in a thousand instances, and naturally connects together our ideas of these interrupted perceptions by the strongest relation, and conveys the mind with an easy transition from one to another" (T 1.4.2.35/204). "The passage betwixt related ideas is . . . so smooth and easy, that it . . . seems like the continuation of the same action" of the mind (T 1.4.2.34/204). The result is that we disguise the interruption of the sensible perceptions of the mountain and believe that we are perceiving a perfectly identical and unchanging continuous object.

However, we cannot completely overlook the fact that we do not continue to perceive the object during the time when it is not observed. To avoid the "contradiction" that results from the way the objects appear to us and the way they are conceived by way of the identity substitution principle, we postulate "the fiction of a continu'd existence" (T 1.4.2.36–7/205 and T 1.4.2.43/209). We suppose that the "interrupted perceptions are connected by a real existence, of which we are insensible" (T 1.4.2.24/199). This supposition is the source of the judgment that the objects of our senses exist independently of us. It is only at the final stage of Hume's account that he argues that "a vivacity" is bestowed "on that fiction" by way of its connection with our memories of constant impressions—for example, the mountain outside his window (T 1.4.2.42/209). The trick has already been performed by the imagination at the second and third stages of his account, where one kind of constancy was substituted for the other and the fiction of the unperceived existence was formed to resolve the contradiction.

Thus, as in his discussion of space, Hume lays out a direct opposition between the conclusion we reach on the basis of the Copy Principle and the conclusion generated through a "fiction" or "illusion" of the imagination. But, unlike that case, he argues that we cannot withhold belief in the natural judgment generated by the imagination.

It is true that this primary belief in the reality of our sense impressions is corrected by philosophers who, on the basis of the "few simple experiments," ascribe the continued and independent existence to a second object of our senses that is the *cause* of our sense impressions:

> They change their system, and distinguish, (as we shall do for the future) betwixt perceptions and objects, of which the former are suppos'd to be interrupted, and perishing, and different at every return; the latter to be uninterrupted, and to preserve a continu'd existence and identity. (T 1.4.2.46/211)

Hume then proceeds with his skeptical critique of this philosophical system, although it must be said, *not* on grounds of its falsity; for it does correct the false claim of the natural direct realist view of common sense—namely that our impressions themselves are external and independent objects. But he stresses that philosophers have no independent way of proving the existence of the external object, now considered a distinct object that causes and (at least in some respects) resembles the impression. They borrow the illusion or fiction generated by the imagination, which makes them believe in the continued and independent existence of the represented object of the senses (T 1.4.2.46–55/211–17). Thus this philosophical or scientific view of the senses *"has no primary recommendation, either to reason or imagination, but acquires all its influence on the imagination"* from the natural judgment.[21]

III HUME'S SKEPTICAL CAUSAL REALISM

The main controversy concerning the interpretation of Hume as a skeptical realist has turned on the claim that he is a realist concerning causal power.[22] Since the publication of an article by Ken Winkler in *The Philosophical Review* in 1991, this interpretation has come to be known as "the New Hume" (Winkler 2007). The name has stuck, although it is historically inaccurate.[23] There is nothing new in the claim that Hume was committed to the existence of objective causal power or necessary connection between cause and effect. Three years after the publication of the work we now know as *An Enquiry Concerning Human Understanding*, his friend Henry Home (later Lord Kames) published an essay in which he argued that Hume's frequent references to secret or unknown causal powers showed that he had "an idea of power as a quality in bodies,"—and that in making these references he acknowledged "the reality of this power" (Kames 1751: 291). The controversy between Kames and Hume turned on the question of whether we have an *idea* of causal power as it exists in objects independently of us, not on the question of the reality of such power. Two years later, another contemporary Scottish critic—John Stewart, professor of natural philosophy at the University of Edinburgh—published an essay in which he assumed that Hume, like

Kames, was committed to the existence of *active powers* in matter, and he argued that Hume had mistakenly ascribed such a view to Newton.[24] Thomas Reid wrote to James Gregory in the 1780s that it is "remarkable that Mr Hume, after taking so many pains to prove that we have no idea of necessary connection, should impute to the bulk of mankind the opinion of a necessary connection between physical causes and their effects" (Reid 2002: 253). Reid says that he cannot understand how Hume could ascribe this belief to people "without an idea of necessary connection." The question for Hume's eighteenth-century critics was *not* whether he ascribed power or necessary connection to objects independent of us, but rather how he thought this could be done without an idea.[25]

As Kames pointed out, throughout his discussion of causality and causal inference in the *Enquiry*, Hume presupposes the existence of the hidden or unknown powers and forces of nature and even asserts that the regularities we perceive in ordinary life depend on their existence. Hume writes of the "ultimate springs and principles [which] are totally shut up from human curiosity and enquiry" (EU 4.12/30), of the hidden "powers and principles on which the influence of . . . objects entirely depends" (EU 4.16/33), of "the power or force, which actuates the whole machine" of nature that "is entirely concealed from us, and never discovers itself in any of the sensible qualities of body" (EU 7.8/63–4), and of our lack of access to "the secret connexion, which binds . . . [cause and effect] together, and renders them inseparable" (EU 7.13/66). In his *Treatise*, he writes of "the ultimate force and efficacy of nature [which] is perfectly unknown to us" (T 1.3.14.8/159). The examples may be multiplied. In his most striking statement in the *Enquiry*, Hume writes that nature has "implanted in us an instinct, which carries forward the thought in a correspondent course to that which she has established among external objects; though we are ignorant of those powers and forces, on which this regular course and succession of objects totally depends" (EU 5.22/55). At the same time as he expresses ignorance of the nature of the powers and forces that underlie the regularity that we observe in nature, he presupposes their existence and claims that the regularity we perceive in nature depends on them.

Hume held that, in experimental science as well as ordinary life, we assume the existence of such powers after finding constant conjunctions of cause and effect. He wrote that "we always presume, when we see like sensible qualities, that they have like secret powers, and expect, that effects, similar to those, which we have experienced, will follow from them" (EU 4.16/33). He cites as examples of these "secret powers" the "force or power" of inertia, as well as the power contained in substances that have the color and consistency of bread. When we observe regularity, we not only draw inferences to similar effects in the future, but we also postulate "like secret powers" that authorize the inference.[26]

At the same time as he admits the existence of these powers, Hume argued that we have no positive impression-derived idea of them. Like absolute space and the independent existence of body, he denied that objective causal power or necessity can be conceived though a clear and distinct idea. In the *Treatise*, his application of the Copy Principle led him to deny that the key component of the idea of causality—namely, the "necessary connection" between causes and their effects—arises from the sensory input of external objects.[27] Our sensory impressions of cause and effect reveal only that they are successive and contiguous in space and time. In the Appendix to the *Treatise*, he argued that "no internal impression has an apparent energy, more than external objects" and that our idea of causality does not arise from reflection on the operations of our own minds (T 1.3.14.12/633). His discussion of the idea of necessary connection in Section 7 of the first *Enquiry* focused on this claim. Here, he wrote that "the power or energy" by which our wills cause the motion of our bodies "like that in other natural events, is unknown and inconceivable" (EU 7.15/67).

Hume traced the idea we have of causal power or necessary connection to a purely subjective impression that arises as a result of our experience of one kind of object followed by another in a number of instances. He stressed that this impression is nothing but an "internal impression, or impression of reflection" that arises from the "propensity, which custom produces, to pass from an object to the idea of its usual attendant" (T 1.3.14.22/165). Because we never perceive any necessity in objects, we must "draw the idea of it from what we feel internally in contemplating them" (T 1.3.14.28/169). It is the feeling of connection arising from constant experience that is the source of our idea of necessary connection; that is, of the power by which the cause produces the effect. However, according to the Copy Principle this idea cannot be legitimately applied to external objects: "The ideas of necessity, of power, and of efficacy" that arise from constant experience "represent not any thing, that does or can belong to the objects, which are constantly conjoined" (T 1.3.14.19/164). In the *Treatise*, Hume sometimes appears to be asserting that we have knowledge of causal power or necessary connection in the operations of the mind itself, but this is not his considered view.[28] He writes that "the uniting principle among our internal perceptions is as *unintelligible* as that among external objects" (T 1.3.14.29/169; emphasis added). The impression-derived idea of power or necessity does not represent the power by which any cause, physical or mental, produces its effect.

Thus, on Hume's view, we have no more of an idea of objective causal power than we do of the existence of absolute space or the independent existence of the objects of our senses. Yet Hume clearly refers to such powers and holds that we naturally believe that they exist. As in those other cases, he attributes the belief in objective power to the workings of the imagination. In the *Treatise*, he explains "why we suppose necessity and power to lie in the objects we consider, not in our mind, that considers them" (T 1.3.14.25/167). The explanation lies in the "great propensity" of our mind "to spread itself on external objects, and to conjoin with them any internal impressions, which they occasion, and which always make their appearance at the same time that these objects discover themselves to the senses." Hume goes on to state that the belief in the objectivity of necessity is "so riveted in the mind" of his readers that they will treat his theory of the subjective origin of the idea of necessity or power as "extravagant and ridiculous" (T 1.3.14.26/167).

Hume's explanation of the natural judgment of objective causal power in the first *Enquiry* dispenses with the projective principle postulated in the *Treatise*. Hume writes that "when one particular species of event has always, in all instances, been conjoined with another . . . we suppose, that there is some connexion between them; some power in the one, by which it infallibly produces the other, and operates with the greatest certainty, and strongest necessity" (EU 7.27/75). Here, it is events that contain the power and necessity, not subjective perceptions. The power is located in the world, not merely in the mind that observes the events. Because in common life we make no distinction between our subjective perceptions and external objects, it makes sense that we would immediately judge that the events themselves are inseparable after we have experienced a universal conjunction of similar events.[29]

The natural supposition of objective power, no less than that of absolute space and the independent existence of body, is based on a systematic confusion of ideas. In his *Treatise*, Hume wrote that when people have found objects constantly united together in their experience, custom makes it so "difficult to separate the ideas, [that] they are apt to fancy such a separation to be in itself impossible and absurd" (T 1.4.3.9/223). That is to say, we mistake a purely associational connection for an objective connection that would give us insight into the relation between the cause and the effect.[30] Habit binds "the objects in the closest and most intimate manner to each other, so as to make us imagine them to be absolutely inseparable" (T 1.3.9.10/112).[31] It is only philosophers who are able to abstract from the effects of association, who come to recognize that "even in the most familiar events, the energy of the cause, is as unintelligible as in the most unusual" (EU 7.21/70).

In the famous skeptical Conclusion to Book 1 of the *Treatise,* Hume considers the question of whether our natural propensity to judge that power exists in objects gives us a legitimate ground of assent—although his answer is not without ambiguity. After explaining the paradoxes resulting from the fact that the idea we have of causal power is derived from a subjective impression (T 1.4.7.5/266–7), Hume states that "this deficiency in our ideas" of cause and effect "is not . . . perceiv'd in *common life*" and that "we are as *ignorant* of the ultimate principle, which binds them together" in the most usual as in the most extraordinary cases (T 1.4.7.6/267; emphasis added). He attributes this inability to recognize our *ignorance* to "an illusion of the imagination," namely the projection of the subjective feeling of inseparability onto external objects (i.e., the propensity that he had explained in Section 14 of Part 3 of Book 1). He then proceeds to ask the question "how far we ought to yield to [such] . . . illusions." He states that this "reduces us to a very dangerous dilemma, which-ever way we answer it" and goes on to argue that although we must reject the trivial qualities that have led to "the flights of imagination" of philosophers, we must in other cases rely on them, as we certainly must do in the case of the belief in the independent and continuous existence of body.[32]

Hume's many references to secret and unknown powers, particularly in his *Enquiry Concerning Human Understanding,* suggest that, just like our belief in the independent and continuous existence of body, our pre-philosophical belief in objective power survives the doubts generated by the Copy Principle. The Humean philosopher, like common sense, is committed to the existence of objective causal power. However, unlike common sense, she believes that its nature is unintelligible to us.

In making a judgment about Hume's own commitment as a philosopher to the reality of objective causal power, it is useful to consider his criticism of those in his day who actually *did* deny the existence of power and necessary connection in matter. It is frequently claimed that Hume only criticized the *occasionalists'* view that the Deity is the only locus of power in the universe and accepted their claim that physical causation only consists in regularity.[33] But a careful attention to Hume's arguments against this view, in both the *Treatise* and the *Enquiry*, indicate that he not only rejected their claim to be able to prove that the Deity is the only power in the universe, but also their claim to prove that there is no power in the material world.

It is well understood that the Cartesians argued on the basis of their idea of matter as pure extension that matter cannot think.[34] But Hume claims that they drew a further conclusion about the physical world from their analysis of the idea of matter as an extended being:

> The *Cartesians* . . . having establish'd it as a principle, that we are perfectly acquainted with the essence of matter, have very naturally inferr'd, that it is endow'd with no efficacy, and that 'tis impossible for it of itself to communicate motion, or produce any of those effects which we ascribe to it. (T 1.3.14.8/159)

I have not been able to find this precise argument in any Cartesian writer,[35] but Malebranche comes pretty close when he writes that

> the idea we have of all bodies makes us aware that they cannot move themselves. . . . Bodies have no action, and when a ball that is moved collides with and moves another, it communicates to it nothing of its own, for it does not itself have the force it communicates to it. . . . A natural cause is therefore not a real and true but only an occasional cause. (1674–5/1997: 448)

Malebranche argues on the basis of the idea of matter that there is no force or power in it. He goes on to claim that one can infer from the idea of God that God is the only power or force in the universe.[36] Hume refutes this argument on the basis of his Copy Principle: "If every idea be deriv'd from an impression, the idea of a deity proceeds from the same origin; and if no impression, either of sensation or reflection, implies any force or efficacy, 'tis equally impossible to discover or even imagine any such active principle in the deity." The Cartesians, he claims, are then left with the conclusion that there is no force or power anywhere in the universe. However, he tells them how they may *avoid* this absurd conclusion:

> If they esteem that opinion absurd and impious, as it really is, I shall tell them how they may avoid it; and that is, by concluding from the very first, that they have *no adequate idea of power or efficacy in any object*; since neither in body nor spirit . . . are they able to discover one single instance of it. (T 1.3.14.19/160; emphasis added)

To say that ideas are *not adequate* is to say that they give "a partial, or incomplete representation of those archetypes to which they are referred" (Locke 1689/1975: 2.13.1).[37] In response to Malebranche's claim that we can infer from our idea of matter that there are only *occasional causes* or, what amounts to the same thing, *regular conjunctions* in the physical world, Hume argues that our idea of matter gives us only a partial or incomplete representation of its object.

Like the question of absolute space, there was an ongoing dispute about the existence of active power or force in matter in Hume's own day (EU 7.25 n16/73n1).[38] In 1733, six years before the publication of his *Treatise*, his neighbor Andrew Baxter published a book in which he argued on the basis of Newtonian physics that matter must be completely passive and can therefore contain no force or power (Baxter 1733).[39] Baxter wrote that "a resistance to any change of its present state is essential to matter, and inconsistent with any active power in it" (1733: 1). Like the Cartesians, he argued that all the effects that people tend to ascribe to inherent powers of bodies are in fact "immediately produced by the power of an immaterial Being" (1733: 36). However, unlike the Cartesians, Baxter argued that we derive knowledge of power from reflection on our own acts of volition. When Hume asks rhetorically in his first *Enquiry* whether it "is more difficult to conceive, that motion may arise from impulse, than that it may arise from volition?" he may well have had the view of Baxter in mind (EU 7.25/73). Hume holds that it is equally possible that there are active powers in matter as well as mind, although we are ignorant of them in both cases. He denies that our ignorance is a good reason to reject the existence of power in either kind of object.

In the original version of the note to this *Enquiry* discussion of *occasionalism*, Hume claimed that Sir Isaac Newton did not mean "to rob Matter of all force and energy" although some of his followers have ascribed that view to him.[40] He commended Newton for putting forward the hypothesis of an "ethereal active Matter" to explain universal attraction. Is this not good evidence that, as a philosopher, Hume himself was prepared to ascribe power to matter, in spite of the contrary evidence of our impression-derived idea of power? He goes on to deny that the *occasionalist* view that there is no power in matter—and thus the view that causality in objects is nothing but regularity—was ever adopted by English philosophers. He mentions in particular the views of Locke, Clarke, and Cudworth, and asks "by what means has it become so prevalent among our modern metaphysicians?" *We* need to ask how this view came to be ascribed to Hume himself.

IV Conclusion

In the 2007 Postscript to his article "The New Hume," Kenneth Winkler (2007: 77) writes that he is "doubtful about the New Hume because it makes Hume too much like Reid." He argues that Reid loses "the critical edge or curiosity" that he (Winkler) "finds so appealing in Hume's philosophy." Reid is satisfied in simply asserting that our ideas of external objects such as extension and hardness are originally *suggested* by sensations without investigating the cause of this connection (Reid 1997: 38 et passim), whereas Hume digs deeper into the cause of the intelligibility we naturally ascribe to the relation between sensations and their corresponding ideas.[41]

I believe that the interpretation of Hume as a skeptical realist gives us a much deeper understanding of the radical difference between the philosophies of Hume and Reid, while at the same time giving us a clear understanding of just how the Common-Sense philosophy of Reid evolved from that of Hume. As is often pointed out, Hume no less than Reid accepted the beliefs of common sense, although he held that they must be corrected through philosophical reflection. Hume wrote in his first *Enquiry* that the mitigated skepticism that he adopts checks Pyrrhonian doubt through "*common sense* and reflection" (EU 12.24/161; emphasis added). But it does so only in a limited way ("in some measure"). For Reid, unlike Hume, both common sense and philosophy have "clear and distinct conceptions" of external bodies that are wholly unlike any impressions.[42] Moreover, he eliminated skepticism by arguing that there is no opposition between the natural judgments of common sense and philosophy.[43] For Hume, on the other hand, that opposition never entirely disappears. It is maintained through the recognition that however much our common-sense beliefs are corrected by reason, they still remain cognitively opaque and directly opposed to conclusions based on our clear and distinct impression-derived ideas.

In denying that we can gain insight into the nature of reality, Hume adopted a major tenet of classical Academic skepticism. In contrast to Pyrrhonian skeptics who simply suspended judgment concerning the external world, the Academics accepted probable judgments while denying that they can be comprehended. Sextus Empiricus wrote that "the adherents of the New Academy . . . differ from the Sceptics [i.e., the Pyrrhonians] precisely in saying that everything is inapprehensible" (1994: I.33: 59.) Similarly, Cicero wrote that the proponent of the New Academy "follows many things probable, that he has not grasped [*non comprehensa*], nor perceived nor assented to but that possess verisimilitude."[44] He went on to note that if one failed to accept such incomprehensible probabilities "all life would be done away with." They provide the Academic philosopher "with a canon of judgment both in the conduct of life and in philosophical investigation" (1933: 508–509). Hume was echoing Cicero when he wrote in his *Abstract* that his aim was to explain "probabilities, and those other measures of evidence on which life and action entirely depend, and which are our guides even in most of our philosophical speculations" (TA 4/646-7).

Hume is a cognitive skeptic: he holds that reality is at bottom unintelligible to human beings. Our clear and distinct ideas are limited by the fact that they originate in our impressions, and our impressions themselves are narrowly circumscribed. At the same time, under the influence of the imagination we naturally form *suppositions* about the nature of reality that take us beyond these impressions and their corresponding ideas.[45] Hume writes that, through an "irregular kind of reasoning from experience" we come to "discover a connexion or repugnance betwixt objects, which extends not to impressions"

(T 1.4.5.20/242). As I have argued in this chapter, it is through such suppositions and irregular reasoning that we come to judge that there is absolute space, that the objects of our senses really exist independently of us, and that there are causal powers that underlie the regularities we perceive. Hume's own texts give us good reason to think that he found the latter two beliefs irresistible and as necessary in philosophy as in common life.

ABBREVIATIONS OF WORKS CITED

EU   *An Enquiry Concerning Human Understanding*. Edited by T. L. Beauchamp. Oxford: Clarendon, 2000.

T   *A Treatise of Human Nature*. Edited by D. F. Norton & M. J. Norton. Oxford: Clarendon, 2007.

TA   *An Abstract of a Treatise of Human Nature*. Reprinted in T.

NOTES

1. The main themes I am stressing here go back to Smith (1905). See Wright (2007b: esp. 18–20).
2. This expression is commonly used in the secondary literature for Hume's principle that ideas must be derived from impressions since Don Garrett (1997: esp. chapter 2) coined it.
3. In his discussion of the ideas of space and time and of the belief in the independent existence of body, Hume uses this term in a technical sense for an idea that is used to represent a perception other than that from which it is derived. Hume explains this use when he writes that "ideas always represent the objects or impressions, from which they are deriv'd, and can never without a fiction represent or be apply'd to any other" (T 1.2.3.11/37).
4. See, e.g., T 1.4.2.56/217, where he attributes the belief in the external world to "a gross illusion," and T 1.4.7.6/267, where he attributes our belief in the objective existence of power or necessary connection to "an illusion of the imagination."
5. This expression is from Hume's letter to Gilbert Elliot of March 10, 1751, where he implies that belief in our senses and experience form a "legitimate Ground of Assent," unlike the belief in the design argument. See Wright (2012: esp. 128–130).
6. However, the Pyrrhonian does not suspend judgment in the *existence* of external objects: Sextus writes that "When we investigate whether existing things are such as they appear, we grant that they appear" (1994, I, 10: 8).
7. Compare the first *Enquiry*: "Though a PYRRHONIAN may throw himself or others into a momentary amazement and confusion by his profound reasonings; the first and most trivial event in life will put to flight to all his doubts and scruples" (EU 12.23/160).
8. Compare EU 12.21/158 and T 1.4.1.7–9/183–4; T 1.4.2.57/218; and T 1.4.7.8–10/268–70.
9. See T 1.4.2.1/187; T 1.4.2.50/50; T 1.4.2.57/218.
10. Hume to Michael Ramsay, August 31, 1737, in Kozanecki (1963: 133–134).
11. Note this unrestricted formulation of the Copy Principle; Hume does not, as he did in the opening pages of the *Treatise*, restrict it to *simple* ideas copying and being caused by *simple* impressions (T 1.1.1.7/4). It has been noted by various commentators that the original principle does not apply to the impressions and ideas of space and time, which are compound.

It is significant that, in the later formulations of the principle in both the *Abstract* and in his first *Enquiry*, Hume no longer restricts it to simple perceptions (TA 6–7/647–8; EU 2.9/21–2). See Coventry (2010) and Falkenstein (1997).

12. This is denied by Kemp Smith who claims that Hume followed Hutcheson's view that space and time are "non-sensational". Hutcheson held that extension is a concomitant idea that accompanies sensations (Smith 1941: 273–281). Against Kemp Smith's interpretation, see also Falkenstein (1997).

13. See Cicero, *Academica*, II (1933: 506–509), Stough (1969: ch.3, esp. 40), and Frede (2005: esp. 300–313).

14. See Descartes, *Principles of Philosophy* II, esp. §§16–18 (1985–91: 229–230), where he denies the existence of a vacuum on the basis of an analysis our idea of space.

15. The view that Hume relies on a "theory of ideas" deriving from his predecessors was originally put forward in Thomas Reid's *An Inquiry into the Human Mind on the Principles of Common Sense* (1764).

16. See, for example, Ayers (1986), Chappell (1994: esp. 31–35), John Mackie (1985: 223), and John Yolton (1984: esp. ch. 5). Contrast Hume's claim that "the reference of the idea to an object . . . [is] an extraneous denomination, of which in itself it bears no mark or character" (T 1.1.7.6/20).

17. He relies solely on the first of these confirming "experiments" in his first *Enquiry* (EU 12.9/152).

18. Berkeley (1710/1949), part I, sect. 2: "As to what is said of the absolute existence of unthinking things without any relation to their being perceived, that seems perfectly unintelligible. Their *esse* is *percipi*, nor is it possible they should have any existence, out of the minds . . . which perceive them."

19. For a complete discussion of "Of scepticism with regard to the senses," including his account of "coherence" as the basis for the belief in independent existence of body, see Wright (2009: 135–156, esp. 142–53). See also Loeb (2002: 177–214).

20. See Wright (2009: esp. 53, 132, 146–51, 156, 158–166).

21. On Hume's acceptance of this philosophical system, in spite of these skeptical arguments, see Wright (2009: 58–60, 151–153).

22. See Wright (1983: esp. ch. 4). This view was given strong support in Strawson (1989).

23. As we have seen, the view that Hume was a causal realist was firmly supported by Kemp Smith who called it a "natural belief." He wrote that the view Hume is "endeavouring to justify" in his sections entitled "Of the Idea of Necessary Connexion" is "not a uniformity view of causation, but a view in which causal agency—power, efficacy, determination—is presupposed throughout" (1941: 393).

24. See my "The Scientific Reception of Hume's Theory of Causation: Establishing the Positivist Interpretation in Early Nineteenth-Century Scotland" (2005b: 329–333).

25. The tradition that holds that Hume denied the existence of objective causal powers and reduced causal power to regularity took root in the nineteenth century after the publication of Thomas Brown's *Observations on the Nature and Tendency of the Doctrine of Mr. Hume, Concerning the Relation of Cause and Effect* (1805) and was taken up by positivist writers of the nineteenth and twentieth centuries who regarded Hume as a forerunner of their own views. Brown himself recognized that his interpretation suppressed the skeptical tendencies of Hume's philosophy. See Wright (2005b: esp. 340–344).

26. Hume added a footnote to this passage in the second edition of 1750, probably in response to Kames's criticism. For a discussion of this note and its reference to another note added

in the same edition, where Hume gives an accurate explanation of his use of the term "power," see Wright (2012:, esp.126–128). These notes are, I believe, misunderstood by Winkler (2007: 54–55), who argues that they authorize a "retrospective reinterpretation" of Hume's references to "secret powers" as references to unknown regularities.

27. He writes that "there is a NECESSARY CONNEXION to be taken into consideration; and that relation is of much greater importance, than any of the other two above-mention'd," namely, priority of the cause to the effect and their contiguity in space and time (T 1.3.2.11/77.

28. He writes, for example, that "upon the whole, necessity is something, that exists in the mind, not in objects" (T 1.3.14.22/165; cf. T 1.3.14.23/166). He even says at one point that there is a "real intelligible connexion" that is to be found in the mind of the experienced observer of a cause and its effect (T 1.3.14.27/168). See Wright (2009: 115–118, 120–122) regarding the ambiguity in Hume's discussion.

29. That is, we are all naturally direct realists in our unreflective lives. See EU 12.7–8/151–2 and T 1.4.2.31–45/201–11.

30. This interpretation of Hume is given by Kant (1783: 7) in his *Prolegomena*.

31. Thus, the nature of belief in causal necessity is similar to belief in necessary truths where, according to Hume, "the person, who assents, not only conceives the ideas according to the proposition, but is necessarily determin'd to conceive them in that particular manner" (see T 1.3.7.3/95).

32. Hume calls the qualities that make us believe in the continued and independent existence of bodes "trivial" at T 1.4.2.56/217.

33. For a recent interpretation of the relation of Hume and Malebranche along these lines, see Ott (2009: part IV, esp. 222–229).

34. See Descartes (1985–1991: II, 64).

35. Perhaps the closest is Louis de la Forge, in his *Treatise of the Human Mind* (1666/1997: 239–240). La Forge writes that there is no way that a body could "move itself or its neighbor" if God removed all motion from matter "because the extension in which consists the nature of body in general, and which is the only quality that remains with it in this state, is in no respect active." I owe this reference to Andrew Platt.

36. Malebranche wrote that "when one thinks of the idea of God, i.e. of an infinitely perfect and consequently all-powerful being, one knows that there is . . . a [necessary] connection between His will and the motion of all bodies, that it is impossible to conceive that He wills a body to be moved and that this body not be moved" (1674–5/1997: 448–449).

37. Hume makes the *adequacy* of ideas a necessary condition for knowledge at T 1.2.2.1/29.

38. Hume asks why the view that matter is without any power has "become so prevalent among our modern metaphysicians." As well as Baxter, he probably had Berkeley in mind. In his *Siris*, published in 1744, Berkeley claimed that the Newtonian attraction does not require "real forces to exist in bodies (1744: §246).

39. For an extensive discussion of Baxter with speculations on his critique of Hume, see Russell (2008: esp. 20–23, 150–154).

40. See EU 7.16 n16/73 n1 and the Editorial Appendix to this note in the Clarendon edition of the *Enquiry*, p. 249. As a result of the criticisms of John Stewart, Hume changed these phrases to "to rob *second causes* of all force and energy" and "ethereal active *fluid*" in the third edition of the *Philosophical Essays* of 1766. See Wright (1983: 162, 183–184 n51).

41. See Hume's discussion of abstraction and distinctions of reason at T 1.1.7/17–25 and especially T 1.1.7.18/25.

42. Reid wrote that "we have clear and distinct conceptions of extension, figure, motion, and other attributes of body which are neither sensations, nor like any sensation" (1765/1997: 76).

43. See Wright (2005*a*).

44. "Etenim is quoque qui a vobis sapiens inducitur multa sequitur probabilia, non comprehensa neque percepta neque adsensa sed similia veri" (Cicero, *Academica*, 1933: 594–595). Compare *Academica*, 1933: 620–621, where Lucullus tentatively accepts the judgments of the Stoics while insisting that they cannot be "'grasped' [comprehendi] and perceived." This passage is quoted in Note A of Bayle's article on "Carnaedes" in his *Dictionary Historical and Critical* (1735: Vol. 2, 326).

45. See Wright (2007*a*: 89–90) and T 1.2.6.9/68; T 1.4.2.56/218; T 1.4.5.20/241–2. Hume's distinction between what we can suppose and what we can conceive was pointed out by Jan Wilbanks (1968: 81–82).

BIBLIOGRAPHY

Ayers, M. R. (1986). "Are Locke's 'Ideas' Images, Intentional Objects or Natural Signs?" *Locke Newsletter* 17, 3–36.

Bayle, Pierre. (1735). *The Dictionary Historical and Critical of Mr. Peter Bayle*, 5 vols., edited and translated by Pierre Des Maizeau, 2nd ed. London.

Baxter, Andrew. (1733). *An Enquiry into the Nature of the human Soul; wherein the immateriality of the soul is evinced from the principles of reason and philosophy.* London: James Bettenham.

Baxter, D. L. M. (2006). "Identity, Continued Existence and the External World," in S. Traiger, ed., *The Blackwell Guide to Hume's Treatise.* Oxford: Blackwell.

Baxter, D. L. M. (2009). "Hume's Theory of Space and Time in Its Skeptical Context," in D. F. Norton and J. Taylor, eds., *The Cambridge Companion to Hume.* Cambridge: Cambridge University Press.

Bayle, Pierre. (1735). *The Dictionary Historical and Critical of Mr. Peter Bayle*, translated and edited by Pierre Des Maizeaux. London: J. J. and P. Knapton, vol. 2.

Bayle, Pierre. (1965). *Historical and Critical Dictionary: Selections*, edited by R. H. Popkin and C. Brush. Indianapolis: Bobbs-Merrill.

Berkeley, George. (1710/1949). *A Treatise concerning the Principles of Human Knowledge, in The Works of George Berkeley, Bishop of Cloyne*, edited by A. A. Luce and T. E. Jessop, vol. 2. London: Nelson.

Berkeley, George. (1744). *Siris: A Chain of Philosophical Reflexions and Inquiries Concerning the Virtues of Tar Water, and diverse other Subjects arising one from another*, 2nd ed. London.

Brown, Thomas. (1805). *Observations on the Nature and Tendency of the Doctrine of Mr. Hume, Concerning the Relation of Cause and Effect.* Edinburgh.

Buckle, S. (2001). *Hume's Enlightenment Tract: The Unity and Purpose of An Enquiry concerning Human Understanding.* Oxford: Clarendon Press.

Chappell, V. (1994). "Locke's Theory of Ideas," in V. Chappell, ed., *The Cambridge Companion to Locke.* Cambridge: Cambridge University Press, 26–55.

Cicero. (1933). *Academica, in Cicero*, 28 vols., translated by H. Rackham. Cambridge, MA: Harvard University Press, vol. xix, 411–658.

Coventry, A. (2010). "Hume's System of Space and Time," in *Logical Analysis and the History of Philosophy*, vol. 13, 76–89.

Craig, E. (2007) "Hume on Causality: Projectivist and Realist," in R. Read and K. Richman, eds., *The New Hume Debate*, 2nd ed. London: Routledge, 113–121.

Descartes, René. (1985–91). *The Philosophical Writings of Descartes*, translated by J. Cottingham et al., 3 vols. Cambridge: Cambridge University Press.

Falkenstein, L. (1997). "Hume on Manners of Disposition and the Ideas of Space and Time," *Archiv für Geschichte der Philosophie* 79, Bd.179–201.

Frede, M. (2005). "Stoic Epistemology," in K. Algra et al., eds., *Hellenistic Philosophy*. Cambridge: Cambridge University Press, 295–322.

Garrett, D. (1997). *Cognition and Commitment in Hume's Philosophy*. Oxford: Oxford University Press.

Kant, I. (1783). *Prolegomena to any Future Metaphysics That Will Be Able to Come Forward as Science*, edited and translated by Gary Hatfield. Cambridge: Cambridge University Press, 2004.

Kozanecki, T. (1963). "Dawida Hume'a Nieznane Listy W Zbiorach Muzeum Czartoryskich (Polska)," *Archiwum Historii Filozofii Spolecznej* 9, 127–141.

Kail, Peter. (2007). *Projection and Realism in Hume's Philosophy*. Oxford: Oxford University Press.

Kames, Lord [Home, Henry]. (1751). *Essays on the Principles of Morality and Religion*. Edinburgh.

La Forge, Louis de. (1666/1997). *Treatise on the Human Mind*, translated and edited by D. M. Clarke. Dortrecht: Kluwer Academic.

Locke, J. (1689/1975). *An Essay Concerning Human Understanding*, edited by P. H. Nidditch. Oxford: Clarendon Press.

Loeb, L. E. (2002). *Stability and Justification in Hume's Treatise*. Oxford: Oxford University Press.

Malebranche, Nicolas. (1674–5/1997). *The Search after Truth*, edited and translated by T. M. Lennon and P. J. Olscamp. Cambridge: Cambridge University Press.

Malebranche, Nicolas. (1688/1997). *Dialogues on Metaphysics and on Religion*, edited and translated by Nicolas Jolley and David Scott. Cambridge: Cambridge University Press.

Mackie, J. L. (1985). "Locke and Representative Perception," in J. L. Mackie, ed., *Logic and Knowledge: Selected Papers*, vol. 1. Oxford: Oxford University Press.

Pierris, G. de. (2002). "Causation as a Philosophical Relation in Hume," *Philosophy and Phenomenological Research* 64 (3), 499–545.

Read, R., and K. A. Richman (eds.). (2007). *The New Hume Debate*, 2nd ed. London: Routledge.

Reid, Thomas (1764/1997). *An Inquiry into the Human Mind on the Principles of Common Sense*, ed. D. R. Brookes. Edinburgh: Edinburgh University Press.

Reid, Thomas. (2002). *The Correspondence of Thomas Reid*, ed. Paul Wood. Edinburgh: Edinburgh University Press.

Russell, P. (2008). *The Riddle of Hume's Treatise: Skepticism, Naturalism, and Irreligion*. Oxford: Oxford University Press.

Sextus Empiricus. (1994). *Sextus Empiricus: Outlines of Scepticism*, edited by Julia Annas and Jonathan Barnes. Cambridge: Cambridge University Press.

Smith, N. Kemp. (1905). "The Naturalism of Hume," *Mind* n.s. 14, 149–173, 335–347.

Smith, N. Kemp. (1941). *The Philosophy of David Hume: A Critical Study of Its Origins and Central Doctrines*. London: Macmillan.

Strawson, G. (1989). *The Secret Connexion: Causation, Realism and David Hume*. Oxford: Clarendon Press.

Strawson, G. (2007). "David Hume: Objects and Power," in R. Read and K. A. Richman, eds., *The New Hume Debate*, 2nd ed. London: Routledge, 31–51.

Stough, C. (1969). *Greek Scepticism*. Berkeley: University of California Press.

Ott, Walter. (2009). *Causation & Laws of Nature in Early Modern Philosophy*. Oxford: Oxford University Press.

Voltaire. (1733). *Letters Concerning the English Nation*. London.

Wilbanks, J. (1968). *Hume's Theory of the Imagination*. The Hague: Martinus Nijhoff.

Winkler, K. P. (2007). "The New Hume," in R. Read and K. A. Richman, eds., *The New Hume Debate*, 2nd ed. London: Routledge, 52–87.

Wright, J. P. (1983). *The Sceptical Realism of David Hume*. Manchester & Minneapolis: Manchester University Press/University of Minnesota Press.

Wright, J. P. (2005a). "Reid's answer to Hume's Scepticism: Turning Science into Common Sense," in E. Mazza and E. Ronchetti, eds., *Instruction and Amusement: Le ragioni dell' Illuminismo brittanico*. Padova: Il Poligrafo, 143–163.

Wright, J. P. (2005b). "The Scientific Reception of Hume's Theory of Causality: Establishing the Positivist Interpretation in Early Nineteenth-Century Scotland," in P. Jones, ed., *The Reception of David Hume in Europe*. Bristol: Thommes-Continuum. 327–347, 396–398.

Wright, J. P. (2007a). "Hume's Causal Realism: Recovering a Traditional Interpretation," in R. Read and K. A. Richman, eds., *The New Hume Debate*, 2nd ed. 88–90.

Wright, J. P. (2007b). "Kemp Smith and the Two Kinds of Naturalism in Hume's Philosophy," in E. Ronchetti and E. Mazza, eds., *New Essays on David Hume*. Milan: Franco Angelli. 17–35.

Wright, J. P. (2009). Hume's "A Treatise of Human Nature": An Introduction. Cambridge: Cambridge University Press.

Wright, J. P. (2012). "Scepticism, Causal Science, and 'The Old Hume,'" *Journal of Scottish Philosophy* 10 (2), 123–142.

Yolton, J. W. (1984). *Perceptual Acquaintance from Descartes to Reid*. Minneapolis: Minnesota University Press.

CHAPTER 6

HUME'S CHIEF ARGUMENT

PETER MILLICAN

I Skepticism, Empiricism, Naturalism, and Irreligion

David Hume's philosophy is complex and multifaceted, generating considerable debate over which themes within it should be seen as dominant. Historically, most of his critics have viewed him as a negative *skeptic* who either deliberately sets out to show the weaknesses and contradictions in human reason,[1] or else is driven to do so by following through the logical implications of his philosophical premises.[2] Prominent among these premises is the *concept-empiricist* assumption inherited from Locke, which Hume expresses as his Copy Principle, that *all ideas are derived from impressions* (T 1.1.1.7/4; EU 2.5/19). But this is not in itself a skeptical principle, and some interpreters have seen it as providing the keystone of a more constructive philosophy.[3] Another very prominent theme in Hume's work is his "Attempt to introduce the experimental Method of Reasoning into Moral Subjects." In accordance with this ambitious subtitle, the *Treatise* aspires to lay the groundwork of a science of human nature that can explain cognitive operations (such as factual belief and the apprehension of external objects) in terms of the association of ideas, enabling Hume to be seen as an *associationist* or early *cognitive scientist*.[4] Although the associationism fades in his later works,[5] Hume's *epistemic-empiricist* commitment to the "experimental" science of man remains a pervasive theme in virtually all of his philosophy, including the two *Enquiries* and *Dissertation on the Passions*, the essays on politics, economics, and aesthetics, and his various contributions to the philosophy of religion. This strong Humean commitment to moral science is often described in terms of his "naturalism."

Hume is a thoroughgoing *naturalist* in at least three senses of that ambiguous word. First, he aims for a *natural* science of human thought and behavior, appealing to down-to-earth causal mechanisms (such as association) rather than any supposed transcendental insight or psychic powers—this has been called *explanatory naturalism*.

Second, his science of man places us squarely in the natural world alongside the other animals, a point emphasized strongly by his explicit comparisons between humans and animals, and by the prominence of these sections within the *Treatise*.[6] Perhaps the most appropriate name for this is *biological naturalism*.[7] Third, Hume argues vigorously against "invisible intelligent powers,"[8] and shows hostility to all forms of established religion: this is *anti-supernaturalism*. He is also commonly thought to be a naturalist in yet a fourth sense, appealing to the naturalness of certain beliefs or methods of reasoning as *vindicating* them against skepticism—what we might call *justificatory naturalism*. But this is controversial, and it is unclear whether Hume sees the resistance of our beliefs to skeptical attack—where this derives from human inability to resist the blind force of nature rather than from our own rational powers—as the *defeat* of skepticism or rather, its *victory*:

> I may, nay I must yield to the current of nature, in submitting to my senses and understanding; and in this blind submission I shew most perfectly my sceptical disposition and principles. (T 1.4.7.10/269)

Here, at least, Hume presents no *conflict* between his skeptical and naturalist orientations, and is perhaps best understood as intending his analysis of the human intellectual condition to give both skepticism and natural instinct their due, without declaring victory for either of them.

Hume's naturalism—in yet a fifth sense which combines various elements of these others—is enduringly associated with Norman Kemp Smith, who played a major role in challenging the previously dominant trend of skeptical interpretation. Taking his cue from Hume's notoriously provocative claim that "Reason is, and ought only to be the slave of the passions" (T 2.3.3.4/415), he argued that "the determining factor in Hume's philosophy" is "the establishment of a purely naturalistic conception of human nature by the thorough subordination of reason to feeling and instinct" (Kemp Smith 1905: 150). On this reading, instinctive practice dominates theoretical reason, and "our ultimate and unalterable tendencies to action are the test of practical truth and falsity" (1905: 156). The primary concern for Kemp Smith's Hume is *moral* philosophy, and the guiding principle of his system—what we might call *sentimentalist naturalism*—is an extension to the theoretical realm of the moral sentimentalism that he learned from Francis Hutcheson. Just as our natural moral sentiments can provide a basis for moral commitment, so our fundamental commitments to the external world and to objective causality are explained as "natural beliefs" grounded on "the ultimate instincts or propensities that constitute our human nature" and which are "thus removed beyond the reach of our sceptical doubts" (1905: 151, 152). In this way, naturalistic feeling trumps skeptical reason.

Kemp Smith's legacy of naturalistic interpretation was developed further by Barry Stroud, who argued explicitly for the predominance of Hume's naturalism over both his skepticism and his concept empiricism (1977: 76–77, 219–224). And Kemp Smith's influence continues to be evident in the work of more recent scholars, some of whom (like Stroud) repeat approvingly his improbable speculation that Hume wrote the bulk of *Treatise* Book 3 before Book 1, his philosophical system having grown from the basis of a Hutchesonian moral theory.[9]

It is a shame that Kemp Smith himself—like most who followed his lead—never carefully analyzed his key term "naturalism" or teased apart its various strands to clarify its relationship with "skepticism" (which also, as Hume himself stressed, comes in several varieties). Hume's explanatory naturalism, manifest in his efforts towards a "science of man," coheres closely with his biological naturalism and anti-supernaturalism. But *justificatory naturalism* fits far less straightforwardly with any of these, because treating beliefs as justified in virtue of their naturalness could easily point towards supernaturalism and the view of humans as semi-divine, both of which apparently come quite naturally to us (if cognitive science of religion is anything to go by, cf. Thornhill-Miller and Millican, 2015). Likewise, Kemp Smith's *sentimentalist naturalism*, subordinating reason to feeling, seems positively contrary to Hume's scientific ambitions.[10] For this crucially privileges "the ordinary consciousness"—embracing the two vulgar "natural beliefs" that our perceptions are independent objects and that external objects somehow contain a "feeling of necessitated transition" (1905: 158–159, 161–162)—in such a way as to make these immune to attack, *even when that attack is in the service of Hume's science of man.* Hume himself is clear that the vulgar belief in independently continuing perceptions is *false* (T 1.4.2.45/210–11; EU 12.9/152), while his account of how the mind "spreads itself on external objects" when ascribing necessity to them is the dismissive explaining away of an erroneous objection to his theory, not a central part of it (T 1.3.14.25/167).[11] If Hume really did view these as privileged "natural beliefs" in the way that Kemp Smith claims, then his declared ambition to lay the groundwork of an objective science that might "discover, at least in some degree, the secret springs and principles, by which the human mind is actuated in its operations" (EU 1.15/14; cf. T Intro. 6–8/xvi–xvii) seems fatally compromised. In short, Kemp Smith's sentimentalist naturalism, by systematically elevating feeling over reason, may "defeat skepticism" to the very minimal extent of insulating our vulgar everyday beliefs, but in the more significant battle between scientific irrationalism (e.g., the claim that science has no more rational warrant than superstition) and naturalistic moral science, it is on the wrong side.

We have seen that there are serious dangers of misrepresentation in categorizing Hume as a "naturalist," and it is also far too simplistic to think of his philosophical orientation as involving a balancing act between "naturalism" and "skepticism." Some of his naturalistic aims conflict with certain types of skepticism but at the same time cohere very well with other types, so we must be sensitive to these nuances and avoid the temptation to pigeonhole Hume into crude contemporary categories. If we seek for a more plausible simple label for Hume's philosophy, combining appropriate elements of both naturalism and skepticism, then Paul Russell (2008) has recently suggested *irreligion,* focusing on the hostility to religion which is central to Hume's anti-supernaturalism, and yet which also counts as seriously skeptical from the point of view of Hume's contemporaries and early critics. Russell's interpretation has considerable merit, for as we shall see, there is plenty of evidence that Hume had religious concerns from early in his life (plausibly providing the main impetus for his interest in philosophy), and much of his writing is either overtly or covertly antitheistic. But "irreligion" is a very broad theme, and my aim here is to capture the *specific* ways in which Hume's philosophy developed and the particular arguments that attracted him. Even though religion is indeed commonly in his sights, he often pursues an independent philosophical agenda of his own, and he is certainly no indiscriminate peddler of anti-religious arguments.

A narrower version of the irreligious interpretation was proposed by Edward Craig (1987), who argued that Hume's primary target is the Judaeo-Christian "Image of God" doctrine or "Similarity Thesis" that man—and most importantly his epistemic faculty of reason—is made in the image of God. Opposition to this thesis nicely combines biological naturalism with skepticism about human reason, and Hume would indeed have been fundamentally opposed to any such assertion of human quasi-divinity. But beyond this obvious point, Craig's interpretation has little solid basis, because although there is a profusion of evidence for Hume's general irreligion, not only in his explicitly anti-religious works but also in the *Treatise*,[12] there are very few of his texts that can plausibly be interpreted as *specifically* targeting the Image of God doctrine.[13] Most of these few, moreover, occur when he is criticizing the Design Argument, whose whole point is to argue for a Deity analogous to the human mind; hence such passages are easily explained by Hume's opposition to that argument without any need to hypothesize some deeper and more general antipathy to the Similarity Thesis. In default of much direct textual support, therefore, Craig's evidence for his interpretation is almost all indirect,[14] but what he supplies looks very insubstantial, especially in the light of subsequent scholarship. Most specifically, he argues (1987: 77–84) that a focus on the Image of God doctrine would naturally lead to Hume's operating with a deductivist conception of reason within the famous argument concerning induction, as was then commonly supposed; but more recent work has convincingly refuted this supposition.[15] Craig goes on to examine three of Hume's other best-known discussions—on the idea of necessary connexion, the two definitions of cause, and personal identity—which he thinks make little sense on the rival interpretation that Hume is an "embryonic positivist" for whom the analytical Copy Principle (rather than the epistemically-focused Similarity Thesis) is of central importance (1987: 121). Again, his case now looks relatively weak in the light of more recent scholarship,[16] and anyway virtually none of what Craig says here points strongly towards the Image of God doctrine: so even if he is right to see Hume's overtly analytical discussions as confused in various ways, his suggestion that the Similarity Thesis lies behind the confusion is mere speculation until backed up with substantial and specific evidence. Meanwhile, we have good reason for distrusting any interpretation that so fundamentally turns on the idea that Hume is muddled in putting such an emphasis on his Copy Principle, a problem which Craig acknowledges:

> it remains obscure what motive [Hume] can have had for being hospitable, even to the extent that he was, to the theory of ideas and impressions, and I am driven to an explanation of the fact in terms of an early enthusiasm for Locke and the "way of

ideas." Hume never got it out of his system, or realised how little, deep down, it actually meant to him. (1987: 123)

Craig thus follows Stroud in taking Hume's concept-empiricist commitments to be relatively shallow, despite Hume's enthusiastic highlighting of his Copy Principle in the *Treatise*, the *Abstract*, and the *Enquiry*, and his continued defence of it (cf. Section III below). There is a strong whiff of philosophical fashion here, whereby just as commentators in the heyday of positivism were inclined to overstress Hume's concept empiricism, so more recent scholars have been inclined to dismiss it as a mildly embarrassing Lockean legacy. Far more satisfactory than either extreme would be a more balanced view that can explain why Hume was so conspicuously attracted to the Copy Principle, even though his interests indeed seem, on the whole, to be epistemological and anti-religious rather than analytical.

II THE BIOGRAPHICAL BACKGROUND OF HUME'S PHILOSOPHY

In attempting to construct a more balanced account of the fundamentals of Hume's philosophy, it will be helpful to start by reviewing briefly what we know of his background and intellectual context, delegating further detail to M. A. Stewart's useful 2005 paper on "Hume's Intellectual Development, 1711–1752." As Stewart illustrates from various sources, Hume's philosophy teaching at Edinburgh University, which he attended from 1721 until 1725 (aged between 10 and 14), would have been traditional and even reactionary, delivered in Latin, thoroughly infused with religion, and generally unlikely to have inspired his interest (2005: 11–16, 19–25). After university, living mainly at the family home at Chirnside (eight miles west of Berwick) and neglecting his intended legal studies, Hume became a voracious reader of classical authors such as Cicero, Virgil, Seneca, and Plutarch (Stewart, 2005: 28–29). These classical interests would have been encouraged by his reading of Shaftesbury's *Characteristicks*, which Hume purchased in 1726 (Stewart 2005: 37–38). At this point his orientation seems to have been broadly Stoical, and it is his efforts towards the introspective Stoic ideal that he blames for the breakdown that followed his enthusiasm for the "new Scene of Thought" which "seem'd to be opened up" to him in 1729 (LET 1.13). Hume's personal experience of the failure of Stoic discipline seems to have encouraged him towards more down-to-earth empirical psychology, in which he apparently made some progress from early in 1731, as he described in his well-known draft letter to a physician of March or April 1734:

I found that the moral Philosophy transmitted to us by Antiquity, labor'd under the same Inconvenience that has been found in their natural Philosophy, of being entirely Hypothetical, & depending more upon Invention than Experience. Every one consulted his Fancy in erecting Schemes of Virtue & of Happiness, without regarding human Nature, upon which every moral Conclusion must depend. This therefore I resolved to make my principal Study, . . . I believe . . . that little more is requir'd to make a man succeed in this Study than to throw off all Prejudices . . . At least this is all I have to depend on for the Truth of my Reasonings, which I have multiply'd to such a degree, that within these three Years, I find I have scribbled many a Quire of Paper, in which there is nothing contain'd but my own Inventions. (LET 1.16)

Perhaps Hume's skepticism towards previous philosophers was also fostered by his reading of Pierre Bayle, who is mentioned in a letter of March 1732 (LET 1.12). Another major factor here seems to have been a loss of religious faith, which we know about principally from a 1751 letter to Gilbert Elliot of Minto and the 1776 deathbed interview recorded by James Boswell. In the letter, which invites Elliot to help in strengthening the theistic arguments of the draft *Dialogues*, Hume tells of having recently "burn'd an old Manuscript Book, wrote before I was twenty; which contain'd, Page after Page, the gradual Progress of my Thoughts on that Head." This began "with an anxious Search after Arguments, to confirm the common Opinion,"[17] while "Any Propensity . . . to the other Side, crept in upon me against my Will," in "a perpetual Struggle of a restless Imagination against Inclination" (LET 1.154). All this suggests that Hume's progressive loss of faith—apparently extending until 1730 or 1731 ("before I was twenty")—was prolonged and difficult, as indeed is typically the case.

In the deathbed interview with Boswell, Hume said that he was "religious when he was young," but that "the Morality of every Religion was bad" and "he never had entertained any belief in Religion since he began to read Locke and Clarke" (Boswell 1931: 76). There is clear irony here, in that Hume lost belief when reading these two *defenders* of theism, and the pairing is suggestive, because both John Locke and Samuel Clarke were prominent advocates of a particular form of Cosmological Argument for God's existence, in which they drew upon the principle that matter and motion alone cannot give rise to thought.[18] This connection is confirmed by the one mention of Clarke in Hume's *Treatise*, in a footnote to T 1.3.3.5/80, which is followed in the very next paragraph by a footnote mentioning Locke. For here Hume attacks their arguments for the Causal Maxim that *"whatever begins to exist, must have a cause of existence"* (T 1.3.3.1/78), which is the other fundamental principle of their Cosmological Argument (e.g., Locke, *Essay* IV x 3; Clarke 1732: 8–9). Although the *Treatise* prudently makes no mention of this irreligious connection, it was not lost on the author of the anonymous 1745 pamphlet to which Hume's *Letter from a Gentleman* was a response: the second "Charge" it lays against him, after "1. Universal Scepticism," is "2. Principles leading to downright Atheism, by denying the Doctrine of Causes and Effects, . . . he maintains, that the Necessity of a Cause to every Beginning of Existence is not founded on any Arguments demonstrative or intuitive" (LG 15).[19]

Hume's interest in Locke and Clarke probably came not from his formal studies (Stewart 2005: 16), but through his friendship with Henry Home, a distant cousin whose family home at Kames was only nine miles southwest of Chirnside. Home—who later became Lord Kames and is now most commonly known by that name—was born in 1696, and as a philosophically minded lawyer, he seems to have taken young David under his wing at Edinburgh. During 1723, Kames will no doubt have talked to the twelve-year-old student about the debates he was then pursuing through correspondence with Samuel Clarke and Clarke's most prominent Scottish follower Andrew Baxter (who also resided in the Scottish borders, six miles west of Chirnside at Duns). We know from Boswell that around that time Kames also grappled with Locke's *Essay*, of which "The chapter on *Power* crucified him" (Boswell 1932: 273). A particular focus of Locke's chapter, as of Kames's correspondence with Clarke, was the topic of free will and necessity, so it seems safe to assume that Kames would likewise have taken a keen interest in the prominent controversy on this topic between Clarke and Anthony Collins, which had occurred in 1717 through the publication of Collins's *Philosophical Inquiry concerning Human Liberty* and Clarke's responding *Remarks*.[20] Some years later, echoes of this debate came to Hume's own doorstep when, in 1732, William Dudgeon, a tenant farmer residing near Coldstream (eight miles south of Chirnside) published *The State of the Moral World Consider'd*, a dialogue promoting necessitarian optimism which was sharply answered by Andrew Baxter, provoking Dudgeon's prosecution for heresy by the Chirnside Presbytery where Hume's uncle George Home was minister.[21] In opposition, Baxter explicitly champions the views of Clarke, a "great Man" and "the best Defender of Liberty" (1732: 27 n.), and insinuates that Dudgeon is an admirer of "Mr. L—z" and "Mr. C—ns" (i.e., Leibniz and Collins) (1732: 35). It seems certain that Hume would have heard of these dramatic events, and the natural expectation that they would leave some mark on him—then just twenty-one but already moving on from his religious crisis to the philosophical thoughts that would lead to the *Treatise*—is at least corroborated by the similarity of his views on "liberty and necessity" to those of Collins.

Dudgeon's prosecution for heretical views on free will and necessity highlights the religious significance of these topics, which were far from narrowly theoretical.[22] Seeing human behavior as causally necessitated generates tensions with religious belief in a number of ways, not only by favoring explanatory and biological naturalism, but, more specifically, by making it hard to absolve any supposed divine Creator of responsibility for the apparent imperfections of His creation (unless, like Leibniz and Dudgeon, one is prepared to see that creation as actually the best of all possible worlds). We know that Hume had an intense early interest in the Problem of Evil from a recently discovered manuscript fragment which seems part of a much longer discussion (Stewart 1994). Moreover, the Free Will Defence is one of the main topics in his "early memoranda" on philosophy, apparently written at about the same time as the *Treatise* was published. One memorandum, for example, says:

> Liberty not a proper Solution of Moral Ill: Because it might have been bound down by Motives like those of Saints & Angels. Id. [King].[23]

To provide a solution to the Problem of Evil, free will must be such that God—in giving it to his creatures—ipso facto becomes unable to ensure in advance that they will be freely virtuous (for otherwise, He has no excuse for failing to ensure this). Hume here points out that if "Saints & Angels" can freely act virtuously from good motives (as orthodoxy maintains, especially in respect of the heavenly afterlife), then God cannot be excused from the problem of "Moral Ill" by appeal to "Liberty," because He could have made *all* His creatures such that they likewise freely acted virtuously from good motives. There seems little doubt that Hume had this point in mind when he came to compose *Enquiry* Section 8, with its compatibilist account of free will that makes it impossible to absolve God from the wickedness of His creation (EU 8.36/103).

III CAUSATION AND THE COPY PRINCIPLE

So far, we have seen that Hume had strong personal reasons to be skeptical about the classical and Christian moralists on whom he had been raised, and that this skepticism gave him a resolve to make "human Nature" his "principal Study" and to base that study on "Experience" rather than "Invention." Contemporary views of human nature were overwhelmingly bound up with the Christian conception of the universe and man's place in it, but by the age of twenty Hume had rejected religion—probably for both metaphysical and moral reasons—and was seeking a science of man that would be quite independent of it. We have here a strong nexus of influences that provide a promising explanation of many of the general tendencies of Hume's philosophy, from *skepticism* about established orthodoxies, *explanatory naturalism* and *epistemic empiricism* in the quest for an observational science of human nature, and *biological naturalism* both from seeing human nature as a subject of empirical study, and from *anti-supernaturalism* consequent on his loss of faith and revulsion for religious ethics. But more specifically, it is remarkable how this intellectual journey had taken him through such a significant cluster of topics associated with *causation*: the Cosmological Argument, the attempts of Locke and Clarke to establish both the Causal Maxim and the principle that thought cannot arise from matter, Kames's correspondence with Clarke and Baxter and his struggles over Locke's "chapter on *Power*," and the prominent and locally salient debates about free will and necessity. All this, I suggest, does much to explain Hume's obvious preoccupation with the idea of causation in his theoretical philosophy.

Turning now to the shape of Hume's early philosophy as we find it in the *Treatise*, we are struck in the very first section by the prominence that he gives to his Copy Principle "that all our simple ideas in their first appearance are deriv'd from simple impressions, which are correspondent to them, and which they exactly represent" (T 1.1.1.7/4). Hume trumpets this as his "first principle" (T 1.1.1.12/7 cf. T App. 6/626) and later extols its philosophical value (T 1.2.3.1/33; cf. TA 7/648). Moreover, he remains equally attached to it in his later writings,[24] although it does not yet fit neatly into the picture we have been building of his philosophy and its background. As we shall see, however, there is a straightforward and elegant way of integrating it into that picture, if we allow ourselves one undocumented—but highly plausible—speculation. Namely, *that Hume was strongly motivated at an early stage by the prospect of applying Locke's concept empiricism to settle the debate over free will and necessity through clarifying and delimiting what could possibly be meant by causal "necessity."* Certainly Hume did in fact so apply his Copy Principle, which he acknowledges to be a reformulation of Locke's denial of innate ideas (TA 6/647–8). What remains to be explained is how such an application would naturally have enticed the young philosopher.

Like most of his British philosophical contemporaries, Hume appears to have accepted Locke's concept empiricism relatively uncritically: in both the *Treatise* and the *Enquiry* he gives arguments to support it, but they are rather perfunctory and unsatisfactory, evincing little inclination to dig deeper.[25] The attraction of the Copy Principle as a weapon against bogus ideas (e.g., of Cartesian or scholastic souls or essences) is obvious enough, but what really excites Hume is the analytical bounty that he intends to draw from it:

> Our author thinks, "that no discovery cou'd have been made more happily for deciding all controversies concerning ideas . . ." Accordingly, wherever any idea is ambiguous, he has always recourse to the impression, which must render it clear and precise. (TA 7/648–9; cf. EU 2.9/21–2)

We shall probably never know which ideas first came under Hume's scrutiny in this way, although his self-quoted words in the *Abstract* passage above—taken from T 1.2.3.1/33— may reflect the joy of new discovery when analyzing our ideas of space and time, most likely in response to Bayle's discussion of Zeno's paradoxes of infinite divisibility.[26] But at some stage early in his philosophical development, as we have seen, it is very likely that Kames would have drawn Hume's attention to Locke's "chapter on *Power*," which begins as follows:

> The Mind, being every day informed, by the Senses, of the alteration of those simple *Ideas*, it observes in things without; and taking notice how one comes to an end, and ceases to be, and another begins to exist, which was not before; reflecting also on what passes within itself, . . . and concluding from what it has so constantly observed to have been, that the like Changes will for the future be made, in the same things, by like Agents, and by the like ways, considers in one thing the possibility of having any of its simple *Ideas* changed, and in another the possibility of making that change; and so comes by that *Idea* which we call *Power*. (*Essay* II xxi 1)

As Hume points out in both the *Treatise* and the *Enquiry*, however, "this explication is more popular than philosophical" (T 1.3.14.5/157) because "no reasoning can ever give us a new, original, simple idea; as this philosopher himself confesses" (EU 7.8 n12/64 n1). Having noticed the flaw in Locke's "explication," Hume would no doubt be keen to develop his own more rigorous account, soon realizing the difficulties involved and the futility of attempting to define *power* using other equally problematic causal terms such as *efficacy*. Ultimately, of course, this led to his now famous analysis in *Treatise* 1.3.14, which begins by observing "that the terms of *efficacy, agency, power, force, energy, necessity, connexion,* and *productive quality,* are all nearly synonimous" (T 1.3.14.4/157),[27] and which then goes on to identify the source of the crucial idea as an impression of reflection before culminating in Hume's two "definitions of cause" (T 1.3.14.31/169–70; cf. T 2.3.2.4/409–10).

Suppose now that Hume, having contemplated this issue at least in general terms, came to consider the debate between Clarke and Collins, perhaps in the context of the Dudgeon affair. This debate involves a *conceptual* disagreement about the meaning of "necessity," Collins equating this with deterministic predictability and ascribing it to human actions as well as physical events (1717: 110–111).[28] In response, Clarke makes clear that his own conception of genuine necessity is very different, involving not mere predictability but something like *mechanical impulse*, whereas by contrast the "moral necessity" which characterizes human behavior

> is not indeed any *Necessity* at all; but 'tis merely a *figurative Manner of Speaking* . . . But now [Collins] makes *Moral Necessity* and *Physical Necessity* to be exactly and Philosophically the same Thing . . . In which Matter, the Author is guilty of a double Absurdity. *First,* in supposing *Reasons* or *Motives* . . . to make the same *necessary Impulse* upon *Intelligent* Subjects, as *Matter in Motion* does upon *unintelligent Subjects*; which is supposing *Abstract Notions* to be *Substances*. And *Secondly,* in endeavouring to impose it upon his Reader as a thing taken for *granted,* that *Moral Necessity* and *Physical Necessity* do not differ intrinsically in their *own Nature.* (Clarke 1717: 15–16)

Hume sides with Collins and has ample motive for doing so, both irreligious and naturalistic (as we saw earlier). But he also wields a novel and powerful weapon, in the form of his own analysis of causation:

> We may learn from the foregoing [two definitions], that all causes are of the same kind, . . . The same course of reasoning will make us conclude, that there is but one kind of *necessity,* . . . and that the common distinction betwixt *moral* and *physical* necessity is without any foundation in nature. This clearly appears from the precedent explication of necessity. 'Tis the constant conjunction of objects, along with the determination of the mind, which constitutes a physical necessity: And the removal of these is the same thing with *chance.* . . . 'tis impossible to admit of any medium betwixt chance and an absolute necessity. (T 1.3.14.32–3/170–1)

In the *Treatise,* Hume does not immediately point out the consequences for human free will, but quickly presents another fruit of his analysis, namely, confirmation that the Causal Maxim—the main foundation of Clarke's Cosmological Argument—cannot be "founded on any arguments either demonstrative or intuitive":

> If we define a cause to be, *An object precedent and contiguous to another, and where all the objects resembling the former are plac'd in a like relation of priority and contiguity*

to those objects, that resemble the latter; we may easily conceive, that there is no absolute nor metaphysical necessity, that every beginning of existence shou'd be attended
with such an object. (T 1.3.14.35/172)

In a similar spirit, he later exploits the same definition to refute that other key principle
of Clarke's Cosmological Argument, that matter and motion could not possibly give rise
to thought:

> we are never sensible of any connexion betwixt causes and effects, and . . . 'tis only by
> our experience of their constant conjunction, we can arrive at any knowledge of this
> relation. Now as all objects, which are not contrary, are susceptible of a constant con-
> junction, and as no real objects are contrary; I have inferr'd from these principles [cf.
> T 1.3.15.1/173], that to consider the matter *a priori*, anything may produce anything,
> and that we shall never discover a reason, why any object may or may not be the
> cause of any other . . . [W]e find by the comparing their ideas, that thought and motion
> are different from each other, and by experience, that they are constantly united;
> which being all the circumstances, that enter into the idea of cause and effect, when
> apply'd to the operations of matter, we may certainly conclude, that motion may be,
> and actually is, the cause of thought and perception. (T 1.4.5.30/247–8)

Thus Hume's analysis of causation has the direct implication that causes and effects can
be discovered only through experience, delivering both a vindication of empirical science and a devastating blow against a priori metaphysics. But an even more important
implication—because hard to establish in any other way—is revealed when he returns to
the territory of Clarke and Collins in *Treatise* 2.3.1–2 on the crucial question of "liberty
and necessity." Here, Hume's two definitions of cause yield parallel definitions of causal
necessity (T 2.3.2.4/409–10; cf. T 2.3.1.4/400–1), capturing all that we can mean by the
term. Then, because human actions satisfy the definitions, it immediately follows that
those actions are as necessary as the motion of billiard balls. Clarke and his allies will
object that human actions lack genuine *physical* necessity, but the upshot of Hume's analysis is that they are using terms without meaning: their supposed distinction between
moral and *physical* necessity (as Hume has already observed at T 1.3.14.32–3) can be con-
signed to the same metaphysical dustbin as scholastic substances:

> this reasoning puts the whole controversy in a new light, by giving a new defini-
> tion of necessity. And, indeed, the most zealous advocates for free-will [e.g. Clarke]
> must allow this union and inference with regard to human actions. They will only
> deny, that this makes the whole of necessity. But then they must shew, that we have
> an idea of something else [i.e. whatever it is that characterises "physical" necessity]
> in the actions of matter, which, according to the foregoing reasoning, is impossible.
> (TA 34/661)

Hume's application of his Copy Principle to the idea of causal necessity thus both
brings human behavior within the reach of deterministic causal science,[29] and

triumphantly solves "the question of liberty and necessity; the most contentious question, of metaphysics, the most contentious science" (EU 8.23/95). We now have a very satisfying answer—firmly rooted in his biography and early writings—to the puzzle of why Hume put such emphasis on his Copy Principle and gave it pride of place as the "first principle" of his philosophy. Through its application to the idea of causal necessity, his concept empiricism turns out to be closely integrated with his other main theoretical commitments and purposes, providing a support for explanatory and biological naturalism, a refutation of causal apriorism in favor of epistemic empiricism, and a further multiple attack on supernaturalism by undermining the principles of the Cosmological Argument and of the Free Will Defence.[30]

In recent years, it has become fashionable to play down Hume's commitment to the Copy Principle, in line with the declining popularity of concept empiricism noted at the end of Section I above. Indeed the "skeptical realist" or "New Hume" interpretation—developed mostly by John Wright, Edward Craig, and Galen Strawson, but since attracting others—centers on the claim that Hume is content to allow meaningful (and potentially truth-apt) thought in the absence of impression-derived ideas. This claim has some textual support in respect of topics such as the external world, where Hume accounts for our thinking in terms of "fictions" that result from associational confusion (rather than bona fide ideas). But in the case of causation, Hume is always very explicit that his analysis delivers both a genuine idea—copied from an impression—and two definitions that are precise enough to yield the host of valuable philosophical results that we have just seen. The "skeptical realist" reading of Hume on causation has, I believe, seemed plausible only because its advocates have systematically avoided addressing those passages where Hume exploits his analysis for philosophical gain, most notably his discussions of materialism (at T 1.4.5.29–33) and "liberty and necessity" (in T 2.3.1–2; TA. 31–4/660–1; and EU 8). If the account just sketched is correct, however, this amounts to a fundamental reversal of Hume's own priorities.[31]

IV THE FORMATION OF TREATISE BOOK 1 PARTS 1–3

Hume's enthusiasm for the Copy Principle explains and structures much of the early content of *Treatise* Book 1. Impressions can arise from either *sensation* or *reflection* (T 1.1.2), with ideas their precise copies (albeit having less "force and vivacity"). It follows that ideas are quasi-sensory and must be determinate; hence thought involving generality requires an appropriate treatment of "abstract ideas" (cf. T 1.1.7.5/19). Combined with Hume's sensory atomism—which provides the basis for his treatment of space and time and his solution to the paradoxes of infinite divisibility—this also means that complex ideas are susceptible of literal division and rearrangement, thus explaining the otherwise puzzling jump from what at first seems like a harmless "second principle, *of the liberty of the imagination to transpose and change its ideas"* (T 1.1.3.4/10), to a full-blown Separability Principle (T 1.1.7.3/18–9) which is far less innocuous and goes on to play a major role in the Part 2 treatment of space and time (and later generates problems in Part 4).

Interleaved with all this analysis and metaphysics is a more epistemological stream of thought, starting with the association of ideas (T 1.1.4) and a taxonomy of relations (T 1.1.5), in preparation for the treatment of "knowledge and probability" in Part 3. Here Hume saw the prospect for another neat theory, based on the observation that all inferences "from one object to another" rely on causation and are at best *probable*, while *demonstrative* inferences tend to be confined to mathematics. This invited the tempting thought that mental operations can be categorized in terms of the relations involved, with *resemblance, contrariety,* and *degrees in quality* corresponding to intuition (T 1.3.1.2/70); *proportions of quantity or number* to demonstration (T 1.3.1.3/70); *identity* and *relations of time and place* to perception (T 1.3.2.2/73–4); and *causation* to probable inference (T 1.3.2.3/74). With this in mind, Hume (T 1.1.5.2/14) shoehorns the multiplicity of relations that Locke had painstakingly identified (*Essay* II xxv–xxviii) into just seven categories.[32] Later in the *Treatise* Hume twice appeals to this taxonomy, to prove the non-demonstrability of the Causal Maxim (T 1.3.3.2/79) and of morality (T 3.1.1.19/463–4). Sadly this whole theory is seriously flawed, but fortunately the bulk of the *Treatise* is unaffected because Hume mostly relies instead on a far more plausible criterion of demonstrability, namely, the Conceivability Principle. However the theory plays a significant role in shaping Book 1 Part 3, which although entitled "Of Knowledge and Probability," is mainly framed by Hume's analysis of the causal relation informed by the Copy Principle (from T 1.3.2.3/74 to T 1.3.15.11/175).[33] Within this overarching framework, Hume inserts his discussions of the Causal Maxim (T 1.3.3) and of causal inference (T 1.3.4–7), but both are presented as "neighbouring fields" (T 1.3.2.13/77–8) to his main analytical business. His famous argument concerning induction in T 1.3.6 shows that the assumption of uniformity which induction presupposes cannot be established on any independent rational basis, instead being taken for granted through the instinctive operation of *custom* (or habit). But it is striking, in view of this argument's subsequent fame, how cursory and relatively muted it is here, set within a section whose main role seems to be to reveal *constant conjunction* as the key to causal ascription, as another step towards analysis of the causal relation (with T 1.3.6.3 echoing T 1.3.2.11). When Hume reassessed the 1739 *Treatise* in his *Abstract* (composed only nine months or so later), the famous argument was elevated from this humble role to become the centerpiece of his theoretical philosophy, as it remained in the *Enquiry* of 1748 and has been considered ever since. So what we find in *Treatise* Book 1 Part 3, apparently, is an organizational structure that reflects the development of Hume's ideas rather than their maturely considered arrangement. And this strongly corroborates our hypothesis, that he came to his theoretical philosophy predominantly through an interest in the analysis of causation rather than in the epistemological assessment of induction.

When Hume does finally turn explicitly to the assessment of "probable reasonings"—again in a long detour (or series of detours) from his search for the source of the idea of necessary connexion—his discussion is scientific rather than skeptical in tone. T 1.3.8 provides experimental support for his analysis of belief in terms of the transfer of vivacity by customary association (typically from the impression of a cause to the idea of its experienced effect); T 1.3.9 explains why the vivacity of belief arises from causation rather than from other relations; T 1.3.10 discusses the mutual influence of belief on the passions and imagination; T 1.3.11 explains "the probability of chances" and T 1.3.12 "the probability of causes," both involving the division of force and vivacity where there is a multiplicity of associational links; while T 1.3.13 discusses "unphilosophical probability" prior to Hume's belated return—at T 1.3.14—to his analysis of the idea of causation (on hold, apparently, since T 1.3.6). These intervening sections include numerous remarks describing the various factors that bear on our judgments of probability, many of which can also be construed as normative: highlighting factors that *ought* (or *ought not*) to bear on such judgments. The overall message here is in favor of basing our beliefs on experience, drawing causal inferences through custom in line with the constant conjunctions that we have observed, and assigning probabilities based on statistical regularities. Probable reasoning accordingly merits categorization amongst what Hume will later call the "general and more establish'd" operations of the mind (T 1.4.7.7/267–8), and beliefs thus formed deserve to be called products of "judgment" or "reason," distinguished from trivial and flighty "whimsies and prejudices, which are rejected under the opprobrious character of being the offspring of the imagination" (T 1.3.9.19 n22/117–8 n1).[34] Irrationalities of the latter kind are particularly associated with religion, which encourages stimulation of the imagination by such things as the "mummeries" of Roman Catholicism (T 1.3.8.4/99–100), saintly relics (T 1.3.8.6/100–1), pilgrimages (T 1.3.9.9/110–11), terrifying sermons (T 1.3.9.15/115), and miracle stories (T 1.3.10.4/120).

V SKEPTICISM: CORROSIVE OR MITIGATED?

So far, we have seen nothing in Hume's formative ideas that is *corrosively skeptical*, in the sense of undermining his scientific ambitions. Many of his views would indeed have been considered skeptical by his contemporaries, such as his denial of the demonstrability of the Causal Maxim, his treatment of induction as founded on instinctive custom (rather than perception of evidential connexions),[35] his analysis of causation in terms of our own inferential behavior (rather than apprehension of objective necessities), and his various criticisms—either explicit or implicit—of religious claims. But none of this seriously threatens *his own* scientific researches, as long as he is content to accept the deliverances of his faculties in a spirit consistent with his theory. A scientist who accepts that his faculties are fallible and his discoveries less than certain does not thereby undermine them, except by the unrealistic standards of a wishful-thinking dogmatist or extreme skeptic who cannot reconcile himself to working within the limits of what human nature allows.

This attitude is most clearly expressed by Hume in the final section of the *Enquiry* of 1748, where he draws attention to the varieties and different degrees of skepticism before himself adopting a *mitigated* or *academic* skepticism (EU 12.24–26/161–3) which recognizes the fallibility of our faculties and is accordingly modest and undogmatic, accepting that there may be limits to the range of our enquiries. He spells this out in respect of induction, responding to his own argument (EU 4, summarized at EU 12.22/153) that our most important method of reasoning about the world rests on a brute assumption—namely, the uniformity of nature—for which no independent justification can be given. The rationalist and the extreme "Pyrrhonian" skeptic will bemoan this lack and demand a more solid basis for induction, but if none is to be had, then we are faced with a stark choice between giving up induction entirely or accepting "the whimsical condition of mankind, who must act and reason and believe; though they are not able, by their most diligent enquiry, to satisfy themselves concerning the foundation of these operations" (EU 12.23/160). Given this pragmatic situation, even the Pyrrhonian can offer no reason for preferring the negative choice, for "he must acknowledge, if he will acknowledge any thing, that all human life must perish, were his principles universally and steadily to prevail" (EU 12.23/160).[36] The upshot is that as long as our investigations do not *undermine* our faculties by showing them to be unreliable, it is entirely reasonable for us to rely on them by default.[37]

Relying on our faculties by default, moreover, is entirely consistent with refining our use of them on the basis of our investigations. Most importantly, although our general presumption of inductive uniformity may have to be taken for granted as indispensable and incapable of further support, this does not require us to accord equal authority to every individual inductive inference, treating thoughtless superstition (e.g., belief in a "lucky charm") with as much respect as careful, disciplined scientific extrapolation. On the contrary, we find by experience that the former is hopelessly unreliable whereas the latter is highly effective, and it is important to notice that there is nothing viciously circular or fundamentally skeptical about such inductive investigation of our own inductive tendencies (any more than there is about empirical cognitive science in general). Much of *Treatise* Book 1 Part 3 can be understood in this scientific spirit, and indeed Hume there seems almost oblivious to the possibility that he might be thought to be raising corrosive skeptical worries about induction.[38] Only in the *Enquiry* does he explicitly acknowledge that his famous argument raises "sceptical doubts concerning the operations of the understanding," before going on to lay these to rest in the way that we have just seen.

The project of the *Treatise* does run into serious trouble, however, when Hume's cognitive investigations ultimately lead to the conclusion that our thought is irremediably incoherent. As we saw earlier (cf. note 34), in analyzing human reasoning he attempts to draw a distinction between the "general" and "universal" principles of the mind that deserve our respect and the "irregular" or "trivial" ones that do not, most explicitly at the beginning of *Treatise* 1.4.4:

> In order to justify myself, I must distinguish in the imagination betwixt the principles which are permanent, irresistable, and universal; such as the customary transition

from causes to effects, and from effects to causes: And the principles, which are changeable, weak, and irregular; . . . The former are the foundation of all our thoughts and actions, so that upon their removal human nature must immediately perish and go to ruin. The latter are neither unavoidable to mankind, nor necessary, or so much as useful in the conduct of life; but on the contrary are observ'd only to take place in weak minds . . . (T 1.4.4.1/225)

But once Hume becomes engaged in the skeptical arguments of Book 1 Part 4, this distinction becomes hard to maintain, as he himself laments retrospectively in the concluding section T 1.4.7.[39] First, at T 1.4.1.10/185, we are saved from extreme skepticism not by the "general and more establish'd" principles of the mind, but by "that singular and seemingly trivial property of the fancy, by which we enter with difficulty into remote views of things" (T 1.4.7.7/268). Second, at T 1.4.2.56/217–8, after a long and fraught discussion of our belief in the continued and distinct existence of external objects, Hume concludes that this belief is founded on "trivial qualities of the fancy" and on "false suppositions," including the "gross illusion . . . that our resembling perceptions are numerically the same." Third, at T 1.4.4.15/231, he finds that standard causal reasoning leads to the conclusion that material objects do not resemble our sensory impressions, which in turn makes it impossible for us to form any "satisfactory idea" (T 1.4.4.9/229) of them;[40] thus causal reasoning and the belief in external objects, "tho' these two operations be equally natural and necessary in the human mind, yet in some circumstances they are directly contrary" (T 1.4.7.4/266). Finally, Hume ultimately finds his account of personal identity in T 1.4.6 to be deeply problematic, based on principles that he "cannot render consistent" (T App. 21/636), although this recognition comes only in the *Appendix* to the *Treatise*, published with Book 3 late in 1740. One major source of the trouble here is Hume's Separability Principle, which he takes to imply the extraordinary claim that his perceptions are independent existences that "may exist separately, without any contradiction or absurdity" (T App.12/634; cf. T 1.4.5.5/233; T 1.4.6.3/252; T 1.4.6.16/259–60).

The conclusion of *Treatise* Book 1 exposes the disastrous breakdown of Hume's would-be distinction between the "general" and "trivial" principles of the mind, making it difficult to mount any consistent defence against corrosive skepticism (T 1.4.7.6–8/267–9). In the end, he can do no more than appeal to our natural tendency to ignore skeptical worries and his own inclination towards metaphysical curiosity despite them (T 1.4.7.9–12/269–71). For those who share such curiosity, he suggests that philosophy can at least be recommended above superstition as the "safest and most agreeable" guide (T 1.4.7.13/271), but this defence appears lame given the obvious retort, that on religious principles Hume's philosophy holds far more danger than Christianity, risking falsehood and eternal hellfire in place of divine truth and salvation.[41] If human reason is as hopelessly inconsistent as Hume has portrayed, then any objective assessment is beyond us, and we seem to be reduced to falling back on personal inclination, with selective "carelessness and in-attention" towards skeptical considerations that would upset our equanimity (as at T 1.4.2.57/218). The upshot is that any Christian who is as attracted towards his faith as Hume is towards philosophy has been given no good reason to reconsider.[42]

From the perspective on Hume's philosophy developed earlier, we have excellent reason to interpret his skeptical despair in the conclusion of *Treatise* Book 1 as entirely genuine: his project has been holed beneath the waterline, and his makeshift defence, by which he attempts to justify the continuation of his investigations, is palpably unconvincing. Hence so far from seeing Hume as a deliberate corrosive skeptic, as so many of his readers have done, there is a lot to be said for Reid's view that he is forced into such skepticism by his own logical rigor and the premises from which he starts.[43]

VI HUME'S CHIEF ARGUMENT AND HIS TAMING OF SKEPTICISM

Barely nine months after *Treatise* Books 1 and 2 were published, Hume was reformulating its "Chief Argument" in the *Abstract*, which was eventually published in March 1740.[44] His choice of topics for inclusion strongly corroborates the account given earlier, whereby it is his views on inductive probability, causation, and free will that are most important to him. He devotes paragraphs 5–7 to the Copy Principle; 8–14 to his argument concerning induction; 15–25 (and 4) to custom, belief, and probability; 26 to the idea of cause (applying the Copy Principle); and 31–4 to free will. By contrast, just one paragraph each is given to skepticism (27), substance and the soul (28), geometry (29), the passions (30), and the association of ideas (35). Hume thus greatly emphasizes the positive aspects of his philosophy, somewhat playing down his skeptical doubts although he seems no closer to resolving them:

> Our author . . . concludes, that we assent to our faculties, and employ our reason only because we cannot help it. Philosophy wou'd render us entirely *Pyrrhonian*, were not nature too strong for it. (TA 27/657)

At much the same time, he was also preparing Book 3 of the *Treatise* for publication, with its *Appendix* bewailing the "labyrinth" into which he had been led by the conundrum of personal identity. So any resolution of the corrosive skepticism of Book 1 Part 4 was still, apparently, some years away.

Such a resolution was finally achieved with the first *Enquiry* of 1748, where Hume puts an even more systematic emphasis on his "chief argument" running from the Copy Principle (Section 2) through induction (4), custom and belief (5), probability (6), causation (7), and free will (8). Section 4 crucially rules out a priori knowledge of the world and thus establishes epistemic empiricism, after which Sections 5 to 8 all strongly support a causal understanding of human thought and behavior. This explanatory naturalism is reinforced by biological naturalism in Section 9 on "the reason of animals," followed by anti-supernaturalism in the next two sections, which illustrate how Hume's inductive theory can undermine superstitious beliefs by first revealing their own dependence on induction and then appealing to methodological consistency.[45] In this spirit, Section 10 explains why the inductive evidence against any reported miracle is almost certain to outweigh the inductive evidence for the report's reliability, while Section 11 points out that induction cannot justify any inference from the observed world to a Designer having qualities (notably justice) that are not manifested in what we observe. The *Enquiry* is rounded off by Section 12, whose calm mitigated skepticism we have already discussed.

It is illuminating to see how the balanced scientific naturalism of the *Enquiry*—whose overall epistemological perspective can seem common sense today—avoids destruction on the skeptical rocks that sank the project of the *Treatise*. First, Hume omits the corrosive skeptical argument of T 1.4.1, perhaps recognizing its serious flaws. That argument depended on the idea that rational judgment must always be *reflexive*, in the sense of requiring a further judgment about our initial judgment's reliability (T 1.4.1.5/181–2). But this requirement, which Hume sees as leading to a vicious regress and a continual diminution of probability,[46] is implicitly challenged in the *Enquiry* by his rejection of antecedent skepticism at EU 12.3/149–50. There, he points out that it is self-evidently hopeless to make reliance on our faculties conditional on a logically prior justification of them, for any would-be justification must itself rely on them. Hence, as we saw earlier, it is entirely reasonable to ascribe them default authority from the start, without tying ourselves in reflexive knots.

Second, in the *Enquiry* Hume omits any discussion of identity over time, and hence has no occasion to repeat his allegations from the *Treatise* that our ascriptions of such identity (either to physical objects, organisms, or persons) are radically incoherent and sustainable only by a "fiction of the imagination."[47] It is tempting to surmise that Hume had come to see the error of his ways here, and was no longer taking for granted that *numerical identity* over time necessarily requires *qualitative invariableness*.[48] Recognition of such an error might explain why he never again discusses identity in any of his works—thus the labyrinth of personal identity is completely unmentioned in the *Enquiry*.[49]

Third, in the *Enquiry* Hume treats our belief in external objects as a natural instinct which is potentially true (as long as we are careful to distinguish objects from our perceptions of them), even though we cannot provide any rational argument to support that belief.[50] We risk incoherence if we try to conceptualize the *nature* of external objects in terms of primary and secondary qualities (EU 12.15/154; cf. T 1.4.4), but apparently there is no harm in thinking of them using the merely relative idea of "a certain unknown, inexplicable *something*, as the cause of our perceptions" (EU 12.16/155; cf. T 1.2.6.9/68).

Finally, although Hume in the *Enquiry* retains his beloved Copy Principle (and its vital application to the issues of causal necessity and free will), he no longer treats ideas so simplistically as sensory images that can be literally divided into independent atomic perceptions and rearranged. Accordingly his Separability Principle disappears, along with the extravagant commitment to the possibility of self-subsisting perceptions which made the metaphysics of the *Treatise* so incredible.[51]

Most of these features of the *Enquiry* involve omission of *Treatise* material, and since Hume does not explicitly disavow what he omitted, we cannot be certain where his editing reflects a genuine change of mind as opposed to pragmatic silence or mere abridgement. In general, the differences seem philosophically well-motivated and hence likely to have resulted from greater maturity and reflection. With respect to the external world, however, the *Enquiry* account is somewhat unsatisfactory in failing to pursue difficult questions raised by the Copy Principle. Part 1 of Section 12 ends by pointing out that if our thinking about external objects is restricted to ideas copied from our sensations, then the merely relative notion that we can have of them as independent entities seems to be "so imperfect, that no sceptic will think it worth while to contend against it" (EU 12.16/155). This subtle phrase, however, is ambiguous, and I suspect deliberately so, reflecting Hume's two minds on the issue. On the one hand, thinking of "the cause of our perceptions" as "a certain unknown, inexplicable *something*" is so pathetically contentless that it hardly qualifies as a thought of a substantial object. But on the other hand, this lack of substantial content perfectly suits Hume's irreligious purposes and his desire to cripple any ambition towards a rival metaphysics based on supposed rational insight into the nature of matter (such as Locke's and Clarke's insistence that matter and motion cannot create thought).[52] Having found a phrase that nicely captures this ambivalence, and without any more satisfactory philosophical resolution to offer, Hume allows his discussion to end here,[53] with a footnote which credits Berkeley for the preceding argument about primary and secondary qualities and observes that such "merely sceptical" arguments typically "*admit of no answer and produce no conviction*" (EU 12.16 n32/155 n1). This observation corresponds with his already-stated pretext for giving so little attention to such arguments: that they "can so little serve to any serious purpose" (EU 12.15/154). Thus Hume apparently wants to rise above extreme skepticism even when he has no satisfactory philosophical answer to it.[54]

VII Conclusion: Hume's Consistent Purposes

If this account is on the right lines, then Hume's philosophy has a consistent underlying core, which probably first started to crystallize when he brought his concept empiricism—the Copy Principle—to bear on a cluster of issues involving causation. But his ultimate aim here was not merely to analyze concepts, and he was motivated more by the valuable corollaries that he saw flowing from his definition of causal necessity: bringing human thought and behavior within the reach of causal science, refuting the supposed apriority of the Causal Maxim, and concluding that causal relations (and hence the properties of matter) can be known only through experience. These results also struck heavily against Christian orthodoxy by undermining the Cosmological Argument, the Free Will Defence, the immateriality of the soul, and more generally the conception of man as radically distinct from the animal creation. Thus we see Hume's explanatory naturalism, epistemic empiricism, anti-supernaturalism, and biological naturalism all fitting together into a coherent system.

This system is also profoundly skeptical by the standards of Hume's day, most notably in regard to its irreligion and denial of the possibility of a priori insight into the nature of things. But Hume does not intend it to be *corrosively* skeptical, in the sense of posing a direct threat to the possibility of a philosophically respectable human science. Thus the extreme skepticism that arises in *Treatise* Book 1 Part 4 is *not* central to his philosophical plans, but derives instead from what he takes to be the logical following-through of his own principles, compelling him towards conclusions with which he is deeply uncomfortable. On this conception of his project, therefore, the dismay that he expresses in the conclusion of Book 1 is genuine rather than a charade, revealing his intense awareness that he has no adequate answer to the corrosive problems that he has unearthed. This extreme skepticism is no part of his intention, let alone a central theme, and the *Abstract* and *Enquiry* therefore reflect his fundamental purposes far more faithfully than does Book 1 of the *Treatise*.[55] The central line of thought made plain in the *Abstract* was in Hume's eyes the "Chief Argument" of the *Treatise* right from the start. His achievement in the *Enquiry* was to refine it further and thus to show how he could avoid the rocks of Pyrrhonism while steering the apparently "leaky, weather-beaten vessel" (T 1.4.7.1/263) of human reason safely towards the possibility of a fruitful, naturalistic science of man.

ABBREVIATIONS OF HUME'S WORKS CITED

D   *Dialogues Concerning Natural Religion*. In D. Coleman, ed. *Dialogues Concerning Natural Religion and Other Writings*. Cambridge: Cambridge University Press, 2007.

EM   *Enquiry Concerning the Principles of Morals: A Critical Edition*. Edited by Tom L. Beauchamp. Oxford: Clarendon, 1998.

EU   *An Enquiry Concerning Human Understanding: A Critical Edition*. Edited by Tom L. Beauchamp. Oxford: Clarendon Press, 2000.

LET   *The Letters of David Hume*, 2 Vols. Edited by J. Y. T. Greig. Oxford: Clarendon Press, 1932.

LG   *A Letter from a Gentleman to His friend in Edinburgh*. Edited by E. C. Mossner and J. V. Price. Edinburgh: Edinburgh University Press, 1967.

NHR   *The Natural History of Religion*. In Tom L. Beauchamp, ed. *A Dissertation on the Passions; The Natural History of Religion*. Oxford: Clarendon Press, 2007.

T   *A Treatise of Human Nature: A Critical Edition*. Edited by D. F. Norton and M. J. Norton. Oxford: Clarendon, 2007.

TA   *An Abstract of a Treatise of Human Nature*. Reprinted in T.

Notes

1. As understood by many hostile critics from Beattie (1770) to Stove (1973), and at least some admirers (e.g., Popkin 1951; Fogelin 1985).
2. A tradition of interpretation begun by Reid (1764) and promoted by Green (1874).
3. Morris (2009), for example, argues that "it is [Hume's] use of [the Copy Principle's] reverse in his account of definition that is really the most distinctive and innovative element of his system."
4. Garrett (1997) interprets Hume's central arguments as contributions to cognitive science.
5. The *Dissertation on the Passions* retains a fair amount of associationism, while the basic principle of *custom*—which Hume sees as *analogous* to the association of ideas (EU 5.20/53–4)—figures strongly in the first *Enquiry*. There is some suggestion in the *Enquiry* (EU 5.9/47) that Hume may have lost confidence in more specific associationist claims, but it seems likely that he continued to think that associationist mechanisms play a major role in human cognition.
6. Three parts of the *Treatise* end with sections on "the reason of animals" (T 1.3.16), "the pride and humility of animals" (T 2.1.12), and "the love and hatred of animals" (T 2.2.12), all of which stress human parallels. Hume ends Part 2.3 without a section on "the will and direct passions" of animals only because, he says, the parallel there is too obvious to require discussion (T 2.3.9.32/448). He also devotes Section 9 of the first *Enquiry* to "the reason of animals."
7. The term *evolutionary naturalism* is tempting, but would be anachronistic as applied to Hume. Darwin's theory of evolution did not appear until 1859, although his note-books of around 1839 show that he was reading Hume's *Enquiry* section on the reason of animals—published more than ninety years earlier—at the time that he came up with his theory.
8. Hume uses this phrase many times in the *Natural History of Religion* (NHR Intro.1, 2.2, 2.5, 3.4, 4.1, 5.2, 8.2, 15.5); at EU 7.21/69 he talks of "some invisible intelligent principle."
9. See for example Stroud (1977), pp. 186, 251 n. 9, 263 n. 10; Craig (1987) p. 71; Noonan (1999), pp. 18–19; Blackburn (2008), p. 108 n. 15. Quite apart from other objections, it is chrono-logically very implausible that Hume left for France in 1734 with his moral ideas signifi-cantly worked out, composed the bulk of the *Treatise* there within three years, and then on his return delayed publishing Book 3 until twenty-one months after the others.
10. Note that the famous hyperbolic statement about reason's being "the slave of the passions" (T 2.3.3.4/415), which so inspired Kemp Smith, does not really involve any *subordination* of reason to passion, for as Hume has just explained in the same paragraph, the two are not (and cannot be) in conflict. His theory of action is essentially that passion sets the *ends* of our action whereas reason works out the *means*. Without some desire to motivate us, we would not prefer one outcome over another, and hence reason would be inert because it has nothing to aim for, not because it is *dominated*.
11. Hume took the mind-spreading metaphor from Malebranche (1674–5/1997, p. 58), but its vividness and apparent fit with various aspects of Hume's own philosophy has contrib-uted to a widespread enthusiasm for characterizing him as a *projectivist*, especially among those attracted to Kemp Smith's view of him as privileging our sentiments in understand-ing the world. The point made here should at least give pause to those inclined to speak of "Humean projection," for it is far from clear that his attitude to causation—where he clearly presents such projection as an *error*—is to be assimilated with his attitude to

morality, where he talks apparently approvingly of the mind's "gilding or staining all natural objects with the colours, borrowed from internal sentiment" (EM App. 1.21/294). The complications involved in ascribing projection to Hume are explored by Kail (2007).

12. As documented at length in Russell (2008).

13. Craig's case for seeing the Similarity Thesis as the "dominant philosophy" of the Early Modern period (1987, chapter 1) also seems to me extremely thin. Given that God is understood as an infinite mind, theist philosophers will almost inevitably draw comparisons with the human mind, but unless these are frequent and pervasive (which Craig's limited citations suggest not), they provide negligible evidence of a "dominant philosophy."

14. Craig's presentation of indirect evidence (1987: 75–128) is fifteen times longer than his direct evidence (1987: 71–74), which cites only T 3.1.1.4/456–7 and various passages from the *Dialogues* (on the Design Argument).

15. See Millican (1995) pp. 123–124, 127–129, 136; (2002) pp. 155–156, 161–163; Garrett (1997) pp. 85–88. Since these appeared, support for the "deductivist" and "antideductivist" interpretations of Hume's argument seems to have vanished.

16. See, for example, Millican (2009) §5 (especially pp. 671–674) on the idea of necessary connexion and §4 on the two definitions, and also Section III of the current paper.

17. The "common Opinion" here seems most likely to mean theism in general, rather than anything more specific.

18. Compare Locke's *Essay* IV x 10 with Clarke (1732: 53).

19. The more general connection between Hume's causal topics and irreligion—to be discussed later—is also strongly corroborated by the references made to *Treatise* Book 1 in the "Sum of the Charge": seven are to T 1.4.5, five to T 1.3.14, one each to T 1.3.2, 1.3.7, 1.3.15, and 1.4.1, and one to the entirety of 1.4.7 (in relation to the first charge of "Universal Scepticism"). T 1.4.5 was clearly far more significant in context than it seems to most commentators today.

20. Kames refers explicitly to the Clarke-Collins debate in his *Essays* (1751: 171). Kames's own debate with Baxter concerned the causation of motion, his views on which were later published in the *Essays and Observations* of 1754.

21. For a useful summary account of this affair, see Russell (2008: 42–45), who speculates (p. 45) that it might have played some role in encouraging Hume to leave Scotland two years later. The free-thinking nephew of a Chirnside minister could certainly expect unwelcome attention and intrusion in such an inquisitorial context.

22. For more on this, see Millican (2007a: §§4–6).

23. The forty philosophical memoranda are in Mossner (1948: 500–503), and, for their dating, see Stewart (2000), especially p. 280, and Stewart (2005: 47). Memorandum 23, quoted here, is one of six that concern the Free Will Defence to the Problem of Evil (the others being numbers 19, 24, 25, 26, and 32).

24. See EU 2.9/21–22 and EU 7.4/62. In a letter to Hugh Blair of July 4, 1762, Hume defends himself against Thomas Reid's suggestion that "I had been hasty, & not supported by any Colour of Argument when I affirm, that all our Ideas are copy'd from impressions" by responding that "I have endeavourd to build that Principle on two Arguments," namely those from EU 2.6/19–20 and EU 2.7/20 (Brookes 1997: 257).

25. For a defence of these arguments, however, see Garrett (1997: 41–48).

26. Writing to Michael Ramsay on August 26, 1737, Hume recommends Bayle's article on Zeno of Elea as one of the readings that will help his friend to "easily comprehend the metaphysical Parts" of the *Treatise* (Mossner 1980: 627). Hume remained proud of his treatment

of space and time until at least 1755, when a noted mathematician, Lord Philip Stanhope, dissuaded him from publishing his treatise "on the metaphisical Principles of Geometry" (LET ii 253).

27. For discussion of Hume's assumption that the idea in question is *simple*, and of his insistence that all the various causal terms in his list are "nearly synonymous," see Millican (2007b) §2.2.

28. For further details of the debate, including relevant quotations, see Millican (2010) §II.

29. For the overwhelming evidence that Hume saw causation (and the universe) as deterministic, see Millican (2010).

30. The last and most dangerous of these implications—although perfectly clear in Hume's early memoranda—was prudently omitted from the *Treatise*. It saw the light of publication only in the *Enquiry*, but even there is expressed as a "mystery" rather than as an explicit threat to theism (EU 8.36/103).

31. For much more on this, see Millican (2009) and (2011). It is revealing how little of the New Hume literature makes any mention whatever of Clarke, Collins, moral and physical necessity, or the application of Hume's definitions to the problems of thinking matter and of "liberty and necessity." These issues are now sufficiently prominent in the literature that readers can draw their own conclusion from New Humean discussions that strategically ignore them.

32. Hence Hume's insistence that all of Locke's "natural" and "instituted" relations (*Essay* II xxviii 2 and 3) should be classed as instances of causation (T 1.1.4.3/11–2 and T 1.1.4.5/12 respectively). Comparison of the two accounts clearly reveals the taxonomic motive here, thus undercutting Kemp Smith's influential claim (1941: 245; cf. Noonan 1999: 18) that Hume's citing of blood and duty relationships as examples of causation is indicative of a predominant interest in moral philosophy. For detailed assessment of Hume's theory of relations, see Millican (forthcoming) §2.

33. So much so that the title word "probability" does not even appear in the main text until T 1.3.6.4/89.

34. This footnote was an afterthought, inserted into the *Treatise* while it was going through the press by means of a "cancel" leaf, which I believe accounts for its placement at the end of the section: it really belongs at the end of T 1.3.9.4/108 and should be read as a comment on T 1.3.9.3–4/107–8. Hume presents it as revealing an ambiguity in "the imagination," although more precisely he is drawing a distinction between two types of *principle* that operate on our ideas in the imagination: those that deserve the accolade of "reason" and those that do not. The same distinction is made more prominently at T 1.4.4.1–2/225–6, between the "permanent, irresistible, and universal" principles and those that are "changeable, weak, and irregular." Allusions to the distinction are also evident at T 1.3.13.11–12/149–50 and especially T 1.4.7.6–7/267–8, where its undermining seems to put Hume's entire philosophical project at risk, as we shall see in Section V of the current paper.

35. Compare Locke's suggestion that "Reason . . . perceives the probable connexion of all the *Ideas* or Proofs one to another" in a discourse that involves probable inference (*Essay* IV xvii 2).

36. If he refuses to acknowledge *anything*, of course, then he can present no reason either way.

37. See §1 of Millican (2012) for a detailed discussion of this response to extreme skepticism, which is more substantial than a crude appeal to *justificatory naturalism*: Hume is not *merely* saying that we cannot help reasoning inductively.

38. Later, at T 1.4.7.3/265 and T 1.4.7.5/266–7, Hume does show concern about the skeptical impact of his conclusions that induction relies on the mind's enlivening of ideas and that the impression of necessity is subjective. But until Part 4, the word "scepticism" and its cognates do not appear at all in the *Treatise*, except for a disapproving comment at T Intro.3/xiv.

39. It is puzzling—and perhaps a symptom of Hume's order of composition and haste in publication—that his most explicit presentation of the distinction, which moreover presents it as unambiguously required in order to "justify" his position, comes *after* two sections (T 1.4.1 and 1.4.2) that cast serious doubt on its tenability.

40. The key causal principle, "from like effects we presume like causes," is applied at T 1.4.4.4/227.

41. Indeed the supposed *eternity* of salvation or hellfire invites Pascal's famous Wager: better to "bet" on religion if the stakes are so high (and ignore the theoretical objections to the Wager as "cold, and strain'd"—T 1.4.7.9/269).

42. I am unconvinced by Garrett's appeal (1997, pp. 233–237) to what he calls Hume's "Title Principle" (at T 1.4.7.11/270) as a solution to this problem. It has no clear basis, gives no solid criterion for discrimination, and seems to be a stage in Hume's train of thought rather than a principle to which he gives enduring weight (e.g., it is not repeated in the *Enquiry*).

43. Hume might also have been motivated to seek out and present skeptical arguments because of their irreligious consequences (a case made strongly by Russell 2008), sometimes perhaps to the detriment of his scientific ambitions.

44. The full title is *An Abstract of a Book lately Published, entituled, A Treatise of Human Nature, &c. wherein the Chief Argument of that Book is farther illustrated and explained.*

45. Note again that Hume considers our inductive beliefs to be subject to rational discipline: as pointed out in Section V and note 37 above, his wholehearted support of induction is not simply an appeal to what we naturally believe.

46. The claim of continual diminution seems unjustified: if I mistake the reliability of my own mathematical judgment, for example, that error might require adjustment *upward* rather than downward, and in any case, my mathematical reliability is quite independent of my reliability in assessing my own faculties. Moreover such reflexive thinking, so far from being a rational duty, might well distract me from the mathematics and thus be ill-advised. On Humean principles, the optimal self-monitoring policy is only discoverable by experience, and cannot be a priori.

47. See, for example, T 1.4.2.26–36/200–5, T 1.4.3.2–4/219–20, and T 1.4.6.5–16/253–60.

48. As stated, for example, at T 1.4.2.31/201–2, T 1.4.3.2/219, and T 1.4.6.6/253–5.

49. In the *Dialogues*, Demea asks "What is the soul of man?" and presents something like the Humean bundle theory, pointing out that this is radically at odds with "that perfect immutability and simplicity, which all true Theists ascribe to the Deity" (D 4.2). But there is no suggestion here—nor in Cleathes's response—that change and complexity are incompatible with identity over time.

50. "It is a question of fact, whether the perceptions of the senses be produced by external objects, resembling them" (EU 12.12/153), but as Hume then explains, we have no observational basis for an inductive argument to decide this question (cf. T 1.4.2.47/212).

51. The atomistic *Treatise* theory of space and time, closely associated with the Separability Principle, is reduced in the *Enquiry* to a tentative "hint" at EU 12.20 n34/158 n1, which clearly acknowledges the motivation "to avoid … absurdities and contradictions,"

so that "lovers of science" will not "expose themselves to the ridicule and contempt of the ignorant."

52. By contrast, Hume presumably considers that even a minimal and relative conception of objects is enough to sustain the inductive science that he himself favors.

53. The final sentence of EU 12.16/155 was added only in the posthumous 1777 edition, perhaps corroborating my speculation that Hume was in two minds, composing his ambivalent conclusion only when his terminal illness was making clear that he would never personally resolve this.

54. To find an answer, I believe Hume would have had to reject his Copy Principle and crude "constant conjunction" view of inductive inference, countenancing both "inference to the best explanation" and postulation of entities with which we are not acquainted. It is unsurprising, in view of Section III above, that he did not explore this avenue.

55. Hence, presumably, the famous 1775 "Advertisement" in which Hume repudiated the Treatise as a "juvenile work" in favor of the *Enquiry* (and the other pieces in Volume 2 of the *Essays and Treatises on Several Subjects*).

Bibliography

Baxter, Andrew. (1732). *Some Reflections On a late Pamphlet, called, The State of the Moral World Considered*. Edinburgh: Hamilton.

Beattie, James. (1770). *An Essay on the Nature and Immutability of Truth; in opposition to Sophistry and Scepticism*. Edinburgh.

Blackburn, Simon. (2008). *How to Read Hume*. London: Granta Books.

Boswell, James. (1931). "An Account of My Last Interview with David Hume, Esq.," in *Private Papers of James Boswell from Malahide Castle, volume 12*, prepared for the press by Geoffrey Scott and Frederick A. Pottle (Mount Vernon NY: William Edwin Rudge, Inc.) and reprinted in Norman Kemp Smith (ed.), *Hume's Dialogues concerning Natural Religion* (London: Nelson, second edition 1947—see "D," Hume 1779, above), 76–89.

Boswell, James. (1932). *Private Papers of James Boswell from Malahide Castle, volume 15*, prepared for the press by Geoffrey Scott and Frederick A. Pottle. Mount Vernon, NY: William Edwin Rudge.

Brookes, Derek. (1997). "The Hume-Reid Exchange," in Thomas Reid (1764), *An Inquiry into the Human Mind on the Principles of Common Sense*, edited by Derek R. Brookes. Edinburgh: Edinburgh University Press, 255–265.

Clarke, Samuel. (1717). *Remarks Upon a Book, Entituled, A Philosophical Enquiry concerning Human Liberty*. London.

Clarke, Samuel. (1732). *A Discourse concerning the Being and Attributes of God*, 8th edition, London.

Collins, Anthony. (1717). *A Philosophical Inquiry concerning Human Liberty*. London.

Craig, Edward. (1987). *The Mind of God and the Works of Man*. Oxford: Clarendon Press.

Dudgeon, William. (1732). *The State of the Moral World Consider'd*. Edinburgh.

Fogelin, Robert. (1985). *Hume's Skepticism in the Treatise of Human Nature*. London: Routledge & Kegan Paul.

Garrett, Don. (1997). *Cognition and Commitment in Hume's Philosophy*. New York: Oxford University Press.

Green, T. H. (1874). "Introduction" to David Hume, *A Treatise of Human Nature*, edited by T. H. Green and T. H. Grose. London: Longman.

Kail, Peter. (2007). *Projection and Realism in Hume's Philosophy*. Oxford: Oxford University Press.

Kames, Henry Home Lord. (1751). *Essays on the Principles of Morality and Natural Religion*. Edinburgh: Kincaid and Donaldson.

Kames, Henry Home Lord. (1754). "Of the Laws of Motion," in David Hume and Alexander Munro (eds), *Essays and Observations, Physical and Literary*. Edinburgh: Philosophical Society of Edinburgh, 1–69.

Kemp Smith, Norman. (1905). "The Naturalism of Hume (I.)." *Mind* 14, 149–173.

Kemp Smith, Norman. (1941). *The Philosophy of David Hume*. London: Macmillan.

Locke, John. (1690/1975). *An Essay Concerning Human Understanding*, edited by P. H. Nidditch. Oxford: Clarendon Press ("*Essay*").

Malebranche, Nicolas. (1674-5/1997). *The Search after Truth*, trans. T. M. Lennon and P. J. Olscamp. Cambridge: Cambridge University Press.

Millican, Peter. (1995). "Hume's Argument Concerning Induction: Structure and Interpretation," in Stanley Tweyman (ed.), *David Hume: Critical Assessments* (London: Routledge), vol. 2: 91–144; reprinted in David W. D. Owen (ed.), *Hume: General Philosophy*. Aldershot: Ashgate, 2000, 165–218.

Millican, Peter. (2002). "Hume's Sceptical Doubts concerning Induction," in Peter Millican (ed.), *Reading Hume on Human Understanding*. Oxford: Clarendon Press, 107–173.

Millican, Peter. (2007a). "Introduction," in Oxford World's Classics edition of Hume's *Enquiry concerning Human Understanding*. Oxford: Oxford University Press.

Millican, Peter. (2007b). "Against the 'New Hume'," in Rupert Read and Kenneth A. Richman (eds), *The New Hume Debate, Revised Edition*. London: Routledge, 211–252.

Millican, Peter. (2009). "Hume, Causal Realism, and Causal Science." *Mind* 118, 647–712.

Millican, Peter. (2010). "Hume's Determinism." *Canadian Journal of Philosophy* 40, 611–642.

Millican, Peter. (2011). "Hume, Causal Realism, and Free Will," in Keith Allen and Tom Stoneham (eds), *Causation and Modern Philosophy*. New York: Routledge, 123–165.

Millican, Peter. (2012). "Hume's 'Scepticism' about Induction," in Alan Bailey and Dan O'Brien (eds), *The Continuum Companion to Hume*. London: Continuum, 57–103.

Millican, Peter. (forthcoming). "Hume's Fork, and His Theory of Relations," in *Philosophy and Phenomenological Research*.

Morris, William Edward. (2009). "David Hume." *The Stanford Encyclopedia of Philosophy* (Spring 2013 Edition).

Mossner, Ernest Campbell. (1948). "Hume's Early Memoranda, 1729-1440." *Journal of the History of Ideas* 9, 492–518.

Mossner, Ernest Campbell. (1980). *The Life of David Hume*, 2nd ed. Oxford: Clarendon Press.

Noonan, Harold W. (1999). *Hume on Knowledge*. Routledge.

Popkin, Richard. (1951). "David Hume: His Pyrrhonism and His Critique of Pyrrhonism." *Philosophical Quarterly* 1, 385–407.

Reid, Thomas. (1764/1997). *An Inquiry into the Human Mind on the Principles of Common Sense*, edited by Derek R. Brookes. Edinburgh: Edinburgh University Press.

Russell, Paul. (2008). *The Riddle of Hume's Treatise: Skepticism, Naturalism, and Irreligion*. New York: Oxford University Press.

Stewart, M. A. (1994). "An Early Fragment on Evil," in M. A. Stewart and John P. Wright (eds), *Hume and Hume's Connexions*. Edinburgh: Edinburgh University Press, 160–170.

Stewart, M. A. (2000). "The Dating of Hume's Manuscripts," in Paul Wood (ed.), *The Scottish Enlightenment: Essays in Reinterpretation*. Rochester, NY: University of Rochester Press, 267–314.

Stewart, M. A. (2005). "Hume's Intellectual Development," in Marina Frasca-Spada and P. J. E. Kail (eds), *Impressions of Hume*. Oxford: Clarendon Press, 11–58.

Stove, D. C. (1973). *Probability and Hume's Inductive Scepticism*. Clarendon Press.

Stroud, Barry. (1977). *Hume*. London: Routledge & Kegan Paul.

Thornhill-Miller, Branden and Peter Millican (2015). "The Common-Core/Diversity Dilemma: Revisions of Humean Thought, New Empirical Research, and the Limits of Rational Religious Belief." *European Journal for Philosophy of Religion* 7, 1–49.

CHAPTER 7

HUME'S PHILOSOPHY OF IRRELIGION AND THE MYTH OF BRITISH EMPIRICISM

PAUL RUSSELL

Most philosophers do not deserve their historical legacy . . .

— Bernard Williams

THROUGHOUT the twentieth century and into the present century, the dominant narrative covering the major thinkers and themes of early modern British philosophy has been that of "British Empiricism." The central figures in this tradition are generally identified as the triumvirate of Locke-Berkeley-Hume. On this view of things, the "British Empiricists" are taken to be primarily concerned to provide an account of the philosophical foundations of human knowledge in general and of modern science in particular. The mighty triumvirate of British Empiricism is positioned in opposition to the rationalists of continental thought, as represented by the equally formidable triumvirate of Descartes-Spinoza-Leibniz. The trajectory of the British empiricist tradition culminates in the work of Hume, who is read as advancing a form of radical skepticism about the scope and limits of human understanding. According to this grand narrative, the whole dialectical process of empiricists versus rationalists reaches its climax with Kant's triumphant synthesis of both empiricist and rationalist elements in his "critical philosophy," in which Kant is taken to have found a middle ground between the skeptical and dogmatical tendencies of the opposing parties. Although it is now common to question this grand narrative and the British Empiricism/Continental Rationalism dichotomy associated with it, it continues to command considerable authority and acceptance and leaves a considerable interpretive void when it is set aside.

There can be little doubt that the empiricist/rationalist schema has done much to shape and entrench the most familiar and well-established interpretations of Hume's philosophy. The view of Hume as an essentially skeptical thinker, drawing out the alarming implications of empiricist assumptions, was already gaining credibility well before Hume's death in 1776. This view, that Hume is fundamentally a philosophical skeptic about the possibility of human knowledge, also contributed to Kant's perspective on Hume's philosophy—famously waking the great German thinker from his "dogmatic slumber" (Kant 1783: 67). By the early twentieth century, however, an alternative reading had emerged that challenged this orthodoxy. Hume should not be read as simply a destructive skeptic but rather as a "naturalist," with constructive ambitions to contribute to "the science of man" (T, Intro 6–7/xx; TA, 1/645) as modeled after Newton's achievements in the natural sciences. Throughout the twentieth century and up to the present time, Hume's philosophy has generally been understood in terms of these two core themes, skepticism and naturalism. The fundamental difficulty we are faced with, however, is how these two themes are related to each other and which one represents Hume's dominant aims and ambitions. Described in more specific terms, the most fundamental problem we are presented with is how to *reconcile* Hume's seeming radical skepticism with his efforts to advance a "science of man"—a tension that pervades Hume's entire philosophy but that is most apparent and acute in his first and most ambitious work *A Treatise of Human Nature*.

In this contribution, I provide an outline of alternative interpretation of Hume's philosophy, one that not only deals with these perplexing challenges of interpretation but that also provides a radically different picture of the way in which Hume's philosophy is rooted in its historical context. The key to solving these difficult interpretive puzzles concerning Hume's philosophy—what one distinguished scholar has referred to as the "*Humesproblem*" (Popkin 1953: 267)—rests with recognizing Hume's fundamental irreligious aims and objectives. This, in turn, requires rejecting some widely accepted claims about the development of Hume's philosophy in relation to problems of religion and, in particular, the suggestion that Hume "castrated" the *Treatise*, removing from it almost all elements that touched on matters of religion and theology. According to the irreligious interpretation, there is an intimate relationship between the myth of castration and the myth of British Empiricism, along with the associated (mis)understanding of Hume's fundamental philosophical concerns. So considered, the irreligious interpretation has far-reaching significance, not only for how Hume's entire philosophical system is to be understood but also for the detailed analysis of his views on a wide and comprehensive range of more specific problems and topics. Beyond this, the irreligious interpretation not only reconfigures our understanding of the unity and structure of Hume's philosophy; in doing this, it also alters our picture of the shape and structure of early modern philosophy as a whole.

I SKEPTICISM, NATURALISM, AND THE RIDDLE

In order to understand the irreligious interpretation of Hume's philosophy, we need to begin with the *Treatise*. The *Treatise* is not only Hume's first work; it is also his most ambitious, judged in terms of both the range of the topics it covers and the depth and detail of the analysis provided. Moreover, as Hume's first and most substantial work—it is by far the longest of Hume's philosophical works—it lays the foundation for Hume's later works and provides an indispensible orientation point for making sense of the trajectory of his subsequent philosophical development and assessing his overall philosophical achievement. The *Treatise* also serves as the principal text around which the established interpretations have been framed and constructed. For all these reasons, from the perspective of the irreligious interpretation, it is the *Treatise* that must serve as the relevant guide for understanding the core features of Hume's philosophical system.

The skeptical reading of Hume's philosophy dates back to its early reception, particularly as provided by two of Hume's most influential Scottish critics, Thomas Reid and James Beattie. Reid and Beattie base their skeptical reading primarily on the *Treatise*, and they present Hume as following lines of thought laid down by Locke and Berkeley in the form of "the theory of ideas" (Reid 1967: I, 95, 101–104, 204–111; Beattie 1770: see esp. 142–156, 455–461).[1] Hume is presented as pursuing an essentially destructive or negative philosophical program, the principal aim of which is to show that our "common sense beliefs" (e.g., in causality, the external world, the self, and so on) lack any foundation in reason and cannot be justified. On this account, Hume is fundamentally concerned to draw out the radical skeptical consequences of adopting "the theory of ideas." This skeptical reading places heavy emphasis on epistemology and metaphysics and relegates his moral philosophy to a secondary or derivative status. Viewed this way, Hume's reputation is well-summed up by Bertrand Russell: "David Hume is one of the most important among philosophers, because he developed to its logical conclusion the empirical philosophy of Locke and Berkeley, and by making it self-consistent made it incredible. He represents, in a certain sense, a dead end: in his direction, it is impossible to go further" (Russell 1947: 685).

Throughout the nineteenth century and most of the twentieth century, the Reid-Beattie skeptical interpretation, as Norman Kemp Smith has calls it (Kemp Smith 1941: 3–8), enjoyed considerable influence and was the dominant account of the central thrust of Hume's philosophy. Although this view continued to enjoy considerable currency throughout the twentieth century, as it still does, it was challenged and brought into question by Kemp Smith's enormously influential study *The Philosophy of David Hume* (1941). According to Kemp Smith, what is crucial to Hume's philosophical system "is not Locke's or Berkeley's 'ideal' theory and the negative consequences that flow from it . . . but the doctrine that the determining influence in human, as in other forms of life, is feeling, not reason" (Kemp Smith 1941: 11). On Kemp Smith's interpretation, the "main thesis" of Hume's philosophy, as presented in the *Treatise* and the first *Enquiry*, is his claim "that belief is more properly an act of the sensitive, than the cognitive part of our natures" (Kemp Smith 1941: 546). Given this, Kemp Smith maintains, Hume's philosophy "can be more adequately described as naturalistic than as sceptical, and that its main governing principle is the thorough subordination of reason to the feelings and instincts" (Kemp Smith 1941: 84).

An important feature of Kemp Smith's naturalistic interpretation is that it presents Hume's basic philosophical strategy as essentially an extension of his views on morals and aesthetics. The key influence here, Kemp Smith claims, was Francis Hutcheson (Kemp Smith 1941: 12–13). More specifically, Hume applied Hutcheson's account of the role of feeling in the sphere of morals to "several of the chief problems to which Locke and Berkeley had drawn attention, but to which they had not been able to give a satisfactory answer" (Kemp Smith 1941: 13). Although this clearly restores a balance between Hume's concern with metaphysics and epistemology, on one side, and morals, on the other, it nevertheless remains focused on the problem of human knowledge as raised in the philosophy of Locke and Berkeley, holding that, contrary to the skeptical account, Hume advances a constructive solution.

Despite the firm emphasis on the influence of Hutcheson and the role of feeling in Hume's philosophy, Kemp Smith is clear that Hume's naturalism has another side to it that was inspired by Newton (Kemp Smith 1941: 53). It was Hume's plan, Kemp Smith suggests, to model his own project of providing a scientific account of the operations of the human mind after the example of Newtonian physics (Kemp Smith 1941: 71). Hume's "science of man" is, on this view, an expression of Hume's ambition to become "the Newton of the moral sciences"—a claim that has been made by a number of other commentators (e.g., Laird 1932: 20–24; Passmore 1980: 43, 131, 156; Mossner 1980: 73–75). Hume's naturalism, so considered, includes his "attempt to introduce the experimental method of reasoning into moral subjects," a theme that is neatly captured in the subtitle to the *Treatise*.

There remains, however, a fundamental difficulty that faces any interpretation that attempts to accommodate Hume's (supposed) ambition to become "the Newton of the moral sciences." The obvious difficulty here is that although Hume is plainly committed to *both* skeptical and naturalistic aims and objectives, these two sides of his thought seem to pull in opposite directions. On the one hand, Hume presents skeptical arguments that are understood systematically to discredit our common-sense beliefs about the world (i.e., undermine even our most ordinary, everyday claims to knowledge). On the other hand, he is understood to aim at being "the Newton of the moral science" by way of introducing "the experimental method of reasoning" into the study of human nature. These two themes do not just diverge from each other; the former defeats the latter. The difficulty is summed-up by Reid in these terms:

> It seems to be the peculiar strain of humour in this author, to set out in his introduction by promising, with a grave face, no less than a complete system of the sciences, upon a foundation entirely new—to wit, that of human nature—when the intention of the whole work is to show, that there is neither human nature nor science in the world.
>
> (Reid 1967: I, 102a).

To the extent that Hume advances extreme skeptical arguments, as he plainly does, Hume "the skeptic" appears to saw off the branch that Hume "the Newton of the moral sciences" is sitting on. Nor will it help if we follow Kemp Smith and appeal to a form of "naturalism" that teaches "that reason, as traditionally understood, has no role in human life." Clearly, this does nothing to answer the skeptic, nor does it serve as a secure philosophical basis on which to make (scientific) claims about the principles and operations of human nature considered as a contribution to human knowledge. These conflicts and tensions between Hume's skepticism and naturalism make up what we may refer to as "the riddle" of Hume's philosophy—which presents itself in the *Treatise* in its most acute and challenging form. In order to solve this riddle, we must look beyond the simple skepticism/naturalism dichotomy that has hitherto dominated the interpretive debate.

II IRRELIGION AND THE RIDDLE'S SOLUTION: THE CORE FEATURES

The solution to the riddle of the *Treatise*, I maintain, begins with a critique of the "castration" hypothesis, which, in its unqualified form, is simply a *myth*. For more than a century, there has been a widely accepted orthodoxy among Hume scholars that the *Treatise* has little direct or substantial concern with problems of religion. According to this view, although the two themes that do dominate the *Treatise*, skepticism and naturalism, are certainly relevant to Hume's views on religion, it is only in his later works that he applies his skeptical and naturalistic principles to this subject in any detail or systematic manner. Before he published the *Treatise*, he may well have intended to include some material that was directly concerned with religion (e.g., his discussion of miracles). Hume decided, however, to "castrate" his work and removed all discussion in it that might give "offence" to the orthodox.[2] As a result of this process, only a few traces of his original concern with these problems are still present in the *Treatise*. Hume's major contributions on the subject of religion are, therefore, to be found in his later writings. This begins with the first *Enquiry*, where he includes a discussion of miracles and the design argument (EU 10 and 11), continues with his *Natural History of Religion* (1757), and culminates with his posthumous *Dialogues Concerning Natural Religion* (1779), which is generally regarded as Hume's greatest work on this subject. Whatever Hume's aims and objectives in the *Treatise* may have been, religion was not central to his philosophical intentions in this work. This view of the *Treatise*, and of the subsequent development of Hume's philosophy in relation to problems of religion, has gone almost entirely unchallenged and continues to enjoy widespread acceptance.

Contrary to the castration hypothesis, Hume's *Treatise* is *systematically* concerned with problems of religion. Important evidence for this comes from the early responses to Hume's *Treatise*, which provide us with a better understanding of the relevant context in which this work was written and published. Early responses to the *Treatise* show that Hume's critics at this time interpreted his various skeptical arguments as being laden with "atheistic" or anti-Christian significance (see, e.g., LG). Hume's early reviewers and critics paid particular attention to his arguments concerning causation and routinely noted that his views on this subject served to discredit a number of fundamental doctrines of natural religion, especially the argument a priori. The most prominent defender of the argument a priori in the eighteenth-century context was Samuel Clarke, who was regularly identified as one of the primary targets of Hume's skeptical arguments throughout the *Treatise*. These and other features of the *Treatise* encouraged Hume's earliest critics to present his work as belonging in the tradition of "freethinkers" and "minute philosophers," such as Hobbes, Spinoza, and Collins—the very same set of thinkers who served as the principal targets of Clarke's effort to demonstrate "the truth and certainty" of the Christian religion in his enormously influential *Discourse Concerning the Being and Attributes of God* (1704–05). In more general terms, the primary context in which Hume's earliest critics assessed and placed his work was within the wider debate between the "religious philosophers" and "speculative atheists," which was the dominant or main philosophical debate throughout the century that preceded the publication of the *Treatise*.[3] It has been a standard practice of proponents of the established interpretations to dismiss Hume's earliest critics as "bigoted" and "silly" (as Hume did for the most part). According to the irreligious interpretation, however, Hume's earliest critics—whatever their other characteristics and qualities—were fully justified in their assessment of Hume's intentions in the *Treatise* and in placing his work in the same general company as "speculative atheists" and others who opposed the "religious philosophers."

Given the responses of Hume's earliest critics, it is evident that we should try to recover an understanding and appreciation of the way in which both Hume's skeptical and naturalistic arguments in the *Treatise* were themselves thoroughly embedded in problems of religion. The right place to begin these investigations is with the overall "plan" of Hume's *Treatise* (see Hume's remarks at TA 1/645). According to the irreligious interpretation, the basic scope and structure of Hume's *Treatise* is modeled or planned after Hobbes's similar project in *The Elements of Law* (1640) and the first two parts of *Leviathan* (1651). The *Treatise* is divided into three books: "Of the Understanding" (Book 1), "Of the Passions" (Book 2), and "Of Morals" (Book 3). This structure almost exactly mirrors the structure of Hobbes's *Elements*, which was first published in 1650 in the form of two treatises, *Human Nature* and *De Corpore Politico*. Moreover, the very title of the *Treatise of Human Nature* appears in Hobbes's work, which is also striking.[4] The significance of these affinities between Hume's and Hobbes's projects goes well beyond their immediate structural similarities and shared title. The common aim of their projects is to develop a secular, scientific account of the foundations of moral and social life. This scientific investigation of moral life, they are agreed, rests on an analysis of human thought and motivation (i.e., the understanding and the passions). The metaphysical foundation for this project is their shared naturalistic and necessitarian conception of human nature—whereby human beings are viewed as part of nature's seamless causal order. Perhaps most importantly, the Hobbist plan of Hume's *Treatise*—what we may describe as the form of his overall project—manifests a general commitment to the autonomy of morality from religion.[5] It is these general claims and objectives that make up the fundamental constructive or positive teachings and lessons of Hume's *Treatise*.

It is evident that this account of Hume's constructive aims and ambitions in the *Treatise* cannot be the whole truth about Hume's philosophy in this work. It leaves out the entire skeptical dimension of his thought—which is clearly negative or critical in content. According to the irreligious interpretation, there is an intimate and intricate relationship between Hume's skepticism and the constructive project of his "science of man." In order to clear the ground to build the edifice of secular morality, Hume had to undertake a systematic skeptical attack on the theological doctrines and principles that threatened such a project. The varied and seemingly unrelated skeptical arguments Hume advances in the *Treatise* are, in fact, held together by his overarching concern to discredit Christian metaphysics and morals. The principal targets of Hume's skepticism in the *Treatise* were the most current and influential arguments presented by various "religious philosophers" who sought to prove (demonstrably) the fundamental articles of the Christian religion: the being and attributes of God, the immortality of the soul, the reality of free will, and so on. So considered, the critical side of Hume's philosophy in the *Treatise* is simply the other side of the same anti-Christian coin that directs and shapes his core Hobbist program concerning the "science of man."

The immediate significance of the irreligious interpretation, as described, is that it accounts for the fundamental unity and coherence of Hume's philosophy in the *Treatise*. This should be understood, in the first place, in terms of the overall (Hobbist) "plan" of Hume's "science of man." Contrary to the accounts suggested by the established interpretations, there is a close and intimate link among all three books of the *Treatise*. (This shows, among other things, that Kemp Smith and those who follow him are seriously mistaken when they treat Book 2 on the passions as of peripheral or marginal relevance to Hume's project.) At the same time, there is a shared or common purpose uniting the skeptical and naturalistic themes that appear throughout the *Treatise*. What holds these dimensions of Hume's thought together, as has been explained, is the aim to discredit religious philosophy and morals and replace them with a secular, scientific understanding of moral and social life. Clearly, then, the irreligious interpretation recognizes the role and importance of *both* Hume's skeptical and naturalistic commitments and identifies a common source for these (distinct) features of his philosophy. It provides, therefore, a more balanced interpretation that avoids emphasizing one side of the skepticism–naturalism dichotomy at the expense of the other.

It would be a mistake to present the philosophical significance of the irreligious interpretation as limited to providing an account of the unity and coherence of Hume's basic intentions in the *Treatise*. This would be too modest and understates what is at stake here with regard to getting an accurate and complete account of Hume's aims and objectives in this work. What Hume aims to provide in the *Treatise* is a *complete system* of irreligion or "atheism." In his various other writings, Hume offers no such complete system or worldview. Only in the *Treatise* do we find Hume's philosophy presented as one complete system (which is not to deny that significant additions and amendments to that system come with his later works). In these respects, the *Treatise* provides us with an insight into the overall structure of his philosophy of a wholly different order.

It is arguable that the irreligious interpretation is just as significant historically as it is philosophically. The irreligious interpretation invites us to place Hume's philosophy in the *Treatise* in an entirely different tradition from those that the established interpretations have identified. The philosophy of Hume's *Treatise* belongs to an irreligious or "atheistic" tradition of thought in which Hume's principal predecessors were Hobbes and Spinoza. What characterizes this tradition—which can be traced back at least as far as Lucretius—is the fundamental aim to free humankind from the yoke of "superstition." Hume's philosophy in the *Treatise* should be recognized as a particularly distinguished and substantial contribution to this tradition of thought. Considered in the more immediate context of the early eighteenth century, Hume's *Treatise* is arguably the single most significant contribution to the philosophical literature of the Radical Enlightenment—however much its significance may be neglected, if not entirely overlooked, in contemporary accounts (see, e.g., Israel 2001). In sum, from both a philosophical and historical perspective, the irreligious interpretation provides a fundamentally different account of the nature and character of Hume's aims and intentions in the *Treatise*. As such, this alternative interpretation has important implications that inevitably resonate far beyond the *Treatise* itself, extending not only to our understanding of Hume's philosophy as a whole, but also to the way we understand the entire period of early modern philosophy.

III THE RIDDLE AND THE ROLE OF PYRRHONISM

In light of the foregoing summary of the core features of the irreligious interpretation, the question may be asked whether this interpretation, whatever its merits, succeeds in providing a satisfactory solution to the riddle? In order to answer this question we need to further refine the problem of the riddle. The first problem that we are faced with is that we need to explain why Hume selects and pursues the particular issues and topics that he takes up in the *Treatise*? Failing any satisfactory answer to this, we are left with a work that pursues a disjointed, fragmented set of topics and problems, presenting us with a Janus-faced work in which the core skeptical and naturalistic concerns are seemingly unrelated and poorly integrated with each other. Let us call this the *unity* problem. Neither the classical skeptical nor naturalistic interpretations provides convincing answers to this question about the unity of Hume's project in the *Treatise*. Both of them lean too heavily on one side or another of the skeptical–naturalist divide and make it very difficult to decipher any clear structure or organization in Hume's arguments and their arrangement. Whatever unity is secured on these accounts involves downplaying, if not neglecting, the other (equally important) dimension of Hume's thought.

In contrast with the established interpretations, the irreligious interpretation provides a detailed and convincing answer to the unity problem. What holds Hume's various skeptical arguments together, as has been explained, is not some unguided philosophical curiosity about an arbitrary set of issues and topics but rather the disciplined, focused aim of discrediting the metaphysics and morals of the Christian religion. More specifically, it is Hume's particular concern to *separate* philosophy and theology, identifying the scope and limits of human understanding in such a way that it excludes the use of philosophy for the purposes of religious doctrine and dogma. The key instrument employed by Hume to achieve this end is his *moderate* skepticism, which discourages theological speculations but permits philosophical investigations in the sphere of common life, most notably in the area of the science of human nature, where we may expect to make some (modest) contribution to human knowledge (T 1.4.2.1, 1.4.7.9–14/187, 269–73; TA 27/657; LG 19–22). To the extent that Hume's skeptical commitments are moderate or "academic" in character, it is a crucial feature of them that they serve the irreligious end of insulating philosophy from the "intangling brambles" of theology and religion (EU 1.11/11).

The irreligious account of Hume's core skeptical intentions also makes sense of another aspect of the unity problem because as it concerns the relationship between Hume's skepticism and his naturalism. Hume's fundamental naturalistic aim is to provide a secular, scientific account of morality, viewed as *autonomous* from religious metaphysics and morals. This project of a "science of man" would be impossible, however, if Hume embraced a stronger, more extreme Pyrrhonist skepticism—because this would require him to throw out "the science of man", along with the theological bathwater. Whatever ambiguities and complexities we may find in Hume's philosophy, he is careful to say that we should not do this. As such, Hume's (irreligious) skeptical efforts to *systematically* discredit Christian metaphysics and morals, suitably contained and constrained, are not just consistent with his ambition to provide a secular, scientific account of moral and political life: it is an essential part of that project. Clearly, then, the irreligious interpretation provides a convincing answer to the unity aspect of the riddle problem as it concerns Hume's various skeptical targets and the relation between his skepticism and his naturalism. His moderate skeptical principles serve as a powerful weapon to discredit the ambitions of "religious philosophers" while leaving his own ambitions to advance the science of man undamaged.

There remains, nevertheless, a further dimension to the riddle problem, lying deep within his system, which is not just a question about the unity of Hume's philosophy but about its very coherence. In the final analysis, this problem concerns the relationship that holds between Hume's moderate, academic skeptical principles and his more extreme Pyrrhonist arguments. More specifically, we require some further explanation for the specific role of Hume's Pyrrhonist arguments within the framework of his (irreligious) philosophy. With reference to Hume's stronger skeptical commitments, critics have argued that Hume's whole project in the *Treatise*, and perhaps throughout his entire philosophy, is not simply Janus-faced (i.e., fragmented and disjointed) but actually *broken-backed*. Hume, his critics point out, not only advances Pyrrhonist skeptical arguments, he also insists in several different contexts that they cannot be refuted—an observation that, famously, reduces him to a state of philosophical "melancholy" and "despair" (T 1.4.7.1/263–4; and 1.4.2.1, 1.4.2.57, 1.4.7.7–10/187, 218, 267–9; TA 27/657). Although Hume also maintains that a skepticism of this extreme kind is unlivable and would be entirely destructive to human life (T 1.4.7.7–9/267–9; cp. EU, 12.23/159–60), considerations of this kind do not (as Hume acknowledges) serve to discredit the skeptics: they can only encourage us to ignore them or simply set them aside. The critical objection remains, therefore, that the *Treatise*, and the rest of Hume's philosophy with it, is indeed broken-backed. The irreligious interpretation, critics argue, still does not provide any solution to *these* concerns—concerns about the coherence of Hume's (core) irreligious intentions.

Hume is certainly alive to the difficulty that faces him here. He openly acknowledges that Pyrrhonist principles would entirely subvert and "cut off" all science and philosophy (T 1.4.7.7/268; D 1.13). He is equally clear that a more moderate skepticism has no such consequences (T 1.4.2.1, 1.4.7.10–14/187, 269–71; LG 19; EU 12.24–30/161–5; D 1.8–9). Hume explains in the conclusion to Book 1 of the *Treatise*, consistent with his remarks on this subject in his later works, that the value of Pyrrhonist reflections is that they serve to expose the weaknesses and narrow limits of human understanding (T 1.4.7.13–4/271–2; cp. EU 12.24–6/161–3; D 1.3–11). The (causal) effect of this is to sustain and support the fundamental tenets of a *moderate* (academic) skepticism. More specifically, as Hume explains in detail in his conclusion to the first *Enquiry*, when we engage in Pyrrhonist reflections, this affects us in two important ways. The first is that it serves to check our tendency to dogmatism (e.g., as manifest in all efforts to demonstrate or prove as certain the doctrines of the Christian religion). The second is that it should encourage us to confine our philosophical investigations to "common life" and to discourage all speculations beyond this sphere—in particular, speculations concerning "the two eternities" (D 1.10; EU 12.25/162). According to Hume, we should turn our philosophical attention away from theological systems and hypotheses and back toward investigations such as the "science of man," which has hitherto been "most neglected" (T 1.4.7.14/278). This is the central lesson of Hume's skeptical observations and exercises in the *Treatise*. On Hume's account, therefore, the benefit we reap from Pyrrhonianism is secured not by adopting its principles and putting them into practice, which would be as damaging as it is impossible, but rather through the way in which it *secures and sustains* our commitments to a more *moderate* skepticism. By providing this form of support for the principles of moderate skepticism, the more extreme form of Pyrrhonist skepticism serves the aims of Hume's fundamental irreligious aims and objectives in both its critical and constructive dimensions.[6]

At this point, the critic may respond that whereas these claims and observations may explain why Hume was motivated to advance Pyrrhonist arguments, they still do not show that his mitigated skeptical principles are well-founded, given his own (unrefuted) Pyrrhonist arguments. That is to say, no convincing argument has been provided that serves to discredit or restrain the extreme skepticism that Hume has unleashed. With regard to this critical response to Hume's (irreligious) position, there are, I suggest, two possible ways of replying on Hume's behalf. One is to note that the critic has not said anything that Hume does not acknowledge himself. Hume makes clear that "the skeptic still continues to reason and believe, even tho' he asserts, that he cannot defend his reason by reason" (T 1.4.2.1/187). If we are looking for secure *rational* foundations for the project of the "science of man," immune from all skeptical doubts, then Hume will agree with the critic that this has not been provided. All that can keep us committed to pursuits of this kind, in face of skeptical doubts, are the practical requirements of human life and the pleasures of philosophy itself. However, it may also be argued, on Hume's behalf, that he provides more resources than this for defeating or at least restraining extreme skepticism. Hume points out, for example, that the "true skeptic will be diffident of his philosophical doubts, as well as his philosophical conviction" (T 1.4.7.14/273). Viewed this way, Pyrrhonism becomes self-subverting. In yielding to "the current of nature," the moderate skeptic shows "most perfectly [his] skeptical disposition and principles" (T 1.4.7.10/269). In contrast with this, the Pyrrhonist is more rash and dogmatic "than even the boldest and most affirmative philosophy" (EU 1.15/15). Given this, it is not surprising that Hume dismisses all forms of "extravagant" or "total skepticism" as mere curiosities that we need not take seriously (T 1.4.1.7, 1.4.2.50, 1.4.7.9–11/183, 214, 269–70; LG 19–20; EU 12.15n/155n, 159–60). To these observations we may add that Hume may also be read as making the more general point about all human reasoning based on experience: that it bears strong resemblance with the reasoning of animals, and, as such, its operations have *natural* foundations, which Hume's own observations explain in some detail (T 1.3.16/176–9; EU 9). Viewed in this way, Hume's skeptical ambitions are not to discredit reason in general but rather to show that we must not misrepresent the operations of reason itself by demanding and seeking rational foundations where there are none. Once we identify the natural foundations of human reason, then we are in a much better position to recognize its limits (e.g., in relation to theological speculations).

These observations concerning Hume's response to the riddle objection make clear that the irreligious interpretation can not only account for the specific role of Hume's skeptical arguments as they concern the unity issue (i.e., how his various skeptical arguments are related to each other and to his naturalism), it can also provide a plausible response to the (further) criticism that Hume's entire project is incoherent or broken-backed. To understand this aspect of the irreligious interpretation involves understanding the way in which Hume maintains that his Pyrrhonist arguments serve to support and sustain his more moderate skeptical principles, consistent with the requirements of his core irreligious aims and ambitions (separating philosophy and theology and securing the autonomy of ethics). Hume's remarks, although they reveal a degree of ambiguity or instability on this matter, nevertheless plainly suggest that this can be accomplished without leaving his irreligious philosophy entirely broken-backed. What is crucial, as he sees it, is that that the *extreme* forms of skepticism that he has unleashed (i.e., Pyrrhonism) can be brought back under control by means of the combined force of naturalism and skeptical reflection itself. On the irreligious account, therefore, Hume holds that there is a way to overcome (if not eliminate) the internal tensions that exist between his (strong) skepticism and his naturalist ambitions.

It is certainly true that some critics of Hume's philosophy may remain unconvinced by this way of responding to the riddle as it concerns the coherence objection. At this point, however, it is important to distinguish between the *interpretive* and *critical* adequacy of the irreligious account of Hume's arguments. Obviously, we may be presented with an interpretation that is entirely adequate, in the sense that it reliably and convincingly captures Hume's intentions and views, even though the position articulated may remain unconvincing from a critical perspective. That is to say, there is no necessary convergence between an accurate (and convincing) interpretation and a true (and convincing) philosophical position—a point that even the most rigid "Humean" will surely concede.[7] Although the irreligious interpretation succeeds in providing a clear and convincing account of how Hume suggests the riddle objection should be handled, his position may well still be judged philosophically vulnerable based on concerns about the success of his efforts to contain his extreme skeptical arguments. Clearly, however, concerns of this kind do not serve to discredit the irreligious interpretation itself. What would discredit the irreligious interpretation, and does discredit the established interpretations, would be an inability to account for why the problem of the riddle even arises for Hume; why Hume's philosophy pursues two themes that stand in such obvious tension with each other; what connects and unites these seemingly opposed strands in his thought; and, finally, how Hume believes that these two strands can indeed be reconciled with each other. In all these pertinent dimensions of the riddle problem, the established interpretations fail where the irreligious interpretation provides clear and credible answers.

IV CAUSATION AND THE LIMITS OF PHILOSOPHY

The irreligious interpretation is by no means limited or restricted to a high-level account of the way in which Hume's skepticism and naturalism are related to each other (as described in the preceding sections). On the contrary, the irreligious interpretation provides systematic, alternative interpretations and analyses of each of the various particular topics that Hume addresses. This includes topics such as space and time, causation and induction, the external world, mind and self, free will, morality, and so on. Although it is not possible to take up each and every one of these topics, there is one topic that demands some specific comment as it concerns Hume's irreligious program. There can be no doubt that Hume's views on the subject of causation serve as the "main pillar" of his philosophical system (Reid 1967: 2, 627–628). According to the irreligious interpretation, Hume puts his views on causation to work to secure his core skeptical and naturalistic objectives understood in terms of his irreligious aims. On one side, he advances his radical and innovative views about causation to establish the limits of human reasoning as it regards religious speculations (i.e., separating philosophy and theology). On the other, he employs his views on causation to serve as the relevant meta-physical foundation for his project of "the science of man"—causal foundations that serve to discredit the opposing philosophical anthropology of the Christian religion. Let us briefly review the central threads of Hume's views on causation as they concern these two dimensions of his thought.

The fundamental issue that separates "religious philosophers" from "speculative atheists" in the context of the seventeenth- and eighteenth-century debate was whether or not an intelligent, immaterial being was the original (necessary) first cause of all that exists. There were two distinct forms of argument that theists generally relied on in support of this hypothesis. The first is the argument a priori or cosmological argument, which was given its classical formulation by Samuel Clarke. Clarke's version of this argument, which was much admired and hugely influential, rests on the general causal principle: "Nothing can come from nothing" [*Ex nihilo, nihil fit*].[8] This princi-ple, which had been employed by Lucretius as a cornerstone for his system of ancient atheism (Lucretius 1951: 43), was now to be turned against atheism. Clarke employed this principle to show, first, that because the material world is not self-existent or a nec-essary being, there must be some further cause of it, distinct from the material world. Second, and related to this, he also employed this principle to argue that matter cannot be prior to mind in existence as no cause can give rise to perfections or excellences it does not itself possess (to suppose otherwise is contrary to the fundamental principle that "nothing can come from nothing"). This was, of course, a familiar form of argument advanced by many others, including Descartes (1984: 2, 28). In refuting this reasoning, Hume offers an alternative fundamental causal principle: *Any thing may produce any thing* (T 1.3.15.1/173; cp. 1.4.5.30/247; TA 11/650; EU 12.29/164). It is, Hume maintains, entirely possible for us to conceive of something beginning to exist without any cause. This is not to say that the world is created or produced by nothing, nor is it to say that the world was produced by itself—these claims would be absurd and contradictory (T 1.3.3.5–6/80–1). All that is claimed is that it is conceivable that the world was not cre-ated or produced or the effect of anything. As far as we can tell a priori, the world may exist or have come into existence without any cause whatsoever.

All that there is to causation as we experience and know it, says Hume, is the constant conjunction or regular succession of resembling objects. In other words, to say X causes Y is to say that, in our experience, we discover that objects resembling X's are always prior to and contiguous with objects resembling Y's (T 1.3.14.28–31/168–70). Our idea of causation as it exists in the world reaches no further than this. On this basis, he con-cludes: "Causation, annihilation, motion, reason, volition; all these may arise from one another, or from any other object we may imagine" (T 1.3.15.1/173). In this way, Hume stands Lucretius on his head with a view to refuting those "religious philosophers" who aimed to refute Lucretius's atheism using his own causal maxim:

> That impious maxim of the ancient philosophy, *Ex nihilo, nihil fit*, by which the cre-ation of matter was excluded, ceases to be a maxim, according to my philosophy. Not only the will of the supreme Being may create matter; but for ought we know a priori,

the will of any other being might create it, or any other cause that the most whimsical imagination can assign.

(EU 12.29n/164n)

Evidently, then, under cover of rejecting Lucretius's general causal principle, Hume has established that, a priori, it is not impossible for matter and motion to produce thought and consciousness. On the contrary, not only is it a priori possible for matter to be as "active" as thought and consciousness and to actually produce thought and conscious- ness, this is exactly what we discover from experience (T 1.3.5.31/248–9). There is, there- fore, no basis whatsoever for the a priori claim that there necessarily exists an original, self-existent being that is an immaterial, intelligent being (i.e., God).

The general conclusion that follows from these interrelated arguments concerning the limits of causal reasoning is that all efforts to demonstratively prove the existence of God are doomed to failure—a point that Hume explicitly makes in the *Treatise* and the *Enquiry* and repeats in the *Dialogues* (T 1.3.7/94; EU 12.28/163–4; D 9.5). It follows from this that the existence of any being can be proved only by arguments from cause and effect and that all arguments of this kind are based entirely on experience. "It is," says Hume, "only experience, which teaches us the nature and bounds of cause and effect, and enables us to infer the existence of one object from that of another" (EU 12.29/164). With respect to the claims of divinity and theology, insofar as it aims to prove the existence of God, all such arguments must be based on causal experience as Hume describes it.

Whereas the cosmological argument, as advanced by Locke, Clarke, and others, aims to prove the existence of God by means of a priori, demonstrative reasoning, the argu- ment from design has at least the merit of being based on experience and analogical reasoning. The essentials of Hume's critique of this argument are first presented in his *Enquiry Concerning Human Understanding* (EU 11) and given a more elaborate state- ment in the *Dialogues*.[9] The design argument begins with the claim that we observe an analogy or resemblance between the world and man-made machines and artifacts (e.g., watches, houses, etc.) in respect of their shared features of order, structure, harmony and the evident way their parts are adjusted to perform some function or serve certain ends (see, e.g., the observations of "Cleanthes," one of the characters of the *Dialogues*, at D 2.5). When we discover an object that has these features (i.e., order, structure, etc.), we infer that these objects have not arisen just by chance but have been produced by human intelligence. We must allow that when we discover resembling effects, we may reason- ably infer that the causes also resemble each other. On this basis, we may conclude, says the proponent of the design argument, that the cause of this world must be "somewhat similar to the mind of man" (D 2.5; EU 11.11/135–6).

The fundamental flaw with this argument, Hume maintains, rests with the weakness of the analogy involved:

In human nature, there is a certain experienced coherence of designs and inclina- tions; so that when, from any fact, we have discovered one intention of any man, it may often be reasonable, from experience, to infer another, and draw a long chain of conclusions concerning his past or future conduct. But this method of reasoning can never have place regard to a Being, so remote and incomprehensible, who bears much less analogy to any other being in the universe than the sun to a waxen taper, and who discovers himself only by some faint traces or outlines, beyond which we have no authority to ascribe to him any attribute or perfection.

(EU 11.26/146; cf. D 2.2–3, 2.7)

In these circumstances, when we reason on the basis of such a weak and overextended analogy, we are vulnerable to the following dilemma. On one side, there is a tendency to anthropomorphize our conception of God and attribute human qualities and attributes to him (e.g., passions, faculties, etc.) without any credible grounds or experimental basis for this (D 3.12–3, 4, 5, 11–12, 59–12, 12, 5–6). We are, in particular, liable to attribute perfections to God that our limited and narrow experience of the universe, in respect of both time and space, cannot possibly justify or license (EU 11.25–7, 12.25–6; D 1.3, 12.7). On the other side, when we are duly and appropriately constrained in these conjectures, we will inevitably collapse into a form of mysticism, which maintains the "mysterious incomprehensible nature of the Deity" (D 4.1). In this way, because the tendency for anthropomorphism is to become a form of "idolatry" and for mysticism to become indistinguishable from a skepticism that claims "that the first cause of All is unknown and unintelligible," both these forms of theism are liable to collapse into plain atheism (D 4.4). It is this general line of argument that serves as a central thread throughout Hume's *Dialogues*.

The crucial lesson to be learned from Hume's account of causation and causal reasoning is that the existence of any being can be proved only on the basis of arguments founded on our experience of cause and effect understood in terms of a constant conjunctions of objects and events. All efforts to establish matter of fact and existence based on a priori, demonstrative reason are flawed and without any foundation. It follows from this that the only plausible basis, methodologically speaking, for the theological claims of religious philosophers is our experience of the world and the analogies this may suggest to us. Hume is equally clear, however, that this line of reasoning takes us well beyond the narrow limits and confines of human understanding and should be rejected. The practical recommendation with which he concludes his first *Enquiry* is that all the volumes of "divinity or school metaphysics . . . contain nothing but sophistry and illusion," and we may, therefore, "commit them to the flames" (EU 12.34/165).

This account of the skeptical implications of Hume's observations concerning the scope and limits of causal reasoning make clear why his own contemporaries regarded his views on this subject, from their earliest statement in the *Treatise* to the arguments published posthumously in the *Dialogues*, as loaded with irreligious significance. This is, however, only the critical or destructive aspect of their irreligious significance. The main debate between religious philosophers and speculative atheists was concerned not just with questions of cosmology but also, as noted before, with issues of philosophical anthropology. More specifically, from any orthodox perspective, the problem of religion was understood as, crucially, a *practical problem*, one concerning our accountability to God in a future state—this being a matter of the greatest importance for human happiness or misery. In this regard, there were two hotly debated issues of particular importance: the immortality of the soul and free will. If the soul is mortal, then there is no basis for either hope or fear concerning a future state. Similarly, unless human beings have free will, it was argued, there is no just basis for any such state—nor even for moral accountability in this world. On both these vitally important issues Hume marshaled his views on causation to devastating effect against various prominent defenses of the Christian religion, such as those advanced by Clarke, Butler, and Berkeley, along with those of many others.

With respect to the question of the soul, since Plato, it has been argued that the best proof of the immortality of the soul is the argument that the soul is immaterial and therefore indivisible and incorruptible. In the *Treatise*, and in his essay "Of the Immortality of the Soul," Hume takes up this topic. Among the many avenues and issues he explores and examines, one line of argument is especially prominent. The most fundamental question for Hume, as for others, is what is the relationship between mind and matter? In particular, what is the *causal* relationship between mind and matter? Clarke and others argued, drawing on the principle of causal hierarchy, that it is absurd and impossible to suppose that mere matter and motion could produce thought of any kind. Hume replies, employing his principle, that "any thing may produce any thing" (T 1.4.5.30/247). It is an empirical question whether we perceive "a constant conjunction of thought and motion," and experience, he argues, confirms a causal dependence of exactly this kind. One implication of this observation is that our existence as thinking subjects depends on our bodily existence. When our bodies die, therefore, it seems reasonable to suppose that mind will also perish. Although Hume does not explicitly draw these obvious conclusions in the *Treatise*, they are openly asserted in his posthumously published essay "Of the Immortality of the Soul."

With regard to free will, it was argued by Clarke, along with many other prominent representatives of Christian orthodoxy (e.g., Butler, Berkeley, Baxter, et al.), that if human beings are simply material beings, then all our actions and activities would be the necessary outcomes of the mechanical laws that govern matter—we would be like clocks.[10] Only immaterial beings, Clarke maintains, have active power, the power of beginning motion or initiating action (Clarke 1738: 2.697, 698). In reply, Hume argued that the basic obstacle to resolving this issue is that proponents of free will suppose that there is something more to causation and necessity in the operations of matter than mere constant conjunction and the inference of the mind that this gives rise to. Once we recognize that this is all that is involved in our experience or idea of causation and necessity, the only relevant question that remains is whether or not we discover similar regularities and inferences with respect to human thought and action. Hume spends much of his discussion showing that human life is as regular and uniform as the "operation of external bodies" (T 2.3.1.3–4/399–400), which allows us to anticipate and predict how other people will act in the future.

Related to this, Hume also rejects any supposed distinction between physical and moral necessity—a distinction that Clarke and others relied on to support their free will views (T 1.3.14.33/171). As for liberty, properly understood, it is entirely compatible with causation and necessity. Liberty should not be understood as the absence of causation and necessity but rather as requiring only an absence of violence, force, or constraint (T 2.3.2.1/407). Agents are at liberty when their actions are determined by their own will and desires (EU 8.3/95). Not only is the doctrine of causation and necessity not a threat to liberty and morality, so understood, it is essential to them. Were actions not subject to causation and necessity, they would be entirely capricious, which would, among other things, erode the basis for all assessment of moral merit or demerit (T 2.3.2.6–7/410–12; EU 8.31/99–100). With these points established, Hume goes on to show, in the *Enquiry*, how the doctrine of necessity, as he describes it, generates a series of serious and intractable difficulties for the theological position (EU 8. 32–6/99–103).

The overall account of human nature provided by Hume, as grounded in his views about causation, is one that presents human beings as part of the seamless order of causes and effects in which there is no categorical divide that distinguishes human beings from the rest of nature, much less presumes their existence for all eternity. Clearly, Hume rejects any form of dualism between thinking, active immaterial beings (that are immortal) and inert, passive, material beings (that are corruptible and mortal). For Hume's contemporaries, this metaphysical picture of human nature, presented in terms of a naturalist and necessitarian framework, was plainly "dangerous" and destructive of core religious doctrine. It is this worldview and perspective on the human condition that is fundamental to Hume's philosophical anthropology, whatever label we may attach to it.[11]

This general analysis of the way in which Hume applied his theory of causation to the various key themes and issues that he takes up in his writings makes clear that this central pillar of his entire philosophy was employed to support both the skeptical and naturalistic dimensions of his irreligious program. His account of the nature and limits of causal reasoning serves to cordon off and discredit the core ambitions of the religious philosophers as they concern various proofs for the existence of God—indeed, all such arguments stand condemned in light of Hume's observations. Similarly, Hume's account of causation serves to systematically naturalize the thoughts and actions of human beings. It rejects any view that presents us as in some way transcending the natural order of things. The metaphysical presuppositions of religious philosophy, as it involves a view of disembodied minds surviving in a future state with peculiar causal powers that distinguish them from the rest of nature, are all thoroughly discredited on Hume's account. Of all the weapons that Hume uses to achieve his fundamental irreligious aims and objectives, none is as effective or wide-ranging as his theory of causation. It could well be said that Hume's theory of causation is the philosophical guillotine upon which he proposes to execute, in a systematic manner, the entire spectrum of theological doctrine and dogma.

V Philosophical "Fox" or
an Irreligious "Hedgehog"?

Given the difficulties and challenges that the established interpretations encounter, especially in relation to the riddle problem, one easy solution is to simply deny that Hume is a philosopher whose diverse and varied concerns are held together by any single linking thread or unifying theme. Hume, it may be suggested, is a thinker who pursues a wide range of distinct and unrelated issues and topics and defies any reductivism of this kind. We should not, therefore, try and force any single framework on his thought—whether this concerns just the *Treatise* or his entire body of philosophical work, considered as a whole. It should be evident, however, that the irreligious interpretation, as I have described it, takes a different view. According to the irreligious interpretation, there are few, if any, "loose ends" in Hume's philosophy that are wholly unconnected with his irreligious program. Just as it is a mistake to treat significant parts of his philosophy—such as his discussions of passions, morals, and even religion itself—as in some way tangential or peripheral to his central concerns, so, too, it is a mistake to suppose that his philosophy lacks any coherent, overarching structure or principle of organization. To this extent, the irreligious interpretation agrees with the established interpretations that it would be a fundamental mistake to simply abandon all efforts to identify and articulate these core features of Hume's philosophy—however much it may disagree with how this has hitherto been done.

One way of explaining this issue is with reference to Isaiah Berlin's celebrated distinction between "foxes" and "hedgehogs" (Berlin 1953). Foxes, Berlin suggests, are those thinkers who "know many things" and have multiple concerns and interests. The hedgehog, in contrast, "knows one big thing," which guides most of what he does. One view, which is perhaps widely accepted at the present time, is that, given this broad distinction, Hume should be classified as a paradigmatic *fox*—pursuing a wide variety of philosophical problems and topics, which are scattered and more or less arbitrarily brought together in his various writings. If Hume is a philosophical fox, some may say, then surely we have reason to question the (hedgehog-like) claims of the irreligious interpretation. Two important and related questions arise out of this. The first is to what extent, when we look beyond the *Treatise*, do Hume's writings taken as a whole reflect a consistent and unifying concern with his irreligious agenda? Second, to what extent does the irreligious interpretation commit us to viewing Hume as better understood as an irreligious hedgehog than a philosophical fox?

Let us begin with the first question. What is the significance of our observations about Hume's irreligious intentions in the *Treatise* for our understanding of the general trajectory and coherence of his philosophy taken as a whole? According to the established interpretations, there is a significant discontinuity between the *Treatise* and his later writings. More specifically, as the castration myth has it, the *Treatise* is more or less unconcerned with matters of religion. This is surprising from any point of view because it generates a sharp schism between Hume's greatest and most substantial work, the *Treatise*, and some of his most significant philosophical contributions and achievements, as found in his (subsequent) critique of religion. The irreligious interpretation reverses this situation by rejecting the castration myth. Whereas the established interpretations find radical discontinuity in the evolution of Hume's philosophical thought and his central concerns in this regard, the irreligious interpretation finds continuity and consistency throughout. Hume's concern with problems of religion begin with the *Treatise* and carry on through his entire philosophy, running from the *Enquiries*, to the *Natural History of Religion*, and finishing with the (posthumously published) *Dialogues*.

When Hume's later works are considered in light of the irreligious interpretation of the *Treatise*, we can make better sense not only of their relations with each other but also of Hume's philosophical development over the course of his life. This is perhaps most striking in the case of the *Enquiries*. Hume, of course, was disappointed by the reception of the *Treatise* in the period that followed its publication. He believed that his "want of success . . . proceeded more from the manner than the matter" of his work, and, to remedy this, he "cast the first part of that work anew in the Enquiry concerning Human Understanding" (MOL, xxxv–vi).[12] The first *Enquiry* was published in 1748 and was followed by the second *Enquiry* in 1751, which cast anew much of the material in the third Book of the *Treatise*, "Of Morals." The fundamental thrust of each of the *Enquiries* corresponds very neatly with the paired core irreligious pursuits of the *Treatise*. In the case of the first *Enquiry*, as Hume's remarks in the first and last sections of that work make clear, it is his fundamental objective to show the limits of human understanding and, in particular, to discredit all efforts to employ philosophy in support of the metaphysical doctrines of the Christian religion (i.e., "superstition"). In the case of the second *Enquiry*, it is Hume's particular concern to show the way in which our moral and social life is founded in basic principles and operations of our human nature or moral psychology—a project that serves the aim of separating morality from any supposed foundation or source in religion. Considered in these terms, taken together, the *Enquiries* simply "cast anew" the two core irreligious themes and elements of the *Treatise*. Clearly, then, although Hume explicitly asks his readers to regard the *Enquiries*, and not the *Treatise*, as the representative statement of his mature philosophy, it would be incorrect to read this as any sort of repudiation of the core irreligious content of the *Treatise* or of its basic aims and ambitions. Those irreligious aims and ambitions resurface in the *Enquiries*, supplemented with further (important) irreligious material. Once the irreligious nature of Hume's ambitions in the *Treatise* is properly identified and articulated, the irreligious content and unifying central themes of the *Enquiries* become even more apparent.[13] The important conclusion that follows from this is that there is very substantial continuity and consistency in respect of Hume's irreligious aims and objectives as they stretch from the *Treatise* to the two *Enquiries*.

With regard to Hume's later works, his preoccupation with irreligious themes is perhaps most apparent in his dissertation *Natural History of Religion* and, especially, in his *Dialogues*.[14] Suffice to note, for our present purposes, that Hume's effort to identify the various natural causes of religion (primarily in problematic features of human existence, such as fear, anxiety, and ignorance) continues a project that was already a prominent feature in the writings of his immediate predecessors, Hobbes and Spinoza (Hobbes 1651: chap. 12; Spinoza 1670: preface). With regard to the *Dialogues*, which Hume was working on for more than a quarter of a century before his death, it is usually regarded as the culmination and fullest statement of his irreligious outlook (an assessment, as has been explained, that generally presupposes the "castration" myth about the *Treatise*). Although there is, of course, considerable debate about what exactly Hume's final position is in the *Dialogues* on the question of the existence of God, there is, nevertheless, little debate or controversy about the undeniable presence of irreligious arguments in this work.[15] In the *Dialogues*, Hume presents in a more compressed form his critique of the cosmological argument (D 9), which draws on material first presented in the *Treatise* and first *Enquiry*. He also presents what is widely regarded as the classic and most forceful statement of the problem of evil—this being an issue he had been thinking about since before the *Treatise* was even published (MEM 2.18, 22–5; see also Stewart 1995). Most importantly, Hume presents, in detail, his critique of the argument from design, which was first presented in a more rudimentary and compressed form in the first *Enquiry* (EU 11). It is evident, therefore, that beginning with the *Treatise*, continuing through the *Enquiries*, the *Natural History of Religion*, and, finally, the *Dialogues*, irreligious concerns, broadly understood, constitute the central thrust and dominant preoccupation of Hume's entire philosophical program.

Does it follow from these observations concerning Hume's systematic commitment to irreligious aims and concerns that we are justified in presenting Hume as an "irreligious hedgehog"? It may be argued that even those who accept the irreligious interpretation in its essentials are not committed to this further claim. To explain this, we need to distinguish between two versions of the irreligious interpretation itself, a weaker and a stronger version. The weaker view rejects the suggestion that the *Treatise* has little interest or concern with issues of religion (as per the castration myth) and is committed to the view that (a) irreligion belongs *among* Hume's central preoccupations in the *Treatise*, an *equal* partner with his skeptical and naturalistic concerns and (b) acknowledges that there is indeed an underlying consistency in respect of Hume's concern with this issue *throughout* his all philosophical writings. These claims are qualified, however, with the further claim that (c) Hume has, nevertheless, a plurality of aims and objectives guiding his philosophy, and irreligion has no claim to being either the dominant or most fundamental feature of his thought. Viewed in this way, Hume remains, a "philosophical fox" and should not be construed as an "irreligious hedgehog." We may, therefore, endorse the first two claims of the irreligious interpretation mentioned earlier without forcing all the major aspects of his philosophy into this framework.

The stronger account holds that this weak view, although it clearly avoids the (more serious) errors of the established interpretations, fails to adequately and sufficiently identify the importance and significance of Hume's irreligious intentions and the role they play in his philosophy. More specifically, in presenting Hume's fundamental aims and objectives as pluralistic, the weaker account underestimates the degree and extent to which Hume's various arguments and discussions are *systematically* woven together, in a disciplined, careful, focused manner, as coordinated and directed by his underlying irreligious concerns. This is, perhaps, most apparent in the *Treatise* but applies to a great extent to the entire body of his philosophical work. The weaker view, although it avoids the error of altogether overlooking Hume's irreligious aims in the *Treatise* and the way this shapes the trajectory of his later work, still misrepresents Hume's concerns as a disjointed, shapeless collection of investigations, held together by little more than Hume's unguided philosophical curiosity. This not only leads to a failure to identify the main thread of Hume's philosophy; it also has a tendency to miss and to misrepresent the way in which *each component* is situated in and attaches to the whole edifice.

There are two further considerations—both of them spurious, in my view—that may encourage some to embrace only the weaker version of the irreligious interpretation. Some may suppose that if we endorse the stronger view, then we must also hold that Hume lacks any independent interest in the various specific topics and problems that he pursues and investigates. Clearly, however, it is entirely possible for the issue of, for example, causation to be of intrinsic interest and importance to Hume while he still, consistently and systematically, uses these investigations and the conclusions he draws from them to serve his central irreligious ends.[16] Another suggestion is that if we endorse the stronger view, then this implies that Hume was willing to advance *any* argument, whatever its merits, so long as it served the purpose of his irreligious agenda. Plainly, once again, no such implication follows. Although it may well be true that some thinkers, who consider their conclusion to be both true and important, may be negligent about the soundness of the arguments they advance in support of these conclusions, Hume is not one of them. (This is a fault, however, that Hume does find in many—although not all—religious apologists.) In sum, it is not necessary to weaken the irreligious interpretation in order to free Hume of either of these vices (i.e., lacking philosophical curiosity beyond his irreligious concerns or negligently producing fabricated and faulty arguments to serve those ends). For all the variety and range that we find in Hume's philosophical contributions, he is, nevertheless, best understood as an "irreligious hedgehog"—albeit in fox's clothing.

VI THE MAIN DEBATE AND THE MYTH OF BRITISH EMPIRICISM

The irreligious interpretation maintains that the primary historical context in which Hume's philosophy belongs, beginning with the *Treatise*, is the debate between "religious philosophers" and "speculative atheists." This debate, which I have referred to as the "main debate," dominated British philosophy from the publication of Hobbes's *Leviathan* in 1651 until well into the middle of the eighteenth century. (For details on this, see Russell 2008: chaps. 3 and 4.) Although the figures and issues involved in this debate clearly overlap with those identified in the British Empiricists versus Continental

Rationalists schema, there are obvious and significant points of difference with respect to which specific figures and issues are of central concern and how they are related to each other. For this reason, it matters a great deal, when identifying and interpreting the central thrust and preoccupations of Hume's philosophy, which one of these contexts we place most emphasis on. When we consider the key set of issues that divided the parties involved in the main debate, it became evident that the very structure of Hume's philosophical thought is fundamentally different from what is suggested by any account that emphasizes Hume's place in the tradition of "British Empiricism."

The philosophy of atheism, as understood in the late seventeenth and early eighteenth centuries, was loosely identified with the metaphysical and moral outlooks of Hobbes and Spinoza—who were almost universally regarded as the most prominent representatives of "modern atheism" (see, e.g., the relevant writings by Clarke, Berkeley, et al.). Although the philosophical systems of atheism, like their theist counterparts, took many different forms, there were, nevertheless, two forms that were especially important for understanding Hume's concerns in the *Treatise* and throughout his philosophy. (These two forms are specifically identified and distinguished by Hume in his "Early Memoranda," which predates the publication of the *Treatise*.) The first of these is "the Pyrrhonian or sceptic" (MEM, 2.40). This mode of atheism is particularly associated with Sextus, Hobbes, and Bayle and insists on the limits of human understanding and philosophy, specifically in relation to theology. In contrast to this form of atheism, the second form of atheism is closely associated with naturalism and is more constructive in its commitments. Hume refers to this form of atheism as "Spinozism," although it resembles what Bayle calls "Stratonic atheism" (Bayle 1705; see also Kemp Smith 1947: 80–86). The key features of this form of atheism are that nature is self-existent, self-ordering, and self-moving. Human beings are part of this natural order of things, and our lives fall entirely within it and are governed by the same laws that regulate all its operations. Clearly, each of the two principal dimensions of Hume's own philosophical system converged on these two notable forms of atheism, as Hume and his contemporaries understood it.

Each of these forms of atheism, falling on either side of the skeptic/naturalist divide, maps onto the core points of contention in the main debate. This may be explained with reference to what we may describe in terms of a triangular set of contested relations, which may also be expanded into a diamond to accommodate a fourth element and a further set of relations that come with this (Figure 7.1).

The three elements of the triangle are Philosophy (P), Religion (R), and Morality (M). The relations that hold among them serve as the crucial points of contention that divide the parties in the main debate. Two of these relations are vital to supporting the aims of religious philosophers. First, in the case of the relation holding between philosophy and religion (P–R), the former was taken to provide secure rational foundations for the latter. The various refutations of "atheism" advanced by the Boyle lecturers and others took this to be the very starting point of their defense of the Christian religion. Second, in the case of the relation between religion and morality (R–M), the latter was understood as depending on the former because no form of morality without religious foundations

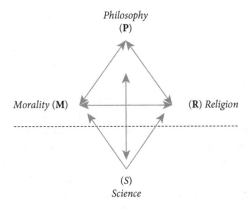

The Pivotal Issues of the Main Debate

FIGURE 7.1 Contested triangle/diamond

could be deemed complete or secure. It is precisely these two vital features of the theists' philosophy that Hume, following his "atheistic" predecessors, struck at. By providing an account of the relationship between morality and philosophy (M–P) that rests the former on the science of human nature and not on religion, these thinkers advanced forms of philosophical naturalism that alarmed their Christian critics and opponents in every way. It is these three relations, which fundamentally divide "religious philosophers" and "speculative atheists," that serve as the essential structure or framework of Hume's entire philosophical system and direct the various complex arguments that he advances.[17]

The triangular analysis may be expanded into a four-cornered diamond to accommodate *science*, considered as a distinct element. This provides us with a further three relations to be considered. Each of them, so considered, also plays a distinct role in accounting for Hume's fundamental irreligious intentions. (One caveat to this is that the science–philosophy distinction was not so clear in the eighteenth century and is, to that extent, anachronistic.) Hume's position concerning each of these further relations may be briefly summarized. The most important of these further relations is the philosophy/science (P–S) relationship. On the familiar "British Empiricism" view, this relationship takes priority over all others because Hume's primary concern is supposed to be with the philosophical foundations of human knowledge and science, in particular (i.e., the same general problem that is supposed to have preoccupied the major early modern philosophers from Descartes to Kant). It is Hume's position on this problem—qua "Empiricist"—that serves to place him in the same company as Locke and Berkeley in opposition to the "Rationalists."

In contrast with this, the irreligious interpretation maintains that it gets things backward to suppose that Hume's primary interest rests with the general problem of the foundations of human knowledge and that his secondary interest is in the relevance of this for the philosophy–religion (P–R) relationship. On the contrary, Hume's particular interest in the foundations of human knowledge, and the limits that these foundations impose on us, is principally motivated by his aim to put an end to the abuse of philosophical speculations by religion. It is the problems of religion, rather than problems of knowledge, that motivate, structure, and direct Hume's philosophical investigations. What matters to Hume is that his conclusions about the scope and limits of human knowledge have application to the main debate—not that they serve as the *terminus* of his own fundamental philosophical concerns.

With regard to the remaining two relations, morality–science (M–S) and religion–science (R–S), both may be understood as corollaries of Hume's views concerning other relations. That is to say, in the case of morality–science (M–S), in line with his irreligious predecessors, Hume is concerned to present a scientific account of morality that severs morality from religious foundations (as per his view on R–M and P–M). This form of naturalism, and all that it involved, was, as we have noted, anathema to the religious philosophers. In the case of religion–science (R–S), it was Hume's concern to show, contrary to all that the Newtonian theologians and their various Christian allies argued for, that the advances of modern science did not serve to support, much less secure, the case for theism. In opposition to all this, following his irreligious predecessors, Hume turned the apparatus of the scientific method onto religion itself, treating it as another item of natural phenomena capable of causal explanation and analysis. In other words, the general apparatus of the natural sciences is turned against religion, with a view to unmasking its origins in (problematic) features of human nature and the human condition. Clearly, then, in each and every major dimension of the structure of the main debate, whether we present it in terms of the triangular or diamond form, Hume decisively sides with the speculative atheists and against their opponents on the side of religious philosophy. It is this general structure that dominates not only Hume's philosophical system in the *Treatise* but also his whole philosophy.

The significance of this analysis for the view that Hume can be comfortably placed in the tradition of "British Empiricism" should now be very clear. It is a myth that Hume belongs in this company, and this myth is itself largely grounded in a deep and systematic misunderstanding of his core intentions in the *Treatise*, which has its own roots in the myth of "castration." When the castration myth is discarded, the irreligious character of the *Treatise* is plain to see. It is no less obvious that all efforts to force Hume's philosophy into the empiricist–rationalist schema comes at great cost. There are three overlapping objections to this perspective on Hume's philosophy that are especially important. First, the empiricist–rationalist framework narrows our perspective in such a way that we are required to marginalize or neglect thinkers who do not fit neatly into this framework. This includes a range of thinkers who, along with their contributions, are absolutely essential to understanding Hume's principal philosophical concerns—most notably Hobbes and Clarke, along with a number of other important figures involved in the main debate and the polemics of the Radical Enlightenment (e.g., Toland, Collins, Tindal, et al.). Second, a related difficulty with the empiricist–rationalist dichotomy, as generally presented, is that it scrambles the groupings of philosophers in this period in a wholly implausible and unconvincing manner. To take just one example of this, Hume is grouped with Berkeley as an opponent of the "Rationalists." The "Rationalists," depending on how these boundaries are delineated, would include Spinoza and perhaps Clarke (who is evidently English, not "continental"). This view of things could hardly be more distorted and confused from the perspective of either Berkeley or Hume. Berkeley, like Clarke, was an Anglican cleric who was primarily concerned to provide a dogmatic defense of the Christian religion, with his arguments aimed directly against the "skepticism and atheism" of Hobbes and Spinoza (see, e.g., Berkeley's subtitle to Berkeley 1713 and also Berkeley 1710: no. 93 and no. 98.) The problem of knowledge is for Berkeley, as it was for Hume, subservient to his primary concern with the problem of religion, as it presents itself in the main debate. Although Hobbes and Spinoza were widely linked together in the late seventeenth and early eighteenth centuries, the empiricist–rationalist dichotomy almost entirely ignores this and makes it difficult to make sense of the relevant basis of this linkage (i.e., with respect to the issue of "atheism"). In general, the empiricist–rationalist schema groups and associates Hume's philosophy in a manner that is not only alien to his own primary concerns and self-understanding but is actually *contrary* to it (and contrary to the way his philosophy was generally received by his own contemporaries).

Arguably the deepest and most significant failing of the empiricist–rationalist schema is the way in which it distorts and misrepresents the core structure and focus of Hume's philosophical interests in terms of epistemological worries rooted in the philosophy–science relationship. On this view of things, what has priority and dominates Hume's philosophical agenda is his concern with the scope and limits of human knowledge, where the immediate target of his skeptical arguments is not religion but our (common-sense) scientific understanding of the world. On this account, the skeptical challenge as it concerns the philosophy–religion relationship is of derived or secondary importance and was not even a significant part of Hume's earliest and most important statement of his philosophy in the *Treatise*. This epistemological slant on Hume's philosophy is manifest in the very label "Empiricism," which gives prominence and priority to matters of epistemology and methodology rather than theology and religion. Obviously, the irreligious interpretation takes the view that this gets Hume's philosophy, from the beginning, the wrong way round. It is the set of issues developed around the philosophical structure or architecture of the main debate (as per Figure 7.1)—not the fabricated, post-Kantian anachronism of the empiricist–rationalist schism—that accurately and adequately captures the relevant structure of Hume's fundamental philosophical aims and objectives.

Whatever merit the empiricist–rationalist schema may have for prying out fragments and segments of Hume's philosophy to illuminate and stimulate subsequent philosophical developments (e.g., post-Kantian concerns regarding the foundations of science etc.), this is not the right framework for appreciating or assessing Hume's overall philosophical contribution and achievement. When we reconfigure Hume's philosophy in these (irreligious) terms, it is evident that the whole edifice of "British Empiricism" is suspect, as is the associated empiricism–rationalism dichotomy. The label and category of "British Empiricism" is, at best, an incomplete and one-dimensional perspective on the far more complex and much richer structures of early modern philosophy. When we rely on this way of dividing up "the great philosophers" of this period—including and especially Hume—we obscure not only what was most important to them, we obscure what is arguably the most interesting and significant features of their philosophy.

ACKNOWLEDGMENTS

In preparing this contribution I have benefited from a number insightful reviews of *The Riddle of Hume's Treatise*, as well as from the comments and criticism provided by participants in several author-meets-critics sessions discussing this book. For this and other helpful conversations, I would particularly like to thank Don Garrett, Jamie Hellewell, Kevin Meeker, Peter Millican, Sam Rickless, and Ken Winkler.

ABBREVIATIONS OF WORKS CITED

D   *Dialogues Concerning Natural Religion*. In D. Coleman, ed. *Dialogues Concerning Natural Religion and Other Writings*. Cambridge: Cambridge University Press, 2007.

EU   *An Enquiry Concerning Human Understanding*. Edited by T. L. Beauchamp. Oxford: Clarendon, 2000.

LET   *The Letters of David Hume*, 2 Vols. Edited by J. Y. T. Greig. Oxford: Clarendon Press, 1932.

LG   *A Letter from a Gentleman to His friend in Edinburgh*. Edited by E. C. Mossner and J. V. Price. Edinburgh: Edinburgh University Press, 1967.

MEM   *Hume's Early Memoranda, 1729–40: The Complete Text*, edited with a foreword by E. C. Mossner, *Journal of the History of Ideas* 9 (1948), 492–518.

MOL   *My Own Life*. Reprinted in *Essays: Moral, Political, and Literary*. Revised edition by E. F. Miller. Indianapolis: Liberty Classics, 1985.

T   *A Treatise of Human Nature*. Edited by D. F. Norton and M. J. Norton. Oxford: Clarendon, 2007.

TA   *An Abstract of a Treatise of Human Nature*. Reprinted in T.

NOTES

1. It is significant, however, that Reid identifies Descartes as the real source of the theory of ideas.
2. What occasioned the process of "castration," according to this account, was Hume's unfulfilled plan, in late 1737, to meet with Joseph Butler, then Dean of St. Paul's Cathedral, and show him his manuscript of the *Treatise*. Hume wanted to avoid causing "offence." See, e.g., Mossner, 1980: 111–113; and also Laird, 1932: 282–283. For Hume's own remarks concerning this episode, see LET 1.24–5/no. 6.
3. The labels and division between "speculative atheists" and "religious philosophers" is one that Hume employs at EU 12.1, where he introduces the concluding section of the first *Enquiry*. For a more detailed description of this debate and its relevance to the early reception of Hume's *Treatise*, see Russell 2008: chaps. 2–5.
4. For more details about Hume's Hobbist plan in the *Treatise*, see Russell 2008: chap. 6. Hume's use of epigrams on the title pages of the *Treatise* also betray his significant

associations with Hobbes's fellow travelers in the freethinking/atheistic camp, most notably Spinoza and Anthony Collins. On this see Russell 2008: chap. 7.

5. It is important to note, however, that these (significant) similarities between the form and structure of Hume's project and Hobbes's do not imply that the *content* of Hume's philosophy is consistently "Hobbist"—which is plainly not the case. As this concerns Hume's views on morals, for example, see Russell 2008: chap. 17.

6. In various passages Hume suggests that there are some significant analogies (and disanalogies) between the philosophical "extravagance" of Pyrrhonism or extreme skepticism and other "excessive" philosophies such as Stoicism, which also demand too much of human nature (D 1.7–8; and cp. T 1.4.1.7, 1.4.7.13/183, 272; LG 20; EU 5.1, 12.23/40–1, 160). Although both "species of philosophy" make demands that are from one point of view unlivable and from another destructive, they may, nevertheless, appear in more moderate forms that have some beneficial and desirable effects.

7. Consider, for example, that we may accept a given interpretation of Hume's views on causation or morals without necessarily endorsing the particular view advanced because these are, obviously, distinct issues.

8. Clarke's argument is still regarded by some of our own contemporaries as "the most complete, forceful, and cogent presentation of the Cosmological Argument that we possess" (Rowe 1998: 8).

9. Although there is no detailed discussion of the argument from design in the *Treatise*, it would be wrong to conclude that in that work Hume's discussion of probable reasoning is unrelated to his irreligious aims and objectives. On the contrary, as I have argued at length elsewhere, at least one key target of his arguments relating to the problem of induction, as this arises in the context of his discussion of causal reasoning, is the doctrine of a future state. The particular view that Hume sets out to discredit is Butler's argument in his *Analogy of Religion* (1736), which aims to show that there is nothing incredible or unreasonable about revealed religion as it advances this doctrine. Butler's *Analogy* was itself a response to Matthew Tindal's *Christianity as Old as Creation* (1730), which had aroused a storm of controversy at the time Hume was writing the *Treatise* (i.e., during the 1730s). For more on this, see Russell 2008: chap. 11.

10. The relevant debates reached Hume's doorstep in the Borders during the 1730s, at the same time he was beginning work on the *Treatise*. The key figures involved were Andrew Baxter (a prominent Clarkean) and William Dudgeon (a radical freethinker). These debates also dragged in Hume's arch-nemesis William Warburton, who was a good and close friend of Baxter's. These figures and the controversies associated with them are of considerable importance and relevance for understanding both Hume's philosophy and its early reception—although they are matters that continue to be neglected and downplayed. See Russell 2008: chaps. 4 and 16 (esp. pp. 230–231); and also Russell 2007/2014.

11. Among the various labels that Hume's own contemporaries employed for doctrines of these kinds were "Spinozism," "pantheism," "atheism," and "Hobbism"—any one of which is a reasonable fit for Hume's general naturalistic program.

12. Hume, famously, later "disowned" the *Treatise*, rejecting it in favor of the *Enquiries* (as stated in the 1777 Advertisement to his *Essays and Treatises*; EU 83/2).

13. It has been a familiar point for some time that the first *Enquiry* has significant irreligious content. On the standard view, this is one notable difference between the *Treatise* and the first *Enquiries* (see, e.g., Flew 1961). More recently, several commentators have helpfully emphasized the full extent of Hume's irreligious intentions in the first *Enquiry* (see, e.g., Millican 2002: esp. 34–48). Clearly, however, it is possible to recognize the presence of

significant irreligious content in the first *Enquiry* without recognizing exactly how this relates this work to the second *Enquiry*, much less how these two works, taken together, are related to the *Treatise*. It is, therefore, the irreligious interpretation of the *Treatise* that, in these respects, secures a full and proper understanding of Hume's irreligious intentions as they inform his philosophy *as a whole*.

14. Mossner presents the standard view on this matter when he says: "*The Dialogues concerning Natural Religion* and 'The Natural History of Religion' are [Hume's] most comprehensive and important contributions to the philosophy and psychology of religion respectively" (Mossner 1980: 319).

15. My own view is that, subject to certain important qualifications, Hume is best understood as defending a form of "hard skeptical atheism" (Russell unpublished; see also Russell 2005/2013: esp. sec. 10). This is a position that lies between dogmatic atheism and agnosticism (or "soft skepticism"). Clearly, however, views differ in these respects, and there is a broad spectrum of views, stretching from some form of (attenuated) deism, through agnosticism, and on to atheism. At the same time, there is also wide agreement that the general thrust of Hume's discussion is one that is plainly hostile to any recognizable form of orthodox theism or religion. The term "irreligion" serves as a general enough label to cover the range of views that fall under this umbrella. The important point is that it is possible to endorse the irreligious interpretation of Hume's philosophy without being committed to any particular view within the broad spectrum that I have described.

16. Compare the parallel case with Clarke's philosophy. There is no conflict between saying that Clarke found issues such as space and time, matter and mind, free will, morality, and so on, all to be of intrinsic interest while at the same time consistently and systematically marshalling his discussions of these topics in defense of the Christian religion.

17. With this in mind, it should also be noted that given the assumptions of the castration hypothesis as it concerns the *Treatise*, since religion is supposed to make little or no appearance in this work, at least two of these relations would simply drop out as irrelevant to Hume's concerns in this work—i.e., the *very opposite* of what the irreligious interpretation maintains.

BIBLIOGRAPHY

Baxter, Andrew. (1733). *An Enquiry Into the Nature of the Human Soul, Wherein the Immateriality of the Soul is evinced from the Principles of Reason and Philosophy*. Edinburgh & London.

Bayle, Pierre. (1705). *Continuation Des Pensées Diverses*. Rotterdam.

Beattie, James. (1770). *An Essay on the Nature and Immutability of Truth*. Edinburgh. Reprint, New York: Garland, 1983.

Butler, Joseph. (1736/1849). *Analogy of Religion Natural and Revealed, to the Constitution and Course of Nature; To which are added Two Brief Dissertations*. Reprinted in Butler, *The Works*, ed. by S. Halifax (vol. 1 of 2 vols.). Oxford: Oxford University Press.

Berlin, Isaiah. (1953). *The Hedgehog and the Fox*, ed. by H. Hardy with a forward by M. Ignatieff. Princeton, NJ: Princeton University Press, 2013.

Berkeley, George. (1710). *A Treatise Concerning the Principles of Human Knowledge*, ed. by J. Dancy. Oxford: Oxford University Press, 1998.

Berkeley, George. (1713). *Three Dialogues between Hylas and Philonous*, ed. by J. Dancy. Oxford: Oxford University Press, 1998.

Clarke, Samuel. (1738/1978). *The Works*. 4 vols. London. Reprint, London: Garland.

Descartes, Rene. (1984). *The Philosophical Writings of Descartes*. 3 vols. Translated by J. Cottingham, R. Stoofhoff, and D. Murdoch. Cambridge: Cambridge University Press.

Dudgeon, William (1765/1994). *The Philosophical Works*. Reprinted with a new introduction by David Berman. London: Routledge.

Flew, Antony. (1961). *Hume's Philosophy of Belief*. London: Routledge.

Hobbes, Thomas. (1640/1994). *Elements of Law*. Originally published as two separate works: *Human Nature* (London: 1650) and *De Corpore Politico* (London: 1650). Reprinted in Hobbes, *Human Nature and De Corpore Politico*, ed. by J. C. A. Gaskin. Oxford: Oxford University Press.

Hobbes, Thomas. (1651/1994). *Leviathan*, ed. by E. Curley. Indianapolis: Hackett.

Israel, Jonathan. (2001). *Radical Enlightenment: Philosophy and the Making of Modernity 1650–1750*. Oxford: Oxford University Press.

Kant, Immanuel. (1783/2004). *Prolegomena to Any Future Metaphysics*, ed. by G. Zöller and trans. by P. G. Lucas and G. Zöller. Oxford: Oxford University Press.

Kemp Smith, Norman. (1941/2005). *The Philosophy of David Hume*, with a new introduction by D. Garrett. Basingstoke, UK: Palgrave.

Kemp Smith, Norman. (1947). Introduction to *Hume's Dialogues concerning Natural Religion*. Edinburgh: Thomas Nelson.

Laird, John. (1932). *Hume's Philosophy of Human Nature*. London: Methuen.

Lucretius. (1951). *On the Nature of the Universe*, trans. by R. E. Latham. Harmondsworth, UK: Penguin.

Millican, Peter. (2002). "Context, Aims and Structure of the Enquiry," in P. Millican, ed., *Reading Hume on Human Understanding*. Oxford: Clarendon, 27–65.

Mossner, Ernest. (1980). *The Life of David Hume*, 2nd ed. Oxford: Oxford University Press.

Passmore, John. (1980). *Hume's Intentions*, 3rd ed. London: Duckworth.

Popkin, Richard. (1953/1980). "Hume's Intentions." Reprinted in Popkin, *The High Road to Pyrrhonism*, ed. by Richard Watson and James Force. San Diego: Austin Hill Press, 267–275.

Rowe, William L. (1998). *The Cosmological Argument*. New York: Fordham University Press.

Reid, Thomas. (1967). *Philosophical Works*, ed. by W. Hamilton. Hildesheim: Olms.

Russell, Bertrand. (1947). *A History of Western Philosophy*. London: Allen & Unwin.

Russell, Paul. (2008). *The Riddle of Hume's Treatise: Skepticism, Naturalism, and Irreligion*. New York: Oxford University Press.

Russell, Paul. (2005/2013). "Hume on Religion," in *The Stanford Encyclopedia of Philosophy* (Winter 2014 Edition), ed. by Edward N. Zalta. http://plato.stanford.edu/archives/win2014/entries/hume-religion/.

Russell, Paul. (2007/2014). "Hume on Free Will," *The Stanford Encyclopedia of Philosophy* (Winter 2014 Edition), ed. by Edward N. Zalta http://plato.stanford.edu/archives/win2014/entries/hume-freewill/.

Russell, Paul. (unpublished.) "Hume's Scepticism and the Problem of Atheism."

Spinoza, Benedict. (1670). *Theological-Political Treatise*, 2nd ed., trans. by S. Shirley and Intro. by S. Feldman. Indianapolis: Hackett.

Stewart, M. A. (1995), "An Early Fragment on Evil," in M. A. Stewart and J. P. Wright, eds., *Hume and Hume's Connexions*. Edinburgh: Edinburgh University Press, 160–170.

Tindal, Matthew. (1730/1978). *Christianity as Old as Creation*. London. Reprint, New York: Garland, 1978.

PART II

METAPHYSICS AND EPISTEMOLOGY

CHAPTER 8

....

HUME'S THEORY OF IDEAS

....

WAYNE WAXMAN

To understand the *theory of ideas* in the manner best suited to Hume's era and philosophical approach, one must distinguish it from both ontology and the theory of language. *Ontology* is concerned with reality in general, and so with objects irrespective of what differentiates them or whether and how they can be given to consciousness. Theory of ideas, by contrast, deals with these same objects insofar as they do or can present themselves to us, whether in sensation, reflexion (as passions, desires, or volitions), or thought (as memories, imaginings, conceptions, judgments, or reasoning). It does so, however, without regard to whether and how ideas can be given linguistic expression. Language, as Hume understood it, depends on communally established conventions (T 3.2.2.10/490; T 3.3.1.15/581–2; EM 5.2.42/228–9; EM App 3.8/306–7) and so goes beyond the individual, isolated conscious mind, whereas theory of ideas is concerned exclusively with the contents present to such minds, regardless of whether these same minds are or are not capable in addition of giving linguistic expression to their ideas (e.g., nonhuman animals). Accordingly, Humean theory of ideas is best understood as a purely psychological program concerned with objects only insofar as they are ideas present to consciousness capable of influencing the understanding, passions, and morals of the individual isolated mind.

Theory of ideas is sometimes criticized for failing to distinguish anything from anything else: if everything we think is ipso facto an idea, be it sensation, memory, fantasy, desire, volition, judgment, or reasoning, what use is the notion? On the ground that anything not an idea is ipso facto unthinkable, and so nothing to us, Hume might well have conceded that the difference between an idea and a nonidea is a distinction without a difference, even while insisting on its indispensability as a corrective in philosophy. For he would have argued that if the history of philosophy proves anything, it is that philosophers are apt to overstep the limits of human understanding in their ontologies and posit objects that, strictly speaking, minds like ours are incapable of thinking. The source of the problem he would likely have traced to the same origin Berkeley did: the misuse of language stemming from a misunderstanding of its relation to thought (ideation). Hence, the importance of distinguishing ideas from words: ideas are the contents present in the consciousness of each individual isolated consciousness, privy only to it, whereas words are public, the common property of all who master the "rules of propriety" (in Locke's phrase) constitutive of their meaning. Their divergence in origin, nature, and role means that words and ideas may not always correspond in content or scope and that even the finest, most scrupulous definition of a word (i.e., "clear and distinct" representation of its meaning) may mislead us regarding the content and scope of the corresponding idea or whether a corresponding idea is even possible for the mind to form. Semantics, in other words, is not a dependable guide either in ontology or psychology. And because, in Hume's view, words are slaves and ideas their masters (LET 2:298–9, n508), philosophers must base their estimations of the nature, powers, and, above all, limitations of the human mind not on the theory of language but on the theory of ideas.

A case in point for Hume is the term "idea" itself. Like Kant after him, Hume thought the use of this term for the subject matter of the theory of ideas too liable to philosophical mischief to be implicitly relied on. In particular, it is so redolent of intellect and reason that its use may tempt one to sideline or even, as with the Rationalists, exclude from the theory such contents and doings of consciousness as sights, smells, sounds, feelings, passions, and desires. To make clear that the scope of his theory of ideas extends to sensations and reflections no less than to thoughts, Hume therefore departed from the practice of Locke and Berkeley and substituted "perceptions" in place of "ideas" (T 1.1.1.1n/2).[1]

I RIVAL INTERPRETATIONS OF HUME'S THEORY OF IDEAS

Before turning to Hume's division of perceptions into impressions and ideas, there is a crucial issue of interpretation that needs to be addressed: did Hume construe perceptions (i.e., impressions, ideas) as representations *of* the objects presented in them, or did he equate them, and thereby psychologize those objects? The principal effect—and appeal—of representationalist readings of Hume's theory of ideas is to preserve the independence of objects vis-à-vis our representations of them. Hume's analyses of our perceptions of bodies, the mind (self, person), space, time, substances, causality, and the like become, on this view, just that: analyses of the *representations* our minds are capable of forming of these things rather than idealist reductions à la Berkeley or Kant of the *things themselves*. Branding these representations fictions, as Hume did implicitly or explicitly, thus does not imply the fictitiousness of the things they represent, but instead merely serves to warn us against assuming a perfect correspondence between them, however natural we may find it to do so. This is because representations of objects, and so, too, all knowledge obtained through their deployment in experience, answer not just to the nature, existence, and relations of their objects, but to human nature, human existence, and human relations as well.

Representationalist hesitations at affirming perfect correspondences between perceptions and objects obviously have no place when Hume's theory of ideas is construed, psychologistically, as equating them. On this reading, Hume's underlying concern was the exclusion of any transcendental component from the theory of ideas on grounds of unintelligibility. For to say that objects are in any literal sense distinct from their perceptions is ipso facto to admit that what is distinct in them is not in any way present to consciousness and that it is therefore impossible to form any idea (positive conception) of what it is. But isn't the admission that something cannot be presented to consciousness in sensation, reflection, or thought tantamount to conceding that it is, and can be, nothing to us? The only objects that can be something for us, and so figure in a theory of ideas tasked to explain the principles of human understanding, passions, and morals, are therefore our own perceptions. Psychologistic readings of Hume's theory of ideas accordingly require that the representation of objects by perceptions be understood entirely nontranscendentally, as exclusively an affair of the conscious relation of perceptions to *one another*. In particular, all perceptions/objects are originally on the same footing: individual, isolated, devoid of all relation. Whatever relation they have to one another, including the representation by some of others, must be understood as entirely the product of our psychology operating in accordance with the prescriptions of human nature. Rather than their relation to objects being taken for granted, effectively treated as intrinsic to perceptions, as on representationalist construals, psychologistic interpreters thus regard it as one of the principal tasks of Hume's theory of ideas to explain how otherwise isolated, independent perceptions acquire the value of representations of one kind or another: how some become memories with respect to others (which then take on the value of recollected objects), how others become imaginings of others (becoming fancied objects), how others become passions for others (loved objects, feared objects, etc.), how others become desires or aversions in respect to others (objects to eat or not eat, mate with or not mate with, etc.), how others become volitions for others (objects that ought to exist), and so on.

Which reading is correct? In the view of this author, the preponderance of evidence favors a psychologistic construal of Hume's theory of ideas. In the very first section of the *Treatise*, after distinguishing perceptions into impressions and ideas and these in turn into simple and complex, Hume oriented his reader thusly: "Having by these distinctions given an order and arrangement to our objects, we may now apply ourselves to consider with more accuracy their qualities and relations" (T 1.1.1.3/2)—whereupon he proceeded to search for a pattern of *temporal priority* and a relation of *causal dependence* derivable from this pattern (of simple ideas on the antecedent simple impressions they resemble: "the Copy Principle" discussed in Section III herein). Hume's statement is uniquely telling because it makes clear right from the start how he understood both the subject matter of the *Treatise* and its task: impressions and ideas are *both equally* the objects it is to deal with; *their* qualities, not those of any other objects (nonperceptions), are what is to be investigated; and *their* relations to *one another,* not to anything else, are what need to be discovered.

Representationalists tend to pass over Hume's statement unremarked and instead cite a variety of texts in the body of the *Treatise* in support of their reading of his theory of ideas. The problem with their evidence is that virtually all these texts fall into either of two categories, neither of which tells us much about Hume's own considered view: (1) characterizations of the views of philosophers Hume was intent on criticizing, and (2) mentions in passing in the course of considering other matters, usually sections or whole parts before the point in the *Treatise* when Hume was ready to bring the full resources of his theory, *developed up to that point,* to bear on the questions of the identity or nonidentity of perceptions and objects and the nature of the representational character of perceptions.

The section that interpreters on both sides of the divide would generally agree is most pertinent to the first question is T 1.4.2, in which Hume analyzed ideas of bodies as products of the fiction of continued, distinct existence. There, he discussed two views: the *vulgar single existence* view, which he rejected as "confound[ing] perceptions and objects" on the ground that "philosophy informs us, that every thing, which appears to the mind, is nothing but a perception" (T 1.4.2.14/193)—subsequently abbreviated as the view that "no beings are ever present to the mind but perceptions" (T 1.4.2.47/212; also T 3.1.1.2/456) and "our perceptions are our only objects" (T 1.4.2.38/206, T 1.4.2.43/209, T 1.4.2.46/211, T 1.4.2.50/213, T 1.4.2.53/216); and the *philosophical double existence view,* which distinguishes "betwixt perceptions and objects, of which the former are suppos'd to be interrupted, and perishing, and different at every different return; the latter to be uninterrupted, and to preserve a continu'd existence and identity" (T 1.4.2.46/211). Representationalist interpreters are committed to showing that Hume espoused a version of the philosophical view but immediately come up against the seemingly insurmountable obstacle of his assertion that "however philosophical this new system may be esteem'd, I assert that 'tis only a palliative remedy, and . . . contains all the difficulties of the vulgar system, with some others, that are peculiar to itself" (T 1.4.2.46/211). Hume's rationale for rejecting the philosophical view may be summarized thusly: because "our perceptions are our only objects," philosophers can form no positive conceptions of the objects they suppose to be distinct from our perceptions except via the qualities met with in perceptions, which means that their "objects" are, in truth, merely a second set of perceptions added in thought (ideas) to those that present themselves to the senses (impressions):

> Philosophers deny our resembling perceptions to be identically the same, and uninterrupted; and yet have so great a propensity to believe them such, that they arbitrarily invent a new set of perceptions, to which they attribute these qualities. I say, a new set of perceptions: For we may well suppose in general, but 'tis impossible for us distinctly to conceive, objects to be in their nature any thing but exactly the same with perceptions. What then can we look for from this conclusion of groundless and extraordinary opinions but error and falsehood? (T 1.4.2.56/218)[2]

Because Hume allows that we may *suppose* objects corresponding to our perceptions to exist even if we cannot *conceive* them without arbitrarily inventing a new set of perceptions, some interpreters ascribe to him a version of the philosophical view that affirms objects *specifically different* from perceptions, that is, which have nothing (quality or relation) in common with them. One version of this interpretation exemplifies the tendency to ascribe to Hume views he entertained in the context of criticizing other philosophers, in this case, Spinoza, whose philosophy of substance he castigated as "gloomy and obscure" and a "hideous hypothesis" (T 1.4.5.19/241). The other widely held version of this reading is more plausible because it at least relies on a text in which Hume was clearly speaking in his own voice: "The farthest we can go towards a conception of external objects, when suppos'd specifically different from our perceptions, is to form a relative idea of them, without pretending to comprehend the related objects" (T 1.2.6.9/68). This, however, seems to be a classic case of mistaking a preliminary statement of Hume's position for his considered view, as articulated in the light of subsequent considerations: "as to the notion of external existence, when taken for something specifically different from our perceptions, we have already shewn its absurdity" (T 1.4.2.2/188). The difference between the first citation, from T 1.2.6, and the second, from T 1.4.2, is T 1.3: Hume's analysis of cause and effect and its key component, the idea of necessary connection. The most plausible interpretation of the T 1.4.2 citation is that the supposition of a causal relation without a relative is rendered absurd by the analysis of T 1.3.[3] And Hume's persistence in this opinion is confirmed by its reaffirmation in the *Enquiry*: "Bereave matter of all its intelligible qualities, both primary and secondary, you in a manner annihilate it, and leave only a certain unknown, inexplicable *something*, as the cause of our perceptions; a notion so imperfect, that no sceptic will think it worth while to contend against it" (EU 12.1.16/155).

These considerations seem to me sufficient to settle the question of the relation of perceptions to objects in favor of their identity, and it is in this psychologistic light that I now address the question of the nature of the representational character of perceptions.

II Impressions and Ideas

Impressions comprise sensations and reflections (passions, desires, and volitions),[4] and ideas thoughts (memories, fantasies, conceptions, judgments, and inferences). Hume left no doubt that the single defining feature that groups these otherwise disparate perceptions into two, mutually exclusive kinds is the high degree of "force and vivacity" that pertains to sensations and reflections but is lacking from thoughts. What is this quality? Hume made clear that it has nothing to do with the strength or violence with which a perception strikes upon the mind, for impressions can be so calm and gentle as to escape notice and, in certain circumstances, may be confused with reason in its supposed contest with the passions. Nor is it a quality whereby perceptions make a strong, lasting impression on the mind because ideas are just as capable of enduringly inscribing themselves in our memories. And impressions are not vivid in the sense of invariably being brighter than thoughts since the sight of a barely discernible gray blur on an otherwise black night (visual sensation) retains the full force of an impression in contrast to the vivacity-lacking visualization of a brilliantly lit, detailed cityscape (visual imagination).

The best guide to what Hume meant by vivacity is his equation of it with the sentiment, feeling, or manner of conception, by which he explicated belief in the real existence of a content present to consciousness. Its primary role in his philosophy is to explain how something present to us merely in thought (idea) comes to be regarded as really existent, as when we believe in the real existence of an unseen fire when we see smoke pouring in through the transom: although the image of the fire in thought is the same whether we merely fantasize it or are prompted to conceive it by the sight of smoke, it is only in the latter case that we believe the fire really to exist and fear being incinerated no less than being asphyxiated. The quality constitutive of the reality attributed to the idea is, according to Hume, the feeling of force and vivacity that distinguishes the manner in which it is conceived thanks to its causal relation to smoke. In other words, we regard the idea/object present to our thought as really existent rather than fictitious, fantastic, or otherwise unreal if and only if something (e.g., causal association) prompts us to conceive it in a forceful and vivacious manner. And a considerable part of the first book of the *Treatise* is devoted to identifying and analyzing the various causes that lead the mind to take objects of thought as real that otherwise would be regarded as merely imaginary, that is, ideas altogether lacking in force and vivacity.

The only difference between the vivacity of ideas and that of impressions of sensation and reflection is that the consciousness of everything present to us in sensation or reflection is ipso facto accompanied by a maximal degree of vivacity affect, automatically, as it were, without requiring additional, special causes. Otherwise, just as the conception of an object accompanied by a high degree of vivacity and belief in the real existence of that object are identical, so, too, the reality we ascribe to any object present to us in sensation or reflection and the high degree of vivacity felt in our consciousness of it are, for Hume, one and the same:

> it appears, that the *belief* or *assent,* which always attends the memory and senses, is nothing but the vivacity of those perceptions they present; and that this alone distinguishes them from the imagination. To believe is in this case to feel an immediate impression of the senses, or a repetition of that impression in the memory. 'Tis merely the force and liveliness of the perception, which constitutes the first act of the judgment, and lays the foundation of that reasoning, which we build upon it, when we trace the relation of cause and effect. (T 1.3.5.7/86)

Sensations and reflections are impressions because human nature determines us to have a maximal feeling of force and vivacity in our consciousness of them, which is just to say that to behold them is to believe them, to hold them for really existent, and thus to treat them as a basis on which to reason and act. Thoughts, by contrast, are mere ideas because, in and of themselves, they lack this feeling and so are never regarded as really existent unless and until some cause intervenes to induce us to conceive them with sufficient force and vivacity to change that (the principal such cause being the association of an idea with an impression in some natural relation, especially cause and effect: see Section III).

Hume also distinguished perceptions according to whether they are simple or complex. An impression or idea counts as simple if it cannot be distinguished into two or more components (different significative uses to which the same simple perception may be put do not compromise its intrinsic simplicity: see Section V). However, a distinguishable perception may still count as simple if its quality would be obliterated by dividing it: "The impressions of touch are simple impressions, except when consider'd with regard to their extension" (T 1.4.4.14/230–1). In general, as with Locke before him, Hume counted any perception as simple that could not be produced in imagination through the combination or separation of perceptions already in one's possession.

III THE COPY PRINCIPLE

Hume's *Copy Principle*, as it is generally known, asserts that "all our simple ideas in their first appearance are deriv'd from simple impressions, which are correspondent to them, and which they exactly represent" (T 1.1.1.7/4). Its importance in Hume's theory of ideas and his philosophy generally can hardly be exaggerated. He deemed it "a new microscope or species of optics, by which, in the moral sciences, the most minute, and most simple ideas may be so enlarged as to fall readily under our apprehension, and be equally known with the grossest and most sensible ideas, that can be the object of our enquiry" (EU 7.1.4/62). Instead of depending on definition to make the ideas we think clear and distinct and being always susceptible to confusing what can be said with what can present itself to consciousness in thought, one has only to produce the impression original of an idea—the sensation or reflexion from which its copy in thought is taken—to eliminate all ambiguity and doubt as to the contents thought in it. That, in a nutshell, is Hume's method, particularly in the first book of the *Treatise*: "instead of searching for the idea in . . . definitions, . . . look for it in the impressions" (T 1.3.14.4/157); if there is none, there can be no idea, and our "words are absolutely without any meaning, when employed either in philosophical reasoning, or common life" (EU 7.2.26/74); but if an impression original can be identified, then it will not only confer perfect clarity on the contents of the idea, but determine its scope of application as well, since "[i]deas always represent the objects or impressions, from which they are deriv'd, and can never without a fiction represent or be apply'd to any other" (T 1.2.3.11/37). Nor need one look further for confirmation of the importance and originality of the thesis than to Kant who, in deriving the problem of his philosophy from Hume's analysis of cause and effect, also adapted his method of solving it from Hume's Copy Principle:

One cannot, without feeling a certain pain, behold how entirely every one of his opponents—Reid, Oswald, Beattie, and lastly Priestly—missed the point of his problem . . . It was not the question whether the concept of cause is correct, serviceable, and in respect of the whole of our cognition of nature indispensable, for this Hume never doubted. Rather, it was the question whether the concept is thought through reason a priori and in this way has an inner truth independent of all experience and therefore also a far more extended employment, not limited to objects of experience: here is where Hume expected a breakthrough. It was indeed only the issue of the origin of this concept, not of its indispensability in use: if only the former were ascertained, then everything concerning the conditions of its use and the sphere in which it can be valid would already of itself have been given.[5]

Commentators of a representationalist bent sometimes construe Hume's Copy Principle as asserting the *intrinsic* representational nature of ideas vis-à-vis impressions and consequently are baffled at the apparent ease with which Hume conceded the existence of cases in which simple ideas can be produced in imagination without any antecedent simple impressions from which to derive them (illustrated by the missing shade of blue case described at T 1.1.1.10/5–6). The alternative reading is that the Copy Principle is an empirical inductive causal inference and so concerns an extrinsic matter of fact pertaining to ideas rather than their intrinsic nature. This reading is strongly supported by the text: foreshadowing the analysis of causal inferences in T 1.3, Hume presented the Copy Principle as a "connexion" inferred from a "constant conjunction of resembling perceptions" on the ground that "a constant conjunction, in such an infinite number of instances, can never arise from chance; but clearly proves a dependence" (T 1.1.1.8/4). Moreover, he let experience decide which depends on which: "That I may know on which side this dependence lies, I consider the order of their *first appearance*; and find by constant experience, that the simple impressions always take the precedence of their correspondent ideas, but never appear in the contrary order" (T 1.1.1.8/5). Clearly, established on this empirical basis, the Copy Principle could have gone the other way had experience showed that simple ideas regularly precede their correspondent simple impression in their first appearance (making ideas the originals and their resembling impressions the copies that represent them); or, in the face of inconstant conjunction (contrariety), gone the way it does only with more probability than the alternative; or, in the absence of all experienced regularity, there would have been no Copy Principle in Hume's theory of ideas at all.

This, to be sure, only shows that experience is required for the *discovery* of the constant conjunction from which the Copy Principle is inferred but does not prove that the causal relation that makes simple ideas representations of simple impressions is not itself, *objectively and in fact*, intrinsic to ideas. There is, accordingly, a long-standing division among interpreters as to whether Hume took the causal relations among perceptions affirmed in the Copy Principle to obtain prior to and independently of associative imagination, and so to be preimaginatively real, or whether the account of causal connections in terms of association in T 1.3 ultimately extends to the Copy Principle as well. Moreover, since the Copy Principle is only one of several causal relations, both representational and nonrepresentational, featuring in Hume's complete theory of ideas, the question needs to be widened to include the causation of impressions of reflection by ideas of sensation, these impressions as causes of their own idea copies, primary ideas as causes of secondary ideas, and custom and association as causes responsible for both the formation of certain ideas in preference to others and the enlivening of these ideas: are these preimaginatively real causal relations taken for granted in Hume's theory of ideas, or does the theory ultimately subject them to the same analysis causal relations generally are given in T 1.3?

There is, I believe, a text that can settle this question. It occurs in T 1.4.6, in connection with Hume's explication of the mind in terms of precisely the same causal relations that feature in his theory of ideas:

> the true idea of the human mind, is to consider it as a system of different perceptions or different existences, which are link'd together by the relation of cause and effect, and mutually produce, destroy, influence, and modify each other. Our impressions give rise to their correspondent ideas; and these ideas in their turn produce other impressions. One thought chaces another, and draws after it a third, by which it is expell'd in its turn. (T 1.4.6.19/261)

In the lead-up to this passage, Hume explicitly recalled the analysis of necessary connection in T 1.3 that explicates causal relations as customary transitions from a given impression to an associated idea: "This question we might easily decide, if we wou'd recollect what has already been prov'd at large, that the understanding never observes any real connexion among objects, and that even the union of cause and effect, when strictly examin'd, resolves itself into a customary association of ideas," that is, a "union of ideas in the imagination when we reflect upon them" rather than "something that really binds our several perceptions together" (T 1.4.6.16/259–60). The implication is that the causal relations that compose Hume's theory of ideas, the Copy Principle included, are as much instances of the customary association of ideas in imagination as the ideas the theory had previously been used to explicate, from space and time in T 1.2, body in T 1.4.2, and substance in T 1.4.3–5, to cause and effect itself in T 1.3.

IV RELATIONS

Of all the principles enunciated in Hume's theory of ideas, he cited none more frequently than the thesis (which holds equally in the reverse direction) that all perceptions (= objects), ideas no less than impressions, are distinct in existence, hence distinguishable from one another and so separable in thought (T 1.1.1.2/2, T 1.1.3.4/10, T 1.1.7.3/18, etc.). According to this *Separability Principle,* no matter how invariably two perceptions may co-occur, whether in the same or in successive times, the ability to separate them in thought suffices to infer that each exists distinctly (outside and independently) of the other. Each distinguishable perception is therefore, for all intents and purposes, a self-subsistent entity, distinct from the mind (T 1.4.2.39–40/207–8) and from nonperceptions no less than from other perceptions (T 1.4.37/222, T 1.4.5.5–6/233-4, T 1.4.5.24/244, T 1.4.6.3/252). Because itches, headaches, passions such as love, volitions, and dreams all qualify as perceptions on Hume's accounting, this means that the Separability Principle obliged him to attribute to these "objects" the same self-subsistence we find it natural to accord to physical objects. Moreover, since successive perceptions, no matter how indiscernible in quality and relations, are likewise distinct under this principle, all perceptions "are interrupted, and perishing, and different at every return" (T 1.4.2.46/211), "a perpetual flux and movement" (T 1.4.6.4/252). As such, no perception can be supposed to have any relation to any other, intrinsic or extrinsic. Relations must instead all be added in thought, so that, in explicating them, Hume had not only to specify the perceptions concerned but the subjective mode of considering them as well.

Hume deemed comparison alone sufficient to relate any pair of ideas, the relation being "that particular circumstance, in which, even upon the arbitrary union of two ideas in the fancy, we may think proper to compare them" (T 1.1.5.1/13). On that basis, even contrariety counts as a relation because it trivially involves a resemblance relation: "no two ideas [objects] are in themselves contrary, except those of existence and non-existence, which are plainly resembling, as implying both of them an idea of the object" (T 1.1.5.8/15). However, it was not arbitrary, trivial relations that interested Hume but those that constitute necessities of thought, or, failing that, are so deeply rooted in human nature that it is not in our power to reason contrary to them. A relation of perceptions constitutes a necessity of thought if it is impossible to conceive any change in their relation without changing one's ideas of them, that is, representing different perceptions than one started with (T 1.3.1.1/69). Because this necessity specifically concerns relations between perceptions that are distinct by the Separability Principle (by contrast with the "relation" of a mountain to a valley, which are only semantically but not ideationally distinct: T 1.2.2.8/32), it is vital to recognize that it is in no sense intrinsic to the perceptions, as it was for Rationalists like Descartes, but instead "lies only in the act of the understanding, by which we consider and compare these ideas" (T 1.3.14.23/166).[6]

It is only when we are *not* necessitated to conceive the ideas we compare to be related in a certain way, yet their relation is neither arbitrary nor trivial, that another relating principle is required (T 1.3.7.3/95). The most important such principle invoked by Hume is *association,* the preferential production of a certain perception upon the appearance of some other (its associate). Although the association of impressions figures prominently in Hume's account of the indirect passions in Book 2 of the *Treatise,* the association of ideas plays a far greater role in his philosophy in general and his theory of ideas in particular. This "uniting principle is not to be consider'd as an inseparable connexion" but "as a gentle force, which commonly prevails" (T 1.1.4.1/10), so that "even in our wildest and most wandering reveries, nay in our very dreams, we shall find, if we reflect, that the imagination ran not altogether at adventures, but that there was still a connexion upheld among the different ideas, which succeeded each other" (EU 3.1/23).

Because the relations with the strongest "associating quality" are resemblance, contiguity, and, above all, cause and effect (T 1.1.4.1–2/10–11), our thoughts tend most easily and naturally to ideas (objects) resembling, contiguous, and/or causally related to those currently before us. What is the associative quality that enables these relations to guide our thoughts in this manner? Here, it is important to distinguish the causes of association, which one may have no consciousness of, from the association itself, whereby one is immediately conscious of a connection between a succession of otherwise distinct perceptions. Resemblance and contiguity, although directly observable in objects (impressions or ideas) (T 1.3.2.2/73 and T 1.3.14.28/168), would nevertheless not connect perceptions in the consciousness of the observing subject if human nature were different and these relations lacked any associating quality (or not they but their opposites possessed it). This is even more obvious in the case of causal relations, which are never observable in objects: "the repetition of perfectly similar instances can never *alone* give rise to an original idea, different from what may be found in any one instance" (T 1.3.14.16/163). Thus, for want of anything immediately observable in the objects, Hume concluded that the associating quality must lie in some feature of the *transition* in thought from one object to another: a quality the subject experiencing the transition cannot fail to be aware of, that ipso facto unites them (relates them, associates them) in its imagination and so marks the transition off from all cotemporary transitions.

What is that quality? Contrary to what one might suppose, Hume's answer was not custom per se, understood merely as "a *tendency or inclination* towards . . . the performance of any action or the conception of any object" (T 2.3.5.1/422). For there is nothing in tendencies to make certain transitions in preference to others *as such* that can be supposed to imbue those transitions with a consciously detectable associating quality capable of uniting the perceptions concerned in the imagination. Experience might supply evidence that such tendencies cause some such quality to appear, but that just goes to prove that the two are not the same. Indeed, human nature might well have been so constituted that associating qualities never appeared when such tendencies operated or dissociating qualities appeared instead. It is thus one thing for a custom to cause us always to think X whenever Y is sensed or thought, quite another for that custom by itself to distinguish the transition to Y "from any new and unusual idea" (T 1.3.9.16/116).

What does serve to distinguish them is a quality that both customary tendencies (T 2.3.5.1/422) and association yield in abundance: "[t]he very nature and essence of relation is to connect our ideas with each other, and upon the appearance of one, to facilitate the transition to its correlative" (T 1.4.2.34/204; also T 1.3.8.3/99). Resemblance, contiguity, and cause and effect associate perceptions in the imagination because "the very essence of these relations consists in their producing an easy transition of ideas" (T 1.4.6.16/260). Facility fills the void left by the absence of any real observable bond in the perceptions present to consciousness, being instead a bond we "only feel . . . among the ideas we form of them" (T 1.4.6.16/259), so that this affect is not just "the effect" but the "essence of relation" (T 1.4.3.3/220). Thus, for Hume, the facility felt in the transition from any object X to any distinct object Y *is* what associates their ideas in the consciousness of the subject that experiences (feels) the transition, so that the relation between X and Y and the consciousness that affectively associates them are one and the same.

Nor is that all. Being a feeling, facility may vary in degree, with its actual strength in any instance fixed by the constancy of experience, the strength of custom, or causes of the kind enumerated in T 1.3.13 ("Of Unphilosophical Probability"). Because facility is the essence of relation, this means that the *stronger this feeling* is in any transition of thought, the *stronger the relation* it produces between the perceptions to and from which the transition is made. Equally, the subject experiencing the transition will be correspondingly more resistant to not relating them, or relating them otherwise, so that any other transition would feel difficult and unnatural to it in direct proportion to the facility of its preferred transition. For example, thanks to the facilitating effect of customary association, the transition from a cause to the idea of the effect that uniformly follows from it (or from the effect to the idea of its cause) becomes so easy and natural that we cannot consider them not to be causally paired or to be causally paired with different objects, "without a sensible violence" (T 1.3.11.4/125), as when thinking of releasing a die from a height we "cannot without violence regard it as suspended in the air" (T 1.3.11.11/128). This is important because it is precisely when feelings of facility acquire the intensity requisite to have this effect that they seem to *determine* our thought;[7] and although a purely affective phenomenon (i.e., not "determination" in any preassociatively real causal sense), it is in just this capacity that feelings of facility constitute a species of impressions of reflexion to which Hume could plausibly trace the origin of ideas of necessary connection:

> This connexion, therefore, which we *feel* in the mind, this customary transition of the imagination from one object to its usual attendant, is the sentiment or impression, from which we form the idea of power or necessary connexion. Nothing farther is in the case. (EU 7.2.28/75; also T 1.3.14.1/156)

Although facility may be essential to those natural relations "by which two ideas are connected together in the imagination, and the one naturally introduces the other, after the manner above-explained [in 1.1.4, "Of the Connexion or Association of Ideas"]" (T 1.1.5.1/13), philosophical relations remain possible in its absence. Nevertheless, in all cases where these relations are not necessary in the strict sense, Hume seems to have regarded them as parasitic on natural relations, most notably in the case of causal relations: "tho' causation be a *philosophical* relation, as implying contiguity, succession, and constant conjunction, yet 'tis only so far as it is a *natural* relation, and produces an union among our ideas, that we are able to reason upon it, or draw any inference from it" (T 1.3.6.16/94). Why are philosophical relations incapable of serving as a basis for reasoning unless there is a corresponding natural relation? In T 1.3.6–10 ff., Hume makes clear that inference always proceeds from something believed to something not believed, where the vivacity of the first is communicated to the second by means of their relation. So, if philosophical relations unsupported by natural relations are unable to serve as a basis for reasoning, it must be because they lack something essential whereby the vivacity of one perception related in them can be communicated to another perception that lacks it. Because facility is the feature that distinguishes the two kinds of relation, the presence of this affect must be what is crucial to the ability of relations to communicate the vivacity of one perception (the believed "premise") to another (the otherwise unbelieved "conclusion"). In other words, only insofar as the transition from an impression or vivid idea X to a vivacity-lacking idea Y feels easy will the vivacity of the former be naturally extended to the latter, and X constitute a *reason* for Y. In order for philosophical relations to be usable as supports for reason, they must first be recognized as analogous to some species of transition-facilitating natural relation (via resemblance, a general rule, or some other circumstance).

Confirmation of the unique idea-enlivening power of natural relations can be found in the paragraph leading up to Hume's first statement of his thesis that facility is the essence of relation, where he sought to establish "it as a general maxim in the science of human nature, *that when any impression becomes present to us, it not only transports the mind to such ideas as are related to it, but likewise communicates to them a share of its force and vivacity*" (T 1.3.8.2/98). Because no perception "transports" the mind to any other unless, and only insofar as, the transition is marked by a feeling of facility (otherwise it lacks the "firm hold and easy introduction [to] distinguish itself from any new and unusual idea," T 1.3.9.16/116), the implication is clear: impressions—and, by extension, memories or other vivid ideas—depend on the facility of the transition in order to communicate their vivacity to the idea thereby related to them. Where there is neither facility nor any foundation in it, as with philosophical relations lacking a corresponding natural relation, impressions and vivid ideas can communicate none of their vivacity to the related ideas. Where facility is present, by contrast, the degree of their vivacity that will be communicated to the related idea will be directly proportional to the degree (intensity) of the facility affect (= the strength of the associative relation). Hume's general maxim of human nature thus boils down to the principle that *vivacity follows facility*: an unbelieved idea will be more or less believed according to the degree of facility felt in the transition to it, up to but not exceeding the degree of vivacity pertaining to the perception from which the transition is made.[8]

V ABSTRACT IDEAS

Having so far considered only representations of one individual perception/object by another, I conclude my account of Hume's theory of ideas with a brief examination of his treatment of general representations, propositions, and language.

Hume's analysis of general representations was adapted from Berkeley, whose concern was to show that the general ideas underlying general terms are not abstract ideas but ordinary, fully concrete perceptions derived from impressions of sensation and reflection. The keystone of his analysis was the Separability Principle. First, it limits abstraction to perceptions capable of distinct existence, such that each can be perceived and conceived in the absence of the other; where this distinctness is lacking, abstraction cannot take place. Second, where language is concerned, the principle prevents semantically independent notions from being cashed out as distinct perceptions. For example, because the distinction between the shape and color of a visible object fails to satisfy the Separability Principle, the notion that the two are distinct perceptions—different abstract ideas, as Locke supposed—has to be rejected as an illusion wrought by the semantic distinctness of the corresponding terms. For although there is indeed a significative distinction to be drawn in the use of the idea of a visible object to designate, on the one hand, things resembling it in shape and, on the other, things resembling it in color, when the idea is considered in and for itself, apart from any significative use to which it may be put, its shape and color are ineluctably one. Thus, the general ideas underlying the general terms "shape" and "color" are not, in truth, distinct perceptions but rather different significative uses of the same perception, according to different resemblances of which it admits.

Yet, it is not resemblance relations alone that constitute generality but their having a basis in custom as well: "If ideas be particular in their nature, and at the same time finite in their number, 'tis only by custom they can become general in their representation, and contain an infinite number of other ideas under them" (T 1.1.7.16/24). The habits instilled by frequently encountered similarities along various axes of resemblance association (e.g., shape, color, material composition, cause, effect, use) are constitutive of generality insofar as they lie in readiness to be triggered by any of the infinitely many possible stimuli (nonabstract impressions or ideas) capable of triggering them. Which of the many habits a given perception may trigger depends on one's present train of thought, the context of its occurrence, or any other "present design or necessity" (T 1.1.7.7/20) that may induce the imagination to invoke one custom in preference to others that may otherwise be just as applicable. Thus, a single, fully determinate (nonabstract) perception of an equilateral triangle one inch in circumference can serve as a general representation of figures, rectilinear figures, regular figures, triangles, or equilateral triangles, according to which custom it triggers in the particular context (T 1.1.7.9/21–2). Finally, with the addition of words to overcome the confusion that may result both from the capacity of the same idea to trigger any of various customary resemblance associations and from the capacity of the same custom to be triggered by quite dissimilar ideas, one arrives at Berkeley's principle "that all general ideas are nothing but particular ones, annexed to a certain term, which gives them a more extensive signification, and makes them recall upon occasion other individuals, which are similar to them" (T 1.1.7.1/17).

Although Hume's intent in T 1.1.7 was to prove that customary resemblance associations, and not abstract ideas, are the general ideas that give meaning to general terms in relation to perceptions/objects (over and above their conventionally grounded meanings), it does not follow that he deemed general ideas impossible independently of language. In other contexts, Hume did not hesitate to attribute to animals incapable of language the same powers of association humans have, including those humans require to form general ideas. Because animals have as much need to sort things as we do if they are to extend properties previously encountered in objects to similar things presently before them, I see no reason to think he would deny a capacity to form general ideas to animals, albeit attenuated. Moreover, given that Hume deemed it one of the cardinal virtues of his account of the understanding that it attributes nothing to humans that cannot also be ascribed to animals, the burden of proof is surely on those who take him to have denied this capacity to animals. So, until someone meets that burden, it seems soundest to conclude that Hume no more supposed that creatures have need of general terms to form general ideas than he supposed that general terms can have a sense in relation to objects (perceptions) even if their conventionally assigned meanings are left unsupplemented with general ideas.

So far as I am aware, Hume never addressed the question of whether thoughts have propositional form, be it linguistic, quasi-linguistic ("mentalese"), or merely logical (e.g., the logical forms of judgments that Kant regarded as constitutive of representation by means of universals). Had he done so, I believe he would have denied it for the following reason. Hume resolved all acts of judgment and reasoning into acts of conception, understood as "the simple survey of one or more objects," that is, "nothing but particular ways of conceiving our objects" (T 1.3.7.5n/96–7n). These ways, as we have seen, are either by association, which is by no means essentially propositional, or by "the arbitrary union of two ideas in the fancy" effected by whatever "particular circumstance . . . we may think proper to compare them" (T 1.1.5.1/13), which also seems neither to imply nor entail propositional form. Thus, on Hume's analysis, there seems to be nothing in human mentation that could not also fall within the powers of creatures that are complete strangers to propositional form.

If true, this implies that Hume's theory of ideas shifts the entire burden of propositional representation onto communally created conventions fashioned to meet the demands of human life, making it a product of collective human artifice rather than individual human nature. The challenge this poses to anyone of a contrary bent is to show that and how propositional form is possible, and indeed necessary, in the individual, isolated mind, prior to and independently of human society and all that depends on it. This is the challenge that Kant would take up by adapting Hume's own theory of ideas to the purpose (see Section III herein). Today, however, with the theory of ideas fallen into desuetude, philosophers and scientists see the problem as one of accommodating propositional form to neural pathways. Yet, even if they should ever succeed in solving it, it would still leave undone the task bequeathed by Hume of showing that and how *conscious* thought can have propositional form completely independently of language.

ABBREVIATIONS OF WORKS CITED

EU   *An Enquiry Concerning Human Understanding.* Edited by T. L. Beauchamp. Oxford: Clarendon, 2000.

T   *A Treatise of Human Nature.* Edited by D. F. Norton and M. J. Norton. Oxford: Clarendon, 2007.

NOTES

1. I know of no substantive difference between T and EU that would affect the treatment of Hume's theory of ideas, and because T, in my judgment, is far more detailed and better argued than EU, my examination will concentrate on Hume's presentation of the theory in that work. The readings presented here have all been distilled from my books *Hume's Theory of Consciousness*, Cambridge: Cambridge University Press, 1994, and *Kant and the Empiricists. Understanding Understanding*, New York: Oxford University Press, 2005.

2. Representationalists sometimes cite Hume's insistence that the existence of body is something that can never be doubted as proof that he espoused a version of the philosophical view that objects are distinct from perceptions: "We may well ask, *What causes induce us to believe in the existence of body?* but 'tis in vain to ask, *Whether there be body or not?* That is a point, which we must take for granted in all our reasonings" (T 1.4.2.1/187). Yet, as an affirmation of *belief*, this poses no problem for exponents of psychologistic interpretations of Hume's theory of ideas. They note Hume's insistence that there can be no belief without an idea on which to confer it (T 1.3.7.1/94, T 1.3.8.7/101, T 1.3.12.22/140, T 1.3.14.36/172), so that the crucial question concerns not the belief that bodies exist but the nature and contents of the *ideas* of bodies on which belief is conferred. In particular, if ideas of bodies are mere fictions of associative imagination, and bodies are nothing distinct from these ideas, our inability not to believe that bodies exist poses no problem for psychologism—it is like the belief attaching to an idea of God that even a skeptic can accept (as with certain readings of Spinoza's equation of God with nature).

3. When confronted with this text, a noted scholar who is an exponent of the view I am criticizing responded in an email that Hume's statement in T 1.4.2 has a footnote referring his reader to T 1.2.6, that there is nothing in T 1.2.6 that proves the absurdity of the notion that objects can be affirmed on the basis of relations without a relative, and therefore Hume could and did espouse that view. Although implausible on its face, my correspondent's argument faces the further obstacle of where Hume chose to place the footnote referring to T 1.2.6: if he had put it after the clause "we have already shewn its absurdity," my correspondent's thesis could at least pass the laugh test; but since Hume attached it to the preceding phrase—"the notion of external existence, when taken for something specifically different from our perceptions"—there is all the more reason to believe that he meant that T 1.3 shows its absurdity.

4. In T 1.3 and 1.4 Hume would add another variety of impression of reflection, one bound up with what is felt in transitions of thought: see Section IV herein.

5. *Prolegomena to any Future Metaphysics*, Preface 258–259 (my translation).

6. Also: "since equality is a relation, it is not, strictly speaking, a property in the figures themselves, but arises merely from the comparison, which the mind makes betwixt them" (T 1.2.4.21/46).

7. "The thought is always determin'd to pass from the impression to the idea, and from that particular impression to that particular idea, without any choice or hesitation" (T 1.3.9.7/110), it "forces us to survey such certain objects, in such certain relations" (T 1.3.11.4/125), and such like.

8. To this I would add the corollary that, for Hume, belief *always* follows facility: even where experience, custom, and relation all support one transition, if facility favors another, as in T 1.4.1, belief will follow facility; and the same is true in the case of the indirect passions, as a consideration of T 2.2.2 shows. We are also now in a position to deal with a question that

some readers may have asked themselves at the end of Section III: how, without vicious circularity, could Hume adapt his associationism to accommodate the very theory of ideas on which associative relations themselves appear to depend? The answer is this: since transitions of thought, the facility felt in them, and the vivacity which follows that facility do not in any way depend on these relations, the explication of the latter through the former cannot be circular.

BIBLIOGRAPHY

Kant, Immanuel. (1902). *Prolegomena zu einer jeden künftigen Metaphysik, die als Wissenschaft wird auftreten können.* Volume IV. Berlin: Walter de Gruyter.

Waxman, Wayne. (1994). *Hume's Theory of Consciousness.* Cambridge: Cambridge University Press.

Waxman, Wayne. (2005). *Kant and the Empiricists. Understanding Understanding.* New York: Oxford University Press.

CHAPTER 9

HUME AND THE MOLYNEUX PROBLEM

HENRY E. ALLISON

In the second edition of *An Essay Concerning Human Understanding*, Locke famously referred to a problem posed for him some months earlier by William Molyneux.[1] The problem is whether a man born blind, who had been able to distinguish between a sphere and a cube by touch, could, immediately on acquiring the power of sight, distinguish these same two figures visually. Molyneux had answered this question in the negative and Locke agreed. Apparently, the issue made its way into the *Essay* because Locke took it as confirming his view that what is usually thought to be simply received by sensation is actually altered by an experientially based judgment, albeit in a habitual way of which the percipient is usually unaware. According to Locke (1694/1975, EHU 2.9.8/145), what is actually seen is "only a Plain variously colour'd," that is, a two-dimensional figure from which the percipient "frames to itself the perception of a convex figure, and an uniform colour." And it follows from this that the newly sighted person would not be able immediately to distinguish the figures due to the lack of any visual experience of the connection between a two-dimensional colored shape and its three-dimensional counterpart.

As a result of Locke's discussion, the "Molyneux problem" became a central issue in eighteenth-century epistemology and psychology. Not only did it provide the starting point for Berkeley's highly influential theory of vision, it was also taken up and further explored by thinkers such as Smith, Voltaire, Diderot, and Condillac, not to mention Leibniz in his response to Locke in the *New Essays*. Indeed, according to Cassirer (1955: 108–118), it posed the central philosophical issue of the time because it necessitated dealing with the question of the relation between sensation and judgment in the formation of experience.

Even if one does not wish to go that far, the significance of this problem for philosophers in the first half of the eighteenth century cannot be gainsaid, and this naturally leads one to ask how Hume stood with respect to it. One might suppose him to answer it in the manner of his fellow empiricists. One might even imagine him responding as he did in his treatment of the role of experience in the generation of our idea of the relation of cause and effect, suggesting that "were a man, such as *Adam*, created in the full vigour of understanding, without experience" (1740/2007 T Abs. 11/650), he would never be able to infer that he was perceiving a three-dimensional, solid figure from his two-dimensional colored perception. But not only does Hume fail to provide an answer of this sort, he fails to provide any answer at all. In fact, apart from a recently rediscovered letter, there is not a single reference to the problem in the Humean corpus.[2] And given the importance of the problem for Hume's empiricistic predecessors, his almost total silence on the matter cries out for explanation.

Although he does not address the issue, a plausible basis for an explanation of this silence has been suggested by Paul Russell. According to Russell (2008: 99–112), Hume's main target in T.1.2, where he presents his account of the ideas of space and time, was Samuel Clarke's defense of Newton's absolute theory in his correspondence with Leibniz, and a focal point of Hume's attack on the Newton-Clarke position was its appeal to the existence of a vacuum. If this is correct, and I assume as a working hypothesis that it is, then we can see why Hume might have ignored the Molyneux problem because his concern, at least in this portion of the *Treatise,* was metaphysical rather than epistemological or psychological.

Nevertheless, this still leaves us with an interesting, if somewhat speculative, question: given his account of space, what would Hume have said about the Molyneux problem had he chosen to address it? My suggestion is that Hume was led, partly by his focus on Clarke and the problem of a vacuum and partly by intrinsic features of his own view, to a relational theory of space that is much closer to Leibniz's than to his empiricist predecessors; one that, if applied to the Molyneux problem, would have led him to a response that is more akin to the former's than to the latter's.

The discussion is divided into three parts. The first sets the stage for the analysis of Hume's position by providing a brief sketch of Berkeley's theory of vision, with a focus on his relation to Locke and their respective treatments of the Molyneux problem. The second is devoted to a presentation of the central features of Hume's two-part system concerning space or extension. The third explores the relevance of Hume's account to the Molyneux problem by arguing that it commits him to the thesis that the visual (as well as the tangible) idea of space is three-dimensional and that this differentiates his position from that of other empiricists and brings it close to Leibniz's.

I BERKELEY'S THEORY OF VISION

Berkeley begins *An Essay Towards a New Theory of Vision* by informing the reader:

> My design is to shew the manner wherein we perceive by sight the distance, magnitude, and situation of objects. Also to consider the difference there is betwixt the ideas of sight and touch, and whether there be any idea common to both senses.
>
> (1709/1964: 171)

Although the bulk of Berkeley's essay is devoted to the topics mentioned in the first sentence, its philosophical weight lies primarily in his treatment of those referred to in the second. In other words, despite what is suggested by the title, it is not so much an essay on vision per se as on the relationship between visual and tactile perception. It is in this context that Berkeley appeals on several occasions to the Molyneux problem and offers a critique of both Molyneux's and Locke's response to it, on the grounds that they failed fully to appreciate the implication of the distinction between ideas of sight and touch.

Berkeley is in essential agreement with Locke and, indeed, a tradition stretching back to Aristotle in maintaining that the distance, magnitude, and situation of objects is a matter of judgment rather than immediate perception.[3] His major innovations lie in his minimalist account of what is immediately perceived or "given" visually and his critique of the geometrically oriented optics of his day. I discuss these in reverse order, focusing mostly on the first.

Limiting ourselves to distance, because similar considerations apply to magnitude and situation, Berkeley (1709/1964: 173) remarks that "it is plain that distance is in its own nature imperceptible, and yet is perceived by sight." And from this seeming paradox he concludes that it must "be brought into view by some other idea that is itself immediately perceived in the act of vision." Since the lines and angles appealed to by the geometrical opticians are not perceived, yet those ignorant of geometry nevertheless "see" distance, Berkeley dismisses that whole approach out of hand. Instead, he attempts to account for the "sudden judgments men make of distance" by factors such as the disposition of the eyes and the confused nature of the retinal image (1709/1964: 175–176). His main point, however, is that these determinations are entirely a matter of custom or habit because there is no necessary connection between these factors and distance. Moreover, as Berkeley points out, it follows from this that the man born blind would, on first receiving sight, be totally incapable of determining distance because he would lack the experience on the basis of which such determinations are made.

This is a consequence of Berkeley's thesis that "what we immediately and properly see are only lights and colours in sundry situations and shades and degrees of faintness and clearness, confusion and distinctness" (1709/1964: 202). Interestingly, he omits flat surfaces or two-dimensional objects from his survey of the contents of immediate visual perception. This contrasts with Locke (1694/1975: 145) who, in his discussion of the perception of a globe, maintains that what is given to the mind is the idea of a "flat circle," which then, by an experientially based judgment, is perceived as a globe.

Berkeley's omission is no accident, however, because he argues against Locke that "plains are no more the immediate object of sight than solids" (1709/1964: 235). This is part of Berkeley's argument against the view that at least plane geometry may be regarded as a science of visual extension, which would entail that visual space of itself yields a geometrical order that is accessible to Molyneux's newly sighted individual. Berkeley denies this on the grounds that the idea of a plain surface presupposes that of a solid, and the latter idea is only accessible through touch.

Underlying this argument is Berkeley's insistence on the radical heterogeneity of vision and touch. Not only are the objects of these senses numerically distinct, they are also specifically different. As Berkeley (1709/1964: 212) queries, "That which I see is only variety of light and colours. That which I feel is hard or soft, hot or cold, rough or smooth. What similitude, what connexion have those ideas with these?"

Berkeley's answer to the first part of this rhetorical question is none and to the second that the connection is acquired through experience of the customary correlation of certain visual and tactile experiences, wherein the former are generally regarded as signs of the latter. On this basis, Berkeley (1709/1964: 231) contends that the objects of vision "constitute an universal language of the Author of nature, whereby we are instructed how to regulate our actions in order to attain those things that are necessary to our bodies, as also to avoid whatever may be hurtful and destructive of them."

Again the target is Locke, who maintained that sight, being the most comprehensive of the senses, conveys to the mind not only "the *Ideas* of Light and Colours, which are peculiar only to that Sense; [but] also the far different Ideas of Space, Figure, and Motion" (1694/1975: 146). Accordingly, whereas Locke suggests that the habitual judgment involved in visual perception is *intra*sensory, Berkeley (1709/1964: 219–220) regards the habitual correlation underlying judgments of distance, figure, and motion as *inter*sensory (between vision and touch).

Berkeley completes his argument for the radical heterogeneity thesis by considering the question of the relation between *particular* extensions, figures, and motions perceived by sight and those perceived by touch (1709/1964: 222–235). Once again, the answer in all three cases is that they share nothing in common except the name, which is itself the result of their customary correlation. Although Berkeley remarks that this follows from what he has previously said, he feels called upon to add some fresh arguments because of the counterintuitive nature of his claim. Of these, I shall here mention only one, which relates directly to the Molyneux problem. Basically, Berkeley argues that Locke's acquiescence to Molyneux's negative conclusion regarding the visual capacities of his newly sighted individual is incompatible with his view that qualitatively identical spatial ideas are accessible to both touch and sight; for if that were the case, then this newly sighted person could use his knowledge of the difference between a cube and a sphere acquired through tactile experience to distinguish between them visually (1709/1964: 225–226). In short, the proper lesson to be learned from the Molyneux problem, one which *both* Locke and Molyneux failed to draw, was that visual and tactile experiences have qualitatively distinct content and there is no inherent connection between them.

II HUME'S VIEW OF SPACE OR EXTENSION

In order to understand how Hume might have responded to the Molyneux problem, it is necessary to review his account of space or extension. Like Berkeley, albeit for different reasons, Hume was deeply suspicious of the doctrine of infinite divisibility and the geometrical proofs cited in favor of it. And, again like Berkeley, he affirmed a doctrine of perceptual minima (visible and tangible) to counter it. Unlike Berkeley, however, Hume made this a central feature of his account.[4] After devoting the first two sections of T 1.2 to attacking the doctrine of infinite divisibility, he turns in the third section to his positive theory, according to which space consists in the "order," "disposition," or "manner of appearing" of extensionless but colored and/or tangible points. Moreover, at the beginning of the next section, he notes that he has presented a two-part system of space (and time), which are "intimately connected together" (1739/2007 1738 T 1.4.1/39). The first part consists in the arguments for the thesis that the constituent parts of space are the above-mentioned points. The second part, which Hume sees as a consequence of the first, maintains that,

> The ideas of space and time are . . . no separate or distinct ideas, but merely those of the manner or order in which objects exist. Or, in other words, 'tis impossible to conceive either a vacuum and extension without matter, or a time, when there was no succession or change in any real existence. (1739/2007 T 1.2.4.2/39–40)

Setting aside the issue of time, Hume's equation of space as an "order or manner in which objects exist" with the denial of a vacuum provides strong support for Russell's thesis that the latter is the real object of Hume's concern. Nevertheless, for present purposes, the question of a vacuum is a side issue that I do not here pursue because the central question concerns Hume's positive thesis about the nature of space and the idea thereof. The problem is exacerbated, however, by the fact that Hume presents this as the logical consequence of the first part of his system in which the sensory data of which the idea of space is composed consist of an array of indivisible colored and/or tangible points. Indeed, Hume himself was keenly aware of the problem of the connection between the two parts of his system and attempted to address it directly in his response to the first of a series of proposed objections to is account. Assuming the voice of a critic, Hume notes:

> It has often been maintain'd in the schools, that extension must be divisible, *in infinitum*, because the system of mathematical points is absurd; and that system is absurd, because a mathematical point is a non-entity, and consequently can never by its conjunction with others form a real existence. (1739/2007 T 1. 2.4.3/ 40)

This is basically a reiteration of Bayle's point that the doctrine of infinite divisibility derives its whole force from the absurdity of its assumed alternatives (Bayle, 1697/1965: 359). Consequently, the critic whom Hume is addressing is Bayle, and the objection takes the form of a reminder that because of the dialectical nature of the argument for infinite divisibility, it is futile to draw any positive conclusions from its rejection. Instead, the proper response, according to Bayle, is to acknowledge that extension "exists only in the mind" (1697/1965: 363).

Hume admits that this conclusion would be unavoidable, "were there no medium betwixt the infinite divisibility of matter, and the non-entity of mathematical points," but he rejects it by offering his own account as just such a "medium." Hume's response to Bayle therefore consists in the introduction of a neglected alternative. Whereas the latter had assumed that there were only three possible positions regarding the composition of the continuum (infinite divisibility, mathematical points, or physical points), Hume suggests a fourth, namely, colored or solid (tangible) points.

This is a bold move on Hume's part, since it requires showing that his view is both distinct from and not subject to the objections raised against the other alternatives. At least at first glance, however, it does not seem very promising. The problem is that, in order to escape the alleged absurdity of physical points, which, qua physical, would be divisible and therefore not points, Hume affirms the reality of his nonextended colored or tangible points. But this subjects him to the obvious objection, already insisted on by Bayle, "that several nonentities of extension joined together will never make up an extension" (1697/1965: 359–360).

Since he was aware of the problem, it is surprising that Hume does not discuss it at any length. Instead, he seems to have assumed that the attribution of color or tangibility to the points somehow ensures their reality, thereby differentiating them from mathematical points, without either compromising their indivisibility or transforming them into physical points.[5] Correlatively, it is the reality of these points that enables an aggregate of them to constitute a determinate line, area, or volume, even though each point by itself is extensionless.

Needless to say, this account has not been well received. In particular, it is unclear how the attribution of color or tangibility to these points makes the difference on which Hume insists and provides the basis for an answer to the classical objection against mathematical points; for whatever nonextensive qualities these points may possess, as far as extension is concerned, it still seems like an attempt to make something out of nothing. And there is, of course, the further question: how could something *tangible* be extensionless?

Nevertheless, without trying to minimize these difficulties, it must be emphasized that there is more to Hume's account of extension than this picture suggests. In fact, what has been omitted is the central feature of this account, namely, that it involves an order or disposition (not simply an aggregate) of points. In short, Hume advances a relational view of space, one in which the relata are these colored or tangible points that possess intensive, but not extensive, magnitude.[6]

This does not, however, suffice to get him out of the woods. The immediate problem is that, although the order or arrangement of the parts can explain shape or configuration and situation, it seems much more difficult to understand how it could explain magnitude. In fact, this is a general problem for relational theories, one that Clarke had raised against Leibniz when he pointed out that space and time are quantities, whereas order and situation (in terms of which Leibniz understood them) are not.[7] Moreover, assuming that Hume was familiar with the Leibniz-Clarke debate and that a central concern of his discussion of space and time in the *Treatise* was to rebut the latter's view, then this is an issue that Hume ought to have addressed in a direct way.

Unfortunately, however, he does not. In fact, if one endeavors to reconstruct the Humean response to Clarke's objection, it seems that, given the resources available to him, he must fall back on sheer aggregation. In other words, Hume seems committed to the view that both the size of an object and the distance between two or more objects is determined by the number of the colored or tangible but extensionless points. And with this we seem to be back to the problem with which we began, namely, how to generate a determinate extension from extensionless points.

In addressing this question, I borrow a suggestion from C. D. Broad concerning Hume's understanding of contiguity. The significance of Hume's treatment of this concept for his views on extension is illustrated by a passage in which he attempts to answer the objection that, on his view, all matter would interpenetrate, since any simple and indivisible atoms that touched one another would do so completely and therefore penetrate. Against this, Hume replies that "A blue and red point may surely lie contiguous without any penetration." And, on this basis, he asks whether one would not perceive "that from the union of these points there results an object, which is compounded and divisible, and may be distinguish'd into two parts, of which each preserves its existence distinct and separate, notwithstanding its contiguity to the other?" (1739/2007 T 1.2.4.6/41).

In analyzing this response, Broad points out first that the difference of the color of the points is irrelevant and second that "contiguity" here cannot mean contact, because, as the objection to which Hume is responding insists, indivisible points would completely coincide with one another if they touched. Consequently, Broad suggests that the contiguity of these points must be understood in terms of an "*intrinsic minimum distance*, such that two points cannot be nearer together than this." And, he goes on to add, "Two points which were at the intrinsically minimal distance apart might be said to be 'contiguous'" (Broad, 1961: 169).

Although Broad took the introduction of the idea of an intrinsic minimum distance as a desperate expedient, it actually provides a solution to Hume's problem. For if we assume such a distance between contiguous points, we can see how the aggregation of these points could produce an extensive magnitude, even though the points, taken singly, are extensionless. Moreover, since contiguity is a relation, this also provides a model for understanding how a relational theory could account for size and distance. Here, the point is not simply that contiguous points are separated by an intrinsically minimal distance, but that the minimal nature of their separation constitutes their contiguity. In short, the relation of contiguity is a limiting case of extensive magnitude.

Apart from the fact that there is no clear evidence that this reflects Hume's actual thinking, there remains the matter of the viability of the conception of an intrinsic minimum distance. This is the target of Broad's critique, and he raises three objections: (1) the conception is inconsistent with the notion of distance; (2) it is impossible, on "general Humean principles" to account for the idea that "there is a certain distance such that no two points can be nearer together than this, and that any two points must be separated either by this distance or by some integral multiple of it"; and (3) the doctrine leads to paradoxical geometrical consequences (1961: 170).

Taking these objections in reverse order, the third can be quickly dismissed on the grounds that Hume would readily admit the charge, but deny its force. Like Berkeley, he fully acknowledges that his account of geometry has consequences that are contrary to the standard view, but he defends it as necessary to avoid the true paradoxes generated by the doctrine of infinite divisibility.

Broad's second objection addresses the modal status of this thesis. He asks, "What would it mean, on Hume's general principles, to say that there is a certain distance such that no two points *can* be nearer together than this, and that any two points *must* be separated either by this distance or by some integral multiplication of it?" (1961: 170). Ruling out analyticity, Broad concludes that, according to Hume's theory, it could only be a belief generated by a regularity in our past experience. But since (as Hume himself admits) we are seldom, if ever, capable of discriminating individual points, which would be required in order to be aware of this minimal distance, it cannot be the latter either (Broad 1961: 170).

I believe that this objection reflects a level confusion on Broad's part. The question is not whether there is an ordinary belief in something like an intrinsic minimum distance, but whether there is an experiential basis for incorporating such a conception into a science of human nature. And here Hume would be in a position to appeal to "experiments" such as the disappearing impression of the ink spot used to support the doctrine of a *minimum visible* (1739/2007 T 2.1.4/27). This is not to defend Hume's position, but merely to suggest that introducing this conception need not create any *new* problems for him because it would simply be a matter of another kind of perceptual minimum.

The first objection appears more serious, since there does seem to be something incoherent in the notion of an intrinsic minimum distance. After all, cannot *any* determinate distance, no matter how small, be conceived as divisible ad infinitum? And does this not preclude the very possibility of such a distance? So formulated, however, it becomes clear that this likewise is not a new problem but merely the old problem of a minimal size applied to distance. In short, if the notion of perceptual minima is coherent, then so is that of an intrinsic minimum distance, and vice versa.

III HUME VERSUS BERKELEY

To understand how, given this account of space or extension, Hume might have addressed the Molyneux problem, it will be useful to consider the major differences between his view and those of Locke and Berkeley, particularly the latter. To begin with, it should be noted that, even though Berkeley shared with Hume the doctrine of perceptual minima, he would have no place for anything like the notion of an intrinsic minimum distance, at least with regard to vision. This is because for Berkeley distance is not, strictly speaking, an object of vision because all that the latter provides is color and light, from which Berkeley does not attempt to construct distance by aggregation (1709/1964: 216). Tactile experience is another matter, however, and it does seem that, inasmuch as he is committed to both tactile experience as the true source of our idea of distance and to a *minimum tangibile*, Berkeley would be committed to something like an intrinsic minimum *tangible* distance in order to construct determinate distances (or sizes) by aggregation.

Moreover, at the phenomenological level, Hume differs sharply from both Berkeley's minimalist account of what is immediately given visually and Locke's richer phenomenology. Hume's phenomenology appears to be motivated by his endeavor to defend the applicability of the copy principle to the ideas of space and time. Not only does he affirm this applicability, he states that his intent is to "apply this principle in order to discover farther the nature of our ideas of space and time" (1739/2007 T 1.2.3.1/33). And, in an attempt to illustrate this application, he suggests that it is essentially a matter of looking. As he initially puts it, "Upon opening my eyes, and turning them to the surrounding objects, I perceive many visible bodies; and upon shutting them again, and considering the distance betwixt these bodies, I acquire the idea of extension" (1739/2007 T 1.2.3.2/33).

Hume illustrates this by the example of the perception of a table:

> The table before me is alone sufficient by its view to give me the idea of extension. This idea, then, is borrow'd from, and represents some impression, which this moment appears to the senses. But my senses convey to me only the impressions of colour'd points, dispos'd in a certain manner. If the eye is sensible of any thing farther, I desire it may be pointed out to me. But if it be impossible to show any thing farther, we may conclude with certainty, that the idea of extension is nothing but a copy of these colour'd points, and of the manner of their appearance. (1739/2007 T 1.2.3.4/34)

Given his commitment to the copy principle and its applicability to the ideas of space and time, this account of how the *idea* of extension is first acquired makes it evident that Hume took the perception of the table from which this idea is derived to be a compound impression. As such, it contains not only a number of discrete colored points but also the manner in which these points are disposed relative to one another. And, as Hume makes clear in his parallel discussion of time, this disposition of the points is not a further impression added to the mix, but simply the manner in which these points present themselves (1739/2007 T 1.2.3.10/36).

It should be clear from this how radically Hume's account differs from both Berkeley's and Locke's. It differs from the former in affirming that the idea of extension is derivable from vision alone and from both in maintaining that the acquisition of the idea does not require any further act of judgment. As we have seen, for Berkeley, determinate visual ideas of extension depend on judgments involving correlations with tactile phenomena, whereas for Locke, they involve judgments based on previously experienced visual experience. By contrast, for Hume, the need for any such act of mind beyond the sheer reception of the visual data is precluded by the fact that spatial relations are already given in a compound impression, a notion that is foreign to both Locke and Berkeley.

This conclusion finds further support in Hume's account of philosophical relations, where, in considering the relations that yield only probabilities (knowledge of matters of fact in the language of the *Enquiry*) he notes that in the relations of time and place (as well as identity) it is a matter of "a mere passive admission of the impressions thro' the organs of sensation," inasmuch as "in none of them the mind can go beyond what is immediately present to the senses, either to discover the real existence or the relations of objects" (1739/2007 T 1.3.2.2/73). Although Hume recognizes that we draw inferences regarding the time and place (as well as the identity) of objects, his point is that all such reasoning is based on causation (T 1.3.2.2/73–74). And it is apparent that no such reasoning is involved in the visual perception of an object such as Hume's table.

If this account of Hume's position is correct, it follows that he could not say that the third dimension is inferred, perhaps on the basis of tactile experience, because at issue is not the dimensionality of physical objects but of visual perceptions *qua visual*, that is, of impressions. Accordingly, if it were inferred, it would have to be from visual evidence, which is just the impression. In fact, the constraints of Hume's theory appear to leave him with only two possible ways of accounting for the perception of a three-dimensional visual space: either it is immediately perceived, in which case we have three-dimensional visual impressions, or the third dimension is a fiction produced by the imagination, presumably on the basis of an associative relation with tactile perceptions. But, despite his fondness for such fictions, Hume nowhere makes any such claim for three-dimensional visual extensions, as he presumably would have done had he regarded the idea as a fiction.

One obvious objection to this reading is that it commits Hume to the existence of three-dimensional visual impressions. The problem was already raised by Reid (1764/1967: 144a) who, with respect to Hume, asked "What kind of thing is the visual figure? Is it a Sensation, or an Idea? If an Idea from what impression copied?" And, in what is obviously intended as a *reductio* of Hume's position, Reid (1764/1967: 144b) remarks that "unless ideas and impressions are extended and figured, it cannot belong to that category."[8] Here, Reid has hit on what is undoubtedly a paradoxical implication of Hume's account, namely, that physical dimensions are assigned to certain impressions and the ideas that supposedly copy them. But the situation here is similar to that concerning the intelligibility of the idea of an intrinsically minimal distance. Simply put, since it is an undeniable fact that Hume regarded visual impressions and their corresponding ideas as *at least* two-dimensional, there seems to be no insuperable difficulty in taking the next logical step and assigning them the third dimension as well.[9]

Admittedly, Hume never explicitly says straight out that our perception of visual space contains three dimensions. In fact, in one place in the *Treatise* he appears to deny it. Thus, in the context of the denial of a vacuum and expressing a view that he appears to endorse, Hume remarks that, "'Tis commonly allow'd by philosophers, that all bodies, which discover themselves to the eye, appear as if painted on a plain surface, and their different degrees of remoteness from ourselves are discover'd more by reason than by the senses" (1739/2007 T 1.2.5.8/56).[10]

Nevertheless, I believe that there are compelling reasons why we *should not regard* this passage as a statement of Hume's considered view on the matter. First, setting aside considerations regarding the retinal image, which for Hume belong to natural rather than moral philosophy, there is phenomenological support for such a view, which would weigh heavily for Hume because, contrary to what the quoted passage suggests, visual experience usually *seems* to be three-dimensional. Thus, the question becomes the basis for this appearance, and if, as just suggested, Hume would not have regarded it as a fiction of the imagination, the only viable alternative is that it is directly perceived.

Second, in his critique of the immaterialist view of the mind, Hume provides an account that strongly suggests (if it does not actually assert) that visual perception is three-dimensional. Referring again to a perceived table, Hume reflects:

> That table, which just now appears to me, is only a perception, and all its qualities are qualities of a perception. Now the most obvious of all its qualities is extension. The perception consists of parts. These parts are so situated, as to afford us the notion of distance and contiguity; of length, breadth, and thickness. The termination of these three dimensions is what we call figure. (1739/2007 T 1.4.5.15/239)

Although Hume does not explicitly say that his perception of the table (unlike his earlier appeal to the same example) is visual, the context certainly suggests as much. And if this is correct, it follows that "thickness," like length and breadth, is an object of vision as well as touch.[11]

The third and perhaps strongest support for this reading is to be found in Hume's account of how the mind proceeds from the particular idea that mirrors a certain disposition of colored points to the abstract idea of space or extension in general.[12] Hume begins by inviting the reader to suppose that the colored points from which the mind supposedly derives its idea of extension are all purple. It follows, he reasons, that with every repetition of this idea (the arrangement of purple points), the mind would not only place the points in the same order but also bestow on them the same purple color. But, he continues, after experiencing points of different colors and "finding a resemblance in the disposition of colour'd points of which they are compos'd," the mind is able to set aside the difference of color and form "an abstract idea merely on that disposition of points, or manner of appearance, in which they agree" (1739/2007 T 1.2.3.5/34). In short, despite the particularity of its ideas, the mind is able to set aside differences of color and attend merely to a structural resemblance in the "disposition" of two or more differently colored sets of points.

This accords with what Hume says in T 1.1.7 regarding "distinctions of reason," where his concern is to show how the mind is capable of distinguishing in thought items that are not separable in imagination or reality (e.g., the color and figure of an object) and, on this basis, take notice of resemblances between distinct objects (e.g., different colored globes). What he is now suggesting is that a similar analysis applies to the disposition of the colored points. Thus, even though this disposition is not separable from the points and their color, the mind (by a distinction of reason) can consider the former separately, thereby framing the idea of a disposition or order shared by distinct sets of points of different colors. And, by parity of reason, by considering that different dispositions of points of various colors resemble each other in being dispositions of colored points, the mind can set aside the differences and arrive at a general idea of extension consisting of an indeterminate disposition of points of indeterminate color. Or, more precisely, it can let one particular set of points disposed in a certain way stand for *any* disposition of points of *any* color.

The crucial point, however, is that Hume carries this generalizing process one step further by extending the analysis to touch as well as vision. As Hume puts it, making sure that the reader is aware that he is making a significant amplification of his argument,

> Nay even when the resemblance is carry'd beyond the objects of one sense, and the impressions of touch are found to be similar to those of sight in the disposition of their parts; this does not hinder the abstract idea from representing both, upon account of their resemblance. (1739/2007 T 1.2.3.5/34)

Whether or not Hume understood it as such, this constitutes a direct challenge to the central tenet of Berkeley's theory of vision and undercuts the latter's response to the Molyneux problem. Whereas Berkeley's theory and his response to this problem were both based on the premise that visual and tactile experience share nothing in common, Hume's account suggests that there is a common spatial order (or manner of disposition) accessible to both sight and touch and, with it, presumably also a common geometry. Otherwise, the resemblance could not be carried over from the visual to the tactile, and the abstract idea of extension could not represent what is common to both.

Although it is possible to interpret this similarity claim in a weaker fashion—for example, as implying that the parts of a visual experience are similar to those of its tangible counterpart in the sense that, in both cases, the parts are disposed above/below and right/left, while the tangible parts are also disposed before/behind—I believe that the most natural reading is to take Hume as claiming that the similarity in the disposition of parts includes the third dimension.[13] Inasmuch as it is an essential aspect of the general idea of space or extension that it contains three dimensions, it would be peculiar if only a disposition of tactile points instantiated this feature.

Finally, if this is the case, it indicates that had Hume chosen to address the Molyneux problem, his response would have been closer to that of Leibniz than to that of either Locke or Berkeley. In his own treatment of the problem in the *New Essays*, Leibniz remarks that in answering the question in the negative both Molyneux and Locke omit a condition that he took to be implicit in the question, namely, that the subject already knows that one of the objects between which he will be asked to distinguish by sight is a cube and the other a sphere. Given this, together with the subject's ability to distinguish such shapes by touch, Leibniz thinks it beyond doubt that said subject "could discern them by applying rational principles to the sensory knowledge which he has already acquired by touch" (1765/1981: 136–37).[14]

Obviously, for Hume, it would be a matter of perception rather than an appeal to "rational principles," and it is unclear what Hume would have said about Leibniz's condition or, more generally, about the capacity of the newly sighted person to distinguish visually a sphere from a cube. What does seem relatively clear, however, and is all that I am here arguing for, is that such a person would be equipped with a necessary condition for such a discrimination, namely, a visual perception of extension in three dimensions.

NOTES

1. See Molyneux's letter to Locke of March 2, 1693 (Molyneux, 1693: 308–312).
2. The letter is to Hugh Blair and dated July 4, 1762. For my discussion of its relevant portion, see note 10.
3. This is noted by Luce (1964: 148).
4. At least in the essay, the doctrine of the minimum visibile is a side issue for Berkeley because it does not form part of his argument for the radical heterogeneity thesis. In fact, Berkeley tells us that he introduces the conception only to fill in his account of vision. See Berkeley (1709/1964: 204).
5. In the *Enquiry*, Hume defends physical points, but he there understands by them indivisible parts of extension, that is, the minima of the *Treatise* (See EU 12.18, 33n/156n). Thus, his change is merely terminological.
6. Those who attribute a relational view of space and/or time to Hume include Mijuskovic (1977), Baxter (1988), and McRae (1980).
7. See the *Leibniz-Clarke Correspondence* (Leibniz, 1956: 32).
8. Reid is here referring to the three-dimensional visible figure, and the "category" is that of being a perception (impression or idea in Hume).
9. I have attempted to provide a charitable reading of Hume's assignment of physical properties to mental items (impressions and ideas) by noting that Humean impressions lack intentionality in the sense that there is nothing of which they are impressions. Thus, rather than speaking of an impression of something red or triangular, Hume is committed to speaking in a proto-Sellarsian manner of a red and triangular impression; see Allison (2008: 14). A vigorous defense of this aspect of Hume's position has been provided by Falkenstein (1997: 191 and 196–201).
10. I am grateful to Falkenstein for calling this passage to my attention in a private correspondence. Pace Falkenstein, however, I opt to downplay it in light of the considerations adduced later, which includes textual evidence pointing in the opposite direction. Although it is possible that Hume was simply inconsistent on the point, I believe that the view I attribute to him best squares with his overall account of space. Moreover, it is noteworthy that in the Appendix to the *Treatise*, Hume abandoned a key element of his thesis, namely, that the distance between bodies supposedly separated by empty space is inferred from the angles of incidence of the light rays that affect our senses on the grounds that these angles are not known to the mind and therefore cannot enable

us to determine the distance (T App. 22/636). More recently, Falkenstein has suggested another passage, which he takes as evidence that Hume assumed that visual (as contrasted with tactile) extension has only two dimensions. The passage is from a recently rediscovered letter of Hume to Hugh Blair (see note 2), in which Hume discusses the portion of the manuscript of Reid's not yet published *Inquiry* that he had been shown by Blair. With respect to the point at issue, Hume writes: "It surpriz'd me to find the Author affirm, that our Idea of Extension is nothing like the Objects of Touch. He certainly knows, that People born blind have very compleat Ideas of Extension[s]; & some of them have even been great Geometers. Touch alone gives us an Idea of Three Dimensions" (1762/1997: 256). I differ from Falkenstein, however, in my reading of this passage. As I see it, the issue is whether Hume is claiming that touch is a necessary or merely a sufficient condition for having an idea of a three-dimensional space. Grammatically, either reading is possible; but I believe that the context speaks strongly in favor of the latter alternative, which leaves the question of the three-dimensionality of visual space entirely open.

11. Falkenstein's treatment of this passage is instructive. Although he discusses it in the context of his rejection of the view that Humean ideas of space and time might be products of distinctions of reason rather than that of the dimensionality of visual impressions (a rejection with which I completely concur), Hume appears to regard the perception of the table as visual rather than tactile, and he explicitly notes that it has three dimensions; see Falkenstein (1997: 189). At the very least, then, this passage, which he describes as "telling," provides a counterpoint to T 1.2.5.8/56.

12. Interestingly, Hume differs sharply from Berkeley on this issue despite his strong endorsement of the latter's critique of the notion of abstract general ideas.

13. This alternative reading, as well as other similar ones, was suggested to me by Falkenstein in private correspondence. Falkenstein's resistance to the stronger reading seems to be based largely, if not entirely, on the weight he places on T 1.2.5.8/56. For reasons given in the body of this paper and note 10, I do not believe that this singular passage should trump the overall considerations that I have attempted to provide.

14. It should be noted, however, that, in contrast to the Leibniz-Clarke Correspondence, Hume could not have been familiar with Leibniz' *New Essays* at the time of the *Treatise* because it was first published in 1765.

BIBLIOGRAPHY

Allison, Henry E. (2008). *Custom and Reason in Hume, A Kantian Reading of the First Book of the Treatise*. Oxford: Clarendon Press.

Baxter, Donald. (1988). "Hume on Infinite Divisibility." *History of Philosophy Quarterly* 5, 133–40.

Bayle, Pierre. (1697/1965). *Historical and Critical Dictionary*. Selections edited and translated by Richard H. Popkin. Indianapolis: Bobbs-Merrill Company.

Berkeley, George. (1709/1964). *An Essay Towards a New Theory of Vision: The Works of George Berkeley, Bishop of Cloyne*, edited by A. A. Luce. London: Thomas Nelson and Sons Ltd., vol. 1.

Broad, C. D. (1961). "Hume's Doctrine of Space." *Proceedings of the British Academy* 47, London: Oxford University Press.

Cassirer, Ernst. (1955). *The Philosophy of the Enlightenment*, translated by Fritz C. A. Koelln and James P. Pettegrove. Boston: Beacon Press.

Falkenstein, Lorne. (1997). "Hume on Manners of Disposition and the Ideas of Space and Time." *Archiv für Geschichte der Philosophie*, 79, 179–201.

Hume, David. (1762/1997). Letter to Hugh Blair, 4 July 1762, in the Appendix to Thomas Reid's *An Inquiry into the Human Mind on the Principles of Common Sense*, edited by Derek R. Brookes. Edinburgh: Edinburgh University Press.

Leibniz, G. W. (1956). *The Leibniz-Clarke Correspondence*, edited by H. G. Alexander. Manchester: Manchester University Press.

Leibniz, G. W. (1765/1981). *New Essays on Human Understanding*, translated and edited by Peter Remnant and Jonathan Bennett. Cambridge: Cambridge University Press.

Locke, John. (1694/1975). *An Essay Concerning Human Understanding*, edited by Peter H. Nidditch. Oxford: Oxford University Press.

Luce, A. A. (1964). "Editor's Introduction," in *The Works of George Berkeley, Bishop of Cloyne*, edited by A. A. Luce. London: Thomas Nelson and Sons Ltd., vol. 1.

McRae, John. (1980). "The Import of Hume's Theory of Time." *Hume Studies* 6, 119–132.

Mijuskovic, Ben. (1977). "Hume on Space and Time." *Journal of the History of Philosophy*, 6, 387–394.

Molyneux, William. (1693). Letter to Locke of March 2, 1693, *in The Works of John Locke*, ninth edition. London, vol. 8, 1794: 208–212.

Reid, Thomas. (1764/1967). *An Inquiry into the Human Mind, on the Principles of Common Sense, in Philosophical Works*, vol. 1 ed. by Sir William Hamilton. Heldesheim, Germany: Georg Olms Verlagsbuchhandlung.

Russell, Paul. (2008). *The Riddle of Hume's Treatise: Skepticism, Naturalism, and Irreligion*, New York: Oxford University.

....

CHAPTER 10

HUME ON SPACE AND TIME

....

DONALD L. M. BAXTER

I SKEPTICISM: SPACE AND TIME
AS THEY APPEAR

....

UNDERSTANDING Hume's theory of space and time requires suspending our own. When theorizing, we think of space as one huge array of locations, which external objects might or might not occupy. Time adds another dimension to this vast array.

For Hume, in contrast, space is extension in general, where being extended is having parts arranged one right next to the other like the pearls on a necklace. Time is duration in general, where having duration is having parts occurring one after another like the notes of a song. Hume's different view stems from his empiricism, his reliance on experience and observation as the foundation of our concepts. Nothing in our experience suggests a single vast array of locations. Rather, we simply notice that bodies are similar insofar as they have lengths that can be compared. Likewise, nothing in our experience suggests a single dimension of time. Rather, we simply notice that different successions are similar insofar as they have durations that can be compared. Theorizing that these observations show there to be a single multidimensional array goes well beyond the evidence for Hume. As a skeptic, he finds himself unable to assent to theories that stray too far beyond the deliverances of the senses.

For Hume, the ideas of space and time are each a general idea of simple—partless—objects arrayed in a certain manner. He argues that the structures of the ideas of space and time reflect the structures of space and time. Therefore, space and time are not infinitely divisible, and they are ways simple objects are arrayed. Consequently, there is no such thing as empty space nor time without change.

Hume's inferences from how their ideas are to how space and time are seem rash. However, as skeptic, his concern is simply with how space and time appear to outer and inner sense. What is rash is to think that we can know any more than that. The ideas we have reflect how space and time appear, and so can ground Hume's inferences.

This approach does not give every opinion about space and time equal weight. Hume distinguishes how space and time apparently appear from how they really appear. The former are views that we can, in the long run, be talked out of by appeal to evidence or consistency; they are akin to superstition. The latter are views that will tend, in the long run, to survive opposition; they are the views that we are naturally constituted to hold when we inquire carefully.[1]

Hume's focus on appearance is the result of his version of the methodology for inquiry employed by the Royal Society.[2] Granting the impossibility of refuting all skeptical challenges, the Society arrived at a mitigated skepticism with the goal of certainty beyond a reasonable doubt. Hume finds even this requirement to mandate suspense of judgment. He is unable to arrive at sufficiently good reason to believe anything. Nonetheless, he finds himself caused to theorize, to believe, and to wish to cause stable agreement in others. He therefore reconceives mitigated skepticism's goal to be assurance beyond a sustainable doubt, where a sustainable doubt is one causally able to remove our assurance over the long term. It strikes Hume that the only ultimate sources of lasting assurance are the vivid experiences of outer or inner sense: hence his concern with space and time as they appear.

Not surprisingly, his views have seemed bizarre to commentators who assumed that he was concerned with space and time as they really are or space and time as they are presupposed to be by our geometry or physics.[3] Focusing on Hume's own concern will reveal his views to be reasonable, even if not convincing. To try to overcome their strangeness and initial implausibility, I focus on his central contentions and the reasonings behind them instead of giving a comprehensive treatment.

Hume's "system concerning space and time" comprises two main claims. First, he argues that finite portions of space and of time are not infinitely divisible. Rather, they are composed of simple and indivisible parts. Second, he argues that these indivisible parts are inconceivable unless occupied by something "real and existent." Consequently, space and time are each a "manner or order, in which objects exist" (T 1.2.4.1–2/39–40).

II SPACE

II.1 Against the Infinite Divisibility of Space

For Hume, to deny the infinite divisibility of a finite spatial interval is both to deny that every part has parts and to deny that the interval has an infinite number of parts. He thought the first denial entailed the second. Current geometers disagree, supposing that a line segment can consist of an infinite number of dimensionless, and therefore indivisible, points. Current thinking is that these points are ordered at least densely—between any two there is another—and in fact form a continuum. Hume, however, argued that the simple parts of an interval could only be ordered discretely—one next to the other—in such a way that the length of the interval was directly proportional to the number of simple parts. So, an infinite number of them would yield a spatial interval of infinite length.

Parts, for Hume, are proper parts. Parthood is irreflexive, asymmetric, and transitive. Nothing is a part of itself; no two things are parts of each other; if one thing is part of a second thing that is part of a third thing, then the first thing is part of the third thing.

Unexpectedly, Hume's argument begins with a preliminary argument concerning ideas (T 1.2.1.2/26–7). Call it the "Minimal Ideas Argument." For Hume, ideas are images, as are impressions (T 1.1.1.1/1; T 1.2.1.3–4/27). Just as an image can have parts, so an idea can have parts. For instance, a mirror image of a chessboard has the images of the squares as parts. On this presupposition, the argument proceeds.

(1) There are ideas in the mind.
(2) Any part of an idea is an idea.
(3) If every idea had parts, then the mind would have an infinite number of ideas.
(4) No mind has an infinite number of ideas.
(5) So some ideas have no parts.

Hume presupposes (1) and (2). Statement (3) follows from them because if every idea had parts, then every idea would have parts with parts, and so on to infinity. Statement (4) is something no one questions for human minds. It follows that there are minimal (i.e., simple) ideas.

Hume thinks that one can verify this conclusion by noticing that one uses exactly similar images, not progressively smaller ones, when imagining a grain of sand, a thousandth part of that grain, and even a ten-thousandth part (T 1.2.1.3/27). A better way to understand his thinking is with his ink spot experiment. Put a tiny spot of ink on a contrasting piece of paper and withdraw slowly until the visual image of the spot disappears. The image just before vanishing is minimal, according to Hume. No smaller image can exist. Therefore, it has no parts, which would have to be smaller images that could exist separately. The image while seeing the spot is what Hume terms an *impression*. Recollecting that experience would require an idea that copies the impression and that is, therefore, simple. Thus, one can verify the conclusion that some ideas have no parts.

It is important not to confuse the ink spot with the impression or idea of it. Hume is not yet arguing that the ink spot or any of its parts are minimal. He is only making an argument that there are minimal impressions and ideas in the mind.

Having established their existence, Hume proceeds to give his main argument that space—extension—is not infinitely divisible (T 1.2.2.1.2/29–30). Call it the "Infinite Extension Argument."[4]

(1) Minimal ideas are too minute to be divided.
(2) Therefore, nothing can be more minute.

(3) Therefore, minimal ideas are "adequate representations" of extremely minute parts of extension however tiny—that is, anything true of minimal ideas qua minute is true of any extremely minute parts of extension.

(4) Minimal ideas arranged one after the other as close together as possible are such that an infinity of them would yield an extension of infinite length.

(5) Therefore, any extremely minute parts of extension arranged one after the other as close together as possible are such that an infinity of them would yield an extension of infinite length.

(6) Therefore, no extension of finite length can have an infinite number of parts.

(7) If every part of an extension of finite length had parts, then the extension would have an infinite number of parts.

(8) Therefore, some parts of extension have no parts.

Hume takes his preliminary argument to have established (1). Statement (2) follows from the assumed fact that anything extended is divisible into parts, and so minimal ideas are extensionless (see T 1.4.5.7/234; T 1.2.3.14/38; T 1.2.4.9/42). The burden of the argument rests on (3). For an idea to be an adequate representation in a certain respect is for everything true of it in that respect to be true of what it represents.[5] For Hume, ideas are images of their objects and so will resemble them in the relevant respect (T 1.4.5.3/233; T 1.4.6.18/260). Here, Hume is concerned specifically with minuteness and with how minute things can be ordered to form an extension. What is true of minute ideas will be true of any minute things, whether in the mind or not.

The trouble is, Hume gives no reason to believe that ideas or images of space resemble it. At best, they show us space as it appears via sensations of extended things—not space as it is in itself. Rather than be troubled, though, Hume would agree entirely. He does not discuss space as it is in itself.

> As long as we confine our speculations to the appearances of objects to our senses, without entering into disquisitions concerning their real nature and operations, we are safe from all difficulties, and can never be embarrass'd by any question. (T 1.2.5.26, n12/638)

He announces in the Introduction that he will rely on experience and observation (T Intro 7/xix). So, "at present I content myself with knowing perfectly the manner in which objects affect my senses, and their connexions with each other, as far as experience informs me of them" (T 1.2.5.26/64). Given Hume's Copy Principle, our ideas of space are copies of sensory impressions and so reflect space as it appears to the senses (cf. T 1.1.1.5–6/3–4). Furthermore, our ideas are the meanings of our words, so if a theory of space is about space in the common acceptation of the word, then it is about space as it appears to the senses (1.4.3.10/224). So, consequences of the minuteness of our minimal spatial images will carry over to the minute parts of space in the common acceptation of "space."

The senses do not, and could not, suggest to us that a line in space is a set of points ordered as a continuum, as our current theory has it. They are not acute enough to discern such points and such an ordering, even aided by microscopes. Given Hume's skeptical approach, his conclusion is plausible that no finite extension as it appears to the senses can have an infinite number of parts.

Note that I am not assimilating Hume to Kant. Hume does not postulate a world of appearance in contrast to a world of things as they are in themselves and about which we can have some a priori knowledge. He is merely confining his descriptions and theories to the ways things in space appear, without taking any stand on the existence of metaphysical realms. As skeptic, he is only giving vent to views about space that strike him forcefully on careful examination of certain ideas copied from certain impressions. These views are ones that he suspects will become the stable views of any careful inquirer who replicates his reasoning and observations. Space as it appears is simply space according to these views.

Note that Statement (3) does not beg the question. Hume does say that minimal ideas are adequate to the "most minute parts of extension" (T 1.2.2.1/29). However, not having proved their simplicity yet, he uses "most minute" not to mean simple, but just to mean being in the general range of the extremely minute. Thus, he draws his conclusion from considering minimal ideas only insofar as they are in that range. Because nothing can be more minute than they are, anything true of minimal ideas qua minute will be true of any extremely minute things, even divisible ones. So, a fact about the possible ordering of minimal ideas will apply to any extremely minute things.

Hume thinks that one can verify Statement (4) by careful manipulation of one's minimal ideas. First, form in the imagination a minimal idea, perhaps by remembering the ink spot just before it vanished from sight. Then form another minimal idea right beside the first, so close that no minimal idea could fit in between. To imagine any sort of distance between them would be to imagine room for a minimal idea. The two adjacent ideas are an idea with the smallest extension. Individually they are extensionless, but together they are extended.

It is hard to understand Hume here. Two questions arise immediately. How can it make sense to say that ideas are themselves extended rather than just of something extended? And how can something extended be formed by adding extensionless things?[6]

The answer to the first question is that ideas are images. Images, such as a mirror image of a chessboard, have parts arranged spatially. That is what it is to be extended for Hume. He says explicitly that ideas can be extended (T 1.4.5.15/240).

As to the second question, understanding requires looking and seeing. Conceptual worries, such as how adding two zero quantities can yield a nonzero quantity, are not relevant. One needs to look and see whether arithmetic addition of zeros is an appropriate model for understanding the length that results from putting a second minimum adjacent to the first. Examining one's ideas shows that it is not. If the ideas are too faint and unsteady, Hume recommends turning to the impressions of the sort that the ideas are copied from. For example, put two grains of sand on a contrasting surface. As in the ink spot experiment, get far enough away that the grains each present a minimal, extensionless impression. Take a single bristle from a broom and slowly move one grain adjacent to the other. There will be a point at which you cannot move it any closer and still discern two grains. Any closer and they will appear as a single grain from your remote viewpoint. When they are at their closest approach, but while still appearing to be two grains, they give you an image with the smallest extension, on Hume's definition, formed from extensionless images.

Let two minimal impressions at their closest approach be said to have one unit of extension. Add a third minimal impression at its closest approach to the second. The result is an impression with two units of extension. Add a fourth minimal impression in the same way. The result is an impression with three units of extension. It is clear that the length of the impression is directly proportional to the number of minimal impressions added. Were the mind capacious enough to allow an infinite number of minimal impressions to be added, the resulting length would be an infinite number of units of extension. As with the impressions, so with the ideas. Hence Statement (4).

Statement (5) follows, given the adequacy claim. If an infinity of extensionless things yields an infinite extension, then an infinity of extremely minute things will do so as well, especially if they are divisible and so extended.

Statement (6), the denial of infinite divisibility in general, follows directly from (5). Statement (7) expresses Hume's particular conception of infinite divisibility. Statement (8) then follows.

Hume is aware that an infinite sum, such as $1/2 + 1/4 + 1/8 + \ldots$ can approach a finite number. However, there is no progression of parts of extension with each of these lengths. That would require that every part of extension be divisible, just as the numbers are (T 1.2.2.2, n6/30 n1).

Following Aristotle, one might object that, at best, Hume's argument only shows that Statement (6) is true concerning actual parts, which does not rule out a finite interval's having an infinity of potential parts. Presumably, the Aristotelian regards the parts as potential when they are merely separable but not separated.[7] However, Hume takes as a principle that separable things are distinct (T 1.1.7.3/18; T 1.4.5.5/233).[8] It is safe to assume that he means that they are actually distinct. So, parts that something potentially has would be actually distinct. It is safe to assume that actually distinct things actually exist. So, the parts something potentially has actually exist. It is hard to see how they could actually exist without being parts. So, something that lacks all parts would also lack potential parts.

This conclusion would follow, even if the potential parts were merely distinguishable. According to Hume's version of the separability principle, even the merely distinguishable are distinct. After all, the distinguishable differ, and nothing can differ from itself without contradiction. So, Hume's principle rules out the Aristotelian objection.

It is tempting to dismiss Hume's Infinite Extension Argument on the grounds that the conclusion is obviously false. The successful application of geometry to space by engineers and scientists is proof enough that finite intervals of space are infinitely divisible.

However, Hume has a reasonable response. Geometric proofs, as they apply to space, are "built on ideas, which are not exact, and maxims, which are not precisely true." We have no standard of geometrical equality other than appearing equal to the senses and imagination. Consequently, we have no way to determine if the axioms of geometry apply at scales too small (or too large) to give a clear appearance. Where they do apply, they apply "roughly, and with some liberty" (T 1.2.4.17/45).[9] The success of applied geometry is no proof of infinite divisibility.

II.2 The Malezieu Argument

It follows from Hume's Infinite Extension Argument that some parts of space are simple. In support, he adds "another argument propos'd by a noted author, which seems to me very strong and beautiful" (T 1.2.2.3/30). It is based on the following passage in Malezieu:

> Moreover when I carefully consider the existence of things, I understand very clearly that existence pertains to units, and not to numbers. I will explain.
>
> Twenty men exist only because each man exists; number is only an extrinsic denomination, or better, a repetition of units to which alone existence pertains . . .[10]

Only units exist. A number of things is not a unit but is, instead, many repeated units. Consequently, a number of things does not literally exist except insofar as the repeated units each exist.

Hume's argument incorporating this insight is as follows:

(1) Anything divisible actually has parts.
(2) Anything with parts is many things, not a single thing.
(3) Only single things really exist.
(4) Anything that is many things can appropriately be said to exist only if those many things each exist.
(5) Anything infinitely divisible is such that all its parts have parts.
(6) So, none of its parts really exist.
(7) So, nothing infinitely divisible can appropriately be said to exist.
(8) So, anything with parts that can appropriately be said to exist has some indivisible parts.

So, any spatial interval has indivisible parts, or, better, the spatial interval simply is those many parts. They are, strictly speaking, what exist.

Hume presupposes (1), and I have already argued against Aristotle for its plausibility. Statement (2) is part of the Malezieu view. Hume takes this assumption to be widely shared as "extension is always a number, according to the common sentiment of metaphysicians" (T 1.2.2.3/30). If something is extended then it consists of parts and so is a number of things. A way to understand (2) is to try to see the strangeness of the contemporary view that the whole is a single thing in addition to its parts. On that view, to hold a six-pack of beer is automatically to hold seven items—the six cans plus the six-pack—even neglecting the plastic yoke. But it would seem that the six-pack simply is the six cans and nothing in addition.[11]

Statement (3) is also part of the Malezieu view and is a version of the ancient tenet that being and unity are convertible.[12] Leibniz thought it could be seen to be true just by paying attention to a shift in emphasis: "That what is not truly *one* entity is not truly one *entity* either."[13] Note that the use of a grammatically singular expression to refer to many things collectively (e.g., "plurality," "multitude," "aggregate") does not entail that a plurality, say, really exists. However referred to, they are many things, strictly speaking.

So, to say that a plurality exists is strictly false. However, saying it can be appropriate if this member of the plurality exists and that one exists and that one exists, and so on, and if, perhaps, these many are related in some salient way. Hence, Statement (4). Statement (5) is the conception of infinite divisibility explicitly considered by Hume. The rest then follow.

One might think that, in his version of the Malezieu argument, Hume meant only that wholes depend on each and all their parts, not that wholes are their parts collectively.[14] However, such a dependence between distinct things, a whole and a part, contravenes Hume's central principle that there are no necessary connections between distinct things; distinct things are separable (T 1.1.7.3/18; T 1.4.5.5/233).

II.3 The General Idea of Space

Having argued to spatial minima from spatially minimal ideas, Hume turns to examining the general idea of space. In accordance with the Copy Principle, he considers the impressions that it is derived from. He will conclude that the idea of space is the idea of colored or tangible points arrayed in a certain manner.

Hume's discussion seems carelessly to shift from characteristics of an impression to characteristics of its object. The shift is licensed by his presupposed account of representation. For Hume, impressions having objects resemble those objects (T 1.4.5.3/233; T 1.4.6.18/260). An impression of a colored point will itself be a colored point; an impression of colored points arrayed in a certain manner will consist of impressions that are colored points arrayed in that manner. By the Copy Principle, the resulting ideas will likewise resemble both the impression and its object. "Every idea of a quality in an object passes thro' an impression" (T 1.4.5.21/243).

The idea of space can be copied only from impressions of sight or touch. They are the only impressions that can occur side by side to form an extended impression (T 1.2.3.3/33; T 1.4.5.9/235). For example, one sees a purple tabletop and forms an impression of the purple expanse. That impression will be a vivid, expansive image made up of simple purple images—"colour'd points"—packed so closely together that there are no gaps of some other color (T 1.2.3.4/34). Hume knows that the expansive image has minimal parts, not because of a granular appearance, but because it is possible to imagine removing some parts and leaving others. The image is visually continuous although not continuous in the mathematical sense.[15]

The impression of a tabletop causes an idea suitable to play the role of the general idea of extension, as do impressions of white doors, black countertops, and the like. The resulting ideas are similar, insofar as they consist of indivisible points arranged one right next to the other. That these ideas are similar causes a word such as "extension" or "space" to be associated with each of them. Use of the word calls one of the ideas to mind to provide an example and readies the rest to be called to mind as needed to provide counterexamples to mistaken general claims. They are present "in power" as Hume says (T 1.1.7.7/20). The idea present to mind in this capacity serves as the general idea. The set of ideas that can play the role of general idea of extension even comes to include ideas of tactile points similarly arranged. For example, when one's arm is on an armrest, one gets tactile impressions of points arranged in just the same manner as the visual points under discussion. So, the general idea of space is the idea of many visual or tactile points arranged one right next to the other, insofar as they are points arranged in that manner (T 1.2.3.5/34).

Hume summarizes this point by saying that the idea of space is the idea of "the manner or order, in which objects exist," where the objects are the points (T 1.2.4.2/40). He is not saying that the idea is of the manner separate from the points. On Hume's account of abstraction, one cannot think of a manner of arrangement without thinking of things so arranged.[16] Although he uses the word "abstract," Hume's idea of space is best thought of as a general idea—a way of thinking of arranged points in general—rather than an abstract idea—a way of thinking of the arrangement somehow mentally separated from the points so arranged.

Hume gives another, "very decisive" argument that the idea of space must consist of simple ideas of colored or tangible indivisible points (T 1.2.3.12–16/38–9). The gist of it, not readily apparent from the text, is as follows:

(1) The idea of space is compounded of indivisible, extensionless ideas.
(2) The idea of space is extended.
(3) The only ideas that can be compounded into extended ones are visual or tactile.
(4) So, these extensionless ideas must be visual or tactile.
(5) So, each one of these extensionless ideas must be of something either colored or tangible as well as extensionless.

In other words, we cannot conceive of the minimal parts of space except as colored or tangible.

Hume's earlier arguments yielded (1). Hume presupposes (2) in this argument, but states it at T 1.4.5.15/240. Statement (3) is arrived at by experience and is plausible given that ideas are images (see T 1.4.5.7/234).

Hume's discussion of (3) is potentially confusing. He says that our ideas are copied from impressions of simple "atoms or corpuscles" and that these simple objects "discover themselves to our senses" by being colored or tangible (T 1.2.3.15/38). However, the ink spot experiment shows that a simple visual impression may be of something complex. Similarly, a simple impression may represent a mite, although the mite has a body and legs. Given the limits of visual acuity that Hume acknowledges, it is unlikely that something giving us a simple impression is really simple (T 1.2.1.4-5/27–8). So, do we have impressions of "atoms" or not? The answer is yes and no, in different senses. Our perception of external objects is mediated by our perception of images (T 1.4.5.15/239). We do not perceive any simple atoms in the external objects, but we do perceive simple atoms in the image. They "discover themselves to our senses" the way the so-called stars do when a blow to the head makes us "see stars." To be both perceived by the senses and imagined, these atoms in the image must be colored or solid.

Hume calls these atoms "mathematical points." His target is theorists who object to mathematical points on the assumption that they are merely simple and indivisible, with no other features. Hume grants that such a point would be a "non-entity" that could not be conjoined with others to form a "real existence." How, then, do they form one? The solution is not to regard points as "physical points," extended but indivisible.[17] That would be absurd because anything extended has parts and so is divisible. The solution is rather to reject those theorists' assumption. Mathematical points are colored or solid (T 1.2.4.3/40). These can be known by experience or imagination to be conjoinable into something.

Hume concludes that the parts of space "are inconceivable when not fill'd with something real and existent," which is just to say that we cannot conceive of them except as colored or tangible (T 1.2.4.2/39). The visible or tangible object said to "fill" a part of space is that part of space. As with the parts, so with the whole. "We have therefore no idea of space or extension, but when we regard it as an object either of our sight or feeling" (T 1.2.3.16/39).

Hume holds that the idea of space is the idea of colored or tangible points disposed in a certain manner, namely, one right next to the other. In other words, it is an idea of "visible or tangible" distance. A consequence is that we have no consistent idea of a vacuum (i.e., empty space). When we are thinking of no points, we are not thinking of that manner in which points are disposed, so we are not thinking of space (T 1.2.5.1/53). Hume does allow for the idea of an "invisible and intangible distance" between nonadjacent points, but this is not an idea of space because it does not have the structure of indivisible parts that space has (T 1.2.5.16/59). The fictitious idea of a vacuum is a conflation of the two incompatible kinds of distance.

Given Hume's concern with space as it appears, one would expect him to conclude that the simple parts of space are colored or tangible. He does not explicitly draw this conclusion, however, despite explicitly drawing a parallel one for time. Nonetheless, a presupposition he makes in "Of the Modern Philosophy" yields the conclusion. He argues there that if the modern philosopher commits himself to the unreality of secondary qualities, then he commits himself to the nonexistence of external objects (T 1.4.4.6, 15/227–8, 231). The argument goes as follows:

(1) If external objects are real, then they do not have secondary qualities.
(2) We cannot help but conceive of external objects as having secondary qualities. . . .

(4) Therefore, external objects are not real.

The argument only works if Hume is presupposing

(3) External objects are as we cannot help but conceive them to be.

The presupposition is appropriate for external objects as they appear.[18] It, plus Statement (2), yields the denial of the consequent of (1). Statement (4) follows by *modus tollens*. So, Hume holds Statement (3). Given (3), if we do conceive of objects in space as colored or tangible and cannot conceive them as not being so, then they are so.

III Time

III.1 Against the Infinite Divisibility of Time

Hume says that the same sort of arguments against the infinite divisibility of space apply to time. There is nothing briefer than the briefest temporally simple ideas. Therefore, *qua* brief, they are adequate representations of anything extremely brief. An infinite number of them in the closest possible succession would yield an idea with infinite duration. So, likewise, an infinite number of extremely brief parts of duration would yield an infinite duration. So, not every part of a finite duration has parts. So, there are temporally simple parts of time (i.e., ones lacking successive parts).

Presumably temporal analogues of the experiment with grains of sand could be conducted. One could experimentally arrive at a temporally minimal impression for a subject by testing the briefest thing detectable. Such an impression would be a temporally minimal impression in Hume's sense: had the stimulus been briefer, it would have caused no impression. Then one could test for the briefest temporal interval between the causes of such impressions without the impressions being simultaneous.[19] The result would be two minimal impressions at their closest temporal approach. The duration of any succession of such impressions so ordered will be proportional to the number of impressions.

Hume's later introduction of steadfast objects—temporal simples that are not brief—does not affect the temporal version of his Infinite Extension Argument against infinite divisibility. The argument works when just using the briefest of temporally simple ideas—ones so brief that no briefer idea could coexist with them.

The Malezieu argument applies to time as well. A temporal interval is just its many simple parts. They are the only parts of time that exist, strictly speaking.

Hume then proposes a supporting argument unique to time (T 1.2.2.4/31).[20]

(1) No two parts of time can be present at the same time.
(2) Suppose there were a moment with distinct parts.

(3) No two parts of that moment could be present at the same time.
(4) When that moment is present, it would be a time at which its parts would all be present.
(5) So, when that moment is present, its parts would all be present and would not all be present.
(6) So, no moment has distinct parts.

Hume takes (1) for granted. It is essential to time that its parts succeed each other (i.e., are successively present, never concurrently present). Statement (2) is the assumption that Hume will disprove by *reductio ad absurdum*. Statement (3) follows. Statement (4) makes the safe assumption that for a moment to be present is for it to be wholly present. The contradiction in (5) follows, yielding (6). So, time consists of simple moments, just as space consists of simple minima.

Hume takes his arguments to be demonstrations that space and time are not infinitely divisible, where demonstrations are decisive, unanswerable arguments causing stable conviction in whomever understands them. He argues that there can be no competing demonstrations of the impossibility of his view. It is "an establish'd maxim in metaphysics" that the clearly conceivable is possible. Hume takes this to entail that the clearly imaginable is possible as well (T 1.2.2.8/32). We can clearly form an image with finite length or duration such that the image is composed of a finite number of simple images. So, it is possible that there exists something with a finite length or duration that is composed of a finite number of simple parts (T 1.2.2.6–10/31–3).

III.2 The General Idea of Time

Having argued to temporal simples, Hume turns to examining the general idea of time or duration. In accordance with the Copy Principle, he considers the impressions that it is derived from. Since any object or perception can be in time, an impression of time will consist of any succession of temporally simple perceptions, whether they themselves are impressions of sensation, impressions of reflection, or ideas.[21] A succession of perceptions is a perception of succession, and the idea of time is a copy of a perception of succession. Because any perceived succession will do, the range of features had by the temporally simple members of the various successions perceived is much broader than for space, including any that we can have an impression or idea of—visual, auditory, affective, and the like. The idea of time will be the general idea of such temporally simple parts arrayed successively, insofar as they are temporally simple parts arrayed successively—first one is present, then another, then another, and so on. So, the idea of time is a succession of ideas with other successions of ideas present in power.

The idea of time can only be derived from a succession. If one has no succession of perceptions, one has no awareness of time: no impression whose copy could serve as an idea of time. For instance, one might have no perceptions, as when in a "sound sleep," or just a single perception unreplaced for a while, as with "a man strongly occupy'd with one thought."[22] The latter case introduces the notion of the steadfast perception or object, which is a peculiarity of Hume's theory of time and which witnesses his adherence to appearance.[23]

When one thought strongly occupies someone, there are other, unnoticed successions. The single thought is steadfast relative to the other successions; it remains while their members are replaced. It is an example of a steadfast object, using "object" in its most general sense. The members of the successions are said to be "changeable"—subject to replacement—whereas the steadfast object is said to be "unchangeable" (T 1.2.3.7, 11/35, 37). The steadfast object and the other successions are "co-existent" (T 1.4.2.29/201). "Coexists with" does not mean the same as "is simultaneous with," which is an equivalence relation. Something's coexisting with successive things does not entail their coexisting with each other, any more than something's spatially overlapping disjoint things entails their overlapping each other.[24] Rather "coexists with" simply means the same as "is neither before nor after." In the example of a man strongly occupied with one thought, his thought is steadfast and unchangeable relative to the coexisting successions he takes no notice of.

Hume gives a second, important example of a steadfast perception, although one hard to understand. He starts out by noting that the same duration seems longer or shorter depending on the rapidity of one's own perceptions. Sometimes exceedingly brief perceptions trip by, rapidly replaced, and sometimes each perception lingers before replacement.[25] A succession in the world seems longer when our thoughts and feelings move faster relative to it and seems shorter when they move more slowly. In some cases, a succession in the world is so quick that it cannot be discerned. For example, a red hot coal on a string can be whirled around so fast that its circuit is complete before successive perceptions of its different positions can be formed. Instead, a steadfast impression of a circle of fire remains unreplaced while the coal itself successively occupies different positions. Without successive impressions of its positions, one is visually unaware of the coal's being in time. A relatively slower succession of perceptions makes elapsed time seem slower, and, at the limit when there is no succession of perceptions, time seems to stop. "Wherever we have no successive perceptions, we have no notion of time, even tho' there be a real succession in the objects" (T 1.2.3.7/35).

But how can we have no notion of time in this case? Although nothing in the path of the whirling coal gives us an awareness of time, successions are perceptible in other places around it. There does not seem to be the same total lack of awareness of time as during occupation with one thought. Hume agrees. His point is that there is no notion of time passing *where the coal is*. "*Wherever* we have no successive perceptions, etc." (emphasis added). Time, for Hume, is a general idea we get from successions. Where there is no succession, there is no source for that idea, even if there are sources elsewhere. So, there is no awareness of time passing in that location, even if there is awareness of time passing in other locations.

We find Hume's point perplexing because we assume that time has a uniform structure across spatial locations. However, we lack any evidence for this assumption. After all, the idea of time is a generalization from perceived successions, and successions at different locations often do not have a uniform structure beyond their successiveness. Just compare the slow tolling of a large bell with the fast tinkling of a little one.[26]

To confirm that the idea of time is copied from perceiving successions, Hume argues that the idea of time cannot be derived from a steadfast object—a nonsuccession (T 1.2.3.8/35–6).

(1) One can conceive of a duration as being longer or shorter.
(2) So, one must conceive it to have parts that can be augmented or removed in order to lengthen or shorten it.
(3) Adding or removing exactly coexistent parts would not lengthen or shorten it.
(4) So, the parts of the conceived duration cannot be exactly coexistent.
(5) A steadfast object causes only exactly coexistent impressions of exactly coexistent parts.
(6) So, an impression of a steadfast object cannot give one the idea of a duration.

The idea of duration must be derived from successions that could have had more or fewer members. A steadfast object has no successive members.

A consequence of this argument is that a steadfast object can be long-lasting or fairly brief without being of greater or lesser duration. There are two kinds of temporal length—duration and steadfastness—just as there were two kinds of distance. For a steadfast object to last longer than another is for it to coexist with more members of some succession than the other. For instance, a stone coexists with more revolutions of the earth than a stick.

One might object to the distinction by arguing that longer steadfastness simply is longer duration. Seemingly, we can distinguish an earlier phase of the stone from a later. Because Hume is committed to the principle that the distinguishable are distinct and separable, the stone would have successive parts—distinct even if perceptually continuous, like the colored points a perceived tabletop. However, the analogy with the tabletop is misleading. A steadfast object is a single, indivisible thing with respect to time.[27] Trying to distinguish an earlier phase from a later is trying to distinguish something from itself. Unlike a duration, then, one cannot conceive of the augmentation or diminishment of a steadfast object. At best, one can imagine a different longer or briefer steadfast object occurring in its place.

In principle, to capture the two kinds of temporal length, one could distinguish intrinsic duration, which requires having successive parts, and extrinsic duration, which requires coexisting with something that has successive parts. However, this nicety goes beyond Hume's purpose of explaining the origin of the idea of time.

Hume's argument concerning steadfast objects raises another possible objection. There is no evidence of temporal complexity at the location of a steadfast object. So, presumably, it occupies a single moment. But a steadfast object coexists with a succession whose members occupy single moments elsewhere. So, some moments coexist. Yet Hume says that none of time's parts are coexistent. However, the objection arises only on the assumption that time is a dimension. Saying that time is structured differently in different locations sounds like saying that time is an even more complex dimension with some coexistent parts. However, for Hume, we have no empirical evidence of dimensions or complex dimensions. We have evidence only of various successions in different places that are similar with respect to their successiveness. Our idea of time is a general idea of these successions as successive. And, clearly, the relevant parts of the succession that make it a succession do not coexist.

A philosopher could go on to form an idea of coexistent successions in general. Such an idea would have a complexity like that of the complex dimension envisioned earlier. However, it would not be the ordinary concept of time, as derived from experience, which is what Hume is concerned to articulate.

So, for Hume, the idea of time cannot be derived from a steadfast object but only from a succession of changeable objects. Furthermore, the idea of time cannot even be applied to a steadfast object without contradiction. That is because one cannot conceive of time without conceiving of a succession of changeable objects. If the idea of time were separable from the ideas of successive things in time, there would be a distinct impression of time along with the impressions of the things in time. But there is not. The experience that gives rise to the idea of time is like hearing five successive notes on a flute. The hearer successively has five impressions, each of a note; there is no sixth impression of their successiveness (T 1.2.3.10/36). So, conceiving of time requires conceiving of a succession. So, the idea of time—the general idea of a succession—cannot be applied to the steadfast without the contradiction that a nonsuccession is a succession.

Thus, all and only successions have duration. The relative lengthiness of steadfast objects is to be distinguished from greater duration. Nonetheless, both ordinary people and philosophers tend naturally to imagine otherwise; they form the fiction that "duration is a measure of rest as well as of motion"; that is, that steadfast objects endure (T 1.2.3.11/37; T 1.2.5.28–9/64–5).[28] This fictitious idea is a conflation of the two incompatible kinds of temporal length.

As with the simple parts of space, we must conceive the simple parts of time, of whatever length, to have some qualities besides indivisibility. Unlike with space, Hume explicitly says that time is as we cannot but conceive it: "the indivisible moments of time must be fill'd with some real object or existence, whose succession forms the duration, and makes it be conceivable by the mind" (T 1.2.3.17/39). The fact that he regards this conclusion as proved by the "same reasoning" confirms that he makes the same conclusion for space as well. That our ideas are of objects as they appear to sense or reflection explains this bold step from how things must be conceived to how things are. Thus, both space and time each consist of indivisible objects arranged in a certain manner with some additional qualities that make them conceivable to the mind.[29]

ABBREVIATION OF WORK CITED

T   A Treatise of Human Nature. Edited by D. F. Norton & M. J. Norton. Oxford: Oxford University Press, 2000.

Notes

1. Cf. T 1.4.4.1, Intro 6-8, 1.2.4.23/225, xvi-xvii, 47.
2. See Van Leeuwen (1963), especially Popkin's preface, p. x, and the conclusion, pp. 143–153.
3. See especially Flew (1976: 257–69); Fogelin (1985: ch. 3); Fogelin (1988: 47–69); and Laird (1931: ch. 3).
4. Hume summarizes the argument at EU 12.18, n. 33/156.
5. Note that an idea cannot be adequate in all respects if it is going to represent objects that are not ideas. There will be things true of an idea *qua* idea that are not true of its objects.
6. Cf. Grünbaum (1967: ch. 3).
7. Aristotle, Physics III.6, 206a8–206b32, and VIII.8, 262a22–263a3; and On Generation and Corruption I.2, 316a20–316a23, in Barnes (1984). For an in-depth discussion of the commitment to actual parts, see Holden (2004).
8. See Aristotle, *Topics*, VII.1, 152b34: "Moreover, see whether the one can exist without the other; for, if so, they will not be the same."
9. See Baxter (2009: 122–123) and Badici (2008).
10. Malezieu (1705), in a section of Book 9 entitled "Réflexions sur les incommensurables." The original, reproduced in Kemp Smith (1941: 341), Laird (1931: 69), and Ryan (2012: 108–109), is as follows:

D'ailleurs quand je considere attentivement l'existence des êtres, je comprens très-clairement que l'existence appartient aux unités, & non pas aux nombres. Je m'explique.

Vingt hommes n'existent, que parce que chaque homme existe; le nombre n'est qu'une dénomination exterieure, ou pour mieux dire, une repetition d'unités auxquelles seules appartient l'existence.

11. See Baxter (1988).
12. Aristotle, *Metaphysics*, XI.3, 1061a16.
13. Mason (1967: 121). See also Baxter (1995).
14. Garrett (2009: 437).
15. Cf. Broad (1961).
16. Cf. Falkenstein (1997).
17. Hume uses the term "physical point" inconsistently. At T 1.3.9.11/112, as well as at EU 12.18 n33/156 n1, he uses it to mean "mathematical point," in the sense here. For background to Hume's discussion, see Bayle (1991), s.v. "Zeno of Elea," note G.
18. As Franklin (1994) points out, a similar assumption is not appropriate for external objects as they are in themselves.
19. Experiments have shown that this closest approach varies by sense modality. See Pöppel (1988: ch. 2).
20. It is likely that Hume is summarizing this argument at EU 12.19/157. See also Bayle (1991), s.v. "Zeno of Elea," note F, for an antecedent version of the argument.
21. Even an idea, when regarded as a "real perception in the mind" can function as an impression (T 1.3.8.15/106).
22. "For one may fix his attention during some time on any one object without looking farther" (T 1.3.6.13/92). Cf. Aristotle, *Physics*, IV.11, 218b30, "the non-realization of the existence of time happens to us when we do not distinguish any change, but the soul seems to stay in one indivisible state."

23. Cf. Van Steenburgh (1977); McIntyre (1976: 87–88); and Costa (1990).

24. Note that "coexists with" is not equivalent to Hume's "perfectly co-temporary," which does mean simultaneous (T 1.3.2.7/76).

25. In a different passage, Hume says that perceptions pass with "an inconceivable rapidity," but this is a different sense of "rapidity" meaning that the transition between two successive perceptions is sudden. If Hume were saying that all perceptions are like the briefest, then he would be wrong to say that our perceptions of thought vary more quickly than our perceptions of sight (T 1.4.6.4/252).

26. Strictly speaking, successions of sounds are not in space, although they are associated with a spatial location. Hume is clear that not everything is in space (T 1.4.5.10/235). Successions of these would be unified by associated location, by resemblance or causation (see T 1.4.6.17/260).

27. Hume thinks that something can be simple in one respect and not simple in another. See T 1.4.4.14/230-31 concerning impressions of touch.

28. Aristotle, Physics, IV.12, 221b6–22. Hume says that our subsequently becoming aware of the contradiction in taking a nonsuccession to endure causes the idea of identity to form, which involves alternating between thinking of something as a single steadfast object and as many successive objects (T 1.4.2.29/200–1).

29. I am grateful for discussion with Jani Hakkarainen, Todd Ryan, and Ruth Weintraub, for translation help from Todd Ryan, John Troyer, and Charlotte Geniez, and for research assistance from Sandra Baxter.

BIBLIOGRAPHY

Badici, Emil. (2008). "On the Compatibility between Euclidean Geometry and Hume's Denial of Infinite Divisibility," *Hume Studies* 34, 231–244.

Barnes, J., ed. (1984). *The Complete Works of Aristotle, Volumes I and II*. Princeton, NJ: Princeton University Press.

Baxter, Donald L. M. (1988). "Identity in the Loose and Popular Sense," *Mind* 97, 575–582.

Baxter, Donald L. M. (1995). "Corporeal Substances and True Unities," *Studia Leibnitiana* 27, 157–184.

Baxter, Donald L. M. (2009). "Hume's Theory of Space and Time in Its Sceptical Context," D. F. Norton, ed., *The Cambridge Companion to Hume*, 2nd ed. Cambridge: Cambridge University Press, 105–146.

Bayle, Pierre. (1991). *Historical and Critical Dictionary: Selections*, trans. Richard H. Popkin. Indianapolis: Hackett.

Broad, C. D. (1961). "Hume's Doctrine of Space," *Proceedings of the British Academy* 47, 161–176.

Costa, Michael J. (1990). "Hume, Strict Identity, and Time's Vacuum," *Hume Studies* 16, 1–16.

Falkenstein, Lorne. (1997). "Hume on Manners of Disposition and the Ideas of Space and Time," *Archiv für Geschichte der Philosophie* 79, 179–201.

Flew, Antony. (1976). "Infinite Divisibility in Hume's Treatise," in D. W. Livingston & J. T. King, eds., *Hume: A Re-Evaluation*. New York: Fordham University Press, 257–269.

Fogelin, Robert J. (1985). *Hume's Skepticism in the* Treatise of Human Nature. London: Routledge & Kegan Paul.

Fogelin, Robert J. (1988). "Hume and Berkeley on the Proofs of Infinite Divisibility," *Philosophical Review* 97, 47–69.

Franklin, James. (1994). "Achievements and Fallacies in Hume's Account of Infinite Divisibility," *Hume Studies* 20, 85–101.

Garrett, Don. (2009). "Difficult Times for Humean Identity?" *Philosophical Studies* 146, 435–443.

Grünbaum, Adolf. (1967). *Modern Science and Zeno's Paradoxes*. Middletown, CT: Wesleyan University Press.

Holden, Thomas. (2004). *The Architecture of Matter: Galileo to Kant*. Oxford: Clarendon Press.

Kemp Smith, Norman. (1941). *The Philosophy of David Hume*. London: MacMillan.

Laird, John. (1931). *Hume's Philosophy of Human Nature*. New York: Dutton/Cambridge University Press.

Malezieu, Nicolas de. (1705). *Elémens de géometrie de Mgr. le duc de Bourgogne*. Trévous and Paris.

Mason, H. T., ed. (1967). *The Leibniz-Arnauld Correspondence*. Manchester: Manchester University Press.

McIntyre, Jane L. (1976). "Is Hume's Self Consistent?" in D. F. Norton, N. Capaldi, & W. L. Robison, eds., *McGill Hume Studies*. San Diego: Austin Hill Press, 79–88.

Pöppel, Ernest. (1988). *Mindworks: Time and Conscious Experience*, trans. Tom Artin. Boston/San Diego/New York: Harcourt Brace Jovanovich.

Ryan, Todd. (2012). "Hume's 'Malezieu Argument,'" *Hume Studies* 38, 105–18.

Van Leeuwen, Henry G. (1963). *The Problem of Certainty in English Thought: 1630–1690*. The Hague: Martinus Nijhoff.

van Steenburgh, E. W. (1977). "Durationless Moments in Hume's Treatise," in G. P. Morice, ed., *David Hume: Bicentenary Papers*. Austin: University of Texas Press.

FURTHER READING

Baxter, Donald L. M. (2008). *Hume's Difficulty: Time and Identity in the Treatise*. London and New York: Routledge.

Frasca-Spada, Marina. (1998). *Space and the Self in Hume's Treatise*. Cambridge: Cambridge University Press.

Garrett, Don. (1997). *Cognition and Commitment in Hume's Philosophy*. Oxford: Oxford University Press.

Jacquette, Dale. (2001). *David Hume's Critique of Infinity*. Leiden, Boston: Brill.

CHAPTER 11

··

HUME'S SKEPTICAL LOGIC
OF INDUCTION

··

KENNETH P. WINKLER

DAVID Hume saw Book 1 of *A Treatise of Human Nature*, "Of the Understanding," as an advance in logic. This may come as a surprise to his twenty-first-century readers, because Book 1 is very different from the sparely written, symbol-filled, problem-laden textbooks used in present-day logic courses. But in the seventeenth and eighteenth centuries, logic was a more spacious subject than it is today—so spacious that Locke's *Essay Concerning Human Understanding*, which ranges widely over topics in epistemology, metaphysics, and the philosophy of language, fell very naturally into it.[1] Hume voices the wide early modern understanding of his subject when he writes, in the introduction to the *Treatise*, that "the sole end of logic is to explain the principles and operations of our reasoning faculties, and the nature of our ideas" (T Intro. 4/xv). He speaks of logic's sole end not to call attention to its narrowness or to confess the modesty of its ambitions, but to mark it off from three subjects whose foundation in human nature he hoped to examine in later volumes of the *Treatise*: morals, criticism, and politics. Together with logic, he explains, these further subjects—he actually calls them "sciences"—embrace "almost every thing, which it can any way import us to be acquainted with, or which can tend either to the improvement or ornament of the human mind" (T Intro. 4/xv).

The subject matter of the present chapter is Hume's logic of our reasoning faculties or *powers*. Hume included the nature of ideas among the topics of logic because ideas were widely viewed as the raw materials of reasoning.[2] This explains why, as he nears the end of the first two parts of Book 1 (Part 1 having been devoted to ideas in general—"their origin, composition, connection, abstraction, &c." and Part 2 to the ideas of space and time in particular), Hume observes that "we shall be the better prepar'd for the examination of knowledge and probability"—our twin objectives in reasoning and the topics of Part 3—"when we understand perfectly all those particular ideas, which may enter into our reasoning" (T 1.2.6.1/66). In providing an inventory of our ideas before taking up the mental operations of judgment and reasoning in which they figure, Hume was following the example of early modern textbooks of logic, in which the bare apprehension of individual terms or notions (typically the subject of the textbook's first part) was treated before judgment (standardly the subject of its second part) and reasoning (standardly the subject of its third part). Hume disapproved of the usual way of understanding judgment and reasoning, as we'll see, but he wrote the *Treatise* in full awareness of the textbook precedent. The textbooks often included a fourth part, on method, the mental operation by which propositions and arguments are arranged into larger discourses or systems. (Geometry was the leading example of such a system.) Here, too, there is a precedent of sorts for Book 1 of the *Treatise*, whose fourth part includes a survey of systems of philosophy, ancient and modern.

Hume examines our reasoning powers in Part 3 of Book 1 of the *Treatise* and in Sections 4 through 6 of the *Enquiry*. These will be our main texts, but we will also touch on Part 4 of Book 1, where Hume reflects on Part 3, and on Section 12 of the *Enquiry*, where he reflects on Sections 4 through 6. Like other early modern logics of reasoning, especially those composed, as Hume's was, under the influence of Locke, these texts are *descriptive*, *explanatory*, and *normative*.[3] They also aspire to be *revelatory*. They are descriptive in documenting how our reasoning actually proceeds, explanatory in telling us why it so proceeds, normative in telling us how it should proceed, and revelatory in using these findings to arrive at larger truths about human nature and human life. This chapter addresses all four aspects of logic. In both the *Treatise* and the *Enquiry*, they are blended in a complex way. This sometimes makes it difficult to pin down Hume's intentions, but I will suggest that the final lessons Hume draws from his logic are, as he himself indicates, "very sceptical" (T Abs. 27/657). According to one of several senses of the word "reason" identified by Locke in the *Essay*, reason is "That Faculty, whereby Man is supposed to be distinguished from Beasts, and wherein it is evident he much surpasses them" (4.17.1). In Hume's less complacent opinion, reason actually unites us very closely with the beasts, and, although we do surpass them in it, this entitles us at best to a very chastened pride.

Before taking up the texts, I want to say a bit more about their context, partly to document some of what I have said and partly to convey a fuller sense of Hume's ambitions as a logician. I begin in 1692 with William Molyneux, an Irish scientist who was Locke's most important philosophical correspondent. In the preface to what became a well-known book on the science of vision, Molyneux compared the logic of his own day to what he saw as the inflexible and impractical logic of the Aristotelians. Logic, he said with satisfaction, "has put on a Countenance clearly different from what it appeared in formerly." As evidence he cited three books: *The Art of Thinking* (also known as the Port Royal *Logic*) by Antoine Arnauld and Pierre Nicole, first published in 1662; *The Search after Truth* by Nicolas Malebranche, first published in 1674–5; and Locke's *Essay*, first published in 1689.[4] Of the three, the *Essay* was his favorite, at least as a college textbook. "I know no Logick that Deserves to be Named" as reading for undergraduates, he wrote, "but the Essay of Humane Understanding."[5]

Leibniz was an appreciative reader of Molyneux, but his own assessment of what he called "our common logic" was less sanguine. He complained that "not... a thought" had yet been given by logicians to the creation of a truly practical logic, "[the] kind of logic which should determine the balance between probabilities, and would be so necessary in deliberations of importance." In his view, logicians had largely confined themselves to codifying rules of deduction; they had little to say about the delicate weighing of evidence pro and con that is vital to the study of nature, the governing of nations, the deliberations of judges and juries, and the decisions of daily life. Leibniz's assessment of recent developments was the opposite of Molyneux's, but, as evidence for his bleaker verdict, he cited the very same books: the *Art of Thinking*, the *Search*, and the *Essay*.[6]

In 1739, in an anonymous pamphlet meant to drum up readers for the *Treatise*, Hume recalled Leibniz's complaint and named the same three books another time:

> The celebrated *Monsieur Leibnitz* has observed it to be a defect in the common systems of logic, that they are very copious when they explain the operations of the understanding in the forming of demonstrations, but are too concise when they treat of probabilities, and those other measures of evidence on which life and action entirely depend, and which are our guides even in most of our philosophical speculations. In this censure, he comprehends *The Essay on Human Understanding*, *Le Recherche de la verité* [*The Search After Truth*], and *L'Art de penser* [*The Art of Thinking*]. (T Abs. 4/646-7).

Hume's echo of Leibniz is, as far as it goes, an excellent indication of his program in Book 1. Hume expands on that program as the anonymous promotional pamphlet continues. Writing in the third person—not as an author in his twenties anxious for the success of his first book, but as an impartial friend of the reading public—he reports that "the author of the *Treatise of Human Nature* seems to have been sensible of this defect in these philosophers, and has endeavoured, as much as he can, to supply it." Hume's attempt to supply or correct the defect is his own system of logic, his fourfold account— descriptive, explanatory, normative, and revelatory—of our powers of reasoning, particularly our powers of probable (or, as we now say, *inductive*) reasoning.

Hume wasn't the only philosopher in mid-eighteenth-century Britain disappointed with the customary logic books. Another was Joseph Butler, Bishop of Bristol and author of *Fifteen Sermons on Human Nature* (1726), a book Hume very much admired. Butler's *Analogy of Religion, Natural and Revealed*, an inductive defense of the Christian religion, was published in 1736, three years before Books 1 and 2 of the *Treatise*. In the introduction to the *Analogy*, Butler points out that when we judge an event to be probable, our judgment rests on a "likeness," or analogy, between the event and some other event—or series of events—that we have observed in the past. Thus, we conclude "that a child, if it lives twenty years, will grow up to the stature and strength of a man; that food will contribute to the preservation of its life; and that the want of it for such a number of days, be its certain destruction." Here, Butler makes a modest contribution to logic in its descriptive aspect. He states a basic fact: having observed how earlier children have grown and prospered, we infer that newborn children will grow and prosper in the same way, or by the same means. More generally, having observed how things of one kind or another have carried on in the past, we infer that they will carry on in much the same way in the future. As a logician, Butler has no more to offer than this. His task in the *Analogy* is not logic but theology. "It is not my design," he explains,

> to inquire further into the Nature, the Foundation, and Measure of Probability; or whence it proceeds, that *Likeness* should beget that Presumption, Opinion, and full Conviction, which the human Mind is formed to receive from it, and which it does necessarily produce in every one; or to guard against the Errors to which Reasoning from Analogy is liable. This belongs to the Subject of Logic, and is a part of that Subject which has not yet been thoroughly considered. Indeed I shall not take it upon me to say, how far the Extent, Compass, and Force, of analogical Reasoning, can be reduced to general Heads and Rules, and the whole be formed into a System. . . . It is enough to the present purpose to observe, that this general way of arguing is evidently natural, just, and conclusive. For there is no Man can make a Question but that the Sun will rise to morrow, and be seen, where it is seen at all, in the Figure of a Circle, and not in that of a Square.[7]

The project Butler sets aside in this passage is the project taken up by Hume. Hume's logic of inductive reasoning will be *descriptive* (in which aspect it will bring the full "extent. . . of analogical reasoning" under convenient "general Heads"); *explanatory* (in which aspect it will inform us "whence it proceeds, that *Likeness* should beget that Presumption, Opinion, and full Conviction, which the human Mind is formed to receive from it"); *normative* (in which aspect it will instruct us in ways of avoiding "the Errors to which Reasoning from Analogy is liable" and furnish us with "general. . . Rules" of reasoning that can be arranged "into a System"); and *revelatory* (in which aspect it will complicate Butler's serene verdict that "this general way of arguing is evidently natural, just, and conclusive").

I The Work of Reason

In Hume's logic of induction, reason plays three different roles. It is the *object* of Hume's investigation, the *vehicle* or *agency* by which he carries out his investigation, and the *source of standards* by which arguments are evaluated. In the present this section, before moving in order through the four aspects of Hume's logic, I want to say a word about what Hume takes the work of reason to be.

For Locke, or for the prevailing opinion he summarizes, reason is (as we've seen) a distinctive and ennobling capacity in human beings. Hume's logic is mainly concerned with a single aspect of this capacity: reason as reason*ing*, the mental act or operation by which conclusions are drawn from premises. A second concern of Hume's logic, as he says as he opens the *Treatise*, is to explain "the nature of our ideas." By this, Hume does not mean the nature of our ideas *as such* (the general features that ideas have in common), but the origin, composition, content, and mutual bearing of various ideas, especially those of philosophical or scientific importance, such as space, time, and cause. The nature of ideas in this sense is a sprawling subject that we cannot enter into here, but we should consider some general remarks Hume makes about the nature of propositions formed from ideas. According to the logical tradition that includes both *The Art of Thinking* and Locke's *Essay*, idea-incorporating propositions are our immediate objects in judgment and inference. Hume takes issue with the tradition in the following passage, where he begins by laying out "a kind of establish'd maxim, . . . universally received by all logicians"—but not, as he is about to explain, by him. The maxim, he explains,

> consists in the vulgar division of the acts of the understanding, into *conception, judgment*, and *reasoning*, and in the definitions we give of them. Conception is defin'd to be the simple survey of one or more ideas: Judgment to be the separating and uniting of different ideas: Reasoning to be the separating or uniting of different ideas by the interposition of others, which shows the relation they bear to each other. (T 1.3.7.5 n.20/96 n.1)

In *conceiving* of God, for example, we contemplate the idea of God in isolation. In judging that God exists, we join the idea of God to the idea of existence. In reasoning that God exists, we join the idea of God to the idea of existence by means of at least one intermediate idea, or "middle term," as in the syllogism *God is supremely perfect; a supremely perfect being cannot fail to exist; hence God exists.*

When he speaks of the established maxim as "vulgar," Hume isn't being condescending or contemptuous. In the early modern sense he's relying on here, "vulgar" means *customary, usual,* or *prevailing,* and the present view, in Hume's opinion, prevails not among ordinary people, but among the learned. Locke, for example, defines a proposition as "the *joining* or *separating* of signs" (*Essay* 4.5.2). Since he recognizes two kinds of signs—*ideas,* which signify things, and *words,* which immediately signify ideas—Locke recognizes two kinds of propositions: *mental* propositions, which join or separate ideas, and *verbal* propositions, which join or separate words. It isn't always clear, when Hume speaks of propositions, whether he has mental or verbal propositions in mind; his usual way of signifying propositions, by means of italicized sentences, is ambiguous. But it is clear that at least in the quoted passage, Hume has mental propositions in mind. He makes two objections to the prevailing view. The first is that the judging mind does not always join or separate *two* different ideas. In propositions "regarding existence," for example, "the idea of existence is no distinct idea" at all (T 1.3.7.5 n.20/96 n.1), because there is no "abstract" idea of existence, "distinguishable and separable" from our ideas of particular things (T App. 2/623). The idea of God is the idea of an *existing God*; to judge that God exists, this is the only idea we need to contemplate. Hume's second objection is that the reasoning mind doesn't always require at least *three* ideas, as Locke for example had insisted. The mind can leap directly from one idea (*existing smoke,* for example) to another (*existing fire*). In view of Hume's first objection, this process can be described in another way: as a leap from a premise (*there is smoke*) to a conclusion (*there is fire*).

The simplifications that Hume is proposing—acts of judgment that take single ideas as their objects; acts of reasoning in which we step directly from idea to idea—are meant to reduce all three acts of the understanding to the act of bare conception, as he goes on to explain. "Taking them in a proper light," he concludes, "[the three acts] all resolve themselves into the first, and are nothing but particular ways of conceiving our objects" (T 1.3.7.5 n.20/97 n.1). Hume nonetheless continues to speak of propositions as the objects of judgment and reasoning. In doing so, he uses the word "proposition" noncommittally, for *whatever structure of ideas it is* (or even, perhaps, for *whatever structure of words it is*) that stands before the judging or reasoning mind. This noncommittal use is especially visible in the *Enquiry*, where Hume's two objections to the logical tradition, although they are not retracted, are not explicitly repeated. The noncommittal use of "proposition" is just what Hume needs to describe the work of reason in a way that everyone will find acceptable. We can all agree, he thinks, that reason's characteristic task is to move from hypothesized or already-accepted propositions, noncommittally understood, to new or enlightening propositions, noncommittally understood.

In the *Enquiry*, speaking noncommittally, Hume describes propositions as "the objects of reason or enquiry." They can be divided, he explains, into two kinds, *relations of ideas* and *matters of fact*. (This division will be important in later sections of this chapter.) "Of the first kind," he writes,

> are the sciences of Geometry, Algebra, and Arithmetic; and in short, every affirmation, which is either intuitively or demonstratively certain. *That the square of the hypothenuse is equal to the square of the two sides*, is a proposition, which expresses a relation between these figures. *That three times five is equal to the half of thirty*, expresses a relation between these numbers. Propositions of this kind are discoverable by the mere operation of thought, without dependence on what is anywhere existent in the universe. Though there never were a circle or triangle in nature, the truths, demonstrated by EUCLID, would for ever retain their certainty and evidence. (EU 4.1/25)

Matters of fact, "the second objects of human reason," differ from relations of ideas on every count. They are "not ascertained in the same manner; nor is our evidence of their truth, however great, of a like nature with the foregoing":

> The contrary of every matter of fact is still possible, because it can never imply a contradiction, and is conceived by the mind with the same facility and distinctness, as if ever so conformable to reality. *That the sun will not rise to-morrow* is no less intelligible a proposition, and implies no more a contradiction, than the affirmation, *that it will rise*. We should in vain, therefore, to attempt to demonstrate its falsehood. Were it demonstratively false, it would imply a contradiction, and could never be distinctly conceived by the mind. (EU 4.2/25-6)

Although I am quoting here from the *Enquiry*, the same division is made in the *Treatise*, implicitly in Part 3 of Book 1 (Sections 1 and 2) and explicitly at various points in Books 2 and 3 (T 2.3.3.2/413–14, T 3.1.1.8/457–8, and T 3.1.1.18/463).

Relations of ideas have, then, four defining features: their "contraries" (or, as we now say, their negations or denials) are—or at least imply—contradictions; their truth can be discovered by "the mere operation of thought"; they do not owe their truth to "what is any where existent in the universe" (which is why we needn't rise from our armchairs to test them); and they are either intuitively or demonstratively certain. In Hume's view, these four features interlock; a proposition with any one of them has them all. Matters of fact are defined by all the opposite features, which again interlock: their contraries or negations are free of contradiction; they cannot be confirmed by thought alone; they do depend for their truth on what exists in nature; and they are neither intuitively nor demonstratively certain. How, then, do we settle on their truth? Hume writes in the *Enquiry* that "it may be replied in one word, EXPERIENCE" (EU 4.14/32). Many matters of fact are known by the senses: that is, by *present* experience. Others are known by memory, or *past* experience. In these cases, the part played by experience seems straightforward—or straightforward enough. But it is "a subject worthy of curiosity," Hume writes, "to enquire what is the nature of that evidence, which assures us of any real existence and matters of fact, beyond the present testimony of our senses, or the records of our memory" (EU 4.3/26). These matters of fact have to do with *future* experience, but we can't now call upon future experience to testify on their behalf. We have only the past and the present to go on. This is what stimulates Hume's curiosity, and, after confessing his interest in the subject, the author of the *Enquiry* repeats, in looser terms, the complaint he had made about the common logics in his anonymous abstract of the *Treatise* (EU 4.3/26).

Hume's distinction between two kinds of propositions yields a distinction between two kinds of reasoning. "All reasonings," he says, "may be divided into two kinds, namely demonstrative reasoning, or that concerning relations of ideas, and moral reasoning, or that concerning matter of fact and existence" (EU 4.18/35). The work of reason, as Hume understood it, probably also included insight into intuitively certain truths, but Hume's logic is primarily a logic of inference or reasoning, and it is his logic of probable reasoning—his distinctive contribution to logic as he understood it—that will occupy us here.

Probable reasoning is a fitting object of philosophical curiosity not only because earlier logicians had neglected it, but because it is inherently perplexing. In demonstrative reasoning as Hume understands it, there is a kind of inevitability. The mind has no option but to conceive of the product of three and five as equal to the half of thirty. We find ourselves unable to conceive of its amounting to anything else. In probable reasoning, by contrast, we *presume* that something is true (as Locke suggests in *Essay* 4.15.5), meaning that we anticipate or "pre-judge" what lies ahead, instead of continuing, in absolute obedience, along a track already laid before us. Each inductive expectation is a more or less daring advance over experience. This going beyond the evidence is what makes probable reasoning worth explaining—and worth bringing under disciplined control. If we are outdistancing the evidence, if we are "adding value" to our premises, why do we add exactly what we do? What right have we to advance beyond our premises at all, and how should we regulate these presumptuous acts of addition or supplementation?

II Hume's Logic in Its Descriptive Aspect

Butler has already given us a very basic descriptive truth about our powers of probable reasoning: we tend to assume that things will carry on in the future very much as they've carried on in the past. Past fires have warmed us, so we assume that the burning logs in a large room's distant corner will have the same comforting effect. Here is Hume's own, more elaborated statement of Butler's basic truth:

> We remember to have had frequent instances of the existence of one species of objects; and also remember, that the individuals of another species of objects have always attended them, and have existed in a regular order of contiguity and succession with regard to them. Thus we remember to have seen that species of object we call *flame*, and to have felt that species of sensation we call *heat*. We likewise call to mind their constant conjunction in all past instances. Without any farther ceremony, we call the one *cause* and the other *effect*, and infer the existence of the one from that of the other. In all those instances, from which we learn the conjunction of particular causes and effects, both the causes and effects have been perceiv'd by the senses, and are remember'd: But in all cases, wherein we reason concerning them, there is only one perceiv'd or remember'd, and the other is supply'd in conformity to our past experience. (T 1.3.6.2/87)

This is an account of what I will call the *leading case* of probable inference. The leading case begins with what Hume calls an "object," perceived or remembered. The inference terminates in a second object, expected or anticipated. Each of these objects, trigger and termination, belongs to a kind or *species*. We can call the kind to which the trigger belongs *kind 1*, and the kind to which the termination belongs, *kind 2*. Hume assigns three main characteristics to the leading case. Here are the first two:

(i)   Objects in kind 1 have, in the remembered past, *always* been followed by objects in kind 2.

(ii) Objects in kind 1 have *frequently* been observed.

What does it mean for us to have witnessed *frequent* instances of kind 1? Hume doesn't offer an exact standard. But it follows from (i) and (ii) that past experience has disclosed *frequent* instances of the first kind's being followed by the second kind, whatever our measure of frequency.

The third characteristic of the leading case is the one that Hume leaves implicit:

(iii) It is *readily apparent* that the triggering object belongs to a kind that we've already recognized.

I take (iii) to be implicit in Hume's statement that the inference proceeds with little ceremony. When a new flame triggers an expectation of heat, it strikes me immediately as *yet another flame.* I don't sift through the evidence for and against that way of sorting it—not consciously, at least.

To sum up the leading case, it includes, first, a *constant* and *frequently repeated conjunction* of temporally ordered kinds and, second, a *triggering object*, appearing to the senses or memory, that falls, uncontroversially, into the kind that is first in the order. Against the background of the conjunction, the triggering object gives rise to a expectation with specific content. We come to expect an object whose kinship with objects in kind 2 will be as obvious as the kinship of the trigger with objects in kind 1. This expectation is not only specific but *confident*, because many past observations speak in its favor and not a single one speaks against it.

The other cases that figure in Hume's inductive logic are, for the most part, departures from (or variations of) the leading case. I list several of them here. My list is meant to be scrupulously descriptive. Making no judgments of value, its only aim is to chart some of the most widespread ways in which we *do in fact* reason from experience. When we turn to the normative aspect of Hume's logic, we will learn that he approves of some of these patterns of reasoning and disapproves of others, but here they are presented with deliberate neutrality. Hume places labels on several of the patterns; in those cases, I've placed his labels in quotation marks. The remaining labels are my own.

Generalization. This is a modest variation on the leading case, in which there's no triggering object, and therefore no particular expectation. We're given a record of one kind's faithful attendance on another, and on that basis we arrive at a general conclusion. Every flame in my experience has, for example, been attended by heat. From that, I infer that all flames are hot: that *every* flame—past, present, or future—is attended by heat.

"The probability of causes" (T 1.3.12, EU 6.4/57–9). This pattern of reasoning takes two forms. One is familiar. The other, for the most part, lies hidden deep in the childhood past of every one of us.

First, the familiar form. "Fire has always burned," Hume reminds us, "and water [has always] suffocated every human creature." Likewise, "the production of motion by impulse and gravity is a universal law, which has hitherto admitted of no exceptions." These are lawful generalizations, arrived at by the generalizing process I've just described. But past experience doesn't always speak with one voice. There are causes, as Hume observes, "which have been found more irregular and uncertain: nor has rhubarb always proved a purge, or opium a soporific, to every one, who has taken these medicines" (EU 6.4/57–8). If I come to expect that a helping of rhubarb will purge me or a dose of opium will make me drowsy, my expectation will be "hesitating" (T 1.3.12.6/132). Rhubarb and opium are *probable* causes rather than certain ones; hence, the name Hume gives to this pattern. I can generalize on the basis of rhubarb's spotty record, just as I generalize on the basis of gravity's spotless record, but when I do, I'll conclude not that rhubarb always purges, but that it usually does.

Hume views the probability of causes in its second form as a distant and virtually irrecoverable part of the our childhood histories. Among all forms of inductive reasoning it is, as he says in the *Treatise*, "the first in order" (T 1.3.12.3/131). It is prior in time even to the leading case, which cannot get a proper grip on us until this more primitive pattern has done its work. Recall that in the leading case, the conjunction between kind 1 and kind 2 must be *frequent*. But it cannot be frequent from the start. At the start and for some time thereafter, there will be, as Hume says, a "want of sufficient number of experiments." A record of frequent co-occurrence has to be built up over time, and, as it accumulates, it's reasonable to suppose that the change it brings about in us is very gradual. A toddler watches as a ball disappears behind a couch and reappears at the other end. It happens again, and a third time. Even now, the conjunction of its disappearance and reappearance may not qualify as frequent, but the child may already be prone to expect (not certainly, but with some degree of assurance) that when the ball disappears the next time, it will reappear soon after. It's just not reasonable to suppose that as the cases of co-occurrence mount, we remain apparently unaffected, only to shift into total confidence when the required threshold of "frequency" is finally reached. Our confidence *accretes*, and, as it does, we are reasoning from the probability of causes, updating as we go along. This reasoning "naturally takes place," Hume says, "before any entire proof can exist." Why he also says that "no one, who is arriv'd at the age of maturity, can any longer be acquainted with it"—why it is lost in our childhood pasts—is a question we'll examine shortly.

"Analogy" (T 1.3.12.15/136, EU 6.1/56). "All kinds of reasoning from causes or effects are founded on two particulars," Hume explains, "*viz.* the constant conjunction of any two objects in all past experience, and the resemblance of a present object to any one of them." (This is a useful summary of the leading case.) "If you weaken either the union or resemblance, you weaken the principle of transition, and of consequence that belief, which arises from it" (T 1.3.12.25/142). In the probability of causes, it's the union that's weakened. In analogy, it's the resemblance. The less perfect the resemblance between the triggering object and earlier objects that I've placed in kind 1, the more hesitant will be my expectation that the triggering object will be attended by an object of kind 2. I've seen a lot of ducks in water before, and they've all tipped over to feed on underwater vegetation. I see a new duck of a different shape—deeper bill, rounder body, tighter neck—and for a moment I wonder what to make of it. I decide that it will dabble, too, but I'm more hesitant than

I would be if its shape exactly matched the familiar pattern. (As it happens, it paddles into deeper water and dives.)

"The probability of chances" (T 1.3.11, EU 6.3/57). We're about to throw a six-sided die. We're confident that it will land—we're assured of that by an instance of the leading case—but we don't know which of its sides will turn up when it does. That, we suppose, is a matter of *chance* (hence the name Hume gives to this pattern). This puts the six sides "upon a footing of equality" (T 1.3.11.6/125–6); each one, in our view, is "alike probable and possible" (T 1.3.11.12/129). Suppose, though, that the die has a single dot on four of its faces and a pair of dots on the other two. 'Tis plain," Hume writes, that we'll "give the preference to that which is inscrib'd on the greatest number of sides" and conclude that a throw of one is more likely than a throw of two (T 1.3.11.9/127). We may even *predict* a throw of one (we might bet on it, for example), but if we do, our expectation will be hesitant, not confident. If the ratio of one-dot sides to two-dot sides increases (if, say, we take up a dodecahedral die, with a single dot on all but one of its twelve sides) our confidence will grow.

"Probability . . . deriv'd from general rules" (T 1.3.13.7/146–7). In coming to terms with new observations, we sometimes rely on conclusions, or "general rules," that we have reached before. For example, an Englishman meeting a Frenchman may have already concluded that "a *Frenchman* cannot have solidity" (Hume's own example at T 1.3.13.7/146). Even if his new acquaintance is "visibly. . . very judicious," the Englishman may set present appearances aside, either because he reflects on his earlier generalization and deliberately applies it to the new case, or because the earlier conclusion, although not recalled to consciousness, makes him blind to the true significance of what he sees. General rules take the form "all *A*'s are *B*'s"; the larger the class of *A*'s, the broader the rule. Hume states several very broad rules, as we'll see. According to one of them, which I'll call Hume's *rule of difference*, "the difference in the effects of two resembling objects must proceed from that particular, in which they differ" (T 1.3.15.8/174). This is broad rule because its *A*'s are resembling objects (or differences between resembling objects) of any kind at all. The rule covers billiard balls and bread loaves as well as it covers Frenchmen. It is also what might be called a *second-order rule*: a rule for arriving at rules, new generalizations about what causes what. The rule of difference doesn't tell us, directly, what to expect in any particular case; it tells us, instead, how to identify causally relevant factors. Suppose that my days have been sedentary and that I've been sleeping fitfully at night. If I take up morning walks and begin to sleep more soundly, I may conclude by Hume's rule that my morning exercise is responsible for the improvement. It's our reliance on broad, second-order rules such as this one that explains why we are, in adulthood, no longer acquainted—or at least no longer well-acquainted—with the second form taken by the probability of causes, in which the strength of an expectation moves up a notch with each confirming "experiment." By using the rule of difference and others like it to zero in on causally relevant factors, we grown-ups can reach perfect confidence much more swiftly than we could when we were young. A toddler may take a long time to learn that soft avocados are

reliably tastier than hard ones. But we can learn this lesson after sampling our first soft avocado.

Reasoning from "one single experiment" (T 1.3.12.3/131). "Nothing is more common," Hume writes in 1.3.12.3, "than for people of the most advanc'd knowledge to have attain'd only an imperfect experience of many particular events." And imperfect experience, as Hume goes on to point out, produces an "imperfect" level of confidence. "But then we must consider," he adds, "that the mind, having form'd another observation concerning the connexion of causes and effects"—another second-order rule along the lines of the rule of difference—"gives new force to its reasoning from that observation; and by means of it can build an argument on one single experiment, when duly prepar'd and examin'd." I make a carefully controlled substitution in a recipe, and when the cake rises higher than before, I conclude that the new ingredient was the cause. "What we have found once to follow from any object, we conclude will for ever follow from it," so from that point on, I stick with the replacement. Here, as in other cases involving the conscious or unconscious use of a general rule, my conclusion is what Hume describes as an *oblique* response to my past experience of ingredients and outcomes, rather than a *direct* one (T 1.3.6.14/93). I do not passively register the brute correlations between them; instead, I bring a second-order rule to bear on them. The rule allows me to *interpret* the correlations, so that I can extract more information from them than a young child (or a less alert baker) ever could. My response is, in a sense, no longer natural, but *artificial*. Even if the crucial experiment I take advantage of isn't one that I arrange, I resort to artifice in drawing information out of it. The artifice needn't be conscious. I may register the superiority of the outcome, unconsciously judge that the new ingredient is the cause, and find myself using the new ingredient from that time forward. Only later may I reflect that I'm using the new ingredient because I made an unconscious judgment based on an unconscious application of a rule. "All Reasoning is search, and casting about, and requires Pain and Application," Locke writes (I ii 10), but Humean reasoning, even reasoning that is oblique or rule-mediated, is sometimes effortless and pain-free, because the act of interpretation—the intellectual straining and lifting—is taking place, unreflectively and automatically, offstage. In adding the extra ingredient, I leap directly from one conception to another.

Recency (T 1.3.13.2/143–4). Recent observations inspire more inductive confidence than do remote ones. "A drunkard, who has seen his companion die of a debauch, is struck with that instance for some time, and dreads a like accident for himself: But as the memory of it decays always by degrees, his former security returns, and the danger seems less certain and real"—even though there's been no change in the number (or proportion) of relevant instances that fall within the drunkard's ken. In general, "an experiment, that is recent and fresh in the memory, affects us more than one that is in some measure obliterated" by time's passage, and it has, as a result, "a superior influence on the judgment."

Salience (T 1.3.12.1). A drop in inductive confidence will follow "a diminution of the impression, and. . . the shading of those colours, under which it appears to the. . . senses" (T 1.3.13.1/143). And inductive confidence will grow as impressions gain in strength. If the pain of a bended knee is unbearable, I'll learn more quickly—and more surely—not to bend the knee than I would if the pain were mild.

Length-sensitivity or inference-weariness (T 1.3.13.3/144). We're less moved by long inductive arguments—long tracings that take us from a cause to a distant consequence or from a consequence back to a distant cause—than we are by short ones. "A man may receive a more lively conviction from a probable reasoning, which is close and immediate, than from a long chain of consequences, tho' just and conclusive in each part." In fact, very few of us can tolerate long and winding causal investigation: "'tis seldom such reasonings produce any conviction," Hume writes, "and one must have a very strong and firm imagination to preserve the evidence to the end, where it passes thro' so many stages" (T 1.3.13.3/144). Sometimes, a great distance between an inductive expectation and its premises does even more to depress our confidence than contrary evidence would.

These, then, are the main headings of Hume's descriptive logic. Of the forms of reasoning I've listed, only two of them—the leading case and generalization—offer what Hume (still speaking descriptively or value-neutrally) calls *proofs* of their conclusions. In the *Treatise*, proof is contrasted with both *knowledge* and *probability*. "One wou'd appear ridiculous," Hume writes there,

> who wou'd say, that 'tis only probable the sun will rise to-morrow, or that all men must dye; tho' 'tis plain we have no farther assurance of these facts, than what experience affords us. For this reason, 'twou'd perhaps be more convenient, in order at once to preserve the common signification of words, and mark the several degrees of evidence, to distinguish human reason into three kinds, viz. *that from knowledge, from proofs, and from probabilities.* By knowledge, I mean the assurance arising from the comparison of ideas. By proofs, those arguments, which are deriv'd from the relation of cause and effect, and which are entirely free of doubt and uncertainty. By probability, that evidence, which is still attended with uncertainty. (T 1.3.11.2/124)

Hume draws the same basic contrast in the *Enquiry*, but in somewhat different terms. Instead of describing the various forms of assurance, he describes the various forms of *argument-based* assurance. Under the heading of knowledge as it was understood in the *Treatise*, assurance includes not only demonstrative certainty, which is argument-based, but intuitive certainty, which isn't argument-based but immediate. In the corresponding passage in the *Enquiry*, intuitive certainty is simply set aside. "Mr. LOCKE," Hume explains in the later work, "divides all *arguments* [my emphasis] into demonstrative and probable." "In this view," he continues, "we must say, that it is only probable that all men must die, or that the sun will rise to-morrow. But to conform our language more to common use, we ought to divide arguments into *demonstrations, proofs,* and *probabilities.* By proofs meaning such arguments from experience as leave no room for doubt or opposition" (EU 6 n.10/56 n.1).

III HUME'S LOGIC IN ITS EXPLANATORY ASPECT

Hume's explanatory logic centers on the leading case. His initial finding about it is negative: our expectations in the leading case are not brought about by reason.

There are, Hume believes, only two ways in which reason could be responsible for our expectations in the leading case. First, as we peer into a triggering object, or closely inspect our idea of it, reason might enable us to see that the expected object is already on its way, much as we see, on peering into the idea of the product of five and three, that it is equal to the half of thirty. Reason, that is, might permit us to infer the expected object, without consulting experience, from the triggering object alone. The constant conjunction of the kinds containing the two objects would then be set aside. Instead, our bare insight into the triggering object would somehow presage or prefigure the advent of the second. According to the second way Hume contemplates, reason infers the expected object not from the triggering object alone, but from the appearance of the triggering object together with our memory of the conjunction of kind 1 and kind 2.

Hume argues that reason can't, in fact, operate in either of these ways. The problem with the first is that our most exhaustive insight into the triggering object *considered in itself*—that is, apart from the conjunction—doesn't supply the slightest clue to the appearance of a second object that is, after all, entirely distinct from it. (It is an object that does not yet exist, and one that can survive, once it arrives, in the absence of the other.) If intense concentration on the triggering object could reveal that a second object is on its way, we could, in principle, infer its appearance *a priori*, on the day of our creation. But Hume holds that even after we got over the daze of a sudden introduction into the world, we would be incapable of such sagacity. As he says in the *Enquiry*, "ADAM, though his rational faculties be supposed, at the very first, entirely perfect, could not have inferred from the fluidity, and transparency of water, that it would suffocate him. No object ever discovers, by the qualities that appears to the senses,... the effects which will arise from it; nor can our reason, unassisted by experience, ever draw any inference concerning matter of fact" (EU 4.6/27). In putting ourselves into Adam's place, we must take care to forget the conjunctions that bind our ideas of causes to our ideas of their effects so firmly that we can hardly imagine the cause without anticipating the effect that follows it. "We fancy," as Hume observes, "that were we brought on a sudden, into this world, we could at first have inferred that one Billiard-ball would communicate motion to another upon impulse"—upon, that is, its colliding with it. "Such is the influence of custom," he adds, "that, where it is strongest, it not only covers our natural ignorance, but even conceals itself" (EU 4.8/28–9). But if (thought-experimentally, of course) we rid our minds of custom's influence, it becomes plain, he thinks, that "the mind can never possibly find the effect in the supposed cause, by the most accurate scrutiny and examination. . . . For the effect is totally different from the cause, and consequently can never be discovered in it" (EU 4.9/29).

Even if it somehow occurred to me that the second billiard ball might move off in a straight line, I can no less easily imagine "that a hundred different events might as well follow from that cause." Both balls might remain at rest. The first might "leap off from the second in any line or direction." The two balls might explode, or fly away. "All these suppositions," Hume concludes, "are consistent and conceivable. Why then should we give the preference to one, which is no more consistent or conceivable than the rest? All our reasonings *a priori*"—our reasonings apart from the constant conjunctions made known to us by past experience—"will never be able to shew us any foundation for this preference" (EU 4.10/29–30; see also T 1.3.6.1/86–7).

Can reason do better when it has more than a present impression—a triggering object—to go on? Will recollecting past conjunctions enable it to see what lies ahead? Here, too, Hume's answer is negative. If reason determined us, Hume claims, it would have to proceed on the following principle: "*instances, of which we have had no experience, must resemble those, of which we have had experience, and that the course of nature continues always uniformly the same.*" But reason cannot arrive at a conclusion of this nature (T 1.3.6.4/88–9). It would have to do so either by demonstrative or probable reasoning. But there can be no demonstrative arguments for the principle, because "we can at least conceive a change in the course of nature; which sufficiently proves, that such a change is not absolutely impossible" (T 1.3.6.5/89). And there can be no probable arguments either, because any probable argument for the principle would, as a probable argument, rest on that very principle, which means that it could not be the source of our commitment to it. "Probability is founded on the presumption of a resemblance betwixt those objects, of which we have had experience, and those, of which we have had none; and therefore 'tis impossible this presumption can arise from probability. The same principle cannot be both the cause and effect of another; and this is, perhaps, the only proposition concerning that relation, which is either intuitively or demonstratively certain" (T 1.3.6.7/90). Hume's causal language makes his explanatory preoccupations very clear.

Hume rounds off the negative part of his explanatory logic of the leading case as follows:

> 'Tis impossible for us to satisfy ourselves by our reason, why we shou'd extend. . . experience beyond those particular instances, which have fallen under our observation. We suppose, but are never able to prove, that there must be resemblance betwixt those objects, of which we have had experience, and those which lie beyond the reach of our discovery. (T 1.3.6.11/91-2)

An inference from one object to another, he concludes, is "not determin'd by reason" (T 1.3.6.12/92).

For Hume, in the *Treatise*, this negative conclusion promptly gives rise to a positive result: our inductive expectations must be produced by what he calls the imagination. This is because the psychological theory of the *Treatise* allows for only four idea-forming or belief-producing mechanisms: the senses, memory, reason, and imagination. The understanding might seem to be a fifth, but in Hume, "the understanding" always refers to reason or imagination (or both). As sources of our inductive expectations, the senses and memory are ruled out from the start, because the expected object is never present to the senses. (It lies, by hypothesis, beyond "the present testimony of our senses and the records of our memory.") Reason is excluded by the present argument. So the imagination is the only remaining candidate. Our inductive inferences must be determined, as Hume says, "by certain principles, which associate together the ideas of these objects, and unite them in the imagination"—by "custom or a principle of association" (T 1.3.6.12/92, T 1.3.7.6/97). "We call everything CUSTOM," he explains, "which proceeds from a past repetition, without any new reasoning or conclusion" (T 1.3.8.10/102).

In the *Enquiry*, Hume's positive conclusion is the same. "If the mind be not engaged by argument to make this step," he writes, "it must be induced by some other principle of equal weight and authority" (EU 5.3/42). That principle, he says a bit later,

> is CUSTOM or HABIT. For whenever the repetition of any particular act or operation produces a propensity to renew the same act or operation, without being impelled by any reasoning or process of the understanding; we always say, that this propensity is the effect of *Custom*. (5.5/43)

"Custom," he then concludes, "is the great guide of human life":

> It is that principle alone, which renders our experience useful to us, and makes us expect, for the future, a similar train of events with those which have appeared in the past. Without the influence of custom, we should be entirely ignorant of every matter of fact, beyond what is immediately present to the memory and senses. (EU 5.6/44–5)

Custom or habit is also at work in all other cases of inductive inference. We will consider only a selection of them here. In the *probability of causes*, past regularities are not absolutely reliable. They hold for the most part, but not always. Hence, they give rise to a more fragile habit or a more hesitant expectation. To account for the fragility of the habit, Hume portrays the mind as a kind of register, faithfully encoding every past instance of the relevant regularity. "Where different effects have been found to follow from causes, which are to *appearance* exactly similar, all these various effects must occur to the mind in transferring the past to the future, and enter into our considerations, when we determined the probability of the event" (EU 6.4/58). The encoding capacity ascribed to us here is remarkable: somehow, we give each observed instance its due. The process by which we do so, Hume seems to think, is generally an unconscious one; this makes its fidelity to the past experience easier to accept. We record past instances in something like the way a hillside records past instances of snowmelt streaming down its slopes. The water is likelier to flow in already well-worn channels. The hillside is a trustworthy indicator of the course of future floods not because of anything the hillside *does*, but because the impressions made on its surface by past floods set the course of future ones.

In the *probability of chances*, it is obviously impossible, as Hume observes, to prove with certainty that the die with a single dot on four sides and no dots on two will, when thrown, reveal a dotted side. Hume's explanation of the case has three parts. First, the mind is determined by custom to suppose that the die with fall and turn up on one of its sides (T 1.3.11.10/128). Custom makes it "almost impossible" for the mind to form an idea of any other outcome. Second, because past experience favors no one side over any other, "the mind [is] in a perfect indifference" between them. Hence, the mind "divides its force"—its total quantity of anticipatory energy—"equally among them" (T 1.3.11.12/128-9). Third,

'tis evident that where several sides have the same figure inscrib'd on them, they must concur in their influence on the mind, and must unite upon one image or idea of a figure all those divided impulses, that were dispers'd over the several sides, upon which that figure is inscrib'd. (T 1.3.11.13/129)

Here, too, hydraulic imagery may be appropriate. We know that water running down a hillside will be moving through one of six channels. Four are filled with leaves and dirt and two pass cleanly over rocks. It's likelier, we conclude, that the emerging water will be cloudy rather than clear.

In all these cases, the expectations formed are direct and unreflective responses to past experience. But we can reflect on past experience and codify it. We may then bring *general rules* to bear. We may dismiss a piece of evidence, as the prejudiced Englishman does. We may hesitate to reach a judgment because our second-order rules urge caution. We may insist on further experiments, which our second-order rules may help us to devise. More than unthinking habit is at work here. Any expectations we form will be oblique rather than direct. But they will remain custom-driven because, were it not for custom, we would form no expectations at all.

The imagination and its idea-enlivening power—its ability to fortify ideas and solidify commitment—also explains the phenomena of *recency, salience,* and *inference-weariness*. Recent and salient triggers have more vivacity than old or tired ones, so they transmit more vivacity to the conclusions that attend them. And when an inference is long and winding, the vivacity of its initiating perception is dissipated. It may peter out before we arrive at the thought of the conclusion, leaving us in suspense and without belief.

Our dependence on custom unites us with the beasts. As Hume indicates most forcefully in *Treatise* 1.3.16 and *Enquiry* 9, both of which bear the provocative title "Of the Reason of Animals," nonhuman animals are, like us, creatures of inductive reason. But they are creatures of reason only insofar as they are creatures of habit. "It is custom alone which engages animals, from every object, that strikes their senses, to infer its usual attendant," he writes in the *Enquiry* (9.5/106). In this, too, they are like us; "no other explication can be given of this operation," Hume writes, "in all the higher, as well as lower classes of sensitive beings" (EU 9.5/106–7).

IV HUME'S LOGIC IN ITS NORMATIVE ASPECT

Hume's logic, as I've so far presented it, abstains from judgments of value. Patterns of reasoning are identified and explained but without being classified as good or bad. Our reasoning powers are investigated with strict scientific neutrality. No pattern is condemned as unreliable or extolled as worthy of our trust.

But the writer who lives and breathes on the pages of *Treatise* 1.3 and *Enquiry* 4–6 is not always a coolly objective scientist. His logic, like its predecessors, has a practical aim, and, especially in 1.3, Hume weaves judgments of value together with his descriptive observations and explanatory inferences.[8] At times, the threads of description, explanation, and evaluation are so closely entwined that it can be hard to pull them apart. My compartmentalized exposition, in which a separate section is devoted to each aspect of Hume's logic is, therefore, unlike his own. In the present section, I will again be enforcing divisions that Hume makes no effort to honor page by page.

IV.1 Philosophical and Unphilosophical Probability

The most basic element in Hume's normative logic is his distinction between philosophical and unphilosophical probability. It is a distinction between patterns of probable reasoning that meet with philosophical approval and patterns of reasoning that do not. Among the patterns of reasoning we surveyed in Section II, some, Hume reports, "are receiv'd"—that is, endorsed or accepted—"by philosophers, and allow'd to be reasonable foundations of belief and opinion." Others "have not had the good fortune to obtain the same sanction" (T 1.3.13.1/143). Because he chooses in these passages to *report*, from a third-person viewpoint, on the seal of approval awarded by a group he calls "the philosophers," Hume himself seems to be hanging back. Readers can fairly wonder whether the philosophers are a club of which Hume considers himself a member. Perhaps he chooses to report because he wants to reserve, or even to conceal, his private judgment. But the verdicts of the philosophers are, as we'll soon see, Hume's own verdicts. In appealing to the philosophers, he isn't expressing a "hands off" attitude but striving instead to be impersonal: to claim *more* authority, rather than less, for the normative judgments he's bringing into play.

Officially speaking, Hume's distinction between philosophical and unphilosophical probability doesn't cover either the leading case or its generalizing variant; when the distinction between the two kinds of probability is first proposed, it applies only to probability in Hume's narrow sense—to inductive reasoning from less than perfect regularities. When, however, the probability of chances, the probability of causes, and analogy are expressly given the seal of approval (T 1.3.11), the leading case and its variant are silently or implicitly endorsed because they are, from any point of view that could be deemed philosophical or "scientific," *at least* as secure as the strictly "probable" (i.e., less than proof-affording) forms of reasoning that Hume explicitly endorses. (The word "scientific," as we now employ it, is a very serviceable substitute for Hume's "philosophical" as it figures in *Treatise* 1.3.) Because the leading case and its generalizing variant represent pure cases from which the merely probable forms are departures, the pure cases are endorsed by default. The forms of unphilosophical probability that Hume condemns include recency, salience, and length-sensitivity. Hume observes that they are "deriv'd from the same principles" as the approved forms, meaning they are derived from the principles of the imagination. They are therefore perfectly normal, but they are, in Hume's view, nonetheless lamentable. They are too distant from the leading case to borrow any of its lustre. We should be guarding ourselves against them, if we can.

Why are some forms of reasoning condemned and others not? Here, we can give the same one-word answer that we gave, at Hume's urging, to an earlier question about the source of our beliefs in matters of fact: EXPERIENCE. In the present case, Hume fills out this one-word answer as follows: the ultimate basis of the distinction between philosophical and unphilosophical probability is "our experience of [the understanding's] operations in the judgments we form concerning objects" (T 1.3.13.11/149)—our experience of its past record of performance, as it relies on one or another method of reasoning. Experience informs us that inferences conforming to chances, causes, and analogy are very often right. They very often lead us to true beliefs. Experience also informs us that inferences guided by recency, salience, and length-sensitivity are very often wrong. They very often entice us into false beliefs. To this it may be objected that no real foundation for the distinction has been provided, because philosophical probability will be vindicated only if its past performance is assessed by its own standards. The suspicion is that if we judge its record by, say, recency or salience, we will get a different—and possibly less reassuring—result. But it is doubtful that recency or salience would allow for more than a fleeting vindication of *any* method, including even recency or salience itself; philosophical probability may well stand alone in its ability to yield both a durable endorsement of itself and an equally durable reproach of its competitors.

IV.2   Rules by Which to Judge of Causes and Effects

In *Treatise* 1.3.15, Hume presents a list of general rules for identifying causes and effects. They provide, he announces, "all the LOGIC I think proper to employ in my reasoning" (T 1.3.15.11/175), but he is not speaking only for himself, any more than Newton was speaking for himself when he introduced, in the *Principia*, such rules as the following: "the causes assigned to natural effects of the same kind must be, so far as possible, the same."[9] We have already met with one of Hume's rules, the "rule of difference" I described in Section II. In the list given below, the rule of difference appears with several of Hume's other rules. Like the rule of difference, they are all second-order rules: rules for forming and refining rules of the first order. The first rule listed (the fourth in Hume's own numbering) incorporates the rule laid down by Newton:

> *Hume's fourth rule.* "The same cause always produces the same effect, and the same effect never arises but from the same cause." (T 1.3.15.6/173)

> *Hume's fifth rule.* "Where several different objects produce the same effect, it must be by means of some quality, which we discover to be common among them. For as like effects imply like causes, we must always ascribe the causation to the circumstance, wherein we discover the resemblance." (T 1.3.15.7/174)

> *Hume's sixth rule.* "The difference in the effects of two resembling objects must proceed from that particular, in which they differ." (T 1.3.15.8/174.; this is what I earlier called the rule of difference.)

> *Hume's seventh rule.* "When any object encreases or diminishes with the encrease or diminution of its cause, 'tis to be regarded as a compounded effect, deriv'd from the union of several different effects, which arise from the several different parts of the cause." (T 1.3.15.9/174)

Although Hume states these rules in *Treatise* 1.3.15, he was already looking ahead to them in 1.3.13 ("Of Unphilosophical Probability"), where he comments as follows on their justification and utility:

> We shall afterwards take notice of some general rules, by which we ought to regulate our judgment concerning causes and effects; and these rules are form'd on the nature of our understanding, and on our experience of its operations in the judgments we form concerning objects. By them we learn to distinguish the accidental circumstances from the efficacious causes. (T 1.3.13.11/149)

This passage makes it plain why Hume's rules for judging of cause and effect are not only part of his logic but part of his *normative* logic: they are rules that tell us how our reasoning "ought" to proceed, just as Hume says. When he states rule (4), he describes it as a "principle we derive from experience" (T 1.3.15.6/173). His point seems to be that it is vindicated by its past success—its tendency to give rise to true belief—in the way we considered just above. The same can be said, we can presume, of the other rules on Hume's list. He also describes rule (4) as "the source of most of our philosophical reasonings," and it is reasonable to assume that this is intended as an endorsement—that it, too, is a normative judgment, at least in part. As the source of most of the reasonings of which philosophers approve, rule (4) is one of which the readers of the *Treatise*, following the example of the philosophers (as the introduction to the *Treatise* bids them to do), should likewise approve.

We have, then, several good reasons for thinking that when Hume presents his rules, he is commending them to us as properly "philosophical." First, they contribute, as he must have known, to an established tradition of laying down laws for the proper conduct of philosophy—a tradition represented most notably by Newton, whose rules were regularly repeated by his many expositors and popularizers. Second, they are rules that Hume tells us we "ought" to follow. Third, they are rules vindicated by their past success—rules that are, as guides to truth, probably, if not provably, correct. Fourth and finally, Hume endorses the possibility of settling empirical questions with single, well-designed experiments, and, to design them, we need rules such as the ones he lists. (By the time the *Treatise* was published, such experiments—known variously as "crucial instances," "crucial experiments," or "instances of the fingerpost"—had been analyzed and advocated by a long line of natural philosophers.) For all of these reasons, proceeding by general rules seems to be a species of *philosophical* probability—not always (because there are faulty rules, such as *all Frenchman lack solidity*), but certainly at times.[10]

I now offer some brief examples of Hume's normative logic in action.

IV.3 The Regulation of Particular Beliefs

Hume's logic is a practical logic that he often puts to work. He makes use of it, for example, in Book 2 of the *Treatise*, a study of the passions in which psychological hypotheses are tested in accordance with his rules. An especially memorable illustration is provided by *Enquiry* 10, where he argues that testimony can never make it reasonable to believe in miracles. His main argument for this conclusion runs as follows:

1. "No testimony is sufficient to establish a miracle, unless the testimony be of such a kind, that its falsehood would be more miraculous, than the fact, which it endeavours to establish" (EU 10.13/115–6).
2. Because a miracle is a violation of the laws of nature, the condition specified by the first premise is never satisfied, and even if it were, the force of the testimony for the miracle would be diminished by the force of the argument against it, which (as an argument for a law of nature) is as strong as any argument from experience can be.
3. Hence, no testimony is sufficient to establish a miracle.

I won't be assessing this formidable argument here. I offer it here as an illustration of the use of Hume's logic, and particularly of general rules, to regulate belief. In the opening paragraph of *Enquiry* 10, where Hume recalls an earlier argument on which his own is modeled, he takes note of the earlier argument's reliance on what he calls "the rules of just reasoning" (EU 10.1/109). Later, he appeals on his own behalf to a "rule" (also called a "maxim") that closely resembles the rules put forward in the *Treatise*: "that the objects, of which we have no experience, resemble those, of which we have; that what we have found to be most usual is always most probable" (EU 10.16/117). Throughout the section, Hume relies on general rules to discriminate between what is "just" in inference and what is unjust. They can all be rolled into one: "a wise man... proportions his belief to the evidence" (EU 10.4/110). In the argument before us, the first premise, a "general maxim" according to Hume, is itself a rule. It can be stated more abstractly, so that it applies to the weighing of any piece of testimony, regardless of its subject matter: *testimony can establish a conclusion only if the falsehood of the testimony is more improbable than the falsehood of the conclusion.* Hume's reliance on this rule is very strong evidence that, in the *Enquiry*, he judged the following of general rules to be securely, even paradigmatically, "philosophical."

IV.4 The Reform of Disciplines

My second example of Hume's normative logic in action shows that it can guide us not only in forming particular beliefs, but in choosing our methods. We can use his logic to assess the conduct of disciplines and (if necessary) to guide their reform.

Hume thought that in the early seventeenth century, or perhaps shortly before, the study of nature was finally set on a secure and more promising path. He indicates this in the introduction to the *Treatise*, where he announces his plan to apply the method that revolutionized natural philosophy—its inductive logic, it seems fair to say—to the study of human nature. In that study, Hume was an innovator. But he was also an innovator, although a more belated one, in the study of history, whose reform accelerated late in the seventeenth century. The reform of history, in which Hume was an active participant, is not a topic usually considered in connection with his treatment on induction, but it is that reform on which I want to comment here.

As a historian, Hume had a professional investment in the assessment of testimony, as he suggests in the following passage from his *History of England*. It prefaces his retelling—his resolutely miracle-free retelling—of the story of Joan of Arc, "the Maid of Orleans."

> It is the business of history to distinguish between the miraculous and the marvelous; to reject the first in all narrations merely profane and human; to doubt the second; and when obliged by unquestionable testimony, as in the present case, to admit of something extraordinary, to receive as little of it as is consistent with the known facts and circumstances. (HE 2.398)

He might also have said: it is the business of history to receive only as much of it as is consistent with the known laws of nature.

In his essay "On the Art of Conversation," published in his *Essays* of 1580, Montaigne defends the willingness of the historian Tacitus to side with tradition in passing on reports of miracles. "When [Tacitus] says that, by favour of Serapis the god, Vespasian cured a blind woman in Alexandria by anointing her eyes with his saliva and also performed some additional miracle or other, he was following the dutiful example of all good historians. . . . Their role is to give an account of popular beliefs, not to account for them: which part is played by theologians and philosophers." In support of this verdict, Montaigne quotes both Quintus Curtius ("[I cannot] omit what I have been told by tradition") and Livy ("These things are neither to be vouched for nor denied: we must cling to tradition"). All this, Montaigne concludes, "is very well said. Let them pass on their histories to us according to what they find received, not according to their own estimate."[11]

Hume's view is very different. He admires these ancient writers, but in writing his *History*, he deliberately departs from their example. Hume takes note of Tacitus's report of the miracles of Vespasian in section 10 of the *Enquiry*. Partly because of the ancient historian's exemplary character, he writes, "no evidence can well be supposed stronger [than this report] for so gross and palpable a falsehood" (EU 10.25/123). Elsewhere in section 10, Hume identifies Livy as a writer who lent his authority to miracles (EU 10.24/122). And Quintus Curtius is mentioned in Section 8, where Hume writes that his veracity "is as much to be suspected, when he describes the supernatural courage of ALEXANDER, by which he was hurried on singly to attack multitudes, as when he described his supernatural force and activity, by which he was able to resist them" (EU 8.8/84). In citing Tacitus, Livy, and Quintus Curtius, Hume needn't be alluding to Montaigne; all three were widely read ancient authorities to whom anyone writing on this topic might refer. But it is clear from these passages that, in Hume's opinion, these ancient models, however worthy of emulation in some respects, fell far short of the defining duty of the historian, because they were unwilling to interrogate their sources—and to do so using the kind of rules (rules of "source criticism," as we call them now) that Hume makes use of in *Enquiry* 10 and in his *History*. As the twentieth-century historian Marc Bloch writes in response to Montaigne, "he obviously does not really understand how it is possible to conduct an examination, specifically a historical examination, of evidence such as [that of Tacitus]. The doctrine of research was worked out later."[12] Hume, in pointed contrast to Montaigne, sees himself as a philosophical historian who has a duty to make source criticism the very foundation of his narrative. In Hume's view, the historical writing of Tacitus and others is unphilosophical in precisely the same sense in which beliefs resting on salience, recency, or inference-weariness are unphilosophical. Hume's *History* aspires, unlike the history of Tacitus, to be philosophical or scientific. In writing it, he was conscious of participating in a modern movement of disciplinary reform—a reform in accord with the rules of his inductive logic.

IV.5 Inductive Skepticism

Hume's normative logic, as I've so far described it, is constructive. Its author has a basic faith in the inductive enterprise. He criticizes beliefs and methods in the bright hope that we can do better. For Hume, as we've seen him so far, logic is—as it was for Aristotle—an *organon* or instrument. His aim (shared by other early modern logicians, as Arnauld and Nicole indicate when they speak of logic as an "art") is to improve this instrument or to strengthen us in our use of it. Yet Hume is best known not for his constructive inductive logic, but for a destructive argument that seems to cast doubt not only on our finest inductive achievements (Newton's laws, for example) but on our most everyday beliefs (e.g., my confidence that tomorrow's breakfast toast will nourish me). This destructive argument is our next topic.

When, in Section II, I outlined the negative argument of *Treatise* 1.3.6, I was careful to present it as an austerely explanatory argument. I offered it as a value-neutral contribution to a science of the mind. Its aim, as I portrayed it, was to establish that reason, considered as a capacity of the mind on which no value judgment had been passed, is not the cause of our inductive expectations. In so portraying it, I was being faithful to many indications in the text. *Treatise* 1.3.6 is not overtly skeptical, and its concerns are not explicitly normative. It simply opens the way for Hume's positive suggestion that custom causes our inductive expectations. This conclusion, so far as 1.3.6 is concerned, is apparently no occasion for disappointment or regret. In 1.3, "custom" doesn't seem to be a derogatory term, and "reason" doesn't seem to be a complimentary one. As Don Garrett has said, "reason" seems to function there as "the name that Hume, as cognitive psychologist, employs for the general faculty of making inferences or producing arguments."[13] Reason in 1.3.6 seems to be a value-neutral mechanism: an indifferent generator of inferences and nothing more.

I believe that this is at best a partial picture. *Treatise* 1.3.6 does stop short of explicit skeptical pronouncements. But the negative argument of 1.3.6 is, in my view, like a tightly wound spring, ready to uncoil at a touch. It has, as I'll try to show, a large store of compressed skeptical *potential*—potential that is, in my view, released in Hume's *Enquiry*. The *Enquiry* will be our main text here.

In the *Enquiry*, Hume seems to me to argue that, from a certain point of view—a point of view whose authority we can never entirely escape—we are unjustified in forming inductive expectations, even when those expectations are in perfect alignment with his rules. He is, in the sense Robert J. Fogelin has identified, a "radical theoretical skeptic" who believes that our inductive expectations are, as Fogelin puts it, "wholly ungrounded" and without warrant.[14] This reading of the *Enquiry* (and of Hume) is traditional, but it has become, especially in recent years, a controversial one. I will defend it vigorously but also (I hope) somewhat cautiously, calling attention to at least some of the reasons why Hume might be read in a different way.[15]

Section 12 of the *Enquiry* is an investigation of the scope and significance of skepticism. As the section begins, Hume asks "what is meant by a sceptic." "And how far," he adds, is it "possible to push. . . philosophical principles of doubt and uncertainty?" (EU 12.2/149). The skepticism under discussion in most of the section is described by Hume as "*consequent* to science and inquiry" (EU 12.5/150). As he indicates throughout the section, but especially in the first of its three parts (where the topic is not inductive skepticism but skepticism concerning the senses), this consequent skepticism, whatever its subject matter, questions whether we are justified or warranted in believing what we do. Its partisans, as Hume points out, claim "to have discovered, either the *absolute fallaciousness* of [our] mental faculties, or their *unfitness* to reach any fixed determination in all those curious subjects of speculation, about which they are commonly employed" (EU 12.5/150; my emphasis). They bring our faculties "into dispute" (EU 12.5/150). The skeptics speak "against" them (EU 12.6/151, 12.10/152), by raising "objections" to their deliverances (EU 12.10/152, 12.16/155, 12.17/155–6, and 12.18/156–7) and by calling their conclusions "into question" (EU 12.13/153). Philosophers may try in response to "justify" the threatened beliefs, as they do in the case of our sense-based belief in body, but the skeptics reply—indeed, they successfully "show"—that this belief is "without any foundation in reasoning" (EU 12.12/153).

The passages I've quoted seem to me to show that whether we are justified in believing what we do is the skeptic's main concern. These passages serve as background to the one I most want to emphasize. It raises "objections" (EU 12.21/158), this time to probable reasoning. They are consequent objections that arise "from. . . profound researches," and these researches turn out to be Hume's own, in earlier sections of the *Enquiry*. "The skeptic," Hume writes in the passage,

> seems to have ample matter of triumph; while he justly insists, that all our evidence for any matter of fact, which lies beyond the testimony of sense or memory, is derived entirely from the relation of cause and effect; that we have no other idea of this relation than that of two objects, which have been frequently *conjoined* together; that we have no argument to convince us, that objects, which have, in our experience, been frequently conjoined, will likewise, in other instances, be conjoined in the same manner; and that nothing leads us to this inference but custom or a certain instinct of our nature; which it is indeed difficult to resist, but which, like other instincts, may be fallacious and deceitful. While the sceptic insists upon these topics, he shows his force, or rather, indeed, his own and our weakness; and seems, for the time at least, to destroy all assurance and conviction. (EU 12.22/159)

Hume goes on to emphasize that the destruction suffered by our opinions is only temporary. I will say more about this in a moment. Of more immediate concern is a recognition provoked by this skepticism, which is that philosophers are "not able, by their most diligent enquiry, to satisfy themselves concerning the foundations of [the] operations" that the skeptic has called into question (EU 12.23/160). Hume's point here isn't that the *causal* or *psychological* foundation of inductive operations eludes philosophers; *that* foundation was laid bare in *Enquiry* 5, where it proved to be custom or habit, as we've seen. It is the *justificatory* foundations that philosophers are unable to unearth, as Hume makes immediately clear. Philosophers, he says, are unable "to remove the *objections*, which may be raised against" our operations (EU 12.23/160, my emphasis). A bit later, when he cautions us against prying into cosmic mysteries—how can we hope to solve them, he asks, if we're baffled by familiar events lying very close to hand?—the dissatisfaction of "philosophers" has apparently spread to all of us. "While we cannot give a satisfactory reason, why we believe, after a thousand experiments, that a stone will fall, or fire burn; can we ever satisfy ourselves concerning any determination, which we may form, with regard to the origin of worlds, and the situation of nature, from, and to eternity?" (EU 12.25/160). Dissatisfaction everywhere awaits us, no matter how commonplace the expectation. That is why the skeptic, as 12.22/159 warns, threatens *all* of our assurance and conviction.

Enquiry 4's main role in this skeptical line of thought is to support 12.22's contention that "we have no argument to convince us, that objects, which have, in our experience, been frequently conjoined, will likewise, in other instances, be conjoined in the same manner." That past conjunctions will be preserved in the future is the "connecting proposition" or "intermediate step" (EU 4.17/34) that the understanding has to establish if it is going to take us from *"I have found that such an object has always been attended with such an effect"* to *"I foresee, that other objects, which are, in appearance, similar, will be attended with similar effects"* (EU 4.16/34). Here, largely in Hume's own words, is his Section IV argument that the understanding is unable to support this proposition.[16]

1. "All reasonings may be divided into two kinds, namely demonstrative reasoning, or that concerning relations of ideas, and moral reasoning, or that concerning matter of fact and existence." (EU 4.18/35)
2. "There are no demonstrative arguments in the case [of the connecting proposition]. . .; since it implies no contradiction, that the course of nature may change." (EU 4.18/35)
3. Hence "if we be. . . engaged by arguments to put trust in past experience. . ., these arguments must be probable only, or such as regard matter of fact and real existence, according to the division above mentioned." (EU 4.19/35)
4. Yet "all our experimental conclusions proceed upon the supposition, that the future will be conformable to the past." (EU 4.19/35)
5. Therefore "to endeavour, the proof of this last supposition by probable arguments, or arguments regarding existence, must be evidently going in a circle, and taking that for granted, which is the very point in question." (EU 4.19/35–6)
6. "It is not reasoning which engages us to suppose the past resembling the future, and to expect similar effects from causes, which are, to appearance, similar" (from (1), (2), and (5). (EU 4.23/39)

There is, as he suggests elsewhere in Section IV, no "logic" that can shelter us in our belief that nature is uniform (EU 4.21/38).

Hume's Section 4 argument closely resembles the argument of *Treatise* 1.3.6, but there is one important difference, brought out clearly in step (5). At the corresponding point in 1.3.6, Hume points out that the belief in the connecting proposition cannot be the cause of itself. But his present point seems to be that the connecting proposition cannot *justify* itself. As he says in another place in Section 4, to classify the connecting proposition as probable would be "begging the question," because all such arguments "suppose, as their foundation, that the future will resemble the past, and that similar powers will be conjoined with similar sensible qualities" (EU 4.21/32). "If there be any suspicion"—that is, any doubt—"that the course of nature may change, and that the past may be no rule for the future, all experience becomes useless, and can give rise to no inference or conclusion." This could perhaps be read as a purely causal observation, but Hume's reference to begging the question makes that unlikely.

Even so, could it be Hume's view in the *Enquiry* that, typically or ideally, reason causes beliefs by justifying them? In that case, he may put forward the claim that reason can't justify the connection proposition only in order to show that reason can't cause our belief in it. He may think that the connecting proposition can be justified in another way, or that we can be justified in our expectations even if the connecting proposition is unjustifiable. Hume never says directly that we can be warranted in forming inductive expectations only if the connecting proposition can itself be justified. It is partly for this reason that some readers doubt he is as radical a skeptic as I've suggested.

I'm doubtful, however, that Hume's interest in the justifying power of reason is a purely instrumental one—an interest pursued only for the sake of reaching a causal conclusion. His interest in it is ultimate—or so the passages I've quoted tend to suggest. Other passages from Section 12 support the same conclusion. The consequent skepticism that triumphs in 12.22 is described by Hume as "PYRRHONIAN." Because "nature," as Hume reassures us, "is always too strong for principle," the undermining effects of Pyrrhonism are only temporary. "Though a PYRRHONIAN," he writes,

> may throw himself or others into a momentary amazement and confusion by his profound reasonings; the first and most trivial event in life will put to flight all his doubts and scruples. . . . When he awakes from his dream, he will be the first to join in the laugh against himself, and to confess, that all his objections are mere amusement, and can have no other tendency than to show the whimsical condition of mankind, who must act and reason and believe, though they are not able, by their most diligent enquiry, to satisfy themselves concerning the foundation of these operations, or to remove the objections, which may be raised against them. (EU 12.23/160)

This passage is significantly critical of Pyrrhonism, but it also credits the Pyrrhonian with an insight: an awareness of our "whimsical" (or, as we would now say, absurd) condition. Hume's objection to Pyrrhonism is not that it is false or that the arguments on its behalf are inconclusive, but that it isn't lastingly or helpfully efficacious. Yet he does say that it *shows* something, just as Berkeley shows something when he argues that our belief in body "carries no rational evidence with it, to convince an impartial enquirer" (EU 12.16/155). Hume's treatment of Pyrrhonian skepticism concerning induction is closely modeled on his treatment of Berkeley's skepticism concerning body. As he observes in Part 1 of the section, although Berkeley's arguments "*produce no conviction*," they also "*admit of no answer*" (EU 12.15/154–5). The same holds for the arguments of the Pyrrhonian. Those arguments may be inefficacious in the long run, since they can't long oppose the force of nature, but, from the viewpoint of a diligent rational inquirer, they are perfectly sound. If they were not, they would not reveal our whimsical condition.

Pyrrhonism, it turns out, does have lasting benefits, even according to Hume. One of them is "the limitation of our enquiries to such subjects as are best adapted to the narrow capacity of human understanding" (EU 12.25/162). "To bring us so salutary a determination," he writes, "nothing can be more serviceable, than to be once thoroughly convinced of the force of the PYRRHONIAN doubt, and of the impossibility, that any thing, but the strong power of natural instinct, could free us from it" (EU 12.25/162). If nothing but natural instinct can free us from it, then we can't be freed by intellectual means: by the discovery that the connecting proposition can be justified by something other than reason or by the discovery that we can be justified in forming expectations even if the connecting proposition can't be justified. Either discovery would be an intellectual remedy for skepticism, rather than a brutely causal one, and according to Hume, no such remedy is available. Implicit in this verdict is the following extension of the six-step argument on p. 216 above:

7. The connecting proposition can only be justified by reason.
8. The connecting proposition cannot be justified (from (6) and (7)).
9. We are justified in forming inductive expectations only if our belief in the connecting proposition can be justified.
10. We are not justified in forming inductive expectations (from (8) and (9)).

I conclude that for Hume, reason is more than an indifferent engine of inference. It has standards of performance built into it. These standards aren't always met, as Hume acknowledges in several places (e.g., at EU 5.22/159), but reason aims to meet them, and, in developing the arguments of *Enquiry* 4, Hume assumes that its aim is fulfilled. This is why he never suggests that reason might defend the connecting proposition in a way that violates those standards—for example, by producing an invalid demonstration. When reason is running as it should, it does more than argue validly. It accepts the deliverances of sense, the records of memory, and our immediate insights into relations of ideas. It is an inferential faculty, but an inferential faculty with a conscience, scrupulous about its inputs as well as its internal operations. (I do not mean to suggest that reason can't argue hypothetically from premises it takes to be unjustified or false. But reason won't give the resulting the conclusions the same unconditional approval it gives to others.) I think it's hard to deny that the author of *Enquiry* 4 accepts reason's standards at least to this extent: he takes it for granted that if reason proves to be the cause of our expectations, we will, owing to the authority of reason's internalized standards, be justified in forming them.

Whether he also believes that we will not be justified in forming them if reason proves not to be their cause is, I grant, a more delicate question, if only because (7) through (10), unlike (1) through (6), make no explicit appearance in Hume's writings. But the considered skeptical sentiments Hume expresses in section 12 make it reasonable to impute (10) to him, along with the extra steps he needs to take to get there.

IV.6 A Second Argument for Inductive Skepticism

The skeptical argument I have just set out is very well-known. Whether or not Hume accepted it, the argument entered the history of philosophy through the *Treatise* and the *Enquiry*, or through the response that readers made to them. I believe the *Treatise* contains a second argument for inductive skepticism. It, too, is well-known, but it is not well-known as an argument for inductive skepticism. This is partly because it can appear to be an undetachable element in an argument that addresses only demonstrative reasoning.[17] But this is not how Hume intended it, as I will now try to show.

The argument, which is presented in *Treatise* 1.4.1, has two parts. In each, Hume considers reason "a kind of cause, of which truth"—that is, true belief—"is the natural effect" (T 1.4.1.1/180). According to the first part, now widely known as the *degeneration argument*, the knowledge produced by demonstration "degenerates into probability" (T 1.4.1.1/180). The basic idea is that although the rules of demonstration are, considered in themselves, "certain and infallible," we sometimes misapply them. However certain they may be in the abstract, in practice we are "very apt to depart from them, and fall into error" (T 1.4.1.1/140). In view of my track record as a demonstrator, if I prove (or *think* I prove) a new theorem, the prudent course would not be to declare it certain, but to assign it some degree of probability.

The second part of the argument is known as the *diminution argument*. Its conclusion is that under the kind of continued inspection mandated by "the rules of logic" (T 1.4.1.6/183), probability eventually vanishes. The diminution argument is more complex than the degeneration argument and its interpretation more controversial, but the animating idea is roughly this. Suppose I've proven a new theorem, after taking the degeneration argument to heart. Based on my judgment that I'm a reliable (although imperfect) instrument for detecting soundness in a demonstration, I cautiously assign it a high degree of probability. The rules of logic now require me to step back and ask how reliable I am as a judge of my reliability as a soundness-detector. I see that my track record in similar cases hasn't been perfect; I've sometimes made more favorable judgments than I should have. In view of this "new uncertainty," as Hume calls it (T 1.4.1.6/182), it seems that I should lower the probability I originally assigned to my theorem. I comply, but the rules of logic aren't finished with me. They advise me to step back once again. I must ask how reliable I am in judging how reliable I am as a soundness-detector. Here, again, I seem "oblig'd," as Hume explains, "to add a new doubt" and to lower my assignment yet again. But after I make this latest adjustment, the rules of logic are still not completely satisfied. They ask me how reliable I am in judging how reliable I am in judging how reliable I am as a soundness-detector. By this time (if not before) the mind boggles, as Hume himself emphasizes (T 1.4.1.10/185). Yet the rules of logic grind on. I now realize that they will confront me with an infinite series of questions. I may have trouble separating the particular content of each new question from its predecessor in the series, but I see clearly enough now how the questions are formed, and I understand that the answer to each will exert some downward pressure on the probability of my theorem—so much so that "at last," as Hume explains, "there [will] remain nothing of the original probability, however great we may suppose it to have been, and however small the diminution by every new uncertainty" (T 1.4.1.6/182).

Hume's argument, in both its parts, is open to many objections that we cannot follow up here.[18] My present intention is to make two interpretive points: that Hume intends the diminution argument to apply to all probabilities (and therefore to all inductive expectations), and that he takes its conclusion to be radically skeptical. If I'm right, it follows that the diminution argument, like the argument of *Enquiry* 4, is an argument for radical inductive skepticism.

My first point is relatively easy to establish. When I stated the diminution argument, I used a theorem—a former certainty, now exposed as a probability—as my example. The structure of 1.4.1, in which the diminution argument is reached through the degeneration argument, makes this a natural choice. But 1.4.1 makes it clear that the diminution argument applies to probabilities *as such* and not only to former or "degenerated" certainties. There is good evidence for this in the very title of 1.4.1, "Of Scepticism with Regard to Reason." Hume recognizes two kinds of reasoning, demonstrative and probable, which means that if 1.4.1 is to be true to its title, each kind should be examined there. (In *Enquiry* 12, Part 2, whose topic is also skepticism concerning reason [see 12.17], each kind is given due consideration.) There is even more compelling evidence in the way Hume shifts from the first part of his argument to the second. "Since therefore all knowledge resolves itself into probability, and becomes at last of the same nature with that evidence, which we employ in common life," he writes, "we must now examine this latter *species* of reasoning, and see on what foundation it stands" (T 1.4.1.4/181; my emphasis). In proposing to examine the *species*, he's proposing to examine probable reasoning *in its fullness*, and his expression of interest in its "foundation" is meant to recall the foundational study of induction he has so far undertaken. *Treatise* 1.4.1 is thereby presented as an extension or continuation of the general inductive logic whose construction commenced in Part 3.

But (turning now to my second point) is the diminution argument radically skeptical? Many recent commentators have argued forcefully that it is not; this is a large issue I can only touch on here.[19] Hume does say that his main purpose in offering the diminution argument is to confirm a cognitive-scientific discovery already defended in Part 3, that belief is the work of "the sensitive part of our nature" (T 1.4.1.8/184). But his dedication to this conclusion doesn't mean that the argument of 1.4.1 cannot also be radically skeptical, and, in the final paragraph of Section 1.4.2 ("Of Scepticism Concerning the Senses"), Hume draws a common skeptical lesson from both of them. So far as I can see, this lesson is neither withdrawn nor moderated later in Book 1:

This sceptical doubt, both with respect to reason and the senses, is a malady, which can never be radically cur'd, but must return upon us every moment, however we may chace it away, and sometimes may seem entirely free from it. 'Tis impossible upon any system to defend either our understanding or senses, but we must expose them farther when we endeavour to justify them in that manner. As the sceptical doubt arises naturally from a profound and intense reflection on those subjects, it always encreases, the farther we carry our reflections, whether in opposition or conformity to it. Carelessness and in-attention alone can afford us any remedy. (T 1.4.2.57/218)

Could it be Hume's view that reason and the senses *needn't* be defended? That's certainly possible, but it seems to me to be at odds with the urgent language of the passage, and with Hume's insistence that carelessness and inattention are our *only* remedies. (Note that neither is a *permanent* remedy. As Hume says, the skeptical malady can never be "radically cur'd"—cured, that is, at its root. The relief they offer, no matter how long-lasting and how much in accordance with our instincts, is only symptomatic.) That a defense is not required would be an *insight*, and there is no hint in the passage that such a curing insight is to come.

The diminution argument is not repeated in the *Enquiry*, and this may help to explain a difference between that work and the *Treatise*. As several commentators have noted, radical skepticism hardly rears its head in Part 3 of Book 1; it is present in Book 1, if present at all, only in Part 4.[20] It's no accident that in presenting the first argument for inductive skepticism, I relied so heavily on the *Enquiry*. In the *Treatise*, the argument of 1.3.6 is never used to serve radically skeptical ends, not even in 1.4. Is this because the author of the *Treatise* was unprepared to draw radically skeptical conclusions from it? I do not think we have to say so. Because the author of the *Treatise* had a second skeptical argument at his disposal, he had no need to give the argument of 1.3.6 a skeptical turn. He could devote Part 3 to his constructive logic and save his skepticism for Part 4.[21] In the *Enquiry*, where the argument of 1.4.1 was no longer available, the argument of 1.3.6 became a vehicle for radical skepticism, but Hume may have been aware of its skeptical potential long before that.

V REVELATIONS

In conclusion, I turn to the final lessons of Hume's logic. The first is that we are not as thoroughly rational as the philosophical tradition suggests we are. It would be misleading to define us as "rational animals," as Plato, for example, was rumored to have done. Like the oxen of old New England, who were yoked together during the work week and then spent their Sundays resting and grazing side by side, we are, at bottom, creatures of custom or habit. Our inductive expectations do not rest on rational insight, but on a natural instinct that we share with other animals. Earlier philosophers, in Hume's view, overestimated reason's power in two ways. Some of them, the dogmatists, thought that reason could build a foundation beneath our most basic beliefs. They were mistaken; any such foundation is beyond reason's powers. Others, the traditional skeptics, thought that this discovery would somehow lead us to abandon our beliefs. They, too, were mistaken, because no philosophical discovery, even one whose supporting arguments are unanswerable, can suppress our belief-forming tendencies.[22]

The second revelation, one we've already touched on, is an insight into our absurd or whimsical condition. Unlike the plow-pulling yoke-fellows, we seek reasons for our beliefs. When we fail to find them—or, even more discouragingly, when we come up with unanswerable arguments that they will never be found—we may suffer "momentary amazement and irresolution and confusion" (EU 4.15/32), but we end up believing no less firmly than we did before. We suffer, as believers, from a kind of double-consciousness. We pride ourselves on having reasons but when we cast about for reasons for our reasons, we come up empty-handed, and yet our pride (in the long run, at least) continues unabated. In spite of the skeptic's transiently disabling arguments, we continue, as Hume says, to "act and reason and believe" (EU 12.23/160), but this actually understates the nature of our commitment. We take ourselves to be *justified* in acting, reasoning, and believing as we do, and, according to the constructive part of Hume's normative logic, in this we are very often right. Yet, according to the destructive part of that logic, in fact, we are always in the wrong. Not all of us are sensible of the collision between our pretensions and our actual achievements; perhaps what I've called double-consciousness is fully present only in those of us who are. But Hume wants it to be present in all of us, or at least in all of us who read his books. Its presence in a wide audience, polite as well as scholarly, is what the *Enquiry* tries to bring about.

What I've called double-consciousness may seem to be a soothing label for inconsistency. How can Hume insist on inductive discrimination—on ranking inductive arguments as better or worse and inductive methods as laudable or lamentable—if all of them rest on the same unjustifiable assumption? Won't all arguments and methods stand equally condemned? How can a normative logic be constructive if it is also skeptical? In Hume's *Dialogues Concerning Natural Religion*, the character Cleanthes, who is following the trail of many of these questions, describes the skeptic's doubts as "undistinguished" or undiscriminating (1.16). How, he wonders, can the Pyrrhonian's doubts be discriminating? Mustn't they apply across the board?

Here, I can do no more than briefly indicate how these understandable worries might be dealt with. It may be that in his philosophical writings, Hume occupies two different points of view: the viewpoint of common life and the viewpoint of foundational philosophy. From the viewpoint of common life, where the deliverances of human nature are unquestioningly accepted, arguments and methods can be rated as better or worse. "Common life" is Hume's own label; for him, it embraces not only what we would call common sense, but also large stretches of what he calls philosophy. We would call these stretches "science"; according to Hume, their "decisions" or conclusions are "nothing but the reflections of common life, methodized and corrected" (EU 12.25/162).[23] So understood, common life includes the natural philosophy of Newton and the descriptive and explanatory portions of Hume's logic. "Foundational philosophy" is not Hume's label but my own; it marks out a viewpoint that we can only fleetingly inhabit. From the viewpoint of foundational philosophy, Pyrrhonian arguments can persuade us that we're wrong to trust in nature's uniformity. But the mandates of human nature will insulate common life from our suspicions. From the security of the common life viewpoint, we can be inductively discriminating. We can prefer Newton's physics to Descartes's, Hume's retelling of "The Maid of Orleans" to (say) Christina de Pizan's, and the wariness of a modern historian to the credulousness of an ancient one. When we occupy that viewpoint, the lessons of skepticism need not be entirely forgotten, as Philo observes in replying to Cleanthes (D 1.8). Enduring memories of our brush with Pyrrhonism may inspire lasting "modesty and reserve" in us and forever discourage us from cosmic inquiries, just as Hume says (EU 12.24–5/161–2). But our basic commitment to induction will remain intact—so long, that is, as the arguments of the Pyrrhonian are not actually relived, but remembered only in the abstract, as most of us remember the demonstrations of geometry.

It's fair to wonder, though, whether this reconciliation of viewpoints goes as far as it should. We might ask, for example, how each viewpoint acquires its authority. Can Hume explain how two viewpoints acquire the authority to pronounce, in apparently incompatible ways, on the justification of belief?

It isn't hard to imagine a Humean account of the authority of the viewpoint of common life. Our belief in nature's uniformity, and the intellectual virtues we exhibit when we adhere to Hume's rules of reasoning, are both very useful. It would be natural for us to approve of them, as we approve of the moral virtues of justice and benevolence.[24] But the authority of the foundational viewpoint is more obscure. Hume says that skepticism mortifies every passion except the love of truth (EU 5.1/41). He adds that the love of truth is a passion that "never is, nor can be carried to too high a degree." Can the authority of foundational philosophy be derived from the influence of this passion? If the love of truth is a love of justification, or a disdain for *un*justification, the answer may be yes.[25] But even then we may wonder why our love of justification can't be completely fulfilled by justifications that terminate in beliefs that human nature renders unavoidable. This is a kind of "relative" justification: justification relative to commitments that we cannot (or cannot for long) suspend. Why shouldn't this be enough for us? At several points in the *Treatise*, Hume appeals to a principle that may provide an answer. "The imagination," he writes, "when set into any train of thinking, is apt to continue, even when its object fails it, and like a galley put in motion by the oars, carries on its course without any new impulse" (T 1.4.2.22/198). In *Treatise* 1.2.4, Hume uses the principle to explain how we arrive at a standard of perfect or absolute equality, given only the roughly equal items that experience puts before us. Perhaps the same principle can be used to explain how, having arrived at a notion of relative justification, we arrive at a notion of justification that is absolute—a notion that will borrow its lustre from the already established lustre of the other.

This leaves us, however, with still another difficulty, because it isn't easy to see how the viewpoint of foundational philosophy can retain its authority once it's been explained in such a manner. This is because the explanation seems to debunk foundational philosophy or disenchant it: it portrays foundational philosophy as deriving its authority from the authority of common life, thereby compromising its ability to enter a disapproving verdict on common life; and, in accounting for that authority, it appeals to a "trivial" imaginative tendency of which foundational philosophy cannot itself approve.

"Human beliefs," wrote George Eliot, "like all other natural growths, elude the barriers of system."[26] It's not unreasonable to suppose that Hume, as a promoter of the science of human nature, must disagree, but I'm far from sure that this is true. The science of human nature would be worth pursuing even if there turn out to be beliefs—or doubts—that it cannot explain. If Hume, as I've contended, is a radical skeptic, he has, it seems to me, at least two choices. He can hope for a naturalistic explanation of the authority of radical skepticism that won't be debunking, or he can say that, even though the authority of skepticism can't be naturalistically explained, its authority is nonetheless genuine.[27] To make the second choice is to confess to a lingering non-naturalism, or to side with Eliot in thinking that nature outruns our ability to explain it systematically. A radical skeptic who is naturalistically inclined may have other choices, but I can sympathize with any reader who thinks that if these two turn out to be the only ones, we should reconsider whether Hume's inductive skepticism can be as radical as I've suggested here.[28]

ABBREVIATIONS OF WORKS CITED

D   Dialogues Concerning Natural Religion. In D. Coleman, ed. Dialogues Concerning Natural Religion and Other Writings. Cambridge: Cambridge University Press, 2007.

ESY   Essays: Moral, Political, and Literary. Revised edition by E. F. Miller. Indianapolis: Liberty Classics, 1985.

EU   An Enquiry Concerning Human Understanding. Edited by T. L. Beauchamp. Oxford: Clarendon, 2000.

HE   The History of England, 6 Vols. Foreword by W. B. Todd. Indianapolis: Liberty Classics, 1983.

T   A Treatise of Human Nature. Edited by D. F. Norton and M. J. Norton. Oxford: Clarendon, 2007.

NOTES

1. On Locke as a logician see Buickerood (1985) and Winkler (2003).
2. "[T]he reflections we can make on our ideas are perhaps the most important part of logic, since they are the foundation of everything else" (Arnauld and Nicole, 1996: 25).
3. For Locke's views on reasoning and their influence on Hume, see Owen (1999). For further discussion of Hume's logic in the Treatise see Boehm (2013).
4. Molyneux (1692), fourth unnumbered page in the dedicatory letter to the Royal Society.
5. Locke (1979: 715).

6. Leibniz (1985), Section 31.

7. Butler (1736: iv).

8. See Loeb (2006).

9. Newton (1999: 795), Book 3, rule 2.

10. Why, then, does Hume say that skeptics take pleasure in observing "that the following of general rules is a very *un*philosophical species of probability; and yet 'tis only by following them that we can correct this, and all other unphilosophcical probabilities" (T 1.3.13.12/150; my emphasis)? I'm not sure I can say, but in the *Enquiry*, where some of Hume's rules are used to explain "how it happens, that men so much surpass animals in reasoning, and one man so much surpasses another" (EU 9.5/106), they are cast in a more optimistic light.

11. Montaigne (1993: 1068).

12. Bloch (1953: 82).

13. Garrett (1997: 92); for the background see pp. 84–85 and 91–94. See also Cohon (2008: 65–73).

14. Fogelin (1985: 5).

15. For a powerfully stated alternative to the interpretation offered here, see Garrett (1997: 76–95 and 205–241) and Garrett (2004).

16. For a fuller and exceptionally revealing reconstruction of the argument of *Enquiry* 4, see Millican (2002).

17. Michael Williams (2008: 90) writes that in *Treatise* 1.4.1, "the topic is demonstrative reasoning." For a corrective see Owen (1999: 183–184) and Fogelin (2009: 40).

18. See Hacking (1978), Fogelin (1985: 13–24), and Fogelin (2009: 44–48).

19. For nonskeptical readings, see Garrett (1997: 22–28), Owen (1999: 175–196), and Allison (2008). For a skeptical reading, see Meeker (2000: 221–238); see also Meeker (2013), chapter 3.

20. See Broughton (1983: 3–18), Garrett (1997: 91–95), and Loeb (2002: 38–59).

21. For a highly suggestive account of the relationship between Parts 3 and 4, see Loeb (2002), especially pp. 1–37 and 177–252.

22. For further development of these themes, see Popkin (1951: 385–407).

23. To methodize a reflection is to reduce it to general principles. See "Of the Standard of Taste" (ESY 236).

24. For details, see Winkler (1999: 183–212).

25. In Hume's view, it may be neither; see *Treatise* 2.3.10.

26. *Silas Marner* (1861), chapter 17, p. 313.

27. This is one apparent sign of tension between Hume's skepticism and his naturalism. For further discussion of the tension, see Broughton (2008: 425–440), Falkenstein (1997: 29–72), Garrett (2004), Russell (2008: 3–11, 266–278), Stroud (2011: 144–166), and Williams (2008: 80–107).

28. I'm grateful to Jani Hakkarainen and Paul Russell for helpful comments on a draft of this chapter.

BIBLIOGRAPHY

Allison, Henry E. (2008). *Custom and Reason in Hume*. Oxford: Clarendon Press.

Arnauld, Antione, and Pierre Nicole. (1996). *Logic or the Art of Thinking*, translated by Jill Vance Buroker. Cambridge: Cambridge University Press.

Bloch, Marc. (1953). *The Historian's Craft*. New York: Vintage.

Boehm, Miren. (2013). "Hume's Foundational Project in the *Treatise*." *European Journal of Philosophy*. http://dx.doi.org/10.1111/ejop.12056.

Broughton, Jane. (1983). "Hume's Skepticism about Causal Inferences." *Pacific Philosophical Quarterly* 64, 3–18.

Broughton, Jane. (2008). "Hume's Naturalism and His Skepticism," in Elizabeth A. Radcliffe, ed., *A Companion to Hume*. Oxford: Blackwell, 425–440.

Buickerood, James G. (1985). "The Natural History of Logic: Locke and the Rise of Facultative Logic in the Eighteenth Century." *History and Philosophy of Logic* 6, 157–190.

Butler, Joseph. (1736). *The Analogy of Religion*. London: Knapton.

Cohon, Rachel. (2008). *Hume's Morality*. Oxford: Oxford University Press.

Eliot, George. (1861). *Silas Marner*. Edinburgh and London: Blackwood and Sons.

Falkenstein, Lorne. (1997). "Naturalism, Normativity, and Scepticism in Hume's Account of Belief." *Hume Studies* 23, 29–72.

Fogelin, Robert J. (1985). *Hume's Skepticism in the* Treatise of Human Nature. London: Routledge.

Fogelin, Robert J. (2009). *Hume's Skeptical Crisis: A Textual Study*. Oxford: Oxford University Press.

Garrett, Don. (1997). *Cognition and Commitment in Hume's Philosophy*. New York: Oxford University Press, 1997.

Garrett, Don. (2004). "'A Small Tincture of Pyrrhonism': Skepticism and Naturalism in Hume's Science of Man," in Walter Sinnott-Armstrong, ed., *Pyrrhonian Skepticism*. Oxford: Oxford University Press, 68–98.

Hacking, Ian. (1978). "Hume's Species of Probability." *Philosophical Studies* 33, 21–37.

Leibniz, Gottfried Wilhelm. (1985). *Theodicy*, translated by E. M. Huggard. LaSalle, IL: Open Court.

Locke, John. (1979). *The Correspondence of John Locke*, E. S. DeBeer, ed., volume 4. Oxford: Clarendon Press.

Loeb, Louis E. (2002). *Stability and Justification in Hume's* Treatise. Oxford: Clarendon Press.

Loeb, Louis E. (2006). "Psychology, Epistemology, and Skepticism in Hume's Argument About Induction." *Synthese* 152, 321–338.

Meeker, Kevin. (2000). "Hume's Iterative Probability Argument: A Pernicious Reductio." *Journal of the History of Philosophy* 38, 221–238.

Meeker, Kevin. (2013). *Hume's Radical Skepticism and the Fate of Naturalized Epistemology*. Basingstoke, Hampshire: Palgrave Macmillan.

Millican, Peter. (2002). "Hume's Sceptical Doubts Concerning Induction," in Peter Millican, ed., *Reading Hume on Human Understanding*. Oxford: Clarendon Press, 107–173.

Montaigne, Michel de (1993). *The Complete Essays*, translated by M. A. Screech. London: Penguin.

Molyneux, William. (1692). *Dioptrica Nova*. London: Benjamin Tooke.

Newton, Isaac. (1999). *The Principia: Mathematical Principles of Natural Philosophy*, translated by I. Bernard Cohen and Anne Whitman. Berkeley: University of California Press.

Owen, David. (1999). *Hume's Reason*. Oxford: Oxford University Press.

Popkin, Richard H. (1951). "David Hume: His Pyrrhonism and His Critique of Pyrrhonism." *Philosophical Quarterly* 1, 385–407.

Russell, Paul. (2008). *The Riddle of Hume's* Treatise: *Skepticism, Naturalism, and Irreligion*. New York: Oxford University Press.

Stroud, Barry. (2011). "Hume's Scepticism: Natural Instincts and Philosophical Reflection," in his *Philosophers Past and Present*. Oxford: Clarendon Press, 144–166.

Williams, Michael. (2008). "Hume's Skepticism," in John Greco, ed., *The Oxford Handbook of Skepticism*. Oxford: Oxford University Press, 80–107.

Winkler, Kenneth P. (1999). "Hume's Inductive Skepticism," in Margaret Atherton, ed., *The Empiricists*. Lanham, MD: Rowman and Littlefield, 183-212.

Winkler, Kenneth P. (2003). "Lockean Logic," in Peter Anstey, ed., *The Philosophy of John Locke: New Perspectives*. London: Routledge, 154–178.

CHAPTER 12

....

HUME AND THE PROBLEM
OF CAUSATION

....

HELEN BEEBEE

IT is in good part due to Hume that causation has been regarded as problematic by analytic philosophers in the past hundred years or so. Hume's own major problem when it comes to causation is that of understanding the idea of "necessary connection"—a crucial component of the idea of causation, he thinks, but one whose impression-source he needs to spend a large part of Book 1 of the *Treatise* attempting to locate. Historically, the majority of commentators have taken at least part of Hume's eventual conclusion to be that an objective, mind-independent, necessary connection between causes and effects is unintelligible. Because the impression-source of the idea of necessary connection turns out to be our own mental activity and not sensation, that idea cannot latch on to any mind-independent feature of reality: necessity turns out to be a product of our own minds. So, whatever we might *think* we are doing when we engage in causal talk and thought, we are not referring to mind-independent necessity.

On the other hand, the objective features that Hume *does* take our causal thought and talk to imply—namely, contiguity, temporal priority, and constant conjunction—are generally agreed to be insufficient to ground the truth of causal claims. Writing exactly a hundred years ago, Bertrand Russell (1912–13) argues that Hume's "constant conjunctions" or exceptionless regularities are, in fact, rarely to be found in nature, and there are standard problems for a "naïve regularity theory" of the kind Hume is sometimes thought to be proposing, even setting aside Russell's complaint. In particular, there is the problem of accidental regularities (where As are constantly conjoined with Bs but As do not cause Bs) and the problem of the common cause (where, again, As are constantly conjoined with Bs, but both are effects of a common cause, so that, again, As do not cause Bs). Coming at the problem from a different angle, Elizabeth Anscombe (1971) famously argues that the conceptual connection between causation and regularity posited by Hume does not, in fact, exist and, contra Hume, that we do have a sensory impression of the relation between causes and effects after all. Other philosophers have argued that causation is really not as indispensable a concept as Hume thought, following Russell's claim that its "complete extrusion from the philosophical vocabulary [is] desirable" (1912–13: 1). Russell's claim here is motivated by the claim that "the word 'cause' is . . . inextricably bound up with misleading associations" (ibid.), chief among these being the associations with necessity and regularity that Hume identifies.

Most recent philosophical positions on the nature of causation can be seen as attempts to maintain the spirit of, or else take issue with, what Hume is alleged to have thought, with "Humean" theorists offering refinements of the idea that causation "in the objects" is, at bottom, merely a matter of constant conjunction or regularity (e.g., counterfactual and probabilistic theories) and "anti-Humean" theorists claiming that, ontologically speaking, there must be more to causation than mere regularity (e.g., necessitarian views and powers-based accounts). In fact, however, Hume's words have proved to be susceptible to differing interpretations that fall on both sides of the "Humean" and "anti-Humean" divide: some commentators take Hume to endorse the claim that there is more to causation "in the objects" than regularity. Indeed, some commentators take Hume to hold that causation is a matter of real, fully mind-independent, necessary connections.

The interpretative problems encountered when we try to make sense of what Hume says about causation are the main focus of this chapter. I begin in Section I by briefly summarizing Hume's journey, as it plays out in the *Treatise*, toward the location of the impression-source of the idea of necessary connection. In Section II, I begin discussion of the interpretative divide just mentioned, which turns in large part on whether we hold Hume to a "meaning-empiricist" position that appears to be entailed by his theory of ideas and in particular by the "Copy Principle" (see, e.g., Winkler 2000, Section I, and Millican, this volume, Section III). In Section II, I focus on the meaning-empiricist interpretative options, which have in common the denial that the idea of causation can succeed in referring to any mind-independent feature of reality beyond contiguity, priority, and constant conjunction. (Hume thus interpreted is sometimes referred to as "Old Hume.") In Section III, I focus on versions of the "skeptical realist" interpretation ("New Hume"), which takes Hume to affirm rather than deny that claim. In Section IV, I briefly discuss Hume's famous two definitions of causation, and, in Section V, I say something about the seemingly intractable nature of the interpretative dispute surrounding Hume's views on causation.

I THE GENESIS OF THE IDEA OF CAUSATION

Early on in the *Treatise*, Hume notes that it is "only *causation*, which produces such a connexion, as to give us assurance from the existence or action of one object, that 'twas followed or preceded by any other existence or action" (T 1.3.2.2/73–4). In other words, if our reasoning concerning "matters of fact"—what is going on out there in the world—is to have any epistemic legitimacy, it must be *causal* reasoning: reasoning from causes to effects or vice versa. It is the causal relation between eating bread and nourishment that assures me that my toast will nourish rather than poison me, and it is the causal relation between a key being turned in the lock and a certain kind of sound—which I can now hear—that assures me that my front door has just been opened.

We therefore need to investigate our idea of causation, and—because Hume subscribes to the "Copy Principle," according to which all our ideas are copies of impressions—our means for doing so is to uncover the impression from which it arises. He quickly concludes that contiguity (causes and effects are right next to each other in space and time) and priority (causes precede their effects) are part of our idea of causation, the impression-sources of these ideas having already been identified in T 1.2. But contiguity and priority cannot be the whole story: "An object may be contiguous and prior to another, without being consider'd as its cause. There is a NECESSARY CONNEXION to be taken into consideration; and that relation is of much greater importance" (T 1.3.2.11/77). Finding no impression of necessary connection when inspecting any individual cause–effect pair, however—the place where one would expect to find it—he proceeds to "beat about all the neighbouring fields" (T 1.3.2.13/78) in the hope that the searched-for impression will be found in an unexpected location, which indeed it is—eventually.

There now follows Hume's famous discussion of inductive or causal reasoning. We've already seen that beliefs about matters of fact that are not currently present to the memory or senses arise as a result of reasoning from causes to effects (or vice versa). Hume argues that that inference cannot be a matter of "demonstration" or a priori inference more generally: just by inspecting a given event in isolation, we cannot draw any conclusions about what will happen next. ("There is no object, which implies the existence of any other if we consider these objects in themselves"; T 1.3.6.1/86.) It is only once we have past experience of As being followed by Bs—that is, once we have experience of a constant conjunction of As and Bs—that we are able to infer that a B will follow on observing an A; and this experienced constant conjunction together with the occurrence of an A still fails to imply the existence of a B. Hume concludes that the inference from cause to effect is a matter of brute psychological association or, as he puts it in the *Enquiry*, "CUSTOM or HABIT" (EU 5.1.5/43): once As and Bs are constantly conjoined in our experience, when confronted with an A, we come to expect a B in just the same way as a dog comes to expect food on hearing the familiar sound of its bowl clanking on the kitchen floor.

How does all this aid our grip on the *idea* of causation, as opposed to the *inference* from causes to effects? Well, Hume's eventual conclusion in the famously contested section "Of the Idea of Necessary Connexion" (T 1.3.14; EU 7) is that it is the inference itself that supplies the impression-source. Hume here repeats his earlier claim that we can discern no necessary connections between objects considered in isolation: I cannot "go any farther" than discerning contiguity and precedence, "nor is it possible for me to discover any third relation betwixt these objects" (T 1.3.14.1/155). However, "where I find like objects always existing in like relations of contiguity and succession," this repetition "produces a new impression, and by that means the idea [of necessary connection]" (ibid.): "I find, that upon the appearance of one of the objects, the mind is *determin'd* by custom to consider its usual attendant, and to consider it in a stronger light upon account of it relation to the first object. 'Tis this impression, then, or *determination*, which affords me the idea of necessity" (T 1.3.14.1/156).

The shape of Hume's argument here is clear enough: there is no impression of necessary connection when we consider two "objects" or events *a* and *b* in isolation, but there *is* such an impression when we consider *a* and *b* *and* have previously observed As and Bs to be constantly conjoined. Hence, the impression cannot be an impression of sensation: repeated observation cannot plausibly be thought to enable us to discern some relation between *a* and *b* that was previously present but somehow invisible to us when we observed As being followed by Bs. The only thing that has changed, and so might serve as the cause of the new impression, is a change *in us*; namely, the acquisition of the expectation of a *B* on observing an *A*. Hence that change—the habitual association of As and Bs—must be responsible for the impression of necessary connection.

Several issues remain rather opaque, however. In particular, what are Hume's grounds for asserting that we "cannot discern any third relation" on first observing our *A*–*B* pair? And if the impression of necessary connection is an impression of reflection—a result of the operation of an internal psychological mechanism, rather than our experience of the external world—how does this affect our apparent ability to deploy the *idea* of necessary connection in our causal talk and thought *as though* we are speaking about the external world and not about our own minds?

I leave the latter question to the next section and here focus on the first, concerning Hume's grounds for asserting that we "cannot discern any third relation" on first observing our *A*–*B* pair. At first sight—and indeed this is how he initially presents the matter in the *Treatise*—he appears simply to be making a brute appeal to phenomenology: "When I cast my eye on the *known qualities* of objects, I immediately discover that the relation of cause and effect depends not in the least on *them*. When I consider their *relations*, I can find none but those of contiguity and succession" (T 1.3.2.12/77). Later, in T 1.3.14, however, it becomes clear that his grounds are not merely phenomenological:

> Now nothing is more evident, than that the human mind cannot form such an idea of two objects, as to conceive any connexion betwixt them, or comprehend distinctly that power or efficacy, by which they are united. Such a connexion wou'd amount to a demonstration, and wou'd imply the absolute impossibility for the one object not to follow, or to be conceiv'd not to follow upon the other: Which kind of connexion has already been rejected in all cases. (T 1.3.14.13/161–2)

Hume's point is made more succinctly right at the outset of his argument in the corresponding section of the first *Enquiry*: "From the first appearance of an object, we never can conjecture what effect will result from it. But were the power or energy of any cause discoverable by the mind, we could foresee the effect, even without experience; and might, at first, pronounce with certainty concerning it, by the mere dint of thought and reasoning" (EU 7.7/63).

It seems, then, that Hume runs together two distinct claims. One is the claim that on first observing a given cause–effect pair we have no impression of any connection whatsoever between them. As he puts it in the *Enquiry*: "The first time a man saw the communication of motion by impulse, as by the shock of two billiard balls, he could not pronounce that the one event was *connected*; but only that it was *conjoined* with the other" (EU 7.28/75). This claim is a straightforward phenomenological claim for which Hume offers no further justification. The second is the weaker claim that on first observing our cause–effect pair we have no impression of a *specific* kind of connection between the two—or, perhaps more perspicuously, no impression of any *feature of the cause* that would enable us to infer with certainty that the effect will follow. (Galen Strawson [1989: ch. 11] calls this feature the "a priori inference-licensing property," or "AP property" for short.) And Hume *does* offer justification for *this* claim, namely, the fact that we can in fact draw no such inference on first observing the cause.

This is an important distinction because, as Mackie (1974: 12–13) notes, we really can distinguish between two different species of possible necessary connection here: what he calls "necessity$_1$," and "necessity$_2$," respectively. (This terminology may not be the most apt, however, since it is unclear why we are forced to think of *all* possible "ties" between causes and effects as kinds of *necessary* connection. Thus, for example, counterfactual analyses of causation characterize causes as necessary rather than sufficient conditions of their effects; such analyses therefore do not require that causes *necessitate* their effects. Perhaps more pertinently, given their overtly anti-Humean agenda, Mumford and Anjum [2011] argue both that causal relations are perceivable [2011: ch. 9], and that causation is not a matter of necessitation [2011: ch. 3].)

Although Hume seems to want to establish the stronger claim (that we have no impression of *any* "tie" on first observing our cause–effect pair) as well as the weaker one (that we have no impression of an AP property), it is clear that his main interest lies in the weaker claim. This is because his main interest in causation is in its connection with inference. Causation, remember, is supposed to be *the* relation by which we (legitimately) form beliefs about what is not immediately present to the senses or memory, and it is doubtful whether a mere observable "tie" between causes and effects would have any connection with our capacity to infer effects from causes. Such a tie between cause and effect would certainly not shed any light on the formation of the expectation of the effect given the impression of the cause because a mere tie could, presumably, only be observed as part of the temporally extended sequence that includes both cause and effects. (I cannot see the dog tied to the lamppost unless I can see both dog and lamppost. I could perhaps see that the dog is tied to *something* if the lamppost were somehow hidden from view and I could only see the dog and the rope; but if my interest was precisely in *what* the dog is tied to, this would not be much help.) Moreover, if we think about extrapolation to other cases, knowing by observation that *this* C caused an E is only going to allow me to infer Es from Cs in other cases if the fact that this C caused an E implies that all other Cs cause Es as well; and this will only be so if the occurrence of a C *guarantees* the occurrence of an E and if, in addition, I can know this to be so on the basis of observing the single case; a weaker connection would not serve to legitimize the inference.

So, although Hume's account provides a positive answer to the question he started with—what is the origin of the idea of necessary connection?—it also establishes an important negative conclusion, namely, that we cannot detect any feature of the cause that would license a priori inference to the existence of the effect. This sets him in direct opposition to the Scholastics, for whom penetration into the essences of objects can be achieved through sensory experience, as well as to the rationalists, for whom the same feat could be achieved through "purely mental scrutiny" (Descartes 1641: 21). Hume takes himself to have shown that neither purely mental scrutiny of the *idea* of a particular cause nor the scrutiny of the cause itself, via sensory impressions, will deliver any knowledge of its effects—because, if such knowledge were delivered, so too would be the idea of necessary connection. And no such idea is forthcoming from these sources: "reason alone can never give rise to any original idea" (T 1.3.14.5/157), and nor—as we have seen—can an impression-source for the idea come from sensory experience.

II Hume as a Meaning-Empiricist

Although the story so far is relatively uncontroversial from an interpretative point of view, we are still a long way short of an account of what features we ascribe to the world when we deploy causal talk. We know the circumstances—both internal and external—that give rise to our ability to "call the one object, *Cause*; the other, *Effect*" (EU 7.27/75), namely, the impression of the cause together with repeated past experience of events similar to the cause being immediately followed by events similar to the effect. But what *is* it to "call" one object a cause and another its effect? The major obstacle to answering this question on Hume's behalf is, precisely, the discovery that the source of the idea of necessary connection is an impression arising from an internal, mental operation—"the determination of the mind, to pass from the idea of an object to that of its usual attendant" (T 1.3.14.25/167). For this *seems* to suggest that in talking about causation we are really talking, at least in part, about our own state of mind and not about the world. Indeed, Hume seems to say as much explicitly. Putting words into an imaginary objector's mouth, he says: "What! the efficacy of causes lie in the determination of the mind! . . . Thought may well depend on causes for its operation, but not causes on thought" (T 1.3.14.26/167). He does not attempt to argue that this interpretation of his position is mistaken; instead, he merely notes that "the case here is much the same, as if a blind man shou'd pretend to find a great many absurdities in the supposition, that the colour of scarlet is not the same with the sound of a trumpet, nor light the same with solidity" (T 1.3.14.27/168).

Hume accounts for the predicted unwillingness of his readers to agree with him on this score—their "contrary biass"—as follows:

'Tis a common observation, that the mind has a great propensity to spread itself on external objects, and to conjoin with them any internal impressions, which they occasion, and which always make their appearance at the same time that these objects discover themselves to the senses. Thus as certain sounds and smells are always found to attend certain visible objects, we naturally imagine a conjunction, even in place, betwixt the objects and qualities, tho' the qualities be of such a nature as to admit of no such conjunction, and really exist no where . . . the same propensity is the reason, why we suppose necessity and power to lie in the objects we consider, not in our mind, that considers them. (T 1.3.14.25/167).

Hume's metaphor of the mind's "propensity to spread itself on external objects" has, as Peter Kail notes (2007: xxiii), spawned a further metaphor—that of *projection*—which looms large in many discussions of Hume's views, not just on causation but also on morality, aesthetics, and (most obviously) secondary qualities.

How might the notion of projection help us to get a handle on Hume's views about causation? Well, in the passage just quoted, projection—the mind's propensity to spread itself—is used to explain an error we are inclined to make: the error of supposing that "necessity and power . . . lie in the objects" and "not in our mind." The most obvious way to understand the nature of this error is as the error of supposing that causes really do have within themselves the AP property: a property such that, were we to be capable of detecting it, would enable us to infer the existence of the effect a priori. And we make the error because we project our own inferential habit—the associative mechanism by which the impression of the cause engenders belief in the effect *in our minds*—onto the cause and effect themselves, so that we conceive (or rather we *think* we conceive) of the cause, just by itself, as the *ground* of the inference to the effect. That is, we conceive (or think we do) of the cause as possessing the AP property when really, given the impression-source of the idea of necessary connection, causes *cannot* "necessitate" their effects in *this* sense because to suppose that they do would be to assume that the idea of necessary connection can latch onto mind-independent necessity—something Hume takes himself to have shown to be impossible, at least for beings like us. We are simply incapable of using the idea of "necessary connection" to refer to such a thing because any such idea would lack the required impression-source.

Is Hume thereby claiming that causation "in the objects"—the world's contribution to the obtaining of causal relations—*could not be* any more than contiguity, priority, and constant conjunction? This is a highly contentious question. Some authors think that he is claiming exactly that and for the reason just given: contiguity, priority, and constant conjunction exhaust the elements of the idea of causation that can refer to mind-independent features of reality, and so the contribution from the world to causation itself—which is, after all, simply whatever it is that our *idea* of causation refers to—can likewise only amount to these three features. This interpretative line holds Hume to a strict meaning-empiricist position, which ties the semantic content of our ideas directly to their impression-sources and so leaves no semantic scope for reference to features of reality that lie beyond our sensory capacities.

I consider some objections to this line of interpretation in the next section, but for now, I briefly rehearse the interpretative options that hold Hume to something like this strict meaning-empiricist line. There are two main lines of thought here. What I have elsewhere called the "traditional" interpretation (Beebee 2006: ch. 5)—largely on the grounds that it is the view most commonly attributed to Hume among philosophers more widely, even if it is less frequently specifically endorsed among Hume scholars—takes Hume to be offering a version of the "regularity theory" of causation (see Psillos 2009): to say that *a* caused *b* is simply to say that As and Bs stand in the relations of contiguity, priority, and constant conjunction (and that *a* and *b* both occur). Versions of this interpretative position are held by, for instance, Mackie (1974), Beauchamp and Rosenberg (1981), Wilson (1986), and Garrett (1997; 2009).

By contrast, the "projectivist" interpretation (Beebee 2006: ch. 6; Coventry 2006), although agreeing with the traditional interpretation that causation "in the objects" is exhausted by contiguity, priority, and constant conjunction, takes Hume's metaphor of the mind's propensity to spread itself on the world not merely to explain an error—that of supposing that causes possess the AP property—but to point toward a positive thesis. When discussing taste, Hume says that taste "has a productive faculty, and gilding and staining all natural objects with the colours, borrowed from internal sentiment, raises in a manner a new creation" (EM App. 1/294). The projectivist interpretation takes Hume to have the same view about our habit of inferring effects from causes: in our causal talk, we judge the world to be a world of necessary connections but not by *representing* it as containing some mind-independent feature; rather, necessary connection is a "new creation" with which we gild or stain. So, the world is, as it were, adequate to our causal talk not by containing genuine necessary connections (indeed, given meaning empiricism, we are not so much as capable of ascribing such features to reality), but by being adequate—via constant conjunction—to the inferential habit that we project onto it.

The central disagreement between these two lines of interpretation, then, is over whether or not Hume takes the idea of necessary connection, which, both sides agree, fails to represent any mind-independent feature of reality, to nevertheless play an essential semantic role in our idea of causation.

II.1 Hume as a Regularity Theorist

Let's start with the traditional interpretation. The major element of disagreement between the different versions thereof concerns the precise role of the idea of necessary connection. Recall that Hume seems to think that this idea is a component of the idea of causation—and, moreover, a component that is distinct from the idea of constant conjunction. How can this claim be squared with the claim that Hume takes causation to be merely a matter of constant conjunction (plus contiguity and priority)? One option (Mackie 1974) is to take Hume to be advocating a revision of the concept of causation:

once we realize how utterly defective the idea of necessary connection is, the idea of causation should be "cleaned up" so that the idea of necessary connection plays no part.[1] A second option (Beauchamp and Rosenberg 1981; Wilson 1986) is to hold that the idea of necessary connection merely plays a role in the assertibility of causal claims and not in their truth conditions. A third option, pursued by Garrett (1997; 2009), is to exploit the thought that the idea of causation is an *abstract* idea; the answer to the question of what role the idea of necessary connection plays in the idea of causation then becomes rather nuanced. I briefly discuss Garrett's view later, but first let's consider some of the textual evidence for and against the traditional interpretation.

The major piece of textual evidence standardly adduced in favor of the traditional interpretation is Hume's famous two definitions of causation, which appear in the *Treatise* as follows:

> We may define a CAUSE to be "An object precedent to and contiguous with another, and where all the objects resembling the former are plac'd in like relations of precedency and contiguity to those objects, that resemble the latter." If this definition be esteem'd defective, because drawn from objects foreign to the cause, we may substitute this other definition in its place, *viz.* "A CAUSE is an object precedent and contiguous to another, and so united with it, that the idea of the one determines the mind to form the idea of the other, and the impression of the one to form a more lively idea of the other." (T 1.3.14.31/170)

The two definitions have spawned a huge amount of interpretative controversy, to which I return in Section IV. For now, however, note that neither definition mentions the idea of necessary connection. Of course, the mental process that gives rise to that idea is mentioned in the second definition, but the idea itself is absent. Moreover, the first definition appears to be a straightforward statement of the regularity theory.

On the negative side, one major alleged source of evidence against the traditional interpretation—and against the projectivist line as well—is Hume's repeated apparent references to secret or unknown powers, forces, or "principles," especially in the first *Enquiry*. Interpreters who cast Hume as a "skeptical realist" take these references to be good evidence that he, in fact, holds that there really is something more to causation "in the objects" than mere regularity, even though that "something more" is something that lies forever beyond our grasp.

I return to this debate in Section III. More important for the purposes of adjudicating between the traditional and projectivist interpretations are Hume's apparent insistence that the idea of necessary connection is a part of the idea of causation and his disinclination to retract that insistence (*pace* Mackie) or to take our causal talk to be irredeemably defective (*pace* Stroud), even once its source in our mental activity has been discovered. After all, his response to "What! the efficacy of causes lie in the determination of the mind!" is not to claim that his view has no such consequence or to agree with his imagined opponent that the idea of causation is indeed, on his own view, absurd; rather, it is to point out that the view attributed to him only seems absurd if we are laboring under the misapprehension that the idea of necessary connection has an external rather than an internal source.

Garrett's position is worth examining in more detail because Garrett attempts to deflect this worry by claiming that there *is* a sense in which the idea of necessary connection can be a "part of" the idea of causation, consistent with causation's being defined in terms that do not appeal to the idea of necessary connection. As I said, Garrett's position takes as its starting point the fact that, for Hume, the idea of causation is an *abstract* idea: an idea capable of representing things that do not perfectly resemble one another. According to Hume, "abstract ideas are really nothing but particular ones, consider'd in a certain light; but being annexed to general terms, they are able to represent a vast variety, and to comprehend objects, which, as they are alike in some particulars, are in others vastly wide of each other" (T 1.2.3.5/34). Garrett explains this as follows:

> Upon noticing a resemblance among objects, Hume claims, we apply a single term to them all, notwithstanding their differences. The term is directly associated with the determinate idea of a particular instance. This determinate idea nevertheless achieves a general *signification*—and hence serves *as* an abstract idea—because the term also revives the "custom" or disposition to call up ideas of other particular instances. (1997: 103)

Garrett calls the set of particular instances to which the relevant term refers its "revival set" (1997: 103).

The contrast here is with Locke, for whom abstract ideas are formed, as the name suggests, by a process of abstraction: we form a single abstract idea of *cat*, say, by abstracting away from all the variations between particular cats so that we are left with an idea that just includes everything that cats have in common. Hume disagrees (as did Berkeley before him [1710: Section 11]), holding instead that our abstract idea *cat* is, in fact, the idea of a *particular* cat, which of course will have various features (size, color of fur, etc.) that are not common to all cats. The *word* "cat" is associated with this idea but in a special way: the word can *also* "call up" other ideas of other particular cats, those cats being the "revival set" of the word "cat." So, for example, although my idea *cat* might be the idea of a medium-sized tabby, I don't come to believe that *all* cats are medium-sized tabbies because the word "cat" calls to mind other members of the revival set—lions, Siamese, and so on—that, of course, consists of cats of various different sizes, breeds, and species.

A *definition* of an abstract idea specifies what it is that all members of the revival set have in common—so, the definition of an abstract idea will coincide with the content of a Lockean abstract idea (four paws, furry, etc.) without actually fully describing the content of *any* idea because, again, any idea of a cat will include specific size, color, and so on.

In the case of the abstract idea of a relation R, Garrett claims that the "revival set" is constituted by all the *pairs* of objects or events (or whatever) that are related by R. In the case of causation, what the members of the revival set have in common is that the first member of each pair stands in the relations of contiguity, priority, and constant conjunction to the second member; this thus constitutes the definition (or rather, as we see in the next section, *one* of two alternative definitions) of causation.

How, if at all, does the idea of necessary connection get in on the act, given Garrett's interpretation of Hume? Well, Garrett (2009: 82–83) distinguishes between an idea's being part of a complex (but nonabstract) *idea* and its being a part of a *concept*, where "concept" is a less misleading name for Hume's abstract idea (because an abstract idea, on Hume's view, is simply a particular idea that plays the special role of "standing for" all other members of the revival set: it has "general signification"). He claims that the sense in which the idea of necessary connection is part of the concept of causation is that the "idea is part of every idea in the revival set" (2009: 83). And it is true, he claims, "that the idea of necessary connection is part [in the above sense] of at least many individuals' concept of CAUSATION" (ibid.). However, "it is not *essential* to the concept of CAUSA-TION itself. For to overcome the projective illusion . . . is not to change the pairs of objects whose ideas constitute the revival set of the idea of cause and effect, but only to correct the way in which those pairs are represented" (ibid.).

Garrett's thought here, I take it, is that the idea of necessary connection is not an "essential" part of the concept of causation, and this is because the abstract idea of causation, for those who have "overcome the projective illusion," has as its revival set ordered pairs of objects (or events). And this gets to count as the *same* abstract idea as that had by those who have failed to overcome the illusion—for whom the idea of necessary connection *is* a part of the concept of causation—because both sets of concept possessors have the very same pairs of objects figuring in their revival sets; it's just that those who are still in the grip of the projective illusion have something extra, but inessential, in there as well.

Garrett is surely right that, for Hume, the idea of causation is an abstract idea and is, thus, a particular idea "consider'd in a certain light." What is less clear is why the abstract idea of a *relation R* is the revival set merely of *pairs* of particular objects or events of the form <a, b>, as opposed to the revival set of pairs of particular R-related events <aRb>. It is the former claim that appears to render it impossible for Hume to think that the idea of necessary connection could be an essential part of the concept of causation because, in that case, the revival set would have to have as members not ordered pairs of events but pairs of events *related by necessary connection*. (Suppose, for the sake of the argument, that necessary connection is both a genuine feature of mind-independent reality and an essential component of causation. Then the world might in principle lack that feature and yet contain the very same pairs of events. Then the concept that *merely* picks out those pairs of events would fail to be the concept of causation because it could apply to pairs of events that are not, in fact, causally related.)

The worry here is this: Garrett's position is, at first sight, hostage to the worry raised earlier against versions of the traditional interpretation generally: it excludes the idea of necessary connection from the idea of causation, contrary to what appear to be Hume's intentions. Or rather, it excludes the idea of necessary connection from a cleaned-up version of the concept of causation—the concept possessed by those who have overcome the projective illusion. And this fits poorly with Hume's apparent disinclination to strip the idea of necessary connection from the idea of causation, even once the projective illusion (of thinking that causes have the AP property) has been uncovered.

Garrett's implicit response to this worry seems to be that once we grasp the fact that, for Hume, the revival set for the abstract idea of a relation consists merely of ordered pairs, there is simply no room for the claim that the idea of causation might have as its revival set pairs *related by necessary connection*. But it is unclear why we should attribute this view of abstract ideas of relations to Hume; and, in any case, Garrett seems to concede that the concept of a relation *can* have as its revival set *R*-related events because this is precisely what seems to be implied by the claim that "the idea of necessary connection is part of at least many individuals' concept of CAUSATION." Of course, Garrett thinks that the inclusion of the idea of necessary connection is "not essential to the concept of CAUSATION itself," but without the claim that the revival sets of abstract ideas of relations are (essentially) sets of mere pairs of objects, this claim is unwarranted. Nonetheless, Garrett's account is an interesting attempt to maintain the spirit of the traditional interpretation while conceding some ground to its rivals by allowing a sense in which the idea of necessary connection might be part of the concept of causation.

II.2 Hume as a Projectivist

Suppose we accept that Hume really does think that the idea of necessary connection is an ineliminable part of the idea of causation and that the former idea fails to latch on to any mind-independent feature of reality. One direction this might take us in is toward a projectivist understanding of his position. On this view, projection—the "spreading of the mind"—functions not merely as a causal explanation of our tendency to think of events as necessarily connected; it also plays an essential role in the semantics of "cause," so that what it *is* to "think of" events as necessarily connected is conceived in nonrepresentational terms. (In fact—borrowing a term from Simon Blackburn and following Angela Coventry [2006]—"quasi-realist" is perhaps a better term than "projectivist"; see Joyce [2009: Section 3] for a useful explanation, in the moral case, of the relevant terms.) So, the "contrary biass" discussed earlier is the inclination to assume that the idea of necessary connection *represents* a feature of mind-independent reality, when, in fact, it does not.

One way to motivate the projectivist interpretation is to note that, arguably, Hume holds that the *impression* of necessary connection is projected onto cause–effect pairs, so that how such pairs *look* once the habit of inference has been acquired (this being responsible for the impression) is different from how they look on first observing them (see Beebee 2006: Section 4.3). Thus, Hume's claim that "[a]ll events seem entirely loose and separate" (EU 7.26/74) is not to be read as a completely general claim but as a claim only about how things seem prior to the establishment of the habit of inference; once the habit has been established, the relevant pairs of events look, precisely, necessarily connected. And this is what prompts us to judge that they *are* necessarily connected: we "then call the one object, *Cause*; the other, *Effect*" (EU 7.27/75).

The distinctive element of the projectivist interpretation is its understanding of what it is for two events to be judged to be necessarily connected. Consider an analogy with Hume's account of aesthetic judgment (discussed at greater length in Coventry 2006: 120–39; see also Beebee 2006: Section 6.2). Hume holds that beauty "is no quality in things themselves: It exists merely in the mind which contemplates them" (ESY 230). And yet Hume himself routinely adopts what (in a related context) Huw Price calls "the objective mode of speech" (1998: 125): Hume talks of "real deformity" (ESY 246), of "beauties and blemishes" having "influence" on individuals (ESY 239), and so on. That is, he clearly takes the fact that beauty is, in some sense, in the eye of the beholder to be no bar to making true aesthetic claims that look for all the world as though they are attributions of aesthetic properties to objects outwith the mind.

A projectivist account of Hume's position on aesthetics squares this apparent circle by holding that aesthetic truth is to be distilled from the normative standards that apply to aesthetic judgments. There are "general rules of art," Hume says, that are "founded only on experience, and on the observation of the common sentiments of human nature" (ESY 232); and the verdicts of the "true judges"—those critics who possess "[s]trong sense, united to delicate sentiment, improved by practice, perfected by comparison, and cleared of all prejudice" and therefore are able to apply the rules appropriately—"is the true standard of taste and beauty" (ESY 241). It is existence of this standard, according to a projectivist line, that makes it appropriate to attribute truth and falsity to aesthetic judgments, despite the fact that those judgments fail to *represent* objects as possessing genuine intrinsic aesthetic properties. In other words, our aesthetic judgments *project* our aesthetic responses onto objects, and the truth or falsity of those judgments is determined by their conformity (or not) to the true standard of taste.

The intended analogy with the case of causation and necessary connection is straightforward. Again, we have something internal—an impression of reflection (rather than a sentiment)—and the corresponding idea projected onto the world. And we have the causal analogue of the "rules of art"—the contiguity, priority, and constant conjunction requirements together with Hume's "rules by which to judge of causes and effects" (T 1.3.15). Those rules, correctly applied (perhaps by somebody akin to Garrett's "idealised spectator"; see Section IV), deliver a "true standard" for causation, which in turn renders our causal judgments truth-evaluable.

Two serious objections to the projectivist interpretation are, first, that there is virtually no direct textual evidence supporting it, and, second, that it ascribes to Hume a view—noncognitivism—that a philosopher writing in the first half of the eighteenth century would hardly have been in a position to so much as formulate. On the positive side, however, the interpretation does succeed in ascribing to Hume three theses for which there *is* evidence that he endorses: meaning-empiricism, the thesis that the idea of necessary connection is an essential part of the idea of causation, and the thesis that our causal talk is not irredeemably defective. (As we have just seen, he does after all offer us "rules by which to judge of causes and effects," and he consistently relies on causal claims elsewhere in his work.) Other interpretations ascribe at most two of these three theses to Hume. Of course, it is a matter of controversy which, if any, of the three theses really are endorsed by Hume but evidence that all three should be ascribed to him is, *a fortiori*, evidence that the projectivist interpretation is correct.

The point about the lack of availability of a noncognitivist position at the time Hume was writing might be mitigated somewhat by the thought that Hume's discussion of aesthetic judgment can reasonably be interpreted as a gesture toward something like a projectivist position in the aesthetic case. Even so, perhaps the best that can be said is that if Hume really does intend to endorse all three of the theses just described, then projectivism is the position he would have embraced, had he been in a position to do so.

III Rejecting
Meaning-Empiricism: Skeptical Realism

Recall from Section I that, in the *Treatise*, Hume apparently uses projection—the mind's propensity to spread itself—to explain an error we are inclined to make: it is "the reason, why we suppose necessity and power to lie in the objects we consider, not in our mind, that considers them" (T 1.3.14.25/167). This strongly suggests, of course, that Hume holds that necessity and power do *not* "lie in the objects we consider." However, in many other places—especially, but not exclusively, in the first *Enquiry*—he makes plenty of realist-sounding claims: "the particular powers, by which all natural operations are performed, never appear to the senses" (EU 5.3/42), "the powers and forces, by which the [course of nature] is governed, [are] wholly unknown to us" (EU 5.21/54), and so on (see Strawson 1989: Sections 16–20, for many more examples). Hume seems, then, to be endorsing a realist position on causation (or at least on "powers")—albeit a realism that is tinged with skepticism. There *are* real causal powers in nature, he seems to be saying, but their nature eludes us. Indeed, in the *Enquiry* section on the idea of necessary connection (Section 7), where he argues for the same view about the impression-source of the idea of necessary connection as in the *Treatise*, he takes that view to reveal "the surprizing ignorance and weakness of the understanding" (EU 7.29/76). (Other interpreters have of course denied that Hume's realist-sounding utterances are to be read as genuine endorsements of realism; see, for example, Jacobson 2000; Winkler 2000; 2010: Section 3.)

Hume thus sometimes sounds more like a "skeptical realist"—someone who believes in real causal powers but accepts that we cannot know their nature (and, in particular, that we cannot perceive or detect them)—than a meaning-empiricist (i.e., someone who holds that to talk of *real*, mind-independent causal powers is to "talk without meaning"). And this is precisely the view that has been attributed to Hume by several commentators (e.g., Kemp Smith 1941; Wright 1983; 2000; Strawson 1989; 2000; Buckle 2001; Kail 2007). A common (although not universal) theme among such interpreters is that whereas Hume's own theory of ideas pushes him toward full-blown meaning-empiricism, he does leave scope for the ability to form a "relative idea" of features of reality whose nature we cannot, thanks to our sensory limitations, fully grasp (see, e.g., Flage 2000) and/or that we can coherently "suppose" or "conceive" that reality has such features despite lacking what Strawson calls "positively contentful" ideas of those features (1989: Section 12.2).

There are interesting and subtle differences between the different versions of the skeptical realist interpretation. For example, Strawson takes Hume to be a subjectivist about necessity (1989: Section 15.3), but to hold nonetheless that our causal talk refers to real causal power, or "Causation," as Strawson calls it, conceived as the feature of the world (nature unknown) that underpins its regularities. Buckle, by contrast, takes Hume to believe in underlying "mechanisms" that endow objects with causal powers. But "[s]ince the mechanisms are inaccessible to perceivers like us, the powers of the objects must remain hidden: all that we can observe are their effects in the world, including their effects on us" (2001: 194). John Wright, by contrast again, takes Hume to believe in the AP property: when we make causal claims, we really do claim that the cause has a power that absolutely guarantees the effect.

A second dimension of variation concerns what kind of attitude Hume has toward real causal powers. One might be interested in showing why Hume himself believes in them—for example, because such a belief would be entirely reasonable given his Newtonian heritage (see Buckle 2001: 210–211) or because he would have been persuaded by a philosophical argument to the effect that nature's regularities can't be a matter of cosmic luck (Craig 2000; Strawson 1989: 21). Or, one might be interested in showing how Hume's own avowed psychology and/or epistemology can deliver belief in real powers, so that the issue isn't whether or not Hume is convinced that they exist, but whether or not he has the resources to explain how *we* come to believe in them, given his story about the operation of the mind. Thus, for example, John Wright holds that belief in the AP property is straightforwardly delivered by our habit of inferring effects from causes: when we come, thanks to the establishment of that habit, to "call the one object, *Cause*; the other, *Effect*," precisely what we do is ascribe the AP property to the cause (and not mistakenly so).

I have argued elsewhere that Wright's is the most convincing version of the skeptical realist interpretation (2006: ch. 7); here, I briefly explain what, on Wright's view, the projective "error" is that Hume attributes to us when we "suppose necessity and power to lie in the objects we consider, not in our mind, that considers them." Wright's answer is that the error is that of thinking that *detectable* necessary connections exist. Because of our tendency to "spread the mind," we mistake an impression of reflection (the impression of necessary connection) for an impression of sensation, and so we are inclined to suppose that we are detecting the AP property when, really, we are merely projecting. Nonetheless, the AP property is what we ascribe in our causal talk. We have an understandable tendency to be mistaken about the impression-source of the idea of necessary connection but not about its content. The skeptical part of Hume's skeptical realism remains in place, however, because what we ascribe to the cause is only its having some feature or other, such that were we to be able to detect it, we would be able to infer the effect a priori. The nature of that feature, of course, eludes us entirely: we cannot detect it and so do not have a grasp of what it is really like (see Wright 2000: Section 4).

IV THE TWO DEFINITIONS

We saw in Section III.1 that Hume's two definitions—stated at T 1.3.14.31/170 and slightly reformulated at EU 7.29/76–7—have been cited as a major piece of evidence in favor of a meaning-empiricist reading and, in particular, the traditional interpretation. On the other hand, Hume's preamble to the statement of the two definitions in the *Enquiry*, which says that "the ideas which we form" concerning the causal relation are "so imperfect" that "it is impossible to give any just definition of cause, except what is drawn from something extraneous and foreign to it" (EU 7.29/76), have been taken by some authors to point not to meaning-empiricism but to the inadequacy of the definitions as reflections of the true nature of real causal powers, thanks to our cognitive limitations.

More generally, there have been various recent attempts to explain the purpose of the two definitions that reject the idea that they are intended to capture the *meaning* of "cause"—an idea that is immediately problematic in any case because they so clearly fail to be even co-extensive, let alone necessarily so. Here are the two definitions of the *Treatise* again:

(1) An object precedent to and contiguous with another, and where all the objects resembling the former are plac'd in like relations of precedency and contiguity to those objects, that resemble the latter.

(2) An object precedent and contiguous to another, and so united with it, that the idea of the one determines the mind to form the idea of the other, and the impression of the one to form a more lively idea of the other. (T 1.3.14.31/170)

(1) and (2) fail to be co-extensive because, first, two events might satisfy the constant conjunction requirement in (1) and yet fail to have been repeatedly observed by anyone, as required for (2) to hold; and, second, As and Bs might have been constantly conjoined in the experience of a particular observer and yet fail to be constantly conjoined *simpliciter*, as required by (1).

One broad line of interpretation has been to think of the two definitions as specifications of the circumstances that prompt causal judgment. For example, Craig says that the definitions characterize the "circumstances under which belief in a causal connection arises, one concentrating on the outward situation, the other on the state of the believer's mind that those outward facts induce" (1987: 108). In similar vein, Garrett says: "we can define 'cause and effect' either in terms of the *constant conjunction* that in fact produces the determination or transition . . . or we can define 'cause and effect' in terms of the *association* and *inference*" (1997: 106).

Garrett also argues that the definitions are in fact co-extensive. We can give (1) either an "absolute" reading—referring to constant conjunction *simpliciter*—or a "subjective" reading, in which "constant conjunction" means "observed constant conjunction." Correspondingly, we can read "the mind" in (2) as the mind of an "idealized" spectator—one who observes all and only representative samples of pairs of events, so that they will satisfy (2) if and only if (1) is satisfied—or, alternatively, as the mind of a normal observer, who may observe unrepresentative samples of pairs of events (a "subjective" reading). Reading both definitions in the absolute/idealized spectator sense delivers co-extensiveness, as does reading both in the subjective sense; the appearance of lack of co-extensiveness is a function of the fact that we are inclined to give (1) the absolute reading and (2) a subjective reading (see Garrett 1997: 108–111).

A second interpretative position, defended in Beebee (2011), construes the two definitions as characterizing two distinct *mental* mechanisms that deliver causal judgment. Hume says that the two definitions "are only different, by their presenting a different view of the same object, and making us consider it either as a *philosophical* or a *natural* relation; either as a comparison of two ideas, or as an association betwixt them" (T 1.3.14.31/170). If we take this claim at face value, the suggestion seems to be that (1), rather than characterizing how the world has to be in order for a causal claim to be true or to generate a causal judgment, in fact characterizes a mental procedure: that of *comparing* the ideas of two events and thereby coming to judge that one caused the other (this being causation "considered as a philosophical relation"). Note here that (1) refers to objects that are "*plac'd* in like relations of precedency and contiguity" (emphasis added) and "placing" is something *we* do. By contrast, (2) characterizes a distinct mechanism that delivers causal judgment—the habit of inference generated by experienced constant conjunction. This is causation "considered as a natural relation."

A third position—that of Strawson—is that "the two definitions of cause give an account of the content of the *idea*'s impression-sources." They give information about what we positively contentfully mean and, indeed, about all we can really (positively contentfully) mean, according to the theory of ideas, when we talk about causes. Strawson's interpretation is closer than the previous two to the thought that the two definitions specify the *meaning* of "cause"; but Strawson distinguishes between what we can "positively contentfully" mean and what the idea of causation *refers* to. So, in Strawson's view, Hume's suggestion that the definitions may be thought to be defective because "drawn from objects foreign to the cause" is a recognition of the fact that a specification of causation's true nature—something one might *want* a definition of causation to do—is beyond our cognitive powers.

What all of these three interpretative positions share is the implication that the two definitions, just by themselves, are in fact neutral between the various interpretative options surveyed earlier concerning Hume's considered view on the nature of causation. Taking the Craig/Garrett line first, the circumstances under which we (or an idealized observer) come to make causal judgment may or may not reflect causation's true nature. The idealized observer is only human and therefore is only idealized in the sense of never observing misleading regularities; he does not possess the superhuman power of ascertaining whether or not there are any secret (to us humans) causal powers. Similarly, my own interpretative take specifies only the mental processes whereby we do (or should) come to make causal judgments; the true nature of causation may or may not be reflected in those processes. (Whether or not there are secret powers, and whether or not Hume takes these to be essential features of causation, makes no difference to how it is that we, who are insensitive to such things, come to make causal judgments.) Finally, Strawson's interpretation of the two definitions themselves (as opposed to Hume's remarks about their being "esteem'd defective"), although part of an argument intended to cast doubt on a meaning-empiricist interpretation of Hume, is fully consistent with that interpretation; the meaning-empiricist line simply makes the further claim that the nature of causation is fully captured by our "positively contentful" idea of it (so that the definitions may be *esteemed* defective but, in fact, are not).

The two definitions just by themselves, then—at least according to several recent interpretations thereof—settle nothing when it comes to the controversy surrounding the nature of causation and the meaning of "cause."

V Conclusion

What explains the fact that Hume's own words lend themselves to such radically different interpretations? Doubtless, the philosophical preferences of his interpreters play a role—generally speaking, interpreters seem to avoid attributing a view to Hume that is obviously false by their own lights, and this is unlikely to be a coincidence. Differences between the *Treatise* and the *Enquiry* play a role, too; Strawson, for example, argues that Hume's considered views are those expressed in the *Enquiry*, where he sounds (to my ears and to Strawson's, too) rather more skeptical-realist than he does in the *Treatise* (see Beebee 2006: Section 7.8; Strawson 2000: Section 2). On the other hand, Peter Millican takes Hume's discussion of free will in Section 8 of the *Enquiry* to deliver "a torpedo into the core of the New Humeans' position" (Millican 2007: 193; 2010), and Peter Kail takes Hume's discussion of the self in the Appendix to the *Treatise* to "tip the balance firmly in favour of realism" (2007: 124).

Another possible explanation of the apparently intractable interpretative dispute might simply be that Hume is not especially interested in many of the issues that divide the interpretative positions. It can be agreed on all sides that his major epistemological interest when it comes to causation is to show that there are no causal principles knowable a priori and that it is only by experience that we can come to discover the causal structure of the world. The success of his arguments against rival philosophical positions—occasionalism in Section 7 of the *Enquiry* and libertarianism in Section 8—and various theological positions (arguments for the existence of God in the *Dialogues Concerning Natural Religion* and the existence of miracles in Section 10 of the *Enquiry*) arguably depend on elements of his position that the various different interpretations agree on—that we cannot draw a distinction between causes and occasions, for example, or that human actions are subject to the same species of necessity as are the movements of billiard balls (although Strawson would disagree when it comes to occasionalism (see Strawson 1989: ch. 20; Beebee 2006: Section 7.3), and Millican would disagree when it comes to libertarianism; see above).

Skepticism of a kind is also present in all of the interpretative positions. Some skeptical realist commentators have complained that the traditional, regularity-theory interpretation of Hume fails to attribute to him a suitably skeptical position because, on that view, there is nothing ungraspable or unknowable about the nature of causation (see, e.g., Craig 1987: 129–30; Strawson 1989: 10–14). But we can resist this claim. It is one thing to hold that our cognitive powers are so limited that we cannot so much as formulate a coherent question about causation's underlying nature ("[w]e have no idea of this connexion, nor even any distinct notion what it is we desire to know, when we endeavour at a conception of it"; EU 7.29/77) and thus to hold that our actual causal talk and thought cannot latch onto any such thing; it is quite another to claim that there definitely is not, or could not be, some further relation between causes and effects that beings with superior cognitive powers might be able to grasp – a claim that neither the traditional nor the projectivist interpretation needs to attribute to Hume. Even *qua* non–skeptical-realist, Hume's position enshrines a kind of cognitive modesty that deserves, I think, to be called "skeptical."[2]

If all this is right, then perhaps it is not so surprising that Hume fails to state the precise semantic content of the idea of causation in a way that would be less susceptible to interpretative disagreement than are his actual words.

Abbreviations of Works Cited

EM   *Enquiry Concerning the Principles of Morals*. Edited by Tom L. Beauchamp. Oxford: Clarendon, 1998.

ESY   *Essays: Moral, Political, and Literary*. Revised edition by E. F. Miller. Indianapolis: Liberty Classics, 1985.

EU   *An Enquiry Concerning Human Understanding*. Edited by T. L. Beauchamp. Oxford: Clarendon, 2000.

T   *A Treatise of Human Nature*. Edited by D. F. Norton and M. J. Norton. Oxford: Clarendon, 2007.

Notes

1. Stroud's (1977) interpretation, according to which Hume is a kind of error theorist about causation, sits somewhere between the traditional and projectivist interpretations. On Stroud's view, the idea of necessary connection is defective, but we cannot help but deploy it. So, Stroud agrees with the projectivist interpretation that the idea of necessary connection plays a semantic role in our causal talk, but agrees with the traditional interpretation that that idea is irredeemably defective.

2. Kail (2008: 455–456) disputes whether a meaning-empiricist line really allows Hume the semantic scope to formulate a genuinely skeptical thought here; see also Kail (2007: Section 4.3).

Bibliography

Anscombe, G. E. M. (1971). *Causality and Determination: An Inaugural Lecture.* Cambridge: Cambridge University Press. Reprinted in E. Sosa and M. Tooley, eds., *Causation.* Oxford: Oxford University Press, 1993.Beauchamp, T. L., and A. Rosenberg. (1981). *Hume and the Problem of Causation.* New York: Oxford University Press.

Beebee, H. (2006). *Hume on Causation.* Abingdon: Routledge.

Beebee, H. (2011). "Hume's Two Definitions: The Procedural Interpretation." *Hume Studies* 37, 243–274.

Berkeley, G. (1710). *A Treatise Concerning the Principles of Human Knowledge,* ed. J. Dancy. Oxford: Oxford University Press, 1998.

Buckle, S. (2001). *Hume's Enlightenment Tract.* Oxford: Oxford University Press.

Coventry, A. (2006). *Hume's Theory of Causation.* New York: Continuum Press.

Craig, E. (1987). *The Mind of God and the Works of Man.* Oxford: Clarendon Press.

Craig, E. (2000). "Hume on Causality: Projectivist and Realist?," in Read and Richman, eds., 113–121.

Descartes, R. (1641). *Meditations on First Philosophy,* trans and ed. J. Cottingham. Cambridge: Cambridge University Press, 1996.

Flage, D. (2000). "Relative Ideas Re-viewed," in Read and Richman, eds., 138–155.

Garrett, D. (1997). *Cognition and Commitment in Hume's Philosophy.* Oxford: Oxford University Press.

Garrett, D. (2009). "Hume," in H. Beebee, C. Hitchcock, and P. Menzies, eds., *The Oxford Handbook of Causation.* Oxford: Oxford University Press.

Jacobson, A. J. (2000). "From Cognitive Science to Post-Cartesian Text: What Did Hume Really Say?," in Read and Richman, eds. 156–166.

Joyce, R. (2009). "Moral Anti-Realism," in E. N. Zalta, ed., *The Stanford Encyclopedia of Philosophy (Summer 2009 Edition).* http://plato.stanford.edu/archives/sum2009/entries/moral-anti-realism/.

Kail, P. (2007). *Projection and Realism in Hume's Philosophy.* Oxford: Oxford University Press.

Kail, P. (2008). "Review of H. Beebee, *Hume on Causation,*" *Mind* 117, 451–456.

Kemp Smith, N. (1941). *The Philosophy of David Hume.* London: Macmillan.

Mackie, J. L. (1974). *The Cement of the Universe.* London: Oxford University Press.

Millican, P. (2007). "Humes Old and New: Four Fashionable Falsehoods, and One Unfashionable Truth." *Proceedings of the Aristotelian Society* Supp. 81, 163–199.

Millican, P. (2010). "Hume, Causal Realism, and Free Will," in K. Allen and T. Stoneham, eds., *Causation and Modern Philosophy,* 123–165. New York: Routledge.

Mumford, S., and R. Lil Anjum. (2011). *Getting Causes from Powers.* Oxford: Oxford University Press.

Price, H. (1998). "Two paths to pragmatism II," in R. Casati and C. Tappolet, eds., *European Review of Philosophy* 3, 109–147.

Psillos, S. (2009). "Regularity Theories," in H. Beebee, C. Hitchcock, and P. Menzies, eds., *The Oxford Handbook of Causation,* 131–157. Oxford: Oxford University Press.

Read, R., and K. Richman, eds. (2000). *The New Hume Debate*. London: Routledge.

Russell, B. (1912–13). "On the Notion of Cause," *Proceedings of the Aristotelian Society* 13, 1–26.

Strawson, G. (1989). *The Secret Connexion*. Oxford: Oxford University Press.

Strawson, G. (2000). "David Hume: Objects and Power," in Read and Richman, eds., 31–51.

Stroud, B. (1977). *Hume*. London: Routledge.

Wilson, F. (1986). "Hume's Defence of Science," *Dialogue* 25, 611–628.

Winkler, K. (2000). "The New Hume," in Read and Richman, eds. 52–87.

Winkler, K. (2010). "P. J. E. Kail's *Projection and Realism in Hume's Philosophy*," *Philosophical Books* 51, 144–159.

Wright, J. P. (1983). *The Sceptical Realism of David Hume*. Manchester: Manchester University Press.

Wright, J. P. (2000). "Hume's Causal Realism," in Read and Richman, eds. 88–99.

CHAPTER 13

HUME ON THE EXTERNAL WORLD

GEORGES DICKER

I THREE ASSUMPTIONS BEHIND HUME'S ACCOUNT

LIKE Descartes, Locke, and Berkeley before him, Hume propounds a theory of the external world or of what, in his case, is better called the belief in the existence of body. He gives a brief version of his theory in Section 12 of the First *Enquiry*, but his fullest account is in T 1.4.2, "Of Scepticism with Regard to the Senses." Regarding this section of the *Treatise*, Jonathan Bennett (1971: 313) wrote:

> It is extremely difficult, full of mistakes, and—taken as a whole—a total failure; yet its depth and scope and disciplined complexity make it one of the most instructive arguments in modern philosophy. One philosopher might be judged superior to another because [s]he achieved something of which the other was altogether intellectually incapable. By that criterion Hume surpasses Locke and Berkeley—because, and only because, of this one section.

This essay expounds Hume's theory and offers an assessment of it.

The theory rests on three assumptions. In calling these "assumptions," I do not mean that Hume never argues for them, but rather that the emphasis of his discussion falls much more heavily on developing their implications than on justifying them—on working *from* them as givens rather than *toward* them as points to be established.

First, Hume holds, like many seventeenth- and eighteenth-century philosophers, that the only things we perceive by our senses are what Berkeley called "sensations or ideas," which Hume calls "impressions" (T 1.2.6.8/67; T 1.4.2.21/197; T 1.4.5.15/239; EU 12.1.9–12/152–3). The motivation for this view is the "Argument from Illusion," which is really a family of several arguments, which I now briefly and uncritically survey.

The *argument from perceptual relativity* holds that when one looks at an ordinary object like a table, what one sees changes as one's distance from the table and angle of view changes. But the table itself does not change. So, what one sees is not really the table, but only a visual image or rather a series of different images or sense impressions (EU 12.1.9/152).

The *argument from the causal facts of perception* holds that when an ordinary object stimulates one's sense receptors, what one perceives depends on the type of sense organs one possesses and the condition of those organs. For example, when the eyes of a near-sighted person and those of a far-sighted person are both stimulated by a US flag, what each sees is different due to the different capabilities of their eyes. But the properties of the stimulus object—the flag—do not causally depend on the capabilities of anyone's sense organs: they are utterly independent of that. So, what one perceives is not the stimulus object itself, but rather an image or a percept whose qualities depend at least partly on the perceiver's sense organs.

The *argument from illusion* (proper) holds that there are illusions in which what we perceive has properties that aren't those of any physical thing that we currently perceive. Yet we do perceive *something* in those cases, so this something must be a mental image of some sort. Furthermore, there is no telltale difference between such an image and what we perceive in normal cases; so, even in normal cases, we perceive only mental images. Hume offers this instance: by pressing one eye with a finger, one can cause oneself to see everything double. In such a case, at least half of the things one sees are merely mental images. But there is no special, telltale, qualitative difference between these images and the other half of the things we see to indicate that whereas the former are merely mental images, the latter are material things. So it follows that all the things we see are just mental images (T 1.4.2.45/210–11).

The *argument from hallucination* holds that, in a hallucination, we perceive only a mental image. But again, there is no telltale difference between what we perceive in such a case and what we perceive in nonhallucinatory cases; therefore, even in the latter, we perceive only mental images. A recent variant of this argument (Smith 2004: 194–197) holds that, in a hallucination, we are aware of something other than a material object—a sensation, idea, or impression. Call this mental item "*I*." *I* is caused by some event in the brain, call it "*X*." But now suppose that the perception is exactly similar, except that it is not a hallucination. Then *X* is still the proximate cause of the perception, but *X* is in turn caused by a chain of events that extends outside the perceiver's body to a stimulus object. But why should the addition of more links to this causal chain mean that we do not perceive *I* anymore?

Finally, there is an *epistemological argument*. Whatever else perception may be, it is a way of picking up or acquiring knowledge of its objects. By perceiving an object, one can come to know that it exists and has certain properties. However, there is good reason to believe that any perceptual experience had when a physical object is stimulating one's sense receptors can be duplicated when there is no object stimulating the sense receptors. Such a duplicate experience can be produced, for example, by directly stimulating the brain, in a drug-induced hallucination, in a vivid dream, or conceivably even by Descartes's evil deceiver or some "scientific" counterpart thereof. So, it seems that the objects whose existence and nature we come to know in any case of perception cannot be physical objects that cause our sensory experiences. Rather, they must be items that we are aware of regardless of how the experiences are caused—something that normal and duplicate experiences have in common. What are these items? The answer given is that they are impressions, Berkeleyan "sensations or ideas," or, to use the modern term, "sense data." Of course, these items are not the physical objects that people naïvely think they perceive. So, how do we know that there are physical objects at all, if we know it? The answer offered is that we know it by causally inferring the existence of physical objects from the impressions or sense data that we immediately perceive.

This last point leads directly to the second assumption governing Hume's theory. Contra Descartes and Locke, Hume holds the view, powerfully defended by Berkeley in his *Principles of Human Knowledge* (Part I, sections 18–20), that we cannot legitimately infer the existence of bodies existing outside our minds from our impressions or ideas. Hume buttresses Berkeley's view with an influential argument of his own, one based on his analysis of causal reasoning. The argument is that we can establish a causal relation between X's and Y's only by observing that X's and Y's have been constantly conjoined, we can observe that X's and Y's have been constantly conjoined only if we can perceive both X's and Y's, and we can perceive impressions but we cannot perceive bodies; therefore, we cannot establish a causal relation between impressions and bodies (T 1.4.2.47/212; EU 12.12/153).

Berkeley claimed to avoid the external world skepticism to which the two foregoing assumptions seem to lead by reducing bodies to ideas; that is, by holding that bodies are nothing but orderly collections of ideas. Hume's third background assumption simply rejects Berkeley's theory, essentially on the grounds that it is too incredible to be believable (EU 12.15, n32/155n).

It is obvious that these three assumptions commit Hume to skepticism with respect to our belief in an external world. For Hume, the belief in the existence of body has no rational basis. Yet, as we shall now see, he has much more to say about it.

II THE GENERAL NATURE OF HUME'S THEORY

Although Hume holds that the belief in body has no rational foundation, he also holds that humans cannot help believing that bodies exist. His main purpose in T 1.4.2 is to give a causal explanation of why we cannot help having this belief. The success or failure of his discussion rests not on any conclusion reached about the status of this belief—its reasonableness or unreasonableness, or its truth or falsity—but only on whether, in accordance with the *Treatise*'s purpose of providing a "science of MAN," his explanation of why we have the belief is convincing. This is why he opens by saying, "We may well ask, *What causes induce us to believe in the existence of body?* but 'tis in vain to ask, *Whether there be body or not* ... [T]he subject, then, of our present enquiry is concerning the *causes* which induce us to believe in the existence of body" (T 1.4.2.1– 2/187–8). This approach is parallel to Hume's treatment of induction, of the belief in objective necessary connections between events, and of the belief in personal identity: when he finds that these cannot be rationally justified, he seeks to give psychological explanations of them. It turns out, furthermore, that Hume identifies two versions of the belief in body: an ordinary or, as he calls it, "vulgar" version that we all hold until we are confronted with arguments that demonstrate its falsity, and a "philosophical" version that we are driven to by those arguments but for which Hume sees no rational foundation and which he ultimately also rejects as false.

III THE "VULGAR" BELIEF IN THE EXISTENCE OF BODY

Hume analyzes the ordinary belief in body into two parts: belief in the *continued* existence of the objects of the senses while they are not being perceived (CE) and belief in the existence of the objects of the senses *distinct* from (independently of) being perceived (DE). He claims that if CE is true, then DE is true; he also says that if DE is true, then CE is true. The former claim is right, but the latter claim needs a defense that Hume does not provide: why could there not be "distinct" objects that coincidentally exist only when they are perceived?[1] But this matters little because the rest of Hume's analysis requires only that CE entail DE: it consists largely in explaining the belief in CE, which would then also explain the belief in DE (T 1.4.2.23/199; T 1.4.2.44/210). The heart of his discussion is his attempt to explain the belief in CE; his central theme is that this belief is false but that certain psychological principles of the imagination can explain it and therefore also explain DE. He begins, however, by arguing that neither the *senses* nor *reason* can give rise to either the belief in CE or the belief in DE.

Hume's reason for denying that the senses could give rise to the belief in CE is very straightforward: this would require that the senses continue to operate when they are not operating—a contradiction (T 1.4.2.3/188). Next, Hume argues that, for the senses to give rise to the belief in DE, they would have to present our impressions either (a) as images or representations of objects or (b) as being themselves those very distinct existences, by "a kind of fallacy and illusion" (T 1.4.2.5/189). Option (a) is excluded because the senses "convey to us nothing but a single perception, and never give us the least intimation of something beyond" (T 1.4.2.4/189). Option (b) is excluded for more complicated reasons. First, the senses would have to present both the impressions and *ourselves*, so that "the difficulty [would become] how far we are *ourselves* the objects of our senses," but "there is no question in philosophy more abstruse than that concerning identity, and the nature of the uniting principle, which constitutes a person . . . [T]hese ideas of self and person are never very fix'd nor determinate. 'Tis absurd, therefore, to imagine the senses can ever distinguish between ourselves and external objects" (T 1.4.2.5–6/189–90). Second, it is *false* that our impressions have a distinct existence, and the senses cannot lie about the "situation and relation" of our impressions anymore than they can lie about their intrinsic nature (T 1.4.2.7/190). Third, the notion of "distinctness" is itself a complex one that has two components: *externality* and *independence*. As one commentator notes, "externality is a spatial notion: X is external to Y if and only if X is located apart from Y. Independence is a modal notion: X is independent of Y if and only if X could exist even if Y did not."[2] Now the belief in externality can't be based on the senses because it would then have to be based on our perceiving things as being external to our own bodies, but this could happen only if the senses had already given rise to the belief in the externality of our bodies, which is just a special case of what we are trying to explain (remember that, for Hume, we do not perceive our bodies but only impressions of our bodies). Nor can the belief in independence be based on the senses because the senses cannot present their objects as having the modal property of *possibly existing independently of us*: "As to the *independency* of our perceptions on ourselves, this can never be an object of the senses" (T 1.4.2.10/191).[3] These points are confirmed, Hume adds, when one remembers that colors, tastes, smells, and sounds have the same status as our pains and pleasures, yet the former "exist after the same manner" as shape, size, solidity, and motion, so that those, too, are not perceived by sense to have a distinct (or a continuous) existence.

Hume's argument for holding that reason cannot give rise to the belief in either CE or DE is brief. First, he argues that "children, peasants, and the greatest part of mankind" obviously do not base their belief in CE or in DE on any arguments because they are ignorant of such arguments. Next, he argues that CE and DE are so easily shown by philosophy to be *false* and "entirely unreasonable" that they "must proceed from some other faculty than the understanding" (T 1.4.2.14/193). He next introduces his theory that the belief in CE and DE is both (a) generated by the *imagination* and (b) false, but here I shall disentangle his exposition by first expounding separately his reasons for thinking that this belief is false.

IV WHY THE ORDINARY BELIEF IS FALSE

To show that belief in DE is false, Hume lists the "experiments, which convince us, that our perceptions are not possest of any independent existence" (T 1.4.2.45/210–11). These "experiments" are basically the arguments from perceptual relativity and from illusion that were expounded earlier. To show that the belief in CE is false, he offers the *modus tollens* argument that because DE is false but is implied by CE, CE must be false too (T 1.4.2.44/210).

Hume, however, has a novel and more fundamental reason for holding that CE is false: our *perceptions* are obviously discontinuous, "broken," or "interrupted." Consider, for example, the perceptions you have when looking at the furniture in a room. Those perceptions are plainly discontinuous: they cease to exist and are replaced by different perceptions every time you glance away from the furniture or leave the room, and they cease to exist without being replaced by other perceptions when you go into a dreamless sleep. This simple and obvious point, Hume thinks, incontrovertibly proves the falsity of the belief in the "continu'd" existence of the objects of the senses—he sees it as a decisive, stand-alone argument for the "gappiness" of sensible objects.

To grasp Hume's thinking, it is crucial to understand that when he says that our perceptions are interrupted or discontinuous, he is not saying merely that our *perceivings*, or acts of perception, or perceptual episodes are discontinuous, which is of course true. Rather, he is also claiming that the *objects of* our perceptions—the things that we perceive—are discontinuous. For Hume does not distinguish between perceptual episodes and the objects perceived in them; his use of the term "perceptions" to stand indifferently for both perceptual episodes and their objects is not just linguistic carelessness, but reflects a genuine collapsing of the distinction between them—one that he attributes even to the "vulgar". The only form in which Hume recognizes a distinction between perception and its objects is that of the philosophical theory of the "double existence of perceptions and objects" advocated by Descartes, Locke, and others—a theory that Hume rejects.

Hume's collapsing of this distinction calls for an explanation, if only because the distinction is so elementary. Even ordinary, unsophisticated common sense would distinguish between perceiving something, or the perception of something, and *what* is perceived; for example, between seeing an apple and the apple that we see. Why, then, does Hume reject this distinction? The reason surfaces when we see that, from Hume's empiricist point of view, the distinction cannot be one between the object perceived and some "act" of perception because such an act would not be something of which we could have any impression: it would have to be, so to speak, diaphanous or "transparent," so that Hume's empiricism would banish it as a meaningless notion. It seems, then, that the *only* thing that could have differentiated between perceptions and their objects is a *temporal* difference between them because objects can outlast the perceptions of them and so must be distinct from those perceptions. This point is at the heart of Kant's "Analogies of Experience," where Kant explicitly distinguishes between the time relations of perceptual episodes and the time relations of their objects, saying that perceptual episodes may be successive even when their objects are co-existent; for example, that while the perceptions of the front of a house may occur before perceptions of the back, the front and back of the house that the observer successively sees co-exist.[4] Hume recognizes the point in his own way when he says that the chief component in our belief in body is precisely that bodies continue to exist unperceived. But, unlike Kant, Hume does not argue that assigning a different set of time relations to objects of perception from those of the perceptions themselves is a condition of the very possibility of experience and is therefore epistemologically warranted.[5] Rather, Hume sees the time relations of perceptual episodes—what some Kant commentators call the subjective time order—as the only one that is necessary for experience: what Kant considers to be the objective time order enters into Hume's thought only as the fictional product of the imagination working in accordance with contingent principles. So, these time relations cannot, for Hume, be appealed to as an epistemically warranted way of distinguishing between perceptions and objects: objects do not *knowably* have different time relations from perceptions. Within the range of what can be known, there are only the time relations of the perceptions themselves and because there is, accordingly, no other set of time relations to appeal to, and yet no way to distinguish between perceptions and objects other than their time relations, the distinction between perceptions and objects collapses.

A possible objection to this explanation of why Hume thinks that sensible objects have an intermittent existence is that it conflicts with his initial account of the ordinary belief in body. For, as we saw, at the very beginning of T 1.4.2, Hume explicitly says that one component of the ordinary belief in body is DE—the belief that sensible objects have a "distinct" existence; he thus seems to embed the distinction between the perception of X and the existence of X within his own analysis of the ordinary belief. But I have just argued that Hume's novel and most basic reason for holding that sensible objects have an intermittent existence—one a dim grasp of which he even attributes to the vulgar—turns on *collapsing* the distinction between perceptions and their objects. Is Hume then committed to saying that the ordinary belief in body is self-contradictory, that it entails that sensible objects both do and do not enjoy an existence independently of being perceived?

It might seem that this objection can be answered by appealing to a striking feature of Hume's position that I have not yet mentioned, namely, his notion of an unowned perception.[6] According to Hume, the core of the ordinary belief in body is that the very same objects one perceives by sense, "perceptions," continue to exist when one no longer perceives them. But, for Hume, this does not mean that they then exist as something other than perceptions. Rather, it only means that they have become detached from the particular bundle of perceptions or Humean "self" to which they formerly belonged—that they have become unowned perceptions. As he puts it:

> What we call a *mind*, is nothing but a heap or collection of different perceptions, united together by certain relations, and suppos'd, tho' falsely, to be endow'd with a perfect simplicity and identity. Now as every perception is distinguishable from another, and may be consider'd as separately existent; it evidently follows, that there is no absurdity in separating any particular perception from the mind; that is, in breaking off all its relations, with that connected mass of perceptions, which constitute a thinking being. . . . If the name of *perception* renders not this separation from a mind absurd and contradictory, the name of *object*, standing for the very same thing, can never render their conjunction impossible. External objects are seen, and felt, and become present to the mind; that is, they acquire . . . a relation to a connected heap of perceptions. . . . The same continu'd and uninterrupted Being may, therefore, be sometimes present to the mind, and sometimes absent from it, without

any real or essential change in the Being itself. An interrupted appearance to the senses implies not necessarily an interruption in the existence. The supposition of the continu'd existence of sensible objects or perceptions involves no contradiction. (T 1.4.2.29–40/207)

I read this passage as implying that, for Hume, DE does not mean that a sensible object can exist distinct from a perception of it, in the sense that it can exist wholly unperceived or unsensed. Rather, DE means only that a sensible object can exist distinct from anything that Hume would call a mind or a person—that it can be, so to speak, a "free-floating" perception, one that exists apart from any bundle of perceptions. On this reading, Humean unowned perceptions should not be confused with Russellian unsensed *sensibilia*.[7] If one rejects the perception/object distinction, then one is thereby committed to the possibility of such unowned perceptions, because just by virtue of anything's being a sensible *object*, it is also a *perception*, so that there is already consciousness "of" it, whether it is perceived by what Hume would call a mind or not. Look at this way: if there is no distinction between an object and a perception of it, then even when the object ceases to be perceived by a mind or self, it must continue to be perceived; it could not cease to be perceived without becoming distinct from what it had been identical with, that is, without undergoing a "real or essential change," which is what Hume denies happens. Unowned perceptions exist apart from any bundle of perceptions, but they do not thereby cease to be consciously sensed; they are, so to speak, suffused with consciousness. This is, of course, an extremely odd notion—one that some philosophers would find incoherent—because it implies both that a sensible object can exist perceived yet not perceived *by* any mind or person, and a kind of panpsychism—but it is what Hume advocates in the quoted passage.

But even waiving the objection that the notion of an unowned perception is incoherent, this notion cannot provide a satisfactory answer to the objection that Hume himself builds the perception/object distinction into his analysis of the ordinary belief in body because it runs afoul of what I have suggested is Hume's most basic reason for thinking that sensible objects have an intermittent existence. For if sensible objects *can* continue to exist as unowned perceptions, then what assures Hume that they *do not* in fact do so—thereby possessing a continuous existence after all?[8] Obviously, he could no longer say that objects exist intermittently on the grounds that they can't outlast perceptions of them, because unowned perceptions need not be intermittent. Indeed, there is an even stronger point to be made here. Of course, if it is logically possible that there are unowned perceptions, then it is also logically possible that they have an intermittent existence. But Hume's only reason for introducing unowned perceptions, their very *raison d'être*, is to serve as continuants that exist when no one has them—when they are not attached to any bundle of perceptions. For Hume, only if they so exist can the ordinary belief in body be true. It would be completely pointless and self-defeating for Hume to suppose that unowned perceptions have an intermittent existence; in order for unowned perceptions to play the role in the ordinary belief that he assigns to them, he must postulate that they *do* exist continuously (according to that belief). As for the *modus tollens* argument that is supposed to demonstrate that sensible objects have a gappy existence, it poses no problem for the believer in unowned perceptions; she will say that one of its premises (DE's denial, viz., that sensible objects do not enjoy a "distinct" existence) is simply false because sensible objects, *qua* unowned perceptions, *do* have an existence distinct and independent of being perceived by a mind.

In brief, whether Hume thinks that the vulgar are committed to saying that unowned perceptions merely can or that they do exist continuously, he cannot appeal to unowned perceptions to answer the objection that the object/perception distinction is built into his analysis of the ordinary belief in body. For such an appeal would ruin his novel argument for the intermittency of sensible objects: if unowned perceptions even can exist continuously, then the premise that perceptions have an intermittent existence is questionable, and if they do exist continuously, then that premise is false. So, he needs to give an answer to the objection that does not appeal to unowned perceptions.

I think he could give such an answer. This objection assumes that, in his treatment of the relationship between CE and DE at the very beginning of T 1.4.2, Hume is already presupposing his view that there is no ontological distinction between X and a perception of X. I suggest, however, that it is wrong to attribute this presupposition to him. For when Hume expounds the relationship between CE and DE at the outset of T 1.4.2, he is not yet assuming his own view about the relation between a perception and its object; he is allowing for the possibility that there is a distinction between perception and *what* is perceived, at least in the sense that he has not yet entertained the question of whether objects and perceptions are distinct. This is confirmed by the fact that only later in the section does he announce that he will "call indifferently *object* or *perception* . . . what any common man means by a hat, or shoe, or stone" (T 1.4.2.31/202). At this later point, he does attribute the collapse of the perception/object distinction to the ordinary person, but that is because now he *is* reading (however mistakenly) this part of his own metaphysics into the ordinary person's view. The ordinary view is, as it were, a moving target in Hume's discussion, and this target does not reach a resting place until at least the passage I have just quoted. It is true that he there adds, "I shall be sure to give warning, when I return to a more philosophical way of speaking and thinking" (T 1.4.2.31/202), but this is an ironical remark that should not to be taken to mean that he regards this "more philosophical way" as superior, because it will turn out to be nothing but the Cartesian/Lockean view of the "double existence of perceptions and objects" that he rejects.

I am not saying that the people Hume calls "the vulgar" *really* hold that there is no distinction between perceptions and objects. Although, of course, such people were not (and are not now) acquainted with G. E. Moore's "Refutation of Idealism," they would presumably have applauded Moore's argument that since a perception of red and a perception of blue differ in color but have something in common, in virtue of which both are perceptions, there has to be a distinction between a perception and its object. (Moore talks of sensations rather than of perceptions, but his point carries over to perceptions.) Nevertheless, Hume simply *attributes* to the vulgar his own view that there is no distinction between perceptions and objects. Perhaps the reason he so easily does so is that he thinks the vulgar would be just as hard-pressed as he is to find introspectively a distinction between perceptions and objects: for the vulgar no less than the philosopher, any putative act of perception gets "swallowed up" by the object perceived.

My reply to the possible objection just considered serves to illustrate one reason why T 1.4.2 is so difficult. When Hume describes what he presents as ordinary or "vulgar" views, he incorporates certain elements of his own metaphysical views into his descriptions, thus leaving the reader with the task of disentangling what really are ordinary views from Humean accretions to those views. Thus, to give another illustration, Hume correctly holds that the vulgar believe that the very objects they perceive by sense continue to exist when they no longer perceive them. But he also mistakenly thinks that the vulgar do not, in cases of nonhallucinatory and nonillusory perception, distinguish between bodies and what are *really* only impressions. So, he thinks, their belief in the continued existence of bodies is really a belief in the existence of unowned perceptions. He thinks that this belief is coherent but false—that perceptions *could* but *do not* exist unowned. So far as I can see, he never gives a reason why the belief in unowned perceptions is false; at best, his arguments show that we cannot *know* that there are unowned perceptions. In any case, Hume's ascription of this belief to common sense is a stark illustration of his penchant for reading his own metaphysical views into what he presents as the ordinary views of humankind.

I have argued that Hume's claim early in T 1.4.2, that the ordinary belief in body implies a belief in the "distinct" existence of sensible objects, should not prevent us from recognizing that, according to the considered view of the ordinary belief that Hume develops as the section progresses, the perception/object distinction gets collapsed. It does not follow, however, that Hume's novel reason for holding that sensible objects have a discontinuous existence—the intermittency of our perceptions combined with the collapse of the perception/object distinction—is compelling. I shall now argue that it is not compelling, thus making an internal criticism of what I take to be Hume's most original and basic reason for that view.

As my earlier reference to Hume's notion of unowned perceptions suggests, there are three relevant possibilities to consider. The first possibility is that there is no perception/object distinction and that there are unowned perceptions. On that option, Hume cannot correctly assert that perceptions have an intermittent existence, because unowned perceptions are precisely ones that he supposes remain uninterrupted or continuous even when they are detached from any mind that could have them. So, on this option, Hume's novel argument against the continuity of sensible objects breaks down because its key premise that perceptions have an intermittent existence is simply false. The second option is that there is no perception/object distinction and that there are no unowned perceptions. On that option, the key premise of Hume's argument is true and the ordinary belief in body is false, just as Hume says. So, it may seem as though this option would give Hume everything that he needs. But that is not the case, for once Hume allows that unowned perceptions are at least possible, he has no way to show that it *is* false that they exist. At best, he may hold that there is no good reason to believe that they exist; but, of course, this does not show that they do not exist. It does not even show that it is reasonable to believe that they do not exist because the principle that if there is no good reason to believe *p*, then it is reasonable to believe not *p* is surely incorrect (rather, it is then reasonable to suspend judgment about *p*—to "withhold *p*," as epistemologists put it). So, even if this second option happens to be the true one, Hume has no warrant for accepting it and thus no warrant for accepting the key premise of his novel argument. The third option is that there is a perception/object distinction after all. On that view, the intermittent existence of our perceptions that serves as the starting point of Hume's argument is preserved, but the argument breaks down because there is no longer any reason why objects cannot outlast our "gappy" perceptions of them, since objects are distinct from those perceptions. I see no way for Hume to escape from this trilemma. I conclude that although he has a striking, novel reason for saying that sensible objects have an intermittent existence, ultimately that reason is not compelling.

V CONSTANCY AND COHERENCE

I turn now to Hume's explanation of how the belief in object continuity is generated. Because it does not arise from either the senses or reason, Hume holds that it is produced by the faculty of *imagination* when that faculty is stimulated by two features of our impressions: *constancy* and *coherence*. Constancy can be defined as follows.

> A series of impressions, *I*, exhibits constancy = *df* I is a discontinuous series of impressions all of whose members exactly resemble each other.

Hume gives this example of constancy and its effect on the imagination:

> I survey the furniture in my chamber; I shut my eyes, and afterwards open them; and find the new perceptions to resemble perfectly those, which formerly struck my senses. This resemblance is observ'd in a thousand instances, and naturally connects together our ideas of these interrupted perceptions by the strongest relation, and conveys the mind with an easy transition from one to another. An easy transition or passage of the imagination, along the ideas of these different and interrupted perceptions, is almost the same disposition of mind with that which we consider one constant and unchanged perception. 'Tis therefore very natural for us to mistake the one for the other. (T 1.4.2.35/204)

Hume then notes that constancy does not characterize all of our perceptions but that, even when it does not, those perceptions

> preserve a *coherence*, and have a regular dependence on each other; which is the foundation of a kind of reasoning from causation, and produces the opinion of their continu'd existence. When I return to my chamber after an hour's absence, I find not my fire in the same situation, in which I left it: But then I am accustomed in other instances to see a like alteration produc'd in a like time, whether I am present or absent, near or remote. This coherence, therefore, in their changes is one of the characteristics of [those perceptions that we equate with] external objects, as well as their constancy. (T 1.4.2.19/195)

Coherence, then, can be defined this way:

> A series of impressions, *I*, exhibits coherence = *df* I is composed of a discontinuous series of impressions whose members occur in the same temporal relations as the resembling members of continuous but altering series of impressions, and those series closely resemble each other.

Harold Noonan (1999: 174) provides this helpful clarification of coherence:

> Thus, Hume's picture is that in [the fire in my chamber case] I observe a sequence of perceptions:
>
> ABCDXXXJHIJ
>
> and on many other occasions have sequences of the form:
>
> ABCDEFGHIJ
>
> or:
>
> ABXXXFGHIJ
>
> and so on. The series of perceptions ABCDXXXJHIJ which I receive from the fire in my study before and after my trip outside is thus a coherent series, not intrinsically [as the case of constancy], but because of its relation to the other series of this kind.

VI WHY COHERENCE IS NOT ENOUGH

Hume argues that coherence alone is much too weak to support the belief in object continuity. He says:

> Any degree . . . of regularity in our perceptions, can never be a foundation for us to infer a greater degree of regularity in some objects, which are not perceiv'd . . . But 'tis evident, that whenever we infer the continu'd existence of the objects of sense from their coherence, and the frequency of their union, 'tis in order to bestow on the objects a greater regularity than what is observ'd in our mere perceptions. We remark a connexion between two kinds of objects in their past appearance to the senses, but are not able to observe this connexion to be perfectly constant, since the turning about of our head, or the shutting of our eyes is able to break it. What then do we suppose in this case, but that these objects still continue their usual connexion, notwithstanding their apparent interruption, and that the irregular appearances are join'd by something, of which we are insensible? But as all reasoning concerning matters of fact arises only from custom, and custom can only be the effect of repeated perceptions, the extending of custom and reasoning beyond the perceptions can never be the direct and natural effect of the constant repetition

and connexion, but must arise from the co-operation of some other principles. (T 1.4.2.21/197–8)

To grasp Hume's argument, suppose that I have a series of what I shall call "type I cases" of viewing a fire my fireplace—cases where I look continuously at the diminishing fire.

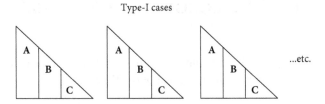

Type-I cases

...etc.

Given that I have observed a sufficiently long series of such cases and no contrary cases, if, in a new case, I have impressions as of stage A of a fire, then, by Hume's theory of causal inference, I may infer that I will have impressions of stage B. This is because my past experience licenses me to rely on the generalization that whenever I have stage A impressions, they are followed by stage B impressions. But now suppose I observe what I shall call a "type II case"—a case in which, at one or more times while the fire is burning, I shut my eyes, turn away, or leave the room:

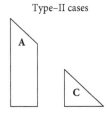

Type–II cases

If I were to infer a stage B impression from the stage A impression in this type II case, I would still be relying on the generalization that whenever I have stage A impressions, they are followed by stage B impressions. But, as this type II case itself shows, I have not observed that generalization to hold in all cases, so the case is a counterinstance to the generalization. Therefore, in inferring a stage B impression from a stage A impression in this type II case, I am imputing to things a greater degree of regularity than I have observed in them. Hume considers several more complex cases of coherence that there is no space to discuss here, but similar reasoning applies to them.[9]

In the end, then, the inference from coherence must be supplemented by what H. H. Price called Hume's "inertia principle," according to which the imagination, stimulated by the coherence of our impressions, adds to them a degree of regularity greater than we ever observe; just as, in Hume's memorable image, the inertia of a galley contributes to its forward motion even between the strokes of the oars (T 1.4.2.22/198). He adds that even with the addition of the inertia principle, coherence "is too weak to support alone so vast an edifice, as is that of the continu'd existence of all external bodies; and . . . we must join the *constancy* of their appearance to the *coherence*, in order to give a satisfactory account of that opinion" (T 1.4.2.23/198–9). This leads directly to the elaborate four-part "system" that he gives to explain how constancy gives rise to the belief in object continuity.

VII The "Vulgar System" and the "Philosophical System"

According to what Hume calls "the vulgar system" (the version of the belief in body held by the common person and by all of us most of the time), the following three propositions are all true:

(1) Sensible objects are bodies.
(2) Sensible objects have a continuous existence.
(3) Bodies have a continuous existence.

These propositions are, of course, perfectly consistent, but Hume thinks that (2) is false. He holds that the vulgar falsely believe that sensible objects have an uninterrupted or continuous existence—that they are deluded in their belief that (2) is true. To explain how the delusion arises, he offers, in addition to coherence, a complicated four-part "system" that turns on constancy, which may be summarized as follows. The first part's operative component is Hume's definition of (diachronic) identity, according to which a thing retains its identity through time if and only if (a) its existence is uninterrupted and (b) the thing does not change during that time.[10] The second part makes four distinct points: (1) a set of impressions exhibiting constancy meets condition (b) because its earlier members exactly resemble its later members; (2) a psychological principle causes us to think, whenever X exactly resembles Y, then X is identical with Y; (3) this principle drives us toward the belief that the earlier impressions are identical with the later ones, but (4) the discontinuity (interruption, gap) between the earlier and later impressions means that they do not meet condition (a), and so drives us toward the opposite belief, thereby generating a mental unease or tension in face of the threatened contradiction. The third part of the system holds that we avoid this contradiction by "feigning" the continued existence of sensible objects during the gaps between our interrupted but exactly resembling impressions. This feigning, which is carried out by the imagination, masks those gaps and thereby frees us to think of sensible objects as also meeting condition (a) and so as possessing identity over time. The fourth part of the system holds that because the feigning consists in a lively idea related to present memories that are "equivalent to impressions," it meets Hume's official definition of belief as "a lively idea related to or associated with a present impression" (T 1.3.7.5/96) and thus amounts to a *belief* in the continuous existence of the objects of the senses; thus, in the fourth part, the "feigning" of the third part is promoted to the status of a belief.

A critic of Hume might object that he attributes to the vulgar the inconsistent position that sensible objects are both continuous and intermittent. But this possible objection, although quite natural, would be incorrect because, in the end, the vulgar deny the intermittency and affirm the continuity. It is true that point (4) of the second part of the system implies that the vulgar are at least dimly aware of the "gappiness" of sensible objects. But this awareness does not rise to the level of a belief; it is akin to a person's being dimly aware that his or her spouse is unfaithful but refusing to believe it. If the activity of the imagination that Hume describes in the third part of his system did not occur, then the vulgar *would* believe that perceptions/sensible objects have an intermittent existence (just as, if the betrayed spouse were not blinded by love or trust, he or she would believe the infidelity). But because this activity of the imagination is for Hume a built-in psychological principle that always operates and that thus kicks in as soon as we are presented with "gappy" but resembling impressions, there is no time at which the vulgar believe that perceptions/sensible objects have only an intermittent existence and hence no time at which they believe that they have *both* an intermittent and a continuing existence.

Although Hume maintains that the vulgar system is consistent, he argues that it is "really false" (T 1.4.2.43/209). For, in addition to his novel argument for the intermittency of sensible objects, he finds that "a very little reflection and philosophy is sufficient to make us perceive" that the objects of the senses do not have a distinct or independent existence and therefore do not have a continuous existence either. Thus, immediately after telling us that his system is "consistent [and] perfectly convincing," Hume attacks Proposition (2) of the system by means of his above-mentioned *modus tollens* argument (T 1.4.2.44/210–11 and T 1.4.2.50/214):

(1) If sensible objects continue to exist while not being perceived, then they exist independently of being perceived.
(2) Sensible objects do not exist independently of being perceived.

∴ Sensible objects do not continue to exist while not being perceived.

To support this argument's second premise, Hume cites the "experiments, which convince us, that our perceptions are not possest of any independent existence," such as pressing one eye with a finger and seeing everything double (T 1.4.2.45/210). Except for the Humean twist, exhibited in the first premise, of linking independence with continuity, this is a standard appeal to the argument from illusion. Thus, Hume appeals to the point that the veridical and the nonveridical perceptions obtained in a case of double vision "are both of the same nature" (i.e., are phenomenologically indistinguishable) to prove that they are both equally "dependent on our sense organs, and the disposition of our nerves and animal spirits" (T 1.4.2.45/211).

If we accept the *modus tollens* argument and continue to hold Propositions (1) and (3) of the vulgar system, however, we fall into the contradiction of accepting:

(1) The objects of perception are bodies.
(not 2) The objects of the senses have a discontinuous existence.
(3) Bodies have a continuous existence.

But Hume holds that people who accept the *modus tollens* argument find a way to avoid the contradiction. They avoid it by devising the "philosophical system" or the theory of "the double existence of perceptions and objects," which denies (1) and affirms the following propositions:

(1a) The objects of the senses are our own perceptions or impressions.
(not 2) The objects of the senses have a discontinuous existence.
(3) Bodies have a continuous existence.

Thus, the realization that the objects of the senses have neither an independent nor a continuous existence does not lead people to give up the belief in body. Instead, they invent the "philosophical system," which distinguishes between perceptions and objects and posits continuous bodies as the causes of their discontinuous perceptions. The contradiction is avoided by ascribing the discontinuity to perceptions and the continuity to bodies.

Hume then proceeds to lambaste the philosophical system as being even worse off than the vulgar system. First, the philosophical system has no rational basis because the causal inference from perceptions to bodies that it relies on is worthless. Second, it derives all of its plausibility from and is thus parasitic on the vulgar system because we would never have devised it had we not been first been convinced by our imagination that the very objects of sense have a continued and distinct existence. Third, because the philosophical system denies what the vulgar system affirms (viz., the continuous existence of the objects of the senses), it even contradicts the very system that it depends on! Finally, in a later section of the *Treatise*, Hume argues that the philosophical system is false, essentially on the Berkeleyan grounds that since "neither colour, sound, taste, nor smell have a continu'd and independent existence," and the primary qualities of shape, size, and motion cannot be conceived to exist without those sensible qualities (nor, he argues, defined in terms of solidity), it follows that "there is nothing in the universe, which has such an existence" (T 1.4.4.15/23).

VIII A CONTEMPORARY CRITICISM OF HUME

As we have seen, Hume shares with many of his contemporaries the assumption that we perceive only impressions—"sensations or ideas" or "sense data"—for he accepts the arguments that are supposed to prove that this assumption is correct. With many contemporary philosophers however, I believe that all such arguments are unsound.[11] Consider only the ones given by Hume himself.

A. Perceptual relativity:

(1) What we see changes when we look at an object from different distances and angles.

(2) The object itself does not change.

∴ (3) What we see is something other than the object—an impression, image, or sense datum.

The objection to this argument is that all (1) really means is:

(1a) When we look at an object from different distances and angles, the object's shape and size *seem* (in one sense of "seem") to change.

But from (1a) and (2), it is obviously invalid to conclude that (3). Such an argument was taken to be sound by philosophers for a long time because they thought that (1a) entails (1). In general, they thought that this form of argument is valid:

S perceives something that seems or appears *F.*

∴ S perceives an appearance (impression, sense-datum, etc.) which really is *F.*

But, as R. M. Chisholm neatly showed, this form of argument, which he dubbed "the Sense Datum Fallacy," is invalid.[12] Much the same point can be made about arguments turning on the causal facts of perception, as can be seen by substituting "with different kinds of eyes" for "from different distances and angles" into (1a).

B. Illusion (seeing double):

(1) When we press one eye with a finger, we see two of every object that we previously saw.

(2) At least one member of every such pair of objects lacks a continuous and independent existence.

(3) Both members of every such pair of objects are of the same nature.

∴ Both members of every such pair of objects lack a continuous and independent existence.

One objection is to premise (1)'s claim that upon pressing one's eye we really see *two* objects for every one that we saw before—that the number of objects then seen literally increases (it doubles). This is to take the element of truth expressed in (1) much too literally. All (1) really commits us to is that, upon pressing one eye, we *seem* to see a "twin" of every object that we previously saw. But *seeming to see* a new object is not the same thing as *actually seeing* a new object; as would happen if, say, the object had undergone mitosis or fission: the argument simply confuses these two different things. Another objection is to premise (3): even if we grant premise (1) and the talk in premises (2) and (3) of pairs of "objects," there is no good reason to accept premise (3), that both members of such a pair of objects are "of the same nature." Why not maintain, instead, that one of the two objects in such a pair is a body or material thing, whereas only the other one is an impression or "perception"? The usual reason given is that there is no special, discernible, telltale difference between the two "objects" that indicates that one of them is a mind-dependent impression while the other is a body; therefore, they must both be of the same nature. Thus, because according to (2) at least one of them must be an impression, both of them must be impressions. But this reason for saying that both "objects" are of the same nature is defective. The fact that two things are visually alike does not show that they are "of the same nature."[13]

IX Concluding Observation

Even if the arguments purporting to show that we perceive only our own impressions or "sense data" are all unsound, this does not mean that there is no epistemological problem about our knowledge of bodies. It is sometimes thought that this problem arises only from the belief that we perceive only our own impressions or "sense data," so that once that belief is rejected, the problem disappears. But this is wrong. The real source of the problem is that the perceptual experiences we have when we perceive material objects can be duplicated when we do not perceive any material object because they can be caused to occur even when no material object is present or stimulating our sense receptors. This shows that even when we *do* perceive a material object, we cannot *know* that we are perceiving it solely on the basis of our present perceptual experience. How then can we know that we are perceiving a material object? It's not enough to say that we can know this simply by appealing to other perceptions for corroboration because the perceptual experiences had in those other perceptions can also be caused to occur even when no material object is present or stimulating our sense receptors, and this point leads to an infinite regress of corroborations. Thus, the problem of our knowledge of the external world that Hume thought to be insoluble remains even when we reject his assumption that we perceive only our own impressions.[14]

Abbreviations of Works Cited

EU   *An Enquiry Concerning Human Understanding.* Edited by T. L. Beauchamp. Oxford: Clarendon, 2000.

T   *A Treatise of Human Nature.* Edited by D. F. Norton and M. J. Norton. Oxford: Clarendon, 2007.

Notes

1. I propose an answer to this question in Dicker (2007), on which many points made in this essay are based.
2. Noonan (1999: 167).
3. See Noonan (1999: 168).
4. See Kant, *Critique of Pure Reason* (1997), A290/B235–A193/B238.
5. Kant does not argue for the thesis that assigning a different set of time relations to objects of perception from those of the perceptions themselves is a condition of the possibility of experience in the "Analogies of Experience," where the distinction between the subjective time order and the objective time order is assumed from the start and serves as a premise of the arguments. Rather, the need to assign a different set of time relations to perceptions and to their objects is supposed to be established earlier, in the "Transcendental Deduction."
6. The term "unowned perceptions" was, to the best of my knowledge, coined by Bennett (1977: 345).
7. This reading differs from Price (1940), where unowned perceptions are throughout equated with unsensed *sensibilia*.
8. This crucial point was called to my attention by Peter Millican.
9. See Dicker (2007: 142–144).
10. The first part also includes a difficult discussion of the relation among unity, multiplicity, and identity, but it is not necessary to analyze that discussion for my purposes. It is analyzed in Baxter (2006: 114–132).
11. I discuss such arguments in depth in Dicker (1980) and in Dicker (2011).
12. See Chisholm (1957: 151–152; 1966: 94–95; 1976: 47–48; 1994: 101–102).
13. See Austin (1962: 50–52).
14. See Dicker (1980: 57–58) and Dicker (2011: 34–35).

Bibliography

Austin, J. L. (1962). *Sense and Sensibilia*. London: Oxford University Press.

Baxter, Donald L. (2006). "Identity, Continued Existence, and the External World," in Saul Traiger, ed., *The Blackwell Guide to Hume's Treatise*. Oxford: Blackwell, 114–132.

Bennett, Jonathan. (1977). *Locke, Berkeley, Hume: Central Themes*. Oxford: Oxford University Press.

Chisholm, Roderick M. (1957). *Perceiving: A Philosophical Study*. Ithaca, NY: Cornell University Press.

Chisholm, Roderick M. (1966). *Theory of Knowledge*, 1st ed. Englewood Cliffs, NJ: Prentice-Hall.

Chisholm, Roderick M. (1976). *Person and Object: A Metaphysical Study*. London: Allen & Unwin.

Chisholm, Roderick M. (1994). "On the Observability of the Self," reprinted in Quassim Cassam, ed., *Self-Knowledge*. Oxford: Oxford University Press, 94–108.

Dicker, Georges. (1980). *Perceptual Knowledge: An Analytical and Historical Study*. Dordrecht/Boston/London: D. Reidel.

Dicker, Georges. (2007). "Three Questions about *Treatise* 1.4.2," *Hume Studies* 33:1 (April), 115–153.

Dicker, Georges. (2011). *Berkeley's Idealism: A Critical Examination.* New York: Oxford University Press.

Kant, Immanuel. (1997). *Critique of Pure Reason,* trans. Paul Guyer and Allen W. Wood. Cambridge: Cambridge University Press.

Noonan, Harold W. (1999). *Hume on Knowledge.* London: Routledge.

Price, H. H. (1940). *Hume's Theory of the External World.* Oxford: Clarendon Press.

Smith, A. D. (2004). *The Problem of Perception.* Cambridge: Harvard University Press.

FURTHER READING

Loeb, Louis. (2001). *Stability and Justification in Hume's* Treatise. Oxford: Oxford University Press.

Stroud, Barry. (1977). *Hume.* London: Routledge and Kegan Paul.

CHAPTER 14

HUME ON PERSONAL IDENTITY

GALEN STRAWSON

"When I enter most intimately into what I call *myself* . . . "

IN this paper, I focus on Hume's initial discussion of personal identity in section 1.4.6 of his *Treatise*. I argue, first, that Hume doesn't think that the mind is just a "bundle" of perceptions; second, that the bundle account of the mind that he expounds in 1.4.6 doesn't involve any sort of denial of the existence of subjects of experience; third, that he never claims that the subject of experience isn't encountered in experience.[1] I don't here consider Hume's partial repudiation of his account of personal identity in the Appendix to the *Treatise*. He doesn't in the Appendix find any fault in his phenomenological account in 1.4.6 of what he comes across when he engages in mental self-examination by "entering intimately into what I call *myself*." Nor, I believe, does he find any fault in his treatment of the other main topic of T 1.4.6: his account of how we come to believe in the existence of a persisting self as a result of the mind's "sliding easily" along certain series of perceptions.[2]

I THE EXPERIENCE/EXPERIENCER THESIS

I begin with a point stressed by many philosophers and taken for granted by many others, including Hume; reasonably so, because it's a necessary truth. Frege puts it straightforwardly: "an experience is impossible without an experiencer" (1918: 27). It's "an obvious conceptual truth that an experiencing is necessarily an experiencing by a subject of experience, and involves that subject as intimately as a branch-bending involves a branch" (Shoemaker 1986: 10).

I'll call this the *Experience/Experiencer Thesis*.[3] Note that it doesn't commit one to any particular metaphysical view about the ultimate nature of the subject of experience. One can be as uncommitted on this question as Descartes is in his *Second Meditation*.[4] One can, for example, fully accept the Experience/Experiencer Thesis without supposing that a subject of experience is something that lasts longer than a single experience or "perception."

One way to mark this point is to say that the Experience/Experiencer Thesis isn't something that Buddhists deny. Another is to say that the notion of the subject that features in the necessary truth doesn't allow that one can say something true by saying that "the existence of experience entails the existence of subjectivity, but not the existence of a subject of experience." The presence of subjectivity already entails the presence of a subject of experience, given the present metaphysically uncommitted notion of a subject of experience.

I'll consider a challenge to this claim at the end of Section II. For the moment, it can be re-expressed by saying that experience is necessarily experience *for*—experience for or on the part of someone or something. Consider pain, an unhappily familiar case of experience. It is, essentially, a feeling, and a feeling is just that, a feel-*ing*, a being-felt, something that can't possibly exist without there being a feel-*er*. The noun "feeler" doesn't import any metaphysical commitment additional to the noun "feeling;" it simply draws one's attention to the full import of "feeling." The sense in which it's necessarily true that there's a feel*ing*, and hence a feel*er*, of pain, if there is pain at all, is the sense in which it's necessarily true that there's a subject of experience if there is experience, and hence subjectivity, at all.

Kant endorses the Experience/Experiencer Thesis when he writes to Herz that "the thinking or the existence of the thought and the existence of my own self are one and the same" (1772: 75) or (a better translation, all in all) "the experiencing or the existence of the experience and the existence of my own self are one and the same." One might call this claim the *Experience/Experiencer Identity Thesis*. Evidently it entails the Experience/Experiencer Thesis.

II THE BUNDLE THEORY OF MIND

The Experience/Experiencer Identity Thesis is endorsed by many philosophers, including Descartes, as I read him,[5] and William James in his *Principles of Psychology*. It seems useful to put it on the table now, if only because it appears to be cognate with an outright ontological claim often attributed to Hume: the claim that the subject, or "self," or "mind," or "person," conceived of as something that persists through time, is identical to a series of experiences and is therefore—presumably—identical to a single (possibly complex) experience at any particular time that it exists.

Hume, however, is a skeptic. If we know anything for certain about his position, it is that *he doesn't claim to know the ultimate nature of things* (other than individual experiences or "perceptions," conceived in the traditional "internalist" way). He's clear on the point that "the essence of the mind" is unknown to us; it is "equally unknown to us with that of external bodies" (T Intro. 8/xvii). His fundamental claim about the mind, accordingly, is the following moderate, skeptical, semantico-epistemological claim: all the empirically warranted content we can give to the idea of a mind or self or person,[6] and hence all the content we can give to these ideas in so far as they have a legitimate employment in philosophy, which must restrict itself to clear and distinct ideas,[7] is the idea of a perception or experience or series of perceptions or experiences. The mind "as far as we can *conceive* it, is nothing but a system or train of different perceptions" (TA 28/657, emphasis added). We have no "*notion* of . . . self . . . , when *conceiv'd* distinct from particular perceptions . . . we have no *notion* of . . . the mind . . . , distinct from the particular perceptions" (TA 18, 19/635, emphasis added).[8] These are explicitly epistemologically qualified statements of what has come to be known as the "bundle theory of mind." They're claims to the effect that this is all we can know or clearly conceive of the mind, they're not claims that this is all it *is*.

However: we also find many epistemologically unqualified ontological formulations of the bundle theory of mind. Minds, or selves, or persons are "nothing but a bundle or collection of different perceptions" (T 1.4.6.4/252). "They are the successive perceptions only, that constitute the mind" (T 1.4.6.4/253); a "succession of perceptions . . . constitutes [a] mind or thinking principle" (T 1.4.6.18/260). It is a "chain of causes and effects, which constitute our self or person" (T 1.4.6.20/262)[9]; a "composition of . . . perceptions . . . forms the self" (TA 15/634). A "train . . . of . . . perceptions . . . compose a mind" (TA 20/635). Hume couldn't be more plain: "what we call a mind, is nothing but a heap or collection of different perceptions, united together by certain relations" (T 1.4.2.39/207). It is a "connected mass of perceptions, which constitute a thinking being" (T 1.4.2.39/207), "a connected heap of perceptions" (T 1.4.2.40/207). It is a "succession of perceptions, which constitutes our self or person" (T 1.4.7.3/265). "It must be our several particular perceptions, that compose the mind. I say, compose the mind, not belong to it" (TA 28/658).[10]

How should we take these statements, given that they're made by a skeptic who denies any knowledge of the ultimate nature of reality, apart from the nature of individual experiences or perceptions? We should step back. We should recall Hume's repudiation of the "positive air" of the *Treatise*, which sometimes led him to couch semantic or epistemological claims in dramatic ontological terms: "Above all, the positive air, which prevails in that book, and which may be imputed to the ardor of youth, so much displeases me, that I have not patience to review it" (LET: 1.187). We should recall that Hume's central project in the *Treatise* and the first *Enquiry* is a "science of man," of "human nature" (T Intro. 6/xvi), a "mental geography, or delineation of *the distinct parts and powers of the mind*" (EU 1.13/13, emphasis added). "It cannot be doubted," he says, "that *the mind is endowed with several powers and faculties,* [and] that these powers are distinct from each other." His hope is that "philosophy . . . may . . . discover, at least in some degree, *the secret springs and principles, by which the human mind is actuated in its operations*" (EU 1.14/13–14, emphasis added). "At least in some degree": he thinks that there is only so much that philosophy can do; for, again, "to me it seems evident, that the essence of the mind [is] equally unknown to us with that of external bodies"; it is impossible to "discover the ultimate original qualities of human nature (T Intro. 8/xvii). It follows that the mind can't be just a series of experiences, on Hume's view, although all we can know of it is a series of experiences. For "the [experiences] of the mind are perfectly known" (T 2.2.6.2/366), and nothing can be both unknown and perfectly known. Nor can a thing have any "secret springs and principles" that are at best only partially discoverable if it's just a series of perfectly known experiences.[11]

Hume regularly makes the point that nothing is hidden so far as experiences are concerned: "since all actions and sensations of the mind are known to us by consciousness, they must necessarily appear in every particular what they are, and be what they appear"; for "consciousness never deceives" (T 1.4.2.7/190; EU 7.13/66). They can't, therefore, be all there is to the mind, as the ontological bundle theory asserts. Hume doesn't for a moment intend to assert the ontological claims quoted two paragraphs back without restriction. They are, again, claims about the mind so far as we have any empirically (hence philosophically) respectable knowledge of it. They're claims about the maximum legitimate content of any claims about the nature of the mind that can claim to express knowledge of the nature of the mind.[12]

I'm going to take it that this is beyond serious dispute—that we are in the twenty-first century sufficiently reconciled with the eighteenth (after the confusions of the nineteenth and twentieth) to have passed beyond the point at which we think that Hume was in his discussion of personal identity concerned to make an outright ontological claim about the ultimate nature of the mind or self. If there's one thing we know about him, it is—again—that he's a skeptic who doesn't claim to know the ultimate nature of any reality, other than the reality of perceptions or experiences.

There are other ways of proving that Hume was no sort of ontological bundle theorist. One proof starts out from his key explanatory theoretical commitment—to the existence of a faculty of the mind called "the imagination." Another related proof starts out from the details of his theory of ideas, and of the association of ideas. These central features of his thought are provably incompatible with the ontological bundle theory. There is, however, no need to consider them further here, because the basic point is secure (I give the proofs in Strawson 2011a: 56–61).

III "WHEN I ENTER MOST INTIMATELY INTO WHAT I CALL *MYSELF*"

With the Experience/Experiencer Thesis in place, consider what is perhaps Hume's most famous remark: "when I enter most intimately into what I call *myself*, I always stumble on some particular perception or other . . . I never can catch *myself* at any time without a perception, and never can observe anything but the perception" (T 1.4.6.3/252).

The word "perception" refers here to an actual occurrence, an actual episode of perceiving that occurs at a particular time, and it's worth varying Hume's wording in a number of ways. The first variation substitutes "episode of perceiving" or "perceiving" for "perception": . . . when I enter most intimately into what I call myself, I always stumble on some particular episode of perceiving or other . . . I never can catch *myself* at any time without an episode of perceiving, and never can observe anything but the perceiving.

The second variation substitutes "come across" for "catch" in the first variation, in the attempt to make things clearer: . . . when I enter most intimately into what I call myself, I always stumble on some particular episode of perceiving or other . . . I never can come across *myself* at any time without [coming across] an episode of perceiving, and never can observe anything but the perceiving.

The third variation substitutes "episode of experience" or "experience" or "experiencing" for "perception": . . . when I enter most intimately into what I call *myself* I always stumble on some particular episode of experience or other . . . I never can come across *myself* at any time without [coming across] an experience, and never can observe anything but the experience (experiencing).

I'll regularly substitute "experience" for "perception" in what follows because one natural use of "experience" in present-day philosophical discourse corresponds very well to what Hume means by "perception," a term he uses in an entirely general way to cover any sort of conscious mental occurrence ("perceptions" subdivide into "impressions" and "ideas," in Hume's terminology). The substitution may help to suspend certain standard interpretative reflex reactions that seem to have sunk into the very words of the text in such a way that we no longer have clear access to the original. "Experiencing" is also helpful because it makes it clear that an actual occurrence of experience is in question.

I believe that Hume's meaning is wholly preserved in these variations of the original passage. What does it say? It's a strictly phenomenological claim. It says that when I consider myself in my mental being, when I engage in a certain kind of mental self-examination, two things are true:

(1) I never catch or come across myself without also catching or coming across an experience (the *No Bare View Thesis*).
(2) I never observe anything other than the experience—the experiencing, the episode of experience (the *Nothing But an Experience Thesis*).

These two claims are linked but different. According to (1), the weaker claim, I never get a *bare view* of the self or subject of experience. That is, I never get a view of the subject alone. I do, of course, always catch *myself*, the subject of experience, as Hume says, when I enter most intimately into what I call myself and observe an experience. For, (a), an experience encountered in this way is indeed an *experience*, an actual concrete episode of experienc*ing*, and therefore always and essentially involves an experienc*er*, because an experiencing is necessarily an *experiencing-by-an-experiencer* (as the Experience/Experiencer Thesis states). And, (b), the claim that an experience or experiencing necessarily involves an experienc*er* isn't just the claim that it presupposes an experiencer, as a possibly unencountered, transcendental condition of its possibility. To think clearly about what an actual experiencing is is to see that it's not possible to encounter an experiencing, in mental self-examination, without also encountering an experiencer.[13] What remains true, nevertheless, is that I never catch or come across myself at any time pure, as it were (i.e. "without a perception" or experience). Nor, therefore, and crucially, given Hume's purposes, do I ever catch anything that presents itself as capable of existing entirely apart from the particular experience in such a way as to have a chance of qualifying for the title "substance" as traditionally understood.[14]

So much for (1). According to (2), the stronger claim, when I catch myself in this way, I never observe anything but the experience—the experience-event, the episode of experience. The experience-event is, to be sure, an experiencing. It's a necessarily-subject-of-experience-involving thing, a thing whose existence is, necessarily, partly *constituted* by the existence of a subject of experience. So I do indeed catch myself, the self or person or subject, in catching the experience. But no self or subject presents in such a manner that it can be taken to be ontically distinct from the overall experience-event in the way that the philosophical tradition of Hume's time uniformly supposes the self or subject (or soul) to be. There's no impression of any such thing to be had, and there is therefore (for a Humean empiricist) no warrant for taking there to be such a thing in one's philosophy when one is aiming to make knowledge claims about the nature of reality. Nothing presents as a subject that is distinct or distinguishable from the episode of experience in such a way that it can be taken to be ontologically separate from the episode of experience on the terms of Hume's fundamental Separability Principle.[15] It's not just that nothing presents as a *simple, unchanging, persisting* (*continuously existing*) subject distinct from the episode of experience, although this—the soul as traditionally conceived—is Hume's principal point and target. It's that no subject of any sort, not even a fleeting one, presents as distinct from the episode of experience in the required way.

One can re-express the point by saying that for any given individual experiencing *e* encountered in reflection on one's mental being, when *e* is strictly examined, no subject presents as in any way *e-transcendent*.[16] To say this, though, is not—not at all—to say that a subject or self is not encountered in any way at all. To say that all that we encounter in mental self-examination, so far as the mind or self or subject of experience is concerned, is a series of experiences or experiencings, is not to say that we don't encounter a subject of experience in any sense at all; for an experience is a necessarily-subject-involving occurrence. Even the outright ontological (and therefore non-Humean) claim that the mind or self is nothing but a series of experiences is not—not at all, not in any way—the claim that it doesn't involve any subject of experience or any subjects of experience. For, once again, the existence of an experience, an actual experiencing, obviously and necessarily involves the existence of a subject of experience.

So much for (2). I think Hume is exactly right about both (1) and (2); he gives an extremely accurate report of what one finds when one engages in this sort of mental self-examination. The phenomenological facts are waiting for anyone to discover and are well recognized in the Phenomenological tradition of philosophy deriving from Husserl. When Kant says that "I do not know myself through being conscious of myself as experiencing, but only when I am conscious of the intuition of myself as determined with respect to the function of experiencing" (1781/7: B406), he has more in mind than Hume, but he is also expressing something like (1), and, in effect, (2). William James affirms (2) when, using "thought" in Descartes's entirely general sense to mean any kind of conscious experience, he says that "the passing Thought itself is the only *verifiable* thinker" (1890: 1.346).[17]

Hume, then, never denies the existence of selves or subjects of experience, contrary to what some have suggested. If, however, one defines a self or subject of experience as something that persists for a considerable period of time—in a way that was then and still is the most common understanding of the term—then Hume does, of course, deny that we can know there to be such a thing; and he also, of course, and connectedly, and centrally, denies that we can legitimately take the idea or term *self* (or *mind* or *person*) to mean such a thing. We can, when doing philosophy, sufficiently characterize what the "metaphysicians" (T 1.4.6.4/252) take themselves to have in mind when they use the term *self* or *person*, even though these terms are not clear and distinct (or therefore "intelligible") by Hume's empiricist standards; Hume offers such a characterization himself (T 1.4.6.1–2/251). But when empirically warranted knowledge claims are in question, the idea of the self, understood to pick out something that persists for a considerable period of time, can on Hume's view have no more legitimate meaning or content than the idea of a (possibly gappy) series of experiences.

IV A TROUBLESOME AMBIGUITY

Of the two readings just suggested, it's the reading of (2) that many philosophers find more difficult, given the existing tradition of Hume commentary. The difficulty derives in part from the fact that words like "perception" or "experience" have a natural dual use, which is harmless in many contexts but potentially misleading in others. The primary use of these words is to denote an actual, particular episode of conscious experience occurring at a particular time. But we can also use expressions like "perception of red" and "experience of red" to denote a type of experience rather than any particular "token" occurrence of experience, and Hume does sometimes use "perception" (or rather, more commonly, "impression" and "idea") in just this way: not as a word for an actual concrete occurrence, occurring at noon, say, or ten to three, but as a word for a type of experiential content—the experience of *red*, say, or *pain*, or *the taste of pineapple*, or the thought *twice two is four*. Of the fifty-nine occurrences of the word "perception" in the passages of Hume's writing that primarily concern us now ("Of Personal Identity," Paragraphs 10–21 of the Appendix, and Paragraph 28 of the Abstract) only two are even prima facie candidates for being type uses.[18] That said, there are type uses elsewhere in the *Treatise* (especially of "impression" and "idea"), cases in which we may naturally think of *a* perception as something independent of any actual (necessarily-experiencer-involving) concrete occurrence of experiencing. It may be that the availability of such uses to mean *red* as a type of experiential content removes a crucial barrier on the route to the false view that Hume's famous claim is that all he comes across, when he comes across a perception or experience in mental self-examination, is, as it were, a mere patch of content, a patch of content that, although occurrent, can somehow be supposed to exist independently of any necessarily-experiencer-involving episode of experiencing, and, hence, independently of any particular subject of experience.

It's not easy to know what to make of this line of thought, but it seems to involve attributing to Hume the idea that one could come across occurrent experiential/perceptual content, an actual occurrence of redness-experience, say, existing at a given particular time, without in any sense coming across a subject of experience. And this idea has been extended into the claim that Hume denies the existence of subjects of experience altogether. Price, however, thinks that it is enough to read and understand the words "when I enter most intimately into what I call *myself* . . . " to be clear on the point that Hume believes in the existence of a subject of experience of some sort.[19] What Hume denies is simply that there is any empirically respectable evidence for the view that there is a subject of experience that lasts longer than any given fleeting necessarily-subject-involving perception, let alone a subject of experience that is metaphysically simple, ontically self-subsistent, and absolutely unchanging through time (T 1.4.6.1–2/251).

Hume is right about this, on his own empiricist terms. But if one thing is certain, it is that the "bundle" account of the mind or self, or subject—which records all the empirically legitimate content that can be given to the idea of the mind or self or subject, and hence all the content that it can be allowed to have in any purported knowledge claim in a strict empiricist philosophy—doesn't conceive the mind, incoherently, as a bundle of subject-of-experience-lacking but nonetheless occurrent experiential-content patches. It conceives it as a bundle of necessarily-subject-involving experiential-content patches. The claim, once again, is that, in so far as we take it that *the self or subject is something that persists through a long stretch of time*, the only empirically warranted and therefore clear and distinct content of our conception of that entity is of a bundle or succession of numerically distinct *selves* or *subjects* experiencing numerically distinct experiential contents: lots of subjects, not just one. One can put this in another way by saying that the empirically warranted content of our conception of a persisting self or subject is a (temporally gappy) bundle of numerically distinct experiences—as Hume does. But if one puts it this way, one must be clear on the point that these experiences are necessarily subject-of-experience-involving experiences. Lots of numerically distinct experiences mean lots of numerically distinct subjects.

Has anyone ever really taken the "no-ownership" view to be the denial that experiences necessarily have subjects at least in the sense that they are necessarily experiences-*for*? I fear so. The view is, for all that, incoherent, and as foreign to Hume as it is to Buddhists.

> The idea that there could be an actual occurrence of redness-experience without any *subjectivity* is indeed and of course incoherent. The idea of an actual occurrence of redness-experience without a *subject* isn't. And this is precisely Hume's point in the passage in question. You've simply laid it down that you're going to use "subject" in a metaphysically noncommittal way, which has the consequence that the existence of subjectivity entails the existence of a subject. To do this, though, is to deprive yourself

of the terms you need to make Hume's point. More seriously, it's to make the correct objection to your claim invisible.

I don't think many participants in the 275-year discussion of Hume's account of personal identity have had this point in mind, but it's worth registering nonetheless, for there's a sense in which it's correct, given that Hume has the then universally accepted idea of a *persisting* mind, self, person, subject, or "thinking being" firmly in mind in his discussion of personal identity. For, relative to that idea of the subject, the suggestion that a fleeting perception involves only subjectivity, and not *a* subject, can be given a reasonable sense. It isn't, however, correct as an interpretation of Hume. That is, he wouldn't have allowed that there could be subjectivity without there being (ipso facto) a subject of experience, once the assumption that subjects are long lived had been cancelled. When he says that a single experience (perception) may qualify as a substance, so far as we have any empirically warranted conception of a substance, he doesn't mean that a single experience—a patch of subjectivity—could exist without a subject of experience for whom it was an experience.

It's helpful to consult Hume's sub-oyster on this issue—the minimal "thinking being" of his Appendix. I'll return to it in the next section.

V What Is Given in Experience

Let me re-present the point using a primitive symbolism in which S stands for a *subject of experience*, E for an *experience* (or perception), and C for a *content*, i.e. an occurrent experiential content (an occurrent perception content). The curly brackets constitute a *phenomenological* context. That is, anything inside the curly brackets is a representation of *what is phenomenologically given, given in experience*.[20]

The No Bare View Thesis, (1), can now be expressed as follows. When I engage in mental self-examination, I do not encounter any experience or impression that can be represented simply as $\{S\}$. I have, in other words, no sort of experience or impression of a subject alone, let alone an experience or impression of some continuing unchanging subject alone. I do, of course (necessarily, trivially), encounter a subject of experience in encountering an experience, but all experiences or impressions of the subject are experiences or impressions of the subject *with*, or *involved in*, an (episode of) experience. That is, they are at the very least of the form $\{S + E\}$ where "E" stands for whatever particular experiential content you encounter when you try to catch yourself in the moment of experiencing something, which cannot be supposed to be simply S, given that $\{S\}$ has been ruled out.

But experiences of the subject aren't really of the additive $\{S + E\}$ form either. According to the Nothing But an Experience Thesis, (2), the experience of the subject that is necessarily involved in any coming upon an actual experience in Humean mental self-examination doesn't present the subject as something distinct from the experience in such a way as to legitimize any sense in which I can be said to encounter the subject *on the one hand* and the experience *on the other hand*. Hume expresses this last point strikingly and accurately by saying that there's a fundamental sense in which what I observe or catch is *just the experiencing*; that is, {E}. And there is a fundamental sense, acknowledged by Kant, in which this claim is phenomenologically correct. It has, however, caused confusion because something that Hume takes for granted—reasonably enough, because it's a necessary truth—has been suppressed by influential commentators and accordingly discounted by many readers.

This (of course, and again) is the Experience/Experiencer Thesis, the point that an experience that is come upon in this way is indeed an *experience* (an experienc*ing*). Such an experience isn't just an experiential content type—it's not just an experiential content understood in a way that allows that an experiential content can concretely occur or be detected without an experiencer also existing and being detected. An experience, once again, is an experiencing, and to come across an experiencing is necessarily to come across an experiencer. (In Hume's terms: a perception—an actual temporally situated occurrence, a concrete mental event—isn't just a perceptual content. A perception is a *perception*, an actual perceiv*ing* of something that necessarily involves a perceiv*er*, a subject of experience.)

A necessary truth needn't, of course, be phenomenologically apparent, even in one who takes it for granted—a point to which I will return. The present claim is not that Hume takes a certain theoretical point (a necessary truth) for granted and automatically applies it in his report of the deliverances of mental self-examination. Nor is it that Hume's experience, when he engages in mental self-examination, is influenced by his theoretical appreciation of the necessary truth in question. The present claim is a very simple one about what he means by the word "perception" ("experience") in this context. One might express it by saying that {E} can be represented as {S:C}, where ":" has some kind of intense-intimacy-intimating function that we need not at present specify further. It's {S:C}—a subject-experiencing-a-content—that I catch or observe, in some way that does not involve any explicit differentiation of S and C, when I catch or observe an experience or experiencing {E} and can observe nothing but {E}. For {E} is {S:C}.[21]

In these terms, one can say that the error in the traditional interpretation (especially its "no ownership" division) is to think that when Hume says he "never can observe anything but the experience," he means that all he encounters when he encounters the experience is {C}, a "mere content," as it were, a visual presentation as of a tiger, say, a mere content that is somehow given wholly independently of its being an actual episode of experiencing on the part of some subject of experience—even though it is given as a concretely occurring phenomenon. But to log a content in this sense is not to log an experience in the sense (in the way) that concerns Hume in this passage. It's not to take notice of an actual episode of experiencing (perception) at all, as one is bound to if one is seriously engaged in the focused exercise of mental self-apprehension that Hume is engaged in. A simple way to see this is to consider the difference between (a) what it is to experience a patch of red in a completely unreflective way, and (b) what it is to consider an experience of a patch of red and consider it specifically as such (i.e. as an experience). In entering intimately into himself in mental self-examination—a thing that can be difficult to do, as Reid points out[22]—Hume is wholly focused on (b). And when you do something of the sort specified in (b), to come upon the experience is necessarily to come upon the subject of experience.

Some may agree that an experience is a necessarily-subject-involving entity, a subject-entertaining-a-content entity or $S:C$ entity, while continuing to insist that it's just the C-ness of the necessarily-S-involving experience that Hume claims to come upon in claiming to come upon nothing but $\{E\}$. The idea is that Hume abstracts away from the necessarily-subject-involving reality of the experience considered as a concrete whole, even when engaged in this specially focused act of investigative entry into his own mental being, and somehow considers only the abstract content(-type) C. The trouble with this proposal is that there is no reason to believe it, and overwhelming reason not to, given Hume's careful investigative project. The view that Hume claims to find nothing but $\{C\}$ seems to be nothing but an old prejudice, facilitated by the fact, already noted, that the word "perception" and other similar words can be understood to have not only a necessarily-subject-involving concrete-occurrence use but also a subject-independent content-type use.

The weight of the traditional interpretation is so great that many may not be convinced. It may help to consult the imagined sub-oyster of Hume's Appendix, a creature that is, Hume supposes, even less sophisticated than an oyster, but is nonetheless a "thinking being" in the wide Cartesian sense of "thinking", an experiencing or conscious being, a subject of experience—even though it has "only one [experience], as of thirst or hunger" (TA. 16/634).[23] "Consider it in that situation," he says. "Do you conceive anything but merely that [experience]?" No, he answers. But you do indeed conceive an experience—something that is a conscious episode by definition, an actual episode of experiencing; you do (trivially) conceive or come upon a thinking-being-involving phenomenon and hence upon a "thinking being," a subject of experience.[24] And Hume's claim is the same as before: nothing more is given to observation or conception, in the thinking being's being given, than the experience. There is nothing that gives reason to believe in any "self or substance" that endures and could possibly exist apart from the experience. But to say this is (once again) in no way to say that you don't come upon a thinking being, a thinking being considered in its mental being, when you come upon the experience—the experiencing.[25]

If I join Hume in the practice of entering intimately into what I call myself, then, I get no view of a bare self—$\{S\}$—a self or subject that is not having any experience. True. Nor do I get a view of a subject having an experience in which the subject is given apart from the overall experience-event as something clearly distinguishable from it—$\{S + E\}$. True. And I certainly don't get a view of some enduring unchanging perfectly simple subject that is fully ontologically distinct from the experience—of $\{*S*\}$, as it were, the subject that is the explicit principal target of Hume's skepticism, the soul beloved of the philosophers he's criticizing. True. What I come upon is $\{E\}$, nothing but $\{E\}$, where $\{E\}$ is $\{S:C\}$, an experiencing-of-a-content-by-an-experiencer.

This is not to say that the subject is encountered as some sort of *personalitied* entity when {*E*} is come upon. It isn't. Nor is it to say that it's encountered as an express object of attention, if this is taken to mean that it has some special, separate salience as object of attention over and above the experience-event considered as a whole. Hume's crucial and wholly correct phenomenological point is, once again, precisely that it isn't. How, then, is it encountered? This is a question that has been well treated in the Phenomenological tradition, and I will shortly say more about it.

Some may think that this account of what Hume is saying is sophistical, or too complicated. It will look sophistical or overcomplicated only to those who have been conditioned by the traditional interpretation of Hume. All that the present account attributes to Hume is great phenomenological perspicacity, honesty, and accuracy of expression. True, he was dead set against immortal souls, but there's no reason to think that his description of his experience of mental self-examination is influenced by any theoretical prejudice, and the point that we have no impression or impression-based idea of an ontically separate self or subject had already been very clearly made by Berkeley.[26]

VI SUBJECT OR SUBJECTIVITY?

Some may still question whether a *subject* is come upon, experientially, when {*E*} is come upon. What is come upon, they may say, what is knowably come upon, is, at bottom, just *subjectivity*. "{*E*} is {*S:C*}" can be allowed to stand as correct, then, only on condition that one read "*S*" simply as "subjectivity." What we have, on this view, is just *C*-flavored subjectivity. Meditators may agree, claiming that an event of experience encountered in attentive, meditative mental self-examination presents merely as something that is intrinsically both subjectivity-involving and content-involving, not as something intrinsically subject-involving.[27]

As before, I think this challenge is worthwhile. There is, however, no reason to think that Hume thought along these lines or ever thought there could be a perception or experience—a subjectivity-event—without a "thinking being." There's a thinking being (a conscious being) even in the case of the sub-oyster. The lesson of the sub-oyster is that a perception (a perceiving) entails a thinking (conscious) being. No thinking (conscious) being, no perception. This, converted into the present terms, says that a subjectivity-involving event entails a subject. No subject, no subjectivity-involving event.

It may be objected that "subject" is a count noun, whereas "subjectivity" is a mass term that is, as such, intrinsically less metaphysically committed. But to say that subjectivity is knowably present or experientially given is already to concede an ineliminable sense in which a subject is knowably present, experientially given. Why is this? Because experience is essentially experience-*for*, and such *for*-ness strictly entails a subject.[28] Hume agrees. He holds that we have to do with a thinking (or conscious) being when we contemplate the sub-oyster's experience, even as he rejects the whole traditional metaphysical framework of substance and accident and, to that extent, anticipates Kant on the point that—in so far as we accept to use the categories of traditional metaphysics at all—we can't even know that the thinking being (which certainly exists) is substantial in nature and not in some way "just" an accident or property.[29]

Hume doesn't, then, think that any particular traditional substantial metaphysical commitment is built into the admittedly grammatically substantival noun phrase "thinking being," and he famously holds that individual experiential episodes themselves pass the traditional test for being a substance, so far as we can understand the notion of a substance at all (T 1.4.5.5/233; TA 19/634).[30] His position is plain: if there is indeed an experience, then there is indeed a thinking being. There is, in other words, a subject of experience. The presence of experience or subjectivity is sufficient for the presence of a subject of experience.[31]

If the view that you can't have experience (subjectivity) without a subject were doubtful, it might seem improper to hang an argument that Hume accepts it on his treatment of the sub-oyster. There is, though, a comfortable, central, metaphysically uncommitted sense in which it's necessarily—trivially—true (experience is necessarily experience-*for*), and the attribution of this view to Hume doesn't hang on the sub-oyster.

VII   METAPHYSICS AND PHENOMENOLOGY

Whatever the phenomenological facts, it is in the present terms a straightforward metaphysical truth that an experience necessarily involves a subject of experience as well as a content. Using square brackets for straightforwardly metaphysical propositions and an arrow to indicate metaphysical entailment, one can represent it as follows: $[E \rightarrow [S \& C]]$.

Having done so, it's natural to ask how this metaphysical claim—I'll call it the *ESC Thesis*—relates to the structurally cognate phenomenological claim $\{E\} = \{S:C\}$, the claim that an event of experience genuinely grasped in mental self-examination presents as both subject-involving and content-involving. It's worth considering this question both for its own sake and for the further light that considering it throws on Hume's position.

Let me first strengthen the representation of the metaphysical ESC Thesis to bring it formally into line with the phenomenological thesis: $[E = S:C]$. This states that an experience consists, metaphysically, of a subject entertaining (experiencing, standing in the relation of haver-of to) a content.[32] I think that this is, in fact, the best thing to say, with Kant in 1772, when the notion of the subject is taken in Hume's way (i.e. narrowly and mentalistically), as it is here. It is, however, a difficult idea, and one needn't accept it in order to consider the question of how the two claims—curly and straight bracketed, phenomenological and metaphysical—relate.[33]

It may first be said that the phenomenological claim can be false even if the metaphysical claim is true. It may be said that even if $[E = S:C]$ is true, it's possible to have an experience—of a tiger, say—and to be aware of it specifically as an experience, an occurring experiential content (so that one is not merely aware of the outside world, but also of one's experience of it), without being in any way aware of a subject of experience or even subjectivity; let alone necessarily aware of it. The idea, then, is that

    (i) one turns one's attention on an experience, so that it's true to say that what is presented to one is an experience, {E},

and

    (ii) the object of one's attention, E, has, in fact, the metaphysical structure [S:C],

but

    (iii) the actual phenomenological content of one's experience of the experience, i.e. {E}, is fully conveyed just by {C}.

I think this claim may still sound plausible to some in the analytic tradition, and some nonphilosophers may agree. But even if it were true its truth wouldn't be relevant to the discussion of Hume, because the question that concerns us at present isn't just about having an—any—experience. It's much more specific. It's about what happens when, like Hume, one sets out in pursuit of a certain very special kind of experience—when one sets out specifically to observe oneself having an experience and, in this way, "enters intimately" and attentively into oneself (this is the point made with (a) and (b) earlier). It's about what one finds, in the way of mental phenomena, when one does this rather unusual thing. And here I think it is quite clear that to log the experiencing properly—genuinely to grasp something as an experience, as an experiencing—is, necessarily, to log the experiencer. The experience consists of an experiencer experiencing a content, and focused attention to the experience—to the experience considered specifically as an episode of experience—is (I propose) bound to involve cognizance of this fact. This is so even if—even though—the focused attention needn't involve any thought or grasp that the experiencer is oneself (i.e. any fully or expressly self-conscious thought).[34]

VIII THETIC AND NONTHETIC

This may still be doubted, so let me restate the point, initially in an intentionally imperfect way. The claim is not that the subject considered specifically as such (the subject-as-such, as it were) must present (verb) as an express object of attention.[35] It's not that the subject must be apprehended in a "thetic" way, in the language of the phenomenologists, i.e. expressly apprehended as an object of attention in the focus of consciousness.[36] On the contrary: the best thing to say, in many contexts of enquiry, *given the way in which the conception of what it would be to apprehend the (mental) subject is set up in those contexts*, is that the subject (considered specifically as such) is not apprehended—not even in a specially attentive act of Humean mental self-examination. For any awareness of the subject-as-such is in this case "nonthetic": not in the focus of attention, in no way "express.". Many sincere self-observers will accordingly truthfully deny that they encounter any such thing as the subject in the Humean thought-experiment, and they will be right. This is the sense in which Hume's phenomenological report, according to which all he finds is {E}, is correct: there is indeed no thetic presentation of the subject as such. The report is correct given the assumption that any such presentation would ipso facto be presentation of the subject as something in some way distinct from the experience as a whole; that this is what a thetic focusing of attention on the subject would inevitably amount to, a singling out of the subject. For this, as Hume rightly says, is precisely what does not happen. And yet there is awareness of the subject. Successful focusing on the whole phenomenon of an experience, an actual episode of experiencing, can't deliver just the content of the experience without delivering any sort of awareness of the subject, any more than successful focusing on the whole phenomenon of a page with words written on it can deliver just the content of the words.

Actually, the last paragraph is too concessive. The concession lies in the supposition that the notion of being apprehended as an *express* or *thetic* object of attention is equivalent to the notion of being apprehended as an express *and distinct* object of attention. One can specifically exclude the distinctness claim from the definition of "thetic," to get "apprehended as an express but not necessarily distinct object of attention," but even then the claim that the subject is not thetically apprehended may be too concessive. This is because there is, after all (I propose), a fundamental sense in which the subject is indeed an express object of my attention, and necessarily so, when I apprehend the experience. The experience I apprehend is indeed an experience, an experiencing, a necessarily-subject-involving thing (not just a content), and I can't possibly genuinely and expressly apprehend it as such, as an experiencing, without also in some way expressly apprehending the subject necessarily involved in the experiencing. I can no more do this than I can fully and carefully and expressly apprehend an actual walking without expressly apprehending a walker.

It may be objected that even if this is so—even if I do necessarily apprehend a subject, in apprehending an experience in focused mental self-examination, and even if there is a sense in which I apprehend the subject *expressly* in so doing, although I do not apprehend it as a *distinct* object of attention—still I do not expressly apprehend the subject *as such* as part of the object of my attention, in expressly apprehending the experience. And it may then be said that this as-such-ness is central to one conception of what expressness or theticity is. In fact, though, this claim, too, is debatable. It brings up the distinctness issue again because there are two readings of "apprehend as." Thus it may be reasonably said that although I do not apprehend the subject expressly as the object of my attention by any process of consciously deploying a concept of the subject, I do nonetheless apprehend the subject expressly as such in apprehending what is in fact the object of my attention—the experience, the experiencing—expressly *as an experience*, an experiencing; and even though I don't apprehend the subject as in any way distinct from the whole experiencing. I think this is right.

> I understand your phenomenological proposal, and I still don't agree with it. The claim that you can't observe an experience without also observing an experiencer is doubtless true when taken merely referentially or "relationally": if an experience consists metaphysically of a subject experiencing a content, then awareness of an experience is necessarily awareness of a subject. But why should I accept the claim when it's taken "notionally,"; i.e. as a phenomenological claim, a claim about the experiential character that my experience has for me when I set out on the Humean project of mental self-examination and deliberately take one of my experiences as the object of my attention?[37]

I do indeed mean it to be taken "notionally" or phenomenologically and not just referentially or relationally. Perhaps it will help to distinguish two versions of the phenomenological claim, i.e. the claim that any conscious episode of mental self-examination whose principal phenomenological content is such that it is

(1) awareness of an experience

(awareness "from the inside," as we say) will also and necessarily be such that its *phenomenological* content involves

(2) awareness of a subject of experience,

even though (2) need not (Hume's point) involve any presentation of the subject as a distinct object of awareness and may amount simply to a genuine grasp of the fact that the experiential content is live, is actually being lived, had, experienced.

The first and weaker version of this two-point claim restricts attention to those cases in which, with Hume, one undertakes to engage in the special attentive activity of entering intimately into what one calls oneself. The second and stronger version has it that any mental episode at all whose primary content is (1) necessarily also involves (2), however nonthetic the awareness of the subject may be. The stronger version greatly increases the number of relevant cases, for mental episodes that include (1), awareness of an experience, often occur when one isn't involved in specially focused and intentionally directed intimate self-examination. There are, for example, cases in which one is aware of the fact that one is experiencing pinkness when looking at a white table under red light and automatically judging the table to be white or in which one looks at oneself in a mirror under fluorescent light and thinks that one isn't really that color. This awareness of experience-as-such may be marginal, *en marge, en parergo*, in Aristotle's phrase,[38] but it is nonetheless real, a real concrete occurrence, part of the actual course of one's experience.

I think we should all grant the weaker version of the two-point claim, and that it is the beginning of wisdom in these matters to see that the second, stronger version is also true.[39] The simplest way to realize this, perhaps, is to consider again the difference between what it is to experience red and what it is to think about an experience (on one's own part) of red.

Some philosophers, including most Phenomenologists, favor an even stronger claim, which I mentioned earlier and put aside. This is the claim that all experiences whatever—not just experiences that involve some kind of concerted or explicit reflection on experience—necessarily involve (2) some sort of nonthetic awareness of the subject simply in so far as they necessarily involve (1) some sort of awareness of themselves.

I think this is true. The question is of great interest when one considers the many issues raised by Hume's discussion of personal identity and mental self-examination. But it is a topic for another time.[40]

IX RUSSELL AND FOSTER

I've been arguing that Hume doesn't claim that the subject of experience isn't encountered in experience. Since taking up this cause,[41] I've found that I'm not alone. If I haven't convinced you, perhaps Russell will. He considers the Humean project of mental self-examination and makes the point helpfully in his own terms in *The Problems of Philosophy*:

> When we try to look into ourselves we always seem to come upon some particular thought or feeling, and not upon the "I" which has the thought or feeling. Nevertheless there are some reasons for thinking that we are acquainted with the "I," though the acquaintance is hard to disentangle from other things. To make clear what sort of reason there is, let us consider for a moment what our acquaintance with particular thoughts really involves. When I am acquainted with "my seeing the sun," it seems plain that I am acquainted with two different things in relation to each other. On the one hand there is the sense-datum which represents the sun to me, on the other hand there is that which sees [has] this sense-datum. All acquaintance . . . seems obviously a relation between the person acquainted and the object with which the person is acquainted. When a case of acquaintance is [itself something] with which I can be acquainted (as I am acquainted with my acquaintance with the sense-datum representing the sun) it is plain that the person acquainted is myself. Thus, when I am acquainted with my seeing the sun, the whole fact with which I am acquainted is "self-acquainted-with-sense-datum" . . . It does not seem necessary to suppose that we are acquainted with a more or less permanent person, the same today as yesterday, but it does seem as though we must be acquainted with that thing, whatever its nature, which sees the sun and has acquaintance with sense-data. Thus, in some sense it would seem we must be acquainted with our Selves as opposed to our particular experiences. (Russell 1912: 27–28)[42]

And when John Foster writes that

> "a natural response to Hume would be to say that, even if we cannot detect ourselves *apart from* our perceptions (our conscious experiences), we can at least detect ourselves *in* them—that when I introspectively detect an experience, what is revealed is the complex of myself-experiencing-something or myself

experiencing-in-a-certain-manner. Indeed, it is not clear in what sense an experience *could* be introspectively detected without the detection of its subject" (Foster 1991: 215)[43]

his only error, in my view, is to think that Hume ever thought otherwise. Hume's target was the simple, unchanging, persisting subject of the philosophers and the church, nothing less and nothing more.[44]

X Is Hume Right About Intimate Entrance?

How does Hume come out of all this? Wonderfully well. He makes an extremely perceptive claim—a completely accurate claim, as far as I can see—about what it's actually like to encounter oneself as a (mental) subject of experience when one has decided to go looking for oneself considered specifically as a (mental) subject of experience.

How does one proceed in such a case? The most natural thing to do at first, I think, is to try to catch oneself on the fly in one's experience in the present moment (it's a familiar claim that the act of trying to take one's present experience as the explicit or thetic object of one's attention inevitably induces a delay that means that what one actually catches is the immediate past experience).[45] And this is probably what Hume did. One may also conduct one's investigation by having, or staging, in expressly introspective mode, an individual, explicitly self-conscious mental episode; by thinking, now, "I'm reading a book" or "I'm bored," "I'm now thinking about my thinking"; and he may also have tried this. The result is the same. There is, as Hume says, (1) no bare or naked view or apprehension of the subject. There is, as he says, (2) no view or apprehension of the subject as something saliently experientially distinct from the episode of experiencing considered as a whole. There is, as he says, (3) nothing that presents both as the subject of the apprehended experience and as an intrinsically persisting (or experience-transcendent) thing. There is, nevertheless, (4) apprehension of the subject, not only "relationally" speaking but also "notionally" speaking (p. 284), in the apprehension of the experience in present-moment mental self-examination. When Hume carries out this exercise, what he apprehends is, as he says himself, "*myself*," by which he means specifically himself considered as mental subject, the mental subject that necessarily exists when experiences exist.

To say that the self or mental subject doesn't present as an intrinsically persisting thing is not, of course, to say that people don't *believe* that it's an intrinsically persisting thing. They do, as Hume knows; and they may well also believe that they have direct experience of there being such a thing, or at least, as Hume remarks, experience that strongly backs up the belief that there is such a thing. If, however, we consider how the mental subject is given in unprejudiced mental reflection of the sort Hume is engaged in, we find nothing of the sort—just as he says. This, after all, is why he devotes most of "Of Personal Identity" to explaining the various mechanisms by which we come to believe in a persisting subject of experience in spite of the fact that no such thing presents itself as such when we engage in reflection of this kind.

Abbreviations of Works Cited

EU   *An Enquiry Concerning Human Understanding.* Edited by T. L. Beauchamp. Oxford: Clarendon, 2000.

T   *A Treatise of Human Nature.* Edited by D. F. Norton and M. J. Norton. Oxford: Clarendon, 2007.

TA   *An Abstract of a Treatise of Human Nature.* Reprinted in **T**

LET   *The Letters of David Hume,* 2 Vols. Edited by J.Y.T. Greig. Oxford: Clarendon Press, 1932.

Notes

1. When I cite a work by someone other than Hume, I give the first publication date or (occasionally) estimated date of composition, whereas the page reference is to the published version listed in the bibliography.
2. I discuss the famously difficult issue of what happens in the Appendix in Strawson (2011a: part 3) and Strawson (2012).
3. In other work, I call it "Frege's Thesis" (Strawson 1994: 129–134) and the "Subject Thesis" (Strawson 2009: 271–276).
4. "I know that I exist; the question is, what is this *I* that I know? I do not know." I do not know that I'm not just a "human body," or "some thin vapour which permeates my limbs—a wind, fire, air, breath." "But whatever I suppose, and whatever the truth is, for all that I am still something" (1641: 18).
5. See e.g. Strawson (2009: 338–349).
6. In his discussion of personal identity in Book 1 of the *Treatise*, Hume uses the words "mind," "self," and "person" interchangeably. So he uses "person" to denote himself considered simply in his mental being (see e.g. Penelhum [1955], Pike [1967], Biro [1993]), and this is also what he refers to when he speaks of "myself." The term "person" builds in the idea of something that has "personality," i.e. (this is the eighteenth-century use of "personality") diachronic continuity considered as a person.
7. For Hume's use of this criterion see e.g. T 1.1.7.6/19, and T 1.2.4.11/43; see also EU 12.20/157, EU 12.28/164, EU 4.18/35.
8. All mental occurrences are perceptions, in Hume's terminology—thoughts, sensations, emotions, ideas, and so on—and they're all (by definition) conscious. The word that now corresponds most closely to Hume's word "perceptions" in this use is "experiences."
9. Here the "causes and effects" are particular perceptions.
10. Six of these eleven quotations are from passages where Hume is discussing something else or summarizing the view and stating it in a particularly compressed form. See also T 2.1.2.2/277.
11. Here Hume takes up a (Newtonian) methodological position parallel to that of the early behaviorists. Just as it didn't occur to the original behaviorists to deny the existence of inner mental states of consciousness—they simply chose to restrict their experimentation

to the recording and measuring of publicly observable phenomena—so too Hume doesn't deny the existence of the mind considered as something more than a series of perceptions. It's just that the essence of the mind is unknown to us and that it's "impossible to form any notion of its powers and qualities otherwise than from careful and exact experiments, and the observation of those particular effects, which result from its different circumstances and situations" (T Intro. 8/xvii).

12. Objection: the outright ontological claims about the mind may be said to be literally true when made strictly within the philosophical framework of ideas constituted by empirically warranted clear and distinct ideas, since they just repeat the definition of the empirically warranted clear and distinct idea of the mind. Reply: true; the point is then that this empirically warranted framework of ideas is, in Hume's philosophy, rightly and crucially embedded within a larger, skeptical framework of ideas. In the larger sceptical framework, it's acknowledged that there may be and indeed is more to reality than what we can form empirically warranted clear and distinct ideas of. Words like "mind" and "bodies" are accordingly used in a larger sense in a way already illustrated: "the essence of the *mind*" is "equally unknown to us with that of *external bodies*" (T Intro. 8/xvii); "the perceptions of the *mind* are perfectly known," but "the essence and composition of *external bodies* are so obscure, that we must necessarily, in our reasonings, or rather conjectures concerning them, involve ourselves in contradictions and absurdities" (T 2.2.6.2/366); "'Tis in vain to ask, Whether there be *body* or not? That is a point, which we must take for granted in all our reasonings" (T 1.4.2.1/187). Note that exactly the same is true of Hume's use of words like "cause," "power," "force," and so on. See e.g. Strawson (2011a: 45n).

13. Phenomenologists should note that this claim is not at odds with Sartre's and Gurwitsch's insistence on the "nonegological" character of experience (see e.g. Gurwitsch 1941).

14. According to one central traditional metaphysical definition, a substance is something that can exist by itself without dependence on any other created or contingently existing thing.

15. "Whatever is distinct, is distinguishable; and whatever is distinguishable, is separable by the thought or imagination . . . and may be conceiv'd as separately existent, and may exist separately, without any contradiction or absurdity" (T App.12/634). See Garrett (1997: ch. 3).

16. One can say the same for any series of experiences E so encountered: nothing presents as in any way E-transcendent.

17. For James's explicit adoption of the Cartesian use of "thought" to mean "every form of consciousness indiscriminately," see e.g. James (1890: 1.224). Compare Reid in a manuscript note of December 1, 1758: "it seems utterly inexplicable how we come by the very Idea of a Subject or to imagin that these thoughts have a necessary Relation to some thing else which we call their Subject. We are onely conscious of the thoughts, yet when we reflect upon them there arises necessarily and unavoidably a Notion of a thinking thing, & that this thought we are conscious of is its Operation or Act. . . . If any Man will affirm that thought may exist without a Subject & that the conceiving it as an Act or Operation of some Being is a vulgar or a Philosophical Prejudice, I do not see how he can be confuted but by appealing to his own Sense or the Common Sense of Mankind" (Reid 1764: 320–1; note the use of the word "notion," following Berkeley's use in his *Principles*). On this view, a subject is a transcendental condition of an experience in Kant's sense, can be known to be so, and, accordingly, can be known to exist when an experience is known to exist, but we don't have any experiential encounter with the subject in being conscious of our thoughts.

18. Note that when Hume talks of the "sub-oyster" that has only "one perception" (T App. 16/634), he could mean that the sub-oyster has only one type of perception, not just one perception.

Hume also holds that there can be complex perceptions (see e.g. T 1.1.1.4/3; T 1.4.5.12/237), and when he considers the case in which "several perceptions . . . mingle" (T 1.4.6.4/253), it's plausible that his idea is that they may mingle in such a way as to form a single complex perception. It's clear enough that "perceptions" still refers to actual occurrences, in the phrase "several perceptions . . . mingle," but if we fix on the idea that there is one complex perception, then, relative to that idea, we may say that "perception" has a type use in describing the different types of content in that single perception (sound, smell, and taste, say, or the ideas *grass* and *green* in the thought that grass is green).

19. Price (1940: 96–97). See also Chisholm (1969: 97).

20. I introduced this scheme in Strawson (2001).

21. Recall that experiential content is wholly "internalistically" conceived, here, as concrete occurrent mental content (for those who know about philosophical "Twins," it's that in respect of which you and your "Twin" on "Twin Earth" are qualitatively identical).

22. See e.g. *Inquiry* §5.2: the "sensation of hardness may easily be had, by pressing one's hand against the table, and attending to the feeling that ensues, setting aside, as much as possible, all thought of the table and its qualities, or of any external thing. But it is one thing to have the sensation, and another, to attend to it, and make it a distinct object of reflection. The first is very easy; the last, in most cases, extremely difficult" (1764: 55–56).

23. This may concern a type or a token of experience. Oysters were a popular example, used also by Descartes and Locke.

24. A subject that you are considering specifically and only in its mental being.

25. As noted (n. 18), the first occurrence of the word "perception" in TA 16 may seem to invite a type reading—the sub-oyster has only one type of perception—whereas the second occurrence seems to be part of an invitation to consider one single particular "token" perception. But this isn't any kind of error on Hume's part.

26. See e.g. Berkeley 1713: 297. Hylas says to Philonous "in consequence of your own principles, it should follow that you are only a system of floating ideas, without any substance to support them." For the suggestion that there might have been a Buddhist influence on Hume, see Gopnik 2009.

27. See e.g. Shear (1998), Rosch (1997). See also Stone (1988; 2005). Hume is not, of course, concerned with some specially trained practice of mental self-examination.

28. Note that if one allows that there is subjectivity where I am, and non-overlapping subjectivity where you are, and again where your friend is, one is in effect committed to a count noun—something like "patch of subjectivity" or "episode" or "stream" of subjectivity— i.e. *a* subject.

29. It is, Kant says, "quite impossible" for me, given my experience of myself as a mental phenomenon, "to determine the manner in which I exist, whether it be as substance or object or as accident or property" (1787: B420). Compare Descartes in note 2 above.

30. Hume likes this point.

31. For a doubt about this approach to the sub-oyster, see Garrett (1997: 180).

32. The "intimacy-intimating colon" is designed to sweep up all these phrases; different theories may give different accounts of its force, which is now metaphysical, not phenomenological.

33. I argue for this view in Strawson (2008: essay 6) and Strawson (2009: part 7). With the William James of *The Principles of Psychology*, I think the best thing to say, when we operate with the "thin," mentalistic notion of the subject, is that every numerically distinct experience has a different subject. As it stands, however, the symbolism does not exclude saying that numerically distinct experiences occurring in a single human being have the same subject. Thus we might have $[E_1 = S_1:C_1]$, $[E_2 = S_1:C_2]$, $[E_3 = S_1:C_3]$, and so on.

34. Full or express self-consciousness is consciousness of oneself that involves grasping oneself expressly *as oneself* and, not, say, just as the child of x and y, or the person obliquely reflected in the glass. It's a familiar point that it is possible for one to be wrong—or unaware—that the person one is thinking about is in fact oneself in every case except the case in which one is thinking about oneself specifically as oneself. See, classically, Castañeda (1966), Shoemaker (1968), Perry (1979).

35. I use "express" where many would use "explicit" because it is helpful to give "explicit" a weaker than normal use in discussions of this topic.

36. It doesn't matter whether this apprehension is supposed to be active or passive.

37. For the relational-notional distinction, see Quine (1955); remember that phenomenological content properly understood is no less cognitive than sensory.

38. "[K]nowledge and perception and opinion and understanding have always something else as their object, and themselves only marginally" (*Metaphysics* 12.9.1074b35–6).

39. This is useful for Hume, because he is well aware of the "refrigerator light" problem that arises when one uses introspection as a tool of scientific enquiry. The science of the mind "has, indeed, this peculiar disadvantage, which is not found in natural, that in collecting its experiments, it cannot make them purposely, with premeditation, and after such a manner as to satisfy itself concerning every particular difficulty which may arise. When I am at a loss to know the effects of one body upon another in any situation, I need only put them in that situation, and observe what results from it. But should I endeavour to clear up after the same manner any doubt in moral philosophy, by placing myself in the same case with that which I consider, 'tis evident *this reflection and premeditation would so disturb the operation of my natural principles, as must render it impossible to form any just conclusion from the phaenomenon.*" (T Intro. 10/xvii–xix).

40. For a brief further treatment, see Strawson (2011a: 89–94) and references therein.

41. In a talk given to the Hume Society in Cork in 1999.

42. Sydney Shoemaker tells me that this passage was the subject of his first paper, and it is worth bearing in mind Shoemaker's demolition of the "view, which motivates 'bundle', 'logical construction', and 'no subject' theories of the self, that from an empiricist standpoint the status of the self (the subject of experience) is suspect compared with that of such things as sensations, feelings, images, and the like" (1986: 24). At the same time, Shoemaker thinks that the standard perceptual model of introspection favored by such empiricists is incorrect, and his claim is accordingly conditional: *if* one accepts such a model at all, then "the view that we have introspective perception of individual mental happenings but not of a self is indefensible" (ibid.).

43. See also 215–19. Compare Margolis (1988).

44. Objection: I still favor the only-{*C*} reading because I think that that Hume might have been happy to agree with what Kant is trying to express when he says such things as that 'the representation of [empirical] apperception . . . is nothing more than feeling of an existence' (Kant, 1783: §46n), or that "the consciousness of myself in the representation *I* is no intuition at all, but a merely *intellectual* representation of the self-activity [*Selbsttätigkeit*]

of a thinking subject" (Kant, 1781/7: B228). Reply: to the extent that this is right, it seems to me to strengthen the rejection of the only-{C} reading.
45. I question this claim in Strawson (2010).

BIBLIOGRAPHY

Aristotle (c. 350 BCE/1924). *Metaphysics*. Trans. with commentary by W. D. Ross. Oxford: Oxford University Press.

Berkeley, G (1734). *Three Dialogues between Hylas and Philonous*, third edition. London: Tonson.

Biro, J. (1993). "Hume's new science of the mind," in D. F. Norton, ed., *The Cambridge Companion to David Hume*, 33–63. Cambridge: Cambridge University Press.

Castañeda, Hector-Neri. (1966). "'He': A Study in the Logic of Self-Consciousness," *Ratio* 8, 130–157.

Chisholm, R. (1969). "On the Observability of the Self," *Philosophy and Phenomenological Research* 30, 7–21.

Descartes, René. (1641/1986). *Meditations in First Philosophy*. Translated by John Cottingham. New York: Cambridge University Press.

Foster, J. (1982). *The Case for Idealism*. London: Routledge.

Foster, J. (1991). *The Immaterial Self: A Defense of the Cartesian Dualist Conception of the Mind*. New York: Routledge.

Frege, G. (1918/1967). "The Thought: A Logical Inquiry," in P. F. Strawson, ed., *Philosophical Logic*, 17–38. Oxford: Oxford University Press.

Garrett, D. (1997). *Cognition and Commitment in Hume's Philosophy*. Oxford: Oxford University Press.

Gopnik, A. (2009). "Could David Hume Have Known about Buddhism? Charles Francois Dolu, the Royal College of La Flèche, and the Global Jesuit Intellectual Network," *Hume Studies* 35, 5–28.

Gurwitsch, A. (1941). "A non-egological conception of consciousness," *Philosophy and Phenomenological Research* 1, 325–338.

James, W. (1890/1950). *The Principles of Psychology*, 2 volumes. New York: Dover.

Kant, I. (1772/1967). Letter to Marcus Herz, February 21, 1772, in *Kant: Philosophical Correspondence 1759–99*. Edited and translated by Arnulf Zweig. Chicago: University of Chicago Press.

Kant, I. (1781-7/1933). *Critique of Pure Reason*. Translated by N. Kemp Smith. London: Macmillan.

Kant, I. (1783/1997). *Prolegomena to any Future Metaphysics*. Edited by G. Hatfield. Cambridge: Cambridge University Press.

Margolis, J. (1988) "Minds, Selves, and Persons," *Topoi* 7, 31–45.

Penelhum, T. (1955). "Hume on Personal Identity," *Philosophical Review* 64, 575–586.

Perry, John. (1979). "The Problem of the Essential Indexical," *Noûs* 13 (December), 3–21.

Pike, N. (1967). "Hume's Bundle Theory of the Self: A Limited Defense," *American Philosophical Quarterly* 4, 159–165.

Price, H. H. (1940). *Hume's Theory of the External World*. Oxford: Oxford University Press.

Quine, W. V. (1955/1966). "Quantifiers and Propositional Attitudes," in *The Ways of Paradox*. New York: Random House.

Reid, T. (1764/2000). *An Inquiry into the Human Mind*. Edited by D. Brookes. Edinburgh: Edinburgh University Press.

Rosch, E. (1997). "Transformation of the Wolf Man," in J. Pickering, ed., *The Authority of Experience*, 3–27. London: Curzon Press.

Russell, B. (1912). *Problems of Philosophy*. Oxford: Oxford University Press.

Shear, J. (1998). "Experiential Clarification of the Problem of Self," *Journal of Consciousness Studies* 5, 673–686.

Shoemaker, S. (1968). "Self-Reference and Self-Awareness," *Journal of Philosophy* 65 (October), 555–567.

Shoemaker, S. (1986/1996). "Introspection and the Self," in *The First-Person Perspective And Other Essays*, 3–24. Cambridge: Cambridge University Press.

Stone, J. (1988). "Parfit and the Buddha: Why There Are No People," *Philosophy and Phenomenological Research* 48, 519–532.

Stone, J. (2005). "Why There Still Are No People," *Philosophy and Phenomenological Research* 70, 174–192.

Strawson, G. (1994). *Mental Reality*. Cambridge, MA: MIT Press.

Strawson, G. (2001). "Hume on Himself," in D. Egonsson et al., eds., *Essays in Practical Philosophy: From Action to Values*. Aldershot: Ashgate Press.

Strawson, G. (2009). *Selves: An Essay in Revisionary Metaphysics*. Oxford: Oxford University Press.

Strawson, G. (2010). "Radical Self-Awareness," in M. Siderits, E. Thompson, and D. Zahavi, eds., *Self, No Self?: Perspectives from Analytical, Phenomenological, and Indian Traditions*, 274–307. Oxford: Oxford University Press.

Strawson, G. (2011a). *The Evident Connexion: Hume on Personal Identity*. Oxford: Oxford University Press.

Strawson, G. (2011b). "Cognitive Phenomenology: Real Life," in T. Bayne and M. Montague, eds., *Cognitive Phenomenology*. Oxford University Press.

Strawson, G. (2012). "All My Hopes Vanish: Hume's Appendix," in A Bailey and D. O'Brien, eds., *The Continuum Companion to Hume*. London: Continuum.

PART III

PASSION, MORALITY, AND POLITICS

CHAPTER 15

....

HUME ON PRIDE AND THE OTHER INDIRECT PASSIONS

....

JACQUELINE TAYLOR

ONE of the most striking features of Hume's account of the passions in the *Treatise* is his starting point: he begins with pride, one in a set of passions he calls "indirect passions." Hume focuses on pride as a positive passion that indicates a self-valuing and on its role as a moral virtue. Although pride may take vicious forms, Hume's concern lies with pride as a passion or virtue that contributes positively to our sense of who we are and, in particular, to our moral identity. "A due degree of pride" is useful to the proud person, giving her a sense of confidence and competence (T 3.3.2.8/596). The "elevated" feelings that characterize pride also make it agreeable to the person possessed of it (T 3.3.2.14/600). Pride is thus useful and agreeable to the proud person. And when a modest demeanor conceals signs of pride that others would find disagreeable, pride becomes potentially more useful and agreeable because others may nevertheless judge that she has good reason for taking pride in some valuable feature or possession and esteem her for the valuable quality, her modesty, and her pride. Although some other moderns, notably Descartes, regard pride as a positive passion, only Hume gives it a central role in his account of the passions. Others, such as Hobbes or Mandeville, who find pride to be a central element in human passionate nature, focus on its tendency to take excessive and vicious forms.

In this essay, I examine those features of pride that make Hume's account of the indirect passions so distinctive. I begin with an examination of his application of the experimental method to explain the origin of the indirect passions. The four main indirect passions are pride, humility, love, and hatred. Pride and humility are crucial to our identity, including our sense of how others regard us, whereas love and hatred are important feelings for or attitudes toward others. In establishing a double relation of ideas and impressions as the efficient causes of these passions, Hume undermines the appeal to final causes so prevalent in the works of his contemporaries and predecessors. Appeals to final causes purport to establish the appropriate objects of the passions, as well as the appropriateness of our having some of the passions we do, and why we should cultivate some passions rather than others.[1] Hume's claim that the causes of the indirect passions are not original—that there are not principles of the mind that lead us to recognize or value particular things as causes of pride—allows him to establish that these passions and their objects have a cultural and historical variability. I next turn to examine the relationship Hume draws among the principle of sympathy, pride, and the causes of pride. I then look more particularly at the role of pride and the other indirect passions in Hume's system of ethics as presented in Book 3 of the *Treatise* and in *An Enquiry Concerning the Principles of Morals*. My aims here are twofold. First, I show that Hume connects pride in virtuous character with moral confidence and competence. Second, I examine a concern Hume raises about a certain conception of pride and the other qualities that comprise greatness of mind. Of special interest here is Hume's more mature attitude in the *Enquiry* about ethical pluralism and the importance of humanity, justice, and benevolence as the central virtues of the modern and enlightened society. In the final part of the essay, I raise and allay a worry that arises from the consideration that the approbation of others, which may produce, confirm, or sustain someone's pride in her character, makes Humean moral agency heteronomous in nature.

I ON PRIDE

In the "Abstract," Hume writes that the *Treatise* volume on the passions "contains opinions, that are altogether as new and extraordinary" as those of Book 1 (TA 30/659). He observes that a wide variety of objects cause the indirect passions. Pride, for example, can arise from mental qualities, such as wit or courage, or qualities of the body, such as beauty or strength, or from external advantages, such as lineage or riches. Hume's aim is thus "to find out that common circumstance, in which all these objects agree, and which causes them to operate on the passions" (TA 30/660). His approach in *Treatise*, Book 2, comprises an exemplary instance of applying the experimental method to "moral subjects." In beginning with pride and humility, Hume notes that because these words are in general use and these are the most commonly experienced passions, everyone can "form a just idea of them" (T 2.1.2.1/277). In appealing to our shared experience of these passions, Hume echoes claims by natural philosophers such as Newton or Boyle that we must begin with the phenomena, rather than with speculative hypotheses. Earlier, in the introduction to the *Treatise*, Hume noted that he could not perform experiments that intervene in nature, such as those carried out in the laboratory, because the "reflection and premeditation" required for this kind of experiment would interfere with the operations of the natural principles of the mind that he had set out to examine. His approach instead relied on "a cautious observation of human life" and experiments gleaned from "the common course of the world" and people's behavior "in company, in affairs, and in their pleasures" (T Intro. 10/ xix). More precisely, Hume's experiments consist of theoretically refined observations that allow him to identify the common object of pride and humility, which is the self, and their causes and the elements the various causes have in common, an associative explanation of the efficacy of these causes, and a series of proofs that provide evidence for Hume's hypothesis.

Hume considers pride and humility as two key passions that concern the self: "Here the view always fixes when we are actuated by either of these passions" (T 2.1.2.2/277). Pride and humility give us an idea of ourselves as "more or less advantageous," so that we are "elated by pride, or dejected with humility" (T 2.1.2.2/277). The affect or feeling of pride is a kind of pleasure, whereas the affect of humility is a form of pain or uneasiness, and this difference in affective quality renders them contrary feelings. Because these contrary feelings have the same object of the self, Hume reasons that the cause of the two passions cannot also be the self; the cause must be something else that produces the distinctive pleasure of pride or uneasiness of humility. Here, then, we may draw a distinction between the cause and the object of these passions: the first is some idea we have that excites the passion, while the idea representing the object is produced when the mind turns to the self once we feel pride or humility. Hewing to his associationist framework, Hume observes, somewhat misleadingly, that the passion of pride or humility is thus a passion between two ideas, one that produces the passion and the other an idea produced by it (T 2.1.2.4/278).[2] Hume next draws another distinction between two properties of the causes, calling the first the subject of the cause and the second its quality. We find a "vast variety of subjects" among those things that produce pride and humility: qualities of mind and body and "whatever objects are in the least ally'd or related to us," such as our possessions or family (T 2.1.2.5/279). The cause must also possess a particular quality, that is, some value or disvalue, which makes the cause of pride something in which we take pleasure, and the cause of humility something that makes us uneasy about ourselves.

With these two sets of distinctions in place, Hume raises the question of what determines each of the properties to be what it is and what assigns each of the object, subject, and quality to the passions of pride and humility. This particular inquiry will help us to determine the origin of pride and humility and invokes a new distinction, namely, between natural properties and original properties. The aim is thus to establish whether these properties are all natural and original or whether human artifice may also play a role in determining one or more of these properties to be what it is. The fact that our mind always turns to consider the self when we experience pride or humility suggests that the object of pride and humility is natural. The self as the object of these passions is also an original property; Hume argues that the mind must possess some original qualities simply "in order to exert itself." That the self, as the object of pride or humility, is the distinctive characteristic of these passions shows that it "proceeds from an original quality, or primary impulse," one that is "most inseparable from the soul" and that "can be resolv'd into no other" (T 2.1.3.3/280).

That the mind actuated by pride always produces a particular idea of the self makes the object of pride natural. A similar point holds for the causes of pride. Certain possessions or advantages, including mental and bodily qualities, wealth, and power, have tended to produce pride in people across history and cultures. Significantly, the causes of pride are not original; again, the analogy is with the original property that makes self an object of pride. Consider, in particular, the external advantages that produce pride and that include possessions such as furniture, transport, clothing, houses, or gardens. Throughout time and across cultures, we find a vast variety in the types of houses, furniture, transportation, gardens, and other causes of pride. It is impossible that the mind would have as part of its "primary constitution" some principle that would recognize each distinctive kind of house or article of clothing as a cause of pride. For these causes to be original would require "a monstrous heap of principles" (T 2.1.3.6/282). In addition, and this helps to explain why there is so much variety among these causes, many such advantages arise from human artifice: from industry, caprice, and good fortune. So, for example, "industry produces houses, furniture, and cloaths. Caprice determines their particular kinds and qualities"; availability of resources for fabrication and the changing trends in fashion will influence which style of house or clothing we find beautiful (T 2.1.3.5/281). If there is not some original quality of the mind that adapts each cause to the passion of pride, there must be some other quality common to all of them and that renders them efficacious in producing pride. This moment in his analysis of the indirect passions is key for Hume, and he likens the reduction of mental principles here to the Copernican revolution, which displaced the ancients' "intricate systems of the heavens" (T 2.1.3.7/282).

To ascertain the common efficacious quality that the various causes share, Hume first turns to "certain properties of human nature" that concern how the mind moves from one perception to the next. These are the association of ideas (by resemblance, causation, and contiguity) and a similar association of impressions (limited to resemblance in terms of pleasure or pain). These "two kinds of association . . . assist and forward each other," and when an association of ideas "concurs" with one of impressions, they unite in one action and "bestow on the mind a double impulse," making the new passion arise with so much more force that "the transition to it must be render'd so much more easy and natural" (T 2.1.4.4/283–4). Hume draws an analogy with Addison's argument that when beauty is aroused by more than one sense, the resultant sounds, fragrance, colors, and so forth heighten the pleasures of the imagination. When related ideas concur with resembling impressions, there is a greater force that facilitates the transition to the new passion.

Hume is now in a position to make two suppositions regarding the qualities and subjects of the causes that produce pride and compare these to the already established properties of the passion. In examining the qualities of a number of causes of pride or humility, Hume observes that they concur in producing either pleasure or pain (respectively), and so he supposes that each cause of pride produces a separate pleasure, whereas each cause of humility produces a separate uneasiness. With respect to the subjects of the causes of pride, Hume had noted that these include features of our mind or body, our possessions, or other advantages, and so he now supposes that all such causes "are either parts of ourselves, or something nearly related to us" (T 2.1.5.2/285). The two properties that Hume has established as belonging to the passions of pride and humility are that they have the self as their object, and they are, respectively, pleasant or painful.

In comparing the established properties of the passions with the supposed properties of their causes, Hume finds that "the true system breaks in upon me with an irresistible evidence. That cause, which excites the passion, is related to the object, which nature has attributed to the passion; the sensation, which the cause separately produces, is related to the sensation of the passion: From this double relation of ideas and impressions, the passion is deriv'd" (T 2.1.5.5/286). The double relation thus comprises the common efficacious circumstance that produces pride.

After next introducing some limitations that set out the conditions for appropriately experiencing pride, Hume turns to the particular categories of causes, qualities of mind and body, external advantages, riches and property, and the seconding sentiments of others that we receive through sympathy with them and that sustain or disconfirm our pride or humility. He shows that, in all cases, we can locate the double relation as the common cause, thereby providing ample proof for his system. He ends Part 1 of Book 2, with an account of the pride and humility of animals and argues that their passions arise in exactly the same way. We observe the pleasure and deportment of pride and vanity in animals such as peacocks and swans; the causes of animal pride are the same as for pride in humans, although, in the case of animals, the causes are limited to the body (e.g., beauty or strength) and there is the same relation of ideas (albeit a more vulgar judgment) and impressions. As Hume explains, "'Tis usual with anatomists to join their observations and experiments on human bodies to those on beasts, and from the agreement of these experiments to derive an additional argument for any particular hypothesis" (T 2.1.12.2/325). That this observation-based experiment with animals corresponds with those with people shows that his "hypothesis is so simple, and supposes so little reflection and judgment, that 'tis applicable to every sensible creature," and this is "a convincing proof of its veracity" (T 2.1.12.9/328).

Let us briefly review what Hume has accomplished. He began with an appeal to the indirect passions of pride and humility as phenomena of which we have a shared experience. He then employed more refined observations to identify various theoretical features of the passions: their causes, including the subject (the various kinds of things that we possess or are related to us that produce pride or humility) and a quality, either pleasure or uneasiness, that inheres in the subject; and their objects, namely, an idea of ourselves as advantaged or disadvantaged in virtue of the cause. He established that the object of pride or humility is both original and natural, and that the causes, although natural, are not original. He then argued that just as ideas may be associated together, so too may impressions, at least, in virtue of resemblance in terms of pleasant or painful feeling. If two resembling ideas concur with two resembling impressions, there is an additional force or vivacity that facilitates the transition of the mind from one perception to another. The two suppositions regarding our idea of the causes of pride as something related to us and the impression of the cause as pleasant or painful resemble the properties of pride as a kind of pleasure and of humility as painful; thus, the idea pride produces of oneself as advantaged or disadvantaged in virtue of one's relation to the object that caused the pride or humility. This double association of ideas and impressions facilitates the mind's transition to pride or to humility and to the affectively infused idea of oneself as advantaged or disadvantaged. Hume's most significant discovery is that the double association of ideas and impressions also comprises the common circumstance that produces pride or humility. In the *Dissertation on the Passions*, he refers to the two sets of ideas and impressions as "the real, efficient causes of the passion" (DP 8). In giving an explanation of the production of these passions in terms of efficient causes, something Locke, Addison, and Hutcheson all found more difficult than making suppositions about their final causes, Hume dispenses with the need to invoke final causes.

In sum, Hume has deployed aspects of the experimental method of the natural philosophers: invoking the phenomena and making refined observations, and drawing analogies with natural philosophy (Copernicus's reduction of explanatory principles), natural history (Addison's Lockean account of the pleasures of the imagination), and with animals. Although natural philosophers conduct artificial experiments, intervening in nature to manipulate the phenomena, for Hume to do so would undermine his aim of examining and explaining the natural operations of the mind. His cautious observations have nevertheless afforded a methodical identification of the more theoretical features of the passions and of their causes and effects. To repeat: Hume's most significant achievement here has been to give an explanation of how the indirect passions are produced in terms of their efficient causes, which are other mental perceptions. Notably, Hume's explanation of the causes of pride as not original accommodates his account of justice as an artificial virtue: a convention first established to serve a mutual interest in stability of possessions, becomes, when a rule-guided and extended sympathy leads to the moral approval of justice and the disapproval of injustice, a moral obligation that may be cultivated as a trait of character, a virtue in which to take pride (T 3.2.2.23–7/499–501). I further examine the relation between pride and justice in Section III.

II PRIDE IN THE APPROBATION OF OTHERS

In the *Treatise*, Hume draws close connections among pride, its cause (with a special emphasis in Book 2 on wealth, and in Book 3 on virtue), and the approbation and esteem of others. That we value and wish to sustain pride reflects the "vast weight and importance" to us of "our reputation, our character, our name" (T 2.1.11.1/316). Although we might create a reputation or name for ourselves, or cultivate our character, we need others to confirm that our reputation or character is, in fact, good. Hume had stipulated as one of the "limitations" on pride that there must be public recognition of the value of what we regard as the cause of pride, although, clearly, different groups of people will have different ideas about what is valuable or praiseworthy (T 2.1.6.6/292). In introducing the principle of sympathy, Hume highlights the importance of others' esteem for those who possess some valuable quality; so others not only discern and endorse the value of the quality that produces the person's pride, but they also esteem her as the possessor of it. Their esteem in turn can produce or sustain the person's pride.[3]

Hume introduces sympathy as a principle of the imagination by which we communicate our sentiments and opinions to one another. Any passion, sentiment, or opinion can be communicated. The sympathizer infers another's passion or opinion through the perceived "external signs in countenance or conversation," for example, by someone's facial expression or bodily deportment or through her voicing her sentiment or judgment (T 2.1.11.3/317). After the sympathizer forms an idea of the person's passion or opinion, sympathy functions to enliven the idea so that the sympathizer herself feels a similar passion or some other response to the person's passion (such as compassion for the other's grief), or the force of the other's judgment. In T 2.1.11, Hume focuses on our sympathy with others' sentiments or opinions about us and the effects of our doing so on our sense of pride or humility. He refers to these sentiments and opinions of others as "seconding sentiments" because others' esteem, approval, or disapproval can second or confirm our own sense of our worth, reflected in our pride or humility. Hume argues that, in addition to the primary causes of pride, such as the qualities of mind and body, the seconding opinions and sentiments of others serve as a secondary cause of pride. When the person proud of some valuable quality sympathizes with the praise of others, she feels a corresponding pleasure that enhances her pride. Others' judgments or attitudes can also leave us "shock'd" when they disagree with our own assessment of ourselves (T 2.1.11.9/321).

Hume makes a deeper point about the importance of sympathy and the sentiments it elicits in others. Although he describes these sentiments as a secondary cause of pride or humility, they not only have an influence equal to that of the primary causes on those passions, but those primary causes will themselves "have little influence, when not seconded by the opinions and sentiments of others" (T 2.1.11.1/316). Hume articulates at least two significant insights here. As we saw earlier regarding the limitations that circumscribe appropriately felt pride, the value of an object I regard as a reason for my pride must also "be very discernible and obvious . . . to others" (T 2.1.6.6/292). Recall that the causes of pride are not original, particularly those that have their origin in human industry, caprice, or fortune. Sympathy here has a unique role in allowing us to exert social pressure on one another, through our judgments and sentiments, so that we achieve a shared sense of the value of things (allowing, of course, for some individual or subcultural differences). Such social pressure is often communicated automatically in the course of educating someone into our language, manners, and valued commitments: the person is thus insensibly inculcated into our shared values and way of life. Hume is particularly clear and descriptive on how this social sympathy or "contagion" works to inculcate us into a shared way of life in his essay, "Of National Characters." The very act of conversing together on a regular basis shapes our manners, characters, desires, language, and dialect. When they are united under the same government and laws, the people will "have a common or national character, as well as a personal one" (ESY 203).

His second insight about sympathy's role in our valuing the primary causes of pride emphasizes our need for this kind of social communication in order to keep the mind lively and not sink into an enervating "melancholy and despair," as well as keeping us attuned to both our own passionate experience and that of others. Company presents us with "a rational and thinking being like ourselves, who communicates to us all the actions of his mind; makes us privy to his inmost sentiments and affections; and lets us see, in the very instant of their production, all the emotions, which are caus'd by any object" (T 2.2.4.4/352–3). Among all the creatures on earth, man "has the most ardent desire of society." "Whatever other passions we may be actuated by," including pride, the "animating principle of them all is sympathy; nor wou'd they have any force were we to abstract entirely from the thoughts and sentiments of others." Hume imagines someone with the powers to make the sun rise and set and to create abundance on earth, but "he will still be miserable till you give him some one person at least, with whom he may share his happiness, and whose esteem and friendship he may enjoy" (T 2.2.5.15/363). A passage suggesting that "the minds of men are mirrors to one another" nicely captures the force of this sympathetic communication when we respond emotionally to one another. The rich man gets pleasure from his possessions; others sympathize with his pleasure, and they feel both the pleasure of his pleasure and esteem for him for possessing this source of pleasure. His sympathy with their esteem adds to his pleasure, and this "secondary satisfaction" is the pleasure of pride. Others in turn sympathize with his pride, which increases their esteem for him and makes the esteem-earning sense of pride "one of the principal recommendations of riches"; to feel pride and earn the esteem of others "is the chief reason, why we either desire them for ourselves, or esteem them in others" (T 2.2.5.21/365). The description of the successive mirroring between the wealthy man and those who esteem him emphasizes a deepening passionate attunement that serves both to create a social bond through their mutual recognition of one another's passions and to second and sustain the sense of shared values—in this case, a well-founded pride, the earned esteem of others, and wealth.

Hume allows that particular values may be shared by some but not all. In particular, we tend to value and to want esteem for the qualities "in which we chiefly excel. A mere soldier little values the character of eloquence: A gownman of courage: A bishop of humour: Or a merchant of learning" (T 2.1.11.13/322). Our profession, nationality, religion, social standing, and talents each provides a different context in which our sense of self-worth may be enhanced or diminished. Thus, two of us may be proud of our nationality, but only one of us has a particular talent that gives further reason for pride and earns additional esteem from others. We are also discerning about who esteems us and for what reason: "we receive a greater satisfaction from the approbation of those, whom we ourselves esteem" and are "mortify'd with the contempt of persons, upon whose judgment we set some value" (T 2.1.11.11/321). On the other hand, "plagiaries are delighted with praises, which they are conscious they do not deserve," but this is an attempt to give stability to their fictions about who they are (T 2.1.11.19/324).

III SYMPATHY AND PRIDE

I now turn to the role of sympathy and the relation Hume draws between pride in virtue and others' approbation of virtuous character. I noted in the beginning of this essay that Hume gives the central place to pride in his Book 2 account of the passions. Pride and, to a lesser extent, the other indirect passions of love, humility, and hatred, also have a special place and role in his Book 3 system of ethics: "the most considerable effect that virtue and vice have upon the human mind" is to excite pride or humility in their possessor, as well as others' love for the virtuous or hate for the vicious person (T 3.1.2.5/473). Those of virtuous character are proud of their virtue. Moreover, the usefulness of a "due degree of pride" or an appropriate "value for ourselves" is itself "a source of virtue" (T 3.3.2.8/596). Although Hume has argued that pride is a pure emotion that does not directly move us to action, a proper pride nevertheless "makes us sensible of our own merit, and gives us a confidence and assurance in all our projects and enterprises" (T 3.3.2.8/597). I think this claim about having an awareness of our own merit, especially an awareness of our competence as moral agents so that we act with confidence and assurance, shows the importance of the role pride has in Hume's overall project in the *Treatise*.

It is worth noting the contrast Hume draws between his system of ethics and two other kinds of eighteenth-century moral theories that regard morality as grounded in some kind of sentiment or pleasure: the selfish theory, for example, of Mandeville, on the one hand, and the moral sense theory, such as that of Hutcheson, on the other. In T 2.1.7, where Hume is considering virtue as one of the causes of pride, he introduces both of these theories and argues that both are compatible with the associationist explanation he has given of pride. Both theories hold that virtue produces pleasure and vice uneasiness, and it follows from both (even if neither theory explicitly recognizes the implication) that both must regard pride and humility as the effects of the original pleasure or uneasiness. Hume's own moral philosophy draws on aspects of both kinds of theory, but the positive role he gives to pride and a proper self-regard makes Hume's account unique. According to Mandeville, good behavior is something into which people must be manipulated, and one of the most important strategies for getting people to act in ways that produce public benefits is by appealing to their vanity, one of the frailties of human nature. People are motivated by their pride to earn the esteem of others; if they believe that conduct benefiting society is regarded as praiseworthy, then such conduct, motivated by the private vice of vanity nevertheless yields social benefits. Pride, for Mandeville, is not a character trait that imparts a sense of moral competence but is rather a distinct kind of pleasure for which human beings have an insatiable craving. In contrast, and with Hutcheson, Hume thinks we have genuinely altruistic motives, such as benevolence or compassion. And for Hume, although we may take pride in our benevolence, when we do act in genuinely benevolent ways, it is to prevent another's distress or promote her well-being and not to flatter our vanity through the esteem of others. Moreover, a due degree of pride reflects a proper sense of self-regard and is valued both by the proud person herself and by others.

On the other hand, Hume is clearly persuaded, at least to some extent, by the arguments of Hobbes and Mandeville that convention and artifice play a necessary role in redirecting human conduct in socially beneficial ways. Although Hutcheson attempts to derive the elements of justice, property, and other rights and obligations from forms of benevolence, Hume argues that justice is not "a natural principle, capable of inspiring men with an equitable conduct toward each other" (T 3.2.2.8/488). Hume's use of the term "natural principle" here is really akin to his use of "original principle" that we examined in Section I of this essay.[4] There we saw that nature has made the self the object of pride and humility by an original principle of the mind. We also saw that, in contrast, the causes of pride are not original because "'tis utterly impossible they shou'd each of them be adapted to these passions by a particular provision and primary constitution of nature"; there are too many such causes, and given that many result from human artifice, they are also constantly evolving (T 2.1.3.5/282). Similarly, those impressions and sentiments "which give rise to justice, are not natural to the mind of man, but arise from artifice and human conventions" (T 3.2.2.21/496).[5] The problem that justice solves arises both from our natural partiality and unstable, scarce resources. Partiality and insecurity feed the avidity of everyone, and each person must fear the avidity of others, making him yet more insecure. The remedy to this problem is found "in the judgment and understanding"; reflection on the benefits of our natural sociability suggest that a better way to secure goods is through rules establishing possession (T 3.2.2.9/489). Self-interest thus restrains itself for long-term advantages, and those participating in this scheme of rules find they share a general sense of common interest. Justice becomes a virtue and injustice a vice when the rules provide a broader scope, so that we extend our sympathy to all those covered by the rules. Sympathy is thus the source of the moral approbation of justice and the disapprobation of injustice.

Through education and public praise and blame, justice acquires greater esteem. The person who cultivates a sense of honor is useful both to herself and to others and thus earns the esteem of others and has a reason for pride (T 3.2.2.25–6/500–1). Once merit is associated with justice and demerit with injustice, people can acquire a reputation for honor, trustworthiness, and just conduct, which serves as a further cause of pride. A virtue useful for both oneself and others, one arising from artifice and convention and not from an original motive of our nature, thus naturally earns the esteem of mankind and is a reason for pride in those committed to acting justly. It is worth noting that Hume claims that "no virtue is more esteem'd than justice, and no vice more detested than injustice; nor are there any qualities, which go farther to the fixing the character, either as amiable or odious" (T 3.3.1.9/577). Moreover, an implication of Hume's views on power and authority as causes of a particularly enhanced sense of pride suggests that the just magistrate has a greater cause for pride than do ordinary citizens. Magistrates both execute the laws of justice and are responsible for decision making when there is controversy.

In T 2.1.10, Hume argues that persons with social power or authority have an ability, one that others lack, to act in ways that benefit or harm others. When the person with social power, such as the magistrate, compares himself with those with less or who lack it altogether, it makes his authority "seem more agreeable and honourable," thus augmenting his sense of pride (T 2.1.10.12/315). Magistrates are also in a position to provide opportunities to promote pride in the members of society by erecting schemes to promote the public interest and coordinating the citizenry to improve society: "Thus bridges are built; harbours open'd; ramparts rais'd; canals form'd; fleets equip'd; and armies disciplin'd; everywhere, by the care of government" (T 3.2.7.8/539). As Annette Baier suggests, the citizenry in an improving society can share in this sense of accomplishment to which they have contributed,[6] and their taking pride in their nation or government reflects the national character of that society.[7]

IV MORAL APPROBATION AND PRIDE

Pride in the natural virtues may also be sustained or enhanced by the moral approbation of others. A due degree of pride is useful and agreeable to the possessor and is itself a natural virtue. Having an appropriate pride, particularly for qualities society deems valuable, such as good character, reputation, or social standing, also tends to earn the respect of others. We love someone for any quality she possesses that is in some way useful or agreeable for her or for others. But some qualities are more significant than others, and these will cause respect rather than simply love. In T 2.2.10, Hume gives as examples riches, genius, and learning. In considering moral character, he observes, "The characters of Caesar and Cato, as drawn by Sallust, are both of them virtuous, in the strictest sense of the word; but in a different way: Nor are the sentiments entirely the same, which arise from them. The one produces love; the other esteem: The one is amiable; the other awful: We cou'd wish to meet with the one character in a friend; the other character we wou'd be ambitious of in ourselves" (T 3.3.4.2/608–8).[8] Respect and its negative counterpart, contempt, are what Hume refers to as mixed passions. They are indirect passions that arise from a comparison between oneself and another. If I see that someone outshines me in her accomplishments or other valuable qualities when I compare myself to her, I experience humility about myself and esteem for her; this mixture of humility and esteem is respect. Contempt, likewise, is a mixture of pride and hate, when comparison shows that I have significant qualities that the other lacks. Hume argues that some qualities that produce love in others are less likely to produce pride, and he gives as examples "good nature, good humour, facility, generosity, beauty" (T 2.2.10.8/392). Such qualities typically elicit love rather than respect. Because they do not typically produce pride, someone who lacks them will not experience humility when she compares herself with someone who has them. This difference between love and respect helps to explain Hume's preference for some natural abilities over some natural virtues. Even simple people may be good-natured and will be loved for it, but one really must possess the respect-earning and pride-producing qualities, such as good sense or industriousness (T 3.3.4.1/607).

So, the different degrees of value that qualities have elicit different attitudes, such as love or respect, hate or contempt. There are also different aspects of traits of character that influence the moral approbation of others. These aspects are the utility and the immediate agreeableness of traits: both aspects may be found in the same trait, and both produce moral approbation, although they do so in different ways. We gauge the usefulness of a trait by reflecting on its tendency to promote or diminish the well-being of the agent or others. Pride is useful to the virtuous or talented person, and its usefulness is a further source of virtue: "nothing is more useful to us in the conduct of life, than a due degree of pride, which makes us sensible of our own merit, and gives us a confidence and assurance in all our projects and enterprises" (T 3.3.2.8/596–7). Pride is also agreeable to the proud person. Hume turns to history to consider the proud heroes of the ancient world as examples of the sublime pleasure of pride. The set of qualities he terms greatness of mind or heroic virtue include "courage, intrepidity, ambition, love of glory, magnanimity," and all are either forms of "a steady and well-establish'd pride and self-esteem" or have "a strong mixture of self-esteem in them" (T 3.3.2.13/599–600). The proud person experiences "an elevated and sublime sensation"; indeed, "nothing invigorates and exalts the mind equally with pride and vanity" (T 3.3.2.14/600, T 2.2.10.6/391). The elevated and sublime sentiment, the invigorated mind, makes the person's pride immediately agreeable to her.

The person with a mind invigorated by pride has the "confidence and assurance" to pursue her projects. But Hume expresses caution about the admiration and approbation of heroic pride and the other virtues comprising greatness of mind. Many consider "heroism, or military glory" as the most sublime kind of merit." But "men of cool reflection are not so sanguine in their praises of it," given "the infinite confusions and disorder, which it has caus'd in the world" (T 3.3.2.15/600–1). The problem is twofold. First, the sympathy with the immediately agreeable aspect of the various traits comprising greatness of mind is unreflective; the spectators cannot help admiring the courageous hero even though a more reflective judgment recalls "the evils, which this suppos'd virtue has produc'd in human society." The elevated sentiment or exalted mind of the proud hero and heroine is precisely what makes their pride immediately agreeable to them. Spectators are dazzled by the character of the hero so that they "cannot refuse it their admiration," and their minds are "over-power'd by a stronger and more immediate sympathy" (T 3.3.2.15/601). In EM, after observing that the utility of courage is a source of its merit, Hume notes that courage also has "a peculiar lustre, which it derives wholly from itself, and from that noble elevation inseparable from it." Poets and playwrights draw the courage of heroes to display "a sublimity and daring confidence; which catches the eye, engages the affections, and diffuses, by sympathy, a like sublimity of sentiment over every spectator" (EM 7.11/254). The grandeur of philosophical tranquility (another form of magnanimity) "seizes the spectator, and strikes him with admiration" (EM 7.16/256). Rather than reflecting on the tendencies of courage, magnanimity, or tranquility, the spectators find the hero's sublimity infectious and are struck with admiration.

Second, Hume views the cultural attitudes that dominate in the heroic society as inconsistent with the values of the modern just society. This is particularly clear in EM. For example, "the martial temper of the Romans, enflamed by continual wars, had raised their esteem of courage so high, that, in their language, it was called virtue, by way of excellence and of distinction from all other moral qualities" (EM 7.13/254-5). Martial bravery among the Scythians "destroyed the sentiments of humanity; a virtue surely much more useful and engaging" (EM 7.14/255). The ancient heroes in both war and philosophy "have a grandeur and force of sentiment, which astonishes our narrow souls, and is rashly rejected as extravagant and supernatural" (EM 7.18/256). A society that values as the chief excellences the martial virtues, magnanimity, or a Stoical tranquility or detachment tends to lack the advantages to be had where "beneficence, justice, and the social virtues," such as humanity or clemency, are most valued (EM 7.15/255). Despite sounding a note of caution about valorizing the heroic conception of the virtues, a well-grounded pride still retains the status of a virtue. But Hume's recognition of a historical and cultural pluralism with respect to different rankings or meanings of virtues, depending on how fixed moral and accidental causes shape ethical outlooks, is tempered by a refusal to endorse the inhumanity of those societies that value the martial virtues to the exclusion of justice, benevolence, and a sense of our shared humanity.[9]

V Conclusion: Heteronomous Moral Agency

Like Francis Hutcheson, Adam Smith and other sentimentalists, Hume emphasizes the sentiment-based responses, such as love or approbation, to qualities of our own and others' character. Humean pride and Smithian propriety are important responses on the part of agents to the passions and sentiments of others. In connecting pride in character and other valuable qualities with reputation, Hume also emphasizes the necessity of our seeing ourselves as others see us if we are to sustain our sense of pride. Pride and humility, as well as the love, respect, hate, and contempt of others are key sources of our ethical and social identity. It matters to us that others recognize, endorse, and esteem us for our valuable qualities. Pride, as we have seen, is an attitude of positive self-assessment that often, at least in part, reflects our valuing of others' seconding sentiments directed toward ourselves. The effects of sympathetic mirroring, especially with self-regarding passions such pride and humility, on the one hand, and the sentiments of others that reflect their attitude toward us, on the other hand, reflect our social interdependence. The Humean moral agent thus contrasts with the Kantian conception of the moral agent, for whom autonomy is the defining attribute that makes possible her morally efficacious conduct. Indeed, one contemporary Kantian, Christine Korsgaard attempts to turn this contrast into a condemnation of the sentimentalist conception of agency. She writes that, for Hume and others such as Hutcheson and Smith, "the approval and disapproval of others is the fundamental moral phenomenon, from which all our ideas spring. There is something obviously unattractive about taking the assessment of others as the starting point in moral philosophy" (Korsgaard 1996: 189).

Bernard Williams makes a similar point about the influence of the Kantian conception of morality on the contemporary rejection of shame as a significant ethical emotion. On the Kantian view, the heroic Greeks whose moral psychology and ethical commitments Williams is exploring and their values are rendered heteronomous because they lose or save face in the eyes of others. Williams rejects the Kantian (or Platonic) interpretation of shame and argues instead that "the basic experience connected with shame is that of being seen, inappropriately, by the wrong people, in the wrong condition" (Williams 1993: 78). Citing James Redfield, Williams observes that shame (*aidos*) and indignation or contempt (*nemesis*) form a pair of reflexive attitudes; we can see that such a description evokes Hume's account of sympathetic mirroring (Williams 1993: 80). Although the hero will be ashamed if he earns the indignation or contempt of others, he internalizes shared attitudes concerning honor, shame, and contempt, so that he will also feel shame when he himself recognizes that his conduct is contemptible. Moreover, what matters about how others can produce shame in someone is that the person respects those who direct their gaze toward him. We saw earlier that Hume makes this point with regards to pride: "we receive a much greater satisfaction from the approbation of those, whom we ourselves esteem and approve of," and "the judgment of a fool" will be "inferior in its influence on our own judgment" compared to the influence of the wise man's judgment (T 2.1.11.11/321). We are susceptible to the approval or blame of particular others precisely because we share values and commitments, and we come to share these both through a sympathy-based education into the ways of our culture and through the kind of moral conversation and debate that the common point of view makes possible and that can lead to changes in values and commitments.

Williams cites Gabriele Taylor, who argues that shame is the emotion of self-protection since fear of shame (what Williams calls "prospective shame") helps us adhere to our deepest convictions and preserves self-respect (Williams 1993: 79). Taylor makes a similar point about pride: the person who has her pride has standards that help to sustain self-respect (Taylor 1985: 50).[10] Another important addition to the account of pride in EM is Hume's argument that pride is important for a sense of dignity that protects us against mean and slavish conduct. He asks, "Who is not struck with any signal instance of greatness of mind or dignity of character; with elevation of sentiment, disdain of slavery, and with that noble pride and spirit, which arises from conscious virtue?" (EM 7.4/252). Indeed, "we never excuse the absolute want of spirit and dignity of character, or a proper sense of what is due to one's self, in society and the common intercourse of life" (EM 7.10/253). The want of dignity is a vice that makes people servile and fawning; and "where a man has no sense of value in himself, we are not likely to have any higher esteem of him" (EM 7.10 n 42/253–4, n4). A "generous pride or self-value," an awareness of the standards of conduct that preserve one's dignity, and an expectation that others give one what is due to one, is thus absolutely requisite in the good character

(EM 7.10/253). Even this generous pride can still be sustained by sympathetic mirroring with others. "Our continual and earnest pursuit of a character" brings our character to the imagined gaze of others, and "this constant habit of surveying ourselves, as it were, in reflection, keeps alive all the sentiments of right and wrong, and begets, in noble natures, a certain reverence for themselves as well as others; which is the surest guardian of every virtue" (EM 9.10/276).

Although Hume emphasizes the necessity of pride for good character, he also stresses a similar need for modesty to mitigate the external signs of pride that tend to produce uneasiness or offense in others. He mediates here between the vicious forms of pride, such as arrogance or conceit, and a genuine pride that may nevertheless produce uneasiness in others by comparison. Sympathy with the pleasures of pride or self-esteem in great or superior persons produces that mixture of humility about oneself and admiration for the superior person that results in respect or esteem. Yet we often automatically sympathize with the pleasure exhibited by the viciously proud person. Although our judgment about his inferior merit blocks respect for him, his evident belief in his own superiority still influences our imagination, making us feel lesser to him by the comparison. In making others uneasy, false pride or conceit is rendered vicious. Because we have a natural partiality to ourselves and pride is so immediately agreeable to the proud person, we condemn most outward signs of pride by a general rule and "establish the rules of good breeding, in order to prevent the opposition of men's pride and render conversation agreeable and inoffensive" (T 3.3.2.10/597).

The delicate concern for others, the desire for mutually agreeable conversation with them, as well as our concern for our own reputation with others and the role their esteem plays in sustaining our pride, all point to the importance for us of sociability and communicating our sentiments and opinions with one another. Nevertheless, the "man of sense and merit is pleas'd with himself, independent of all foreign considerations" (T 3.3.2.7/596). Because he does not crave the flattery of others, as the fool or conceited person does, he is not so apt to engage in comparisons with others to shore up his self-esteem. The person of sense and merit has a well-grounded pride. I noted earlier the importance of pride for protecting self-respect, where that is grounded in the standards one has set for conduct and character. The betrayal of such standards may involve a self-degradation that diminishes a person's respect for herself. This point about the role of pride in protecting one's core values and commitments mitigates the criticism of those, such as Korsgaard, who regard the Humean agent as heteronomous. If Hume is right about the role of sympathy and pride in achieving a sense of moral identity—and contemporary research on empathy and self-conscious emotions such as pride suggests that he is—then we are fundamentally interdependent.[11] To have any sense of self, to have a sense of moral identity and agency, we must subject ourselves to others' attitudes and opinions about us. But this essential susceptibility to and mutual scrutiny of one another does not preclude critical reflection on and debate about the meanings and values we find most important for a well-founded sense of pride.

Abbreviations of Works Cited

EM   *Enquiry Concerning the Principles of Morals*. Edited by Tom L. Beauchamp. Oxford: Clarendon, 1998.

ESY   *Essays: Moral, Political, and Literary*. Revised edition by E. F. Miller. Indianapolis: Liberty Classics, 1985.

EU   *An Enquiry Concerning Human Understanding*. Edited by T. L. Beauchamp. Oxford: Clarendon, 2000.

T   *A Treatise of Human Nature*. Edited by D. F. Norton and M. J. Norton. Oxford: Clarendon, 2007.

TA   *An Abstract of a Treatise of Human Nature*. Reprinted in **T**

Notes

1. Francis Hutcheson, following a strategy pursued by Locke to explain why we perceive secondary qualities as we do, and also by Joseph Addison to explain why we experience the pleasures of the imagination, appeals to final causes and to the wisdom and goodness of the Deity to explain why our perception of certain ratios of uniformity and variety produce in us the pleasures of beauty (Hutcheson 2004). See also Addison (1711).
2. For helpful critical discussion, see Davidson (1976) and G. Taylor (1985).
3. See also Alanen (2005).
4. That Hume means original in this sense seems evident at T 3.2.1.19/484, T 3.2.2.8/488, and T 3.2.2.21/496.
5. Hume's claim that justice is, in one sense, natural corresponds to his use of "natural" in T 2.1.3, where what is natural is what normally or necessarily occurs: "No virtue is more natural than justice. Mankind is an inventive species; and where an invention is obvious and absolutely necessary may as properly be said to be natural as any thing that proceeds immediately from original principles, without the intervention of thought or reflection" (T 3.2.1.19/484).
6. See Baier (1980) for arguments for the virtues of magistrates, monarchs, and well-governed citizens, and Baier (2010).
7. Hume thought the English had special reason for national pride in their form of government, their industriousness, and the balanced social relations between men and women. For further examples, see "Of National Characters," "Of the Rise and Progress of the Arts and Sciences," "Of Refinement in the Arts," all in ESY, and "A Dialogue" in EM.
8. Interestingly, Hume observes in this section, "Each of the virtues, even benevolence, justice, gratitude, integrity, excites a different sentiment or feeling in the spectator" (T 3.3.4.2/607).
9. I explore Hume's criticism of martial societies in more detail in Taylor (2013) and Taylor (2015).
10. Taylor confines her examination of Hume on pride and humility to the *Treatise*, and so she misses that he makes this same point in the more subtle account of EM (see Taylor 1985).
11. I explore some of the contemporary research on empathy and self-conscious emotions in Taylor (2011).

Bibliography

Addison, Joseph. (1711). "The Pleasures of the Imagination," in *The Spectator*.

Alanen, Lilli. (2005). "Reflection and Ideas in Hume's Account of the Passions," in J. Jenkins, J. Whiting, and C. Williams, eds., *Persons and Passions: Essays in Honor of Annette Baier*. Notre Dame, IN: University of Notre Dame Press, 117–142.

Árdal, Páll. (1966/1989). *Passion and Value in Hume's Treatise*. Edinburgh: Edinburgh University Press.

Baier, Annette C. (1980). "Master Passions," A. O. Rorty, ed., in *Explaining Emotions*. Berkeley: University of California Press, 403–424.

Baier, Annette C. (2010). *The Cautious Jealous Virtue: Hume on Justice*. Cambridge, MA: Harvard University Press.

Davidson, Donald. (1976). "Hume's Cognitive Theory of Pride," *Journal of Philosophy* 73 (19), 744–757.

Hume, David. (1985). *Essays: Moral, Political, and Literary*. Eugene F. Miller, ed. Indianapolis: Liberty Fund.

Hume, David. (1998). *Enquiry Concerning the Principles of Morals*. Tom Beauchamp, ed. Oxford: Clarendon Edition, Oxford University Press.

Hume, David. (2007a). *A Treatise of Human Nature*. David Fate Norton, Mary J. Norton, eds. Oxford: Clarendon Edition, Oxford University Press.

Hume, David. (2007b). *A Dissertation on the Passions and The Natural History of Religion*. Tom L. Beauchamp, ed. Oxford: Clarendon Press.

Hutcheson, Francis. (2004). *An Enquiry into the Original of Our Ideas of Beauty and Virtue*. Wolfgang Leidhold, ed. Indianapolis: Liberty Fund.

Korsgaard, Christine M. (1996). "Creating the Kingdom of Ends: Reciprocity and Responsibility in Personal Relations," in *Creating the Kingdom of Ends*. Cambridge: Cambridge University Press, 188–223.

Taylor, Gabriele. (1985). *Pride, Shame, and Guilt: Emotions of Self-Assessment*. Oxford: Oxford University Press.

Taylor, Jacqueline. (2011). "Moral Sentiment and the Sources of Moral Identity," in C. Bagnoli, ed., *Morality and the Emotions*. Oxford: Oxford University Press, 257–74.

Taylor, Jacqueline. (2013). "Hume on the Importance of Humanity," in *Revue internationale de philosophie*, 81–97.

Taylor, Jacqueline. (2015). *Reflecting Subjects: Sympathy, Passion and Society in Hume's Philosophy*. Oxford: Oxford University Press.

Williams, Bernard. (1993). *Shame and Necessity*. Berkeley: University of California Press.

CHAPTER 16

··

THE NATURE AND
FUNCTIONS OF SYMPATHY
IN HUME'S PHILOSOPHY

··

RICO VITZ

THE concept of sympathy in Hume's philosophy is particularly intriguing for two reasons. First, Hume's texts pose a number of interpretive puzzles that make it rather challenging to understand the nature of sympathy. These puzzles prompted one of Hume's most prominent commentators to note, "How it is possible to find room for sympathy in so atomistic or individualistic a psychology as Hume's, is one of the most interesting questions which are raised by his system" (Selby-Bigge 1893, xxi). Second, given the various functions of sympathy, the concept plays a deeply important role not only in Hume's ethics and his social philosophy, but also in his cognitive psychology and, hence, in his epistemology, as well as his philosophy of religion. Thus, understanding Hume's account of sympathy is critical to understanding his philosophical system, but not easy to achieve.

My aim in this chapter is to outline the key details of this particularly interesting aspect of Hume's philosophical system. My presentation will be threefold. In the first section of the paper, I will elucidate the *nature* of sympathy, drawing on some of the more recent ways in which Hume's commentators have attempted to resolve the interpretive puzzles Hume's works present. In the second section, I will explicate some of the *functions* sympathy has in Hume's philosophy, including not only three that have been particularly prominent in the secondary literature, but also two others that have received considerably less attention. In the final section, I will summarize Hume's account of the nature and functions of sympathy and briefly suggest some of the ways in which these aspects of Hume's moral psychology seem to be supported by contemporary psychological research.[1]

I The Nature of Sympathy

My explanation of the nature of sympathy in Hume's philosophy will proceed in two stages. First, I will elucidate three different aspects of sympathy, which Hume identifies in the *Treatise* and the second *Enquiry*. Second, I will summarize and clarify an interpretive controversy concerning whether the account of sympathy in his earlier work differs from the account in his later work.

I.1 Three Aspects of Sympathy

Hume claims that to sympathize with others is, in general, to receive by communication the inclinations and sentiments of others "however different from, or even contrary to, our own" (T 2.1.11.2/316; cf. T 2.2.5.6–7, 14/359–60, 362; T 2.2.9.13–7/385–8). He uses the term "sympathy" more specifically, however, to refer to three different aspects of the way in which a person "receives" or "enters into" the sentiments of others.[2]

First, Hume uses the term "sympathy" to identify a psychological *mechanism*: namely, the *principle of sympathy*, by which one "enters into" the sentiment(s) of another.[3] In the *Treatise*, for instance, he claims that it is "the principle of sympathy, by which we enter into the sentiments of the rich and poor, and partake of their pleasure and uneasiness" (T 2.2.5.14/362; cf. T 2.2.5.2/358) and that one person who sees another in danger would enter into the suffering of the other by the "principle of sympathy" (T 2.2.9.13/385). Moreover, he claims that the principle of sympathy is the animating source of most of one's passions and sentiments (T 3.3.2.3/593).[4] In the *Enquiry*, Hume uses the term "sympathy" differently from the way he uses it in the *Treatise*, but he continues to use it to refer to the principle, or psychological mechanism, described in the *Treatise*. For instance, he uses the term for the very first time in the *Enquiry* in a discussion of character traits, such as beneficence and humanity, "or whatever proceeds from a tender sympathy with others" (EM 2.5/178; cf. T 3.3.3/602–6). He regularly uses the phrase "proceeds from" to refer to a thing's origin, cause, or principle (see, e.g., T 1.3.12.5/132; T 1.3.13.8/147; T 1.3.15.8/174; T 2.1.3.3/280; T 2.2.12.5–7/398; EU 8.13, 30–1/87, 98–9) and repeatedly uses it to refer to the psychological mechanism of sympathy, which causes certain passions (see, e.g., T 2.2.6.20–1/365; T 2.2.7.5/371–2; T 2.3.6.8/427; T 3.3.2.2–3/592–3; cf. EM 2.5/178).

So, the earliest occurrence of the term "sympathy" in the *Enquiry* is consistent with Hume's use of the term in the *Treatise* to refer to the principle and so are latter occurrences of the term. For example, he claims that people "enter into" the sentiments of others by means of a "natural sympathy" (EM 7.2/251; cf. EM 7.11, App 3.2/254, 303; T 2.2.5.6–7, 14/359–60, 362) and identifies sympathy as a principle that enters deeply into all human sentiments (EM 5.45/231). Thus, he uses the term "sympathy" to refer to a cognitive mechanism, or "principle."

Second, Hume uses the term "sympathy" to identify a psychological *process*: namely, the *sympathetic conversion* of an idea of another's sentiment into an impression of one's own. In the *Treatise*, for instance, he says, "[W]hen we sympathize with the passions and sentiments of others, these movements appear at first in *our* mind as mere ideas, and are conceiv'd to belong to another person, as we conceive any other matter of fact. 'Tis also evident, that the ideas of the affections of others are *converted into* the very impressions they represent, and that the passions arise in conformity to the images we form of them" (T 2.1.11.8/319; cf. T 3.3.2.5/595).[5] As this example suggests, on Hume's account, when a person "enters into" the sentiment of another, he or she begins by forming an idea of the other's sentiment. This idea of the other's sentiment is "converted into" an impression by the principle of sympathy (cf. T 2.2.9.13/385–6). This impression "acquires such a degree of force and vivacity" that he or she experiences the same kind of passion as the other (T 2.1.11.3/316–7). Thus, he uses the term "sympathy" to refer not only to a psychological mechanism, or "principle," but also to a psychological process by which an idea is converted into an impression "by the force of imagination" (T 2.3.6.8/427).

Third, he uses the term "sympathy" to identify the affective *product* of this conversion process: namely, the *sentiment of sympathy*.[6] In the *Treatise*, for instance, he says that sympathy is "nothing but a lively idea converted into an impression" by which we may "enter into" the sentiments of another person "with so vivid a conception as to make it our own concern; and by that means be sensible of pains and pleasures" that do not belong to ourselves (T 2.2.9.13/385–6). Elsewhere, in the same work, he refers to the "agreeable sympathy" that is produced in those who esteem the rich (T 3.3.5.5/616). In a similar passage in the second *Enquiry*, he refers to the "sentiment of sympathy" that is produced in someone contemplating the character of a virtuous person (EM 6.3/234). Likewise, in a footnote in the second appendix of the text, he identifies sympathy as a sentiment, specifically, as the sentiment of general benevolence (EM App 2.5 n60/298). Thus, he also uses the term "sympathy" to refer to a psychological product, more specifically, to the sentiment that is the result of the psychological process caused by the psychological mechanism, or "principle," of sympathy.

I.2 Interpretive Difficulties

Notice, though, what Hume does in the last passage that I cited from the second *Enquiry*. Not only does he identify sympathy as a sentiment, he also identifies benevolence and humanity as sentiments and seems to equate the three. This type of usage of the term "sympathy" in Hume's latter work has led to a debate among Hume's commentators about the relationship between his account of sympathy in the *Treatise* and his account of sympathy in the second *Enquiry*. Participants in the debate hold a rather wide variety of views concerning Hume's account of the nature of sympathy in the second *Enquiry*. For ease of presentation, let me divide these into three groups.

The first group—represented, for example, by Selby-Bigge and Capaldi—claims that the accounts of sympathy presented in the *Treatise*, on the one hand, and in the second *Enquiry*, on the other, are markedly different. Selby-Bigge (1893: xxi) suggests that there is a significant difference between the moral psychology of the *Treatise* and that of the second *Enquiry* and claims that the psychology of sympathy, which plays such a central role in the second and third books of the *Treatise*, is "almost entirely ignored in the *Enquiry*." On his reading, Hume may have been so displeased with his account of sympathy in the *Treatise* that he abandoned it in his later work. Specifically, he claims that in the *Enquiry* sympathy is simply "another name for social feeling, humanity, benevolence, [or] natural philanthropy, rather than the name of the process by which the social feeling has been constructed out of non-social or individual feeling" (Selby-Bigge 1893: xxvi). Capaldi (1975: 180–187) seems to take a similar view, claiming that Hume is not merely reticent about identifying sympathy as a principle but that he rejects it as a psychological mechanism from which benevolence is derived.

The second—represented, for example, by Laird and Penelhum—expresses partial agreement with Selby-Bigge and Capaldi. Laird accepts Selby-Bigge's claim that the "sympathy" of the *Treatise* becomes "natural philanthropy or fellow-feeling" in the *Enquiry*. He rejects, however, Selby-Bigge's "suggestion that Hume became intentionally reticent concerning the 'machinery' of sympathy," claiming that such a thesis "is difficult to sustain" (Laird 1932/1967: 238–239). Penelhum is ambivalent about the accuracy of Capaldi's reading. He contends, however, that if Capaldi's interpretation is not correct, then Hume's reference to the sentiment of humanity in the second *Enquiry* "has to be construed as a shorthand for the details of sympathy that are spelled out in the *Treatise*" (Penelhum 1992: 156).

The third—represented, for example, by Altmann, Abramson, and Debes[7]—claims that the accounts of sympathy presented in the *Treatise*, on the one hand, and in the second *Enquiry*, on the other, are substantially the same. Altmann (1980: 133–5) notes that simply because "the notions and jargons of the *Treatise* do not reappear in the *Inquiry*, this does not entail that the sympathy mechanism has been rejected" and argues that "the principle of sympathy is not rejected by Hume in either Book III of the *Treatise* or in *An Inquiry concerning the Principles of Morals*." Abramson (2001: 48) contends that, contrary to what those in the first group "would have us believe, all the essential details of Hume's doctrine of sympathy can in fact be found" in the second *Enquiry*. Similarly, Debes defends what he calls "a no-change hypothesis" (2007b: 314)[8] and argues that "there is no real inconsistency between Hume's position in the *Enquiry* and the *Treatise* regarding humanity, sympathy, and the source of our moral sentiments" (2007a: 29).

The interpretation of the first group might seem to be supported both by the fact that, in the *Enquiry*, Hume identifies sympathy with the sentiments of benevolence and humanity (see, e.g., EM 6.3/234, EM 9.12/276, EM App. 2.5 n60/298n), as I noted earlier, as well as by Hume's apparent lack of concern in the *Enquiry* to provide a detailed account of the principle of sympathy. Moreover, according to Capaldi, there are two particular passages that evince the change in Hume's accounts from the *Treatise* to the second *Enquiry*.

I.2.1 *The First Passage: EM 5.13*

The first passage is from the fifth section of the second *Enquiry*. Hume says,

> It is but a weak subterfuge, when pressed by these facts and arguments, to say, that we transport ourselves, by the force of imagination, into distant ages and countries, and consider the advantage, which we should have reaped from these characters, had we been contemporaries; and had any commerce with the persons. It is not conceivable, how a *real* sentiment or passion can ever arise from a known *imaginary* interest; especially when our *real* interest is still kept in view, and is often acknowledged to be entirely distinct from the imaginary, and even sometimes opposed to it. (EM 5.13/217)

On Capaldi's interpretation, this passage contains "a perfect description of the sympathy mechanism" and "leaves us in no doubt" that Hume rejects the principle of sympathy, as described in the *Treatise* (1975: 181). If, however, Hume's intention in this passage is to *reject* the principle of sympathy, then his argument is rather blatantly inconsistent since Hume uses the passage to introduce an *affirmation* of the principle. In fact, in the latter part of the section, he attempts to show that the *"principles of humanity and sympathy* enter so deeply into all our sentiments, and have so powerful an influence, as may enable them to excite the strongest censure and applause" (EM 5.45/231, emphasis added; see also, e.g., EM 5.18/220).

In the passage that Capaldi cites as evidence of Hume's rejection of the principle of sympathy, Hume is merely claiming that *certain kinds* of imagined interests are not the source of the pleasure of utility, not that *no* imagined interest *per se* can affect a person. In fact, in the very next paragraph, he offers an example of a way in which an imagined interest can do so. He says, "A man, brought to the brink of a precipice, cannot look down without trembling; and the sentiment of imaginary danger actuates him, in opposition to the opinion and belief of real safety" (EM 5.14/217). He then goes on to explain that, in such a case, the imagination is aided by other factors. His aim is to elucidate the role the imagination plays as the source both (1) of the pleasure people get from utility and (2) of their moral approbations (cf. EM 5.15/218). Later, he identifies sympathy as a psychological principle that keeps people from being "totally indifferent" to the interests of others. Thus, Hume may be guilty of writing unclearly, as Selby-Bigge (1893: vii) suggests—and hence, of inviting the kind of reading that Capaldi offers—but the first passage to which Capaldi appeals is not evidence that Hume rejects the principle of sympathy.

I.2.2 *The Second Passage: EM 5.17 n19*

The second passage occurs in a footnote later in the same section. Hume says,

> It is needless to push our researches so far as to ask, why we have *humanity* or a fellow-feeling with others. It is sufficient, that this is experienced to be *a principle in human nature.* We must stop somewhere in our examination of causes; and there are in every science, some general principles beyond which we cannot hope to find any

principle more general. No man is absolutely indifferent to the happiness and misery of others. The first has a natural tendency to give pleasure; the second, pain. This every one may find in himself. It is not probable, that these principles can be resolved into principles more simple and universal, whatever attempts may have been made to that purpose. But if it were possible, it belongs not to the present subject; and we may here safely consider these principles as original: happy, if we can render all the consequences sufficiently plain and perspicuous! (EM 5.17n19/219-20n; emphasis added)[9]

On Capaldi's (1975: 181) reading, Hume's intention in this passage is to make clear that "there will be no attempt to explain our humanity by reducing it to the sympathy mechanism." The focal point of this footnote is the principle of humanity. Thus, in order to assess Capaldi's interpretation of the passage, it is necessary to have an accurate understanding of the relationship between the principle of sympathy and the principle of humanity. I provided a brief description of the nature of sympathy earlier. So, in what follows, I will focus on Hume's accounts of the nature of humanity[10] and of the relationship between the principle of sympathy and the principle of humanity—both in the *Treatise* and in the second *Enquiry*.

In the *Treatise*, Hume uses the term "humanity" to refer to three things. First, he uses it, as he uses the term "sympathy," to refer to a *psychological mechanism*: namely, the *principle of humanity* (T 3.2.1.6/478).[11] Second, he uses it to refer to an *affective product* of this principle: namely, the *sentiment of humanity*. For instance, he identifies humanity as a passion that helps to provide the motive for fathers to care for their children and for people "to relieve the miserable" (T 3.2.5.6/518-9). Third, he uses the term to refer to a *dispositional product* of this principle: namely, the *virtue of humanity*, which is a tender and caring quality of character (see, e.g., T 3.3.1.12, 24/579, 587; T 3.3.3.3-5/603-5). For instance, he speaks of "generosity, humanity, compassion, gratitude, friendship, fidelity, zeal, disinterestedness, liberality, and all those other qualities, which proceed from the character of good and benevolent" (T 3.3.3.3/603).[12]

So, on the account Hume provides in the *Treatise*, both the principle of sympathy and the principle of humanity are aspects of the human mind by which people desire to care for the interests of others. The principle of sympathy, however, can activate a wider range of affective states. For instance, it could be the cause of hatred or contempt (T 2.2.9.15/387). The principle of humanity, on the other hand, could not be the cause of negative sentiments such as these because there is always a mixture of anger with hatred or contempt, and anger is "a desire of the misery of the person hated, and an aversion happiness" (T 2.2.9.1-3/381-2). Thus, the principle of sympathy, unlike the principle of humanity, could be the cause of benevolent or malevolent motives. Therefore, in the *Treatise*, the principle of sympathy and principle of humanity are not identical.

In the second *Enquiry*, however, it is difficult to tell what, if any, difference there is between the two. In this latter work, Hume does not describe the principle of sympathy as a cause of malevolent motives. From the absence of a description of sympathy as a cause of ill-will, however, it does not follow that Hume intends the principle to be a psychological mechanism that is solely inclined to benevolence. What is more interesting is that he does refer to sympathy and humanity as *two principles*, not *a principle*, of human nature (see, e.g., EM 5, 45/231).[13] The significance of this evidence, however, is difficult to assess given Hume's imprecise practice of differentiating principles. In one footnote, for instance, he refers to "humanity or a fellow-feeling with others" as "*a principle* of human nature." A little later in the same footnote, he says that "we may here safely consider *these principles* as original" (EM 5.17 n19/219–20n; emphasis added). It is not clear whether the phrase "these principles" refers (1) solely to "some general principles" that are found in every science; (2) both to "some general principles" that are found in every science and to the principle of humanity, which is also known as the principle of fellow-feeling; (3) not to "some general principles" that are found in every science, but both to the principle of humanity and to a different principle—namely, the principle of fellow-feeling; or (4) to "some general principles" that are found in every science, and to the principle of humanity and to the principle of fellow-feeling. The fact that the referent of the phrase "these principles" in the footnote is ambiguous evinces Hume's failure to differentiate principles clearly.

What might seem more problematic, however, is that Hume refers to original principles *at all*. Given his assertion that "any hypothesis, that pretends to discover the ultimate original qualities in human nature, ought first to be rejected as presumptuous and chimerical" (T Intro. 8/xvii), how can he claim to explain *any* original principle, particularly sympathy (T 2.1.3.1–3/280; T 2.1.11.1–2/316) or humanity (EM 5.17 n19/219n)?

Let me suggest one possible way of answering this question by drawing on a comparison between Hume's "moral philosophy" and his "natural philosophy." Regarding the activity of the human mind, Hume says, "To explain the ultimate causes of our mental actions is impossible" (T 1.1.7.11/22; cf. T Intro. 9/xvii–iii). In a similar vein, regarding the activity of the operations of natural bodies, he claims that "no philosopher, who is rational and modest, has ever pretended to assign the ultimate cause of any natural operation" (EU 4.12/30). Thus, there is a similarity between Hume's skeptical attitude regarding our ability to describe the ultimate causes in the realm of "moral philosophy" and his attitude regarding our ability to describe the ultimate causes in the realm of "natural philosophy." In light of this similarity, one might reasonably wonder whether an analysis of Hume's exposition of our inability to describe the original qualities of natural phenomena might help us to understand his moral psychology. I submit that it can, as follows.

In his account of the ultimate causes of the operations of natural bodies, Hume asserts that

> the utmost effort of human reason is to reduce the principles, productive of natural phenomena, to a greater simplicity, and to resolve the many particular effects into a few general causes, by means of reasonings from analogy, experience, and observation. But as to the causes of these general causes, we should in vain attempt their discovery; nor shall we ever be able to satisfy ourselves, by any particular explication of them. These ultimate springs and principles are totally shut up from human

curiosity and enquiry. Elasticity, gravity, cohesion of parts, communication of motion by impulse; these are probably the ultimate causes and principles which we shall ever discover in nature. (EU 4.12/30)

In this passage, he makes a distinction between the *ultimate springs and principles* and the *general principles* that are productive of natural phenomena. This distinction is critical for the following reason: although he notes that people cannot know the ultimate springs and principles, he claims that they can form reasonable beliefs about general principles, such as gravity and communication of motion by impulse. Intriguingly, he refers to these general principles as "*probably* the ultimate causes and principles *which we shall ever discover*" (EU 4.12/30–1; emphasis added) and, elsewhere in his work, adopts the practice of referring to the general principles as ultimate principles—at least, the ultimate principles that people may discover. For instance, in the passage to which Capaldi refers, in the footnote of EM 5.17/219–20n, he says *that we can safely consider* the principle of humanity or fellow-feeling as original.[14]

How, though, could recognizing sympathy and humanity as principles that can be "considered as original" help to elucidate the nature of the relationship between them? In the field of natural philosophy, Hume claims that "we may esteem ourselves sufficiently happy, if, by accurate enquiry and reasoning, we can trace up the particular phenomena to, or *near to* . . . *general principles*" such as gravity, cohesion of parts, and communication of motion by impulse (EU 4.12/30–1; emphasis added). Similarly, in the field of moral philosophy, he suggests that we can esteem ourselves sufficiently happy if we can trace up the particular phenomena of human behavior to, or near to, the general principles of sympathy and humanity—principles that we can safely consider as original and that, at least on Hume's account, may be the ultimate causes of human behavior that we will ever discover (cf. EU 4.12/30–1). Notice that this is exactly the attitude he takes in his discussion of the principle of humanity. Consider the footnote at EM 5.17 again, focusing not, specifically, on what Hume says about humanity but, more generally, on what he says about explanatory principles in science. He says,

> We must stop somewhere in our examination of causes; and there are in every science, some general principles beyond which we cannot hope to find any principle more general. . . . It is not probable, that these principles can be resolved into principles more simple and universal, whatever attempts may have been made to that purpose . . . we may here safely consider these principles as original: happy, if we can render all the consequences sufficiently plain and perspicuous! (T 5.17/219–20n)

So, how can Hume claim to explain *any* original principle, particularly sympathy (T 2.1.3.1–3/280; T 2.1.11.1–2/316) or humanity (EM 5.17n19/219n)? He can do so for the very reasons he gives at EU 4.12/30–1 and EM 5.17 n19/219–20n.

Thus, Capaldi is right that Hume does not attempt to reduce the principle of humanity to the principle of sympathy in the *Enquiry*. Hume makes no such attempt at reduction in his later work because he treats these principles as original. The treatment he gives these principles in the *Enquiry*, however, is consistent with the one he gives them in the *Treatise*: he consistently regards each as a general principle and uses each to explain moral motivation and moral assessment.[15]

I.3 Summary

In short, in his earlier work, Hume uses the term "sympathy" to refer to three different aspects of human moral psychology: a *mechanism*, a *process*, and the affective *product* of this process. The first is the *principle of sympathy*, by which one "enters into" the sentiment(s) of another. The second is the *sympathetic conversion* of an idea of another's sentiment into an impression of one's own. The third is the *sentiment of sympathy*. Between his earlier work and his later work, however, he seems to use the term "sympathy"—and related terms, like "humanity"—equivocally. This equivocal use of terms has led to a variety of views among Hume's commentators about the nature of sympathy in Hume's later work. Traditionally, Hume scholars suggested that the apparent changes in Hume's use of terms evinces an abandonment—or, at the very least, a substantial revision in Hume's moral psychology. More recently, Hume scholars have argued that the changes in Hume's account of sympathy are merely stylistic. On the latter readings, the nature of sympathy and its place in Hume's moral psychology remain essentially unchanged from the *Treatise* to the second *Enquiry*.

II THE FUNCTIONS OF SYMPATHY

Having discussed what sympathy *is*, let us now consider what it *does*.[16] I will begin this section by elucidating three of the functions of sympathy in Hume's philosophy that have been discussed more frequently in the secondary literature. I will then elucidate two of the functions that have been discussed less frequently or less elaborately.

II.1 Three More Frequently Discussed Functions

The three functions of sympathy that are more frequently and elaborately discussed by Hume's commentators are elements of his ethics and his aesthetics.[17] The first concerns sympathy's role in moral motivation; the second, its role in moral evaluation; the third, its role in aesthetic evaluation.

II.1.1 *Sympathy as a Source of Prosocial Motivation*

There is a great deal one could say—and, in fact, many have said—on sympathy as a source of moral motivation. For the sake of clarity, I will focus on two cases in which sympathy causes benevolence, or a desire for the well-being of another[18] (cf. T 2.2.6.1–6/366–8; T 2.2.9.1–20/381–9).[19] Focusing on these cases of sympathy as a cause of benevolent motivation is particularly apt for present purposes both because benevolence is an archetypical prosocial motive and because, in Hume's philosophy, it bears a striking resemblance to other types of prosocial motives, like pity (cf. T 2.2.7.1/369; T 2.2.9.3–4/382).[20]

The first case is that of a person who feels benevolence for a beggar. In this case, Hume suggests that sympathy gives rise to moral motivation in the following way. The process of sympathetic conversion begins when a person sees a beggar and, consequently, acquires the idea of a passion, such as misery. The person acquires this idea from an impression of the beggar's misery, which she knows by the effects and "external signs" of the sentiment—for example, the beggar's worn clothes and malnourished physique.[21] The principle of sympathy then operates on the faculty of imagination to increase the "force" or "liveliness" of the idea of the beggar's misery to such a degree that the idea becomes an impression: namely, a sentiment of sympathy. Thus, the person "enters into" the sentiment of the beggar, experiences a sentiment of sympathy, and, consequently, experiences benevolent motivation.

The second case is more complex. According to Hume,

'Tis certain, that sympathy is not always limited to the present moment, but that we often feel, by communication, the pains and pleasures of others which are not in being and which we only anticipate by the force of imagination. For, supposing I saw a person perfectly unknown to me, who, while asleep in the fields, was in danger of being trod under foot by horses, I should immediately run to his assistance and in this I should be actuated by the same *principle of sympathy* which makes me concerned for the present sorrows of a stranger. The bare mention of this is sufficient. (T 2.2.9.13/385; emphasis added)

How does sympathy work in a case such as this one? How does a person "enter into" sentiments that another is not currently experiencing (cf. T 2.2.9.13/385–6)? To explain cases such as this, Hume distinguishes among three kinds of sentiments of sympathy—first sympathy, extensive sympathy, and limited sympathy. When the spectator sees the man asleep in the field, the man apparently has no negative feelings. Thus, the sentiments with which the spectator sympathizes do not yet exist. Nonetheless, he is able to "extend" his sympathy to those sentiments that he anticipates will follow from the man's present condition, as Hume notes:

When the present misery of another has any strong influence upon me, the vivacity of the conception is not confin'd to its immediate object, but diffuses its influence over all the related ideas, and gives me a lively notion of all the circumstances of that person, whether past, present, future; possible, probable, or certain. By means of this lively notion I am interested in them; take part with them; and feel a sympathetic motion in my breast, conformable to whatever I imagine in his. (T 2.2.9.14/386)

Lest we misunderstand Hume's point, it is important to note that as he is using the phrase in this passage, "the present misery of another" does not necessarily refer to a sentiment that a person is feeling at a given moment. For instance, the "present misery" of the man asleep in the field is not a sentiment the man is currently experiencing; rather, it is the pain the spectator anticipates the man will experience in the near future. The *first sympathy* a person feels is simply the initial sentiment of sympathy that she has upon considering the condition of another. *Extensive sympathy* is the sympathetic sentiment a person has when the force of the first sympathy is strong enough to provide a lively notion not only of the present circumstances of the person who is the object of her interest but of "all the circumstances of that person, whether past, present, future; possible, probable, or certain," such as the pain that the man in the field will experience if no one comes to his aid. A person has *limited sympathy* when the first sympathy is weak (cf. T 2.2.9.14/386).

On Hume's account, the "force" of the first sympathy is particularly significant for two reasons. First, it determines whether a person will experience extensive or limited sympathy. A person will experience extensive sympathy if the first sympathy is strong; limited sympathy if the first sympathy is weak. Second, it determines whether a person will have a strong prosocial motive. A person will have such a motive if the first sympathy is strong, and lack such a motive if the first sympathy is weak.[22]

II.1.2 *Sympathy as a Source of Moral Evaluation*

In addition to its role as a source of moral motivation in Hume's philosophy, sympathy also functions as a source of moral evaluation. There is a good deal of debate about just *how* sympathy functions in this regard, but *that* it has this role is a point on which Hume's commentators agree.

Hume famously argues that people's moral judgments are not derived from reason. Rather, he contends, "[m]orality . . . is more properly felt than judg'd of" (T 3.3.2.1/470; cf. T 3.3.5.1/614). On his account, when people pronounce any action or character to be virtuous or vicious, they mean nothing but that from the constitution of their natures they have a feeling or sentiment of approbation or of blame, respectively, from the contemplation of it (T 3.3.1.26/469; cf. EM App. 1.10/289). He recognizes that these sentiments vary both according to people's particular relations to the object of their moral assessments and according to the present disposition of their minds. Moreover, he notes that this kind of partiality would remain were people to evaluate, from their particular points of view, the actions or character of others (cf. T 3.3.1.15/581–2). To correct for this partiality, he provides "a method of correcting [people's] sentiments, or at least correcting [their] language, where the sentiments are more stubborn and inalterable" (T 3.3.1.16/582). In his discussion of the nature of goodness and "whence its merit is deriv'd," he describes it as follows:

> When experience has once given us a competent knowledge of human affairs, and has taught us the proportion they bear to human passion, we perceive, that the generosity of men is very limited, and that it seldom extends beyond their friends

and family, or, at most, beyond their native country. Being thus acquainted with the nature of man, we expect not any impossibilities from him; but confine our view to that narrow circle, in which any person moves, in order to form a judgment of his moral character. When the natural tendency of his passions leads him to be serviceable and useful within his sphere, we approve of his character and love his person, *by a sympathy with the sentiments of those, who have a more particular connexion with him.* (T 3.3.3.2/602; emphasis added; cf. T 3.2.1.6/478; T 3.3.1.15–17, 20/581–3, 591)

Thus, on Hume's account, sympathy is a cause both of people's initial assessments and of their refined assessments of the actions and characters of others.

As I noted previously, Hume's commentators disagree about a number of the finer points of his view; for example, whether refined moral judgments are based on the sentiments of actual persons or on those of an idealized spectator, how significant a factor sympathy (as opposed to reason or social discourse) is in the process of refining people's moral judgments,[23] and so forth. On this much, however, they seem to have reached a consensus: on Hume's account, people's moral evaluations of others are derived, in part, from sentiments caused by the principle of sympathy.

II.1.3 *Sympathy as a Source of Aesthetic Evaluation*

A third, related role of sympathy in Hume's philosophy is its function as a source of aesthetic evaluation. As Hume notes, sympathy is "a very powerful principle in human nature" that has a great influence not only on our moral sentiments but also on "our *taste of beauty*" (T 3.3.1.10/577; emphasis added). As in the case of moral evaluation, this influence operates in two ways.

First, sympathy allows people to enter into the sentiments of others, thereby giving rise to certain aesthetic sentiments. For instance, Hume claims that a man who goes to the theater "is immediately struck with the view of so great a multitude, participating of one common amusement; and experiences, from their very aspect, a superior sensibility or disposition of being affected with every sentiment, which he shares with his fellow-creatures" and that "[e]very movement of the theatre, by a skilful poet, is communicated, as it were by magic, to the spectators; who weep, tremble, resent, rejoice, and are inflamed with all the variety of passions, which actuate the several personages of the drama" (EM 5.24–6/221–2). In fact, as Hume notes in his essay "On Tragedy," "The whole art of the poet is employed, in rouzing and supporting the compassion and indignation, the anxiety and resentment of his audience. They are pleased in proportion as they are afflicted, and never are so happy as when they employ tears, sobs, and cries to give vent to their sorrow, and relieve their heart, swoln with the tenderest sympathy and compassion" (ESY 216–7). The source of these aesthetic sentiments is sympathy (T 2.2.7.3/369).

Second, Hume claims that people's normative assessments of works of art follow from the aesthetic sentiments they derive from sympathy. For instance, in his essay "The Sceptic," in discussing our assessments of beauty and deformity, he says,

[T]he case is not the same with the qualities of *beautiful and deformed, desirable and odious*, as with truth and falsehood. In the former case, the mind is not content with merely surveying its objects, as they stand in themselves: It also feels a sentiment of delight or uneasiness, approbation or blame, consequent to that survey; and this sentiment determines it to afix the epithet *beautiful or deformed, desirable or odious*. Now, it is evident, that this sentiment must depend upon the particular fabric or structure of the mind, which enables such particular forms to operate in such a particular manner, and produces a sympathy or conformity between the mind and its objects. Vary the structure of the mind or inward organs, the sentiment no longer follows, though the form remains the same. The sentiment being different from the object, and arising from its operation upon the organs of the mind, an alteration upon the latter must vary the effect, nor can the same object, presented to a mind totally different, produce the same sentiment. (ESY 164)

Elsewhere, for example in "Of the Delicacy of Taste and Passion" and "Of the Standard of Taste," Hume goes into detail about the requisite conditions for reconciling the diverse aesthetic sentiments of a variety of people. As interesting and important as those details are to understanding Hume's account of taste as it relates to art and beauty, they are ancillary to the central aim of this chapter. So, for present purposes, let me simply highlight the fact that, on Hume's account, the role sympathy plays in people's aesthetic evaluations is roughly similar—although certainly not identical—to that which it plays in people's moral evaluations.[24]

II.2   Two Less Frequently Discussed Functions

Let us turn, next, to two of the less frequently discussed functions of sympathy in Hume's philosophy. The first concerns its role as a source of belief in the existence of other minds; the second, its role as a source of a variety of beliefs acquired by "contagion."

II.2.1   *Sympathy as a Source of Belief in the Existence of Other Minds*

As the previous sections suggest, Hume recognizes that people believe in the existence of other minds. How, though, does he account for such belief? One way for him to do so would be to show how it is founded in reason. Another way would be to show how it is grounded in human nature. Hume's commentators disagree about whether he attempts to offer an explanation of the former type.[25] The latter, however, is exactly the kind of explanation he suggests in his introduction of sympathy in the *Treatise*. He says,

No quality of human nature is more remarkable, both in itself and in its consequences, than that propensity we have to sympathize with others, and *to receive by communication their inclinations and sentiments*, however different from, or even contrary to our own. This is not only conspicuous in children, who implicitly embrace every opinion propos'd to them; but also in *men of the greatest judgment and understanding, who find it very difficult to follow their own reason* or inclination, in opposition to that of their friends and daily companions. . . . A good-natur'd man *finds himself* in an instant of the same humour with his company; and even the proudest and most surly take a tincture from their countrymen and acquaintance. A chearful countenance *infuses* a sensible complacency and serenity into my mind; as an angry or sorrowful one *throws a sudden* damp upon me. Hatred, resentment, esteem, love, courage, mirth and melancholy; all these passions I feel more *from communication* than from my own natural temper and disposition. (T 2.1.11.2/316; emphasis added)

Let me highlight three particularly salient things about this passage. First, Hume suggests that people properly acquire beliefs about the minds of others by means of a particular psychological mechanism: namely, sympathy. Second, he immediately goes on to contrast the principle of belief acquisition in such cases with a different principle: namely, reason. Third, he suggests not only that people can properly acquire beliefs about the minds of others and that the cause of these beliefs is sympathy, but also that they acquire such beliefs unreflectively. People simply *find* themselves with such beliefs rather than *persuade* themselves by means of an argument.

He offers a similar kind of causal explanation of belief in other minds in a discussion of "the nature and force of sympathy." He says,

We may begin with considering a-new the nature and force of *sympathy*. The minds of all men are similar in their feelings and operations, nor can any one be actuated by any affection, of which all others are not, in some degree, susceptible. As in strings equally wound up, the motion of one communicates itself to the rest; so all the affections readily pass from one person to another, and beget correspondent movements in every human creature. When I see the *effects* of passion in the voice and gesture of any person, my mind immediately passes from these effects to their causes, and forms such a lively idea of the passion, as is presently converted into the passion itself. In like manner, when I perceive the *causes* of any emotion, my mind is convey'd to the effects, and is actuated with a like emotion. Were I present at any of the more terrible operations of surgery, 'tis certain, that even before it begun, the preparation of the instruments, the laying of the bandages in order, the heating of the irons, with all the signs of anxiety and concern in the patients and assistants, wou'd have a great effect upon my mind, and excite the strongest sentiments of pity and terror. No passion of another discovers itself immediately to the mind. We are only sensible of its causes or effects. From *these* we infer the passion: And consequently *these* give rise to our sympathy. (T 3.3.1.7/576)

This passage provides a particularly helpful opportunity for clarifying Hume's position because of its ambiguity. At first glance, it might seem to suggest that sympathy is a mechanism that provides evidence from which people reason to the existence of other minds. After all, Hume concludes the passages by noting that it is from the causes and effects of their sentiments that people "*infer* the passion."[26] The temptation to read the passage in this way is misleading for two reasons. First, the word "infer" itself is ambiguous. Given its etymology—from the Latin *inferre*—it is natural to read the term in a causal, rather than in an inferential sense. In fact, in the *Oxford English Dictionary*, the *primary* sense of the term is causal;[27] the *tertiary* sense of the term is inferential.[28] Second, the language leading up to the conclusion suggests that the term is used in a causal sense. Hume says that a person's mind is "convey'd" and "immediately passes" to the sentiments of another, and this movement is described with a causal metaphor: "As in strings equally wound up, the motion of one communicates itself to the rest; so all the affections readily pass from one person to another, and beget correspondent movements in every human creature." Thus, Hume's point in this passage is that the causes and effects of people's sentiments trigger one's principle of sympathy, initiating the process by which one enters into the minds of others and, thereby, is caused to believe in the existence of other minds.[29] In short, as Pitson (2002: 269 n11) suggests, belief in the existence of other minds satisfies a number of the criteria for being a kind of Humean "natural" belief: for example, it is non-theoretical, inevitable and indispensable, an inevitable product of the mechanisms of association, and so forth.[30] Hence, on Hume's account, sympathy has an important epistemic function not only as a source of people's moral and aesthetic judgments but also as a source of belief in the existence of other minds.

II.2.2 *Sympathy as a Source of Beliefs Acquired by "Contagion"*

In fact, the scope of sympathy's epistemic effects is not even limited to moral evaluations, aesthetic evaluations, and beliefs about other minds. It extends to a wide variety of beliefs that people can acquire by "contagion," as I will show presently.[31]

Throughout his work, Hume makes a number of references to "contagion." Many of these references concern the passions. In the *Treatise*, for instance, he says, "The passions are so contagious, that they pass with the greatest facility from one person to another, and produce correspondent movements in all human breasts" (T 3.3.3.5/605). Similarly, in the second *Enquiry*, he discusses people's ability to "catch" sentiments "by a contagion or natural sympathy" (EM 7.2/251; cf. EM 7.21/257–8). Likewise, in his *Essays*, he discusses people's "propensity to company and society" and notes that the dispositional aspect of human psychology that causes human beings to "enter deeply into each other's sentiments" also "causes like passions and inclinations to run, as it were, by contagion, through the whole club or knot of companions" (ESY 200–4).[32] In each of these examples, Hume uses the term "contagion," or one of its cognates, to refer to *sympathetic conversion*, or the psychological process by which an idea of another's sentiment is enlivened such that it becomes an impression of one's own.

The product in each of these cases is an affective state, but Hume does not restrict the product of sympathetic conversions to these kinds of states alone. He also claims that people's opinions, or beliefs, can be contagious. In the *Treatise*, for instance, he notes that by means of the *principle of sympathy*, people enter "into the opinions and affections of others" (T 2.1.11.7/319) and suggests that

[n]o quality of human nature is more remarkable, both in itself and in its consequences, than that propensity we have to sympathize with others, and to receive by communication their inclinations and sentiments, however different from, or even contrary to, our own. This is not only conspicuous in children, who implicitly embrace every opinion proposed to them; but also in men of the greatest judgment and understanding, who find it very difficult to follow their own reason or inclination, in opposition to that of their friends and daily companions. (T 2.1.11.2/316)

Thus, on Hume's account, both sentiments *and beliefs* can be acquired by the principle of sympathy. In this respect, he suggests, the operation of sympathy is strikingly similar, if not "exactly correspondent to" the operation of the understanding, insofar as each functions to enliven ideas (cf. T 2.1.11.3, 8/317, 320).

III CONCLUSION

Let me close with a brief summary and an observation. In the foregoing sections, I explained the nature and functions of sympathy in Hume's philosophy. In the first, I elucidated three different aspects of sympathy and clarified an interpretive controversy concerning Hume's presentations of sympathy in the *Treatise* and in the second *Enquiry*. In the second, I elucidated three of the functions of sympathy in Hume's philosophy that have been discussed more frequently in the secondary literature—namely, its roles in moral motivation, in moral evaluation, and in aesthetic evaluation—and, then, elucidated two of the functions that have been discussed less frequently or less elaborately—namely, its roles as a source of belief in the existence of other minds and as a source of a variety of beliefs acquired by "contagion."

What makes the nature and functions of sympathy in Hume's philosophy intriguing is not merely the significance of each in the system of one of the seminal figures in the history of philosophy. That alone might make the study of Hume's conception of sympathy important. What makes these aspects of his moral psychology so intriguing, however, is the support they seem to have received in contemporary psychology and cognitive science. To take but a few examples: the work of Daniel Batson and others seems to support Hume's account of sympathy as a source of prosocial motivation. The works of Martin Hoffman and of Jesse Prinz seem to provide evidence for Hume's views about the role of sympathy in moral assessment and moral development, respectively. The work of Arie Kruglanski and a variety of other social psychologists seem to buttress Hume's views about the contagious nature of beliefs.[33] These are merely some general observations about the relationship between Hume's work and contemporary scientific research. They suggest, however, that aside from having interesting opportunities for philosophical research on the nature and functions of sympathy in Hume's work, there may very well be promising and significant interdisciplinary opportunities as well. That possibility, it seems to me, is not simply intriguing; it is fascinating.

ABBREVIATIONS OF WORKS CITED

DP   *A Dissertation on the Passions*. In T. Beauchamp, ed. *A Dissertation on the Passions; The Natural History of Religion*. Oxford: Clarendon Press, 2008.

EM   *Enquiry Concerning the Principles of Morals*. Edited by Tom L. Beauchamp. Oxford: Clarendon, 1998.

ESY   *Essays: Moral, Political, and Literary*. Revised edition by E. F. Miller. Indianapolis: Liberty Classics, 1985.

EU   *An Enquiry Concerning Human Understanding*. Edited by Tom L. Beauchamp. Oxford: Clarendon, 1998.

T   *A Treatise of Human Nature*. Edited by D. F. Norton and M. J. Norton. Oxford: Clarendon, 2007.

NOTES

1. Given the nature of my aim, I will only be able to touch briefly on the works of the commentators that I discuss. So, there is a great deal of interesting and influential work on Hume that I simply will not have the space to address. Nonetheless, my hope is that what follows will be not only a helpful survey of some of the more significant work that has been done on the nature and functions of sympathy in Hume's philosophy, but also a helpful guide for potentially fruitful areas of future research on the topic.

2. I do not mean to imply that Hume was aware of his varying uses of the term "sympathy." In fact, I suspect that he was not and that his failure to distinguish clearly (perhaps, to notice) the varying ways in which he uses the term is one of the fundamental reasons that there is significant disagreement among Hume's commentators about his account of sympathy.

3. Hume uses phrases of the form "principle of x" to identify the cause of x or the origin of x—see, e.g., T 1.4.5.31/248; T 2.1.1–3/275–82; T 2.2.5.5/359; cf. EM 8.13, 30–1/87, 98–9, as well as T 1.3.2.7–3.5/76–81; T 1.3.12.5/132; T 1.4.2.37/205; T 2.2.2.7/335; T 2.2.5.12–4/362; T 2.2.7.5/371.

4. I take it that Hume is speaking hyperbolically when he claims that sympathy is the source of all of the passions by which people are actuated (T 2.2.5.15/363).

5. The emphasis on "our" is Hume's; the emphasis on "converted into" is mine.

6. A number of Hume's commentators deny that sympathy is a passion, on Hume's account—see, e.g., Chismar (1988–9: 238), Mercer (1972: 21), Roberts (1973: 97), Wand (1955: 276).

7. In the interest of full disclosure, I should note that my own work on Hume's moral psychology puts me in the third camp as well. In fact, what follows in this section is, in large part, a development of arguments that I offer in Vitz (2004: 261–275); see also Vitz (2002: 271–295).

8. Jacqueline Taylor seems to endorse a contrary view; see, e.g., Taylor (2002: 56). In more recent work, however, she claims not that Hume "drops" the associative account of sympathy but that he "sets the theory of association aside without abandoning it altogether" (Taylor 2008: 292 n5); cf. Taylor (2009: 321). See also Taylor (2013).

9. The term "fellow-feeling" is used only twice in the *Enquiry*. In the first occurrence, from the footnote just cited, the term "fellow-feeling" is used to refer to a principle. In the second occurrence, from the section entitled "Of Qualities Immediately Agreeable to Ourselves," he refers to "social sympathy . . . or fellow-feeling with human happiness or misery" as a sentiment (EM 7.29/260). Thus, the term "fellow-feeling" is used, as are the terms "sympathy" and "humanity," to refer both to a sentiment and to a principle.

10. As Debes (2007*a*) rightly notes, elucidating Hume's account of humanity is key to sorting out the interpretive problems concerning sympathy in the second *Enquiry*.

11. Recall, as I noted earlier, that Hume uses phrases of the form "principle of x" to identify the cause of x or the origin of x.

12. Cf. Debes (2007*a*).

13. Cf. Debes (2007*a*).

14. Hume uses the phrases "ultimate causes," "ultimate principles," "ultimate original qualities," and "original quality(-ies)" interchangeably (cf. T Intro. 9/xvii–iii; T 2.2.7.3/369-70; T 3.1.2.6/473).

15. I will elucidate Hume's use of the principle of sympathy to explain each of these later, in Section II.

16. In what follows, I will adopt the standpoint of the third group of interpreters and refer to Hume's position on sympathy as if it is essentially unchanged from his earlier to his later work.

17. In addition to the works mentioned in Section I.2, see also, Ardal (1966), Baier (1991), Bricke (1996), Cohon (2008), Garrett (1997), Darwall (2004), Kail (2007), Mackie (1980), Russell (1995), and Stroud (1977). In addition, see, e.g., Brown (1988, 2001, and 2008), Korsgaard (1999), Radcliffe (1994, 1996, and 2008), Taylor (2002 and 2009).

18. As I argue elsewhere, on Hume's account, the scope of benevolent motivation is very broad, extending beyond one's family and friends, beyond one's fellow citizens, and even beyond human beings to any thinking being, including animals. See Vitz (2002); cf. Hacking (2001).

19. In both this and the following section, I will focus on examples from the *Treatise*. As I noted earlier, however, the differences between the *Treatise* and the second *Enquiry* concerning Hume's accounts of sympathy and of humanity are basically in the manner of his presentation, not in the essential details of the matter he presents. In both works, he identifies sympathy both as a source of moral evaluation and as a source of moral motivation.

20. These two cases are from the *Treatise*. For similar discussions of Hume's account of moral motivation in the second *Enquiry*, see Abramson (2001), Debes (2007*a* and 2007*b*), as well as Vitz (2004).

21. Notice that Hume's account of moral motivation implies that people have knowledge of—or, at least, reasonable beliefs about—other minds. I will discuss this issue, specifically, in Section II.2.1.

22. In fact, if the first sympathy is weak, the person is likely to experience contempt for the object of his or her attention (cf. T 2.2.9.15/387).

23. On this latter point, see, especially, Taylor (2002) and Taylor (2009).

24. For more detailed discussions of the function of sympathy in Hume's aesthetics, see, e.g., Dadlez (2004), Jones (1976), Kirby (2003), Mothersill (1989), Neill (1997), Saccamano (2011), and Taylor (2008).

25. In keeping with his epistemological commitments, he does not attempt to account for the existence of other minds by appealing to a demonstrative argument (cf. EU 4.1–2/25–6; ESY 591; DP 9). His commentators disagree on whether he offers a probable argument, like the one Mill makes in *An Examination of Sir William Hamilton's Philosophy* (1865: 208–210). Regarding the debate among Hume's commentators, see, e.g., Pitson (2002), as well as Pitson (1996) and Waldow (2009a and 2009b).

26. See, e.g., Gordon (1995: 727–728), Kirby (2003: 310–314, 322–323), Mercer (1972: 31), Waldow (2009a: 73–74).

27. "To bring on, bring about, induce, occasion, cause, procure."

28. "To bring in or 'draw' as a conclusion; *spec.* in *Logic*, To derive by a process of reasoning, whether inductive or deductive, from something known or assumed; to accept from evidence or premises; to deduce, conclude."

29. cf. Pitson (2002); as well as Pitson (1996); see also Waldow (2009a and 2009b).

30. cf. Kemp Smith (1941: 76, 86–87, 94, 114, 170, 176, 454, 549).

31. In what follows, I offer a very brief description of Hume's position. I provide a more detailed account in Vitz (2014).

32. See also "Of the Rise and Progress of the Arts and Sciences" (ESY 111–2) and "Of the Liberty of the Press" (ESY 604), where Hume makes similar and related comments on the nature of contagion.

33. In the interest of brevity, I will limit my examples to some of the major works of the authors I have highlighted. See, e.g., Batson (1991), Hoffman (2001), Prinz (2007), Kruglanski (1989). Cf. Prinz (2004).

Bibliography

Abramson, Kate. (2001). "Sympathy and the Project of Hume's Second *Enquiry*," *Archiv Für Geschichte Der Philosophie* 83 (1), 45–80.

Altmann, R. W. (1980). "Hume on Sympathy," *Southern Journal of Philosophy* 18 (2), 123–136.

Ardal, Pall. (1966). *Passion and Value in Hume's Treatise*. Edinburgh: Edinburgh University Press.

Baier, Annette. (1991). *A Progress of Sentiments*. Cambridge, MA: Harvard University Press.

Batson, Daniel C. (1991). *The Altruism Question: Toward a Social-Psychological Answer*. Hillsdale, NJ: Lawrence Erlbaum Associates.

Bricke, John. (1996). *Mind and Morality*. Oxford: Oxford University Press.

Brown, Charlotte. (1988). "Is Hume an Internalist?" *Journal of the History of Philosophy* 26, 69–82.

Brown, Charlotte. (2001). "Is the General Point of View the Moral Point of View?" *Philosophy and Phenomenological Research* 62, 197–203.

Brown, Charlotte. (2008). "Hume on Moral Rationalism, Sentimentalism, and Sympathy," in E. S. Radcliffe, ed., *A Companion to Hume*, 219–239. Oxford: Blackwell.

Capaldi, Nicholas. (1975). *David Hume: The Newtonian Philosopher*. Boston: Twayne.

Chismar, Douglas. (1988–9). "Hume's Confusion About Sympathy," *Philosophical Research Archives* 14, 237–246.

Cohon, Rachel. (2008). *Hume's Morality: Feeling and Fabrication*. Oxford: Oxford University Press.

Dadlez, E. M. (2004). "Pleased and Afflicted: Hume on the Paradox of Tragic Pleasure," *Hume Studies* 30, 213–236.

Darwall, Stephen. (2004). *Welfare and Rational Care*. Princeton, NJ: Princeton University Press.

Debes, Remy. (2007a). "Humanity, Sympathy and the Puzzle of Hume's Second Enquiry," *British Journal for the History of Philosophy* 15 (1), 27–57.

Debes, Remy. (2007b). "Has Anything Changed? Hume's Theory of Association and Sympathy After the Treatise," *British Journal for the History of Philosophy* 15 (2), 313–338.

Garrett, Don. (1997). *Cognition and Commitment in Hume's Philosophy*. Oxford: Oxford University Press.

Gordon, Robert. (1995). "Sympathy, Simulation, and the Impartial Spectator," *Ethics* 105, 727–742.

Hacking, Ian. (2001). "On Sympathy: With Other Creatures," *Tijdschrift voor Filosofie* 63, 685–717.

Hoffman, Martin. (2001). *Empathy and Moral Development: Implications for Caring and Justice*. Cambridge: Cambridge University Press.

Jones, Peter (1976). "Hume's Aesthetics Reassessed," *Philosophical Quarterly* 26, 48–62.

Kail, P. J. E. (2007). *Projection and Realism in Hume's Philosophy*. Oxford: Oxford University Press.

Kemp Smith, Norman. (1941). *The Philosophy of David Hume*. London: Macmillan.

Kirby, Brian. (2003). "Hume, Sympathy, and the Theater," *Hume Studies*, 315–322.

Korsgaard, Christine. (1999). "The General Point of View: Love and Moral Approval in Hume's Ethics," *Hume Studies* 25, 3–41.

Kruglanski, Arie. (1989). *Lay Epistemics and Human Knowledge: Cognitive and Motivational Bases*. New York: Plenum.

Laird, John. (1932/1967). *Hume's Philosophy of Human Nature*. London: Methuen and Co., 1932; reprint, Hamden: Archon Books.

Mackie, J. L. (1980). *Hume's Moral Theory*. Oxford: Routledge.

Mercer, Philip. (1972). *Sympathy and Ethics*. Oxford: Oxford University Press.

Mill, J. S. (1865). *An Examination of Sir William Hamilton's Philosophy*. London: Longmans.

Mothersill, Mary. (1989). "Hume and the Paradox of Taste," in G. Dickie, R. Sclafani, and R. Ronald, eds., *Aesthetics: A Critical Anthology*. New York: St. Martin's Press.

Neill, Elizabeth. (1997). "Hume's Moral Sublime," *British Journal of Aesthetics* 37, 246–258.

Penelhum, Terence. (1992). *David Hume: An Introduction to His Philosophical System*. West Lafayette: Purdue University Press.

Pitson, A. E. (1996). "Sympathy and Other Selves," *Hume Studies* 22, 255–271.

Pitson, A. E. (2002). "Hume and Other Minds," in *Hume's Philosophy of the Self*, 142–159. London: Routledge.

Prinz, Jesse. (2004). *Gut Reactions: A Perceptual Theory of Emotion*. Oxford: Oxford University Press.

Prinz, Jesse. (2007). *The Emotional Construction of Morals*. Oxford: Oxford University Press.

Radcliffe, Elizabeth. (1994). "Hume on Motivating Sentiments, the General Point of View, and the Inculcation of 'Morality,'" *Hume Studies* 20, 37–58.

Radcliffe, Elizabeth. (1996). "How Does the Humean Sense of Duty Motivate?" *Journal of the History of Philosophy* 34, 383–407.

Radcliffe, Elizabeth. (2008). "The Humean Theory of Motivation and its Critics," in E. S. Radcliffe, ed., *A Companion to Hume*, 477–492. Oxford: Blackwell.

Roberts, T. A. (1973). *The Concept of Benevolence*. New York: Macmillan.

Russell, Paul. (1995). *Freedom and Moral Sentiment: Hume's Way of Naturalizing Moral Responsibility*. Oxford: Oxford University Press.

Saccamano, Neil. (2011). "Aesthetically Non-Dwelling: Sympathy, Property, and the House of Beauty in Hume's Treatise," *Journal of Scottish Philosophy* 9, 37–58.

Selby-Bigge, L. A. (1893/1975). "Introduction," in David Hume, *Enquiries Concerning Human Understanding and Concerning the Principles of Morals*, L. A. Selby-Bigge, ed., third edition, P. H. Nidditch, vii–xxxi. Oxford: Oxford University Press.

Stroud, Barry. (1977). *Hume*. London: Routledge.

Taylor, Jacqueline. (2002). "Hume on the Standard of Virtue," *Journal of Ethics* 6, 43–62.

Taylor, Jacqueline. (2008). "Hume on Beauty and Virtue," in E. S. Radcliffe, ed., *A Companion to Hume*. London: Routledge.

Taylor, Jacqueline. (2009). "Hume's Later Moral Philosophy," in D. F. Norton and J. Taylor, eds., *The Cambridge Companion to Hume*, 2nd ed. Cambridge: Cambridge University Press.

Taylor, Jacqueline. (2013). 'Hume on the Importance of Humanity'. *Revue Internationale de Philosophie* 67, 81–97.

Vitz, Rico. (2014). "Contagion, Community, and Virtue in Hume's Epistemology," in *The Ethics of Belief: Individual and Social*, edited by Jonathan Matheson and Rico Vitz. Oxford: Oxford University Press.

Vitz, Rico. (2002). "Hume and the Limits of Benevolence," *Hume Studies* 28 (November), 271–295.

Vitz, Rico. (2004). "Sympathy and Benevolence in Hume's Moral Psychology," *Journal of the History of Philosophy* 42 (July), 261–275.

Waldow, Anik. (2009a). *David Hume and the Problem of Other Minds*. London: Continuum.

Waldow, Anik. (2009b). "Hume's Belief in Other Minds," *British Journal for the History of Philosophy* 17, 119–132.

Wand, Bernard. (1955). "A Note on Sympathy in Hume's Moral Theory," *Philosophical Review* 64.2, 275–279.

CHAPTER 17

....

REASON, BELIEF, AND THE PASSIONS

....

DAVID OWEN

One is tempted to define man as a rational animal who always loses his temper when he is called upon to act in accordance with the dictates of reason.

— Oscar Wilde

I BACKGROUND

....

[I]t seems to me certain that a great light in the intellect is followed by a great inclination in the will; so that if we see very clearly that a thing is good for us, it is very difficult—and on my view, impossible, as long as one continues in the same thought—to stop the course of our desire.

(Descartes 1644: 233–234)

IN this letter, Descartes seems to be expressing the view that a really clear grasp of the good determines the will. This grasp of the good is intellectual, not sensory, and "the course of our desire" is simply the inclination of the will. Desiring is an activity of the will. If one makes a few obvious changes, the picture that emerges is the one I would like to attribute to Hume when he speaks of the springs and activating principles of action. It is a fundamental, original principle of human nature, empirically discovered, that an impression or an idea of pleasure is frequently followed by an action

Nature has implanted in the human mind a perception of good or evil, or in other words, of pain and pleasure, as the chief spring and moving principle of all its actions. But pain and pleasure have two ways of making their appearance in the mind; of which the one has effects very different from the other. They may either appear in impression to the actual feeling and experience, or only in idea, as at present when I mention them. 'Tis evident the influence of these upon our actions is far from being equal. Impressions always actuate the soul, and that in the highest degree; but 'tis not every idea which has the same effect. (T 1.3.10.2/118)[1]

In Hume, the contingent but perfectly general connection between pleasure and action plays the role that, in Descartes, was played by the connection, known a priori, between the perception of the good and the inclination of the will. This aspect of Hume's psychology is far more important to his overall account of motivation than his better known views on reason and the passions. Indeed, once the centrality of the influence of impressions and ideas of pleasures and pains is acknowledged, many common ways of understanding Hume's claims about the reason and the passions must be corrected.[2] Let's call the principle stating the link between action and pleasure the Pleasure Principle.

To investigate Hume on action, the will, the passions, and reason, one should first think about, quite literally, what he is talking about. With the exception of "action," all of the terms just used to demarcate the topic of this aspect of Hume's psychology are faculty terms. The faculty of the will has volitions as its product; the faculty of the passions produces the individual passions, such as hope and fear, desire, pride, and hatred; while the faculty of reason is the faculty responsible for inferences or pieces of reasoning, both demonstrative and probable.[3]

In spite of the centrality of faculty talk in Hume, he has a rather thin view of faculties.[4] Any appeal to faculties has to be cashed out in terms of patterns of causal connections between perceptions of the mind. An appeal to the faculty of reason or the will has no explanatory value on its own. Suppose that a person "who concludes somebody to be near him, when he hears an articulate voice in the dark, reasons justly and naturally." We do not explain the belief and its justness by saying it derives from the faculty of reason. We explain it by showing that it "be deriv'd from nothing but custom, which infixes and enlivens the idea of a human creature, on account of his usual conjunction with the present impression" (T 1.4.4.1/225). Similarly, suppose a thirsty person reaches for a glass of water. The action is not explained by citing that it was preceded by an act of will or volition that derived from the faculty of the will. It is explained by citing the person's thirst as a painful impression of a certain sort, together with the belief that a drink from the glass of water will relieve that thirst. That is explanatory because "[t]he mind by an *original* instinct tends to unite itself with the good, and to avoid the evil" (T 2.3.9.2/438). Such a general principle is present in most Humean explanations of action, and it can be expressed in many ways. One such way is the claim that "all men desire pleasure" (T 2.1.10.8/314). It is the general link between pleasure and action that is explanatory here, not the presence of a desire.[5]

Here, as elsewhere, it would be difficult to overemphasize the importance of Hume's division of the perceptions of the mind into impressions and ideas, and his Copy Principle, that "all our simple ideas in their first appearance are deriv'd from simple impressions, which are correspondent to them, and which they exactly represent" (T 1.1.1.7/4). This principle colors virtually every major thesis put forward by Hume.

Think of causal inference, the nature of belief, skepticism with regard to reason and the senses, personal identity, sympathy, the indefinability of the passions, and the complex double relation of ideas and impressions that is so distinctive of his account of the indirect passions.[6] In this paper, I want to investigate a few aspects of Hume's account of reason, belief, the passions, and motivation in light of these two general principles.

One constraint that immediately arises is this: no faculty can produce a new (simple) idea. All simple ideas are derived from impressions. In particular, the faculty of reason cannot produce a new idea. This follows from the Copy Principle. And Hume is explicit about it: "reason alone can never give rise to any original idea" (T 1.3.14.5/157). (See also T 1.3.6.3/88; T 1.3.14.17/164; TA 4/625). Unlike many other faculties, reason cannot produce impressions either.[7] Reason produces inferences, and an inference always finishes with a belief (an idea) or a relation of ideas. Such ideas must always have been experienced at some earlier time as impressions. The faculty of sensation produces impressions of sensation; the faculties of the will and the passions produce secondary impressions or impressions of reflection. The faculties of the imagination, reason, and memory produce only ideas, not impressions, although the beliefs produced by the latter two faculties are ideas with such force and vivacity that they approximate to impressions. These ideas, of course, are available to the imagination, reason, and memory only because they have been derived from previously experienced impressions.

II An Example

Although this paper is primarily about reason, belief, the passions, and motivation, I want to further illustrate the importance of the doctrine of impressions and ideas on these topics with a point about the beginning of Book 3 and the moral sentiments. In the advertisement for Book 3, after claiming that the book "is in some measure independent of the other two," Hume says

> It must only be observ'd, that I continue to make use of the terms, *impressions* and *ideas*, in the same sense as formerly; and that by impressions I mean our stronger perceptions, such as our sensations, affections and sentiments; and by ideas the fainter perceptions, or the copies of these in the memory and imagination. (T 292/455 facing)

The only thing Hume asks his new readers to bring to Book 3 is the distinction and relation between impressions and ideas. He then goes on to structure T 3.1.1 in terms of that distinction:

> this distinction gives rise to a question, with which we shall open up our present enquiry concerning morals, *Whether 'tis by means of our ideas or impressions we distinguish betwixt vice and virtue, and pronounce an action blamable or praiseworthy?*

This will immediately cut off all loose discourses and declamations, and reduce us to something precise and exact on the present subject. (T 3.1.1.3/456)

It is immediately apparent that "[t]hose who affirm that virtue is nothing but a conformity to reason ... concur in the opinion, that morality, like truth, is discern'd merely by ideas, and by their juxta-position and comparison" (T 3.1.1.4/456). We need to "consider, whether it be possible, from reason alone, to distinguish betwixt moral good and evil." Now, if the idea of "moral good" is derived from an impression in the same way that the idea of "natural good" is derived from an impression of pleasure, we know in advance that it cannot come from reason alone. Reason can never produce an impression or a new idea. Those who have read Books 1 and 2 will see this right away. More discussion is required for others, and Hume proceeds to give it. The ensuing discussion (T 3.1.1.5–16) also uses earlier material, concerning motivation, and we will get back to that material shortly. Only one possibility remains open to those who would find moral distinctions in reason alone. Although the faculty of reason cannot discover a new idea, it can, roughly speaking, discover a new *relation* of ideas. Hume argues against this possibility in the (bulk of the) rest of this section, T 3.1.1.17–25. T 3.1.1.26 segues into the discussion, found in T 3.1.2, of moral distinctions being derived from sentiments. Interestingly, Hume does *not* here directly argue that the impression from which virtue (or vice) is derived is not a sense impression but rather a sentiment of (dis)approbation, a feeling, an impression of reflection. Nor does he argue against the possibility that virtue and vice might actually be causal relations. Instead, he argues that "vice and virtue are not matters of fact, *whose existence we can infer by reason*" (emphasis added). This, too, would have been obvious to a reader of Book 1; causal reasoning can only lead us to an unobserved matter of fact *of a sort we have previously experienced*. Causal reasoning always ends with an idea, and we must previously have experienced an impression from which that idea is derived.

Hume's claim that the "rules of morality ... are not conclusions of our reason" (T 3.1.1.6/457) is a claim about the origin of the ideas of virtue and vice. He does not mean that we cannot conclude that someone is virtuous by means of an argument; such an argument is possible as long as we have experienced the relevant impression from which we have derived the idea of virtue; once we have the idea of virtue, it can occur in arguments just like any other idea And when he says that "[m]orality, therefore, is more properly felt, than judg'd of" (T 3.1.2.1/470), he is not denying that moral claims are beliefs. He is saying something about both the origin and nature of such beliefs. Admittedly, this is a lot clearer if one has read Book 1, something Hume did not expect all his readers to have done. But for those who have, it is difficult to read "[m]orality, therefore, is more properly felt, than judg'd of" without hearing "belief is more properly an act of the sensitive, than of the cogitative part of our natures" (T1.4.1.8/183) and "all probable reasoning is nothing but a species of sensation" (T1.3.8.12/103). Hume is locating moral judgments squarely in the middle of his account of belief and probable reasoning, not denying that they belong there.

Now consider Hume's characterization of reason in T 3.1.1:

Reason is the discovery of truth or falshood. Truth or falshood consists in an agreement or disagreement either to the *real* relations of ideas, or to *real* existence and matter of fact. Whatever, therefore, is not susceptible of this agreement or disagreement, is incapable of being true or false, and can never be an object of our reason. Now 'tis evident our passions, volitions, and actions, are not susceptible of any such agreement or disagreement; being original facts and realities, compleat in themselves, and implying no reference to other passions, volitions, and actions. 'Tis impossible, therefore, they can be pronounc'd either true or false, and be either contrary or conformable to reason. (T 3.1.1.9/458)

Reason is the faculty (thought of suitably austerely) that produces truths or falsehoods. That is to say, chains of ideas, which constitute pieces of reasoning or inferences, result in beliefs (or relations of ideas), which are true or false. Inferences cannot result in impressions, either of sensation or reflection. "Passions, volitions, and actions" just do not appear as the conclusions of inferences. But inferences do result in beliefs (ideas) and, as far as I can tell, there are no constraints on what the content of a belief might be that are not exhausted by the Copy Principle. There is nothing to prevent a belief, as the conclusion of the piece of probable reasoning, from having virtue or vice as part of its content. To deny this would be to saddle Hume with the view that one could never have an idea of a passion but only the actual passion. Whatever else Hume might mean by his claim that "morals . . . cannot be deriv'd from reason" (T 3.1.1.6/457), he cannot mean that a moral judgment is not a belief or that a moral judgment cannot be the result of probable reasoning. Part of what he means is that ideas with moral content are not derived from demonstrative or causal relations. And another part of what he means is that the faculty of reason never results in an impression. It follows from this that ideas with moral content have to be derived from impressions. And, unless there are sense impressions with moral content, moral ideas must be derived from impressions of reflection, or sentiments.[8]

III BELIEF

In the passage from T 3.1.1.9 just quoted, Hume spoke of "passions, volitions, and actions." This is a useful grouping because often in Hume it is irrelevant whether one talks of a passion, which causes a volition and hence an action, or a volition, which causes an action, or, simply, of an action. I'll use the term "PVA" for this grouping.

Beliefs motivate by causing PVAs, primarily by locating pleasure and pain, according to the Pleasure Principle. Beliefs can motivate because they are ideas that share with impressions the extra force and vivacity that makes them causally efficacious:

The effect, then, of belief is to raise up a simple idea to an equality with our impressions, and bestow on it a like influence on the passions. This effect it can only have by making an idea approach an impression in force and vivacity. (T 1.3.10.3/119)

We are "more actuated and mov'd" by beliefs compared to ideas of the fancy. They have "more force and influence" and "appear of greater importance." They are "the governing principles of all our actions."[9] "[B]elief is almost absolutely requisite to the exciting of our passions" (T 1.3.10.4/120). Hume is explicit that this feature of beliefs "may give us a notion after what manner our reasonings from causation are able to operate on the will and passions" (T 1.3.10.3/120).

Beliefs are ideas and are typically produced by causal inferences. If they have the right sort of content, typically pleasure and pain, they can cause PVAs. In fact, this was clear as early as the second section of the *Treatise*:

> An impression first strikes upon the senses, and makes us perceive heat or cold, thirst or hunger, pleasure or pain of some kind or other. Of this impression there is a copy taken by the mind, which remains after the impression ceases; and this we call an idea. This idea of pleasure or pain, when it returns upon the soul, produces the new impressions of desire and aversion, hope and fear, which may properly be called impressions of reflection because deriv'd from it. (T 1.1.2.1/8)

The Pleasure Principle is the fundamental principle of human nature that perceptions of pleasure and pain concern, affect, and weigh with us and thereby cause PVAs. And in an early discussion of this point, already quoted, Hume is explicit that such a productive perception can be either an impression or an idea:

> Nature has implanted in the human mind a perception of good or evil, or in other words, of pain and pleasure, as the chief spring and moving principle of all its actions. But pain and pleasure have two ways of making their appearance in the mind; of which the one has effects very different from the other. They may either appear in impression to the actual feeling or experience, or only in idea, as at present when I mention them. (T 1.3.10.2; SBN 118)

I think it is significant that although Hume, as often as not, links pleasure with action via a passion, especially desire and aversion, he doesn't always, and he doesn't have to. The important point is the original, basic connection between the perception of pleasure and pain and PVAs:

> The mind by an *original* instinct tends to unite itself with the good, and to avoid the evil, tho' they be conceiv'd merely in idea, and be consider'd as to exist in any future period of time. (T 2.3.9.2/438)

Desire is one way that the Pleasure Principle can be instantiated, but it is not the only way. Hume doesn't need desire or any other passion to bridge the gap between the perception of pleasure or pain and action or inclination to act. There is no gap because the principle is a fundamental fact about human nature.[10] This is a controversial claim, and we shall return to it.

Now Hume famously says that reason alone cannot produce or prevent PVAs: "reason alone can never be a motive to any action of the will" (T 2.3.3.1/413). Whatever else Hume might mean by the claim that reason doesn't produce PVAs, he can't mean that beliefs don't cause these things. It is manifestly obvious that he thinks they do.[11]

IV MOTIVATION

The claim that beliefs—typically beliefs about pleasure—can cause PVAs is enough to show that Hume is not a "Humean" about motivation and action. The Humean theory of motivation holds that both a belief and a desire (more generally, both a cognitive and a conative component) are needed, jointly, to cause an action. In this model, the desire is conative in that it provides the goal of behavior, whereas the belief just guides and directs the behavior in achieving that goal. I desire a glass of water, and my beliefs, formed by causal reasoning, direct my behavior so that I can fulfill that desire. I get a glass from the cupboard, I retrieve a pitcher of water, and so on.[12]

It is not difficult to see why this picture has been found in Hume. It is a natural enough way to read "Of the influencing motives of the will" (T 2.3.3/413–18) and almost irresistible if one reads that section in isolation from the rest of *Treatise* and with the belief/ desire theory of action in mind:

> It can never in the least concern us to know, that such objects are causes, and such others effects, if both causes and effects be indifferent to us. Where the objects themselves do not affect us, their connexion can never give them any influence; and 'tis plain, that as reason is nothing but the discovery of this connexion, it cannot be by its means that the objects are able to affect us (T 2.3.3/414).

If we are indifferent to features of the world, if beliefs about them in no way affect us, they will not influence us or cause PVAs. It may look here as if we need to appeal to independent desires to get to something that does weigh with us, concern us, or influence us.

The belief/desire model isn't Hume's because it leaves out the crucial role of pleasure and the Pleasure Principle. The two sentences that precede the passage just quoted read:

> 'Tis from the prospect of pain and pleasure that the aversion or propensity arises towards any object: And these emotions extend themselves to the causes and effects of that object, as they are pointed out to us by reason and experience.

Hume does not think that all objects in the world and their properties leave us indifferent and fail to affect us. If objects give us pleasure or pain, or if we believe that in easily instantiated circumstances they will give us pleasure or pain, then we are far from indifferent to them. Such objects weigh with us, are a matter of concern to us, and affect us. In

Hume's psychology, the Pleasure Principle provides a firm link between perceptions of the mind with a certain content and action.[13]

Although not entirely without supporters, this is still a minority view about Hume on motivation.[14] In general, the main feature of this account is the Pleasure Principle: the perception of pleasure or pain weighs with us and causes PVAs. Let us call this picture of Hume the Motivating Belief Account, or MBA, and proceed to look at various ways one might fill in its details.

How should one see the precise role of passions, volitions, and actions in the MBA? In particular, does desire (or aversion) play a special role? One might hold that desire (or aversion) is still necessary for one to be moved to act. For the belief in soon-to-be-instantiated pleasure or pleasure in store, to motivate, one might think that Hume also requires a desire, not only for the means to obtain the pleasure, but for the pleasure itself.

I think this is Karlsson's view, who is the creator of the lovely expression "pleasure in store":

> Now Hume evidently maintains that a person forms a desire or aversion for something when, and only when, she judges that it has (or is likely to have) pleasure or pain in store for her (T 2.3.3.3/414; T 2.3.3.7/416–17; T 2.3.9.1/438; T 2.3.9.7/439; T 3.1.1.12/459), and this desire or aversion moves her to pursue or avoid the thing in question. (Karlsson 2006: 246–247)[15]

If by "desire," Karlsson means a particular sort of direct passion, I don't think any of the passages he cites provides decisive evidence for the thesis that when the belief in pleasure in store influences action, it typically does so by causing a desire that causes the action. The second passage only mentions desire as an example of one of the passions that "yield to our reason without any opposition" upon the perception of falsehood or insufficient means. That passage places as much emphasis on willing as desiring, as do the passages from T 2.3.9, "Of the direct passions."[16] T 3.1.1.2, from "Moral distinctions not deriv'd from reason," is a repetition of T 2.3.3.7, from "Of the influencing motives of the will." Each of these two paragraphs is, *inter alia*, about the two ways in which a passion may be said to be unreasonable (T 2.3.3.7) or, alternatively, the two ways in which reason may influence conduct (T 3.1.1.12). Reason, here causal reasoning, which issues in belief, may inform us of the existence or nonexistence of the object of a passion or may inform us of the sufficiency or insufficiency of the means chosen to obtain the perceived pleasure in store. Reason, passion, and actions are frequently talked about in these paragraphs, whereas a desire (desire for a "fruit of an excellent relish") is referred to only once. The expression "desir'd good" is used in both paragraphs. But this needn't flag the presence of a desire; it might flag the presence of a belief in perceived pleasure in store.[17] This is a possibility we now explore.

Suppose expressions such as "desir'd good" don't refer to a particular direct passion but rather to the presence of a belief in pleasure in store that may cause any one of the motivating or direct passions. Then it looks as if Hume might use the term "desire" and its cognates in more than one way. In one usage, "desire" refers to a particular sort of motivating passion, which stands alongside volition, hope, fear, grief, joy, and the like. In the other usage, "desire" is used to indicate the presence of *any* of the particular direct passions. This usage often draws attention to the close causal link between perceived pleasure and the subsequent presence of one of the motivating passions, which in turn causes action. So we have not only "desir'd good" but such expressions as "All men desire pleasure."

It is what Cohon calls the key passage, from which I have already quoted, that provides what many think to be decisive evidence that Hume thinks a desire, in particular, is needed to complete the causal link between belief and action. The key passage is the first one cited by Karlsson:

> 'Tis obvious, that when we have the prospect of pain or pleasure from any object, we feel a consequent emotion of aversion or propensity, and are carri'd to avoid or embrace what will give us this uneasiness or satisfaction. 'Tis also obvious, that this emotion rests not here, but, making us cast our view on every side, comprehends whatever objects are connected with its original one by the relation of cause and effect. Here then reasoning takes place to discover this relation; and according as our reasoning varies, our actions receive a subsequent variation. But 'tis evident, in this case, that the impulse arises not from reason, but is only directed by it. 'Tis from the prospect of pain or pleasure that the aversion or propensity arises towards any object: and these emotions extend themselves to the causes and effects of that object, as they are pointed out to us by reason and experience. It can never in the least concern us to know, that such objects are causes, and such others effects, if both the causes and effects be indifferent to us. Where the objects themselves do not affect us, their connexion can never give them any influence; and 'tis plain, that as reason is nothing but the discovery of this connexion, it cannot be by its means that the objects are able to affect us. (T 2.3.3.3/414)

One has to read this with an unjaundiced eye to realize that it doesn't mention desires at all. The emphasis is all on the prospect of pleasure and pain, and the impulse (i.e., the propensity or aversion) to which it gives rise. But isn't "propensity or aversion" just a synonym for "desire"? Hume sometimes talks this way, as in the following list of direct passions in T 2.3.9.2: "desire and aversion, grief and joy, hope and fear, along with volition." But consider the following passage:

> The chief spring or actuating principle of the human mind is pleasure or pain; and when these sensations are remov'd, both from our thought and feeling, we are, in a great measure, incapable of passion or action, of desire or volition. The most immediate effects of pleasure and pain are the propense and averse motions of the mind; which are diversify'd into volition, into desire and aversion, grief and joy, hope and fear. (T 3.3.1.2/574)

Here, the direct passions are described as "the propense and averse motions of the mind." This seems to me to be just another way of saying that they are motivating, that they give rise to action. But later in the very same sentence, Hume speaks of "desire and aversion" as one of the particular passions into which the general category is "diversify'd."

It seems to me that one (not the only) promising way to read all this is to say that "desire," "aversion," and "propensity," and their cognates are sometimes used to refer to the class of direct passions as a whole. Alternatively, these terms are sometimes used to pick out just one particular sort of motivating passion. As an instance of a particular sort of direct passion, a desire has a unique phenomenology. And different desires have different phenomenologies. It just seems empirically false that an instance of (some) desire (or other) is always present as a causal antecedent of action. In fact, desires, as particular sorts of direct passion, are only really needed in special circumstances, although they may in fact occur in many others.[18] It is all right to use "desire" as a synonym for "the propense and averse motions of the mind," or "the direct passions," or "the motivating passions" as long as it is clear what one is doing.

V THE WILL AND THE DIRECT PASSIONS

We are still investigating the details of how to fill out the MBA, as found in Hume. We have now rejected the view that a belief about pleasure in store, in order to cause an action, needs first to cause a desire, which in turn causes an action. Desires are, for Hume, just one sort of motivating passion; any direct passion can be motivating—that is, can be a passion that causes action. And a perception (impression or idea) of pleasure or pain can cause any one of the direct passions. So now let us consider MBA as claiming that beliefs about pleasure and pain cause direct passions of any sort, which in turn cause actions. It is possible that, all things considered, this is the thesis that best accords with the bulk of the texts. But it leaves out any significant role for the will and volitions. There is just enough in Hume about the will and its products to make it worthwhile for us to see how MBA can be filled out in a way that makes crucial use of the will. Once one finds a place for the will and its volitions, it is not so clear that Hume needs to *always* appeal to direct passions as well as to beliefs about pleasure in his account of the antecedents of action. I want to consider the radical view that Hume's psychology didn't require a direct passion to be inserted between a belief concerning pleasure in store and action.

Even if one thinks that, for Hume, it is completely unproblematic to treat volition as a direct passion along with desire, hope, fear, and the like, there is still room in Hume for something very much in the spirit of the radical view I want to explore. No one who wants to treat Hume as committed to the claim that an action is always caused by a passion would be happy with counting a sequence that contained a belief about pleasure and a volition—but no other direct passion—as an adequate cause of action. We will explore why this is so shortly. But for the moment, let us treat volitions not as direct passions, but as *sui generis* secondary impressions that are the product of the will.

The first three sentences of Book 2, Part 3, "Of the Will and Direct Passions," read:

We come now to explain the *direct* passions, or impressions, which arise immediately from good or evil, from pain or pleasure. Of this kind are, *desire* and *aversion, grief* and *joy, hope* and *fear*. Of all the immediate effects of pain and pleasure, there is none more remarkable than the WILL; and tho', properly speaking, it be not comprehended among the passions, yet as the full understanding of its nature and properties, is necessary to the explanation of them, we shall here make it the subject of our enquiry.

Let us first make what I take to be an obvious correction and engage in some clarification. "Will" is a faculty term, so, strictly speaking, what Hume is talking about here is what the will produces, not the will itself. The impressions that the will produces are usually called "volitions," and Hume uses this term elsewhere.[19] With this correction, we can read the rest of the sentence as claiming something like this: Volitions, properly speaking, are not passions. But they are secondary impressions and will be treated along with the direct passions for the purposes of discussion in Book 2, Part 3.[20]

A natural way of reading these three sentences is that volitions are perhaps the most significant items to be immediately caused by perceptions of pain and pleasure, where "immediately caused" rules out the intervention of some (other) direct passion.[21] Since, traditionally, volitions are the immediate causes of actions, it looks as if there can be a causal chain from perceptions of pleasure to action via no perception of the mind other than volition. One characterization of volitions as immediate causes of action is Locke's:

> Volition . . . is an act of the Mind directing its thought to the production of any Action, and thereby exerting its power to produce it. (*Essay* 2.21.28)

Hume's characterization echoes this:

> By the *will*, I mean nothing but *the internal impression we feel and are conscious of, when we knowingly give rise to any new motion of our body, or new perception of our mind.* This impression, like the preceding ones of pride and humility, love and hatred, 'tis impossible to define. (T 2.3.1.2/399)[22]

As Cohon notes (2008: 34), there is a hint of the epiphenomenal about this. But Hume usually speaks of volitions and actions as pairs, with the former causing the latter. For example, in paragraph 4 of "Of the Influencing Motives of the Will," Hume argues that

> Since reason alone can never produce any action, or give rise to any volition, I infer that the same faculty is as incapable of preventing volition, or of disputing the preference with any passion or emotion.

The term "volition" is used several times in this paragraph. The point seems to be that if reason were to prevent a passion from issuing in action, it would have to prevent the volition that would have been the proximate cause of action if reason hadn't intervened. But if reason had "an original influence on the will, . . . [it] must be able to cause, as well as hinder, any act of volition."

Although Hume sometimes talks, like Locke, of volitions as *acts* of mind or will, more often he treats them simply as impressions that cause actions. So, the natural reading of the first three sentences of Part 3 of Book 2 gives us something like the following: the most significant immediate effect of the perception of pleasure in store is the activation of the will, or the production of a volition; a volition is the immediate cause of an action. At the very least, it seems that Hume is happy with the thought that a belief and volition can serve as an adequate explanation of some actions, even if it is more typical for the beliefs to cause direct passions first. Let us see how volitions might enter into the picture in a typical case, in which the belief in pleasure in store causes a direct passion, such as desire or aversion, hope or fear. For example, suppose that the belief that eating the apple will give me pleasure causes a desire to eat the apple. In most cases, I can't simply eat the apple; I must do something as a means toward the end of eating it. A little bit of causal reasoning leads to the belief that if I reach out my hand just so, I can grasp the apple, bring it to my mouth, and eat it. The desire to eat the apple, plus the belief that an action of a certain sort will bring about my eating the apple, puts the will into gear and causes a volition, which in turn causes an instance of that sort of action.[23]

Although this example collapses a whole theory of action and practical reasoning into a few sentences, it is accurate enough about a typical sort of account of the antecedents of action that Hume might give. The belief in pleasure in store causes a desire for that pleasure. That desire may combine with a belief about how to satisfy that desire, causing a volition. The volition in turn causes an action. The volition needn't be considered epiphenomenal because it ensures that the action is intentional.[24] The belief that eating the apple will give me pleasure may be false. The belief that moving my hand just so will bring about my eating the apple may be false. These are the two ways the desire or the action may be considered unreasonable, although it is clear that, in each case, the problem lies with the belief, not the volition, desire, or action.

This picture, an instance of the MBA account, differs from the traditional picture mainly in allowing a belief in pleasure to cause a desire. On the MBA, a belief can be causally efficacious, whereas the traditional picture holds belief, as the product of reason, to be inert. In Section III just quoted, we argued that it was clear from the text that Hume held that beliefs about pleasure could be causes of PVAs. I now want to indicate that Hume's whole account of impressions, ideas, beliefs, and vivacity points in the direction of the causal efficacy of beliefs. Impressions, whether of sensation or reflection, are characterized by their feeling, emotion, sensation, or sentiment.[25] We initially grasp the distinction between impressions and ideas because everyone knows "the difference between feeling and thinking" (T 1.1.1.2). It is a crucial part of Hume's theory that belief is a feeling, and that the nature of that "*feeling or sentiment*" is analogous to some "*other sentiment of the human mind.*" That sentiment is, of course, the feeling characteristic of impressions. In the body of the *Treatise*, Hume describes this feeling in terms of force and vivacity. In the "Appendix," he tries to be more accurate and describes beliefs, in contrast to "the loose and indolent reveries of a castle-builder," this way:

They strike upon us with more force; they are more present to us; the mind has a firmer hold of them, and is more actuated and mov'd by them. It acquiesces in them; and, in a manner, fixes and reposes it self on them. In short, they approach nearer to the impressions, which are immediately present to us; and are therefore analogous to many other operations of the mind. (TA 3/624–5)

If belief did not bear this analogy with impressions, "we must despair of explaining its causes," Hume says in the same passage. Beliefs are the product of causal reasoning. Hume's explanation of belief, as approximating to impressions, is part of his explanation of causal reasoning. This explanation is summed up in the following "general maxim in the science of human nature":

when any impression becomes present to us, it not only transports the mind to such ideas are related to it, but likewise communicates to them a share of its force and vivacity. (T 1.3.8.2/98)

Hume was very proud of his account of belief in terms of its feeling, sentiment, emotion, or sensation. That theory has many important features. One of them is the unified account of memory, sense impressions, and belief. All of these are characterized in terms of force and vivacity; the main items of our cognitive experience are thus rendered uniform. Another feature of Hume's account is that it preserves belief from the otherwise unassailable force of skeptical arguments, as in "Scepticism with regard to reason." It is the vivacity of ideas, and its characteristics, that drive many of the arguments of "Conclusion to This Book."

Hume's account of belief has many parallels to his account of the passions. He explicitly draws analogies between them. The first analogy is between belief formation and the formation of the indirect passions. In the formation of causal beliefs,

the present impression gives a vivacity to the fancy, and the relation [of association] conveys this vivacity, by an easy transition, to the related idea . . . There is evidently a great analogy betwixt that hypothesis [the formation and nature of causal beliefs], and our present one of an impression and idea, that transfuse themselves into another impression and idea by means of their double relation: Which analogy must be allow'd to be no despicable proof of both hypotheses. (T 2.1.5.11/290)

The second analogy is between belief and sympathy. The association of ideas plays a crucial role in both belief and sympathy, and, in each case, an idea is enlivened by the addition of extra force and vivacity. In the case of belief, the source of the extra force and vivacity is the associated impression; in the case of sympathy, the source is the impression of the self. Hume says: "Let us compare all these circumstances, and we shall find, that sympathy is exactly correspondent to the operations of our understanding; and even contains something more surprizing and extraordinary" (T 2.1.11.8/320). Sympathy is more extraordinary than belief because, in the latter case, an idea is enlivened so that it approximates to an impression whereas, in the former case, it actually turns into an impression.[26]

Cohon emphasizes that, for perceptions of pleasure to cause motivating passions, those perceptions need to be seen as active, not inert: "Hume does not think the sensation of pain itself an 'indolent judgment of the understanding.' Rather pain is the sort of experience that inherently generates an impulse to retreat . . . the believed idea of pain has an influence on the passions similar to that of an actual feeling of pain" (2008: 48). Once one allows beliefs to be causally active, there is no reason to think that they can only cause passions rather than volitions or actions. The following distinct sequences all seem to me to be very common:

- the sensation of pain (putting one's hand on a hot burner) directly causes an involuntary "reflex" action of the withdrawal of the hand (sensation causes action);
- a less painful sensation causes the intentional action of withdrawing one's hand (sensation causes volition causes action);
- an even less painful sensation causes a desire for the pain to stop, which, combined with a belief about how to stop the pain, causes a volition, which causes an action (sensation causes passion which, together with belief, causes volition and action).

It is just as easy to construct distinct cases with ideas of pain rather than sensations. The moral seems to be that, once one allows beliefs to cause passions, one is committed to allowing them to cause volitions and actions as well. The MBA maintains that beliefs about pleasure cause PVAs. That claim now appears to be distributive: beliefs about pleasure can cause passions, or cause volitions, or cause actions.[27]

VI "REASON ALONE"

When Hume claims that "reason alone can never be a motive to any action of the will" (T 2.3.3.1/413; i.e., doesn't cause passions, actions, or volitions), what does he mean? We have already argued that he doesn't mean that beliefs don't cause such things. The Pleasure Principle is a general principle of human nature that provides a firm link between beliefs about pleasure or pain, and passions, actions, or volitions. That is to say, the Pleasure Principle leads to the MBA, in any one of its many forms. But anyone who finds that account in Hume is faced with a problem. The faculty of reason produces beliefs; beliefs cause PVAs. If "produce" is a causal concept, and if causation is a transitive concept, then it looks as if the faculty of reason causes PVAs. This appears to be incompatible with the claim that reason alone doesn't provide a motive to the will. The seeming incompatibility is even more apparent with this other (I think more accurate) formulation of Hume's claim: "reason alone can never produce any action, or give rise to volition" (T 2.3.3.4/414). Inferences, items of reasoning, or exercises of the faculty of reasoning, end with beliefs. Some beliefs "give rise to volition."[28] So, inferences or reasonings produce or give rise to things that give rise to volitions and, hence, actions.

Speaking of the faculty of reason requires us to rethink what appears to be obvious on the traditional view.[29] On that view, it was assumed that "reason alone doesn't provide a motive" simply meant—or straightforwardly implied—that "beliefs on their own don't motivate," that is to say, beliefs on their own do not cause PVAs.[30] But if "reason" is a faculty term, then there is at least a little work to do to get from "reason alone doesn't motivate" to "beliefs don't motivate" via the uncontroversial "reason produces beliefs."

Consider just a few of Hume's formulations of the thesis we are considering: "reason alone can never be a motive to any action of the will" (T 2.3.3.1/413); "reasoning . . . never influences any of our actions, but only as it directs our judgment concerning causes and effects" (T 2.3.3.2/414); "the impulse arises not from reason, but is only directed by it" (T 2.3.3.3/414); "as reasoning is nothing but the discovery of this [causal] connexion, it cannot be by its means that the objects are able to affect us" (T 2.3.3.3/414); "reason alone can never produce any action, or give rise to volition" (T 2.3.3.4/414); "reason has no original influence" (T 2.3.3.4/415). Because "reason" is a faculty term, we can distinguish the faculty (reason), the characteristic activity of the faculty (reasoning or inference), and the result or outcome of that activity (conclusion or object of reason, belief).[31] The characteristic activity of the faculty of reason is reasoning or inference, and Hume is clear that "All kinds of reasoning consist in nothing but a *comparison*, and a discovery of those relations . . . which two or more objects bear to each other" (T 1.3.2.2/73). He is equally clear that the outcome of reasoning is a belief.[32] What reason produces is beliefs. Once the activity of reasoning produces a belief as the termination of that activity, the faculty of reason has done its job. PVAs are not produced by reason because they are not the outcome of the reasoning process. They are not conclusions of reason. Reason doesn't produce impressions of reflection or passions any more than it produces impressions of sensation. An argument or piece of reasoning doesn't have as its conclusion either a feeling of anger or the gustatory sensation of roast beef. Of course, the belief with which the argument concludes might *cause* such an impression, but such an impression is not the outcome of a piece of reasoning.[33]

On Hume's view, in an instance of probable reasoning, a present impression causes an idea with which it is associated and communicates to that idea a share of its force and vivacity. That is what turns the idea into a belief. This belief, if it has the right sort of content, can give rise to a passion and/or a volition and, hence, an action. This is a straightforward causal chain. So what is Hume denying when he claims that "reason alone can never produce any action, or give rise to volition" (T 2.3.3.4/414)? Passions or volitions are impressions, not ideas. But the conclusion of any argument or piece of reasoning is an idea, not an impression. The faculty of reason produces ideas, not impressions. But an action requires a volition, not an idea of a volition, as its cause.

Some faculties, such as the senses, produce impressions. But other faculties, such as reason and the imagination, produce only ideas. Contrary to long-standing tradition, Hume thinks that reason is just the wrong sort of thing to produce passions, volitions, or actions. It is the same sort of mistake as it would be to claim that the imagination produces impressions of sensation. But just as a piece of reasoning (an inference, or argument) can produce a belief that causes the holder of that belief to become angry, so, too, can it produce a belief that causes a volition (or a passion and then a volition), which in turn causes an action. But none of the anger, the volition, the passion, or the action is the outcome of a piece of reasoning or a conclusion to an argument. That is just not the way the faculty of reason works. There is a partial analogy here with reason and the moral senses; the faculty of reason is such that it cannot produce an impression as a conclusion to argument or the end point of an inference. A fortiori, it can produce neither an impression from which the idea of virtue is derived nor a volition (or passion) that brings about an action.

This is only part of the story. For one thing, on the account just sketched, Hume could be accused of simply changing the subject.[34] On the traditional account, the faculty of reason can produce volitions. Hume gives us an account of reason in which it produces only beliefs, so that it is virtually a category mistake to suggest that reason produces volitions. I don't think that this is a decisive objection. Hume would be happy, I suggest, to let the matter that concerns us come down to a choice between different accounts of reason to be decided on empirical and theoretical grounds. Nonetheless, the arguments of T 2.3.3, like the arguments of T 3.1.1, are meant to make a contribution on their own and not merely follow from Hume's general picture.[35] Another limitation of this account is this: the point of beliefs was to approximate to impressions (T 1.3.10.3/119); in order to survive, we need to act on the belief that something is about to happen. We can't wait for the impression of colliding with a train; we have to act on the belief *before* the event actually occurs. But if beliefs can stand in for impressions, then reason can produce, not impressions, but the simulacrum of impressions. The claim that reason produces ideas, not impressions, is not enough to enable us to understand what Hume is ruling out when he says that reason, acting alone, doesn't cause passions, volitions, or actions.

We need to remember the original point of arguing that "reason alone can never be a motive to any action of the will." Hume wanted to undermine the traditional "talk of the combat of passion and reason and passions" where it was "usual in philosophy, and even in common life . . . to give the preference to reason, and assert that men are only so far virtuous as they conform themselves to its dictates" (T 2.3.1.1/413). Hume's attack on this picture was part of his overall attack on the picture of human nature that saw "reason" as the faculty responsible for all the elevated things in life (truth, beauty, the good), whereas the faculty that is the passions, which include desires, especially the desire for pleasure, was responsible for all that was base in human nature. Hume wanted to replace this picture of human nature with one in which the faculty of reason did not play a dominant role. Human nature is such that the faculty of reason can be understood, not as an independently functioning faculty, but only as a faculty functioning together with the senses, the passions, and the imagination. It is only because we are *feeling* creatures that reason can function at all. Hume's claim that "Reason is, and ought only to be the slave of the passions" is a very provocative way of summing up his opposition to the traditional picture of reason as dominant in the combat between reason and the passions.

Hume's goal with respect to reason and the passions is not adequately or appropriately represented by the modern belief/desire theory of action, and his claim that "reason alone can never be a motive to any action of the will" does not translate into "beliefs alone don't motivate." Hume's position on reason and the passions is part of his overall account of reason and human nature, which includes the following claims:

- the activity of probable reasoning cannot be understood as the activity of an independently functioning faculty of reason; it requires an appeal, *inter alia*, to an account of beliefs as feelings (T 1.3.6);
- such beliefs survive skeptical scrutiny only because belief is an act of the sensitive side of our nature (T 1.4.1);
- "Where reason is lively, and mixes itself with some propensity, it ought to be assented to. Where it does not, it never can have any title to operate on us" (T 1.4.7.11/270).[36]

Seen in this context, the claim that "reason alone" doesn't motivate is the claim that reason, as a faculty of human beings, can only function, not on its own, but in harmony with our feelings and passions. The picture of reason as potentially triumphing over the passions is an empirically false picture of human nature. Seen in this light, the fact that some beliefs (i.e., beliefs about pleasure) can motivate us to act, either directly or by causing some passion, far from being a problem for his theory instead becomes an integral part of it.

Given human nature as it is, two things are required for the result of a piece of reasoning to produce passions or volitions: the idea so produced must have the right sort of content (i.e., pleasure or pain), and it must have sufficient force and vivacity to have the sort of causal impact impressions have. These are just general features of human nature, discovered empirically. If we consider reason and belief in abstraction from these features, that is, if we consider reason alone, we cannot account for what belief is, how the faculty of reason produces beliefs, nor how beliefs survive skeptical arguments. Nor could we understand how certain beliefs are motivating (i.e., produce PVAs). Once those features are taken into account, we have a rather different picture of the faculty of reason from that with which we are likely to have started. We believe and act, but we do neither because of reason alone. The faculty of reason does not, and cannot, function in isolation from the sensitive and imaginative parts of our natures.

ACKNOWLEDGMENTS

This paper has been presented at several different forums, including the department colloquium at Uppsala, the Humean Readings Group in New York, the Third Hume Conference in Belo Horizonte, a graduate seminar in Oxford, the Hume Society Conference in Boston, and a Hume conference in Cambridge organized by Peter Kail and Marina Frasca-Spada. I thank audiences at and organizers of all these. Special thanks to Rachel Cohon, Don Garrett, and Michael Gill for extensive discussion over the years and detailed comments. Thanks also to Elizabeth Radcliffe, Kate Abramson, Peter Kail, and Michael Karlsson for criticism and support.

ABBREVIATIONS OF WORKS CITED

DP   *A Dissertation on the Passions.* In T. Beauchamp, ed. A *Dissertation on the Passions; The Natural History of Religion.* Oxford: Clarendon Press, 2008

EM   *Enquiry Concerning the Principles of Morals.* Edited by Tom L. Beauchamp. Oxford: Clarendon, 1998.

EU   *An Enquiry Concerning Human Understanding.* Edited by T. L. Beauchamp. Oxford: Clarendon, 2000.

NOTES

1. See also T 2.1.10.8–10/314–15; T 2.3.1.1–2/399; T 2.3.3.3/414; T 2.3.3.9.1–7/438–9; T 3.3.1.27/589–90; T 3.3.1.2/574.
2. What used to be the standard view is well represented by Stroud (1977), Mackie (1980), and Bricke (1996). Radcliffe (1999) presents an important development of the standard view. Important new work can be found in Baier (1991), Persson (1997), Karlsson (2006), Kail (2007), and Cohon (2008). There are all sorts of questions, especially about practical reason and Hume's claim that a passion "contains not any representative quality, which renders it a copy of any other existence" (T 2.3.3.5/415) that I only touch on here. Much other good work (e.g., Sturgeon 2001; Setiya 2004) is available, and more is being produced all the time.
3. The characteristic activity of the faculty of the will is willing. That activity terminates in volition. Volitions are the proximal causes of actions. The will can be pushed into activity by a passion (i.e., passions can cause volitions). The characteristic activity of the faculty of reason is inferring or reasoning. A demonstrative inference is made up of intuitions. So, by a minor extension, intuitions also count as the results of the characteristic activity of the faculty of reason, even though they are not inferences. The activity of probable or causal inference results in beliefs. For the purposes of this paper, I ignore the complications that arise from considering demonstrative inferences and the items of knowledge (objects of reason, relations of ideas) with which they terminate.
4. This issue might be controversial. Don Garrett advocates what may be a more robust view of Hume on faculties:

    Hume himself makes central and extensive use of the term "faculty" in the *Treatise*. ... His objection is not to characterizing things as having faculties; rather, it is to supposing that by doing so one has already isolated and provided ultimate explanations. (Garrett 2006: 153)

I agree that Hume's use of faculty talk is central to the way he expresses his views, and it is important for us to understand that. I think it is equally important to realize that, for

Hume, the mention of faculties carries no explanatory weight. I think Garrett and I both have pretty much the same view of Hume's objection to the explanatory fruitfulness of faculties. Pages 152–158 of Garrett's (2006) article present excellent guidance on how to understand Hume on the faculty of reason.

5. See the discussion about the different uses of "desire" in Section IV of this paper.

6. See Owen (2008).

7. Don Garrett reminds me that there is a sense in which the faculty of reason produces the impression of necessary connection. It is even true, I suppose, that having produced that impression, it then goes on to make use of the idea derived from that impression in subsequent inferences. But it doesn't produce that impression as the conclusion of an inference; it is the activity of the exercise of the faculty of reason, the actual experiencing of an inference taking us from something observed to something unobserved, that produces the impression of determination or necessity. The point is that we need an account of the mechanism of causal inference that doesn't rely on our already having the idea of necessary connection. As Hume famously quips, "perhaps 'twill appear in the end, that the necessary connexion depends on the inference, instead of the inference's depending on the necessary connexion" (T 1.3.6.3/88).

8. As the title of this section of my paper indicates, I am not trying to give an account of T 3.1.1. I am just using one aspect of it as an example of the importance of the Copy Principle.

9. The full passages come from the "Appendix": "They strike upon us with more force; they are more present to us; the mind has a firmer hold of them, and is more actuated and mov'd by them. It acquiesces in them; and, in a manner, fixes and reposes itself on them" (T A2/624–5). What "distinguishes the ideas of the judgment from the fictions of the imagination . . . gives them more force and influence; makes them appear of greater importance; infixes them in the mind, and renders them the governing principles of all our actions" (T 1.3.7.7/629). See also the first Enquiry (EU 5.12/49–50), which contains almost exactly the same wording.

10. There is one place where Hume suggests an almost evolutionary account of the Pleasure Principle: "We are conscious, that we ourselves, in adapting means to ends, are guided by reason and design, and that 'tis not ignorantly nor casually we perform those actions which tend to self-preservation, to the obtaining pleasure, and avoiding pain" (T 1.3.16.2/176).

11. If one wants to maintain a traditional reading of "reason alone can never be a motive to any action of the will," then one will have to deny that the perception of a future pleasure is a belief. Elizabeth Radcliffe was prepared to do this in 1999:

> Thus, we can conclude that the prospect of pleasure or pain, which is the basis of our concern, is not discerned by reason. So it follows on my argument that "the prospect of pleasure or pain" should not be regarded as a belief. (Radcliffe, 1999: 112)

I admire the consistency such a position shows, but it is rather quixotic. I think it is more plausible to rethink what the claim "reason alone can never be a motive to any action of the will" might mean. See Section VI of this chapter. Radcliffe has significant insights and important arguments, which can't be addressed here.

12. See Smith (1994), pp. 8–9 and *passim*. The Humean theory is not just a theory of motivation or motivating reasons; it is also a theory about what constitutes a reason for action. I am not concerned with the question of what constitutes a reason for action here; indeed, I suspect that it is largely irrelevant to Hume's discussion of reason and the passions.

13. Cohon (2008: 38) calls T 2.3.3.3 "the key paragraph." She supports the interpretation of this paragraph given here with, *inter alia*, further textual evidence from the *Dissertation of the Passions* (DP 5.1) and the second *Enquiry* (EM 1.7/172). See Cohon (2008: 50–51). These texts seem to me decisive. They are, respectively:

> It seems evident, that reason, in a strict sense, as meaning the judgment of truth and falsehood, can never, of itself, be any motive to the will, and can have no influence but so far as it touches some passion or affection. *Abstract relations* of ideas are the object of curiosity, not of volition. And *matters of fact,* where they are neither good nor evil, where they neither excite desire nor aversion, are totally indifferent, and whether known or unknown, whether mistaken or rightly apprehended, cannot be regarded as any motive to action.

And,

> inferences and conclusions of the understanding, which of themselves have no hold of the affections, nor set in motion the active powers of men, . . . discover truths: But where the truths which they discover are indifferent, and beget no desire or aversion, they can have no influence on conduct and behaviour.

14. In one form or other, all of Cohon (2008), Karlsson (2006), Baier (1991), Persson (1997), and Kail (2007) hold this minority view. Both Karlsson and Cohon patiently provide a sympathetic account of Hume as holding that any belief, even one about pleasure or pain, needs to be supplemented by an independently held desire in order to cause a PVA. They both reject that view of Hume, but nonetheless think that such a belief must give rise to a desire (Karlsson) or, more generally, a motivating passion (Cohon) in order to influence action.

15. This fine article (Karlson 2006) discusses not just motivation, but also practical reasoning, in Hume and his critics. It covers much more ground than my effort here, which concentrates primarily on the importance of belief and the Pleasure Principle.

16. We'll discuss T 2.3.9 in the next section of this paper.

17. There is a way of making the notion of pleasure as a desired good the center of Hume's account of motivation. See Kail (2007), chapter 8. I hope to explore that in another place.

18. The sort of thing I have in mind are actions that result from those direct passions that arise, not from the perception of pleasure or pain, but

> from a natural impulse or instinct, which is perfectly unaccountable. Of this kind is the desire of punishment to our enemies, and of happiness to our friends; hunger, lust, and a few other bodily appetites. These passions, properly speaking, produce good and evil, and proceed not from them, like the other affections. (T 2.3.9.8/439)

Desires are needed in these cases precisely because there is no belief in pleasure in store, and the Pleasure Principle doesn't apply.

19. Although never, interestingly enough, in the sections on liberty and necessity. It is worth noting that in T 1.3.14.12/632 and again in T 1.3.15.1/173, volitions are used as an example of the sort of thing that can be caused by anything. And, of course, Hume denies that a volition is an impression that can serve as the source of our idea of power or necessary connection.

20. In T 2.3.9.2/438, Hume phrases his list of indirect passions so as to make it appear that volitions are somewhat different from the others: "the *direct* passions of desire and aversion,

grief and joy, hope and fear, along with volition." But two paragraphs later, volition is mentioned along with other direct passions without any hint of difference: "the direct passions, or the impressions of volition and desire," "the direct affections . . . desire of volition, joy or hope." The passage from T 3.3.1.2/574, quoted earlier, also seems to separate volitions from desire, aversion, hope, fear, grief, and joy as different sorts of impressions into which "the propense and averse motions of the mind" are diversified.

21. Don Garrett suggested to me that Hume might just be saying that, of all the direct passions, none is more remarkable than the will.

22. This passage also needs to be corrected, replacing "the will" with "a volition, the product of the faculty of the will."

23. It took me far too long, and required reading Cohon (2008: 41–42), to see that this is the picture Hume is sketching in T 2.3.9.7/439. I think Tito Magri may have tried to explain this to me as well. The passage reads:

> DESIRE arises from good consider'd simply, and AVERSION is deriv'd from evil. The WILL exerts itself, when either the good or the absence of evil may be attain'd by any action of the mind or body.

Cohon, using "Spontaneous Creation view" where I use "MBA," goes on to say:

> Since desire *arises* from the consideration of good (that is, pleasure), then, says the Spontaneous Creation view, it is not present all along, but comes into existence anew when one considers the prospect of pleasure. When one also believes that one may acquire the good or avert the evil by acting, the will exerts itself.

24. Cohon (2008: 34) recognizes that volitions may play this role in Hume.

25. Hume often uses these terms interchangeably. See T 2.2.8.4/373–4 and T 2.3.3.8/417.

26. Stroud (1977), chapter 7, argues that Hume's account of belief as an act of the sensitive part of our natures sits badly with the claim that beliefs, arrived at by reasoning, can never be a motive to any action of the will. It is unarguable that Hume's account of belief is in tension with any account of belief that leaves it inert. The tension is irresolvable as long as one thinks "reason alone doesn't motivate" implies "beliefs are inert."

27. The difference between this distributed claim and the claim that beliefs about pleasure can only cause passions (and hence volitions and actions) is why those who hold the latter would be unhappy with allowing volitions to count unproblematically as direct passions.

28. For the purposes of the discussion in this section, it doesn't matter whether one thinks that beliefs can cause passions, which in turn causes volitions, or whether it is possible that beliefs can produce volitions directly.

29. Understanding Hume on reason in just about any context requires recognition that the term "reason" is, for Hume, primarily a faculty term. See note 4. Understanding the centrality of Hume's use of faculty language is quite compatible with maintaining, as I do, that Hume has a very thin view of faculties.

30. See Stroud (1977), Mackie (1980), and Bricke (1996). See Cohon (2008), chapters 1–3, for countless other references.

31. Pervasive use of faculty terminology results in usages that we regard as rather odd, and some care is required when interpreting them. See notes 3 and 4.

32. See T 1.3.4–10/82–123. Again, I leave out demonstrative reasoning and its outcome for ease of presentation. Cohon (2008: 65–68) provides an excellent summary of this way of looking at Hume on reason.

33. This point simply follows from the Copy Principle and the nature of the faculty of reason. It is analogous to the point made about reason and moral distinctions in Section II. It is part of Cohen's position, and she articulates it toward the end of a long and thorough discussion of the issue: "when Hume says that reason alone cannot produce a passion, what he means is that a passion is not the outcome of a reasoning process" (Cohon 2008: 77). Persson (1997) is on to something similar when he talks about belief being a manifestation of reason. Garrett finds it an uncontroversial thing to say about Hume in an encyclopedia article on Hume: "For him, the outcome of reasoning itself is belief, not desire or action; and although reasoning can, in concert with other aspects of one's nature, contribute to the production of new desires and actions, this process of production is not itself one of reasoning" (Garrett 2005). Garrett uses this, however, to support the controversial claim that Hume rejects even a limited, means–ends conception of practical reasoning. An investigation of Hume on practical reasoning is beyond the scope of this paper, as is an investigation of what is at stake when Hume denies that a passion has any representative quality. Nor will I talk about the calm versus the violent passions, a conflict that Hume thinks replaces the alleged conflict between reason and the passions. But I think this much follows straightforwardly. Something can be contrary to reason only if it is (or is suitably related to) the outcome of a piece of reasoning, a belief. But only other beliefs (or things suitably related to beliefs) are capable of this. So, just as PVAs cannot be the conclusions of arguments, neither can they be contrary to conclusions of arguments, except in the two relevant ways Hume mentions.

34. Don Garrett reminded me of this. The same point is made by Stroud (1977: 157).

35. One of the original contributions made by T 2.3.3 is the argument from the nonrepresentational nature of the passions and the related argument concerning just what it means to call an action "unreasonable." As mentioned before, I cannot go into these important arguments here.

36. For my views on the first two of these points, see Owen (1999). For a thorough discussion of the third point, see Garrett (1997), chapter 10.

Bibliography

Baier, Annette. (1991). *A Progress of Sentiments*. Cambridge: Harvard University Press.

Bricke, J. (1996). *Mind and Morality*. Oxford: Clarendon Press.

Cohon, Rachel. (2008). *Hume's Morality: Feeling and Fabrication*. Oxford: Oxford University Press.

Descartes, Réne. (1644/1991). "Letter to Mesland, 2 May, 1644," in J. Cottingham, D. Murdoch, R. Stoothoff, and A. Kenny, eds., *The Philosophical Writings of Descartes*, vol. 3. Cambridge: Cambridge University Press.

Garrett, Don. (1997). *Cognition and Commitment in Hume's Philosophy*. New York: Oxford University Press.

Garrett, Don. (2005). "Hume," in E. Craig, ed., *Routledge Encyclopedia of Philosophy*. London: Routledge. Retrieved May 21, 2009, from www.rep.routledge.com/article/DB040SECT10

Garrett, Don. (2006). "Hume's Conclusions," in Saul Traiger, ed., *The Blackwell Guide to Hume's Treatise*. Oxford: Blackwell, 151–176.

Kail, Peter. (2007). *Projection and Realism in Hume's Philosophy*. Oxford: Oxford University Press.

Karlsson, Mikael. (2006). "Reason, Passion, and the Influencing Motives of the Will," in Saul Traiger, ed., *The Blackwell Guide to Hume's Treatise*. Oxford: Blackwell, 235–255.

Mackie, J. L. (1980). *Hume's Moral Theory*. London: Routledge.

Owen, David. (1999). *Hume's Reason*. Oxford: Oxford University Press.

Owen, David. (2008). "Hume and the Mechanics of the Mind: Impressions, Ideas and Association," in David Fate Norton, ed., *Cambridge Companion to Hume*, 2nd ed. Cambridge: Cambridge University Press, 70–104.

Persson, Ingmar. (1997). "Hume—Not a 'Humean' About Motivation," *History of Philosophy Quarterly* 14, 189–206.

Radcliffe, Elizabeth. (1999). "Hume on the Generation of Motives: Why Beliefs Alone Never Motivate," *Hume Studies* 25, 101–122.

Setiya, Kieran. (2004). "Hume on Practical Reason," *Philosophical Perspectives* 18, 365–389.

Smith, Michael. (1994). *The Moral Problem*. Oxford: Blackwell.

Stroud, Barry. (1977). *Hume*. London: Routledge.

Sturgeon, Nicholas. (2001). "Moral Skepticism and Moral Naturalism in Hume's Treatise," *Hume Studies* 27, 3–83.

Traiger, Saul. (2006). *The Blackwell Guide to Hume's Treatise*. Oxford: Blackwell.

CHAPTER 18

....

HUME ON
PRACTICAL REASON

Against the Normative Authority of Reason

....

KARL SCHAFER

As deep and pervasive as Hume's influence is, there is perhaps no area in which it is more comprehensive than the study of practical reason. Indeed, even today much of the debate about these issues revolves around positions that are generally taken to be true, if not to the letter of Hume's views, then at least to their spirit. This is clearest insofar as Hume is often taken to be the father of what is sometimes called "double Humeanism" about practical reason. The double Humean combines together two views often attributed to Hume: a view about motivational psychology, often referred to as the Humean Theory of Motivation (HTM), and a view about normative reasons for action, often called the Humean Theory of Practical Reasons (HTR).[1]

In broad outlines, the first of these claims that beliefs and other cognitive states, on their own, can never motivate a new desire, intention, or action. Rather, on this view what motivates us to desire, intend, or act is always the cooperation of some desire (or other conative state) with such cognitive states. Thus, on the HTM, practical motivation is always the product of two fundamentally distinct categories of mental state operating in conjunction with one another.[2]

The HTR, on the other hand, concerns *normative* reasons for action (and, by extension, normative reasons to desire or intend).[3] In particular, the HTR claims that an agent's reasons for action are always the product of his desires, properly weighed against each other. So, for example, in its classical form, the HTR claims that one has a reason to perform some action just in case this action will promote the fulfillment of one's basic or underived desires, given what one believes (or ought to believe) is the case.[4]

When appropriately developed, many philosophers have taken the combination of these two views to be an extremely elegant and attractive theory of practical reason. According to this theory, the sole function of practical reasoning is the selection of the means that will best fulfill an agent's basic or underived desires, properly weighed against each other. Such desires are taken by this theory as given and thus as not subject to rational evaluation. Rather, according to this theory, when we ask whether someone's actions are supported by their reasons for action, we are simply asking whether these actions are among those that best promote the fulfillment of these basic desires. On this view, practical rationality (in the sense of being responsive to one's reasons for action) is simply a matter of deciding on the course of action that will best serve one's basic desires, appropriately weighed.

As the "Humean" label indicates, the contemporary association of these two views with Hume remains very strong. And yet, as readers of Hume have increasingly begun to recognize, there is good reason to be suspicious about whether Hume was a Humean in either of these two senses.[5] Here, I argue that these suspicions are well founded in both cases. As a result, we do Hume a disservice when we characterize his relevance to the contemporary debates about practical reason in terms of his status of as the alleged father of "double Humeanism." But while Hume is not relevant to the contemporary debate *in this way*, he is highly relevant to it all the same. Or so I hope to show.[6]

I HUME'S THEORY OF MOTIVATION

In considering these issues, I'll take up Hume's relationship to the HTM and the HTR in turn, beginning—as is natural—with the first. To understand Hume's motivational psychology, it is important to begin by sketching the basic elements that make up Hume's conception of the human mind.[7] For Hume, the mind, at least insofar as we are aware of it, is composed of a set of perceptions, which are connected together by relations of causality and resemblance. These perceptions are themselves divided into two broad classes: impressions and ideas. Impressions are more vivacious than ideas—and, although all our (simple) ideas are copied from preceding impressions, no impression is copied from any preceding perception in the mind.

The broad class of impressions may, in turn, be divided into two further classes. First, there are impressions of sensation, which are the product of our external senses. And second, there are impressions of reflection, which are caused by preceding perceptions in the mind. This latter class of impressions is dominated by the passions—which include our desires, but also include many other states, such as pride, humility, love, hate, curiosity, and the like. Hume's discussion of the passions is, of course, one of the richest elements in his philosophy. But, for our purposes here, what is most important to note is simply that the passions, together with the closely associated impression of reflection that Hume calls "volition," are *roughly* equivalent to the contemporary class of conative states.

Finally, for Hume, beliefs are simply ideas that have reached a level of vivacity that, although lower than that possessed by impressions, is still sufficient to allow them to approximate the causal role that impressions play in the mind. Taking all this together, we may treat the question of whether Hume accepts the HTM as equivalent to the question of whether he believes that it is possible for an idea or belief to motivate a new passion, volition, or action without the cooperation of some preexisting passion or volition. If Hume does answer this question negatively, it seems reasonable to regard him as a Humean in the manner in which much of the tradition has done. But if he answers affirmatively, then we should be suspicious of attributing such a view to him.

I.1   The Humean Theory of Motivation: The Inertia of Belief

Why might one think that Hume answers this question negatively? Here, the central issue is what Hume means when he states that reason is "perfectly inert and can never either prevent or produce any action" (T 3.1.1.8/458). It is traditional to read this claim as an endorsement of some form of the HTM.[8] And this is in fact a very natural reading of it, especially within a contemporary context that tends to focus on the motivational efficacy of *mental states* like beliefs and desires. For, in this context, it is very natural to interpret the claim that reason is inert to mean that the *products* of reason—that is, ideas and beliefs—are inert.[9]

On this interpretation of Hume, the role of beliefs in motivation is simply to direct the motivational force possessed by preexisting passions and volitions toward the actions that will be likely to satisfy them. Thus, on this view, a belief on its own can never motivate a new passion or action.[10] At most, a belief can combine with preexisting passions to produce new passions—passions whose motivational force derives entirely from the motivational force of those preexisting passions.

Such a reading of Hume does fit well with a natural reading of much of what Hume says about these issues, so it is not difficult to understand why it has dominated traditional Hume interpretation. For instance, when Hume considers the manner in which we are motivated by the prospect of pleasure or pain, he writes,

> 'tis evident in this case, that the impulse [to action] arises not from reason, but is only directed by it. 'Tis from the prospect of pain or pleasure that the aversion or propensity arises towards any object: And these emotions extend themselves to the causes and effects of that object, as they are pointed out to us by reason and experience. It can never in the least concern us to know, that such objects are causes, and such others effects, if both the causes and the effects be indifferent to us. Where the objects themselves do not affect us, their connection can never give them any influence.
> (T 2.3.3.3/414)

It is not unnatural to read Hume's reference to "indifference" in this passage to mean the following: we are "indifferent" to some possibility just in case we have no preexisting passion that relates to this possibility. And, if we read this passage in this way, it does appear to claim that new passions or actions can never arise from an idea or belief considered on its own. Rather, on this reading, the "impulse to action" must (at least in part) be the product of a preexisting passion that makes us more than "indifferent" to the objects of these ideas or beliefs.

Read in this way, then, this passage appears to support the attribution of the HTM to Hume. And this is hardly the only passage that might be taken in this way. But despite this, there are several serious problems facing any such interpretation.

First, it is important to ask what the status of the claim that all beliefs are motivationally inert is supposed to be on this interpretation. Many contemporary proponents of a form of the HTM, such as Michael Smith, take some claim of this sort to be an a priori truth that is "built into" our folk understanding of the basic categories of motivational psychology, such as belief and desire. But it is quite clear that Hume cannot understand it in this way, since he regards beliefs and passions to be "distinct existences" between which it is impossible to establish any causal connections a priori.[11] Thus, given Hume's views about the nature of beliefs and passions, any claim he makes about the connections between them must be understood to be empirical in character.

Unfortunately, if we read the claim that reason is inert as an empirical claim concerning the motivational efficacy of our beliefs, it hardly seems sufficient for Hume's purposes. After all, if this is the nature of Hume's claim, there are plenty of cases that Hume's rationalist opponents will point to as prima facie disconfirming it. So, it is hard to see how this claim would gain much dialectical traction without much greater empirical support than the rather offhand observations Hume offers in the *Treatise*. Moreover, in arguing for the claim that reason is inert, Hume appears to be arguing for something stronger than a mere empirical generalization. That is, he appears to want to argue—not just that human reason is, as a matter of empirical fact, inert—but rather that reason *by its very nature must be inert*. And this claim plainly requires something stronger than an empirical generalization about the contingent facts of *human* motivational psychology.

Moreover, given Hume's general views about the nature of belief, it would be extremely odd for him to make even the empirical claim that no human belief is motivationally efficacious. After all, for Hume beliefs are simply slightly less vivacious copies of impressions—including both impressions of sensation and impressions of reflection (including passions). And Hume clearly believes that a belief will generally mimic the causal properties of the impression from which it is derived, at least to a large degree.[12] Thus, given that some beliefs are copied from motivationally efficacious passions, it would be odd for Hume to claim that these beliefs are *entirely* motivationally inert—since this would, in effect, present a counterexample to his general account of the relationship between the causal properties of beliefs and the causal properties of the impressions from which these beliefs are copied.

As we will see in a moment, we can avoid this problem and better capture the force of the claim that reason is inert by reading it as a claim about the *faculty* of reason as opposed to a claim about the *products* of this faculty, such as beliefs. But these problems are far from the most serious ones for a reading of Hume that seeks to attribute to him a version of the HTM along these lines. Far worse are the many examples of ordinary human motivation in which Hume appears to claim that an idea or belief *can* cause a new passion without the cooperation of any preexisting passion or volition. For, if these passages are taken at face value, Hume appears to offer and endorse, as basic to human psychology, a variety of counterexamples to the HTM, as characterized here.[13]

This is clearest in those passages in which Hume discusses the motivational efficacy of our beliefs about future pleasure and pain.[14] For example, immediately before the famous "indifference" quote discussed earlier, Hume writes that:

> when we have the prospect of pain or pleasure from any object, we feel a consequent emotion of aversion or propensity, and are carry'd to avoid or embrace what will give us this uneasiness or satisfaction. (T 2.3.3.3/414)

And at the very beginning of the *Treatise*, when discussing the basic distinction between impressions and ideas, he writes:

> An impression first strikes upon the senses, and makes us perceive heat or cold, thirst or hunger, pleasure or pain, of some kind or other. Of this impression there is a copy taken by the mind, which remains after the impression ceases; and this we call an idea. This idea of pleasure or pain, when it returns upon the soul, produces the new impressions of desire and aversion, hope and fear, which may properly be called impressions of reflection, because derived from it. (T 1.1.2.1/7–8)

Both of these quotes appear to describe the normal course of human motivation as having the following basic structure.[15] First, we come to form a vivid idea (or belief) concerning some future pleasure or pain. Then this idea, on its own, produces in us a consequent desire to seek out or avoid the objects that are connected with the object of this idea. And then these desires, everything else being equal, move us to act in the desired manner. If this is correct, then Hume cannot be read as claiming that ideas, on their own, are incapable of causing the formation of new passions. For, in fact, if these passages are taken at face value, his view appears to be that just this occurs all the time during the course of ordinary human motivation. If this is right, then whatever Hume means when he claims that reason is inert, he cannot mean that all ideas are inert in the manner the HTM claims.[16]

There are two natural avenues of resistance to this point. First, one might argue that our "beliefs" about pleasure and pain are not purely cognitive states. As a result, one might insist that the fact that these "beliefs" can (on their own) produce new passions does not count in any way against the HTM. Such a reading of Hume might take solace from the fact that Hume, following the common English usage of his time, often refers to pleasure and pain as "good" and "evil"—which might be taken to suggest that these ideas involve some sort of non-belief-like component. But there is no suggestion in Hume that anything like this is the case. In fact, Hume commits himself to the view that beliefs about pleasure and pain are beliefs of a straightforwardly factual sort in passages such as T 3.1.1.12/459, where he includes facts about pleasure and pain among the matters of fact that are insufficient to make an action "unreasonable."

For these reasons, a far more promising way of defending the attribution of the HTM to Hume is to do what most attributers of the HTM to him have done: attempt to render these passages compatible with the HTM by insisting that Hume takes all human beings to possess a general background desire to seek pleasure and avoid pain—a desire that is the real source of the apparent motivational efficacy of beliefs about pleasure and pain in cases like those presented earlier.

Such a view is very common in the literature on these issues. But, to my mind, it represents a fundamental misinterpretation of what Hume means when he speaks of passions and other perceptions. On this reading, we possess a constant and ever-present desire to seek pleasure and avoid pain. Now, for this reading to be remotely plausible, this desire must be understood to be one of Hume's "calm desires and tendencies, which, tho' they be real passions, produce little emotion in the mind" (T 2.3.3.8/417). For, surely, we are not generally conscious of such a desire in the manner we are conscious of our more violent passions and sentiments. But, even if this desire is understood on the model of Hume's calm passions, its existence conflicts with another of Hume's core philosophical commitments. In particular, although a calm passion produces "little emotion in the mind," this does not mean that it produces none at all. Rather, for Hume, all of the passions (and other perceptions) that are part of my mind possess phenomenal force and vivacity and so make some contribution to my consciousness.[17] In this way, when Hume speaks of passions, he always has in mind a state that—in the contemporary lingo—has an affective as well as a dispositional component. Thus, when Hume speaks of calm passions, he is not referring to a class of passions that are merely dispositional and so completely absent from our consciousness—rather, he is referring to a class of passions that make a modest contribution to my consciousness (or, perhaps better, my conscious attention) when compared to our more violent passions and sentiments.

The difficulty this raises is that there is no textual evidence that Hume believes that even a very calm desire for pleasure is constantly present within our mind. In fact, there is fairly decisive evidence against the attribution of any such view to Hume. For example, consider Hume's famous discussion of the idea of the self, where he writes:

> If any impression gives rise to the idea of self, that impression must continue invariably the same, thro' the whole course of our lives; since self is suppos'd to exist after that manner. But there is no impression constant and invariable. (T 1.4.6.2/251)

A constant and invariable desire for pleasure, no matter how calm, would be just the sort of impression that Hume here explicitly rejects. Thus, it is difficult to see how this way of defending the attribution of the HTM to Hume might be reconciled with Hume's understanding of the nature of the passions and his conception of the self.[18]

I.2 The Motivational Power of the Faculty of Reason: The Inertia of Reason

Far better, then, to rest content with the natural reading of these passages—a reading that makes it clear that Hume would not endorse the HTM, at least in an unqualified form.[19] But, if this is right, how should we interpret the claim that reason is inert?

As I noted earlier, the attribution of the HTM to Hume rests on a natural inference from the claim that reason is inert to the claim that the products of reason are inert. But we need not accept this inference—or anything like it—to preserve the intended force of Hume's inertness claim.

To see why, it will be helpful to consider in more detail why Hume believes that reason is inert and why he thinks this claim is philosophically significant. In the first instance, Hume believes that reason is inert because he believes that reason consists in the "discovery of truth and falsehood" (T 3.1.1.9/458). Or, in other words, he believes that when reason produces or prevents something via one of its characteristic operations, it does so via the discovery of its (likely) truth or falsehood. But Hume also takes himself to have shown that passions and actions are not, strictly speaking, true or false. Thus, he concludes, reason alone cannot prevent or produce a new desire or action via one of its characteristic operations—because it could only do so via approving of that desire or action as true or disapproving of it as false.

There's a great deal to unpack in this quick summary of Hume's argument—more, sadly, than there is space to explore here. But let's pause to emphasize a few key ideas that lie behind it. [20]

First of all, it is crucial to note that Hume takes the "truth or falsehood" that reason discovers to fall into two basic categories: what he calls "real relations of ideas" and "real existence and matters of fact":

> Truth or falsehood consists in an agreement or disagreement either to real relations of ideas or to real existence and matters of fact. What . . . is not susceptible of this agreement or disagreement, is incapable of being true or false, and can never be an object of our reason. (T 3.1.1.9/458; cf. T 2.3.3.2/413)

As a result, Hume takes the following three characterizations of the faculty of reason to pick out one and the same faculty:

(1) reason as the faculty for inference in general;
(2) reason as the faculty for demonstrative and probable inference; and
(3) reason as the faculty for the "discovery of truth and falsehood" (insofar as this extends beyond the senses and memory).

In other words, Hume takes our inferential abilities to be exhausted by our ability to perform demonstrative and probable inferences. And he takes this ability to be co-extensive with the ability to discover truths and falsehoods—at least insofar as these extend beyond the immediate deliverances of the senses and of memory.[21]

It is plain that Hume does not regard this conception of reason as particularly controversial.[22] But, in the present context, it is worth stressing that, by equating our general inferential faculty with our faculty for making theoretical inferences of these two sorts,

Hume's use of the term "reason" excludes from consideration conceptions of reason like those found in the Aristotelian tradition and in Kant, which give equal significance to theoretical *and* practical inference.[23] Just how substantive this issue is will depend somewhat on how important we take the category of "inference" to be. And, as we will see later on, if Hume's arguments are successful, the question of how to conceive of the faculty of reason will be far less significant than it might seem, since one of Hume's ultimate aims is to undermine the normative authority of reason in general. Thus, if he is successful in this, how we draw the line between "reason" and other aspects of the mind will be of much less significance than it is often taken to be. Nonetheless, this feature of Hume's conception of reason is crucial to keep in mind in considering the relationship between his views and those of figures like Kant.

In any case, once this conception of reason is on the table, in order to establish the inertness of reason, all that remains to be shown is that passions, volitions, and actions are incapable of either of the forms of agreement or disagreement on which the operations of reason rest.

This claim is likely to be most controversial in the case of passions (and volitions). What prevents passions (and volitions), according to Hume, from entering into either of these forms of agreement or disagreement is, most fundamentally, that they are impressions as opposed to ideas. This has two important consequences for Hume. First, although reason can compare ideas with one another in order to discover their "real relations," it is not capable of performing this task with respect to our impressions.[24] Thus, reason is incapable of discovering the first form of agreement or disagreement in a passion (or volition).

Second, as an impression of reflection, a passion is "an original existence . . . [and] contains not any representative quality, which renders it a copy of any other existence" (T 2.3.3.5/415).[25] But, according to Hume, the second sort of agreement or disagreement requires just this—since, "this contradiction consists in the disagreement of ideas, considered as copies, with those objects which they represent" (T 2.3.3.5/415).[26] Thus, Hume concludes that it is impossible to discover either of these two forms of agreement or disagreement in any passion: "'Tis impossible, therefore [that our passions] can be pronounced either true or false, and be either contrary or conformable to reason" (T 3.1.1.9/458).[27]

Much the same is true, according to Hume, of actions. In fact, for just these reasons, Hume concludes that a piece of reasoning can *only* conclude in the formation of a new idea or belief—as opposed to a passion, volition, or action. And, crucially, this is not merely an empirical claim about *our* faculty of reason—rather, it is something that is true of *any* faculty of reason as such. For, unlike ideas and impressions, the *faculty of reason is* individuated by its characteristic activities and products for Hume.[28]

Crucially, if this is true, there is no reason to interpret the claim that reason is inert as an endorsement of any form of the HTM. Once we recognize that reason for Hume is identical with the faculty for demonstrative and probable inference, it is most natural to read the inertness claim as a claim about this faculty—namely, that its characteristic *operations* can never (on their own) produce new passions, volitions, and actions.

And we can accept this claim without accepting the further claim that the products of reason—that is, ideas and beliefs—can never (by themselves) cause new passions, volitions, or actions. For the claim that *reasoning* can never (on its own) produce new passions, volitions, or actions is perfectly compatible with the claim that ideas can produce new passions and the like so long as ideas do so via a process that cannot itself be regarded as a piece of reasoning.[29]

Read this way, Hume's claims about the inertness of reason are not claims about the motivational power of ideas or beliefs. Instead, they are claims about the motivational power of a *faculty*.[30] For the reasons just alluded to, such a reading easily avoids the issues we noted earlier for the attribution of the HTM to Hume. And, for the reasons we have already discussed, it also fits very naturally with Hume's arguments in favor of the claim that reason is inert.[31] Moreover, it is easy to interpret the passages that are often taken to support the attribution of the HTM to Hume so as to support this interpretation. For example, the famous "indifference" passage that we discussed earlier only supports the attribution of the HTM if we read its references to "indifference" to involve a conception of indifference whereby we are indifferent to some object whenever we do not possess some preexisting passion related to this object. But, in fact, given how Hume generally uses this term, it is far more natural to understand his references to "indifference" so that we are indifferent to some object just in case the idea of that object would not *excite* in us a new passion. And, of course, when read in this way, this passage supports a very different view of Hume than the one involved in the HTM.

For example, when Hume reworks the "indifference" passage in the *Dissertation on the Passions*, he writes that:

> matters of fact, where they are neither good nor evil, where they neither excite desire nor aversion, are totally indifferent; and whether known or unknown, whether mistaken or rightly apprehended, cannot be regarded as any motive to action. (DP 5.1)

And similarly, when discussing these issues in the *Enquiry*, he writes:

> where the truths which [reason or the understanding's inferences] discover are indifferent, and beget no desire or aversion, they can have no influence on conduct or behavior. (EM 1.7/172)

Both of these passages fit far better with the second reading of "indifference" just proposed, and because they are reworkings of the original *Treatise* passage, it is natural to conclude that *none* of these passages gives any real support to the attribution of the HTM to Hume.

Finally, this way of reading the claim that reason is inert fits perfectly with Hume's intended usage of this claim. For in making this claim, Hume's primary target was the sort of moral rationalism that represented the main alternative to sentimentalist views like Hume's within English-language philosophy during his lifetime. This sort of view—represented by William Wollaston, Samuel Clarke, and (arguably) John

Locke—claimed that facts about morality could be discovered by the operations of reason alone, in much the same manner as facts about mathematics or (perhaps) God.[32] The main purpose of Hume's claim that reason is inert is to establish a basis for arguing against views of this sort:

> Since morals . . . have an influence on actions and affections, it follows, that they cannot be derived from reason . . . because reason alone . . . can never have such an influence. Morals excite passions, and produce or prevent actions. Reason of itself is utterly impotent in this particular. (T 3.1.1.6/457; cf. T 3.1.1.12/459)

Now, if these claims are correct, to properly understand this argument, we need to realize that it is ultimately concerned, not with the motivational efficacy of moral judgments or attitudes, but instead with the motivational efficacy of our *moral faculty*. Thus, just as we need to understand Hume's claims about reason to be claims about a certain faculty—as opposed to claims about the products of this faculty—we also need to read his claims about the motivational efficacy of "morals" to be concerned with the motivational efficacy of a faculty—namely, our faculty for making moral distinctions.[33] Otherwise, Hume's arguments concerning these matters would simply be fallacious—because, as we have seen, there is no conflict between the claim that reason is inert and the claim that the products of reason are sometimes very "ert" indeed. Thus, Hume's point against the rationalist cannot be that the rationalist allows reason to produce beliefs that in turn can motivate new passions and actions, because Hume himself allows for this possibility in the case of ordinary beliefs about pleasure and pain.

As such, although Hume does describe what is at issue in these passages in a variety of ways, what ultimately concerns him in them is the relationship between two faculties: the faculty of reason and our moral faculty. On this way of reading Hume, his argument against the moral rationalist has the following structure:

(1) The faculty of reason (on its own) can never produce passions or actions by approving or disapproving of them.

(2) Our faculty for making moral distinctions (on its own) can produce passions and actions by approving or disapproving of them.

(3) Thus, our faculty for making moral distinctions cannot be explained solely through an appeal to the faculty of reason. Our moral faculty is not merely one of the manifestations of the faculty of reason, and moral distinctions are not derived from reason alone.

This argument is valid—and, given the correctness of Hume's previous arguments, its first premise is true. Moreover, given Hume's own views about the moral sense, its second premise will be true as well. After all, given these views, it is clear that our moral faculty can (on its own) produce new passions. And in virtue of producing these passions, our moral faculty also approves and disapproves of actions as well. Thus, unlike the faculty of reason, which can never produce a passion or action by approving or disapproving of it without the cooperation of some other faculty, our moral faculty is capable of producing new passions and actions *by approving or disapproving of them* without relying on any faculty other than itself.[34]

So, at least given Hume's views about these matters, this argument is sound as well as valid. And it is sufficient to refute the moral rationalism that is Hume's target. For the moral rationalist's distinctive claim is precisely that our faculty to make moral distinctions is just one particular manifestation of our general faculty of reason. Thus, this reading of the inertness of reason vindicates the main use that Hume wishes to put this claim to without thereby taking on the problematic interpretative commitments discussed earlier.

II HUME ON PRACTICAL REASONS: 'TIS NEVER CONTRARY

II.1 The Humean Theory of Practical Reasons

For these reasons, we should be dubious of the claim that Hume accepted the first component of the "double Humeanism" about practical reason that is often ascribed to him. But perhaps things stand better with respect to the second prong of the Humean account: the HTR?

Much as was the case with respect to the HTM, it is not difficult to find passages that can be read to support attribution of some form of the HTR to Hume.[35] For example, the following famous passage is often read as an explicit endorsement of some form of this view:

> What may first occur on this head, is, that as nothing can be contrary to truth or reason, except what has a reference to it, and as the judgments of our understanding only have this reference, it must follow, that passions can be contrary to reason only so far as they are accompany'd with some judgment or opinion. According to this principle, which is so obvious and natural, 'tis only in two senses that any affection can be called unreasonable. First, when a passion such as hope or fear, grief or joy, despair or security, is founded on the supposition of the existence of objects, which really do not exist. Secondly, when in exerting any passion in action, we choose means insufficient for the design'd end, and deceive ourselves in our judgment of causes and effects. Where a passion is neither founded on false suppositions, nor chooses means insufficient for the end, the understanding can neither justify nor condemn it. 'Tis not contrary to reason to prefer the destruction of the whole world to the scratching of my finger. (T 2.3.3.6/415–16)

When viewed through the lens of the contemporary debate about *normative* reasons for action, it is very natural to read Hume's references in this passage to when a passion is "unreasonable" or "contrary to reason" to be expressions of a theory of normative reasons for action—a theory according to which an agent may be said to have a reason not to have a desire (or, by extension, not to perform an action) *only* insofar as this desire is either the product of a false belief or a failure of means–ends reasoning. According to this interpretation of Hume, where neither of these two features is present, there is simply no space to engage in the evaluation of an agent's desires in terms of her conformity with what she has normative reason to do. Thus, according to this version of Hume, our underived desires can never be evaluated in terms of their responsiveness to our reasons for action. Rather, to evaluate a desire in terms of an agent's reasons for action just is to consider whether it was derived from some prior desire via a process that involved a faulty (theoretical) inference or false belief.

In such a reading of this passage, we can easily recognize the Hume who is often regarded by contemporary proponents of the HTR as their intellectual forefather. And there are many other passages which, if read in this manner, naturally support the attribution to Hume of a theory of this sort. But there are also good reasons to be skeptical that this is, in fact, the correct way to interpret Hume's discussion of these issues.

To begin to see why, consider the following passage:

> For it proves directly, that actions do not derive their merit from a conformity to reason, nor their blame from a contrariety to it; and it proves the same truth more indirectly, by showing us, that as reason can never immediately prevent or produce any action by contradicting or approving it, it cannot be the source of the distinction betwixt moral good and evil. Actions may be laudable or blameable; but they cannot be reasonable or unreasonable: Laudable or blameable, therefore, are not the same with reasonable or unreasonable. (T 3.1.1.10/458)

There are two things about this passage that are highly significant for any attribution to Hume of the HTR. First, Hume here claims that *no* action can be called "reasonable or unreasonable." Thus, if his use of these terms is meant to address the normative question of whether an action is in conformity with an agent's reasons for action, here he appears to be claiming that it *never* makes sense to speak of actions in these terms at all. And this, of course, would rule out the HTR—along with any other theory that accepts that there are any reasons for action at all.[36]

For this reason, a defender of the attribution of the HTR to Hume must read his references to what is "reasonable or unreasonable" in passages such as this one in some other way. But once one does so, the primary evidence for the attribution of the HTR to Hume quickly disappears. For note that Hume, in this passage, equates the question of whether some action is "reasonable or unreasonable" with the question of whether the faculty of reason can "immediately prevent or produce any action by contradicting or approving of it." And, similarly, in the first passage under discussion, Hume treats the question of whether a desire is "unreasonable" as equivalent to the question of whether this desire might be contrary to the faculty of reason.[37] Thus, Hume's immediate concern in these passages is not whether a desire or action is contrary to an agent's *reasons for action* in the contemporary sense of this phrase. Instead, his primary concern is whether a desire or action can be said to be contrary to the *faculty of reason* as Hume understands it. Or, in other words, when Hume asks whether a desire is "contrary to reason" or "unreasonable," he is concerned with whether this desire could ever be prevented by one of the operations of the faculty of reason (operating on its own).

Once we recognize that Hume's main concern in these passages is *this* issue in faculty psychology, it is hardly surprising that he reaches the conclusions that he does. For, as we have already discussed, Hume conceives of reason as the faculty for demonstrative and probable inference, so it is entirely natural for him to claim that a desire can be "contrary to" this faculty only insofar as it is based on faulty reasoning or false belief. Thus, as is in general true of Hume's claims about reason in the *Treatise*, the claim Hume is arguing for in these passages is not primarily a normative claim but rather a psychological one about a particular mental faculty. And, much as it was a mistake to quickly infer anything about the inertness of the *products of reason* from Hume's claims about the inertness of the *faculty of reason*, it is also a mistake to quickly infer normative conclusions from Hume's psychological discussion of whether actions and passions may be "contrary" to the faculty of reason. For in fact—as we will see in moment—one of Hume's main aims in his discussion of the faculty of reason is to undermine the traditional idea that this faculty *as such* has any special sort of normative authority. Thus, there is no simple path from Hume's psychological claims about the faculty of reason to normative claims about what we have most reason to do or desire.

If this is right, then the passages that are often taken to support the attribution to Hume of the HTR are actually concerned with a different issue entirely—namely, the question of the relationship between our passions and actions and the faculty of reason as Hume understands it. But where does this leave the task of interpreting Hume's views with respect to the normative questions that the HTR addresses? In other words, what—if anything—does Hume say about when one has a reason for action in the contemporary, normative sense?

In response to this question, Derek Parfit has suggested that Hume simply lacks any conception of a reason for action in the normative sense of this term.[38] But although I agree with Parfit that Hume's discussion of "reason" is not directly concerned with such issues, this does not mean that Hume has nothing of interest to say about these sorts of normative questions. In particular, although Hume does not make use of the contemporary concept of a reason for action, he does have much to say that speaks to which sorts of considerations an agent's feelings and actions *ought* to be responsive to. And, insofar as he addresses this question, he is providing us with a picture of how we ought to feel and act that addresses the same basic questions that contemporary theories of reasons for action are meant to.

But what is the picture of these issues that we find in Hume? One answer to this question, of course, is provided by the traditional attribution to Hume of the HTR. But we have already undermined the grounds on which this attribution rests. And, as we will see in a moment, there are crucial aspects of Hume's positive views about these issues that are inconsistent with the HTR.[39] But if Hume is not a proponent of the HTR, what *are* his views about these issues? In a moment, I'll discuss my own view of this issue, but first I want to briefly discuss an important alternative view that also challenges the traditional attribution of the HTR to Hume.

To see what this view involves, remember the passage in which Hume claims that actions are never "reasonable or unreasonable." As we noted earlier, if we read "reasonable or unreasonable" in this passage as meaning *in conformity with or contrary to one's reasons for action*, then this passage seems to claim that there are, strictly speaking, *no* reasons for action. This is a very radical claim indeed, but that—of course—is no reason not to attribute it to *Hume*. And, in fact, a number of authors have recently suggested that Hume should be read in just this manner. Thus, on these views, Hume is not a Humean about reasons for action because he is in fact a skeptic about reasons for action of all sorts.[40] As Elijah Millgram puts the point, on this reading, Hume is not a Humean because he believes that whenever and however our passions and desires are sensitive to changes in our beliefs, "this sensitivity is not itself an aspect of rationality, and a failure of such sensitivity does not expose one to the criticism that one is being irrational."[41] Thus, for authors such as Millgram, Hume should be read as attacking the idea that there is any interesting sense in which any passions, desires, or actions can be evaluated in terms of their responsiveness to an agent's reasons for action.

When presented in this way, it is easy to see that Millgram's view represents a natural development of the traditional Humean reading of Hume. In short, Millgram has simply extended the Humean's claims about the status of *underived* desires so that these claims apply to *all* desires, passions, and actions—be they derived or underived. Unfortunately, once characterized in this way, it is not difficult to see that this interpretation suffers from some of the same basic interpretative issues that are at the root of the traditional Humean reading of Hume. In particular, both of these interpretations draw most of their plausibility from the attempt to read Hume's references to what is "contrary to reason" or "unreasonable" as concerned with the normative question of what one's reasons for actions support or oppose.[42] Thus, both of these interpretations lose much of their attractiveness once we recognize that these passages are directly concerned with psychological issues relating to the Humean faculty of reason—as opposed to normative questions about reasons for action.[43]

For instance, when Hume writes that "'tis not the passion, properly speaking, which is unreasonable, but the judgment," he might very naturally be read as endorsing some sort of global skepticism about reasons for action (T 2.3.3.6/416). But, in fact, he is simply endorsing a familiar claim about the relationship between the passions and the faculty of reason—namely, that our passions are never "contrary" to this faculty in the sense already discussed. So, while it is surely true that Hume rejects the idea that the faculty of reason has a practical dimension, this does not have any immediate implications for the normative question of whether there are reasons for action.

II.2 Virtue, Reasons, and the Authority of Reason

So what *would* Hume say about reasons for action in the contemporary, normative sense of the phrase? Earlier, I suggested that it is easiest to approach this question by considering what Hume has to say about the considerations that our desires, passions, and actions *ought* to be responsive to. For whenever we have such a consideration—that is, whenever we have a consideration that one's actions ought to be responsive to—we have something that has the essential properties of what we refer to today as a *reason for action* in at least the most basic normative sense of this term.[44]

Of course, as noted earlier, Hume does not use the phrase "reason for action" in this way. Thus, the question facing us is how to translate what Hume does say about these issues into a contemporary philosophical idiom in which talk of "reasons" plays a central role. But, once we do so, I think it is relatively clear that Hume would endorse neither the Humean account of reasons for action nor a general skepticism about the same.

What is most important in this regard is Hume's conviction that there are considerations, to which any normal agent ought to be responsive, but which are not amenable to a "Humean" account.[45] Consider, for example, Hume's attitude toward morality as summed up at the conclusion of the *Treatise*. There, Hume describes the *Treatise*'s project as an "anatomical" one that is focused mainly on describing and explaining the functioning of the mind—as opposed to making normative claims about how it ought to function. But, nonetheless, Hume stresses that nothing in this discussion is meant to undermine what Hume calls "practical morality." Rather, he believes that his discussion will only strengthen our pretheoretical commitment to morality in this sense. And, when it comes to this *normative* branch of philosophy, it is quite clear that Hume accepts that the desires and passions of individuals *ought* to be responsive to moral considerations in ways that go beyond any sort of responsiveness to instrumental considerations.

After all, the ultimate basis of these moral distinctions lies, for Hume, in the moral sense. And, as Hume himself notes, the moral sense cannot itself be accounted for through an appeal to purely instrumental considerations.[46] But, nonetheless, we are willing to judge that those who lack a moral sense—as well as those who lack any of the Humean virtues—are not functioning in the manner they *ought* to be. Thus, the pattern of normative evaluation of others as virtuous or vicious that Hume endorses does not vary with the desires of the subject being evaluated in the manner one would expect if Hume endorsed a desire-based or instrumentalist account of reasons for action. For Hume, the absence of certain moral responses counts against one practically, whatever one's background set of desires and preferences. And so, although it may not be contrary to *Humean reason* (in the sense of demonstrative and probable inference) "to prefer the destruction of the whole world to the scratching of my finger," there certainly are *good reasons* not to do so—that is, considerations which men who are fully rational *in the substantive sense of being responsive to all the reasons for action* will be responsive to.[47]

In this way, Hume would readily accept that there are many non-Humean considerations that an agent ought to be responsive to in deciding what to do. Or, in other words,
there are many non-Humean considerations to which a virtuous agent, in Hume's sense,
will be responsive. In considering this last way of capturing Hume's views about these
issues, it is crucial to remember that Hume uses terms like "virtue" very expansively.
In particular, it is clear that Hume means his account of virtue and vice to apply not
just to the moral virtues in a narrow sense, but also to qualities like prudence or wisdom, which we today would generally be inclined to view as manifestations not of good
moral character, but rather of *practical or epistemic rationality*.[48] Thus, Hume intends his
account of virtue and vice to provide the outlines of an account, not just of the moral virtues in a narrow sense, but rather of meritorious character traits of *any* kind, including
those that we today would group together under the headings of practical and epistemic
rationality.

In this way, for Hume, being properly responsive to practical reasons is one aspect
of what it is to be virtuous in his expansive sense of the term. As such, Hume's understanding of the relationship between reasons for action and morality is actually much
closer to that of contemporary virtue ethicists like Philippa Foot than it is to the instrumentalism that has taken up Hume's name.[49] In particular, once we translate Hume's
views about how we ought to feel and act into the contemporary idiom of "reasons for
action," we can see that Hume would agree with these virtue-ethicists that the question
of whether someone has been responsive to her reasons for action cannot be separated
from the evaluation of this responsiveness as virtuous or vicious. Thus, Hume would
join these theorists in denying that there is any *normatively authoritative* standard of
practical rationality that is fully independent of the standards of virtue and vice.[50]

Of course, Hume would give a very different account of the origins of our standards
of virtue and vice than the account offered by contemporary neo-Aristotelians. After
all, Hume has no interest in the project of grounding facts about virtue and vice in an
Aristotelian conception of human nature or an Aristotelian conception of man's proper
function. Rather, according to Hume, for a character trait to be a virtue is just for us to
approve of this character trait in a certain sort of way when we view it from a certain
point of view.[51] More precisely, for Hume a character trait is a virtue just in case it is
approved of by the moral sense when viewed from what Hume describes as the "general
point of view."[52] Thus, for Hume, a consideration will be something that we ought to be
responsive to just in case being responsive to it is something that elicits our passionate
approval when such responsiveness is viewed from the general point of view. In this way,
remembering the expansive sense in which Hume speaks of virtue, we can extract from
Hume's account of virtue and the moral sense an implicit (and admittedly very rough)
account of when some consideration should be considered a normative reason for an
agent to act:

(REASONS) Some consideration C is a reason for X to A just in case the moral sense
approves of X's A'ing being positively responsive to (the belief that) C when we view
this behavior from a reflective "general point of view."[53]

For the reasons already noted, I believe that something like this principle provides the most natural way to translate contemporary talk about reasons into Hume's own discussion of the various "virtues" and "vices" that make up good Humean character.[54] Crucially, although the account of reasons for action that follows from REASONS is not Humean in the traditional sense, it is deeply rooted in the passions in two important respects. First, according to REASONS, it is our passionate responses of approval and disapproval that determine what is or is not a reason for someone to act. And second, although REASONS does not generate a fully desire-dependent account of reasons for action, it does produce an account according to which an agent's passions will often play a large role in determining what she has reason to do. For, as Hume often stresses, whether we approve of some response in a particular individual from the "general point of view" will be heavily influenced by that individual's own passionate makeup. Thus, although REASONS is not a fully Humean account, it is an account according to which there is a good deal of "subject-sensitivity" (in the sense of this term familiar from contemporary epistemology) built into our understanding of reasons for action.[55] For, on this account, what I have reason to do will often differ from what you have reason to do precisely because of differences in our passionate makeup.

As I have already noted, there is much in this account of reasons for action that is similar to contemporary virtue-theoretical accounts of these issues. But Hume's views about these questions are, in one important respect, far more radical than the views of most such theorists. In particular, one of the central lessons of Hume's discussion of the place of reason in the theoretical and practical spheres is that the faculty of reason *as such* has no intrinsic normative authority in *either* case. This is clearest, of course, in Hume's discussion of the manner in which reason completely undermines itself when it reflects on the question of its own reliability.[56] As the conclusion of Book 1 of the *Treatise* makes clear, Hume believes that it is only possible to avoid the skeptical consequences of this fact by rejecting the idea that *all* the operations of the faculty of reason should be *equally* authoritative with respect to the question of what we ought to believe. Instead, if we are to avoid both skepticism and the dull rejection of all reasoning as such, we must allow the operations of our reason to be guided and moderated by the more sensitive parts of our nature—including the passions of curiosity and ambition.

In this way, the single most important upshot of Hume's discussion of reason in the theoretical sphere is the denial that there is any sort of universal or necessary connection between what our *faculty of reason* approves of and what we have normative *reason to believe*. For the second, normative question cannot be settled by any appeal to the operations and standards of the faculty of reason alone. As we have just been discussing, much the same is true in the practical case as well. For, as we have just seen, one of the primary purposes of Hume's discussion of reason in the practical sphere is to systematically undermine the idea that the faculty of reason should have any sort of special authority with respect to questions of how we ought to act. Rather, much as in the theoretical case, Hume believes that reason ought to play a role in determining what we do only insofar as its influence is moderated and guided by our passions and sentiments.

Thus, here, too, we find Hume severing the traditional connection between what our faculty of reason approves of and what we have normative reason to do.[57]

It seems to me that it is here, as much as anywhere else, that the historical significance of Hume's discussion of theoretical and practical reason rests. For the most fundamental difference of opinion between Hume and Kant on these issues is not a matter of how they conceive of the faculty of reason—although, of course, they do conceive of this faculty in quite different ways. Rather, what separates Hume from Kant most deeply on these issues is that Kant accepts, while Hume rejects, the traditional idea that the faculty of reason has a special sort of normative authority. In this respect, at least, Kant is thoroughly more traditional than Hume—for on this point it is clear where the weight of traditional opinion lies. After all, in their very different ways, the idea that the faculty of reason should have a special normative status is shared by figures as diverse as Plato, Aristotle, Aquinas, Descartes, Locke, and Kant. And, more importantly for present purposes, this is also an assumption that is shared by most contemporary Humeans as well. In this way, the most radical aspect of Hume's discussion of reason is the quite simple and radical idea that the question of what we ought to believe and how we ought to act is *never* settled by what our faculty of reason (on its own) approves of.[58] It is this general challenge to the authority of reason, as much as Hume's discussion of (say) the concept of a cause, that sets the stage for Kant's attempt to answer his famous questions *quid juris*. For Kant is concerned with this question—not just with respect to this or that particular concept—but also with respect to the use of our faculty of reason *in general* in both the theoretical and practical spheres. But that is a story for another time.

Abbreviations of Works Cited

DP   *A Dissertation on the Passions*. In T. Beauchamp, ed. *A Dissertation on the Passions; The Natural History of Religion*. Oxford: Clarendon Press, 2008.

EM   *Enquiry Concerning the Principles of Morals*. Edited by Tom L. Beauchamp. Oxford: Clarendon, 1998.

SBN   *A Treatise of Human Nature*, Edited by L. A. Selby-Bigge, 2nd edition revised by P. H. Nidditch, Oxford: Clarendon Press, 1975.

T   *A Treatise of Human Nature*. Edited by D. F. Norton and M. J. Norton. Oxford: Clarendon, 2007.

Notes

1. For the sake of simplicity, I'll avoid speaking of "motivating reasons for action" and reserve the phrase "reasons for action" to capture claims about what some authors call "normative reasons for action." But if one prefers such terminology, one can regard HTM as a theory about the first of these sorts of reasons and HTR as a theory about the second.

2. The phrase "Humean Theory of Motivation" is used in a variety of different ways, leading to a good deal of unnecessary confusion. For instance, consider Michael Smith's (1994) version of the Humean theory of motivation. Smith does accept that a desire can only be *motivated* by a set of mental states that includes a prior desire. But, at the same time, he believes that a belief (plus background facts about rationality) can *give rise to* a new desire. Thus, for Smith, at least as I read him, not all cases of the latter are cases of the former—because motivation always involves a teleological element, which need not be present in every case in which one state gives rise to another. If this is correct, Smith accepts HTM only as applied to the special case of *motivation* in this restricted sense of the term. Still, if the reading given here is correct, Hume does not endorse the HTM even in this restricted sense.

3. To be clear, when I speak of practical reasons here and in what follows, I have in mind reasons for action—that is, what are sometimes referred to as "object-given" as opposed to "state-given" reasons for desire.

4. Many contemporary views that are influenced by these ideas contain significant non-Humean elements as well. For an important example, see Schroeder (2007). For the importance of the distinction between underived and derived desires see the discussion in Nagel (1974).

5. See the following discussion for some of the authors who have called this assumption into question.

6. In discussing these issues, I focus primarily on Hume's views as presented in the *Treatise*—although I will occasionally refer to his discussion of them in his later work. In part, this is the product of the fact that Hume's arguments concerning these questions are much more fully stated in the *Treatise* than they are elsewhere. But I also believe that Hume's views about these questions remain relatively constant throughout his lifetime. For some discussion of what is novel about Hume's later moral philosophy, see Baier (2008).

7. For a much more detailed discussion of these issues, see David Owen's essay in this volume.

8. For examples of this reading, see Bricke (1996), Mackie (1980), and Stroud (1977).

9. A point made nicely by Cohon (2008). Much of the following discussion draws on Cohon's important work on these issues.

10. Such a view, of course, need not insist that beliefs (on their own) never *cause* the formation of new desires—it need only insist that beliefs (on their own) never cause the formation of new desires in the manner that is characteristic of ordinary human *motivation*. Just how this distinction is drawn will vary somewhat from theory to theory, but, for the purposes of the discussion to follow, we need not settle on any particular account of it because the examples to be discussed are plainly instances of ordinary human motivation as Hume understands it. Thus, consideration of these cases is sufficient to refute the attribution of the HTM to Hume.

11. In this way, although much of Hume's discussion is concerned with what we would today call the functional role of ideas and passions, his conception of these perceptions as fundamentally "distinct existences" means that the functional characteristics and interconnections of these states must be regarded as contingent features of them. This is one way in which Hume's approach to these issues is quite different from the analytic functionalism about desire that one finds in, say, Smith (1994).

12. T 1.3.10.

13. And, unlike in the case of the "missing shade of blue," he offers these apparent counterexamples in describing the course of human motivation under *normal* conditions.

14. Although it is plain that Hume takes the most common form of human motivation to be motivation by pleasure and pain, I think it is also relatively clear that he accepts that other forms of human motivation exist. But this is not uncontroversial.

15. For other similar passages, see T 1.3.10.3/119–20, T 3.1.1.12/459, and T 2.3.9.7/439.

16. An interesting question of detail concerning Hume's account is whether the motivation of an action by a belief of this sort must always go *via* a direct passion of some sort. To me, the textual evidence suggests that it need not, but I will leave this question to the side here. For more discussion of this issue, see Cohon (2008) as well as Karlsson (2005).

17. This, of course, is not entirely uncontroversial. Unfortunately, there is no space here to discuss the nature of Humean perceptions in detail. For more discussion, see again David Owen's essay in this volume.

18. None of this means, of course, that we can't attribute to the human mind a general tendency to seek pleasure and avoid pain. After all, Hume does just this. But this general tendency would not considered a desire in the strict sense by Hume—nor would it necessarily be a desire in anything but a fairly trivial sense of this term.

19. One option here would be to restrict the claim that beliefs are "inert" to those beliefs that are the product of reason. (Compare Pigden (2009).) Unfortunately for this line of interpretation, Hume seems to treat any and all beliefs about pleasure and pain as equally capable of causing new desires, no matter what their source. What might be more plausible is restricting these claims to claims about beliefs that are the product of reason *alone*—which, given Hume's views about the role of experience in probable inference, would be limited to beliefs that we can arrive at via *deductive reasoning alone*. I think that Hume would probably agree that such beliefs are inert, but I believe that his claims about the inertness of reason extend beyond this point to include the points discussed later.

20. My treatment of these topics will be relatively brief—for a more detailed discussion of them, see David Owen's essay in this volume, with which I am in broad agreement on most of these issues. For excellent discussion of these issues, see chapter 3 of Cohon (2008) and Sayre-McCord (2008). Compare Karlsson (2005).

21. For helpful discussions of Hume's understanding of the faculty of reason, see Owen (2002) and Garrett (2005). Note that I follow these authors in taking Hume to use "reason" in a relatively unambiguous fashion throughout the *Treatise*. (For a dissenting view on this issue, see Baier (1991).)

22. In particular, he appears to regard this definition of reason as one that all parties to the debate should accept. And he takes his definition of reason to be a natural development of Locke's conception thereof.

23. So, for example, Kant would deny *both* that there is nothing to reason beyond a capacity for Humean demonstrative and probable inference *and* (in a sense) that every instance of demonstrative inference involves the discovery of a theoretical truth or falsehood. As such, he would deny both the equation of the first and second definitions of reason just noted *and* the equation of the second and third of these definitions.

24. Why exactly this is the case is a complicated question, although it is plain that it must in part be a product of impressions' high level of force and vivacity.

25. I've phrased this carefully to sidestep the vexed issue of whether impressions of reflection represent anything beyond themselves.

26. One of the most important questions in Hume interpretation is why Hume feels entitled to make this claim. For more on this issue, see Schafer (2013).

27. These arguments are often broken down into two distinct arguments—the "representation argument" and an argument by "division of the faculty of reason." In my brief comments here, for reasons of space, I have tried to emphasize the connections and commonalities between these two arguments.

28. Of course, this is not meant to suggest that there are brute metaphysical necessities lurking behind Hume's discussion of the faculty of reason. The fact that this is true of any instance of this faculty is, for Hume, a simple consequence of the manner in which we use the term "reason."

29. Of course, these further processes will then be the product of some faculty or tendency of the mind other than the faculty of reason, but it would be a mistake to conflate Hume's anti-rationalistic insistence that motivation involves *faculties* other than reason with the claim, characteristic of the HTM, that cognitive *states* alone cannot motivate.

30. Interestingly, on this point, Hume is actually more radical than many contemporary Humeans like Smith.

31. Interpreting these claims as claims about the causal powers of faculties also allows us to avoid some of Cohon's (2008) controversial claims about the intransitivity of the production relation.

32. See, in particular, Clarke (1706) and Wollaston (1724).

33. Thus, contrary to some noncognitivist interpretations of Hume, when Hume claims that "morals" are motivationally efficacious, he is, in the first instance, making a claim about our moral faculty and not a claim about the products of this faculty (however we understand them). For more on whether Hume should be read as an expressivist about moral discourse, see note 51.

34. This is, of course, an extremely compressed version of a much more complicated set of issues. Hopefully, it will give the reader a sense of the relevant line of thought here. (A fuller discussion of these issues would require careful attention to the phrase "derived from reason" in the context of both Hume's discussion of causality and his discussion of morality.)

35. For some examples of this reading of Hume, see (arguably) Williams (1981), Sobel (2001), Rawls (2000), and Darwall (1995).

36. For this point see, for example, Millgram (1995) and Hampton (1995).

37. For related arguments, see Setiya (2004), Zimmerman (2007), and Schafer (2008).

38. See Parfit (2011).

39. For further objections to the attribution of such a view to Hume see Setiya (2004), Zimmerman (2007), and Schafer (2008).

40. Compare Korsgaard (1986), as well Millgram (1995) and Hampton (1995).

41. Millgram (1995: 81).

42. Although, to be sure, the reading of these passages provided by Millgram (et al.) is much more consistent than the traditional Humean interpretation. Moreover, as will become clearer, I agree that Hume is a skeptic about "reasons for action" in the sense of "reasons for action" that builds a strong constitutive connection between reasons for action and *reasoning* (in a faculty-dependent sense) into the very notion of "reasons of action". But Hume's rejection of this view is, I think, best understood in terms of the rejection of a particular theory of *what reasons for action are*, as opposed to being a rejection of the very existence of reasons for action in general.

43. Millgram (1995) argues that Hume was forced into this sort of skepticism by an impoverished conception of the intentional content of the passions. For a reply to this argument, see Schafer (2008). See also Radcliffe (1997).

44. As astute readers will have noticed, this formulation is too crude in certain respects. But the basic idea is sufficient for our purposes here. Once again, I focus on reasons for action to avoid some delicate issues about different species of potential reasons for desire.

45. See Setiya (2004) and Schafer (2008) for further discussion of this issue.

46. EM 6.23–5/244.

47. Something very similar is true of many considerations that are not moral in a narrow sense of this term, such as prudential and aesthetic reasons of various sorts.

48. See the whole discussion of T 3.3.4 and, in particular, the lists at T 3.3.4.7–8; SBN 610–11. There, Hume mentions the following virtues (in a broad sense): industry, perseverance, patience, activity, vigilance, application, constancy, temperance, frugality, economy, resolution, wit, eloquence, and good humor. For further discussion of the epistemic case, see Schafer (2014).

49. For different versions of this conception of practical reason, see Foot (2001), McDowell (1998), Quinn (1993), and Setiya (2007).

50. Here, it is important not to be misled by Hume's discussion of the "interested obligation" to morality, which concerns the question of whether self-interest can *motivate* us to be moral.

51. See, in particular: "So that when you pronounce any action or character to be vicious, you mean nothing, but that from the constitution of your nature you have a feeling or sentiment of blame from the contemplation of it. Vice and virtue, therefore, may be compar'd to sounds, colours, heat and cold, which, according to modern philosophy, are not qualities in objects, but perceptions in the mind." (T 3.1.1.26; SBN 468)

   Passages like this one make it clear, I think, that there is a factual component to claims about vice and virtue for Hume. But this leaves open the question of whether such claims might, in addition, express certain passions or volitions. Thus, although I think it is relatively clear that Hume is not a "pure" expressivist about moral discourse, nothing I say here is meant to rule out the possibility that he accepts a form of "hybird expressism" on which moral terms sometimes express states that involves *both* a belief-like and passion-like component.

52. For an excellent discussion of just what the "general point of view" involves and how it differs from an ideal observer's point of view, see Sayre-McCord (1994).

53. It is worth noting here that it remains open for someone who accepts REASONS to interpret its reference to "approval" differently in, say, the epistemic and the practical cases. For example, whereas the moral virtue of a faculty is determined, for Hume, by its ability to stand up to the scrutiny of the moral sense, one might claim that the epistemic merit of the same faculty is determined by its ability to win the approval of the passions that Hume focuses on at the close of Book 1 of the *Treatise*—namely, the "intellectual passion" of curiosity or "the love of truth" from a reflective point of view. Such a view would allow one to derive several distinct species of "reasons for X" from the basic picture of "considerations one ought to be responsive to" sketched earlier.

54. For similar suggestions about how to translate Hume's views into the contemporary language of "practical reasons," see Setiya (2004), as well as the conclusion to Mason (2005).

55. For "subject-sensitive" views in epistemology, see Hawthorne (2004).

56. T 1.4.1.

57. This is why it seems to me to be a mistake to attempt to translate Hume into contemporary terms via a conception of normative reasons that focuses on *the faculty of reason*. For this would actually distort one of the main thrusts of Hume's arguments about these matters in a quite fundamental way. So, we should not, for example, translate Hume into contemporary terms via a principle like: (REASONS') Some consideration C is a reason for X to A just in case it is possible to move via *sound reasoning alone* from the belief that C to a motivation to A.

58. Of course, there are dissenting voices on this point in the tradition prior to Hume—but isn't that always the case?

BIBLIOGRAPHY

Baier, Annette. (1991). *A Progress of Sentiments*. Cambridge: Harvard University Press.

Baier, Annette. (2008). "Enquiry Concerning the Principles of Morals: Incomparably the Best?" in E. Radcliffe, ed., *A Companion to Hume*. Malden: Blackwell Publishing, 293–320.

Bricke, J. (1996). *Mind and Morality*. Oxford: Clarendon Press.

Clarke, Samuel. (1706/1897). *A Discourse Concerning the Unchangeable Obligations of Natural Religion, in British Moralists, being Selections from Writers Principally of the Eighteenth Century*, L. A. Shelby-Bigge, ed. Oxford: Clarendon Press, vol. 2.

Cohon, Rachel. (2008). *Hume's Morality*. Oxford: Oxford University Press.

Darwall, Stephen. (1995). *British Moralists and the Internal "Ought" 1640–1740*. Cambridge: Cambridge University Press.

Foot, Philippa. (2001). *Natural Goodness*, Oxford: Clarendon Press.

Garrett, Don. (2005). "Hume's Conclusions," in S. Traiger, ed., *The Blackwell Guide to Hume's Treatise*. Oxford: Blackwell, 151–176.

Hampton, Jean. (1995). "Does Hume Have an Instrumental Conception of Practical Reason?," *Hume Studies* 21, 57–74.

Hawthorne, John. (2004). *Knowledge and Lotteries*, Oxford: Oxford University Press.

Karlsson, Mikael. (2005). "The Influencing Motives of the Will," in S. Traiger, ed., *The Blackwell Guide to Hume's Treatise*. Oxford: Blackwell, 235–255.

Korsgaard, Christine. (1986). "Skepticism about Practical Reason," *Journal of Philosophy* 83 (1), 5–25.

Mackie, J. L. (1980). *Hume's Moral Theory*. London: Routledge.

Mason, Michelle (2005). "Hume and Humeans on Practical Reason," *Hume Studies* 31 (2): 347–378.

McDowell, John. (1998). *Mind, Value, and Reality*, Cambridge, MA: Harvard University Press.

Millgram, Elijah. (1995). "Was Hume a Humean?," *Hume Studies* 21, 75–93.

Nagel, Thomas. (1974). *The Possibility of Altruism*. Oxford: Oxford University Press.

Owen, David. (2002). *Hume's Reason*. Oxford: Oxford University Press.

Parfit, Derek. (2011). *On What Matters*. Oxford: Oxford University Press.

Pigden, Charles R. (2009). "If not Non-Cognitivism then What?" in Pigden, ed. *Hume on Motivation and Virtue*, New York: Palgrave Macmillan, 80–104.

Quinn, Warren. (1993). *Morality and Action*, Cambridge: Cambridge University Press.

Radcliffe, Elizabeth. (1997). "Kantian Tunes on a Humean Instrument: Why Hume is not Really a Skeptic About Practical Reason," *Canadian Journal of Philosophy* 27: 247–270.

Radcliffe, Elizabeth. (1999). "Hume on the Generation of Motives: Why Beliefs Alone Never Motivate," *Hume Studies* 25 (1–2): 101–122.

Rawls, John. (2000). *Lectures on the History of Moral Philosophy*. Cambridge: Harvard University Press.

Sayre-McCord, Geoffrey. (1994). "On Why Hume's 'General Point of View' Isn't Ideal—and Shouldn't Be," *Social Philosophy and Policy* 11(1): 202–228.

Sayre-McCord, Geoffrey. (2008). *Hume on Practical Morality and Inert Reason*. In Russ Shafer-Landau (ed.), Oxford Studies in Metaethics: Volume III. Oxford: Oxford University Press.

Setiya, Kieran. (2004). "Hume on Practical Reason," *Philosophical Perspectives* 18, 365–389.

Setiya, Kieran (2007). *Reasons Without Rationalism*, Princeton: Princeton University Press.

Schroeder, Mark. (2007). *Slaves of the Passions*. Oxford: Oxford University Press.

Smith, Michael. (1994). *The Moral Problem*. Oxford: Blackwell.

Schafer, Karl. (2008). "Practical Reasons and Practical Reasoning in Hume," *Hume Studies* 34 (2), 189–208.

Schafer, Karl. (2013). "Hume's Unified Theory of Representation," *European Journal of Philosophy* 21(3).

Schafer, Karl. (2014). "Curious Virtues in Hume's Epistemology," *Philosopher's Imprint* 14(2): 1–20.

Sobel, David. (2001). "Subjective Accounts of Reasons for Action," *Ethics* 111 (2001): 461–492.

Stroud, Barry. (1977). *Hume*. London: Routledge.

Williams, Bernard. (1981). "Internal and External Reasons," in *Moral Luck*. Cambridge: Cambridge University Press, 101–113.

William, Wollaston (1724/1897). *The Religion of Nature Delineated, in British Moralists, being Selections from Writers Principally of the Eighteenth Century*, L. A. Shelby-Bigge, ed. Oxford: Clarendon Press, vol. 2.

Zimmerman, Aaron. (2007). "Hume's Reasons," *Hume Studies* 33 (2), 211–256.

....

CHAPTER 19

HUME, FREE WILL, AND MORAL RESPONSIBILITY

....

TONY PITSON

HUME's discussions of liberty and necessity are often cited as classic expressions of compatibilism or reconciliationism regarding the notions of freedom and determinism. But, quite apart from whether this is a fair representation of Hume's position, there is a danger here of ignoring the distinctive contribution to that position of central themes of Hume's philosophy more generally. These include his accounts of causation, of the basis for the distinction between virtue and vice, and of the nature and structure of the self; and also his naturalistic response to philosophical skepticism. We will see that when Hume's treatment of liberty and necessity is considered from this wider perspective, it reveals many features that provide striking points of contact with contemporary discussions of free will and moral responsibility. In doing so, it also promises to provide a more robust conception of what it is to be a free and responsible agent than might be expected from any standard form of compatibilism. Before proceeding to this aspect of Hume's position, however, I begin by looking in some detail at the position itself, as it emerges from Hume's discussions of liberty and necessity.

I HUME ON LIBERTY, NECESSITY AND MORAL RESPONSIBILITY

....

I.1 Hume on Liberty and Necessity

What, then, does Hume have to say about liberty and necessity in the *Treatise* (T 2.3.2–3) and first *Enquiry* (EU 8)? The outlines, at least, are familiar. On the one hand, Hume is an advocate of necessity as a feature of both the natural world and also the moral world of human action. At the same time, Hume recognizes a conception of liberty that is consistent with the view that our actions are necessitated or determined and that provides the basis for regarding us as morally responsible agents. This conception of liberty, however, is to be distinguished from the scholastic doctrine of free will (T 2.1.10.5/312), which equates liberty with *indifference* of the will. Let us then look more closely at Hume's position beginning with what he says about liberty.

I.1.1 *Liberty*

Hume recognizes that an important argument on behalf of the notion of liberty of indifference is provided by an appeal to introspection and the experience associated with performing an action that is not compelled or constrained.[1] Hume, however, dismisses this appeal to ordinary experience, not because it is inappropriate to consult the sense or understanding of nonphilosophers, but simply because the claimed experience provides no real evidence of the existence of liberty of indifference. In fact, we have only a "false sensation of liberty," one that makes us imagine that whatever voluntary action we perform, we could have done otherwise—or, in other words, that the will itself is undetermined or "subject to nothing" (T 2.1.10.9/314; T 2.3.2.2/408). If we attempt to demonstrate this liberty of indifference by performing some capricious or irregular action, this evidently fails to show that we could have so acted when we were *not* motivated by the "fantastical desire of showing liberty" (EU 8.22, n18/94). We are in the grip of an illusion here arising from our ability to imagine willing an alternative action from the one performed, as if this showed that the will really is indifferent between the one action and the other. Hume stresses the difference, in this context, between the first- and third-person perspectives: while the former reflects the supposed feeling of liberty of indifference, the latter assumes that our actions may be inferred from our motives and character, provided that our circumstances and nature are sufficiently well known.

Hume's repudiation of free will, as involving liberty of indifference, does not prevent him from ascribing to us a certain kind of freedom or liberty: what he refers to in the *Treatise* as "liberty of spontaneity" (T 2.3.2.1/407). The contrast Hume draws between the two kinds of liberty he has distinguished amounts to this: that indifference is opposed to causation or necessity, whereas spontaneity is opposed to "violence."[2] In other words, I am free in the former sense to the extent that my voluntary actions are undetermined and, in the latter sense, to the extent that nothing prevents me from doing what I want to do or forces me to act contrary to my wants.

The difference between the two notions of liberty is all-important. The idea of liberty of indifference amounts to a form of incompatibilism regarding freedom and determinism. If the will is "indifferent" or uncaused in its operations, then our voluntary actions are not determined. Liberty of spontaneity, on the other hand, appears to be consistent with determinism: being able to act in accordance with our wants or choices does not exclude the possibility that they themselves are determined. The doctrine of liberty to which Hume refers critically throughout his discussion in T 2.3.2 is plainly that of liberty of indifference; it is equivalent to the idea of free will. In his discussion of liberty in section 8 of the first *Enquiry*, Hume is more anxious to stress the point that there is an idea of liberty on which we are all agreed and that does not prevent us from also applying the doctrine of necessity to the actions of the will; hence, his description of what he is doing as a "reconciling project with regard to the question of liberty and necessity" (EU 8.23/95). The idea of liberty Hume has in mind "can only mean *a power of acting or not acting, according to the determinations of the will*" (Hume's emphasis).[3] Hume refers to liberty, so characterized, as "hypothetical."

I.1.2 *Necessity*

Leaving aside the question of the relation between liberty of spontaneity and "hypothetical" liberty, the crucial point remains that although these conceptions of liberty allow for the compatibility of free action with determinism (or "necessity"), liberty of indifference clearly does not. According to the conceptions of liberty endorsed by Hume, whether we act freely depends on how the action is caused. Is it a product of our own volition or of "violence" in the form of constraint or coercion? It is a question of the *way* in which the action is necessitated or determined, not of the absence of any such causal influence.

Hume recognizes that we might well think otherwise and attempts to account for this from the perspective of his account of causal necessity (in T 1.3.14 and EU 7) and the new definition of "necessity" to which this gives rise. A central theme of Hume's discussion of liberty and necessity in the first *Enquiry* is that "all men have ever agreed in the doctrines both of necessity and liberty . . . and that the whole controversy has hitherto turned merely upon words" (EU 8.3/81). Hume attempts to illustrate this through his definitions of the crucial terms involved, with the emphasis on his account of necessity.[4] His strategy in establishing the truth of determinism as an account of human action is to begin with the necessity exhibited by the operation of bodies (EU 8.4/82; T 2.3.1.2/399). The gist of this account is that the idea of cause and effect arises from our experience of the constant conjunction of certain objects or events and that the resulting idea of causal necessity is nothing but the determination of the mind to infer the existence of one such object from that of the other (EU 8.5/82; T 2.3.1.4/400). The next step is to establish that a similar account may be given of our actions and the causes from which they typically proceed. According to Hume, a "general view of the common course of human affairs will be sufficient" to confirm this (T 2.3.1.5/401). In sum, "There is a general course of nature in human actions, as well as in the operations of the sun and the climate" (T 2.3.1.10/402; cf. EU 8.7–9/83–5).

Hume recognizes that his claim about the uniformity of human actions is liable to be disputed. The actions of human beings often appear wayward and at odds with their known characters and dispositions. Although "Necessity is regular and certain," it appears that "Human conduct is irregular and uncertain" (T 2.3.1.11/403). Hume's response is to note that apparent irregularities also occur in the operations of nature but that, when we approach this as philosophers, we are prepared to ascribe this to our imperfect knowledge of these operations. We do so while acknowledging that natural events may be governed in these cases by "contrary and conceal'd causes" (T 2.3.1.12/404; cf. EU 8.13/87). According to Hume, similar considerations apply in the case of human behavior; in this respect, physical nature and human nature are on a par. And, just as the uniformity we find in nature enables us to make inferences about objects or events that lie beyond our immediate experience, so "this experienced uniformity in human actions is a source, where we draw *inferences* concerning them" (EU 8.16/88; Hume's emphasis). Thus, in addition to natural evidence, we are also provided with a kind of moral evidence about human actions derived from a consideration of people's "motives, temper and situation." This enables us to arrive at conclusions about the actions of others in ordinary life, as well as in such spheres as politics, war, and commerce (T 2.3.1.15/405; EU 8.7–9/83–5; EU 8.17–18/89–90). The affinity between the two kinds of evidence, natural and moral, is illustrated by the way that they may provide a single chain of argument derived from the same principles (T 2.3.1.17/406–7; EU 8.19/90–1).

If we have failed to acknowledge the application of the doctrine of necessity to human actions, then Hume has a ready diagnosis. In brief, although we do not feel any necessary connection between motive and action, we have a propensity to suppose that we do perceive a connection of this kind between causes and effects in the natural world (EU 8.21/92). This is at least part of the reason why Hume stresses the importance of his "new definition" of necessity for his treatment of the issues involved here (TA 34/661). There is also the point that the doctrine of necessity, as it applies to human behavior, might be thought damaging to religion and morality (T 2.3.2.3/409; EU 8.26/96). According to Hume, however, far from this being so, both liberty and necessity, as he understands these notions, are essential to these institutions—and, in particular, to the practices of reward and punishment, with their presumption that human beings are accountable for their actions both to each other and even to God (T 2.3.2.5–6/410–11; EU 8.28–31/97–9). Reward and punishment function as motives that have a regular and uniform influence on the mind, in accordance with the doctrine of necessity. At the same time, liberty of the spontaneous or "hypothetical" kind is essential to morality because human actions give rise to praise and blame only in so far as they proceed from internal qualities of the agent rather than from "external violence" (EU 8.31/99).

I.2 Hume and Moral Responsibility

So far, we have considered some basic aspects of Hume's accounts of liberty and necessity and his attempt to establish not only that these notions are mutually consistent, when properly understood, but also that both are essential to morality and to the practices of praise and blame, reward and punishment. The time has now come to look more closely at the implications of Hume's compatibilism for his view of moral responsibility. We know, roughly, what it is on Hume's account for an action to be free (i.e., that it is a product of our choice or volition rather than external constraint). But under what circumstances is the agent to be considered morally responsible for his action as an instance of virtue or vice? It seems evident that not every action that is free in accordance with the notion of liberty of spontaneity or "hypothetical" liberty is subject to moral appraisal. Many of our voluntary actions appear to be free of moral implications. As we shall see, the question about moral responsibility is equivalent, for Hume, to the question of the circumstances under which someone's action is liable to give rise to moral approbation or disapprobation.

Hume, as a moral sense theorist, regards approbation and disapprobation as *sentiments* that occur in association with the indirect passions.[5] Thus, virtue and vice, according to Hume, are attended with the same circumstances as those in which pride and humility, love and hatred, are excited (T 3.1.2.5/473). In fact, virtue as a mental quality is equivalent to the power of producing love or pride, and vice to the power of producing humility or hatred (T 3.3.1.3/575). So far as the moral sentiments are concerned, the impression arising from virtue is agreeable or pleasurable, whereas that arising from vice is painful or "uneasy" (T 3.1.2.2/471). This reflects Hume's view of virtue and vice themselves as mental qualities of agents that, in the former case, are a source of pleasure or benefit either to their possessor or to those affected by her actions, and, in the latter case, are a source of pain or uneasiness to the subject or to others. The distinction between virtue and vice is founded in the resulting moral sentiments, bearing in mind that, on Hume's account, these sentiments, as distinctive forms of pleasure and pain, arise only when agents and their moral qualities are considered from a general point of view and not simply from that of our own particular interests (T 3.1.2.4/472; EM 5.42/228; EM 9.6/272; EM 9.8/274). Hume even identifies the pleasure or pain arising from the general survey of any action or quality of mind with its virtue or vice, whereas the approbation or blame we feel is declared to be "nothing but a fainter . . . love or hatred" (T 3.3.5.1/614).

Hume appears, then, to be offering the following account of what it is for an agent to be morally responsible for his action: namely, that the action is an instance of virtue or vice considered as a quality of the agent conducive to pleasure or pain; that we respond to this quality with pleasurable or painful sentiments belonging to the indirect passions of love or pride, hatred or humility; and that these sentiments, in turn, are associated with the moral sentiments of approbation or disapprobation. A crucial consideration is that for an action to elicit the moral sentiments it must be connected to the agent in a certain kind of way. Beyond the bodily movements involved, it must be an *intentional* action, for an intention reveals qualities that endure beyond the action itself and thereby connect it with something durable in the agent (T 2.2.3.4/349). In Hume's terms, for someone to be considered responsible for an action, that action must "infix" itself upon him by having some cause in his character or disposition (T 2.3.2.6/411; T 3.3.1.4, 5/575; EU 8.29, 31/98, 99). Our judgment that the person is thereby responsible for what he has done rests in the sentiments to which his action gives rise. In this sense, we may be said to *feel* that he is responsible, whereas his *being* morally responsible is to be understood in relation to the sentiments that provide our response to his action when it is related to him in the right kind of way.[6]

A comparison may be drawn here with one of the more important recent contributions to the topic of freedom and responsibility, namely, that of Peter Strawson.[7] The essence of Strawson's account of moral responsibility is that this notion may be understood only by attending to reactive attitudes and feelings like gratitude and resentment; for, according to Strawson, such attitudes and feelings are intrinsic to the sense of freedom and responsibility we feel in ourselves and attribute to others.[8] Strawson also refers to our morally reactive attitudes, such as the moral indignation we may feel on behalf of another as a vicarious analogue of resentment. In addition, there are self-reactive moral attitudes, such as feeling obliged or guilty, that reflect demands made on us by others. Strawson thus appeals to the "moral sentiments" as providing the basis for the distinction we draw between those cases in which agents are considered responsible for their actions and those in which they are not or at least not fully so.[9]

Hume's own account of the way in which the moral sentiments arise from our experience of the beneficial or harmful consequences of people's actions makes reference to passions belonging to the reactive attitudes to which Strawson refers. Thus, moral approbation is associated not only with love as an indirect passion, but also such positive attitudes as gratitude, admiration, and esteem; moral disapprobation, conversely, is attended with hatred, anger, and other such negative attitudes as resentment, indignation, contempt, and disgust. These different attitudes reflect the fact that we respond to beneficial or harmful actions as they affect others as well as ourselves. So far as the moral sentiments are concerned, it appears that, for Hume, they are a sympathetic analogue of the participant reactive attitudes, distinguished by the fact that they are experienced from a relatively unbiased and disinterested point of view (T 3.1.2.11/475–6; T 3.3.1.15, 23/581–2, 587; EM 5.42/229).

In the case of the self-reactive attitudes—feeling obliged, remorseful, and the like—we are reminded of the significance for Hume of our concern with *reputation* (T 3.2.2.27/501; EM 8.11/265) as manifested in our "constant habit of surveying ourselves, as it were, in reflection" (EM 9.10/276). We are able imaginatively to view ourselves as we appear to others, as well as considering others as they feel themselves, as part of the process of sympathy by which the sentiments of those around us become our concern (T 3.3.1.26/589). One's character is favorably regarded by others in so far as it manifests the social virtues; and this is also the basis for peace of mind, to the extent that self-survey is bearable only for someone who displays a regard for mankind and society (T 3.3.6.6/620). This aspect of self-concern enables Hume to account for the self-reactive attitude of feeling obliged to act in a certain kind of way. Thus, Hume refers to the person who performs an action from a sense of duty because he lacks a virtuous motive that is common in human nature and hates himself on this account (T 3.2.1.8/479).[10]

An important aspect of Strawson's position as one that locates moral responsibility in the reactive attitudes and feelings is that it provides a response to *skepticism* about the very possibility of freedom and responsibility.[11] This might be compared with what Hume himself has to say in other contexts where skeptical arguments arise. In his well-known discussion of belief in the existence of body, for example, Hume distinguishes between the questions of what it is that causes us to have this belief and whether or not the belief is true. The latter question is one that it is "in vain to ask" (T 1.4.2.1/187). We cannot help but take for granted that bodies exist no matter the arguments by which the skeptic might seek to undermine the belief. As Hume puts it in the first *Enquiry*, we are carried by "a natural instinct" to repose faith in our senses; belief in an independent and external world is not a product of reason and, indeed, carries no rational evidence with it (EU 12.7/151). The antidote to skepticism is provided not by philosophical argument but by the propensities to belief that belong to human nature. "Nature, by an absolute and uncontrollable necessity has determin'd us to judge as well as to breathe and feel" (T 1.4.1.7/183). This provides the model for those who would doubt the reality of moral distinctions for no one could seriously believe that all characters and actions are alike (EM 1.2/169–70). The distinction between virtue and vice is made by nature in so far as it is founded on the original constitution of the mind (EM 5.3/214). Thus, it is impossible to deny all distinctions of manner and behavior: there are many qualities to which even the most determined skeptic cannot fail to respond with praise and approval (and, we might add, the full range of reactive attitudes described earlier). But, to the extent that all this is true, we will recognize people as being responsible for their actions when they are the product of certain qualities of character, whatever the skeptical arguments of some philosophers.[12]

I.3   Responsibility and Excusing or Extenuating Conditions

I now turn to Hume's account of those circumstances under which a person is not praised or blamed for his action and, to this extent, not considered responsible for it, even when that action may have beneficial or harmful consequences of a kind that would normally generate the moral sentiments. Although Hume refers only rather briefly to the various kinds of circumstance in which we withhold, or at least qualify, ascriptions of responsibility, it is clear that they fall into a number of interestingly different categories. First, there are those cases in which someone is subject to violence or constraint and is thus prevented from acting in accordance with his choice or volition. Apart from the example of the person who is imprisoned or in chains (EU 8.23/95) and thus prevented from escaping his confinement, there is the interesting case of the man who is unable to act because he is suddenly struck with a palsy (EU 7.13/66).[13] We should also note the rather more problematic example of "violence" in which someone is acting under duress. Even if this person is choosing to act as instructed, he is presumably not exercising the kind of liberty required for him to be held responsible or at least not fully so. From a Humean perspective, what he is being forced to do is not a reflection of the kind of person we know him normally to be.

Second, there is the case of subjects who appear to lack the capacity for the kind of agency necessary for moral responsibility. "'Tis commonly allow'd that mad-men have no liberty" (T 2.3.1.13/404).[14] Their actions lack the kind of regularity that would enable us to ascribe to them any durable or constant qualities of character. In this respect, their actions are further removed from necessity than those of the ordinary agent. It seems clear that the category of the nonmoral agent would have to be extended to include non-human animals and young children.[15] Hume seems committed to denying that animals are moral agents even when they engage in the same relations which, in human beings, would be condemned as wrong and even criminal. This, at least, is the message that might be taken from Hume's discussion of animal incest and his claim that such rela-tions in animals "have not the smallest moral turpitude and deformity" (T 3.1.1.25/467). A similar point evidently applies also to plants (T 3.1.1.24/467). These kinds of case remind us of the distinction to be drawn between those who lack the capacity for mor-ally responsible agency and those who possess the capacity but whose actions may in certain cases fail to give rise to either praise or blame.[16]

Third, there is the category of actions in which ascriptions of responsibility may be withheld on account of factors such as ignorance or accident. Thus, according to Hume, people are not blamed for "evil" actions that are performed ignorantly and "casually" (T 2.3.2.7/412; EU 8.30/98). Ignorance plays a part in Hume's illustration of the distinc-tion between a mistake of fact and a mistake of right. When Oedipus killed Laius, he did so in ignorance of the fact that he had killed his own father. This is to be contrasted with Nero's killing of his mother, Agrippina, in full awareness of their relation to each other (EM App. 1.12/290). So far as the case of "casual" or accidental actions is concerned, Hume suggests that "A man, who wounds and harms us by accident, becomes not our enemy upon that account, nor do we think ourselves bound by any ties of gratitude to one, who does us any service after the same manner" (T 2.2.3.3/348).

Of course, matters are not quite so straightforward: as Hume goes on to acknowledge, "men often fall into a violent anger for injuries, which they themselves must own to be entirely involuntary and accidental," even if such anger is not sustained (T 2.2.3.6/350). But there is a more important problem. If, while cleaning your gun you inadvertently fire it in my direction, I might well condemn you for carelessness even while recogniz-ing that any resulting injury was caused by accident. Evidently, some accidents are more blameworthy than others. But leaving aside cases of this kind, we can see that there may be acts of inadvertent or accidental wounding in which no blame attaches to the agent given the absence of any intention to cause injury and the difficulty of foreseeing any such outcome.

Hume also refers to hasty or unpremeditated actions as ones in which less blame attaches to the agents than would be so if any harmful consequences had been foreseen and intended (T 2.3.2.7/412). In contrast to cases of the previous kind, the agent is still considered to a degree responsible and blameworthy, but to a lesser extent than if his "evil" action had been performed with deliberation and forethought. Although Hume does not spell this out, we clearly need to distinguish between cases in which a person is excused responsibility for an "evil" action altogether and others in which responsibility is mitigated by extenuating circumstances. Nor is this the only kind of distinction that might be drawn here. Someone may, for example, admit that his action would normally be considered blameworthy but claim that it was, in the circumstances, justified or at least permissible—so accepting responsibility, but denying that what he did was wrong. Or again, someone might plead provocation as an excuse or perhaps justification for his action without disclaiming responsibility for it.[17] Evidently, the issues involved here are considerably more complex than Hume's rather cursory treatment of them would suggest.

There is a fourth and final, category of actions to be considered in this context: namely, ones that are followed at some point by repentance or a "change of life"—something that, according to Hume, "wipes off every crime," especially where there is evident reform (T 2.3.2.7/412). This reflects the fact that actions render a person criminal only in so far as they are proofs of criminal passions or principles. If a change of character really does occur, so that the agent is no longer motivated by such passions or principles, then he ceases to be morally responsible for his past criminal actions. In other words, he would cease to be blameworthy for these actions or to be punishable for them. Thus, continued responsibility requires more than merely that the *same person* is still involved, although to the extent that this is so we might also think that it would be appropriate for this person to make restitution for what is, after all, his past offence.[18]

The rationale for these various kinds of case in which, according to Hume, persons are excused responsibility for their actions lies in the crucial distinction between an action and its causes—in particular, those that relate to the mind of the agent. As we have seen, on Hume's account, what is required for a person to be responsible for his action is that it should proceed from some durable feature of his character. Even when an action is contrary to the rules of morality, the agent is held responsible for it only to the extent that his action reflects some trait of character that arouses hatred and disapprobation in the spectator (T 2.3.2.6/411). Strictly speaking, virtue and vice belong not to actions themselves but rather to the traits or dispositions they manifest. The agent is morally responsible, or liable to praise or blame, precisely where a beneficial or harmful action arises from this kind of internal cause rather than one that fails to reflect the kind of person the agent is. This position is summarized by Hume at various places: for example, T 3.3.1.4–5/575; and EU 8.29/98.

As for the question of why certain traits of character evoke the indirect passions and thus also the moral sentiments of approbation and disapprobation, this must be ascribed to the fact that the actions typically associated with those traits affect either the agent himself or others in ways that resonate with the spectator. In the *Treatise*, the spectator's response to those benefited by virtue or harmed by vice is explained by reference to the mechanism of sympathy (T 3.3.1.14–18/580–4; T 3.3.2.3/593; T 3.3.3.2/602–3). In the second *Enquiry*, on the other hand, Hume seems content to appeal to humanity, as "a concern for others" (EM 5.46/231), in explaining the spectator's engagement with those affected by the actions to which virtue and vice give rise. The important point is that Hume continues to hold that there is such a thing as fellow-feeling or a disinterested concern for others, even if he no longer wishes to identify some further principle or mechanism that would account for this (EM 5.17, n19/219, n1).

II ISSUES ARISING: FREE WILL AND MORAL RESPONSIBILITY

Hume's discussion of the debate surrounding free will ("liberty") and determinism ("necessity") is relevant to a variety of issues in the wider philosophical literature on this topic. Under the general heading of "moral responsibility," we might distinguish such particular ideas as those of autonomy, agent causation, character, and the self. But let us begin with the notion of moral responsibility itself.

I mentioned earlier the view implicitly repudiated by Hume that a person is a free agent only to the extent that whatever voluntary action he performs, he could, at the time in question, have chosen to act differently. Indeed, this appears to be what it is to have free will or what Hume refers to as liberty of indifference. Furthermore, this might be considered to provide a crucial condition for moral responsibility. Is the ordinary shoplifter not distinguished from the kleptomaniac precisely by the fact that the former *could* choose to act differently when the opportunity for stealing arises whereas the latter is *compelled* so to act? According to Hume, however, the idea that responsible agency consists in the ability to choose differently from the way one actually does is no more than an illusory product of the imagination. Yet there does appear to be a powerful intuition in favor of the assumption that we are free only in so far as we are able to choose between alternative courses of action, even if this commits us to rejecting a deterministic account of human agency.

Hume, to the contrary, argues that we may recognize the truth of determinism or necessity while retaining a legitimate idea of liberty: that of spontaneity or "hypothetical" liberty. It is important, therefore, that he should be in a position to reject the view that a person is morally responsible for what he has done only if he could, in that situation, have chosen to act differently.[19] He receives support, in this respect, from another important contribution to the recent literature on this topic, in which the principle of alternative possibilities as a condition for free and responsible action is rejected by appeal to counterexamples.[20] One such counterexample reflects the notion that human beings are distinguished by their ability to form second-order desires regarding those first-order desires that move them to action (Frankfurt 1971: 6–7). This enables us to recognize the possibility of a case such as that of the willing addict whose first-order desire to take the drug is overdetermined: the desire is effective both because of his physiological addiction but also because of his second-order desire that it should be so. In this way he is, according to Frankfurt (1971: 20), morally responsible for taking the drug in spite of the fact that he is prevented by his addiction from acting or desiring otherwise.

Rather than seek support for Hume's rejection of the alternative possibilities condition from Frankfurt-type counterexamples—ones that raise many controversial issues of their own—we may appeal to aspects of Frankfurt's position that bring us closer to that of Hume. Frankfurt's account of free will and moral responsibility focuses on the mind of the agent, his motives or the reasons for which he acts, and the extent to which the agent identifies with the desire that moves him to action. It is this kind of consideration, rather than what else the agent could have done in the circumstances, that is relevant to assessing the agent's responsibility for his action (Frankfurt 1971: 18–20). Now we might derive a moral of a broadly similar kind from Strawson's account of the conditions for moral responsibility. For the interpersonal reactive attitudes to which he refers are, as Strawson (1974: 14) himself makes clear, responses to the good or ill will reflected in the agent's conduct. In this respect, Strawson and Frankfurt might be said to share a "quality of will" thesis regarding the grounds of responsible agency.[21] Not only this, but we find here an important link with Hume's own view of what it is to be a morally responsible agent. This is illustrated by the fact that the kinds of excuse and exemption referred to earlier serve to relieve the agent of responsibility precisely because they provide cases in which his behavior is not the product of a blameworthy will or motivation to which we would respond with attitudes like indignation and moral disapproval.

II.1 Autonomy and Agency

We can now, then, consider Hume's position in light of various issues relating to the agent as the focus of moral praise and blame, beginning with the idea of autonomy.[22] We encounter here many ideas that are of interest from Hume's philosophical perspective: in particular, to do with the self, the relations among its passions or desires, the extent to which it is able to determine its own formation and the dispositions arising from it, and its self-directed reactive attitudes.

The autonomous agent might be thought of as the person whose actions are not the product of coercion or constraint: as someone who, to that extent, enjoys Hume's liberty of spontaneity. But reflection suggests that autonomy involves a good deal more than simply being able to do what one wants. It seems apparent, for example, that liberty of spontaneity provides a notion of agency that may be applied to nonhuman animals, as well as to human beings. Hume himself acknowledges that "the will and the direct passions" as they appear in animals "are of the same nature, and excited by the same causes as in human creatures" (T 2.3.9.32/448). Animals can therefore satisfy the condition for liberty of spontaneity, of being able to act in accordance with their desires and volitions unless prevented from doing so. Yet, it appears that, in the case of animals—and also young children—we are concerned with agents who are not held morally responsible for their actions.

There is another direction from which we might approach the point that the kind of autonomy required for moral agency transcends Hume's notion of liberty of spontaneity (or "hypothetical" liberty). One may, after all, be acting on wants that one would like to be able to resist; we might even refer here to the possibility of alienation from certain wants.[23] Again, the idea of desires by which the agent is constrained is a familiar one, as in the example of the kleptomaniac.[24] Even in this last case, however, we might want to distinguish between the subject who yields without reluctance to his shoplifting propensities and the one who attempts, perhaps in vain, to resist them. How far, then, is Hume able to accommodate this kind of distinction within an agent's wants or desires, between those that are embraced or identified with and those that are experienced as a constraint on behavior?

One aspect of Hume's discussion that bears directly on this question is the distinction he draws among our impressions of reflection between the *calm* and the *violent* passions (T 2.1.1.3/276; DP 5.2, 4).[25] This enables Hume to explain why some philosophers should mistakenly think that our mental lives are marked by a conflict between reason and passion, with the apparent implication that we are free and morally responsible agents only in so far as our actions proceed ultimately from reason or the understanding rather than passion. Because neither the calm passions nor reason as "actions of the mind" produce much "sensible emotion," we are apt to confound our calm desires—including "the general appetite to good, and aversion to evil"—with the determinations of reason (T 2.3.3.8/417; cf. T 2.3.4.1/418–9; T 3.3.1.18/583). Crucially, the calm passions "often determine the will" (T 2.3.3.9/417), and they may do so in opposition to a violent passion whose indulgence would run counter to our interests. Thus, we may identify "strength of mind"—the other side of the coin from weakness of will—precisely with the tendency of the calm passions to prevail over the violent (T 2.3.3.10/418; EM 6.15/239; DP 5.4), acknowledging, of course, that no one is immune to the influence of the latter. As Hume goes on to argue, it is therefore important not to confuse the distinction between the calm and the violent passions with that between passions that are weak and passions that are strong (T 2.3.4.1/418–9). Although violent passions generally have a more powerful influence on the will, it is often the case that we act in accordance with the calm passions when they are supported by reflection and resolution. This struggle between passion and reason, as it is often mistakenly characterized, not only marks off one person from another but also the same person at different times (T 2.3.8.13/438).

The idea that autonomy is associated with a certain kind of self-determination or self-mastery (Hume's "strength of mind") sometimes gives rise to talk of the "real" or "true" self as the responsible agent.[26] An extreme version of this view of free and responsible agency is provided by Chisholm in his version of Thomas Reid's doctrine of agent causation (i.e., that the agent is an uncaused cause of those decisions or actions that exhibit free will).[27] This appears to amount, in effect, to the idea of liberty of indifference rejected by Hume; it also falls foul of Hume's principle that "all causes are of the same kind" (T 1.3.14.32/171). But it does not seem that we have to go as far as the idea of agent causation, so understood, to attach some sense to the view that the human agent is capable of the kind of autonomy associated with self-determination or self-mastery. As we have seen, the latter, in Hume's terms, would consist in the predominance of the calm passions. The resulting quality of character, strength of mind, belongs to the category of the "personal" virtues, including those qualities useful to the person himself (EM 6.15/239). We praise the person who is capable of resisting the temptation of present pleasure in favor of more distant enjoyment, just as we also blame the person who fails to act in accordance with his perceived longer term interest.

All this has important implications for Hume's position in regard to autonomy and moral agency. Hume would have to reject any notion of self-determination that implies that it is a simple matter of choice for the agent which kinds of quality will be expressed in his action, and, accordingly, whether he will be the subject of praise or blame. This does not mean, however, that we are unable to exert any control over the motives or dispositions that underlie our voluntary actions. Even if the capacity to which Hume refers as "strength of mind" tends to vary in degree from one person to another, the same agent, on different occasions, may be more or less successful in exercising it. As for the idea of the "real" or "true" self being revealed in our praiseworthy or blameworthy actions, we should bear in mind that Hume recognizes different ways of thinking about the self corresponding to the distinction between personal identity "as it regards our thought and imagination, and as it regards the passions or the concern we take in ourselves" (T 1.4.6.5/253). For the purpose of Hume's view of moral responsibility, the crucial role is the one played by the latter aspect of personal identity: the self considered from this perspective is the one associated with a certain character and disposition.[28]

According to Hume, as we have seen, actions "infix" themselves on the agent so as to make him responsible for them only if they proceed from his character or disposition as something durable or constant (T 2.3.2.6/411).[29] We would expect, then, that if a person acts in a way that is out of character, Hume would hesitate, at least, to regard this as an action for which he is responsible (even though the action may be voluntary and uncoerced). This is illustrated by his claim that we are less blamed for hasty and unpremeditated actions because a hasty temper "infects not the whole character" (T 2.3.2.7/412). Again, we may seek to explain, rather than to blame, an uncharacteristic action, as in the case of the person of an obliging disposition who gives a peevish answer because he has toothache or has not dined (EU 8.15/88). On this view, unqualified judgments of moral responsibility are reserved for those cases in which we respond with praise or blame, approval or disapproval, as well as the associated indirect passions. As for the notion of autonomy, this would become a matter of how far the agent is susceptible to the calm, as well as the violent passions, and to that extent able either to resist or to acquiesce in his immediate desires or impulses.[30]

An important source of skepticism about moral responsibility lies with our apparent absence of choice as to the kinds of character we possess.[31] But, even if we did not originally *choose* our character, it does not follow that we are unable to change it in any respect. The possibility of a change in character for which the person himself is responsible seems to be implied in Hume's view, referred to previously, that repentance with evident reform "wipes off" past crimes. We should, however, distinguish here between being able to change one's character *directly*, simply by willing or choosing to do so, and being able to change it *indirectly*: for example, by holding in mind a model of the kind of character of which we approve and then allowing ourselves to be influenced by this model (Bricke 1984: 83–93). We can form a conception of a praiseworthy character, one which is a model of perfect virtue (EM 9.2/269–70; cf. EM 5.10/216). Provided that one is already "tolerably virtuous," it is possible to aspire to a character of this kind and, by its continued pursuit, bring about an alteration in one's own character (ESY 170).[32] This reflects the fact that the mind exhibits a degree of flexibility and that it is subject in particular to the influence of moral causes as "circumstances, which are fitted to work on the mind as motives or reasons, and which render a peculiar set of manners habitual to us" (ESY 198).

The "pessimist" to whom Peter Strawson refers is unlikely to be satisfied with this.[33] To achieve a change of character, we must already be disposed to be influenced by the factors that bear on our choice—and this in itself may not be something for which we could be considered responsible. On this basis, it may be claimed that if determinism is true—in accordance with Hume's own account of necessity—then we cannot justifiably regard ourselves as free and responsible beings. In particular, it is the impossibility of self-determinability, of our being *ultimately* responsible for the way we are, that prevents us from being morally responsible for the actions resulting from our character.[34] Even if we are psychologically incapable of giving up the practices associated with the reactive attitudes, the result will be a conflict of commitment: to the metaphysical truth, on the one hand, and to the reactive attitudes on the other.[35]

The premise that moral responsibility depends on the possibility of ultimate self-determination is common both to the kind of pessimism represented by Galen Strawson and also to certain forms of libertarianism.[36] In each case, this premise is used in support of an incompatibilist position; but whereas in the former it leads to the conclusion that we are incapable of "true" responsibility, in the latter it leads to the rejection of determinism in favor of the view that moral responsibility is a reality. Libertarianism based on the possibility of ultimate self-determination ascribes to us a contracausal freedom in which we are able to breach the continuity between character and conduct (Campbell 1966: 129). On this account, those of our actions that are a product of our character fail to exhibit free will or, hence, moral agency; in direct contrast to Hume's view, we are responsible only for those actions that do not arise in this way but rather are caused by the self when it transcends its character.

There is a further point of agreement between Galen Strawson's position and that of the libertarian. Strawson (1993: 91) recognizes that we do have a sense of ourselves as self-determining agents—one that derives from our ordinary intentional actions—and that this is, arguably, a source of our "natural" inclination toward incompatibilism. Campbell's libertarianism also appeals to the "inner standpoint" in developing the idea of self-determination (1966: 132); but, unlike Strawson, he takes our apparent consciousness of self-determining activity at face value and claims to find it only where we are *not* simply following the desires that belong to our character but rather resisting them from a sense of duty (1966: 130–131; 1957: 177). This, according to Campbell (1957: 170), provides "the phenomenological analysis that supports Libertarianism." It is, however, possible to provide a different account of the phenomenology of this kind of conflict—as in Hume's treatment of the circumstances in which we act from a sense of duty in opposition to our natural inclination (T 3.2.1.8/479). Here, the conflict is represented as one between a calm desire and an opposing violent passion. But, so regarded, it fails to provide an instance of the kind of self-determination that a libertarian like Campbell has in mind.

What of Galen Strawson's antilibertarian position: one that nevertheless concurs with libertarianism in rejecting the reconciliationist or naturalist account of our capacity for free and responsible action? Hume would evidently agree about the impossibility of ultimate self-determinability. Although he accepts that the self may be distinguished from its character to the extent that it may remain the same even where a change of character occurs, this is not to say that the self is capable of transcending character in the way envisaged by a libertarian like Campbell. It is also clear, however, that Hume would resist Galen Strawson's move from non–self-determinability to the impossibility of free and responsible action. The assumption is that if one's character originates in factors that are not themselves a matter of choice, it follows that one cannot be responsible for the actions that flow from that character. But however one's character originates, Hume has shown that it need not be experienced simply as something given, whose influence is beyond one's control. For this sort of reason, it may be argued that the causal origin of a person's character is not in itself relevant to our ascriptions of moral responsibility to the actions arising from it.[37]

Now this, by itself, might not be considered to meet the point that we do not, after all, really make ourselves the way we are—that this has to do with aspects of our heredity and environment that are beyond our control. To this extent, we cannot be considered *truly* responsible for what we do even if we find it difficult, if not impossible, to adopt a radically objective attitude either toward ourselves or others (Strawson 1993: 81).[38] It seems clear from Hume's treatment of theodicy in the final paragraphs of section 8 of the first *Enquiry* that he would be unable to take seriously a notion of "true responsibility" that would result in the view that human actions are devoid of any moral quality.[39] This is because the mind is so formed that we cannot help responding with the moral sentiments to certain characters and actions, especially when they have obvious social benefits or detriments. Any philosophical speculations that suggest that we are wrong to do so are unable to "counterbalance" these sentiments (EU 8.35/102). Hume draws from this an important moral about the nature of philosophy itself, namely, that, in order to escape from the "inextricable difficulties" to which such speculations give rise, philosophy must return to its "true and proper province," namely, "the examination of common life" (EU 8.36/103).[40] Hume's view of philosophy is expressed in the dictum that "philosophical decisions are nothing but the reflections of common life, methodized and corrected" (EU 12.25/162; cf. D 134). Although common life provides the data on which Hume's account of the passions and morals is based, philosophy, as Hume conceives of it, involves ordering and drawing conclusions from these data so that we arrive at the general principles of human nature (EM 5.43/230). The danger of philosophical speculation that departs from common life is that it subverts itself by depriving us of the evidence for any proposition (T 1.4.7.7/267) and leads to conclusions sufficiently remote from ordinary experience that we can no longer trust our common methods of argument (EU 7.24/72). Hume's own account of moral responsibility is thus rooted in our ordinary practices as the only context from which we might expect to derive any just or meaningful notion of "true" responsibility.[41]

III Conclusion

We have seen that Hume's account of liberty and necessity is intended to establish both that the doctrine of necessity applies to the actions of human beings, as well as to events in the natural world, and also that our actions may be free in a sense that allows for moral responsibility. The crucial requirement is that what we do should proceed from a certain kind of internal cause—namely, our character and the kinds of motive with which it is associated—rather than from any form of "violence." In the latter case, our actions fail to excite the moral sentiments, at least in any unqualified way, and this is tantamount to regarding us as being less than fully responsible for these actions or perhaps not responsible at all. On this view, moral responsibility is constituted by the practices associated with the moral sentiments and the indirect passions, and this provides a naturalistic response to skepticism about responsibility that may be compared with Hume's response to epistemological forms of skepticism. Hume's position eschews attempts to found moral responsibility in metaphysical notions, such as that of a substantial self that stands apart from its "perceptions." At the same time, however, it provides an idea of the self that explains how it may retain a kind of identity that allows for ascriptions of responsibility. It is the idea of a self with a certain structure among its perceptions: one that may be said to make someone the kind of person he or she is. This, in turn, enables us to understand what it is for a person to be a moral agent and to be the legitimate object of reward and punishment, praise and blame. What we have, then, is an account of freedom and responsibility that draws from important aspects of Hume's epistemology, as well as from the moral psychology embodied in his theory of the passions. It is an account that fully deserves to stand alongside contributions to the current vigorous debate surrounding the problem of free will.

Abbreviations of Works Cited

D   *Dialogues Concerning Natural Religion*. In D. Coleman, ed. *Dialogues Concerning Natural Religion and Other Writings*. Cambridge: Cambridge University Press, 2007.

DP   *A Dissertation on the Passions*. In T. Beauchamp, ed. *A Dissertation on the Passions; The Natural History of Religion*. Oxford: Clarendon Press, 2008.

EM   *Enquiry Concerning the Principles of Morals*. Edited by Tom L. Beauchamp. Oxford: Clarendon, 1998.

ESY   *Essays: Moral, Political, and Literary*. Revised edition by E. F. Miller. Indianapolis: Liberty Classics, 1985.

EU   *An Enquiry Concerning Human Understanding*. Edited by T. L. Beauchamp. Oxford: Clarendon, 2000.

LET   *The Letters of David Hume.* 2 Vols. Edited by J. Y. T. Greig. Oxford: Clarendon Press, 1932.

T   *A Treatise of Human Nature.* Edited by D. F. Norton & M. J. Norton. Oxford: Oxford University Press, 2000.

Notes

1. See, for example, King (1739: 322–323). Descartes (1986: 39) also claims to know by experience that the will is unrestricted. For some discussion of the philosophical background to the idea of liberty of indifference, see Norton and Norton, editors, *Treatise*, vol. 2, 865, annotations for T 2.3.2.2/408.

2. See Chambers's *Cyclopedia*, and the entry under "SPONTANEOUS": that is, "in the Schools, a term applied to such Motions of the Body and Mind as we perform of our selves, without any constraint. Thus, in Morality, Those Actions . . . excluding all Constraints but not excluding Necessity, are called *Spontaneous Actions*" (1728: 2.114).

3. Compare Locke: "the *Idea* of *Liberty*, is the *Idea* of a Power in any Agent to do or forebear any particular Action, according to the determination or thought of the mind" (1975: bk 2, ch. 21, sec. 8).

4. There are also indications in the *Treatise* discussion that the controversy concerning liberty and necessity has to do with the meanings of these words and their definitions: see T 2.3.1.2/399; T 2.3.1.16–18/406–7; T 2.3.2.4/409.

5. In each case, we are concerned with impressions of reflection, as Hume classifies them (T 2.1.1).

6. There is obviously a large question here about how we are to understand this notion of the "right kind of way." There is a further question as to whether the fact that an action is a product of the agent's character provides a sufficient explanation of what this way is. See Schauber (2009) for a discussion of these issues.

7. See Strawson (1974) and Strawson (1985). The comparison provides an important theme of Russell (1995); see, especially, chapter 5.

8. Strawson (1974: 23); Strawson (1985: 31).

9. Strawson (1974: 24); Strawson (1985: 31).

10. A further case in point is that of the person who is blamed for neglecting his children because it shows a want of natural affection "which is the duty of every person" (T 3.2.1.5/ 478). If Hume is right, then a parent who is not so motivated will come to feel badly about himself in light of the disapproval of others and so take care of his children out of a sense of obligation. Hume's view that acting from a sense of duty is a substitute for acting from a virtuous natural motive stands in contrast to what Kant (1963: 66) says about an action having genuine moral worth only when it is done for the sake of duty alone.

11. Strawson (1985: 32).

12. In Strawson's terms, the contrast that underlies skepticism regarding moral responsibility is between our ordinary participant reactive attitudes and the "objective" attitude in which we respond to others as subjects for treatment rather than as people to be praised and blamed, approved or disapproved (Strawson [1974: 9]; Strawson [1985: 34]). Although we tend to adopt this latter attitude only in certain special sorts of case, it might be thought that a theoretical conviction of the truth of determinism should lead to the adoption of the objective attitude toward *everyone*: we are all equally at the mercy of forces that prevent us from being considered morally responsible for our actions. According to Strawson

(1974: 11), however, even if we can make sense of this possibility, it is something that is *practically inconceivable* for us, given our commitment to ordinary interpersonal relationships and the reactive attitudes to which we are thereby exposed.

13. Palsy is "a disease, wherein the Body or some of its Parts, lose their Motion, and sometimes their Sensation" (Chambers 1728: 2.740).

14. Also worth noting in this context is Hume's reference to the possibility of someone being seized with a sudden and unknown frenzy—the human equivalent to an unpredictable event like a sudden earthquake (EU 8.20/91). This is not, however, a case of someone who is generally incapable of responsible agency.

15. So far as the latter are concerned, Hume refers to crimes being punished "when the person is come to the full use of reason" (T 3.2.8.9/548).

16. Cf. Strawson (1974: 7).

17. For more on these distinctions see Austin (1961: 123–125).

18. Hume allows that "the same person may vary his character and disposition, as well as his impressions and ideas, without losing his identity" (T 1.4.6.19/261).

19. Hume's "hypothetical" liberty does not require that the alternative of *choosing* to act differently should have been available: only that *if* such a choice had been made, then the agent would have been able to act accordingly.

20. See Frankfurt (1969: 835–836).

21. See McKenna (2005: 175). This kind of claim should not prevent us from recognizing the very different approaches of Strawson and Frankfurt to the issue of free will and moral responsibility: in particular, Strawson's concern with interpersonal reactive attitudes as a source of the moral sentiments in contrast to Frankfurt's emphasis on the agent's attitude toward his own motives as the determinant of his moral standing.

22. Although Hume does not use the term "autonomy" in his philosophical writings, the notion of self-government that it signifies is endorsed by Hume in reference to the secession of the American colonies (LET 2:303). The notion of autonomy thus also connects with our ascriptions of freedom and responsibility to individual agents whose behavior exhibits the capacity for self-control. In this respect, our ordinary thinking about both ourselves and others as agents reveals an intuitive idea of autonomy, although it is one that is somewhat removed from the use of this idea in certain philosophical accounts of freedom of the will (such as that of Kant).

23. See Ekstrom (2005: 47); see also Frankfurt (1993: 176).

24. See Wolf (1993a: 155).

25. Hume initially presents this as a distinction between two kinds or classes of passion (T 2.1.1.3/276; Hume further elaborates on the class of calm passions at T 2.3.3.8/417). But Hume then immediately uses the calm–violent distinction to refer also to different ways in which the same passion, of whichever class, may be experienced (T 2.1.1.3/276; cf. T 2.3.8.13/437–8). In what follows, I will be taking Hume's distinction to mark a class or category difference acknowledging that there is also a sense in which any passion may be experienced more or less calmly or violently.

26. See Ekstrom (2005: 58); Wolf (1993a: 158–168).

27. See Chisholm (1982: 32): "each of us, when we act is a prime mover unmoved." Reid (1788: 265) argues that "moral liberty" requires that the agent should be the cause of the determination of his own will.

28. There remain questions about Hume's understanding of the notion of personal character as something that may be considered "peculiar to each individual" (ESY 203; cf.

T 2.3.1.10/402–3). How, for example, is character as a comparatively durable feature of the person qua moral agent to be accommodated within Hume's account of the self as a bundle or collection of perceptions (T 1.4.6.4/252)? Perhaps the most promising suggestion is to be found in McIntyre (1990: 198–199); for a critical response, see Kinneman (2005: 18).

29. It has been suggested that the presence of motives reflecting character as something constant and stable is not sufficient for responsible agency because we may be quite passive in respect of these motives; see Schauber (2009: 35). But although we may be said to suffer "violent" passions like anger and hatred, it seems to make little sense to say this about a "calm" passion such as our concern for our longer term interests. As we have seen, it is the fact that we are capable of being motivated by passions of the latter kind that appears crucial to our status as autonomous moral agents.

30. This provides a context in which it is possible for the agent to display such "private" or "selfish" virtues as prudence (EM 6.20–2/242–3), bearing in mind that while it is sometimes classified as an intellectual rather than a moral virtue, prudence can have "a considerable influence on conduct" (EM App. 4.2/313; cf. T 3.3.4.4–6/609–10).

31. In a well-known paper, John Hospers (1996: 33) raises the question as to whether we can be responsible for *any* of our actions if we are not responsible for the character from which they arise.

32. That someone might seek to bring about a change for the better in his character in this way would be explained by the concern for reputation to which Hume has referred. This concern leads to a process of self-survey by which one becomes aware of how one's is viewed by others; and, if Hume is right, this process is bearable only to the extent that one's character meets with approval.

33. Strawson's pessimist is someone who holds that if determinism is true, then concepts such as moral obligation and moral responsibility have no application—and, correspondingly, the practices of praise and blame, reward and punishment, are unjustified (1974: 1).

34. See Galen Strawson (1993: 84, 87); Galen Strawson (1994: 19–21).

35. See Strawson (1994: 71–73). We might also compare here the position of Nagel (1986: ch. 6, esp. 110–126) who, while admitting that we cannot get rid of our sense of autonomy and responsibility, argues that neither appears to be available to us when we consider our actions from an external perspective and in light of the impossibility of choosing everything about ourselves given the influences of both heredity and environment.

36. As endorsed by Campbell (1957; 1966).

37. See Frankfurt (1975: 120–122).

38. See also Nagel (1986: 127) on the impossibility of developing a *completely* objective view of ourselves.

39. In the case of theodicy, it seems that if we accept that the causes of our actions lead back ultimately to God, then the only way of avoiding the conclusion that God is to blame for our criminal actions is to suppose that none of our actions possesses any moral turpitude.

40. Hume refers frequently throughout his philosophical writings to "common life" in distinguishing his own philosophical position from the kind to which he is opposed (see, for example, EU 11.27/146; EU 12.21/158; EM 1.5/171; EM 5.43/230; T 1.3.7.7/629; T 2.1.10.5/312; and ESY 172).

41. The model here is provided by Hume's treatment of the idea of causal efficacy: we can arrive at a "just idea of this efficacy" only by producing instances where its operations are revealed to us in experience; otherwise, the idea is "impossible and imaginary" (T 1.3.14.6/157–8). The challenge for the pessimist is to show that his idea of responsibility should not be dismissed in similar fashion.

Bibliography

Austin, J. L. (1961). "A Plea for Excuses," in J. O. Urmson and G. J. Warnock, eds., *Philosophical Papers*. Oxford: Clarendon Press, 123–152.

Bricke, J. (1984). "Hume's Volitions," in V. Hope, ed., *Philosophers of the Scottish Enlightenment*. Edinburgh: Edinburgh University Press, 70–99.

Campbell, C. A. (1957). *On Selfhood and Godhood*. Aberdeen: Allen and Unwin.

Campbell, C. A. (1966). "Is 'Free Will' a Pseudo-Problem?" in B. Berofsky, ed., *Free Will and Determinism*. London: Harper and Row, 112–135.

Chambers, E. (1728). *Cylcopaedia; or an Universal Dictionary of Arts and Sciences*, in two volumes. London: J. and J. Knapton.

Chisholm, R. (1982). "Human Freedom and the Self," in Gary Watson, ed., *Free Will*. Oxford: Oxford University Press, 24–35.

Descartes, R. (1986). *Meditations on First Philosophy*. Translated by J. Cottingham with an introduction by B. Williams. Cambridge: Cambridge University Press.

Ekstrom, L. W. (2005). "Alienation, Autonomy, and the Self," in P. A. French and H. K. Wettstein, eds., *Free Will and Moral Responsibility*. Oxford: Blackwell, 45–67.

Frankfurt, H. (1969). "Alternate Possibilities and Moral Responsibility," *Journal of Philosophy* 66, 829–839.

Frankfurt, H. (1971). "Freedom of the Will and the Concept of a Person," *Journal of Philosophy* 68 (1), 5–20.

Frankfurt, H. (1975). "Three Concepts of Free Action," *Proceedings of the Aristotelian Society* Supp. Vol. 2, 113–125.

Frankfurt, H. (1993). "What We Are Morally Responsible For" in J. M. Fischer and M. Ravizza, eds., *Perspectives on Moral Responsibility*. Ithaca: Cornell University Press, 286–295.

Hospers, J. (1996). "What Means This Freedom?" in B. Berofsky, ed., *Free Will and Determinism*. New York: Harper and Row, 26–45.

Kant, I. (1963). *The Moral Law*. Translated and analyzed by H. J. Paton. London: Hutchinson.

King, W. (1739). *An Essay on the Origin of Evil*, 3rd ed., translated with notes by Edmund Law. Cambridge: printed for William Thurlbourn.

Kinneman, T. (2005). "The Role of Character in Hume's Account of Moral Responsibility," *The Journal of Value Inquiry* 39, 11–25.

Locke, J. (1975). *An Essay Concerning Human Understanding*. Edited with an Introduction by P. H. Nidditch. Oxford: Oxford University Press.

McIntrye, J. (1990). "Character: a Humean Account," *History of Philosophy Quarterly* 7 (2), 193–206.

McKenna, M. (2005). "Where Frankfurt and Strawson Meet," in P. A. French and H. K. Wettstein, eds., *Free Will and Moral Responsibility*. Oxford: Blackwell, 163–180.

Nagel, T. (1986). *The View from Nowhere*. Oxford, Oxford University Press.

Reid, T. (1788/1969). *Essays on the Active Powers of the Human Mind*. Cambridge, MA: MIT Press.

Russell, P. (1995). *Freedom and Moral Sentiment*. Oxford: Oxford University Press.

Schauber, N. (2009). "Complexities of Character: Hume on Love and Responsibility," *Hume Studies* 35 (1 & 2), 29–55.

Strawson, P. (1974). "Freedom and Resentment," in *Freedom and Resentment and Other Essays*. London: Methuen, 1–25.

Strawson, P. (1985). *Skepticism and Naturalism*. London: Methuen.

Strawson, G. (1993). "On 'Freedom and Resentment'" in J. M. Fischer and M. Ravizza, eds., *Perspectives on Moral Responsibility*. Ithaca: Cornell University Press, 67–100.

Strawson, G. (1994). "The Impossibility of Moral Responsibility," *Philosophical Studies* 75 (1), 5–24.

Wolf, S. (1993*a*). "The Importance of Free Will," in J. M. Fischer and M. Ravizza, eds., *Perspectives on Moral Responsibility*. Ithaca: Cornell University Press, 101–118.

Wolf, S. (1993*b*). "The Real Self View," in J. M. Fischer and M. Ravizza, eds., *Perspectives on Moral Responsibility*. Ithaca: Cornell University Press, 151–169.

CHAPTER 20

....

HUME ON *IS* AND *OUGHT*

Logic, Promises, and the Duke of Wellington⃰

....

CHARLES PIGDEN

I INTRODUCTION

....

HUME is widely supposed to have argued that you can't get an *ought* from an *is*, moral or evaluative conclusions from non-moral or "factual" premises (T 3.1.1.27/469–70). John Searle is supposed by some to have proved otherwise, to have shown that it is possible to derive an *evaluative*—though not, perhaps, a *moral*—conclusion from purely "factual" or descriptive premises. The idea that such derivations are *impossible* is in Searle's view a fallacy—the *Naturalistic Fallacy Fallacy* (Searle 1964: 125). Searle's basic idea is that certain kinds of performative speech acts—such as saying "I will" in the course of a properly constituted marriage service—involve undertaking duties or obligations. That the bride and the bridegroom are undertaking certain duties is *analytic*, at least in the sense that if you don't understand at least roughly what the bride and the bridegroom are now supposed to do, you don't understand either the relevant speech acts or the language game in which they are embedded. Thus to say that someone has performed a speech act such as getting married or making a promise—surely a factual, descriptive, or empirical claim—entails that they have certain duties or obligations and thus, at least *prima facie*, that there are certain things that they ought to do. More generally, human institutions have a normative dimension to them. To understand the game of chess is to understand that if I put you in check, you ought to move your king, to block my attack or to take the attacking piece. Thus it *follows* from the factual or descriptive claim that Carlsen has just checked Anand that Anand is obliged to move his king, to block the attack or to take the attacking piece.

⃰ Earlier versions of this chapter were read at Nottingham, Otago, Cambridge, Oxford, and Düsseldorf. I thank the audiences for their comments, especially the Düsseldorf logicians.

I have several aims in this chapter. Firstly I want to insist on a distinction that Searle and his contemporaries generally failed to make: the distinction between the *Logical* Autonomy of Ethics and the *Semantic* Autonomy of Ethics. Several versions of the Logical Autonomy of ethics are provable (and thus true) but none implies the Semantic Autonomy of Ethics, which is a much more debatable claim. Secondly, I shall be arguing that Hume only subscribed to the *Logical* Autonomy of Ethics and that he was committed to claims that implicitly contradict *Semantic* Autonomy. Thus Hume thought, or at least implied, that with the aid of the relevant observations and explanations it is indeed possible to deduce an *ought* from an *is*, moral conclusions from "observations concerning human affairs," although the deductions in question require analytic bridge principles that are, in fact, false. If the Naturalistic Fallacy Fallacy is indeed a fallacy, it is a fallacy that Hume did not commit. Thirdly I shall argue that Searle's views are not incompatible with Logical Autonomy but only Semantic Autonomy, which is fortunate for him since if they *were* incompatible with Logical Autonomy, they would be provably false. Fourthly, I shall argue that, in so far as Searle succeeds in deriving evaluative conclusions from factual or descriptive sentences, the conclusions are not genuinely moral. The *oughts* in question are not moral or unqualified *oughts*. In so far as I can derive the conclusion that I ought to keep a promise from a set of non-moral premises, the conclusion won't be that I ought to keep the promise *tout court*, nor even that I ought to keep the promise *other things being equal*, but that *other things being equal*, I ought to keep the promise *according to the rules of the promising game*. Similarly, in so far as the premise that Carlsen has just checked Anand implies that Anand ought to move his king, to block the attack or to take the attacking piece, it only implies that Anand ought to do one of these things *according to the rules of chess*. Finally, Hume subscribed to analytic bridge principles that would license us to move from institutionally qualified *oughts* (what you ought to do according to the rules of some institution) to moral *oughts*. Indeed, some parts of the *Treatise* can be read as an attempt to develop such deductions, though, as I contend (but do not argue), the analytic bridge principles required are all false.

II TWO TYPES OF AUTONOMY: LOGICAL AND SEMANTIC

Let's start with the distinction between Logical and Semantic Autonomy. Consider the following inference F:

(1) Fritz is a bachelor;

therefore

(2) Fritz has no wife.

Is this a valid argument? In one sense "yes" and in another sense "no." It is not a *logically* valid argument, such that *given its structure* and *whatever the meanings of the non-logical words*, the premises cannot be true and the conclusion false. For there are many arguments with the same logical structure in which the conclusion is false but the premise is true. For example:

(1) Obama is a Democrat;

therefore

(2) Obama has no trousers.

But though the inference F is not *logically* valid, it is *analytically* or *materially* valid, since given the meanings of "bachelor" and "wife" it is impossible for the premise "Fritz is a bachelor" to be true and the conclusion "Fritz has no wife" to be false. When a set of premises *analytically entails* a conclusion in this way, it is generally possible to convert the inference into a logically valid argument by adding in an extra premise, namely, an *analytic bridge principle*, true by definition, which expresses the meaning links between the original premises and the conclusion. Thus the *analytically valid* inference F can be reformulated as the *logically valid* F':

(1)   Fritz is a bachelor;
(1a) No bachelor has a wife;

therefore

(2) Fritz has no wife.

Now, the distinction between formally and materially valid arguments or between logical consequence and analytic entailment is not only rough and ready, but also, perhaps, a pragmatic one, since it depends on a prior partition of the vocabulary into *logical* symbols whose meaning is kept more or less constant in determining the consequence relation and *non-logical* or schematic terms whose interpretation is allowed to vary. And where exactly you draw the line is determined, in part, by pragmatic considerations. Nonetheless, given such a partition, we can distinguish between *logically* or *formally* valid arguments and materially valid arguments. Furthermore, this was a distinction available to Hume since it was implicit in the teachings of his logic professor at Edinburgh, Colin Drummond. "How does the conclusion [of a valid syllogism] follow from the premises?" he asked his students rhetorically. Answer: "Not materially but formally, since there is no new matter in the conclusion that is not in the premises, but the terms are merely arranged in a different way" (Drummond 1725: 49–50). Now, given this distinction (which goes back at least to medieval times[1]), we can make a further distinction between two variants of Hume's No-Ought-From-Is thesis (hencefoward

NOFI)—*Logical* Autonomy, the claim that there are no *formally* valid inferences from non-moral premises to moral conclusions, that you can't get moral conclusions from non-moral premises by logic alone, and *Semantic* Autonomy, the claim that there are no *materially* valid arguments from non-moral premises to moral conclusions, that you can't get moral conclusions from non-moral premises with the aid of logic plus analytic bridge principles (because there *are* no such bridge principles). Now Logical Autonomy does not imply Semantic Autonomy. If you can't get moral conclusions from non-moral premises by logic alone, it does not follow that you can't get moral conclusions from non-moral premises by logic plus analytic bridge principles. But Semantic Autonomy implies Logical Autonomy. If you can't get moral conclusions from non-moral premises by logic plus analytic bridge principles, *a fortiori*, you can't get moral conclusions from non-moral premises by logic alone. However, the *negation* of Logical Autonomy implies the *negation* of Semantic Autonomy. If you *can* get moral conclusions from non-moral premises by logic alone it follows, *a fortiori*, that you can get moral conclusions from non-moral premises with the aid of logic plus analytic bridge principles. Thus, for anyone interested in the autonomy or otherwise of ethics, Logical Autonomy comes first.

As I have argued elsewhere,[2] what Hume was insisting on in his famous Is/Ought passage was the *Logical* Autonomy of Ethics. His argument depends upon the *conservativeness of logic*, the meta-logical principle, widely believed in the Eighteenth Century, that in a logically valid argument you can't get out what you have not put in; more specifically, that there can be no *matter* or non-logical content in the conclusion that is not contained in the premises. As Prior (1960) pointed out, this principle is (strictly speaking) false. Fortunately for Hume, I have in my back-pocket a proof of a more sophisticated version of conservativness, namely, that if there is non-logical content in the conclusion of a valid inference that does not appear in the premises, that content suffers from *inference-relative vacuity* (Pigden 1989). This means that the novel expressions in the conclusion can be uniformly replaced *salva validitate*, that is, without prejudice to the validity of the resulting inference. So if "ought" is *not* treated as a logical word (perhaps an important proviso), you cannot *logically* derive a non-vacuous *ought* from an *is*, a substantively moral conclusion from non-moral premises. Note, however, that this tells us nothing whatsoever about the nature of morality since, by the same token, you can't derive non-vacuous "hedgehog" conclusions from "hedgehog"-free premises. No-Non-Vacuous-Ought-From-Is does not imply that there is any fundamental semantic divide between the non-moral and the moral or between fact and value.[3] It's a meta-ethically neutral thesis. If there is such a divide, other arguments are required to prove its existence.

However, my argument only works with the proviso that "ought" is not (or should not be treated as) a logical symbol. What if there are logical principles governing "ought" and related concepts, deontic "logics" that are genuine logics? Even if there are such principles, it turns out that we can formulate and prove another version of Logical Autonomy. Gerhard Schurz accepts that some among a large range of deontic logics may be correct, and thus that it is possible to derive the theorems of (the correct) deontic logic from non-moral premises—a logical *ought* from an *is*. But Schurz has a proof of a *different* version of Logical Autonomy. The idea is roughly this. So long as a certain *kind* of analytic bridge principle for that operator is not included in the logic—formally, a principle that contains at least one schematic letter that has at least one occurrence *within* the scope of the deontic operator O and at least one occurrence *outside* the scope of any O—then we can distinguish between arguments that derive moral conclusions from non-moral premises by deontic logic alone and arguments that derive moral conclusions from non-moral premises with the aid of deontic logic plus analytic bridge-principles. Furthermore, we can show that if an ought-operator occurs in the conclusion of a logically valid argument but not in the premises, any predicate occurring in the scope of such an operator can be uniformly replaced with any other predicate of the same grammatical type *salva validitate*, that is, without prejudice to the validity of the resulting inference. This means that if it is possible to derive a partly moral conclusion *A* from non-moral premises **D**, which includes a subformula saying that we ought to smite the godless, you can also derive parallel conclusions *A'* and *A"* including corresponding subformulae saying respectively that we ought to smite the godly and that we ought *not* to smite the godless. Thus you can't get a substantively moral *ought* from an *is*; that is, an *ought* that tells you to do something as opposed to something else.

Does Schurz's result support any meta-ethical conclusions, for instance, non-cognitivism or expressivism? I used to think so, but now I have changed my mind. Schurz's result holds for *all* modal operators that are *not* characterized by bridge principles and only applies to "ought" in so far as it is such an operator. What Schurz shows is that for any modal logic L and for any modal operator M, so long as L is axiomatizable without bridge principles for M, then if M appears in the conclusion of an L-valid inference $K \Vdash_L X$ but not in the premises, we can uniformly replace any predicate F occurring within the scope of M in **X** with any other same-placed predicate G, *salva validitate*. Thus Schurz's result holds for the belief operator B ("X believes that") as well as the deontic operator O. In deontic logics, O*A* does not imply *A*, and *A* does not imply O*A*. So too with the logic of belief: "X believes that P" does not imply P nor does P imply that X believes that P. (Contrast the knowledge operator K and the necessity operator $\square$: both K*p* and $\square p$ imply *p*.) Thus a version of conservativeness holds for a wide class of modal operators M, of which the deontic operator O happens to be a member. *If there are no bridge principles applying to M, you cannot logically derive M-relevant conclusions from non-M premises.* Schurz's proof does not depend on any *special* features of the deontic *ought* apart from the fact that (in his opinion) it should be construed as a modal operator without bridge principles. Hence, Schurz's proof does not support expressivism or non-cognitivism about ought-claims unless it *also* supports expressivism about (for example) statements of belief.

III AUTONOMY DENIED: LOGICAL OR SEMANTIC

Searle takes himself to be contradicting Hume's supposed claim that "no statement of fact by itself entails any statement of value" (Searle 1964: 120). But he fails to distinguish between Logical and Semantic Autonomy, partly because he fails to distinguish between logical consequence and analytic entailment. Indeed, in the Sixties debate, terms like "tautology" and "entails" were chucked around with a cheerful imprecision that is truly distressing to logically sensitive souls such as myself. Because Searle fails to distinguish between Logical and Semantic Autonomy, he fails to ask himself which of the two claims he is trying to disprove. Once you *do* ask the question, however, it becomes pretty obvious that it is the *second* thesis, *Semantic* Autonomy, that he must have had in mind. Simplifying somewhat, his claim appears to be this:

> Thesis (A)
> "Smith promised to pay Jones $500"
> *analytically entails*
> Thesis (B)
> "Smith *ought* / *is obliged* to pay Jones $500,"
> with the possible aid of some *ceteris paribus* clause.

It must be analytic entailment that he is thinking of since it is obvious that (B) is not a logical consequence of (A). For there are interpretations of the non-logical vocabulary according to which (A) is true and (B) false. Thus, in so far as Searle's argument succeeds, it only refutes Semantic Autonomy: *Logical* Autonomy remains intact. But does it succeed? Are there analytic bridge principles that enable you to move from Thesis (A) to Thesis (B)? To prove the point, Searle has to come up with an analytic bridge principle K, such that (B) follows *logically* from K in conjunction with (A).

Looking back at the debate, we can see two lines of criticism of Searle's "proof": the Ceteris Paribus Critique and the Promising Game Critique. Let's take them in turn.

IV THE CETERIS PARIBUS CRITIQUE: THOMSON AND THOMSON

Nobody thinks that the fact that you have made a promise analytically entails that you ought to keep it. It is generally supposed that you ought not to keep a promise that it was wrong to make and that other obligations can trump a promise, especially if the other obligations are morally pressing and the promise is relatively trivial. Thus the bridge principle cannot be of the form:

> (K)   If Smith promises to pay Jones $500, then Smith ought to pay Jones $500.

Rather, the bridge principle should be something like this:

> (K')   If Smith promises to pay Jones $500 and *other things are equal,* then Smith ought to pay Jones $500.

But the second conjunct in the antecedent looks awfully like a *moral* proposition since in order for other things to be equal, there would have to be nothing that might reasonably be regarded as voiding or invalidating the promise (such as a prior promise to pay the $500 to somebody else) nor any obligation that might reasonably be regarded as trumping Smith's duty to pay up, such as the obligation to help a needy relative who can only be saved from death or destitution by the gift of five hundred dollars. Indeed, what (K′) really amounts to is this:

(K″)   If Smith promises to pay Jones $500 and it is *not* the case that there is a factor F (from a range of factors M) such that, given F, it is not the case that Smith ought to pay Jones $500 (when the promise falls due), then Smith ought to pay Jones $500 (when the promise falls due).

But from

(A) Smith promised to pay Jones $500

and

(K″)   If Smith promises to pay Jones $500 and it is *not* the case that there is a factor F (from a range of factors M) such that, given F, it is not the case that Smith ought to pay Jones $500 (when the promise falls due), then Smith ought to pay Jones $500.

we cannot derive

(B)   Smith ought to pay Jones $500.

To derive *that* conclusion we need the further, rather moral-looking premise:

(A#)   It is *not* the case that there is a factor F (from a range of factors M) such that, given F, it is not the case that Smith ought to pay Jones $500 (when the promise falls due).

But in that case we don't really have an Is/Ought inference. For one of the premises required to derive (B) from (A) is not empirical or analytic but moral. Hence Searle's counterexample to NOFI is defused. He has not succeeded in deriving a moral conclusion from entirely non-moral premises with the aid of analytic truths. That, in a nutshell, is the Ceteris Paribus Critique of Thomson and Thomson in their well-known paper "How Not to Derive 'Ought' from 'Is'" (1964). But although Thomson and Thomson manage to defuse Searle's counterexample, they fail to defuse his argument. For what we *can* infer from (A) with the aid of (K″) is this:

(B#)   If it is *not* the case that there is a factor F (from a range of factors M) such that, given F, it is not the case that Smith ought to pay Jones $500 (when the promise falls due), then Smith *ought* to pay Jones $500 (when the promise falls due).

And (B#) is a non-trivial and authentically moral conclusion. It's not a categorical *ought*, of course, but neither are many authentically moral propositions. "You ought to obey the sovereign's commands," despite its categorical appearance, is really a conditional: "If the sovereign commands you to do something, then you ought to do it." But that does not mean that it is not a contentious, and consequently, a substantive moral claim. So too with (B#). The fact that it is a conditional does not mean that it is not a substantive moral proposition.

V Hare, Godwin, and the Promising Game Critique

But is (K″) genuinely analytic? A genuinely analytic truth is one that you cannot deny without manifesting either a misunderstanding of the words of which it is composed or a misunderstanding of the language game from which they derive their meaning. But (K″) is not a proposition of that kind. If it is analytic, it is analytic because it is a substitution instance of the following principle (which must itself be analytic):

(K‴)   If a person P promises to X and it is *not* the case that there is a factor F (from a range of factors M) such that, given F, it is not the case that P ought to X (when the promise falls due), then P ought to X.

Is it possible to deny (K‴) without manifesting a misunderstanding of "promise" or of the language game from which the word derives its meaning? The answer is, obviously, *yes*. For you can deny (K‴) without manifesting either a misunderstanding of the word "promise" or a misunderstanding of the promising game itself, if you reject or condemn the institution of promising. Hence (K‴) is not analytic. And if (K‴) is not analytic, (K″) is not analytic either.

What do I mean by "rejecting the institution of promising" or "rejecting the promising game"? You reject the promising game if it is a game you refuse to play or if you refuse to be bound by its rules. More importantly for present purposes, you reject the promising game if you think that we are not in general obliged to keep our promises and that the institution of promising is a morally suspect affair. (You don't have to think that we should *never* keep our promises, but you do have to think that we are not obliged to keep them simply *because* they are promises.) This attitude is eccentric but not incoherent, and it is quite compatible with *understanding* the rules of the language game that you reject. You can understand very well that *according to the rules of the Promising Game* you generally ought to keep your promises whilst believing that, in fact, you have no obligation to do so. This was, at least in theory, the attitude of Hume's near contemporary, William Godwin (husband of Mary Wollstonecraft and father of Mary Shelley) whose *Enquiry Concerning Political Justice* was the radical-*chic* smash-hit of the early 1790s:

What I have promised is either right, or wrong, or indifferent. There are few articles of human conduct that fall under the latter class [a point which follows from Godwin's act-consequentialism]. Omitting these, let us then consider only the two preceding classes. "I have promised to do something just and right." This certainly I ought to perform. Why? Not because I promised, but because justice prescribes it. . . . If we discover any thing to be unjust, we ought to abstain from it, with whatever solemnity we have engaged for its perpetration [that is, whether or not we have promised to do it]. We were erroneous and vicious when the promise was made; but this affords no sufficient reason for its performance. (Godwin 1793, 3.3)

Thus, according to Godwin, what we promise to do is either already right (just) or already wrong (unjust). If it is already right, then we ought to do it whether we have promised to do it or not. And if it is already wrong, we ought *not* to do it whether we have promised to do it or not. Either way, it is not the case that, generally speaking, we ought to keep our promises (i.e., it is *not* the case that we are obliged to keep our promises unless there is something specific from a vague but not entirely open-ended range of moral factors that invalidates the obligation). Thus Godwin denies (K‴). But, weird though this is, it is abundantly clear from his discussion that he not only understands the concept of a promise but is perfectly familiar with the Promising Game from which it is derived. Now if you can deny a purportedly analytic truth without manifesting a misunderstanding of either the words involved or the relevant language games, then the "truth" in question is either not analytic or not true (and *a fortiori* not analytic). Hence, true or not, (K‴) is not analytic. This is the good idea, lurking behind the prescriptivist rhetoric in Hare's famous paper "The Promising Game" (1964).

VI Winchelsea, Wellington, and the Dueling Game

What obscures the point for most of us is that we are, in fact, conscientious (if not enthusiastic) players of the Promising Game, which means that we subscribe to its rules. But the non-analytic nature of (K‴) becomes clearer once we consider a parallel case in which the game is no longer played. Consider the following derivation, which closely parallels Searle's:

(1*a) The Earl of Winchelsea (a gentleman) publicly accused the Duke of Wellington (another gentleman, then serving as Prime Minister) of a policy of deliberate deception: "Under the cloak of some colored show of zeal for the Protestant religion" he is carrying on "an insidious design for the infringement of our liberties and the introduction of Popery." [Wellington was at that time endeavoring to pass the Bill for Catholic Emancipation.] Lord Winchelsea declined to apologize for this insult.

(1*b)   The Duke of Wellington called on Lord Winchelsea to give him "that satisfac-
        tion [for his conduct] which a gentleman has a right to require and no gentle-
        man ever refuses to give."

(2*)   Wellington issued a valid challenge to a duel (from (1*b).)

(3*)   Wellington placed Winchlesea under an obligation *either* to apologize to
        Wellington *or* to accept his challenge.

(4*)   Winchelsea was under an obligation *either* to apologize to Wellington *or* to
        accept his challenge.

(5*)   Thus, Winchlesea ought either to have apologized to Wellington *or* to have
        accepted his challenge. [In fact he did both, apologizing after having fired
        into the air during the duel, a practice known as "deloping."[4]]

Of course, even if we accept the rules of the Dueling Game, (2*) does not analytically
entail (3*). Given these rules, Winchelsea would not have been obliged to fight or apologize if he had been blind, infirm or crippled (or if Wellington had been blind, infirm
or crippled). And there are, no doubt, other circumstances (such as being Wellington's
commanding officer whilst on active service) that would have relieved Winchelsea of
the obligation to respond. Nonetheless, the following thesis

(K*)   If after a public insult Wellington challenged Winchelsea to a duel and if it
        was *not* the case that there was a factor F (from a range of factors N) such, that
        given F, it was not the case that Winchelsea ought to have dueled or apolo-
        gized, then Winchelsea ought to have dueled or apologized.

has the same kind of status as

(K″)   If Smith promises to pay Jones $500 and it is *not* the case that there is a factor
        F (from a range of factors M) such, that given F, it is not the case that Smith
        ought to pay Jones $500 (when the promise falls due), then Smith ought to
        pay Jones $500 (when the promise falls due).

And if (K*) is not analytic—as surely it is not—then (K″) is not analytic either. Thus,
Searle's Is/Ought inference is a failure since the bridge principle on which it relies is not
really analytic. But although (K*) and K″) are *not* analytic, the same cannot be said for
their game-relative transforms (K*R) and (K″R):

(K*R)   If after a public insult Wellington challenged Winchelsea to a duel and if it
        was *not* the case that there was a factor F (from a range of factors N) such that,
        given F, it was not the case that according to the rules of the Dueling Game,
        Winchelsea ought to have dueled or apologized, then *according to the rules of
        the Dueling Game*, Winchelsea ought to have dueled or apologized.

(K″R)   If Smith promises to pay Jones $500 and it is *not* the case that there is a factor F
        (from a range of factors M) such that according to the rules of the Promising
        Game, given F, it is not the case that Smith ought to pay Jones $500 (when the
        promise falls due), then, *according to the rules of the Promising Game*, Smith
        ought to pay Jones $500 (when the promise falls due).

What (K*R) amounts to is the thesis that, *ceteris paribus*, if a gentleman such as Winchelsea had insulted a gentleman such as Wellington and if Wellington had challenged Winchelsea to a duel, then *according to the rules of the Dueling Game* Winchelsea ought to have fought or to have apologized. A person who doubted or disputed this claim would indeed show that they did not really understand the Dueling Game as it was (sometimes) played in the early nineteenth century and thus that they did not really understand the relevant speech acts. What (K″R) amounts to is the thesis that, *ceteris paribus*, if Smith promises to pay Jones $500, then *according to the rules of the Promising Game* Smith ought to pay Jones $500. A person who doubted or disputed this claim would indeed show that they did not really understand the Promising Game as we play it today and thus that they did not really understand the relevant vocabulary. But you can accept (K*R) whilst being of the opinion that it is wrong to fight duels or to coerce an apology under the threat of a duel. And you can accept (K″R) whilst agreeing with Godwin that the Promising Game is a pernicious practice.

VII Ought/Ought Inferences: Institutional to Moral

Now what extra premise would be required to derive something like the authentically moral *ought* of (B#) from the non-moral (A) and the genuinely analytic (K″R)? Something like this:

(OPG)   We (morally) ought to obey the rules of the Promising Game.

This conveys the general idea that the Promising Game is a good game to play and that we ought to abide by its rules, but to convert Searle's argument into a logically valid deduction, we need something more specific:

(OPG′)   If, *according to the rules of the promising game*, Y ought to do X, then *morally* Y ought to do X.

This gives us:

(A)   Smith promised to pay Jones $500.
         [Assumption.]

(K″R)   If Smith promises to pay Jones $500 and it is *not* the case that there is a factor F (from a range of factors M) such that *according to the rules of the Promising Game*, given F, it is not the case that Smith ought to pay Jones $500 (when the promise falls due), then, *according to the rules of the Promising Game*, Smith ought to pay Jones $500 (when the promise falls due).

[Analytic Truth.]

(OPG′) If *according to the rules of the promising game* Y ought to do X, then *morally* Y ought to do X. [Assumption.]

    (K″) If Smith promises to pay Jones \$500 and it is *not* the case that there is a factor F (from a range of factors M) such that, given F, *according to the rules of the Promising Game*, it is not the case that Smith ought to pay Jones \$500 (when the promise falls due), then Smith *morally* ought to pay Jones \$500 (when the promise falls due). [From (K″R) and (OPG′).]

    (B#) If it is *not* the case that there is a factor F (from a range of factors M) such that, given F, *according to the rules of the Promising Game*, it is not the case that Smith ought to pay Jones \$500 (when the promise falls due), then Smith *morally* ought to pay Jones \$500 (when the promise falls due).

[From A) and K″).]

(*Ceteris paribus*)

    It is not the case that there is a factor F (from a range of factors M) such that, given F, *according to the rules of the Promising Game*, it is not the case that Smith ought to pay Jones \$500 (when the promise falls due).

    [Non-moral assumption, depending on (a) the rules of the Promising Game and (b) contingent matters of fact.]

(B) Smith *morally* ought to pay Jones \$500 (when the promise falls due).

[From (B#) and (*ceteris paribus*) resting on (A), (K″R), (OPG′), and (*Ceteris paribus*).]

This is a bit rough, but I take it that it can be converted into a formally valid argument without too much trouble. But, of course, it is not an Is/Ought inference. The problem lies with (OPG′), which obviously expresses a moral principle. But perhaps we can get an Is/Ought inference by deriving (OPG) or (OPG′) from factual premises with the aid of analytic bridge principles?

VIII Hume's Own Is/Ought Deductions: From Feelings to Duties

Interestingly enough, this is pretty much what Hume tries to do in *Treatise* 3.2.6. For Hume, it is analytic that a trait is a virtue if it gives to a suitably qualified spectator the pleasing sentiment of approbation (EM App. 1.10/289), and it is likewise analytic that we have an obligation to do—and hence ought to do—those actions whose neglect or non-performance would displease us after a certain manner (T 3.2.5.4/517). Now keeping promises is a practice that gives to suitably qualified spectators the pleasing sentiment of approbation (where being suitably qualified involves taking the general point of view and *not* being misled by factual error or the delusive glosses of superstition or false religion). Indeed, approbation persists or is intensified in those ideally qualified spectators who have had the origin and utility of promises explained to them by Hume. Hence fidelity to promises is a virtue. Indeed, we have an *obligation* to keep our promises since the neglect or non-performance of promises displeases us, giving rise to the sentiment of disapprobation (T 3.2.6/516–25). Thus Hume deduces an *ought*—that we *ought* on the whole to keep our promises—from factual observations concerning human affairs (specifically a set of facts about how we are inclined to feel, together with a speculative theory that endeavors to explain those facts) with the aid of two supposedly analytic bridge principles. But this is (OPG), the principle that has to be derived from facts if Searle's argument is to work as an inference from non-moral observations to authentically moral conclusions. Of course, the fact that Hume relied on analytic bridge principles to deduce moral conclusions from observations concerning human affairs (and more specifically human feelings) does not prove that his deductions were a success. In my view, they fail since the principles in question are not analytic. It is conceptually possible for an informed human spectator, taking the general point of view, to approve of non-virtues or to *dis*approve of the neglect or non-performance of acts which ought not to be done.[5] But believing or presupposing analytic principles that are not really analytic is one of the ills that philosophical flesh is heir to, and even Hume is no exception in this regard.

IX Conclusion

What is the upshot? Firstly that Searle has not managed to provide a counterexample to Semantic Autonomy since the bridging principles he requires are not analytic. There are analytic truths in the general area, but they won't allow him to derive authentically moral conclusions without the aid of a moral premise (OPG). Secondly, that Hume himself derives the moral premise that Searle requires from factual premises with the aid of a supposedly analytic bridge principle. Thus Hume did not subscribe to Semantic Autonomy. Finally, that these issues become a lot clearer if you make the necessary distinctions. To say that you cannot derive moral conclusions from non-moral premises with the aid of logic alone is one thing; to say that you cannot derive moral conclusions from non-moral premises with the aid of logic plus analytic bridge principles is quite another. Hume believed the first but not the second. Searle confuses the two and fails to prove that either one is false.

ABBREVIATIONS OF WORKS CITED

EM   *Enquiry Concerning the Principles of Morals.* Edited by Tom L. Beauchamp. Oxford: Clarendon, 1998.

T   *A Treatise of Human Nature.* Edited by D. F. Norton and M. J. Norton. Oxford: Clarendon, 2007.

Notes

1. See Broadie (1993). The distinction was not forgotten in the Early Modern Period despite the decline of logic, but, by the 1960s, many philosophers had become a bit hazy about it.

2. See Pigden (1989), (2010a), (2010b), (2010c), and especially (2010d). Why was Hume insisting on Logical Autonomy in the No-Ought-From-Is (or NOFI) passage? Well, the point of *Treatise* 3.1.1. (as its title suggests) is to argue that moral distinctions are not derived from reason and, in particular, to prove that the basic principles of morality are not demonstrable. Now for moral truths to be demonstrable, they would have to be either self-evident in themselves or logically deducible from self-evident truths. By the end of 3.1.1, Hume believes himself to have proved that no (non-trivial) moral truths are self-evident. This still leaves open the possibility that the truths of morality might be deducible from self-evident truths of some other kind (proofs of the being of God, observations concerning human affairs—whatever), a possibility mooted by Locke (*Essay* 4.3.1.18: 549) and suggested by philosophers such as Hobbes and Spinoza. The point of NOFI is to foreclose this option. If no (non-trivial) moral proposition is self-evident and no (non-trivial) moral proposition is logically deducible from non-moral propositions, then no (non-trivial) moral proposition is demonstrable.

3. As Frank Snare (1991) pointed out, it is obvious that NOFI follows from non-cognitivism plus the conservativeness of logic, but not non-cognitivism from NOFI. So how can NOFI support non-cognitivism? Perhaps by an inference to the best explanation. If moral judgments express attitudes rather than beliefs, and if, in a logically valid argument, you don't get out what you haven't put in, then NOFI would appear to follow—that is, it won't be possible to derive moral conclusions from non-moral or descriptive premises. Thus, if noncognitivism is part of the best explanation of NOFI, and if NOFI is true, then probably non-cognitivism is true too! This inference fails, however, since there is a better, because simpler, explanation of NOFI; namely, the conservativeness of logic by itself. The problem persists with the variants of NOFI proved by Schurz and myself since both derive NOFI, in the form of Logical Autonomy, from different versions of conservativeness. Hence NOFI provides no support for non-cognitivism, whether deductive or abductive. See Pigden (2010a) and (2010d).

4. For more on this encounter, see Hibbert (1997: 274), and Appiah (2010: ch. 1). Appiah's discussion is both relevant and interesting and abounds with fascinating historical detail.

5. See Pigden (2007), in which I criticize a similar set of principles due to another famous David, namely David Lewis.

Bibliography

Appiah, Kwame Anthony. (2010). *The Honor Code: How Moral Revolutions Happen*. New York and London: Norton and Norton.

Broadie, Alexander. (1993). *Introduction to Medieval Logic*, 2nd ed. Oxford: Clarendon Press.

Drummond, Colin. (1725). *Compendium Logicae*. Edinburgh: Edinburgh University Library, MS 2651.

Godwin, William. (1793). *An Enquiry Concerning Political Justice*, vol. 1, Indianapolis: Online Library of Liberty.

Hare, R. M. (1964). "The Promising Game," in *Revue Internationale de Philosophie* 70, 398–412, reprinted in W. D. Hudson (ed.), *The Is-Ought Problem*. London: Macmillan, 1969, 144–156; all references to this reprint.

Hibbert, Christopher. (1997). *Wellington: A Personal History*. London: Harper Collins.

Hudson, W. D. (ed.) (1969). *The Is-Ought Problem*. London: Macmillan.

Pigden, Charles R. (1989). "Logic and the Autonomy of Ethics." *Australasian Journal of Philosophy* 67(2/1989), 127–151.

Pigden, Charles R. (2007). "Desiring to Desire: Russell, Lewis and G. E. Moore," in S. Nuccetelli and G. Seay, eds., *Themes from G. E. Moore*. Oxford and New York: Oxford University Press.

Pigden, Charles R. (ed.) (2010). *Hume on Is and Ought*. Basingstoke: Palgrave Macmillan.

Pigden, Charles R. (2010a). "Introduction," in C. R. Pigden, ed., *Hume on Is and Ought*. Basingstoke: Palgrave Macmillan, 1–38.

Pigden, Charles R. (2010b). "Letter From a Gentleman," in C. R. Pigden, ed., *Hume on Is and Ought*. Basingstoke: Palgrave Macmillan, 76–91.

Pigden, Charles R. (2010c). "Comments on 'Hume's Master Argument,'" in C. R. Pigden, ed., *Hume on Is and Ought*. Basingstoke: Palgrave Macmillan, 128–142.

Pigden, Charles R. (2010d). "Snare's Puzzle/Hume's Purpose: What Hume Was Really Up to with No-Ought-From-Is," in C. R. Pigden, ed., *Hume on Is and Ought*. Basingstoke: Palgrave Macmillan, 169–191.

Prior, A. N. (1960). "The Autonomy of Ethics" *Australasian Journal of Philosophy* 38, 199–206.

Schurz, Gerhard. (1997). *The Is-Ought Problem. A Study in Philosophical Logic*. Dordrecht: Kluwer.

Schurz, Gerhard. (2010). "Non-Trivial Versions of Hume's Is-Ought Thesis," in C. R. Pigden, ed., *Hume on Is and Ought*. Basingstoke: Palgrave Macmillan, 198–216.

Searle, John. (1964). "How to Derive 'Ought' from 'Is.'" *Philosophical Review* 73(1964), 43–58; reprinted in W. D. Hudson (ed.), *The Is-Ought Problem*. London: Macmillan, 120–134; all references to this reprint.

Snare, Francis. (1991). *Morals, Motivation, and Convention*. Cambridge: Cambridge University Press.

Thomson, James, and Thomson, Judith. (1964). "How Not to Derive 'Ought' from 'Is.'" *The Philosophical Review* 73(1964), 512–516; reprinted in W. D. Hudson (ed.), *The Is-Ought Problem*. London: Macmillan, 1969, 163–167; all references to this reprint.

CHAPTER 21

HUME, MORALITY, AND SKEPTICISM

SIMON BLACKBURN

I THE EXPLANATION OF ACTION

BEFORE thinking about Hume's account of morality and moral reasoning, we need to have a clear view of his theory of the explanation of action. This has prompted a large and, in my view, unnecessarily convoluted literature. Rather than offering detailed commentary on the complexities to which others have felt themselves forced, I shall simply give my own account (and defense) of the way in which Hume thinks that reason is inactive on its own. And then I do the same for morality and his alleged skepticism about practical reason. Good commentaries have made many of the points I make in different places, but it is salutary to bring them together.

Many commentators have pointed out that Hume clearly has no a priori right to lay down principles about what causes what. The direct opposite is one of the non-negotiable, central pillars of his whole empiricism: "Any thing may produce any thing. Creation, annihilation, motion, reason, volition; all these may arise from one another, or from any other object we can imagine" (T 1.3.15.1/173). Yet he might appear to be offering just such an argument in T 2.3.3, precisely denying that reason alone can cause volition—denying one of his very own examples of "any thing may produce any thing." The contradiction would indeed be blatant, but it only arises from the thought that his claim is made a priori, and it employs a quite general notion of causation. Yet, on the face of it, there are endless cases where beliefs cause actions or passions, where thinking things through cause beliefs, and, in general, where it is natural to think that ratiocinative activity controls and directs our practical decision making, actions, and behavior (contra Cohon 2008a; 2008b). The thought of imminent pain typically triggers fear, the sight of an unexpected face at the window makes me jump (Anscombe 1957: 9), the awareness of someone suffering typically causes distress, and, as Hume tells us, merely reflecting on sex "suffices to excite the appetite" (T 2.2.11.6/396).

However, there is no need to make heavy weather of any of this. Let us immediately concede that reasonings, cognitions, beliefs, and reflections do affect passions and actions. The first question is whether they do so *alone*. Aristotle thought that, in the relevant sense, they do not:

> Understanding evidently does not move anything without desire—for wish is a desire, and when movement is in accord with calculation, it is in accord with wish. (*De Anima* III 10.433ª.22–9)[1]

The second question concerns this notion of an action "according" with calculation and wish. This suggests that sheer brute causation, as when the face at the window makes you jump, is not to the point. There is no clear sense in which the behavior is "in accordance with" the information, in the way, for instance, that eating something is in accordance with believing it is palatable and being hungry. In the cases that interest Hume (and Aristotle and their rationalist opponents), it is psychological explanation that is the topic, and here there is endless variation, in which the same calculation or the same perceptions or the same causal inferences or beliefs generate very different results in different subjects or even in the same subject at different times. Where there is such variation, Hume thinks it is wrong, strictly speaking, to select just one element in a causal field as "the" cause—this is the third of his rules by which to judge of cause and effect (T 1.3.15.2/173). Instead, there will be factors responsible for it: "philosophers form a maxim, that the connection betwixt all causes and effects is equally necessary, and that its seeming uncertainty in some instances proceeds from the secret opposition of contrary causes" (T 1.3.12.5/132). Folk psychology and psychological theory alike put these differences down to intervening theoretical variables, and this is how desires, inclinations, temperament, values, emotions, and passions in general take their place in the explanatory story of human choice.

We are virtuosi at using these to explain, to predict, and to control and intervene, altering peoples' choices or contouring around them as we need. As children, we learn to describe the difference between one person and another in these respects. We learn not only of the direction of the passions, but also of their strength or weakness, their susceptibility to alteration or their relative fixity. We learn what we can rely on from most people and what seems idiosyncratic to some and not others. In short, we grow into the human world. It is complex, because there are both change and speed limits to change, similarity and variety, and interactions and adjustments without end (EU 8.7–16/150–4). Hume's general term is the "passions." "Feelings" might be a better modern translation, and although the phrase "the web of belief" has passed into the language, it is a pity that its equivalent, "the web of feeling," has not done so.

It is also said in the literature that if this is how we read Hume, his point is trivial or tautological: given that the passions need have no phenomenology, as is implied by the category of calm passions, then they simply become shadows cast by our explanatory practices. Is he simply postulating a "something we know not what" to fill the gap between whatever reason supplies and whatever action or choice ensues, telling us, in effect, that only motives motivate?

This accusation relies on bad philosophy of science. You might as well charge that Newton just postulates mass as "something we know not what" to fill the gap between applied force and ensuing acceleration, or force as "something we know not what" to fill the gap between mass and acceleration, and then announce triumphantly that Newton's laws of motion are vacuous. The point that is overlooked is that these intervening variables have a high degree of constancy and thus create the theory that enables us to know what to expect and how to control the order of events. If someone's route from cognition to action seems to suggest a passion, such as love of music, one day, we may reasonably expect the same another day. Human beings are, of course, more variable than simple natural systems, but the principles are exactly the same. Your love of music indeed fills the gap between your hearing a concert announced and your buying a ticket, but it also enables me to predict what you are likely to do next time around, or to know how to intervene to bring you pleasure, and so on.

As it stands, Hume's claim depends on a division between cognition and other world-directing states of mind. It might be suggested that in our actual psychologies the distinction becomes blurred, primarily by those perceptions that carry "affect" with them: the perception that someone needs comforting, that something has to be done, or that some clothes are simply impossible. Although the phenomenology is interesting enough, it does not undermine Hume's point because it would need to be argued that the affective perception is itself a function of pure cognition. But there is no reason for thinking that. It has blended cognition with affect, so is itself the resultant of contingent profiles of concern and desire.

Although this much should be beyond doubt, it leaves a deep and interesting residual question: is it then contingent that we need both the cognitive and the conative in these explanations? Could there be a race of superrational creatures who can get by with just one? There could certainly be creatures in whom there is much less variation in the route from cognition to action. But it may be a priori that for any creatures susceptible of even quite primitive versions of psychological explanation, it is necessary to distinguish the world-guided part and the world-directed, goal-seeking part.

In his seminal exploration of this issue, Jonathan Bennett showed in detail how any theory of explanation of action will see it in terms of identifying, first, a creature's goals and then, second, its registrations of aspects of its environment, it being only these together that provide an explanatory and predictive theory of what it will do (Bennett 1976). It seems, then, to be a priori that we need elements with each "direction of fit." The rationale for thinking this is that we would actually not need or have a psychological theory at all for any imagined "superrational" creatures for whom there is no evidence of goals, variation in goals, and variation in means taken to achieve goals. They would be much more simply describable in pure stimulus–response terms—not superbly minded, but not minded at all; not acting especially rationally, but merely moving, not acting at all. Hume cannot perhaps be directly credited with anticipating this thought, but it is significant that what he says chimes in so well with it. He is, after all, very sure that the empirical science is going to fall out as he says, and Bennett's development excuses his certainty. This is also the moral of the idea of two different directions of fit: cognitions must conform to the world, but in action, we set about making the world conform to our goals or desires (Anscombe 1957: 56; Smith 1987).

Now we can revisit the second question I raised about Hume's argument concerning which *kind* of explanation we are to consider. This was anticipated earlier in Aristotle's talk of action being "in according with" calculation only when it is in accord with desire or wish, and it is properly emphasized in Sayre McCord (2007). Like Aristotle, Hume is not really interested in causation in general, as when a piece of reasoning gives me a headache or thinking about some truth or falsity makes me angry or excited. In a variation on Aristotle's words, he is explicitly talking of whether a passion can be "opposed by or contradictory to" truth and reason (T 2.3.3.5/415). It is the denial of this that separates him from the rationalists. He is interested in psychological explanation, with its proprietary role of answering a certain kind of "why?" question by bringing to light what it was about an action that inclined us toward it or motivated us to perform it. It is the structure of that explanation that interests him, and the division of it into its two different kinds of component differentiates him from those who think that world-guided states of mind, with their one dimension of truth and falsity, are sufficient. I defer further discussion of this until the following section, considering the notorious "passion is an original existence" passage (T 2.3.3.6/416).

II The Offensive Against Rationalism

Hume is quite commonly described as a skeptic about practical reason, especially by those philosophers who think that this is a bad thing to be (Korsgaard 1986; Millgram 1995; Nagel 1970: 64; for a more accurate view, see Zimmerman 2007). Those who do not accept the charge are more apt to describe him as a naturalist—a psychologist primarily concerned with describing the desires and concerns that actually move us, although also quite capable of bestowing admiration on some of these or expressing aversion to others. The standards for his admiration or aversion, of course, reflect his views about whether any particular trait is useful or agreeable to ourselves or others. It is this that makes the difference between objects of Hume's admiration, such as dignity of mind, courage, or perseverance, and those that he scorns, such as the "monkish virtues" of penance, mortification, and humility. Hume wields those standards very seriously: there is nothing skeptical in his commitment to them and to the judgments they support.

In other words, he gives his own account of what practical reasoning is and why it is so important. For this reason alone, it is misleading to describe him as a skeptic about it. As we shall shortly see, he was, indeed, a skeptic about a particular *version* of practical reasoning or philosophical *account* of practical reasoning, but, unless it is evident that this version or account is compulsory, that is not the same thing. And this is so far from evident, so far from solidly argued, and indeed so far from even faint plausibility, that it is a sociological puzzle why so many philosophers continue to take it seriously.

Hume was obviously skeptical about the versions of practical reason that were offered by rationalists of his day: William Wollaston, Ralph Cudworth, John Locke, or Samuel Clarke. He himself says of Montesquieu:

> This illustrious writer, however, sets out with a different theory, and supposes all right to be founded on certain RAPPORTS or relations; which is a system, that, in my opinion, never will be reconciled with true philosophy. Father Malebranche, as far as I can learn, was the first that started this abstract theory of morals, which was afterwards adopted by Cudworth, Clarke, and others; and as it excludes all sentiment, and pretends to found everything on reason, it has not wanted followers in this philosophic age. (EM 12.n3/93)

And he refers us to the first Appendix of EM for his own rebuttal. He would also, one supposes, have been skeptical about the existence of "pure practical reason" in the form in which it was later defended by Kant. Here is why he might have been: let us call a "conative standpoint" one that is occupied by people not merely insofar as they are capable of agency informed by cognition and inference, but just insofar as, in addition, they have some desire, aim, inclination, motivation, concern, or feeling. Then the Kantian holds that there are imperatives of reason, such as confining your maxims to those that pass the categorical imperative test, that can be known to be compulsory either without any assistance of conation or, equivalently, from any conative standpoint whatsoever. Hume believes in no such thing. The discussion of the artificial virtues in the *Treatise* and the combination of consequentialism and virtue theory in EM show that, for Hume, principles must earn their living by being conducive to things we value. In turn, to see things as valuable is partly a function of the conative part of our natures, and so it is only because of that nature that we see principles themselves as compulsory. We do so only on the grounds that they build the "vault" within which we shelter (EM App. 3, 5/171). Were they generally not to guide us, we would lose the chance of things we value, such as cooperation, security, and trust, and whose absence would give us pain.

Hume would doubtless have agreed with Mill that Kant's attempt to prove otherwise is a "grotesque" failure (Mill 1861/2001: 4).[2] The derivation of the "formula of universal law" only shows that the worlds of the universalized maxim are not such as we would choose on other grounds—grounds that we care about, such as utility. Otherwise, the fact that a maxim cannot be universalized is indifferent to us or even desirable. A pleasant example of this latter is visible in today's American politics. An engaged and rightly angry satirist may excoriate as effectively as he can the pride that Republicans especially take in their indifference to facts and truth, and, in doing so, he is, let us say, acting on the maxim that barefaced chicanery always needs ridicule and condemnation. However, in the world where this maxim is universalized, there would remain no such targets, and his way of acting on the maxim would evaporate. This is no different, formally, than the argument about lying promises, let alone the other examples alleged to illustrate the formula of universal law, and the only difference is that, in those cases, the upshot would be undesirable whereas in this case it is quite the reverse.

Contemporary proponents of rationality as a self-propelling faculty, one needing no assistance from passions, tend to suppose that Hume or Humeans must think that our desires or feelings are themselves our reasons for acting (Nagel 1970: 10). This then quickly translates into it being impossible that other peoples' desires or feelings are ever reasons for me, the idea being that since my whole motivational tank is full of my own desires and feelings, there is no room for those of anybody else. With this one move, Hume is turned into a conative solipsist and moral imbecile. But the move is wholly misguided for at least two reasons. First, there is the old point from Butler, which Hume repeats, that my own desires might perfectly well include a concern that your desires and feelings are gratified (EM App. 2/168). And, second, my own passions are typically not reasons. They are the matrix within which other things become my reasons (Blackburn 1998: 254; Pettit & Smith 1990). When Augustine says that "in the pull of the will and of love appears the worth of every-thing to be sought or avoided, to be thought of greater or less value" (1982: 4.4.1/109), he is not saying that the pull is itself a reason for anything. He is saying that it is in the light of the pull, or the perspective afforded by the pull, that features of the case are taken in and made into our own reasons for action and preference—just as Aristotle said that a person's "character controls how the end appears to him" (NE III.5. 1114^{a}31–^{b}3). Given the Humean ubiquity of sympathy, those other features will, of course, include what we take to be the desires and feelings of other people. Most contemporary rationalists and intuitionists remain innocently silent about why or when "normative reasons" actually influence us: some substitute the question of why they ought to influence us, and they can then reply that this is not an open ques-tion (Parfit 2011: v. II: 413). But this sidesteps the really open question, which is why they do influence us. Were they to confront this, rationalists might do well to adopt Augustine's model, which at this point is exactly the same as Aristotle's or Hume's. Even Kant might, insofar as it is one thing to know that an imperative is compulsory but another distinct thing to feel compelled.

So we have two kinds of rationalism about which Hume might indeed have been skeptical. But those who think he is skeptical about practical reason as such fear more than that. The notorious texts for the prosecution include:

> It is not contrary to reason to prefer the destruction of the whole world to the scratching of my finger. It is not contrary to reason for me to chuse my total ruin, to prevent the least uneasiness of an Indian or person wholly unknown to me. It is as little contrary to reason to prefer even my own acknowledged lesser good to my greater, and have a more ardent affection for the former than the latter. (T 2.3.3.6/416)

And

> In short, a passion must be accompanied with some false judgment in order to its being unreasonable; and even then it is not the passion, properly speaking, which is unreasonable, but the judgment.

> The consequences are evident. Since a passion can never, in any sense, be called unreasonable, but when founded on a false supposition, or when it chuses means insufficient for the designed end, it is impossible, that reason and passion can ever oppose each other, or dispute for the government of the will and actions. (T 2.3.3.6/416)

Here is Hume, allege his opponents, hanged by his own words! But the context of these discussions is entirely that of heavy-duty anatomical studies, not one of evaluative reflections upon human life. "Reasonable" here means "issuing from reason (our cognitive and inferential powers) alone," or, in other words, regardless of conative standpoint. Seeing us as motivated solely by reason would demand the causal rigidity that we discussed in the prior section. Similarly, when Hume says provocatively that "tis not contrary to reason to prefer the destruction of the whole world to the scratching of my little finger," he is not denying that such a preference would be absurd, immoderate, appalling, insane, inhumane, or ridiculous. He is just denying one explanation, first, of why we do not have such a preference and, second, of why we find it so appalling, in order to make room for his own.[3]

It will be appropriate here to insert a short aside about the notorious argument for his position that Hume advances. Reason cannot alone produce passions and actions, as we have seen, but neither can it stand in logical relations to them, such as, for instance, contradicting them. The argument for this is simple:

> A passion is an original existence, or, if you will, modification of existence, and contains not any representative quality, which renders it a copy of any other existence or modification. When I am angry, I am actually possest with the passion, and in that emotion have no more a reference to any other object, than when I am thirsty, or sick, or more than five foot high. It is impossible, therefore, that this passion can be opposed by, or be contradictory to truth and reason; since this contradiction consists in the disagreement of ideas, considered as copies, with those objects, which they represent. (T 2.3.3.5/415)

An extreme view of this, perhaps set afoot by Anthony Kenny (1963), interprets Hume as denying or ignoring the intentionality of passions or emotions, as if Hume thought that you can desire, but not desire anything, or take pride, but not take pride in any particular thing. This is quite gratuitous: after all, Hume devotes most of Book 2 of the *Treatise* to considering the various objects of the various passions. It is slightly more reasonable to protest that because passions have intentional objects, their "fit" with these objects may be appropriate or inappropriate and thereby opens up a field on which reason may be deployed. The response, again, is that whereas a passion such as fear might indeed have a particular object, and whereas we may indeed make judgments about whether it is appropriate to that object, neither the fear itself nor our onlooking judgments are the progeny of reason alone or stand to be contradicted by or in accordance with truths. The arachnophobe is terrified at the spider in the bath; the entomologist is not and neither does he think the spider is an appropriate object of fear. But the problem with the fear is not a representative failure, like color blindness. It represents the spider no more nor less than the entomologist's interest in it. He is lucky in his calm, and she is unlucky in her fearfulness, and as far as that goes, it is just as one of us might be lucky and the other not in our height or thirst or hunger. These are all "original existences." The only difference is that we hope that passions are susceptible to alteration by persuasion and experience, mobilizing other things about which we care, and sometimes they are.

Hume is correct that the fear itself is not a state of mind representing any fact about the spider. It might be triggered by the false belief that it is capable of causing pain or death, but then it is the falsity of this supposition that clashes with the truth, not the consequential fear. The fear itself does not represent it as being dangerous (although it may be responsible for perceptions saturated with affect, as described earlier). The arachnophobe may, wrongly, believe that the spider is dangerous, but her fear might equally coincide with knowledge that it is not—it may be merely the sight of it that triggers the panic, just as the thought of appearing in public might terrify a young person. As Hume describes, imagination can trigger fear as effectively as belief (T 1.3.13.11/148). On the other hand, an entomologist may know that a spider is dangerous but feel no fear because he is confident of his ability to avoid its bite.

A final canard that has gained some currency is not so extreme as the view that Hume permits no practical reasoning, but holds instead that he can only admit "means–end" practical reasoning or "hypothetical imperatives" in which the end is given and we argue about the means. On the face of it, this is simply untrue: Hume frequently tries to persuade us of the value of certain ends in life (tranquility, the pleasures of the well-stocked and well-practised mind "cultivating of that higher and more refined taste, which enables us to judge of the characters of men, of compositions of genius, and of the productions of the nobler arts" (ESY 1.1.4/6) and the trumpery nature of others, nor is there the least obstacle to his doing so. One might try arguing that because such reasoning must, in accordance with his own view, activate some "passion" to be effective, then it can always be represented as a means to satisfying whatever desire is involved in that passion. But that falsely supposes that Hume's passions are all and only desires, whereas he is explicit that many other things are (T 2.1.1.4/276–7). Sometimes, we may be drawn to some course of action because we imagine it to be conducive to a certain end that we desire. But we may equally be drawn to it in the same way that we might be drawn to the company of a friend simply because it is agreeable or drawn to an action because gratitude suggests it. There is no reason for Hume either to deny the phenomena or to describe it differently (Gill 2011; Russell 2009).

The related charge, that Hume cannot even certify the irrationality of failing to take known means to genuinely intended ends, seems no better. First of all, it is not easy to make out just what the "norm" here is: there are states of mental paralysis, vacillation, irresolution, depression, self-doubt, and inertia that may on occasion be unfortunate ("irrational") but any of which may, in a different context, be a thoroughly good thing, perhaps even the work of an on-board guardian angel saving you from yourself. Kant himself sometimes pronounces it to be analytic that if you fully will the end, then you also will the known necessary means, in which case there is no space for a "norm" to be needed or to apply.[4] In other words, although there are norms of rationality, and they can be broken, it is much more doubtful whether this is one, for failures here force reinterpretation (contra Dreier 2001). If we find you are not taking what you must know to be the necessary steps, then we no longer know where you stand on the end.[5] You may have simply resigned yourself to the end being out of your current reach. The only norm in the case is that, from the standpoint of desire for the end, the subject failing to take the means is doing the wrong thing.

III REASONABLE PEOPLE

Hume never changed his mind about the fundamentals of his view of morals and practical reason. There is, at most, a shift in his principal interests, but that is quite consistent with complete constancy of doctrine. The shift I have in mind is from the *Treatise*, with the passages I have quoted, to his own moral, political, and historical works and essays, where he is less concerned to distinguish the different parts of the soul and more concerned to describe and comment upon the doings of people.

Although in the *Treatise* passages he is concerned, as a strict anatomist of the mind, to circumscribe the role of reason and its relation to the passions, in his other writings, he is quite happy to talk of reasons as any kind of consideration for or against something, and he similarly talks freely of reasonable people, plans, desires, precautions, policies, or inclinations, allowing himself the senses that the Oxford Dictionary offers: having sound judgment, sensible, sane, not asking too much, moderate in demands or amount, not absurd or ridiculous.[6] This actually implies that he need not have made his anatomical points by putting the word "reason" so much in the center—and had he not done so, he might have avoided a good deal of misunderstanding. The important point about the will and morality is that cognizing the relations of ideas (i.e., making correct logical and mathematical inferences) and exercising causal and inductive habits on the data of the senses, even when they are acting in concert, do not by themselves suffice to explain actions. They need the assistance of the active states of passion and concern. There is a point that can be made without involving any notion of reason, yet it contains the essence of Hume's view.

Revisiting the person who prefers his own acknowledged lesser good to his greater, Hume the moralist could perfectly well describe him as unreasonable, just as he can see the erection of the vaults of principle and justice as exercises of reason; that is, as deployments of admirable human traits such as foresight, prudence, and cooperation. It is with this hat on that he says:

Whatever we may imagine concerning the usual truth and sincerity of men who live in a rude and barbarous state, there is much more falsehood, and even perjury among them, than among civilized nations; virtue which is nothing but a more enlarged and more cultivated reason, never flourishes to any degree, nor is founded on steady principles of honour, except where a good education becomes general; and where men are taught the pernicious consequences of vice, treachery, and immorality. (HE 3, App. 1)

When our humanity condemns traits of mind, then, if we so choose, the word "unreasonable" is at hand, although in my own view the other words that name their vice are both stronger and more precise. What is the authority, or what Mill would have called the ultimate sanction of the humane sentiments? Why can humane feelings be a standpoint from which to condemn envy, whereas envy is not a standpoint from which to condemn humane feelings? The ultimate sanction lies in the weight of our own feelings, no more, but certainly no less. When these fail, as with the sensible knave, there is no skyhook dragging him out of himself into the ambit of humanity. There is only our own aversion, perhaps a resolution to improve education to prevent his like from emerging, and a sad prediction of his ultimate failure to live a life that is satisfying even to himself.

It is hard to read much of the literature of the past forty years, from Murdoch (1970) to Parfit (2011), without fearing that a kind of fog has drifted over the landscape of moral philosophy. A multitude of writers have felt that they see "normativity" deep in the recesses of the heavens, whereas in our minds there live not only desires and other passions, but something greater, some perception of the sun with the authority to stamp some desires, but possibly not others, as the darling creatures of reason. When writers feel they can do this, they can then excoriate Hume for not having done the same. But I know of no argument suggesting that this is more than an illusion and, by philosophical standards, a dangerous one. Relegating those whose concerns we wish to oppose to being irrational is a way of objectifying them rather than one of engaging with them. We should be careful about using it as the default diagnosis.

IV Value and Morality

A remark of the historian Margaret Wilson illuminates Hume's approach to values. Talking in general of philosophers of the seventeenth century, including Galileo, Descartes, Hobbes, Boyle, and Malebranche, Wilson says:

also common to most of these writers is a tendency to vacillate, just as Locke does, over whether terms like "color" and "red" denominate physical structures, or the "powers" that (partly) result from the structures to cause sensations, or (as Locke seems usually to suppose) the sensations themselves.

(Wilson 1992: 229)

In other words, these writers were unable or unwilling to decide between three theories:

1. Colors are microphysical structures (possibly including relationships with other surrounding physical structures).
2. Colors are the powers or dispositions that objects have, in virtue of their microphysical structures, to cause particular sensations in us.
3. Colors are sensations (*qualia*) in us.

There have been defenses of these philosophers, but everyone will recognize the same three candidates for virtues in Hume: here, I pick only three out of many illustrative remarks:

1. They are useful or agreeable qualities in persons.

   Temperance, sobriety, patience, constancy, perseverance, forethought, considerateness, secrecy, order, insinuation, address, presence of mind, quickness of conception, facility of expression, these, and a thousand more of the same kind, no man will ever deny to be excellencies and perfections. As their merit consists in their tendency to serve the person, possessed of them, without any magnificent claim to public and social desert, we are the less jealous of their pretensions, and readily admit them into the catalogue of laudable qualities. We are not sensible that, by this concession, we have paved the way for all the other moral excellencies, and cannot consistently hesitate any longer, with regard to disinterested benevolence, patriotism, and humanity. (EM 6.1.21/126)

2. They are the powers that persons have, through possessing such qualities, to excite pleasure, love, and admiration, or their opposites, in those who contemplate them.

   Now since every quality in ourselves or others, which gives pleasure, always causes pride or love; as every one, that produces uneasiness, excites humility or hatred: It follows, that these two particulars are to be considered as equivalent, with regard to our mental qualities, virtue and the power of producing love or pride, vice and the power of producing humility or hatred. In every case, therefore, we must judge of the one by the other; and may pronounce any quality of the mind virtuous, which causes love or pride; and any one vicious, which causes hatred or humility. (T 3.3.1.3/575)

3. They are these passions themselves, lying in the mind of the person contemplating them.

   Take any action allowed to be vicious: Wilful murder, for instance. Examine it in all lights, and see if you can find that matter of fact, or real existence, which you call vice. In which-ever way you take it, you find only certain passions, motives, volitions and thoughts. There is no other matter of fact in the case. The vice entirely escapes you, as long as you consider the object. You never can find it, till you turn your reflection into your own breast, and find a sentiment of disapprobation, which arises in you, towards this action. Here is a matter of fact; but it is the object of feeling, not of reason. It lies in yourself, not in the object. So that when you pronounce any action or character to be vicious, you mean nothing, but that from the constitution of your nature you have a feeling or sentiment of blame from the contemplation of it. (T 3.1.1.26/468–9)

EUCLID has fully explained every quality of the circle, but has not, in any proposition, said a word of its beauty. The reason is evident. Beauty is not a quality of the circle. It lies not in any part of the line *whose* parts are all equally distant from a common center. It is only the effect, which that figure produces upon a mind, whose particular fabric or structure renders it susceptible of such sentiments. In vain would you look for it in the circle, or seek it, either by your senses, or by mathematical reasonings, in all the properties of that figure. (ESY 1.18.16/165)

It may seem unpardonable, by modern analytic standards, to sit quiet about such an apparently momentous choice: in the object, in its powers, or in us? But Hume, at least, has a compelling excuse. The vacillation is over a "metaphysical" question: "what colours are" or "what virtues are." But this is not Hume's question. Hume is the philosopher of human nature, and his enquiries are entirely concerned with what underlies our *experience* of virtue or our *thoughts* or *talk* about virtue. As far as that goes, he need not be troubled about the vacillation. From his perspective, the tripartite story is quite enough in the way of metaphysics. On the one hand, we have the qualities of character. These are able to excite our admiration and esteem. And those feelings gain expression in our moral approval. Were any of the three stages missing, we would not be valuing qualities of character as we do.

The same tripartite structure underlies Hume's philosophy of causation:

(1) Causes are temporarily prior elements in regular patterns of events.
(2) They are the powers such patterns have to prompt inferential dispositions in the mind.
(3) They are the inferential dispositions themselves or other stances of the mind, such as our disposition to make practical interventions to achieve results.

The second element is not so prominent here, presumably because it would be a poor attack on the concept of causation simply to cite the causal powers described therein. But it truly describes the relation between the first and third elements. In each case, then, there is, on the one hand, the contribution of the world insofar as we can understand it and, on the other hand, the functional change in the mind that is aware of that contribution. And Hume is just as forthright about the third element:

The necessity of any action, whether of matter or of the mind, is not properly a quality in the agent, but in any thinking or intelligent being, who may consider the action, and consists in the determination of his thought to infer its existence from some preceding objects. (T 2.3.2.2/408)

If Hume is by contemporary standards regrettably relaxed about the metaphysics, he is equally so about the semantics. There is bound to be an anachronistic element in shoehorning his views into our own semantic categories, although it is quite proper to argue that one or another view of the meaning of evaluative sentences is the best descendant of his insights.

The recent weight of critical opinion seems to have been that the most legitimate or direct heir is a secondary quality theory, thinking of the moral sense as analogous to our sense of color. Yet he makes no use of the idea of a moral sense outside T 3.3.1, where it is simply a notational variant of moral sentiment, and although he certainly notes an analogy with secondary qualities, there are disadvantages in offering him this comparison by way of a substantial theory (Blackburn 1993). This is because Hume does not think there exists a stable and defensible theory of the way in which our experience of any sensible quality relates to the quality itself. The whole of *Treatise* 1.4, with its culminating cries of despair, shows that the last thing he should be happy to do is to "model" the philosophy of the passions on the catastrophic absence of tenable theory that surrounds the perception of sensible qualities. It would be like using an Escher drawing as an architectural blueprint.

Even if we thought something more positive emerged from Book 1, there would still be obstacles in the comparison with color. A passion in the case of ethics and an inferential disposition in the case of causation are neither of them much like a bare experience of color. A real passion, for instance, requires no sensory contact with its object. It can be aroused by a true or false narrative in a way that a color experience cannot. It is active in the way that a color experience is not. Having or changing a passion or inclination is making a response to an object, and in that sense the phenomena we are talking about are all of them "response dependent." But this is not to say that in voicing our response we describe it, saying something that will be true if we are sincere and false if we are not. The expression of a passion, like the expression of an inferential disposition, is most certainly not the description of how its object strikes one, let alone how it strikes some population or subset of the population. There is a world of difference between "I love her!" and "she is such as to excite love in population P"—for any population at all, including the set with only myself in it.

Wittgenstein saw this clearly:

> If someone asks me: "What colour is this book?" and I reply: "It's green"—might I as well have given the answer: "The generality of English-speaking people call that 'green'"?
>
> Might he not ask: "And what do you call it?" For he wanted to get my reaction.
>
> (Wittgenstein 1956/1978, III, §71, 197)

Wittgenstein's listener gets what he wants only when we say out of our own mouths that something is beautiful, or good, giving our own reactions. The first two elements in our trio are not forgotten, for that reaction will be grounded in the qualities of objects, and it will be the result of the power those qualities have to excite love and pride or, alternatively, aversion and shame. Nevertheless, it is our own state of mind and its expression that take primary place in locating the semantics of our expressions. They are,

I should say, the semantic anchorage points of the most general forms of evaluative language (so-called *thick terms* with which we express warm or cold feelings about a trait have this anchorage point, but also have another in the kind of trait to which we are referring). Hume was not concerned with the niceties that divide expressivists and secondary-quality theorists, and perhaps he was wise not to be. But he locates the key to understanding the phenomena of morality in exactly the same place as do expressivists. The rest is detail about how exactly to cross from simple expression of attitude to the propositonal reflection of that attitude as it occurs in the elaborated activity of making judgment.

V EXPRESSION AND THE COMMON POINT OF VIEW

This brings us to a further important wrinkle. Does Hume ignore Wittgenstein's point when he introduces the "general point of view" in the *Treatise* or "common point of view" in EM? The concept is not entirely easy to fit with the simple idea of voicing our own reactions to things. Indeed, Hume introduces it in response to two "remarkable circumstances in the affair, which may seem objections to the present system" (the other is the virtue-in-rags problem, which he easily handles). When we "take up" the point of view "of those who have an intercourse with a person," it might seem that we leave behind our own sentiments entirely, but confine ourselves to what those would have been had we been in a quite different situation. In which case, the idea that it is our sentiments of approbation or disgust that excite our applause or condemnation is no longer true—we issue the verdicts but do not have the sentiments. This is perhaps the most significant objection to an expressivist reading of Hume on morality and aesthetics; it is directly parallel to the problem in the discussion of causation when we meet the idea of causal connections of which we have no inkling and which we cannot therefore use in making inferences.

Hume answers the problem quite confidently in the *Treatise* ("But to consider the matter a-right, it has no force at all; and it is the easiest matter in the world to account for it"), although the analogy he uses might be thought not to come to terms with the problem:

> In like manner, external beauty is determined merely by pleasure; and it is evident, a beautiful countenance cannot give so much pleasure, when seen at the distance of twenty paces, as when it is brought nearer us. We say not, however, that it appears to us less beautiful: Because we know what effect it will have in such a position, and by that reflection we correct its momentary appearance. . . . It is therefore from the influence of characters and qualities, upon those who have an intercourse with any person, that we blame or praise him. (T 3.3.1.14/582)

This is correct as far as it goes. Hume is clearly within his rights to notice the privilege some positions enjoy. We have to be in the "right" position to respond to beauty, taste, causation, or virtue and vice. If a meal gains applause because *when* you taste it you find it pleasurable, you cannot argue that it fails to deserve the applause because you yourself, not tasting it, are gaining no pleasure. You recognize what would be needed to make the verdict in propria persona (similar themes recur in "Of the Standard of Taste," ESY 1.23.11/233–4).

But what account does Hume have of the verdict when it is unaccompanied by the pleasure? One natural suggestion would rely on the second element of the three I have been distinguishing: the face is such as to excite pleasure, but only on subjects well placed to appreciate it. But if this is just an empirical judgment, there seems to be a disengagement from actual passion. If we carry that over to the moral case, it would seem that our judgment that someone's character is such as to serve those closer to him might be a purely intellectual assessment, again disengaged from feeling and therefore incapable on its own of engaging our own emotions. And that would strip moral judgments of their practical identities.

This overlooks the role of sympathy in Hume's system. The service done to those others with whom the agent does have a close positive relation does excite a sentiment in us as we contemplate the service. It excites our sympathetic approval and thence our praise or blame. In other words, taking up the "common point of view" is not a matter of leaving passion behind. Imagining the pleasure of those who have intercourse with the virtuous character, we feel a corresponding pleasure on their behalf, as it were, and that excites our admiration, our tendency to praise or blame, and perhaps our own motivations if we are then minded to emulate this character or encourage others to do so. The continued involvement of the passions is made especially clear in EM:

> While the human heart is compounded of the same elements at present it will never be wholly indifferent to public good, nor entirely unaffected with the tendency of character and manners . . . the humanity of one man is the humanity of every one; and the same object touches this passion in all human creatures. (EM 9.6/148)

Similarly, the lover dwelling on how lovely his mistress looked last night or imagining how she will look tonight is pleasurably reliving or imagining a pleasure, and to the art lover thinking of those lucky people in the National Gallery itself conjures a pleasure. With sympathy, we imagine ourselves in the position of anyone contemplating the mistress or the paintings; knowing the pleasure we would then receive, we give, as it were a displaced or "de-centered" verdict—the one that these objects deserve. And the word "deserve" is no problem here because we have already seen that the traits and dispositions of character we admire only get fully manifested in some circumstances. Prioritizing the position of one tasting the meal (seeing the beauty, being within the ambit of the agent), imagining how we would feel in that situation, and thence feeling a vicarious pleasure or pain, we have the sentiments that get expressed in our "corrected" moral judgments (Radcliffe 1994).

At this point, we might raise the question of just how practical Hume thinks that morality is. Is he what, in contemporary terms, is sometimes called an "internalist," thinking that a moral commitment necessarily motivates the one who has it? Or is he more of an "externalist," holding that although it is practical in one sense or another, nevertheless, it is contingent whether an appreciation of what morality requires motivates us on any particular occasion? On this latter view, thinking that morality requires something would be like thinking that such-and-such represents better value for money. Such a consideration doubtless motivates most people most of the time but bears marks of contingency upon it. You can ignore it, if you wish.

There is every evidence that Hume adopted the second, more externalist, position. All that he requires is that passion alone *can* motivate us to act, once reason has indicated how to act to satisfy it, not that it *must* do so. Morality, especially, is not exempt from variation in this respect:

> Hence we naturally desire what is forbid, and take a pleasure in performing actions, merely because they are unlawful. The notion of duty, when opposite to the passions, is seldom able to overcome them; and when it fails of that effect is apt rather to increase them, by producing an opposition in our motives and principles. (T 2.3.4.5/421)

> My sympathy with another may give me the sentiment of pain and disapprobation, when any object is presented, that has a tendency to give him uneasiness; tho' I may not be willing to sacrifice any thing of my own interest, or cross any of my passions, for his satisfaction. (T 3.3.1.19/586)

Hume is well aware that we are contrary beings, as well as short-sighted, hard-hearted, jealous, envious, and all the rest. There is only a small particle of dove mingled in with the wolf and the serpent. But, of course, all that is consistent with the passionate nature of moral commitment because none of our other passions sits in the motivational saddle all the time, either. Life is a constant exercise of balance and compromise. When duty does not strike us as all that attractive compared to, say, the temptations of the moment or even long-term worldly interest, it can recruit allies: public opinion, reputation, the fear of discovery, the anticipated pain of not being able to bear our own survey. Sometimes, with extra pull, it gains the day, and sometimes it does not.

The comparison with money may be useful. It may be contingent that money motivates, but it is a contingency with very deep roots. Certainly, it does not motivate everyone all the time. We don't feel like working, or we do things freely, we waive away proffered payments, we are generous and careless. But given the functional role of money in recompensing the goods and services we supply so that we are able to command goods and services in return, it cannot be contingent that it matters to us. Nothing could count as money unless it did so. It is doubtless contingent that we use money: contingent on the "circumstances of justice"—the fact that goods are in short supply, that human beings need to work for them, that they will be self-interested enough only to work for a return, and that they can contrive stable enough circumstances to take a token for that future return. Money, too, might be compared to a vault, built on trust in reciprocity, where individual transactions may be against the public interest, but where the shelter of the whole system is incomparably useful. To perform this function, money must motivate, and occasions on which it is ignored must be exceptional. In fact, motivation by a sense of justice and motivation by money are not as distinct as we might, high-mindedly, like to think. Hume's comparison (EM App. 3, 8) is deeply apt.

It is here that the practical nature of morality rests. It involves a set of thoughts and feelings that both emerge from what gives us pain or pleasure, and it provides a new direction, a new set of objects of pain and pleasure: the traits that we despise or hate and those that we admire and of which we might feel proud. This is the "new creation" of which Hume talks. It does not follow at all that those pleasures and pains motivate us all the time, although they will have their voice heard, if sometimes only faintly, in our practical inclinations. A society in which this is not so could not long continue to exist, and that is enough to ensure the continued public interest in admonishing the villains and shoring up the tottering virtue of the weak.

ABBREVIATIONS OF WORKS CITED

EM   *Enquiry Concerning the Principles of Morals.* Edited by Tom L. Beauchamp. Oxford: Clarendon, 1998.

ESY   *Essays: Moral, Political, and Literary.* Revised edition by E. F. Miller. Indianapolis: Liberty Classics, 1985.

EU   *An Enquiry Concerning Human Understanding.* Edited by T. L. Beauchamp. Oxford: Clarendon, 2000.

HE   *The History of England,* 6 Vols. Foreword by W. B. Todd. Indianapolis: Liberty Classics, 1983.

T   *A Treatise of Human Nature.* Edited by D. F. Norton and M. J. Norton. Oxford: Clarendon, 2007.

NOTES

1. Also, theoretical understanding "never contemplates what is done in action and says nothing about what is to be avoided or pursued" (*De Anima* III 9 432^{b}27–9). I am indebted here to Reeve (2012).
2. Of course, neither Hume nor Mill need disapprove of the "formula of humanity" taken purely as a piece of practical morality.
3. A similar distinction between cognitive psychology and evaluative epistemology informs Hume's wider philosophy. See Garrett (2002: 214).
4. It is true that Kant qualifies this in some passages, adding that it is "only insofar as reason has a decisive influence on his actions," but he also says it outright, omitting the qualification, sometimes in the same paragraph (*Groundwork* 1998: 4.417).

5. For accuracy, one must be very careful about knowing the necessary means. If I intend to lose weight and know that a necessary means is to eat less, I can nevertheless rightly hold that on each occasion of a meal, it is not necessary to diet just now: there is a paradox here akin to that of the paradox of the preface.

6. For example: "One that has a real design of harming us, proceeding not from hatred and ill-will, but from justice and equity, draws not upon him our anger, if we be in any degree reasonable" (T 2.2.3.7/350). "But all prospect of success in life, or even of tolerable subsistence, must fail, where a reasonable frugality is wanting" (EM 6.11/237). "Your precaution" says Philo, "of seasoning your children's minds with early piety, is certainly very reasonable; and no more than is necessary in this profane and irreligious age" (D 3). There are endless other examples.

BIBLIOGRAPHY

Anscombe, G. E. M. (1957). *Intention*. Oxford: Blackwell.

Augustine of Hippo. (1982). *De Genesi ad Litteram*, in *Ancient Christian Writers*, Quasten, J. Burghardt, W. J. and Lawler T. C., eds. Mahwah NJ: Paulist Press.

Bennett, J. (1976). *Linguistic Behaviour*. Cambridge: Cambridge University Press.

Blackburn, S. (1993). "Hume on the Mezzanine Level," *Hume Studies* 19, 273–288.

Blackburn, S. (1998). *Ruling Passions*. Oxford: Oxford University Press.

Cohon, R. (2008a). *Hume's Morality: Feeling and Fabrication*. Oxford: Oxford University Press.

Cohon, R. (2008b). "Reply to Radcliffe and Garrett," *Hume Studies* 34(2), 277–285.

Dreier, J. (2001). "Humean Doubts about Categorical Imperatives," in Millgram, E. ed., *Varieties of Practical Reasoning*, Cambridge, MA: MIT Press, 27–47.

Garrett, Don. (2002). *Cognition and Commitment in Hume's Philosophy*. Oxford: Oxford University Press.

Gill, M. (2011). "Humean Moral Pluralism." *History of Philosophy Quarterly* 28(1), 45–64.

Kant, Immanuel. (1998). *Groundwork*. Mary J. Gregor, trans. and ed. Cambridge: Cambridge University Press.

Kenny, A. (1963). *Action, Emotion and Will*. London: Rougledge & Kegan Paul.

Korsgaard, C. (1986) "Skepticism about Practical Reason" *J. Phil* 83 (1) 5–25.

Mill, J. S. (1861/2001). *Utilitarianism*. George Sher, ed. Indianapolis: Hackett.

Millgram, E. (1995) "Was Hume a Humean?" *Hume Studies* 21 (1) 75–93.

Murdoch, I. (1970). *The Sovereignty of Good*. London: Routledge & Kegan Paul.

Nagel, Thomas. (1970). *The Possibility of Altruism*. Princeton, NJ: Princeton University Press.

Parfit, D. (2011). *On What Matters*. Oxford: Oxford University Press.

Pettit, P., and M. Smith. (1990). "Backgrounding Desire," *Philosophical Review* 99, 565–92.

Pigden C. R., ed. (2009). *Hume on Motivation and Virtue*. London: Palgrave Macmillan.

Radcliffe, E. (1994). "Hume on Motivating Sentiments, the General Point of view, and the Inculcation of Morality," *Hume Studies* 20, 37–58.

Radcliffe, E. (2006). "Moral Internalism and Moral Cognitivism in Hume's Metaethics," *Synthèse* 152, 353–70.

Reeve, David. (2012). *Action, Contemplation, and Happiness: An Essay on Aristotle*. Cambridge: Harvard University Press.

Russell, L. (2009). "Two Kinds of Normativity: Korsgaard vs. Hume," in C. R. Pigden, ed., *Hume on Motivation and Virtue*. London: Palgrave Macmillan: 208–225.

Sayre-McCord, G. (2007). "Hume on Practical Morality and Inert Reason," in Russ Shafer-Landau, ed., *Oxford Studies in Metaethics* . Oxford: Oxford University Press: 299–320.

Smith, M. (1987). "The Humean Theory of Motivation," *Mind* 96, 36–51.

Wilson, M. (1992). "History of Philosophy in Philosophy Today; and the Case of the Sensible Qualities," *Philosophical Review* 101, 191–243.

Wittgenstein, Ludwig. (1956/1978). *Remarks on the Foundations of Mathematics*, G. H. von Wright, R. Rhees, and G. E. M. Anscombe, eds.; translated by G. E. M Anscombe. Oxford: Basil Blackwell.

Zimmerman, A. (2007). "Hume's Reasons," *Hume Studies* 33, 211–256.

CHAPTER 22

HUME ON THE ARTIFICIAL VIRTUES

GEOFFREY SAYRE-MCCORD

I INTRODUCTION

My aim in this chapter is to make sense of Hume's account of the artificial virtues. According to virtually everyone, Hume's discussion of the artificial virtues—and especially of the conventions on which he argues they depend—is inspired, rich, and subtle. At the same time, also according to virtually everyone, Hume's discussion is deeply puzzling. Some have thought the puzzles so deep as to render Hume's position internally inconsistent or, if not, at least disingenuous.[1] Puzzling though Hume's discussion is, I hope to show that his account of the artificial virtues is not just consistent and sincere but plausible and attractive.

II BACKGROUND

Hume begins his discussion of morals, in the *Treatise of Human Nature*, arguing that our capacity to mark moral distinctions is not due to reason alone, but depends crucially on our ability to feel moral approbation and disapprobation. Just as we would not be able to distinguish things by their color, were we entirely color blind, so too, Hume maintains, we would not be able to distinguish actions, sentiments, or characters morally, were we entirely disengaged affectively.[2] "[V]irtue," Hume writes, "is distinguished by the pleasure, and vice by the pain, that any action, sentiment or character gives us by the mere view and contemplation" (T 3.1.2.11/475). And, pressing the same idea, he claims that "To have the sense of virtue is nothing but to *feel* a satisfaction of a particular kind from the contemplations of a character" (T 3.1.2.3/471).[3] That "particular kind" of satisfaction, on Hume's account, is a distinctive feeling of moral approval, which one feels thanks to the workings of sympathy when one sets aside considerations of self-interest.

Significantly, although Hume appeals generally to feelings of moral approval and disapproval, he refines his view of which moral approvals and disapprovals are relevant to moral distinctions and why. He does this in order to capture accurately the moral judgments we actually make while also explaining the differences between (1) our merely feeling approval of some trait and our judging it to be a virtue and (2) our judging a trait to be a virtue and it actually being a virtue. In places, Hume does write as if thinking that something is a virtue is simply a matter of feeling approval toward it, holding, for instance, that morality "is more properly felt than judg'd of" (T 3.1.2.1/470).[4] Yet, as Hume recognizes, the plausibility of his theory depends on it respecting, and being able to explain, the fact that we distinguish between *feeling* approving of someone and *judging* her to be virtuous (just as we distinguish between something appearing blue and our judging it to be blue). And he takes great care in doing so. One of the important refinements involves distinguishing moral approval (which is felt "only when a character is considered in general, without reference to our particular interest" [T 3.1.2.4/472]) from other kinds of approval. Another is the identification of a privileged set of circumstances, distinctive of what Hume calls the "General Point of View," in which feelings of moral approval set the standard for whether something counts as virtuous and so a standard for moral judgment. Some trait is a virtue, on Hume's view, if, but only if, it would garner moral approval from the General Point of View. With that standard in place, we can distinguish between what we happen to approve of, given our actual situation, and what we would approve of, were we to take up the General Point of View. For our purposes, though, we can leave aside these refinements and the details of Hume's account of moral judgment in order to focus on what, according to Hume, secures the relevant moral approval.[5]

III Virtuous Actions and Virtuous Motives

According to Hume, the relevant feelings of moral approval and disapproval are directed fundamentally not at actions (even though we do evaluate actions morally) but at the motives and durable traits of mind and character that give rise to action. "'Tis evident," he maintains, "that when we praise any actions, we regard only the motives that produced them, and consider the actions as signs or indications of certain principles in the mind and temper. The external performance has no merit. We must look within to find the moral quality" (T 3.2.1.2/477).[6] This view is as old as Plato and Aristotle, who emphasized that the moral standing of one's actions depends not merely on what one does but on why one does it. The same idea, of course, is at the heart of Kant's moral philosophy, which holds that the moral worth of an action depends exclusively on the agent's intention.[7] Just as there is a crucial difference between those who merely act like friends and those who are truly one's friends (a difference that turns on why they act as they do) there is a crucial difference—a moral difference—between those who merely act in the way a generous, kind, or just, person would act and those who are truly generous, kind, or just (a difference that turns on why they act as they do, and one that affects the moral standing of the action performed).[8] The "ultimate object of our praise and approbation," Hume claims, "is the motive, that produced them" (T 3.2.1.2/477).

Similarly, Hume sees our evaluation of characters as tied to the motives with which we associate them. Thus, for instance, those who are genuinely benevolent are those of whom being motivated by a concern to help others is characteristic, and those who are genuinely cruel are those of whom being motivated by a desire to hurt others is characteristic. As a result, distinctions among the various virtues and vices are, as Hume sees things, ultimately distinctions among corresponding motives, thought of broadly as "principles in the mind and temper" (T 3.2.1.2/477), which include not simply preferences or desires, but also passions, dispositions, and the other aspects of personality that give rise to actions.

What marks a person as benevolent or cruel, just or selfish, courageous or manipulative, Hume is emphasizing, is not what they do but why they do it—the features of their personalities that lead them to act as they do. For this reason, if we blame a person for failing to perform some action and then discover "that the virtuous motive was still powerful over his breast, tho' check'd in its operation by some circumstances unknown to us, we retract our blame, and have the same esteem for him, as if he had actually perform'd the action, which we require of him" (T 3.2.1.3/477–8).

Indeed, it is a central tenet of Hume's account that a person's actions are merely "external signs" of what matters to virtue.[9] For each kind of action that we might see as virtuous, and each character trait we might count as a virtue, Hume holds that there must be "in human nature" some corresponding motive (i.e., preference, desire, disposition, or other principle of mind of temper) that would lead to that action, that is characteristic of that virtue, and that secures our moral approval from the General Point of View.

IV THE SENSE OF DUTY AND THE REGARD
TO THE VIRTUE OF AN ACTION

Once we have such a motive in sight, along with an understanding of the sorts of actions to which it would give rise, we can identify that kind of action as, say, benevolent, just, or courageous, even in cases in which the corresponding motive is actually absent. And a person might perform that kind of action without the virtuous motive. Yet, in acting without the virtuous motive, that person will not be acting as a benevolent, just, or courageous person would—that is, not benevolently, justly, or courageously—even though she does what a benevolent, just, or courageous person would have done. In lacking a virtuous motive, the person's action will not be virtuous, even if it is the *kind* of action a virtuous person would have performed (albeit with different motives).

As Hume notes, someone might actually be moved to perform the kind of action by a "regard to the virtue" of the action, that is, from the recognition that it is the kind of action a virtuous motive would lead one to perform. With this in mind, Hume points out that

> When any virtuous motive or principle is common in human nature, a person, who feels his heart devoid of that principle, may hate himself upon that account, and may perform the action without the motive, from a certain sense of duty in order to acquire by practice, that virtuous principle, or at least, to disguise to himself, as much as possible, his want of it. (T 3.2.1.8/479)[10]

Hume here talks specifically of a sense of duty, which (according to Hume) is the sense that a failure to perform an action would show a blameable lack of a virtuous motive.[11] Yet presumably not every action that would result from a virtuous motive is such that absence of the motive would be blameable. So not every virtuous action will be a duty, although all actions that are a duty are virtuous. This means that a person might recognize of some motive that it is virtuous, but not a duty. If this recognition were to move the person to act as those with that motive would act, this would not be a case of acting from a sense of duty. Hume captures both possibilities by talking about "a regard to the virtue" of an action (T 3.2.1.6/478 and T 3.2.1.9/480) or "a sense of its morality" (T 3.2.1.7/479), which involve seeing the action as one a person with a virtuous motive would perform (whether or not failing to have the motive is blameable). Although Hume in the quoted passage highlights a case in which a person notices his lack of a virtuous motive, it is worth registering that a person might actually have the relevant virtuous motive while also recognizing that it is a virtuous motive, thus finding himself with both the first virtuous motive and the motive provided by a regard to the virtue of the action.

Importantly, acting from the sense of duty or a regard to the virtue of the action may well secure the relevant approval and so itself count as a virtuous motive, at least when people are right about what is virtuous.[12] Taking advantage of this, "the public instructions of politicians, and the private education of parents, contribute to the giving us a sense of honour and duty" that provides a motive to act as virtue requires (T 3.2.6.11/533-4; see also T 3.2.2.25/500, T 3.2.5.12/523, T 3.2.8.7/545-6).[13] In fact, Hume claims, "every one, who has any regard to his character, or who intends to live on good terms with mankind, must fix an inviolable law to himself, never, by any temptation, to be induc'd to violate those principles, which are essential to a man of probity and honour" (T 3.2.2.27/501).

V The Need for a First Virtuous Motive

Although a motive of duty or a (motivating) regard to the morality of an action may sometimes itself be virtuous, Hume argues that it is necessarily a secondary motive[14]—one that relies, for its intelligibility, on there being in human nature (even if not in the person in question[15]) some *other* motive to perform the act in question. The motives of duty and more generally of regard to the morality of an action, according to Hume, always presuppose some *other* motive in light of which the action in question counts as one's duty or as virtuous. Indeed, Hume advances the following as an "undoubted maxim": *"that no action can be virtuous, or morally good, unless there be in human nature some motive to produce it, distinct from the sense of its morality"* (T 3.2.1.7/479).[16]

Why accept that maxim? Hume offers a fairly simple argument: to see some action as one's duty, as virtuous, or as morally good, is to see it as a sign of a virtuous motive. To see a motive as virtuous is to think it would secure the relevant approval (i.e., approval from the General Point of View). Whereas the regard for the virtue of an action or a motive of duty might well secure that approval (and be seen as securing it), to have such motives involves seeing some motive for an action as being such that it would secure the relevant approval. And, on pain of circularity, that must be some motive other than a regard for the action's virtue or the sense that so acting is one's duty: "To suppose, that the mere regard to the virtue of the action, may be the first motive, which produc'd the action, and render'd it virtuous, is to reason in a circle" (T 3.2.1.4/478). (This has come to be called the "circle argument.")

Hume does not say why the circularity would be a problem, taking for granted that it obviously is. But it is worth noting that the circularity poses two distinct problems.

First, if we were caught in the circle, the regard to the virtue of an action (or the motive of duty) would have no determinate content and so no particular actions that it would serve to motivate. Which actions are virtuous? Which are our duty? If, as Hume has argued, these questions are answered by appeal to the virtuous motive one might have in performing them, and that motive is simply a regard to the virtue of the action, we would have no way to identify which actions are to be so regarded and so no motive, yet, to do anything in particular. The problem is much like the one I would face if my sole desire were to fulfill the desires of my beloved while her sole desire was to fulfill mine. With nothing more to go on, I would have no motive, yet, to do anything in particular. For me to have a motive to do something, my beloved needs to have some desire that does not refer exclusively back to my desire to satisfy her desires (or, at least, I have to think she has such a desire).[17] What is needed is some desire of hers (that I might act to satisfy) other than a desire to satisfy my desire to satisfy hers. Similarly, when it comes to a regard for *the virtue of an action* (which involves seeing the action as one a person with a virtuous motive would perform), what is needed is some motive to perform an action, other than a regard to the virtue of that action—a motive that is virtuous (or, at least, such that I think it is virtuous). Once another motive is in play, in light of which I might see some particular action as virtuous, a regard for virtue will have a focus and direction, whereas without it, it would have neither.[18]

Second, if we were caught in the circle, we would find ourselves with no account of the virtuousness of the actions we are hoping to explain. The virtuousness of those actions, Hume maintains, depends on the virtuousness of the motive we have to perform them, but the motive on offer—the sense of duty (or a regard to the virtue of the action)—will be an approvable motive (i.e., a virtuous motive) only if (Hume assumes) it is accurate—that is, only if the action in question is really a duty or virtuous. In order for a regard to the virtue of an action to be virtuous, "the action must be really virtuous; and this virtue must be deriv'd from some virtuous motive: And consequently the virtuous motive must be different from the regard to the virtue of the action" (T 3.2.1.4/478).[19] But that means we need an independent explanation of the virtue of the action, an explanation that appeals to something other than a regard to the action's virtue.

Despite Hume writing, at one point, that an "action must *be virtuous*, before we can have a regard to its virtue" (emphasis added), the argument does not require this. If it did, then a fair response would be to point out that people often seem to regard some action as virtuous and perform it for that reason, but be wrong. Examples of misguided acts of duty are legion.

Yet this response mistakes how Hume's argument works. It does not assume that when we regard some action as virtuous we are always right. Hume can easily acknowledge that people may mistakenly think that an action is virtuous and perform the action out of a (mistaken) regard for its (supposed) virtuousness. What Hume is assuming, reasonably, is that a mistaken regard for the virtue of an action would not secure the relevant approval and so would not count as a virtuous motive.[20]

But imagine that Hume is wrong and that a mistaken regard for the virtuous of an action is virtuous. Even then, appealing to the mere regard for the virtue of an action will not work to explain the standing of a whole range of virtues as virtues.

On the one hand, that regard, precisely because it can be inaccurate, often leads people to act contrary to these virtues. The regard to virtue or the motive of duty, if not restricted to instances when the agent has things right, will lead to actions a person with the relevant virtue would never perform. To make a mistake about what a benevolent, prudent, just, or honest person would do, and to act accordingly, is to fail to act as a courageous, kind, generous, or honest person would. So this (mistaken) regard cannot be the motive that explains the virtuousness of the actions that are distinctive of the virtues we are trying to explain. This is true even if a regard to the virtuousness of an action renders that action, whichever action it is and however mistaken the regard, virtuous. In that case, although there would be a virtue of, as we might put it, dutifulness, we would still have no explanation of the virtuousness of benevolence, prudence, justice, fidelity to promises, and the like, as contrasted with all the traits that are not virtues. At the same time, it is plausible to think, as Hume seems to, that being moved by a regard to the virtuousness of actions where that regard goes astray (especially if it goes far astray, to the point of counting deeply vicious actions as virtuous) is no virtue at all.

On the other hand, if we restrict ourselves to cases where the regard is accurate—where the action really is a virtuous one—we need an account of what makes the action virtuous, an account that cannot appeal to the (as yet not established as accurate) regard. And, again, the appeal to the regard for the virtuousness of the action leaves us without the explanation we need.

Although Hume's argument invokes his account of what it is to see a motive as virtuous, the argument carries over to other views. Consider Kant, who famously maintains that we can and should act from the motive of duty, not from inclination. Significantly, Kant didn't hold that what matters is, as Hume would characterize it, a "mere regard to the virtue of an action." Instead, Kant sought a standard of duty that would give content and direction to the thought that some action is one's duty. To that end, he argued that the standard of duty requires that our maxims meet certain formal and substantive requirements: that they be universalizable and such that, in acting on them, we treat humanity as an end. To regard an action as one's duty, according to Kant, is to see it as conforming to this standard. Yet this means that we are not talking about "a mere regard for duty," but rather a concern for whether one's maxims are universalizable and compatible with treating humanity, whether in oneself or others, as an end (and never solely as a means). This concern provides a way to avoid the circle Hume identified and so the two problems that circle poses. At the same time, though, Hume would hold that it does so by offering a motive that goes beyond a (mere) regard for the virtue of the action in question: a regard to whether one's maxims are universalizable and such that acting on them involves treating humanity as an end. Whether such a concern is a virtuous motive, let alone (as Kant seems to hold) the only, or most fundamental, virtuous motive, is of course controversial. What is important here, though, is that Kant's defense of the motive of duty involves identifying (what in Hume's terms would be) *another* motive, one that is not a mere regard to duty.[21]

In any case, Hume's argument is that if actions count as virtuous thanks to the motives of which they are a sign, and the motives count as virtuous because they would secure the relevant approval, for each virtuous action there must be some corresponding motive (other than a sense of duty or a regard for its morality), of which the action is a sign, that secures the relevant approval.[22] And the argument generalizes to those who reject the idea that motives count as virtuous because they secure the relevant approval. As long as one offers an account of what makes motives virtuous that does not reduce to holding that thinking a motive virtuous makes it so, a version of Hume's argument will loom. It establishes the need for some virtuous motive—other than the motive of duty or a regard to the virtue of the action—in order to account for the virtuousness of the action and the virtuousness of the corresponding character trait (assuming that the virtuousness of actions and of character traits are a function of the virtuous motives they reflect).

VI Natural and Artificial Virtues

Hume holds that we can distinguish, among virtuous motives (i.e., motives that secure the relevant approval), between those that are artificial and those that are natural. This difference turns on whether people can have the relevant motives absent the existence of various conventions and artifices that reflect the "designs, and projects, and views of men" (T 3.1.2.9/474); if they can, if the motives "have no dependence on the artifice and contrivance of men" (T 3.3.1.1/574), then they are natural; otherwise, the motives are artificial.[23] This difference among the motives underwrites a distinction among corresponding virtues between those that are natural and those that are artificial.

According to Hume, all virtues fall into (at least) one of four categories: they are all either useful, or immediately agreeable, to the person who has the virtue, or to others. And he argues that they all secure the relevant moral approval because, thanks to sympathy, our idea of the pleasure the virtues produce (by being either useful or immediately agreeable) are transformed into a pleasure that, in turn, gives rise to approval from the General Point of View. "When any quality, or character, has a tendency to the good of mankind, we are pleas'd with it, and approve of it; because it presents a lively idea of pleasure; which idea affects us by sympathy, and is itself a kind of pleasure" (T 3.3.1.14/580). Hume offers a detailed account of how this works. But we can leave aside the detailed story. What is important here is the difference, among the qualities or characters that (via sympathy) give rise to the relevant moral approval, between those that are *natural* and those that are *artificial*.

The natural virtues Hume has in mind include "beneficence, charity, generosity, clemency, moderation, equity" (all of which count as social virtues because of "their tendency to the good of society" [T 3.3.1.11/578–9]), as well as "prudence, temperance, frugality, industry, assiduity, enterprize, dexterity"[24] (which make those who have them "serviceable to themselves, and enable them to promote their own interest" [T 3.3.1.24/587–8]) and also good humor, wit, and eloquence (which are immediately agreeable either to the person himself or to others [T 3.3.4.8/611]). What makes these virtues natural is that the motives characteristic of people with them are available, and secure the relevant approval, independently of what particular artifices and contrivances, if any, might be in place. (Of course, how a charitable person acts will depend, among other things, on the various conventions she finds in place. But her virtuous motive—her concern to help those in need—is available and secures approval regardless of those conventions. The same is true, Hume holds, of all the other natural virtues and their corresponding motives.)

In contrast, Hume maintains, there are a number of virtues that depend on motives that we can have only thanks to human "artifice and contrivance" and, in particular, only in the context of voluntary conventions, and he thinks that once present, they secure the relevant approval only in the context of the conventions that made them possible. Hume has in mind, as paradigms of the artificial virtues, justice concerning property, the performance of promises, and allegiance to government, although he also discusses, more briefly, the duties of princes and political ministers, chastity, and modesty. Despite their evident differences, Hume considers them all to be matters of justice. (The title of the section in which all the artificial virtues are discussed is "Of Justice and Injustice.")

Exactly what leads Hume to this broad conception of justice is unclear. But the conception in play seems to be one of justice as requiring restraint in the face of what, absent the appropriate conventions and the motives they make possible, would be temptation, where the conventions depend on mutual restraint, and the failure of restraint is blameable. Noting that "the avidity and partiality of men wou'd quickly bring disorder into the world if not restrain'd by some general and inflexible principles," Hume argues that it was "with a view to this inconvenience, that men have establish'd those principles, and have agreed to restrain themselves by general rules, which are unchangeable by spite and favour, and by particular views of private or public interest" (T 3.2.6.9/531–3).[25] This general story fits his account not simply of justice as it relates to property, but also his accounts of the other artificial virtues. In each case, Hume argues, the virtues consist in a regard for principles or general rules that "men have establish'd" through convention, as mutually advantageous restraints.[26] What makes all these virtues *artificial* is that the motives characteristic of people with them are available, and secure the relevant approval, only in contexts shaped by particular artifices, inventions, and conventions.[27]

It is worth emphasizing that when it comes to the artificial virtues both the motives characteristic of those with the virtues, and the approval those motives garner from the General Point of View, depend on the existence of conventions. The motives are not even available, Hume argues, absent established conventions—there is nothing in particular one is required to do, for instance, concerning property, until there are rules in place establishing what belongs to who. But even when they are in place, Hume argues, their "tendency to the good of mankind" depends on "the whole plan or scheme," that is, on the convention, of which they are a part (T 3.2.2.22/497–8). The benefits they secure are a product of collective action, not available absent the collaboration of others. In contrast, the natural virtues are such that both the motives characteristic of those with them, and the approval these motives garner from the General Point of View, do not depend on conventions.

Although the artificial virtues depend, for their possibility, on human conventions, Hume emphasizes that those conventions are nearly inevitable. "Mankind is an inventive species; and where an invention is obvious and absolutely necessary, it may as properly be said to be natural as any thing that proceeds immediately from original principles, without the intervention of thought or reflexion. Tho' the rules of justice be artificial, they are not *arbitrary*" (T 3.2.1.19/484).

As becomes clear, a crucial feature of all the artificial virtues is that they each solve salient shared problems that we would otherwise face.[28] The differences among the particular artificial virtues reflect differences among the problems and so differences in how they might be solved. Thus, for instance, justice concerning property addresses the need we have for stable possessions and an effective way to transfer goods, whereas fidelity to promises enables us undertake commitments to future performance that others can trust, and the allegiance to political authority makes stable government possible in a way that it otherwise would not be.[29]

To make the case that justice, understood specifically as respect for the property of others, is an artificial virtue, Hume first considers the natural motives one might think of as candidate motives to justice: private interest, public benevolence (or regard to "publick interest"), and private benevolence. Each of these motives do often prompt people to perform just acts (i.e., the kind of acts a just person would perform). However, Hume points out, they are each such that under familiar circumstances people acting on these motives would act contrary to the requirements of justice. Sometimes acting *un*justly is in one's self-interest, sometimes it will promote the general welfare, and sometimes it will be advantageous for those about whom one cares. Moreover, it is worth noting, even when these motives lead one to act as justice requires, a person so motivated is not one whom we admire *as just*, but rather (if we admire the person at all) as prudent, public spirited, or kind, respectively. Hume does not emphasize this second point. But a crucial requirement on any motive that might be the first virtuous motive to justice is that it is the motive we admire as characteristic of those who are just.[30] In light of this, and assuming he has canvassed, and found wanting, all the plausible natural motives to justice, Hume concludes "that we have naturally no real or universal motive for observing the laws of equity but the very equity and merit of the observance" (T 3.2.1.17/483).[31] What is needed is some motive for just actions—other than a regard for their morality—that is both such that it would consistently lead people to act in ways we recognize as just and is the motive we admire as the motive of a just person.[32] And that motive, Hume has argued, must be a non-natural—that is, an *artificial*—motive since no natural motive fits the bill.

Similar considerations would establish, too, that the keeping of one's promises is an artificial virtue. After all, it is clear that the motives Hume considered in discussing justice would likewise fail consistently to lead one to keep one's promises. And it is clear, too, that these are not the motives we approve of when we admire someone for keeping her promise (even if, when these motives lead someone to keep her promise, we are grateful she did). When these motives lead someone to keep her promises, we would not see her actions as a reflection of the virtue of someone who is true to her word (T 3.2.5.11/522–3). It is one thing to keep one's promise because it happens to be in one's interest; quite another to do it because one gave one's word.

When it comes to promises, though, Hume focuses his attention not on these points, but on arguing "*that a promise would not be intelligible, before human conventions had establish'd it; and that even if it were intelligible, it would not be attended with any moral obligation*" (T 3.2.5.1/516). In defense of the first claim, Hume maintains that "If promise be natural and intelligible, there must be some act of the mind attending these words, *I promise*; and on this act of the mind must the obligation depend" (T 3.2.5.2/516).[33] He is thinking of the act of the mind, whatever it might be, as what would provide the necessary "*inclination to perform [i.e. motive], distinct from a sense of duty*" (T 3.2.5.7/519) that would in turn secure the relevant moral approval. Hume then argues that whatever is involved in making a promise, no particular act of the mind is required. Making a promise is not a matter of resolving, Hume points out, nor of desiring, nor of willing, to act in a certain way. On the one hand, a person might perform any of these acts and yet manifestly not have made a promise; on the other hand, a person might well have made a promise without actually resolving, desiring, or willing, to perform as promised. These acts of the mind are neither necessary nor sufficient for having made a promise.

What candidates are left? Perhaps, Hume suggests, one might think that it is "the *willing* of that *obligation*, which arises from the promise" (T 3.2.5.3/516). Against this possibility, he argues that a mere act of will can change neither our own nor anyone else's sentiments of approval. Yet a "change of the obligation supposes a change in sentiment; and a creation of a new obligation supposes some new sentiment" (T 3.2.5.4/517). As a result, he holds, it would be absurd "to will any new obligation... nor is it possible," he thinks, "that men cou'd naturally fall into so gross an absurdity" (T 3.2.5.4/517). In putting his argument in this way, Hume suggests that whereas men couldn't *naturally* fall into so gross an absurdity, they might so fall thanks to the "artifices and contrivances of men." And, in fact, it seems clear that Hume believes that we can and do fall into the absurdity of thinking we can will an obligation. Yet, precisely because willing an obligation is an absurdity, it cannot be the act of mind on which a promise actually depends. Nor, even supposing such an act of the mind, could it actually establish an obligation, for the same reason: a new obligation would require new sentiments, but (Hume holds) an act of willing, by itself, creates no new sentiments.[34]

Again assuming he has canvassed, and found wanting, all the plausible *natural* motives to keep one's promise, Hume concludes: "as there is naturally no inclination to observe promises, distinct from a sense of their obligation; it follows, that fidelity is no natural virtue, and that promises have no force, antecedent to human conventions" (T 3.2.5.6/518–19).[35] What is needed is some motive to keep promises—other than a regard for their morality or a sense of duty —that would consistently lead people to keep their promises while also being the motive we admire as the motive of a person who is true to her word. And that motive, Hume has argued, must be a non-natural—that is, an *artificial*— motive, since no natural motive fits the bill.

Although Hume spends much less time discussing the other artificial virtues— allegiance to government, the morality of princes and political ministers, chastity, and modesty—considerations of the same sort apply. In each case, as with justice and fidelity to promises, Hume holds that there is no *natural* motive (other than a regard to their virtue) that would consistently lead people to perform the actions we recognize as virtuous. Moreover, the natural motives that do sometimes prompt such actions are not the motives we admire as characteristic of those with the relevant virtues. For these virtues, as for justice and fidelity to promises, the corresponding virtuous actions require *artificial* motives.

If it is virtuous to act justly, to keep one's promises, to give allegiance to one's government, and so forth, and if each virtuous action requires a virtuous motive, then there must be some virtuous motive, other than regard to the virtue of so acting, to perform such actions. Yet there is no natural motive that consistently leads people to act as the virtue requires, that is seen as characteristic of those with the virtue in question, and that secures approval from the General Point of View. Since the motive of duty (or a regard to the morality of the actions) won't do (in light of "the circle argument"), and there is no suitable natural motive, then there must be other—artificial—motives, motives due to "the artifice and contrivance of men," that serve as the first virtuous motives for the corresponding virtues.

VII WHICH ARTIFICES?

Hume's discussion of which artifices matter to the artificial virtues is both lovely and seminal.[36] In it, Hume identifies the relevant conventions as depending on "a general sense of common interest; which sense all the members of the society express to one another, and which induces them to regulate their conduct by certain rules" (T 3.2.2.10/490). As Hume turns his attention from one artificial virtue to the next, he identifies the (different) interests we have in common that are served by having various conventions; some to define property, some to make promising possible, some to establish governments to which allegiance might be due. In each case, Hume argues, we are all better off with the conventions than we would be without, and we all have an interest in conforming to the conventions provided others do so as well. Precisely which conventions we happen to put in place matters much less, he thinks, than that we have some conventions rather than none. And we can have the conventions at all only if people succeed in regulating their conduct by common rules or principles.

Thinking specifically of the rules of justice concerning property, Hume offers this description:

> I observe, that it will be for my interest to leave another in the possession of his goods, *provided* he will act in the same manner with regard to me. He is sensible of a like interest in the regulation of his conduct. When this common sense of interest is mutually expressed, and is known to both, it produces a suitable resolution and behaviour. And this may properly enough be called a convention or agreement betwixt us. . . since the actions of each of us have a reference to those of the other, and are performed upon the supposition, that something is to be performed on the other part. (T 3.2.2.10/490)

When it comes to property, the common interest is based, he argues, on the fact that we find ourselves in a situation in which there is moderate scarcity (of the things we need and want), as well as limited generosity among our fellows. This combination gives point to finding a way to make possessions secure, which an effective system of property will do. If either we enjoyed a superabundance of goods or a community of people who were completely unselfish, he argues, the need for property would disappear. But we are not so lucky, and justice finds its place.

Parallel accounts hold for the other artificial virtues, each finding its place thanks to our being in circumstances in which establishing a convention offers the possibility of mutual advantage. In the case of promises, the circumstances are those in which we would benefit not only by being able to express a willingness or an intention to do something in the future, but by being able to make a commitment to future performance that others can count on. This requires, Hume argues, a convention that enables us to undertake a commitment (e.g., give our word) in a context that makes us liable to a penalty of some sort for a failure to perform. In the case of allegiance, the circumstances—different from those required for property and promises but (Hume thinks) largely motivated by problems they render salient—are those that make establishing a government advantageous. In particular, and most importantly, the circumstances that matter are those we find ourselves in when we notice that while the conventions of property and promises are advantageous, we are liable to temptation to act unjustly and to break our promises. This liability, Hume thinks, is due primarily to the "natural infirmity" we all suffer of giving way "to the sollicitations of our passions, which always plead in favour of whatever is near and contiguous" (T 3.2.7.2/534–5). As a result, we are often seduced by the prospect for short-term benefits at the cost of long-term advantages, not least the long-term advantages that come from successfully sustaining conventions that are mutually beneficial. The demands of justice, the obligation to keep promises, and the duties of allegiance, Hume maintains rest "exactly on the same footing, and have the same source both for their *first invention* and *moral obligation*. They are contriv'd to remedy like inconveniences, and acquire their moral sanction in the same manner, from their remedying those inconveniences" (T 3.2.8.4/542–3).[37]

At the heart of the conventions that make the artificial virtues possible is their being mutually advantageous and recognized as being so. Also crucial, though, is that the conventions, and so their advantages, are available only when others will act accordingly as long as one does one's part. Both the mutual advantage and the reciprocal performance are crucial to these conventions working to underwrite moral *virtues*.

Hume is, of course, well aware that not all conventions are mutually advantageous. Fashion comes to mind, as does (more significantly) slavery. Both take the shapes they do, and lead to the actions they do, only thanks to the "the artifice and contrivance of men." Yet these artifices and contrivances work their effects in ways that do not depend on *mutual* advantage, even as they promote the advantage of some. And this, for Hume, disqualifies them from making a virtue of conformity. A similar point holds for societies in which there is a permanent underclass, forced to comply with conventions from which they do not benefit. On Hume's account, those in the underclass have no duties of justice with regard to the established property of others.[38] For Hume, the conventions that underwrite artificial virtues are restricted to those that are mutually advantageous (where the advantages in question depend on people coordinating their behavior and acting on the "supposition, that something is to be performed on the other part").[39]

Significantly, on Hume's view, it matters that the conventions in question actually be in place. That a convention *would* be advantageous, if only we had it, may be reason to work to establish it, but it is no reason to act according to it absent the participation of others. Although there are any number of different conventions of, say, property, that *would* be advantageous, the actual benefits of conforming to one or another convention usually depend on which happens to have been established. Of course, acting in accordance with rules that *would* be part of an advantageous convention may be a way of helping to establish the convention. If so, then one would have some reason to do so. But in acting so as to bring about the mutually advantageous convention one would so far be acting from benevolence or self-interest, not (yet) from justice (since, absent the convention, so acting will not count as an instance of justice).

In the telling, Hume often writes as if each of the relevant conventions are established self-consciously, and voluntarily, by all who are subject to them. And he clearly thinks that those who found themselves without conventions defining property, making promises possible, and establishing governments, would, realizing their advantages, put them in place and would then voluntarily conform to them—assuming others did so as well. The obvious value of such conventions, properly designed (as to be mutually advantageous), makes them something that people would all willingly establish and work to support.

Yet Hume is very sensitive not only to the fact that many conventions are not mutually advantageous, but also to the fact that many that are advantageous emerge slowly, often without conscious planning, even as their perpetuation depends on an (often nebulous) appreciation of their value.[40] And they develop in ways that leave choices among different conventions as something we rarely face without finding ourselves already within conventions from which we have benefitted from the willing conformity of others. Yet once we find ourselves within mutually beneficial conventions, the range of available options is constrained by our established obligations. Within those bounds, what matters most, Hume emphasizes, is that there actually be a mutually advantageous convention. After all, without one, all sorts of significant advantages will be lost to all.

At the same time, Hume largely leaves to one side the significant complications that come with recognizing that different conventions would bring different advantages to different people, a fact that might be expected to introduce more than a little friction among different factions. Such problems would be especially pressing if the parties to the convention are supposed to settle on a convention together through deliberation or bargaining. That our actual conventions are largely ones we find ourselves in and benefitting from, rather than ones that we establish *ex nihilo*, plays an important role in explaining why so much is taken for granted in practice.

Of course, sometimes clearly better conventions are so close to hand that an established convention might begin to lose its grip. Under such circumstances, I suspect, Hume's view would be that we should work to establish the better convention but that, until we succeed, we have a duty to act according to the less than optimal arrangement that is in place as long as it is mutually advantageous and has been sustained thanks to others doing their part on the expectation that we would as well.[41]

That actions are performed as part of an established—and actually mutually beneficial—scheme is essential to their counting as virtuous. At the same time, however,

Hume emphasizes that the particular virtuous actions need not themselves be beneficial. "Taking any single act," Hume notes, "my justice may be pernicious in every respect. . ." (T 3.2.2.22/497–8). Specifically, he recognizes, it may be disadvantageous both to the person who performs it and to others:

> When a man of merit, of a beneficent disposition, restores a great fortune to a miser, or a seditious bigot, he has acted justly and laudably, but the public is a real sufferer. Nor is every single act of justice, consider'd apart, more conducive to private interest, than to public. (T 3.2.2.22/497–8)

What renders justice a virtue is that "however single acts of justice may be contrary, either to public or private interest, 'tis certain, that the whole plan or scheme is highly conducive, or indeed absolutely requisite, both to the support of society, and the well-being of every individual" (T 3.2.2.22/497–8). It is with an eye to the utility of the scheme, of which the act is seen as an integral part, that acts of justice garner the moral approval that constitutes them as virtuous.[42] Consider them apart from the mutually advantageous scheme, or consider acts that are a part of a scheme that is not mutually advantageous, and the grounds of approval disappear.

Stressing this idea, Hume contrasts the natural virtues with the artificial virtues claiming "that the good, which results from the former, arises from every single act, and is the object of some natural passion: Whereas a single act of justice, considered in itself, may often be contrary to the public good; and it is only the concurrence of mankind, in a general scheme or system of action, which is advantageous" (T 3.3.1.12/579–80). But this is, at least, misleading. Hume himself emphasizes that the natural virtues, no less than the artificial virtues, do not always produce the good at which they aim. Sincere acts of benevolence, for instance, do not always succeed in helping others, although they are virtuous. On Hume's account, while benevolence secures moral approval thanks to its *usual* effects, we approve of that motive in particular cases even when it fails to have those effects. As Hume emphasizes, "virtue in rags is still virtue; and the love, which it procures, attends a man into a dungeon or desart, where the virtue can no longer be exerted in action, and is lost to all the world" (T 3.3.1.19/584). Hume's point here, in contrasting the natural with the artificial virtues, is that the advantages, in light of which the artificial virtues secure approval, emerge only thanks to "the concurrence of mankind, in a general scheme or system of action"—a convention—whereas the advantages, in light of which the natural virtues secure approval, are available without recourse to conventions.

VIII The Missing Motive

A striking and puzzling fact about Hume's discussion of the artificial virtues is that he never explicitly identifies the first non-moral yet virtuous motive(s) to act as the artificial virtues require. This is despite having taken a lot of time to argue against various candidate motives while also arguing that for every virtue there must be some such motive—that is, a motive other than a motive of duty (or a regard for the virtue of the action). Hume doesn't, of course, doubt that we can be motivated by a sense of duty (or the regard for the virtue of an action). But he does think that the motive of duty (or the regard for the virtue of an action), if not misguided, requires that there be some other, non-moral, motive that itself secures the approval that constitutes the action as one's duty (or as virtuous). Hume never clearly and explicitly tells us what that motive is.[43]

This has led people to offer a range of interpretations. According to one: *There are no first, non-moral yet virtuous, motives for the artificial virtues.* On this view, Hume is silent about the first—non-moral yet virtuous—motives for the artificial virtues because he thought no such motives exists. Recommending this idea is not just the fact that Hume seems never to identify explicitly such motives but that he works so carefully to rule out what look to be all the viable candidates.

If this is right, then there are two paths to follow. The first is to argue that *the artificial virtues are not genuine virtues.* This involves holding firm to Hume's claim that for each virtue there must be a corresponding non-moral, yet virtuous, motive that renders the corresponding acts virtuous, and concluding that Hume's view must have been that the artificial "virtues" are *not actually virtues at all.* They may, in various ways, resemble virtues—not least in being useful to society—but (on this interpretation) they are, nonetheless, not genuine virtues, precisely because there is no first virtuous motive to their performance. No doubt people are (sometimes) motived to act as the "virtues" would require, but (again on this interpretation) this is always either because of one of the motives that Hume has rightly rejected as candidate motives for the "virtue" in question, or because they have been convinced by politicians, educators, and parents, that so acting is a duty.[44] Still, that people act justly regularly benefits society. So it is no wonder that politicians and others encourage the (false, on this interpretation) idea that so acting is virtuous. In fact, the benefits that come from convincing people that justice is a virtue might help explain why Hume was reticent to emphasize that there was no non-moral yet virtuous motive.

One might have expected Hume to make this point if it were his view. He doesn't. Yet, as defenders of this interpretation point out, the subversive nature of the thesis—that justice is not (actually) a virtue—may have led Hume to downplay the point in favor of joining the forces of those who are promulgating the fiction that it is a virtue.[45] Hume does, after all, argue that "though the philosophical truth of any proposition by no means depends on its tendency to promote the interests of society; yet a man has but a bad grace, who delivers a theory, however true, which, he must confess, leads to a practice dangerous and pernicious" (EM 9.14/278–9). He may well have been concerned that the truths he uncovered would be dangerous and pernicious were he to make them explicit.

Yet this interpretation strikes me as not especially plausible. To think that kindness, benevolence, and the other natural virtues, are genuine virtues, and are virtues because they are useful or agreeable to self or others, while holding that justice, which is useful to others, would fail to be a virtue, seems just the wrong way to go. If Hume really thinks there is no first non-moral, yet virtuous, motive to justice, then the most plausible move is to reject Hume's claim that every virtue is such that there is such a corresponding motive.

This reaction recommends the second path one might follow if one believes Hume thought there was no first non-moral yet virtuous motive for the artificial virtues. On this interpretation *not all virtues require a first, non-moral yet virtuous, motive*. Perhaps the mark of the artificial virtues, as opposed to the natural virtues, is that there is no such motive, and the mistake is to think that what is true of an important class of virtues—the natural virtues—is true of all. The suggestion involves holding that, when it comes to the artificial virtues, Hume abandons, or at least should have abandoned, the "undoubted maxim" mentioned earlier: "*that no action can be virtuous, or morally good, unless there be in human nature some motive to produce it, distinct from the sense of its morality*" (T 3.2.1.7/479).

What is striking here is that Hume seems never to have rejected this maxim. Nor is it clear what in his argument for the maxim he could consistently reject, given his over-all account of the nature of virtue. Embracing this second interpretation requires not simply restricting his maxim to the natural virtues, but also explaining how his general account of virtue survives the restriction. There are two elements of his general account that might be jettisoned: either (1) Hume's commitment to the virtue of an action depending on the motive with which it is performed or (2) his view that the motive of duty (or a regard to the virtue of an action) cannot be the motive the approval of which constitutes an action as virtuous. At least one would have to go.

The first commitment is one that Hume never argues for, yet it is deeply intuitive and has a long and respectable pedigree going back to the ancients. The second view is more distinctive of Hume, but it rests on an explicit argument—the circle argument—for thinking that neither a motive of duty nor the regard to the virtue of an action can be the first virtuous motive that renders an action virtuous.

In any case, we face two options, neither outlandish. One is to hold that Hume thought that what matters, in the case of the artificial virtues, is not *why* one acts in conformity to the relevant conventions, but just that one does. The other is to hold that Hume thought that, in the case of the artificial virtues, the motive still matters, but that the motive of duty (ungrounded though it is) is the motive that matters.[46]

In favor of the first option, one might think, is that we count people as having done the just thing (e.g., as having properly returned someone else's property, as having kept their promise, as having given allegiance to their government) without having to investigate their motives. And we regularly approve of their having done so, again without having to investigate their motives. This is in contrast with the natural virtues, it seems, in that we count acts as benevolent, kind, courageous, and the like, only in light of the motive with which they were performed. And it might seem we regularly approve of what they have done only in light of their motives. This contrast suggests that, with the artificial virtues, what matters is the performance, not the motive, and that the performance is what secures the relevant approval. Against this, though, is the observation that our moral *admiration* of the actions in accord with the artificial virtues seems, as in the case of the natural virtues, to depend on the motive. We might be glad that a person did the just thing, regardless of her motives, but our admiration for her, and our regard for her as a virtuous person, depend on the action not being, say, a part of a plan to willfully deceive others or a reflection merely of fear of punishment. So, although it seems that we recognize acts as, for instance, the acts demanded by justice independent of the motive of the agent, we count conformity with those demands as virtuous only in light of the agent's motive.

At the same time, though, if we are in fact able to recognize acts as just, or as instances of keeping one's promise, or as being demanded by allegiance, all without appeal to the motives of the agents, we find some reason in favor of the second option, according to which (contra the circle argument) the motive of duty is the first (albeit moral) motive for the artificial (but not the natural) duties. Recall that the circle argument depends on the idea that we cannot identify an action as virtuous, in a particular context, unless and until we find a non-moral motive that would both prompt that action and secure approval from the General Point of View. Having found such a motive, a person might recognize that the motive would lead to a particular action and then perform that action from some other motive (including a motive prompted by recognizing that the action would be virtuous). But, absent such a motive, the circle argument supposed, there is no way to identify which actions would be virtuous, and so no way successfully to do a virtuous action because one recognizes it to be virtuous. Yet if, as this interpretation suggests, we can identify which actions are virtuous, in the case of the artificial virtues, without appeal to virtuous motives, the circle argument loses its force, at least with regard to the artificial virtues. And room is left for people to perform such actions from duty—that is, from the recognition that they are virtuous—without having to suppose a non-moral motive to perform such actions.[47]

Of course, this stands as an interpretation of Hume only if there is reason to think Hume rejected the circle argument when it came to the artificial virtues. If he did, it was—remarkably—without any comment whatsoever. And he gives no indication of thinking that, in the case of the artificial virtues, we can identify actions as virtuous without regard to the motives with which they might be performed.[48]

This should give pause when it comes to accepting this interpretation. Moreover, as I will argue, there are in fact non-moral yet virtuous motives that play the role Hume argues needs to be played, which provides additional reason to treat this interpretation as suspect. Specifically, I will argue, people count as acting justly (as a just person would) if they act as they do from a concern to do their share (in a mutually advantageous enterprise), which they may do without thought of duty (or morality more generally). The concern in question, it is worth noting, is with doing one's share as specified by the mutually advantageous convention, not (yet) with doing one's fair share.[49]

Once we have identified such a concern, we are in a good position to distinguish those who conform to conventions from some motive other than a concern to do their share, from those who conform from such a concern. We are also well placed, in a way that this interpretation is not, to recognize that a person may be just, and act accordingly, without thinking in moral terms at all. In the case of benevolence, people count as acting benevolently (and as a benevolent person would) if they act as they do from a concern to help others, which they may do without thought of duty. Similarly, it seems to me, in the case of justice, people count as acting justly (and as a just person would) if they act as they do from a concern to do their share (in a mutually advantageous enterprise), which they may do without thought of duty. Importantly, the concern is with doing one's share as specified by the mutually advantageous convention, not (yet) with doing one's fair share.

It is the presence of such a concern, not the mere conformity with a convention (even a mutually advantageous convention) nor the motive of duty, that is distinctive of those with the artificial virtues. Needless to say, to make good on this suggestion it is important to show that a concern to do one's share (in a mutually advantageous enterprise) is (1) a motive a just person might act on, (2) a motive in light of which she is properly admired as just, and (3) a non-moral motive (i.e., a motive that need not involve a regard to virtue). In other words, we need to defend such a concern as a non-moral, yet virtuous, motive that is characteristic of just people.

Before turning to that task, it is worth mentioning two alternative interpretations that take seriously Hume's "undoubted maxim" ("that no action can be virtuous, or morally good, unless there be in human nature some motive to produce it, distinct from the sense of its morality" [T 3.2.1.7/479]) while retaining the idea that Hume thinks the artificial virtues are genuine virtues. On the first, *the first, non-moral yet virtuous, motive is enlightened self-interest.* This interpretation involves contrasting enlightened self-interest with the self-interest that Hume earlier rules out as not being the motive to justice. The contrast between the two turns on enlightened self-interest being informed by, and available only within contexts shaped by, conventions that make new possibilities available. The enlightenment involved is not just that provided by taking a long and informed view of one's interests, but also, crucially, by appreciating the benefits collective action makes possible. The idea is that once conventions are in place, self-interest is reshaped by an appreciation of the individual benefits we each enjoy by being willing participants in mutually advantageous conventions. "There is," Hume notes, "no passion. . . capable of controlling the interested affection, but the very affection itself, by an alteration of its direction. Now this alteration must necessarily take place upon the least reflection; since 'tis evident, that the passion is much better satisfy'd by its restraint, than by its liberty, and that by preserving society, we make much greater advances in the acquiring possessions, than by running into the solitary and forlorn, condition, which must follow upon violence and an universal licence" (T 3.2.2.13/492). Lending support to the contrast is the fact that when Hume rejects self-interest as the relevant motive, he concentrates on "self-love, *when it acts at its liberty*" (T 3.2.1.10/480; emphasis added), whereas the self-interest advanced here is under restraint, albeit by "the very affection itself, by an alteration of its direction."

In favor of this interpretation are the many places in which Hume emphasizes, first, the extent to which the various conventions he has in mind are in the interest of those who participate in them and, second, the extent to which a recognition of this in fact leads many people to establish and then conform to the conventions. Indeed, there is no question, as a matter of interpretation, that Hume thinks that the relevant conventions owe their existence to people's pursuit of self-interest. Hume claims, for instance, that "the rules of justice are establish'd merely by interest" (T 3.2.2.22/497–8),[50] and he insists that "To the imposition then, and the observance of these rules [of justice], both in general, and in every particular instance, they are at first mov'd only by a regard to interest; and this motive, on the first formation of society, is sufficiently strong and forcible" (T 3.2.2.24/498–500).[51]

The question is whether the motive of self-interest, enlightened and restrained by an appreciation of the benefits that flow from the conventions, is the first non-moral yet virtuous motive *that secures approval from the general point of view*.[52] Might enlightened self-interest be not just the motive that explains why the conventions at the heart of the artificial virtues are established but also "the first virtuous motive" that "is requisite to render an action virtuous" (T 3.2.1.4/478)? Here, Hume's arguments against seeing (unenlightened) self-interest as the first non-moral yet virtuous motive appear to stand equally against enlightened self-interest.

The first of these arguments is that self-interest will not always lead someone to act as the artificial virtues would require, which is true of enlightened self-interest as well. Although enlightened self-interest might well prompt one to greater compliance than would self-interest "at its liberty," there will be cases where a person's interest, however enlightened, is clearly best served by acting contrary to justice. As Hume notes, "'tis easily conceiv'd how a man may impoverish himself by a single instance of integrity, and have reason to wish, that with regard to that single act, the laws of justice were for a moment suspended in the universe" (T 3.2.2.22/497–8). A person motived by enlightened self-interest will predictably be moved, in such circumstances, to suspend the laws of justice for himself, however they stand in the universe.

Admittedly, at points in the *Treatise* Hume seems not to recognize this, writing as if he thinks conforming to the rules of justice is always, on balance, advantageous. So, for instance, concerning the rules of justice, Hume writes that when "society has become more numerous, and has encreas'd to a tribe or nation" people "do not so readily perceive, that disorder and confusion follow upon every breach of these rules" (T 3.2.2.24/498–500). This suggests that Hume might think that *every* breach does in fact cause disorder and confusion and that the problem is just that people have trouble seeing this.[53]

But this suggestion seems wrong for two reasons. First, it is obvious, and would have been obvious to Hume, that "disorder and confusion" do not "follow upon every breach" of the rules of justice. When discovered, breaches may prompt anger and resentment, but they might well not be discovered, and, even when they are, anger and resentment are not the same as disorder and confusion. Neither a single act, nor even several acts, of injustice will work to undermine the whole scheme. Second, Hume clearly recognizes this, observing just one page earlier that "Taking any single act, my justice may be pernicious in every respect [both to my own interest and to the public interest]; and 'tis only upon the supposition, that others are to imitate my example, that I can be induc'd to embrace that virtue" (T 3.2.2.22/497–8). Yet this is a supposition that Hume knows to be false in certain cases, as when the breach is entirely private.

What is advantageous to all, Hume makes clear, is the "whole plan or scheme" constituted by the rules of justice, which "is requisite, both to the support of society, and the well-being of every individual" (T 3.2.2.22/497–8), not the particular acts required by those rules. Needless to say, the scheme would collapse if people too regularly violated the rules. And people's interests are well advanced by performing the actions that are important to sustaining the "whole plan or scheme." Yet performing those acts that are crucial to maintaining the relevant conventions is compatible with performing some unjust acts, and a person concerned solely with enlightened self-interest, rather than justice, will presumably take advantage of the opportunities if she sees them. Hume notes this explicitly in the *Enquiry*: "though it is allowed that, without a regard to property, no society could subsist; yet according to the imperfect way in which human affairs are conducted, a sensible knave, in particular incidents, may think that an act of iniquity or infidelity will make a considerable addition to his fortune, without causing any considerable breach in the social union and confederacy."[54] Hume does go on to argue that the sensible knave is the true loser, but the loss in question comes only because the sensible knave misses out on the "invaluable enjoyment of a character, with themselves at least, for the acquisition of worthless toys and gewgaws"—a benefit that depends on being someone who values being just and has an "antipathy to treachery and roguery" (EM 9.23/283).[55]

The second argument Hume offers for thinking self-interest is not the relevant motive is that *that* motive is not the motive that secures approval from the General Point of View as the motive of justice. This holds true as well of enlightened self-interest, even if enlightened self-interest were to lead one always to conform to the demands of justice. A person who cautiously and successfully pursues her enlightened self-interest may well be admirable as prudent, but the prudence she exhibits does not make her a just person, even if she behaves exactly as a just person would. With the difference in motive comes a difference in the virtue, although virtue may still be there to be found. No matter how enlightened the self-interest and no matter how successfully it leads one to conform to the rules of justice, the just person is set apart from the prudent person by *why* she acts as she does. And the key difference is that a just person's concern, in acting as she does, is not with her self-interest (enlightened or not) but (on Hume's view) with the rules or principles established by the mutually advantageous conventions within which she finds herself.

This crucial fact is nicely picked up by those who see Hume as identifying the just person as the person within whom the rules of justice (broadly construed to cover property, promise, allegiance, etc.) serve as an "inviolable law" that resists "any temptation, to be induc'd to violate those principles, which are essential to a man of probity and honour" (T 3.2.2.27/501).[56] And this brings us to a second and more attractive interpretation, according to which *the first non-moral yet virtuous motive is provided by accepting the rules of property, promising, and allegiance, as inviolable laws.*

It may well be that self-interest would lead one to become such a person. For it might be that the benefits of "the whole plan or scheme" made possible by certain conventions are (or are thought to be) available only to those who embrace the conventions's rules as settled principles for action. But the (potentially self-interested) motive to become such a person is importantly distinct from the motive one has, if one is such a person. And it is the latter motive that seems an especially plausible candidate for the first non-moral yet virtuous motive to justice.[57]

In support of this interpretation are the several places where Hume maintains that a just person will regard the rules of property, promises, allegiance, and the like, as "inviolable." To take just one example, Hume writes that "every one, who has any regard to his character, or who intends to live on good terms with mankind, must fix an inviolable law to himself, never, by any temptation, to be induc'd to violate those principles, which are essential to a man of probity and honour" (T 3.2.2.27/501; see also T 3.2.1.15/482–3, T 3.2.6.10/533, T 3.2.10.15/562–3).[58] The just person, it seems, is one who treats such principles as inviolable. Although a person might do so for self-interested reasons, it is worth noting that one might be concerned not to violate such principles without having acquired that concern for self-interested reasons. Indeed, as Hume emphasizes, educators and politicians, parents and friends, often encourage justice without appealing to self-interest or recommending it as part of an advantageous plan. Thus, parents "are induc'd to inculcate on their children, from their earliest infancy, the principles of probity, and teach them to regard the observance of those rules, by which society is maintain'd, as worthy and honourable, and their violation as base and infamous. By this means the sentiments of honour may take root in their tender minds, and acquire such firmness and solidity, that they may fall little short of those principles, which are the most essential to our natures, and the most deeply radicated in our internal constitution" (T 3.2.2.26/500–1).[59]

So, although some people might embrace certain rules as inviolable for self-interested reasons, and so come to have the motive in question, the motive itself does not require consciously embracing such a plan and it may well find its firmest place among those who acquired the disposition to treat certain rules as inviolable in some other way. Thus, although Hume puts the point saying that a person "*must fix an inviolable law to himself*" (T 3.2.2.27/501; emphasis added), the disposition is found in anyone within whom the principles of justice have, in the appropriate way, taken hold, whether or not he has put them there himself.[60] And, in fact, those who have consciously embraced such a plan out of a regard for their enlightened self-interest might well find themselves wondering whether treating the laws as inviolable is really necessary.[61]

A person within whom the principles of justice have taken hold (however that happens) is moved by the thought that something is another's property, the thought that she has given her word, and the thought that something is required by her country's law, and not just by self-interest or benevolence. Moreover, in a genuinely just person, these thoughts are not simply among the many motives she may have for acting; they take precedence over "particular views of private or public interest" and stand against "spite and favour" (T 3.2.6.9/531–3). Importantly, such motives can play a preeminent role in guiding a person's actions without the person thinking in terms of virtue, or of duty, or of what might garner approval from the General Point of View. They are *non-natural* motives (in the relevant sense) because they require conventions to give them the content and direction they need to prompt action, and they are *non-moral* motives (again, in the relevant sense) because an agent may be moved by a concern with property, promises, the laws of one's country, without thinking in moral terms at all.[62] At the same time, under the right circumstances—when the rules in play are part of a mutually advantageous convention—being moved by such thoughts does secure the approval that constitutes them as virtuous.

The caveat "under the right circumstances" is crucial, however, and provides reason to worry about overstressing the idea that a person with the artificial virtues will regard any rules as "sacred and inviolable." Hume's talk of inviolable laws, as well as his characterization of people imposing "general inflexible rules" on themselves that lead them to see property as "sacred and inviolable" (T 3.2.6.10/533), risks being misleading when thinking about Hume's conception of the artificial virtues. Specifically, it risks masking the fact that, on Hume's view, the rules that "a man of probity and honour" will be concerned to comply will vary according to which conventions (if any) happen to be in place. It is no virtue, according to Hume, to stick to the rules in a context where the relevant convention has no point or place (e.g., where others cannot be counted on to do their part). "Suppose," Hume asks, "it should be a virtuous man's fate to fall into the society of ruffians, remote from the protection of laws and government; what conduct must he embrace in that melancholy situation?" He answers: the virtuous man "can have no other expedient than to arm himself, to whomever the sword he seizes, or the buckler, may belong: And his particular regard to justice being no longer of USE to his own safety or that of others, he must consult the dictates of self-preservation alone, without concern for those who no longer merit his care and attention" (EM 3.9/187).[63] Moreover, a virtuous person will take the "inviolability" of the rules in question to be conditional on the conventions of which they are a part being *mutually* advantageous. In cases where they are not, "a man of probity and honour" need have no disposition at all to comply with the conventions (and may have reason to resist them).

So it is important to see that the first non-moral yet virtuous motive for the artificial virtues cannot plausibly be tightly bound up with a disposition to regard some set of rules (either a single set of rules for all situations, or whichever rules are established by the conventions in which people find themselves) as genuinely "sacred and inviolable." Even the rules of a convention that is mutually advantageous lose their force, on Hume's account, if the circumstances change in ways that make complying with them no longer an integral part of a mutually advantageous plan or scheme.[64] As a result, treating the rules of any convention as "sacred and inviolable" will reflect a (presumably vicious) rule fetishism and not the virtue of justice.

Thus, the first non-moral yet virtuous motive underlying the artificial virtues is found not in the virtuous person's taking certain rules as inviolable, but in her commitment to conform to general rules established by conventions, *given* that the conventions are mutually advantageous, and that others are doing their share as well. This commitment requires that one will "never, by any temptation, be induc'd to violate those principles, which are essential to a man of probity and honour." Yet just what those principles are will vary in significant ways across time and culture. In an important respect, then, on Hume's view (I am suggesting) the only "inviolable law" recognized by a man of probity and honor is found in the commitment not to violate the general rules of mutually advantageous conventions, *whatever, given the circumstances, such rules turn out to be.* Such a person is not willing, *unconditionally*, to conform to actual conventional rules that happen to be advantageous. Her willingness is conditional.

Yet when the conditions are met, the virtuous person's compliance is unstinting—specifically it is "unchangeable by spite and favour, and by particular views of private or public interest" (T 3.2.6.9/531–3).[65] Indeed, the just person's unwillingness to make exceptions for herself, her commitment to the general rules established by the (mutually advantageous) conventions, is central, Hume argues, to securing the benefits the conventions make available. Were people regularly to treat honesty "as the best policy. . . but one liable to many exceptions," as the sensible knave recommends, our capacity to trust each other—and the benefits such trust makes available—would evaporate. A willingness not to make exceptions in light of "of particular views of private or public interest," assuming others are likewise willing, is essential to securing the benefits justice makes available.

Still, a central and attractive feature of Hume's account of the artificial virtues is that people with them are concerned not, in the first instance, with conventional rules (which might change with changing circumstances). They are concerned, rather, with doing their share in mutually advantageous enterprises in which others are likewise willing participants. Such a person will willingly do her share, provided others do as well, while resisting temptations offered by opportunities to exploit the cooperation of others.[66] The role of the conventional rules is secondary, but essential: they work to specify what a person's share is under the circumstances.

This concern—to do one's share (as defined within a mutually advantageous convention), given that others are (or will) as well—gets content, and so direction, only in contexts of specific conventions that are mutually advantageous. So the concern serves as a motive to action only in such contexts: "the conventions of men. . .," as Hume puts it, "create a new motive" (T 3.2.5.10/522). In the context of mutually advantageous conventions, the concern to do one's share finds expression in actions that conform to the relevant rules in a way that lets us distinguish those who simply conform to the rules (because of fear, self-interest, or a fetish for the rules) and those who are, in conforming, being just (i.e., exercising an artificial virtue). The difference is found in the just person's willingness to do her share (unmoved "by particular views of private or public interest") in mutually advantageous arrangements, provided others are as well. Others might be willing to conform to the rules, but if the conditions of their willingness are not that others, too, are willing to do their share within conventions that are mutually advantageous, they may be doing what justice requires but they will not be manifesting the virtue of justice.

People who are concerned to do their share, as specified by mutually advantageous conventions (provided others are willing as well), have *a motive* (when the conventions are available) that is *artificial*—depending as it does on conventions and artifices that reflect the "designs, and projects, and views of men" (T 3.1.2.9/474). At the same time, it is *non-moral* because a person may be disposed to do her share, in this way, and yet not "annex the idea of virtue" to doing so. Yet it is *virtuous* because "a sympathy with public interest" (T 3.2.2.24/498–500) naturally secures approval for this motive from the General Point of View.

The approval, it is worth emphasizing, differs from the approval enjoyed by the natural virtues precisely because the public interest justice serves depends on appreciating "the whole plan or scheme" (T 3.2.2.22/497–8) realized by acting on a reciprocal willingness to constrain the pursuit of interest (public and private) by mutually advantageous rules. It's not that there is no virtue in the pursuit of interest (public and private)—Hume holds that there is. It's that one has missed the distinctive virtue of justice until one appreciates that justice works by constraining the pursuit of particular interest by rules with the following credential: a willingness to comply with them, on the condition that others do so as well, offers mutual advantage.[67]

IX Conclusion

A striking and important feature of Hume's account of the artificial virtues—justice, broadly construed—is that it recognizes, and explains, the huge variety of things just people will do, depending on their circumstances and the conventions that are in place, while capturing the distinctive character of what will be motivating them. Indeed, it offers a unified account of what all such people have in common: a willingness to regulate their behavior by general rules established by shared conventions, *given* that the conventions are mutually advantageous and that others are doing their share as well. On Hume's account (as I understand it) such a willingness is the non-moral yet virtuous motive that we admire as distinctive of those who are genuinely just. To recognize justice as a virtue (or a duty) is to recognize the moral importance of acting on this motive.

It is worth noting that Hume's account of the artificial virtues fits well not simply with our admiring as just those who willingly regulate their behavior by the appropriate rules, but with our thinking that, in doing so, they should be sensitive to whether the conventions that establish the rules are advantageous to all who are subject to them. In fact, there is room to argue, although Hume does not pursue this idea, that a genuinely just person will be especially sensitive to whether the rules in place are advantageous to the most vulnerable. After all, the conventions are most likely to lose their authority (as established by what will secure approval from the General Point of View) by failing to address the interests of the vulnerable.[68]

Acknowledgments

I am grateful to Lorraine Besser-Jones, Don Garrett, and Gerald Postema for very helpful discussions of Hume on the artificial virtues.

ABBREVIATIONS OF WORKS CITED

EM   *Enquiry Concerning the Principles of Morals*. Edited by Tom L. Beauchamp. Oxford: Clarendon, 1998.

T   *A Treatise of Human Nature*. Edited by D. F. Norton and M. J. Norton. Oxford: Clarendon, 2007.

NOTES

1. Marcia Baron, David Gauthier, Rachel Cohon, Stephen Darwall, J. L. Mackie, and Barry Stroud all find inconsistent commitments in Hume's position. Baron (1982) argues that the problems run deep enough that we should see Hume as perpetuating the noble lie that justice and the other artificial virtues are virtues when he thinks they are not. Along similar lines, Gauthier (1992) argues that Hume's account commits him to an error, which Gauthier suspects Hume realized but worked to keep in the shadows. Meanwhile, Cohon (2008), Darwall (1995), and Mackie (1980) each argue that Hume must have silently dropped or restricted one of the commitments that otherwise, together, cause problems.

2. Of course, assuming that there are differences between what is virtuous and what is vicious, and what is red and what is green, beyond their moral and color qualities, a person sensitive to those differences might well be able to distinguish among them. But the distinctions thus drawn will not be in terms of the moral or color differences.

3. The particular kind of satisfaction or pleasure he has in mind is that of moral approval, which arises "only when a character is considered in general, without reference to our particular interest" (T 3.1.2.4/472).

4. These are all places where Hume is emphasizing the essential role of feeling or sentiment in our capacity to make moral distinctions against those who think that reason alone would be sufficient.

5. In what follows, when I write, for instance, of something securing the "relevant approval," I have in mind distinctively moral approval felt when taking up the General Point of View. An important feature of Hume's account is that we can think about whether some motive, action, or character trait would secure that approval without ourselves actually feeling approval. See Sayre-McCord (1994) for a discussion of Hume's account of moral judgment, and Sayre-McCord (2008) for a discussion of the important, but I think often misunderstood, connection Hume claims to hold between morality and motivation.

6. Although we often "fix our attention on actions... these actions are still considered as signs; and the ultimate object of our praise and approbation is the motive, that produced them" (T 3.2.1.2/477).

7. Kant (2002) begins the *Groundwork* claiming that the only thing that can even be conceived of as unconditionally good is a good will; everything else of value, he maintains, depends for its value on being compatible with such a will. Of course, Kant has a distinctive view of what constitutes a good will, but the driving intuition is that various actions, whatever their actual effects, count as valuable, if they are, only in light of why they were performed.

8. Hume is well aware that we might be pleased that someone has acted even when the action is not virtuous, as when, for instance, the action benefits us or those for whom we are

concerned. But there is an important difference, according to him, between being pleased something was done and seeing it as virtuous. And his point is that we will see the action as virtuous only if we would approve of the motive behind it as virtuous.

9. "If any *action* be either virtuous or vicious, 'tis only as a sign of some quality or character. It must depend upon durable principles of the mind, which extend over the whole conduct, and enter into the personal character" (T 3.3.1.4/575).

10. Although Hume recognizes the motivating force of the sense of duty, he also appreciates, and offers an explanation of, the fact that something being forbidden often makes it more attractive. This happens, he argues, when what is forbidden is something we have an independent motive to do; the opposition of the passions involved "commonly causes a new emotion in the spirits. . . This new emotion is easily converted into the predominant passion and increases its violence. . . Hence we naturally desire what is forbid, and take a pleasure in performing actions, merely because they are unlawful" (T 2.3.4.5/421).

11. Hume observes that "we blame a father for neglecting his child. Why? because it shews a want of natural affection, which is the duty of every parent" (T 3.2.1.5/478).

12. Presumably, if a person's sense of duty goes too far wrong, leading people to do what is actually contrary to duty, our approval of their acting on their sense of duty will find its limits.

13. At the same time, Hume rejects the idea that our sense of virtue is entirely the product of educators and politicians on the grounds that their efforts have an effect only because people already have an independent sense of virtue (T 3.2.2.25/500). He also argues that the range of virtues we recognize, which includes virtues that do not redound to the public interest, are not well explained by appeal to the efforts of educators and politicians alone (T 3.3.1.11/578–9).

14. Considering actions prompted by humanity, Hume claims that the motive of "humanity bestows a merit on the actions. A regard to this merit is, therefore, a secondary consideration, and deriv'd from the antecedent principle of humanity, which is meritorious and laudable" (T 3.2.1.6/478).

15. Hume makes clear that while the motive needs to be one humans can and do have—a motive in human nature—a particular person might well lack the motive while still having a duty to act as the motive, if only he were to have it, would lead him to act.

16. Focusing on duty, he later makes the same point, writing that "No action can be requir'd of us as our duty unless there be implanted in human nature some actuating passion or motive, capable of producing the action. This motive cannot be the sense of duty" (T 3.2.5.6/518–19).

17. Alternatively, I might have some other desire with determinate content, that she might work to satisfy with my help; then I would have a motive to do what would help her do what she can to satisfy that desire of mine. Either way, neither of us will have a motive to do anything in particular until there is some other desire in play.

18. One way to avoid the force of this argument is to reject the idea that in order to regard an action as virtuous we need to see it as a sign of a virtuous motive. So, for instance, one might hold that, when it comes to the artificial virtues, conventionally established rules put us in a position to identify the virtuous actions without having to appeal to any virtuous motives. More about this later, when we turn to the puzzling aspects of Hume's account of the artificial virtues.

19. The first is an epistemological difficulty and would be solved if only there were a way to identify which actions are virtuous other than by appeal to the virtuous motive. The second is an explanatory or metaphysical difficulty.

20. It might also be reasonable to hold that if one acts as one sincerely believes to be required by duty one is acting virtuously. So, it is important that the force of Hume's argument does not depend on accepting what he assumes, as I go on to note.

21. The point is complicated by the fact that Kant treats thinking that an action meets this standard as one and the same with thinking, at least in the context of an imperfectly rational will, that it is one's duty. Likely, Hume would argue both (1) that one might regard something as a duty without thinking it meets Kant's standard and (2) that one might recognize, and be moved by the fact, that some action would meet the standard, without thereby thinking that so acting is one's duty. If Kant is right, Hume would argue, it is in being moved by such a thought that one does one's duty, not in being moved by what one believes is one's duty.

22. One might think that Hume supposes that for each type of virtuous action that we recognize there is a distinctive virtuous motive that is not also the motive that underwrites the virtuousness of other kinds of actions. Yet Hume's views don't commit him to this. It might be that the very same motive—say, the motive provided by a concern for the welfare of others—finds expression in a number of ways that we end up distinguishing as distinct virtues. There must be a virtuous motive—that is, a motive of which we approve—in order for the actions to count as virtuous, but (for all Hume argues) it might be that different kinds of actions get their standing as being virtuous from the same motive.

23. Mackie (1980: 77) suggests that the artificial virtues are also such that "it is only by some artifice or invention that people have come to feel approval" of the motives characteristic of those with the artificial virtues. Yet Hume explicitly denies this, holding that after the motives become available (thanks to the artifice and invention of man) "it is *naturally* attended with a strong sentiment of morals" (T 3.3.1.12/579–80). At the same time, Hume clearly thinks that politicians and educators work to strengthen the sentiments. Speaking of the rules of justice, Hume notes that although "the sense of morality in the observance of these rules follows *naturally*, and of itself; tho' 'tis certain, that it is also augmented by a new *artifice*, and that the public instructions of politicians, and the private education of parents, contribute to the giving us a sense of honour and duty in the strict regulation of our actions with regard to the properties of others" (T 3.2.6.11/533–4).

24. As well as ". . . *perseverance, patience, activity, vigilance, application, constancy*" and "other virtues of that kind, which 'twill be easy to recollect. . ." (T 3.3.4.7/610–11).

25. Although the rules are "unchangeable by spite or favour, and by particular views of private or public interest," they are otherwise changeable as circumstances and mutual interest might recommend. This sensitivity to circumstance, including history and mutual interest, explains why the specific actions that might count as virtuous can differ dramatically through time and across communities.

26. One might think that the failure of restraint is blameable because others have a right to the restraint. This fits well with Hume's discussion of property, promises, allegiance, and even the duty of princes and political ministers, where it is easy to identify those who have a right to restraint. But it fits less well with his account of the virtues of modesty and chastity, which do not seem tied to someone having any particular right to expect the restraint. Although restraint is key, it seems that the restraint is not something to which others always have a right, even if a failure to exercise it is, in Hume's view, blameable.

27. Needless to say, it is possible to imagine situations in which the motives characteristic of, say, charitable people will prove to be neither useful nor agreeable to those who are charitable nor to others. Were the world such that this was generally true, Hume would hold (most likely) that, in such a world, charity is not virtuous or (less likely, but still consistently) that such a world would be one in which virtue turns out not to be either useful nor agreeable. What is important to Hume's account of morality is that, as the world is, the virtues are useful or agreeable either to the possessor or to others. It is this feature of them that allows him to explain the moral distinctions we draw (between, say, virtue and vice) by appeal to our moral sentiments of approval and disapproval.

28. This is true, as well, of the natural virtues (at least those that are useful either to the possessor or to others). But how they solve the relevant problems is importantly different. The natural virtues work to solve the problems unilaterally, so to speak, independently of what others might do, whereas the artificial virtues work to solve the problems they do only thanks to the collaboration of others. See Sayre-McCord (1996) for a discussion of the connection, on Hume's view, between salient practical problems and the virtues.

29. And the virtue of chastity, on Hume's telling, encourages confidence in men that certain offspring are their own, thus inducing them to provide support and protection both for those children and for their mothers.

30. Rachel Cohon (1997: 104–105) rightly emphasizes this point.

31. This passage continues by rejecting a regard for the equity and merit of observance as a motive: "as no action can be equitable or meritorious, where it cannot arise from some separate motive there is here an evident sophistry and reasoning in a circle." The "naturally" in this conclusion did not appear in the first edition of Book 3 of the *Treatise*, although Hume added it in his own copy. See P. H. Nidditch's "Textual Notes" to his revised edition of Selby-Bigge's edition, p. 669. There is a parallel passage, regarding the motive to the performance of promises—"'tis evident we have no motive leading us to the performance of promises, distinct from a sense of duty" (T 3.2.5.6/518–19)—in which "naturally" was not indicated by Hume to be missing. Yet, a few sentences later, "naturally" shows up: "as there is naturally no inclination to observe promises, distinct from a sense of their obligation" (T 3.2.5.6/518–19). It's clear, I think, that "naturally" belongs in all three places.

32. It is worth noting that a regard to equity, as Hume is setting things out here, is not a moral motive, although a regard to the *merit* of observing equity is. A regard to equity is a recognition that certain actions are called for, or required by, certain principles or general rules. Having discussed the origin of such principles and rules, Hume turns separately, and later, to the question of "*Why we annex the idea of virtue to justice*" (T 3.2.2.23/498), making clear that he thinks we might recognize something as just or a matter of equity without thereby seeing it as virtuous. The idea of virtue is annexed to the idea of justice, not contained in it, although justice is indeed, Hume thinks, a virtue.

33. Importantly, Hume's point is not that the meaning of "I promise" is fixed by conventions (although its meaning is fixed by conventions). His point is that the virtuous motive a person acts on, if she has the virtue of being true to her word, itself depends on there being certain conventions. The alternative he considers, and argues against, is that there is some state of mind, available independently of conventions, that constitutes the making of a promise and that gives rise to a motive to keep the promises made.

34. "A new obligation supposes new sentiments to arise. The will never creates new sentiments. There could not naturally, therefore, arise any obligation from a promise, even supposing the mind could fall into the absurdity of willing that obligation" (T 3.2.5.5/518).

35. Here, "naturally" does appear in the first edition, lending support to the thought that it belongs in the passage concerning justice that Hume amended in his copy and belongs as well in a passage concerning promises a page earlier, where Hume writes "'tis evident we have [naturally] no motive leading us to the performance of promises distinct from a sense of duty" (T 3.2.5.6/518–19), although it doesn't appear there and was not added later by Hume. This matters, as will become clear, to whether Hume is arguing that there is *no motive whatsoever* to act justly or to keep one's promise, other than the motive of duty, or that there are *no natural motives* to perform such actions. For now, I just note that, as I interpret Hume's position, the restriction to natural motives belongs in and is important.

36. Modern game theory has its roots in Hume's discussion of the "origin of justice and property" and more generally in his account of the origin of the conventions associated with the various artificial virtues. Although Hume sometimes writes as if the problems that give rise to the conventions are simply matters of coordination, especially as he emphasizes that all can expect to benefit from having some convention or other in place, he is clearly sensitive both to the differential impact of different conventions on people's interests and on the incentives people will have to fail to comply (perhaps secretly) when others are complying. Concerning the latter, he recognizes various forms of enforcement as crucial to the stability of the conventions, even as he emphasizes that, compared to life without the conventions, everyone can expect to benefit by compliance, as long as others are complying as well. David Lewis's *Convention* (1969) is a careful articulation, development, and defense of Hume's insights.

37. Here, Hume is arguing that our duty of allegiance to government is not founded on our having made a promise on the grounds that our obligations of fidelity to promises and of allegiance to government are "built on the very same foundation." He allows that we can establish a convention that makes promising possible and fidelity to promises obligatory absent a government. That means we might actually promise allegiance. But whether we do or not, the account of our obligation to keep our promises carries over directly, without the interposition of a promise, to our obligation of allegiance to established governments (if they are suitably mutually advantageous).

38. Whereas it is clear Hume thinks that those who do not benefit from the convention have no duty of justice, it is unclear whether he thinks the convention establishes duties of justice among those who have benefitted, as long as their benefit comes from the willing compliance of others (where that compliance depended on the expectation of mutual compliance). It may be that he thinks that those who enjoy the benefits have duties to each other in light of the mutual, and mutually dependent, advantages they've secured. Whether or not they do, they would have responsibilities—presumably weightier responsibilities—to those who have been exploited by the conventions in place. Yet it seems that, on Hume's view, these responsibilities would not be matters of justice, at least if those who have been exploited can neither make their resentment felt nor enter into alternative arrangements that would benefit others. Consider Hume's example of "a species of creatures intermingled with men, which, though rational, were possessed of such inferior strength, both of body and mind, that they were incapable of all resistance, and could never, upon the highest provocation, make us feel the effects of their resentment." In that case, he concludes, "that we should be bound by the laws of humanity to give gentle usage to these creatures, but should not, properly speaking, lie under any restraint of justice with regard to them" (EM 3.18/190–1).

39. He pretty clearly holds that wherever actual conventions have provided mutual advantage, even if not equal advantage, duties of justice are found.

40. When it comes to property, this easy establishment is due in large part, Hume thinks, to there being an obvious rule for settling, in the first instance, what belongs to whom: "it must immediately occur, as the most natural expedient, that every one continue to enjoy what he is at present master of, and that property or constant possession be conjoin'd to the immediate possession." Strikingly, Hume appeals to what has come to be called "the endowment effect" to explain the comfort we would feel with this solution: "Such is the effect of custom, that it not only reconciles us to anything we have long enjoy'd, but even gives us an affection for it, and makes us prefer it to other objects, which may be more valuable, but are less known to us" (T 3.2.3.4/503–4).

41. The case of revolutions is nicely complicated. Hume thinks that there will likely be no rule within established governments giving permission to revolt. That means, on his account, that we will not have a right to revolt. But a government can nonetheless lose its claim to allegiance (T 3.2.9.4/552–3). And if the government is bad enough, and if we can succeed in replacing it with something enough better to justify the significant hardships revolution imposes on a people, then we may be right to revolt even if we do not have a right to revolt.

42. Of course, not every act of justice is actually needed to sustain the advantageous scheme. What is at stake here is how we conceive of the act when we take up the General Point of View. Just as, from the General Point of View, we think of benevolent acts as *a kind of act that is beneficial* and so approve of particular instances of that kind regardless of whether they are actually beneficial, so, too, we think of just acts as *a kind of act that is an integral part of a scheme that is (mutually) advantageous* and so approve of particular instances of that kind regardless of whether they are actually (mutually) advantageous. For a discussion of why, from the General Point of View, the focus is the usual effects of what is being judged—that is, on the effects of the kind in question, rather than the actual effects of the specific instances—see Sayre-McCord (1994).

43. For a detailed discussion of this puzzle, see Garrett (2007).

44. See T 3.2.2.25/500.

45. Baron (1982) defends this interpretation.

46. This interpretation has been advanced by Cohon (2008).

47. Indeed, at one point, Hume himself claims that "'tis evident we have no motive leading us to the performance of promises, distinct from a sense of duty" (T 3.2.5.6/518–19). But there is reason to think (see footnote 32) that what Hume had in mind was that there is no *natural* motive leading us to the performance of promises (other than a sense of duty). And the point Hume seems to be making, in context, is that the circle argument establishes that there must be some non-natural—that is, artificial—motive in play.

48. Needless to say, even if Hume actually held tight to the circle argument and so to the undoubted maxim that it supports, one might think that he should have put them aside and that, if he had, the resulting account of the artificial virtues would be the stronger for it. I think this would be a mistake, given that (as I argue) there is a non-moral yet virtuous motive that is part of a unified and compelling account of what is motivationally characteristic of people who have the artificial virtues.

49. The differences among the various artificial virtues that fall within the broad category of justice are found in the different sorts of problems the mutually advantageous conventions serve to address.

50. Hume goes on immediately to stress that the connection between the rules of justice and self-interest is "somewhat singular." Our interests are not served by each act required by a rule of justice, he notes, but by "the steady prosecution of the rule, and by the peace and order, which it establishes in society" (T 3.2.2.22/497–8).

51. "*Thus self-interest is the original motive to the* establishment *of justice: but a* sympathy *with public interest is the source of the* moral approbation, *which attends that virtue*" (T 3.2.2.24/499–500). Hume says something similar concerning the convention of promising. See T 3.2.5.11/522–3.

52. This interpretation is pressed by Gauthier (1992), even as he ultimately argues that Hume was committed to an error theory to the effect that our taking justice to impose a duty is a mistake (because, Gauthier argues, the motive required by Hume's "undoubted maxim" is not actually available).

53. Gauthier, in fact, makes just this suggestion.

54. Gauthier holds that, in the *Treatise*, Hume mistakenly assumed that the whole scheme of justice depended on each performance and that this assumption was crucial to his thinking that the first virtuous motive to justice was enlightened self-interest. On this reading, the sensible knave of the *Enquiry* comes on the scene as a revelation and a new challenge to the adequacy of the account advanced in the *Treatise*. Against this proposal stand the passages in the *Treatise* that seem to recognize explicitly that individual acts of injustice may well be in one's self interest.

55. It is worth noting that this observation is compatible with advancing an argument from self-interest for valuing justice and having an antipathy to treachery and roguery, as long as, compared to the alternatives, their contribution to one's overall interest is greater. But this will be true only if there are already some other interests in place that are better served by cultivating a concern for justice and an antipathy to treachery and roguery. As Hume acknowledges, for a person tempted by the thought "That *honesty is the best policy. . .* but is liable to many exceptions," (EM 9.22/282–3) and who holds "that this reasoning much requires an answer, it would be a little difficult to find any which will to him appear satisfactory and convincing" precisely because his actual interests might not be well served by an alteration of his interests (EM 9.23/282–3).

56. Darwall (1995) and Garrett (1997) both emphasize, correctly to my mind, the importance of recognizing that a proper account of justice will find a place for people being motivated by the principles that are "essential to a man of probity and honour."

57. Darwall (1995: 294) thinks this is the right motive but argues that Hume's account of the will cannot accommodate the motive. This is because (according to Darwall) Hume's theory of the will commits Hume to a hedonistic version of psychological egoism that rules out accepting the rules as guides to behavior for their own sake. I think this mistakenly saddles Hume with a moral psychology to which he is—fortunately—not committed. Consider, especially, Hume's discussion "Of Self-Love," which appeared as an appendix to *An Enquiry Concerning the Principles of Morals*, for evidence that Hume recognizes people as having concerns beyond their own interests and pleasures. (See Garrett [1997] for a nice defense of Hume against Darwall's charge.) Garrett, in contrast, defends this motive not just as one that Hume can consistently recognize, but as the first virtuous motive Hume thought was characteristic of justice.

58. After arguing that self-interest, expressed in the adoption of a policy to comply with the rules of justice, constitutes "the original non-moral motive to justice," Garrett (1997: 271) distinguishes that motive from the "first virtuous motive, which bestows a

merit" on the actions performed by a just person. What is important to keep in mind here is that the "first virtuous motive, which bestows a merit" must itself, by Hume's argument, be a non-moral motive—and a non-moral motive that leads consistently to the performance of just actions while being the motive we admire as constituting the justice of the person in question. Self-interest, even enlightened and redirected, does not fit that bill. Still, there is no mistaking the fact that Hume recognizes self-interest as the (or, as I think, *a*) motive that initially leads people to establish, and to conform to, the conventions at the heart of the artificial virtues. In this sense, self-interest is an original non-moral motive to justice but not the motive that is required by the circle argument.

59. Hume argues that however effective these efforts, to the extent they depend on talk of what is "*honorable* or *dishonourable, praiseworthy* or *blameable*," they presuppose another "cause of the distinction we make betwixt vice and virtue" (T 3.2.2.25/500).

60. This isn't the only place where Hume characterizes the restraint as self-imposed: "when any man *imposes on himself* general inflexible rules in his conduct with others, he considers certain objects as their property, which he supposes to be sacred and inviolable" (T 3.2.6.10/533; emphasis added).

61. This is true even for someone who cares about maintaining his character as a "man of probity and honour" or has a concern for "living on good terms with mankind" because these interests might compete with others better served by making an exception to the plan.

62. Hume makes clear that, as he is thinking of things, one might recognize actions as required by justice (or equity) without taking them to be virtuous, although he thinks we do usually annex the idea of virtue to that of justice. (See footnote 33.) Similarly, one might think of actions as required by a convention (or the laws of a country) without thinking of them as virtuous. In the same way, one might have the motives involved in being willing to do one's share, as specified by a convention, without thinking of doing so as virtuous (or as one's duty); although, of course, one might also think that so acting is virtuous (or one's duty).

63. Hume emphasizes as well that under conditions of extreme scarcity "the strict laws of justice are suspended... and give place to the stronger motives of necessity and self-preservation." And he goes on to ask rhetorically "Is it a crime, after a shipwreck, to seize whatever means or instrument of safety one can lay hold of, without regard to former limitations of property?" (EM 3.8/186–7).

64. This will happen under two conditions. It might be that others are not willing to do their part. Or, even if they are, it might be that a willingness to comply, as long as others are, stops being *mutually* advantageous—either because mutual compliance does not yield the advantages or because the advantages do not depend on a mutual willingness to comply.

65. This may reasonably be seen as a mitigated inviolability. One could try to reclaim a more robust inviolability by supposing that each of the relevant rules contains in some way "the condition of its authority" (as one might put it). Then the rule would not be, say, "respect property as defined in the following way," but, instead, something like "when property is defined in the following way within a mutually advantageous convention of which one is a member, respect property so defined." Thought of in this way, the rule itself might be treated as inviolable in a straightforward sense, even if it was, in effect, often irrelevant under actual circumstance. Pursuing this, however, ends up bringing one very close to the idea, suggested earlier, that the one truly inviolable rule in Hume's account is that one not violate the general rules of mutually advantageous conventions, *whatever, given their circumstances, such rules turn out to be.*

66. Hume does not wrestle with the important questions of how the justice of an arrangement depends not merely on it being mutually advantageous but on how those advantages are distributed. Nor does he address worries about how the conditions under which a convention may prove mutually advantageous might themselves be exploitative and so not an appropriate baseline for determining what might be just. The latter concern motivates the idea that the relevant advantage must be one compared to how one would fare absent both force and fraud.

67. Any account of justice that treats its demands as dependent on convention faces two familiar worries. The first is that it will be excessively conservative—recommending that a just person embrace whatever conventions happen to be in place. The second is that it will be unsatisfyingly relativistic—leaving out of the picture any sense of there being standards for justice independent of the particular practices one finds in different societies. I hope that it is clear that Hume's account resists quick versions of these worries. First, Hume's defense of conventions has at its core an insistence that the relevant conventions are only those that are mutually advantageous. So, although a convention must be in place for justice to require compliance, the mere fact that a convention is in place does not mean justice requires compliance with it. (It is true, though, that Hume's theory does imply that if a mutually advantageous convention is in place, justice requires compliance with it, assuming one has benefitted by the compliance of others, even if there are other conventions in prospect that one would prefer or that offer, say, a more equal distribution of advantages.) Second, the non-moral yet virtuous motive to justice—the conditional willingness to comply with mutually advantageous conventions, assuming others will as well—in effect embodies a standard of justice that is independent of particular practices found in different societies by requiring that these practices, in order to establish duties of justice, must provide benefits to all who are subject to them.

68. There is, as I say, room to make this argument. The details of how such an argument would go, though, are complicated by the fact that to fall within the ambit of justice at all people must be such that their compliance with conventions would be advantageous to others. Those who don't meet this requirement will still be proper objects of moral concern as long as they are sentient, Hume emphasizes; but, on his account, that concern will not be a matter of justice. So, the vulnerable who are covered by this sort of argument may well not be the most vulnerable people. As a result, part of the complication involved in arguing that justice requires being sensitive especially to the way in which a convention affects the vulnerable is distinguishing that demand of justice, with its focus on those who might participate in the conventions in a way that benefits others, from the demands of humanity that require a concern for those who might not. See footnote 39.

BIBLIOGRAPHY

Baron, Marcia. (1982). "Hume's Noble Lie: An Account of His Artificial Virtues." *Canadian Journal of Philosophy* 12 (3/September), 539–555.

Cohon, Rachel. (1997). "Hume's Difficulty with the Virtue of Justice." *Hume Studies* 23 (1), 91–112.

Cohon, Rachel. (2008). *Hume's Morality: Feeling and Fabrication*. Oxford: Oxford University Press.

Darwall, Stephen. (1995). *The British Moralists and the Internal 'Ought.'* Cambridge: Cambridge University Press.

Garrett, Don. (2007). "The First Motive to Justice; Hume's Circle Argument Squared." *Hume Studies* 33(2), 257–288.

Gauthier, David. (1992). "Artificial Virtues and the Sensible Knave." *Hume Studies* 18(2/November), 401–428.

Kant, Immanuel. (2002). *Groundwork for the Metaphysics of Morals*, ed. Thomas E. Hill, trans. Arnulf Zweig. Oxford: Oxford University Press.

Lewis, David. (1969). *Convention*. Cambridge, MA: Harvard University Press.

Mackie, J. L. (1980). *Hume's Moral Theory*. London: Routledge.

Sayre-McCord, Geoffrey. (1994). "On Why Hume's General Point of View Isn't Ideal—and Shouldn't Be." *Social Philosophy & Policy* 11(1/Winter), 202–228.

Sayre-McCord, Geoffrey. (1996). "Hume and the Bauhaus Theory of Ethics," in *Midwest Studies in Philosophy*, vol. 20. University of Notre Dame Press, 280–298.

Sayre-McCord, Geoffrey. (2008). "Hume on Practical Morality and Inert Reason," in Russ Shafer-Landau, ed., *Oxford Studies in Metaethics*. Oxford University Press, 299–320.

Stroud, Barry. (1977). *Hume*. London: Routledge.

CHAPTER 23

......

HUME AND VIRTUE ETHICS

......

CHRISTINE SWANTON

I Hume and Virtue Ethics

OUR main task in this chapter is to show how Hume's "sentimentalist" moral theory can be a version of virtue ethics and to elaborate the kind of virtue ethics that best describes Hume's moral philosophy. To accomplish this task, we need a definition of virtue ethics, an account of types of virtue ethical theory, and to locate Hume within this taxonomy. That is the task of the remainder of this section. Sections II–IV elaborate Hume's sentimentalist virtue ethics while Section V explores his pluralistic view about the grounds of virtue.

In recent times, Hume has been interpreted as having a virtue ethical normative ethics; indeed, since virtue and vice feature so prominently in his moral theorizing, this interpretation has plausibility. Taylor (2006: 276), for example, claims that "Hume's moral philosophy may plausibly be construed as a version of virtue ethics" for "among the central concepts of his theory are character, virtue and vice, rather than rules, duty, and obligation." Baier (2010: 135), too, claims that "Hume does make the concept of a virtue, not that of either obligation or duty, the primary one in his moral theory and does not, like Hobbes, take a virtue to be the same as obedience to some general rule." It may be thought that two broad features undermine a virtue ethical reading of Hume. First, Hume is the foremost exemplar of the "sentimentalist" tradition, according to which moral properties are somehow constituted from a "moral sense" that is a "sentiment" (T 3.1.2.1/470). Hume's sentimentalism has been interpreted in what Cohon (2008: 12) calls the "common reading" of Hume as a kind of subjectivist and noncognitivist position incompatible with standard forms of virtue ethics. This problem is addressed in Section III.

Second virtue ethics has been associated, often by definition, with virtue ethics in the Aristotelian or more broadly ancient Greek *eudaimonistic* tradition. Because Hume's moral theory is not best interpreted as *eudaimonistic*, it may be thought that he should not be interpreted as a virtue ethicist. However, as Taylor (2006: 276) suggests, Hume can be seen as a virtue ethicist since virtue notions are "central" in his moral theorizing. Indeed, I have defined virtue ethics in terms of the centrality of virtue notions, allowing for the possibility of several genera of virtue ethics, such as Aristotelian, Humean, and Confucian (Swanton 2003; 2013). Of course, it is fuzzy and controversial just how central virtue notions should be for a theory to be called virtue ethical; my hope is to show that Hume's ethics is a very plausible candidate for membership in the genre.

My definition allows for at least three main forms of virtue ethics. First, on the Aristotelian approach, a virtue is necessarily good for the agent (at least in the absence of bad luck) because it contributes to or is partially constitutive of her *eudaimonia* or flourishing. The theory conforms to my definition since virtue is central in the following way. *Eudaimonia* itself is not defined wholly independently of virtue, even for Aristotle. As he makes clear, a "good" such as pleasure is not good "without qualification" since it needs to be suffused with virtue if it is to be such a good. Sadistic pleasure, for example, is not good for an agent *simpliciter* for it is not good for a virtuous agent, and, as Aristotle also states, goodness of character is the greatest good for an individual. Similarly, friendship as such is not good without qualification because being friends in crime is not good for one. The same point applies to other goods on traditional list theories of goods, such as play and achievement. Hume should not be read as a *eudaimonist* for one simple reason: he does not believe that, at bottom, a necessary condition for a trait being a virtue is that it be characteristically good for the agent. As I shall argue, what makes traits virtues for Hume is a variety of features.

A second major type of virtue ethics is what Slote (2001) calls "agent-based." For him, virtue or a key component of virtue is ethically fundamental and not merely central. According to Slote, the admirability of virtue is wholly dependent on the admirability of motives. In sentimentalist agent-based virtue ethics, such as a morality of what Slote calls universal benevolence, the admirability of benevolence as a virtue is judged "by reference to universal benevolence as a *motive that seeks* certain ends instead of by reference to the actual or probable *occurrence* of those ends" (2001: 25). Furthermore, one can seek certain ends without being wise in that seeking: practical wisdom is not necessary for virtue on the agent-based view. On that view, rightness or acceptability of action is understood, too, by reference to motive.[1]

Should Hume be understood as possessing an agent-based virtue ethics? It may appear so because he claims that unless actions proceed from something "durable or constant" in the person (i.e., character), they cannot "redound to infamy" or merit punishment (T 2.3.2.6/411). What is required for redounding to honor or infamy is quality of motive ("when we praise any actions, we regard only the motives which produced them"; T 3.2.1.2/477). However, it does not follow from this that, for Hume what makes actions right (as opposed to praiseworthy) or what makes a trait a virtue is solely quality of motive. Indeed, for Hume, as we shall see, morality's practices, notably virtuous conduct, must meet the criteria of success in the external world. The criteria of virtue, I shall argue, are not, however, for Hume exhausted by their systematic consequences. (I thus do not interpret Hume as a virtue consequentialist: success is a broader notion).

In short, Hume allows for two broad modes of moral approval: both the motives from which actions flow and forms of success. We might compare Hutcheson (1969: 127) who claims both that "the actions which we approve, are useful to Mankind; but not always to the Approver" and that "every Action which we apprehend as either *morally good* or *evil*, is always suppos'd to flow from our Affection toward sensitive natures; and whatever we call *Virtue* or *Vice*, is either some such affection, or some action consequent upon it" (1969: 132). Thus, for Hutcheson, we never call a person benevolent if he is "in fact useful to others" but only "intends his *own Interest*, without any ultimate desire of the *Good* of *others*" (136). Similarly for Hume virtue is constituted both by goodness of passion or motive and forms of success: one of the criteria of virtue being that it is a trait having a tendency to the good of mankind. Benevolence is such a trait, but at the core of that virtue is benevolence as a passion; namely, the *desire* for another's good.[2]

Hume then subscribes to a third kind of virtue ethics. On this third view, the emotional dispositions constituting states of virtue have to be fitting to the world. As elaborated further below, Hume's virtues are understood through notions such as proper objects and manner of love; proper objects and manner of pity, hope, and joy; proper objects of wit and ways of being witty (Hume indeed distinguishes false and true wit; T 2.1.7.7/297); proper objects and manner of pride; decorum fitted to one's age and station (T 3.3.4.12/612); and so on. Determining what is fitting may be quite sophisticated and controversial: Hume says, for example, that not all the angry passions are vicious "tho' they are disagreeable". Indeed the want of anger (and even hatred) may betoken "weakness and imbecility" (T 3.3.3.7/605). Again, the expression of a virtue of affection must be, as Hume puts it, "naturally fitting" to the kind of lovability that is exhibited by one's child, for example, and to the kind of love that is appropriate to a parental relation. The "appetite of generation" (T 2.2.11.1/394) makes appropriate a different kind of love.

In general, for Hume, some virtues are naturally fitting because of their systematic beneficial consequences, some because they are dispositions to respect in a fitting way socially useful "artifices," and some because they are constituted by agreeable "enduring" and "stable" passions whose expression is characteristically naturally fitted to their objects and for a variety of reasons. As Hume claims:

> For we reap a pleasure from the view of a character, which is naturally fitted to be useful to others, or to the person himself, or which is agreeable to others or to the person himself. (T 3.3.1.30/591)

Would virtue notions be central on this third view? What makes responses naturally fitting is captured through notions that are ineliminably thick evaluative virtue notions, such as decent, well-bred, tasteful, humane, noble, and honorable. Nor should these notions be seen as violating empiricist principles, for their proper applicability demands knowledge of human psychological, social, and cultural nature. For example, we may claim that a person's charity is not genuinely humane or noble because her apparent virtuous selflessness is not based on a healthy self-love but on self-contempt, expressing escape into others. Hume claims:

a genuine and hearty pride, or self-esteem, if well-concealed and well-founded, is essential to the character of a man with honour. (T 3.3.2.11/598)

By contrast:

An abjectness of character . . . is disgustful and contemptible in another view. Where a man has no sense of value in himself, we are not likely to have any higher esteem of him. (EM 7.11/254)

Again, for Hume, a person's joyfulness may not be naturally fitting because it is "disordered by the frenzies of enthusiasm" (ESY 2.2/268). It may lack good breeding, expressing excessive emotion inappropriate to time or place or a lack of modesty betraying overweening pride or obtuseness about social norms.

Hume's version of this third kind of virtue ethics will be elaborated in three stages. The first stage explicates its response-dependent nature; the second demonstrates its objectivity; the third discusses the grounds of virtue status in Hume and the notion of natural fittingness itself.

II THE INTELLIGIBILITY OF ETHICS IN HUME

Hume has certainly been interpreted as a moral sense theorist (Pigden 2009: 95–6) and in recent times this formerly standard interpretation of Hume has been moved from the realm of subjectivist interpretation to a virtue ethical framework (see, e.g., Cohon 2008; Swanton 2007). For Hume, the moral sense (in its manifestation as a sense of virtue) is defined by the sentiment of approbation proper to that sense, and ethical facts are understandable as facts only as "lit up" by, made intelligible by, that sense. Through the "moral sense," we discern qualities *as* virtues and vices. Virtues as properties of persons are understood as "stable" and "enduring" qualities of mind that have a "power" to produce love or pride:

these two particulars are to be consider'd as equivalent, with regard to our mental qualities, *virtue* and the power to produce love or pride, *vice* and the power of producing humility or hatred. (T 3.3.1.4/575)[3]

Hume's account of virtue and vice is a form of property response-dependence view. This kind of view is described thus by John McDowell (1998: 146) in relation to values. Values are not "brutely there" "independently of our sensibility—any more than colours are, though as with colours, this does not prevent us from supposing that they are there independent of any particular apparent experience of them." Hume makes exactly the same point at T 3.1.1.26/469 in relation to virtue and vice when he claims that "Vice and virtue . . . may be compared to sounds, colours, heat and cold, which, according to modern philosophy, are not qualities in objects, but perceptions in the mind." Here, Hume is claiming that just as redness is not there independent of our sensibility, neither is virtue. Once the requisite sensibilities make virtue and vice properties intelligible as ethical properties, we can then understand them as monadic properties of persons just as redness can be understood as an external monadic property of a British postbox (Wiggins 1987: 107).

A property response-dependence view does not entail that the meaning of moral terms is understood in terms of the responses of agents or observers. According to this latter view, when we say that V is a virtue, we mean that, for example, experts, ideal observers, or qualified agents, judge that V is a virtue, or approve of V, or would choose to cultivate V and so on. However, as Blackburn (1998) points out, this is not what we *mean* by moral or aesthetic judgments.

Hume's claim in *The Treatise of Human Nature* (in a section entitled "Moral Distinctions Deriv'd from a Moral Sense") that "since vice and virtue are not discoverable merely by reason, or the comparison of ideas, it must be by some impression or sentiment they occasion, that we are able to mark the difference betwixt them" (T 3.1.2.1/470) is a claim about the very intelligibility of ethics. "Reason," here understood by Hume as the inferential capacity of the "faculty of understanding" operating without any input from sentiment, is necessary for the moral sense to be authoritative. But it is not sufficient: virtue and vice are not discoverable "*merely*" by reason. In particular, without a moral sense, we have no basis for assessing our ends as those of a reasonable person or as those of a moral monster because "reason," in the above sense, is powerless to assign morally intelligible weightings to ends. Hence, Hume claims: "Tis not contrary to reason to prefer the destruction of the whole world to the scratching of my finger" (T 2.3.3.6/416).

It is the moral sense that makes weightings morally intelligible. But what is it about the moral sense that makes this so? First, the moral sense is not defined merely by the capacity to approve or disapprove. Consider an individual who possesses merely the faculty of understanding. He can compare ideas and assess means to ends, but he entirely lacks the ability to experience pleasure and pain and has no empathy or emotions in general. He is like the person who is the "fancied monster" in the *Enquiries*:

> Let us suppose, if the prosperity of nations were laid on the one hand, and their ruin on the other, and he were desired to choose; that he would stand like the schoolman's ass, irresolute and undetermined, between equal motives. (EM 6.4/235)

Second, consider a person who has empathy but only of the kind that takes delight in pain and suffering apart from her own. She prefers the suffering of millions to the painful scratching of her finger. She is another kind of moral monster. The moral sense is defined neither by the ability to be motivated by one's emotions nor by the ability to love or hate in general.

What, then, does define the moral sense? To have the *sense* of virtue "is nothing but to *feel* a satisfaction of a *particular kind* from the contemplation of a character" (T 3.1.2.3/471). The *"particular kind"* of satisfaction is one distinguishable from satisfaction from the contemplation of beauty and other types of satisfactions. As Hume says at T 3.1.2.4/472, the pleasures of approval of characters is of a "peculiar" kind distinct from the approval of musical compositions or of a good wine. The moral sense, to be a *moral* sense, involves sensitivities due to the excitement of "sympathy" but a sympathy driven by or operating within the background of sufficiently extensive desires for the good of others (albeit desires constrained by self-love, as we saw earlier). That is not distinctive of the appreciation of wine or music. The desire for the good of another is benevolence, but the benevolence must be capable of being transferred through sympathy sufficiently extensively if we are to have a moral sense. The capacity for empathy (what Hume calls in the *Treatise* "sympathy") necessary for a *moral* sense is fundamentally empathic benevolence. The moral sense, then, that which makes ethics intelligible as *ethics*, is not merely the capacity to approve or disapprove, or even love or hate, traits of character. The love of virtue and hatred of vice constituting the moral sense is not just bare love or hatred but love and hatred within a sensibility that is fundamentally humane.

It is important to appreciate that the moral sense itself is a passion, not a sensation. Response-dependence views have traditionally been thought to be perceptual, but because the idea of a perceptual moral sense analogous to sense perception is rightly thought suspect, so, too, have response-dependence views of ethics. The root of the problem is the association of secondary properties with perceptual appearance and the association of response-dependence in ethics with that analysis. Conceiving moral properties as secondary properties has resulted in conceiving them in terms of *perceptual* appearance. Here, for example, is McDowell's notion of a secondary property:

> A secondary quality is a property the ascription of which to an object is not adequately understood except as true, if it is true, in virtue of the object's disposition to present a certain sort of perceptual appearance: specifically, an appearance characterizable by using a word for the property itself to say how the object perceptually appears. (1998: 133)

Unfortunately the "perceptual appearance" account of secondary properties renders less visible an interpretation of "perception" (or some related notion) in terms of, for example, Hume's notion of "impressions," which are a subclass of "perceptions" and include pleasure and pain, desire and aversion, passions (emotions) that are not desires, and even the will (which for Hume is not strictly comprehended among the passions and is undefinable; T 2.3.1.2/399). It therefore obscures the possibility of emotional response-dependence views of ethics.

However, there is a problem with this account of Hume's moral sense as a "sense" constituted by a certain type of love and hatred of character traits: namely, love and hatred within a sensibility characterized by sufficiently extensive benevolence constrained by self-love. Such a view, it appears, cannot account for the intelligibility of ethics as essentially practical for, on Hume's own account, love and pride are not motivating passions. They are "pure emotions in the soul, unattended with any desire, and not immediately exciting us to action" (T 2.2.6.1/367). Yet Hume claims morality has an intimate connection with practice and motivation:

> Extinguish all the warm feelings and prepossessions in favour of virtue, and all disgust or aversion to vice: render men totally indifferent towards these distinctions; and morality is no longer a practical study, nor has any tendency to regulate our lives. (EM 1.8/172)

Notice though that this feature of the practicality of 'morality' in general is compatible with Hume's view that "Tis one thing to know virtue, and another to conform one's will to it" (T 3.1.1.22/465–6).[4] We can "know virtue" through the moral sense, but we need not *have* virtue. However, it would be unsatisfactory if, for Hume, there was a disconnection between the moral sentiments of approval and motivations to behave virtuously, and, in fact, there is for him a causal connection between the sentiments of love and hate and motivating sentiments. Hume claims: "love and hatred are not compleated within themselves" and "carry the mind to something further" (T 2.2.6.1/367). In that way, love and hate are characteristically conjoined through the imagination, with, respectively, the motivating desires of benevolence and anger. Hence, the "spectator" sentiments of love or hatred (of virtue and vice) are causally connected to the "participant" perspective of engaged moral life.[5]

Virtues as traits essential for engaged, competent participation in the moral life are constituted by emotional motivating propensities. Without the appropriate emotions, there would be no such virtue and no such competence. As Hume says:

> If I have no vanity, I take no delight in praise: if I be void of ambition, power gives me no enjoyment: if I be not angry, the punishment of an adversary is totally indifferent to me. (EM App., 2.12/301)

There is a large array of emotional response-dependent properties that make the lived world of ethics intelligible for beings such as ourselves. When refined, stable, enduring, and fitting to their objects, they become virtues. Before saying more about the nature of the virtues in Hume, we need to explain further the grounds for judgments of virtue in Hume.

III   THE OBJECTIVITY OF ETHICS IN HUME

Those with a moral sense are capable of making judgments about virtue and vice and their manifestations in different individuals on different occasions. That is, a person might claim that overweening pride is a vice; that Jo's pride, far from being a type that is modest (and virtuous) is, in fact, overweening and that Jo is manifesting overweening pride right now. However, how can we say that such judgments are objective and warranted? How can a moral sense theory account for the fact that Jo's pride *merits* the response of disapprobation? Such judgments, if warranted and true, rely on

(a) an understanding of the criteria of virtue;
(b) an accurate application of those criteria to specific character traits; and
(c) an accurate assessment of whether or not those traits are possessed by specific individuals and are expressed on specific occasions.

Issues of justification and objectivity apply to all these features.

Although individuals possessing a moral sense are capable of making intelligible judgments about overweening pride, for example, that moral sense may not be authoritative. One with an authoritative moral sense is in a good position to make judgments about the criteria of virtue and to apply those criteria accurately. Consider first the criteria of virtue themselves. If a trait is to be naturally fitting, it must conform to one or other of the various criteria of virtue. To determine what constitutes the criteria of virtue for Hume, we need to determine the causes of the moral sense; otherwise, the theory of virtue would not be empirically grounded. There are for Hume two broad kinds of powers of traits to affect the moral sense: the giving of pleasure or pain from reflections on consequences and the giving of pleasure and pain from the immediate impact of "species or appearances":

> Moral good and evil are certainly distinguish'd by our *sentiments*, not by *reason*: But these sentiments may arise either from the mere species or appearances of characters and passions, or from reflexions on their tendency to the happiness of mankind, and of particular persons. My opinion is, that both these causes are intermix'd in our judgments of morals; after the same manner as they are in our decisions concerning most kinds of external beauty: Tho' I am also of opinion, that reflexions on the tendencies of actions have by far the greatest influence, and determine all the great lines of our duty. There are, however, instances, in cases of less moment, wherein this immediate taste or sentiment produces our approbation. (T 3.3.1.27/589–90)

The fact that there are these two aspects to the moral sense suggests that "tendencies" of traits do not exhaust the class of features that make traits virtues. If this is so, Hume should not be read as a virtue consequentialist. Indeed, the causes of the activation of the moral sense suggest two general criteria of virtue:

C1. A trait is a virtue if it tends to the happiness of mankind.
C2. A trait is a virtue if it has properties, not reducible to consequences for happiness, that make it naturally fitting that its species or appearance causes "this immediate taste or sentiment that "produces ourapprobation".

Hume classifies traits that are virtues within his famous taxonomy of useful or agreeable to self or other.[6] In this way, as Taylor (2006) notes, Hume allows for a far greater array of virtues than does Hutcheson: not only are there nonconsequentialist virtues (see further discussion in Section V), but there are also virtues that are self-regarding or primarily so.

Consider now the application of the criteria of virtue. Can Hume account for the possibility of objectivity in the attribution of traits to persons and in their manifestation on particular occasions? He argues that there are a number of well-known propensities in our attributions, tendencies that make for bias and consequent error. In partial individuals, where the sentiments of "morals" and "interest" do not remain "distinct," these sentiments "naturally run into one another" (T 3.1.2.4/472), leading to self-serving judgment. Such individuals may also lack objectivity in the ascription of character traits if the persons evaluated are their enemies rather than their friends, their countrymen rather than foreigners. There are also "illusions" caused by biases of proximity: one cannot feel the same "lively pleasure" from contemplating the virtues of persons remote in time as one does from contemplating those of a familiar friend or acquaintance (T 3.3.1.15/581). Yet the "judicious spectator" (T 3.3.1.14/581) esteems alike, like virtues. To avoid biases of partiality and distance, sentiments need correcting by the adoption of "*steady* and *general* points of view" (T 3.3.1.15/581–2), such that a person of "temper and judgment" (T 3.1.2.4/472) is able to "preserve himself from [the] illusions" (T 3.1.2.4/472) caused by "variations" in sentiment (T 3.3.1.14/581).

It is clear that Hume allows for the correction of our sentiments in a direction that allows for greater objectivity. What about the correction of belief? Because beliefs are "almost absolutely requisite to the exciting our passions" (as well as passions being "very favourable to" belief) (T 1.3.10.4/120; see also T 1.3.13.9–10/148), we need to discuss the evaluation of belief and, in general, the assessment for that evaluation of the mutual reinforcing tendencies of affections and the ideas of the imagination (including belief). Beliefs, for Hume, are those ideas that are "lively" and in particular "enlivened by force and vivacity transferred from an associated impression" (Morris 2006: 81). Does Hume possess the resources for criticizing belief as ill- or well-founded? Is he able to criticize as doxastically vicious certain kinds of mutual reinforcing of passion and imagination? Book I of the *Treatise* explains a number of doxastic and imaginative vices, all of which undermine the credentials of our ascriptions of traits to individuals. Doxastic vices include credulity, obstinate incredulity, and prejudice; imaginative vices in general include the tendency for the imagination to be affected in a deleterious way by distorting passions: "a person of a sorrowful or melancholy disposition is very credulous of everything that nourishes his prevailing passion" (T 1.3.10.4/120).

Just as sentiments need to be corrected by adopting a general and steady point of view in order to achieve greater objectivity, so, too, various natural propensities to bias in the formation of belief need to be corrected. For example, credulity understood as a "too easy faith in the testimony of others" (T 1.3.9.12/112) is a "remarkable propensity to believe whatever is reported." This propensity to inaccurate belief needs to be checked by the testimony of experience, including, of course, one's experience of the caliber of those providing the reports.

Obstinate incredulity is a doxastic vice nurtured by our propensities to adhere to *systems* of beliefs founded on superstition.[7] These tendencies to systematize make us remarkably resistant to the testimony of experience and normal causal reasoning. Again, such propensities need to be checked against experience, difficult though that may be. Note the influence of passion on the imagination, which makes the eradication of both credulity and obstinate incredulity even more difficult.

Another doxastic weakness emphasized by Hume is our propensity for rash adherence to general rules, which themselves are the products of custom and experience. Like all such products, they need to be refined by further experience, and care must be taken in applying them. The "vulgar" are "commonly guided" by general rules formed by "accidental circumstances," whereas the "wise" are guided by those formed by the observance of "efficacious causes" (T 1.3.13.12/149–50). As a consequence, we are vulnerable to prejudices such as the belief that the conversation of Frenchmen "cannot have solidity" (T 1.3.13.7/146). If people dislike Frenchmen because of the (eighteenth-century) Anglo-French wars, then prejudice based on "accidental circumstance" and reinforced by prevailing passion will be nourished and acquire greater force. There is thus no objectivity in the attribution of conversational vice to Frenchmen and in the interpretation of particular conversations through such vice ascription.

We might conclude that those with an authoritative moral sense are "wise" and "sagacious." They are people who are not only knowledgeable about human nature in general, but also have corrected for prevalent infirmities of the imagination's belief-forming mechanisms and of the sentiments.

IV Virtue and the Moral/Nonmoral Distinction

Now that we understand the basic features of Hume's moral sense theory of virtue, we are in a position to tackle head-on a familiar criticism of Hume's conception of virtue and of "morality" in general. This is the criticism that, for Hume, there is no clear demarcation between the moral and the nonmoral *virtues* (as opposed to the moral sense and other "senses") and between virtues and "mental qualities" that are talents. For Hume, there is no clear distinction to be drawn. As we have seen, virtues in general are traits of character that are approved by the "*moral* sense" as opposed to the sense, for example, that detects harmony in musical compositions, and what is "peculiar" or distinctive about the moral sense is that it is animated by benevolence, a passion that is "original" to our "frame and constitution." Indeed, this is what is "moral" about the moral sense. Hence, claims Hume, the moral sense does not approve courage and ambition unless "regulated" by benevolence: "Courage and ambition, when not regulated by benevolence are fit only to make a tyrant and public robber" (T 3.3.3.3/604).

The moral sense approves or otherwise character traits *in general*, and the underlying sympathy and benevolence allows us to distinguish not only justice from knavery but also dispositions to "true" "delicate" wit from "false" wit (T 2.1.7.7/297)[8] and (virtuous) cheerfulness of disposition from tendencies to "dissolute mirth" (EM 7.22, n22/258, n1). These latter virtues do not constitute the "great lines of our duty" (T 3.3.1.27/589–90), but that does not make them less likely to be approved by the benevolent, humane individual. What is important is that the moral sense is able to sort character traits that are good from those that are bad: Hume does not provide us with a further distinction between the moral and the nonmoral within the class of traits approved by the moral sense.

One may argue that there is some kind of significant distinction between moral and nonmoral virtue to be drawn, but, once the moral sense is in place, there is no significant, uncontentious distinction. In his reply to critics (of his *Human Morality*), Scheffler (1995: 974) opposes Susan Wolf's claim that "it is natural to think of the impersonal point of view as *generating* moral requirements and to think of the personal point of view (or, rather respect for it) as constraining or limiting the extent of morality's demands."[9] Scheffler replies that this does not seem natural to him; rather, "it seems natural to think of morality as addressed to the question of how one should live one's life, taking into account both one's personal well being and the interests of others" (974). It seems to me that Hume's virtue-centered conception of the concerns of morality and his classing both "small" and primarily self-regarding virtues as virtues approved by the moral sense fits well with Scheffler's view. We might also include within that conception what Hume calls "faults" that "are nothing but smaller vices," such as being disposed to "negligence" in regard to cleanliness, dubbed by Hume a virtue (T 3.3.4.10/611).

On this conception, the sphere of *virtue* embraces all those good character traits that are of greater or lesser importance in *all* those areas characteristic of a human life: for example, cooperation, sociability, meeting danger, leisure, parenting, friendship, and hygiene. Psychological theories of a good life for human beings, such as attachment theory, recognize a human need for bonding and a secure base, which is the very antithesis of an impersonal perspective. Those needs are not only recognized by virtues such as being a good parent, but also in what Kant (1996: 218) calls "virtues of social intercourse" (*virtutes homileticae*).

In general, Hume's methodological empiricism[10] would sanction deploying all the empirical resources at our disposal to determine what is naturally fitting in the expression of, for example, pride, joy, hope, love, ambitiousness, or benevolence, in order to determine what is virtuous in these areas. We might still object that common usage has a narrow conception of morality, eliminating for some even amiability from the class of moral virtue.[11] Even though it may be hard to find a principled reason for such limitation, it may be that the usage of the "person on the street" is authoritative if there is an uncontested common usage, which I very much doubt. However, I prefer to leave the last word with a generally more educated individual, Hume, who, in a conciliatory mood and in relation to a similar problem of demarcation (that between mental qualities that are virtues and those that are talents), allows for the possibility of a distinction in ordinary language while claiming that it is vague, imprecise of definition, and unimportant:

> I do not find that in the English or any other modern tongue, the boundaries are exactly fixed between virtues and talents, vices and defects, or that a precise definition can be given of the one as contradistinguished from the other. (EM App. 4, 2/313).

Furthermore, he claims, the problem of where to draw the line is of no great moment because different contexts, personalities, cultures, and even personal preferences about what virtues one prefers to have oneself and what virtues one would "rather pass with the world" (EM App. 4.5/316) will govern the way the line is drawn.

V THE PLURALITY OF THE GROUNDS OF VIRTUE

In this section, I argue that Hume grounds the virtues in a plurality of features. To understand this plurality, we need three basic distinctions: consequentialist versus non consequentialist criteria of virtue; natural versus artificial virtues; and within the class of natural virtues, the different passions around which the virtues "cluster" (passions such as pride, love, benevolence, joy, hope)[12]

I concentrate here on the more contentious class of virtues for Hume: those that are nonconsequentialist. The criterion of virtue, (C2) (Section III), embraces two broad types of nonconsequentialist virtue: those that are artificial (discussed now) and those that form a subclass of the natural virtues (such as the various virtues of love). It is well known that Hume divides virtues into the natural and the artificial (notably justice and fidelity). The distinction is important for a reason highlighted by Baier (2010: 130):

> In the important section "Some further reflexions concerning justice and injustice" Hume contrasts the "entire" rights and obligations of property and promise, whose entirety and strictness are taken as a mark of artifice, with "half rights and obligations, so natural in common life" (T 3.2.6.8/531), but this occurs only in "our common and negligent way of thinking" (T 3.2.6.8/530, my emphasis).

Justice as a personal virtue consists in the motivational disposition of "respect for rights, and for the authority of the customary rules which confer such rights" (Baier 2010: 27). The idea of a right is founded on artifice, of which Baier identifies three that concern justice in relation to property rights: "property, its transfer by consent, and binding agreement" (2010: 22).

The "artificial" nature of justice has resulted in two problems in the interpretation of Hume in particular and virtue ethics in general. First, as Baier notes (2010: 22), it is sometimes thought that justice is not for Hume a personal virtue at all but merely a virtue of institutions. However, as a personal virtue, justice is understood by Hume as a disposition to *respect* the artifices of justice, and that involves understanding and acting on one's *obligations* to be just. The truly virtuous, just person is not even tempted to be a "sensible knave," even were it in her pecuniary interest to be so, for being a knave is registered by such a person as "base." Justice as a personal *virtue* is thoroughly nonconsequentialist, as Hume makes clear. However, the institutions of justice, the rules of justice, have at a deep level a consequentialist justification. Were they in the long term to not serve human good, they should over time be changed.

The second problem is this: it is sometimes thought that virtue ethics in general cannot accommodate duty. There is a view that there is a distinction between duty-imposing reasons and reasons of virtue in which the former "define acts as prohibited, permissible or obligatory," whereas the latter "classify behaviour as suberogatory, neutral or supererogatory" (Stohr and Wellman 2002: 69). However, just as Hume speaks of our "great lines of duty" (i.e., relatively stringent duties of virtue), so we can speak of, for example, an egregious failure of benevolence as a violation of a requirement or duty. By contrast, being witty would not be a stringent duty for Hume and would normally be regarded as desirable only, even though wit for Hume is a virtue. I disagree, then, with Baier (2010: 135) when she claims that "role independent natural virtues" such as fortitude, good temper, and benevolence are merely to be "encouraged and welcomed." Some manifestations of benevolence, good temper, and so on may merely be welcome; others are required as duties.

Baier is, however, right to think that, for Hume, the scope of obligation (or even the broader notion of duty or requirement) is not coextensive with "action expressive of virtue or the absence of vice" (132), but that does not mean that, in certain circumstances, the stringency of one's duty to manifest benevolence or be a good parent for example may be stronger and weightier than a specific but relatively trivial obligation of justice (returning a book within a week for example).

What is at stake here is a deep-seated pluralism in the nature and sources of virtue, but it would be a mistake to think that the distinction between the natural and artificial virtues is the only significant pluralism in Hume's substantive philosophy. Another is the pluralism in the nature and sources of the natural virtues themselves: concern for the good of people manifested in benevolence and compassion, the expression of the bonds of love manifested in the many virtues of love, and responsiveness to value in our joyous appreciation of beauty and nature. Many of these virtues, such as tenderness, are nonconsequentialist in nature:

> 'Tis certain that we are infinitely touch'd with a tender sentiment, as well as with a great one. The tears naturally start in our eyes at the conception of it; nor can we forbear giving a loose to the same tenderness towards the person who exerts it. All this seems to me a proof, that our approbation has, in those cases, an origin different from the prospect of utility and advantage, either to ourselves or others. (T 3.3.3.4/604)

The difficulty with the nonconsequentialist natural virtues lies in justifying their natural fittingness to be regarded as virtues. How do we distinguish such virtues from closely related vice? The difficulty is highlighted in the following passage, where the application of (C1) (see Section (III)) in distinguishing virtue from vice is clear, but the application of (C2) less clear:

> We easily gain from the liberality of others but are always in danger of losing by their avarice: Courage defends us, but cowardice lays us open to every attack. . . . Humility exalts; but pride mortifies us. For these reasons the former qualities are esteem'd virtues and the latter regarded as vices. (T 2.1.7.3/295)

Liberality, for example, is justified as a virtue by (C1); humility by (C2). Humility is a trait of which it is naturally fitting that its "species or appearance" causes "this immediate taste or sentiment" (namely, exaltation), whereas (nonvirtuous) pride is fitted for mortification. But what is it about humility that merits exaltation? By the same token, what is it about tenderness that merits being touched? As Hume claims, the tenderness expressed in grief for a friend bestows "a merit as well as it does a pleasure, on his melancholy" (T 3.3.3.6/605).

I shall suggest that the way to understand the natural nonconsequentialist virtues for Hume is this: such virtues are "stable," "enduring" dispositions that are fitted to cause immediate approbation on the witnessing of their manifestations ("species or appearances"), and what makes them fitted to cause this approbation is that they are dispositions to feel and act expressively in a fitting manner from emotions which are, in the circumstances, "fitting" to their objects. In this way, the virtues merit the approbation as well as cause the pleasures of approval. The virtue of joyfulness, for example, is a disposition to express and feel a joy of which it is *fitting* that its "species or appearance" cause delight (as opposed to, e.g., mortification, embarrassment, or disgust). The kind of joyfulness expressed merits that delight on account of its fittingness to its object and the fittingness of its manner and occasion of expression. By contrast, tendencies to "dissolute mirth" are not, for Hume, a virtuous kind of joy because such mirth is not fitting in manner (being expressive of folly) and does not merit approval:

> Cheerfulness could scarce admit of blame from its excess, were it not that dissolute mirth, without a proper cause or subject, is a sure symptom and characteristic of folly, and on that account disgustful. (EM 7.22, n49/258, n1)

The "monkish virtues"—e.g., fasting, celibacy, mortification, solitude (EM 9.3/270)—are, for Hume, by contrast vices of deficient joy: they are expressive of a generalized joylessness even where objects (such as conversation with convivial friends) merit joy. The joylessness is not fitted to its objects.

This, of course, raises the issue: What makes an emotion fitting? According to D'Arms and Jacobson (2000: 65), to say that an emotion is fitting and appropriate in that sense is to say that "it accurately presents its object as having certain evaluative features." On this view, emotions "involve evaluative presentations," and this means that they "present the world to us as having value-laden features" (66). They further argue, however, that "moral considerations about the propriety of having an emotional response are irrelevant to whether the associated evaluative property obtains" (68). For example, the wrongness of being amused by a joke does not count against the joke being funny (66). To move from moral inappropriateness to unfittingness is to commit the "moralistic fallacy."

This distinction between the "moral" and the "fitting" is not made by Hume. He distinguishes between the intelligibility of an emotion (e.g., being enviable in the sense of able to be envied) and its fittingness (e.g., being fit to be envied). On his virtue ethical view of fittingness, the considerations that make an emotion fitting in a circumstance are precisely those that make it virtuous in that circumstance—or at least nonvicious. We have already seen that he does not equate virtue with a narrow taxonomic sense of "moral" virtue. On his account, prudential considerations may make a response fitting on an occasion if that response manifests "prudential" virtue (i.e., a virtue within the broad class of virtuous traits agreeable or useful to the self) and is not a sleazy, indecent kind of self-interested response.

To illustrate the point, let us discuss D'Arms and Jacobson's examples of envy and grief, which they deploy to highlight the alleged fallacy. Consider d'Arms and Jacobson's example of Susan's good fortune in getting tenure as enviable in the sense of fit to be envied as opposed to being able to be envied (2000: 71). To determine what it is to be *fit* to be envied, and in particular whether anything is fit to be envied, it is useful to consider Hume's own account of "enviable" in the sense of *able* to be envied. Hume shows how envy, on the face of it a very strange if not irrational emotion, is psychologically possible and indeed common. He claims first that "envy is excited by some present enjoyment of another, which by comparison diminishes our idea of our own" (T 2.2.8.12/377). Second, he shows that envy requires a certain "proximity" rather than "great disproportion" between ourselves and the one envied. A common soldier, for example, does not envy his general (T 2.2.8.13/377). Third, he argues that "the proximity in the degree of merit is not alone sufficient to give rise to envy, but must be assisted by other relations" (T 2.2.8.15/378). Hume has shown how envy is intelligible as a human emotion, but he has not thereby shown that it is fitting. If envy turns out to be a vice, then envy does not fit its object. What kind of accurate evaluations make it fitting that an academic envy the good fortune of another academic? Are there any? It is not committing the moralistic fallacy to claim that there are not, on the grounds that envy is based on psychologically problematic self-referential comparisons (as Hume's account suggests). Hume's psychological principle of comparison *explains* many emotions, even malice, which Hume describes as "the unprovoked desire of producing evil to another, in order to reap a pleasure from the comparison" (T 2.2.8.12/377). Yet malice is a vice: no object is fit to be treated with malice for the purpose of enhancing one's own pleasure.

It is unclear, however, to what extent Hume regards envy as a vice because he makes allowances for what is common and usual in human nature: "We make allowance for a certain degree of selfishness in men because we know it to be inseparable from human nature, and inherent in our frame and constitution" (T 3.3.1.17/583). We could take this to mean either that the delineation of unselfishness as a virtue must make allowances for this weakness, or that, if it does not, virtue is a threshold or *satis* concept, such that one possesses unselfishness as a virtue if one is unselfish enough. The same applies to the disposition to be unenvious.

Another example is one that Hume also discusses: grief, which is sometimes deemed fitting for Hume albeit "excessive" in view of its disutility (T 3.3.3.6/605). This claim may seem to suit D'Arms and Jacobson's position, although Hume does not suggest that to feel such grief is wrong and vicious, albeit fitting to its object. In D'Arms and Jacobson's example of excessive grief, it is suggested that it is wrong to "fall apart" (77) with grief when one is widowed with young children to take care of, even though such grief is fitting given the sadness of the loss. However, what are the evaluative reasons that support this judgment of fittingness? I cannot think of any such reasons, although we may find explanations for and even sympathize with the breakdown. Again, however, such explanations do not show that the grief is fitting either to the object or to the circumstances. As we have seen, for Hume, the virtue of tenderness allows for the meritoriousness of "excessive" grief that expresses that tenderness, but (I doubt) not to the point of breakdown in circumstances where it is vital one show the necessary resoluteness and strength.

There is much of interest in Hume's texts germane to the fittingness of a wide range of virtues, ranging from meekness and modesty to the "awful" virtues of "great-mindedness." Space has precluded discussion of many of these most interesting virtues.[13]

ABBREVIATIONS OF WORKS CITED

EM   *Enquiry Concerning the Principles of Morals.* Edited by Tom L. Beauchamp. Oxford: Clarendon, 1998.

ESY   *Essays: Moral, Political, and Literary.* Revised edition by E. F. Miller. Indianapolis: Liberty Classics, 1985.

T   *A Treatise of Human Nature.* Edited by D. F. Norton and M. J. Norton. Oxford: Clarendon, 2007.

NOTES

1. For example: "an act is morally acceptable if and only if it comes from good or virtuous motivation involving benevolence or caring (about the well being of others) or at least doesn't come from bad or inferior motivation involving malice or indifference to humanity" (Slote 2001: 38).

2. It should not be simply assumed that benevolence is a virtue "useful to mankind." As Russell (2008) notes, "Mandeville argues that our private vices—indulging our passions

such as greed, ambition and lust—in fact serve the public interest and make for a more prosperous and thriving society. Virtue, on the other hand, becomes an impediment to greatness, empire and achievement" (246). As part of a "science" of morals, for Hume, tendencies of traits need to be assessed: if the private "vices" were indeed "useful to mankind," they should be approved as virtues.

3. Love (in a broad sense) includes for Hume "esteem."

4. For an excellent defense of a noninternalist reading of Hume and Hume's so-called "Motivation Argument," see Norva Y. S. Lo (2010).

5. See also Abramson (2008).

6. At EM 9.3/270, Hume appears to offer the taxonomy as a disjunctive criterion: "as every quality which is useful or agreeable to others is, in common life, allowed to be a part of personal merit") whereas the more cautious and sensible T 3.3.1.28/590 claims that "some qualities acquire their merit from their being *immediately agreeable* to others, without any tendency to public interest; . . . some are denominated virtuous from their being *immediately agreeable* to the person himself, who possesses them." This formulation allows for the possibility that some immediately agreeable properties are not virtues; namely, those that are not naturally fitted for approval. Let us then stick to T 3.3.1.28/590, which merely offers a taxonomy of virtue.

7. Morris (2006) criticizes Owen (1999) for thinking that Hume does not have the resources for criticizing self-consistent systems of belief such as augury. According to Morris, systems on Hume's view, like individual beliefs, should be assessed by the empirical standards that govern causal reasoning and the verdict of experience, because such systems of superstition involve prediction, and claims about matters of fact.

8. Jacobson (2011: 17) cites Gaut's (2007: 241) claim that a comedy full of "hilarious" but really cruel and vicious jokes would not be found amusing by a virtuous audience. For Hume, such jokes would not be a *fitting* object of amusement since they would be a form of "false wit" and not amusing to someone of "delicate" and unprejudiced taste. Hence, they could not be "hilarious."

9. This is part of Scheffler's reply to Wolf (1995).

10. See Garrett's five senses of "empiricism" including "methodological empiricism" described in his 1997 work.

11. van Hooft (2006: 9) claims, indeed, that not only amiability, but also punctuality and courteousness lie outside the class of moral qualities. I disagree; however, it turns out that for him the scope of the moral is defined by the commands of the moral law (9). A conception of the scope of the moral as defined by the "moral law," however that is to be understood, does not sit well with virtue ethics and certainly not with Hume's virtue ethics.

12. See also Swanton (2009). I do not have space to discuss a fourth distinction, that between two broad categories of virtues—the virtues of "goodness and benevolence" and the virtues of "greatness of mind" illustrated by Cato and Caesar, respectively:

> The characters of Caesar and Cato . . . are both of them virtuous in the strictest sense of the word; but in a different way: Nor are the sentiments entirely the same, which arise from them. The one produces love; the other esteem: The one is amiable; the other awful. (T 3.3.4.2/607–08; EM App. 4.6/316)

On this distinction, see also Russell (2013).

13. For a fascinating discussion of meekness, including Hume's view of this trait, see Pettigrove (2012).

Bibliography

Abramson, Kate. (2008). "Hume's Spectator-centered Theory of Virtue," in Elizabeth S. Radcliffe, ed., *A Companion to Hume*. Oxford: Blackwell, 240–256.

Baier, Annette C. (2010). *The Cautious Jealous Virtue: Hume on Justice*. Cambridge Mass.: Harvard University Press.

Baron, Marcia. (2011). "Virtue Ethics in Relation to Kantian Ethics: An Opinionated Overview and Commentary," in Lawrence Jost and Julian Wuerth, eds., *Perfecting Virtue: New Essays on Kantian Ethics and Virtue Ethics*. Cambridge: Cambridge University Press, 8–37.

Blackburn, Simon. (1998). *Ruling Passions*. Oxford: Clarendon Press.

Cohon, Rachel. (2008). *Hume's Morality: Feeling and Fabrication*. Oxford: Oxford University Press.

D'Arms, Justin, and Daniel Jacobson. (2000). "The Moralistic Fallacy: On the Appropriateness of Emotions," *Philosophy and Phenomenological Research* 61, 65–90.

Garrett, Don. (1997). *Cognition and Commitment in Hume's Philosophy*. Oxford: Oxford University Press.

Gaut, Berys. (2007). *Art, Emotion and Ethics*. Oxford: Oxford University Press.

Hutcheson, Francis. (1969). *An Inquiry into the Original of Our Ideas of Beauty and Virtue*. Westmead: Gregg International.

Jacobson, Daniel. (2011). "Fitting Attitude Theories of Value," in Edward N. Zalta, ed., *The Stanford Encyclopaedia of Philosophy* (Spring 2011 Edition), 1–22.

Kant, Immanuel. (1996). Mary Gregor, ed. and trans., *Metaphysics of Morals*. Cambridge: Cambridge University Press.

McDowell, John. (1998). "Values and Secondary Qualities," in John McDowell, *Mind, Value, and Reality*. Cambridge MA: Harvard University Press, 131–150.

Morris, William Edward. (2006). "Belief, Probability, Normativity," in Saul Traiger, ed., *The Blackwell Guide to Hume's Treatise*. Oxford: Blackwell, 77–94.

Norva, Y. S. Lo. (2010). "Is Hume Inconsistent?—Motivation and Morals," in Charles R. Pigden, ed., *Hume on Motivation and Virtue*. Basingstoke: Palgrave McMillan, 57–79.

Owen, David. (1999). *Hume's Reason*. Oxford: Oxford University Press.

Pettigrove, Glen. (2012). "Meekness and Moral Anger," *Ethics* 122(2), 341–370.

Pigden, Charles R. (2009). "If not non-cognitivism, then what?" in Charles R. Pigden, ed., *Hume on Motivation and Virtue* 80–104.

Russell, Paul. (2008). *The Riddle of Hume's Treatise: Skepticism, Naturalism, and Irreligion*. Oxford: Oxford University Press.

Russell, Paul. (2013). "Hume's Anatomy of Virtue" in Daniel C. Russell, ed., *Cambridge Companion to Virtue Ethics*. Cambridge: Cambridge University Press, 92–123.

Scheffler, Samuel. (1995). "Reply to Three Commentators," *Philosophy and Phenomenological Research* 55, 963–75.

Slote, Michael. (2001). *Morals from Motives*. Oxford: Oxford University Press.

Stohr, Karen, and Christopher Heath Wellman. (2002). "Recent Work on Virtue Ethics," *American Philosophical Quarterly* 39, 49–72.

Swanton, Christine. (2003). *Virtue Ethics: A Pluralistic View*. Oxford: Oxford University Press.

Swanton, Christine. (2007). "Can Hume be Read as a Virtue Ethicist," *Hume Studies* 33, 91–113.

Swanton, Christine. (2009). "What Kind of Virtue Theorist Is Hume?" in Charles R. Pigden ed., *Hume on Motivation and Virtue* 226–248.

Swanton, Christine. (2013). "The Definition of Virtue Ethics," in Daniel C. Russell, ed., *Cambridge Companion to Virtue Ethics*, 315–338.

Swanton, Christine. (2015). *The Virtue Ethics of Hume and Nietzsche*. Oxford Wiley Blackwell.

Taylor, Jacqueline. (2006). "Virtue and the Evaluation of Character," in Saul Traiger, ed., *The Blackwell Guide to Hume's Treatise*. Oxford: Blackwell, 276–295.

van Hooft, Stan. (2006). *Understanding Virtue Ethics*. Chesham: Acumen.

Wolf, Susan. (1995). "Moral Judges and Human Ideals: A Discussion of Human Morality," *Philosophy and Phenomenological Research* 55(4), 957–962.

Wiggins, David. (1987). "A Sensible Subjectivism," in David Wiggins *Needs, Values, and Truth*. Oxford: Clarendon Press, 184–214.

CHAPTER 24

···

HUME'S POLITICAL PHILOSOPHY

···

NEIL MCARTHUR

DAVID Hume never wrote the "book" on politics that, in the preface to the initial section, he promised he would add to the three others that make up his *Treatise of Human Nature*. But we are not short of evidence for his views on the topic. In addition to his extended discussion of the origins and nature of government in the completed text of the *Treatise*, he wrote numerous essays devoted to political questions, and his six-volume *History of England* contains extensive reflections on issues relevant to political philosophy. These diverse writings reflect a coherent set of interests and convictions, and it is thus quite legitimate to speak of Hume's political philosophy. There is little agreement among scholars, however, about the precise nature of this philosophy or its implications for modern thought. Some interpret Hume as a reformer, in tune with the progressive spirit of the Enlightenment; others, as a conservative who applies his skeptical principles to political questions. This chapter attempts to survey the full diversity of Hume's writings on political themes in order to allow for a clearer understanding of his importance to the history of political thought.

I THE SOCIAL CONTRACT AND THE QUESTION OF ALLEGIANCE

···

Hume published the third "book" of the *Treatise*, the section of the larger work devoted to morality, the nature of justice, and the foundation of government, in 1740, a year after the publication of the work's initial two sections. After its release, the French journal *Bibliothèque raisonnée* ran a stinging review that claimed: "here, as you can see . . . is the system of Hobbes dressed up in a new taste" (Mossner 1982: 139). This is unfair. Like Frances Hutcheson, to whom he sent a copy of the Treatise, Hume rejects Hobbes's strictly egoistic account of human nature. He readily grants that we naturally possess benevolent sentiments and frequently act on them. However, as the French reviewer notices, Hume thinks that, for the purposes of law and politics, we must assume people will act selfishly, just as Hobbes tells us they will. Because property must be perfectly secure in order for society to thrive, the state and its laws must protect us from one another when we are at our worst, rather than depending on us to act our best. "A man's property," Hume says, "is supposed to be fenced against every mortal, in every possible case" (T 3.2.1.17/483).

Hume rejects another idea that is central to Hobbes's political theory: that of the social contract. He thinks Hobbes's basic premise, that society is founded by a deliberate act of contracting, runs contrary to the evident historical facts. As he points out, in most nations, we have no record of any such founding act of contract. And, even had such an event occurred, every nation's rulers have changed so often that we cannot possibly assert a continuous line of legitimacy between any existing regime and the one to which the people originally pledged their allegiance (ESY 471). Hume argues that government instead results from a process of gradual, unplanned evolution. As he puts it, the state "must be esteemed in a manner accidental, and the effect of many ages" (T 3.2.2.14/492).

Hume provides a brief (and admittedly speculative) overview of how this process takes place. He says that people in a "wild uncultivated state" acquire what he calls an "early education in society" by forming bonds of family, and these bonds have the effect of making them "sensible of the advantages which they may reap" from living together with their fellows—what Hume calls "the sweets of society and mutual assistance" (T 3.2.2.4/486; T 3.2.2.9/489; T 3.2.8.8/538). But before they can actually come together in large numbers, they need to determine "how to separate their possessions, and assign to each his particular portion"—or, in other words, how to govern "the stability of possession" and "the transference of property" (T 3.2.3.4/503; T 3.2.4.1/514). Although the rules to do so are easily arrived at—"the shortest experience of society discovers them to every mortal"—they are not as easily enforced (T 3.2.5.11/522). People may know the benefits that accrue to them when everyone follows the rules. However, we are impulsive creatures, and the temptations to free-ride are strong. "The consequences of every breach of equity seem to lie very remote," Hume says, "and are not able to counterbalance any immediate advantage that may be reaped from it" (T 3.2.7.3/535). He says that people therefore need to place restraints on themselves, and they require a neutral third party to enforce them. They do not, however, deliberately select magistrates with this end in mind. Instead, Hume says that the first rulers in societies tend to be chieftains who acquire authority as war leaders (T 3.2.8.2/540–1). Once such a chieftain is in power in a society, however, the people quickly see "the sensible utility" of having a single authority that can enforce the conventions governing property. And the utility of this early government produces, over time, "an habitual, and, if you please to call it so, a voluntary . . . acquiescence in the people" (ESY 468–9). Government serves the need we all have for security of property, and, once it has come about through historical accident, it earns our allegiance for this reason. But it is not the result of a deliberate choice or plan by any individuals.

In criticizing the social contract, Hume has in mind not only Hobbes, but also, perhaps primarily, Locke. Locke anticipated that his version of the contract might be challenged on grounds of historical accuracy. He called such a challenge a "mighty objection" to his theory (1994: 276; cf., 333–4). The concern is not simply academic. If we claim that governments are legitimate just because their people have consented to them, then, where the facts suggest that the people have *not* consented, it follows that such governments—nearly all existing ones, Hume says—are not legitimate. This means that no one need feel any obligation to obey them, a conclusion that threatens to create social chaos. Locke tries to answer the objection by claiming that the people of a commonwealth tacitly consent to its government by living in the society and benefitting from it and that this generates an obligation to obey. Hume rejects such "tacit consent," however, on the grounds that few citizens have the ability to quit their native country if they do not approve of its leaders (ESY 475).

Hume's criticisms of the social contract have been taken by many readers as decisive against it. However, there is a good reason why contract theories have remained an enduring feature of Western political thought. They provide us with a very effective technique for clarifying the conditions under which we should consider an existing regime to be legitimate. By imagining ourselves in a state of nature, we can see more clearly what we consider to be the true purpose of government by asking what sort of government we would acquiesce to if we lacked one altogether. The answer to this question then gives us a means of addressing what both Hobbes and Locke see as the central problem of political philosophy: when does an actual, existing regime deserve our allegiance, and when may the people consider themselves justified in resisting it? If we are to consider Hume not just as a gadfly critic finding flaws in the logic of his predecessors, but also as a political theorist in his own right, we should ask whether he can provide us with an answer to this question of allegiance to government. In fact, Hume considers himself to have done so, and his answer is original and important.

Although Hobbes and Locke both use the contract technique, they produce different answers to the question of allegiance. Hobbes's doctrine of obedience is very stringent. Because he believes that the essential purpose of government is to provide us with personal security, he thinks that we must recognize the legitimacy of any regime that can maintain a minimal level of public order and does not directly threaten our survival. He says that only a direct threat to our life, which we have a natural right to protect, justifies resistance. Locke wants to say that government exists to protect a more extensive set of natural rights: not only to life but also to liberty and property (or "estate"). Its duty to protect the latter implies, as the American colonists were later famously to insist, that it cannot even tax citizens without their consent (1994: 362). Locke thinks that if a particular regime ignores or invades any of these rights, resistance is legitimate. His theory is clearly more radical that that of Hobbes. Both men's accounts share one feature in common, however: they both appeal to a notion of natural rights to determine the limits of state power. They agree that the state is legitimate just to the extent that it respects our basic rights. Hobbes simply defines these rights more austerely than Locke does. In place of the natural rights of Hobbes and Locke, Hume offers something very different: the standard of utility. He says that "government binds us to obedience only on account of its tendency to public utility" (ESY 489). (Hume uses "utility" in its colloquial sense, meaning usefulness, rather than in the technical sense Bentham later gave it, of measurable units of pleasure.) Hume's purpose here is to change the terms of the debate entirely. Rather than asking the abstract question, when are we justified in overthrowing an existing government, he wants us to ask, more practically, when do we benefit from doing so? "We ought always," he says, "to weigh the advantages which we reap from authority, against the disadvantages" (T 3.2.10.1/554).

Once we make such calculations, we should see that we nearly always do better to keep with the government we have, assuming that it is well-established and is able to accomplish its basic purpose. "It is not with forms of government," Hume warns, "as with other artificial contrivances; where an old engine may be rejected, if we can discover another more accurate and commodious, or where trials may safely be made, even though the success be doubtful" (ESY 512). On the contrary, he says of "violent innovations" in politics: "more ill than good is ever to be expected from them" (ESY 477). He gives several arguments to support this cautious conclusion. First of all, he says that insurrection is "unavoidably attended with bloodshed and confusion," and very often ends in a state of complete anarchy—an outcome that is worse than life under even the most oppressive government (T 3.2.10.6/557). "There is not a more terrible event," he says, "than a total dissolution of government" (ESY 472). He also says that when rulers perceive "a disposition to rebellion" among their subjects, they will become more oppressive out of self-defense, applying "many violent measures which they never would have embraced, had every one been inclined to submission and obedience" (ESY 490). Finally, he says that a rebellion in one country undermines people's respect for authority in others and can thus lead to "the subversion of all government, and . . . an universal anarchy and confusion among mankind" (T 3.2.10.1/553).

Hume's caution in such matters entails a doctrine of allegiance that is markedly more strict than that of Locke. "The common rule requires submission," he says, "and 'tis only in cases of grievous tyranny and oppression, that the exception can take place" (T 3.2.10.1/553). However, he remains very far from Hobbes as well, and he rejects the Tory principle of passive obedience, which he calls "an absurdity" (T 3.2.9.4/552). Hume thinks that we can point to more than a few cases of "grievous tyranny and oppression" where rebellion is warranted, and he admits that "many constitutions, and none more than the British, have been improved even by violent innovations" (T 3.2.9.4/552).[1] Because obedience is always a matter of weighing costs and benefits in individual cases, Hume is unwilling to formulate a general criterion that could tell us definitively when insurrection is warranted. He says that "it is certainly impossible for the laws, or even for philosophy, to establish any particular rules by which we may know when resistance is lawful, and decide all controversies which may arise on that subject" (T 3.2.10.16.360).

Hume's rejection of the social contract is of a piece with his critiques of various metaphysical and theological views in the earlier sections of the *Treatise*. In all these cases, he wants us to be suspicious of abstract speculation when such speculation can only have negative consequences for our everyday lives. He thinks that the convictions of both Whigs, who appeal to the "original contract," and Tories, who urge passive obedience, may be summarized by the old Latin maxim, "*fiat Justitia et ruat Coelum*"—as he translates it, "let justice be performed, though the universe be destroyed." He insists that this maxim "is apparently [i.e. obviously] false, and by sacrificing the end to the means, shews a preposterous idea of the subordination of duties" (ESY 489). Hume thinks that there is no principle of right or justice that, viewed in the abstract, can justify us in undermining society's ultimate end, peace and stability. To put the matter in modern terms, he calls on us to abjure "rights talk" in favor of a cautious consequentialism that looks always to the impact of our actions on the overall public good.

II HISTORY AND THE SCIENCE OF POLITICS

Hume's attempt to carve a middle path on the question of allegiance between Whigs and Tories reflects his life-long project of seeking moderation in politics. "I have the impudence to pretend that I am of no party," he told a friend, "and have no bias" (LET 1.184). He was amused to see that some readers of his *History of England* accused him of obviously favoring the Whig, and others, the Tory point of view. We can also see his negative critiques as serving a larger, constructive purpose: to change the focus of political philosophy, turning philosophers away from the problem of allegiance and toward the more practical question of how society should be organized. If his discussion of the social contract and the question of obedience is one that we would now recognize as belonging to political philosophy proper, the bulk of Hume's writings on political themes are closer to what we would now call political science. Something like this distinction was recognized at the time. Locke says that there are two parts to political philosophy: "the one containing the original of societies and the rise and extent of political power, the other, the art of governing men in society" (Locke 1994: 400). Having offered his view on the first question in the *Treatise*, Hume spent a sizable portion of his working life trying to produce insights that would be of use to those concerned with the second.

One scholar has termed Hume's approach "scientific Whiggism" (Forbes 1985: 125–92). And, indeed, Hume devotes an entire essay to arguing that "Politics May Be Reduced to a Science" (ESY 14–31). With this end in mind, he gathers together data on different regimes throughout the world and throughout history and tries to infer general maxims based on this data. Although he was not the first person to apply such empirical methodology to political questions, he was certainly a pioneer in the practice, and this forms an important, if often neglected, aspect of his legacy. In developing his "science of politics," Hume was clearly influenced by Montesquieu. However, he rejects the Frenchman's conviction that the character of a people is determined by its environment. Hume sees a more complex dynamic at work, with the economy, law, government, technology, and the arts all mutually interacting to shape the culture and morality of a particular nation (see ESY 111–37). He does not adopt the "four-stage" view that was popular among other thinkers of the Scottish Enlightenment. Instead, he makes a somewhat rough division between those cultures he calls "barbarous" and those he calls "civilized." Although he thinks that the nations of Europe have generally progressed from one to the other, this progress has been neither steady nor linear. He suggests that the most civilized society in history was that of Augustan Rome, and he expresses sympathy with Machiavelli's pessimistic view that all societies rise and fall in cycles (HE 2.519, 508; cf. LET 1.273). And, like government itself, he sees social progress, when it happens, to be unplanned, the result of individuals responding to their immediate circumstances.

We can see Hume's method at work in the *History of England*. As he tells the story, after the end of Roman rule, Britain went through a long feudal period when the power of the crown depended on the energy and ability of the individual who wore it. A strong monarch could wield near absolute power, whereas a weak one could do nothing to restrain the great magnates. "Thus," he says, "all was confusion and disorder" (HE 1.361–2). Gradually, however, the nation was able to develop what Hume calls "a more regular plan of liberty" (HE 5.40). By this, he means, first of all, that the laws came to be enforced reliably and impartially and "were not supported singly by the authority of the sovereign" (HE 5.40). Second, the laws came to place restraints on the rulers themselves: the monarch, his ministers, and his "inferior magistrates" such as judges. However, this legal change happened only over many centuries and was the result of various causes. Enlightened monarchs, such as Edward I, played a role by making wise laws that, through their evident utility, endured through time (HE 2.141). The increasing sophistication of law and politics on the continent also contributed, by providing examples and principles (HE 2.521; HE 1.372). Economic development, especially as a result of the colonization of North America, created a prosperous "third estate" that demanded both liberty and stability (HE 2.108–9; HE 3.80). Religion also contributed, as people seeking religious liberty moved to demand broader freedoms. Hume says that the process culminated in the 1689 Revolution Settlement, when the monarchy's last prerogative powers were dispensed with, and the crown and people "were finally taught to know their proper boundaries": the former to make laws that were "inflexible either by spite or favour" and the second to maintain a "watchful jealousy" over the magistrates without undermining their authority (HE 4.476; T 3.2.3.3/502; ESY 12). Following the Revolution, Britain achieved a happy balance between central power and popular freedom, although only as the result of a series of perilous struggles and larger cultural shifts.

Hume decided not to continue his *History* past the final volumes, which culminated in the Glorious Revolution. (The volumes covering this later period were actually written and published first.) He feared that the rancor of contemporary debate would make it impossible for any work on more recent times to receive a fair hearing. However, in his political essays, he offers observations on the politics of his day, including reflections on the party system itself. I have already said that Hume boasted of being without partisan bias. This in itself was not original—it was, in fact, common for people to eschew partisan labels at the time. During this era, political parties were dismissed as "factions" that threatened the unity of the nation and thereby weakened it. According to conventional wisdom, what was supposedly needed instead was impartial "patriotism." Despite the pride he took in his own impartiality, however, Hume did not accept this conventional disdain for parties themselves. He was highly original in recognizing that Britain's two main parties each represented a principle that was important to the health of the British government and that the constant competition between them, so long as it could be kept within reasonable bounds, had genuine value. Hume says:

> in all governments, there is a perpetual intestine struggle, open or secret, between AUTHORITY and LIBERTY; and neither of them can ever absolutely prevail in the contest. A great sacrifice of liberty must necessarily be made in every government; yet even the authority, which confines liberty, can never, and perhaps ought never, in any constitution, to become quite entire and uncontroulable. (ESY 40)

It is the two parties in Great Britain that ensure the balance between liberty and authority that marks a stable, civilized government—the Tories by defending authority, the Whigs by defending liberty. Hume thinks that matters were confused somewhat in Britain by lingering divisions over the legitimacy of the House of Stuart, as well as by residual religious disputes. It was, above all, religious divisions, rather than the spirit of party itself, that had in the past allowed political disputes to become violent confrontations. He speculates that the two parties might be better replaced by Court and Country parties, which would more clearly represent the basic, and necessary, division in public life. And, with the growing acceptance of the 1689 settlement as the basis for the constitution, he saw evidence that this was happening. If he failed to predict the durability of the labels "Whig" and "Tory," he was certainly right to see that the party divisions in Britain were stabilizing around a core set of issues concerning the powers of the Crown and Parliament, with religion playing a minor and steadily decreasing role. And he was also correct, and highly original, in realizing that the party system had come to represent a force for stability in British politics rather than its opposite.

Hume says that only a few small changes would be necessary to make Britain "the most perfect model of limited monarchy." First of all, he says he would like to see the Commons reformed, according to "the plan of Cromwell's parliament," to give each constituency an equal number of voters (ESY 526). Second, he says he would like to do away with bishops and hereditary peers in the House of Lords, with new peers appointed by the existing body of life peers, so that the upper house could "consist entirely of the men of chief credit, abilities, and interest in the nation" (ESY 527). This would establish an aristocracy of talent. Such an aristocracy can give stability to the government by providing steady guidance that protects against the dangers of both tyranny and royal weakness.

As a speculative exercise, Hume offers a scheme for what he calls a "perfect commonwealth" (ESY 5612–29). Despite his admiration for Britain's mixed government, Hume in fact proposes a republic as his ideal state, with neither a monarch nor a hereditary aristocracy. He tries to design a republican government that could govern a large territory by means of a system of representative democracy that preserves strong elements of local autonomy. He gives a vote to adult male freeholders and householders—subject to a property qualification, modest for country landowners although high for urbanites. They elect county representatives, who then elect county magistrates and senators. Power is divided among these various officials, with county representatives meeting locally in groups of one hundred to propose legislation that is then debated in the national senate before being voted on at the county level (although subject to a senate veto). The scheme is intricate, and we can only suspect it would prove unworkable in practice. But its importance lies not in its details but in the conventional view that it challenged.

Hume believes that by giving so much power to the counties—he says that "every county is a kind of republic within itself"—he has solved the problem of how to achieve the republican scheme on a large scale (ESY 520). It had long been an axiom of political thought—one found in numerous ancient authors, as well as modern ones such as Machiavelli and Montesquieu—that (as Hume elsewhere puts it) republicanism "is only fitted for a small State" (LET 2.306). Hume was perhaps the first major thinker to challenge the conventional view that a large republic was unfeasible and to consider how one might be structured. Scholars have speculated that his plan for a large-state republic may have influenced James Madison, who in his tenth "Federalist" paper also outlines a plan to make republicanism workable on a large scale. There are significant differences between Madison's views and Hume's. However, Madison certainly read Hume's work, as did many in revolution-era America, and it is plausible to suggest that his essay helped convince at least some people in the Colonies that a new, representative federalism was a realistic form of political organization, one that could overcome the problems past republics had encountered in trying to rule over large, populous territories.

Although Hume devotes considerable attention to the merits and drawbacks of different forms of government, ultimately, he thinks a country's constitutional structure is less important than the sorts of laws it implements. With the right sort of laws, either a republic, a monarchy, or a mixture of the two may qualify as a civilized government. In a truly civilized state, the ruler (or rulers) establishes a system of "general laws" that treat similar cases consistently, treat all citizens the same, restrict the discretionary powers of the magistrates, and subject these magistrates themselves to the laws (ESY 125; ESY 12; EM App. 3.10/99). Such a system of laws allows commerce to thrive, and this in turn stimulates broader changes in technology and culture.

III Conservatism, Reform, and Revolution

I have already observed that Hume considered himself to be above the partisan divisions of his time. However, the terms of political debate changed dramatically in the decades after Hume's death. We can only speculate how he would have reacted to the "age of revolution" that began in the last years of his life. He did comment on the early stages of the colonial rebellion, surprising his friends by supporting the American rebels. However, his support was the exception that proves his general rule concerning revolution. As he saw it, the revolt had very quickly reached the point at which any attempts to suppress it would generate social chaos, and so the need for stability required the British government to seek an amicable solution. Had Hume lived long enough to witness the French Revolution, it is difficult to imagine him giving it any support, at least once it had moved beyond its early, peaceful stage, and its leaders had abandoned any pretense of following established constitutional processes.

If such speculation is inevitably a perilous business, it is obviously still more fanciful to imagine what Hume would have made of political disputes in our own era. However, it does not follow from this that we must see Hume as having nothing to contribute to these disputes. As I have said, he himself sought to reach generalizations that would, ideally, be valid at all times and in all places, and if we are to recognize him as an important political philosopher, it must be because we think that he has to some extent succeeded. Although scholars who work on Hume's political theory are generally agreed on this point—that his work can be mined for durable insights into political questions—there is no consensus about what specifically Hume has to offer to contemporary debates. Some interpreters have argued that the significance of his political theory lies in the fact that he offers no specifically normative claims at all. On this reading, Hume applies to politics a thorough-going naturalism consistent with his approach to metaphysics. We should see him (to use Hume's own analogy, justifying his approach to morality in the *Treatise*) as an "anatomist" rather than a "painter," which is to say as someone who lays out systematically the sorts of motivations people have and the sorts of emotions and thought patterns that determine their behavior, rather than as someone who attempts to dictate the sort of ends they should have or the sort of society they should want (T 3.3.6.6/621; LET 1.32).[2]

Many scholars have found this naturalist reading difficult to square with the many passages in which Hume explicitly offers opinions and recommendations with regards to politics and law. Some scholars have read him differently—as a conservative philosopher whose ideas anticipate, in important ways, those of modern conservatives. Some, indeed, consider Hume to be the first great conservative philosopher. Naturally, our opinion on this matter depends heavily on how we define the term "conservative." Hume is certainly conservative in one sense of this term. As we have seen, he prescribes extreme caution in attempting to change an established political system. He says: "in the general distribution of power among the several members of a constitution, there can seldom be admitted any other question, than What is established?" (HE 4.354). He thinks that even when reform is more limited, such that the basic constitutional structure of the nation is not threatened, we must proceed slowly and humbly (ESY 124). Describing Henry I's cautious approach to legal reform, he says: "All advances towards reason and good sense are slow and gradual" (HE 1.359; cf. ESY 116).

Hume's conservative interpreters want to attribute to him something stronger than a mere disposition toward caution, however. They argue that his epistemological skepticism provides the philosophical basis for rejecting certain basic principles of progressive thought. Specifically, it leads us to rule out all forms of political rationalism and foundationalism. Rationalists and foundationalists are distinguished by their willingness to transform society according to abstract ideals of perfection or according to the supposed truth about human nature or human history. But, on this reading, no such ideals or truths can survive Hume's skeptical critique of various forms of "false philosophy." A Humean must reject the possibility of formulating, through rational reflection, any conception of the good society that departs dramatically from the actual practice of existing ones (Livingston 1984: 306–42). Those who read Hume in this way find support in comments such as that the "wise magistrate" bears in mind that "habits more than reason" are "in everything . . . the governing principle of mankind" (HE 3.116).

Many eighteenth-century radicals are certainly guilty of the sort of abstract, utopian thinking that Hume's conservative readers deplore. Such writers as Condorcet and Godwin believed that society should drastically reform or even do away with such institutions as the state and the family in order to liberate our "true" human nature. If we accept Hume's central epistemological claim—that we are so constituted as to be denied any direct insight into ultimate reality, including the reality about ourselves—it becomes difficult to defend many of the proposals made by these radicals. We can take as an example Godwin's claim that marriage is an "evil" that goes against our natural inclinations (1793: 850–1). As we see from the "Dialogue" that concludes the *Enquiry Concerning the Principles of Morality*, Hume is alive to the great diversity of cultural practice, and so he would have little trouble accepting the idea that the institution of marriage, as practiced in Western European societies, is a cultural contrivance with no special basis in nature (EM 110–23/324–43). Nevertheless, a Humean could hardly accept the sudden abolition of this institution, which is rooted in the history and habits of the people, in the name of some more "pure" conception of human nature. If a practice is well-established and seems to serve a purpose, we cannot justify its sudden abolition, and we certainly cannot appeal, as Godwin does, to some special insight about what would constitute a more natural way of living.

Before we accept the label of "conservative" for Hume, however, we must consider two issues. First of all, we must ask whether contemporary progressives are guilty of the same sort of rationalism and utopianism that characterizes the thinking of eighteenth-century radicals such as Godwin. Donald Livingston (1994: 339), one of the scholars who sees Hume as anticipating modern conservatism, cites the philosophy of John Rawls as exemplifying the dependence of modern liberalism on radical foundationalist premises. Yet, at least in his later book *Political Liberalism*, Rawls (1996: 100) says that he considers his theory to depend only on "shared fundamental ideas implicit in the public political culture"—which is to say, conceptions of liberty and equality that most members of a democratic society already accept. It is based, in other words, on beliefs and habits that are well established among citizens. Many feminists and advocates for racial equality would equally claim that their demands do not spring from any utopian ideal or radically revisionist conception of human nature, insisting instead that they simply want to see realized the liberal ideal of equal rights long recognized as basic to Western democracy. They would argue that it is impossible to mount a specifically skeptical challenge to their program that does not also implicate this more basic ideal. And many liberals would argue that liberalism at its best entails, in fact, a kind of mitigated skepticism toward all forms of foundationalism because the project of a liberal society is precisely to establish a framework capable of accommodating a full diversity of views, foundational or otherwise. If we accept such a reading of modern liberalism, it begins to look very Humean.

Second, we must address Hume's own reformist program and, more specifically, his attitude toward what he called "superstition." If Hume's contemporaries were unsure how to classify him politically, in one respect they were agreed: he was a radical when it came to religion. Throughout his life, he bravely and tenaciously criticized what he termed the "prevailing systems of superstition," and, although he did not openly admit it, this clearly included nearly all accepted forms of Christianity (LET 2.451). This is despite the fact that the Christian faith was obviously deeply rooted in the habits of the people. Here, the contrast with Edmund Burke, perhaps the Enlightenment thinker most admired by modern conservatives, is revealing. Burke does not seem to have had passionate religious convictions of his own. Rather, he declared himself willing to accept whatever body of doctrine "seems to me to come best recommended by authority" (Burke 1889: 7.25). But he saw religion as a pillar supporting the authority of the state, and he saw a challenge to religious orthodoxy as tantamount to an attack on the established government. Given Hume's attacks on such orthodoxy, it is not surprising that Burke told James Boswell that "keeping company with David Hume, in a strict light is hardly defensible" (Boswell 1928–34: 6.268). If Hume really was a conservative of the sort scholars such as Livingston propose, we might expect him to take a line similar to Burke's on questions of religion. The views of the two men did share an important point in common. Hume thinks that, given the reality of people's faith in Christianity, a state church is the best way to channel this faith so as to prevent it becoming a threat to the social order. But he ultimately hopes people will abandon their religious beliefs more or less altogether. Hume's discussion of religious questions show that he is less concerned about deferring to established customs than he is about preserving social stability. The former often, but not always, serves as a means to the latter. When it comes to religion, the two can pull in opposite directions, and, in such cases, he feels no need to defer to even the most deeply rooted of social customs.[3]

The third main alternative reading has been to see Hume as a reformer, in tune with the overall progressive spirit of Enlightenment philosophy. His attacks on religion are read by (what we might call) his liberal interpreters as part of a broader assault on both popular prejudices and institutional structures that stand in the way of a better society: one that is marked by personal freedom, legal equality, limited state power, and open trade. These interpreters do not deny Hume's caution about reform. It is clear that he does not want to transform society precipitously, in such a way as might undermine its overall stability. However, they see him as ever watchful for opportunities to change it incrementally, according to his own normative ideal. The philosopher is well placed to bring about such incremental change, if not directly then by educating both the public and the legislators. He can show the iniquities that result from bad laws and bad government, as well as provide models for good ones, and he can argue for the principles on which a good society should be based. And, on this reading, this is precisely what we see Hume doing in his political essays and in the *History*.[4]

IV THE ROLE OF THE STATE

Hume is certainly a liberal in one sense of the term: he believes that government must allow people to form their own private conceptions of the good and give them the freedom to pursue these conceptions in the context of an open society and a free market. He is an early and important defender of this distinctively liberal vision of the state. Earlier in the century, Britain had witnessed a series of movements, endorsed by the monarchs William and Mary, to reform the manners of the people in the hopes of making them less materialistic and more public-spirited. Although these movements had little tangible success, both Christian moralist and civic republican authors continued during Hume's day to call on the state to promote virtue and discourage selfishness among citizens. Hume insists that all attempts by the state to reform the morals of the people are misguided. "All plans of government," he says, "which suppose great reformation in the manners of mankind, are plainly imaginary" (ESY 514). Such projects can only succeed by transforming our natural sentiments, which are simply too strong to be molded in this way. "Sovereigns must take mankind as they find them," he says, "and cannot pretend to introduce any violent change in their principles and ways of thinking" (ESY 260).

Hume here follows Bernard Mandeville who savagely mocks the movements for moral reform in his *Fable of the Bees*. Like Mandeville, Hume thinks that such "reformation" is not just hopeless; it is also unnecessary. He believes that society thrives through the selfish actions of its members. But Hume also breaks with Mandeville in an important way by arguing that a commercially thriving society will become, as a result of its economic development, not just a wealthier but also a more moral one. Comparing an inhabitant of feudal England to a modern resident of commercial society, Hume says that the latter is "a better man and a better citizen" than the former and that his life is a "more laudable" one (HE 3.76–7). This is because commerce, by fostering contacts between people, promotes sociability, and he thinks people become more benevolent and humanitarian as they broaden their range of social contacts beyond their immediate circle. The material rewards made available by commerce also act as an incentive to stimulate what Hume calls people's "industry" or, in other words, their desire to labor and improve their condition. This increase in industry in turn stimulates the sciences and the arts, which further heightens people's sense of "humanity" or general benevolence. By binding foreign nations together economically, more widespread commerce also makes for a more peaceful world.

Because commerce serves both the material and moral interests of the nation, Hume thinks the state should be prepared to do what it can to promote it. Its chief role lies in making laws to protect property. Without such laws, people will have no motive to work to improve their lot, since they cannot be certain they will be able to realize the gains from their labor. Beyond this, however, the state must exercise caution in interfering with the market. Hume bears a general presumption in favor of free and open trade with minimal government interference. He details numerous instances throughout history where the state has damaged commerce by trying to manage it (HE 3.77; HE 3.330).

Reading Hume's attacks on government intervention in the economy, we might ascribe to him a minimalist view of the state overall. And, indeed, he seems to confirm this when he says that "we are . . . to look upon all the vast apparatus of our government, as having ultimately no other object or purpose but the distribution of justice" (ESY 37). However, he makes it clear that he is not simply advocating laissez faire. He says elsewhere that the "execution of justice, though the principal, is *not* the only advantage of government" (T 3.2.7.7/537; emphasis added). Rather, he says that "government extends further its beneficial influence; and, not contented to protect men in those conventions they make for their mutual interest, it often obliges them to make such conventions, and forces them to seek their own advantage, by a concurrence in some common end or purpose" (T 3.2.7.8/538).

To defend this claim, Hume makes an argument familiar in modern public economics: that the state can play a role in addressing market failures, where a project would benefit everyone but is not pursued due to the difficulty of coordinating common action and the disincentive effects created by the fear of free-riding. Using the example of draining a common meadow, he says:

> 'Tis very difficult, and indeed impossible, that a thousand persons shou'd agree in any such action, it being difficult for them to concert so complicated a design, and still more difficult for them to execute it; while each seeks a pretext to free himself of the trouble and expence, and wou'd lay the whole burden on others.

To address such market failures and promote the greater good, Hume envisions public-spirited magistrates engaging in ambitious programs of public works. He says that through the intervention of such public officials:

> Bridges are built, harbors opened, ramparts raised, canals formed, fleets equipped, and armies disciplined, every where, by the care of government, which, though composed of men subject to all human infirmities, becomes, by one of the finest and most subtle inventions imaginable, a composition which is in some measure exempted from all these infirmities. (T 3.2.7.8/538–9)

Hume does not provide a detailed program for state action, although he does make a number of somewhat ad hoc proposals. He calls the aiding of "beggars and vagrants" "one of the circumstances in government, which humanity would most powerfully recommend to a benevolent legislator," and he gives the state a role in alleviating the condition of the poor in times of scarcity by addressing shortages in food distribution (HE 3.331). He says that when people are facing hunger, even when this does not reach the level of what he calls "urgent necessity," public officials may "[open] granaries, without consent of proprietors; as justly supposing that the authority of magistracy may, consistent with equity, extend so far" (EM 3.1.8/15). In discussing James's reign, Hume says that his general bias against monopoly allows for an "exception in favour of new inventions"—thus permitting, in modern terms, protection for infant industries (HE 5.231). And, notwithstanding his view that people should be free to choose their professions, Hume also thinks the state can take a role in guiding people into particular professions where these provide services in the national interest (HE 3.135).

In light of these various examples, we can see that Hume takes a pragmatic approach to the question of how the state should manage its relationship to the free market. It can normally promote commerce very successfully merely by establishing a system of equitable laws. However, governors must be willing to intervene more directly when they believe they can do so effectively, either to promote prosperity or for other reasons of clear public interest. But Hume does place a constraint on public action. He believes that the state should create incentives to encourage people to behave in the desired way, rather than coerce them into doing so or try to reshape their character to give them the right sorts of motives.

We can see evidence for Hume's aversion to coercive measures in his discussion of the state's role in religious matters. Despite his concerns about the often-pernicious effects of religious faith, he is nevertheless reluctant to prescribe outright persecution. He thinks such persecution is inherently "iniquitous"; it is also unlikely to be effective (HE 4.123; HE 6.324). He says that it "serves only to make men more obstinate in their persuasion, and to encrease the number of their proselytes" (HE 3.432–3). He argues that a wise magistrate will see fit to intervene in matters of faith only when religious leaders are preaching outright sedition and when that magistrate thinks that a campaign of suppression can succeed. Such a campaign must not risk causing greater disorder than is likely to result from simply tolerating the dissenting views (HE 3.356–7).[5]

In place of suppression and persecution, Hume offers what he thinks is a more lasting solution to the perpetual risk of disorder caused by religious faction: a "fixed establishment" that would place priests under some form of single ecclesiastical structure, with salaries paid from the public purse (HE 3.136). This solution earned him the consternation of Smith and other Whigs, who wanted to see a greater separation of church and state. Hume supports an ecclesiastical establishment for two chief reasons. First of all, it prevents the churches from existing as parallel authorities to the state, with the capacity to undermine its edicts (HE 1.311). Second, when the clergy draw a salary from the state, they are thus its dependents—and this dependency tends to cool their passions because they no longer need to compete for followers. This is not to say that Hume think the state should monopolize religious opinion or repress competing visions. As he puts it, it should not "settle an entire uniformity of opinion" on its subjects (HE 3.432). On the contrary, he says that once the state has ensured that none of the disputants' views overtly threaten the social order, it should quit the field of theology entirely, lest its attempts at imposing any particular set of views itself disrupt social peace.

Hume suggests in his "Perfect Commonwealth" that the Scottish national church provides a model for the ideal ecclesiastical establishment (ESY 520). Scholars have doubted Hume's seriousness here, and, in any case, he is willing to concede that the Church of England has much to recommend it. It possesses enough ceremony to "allure, and amuse, and engage the vulgar . . . without distracting men of more refined apprehensions" (HE 4.122–3). Also, it has normally taken a moderate, tolerant approach to dissenting views (HE 4.119).

V Conclusion

During the decades following his death, Hume's views on political questions were widely read and discussed. Perhaps the most eloquent testimony to his standing is the vehemence with which people such as Thomas Jefferson posthumously attacked him. Objecting to what he saw as Hume's assaults on the true principles of liberty, Jefferson called him "this degenerate son of science, this traitor to his fellow men" (1903–4: 16.44]). In our time, however, Hume's place in the canon of political philosophy is by no means secure. He has arguably fallen victim to the sheer diversity of his insights into political questions, as well as to his failure to bring these all together into a single systematic treatise. It is difficult to hold him up as a paradigmatic representative of any school of thought or to identify specific texts that concisely encapsulate the full range of his views. However, this chapter has attempted to show that many of his insights are original and important and that they should be of interest to readers today—even if their implications for contemporary problems must continue to be debated.

Abbreviations of Works Cited

EM   *Enquiry Concerning the Principles of Morals.* Edited by Tom L. Beauchamp. Oxford: Clarendon, 1998.

ESY   *Essays: Moral, Political, and Literary.* Revised edition by E. F. Miller. Indianapolis: Liberty Classics, 1985.

HE   *The History of England,* 6 Vols. Foreword by W. B. Todd. Indianapolis: Liberty Classics, 1983.

LET   *The Letters of David Hume,* 2 Vols. Edited by J. Y. T. Greig. Oxford: Clarendon Press, 1932.

T   *A Treatise of Human Nature.* Edited by D. F. Norton and M. J. Norton. Oxford: Clarendon, 2007.

NOTES

1. See also ESY 489, HE 4.355.
2. See Hardin (2007: 7–15).
3. See HE 5.526, and HE 5.121, for instance, on its effects during the civil war period.
4. See Stewart (1992), McArthur (2007).
5. See Sabl (2009).

BIBLIOGRAPHY

Berry, Christopher J. (2011). "Science and Superstition: Hume and Conservatism," *European Journal of Political Theory* 10, 141–155.

Boswell, James. (1928–34). *Private Papers of James Boswell from Malahide Castle.* Geoffrey Scott and Frederick A. Pottle, eds., 18 vols. Privately printed.

Burke, Edmund. (1889). *The Works of the Right Honorable Edmund Burke.* Boston: Little, Brown.

Forbes, Duncan. (1985). *Hume's Philosophical Politics.* Cambridge: Cambridge University Press.

Godwin, William. (1793). *An Enquiry Concerning Political Justice.* London: G. G. J. and J. Robertson.

Haakonssen, Knud. (1989). *The Science of a Legislator: The Natural Jurisprudence of David Hume and Adam Smith.* Cambridge: Cambridge University Press.

Hardin, Russell. (2007). *David Hume: Moral and Political Theorist.* Oxford: Oxford University Press.

Jefferson, Thomas. (1903–4). *Writings.* A. A. Lipscombe and A. E. Bergh, eds., 20 vols. Washington, DC: Thomas Jefferson Memorial Association of the United States.

Livingston, Donald W. (1984). *Hume's Philosophy of Common Life.* Chicago: University of Chicago Press.

Locke, John. (1994). *Two Treatises of Government.* Peter Laslett, ed. Cambridge: Cambridge University Press.

Locke, John. (1997). "Some Thoughts Concerning Reading and Study for a Gentleman," in M. Goldie, ed., *Political Essays.* Cambridge: Cambridge University Press, 348–355.

McArthur, Neil. (2007). *David Hume's Political Theory.* Toronto: University of Toronto Press.

Miller, David. (1981). *Philosophy and Ideology in Hume's Political Thought.* Oxford: Oxford University Press.

Mossner, E. C. (1982). *The Life of David Hume.* Oxford: Oxford University Press.

Rawls, John. (1996). *Political Liberalism.* New York: Columbia University Press.

Sabl, Andrew. (2009). "The Last Artificial Virtue: Hume on Toleration and its Lessons," *Political Theory* 37, 511–538.

Stewart, John B. (1992). *Opinion and Reform in Hume's Political Philosophy.* Princeton, NJ: Princeton University Press.

Whelan, Frederick G. (1985). *Order and Artifice in Hume's Political Philosophy.* Princeton, NJ: Princeton University Press.

PART IV

AESTHETICS, HISTORY, AND ECONOMICS

....

CHAPTER 25

HUME, KANT, AND THE STANDARD OF TASTE

....

PAUL GUYER

I DIFFERENCES AND SIMILARITIES

....

THERE seems to be a glaring difference between Hume's theory of taste and Kant's: for Hume, who originally intended to treat "Criticism" as part of a "science of MAN" grounded entirely on "experience and observation" (T Intro. 5, 4.7/xv–xvi), the premise of a sufficient degree of uniformity in human aesthetic response to make the works of art identified by qualified critics as collectively comprising the standard of taste canonical for others can only be empirically confirmed, whereas for Kant the possibility of judgments of taste that speak with a "universal voice" (1790, §8, 5:216)[1] is supposed to rest on "conditions of the power of judgment" that "must be able to be assumed to be valid for everyone a priori" "as requisite for possible cognitions in general" (1790, §38, 5:290), a premise that neither needs nor admits of empirical confirmation. If one is not convinced of one or both of the two assumptions that Kant is hereby making—namely, first, that the conditions for making judgments of taste are the same as those for knowledge in general and, second, that one knows a priori that other human beings are capable of acquiring knowledge in the same way as one does oneself and therefore must also make judgments of taste in the same way one does oneself—then this difference, although glaring, might not seem very important.[2] Instead, two other comparisons between Hume's and Kant's aesthetics could turn out to be more interesting.

First, it may seem to be a striking difference between the two authors that although Hume aims to provide psychological explanations of characteristic concepts and kinds of judgment elsewhere in his philosophy (e.g., his psychological explanations of the origin of our idea of "necessary connexion" and our proclivity to making causal inferences in spite of the absence of a strictly rational basis for them), he apparently tries to argue for the possibility of a standard of taste without ever offering a theory of aesthetic response itself, whereas Kant clearly grounds his argument for the "subjective universal validity" or "common validity" (1790, §8, 5: 214) of judgments of taste on such a theory: namely, his account of the "free play" of the "powers of cognition," imagination, and understanding, "that are set into play" by the representation of a beautiful work of nature or art (1790, §9, 5: 217). Second, although Hume and Kant, in spite of their difference over whether judgments of taste are founded on an a priori principle, nevertheless agree that a standard of taste can never take the form of a set of rules specifying predicates that are necessary and sufficient conditions for beautiful objects but only a canon of paradigmatically successful aesthetic *objects*, they differ on the function of such a canon. For Hume, the function of a standard of taste understood as a canon of tasteful objects is to guide *appreciation*: the canon identified over time by the best qualified critics directs the rest of the audience for art to works that they will enjoy even if they might not have been able to discover or appreciate them on their own because "Many men, [who] when left to themselves have but a faint and dubious perception of beauty, . . . yet are capable of relishing any fine stroke, which is pointed out to them" (ESY 243). For Kant, however, although Friedrich Nietzsche famously accused him of having "just considered art and beauty from the position of the 'spectator,' instead of viewing the aesthetic problem through the experiences of the artist (the creator)" (1887: 73–74),[3] the role of canonical objects of art or classics is primarily to serve as models for subsequent artists who should be stimulated by them, although stimulated not to copy them but rather, paradoxical as this may sound, to imitate the genius of their creators by discovering their own originality (Kant 1790, §47, 5: 309–310).

It is argued here that although Hume does not offer any general theory of aesthetic properties and our response to them in his 1757 essay "Of the Standard of Taste," he does offer elements of such a theory in other works, beginning with the *Treatise of Human Nature*, and that although he does not anticipate Kant's famous concept of free play (that honor being reserved for his compatriot Alexander Gerard), there are many other and important affinities between his general theory of beauty and Kant's. So, once again, the difference between Hume and Kant might not be as great as initially appears. On the question of the function of a standard or canon for taste, however, there is a real difference: although Nietzsche's charge that he offered an aesthetics of or for the spectator rather than the artist may have missed the mark when aimed at Kant, it would not have missed the mark had it been aimed at Hume. Hume, like many writers on taste and criticism in the eighteenth century,[4] was indeed primarily concerned with questions about aesthetic appreciation, whereas Kant's consideration of the role of a canon in artistic production may be considered to prepare the way for the greater emphasis on artistic production that is characteristic of idealistic and Romantic aesthetics in the nineteenth century. In the end, however, we shall see that because Kant's conception of artistic genius mirrors his conception of aesthetic response as free play, his conception of canonical works of art as models for the originality of artistic successors must be carried over to their role for audiences as well—so Hume's failure to include an explicit conception of free play in his account of aesthetic experience will constitute an important limitation on his conception of the standard of taste.

II Hume's Standard of Taste

In "Of the Standard of Taste," the essay hastily added to make *Four Dissertations* out of *Five* in 1757 when Hume's publisher backed away from publishing "Of Suicide" and "Of the Immortality of the Soul,"[5] Hume poses the problem of the possibility of such a standard by opposing a "species of philosophy" and a "species of common sense," the former according to which it is "fruitless to dispute concerning tastes" because "All sentiment is right," having "reference to nothing beyond itself" and the latter, "which opposes it, at least serves to modify and restrain it," by dismissing "without scruple the sentiment of [some] pretended critics as absurd and ridiculous" while accepting that of other critics who should be taken seriously. He then resolves the problem by arguing that although "It is evident that none of the rules of composition" (or other arts) "are fixed by reasonings a priori" (ESY 230–1), nevertheless there are facts that distinguish good critics from "pretended" ones and qualify their preferences as canonical for others. But, on the way from posing the paradox to resolving it, Hume pauses to say very little about any mechanism of aesthetic response that would underlie aesthetic preferences and any properties in objects that would induce such responses. All that Hume says is that "It appears then, that, amidst all the variety and caprice of taste, there are certain general principles of approbation or blame, whose influence a careful eye may trace in all operations of the mind" because "Some particular forms or qualities, from the original structure of the internal fabric, are calculated to please, and others to displease" (ESY 233). Apparently, there is nothing informative to be said about what good critics and the audiences that follow their suggestions find pleasing or why they find that pleasing, although there is much to be said about what makes a critic qualified rather than a pretender.

There is another passage in Hume that also suggests that there is little that can be informatively said about aesthetic properties and our response to them. In fact, Hume liked this passage so much that he used it twice, in the essay "The Sceptic" included in the second volume of the *Essays Moral, Political, and Literary* in 1742 and in the *Enquiry Concerning the Principles of Morals* published nine years later. In this passage, Hume says that

> A man may know exactly all the circles and ellipses of the COPERNICAN system, and all the irregular spirals of the PTOLOMAIC, without perceiving that the former is more beautiful than the latter. EUCLID has fully explained every quality of the circle, but has not, in any proposition, said a word of its beauty. The reason is evident. Beauty is not a quality of the circle. It lies not in any part of the line *whose* parts are all equally distant from a common center. It is only the effect, which that figure produces upon a mind, whose particular fabric or structure renders it susceptible of such sentiments. In vain would you look for it in the circle, or seek it, either by your senses, or by mathematical reasonings, in all the properties of that figure. (ESY 165)[6]

There can be no a priori principles of taste, it seems, because aesthetic preferences are just effects caused by certain properties of bodies, and there can be no rational or a priori explanation of such causal relations. All we can do is determine what conditions are optimal for their occurrence, determine which critics best satisfy those conditions, and then model our preferences on theirs because we will be sure to relish the fine strokes they point out to the rest of us.

However, Hume has more to say elsewhere about what produces aesthetic response and how it does so. Although he does not devote a book of the *Treatise of Human Nature* to "criticism," as the remark previously quoted from its Introduction might have suggested he would, Hume nevertheless discusses the topic of beauty at several points in the work.[7] He discusses it primarily to illustrate his conception of the all-important phenomenon of sympathy. Beauty can illustrate sympathy because sympathy is essential to many if not most of our experiences of beauty. This is because there are two types of beauty, beauty of "*species* and appearance" and beauty connected with an idea of the "utility" of objects, and the enjoyment of the latter in turn typically involves sympathy: "the beauty of all visible objects causes a pleasure pretty much the same, tho' it be sometimes deriv'd from the mere *species* and appearance of the objects, sometimes from sympathy, and an idea of their utility" (T 3.3.5.6/617). In fact, Hume supposes, the majority of our experience of beauty is experience of beauty connected with an idea of the utility of its object, and thus the majority of our experience of beauty involves sympathy. Hume makes this point in his initial exposition of the difference between "beauty and deformity":

> If we consider all the hypotheses, which have been form'd either by philosophy or common reason, to explain the difference betwixt beauty and deformity, we shall find that all of them resolve into this, that beauty is such an order and construction of parts, as either by the *primary constitution* of our nature, by *custom*, or by *caprice*, is fitted to give a pleasure and satisfaction to the soul. This is the distinguishing character of beauty, and forms all the difference betwixt it and deformity, whose natural tendency is to produce uneasiness. Pleasure and pain, therefore, are not only necessary attendants of beauty and deformity, but constitute their very essence. And indeed, if we consider, that a great part of the beauty, which we admire either in animals or in other objects, is deriv'd from the idea of convenience and utility, we shall make no scruple to assent to this opinion. That shape, which produces strength, is beautiful in one animal; and that which is a sign of agility in another. The order and convenience of a palace are no less essential to its beauty, than its mere figure and appearance. (T 2.1.8.2/299)

Once again, it seems that there is little that can be said about how figure and appearance produce pleasure through the primary constitution of our nature: it is just an observed fact that some figures do cause pleasure. However, pleasure in convenience and utility admit an elaborate explanation that involves sympathy and, more generally, imagination: objects that possess convenience and utility are immediately pleasing to someone (often a "rich man") (T 3.3.5.5/616) who can use them to fulfill some specific purpose, but they can indirectly please the rest of us because of our sympathetic enjoyment of the direct enjoyment of their actual users. In cases in which there is no direct enjoyment of utility at all, as with a mere painting of a "justly balanc'd" figure, we nevertheless imagine the well-being a person who really had such a figure would enjoy, and then ourselves enjoy the idea of the imagined person's pleasure "when by sympathy [it] acquire[s] any degree of force and vivacity." Actual "utility, and . . . fitness for that purpose" is an "advantage that concerns only the owner," but sympathy can nevertheless "interest the spectator" and transmit to him the owner's pleasure (T 2.2.51.19/364–5), to which "principle, therefore, is owing the beauty, which we find in everything that is useful," a "considerable" part of our experience in general (T 3.3.1.8/576), whereas merely apparent utility is enjoyed through the intervention of imagination as well as sympathy. Likewise, merely apparent disutility causes pain because of the inevitable operation of the imagination: "When a building seems clumsy and tottering to the eye, it is ugly and disagreeable; tho' we be fully assur'd of the solidity of the workmanship" (T 3.3.1.23/586).

Several points should be noted about Hume's bipartite account of beauty in the *Treatise*. First, although Hume always employs "*species* and appearance" or "figure and appearance" as a hendiadys, the latter concept could be broader than the former: whereas "*species*" or "figure" might be taken to refer solely to the spatial form of a visual object (or the temporal pattern of an auditory object), "appearance" could be supposed to include other properties of a visual object such as color and shine, other properties of something audible such as timbre, and so on. This is noteworthy because properties such as colors, although Hume does not explicitly mention them in the *Treatise*, seem well-suited for his explanation that certain properties of objects immediately trigger pleasure either through the "primary constitution" of our nature or through "custom" or "caprice"; that is to say, through the association of ideas, as when green makes us think of the pleasant ideas of springtime and youth.[8] Thus, when Alexander Gerard—whose *Essay on Taste* was presented to the Edinburgh Society for Encouraging Arts, Sciences, Manufactures, and Agriculture in 1757 and thus could not have been influenced by Hume's simultaneous "Of the Standard of Taste," but which clearly was influenced by Hume's earlier *Treatise*[9]—recognized not two but three species of beauty in visual objects, namely beauty of "figure," of "utility," and of "colours" (1759: 31, 38, 42), he may not have been departing from Hume's classification but only making explicit a possibility that was implicit in it. And in "Of the Standard of Taste," Hume himself notes that "The coarsest daubing contains a certain lustre of colours and exactness of imitation, which are so far beauties, and would affect the mind of a peasant or Indian with the highest admiration" (ESY 238). Here, Hume does acknowledge the possible beauty of colors, which we might consider material rather than formal features of appearance.

The second point to be made here is that although Hume says much about the beauty of *artifacts* in the *Treatise*, he has little to say about beauty in the *fine arts*. He frequently employs the example of architecture, in which the role of utility as well as mere appearance is obvious,[10] as well as decorative arts such as furniture, "tables, chairs, scritoires," and so on (T 2.2.5.17/364). But he mentions painting only in passing, to illustrate the role of imagination in response to well- or ill-balanced figures; fiction only in passing, in his discussion of the force and vivacity as the basis of belief (T 1.2.10 passim.); and music even more briefly, in arguing (in contemporary lingo) that his sentimentalist account of moral judgment does not reduce moral judgment to aesthetic judgment because our sentiments in response to a "good composition of music," a "bottle of good wine," and a good "character or sentiments" in an agent, although all forms of pleasure, "are very different from each other, and . . . have only such a distant resemblance, as is requisite to make them be express'd by the same abstract term" (T 3.1.2.4/472).[11] However, there are other places where Hume more explicitly considers the fine arts.

In one of these, namely the essay "Of Tragedy" that accompanied "Of the Standard of Taste" in the 1757 *Four Dissertations*, Hume resolves the "paradox of tragedy" that had been widely discussed since Jean-Baptiste Du Bos's (1719) *Critical Reflections on Poetry, Painting, and Music*[12]—the paradox, namely, of "our attachment to objects of distress"[13]—by arguing that the energy aroused by our "melancholy" response to the unpleasant events that constitute the content of tragedy is redirected to and amplifies our pleasure in what are essentially the formal features of such a work of art. Hume offers this theory first for the case of oratory, where the events reported are (supposedly) facts and then applies his explanation to the case of tragedy, which presents fictions. First, he argues that oratory "raises a pleasure from the bosom of uneasiness" because

> This extraordinary effect proceeds from the very eloquence, with which the melancholy scene is represented. The genius required to paint objects in a lively manner, the art employed in collecting all the pathetic circumstances, the judgment displayed in disposing them: the exercise, I say, of these noble talents, together with the force of expression, and beauty of oratorial numbers, diffuse the highest satisfaction on the audience, and excite the most delightful movements. By this means, the uneasiness of the melancholy passions is not only overpowered and effaced by something stronger of an opposite kind; but the whole impulse of these passions is converted into pleasure, and swells the delight which the eloquence raises in us.

Then Hume extends this theory to the case of tragedy:

> The same principle takes place in tragedy; with this addition, that tragedy is an imitation; and imitation is always of itself agreeable. This circumstance serves still farther to smooth the motions of passion, and convert the whole feeling into one uniform and strong enjoyment. Objects of the greatest terror and distress please in painting, and please more than the most beautiful objects, that appear calm and indifferent. The affection, rouzing the mind, excites a large stock of spirit and vehemence; which is all transformed into pleasure by the force of the prevailing movement. (ESY 219–21)

Following a suggestion from Alex Neill (1992: 151–154), we may call what Hume offers a "conversion" theory: the paradox of tragedy is resolved by the claim that feelings that would be unpleasant if experienced in response to real and present objects of distress are fully converted into pleasure by the formal features of a work of art, in which case the paradox disappears. Hume's suggestion is thus that the beauty of art, even tragic art, is essentially a beauty of "figure" or "*species*" rather than a beauty of sympathetically shared or imagined utility.

Perhaps that interpretation is too narrow, and what we should extrapolate from "Of Tragedy" is that Hume conceives of the beauty of fine art as beauty of "appearance" and not just "figure" or "*species*." After all, he speaks of "painting," both metaphorically as a feature of oratory and literally after his initial claim about tragedy; moreover, painting deals with color as well as figure or form. So, perhaps his idea is that we take pleasure in material features of works of art, such as color, as well as in formal features, such as selection and organization of actions and events, and that our pleasure in both of these kinds of features is invigorated by our emotional response to otherwise terrifying tragic events and converts that response into more pleasure. We should also note that, just as he had alluded to imitation in a passage earlier cited from "Of the Standard of Taste," here, too, Hume mentions imitation as a distinct source of pleasure in the case of tragedy as opposed to oratory, and he might mean to recognize this as a distinct source of pleasure in fine art—something that would hardly be surprising because a decade before "Of Tragedy" another widely read French author, Charles Batteux (1746), had gone so far as to have declared imitation to be the "single principle" of all the fine arts. But how our pleasure in imitation should be explained was an open question: whereas Gerard (1759: 48–58) would distinguish it from our pleasure in beauty, attributing it to our pleasure in successfully making comparisons rather than our pleasure in readily grasping the object before us,[14] Francis Hutcheson (1725: 42), the father of all the Scottish aestheticians, had previously considered imitation a special case of beauty, "Relative or Comparative Beauty" rather than "Original" or "absolute" beauty, and he explained our pleasure in imitation as a response to the "Unity between the Original and the Copy," a special case of the relation of "unity amidst variety" that he supposed to be the object of all our experiences of beauty and that we might interpret as a kind of form. That is to say, on Hutcheson's account, our response to imitation seems to be a pleasure in form because it is neither an affective response to the content of a work of art nor to material features of the work as such, such as its colors, timbres, and so on. If Hume understood imitation along Hutcheson's lines, he might still have understood the beauty of imitation as a kind of beauty of figure or *species*.

In any case, we can see from "Of Tragedy" that Hume recognizes in fine art beauty of form, beauty of imitation that may or may not be a special case of beauty of form, and perhaps beauty in other features of appearance as well; of course, examples of beauty in the appearance of utility can also be found in works of fine art, although that may not be one of their typical or central features. Does "Of the Standard of Taste" have anything to add to this conception of the beauty of fine art beyond the allusion to colors and imitation already noted? This essay will be more fully discussed in a moment, but here we may observe that in his discussion of the critical virtue of "good sense" Hume states that

> Every work of art has also a certain end or purpose, for which it is calculated; and is deemed to be more or less perfect, as it is more or less fitted to attain that end.

> The object of eloquence is to persuade, or history to instruct, or poetry to please by means of the passions and the imagination. These ends we must carry constantly in our view, when we peruse any performance; and we must be able to judge how far the means employed are adapted to their respective purposes. (ESY 240)

The first thing to note about this passage is that Hume's conception of "art" here is considerably broader than the standard modern conception of "fine art":[15] Kant, for example, will argue that whereas poetry (literature) is a fine art, rhetoric or oratory is a "business of the understanding" and not a fine art (1790: 321), whereas even in antiquity Aristotle had famously contrasted poetry and history, the latter being a mere report of particular facts (*Poetics* 1451b/234). But what is important for our purposes is Hume's recognition that each of the fine arts, whatever the actual extension of that concept might be, has a purpose of its own; for example, poetry has the purpose of pleasing "by means of the passions and the imagination," and so we may assume that pleasure in the successful accomplishment of that end is additional to the pleasure that we may take in figure, in other features of appearance, in the appearance of utility, and in imitation as such. Thus, Hume ultimately suggests that there are multiple sources of pleasure in any medium of art, some shared with all media and some media-specific, and that our experience of art and its pleasures is complex—even if some of that pleasure cannot be explained as more than the typical effect of certain irreducible causes.

That being said, let us now turn at last to Hume's argument about the standard of taste and his conception of the role of a critical canon. As previously mentioned, Hume begins the essay by opposing two positions, one summed up by the slogan *de gustibus non disputandum est* and the other by its rejection (ESY 229–31). As he has also made clear in "The Sceptic" and the second *Enquiry*, Hume accepts the premise on which the first thesis of this antinomy (to borrow the term Kant uses when he reproduces Hume's contrast)[16] is based, namely "Beauty is no quality in things themselves" but only "a certain conformity or relation between the object and the organs or faculties of the mind" (ESY 230), and he further accepts that there are no rules for composition or other arts "fixed by reasonings a priori" (ESY 231); but he also accepts the idea that there are intersubjective standards in taste, such that "Whoever would assert an equality of genius and elegance between OGILBY and MILTON, or BUNYAN and ADDISON, would be thought to defend no less an extravagance, than if he had maintained a mole-hill to be as high as TENERIFFE" (ESY 230–1), and that "The same HOMER, who pleased at ATHENS and ROME two thousand years ago, is still admired at PARIS and at LONDON" (ESY 233). His argument is that even though beauty is a matter of sentiment, not an objective property, there is nevertheless considerable uniformity among the sentiments of the best qualified critics throughout history, and the works that have withstood the test of critical time and come to constitute a canon will indeed be found enjoyable by the rest of us even though we do not have all of the attainments of those critics—once again, the many are "capable of relishing any fine stroke, which is pointed out to them" (ESY 243). The heart of the essay is then the enumeration of the qualifications of those qualified critics who are to identify the canon of artistic masterpieces for the rest of us who may not have the talent and certainly do not have the resources to develop our own critical faculties to the same degree as these critics have but who will appreciate the results of their labors—unlike many of his contemporaries, for example Alexander Gerard (1759: Part 2) and James Beattie (2004: 161–182), Hume does not suppose that anyone can become an ideal critic but does suppose that we can all enjoy the canon identified by those who can.[17]

Hume lists what seem to be five criteria for qualified critics, although the list might be reduced to four. The first qualification is "*delicacy*" of sensory perception and imagination, necessary because the pleasing effects of "particular forms or qualities" in objects may easily be disrupted by even small "defects in the internal organs" of perception and imagination through which those properties produce their effect (ESY 233-4). "Where the organs are so fine, as to allow nothing to escape them, and at the same time so exact as to perceive every ingredient in the composition: This we call delicacy of taste" (ESY 235). Hume illustrates this qualification with the well-known story from *Don Quixote* of the two kinsmen of Sancho Panza who are ridiculed when one detects a slight taste of iron in a sample of wine and the other a slight taste of leather but who are vindicated when the hogshead is emptied and "an old key with a leathern thong tied to it" found at the bottom (ESY 234-5). This example leaves it open whether delicacy of taste can or must be improved by experience, which in an example such as that of wine tasters one might think to be necessary, but Hume's primary point seems to be that delicacy of taste is a natural gift that is not bestowed on everyone. Of course, his thesis that the judgments of critics with delicacy of taste should be canonical for the rest of us assumes that, even with the cruder instruments of taste that most of us have, we will nevertheless enjoy what the more delicate critics pick out for us.

If Hume is conceiving of delicacy of taste as essentially a natural endowment, then when he identifies "*practice*" as the second qualification of a good critic, he means to be identifying a separate criterion. What he has in mind is twofold: first, "*practice* in a particular art, and the frequent survey of a particular species of beauty," or wide "experience" of objects in a particular art form, but, second, close study of any particular work to be judged so "that that very individual performance be more than once perused by us, and be surveyed in different lights with attention and deliberation" (ESY 237-8). Here, Hume's point is that the merits of an individual work may fully emerge only after repeated experience and careful study of that work. Hume then adds that, in order to assign a work "its proper rank among the productions of genius," qualified critics must also have formed "*comparisons* between the several species and degrees of excellence, . . . estimating their proportion to each other" (ESY 238). By this he means that, in addition to having sufficiently studied an individual work and others in its genre or medium to properly assess the degree of that work's realization of the potential for beauty in that genre or medium, thereby having made a sound judgment of the beauty of the work relative to that, good critics must also be experienced in multiple genres or media so that they can make more absolute judgments of quality, not mistaking the "highest excellence" of one kind for the highest excellence possible in any (ESY 238). The role of the good critics is thus not simply to rank works within particular classifications, but also to lead the rest of us to those objects that will afford the best aesthetic experiences overall—presumably taking into account the fact, which Hume is now about to mention, that different arts may also have different ends or purposes (ESY 240).

Finally, Hume adds that the good critic must also "preserve his mind free from all *prejudice*" (ESY 239), something which requires "*good sense* to check its influence" (ESY 240). By the requirement that the critic should free his mind of all prejudice Hume does not mean that the critic should approach the work with a blank mind, but rather he should have a regard to the "particular genius, interests, opinions, passions, and prejudice" of the originally intended audience of the work and "place himself in the same situation as" that audience; in other words, the critic should replace his own prejudices with those of the original audience, forgetting, "if possible," his own "individual being and . . . peculiar circumstances" in order to be able to appreciate the effect the work would originally have had (ESY 239). Hume does later add that neither good critics nor good audiences should replace their own prejudices with those of an originally intended audience at the cost of taking on board inappropriate "ideas of morality and decency" (ESY 246) as opposed to merely outmoded fashions or beliefs, a claim that has spawned a large debate about "moralism" and "immoralism" in aesthetics.[18] He does not discuss why critics or audience should care about works whose beauty can be appreciated only once they have exchanged their own prejudices for the (not morally unacceptable) prejudices of another place or time; presumably, his assumption is that there are beauties to be found in such works that can neither be enjoyed in any other way nor be replaced in an aesthetically full life by other beauties.

If good sense serves merely to check prejudice, then the requirement of good sense is not distinct from the requirement of freedom from prejudice but is the condition of its possibility, and Hume's list would consist of four criteria for qualified critics, not five. However, Hume does say that good sense "is requisite to the operations" of taste in "this respect, as well as in many others," and it is in this context that he observes that different arts have different purposes and that proper judgments can be made only if the purposes of each art are properly understood. Good sense seems to be a general qualification for good critics; in fact, something like the intellectual complement to the more purely sensory qualification of delicacy. Thus, "the same excellence of faculties which contributes to the improvement of reason, the same clearness of conception, the same exactness of distinction, the same vivacity of apprehension, are essential to the operations of true taste" (ESY 240-1); aesthetic response involves both our sensory and our intellectual faculties, so both of those must be strong in good critics. And, like delicacy of taste, good sense would also seem to be something that can be cultivated by practice to a degree but is also a natural endowment that some people simply have to a greater degree than others, although the latter are capable of benefiting from the good sense of the former, in the aesthetic domain as well as elsewhere.

Hume famously concludes his enumeration of the qualifications of good critics with the claim that even though beauty itself is a matter of sentiment and thus there would seem to be no prospect for resolution in disputes about judgments of taste, whether critics have these qualifications is a question "of fact, not of sentiment" (ESY 242); thus, debates about who the qualified critics are can be resolved, and their judgments can be recognized as canonical. Hume's claim might seem to be open to a charge of circularity: how can we judge that a good critic has delicacy of taste and all the rest unless we already accept his judgments of taste, in which case we are right back where we started? Hume is not worried by such a charge and asserts that "Though men of delicate taste be rare, they are easily to be distinguished in society, by the soundness of their understanding and the superiority of their faculties above the rest of mankind" (ESY 243). He must be assuming that good critics demonstrate the superiority of their faculties in other ways than by their particular judgments about contestable cases, perhaps in areas of activity other than the aesthetic altogether, so that there is no danger that we must already accept their judgments of taste in order to declare them qualified. This does not seem an implausible assumption. There might also seem to be a danger of circularity in the specific criteria of practice and comparison: would we not have to know that the critics have practiced with and made comparisons among the right objects, the most beautiful ones, in order to know that their taste has not in fact been warped by excessive exposure to poor work rather than refined by adequate exposure to good ones? Hume does not address this worry, but presumably he simply assumes that the more one studies a particular work and the more works one studies, the more apparent the real merits of the work become—practice will not distort the critic's judgment but will allow it to perform its natural function more fully. This, too, seems a plausible assumption.

It thus looks as if Hume's criteria for qualified critics may be defended.[19] The larger issue seems to be the intended role of Hume's qualifications for critics. As earlier noted, the issue is whether they are supposed to be goals that anyone could aim to realize in order to improve her own taste, or whether they are supposed to be criteria for identifying those actual critics whose preferences should be canonical for the rest of us as the audience for art, as well as for their criticism. Now that we have examined Hume's actual list of criteria, reasons for taking the latter position should be clear. For one, even if the complementary qualifications of sensory delicacy and intellectual good sense can to some extent be improved by practice, they are at bottom natural endowments that not everyone enjoys to the same degree. Nothing I can do will ever give me the same eye for painting that (we suppose) Bernard Berenson enjoyed. Second, achieving sufficient practice and comparison will clearly be time-consuming and expensive, requiring much time and money for travel, training, and so on. Indeed, it may take either an independent income or a professional position as a critic, for even someone in another profession who has enough leisure time and money to go to museums or concerts or movies with some frequency will not be able to devote the same time and money to such pursuits as the rich or professional critic. For both of these sorts of reasons, only a small number of people in any society will be able to become qualified critics. Finally, Hume clearly supposes that the standard of taste is not a set of rules nor even the set of qualifications for ideal critics but the actual body of works that has withstood the test of time—the works of the same Homer who once pleased in Athens and Rome and now pleases in Paris and London and the other works that fall into this category (although there is nothing in Hume's argument to preclude that this category also grows over time, even if, presumably, slowly). Such a body of actual works must be preserved and transmitted over time.

This requires a body of editors, translators, interpreters, curators, critics, and other specialists who make these works accessible to the rest of us, who are clearly actual persons and not idealized roles to which we can all aspire.

The role of Hume's critics is thus the historical function of identifying canonical works of taste and identifying the fine strokes in them so that the rest of us can enjoy them. Let us now see how Kant understands the function of a standard of taste.

III Kant's Models for Posterity

In the introduction to his "Deduction of Judgments of Taste" (1790, §38, 5:289–290), in a section entitled "No Objective Principle of Taste Is Possible," Kant endorses what appears to be an assertion of the limited value of criticism in aesthetic disputes by Hume:

> By a principle of taste would be understood a fundamental proposition under the condition of which one could subsume the concept of an object and then by means of an inference conclude that it is beautiful. But that is absolutely impossible. For I must be sensitive of the pleasure immediately in the representation of it, and I cannot be talked into it by means of any proofs. Thus although critics, as Hume says, can reason more plausibly than cooks, they still suffer the same fate as them. They cannot expect a determining ground for their judgment, but only from the reflection of the subject on his own state (of pleasure or displeasure), rejecting all precepts and rules. (1790, §34, 5: 285–286)

Kant assumes that critics attempt to enunciate general principles and derive their particular judgments from them but that this enterprise is doomed to failure because aesthetic response itself—our pleasure or displeasure in particular objects—is not founded on rules in the first place.

Kant is referring to a passage in Hume's essay "The Sceptic" but may be condemning critics more than Hume intended. Here is what Hume had said:

> even when the mind operates alone, and feeling the sentiment of blame or approbation, pronounces one object deformed and odious, another beautiful and amiable; I say, that, even in this case, those qualities are not really in the object, but belong entirely to the sentiment of that mind which blames or praises. I grant, that it will more difficult to make this proposition evident, and as it were, palpable, to negligent thinkers; because nature is more uniform in the sentiments of the mind than in most feelings of the body. . . . There is something approaching to principles in mental taste; and critics can reason and dispute more plausibly than cooks or perfumers. We may observe, however, that this uniformity among human kind, hinders not, but there is considerable diversity in the sentiments of beauty and worth, and that education, custom, prejudice, caprice, and humour, frequently vary our taste of this kind. You will never convince a man, who is not accustomed to ITALIAN music, and has not

an ear to follow its intricacies, that a SCOTCH tune is not preferable. You have not even any single argument, beyond your own taste, which you can employ in your behalf: And to your antagonist, his particular taste will always appear a more convincing argument to the contrary. (ESY 163)

Hume starts off by asserting that there is considerable uniformity in the operations of the human mind, which Kant is about to attempt to establish on a priori grounds, but then suggests that this is sufficient to establish "something approaching to principles in mental taste," which the title of Kant's section quoting Hume denies. Yet, although Hume allows that critics can reason more plausibly than cooks, he denies that their arguments are ever persuasive against the likes of those with the presumably poor taste to prefer Scottish ditties to the glories of Italian music (which sounds like preferring Ogilby to Milton). This conclusion must be what Kant has in mind in saying that even though critics might appear to reason more plausibly than cooks, ultimately, they must share the same fate, that their reasonings are unpersuasive to those who have a different taste. However, Kant may be attributing to Hume a more negative attitude toward critics than is warranted, for not only, of course, has the (later) "Of the Standard of Taste" defended the authority of qualified critics, although to be sure without discussing their actual methods of communication, but even in "The Sceptic" Hume ultimately defends the real methods of criticism, although not the pretense of inferring particular judgments from general rules. In a passage to which Kant does not allude, Hume writes:

> But though the value of every object can be determined only by the sentiment or passion of every individual, we may observe, that the passion, in pronouncing its verdict, considers not the object simply, as it is in itself, but surveys it with all the circumstances, which attend it. A man transported with joy, on account of his possessing a diamond, confines not his view to the glittering stone before him: He also considers its rarity, and thence chiefly arises his pleasure and exultation. Here therefore a philosopher may step in, and suggest particular views, and considerations, and circumstances, which otherwise would have escaped us; and by that means, he may either moderate or excite any particular passion. (ESY 172)

Here, Hume is explicitly talking about "philosophers" intervening in disputes about practical or moral value, not about critics intervening in disputes about taste, but the point is the same: critics can communicate their judgments persuasively, not by pronouncing general rules and deducing particular judgments from them, but by contextualizing the objects under discussion, drawing attention to particular features of them that might otherwise be underappreciated (which will be facilitated by their extensive "practice" with those objects), making comparisons with other objects in similar or different genres or media (which will be facilitated by their extensive "comparison"), and so on—all of which will allow their audience to more fully appreciate the merits or demerits of the objects concerned and will presumably increase the likelihood of agreement in taste even if not ending disputes by deductive arguments.[20]

None of this does Kant mention. On the contrary, he seems to reject any role for critics in the formation of individual taste. Thus, in the section preceding the one we have just been discussing, he says that "If someone does not find a building, a view, or a poem beautiful, then, first, he does not *allow approval to* be internally imposed upon himself by a hundred voices who all praise it highly," and

> Second, an a priori proof in accordance with determinate rules can determine the judgment on beauty even less. If someone reads me his poem or takes me to a play that in the end fails to please my taste, then he can adduce Batteux or Lessing, or even older and more famous critics of taste, and adduce all the rules they established ... I will stop my ears, listen to no reasons and arguments, and would rather believe that those rules of the critics are false or at least that this is not a case for their application than allow that my judgment should be determined by means of a priori grounds of proof, since it is supposed to be a judgment of taste and not of the understanding or of reason. (Kant 1790, §33, 5:284–285)

Kant does not deny that individuals may come to revise their judgments of taste, but suggests that they must come to do this only by the improvement of their own taste, without any assistance from critics: "Hence a young poet does not let himself be dissuaded from his conviction that his poem is beautiful by the judgment of the public nor that of his friends.... Only later, when his power of judgment has been made more acute by practice, does he depart from his previous judgment by his own free will" (Kant 1790, §33, 5: 282). For Hume, practice is one of the qualifications of good critics, but for Kant it is not something that lends authority to the judgments of critics but something that individuals can and must undertake to improve their own taste. Kant seems to fall into the camp of those who hold that the qualifications for good taste are ideals to which all individuals can aspire, not the qualifications of actual critics whose judgments should be canonical for the rest of us because they will lead us to "strokes" we can all appreciate.

Kant thus seems to reject any role in the formation of good taste for the kind of general rules supposedly offered by critics. Does that mean that he rejects any role whatever for what Hume had actually identified as the product of qualified criticism in "Of the Standard of Taste," namely, not a body of rules at all, but a canon of exemplary *objects* of taste that have withstood the test of time and found to please from Athens to London? In fact, he does not, but emphasizes the role of such a canon in artistic *production* rather than *appreciation*—indeed, Kant's concern with production rather than appreciation is already evident in the passage we have just been discussing, where he has actually been considering the role of criticism on the young *poet* rather than on young *readers* of poetry.

Before we reach this conclusion, however, let us briefly compare Kant's underlying account of beauty to Hume's—for, to make the comparison of their theories of the role of critical canons relevant, we ought to see that their theories of beauty are not entirely incommensurable. The heart of Kant's account of judgments of taste is that our pleasure in beauty is the result of a harmonious "free play" between our cognitive powers of imagination and understanding induced by our representation of the beautiful object and that because we can deduce an a priori assurance that our cognitive powers all function in the same way, as the condition of possibility of shared human cognition in general, we are justified in speaking with a universal voice or judging that any object that has really triggered this state in one person can reasonably be expected to do so in all. The outline of Kant's theory is stated in the Introduction to the *Critique of the Power of Judgment*, where he writes that one's pleasure in a beautiful object

> can express nothing but its suitability to the cognitive faculties that are in play in the reflecting power of judgment, insofar as they are in play, and thus merely a subjective formal purposiveness of the object. For that apprehension of forms in the imagination can never take place without the reflecting power of judgment, even if unintentionally, at least comparing them to its faculty for relating intuitions to concepts. Now if in this comparison the imagination (as the faculty of a priori intuitions) is unintentionally brought into accord with the understanding, as the faculty of concepts, through a given representation . . . a feeling of pleasure is thereby aroused. . . . That object the form of which (not the material aspect of its representation, as sensation) in mere reflection on it (without any intention of acquiring a concept from it) is judged as the ground of a pleasure in the representation of such an object—with its representation this pleasure is also judged to be necessarily combined, consequently not merely for the subject who apprehends this form but for everyone who judges at all . . . whose a priori conditions are universally valid. (1790, Intro., section VII, 5: 189–190)

Now, of course, there are glaring differences between this account of beauty and Hume's: Hume never mentions the idea of a "play" among our cognitive powers, instead leaving unexplained why certain qualities of objects produce pleasure in us; Hume does not explicitly exclude either sensations or concepts from the sources of our pleasure in beautiful objects, thus restricting the source of beauty solely to form; and, of course, Hume trusts to experience and observation for his conviction of the similarity of human responses to beauty, never countenancing any idea of an a priori principle that all human minds work alike.

The last difference between the two accounts is undeniable, although it may be less important than it seems—after all, Hume is more confident than Kant of the paradigmatic power of a well-established critical canon for all of us, even if he assumes no a priori guarantee that our minds all work alike. On the first two points, I would suggest that there are important similarities as well as the obvious differences between the two theories. To be sure, Hume does not use the term "play," and we will see at the end of this chapter that this fact has an important consequence. Nevertheless, as we have seen, in the course of his account of the qualifications of the critic, Hume does assume that aesthetic response involves perception, imagination, and conceptions of the contents, presuppositions, and purposes of particular works of art—in other words, both imagination and understanding—but all functioning without any rules. Because Kant himself says little about what free play really is beyond suggesting that in this state the underlying goal of cognition—the unification of our manifolds of representation—is achieved without the application of any rule derived from a concept,[21] it is not clear that their conceptions of the mental response leading to the sentiment of pleasure in beauty are completely unrelated.

Second, over the course of the *Critique of the Power of Judgment* Kant expands the restrictive conception of beauty as the pure form of a priori intuitions that he initially states and ends up with a catalogue of types of beauty that is in many if not all ways similar to Hume's. As we have seen, Hume ended up with a tripartite or even quadripartite taxonomy of beauty: first, beauty of "*species* or appearance," which might be counted as one type of beauty if equated with beauty of form but as two types if there is a contrast between beauty of form and beauty in other aspects of appearance, such as color; second, the beauty of utility, whether actual and sympathetically shared or merely apparent and imagined; and third, the several beauties of art, connected with the various ends of art, although also including one or more of the previous kinds of beauty. Kant ultimately offers a similar list of types of beauty. He begins his "Analytic of the Beautiful" with cases of "pure" or "free" beauty, which are supposed to involve pleasure in mere form, excluding all pleasure in the matter of objects, in their purposes, or in emotions associated with them, thus for example pleasure in "drawing" rather than color in the visual arts and "composition" rather than instrumentation and coloration in music (1790, §14, 5: 225) or "designs *à la grecque*, foliage for borders or on wallpaper, etc.," all of which "signify nothing but themselves" (1790, §16, 5: 229). Colors in particular are excluded from the proper objects of pure judgments of taste because human affective response to them seems, at least to Kant, to be too variable—"For one person, the color violet is gentle and lovely, for another dead and lifeless" (Kant 1790, §7, 5: 212). On this point, Kant never relents, although as we have seen Hume does allow color to count as one of the beauties of painting (and as we also saw, Alexander Gerard, Kant's probable target on this point, explicitly elevated beauty of color to one of the three main species of beauty.) But no sooner has Kant completed his restrictive account of pure beauty than he recognizes a second kind of beauty, "adherent" beauty, which does presuppose a "concept of what the object ought to be" and "the perfection of the object in accordance with it," for example "the beauty of a horse, of a building (such as a church, a palace, an arsenal, or a garden-house)," each of which presupposes "a concept of the end that determines what the thing should be" (1790, §16, 5: 229–230). These are the same kinds of examples Hume offered of the beauty of utility—animals and houses. And, perhaps contrary to what Kant's argument to this point might have led the reader to expect, Kant does not mention adherent beauty only to deny that it is a proper form of beauty at all; on the contrary, perhaps merely having started with the simple case of pure beauty in order to isolate the free play of imagination and understanding as essential to all beauty, Kant now means to allow more complex cases by suggesting that in the case of adherent beauty we can become pleasurably aware of a free play within the constraints imposed by a purpose or even between the form of objects and their purposes, where the form is not determined by the concept of the purpose of the object but nevertheless seems harmonious with it.[22] Kant does not actually offer as much of an explanation of what is clearly his version of the beauty of utility as Hume had with his explanation of our vicarious enjoyment of utility directly enjoyed by others or our imaginative enjoyment of the mere appearance of utility, but he nevertheless clearly recognizes it as a genuine category of beauty.

Finally, Kant recognizes the distinctive character of the beauty of fine art, different from the adherent beauty of useful artifacts (perhaps even highly bred animals such as racehorses can be considered a kind of artifact). Kant turns to the beauty of fine art only after the "Analytic of the Beautiful," but when he does, in his account of genius, he locates the beauty of works of fine art in the free play of the mind between the more formal features of works of art and their contents, which combination of form and content he calls "aesthetic ideas." Kant writes that the poet, for example, "ventures to make sensible rational ideas of invisible beings, the kingdom of the blessed, the kingdom of hell, eternity, creations, etc., as well as to make that of which there are examples in experience, e.g., death, envy, and all sorts of vices, as well as love, fame, etc., sensible beyond the limits of experience" (1790, §49, 5: 314). He then describes the kind of free play that in his original discussion of the pure beauty of nature or merely decorative art he had restricted to form alone as involving in the case of fine art such contents as well as form:

> Now if we add to a concept a representation of the imagination that belongs to its presentation, but which by itself stimulates so much thinking that it can never be grasped by a determinate concept, hence which aesthetically enlarges the concept itself in an unbounded way, then in this case the imagination is creative, and sets the faculty of intellectual ideas (reason) into motion . . . (1790, §49, 5: 315)

The key to Kant's account of the experience of fine art as genuinely aesthetic experience is that the kind of ideas that furnish the typical contents of art do not function as concepts that determine all the other aspects of the works of art—in other words, as rules—but rather enter into a free play with the forms and other aspects of the works—for example, the symbols that Kant calls "attributes"—that we clearly enjoy in the same way that we can enjoy a play with form alone. Now clearly Kant has representational art in mind here, and he seems to be over-generalizing when he asserts that all beauty, indeed not only all beauty in art but even all beauty in nature, involves the "expression of aesthetic ideas" (1790, §51, 5: 320); his subsequent ranking of "the arts of **speech, pictorial** art, and the art **of the play of sensations**" (music and dance) by the sole criterion of their potential for expressing aesthetic ideas may likewise seem too narrow. But for our purposes the point is just that in recognizing that in much art beauty may lay in our experience of the interplay between form and content Kant is taking an approach to fine art that is not dissimilar to Hume's. Recall how Hume explained our response to tragedy as an invigoration of our pleasure in the form of the work of art by the intensity of our emotional response to its content; in line with his general exclusion of emotion from his account of aesthetic experience, Kant does not mention the emotional response we might have to the kind of ideas that he has identified as the typical content of art, but he has nevertheless also explained our response to art as an interplay between form and content as Hume had done.

So in spite of their differences, there are also deep similarities between Kant's and Hume's catalogues of types of beauty. But now let us return to their differences on the role of a canon for good taste. We can smoothly return to this question from our discussion of Kant's account of fine art, because he discusses the role of canonical works in his account of artistic production rather than aesthetic appreciation, that is, in his account of genius. And although, as we have seen, Kant dismisses the function of criticism in the formation of taste as aesthetic appreciation, he emphasizes the importance of exemplars, thus of a critical canon, in the production of fine art.

This approach is already evident in the discussion of criticism preceding the "Deduction of judgments of taste" on which we have already touched. There Kant had quickly slid from discussing the role of "the works of the ancients . . . rightly praised as models, and . . . called classical" in the formation of taste in general, or in audiences, to the role of such models in artistic production, writing that

> Succession, related to a precedent, not imitation, is the correct expression for any influence that the products of an exemplary author can have on others, which means no more than to create from the same sources from which the latter created, and to learn from one's predecessor only the manner of conducting oneself in so doing. But among all the faculties and talents, taste is precisely the one which, because its judgment is not determinable by means of concepts and precepts, is most in need of what in the progress of culture has longest enjoyed approval if it is not quickly to fall back into barbarism and sink back into the crudity of its first attempts. (1790, §32, 5: 283)

Precisely because taste does not have precepts it needs precedents, a body of exemplary works, no doubt identified and passed on with the assistance of critics functioning as both judges and curators.

That would seem to be a general point, applicable to audiences as well as to artists, but at both the beginning and the end of this passage Kant seems to have his eye primarily on artists, and to be endorsing the importance of a canon of exemplary works for the stimulation of the originality of artists. He continues this theme in the subsequent discussion of genius, although he adds two points there: one, that artists have to learn from precedents the techniques of their media as well as the possibility of their originality, and two, that artists have to learn from precedents the need for taste as well as originality to create works that can appeal to an audience. But even in making the latter point, it is on the taste of artists rather than audiences that Kant focuses. Kant's conception of genius follows straightforwardly from his conceptions of aesthetic response and aesthetic judgment: if the experience of beauty is a pleasure due to the free play of our cognitive powers that can nevertheless be expected to occur in all others who experience the object under optimal circumstances, then, insofar as the experience of beauty can be occasioned by fine art, that art must also be the product of a free play that cannot be fully determined by rules yet is valid for others, indeed communicated to them by the work of art. Thus for Kant genius "(1) is a **talent** for producing that for which no determinate rule can be given, not a predisposition of skill for that which can be learned in accordance with some rule, consequently . . . **originality** must be its primary characteristic," but at the same time, "since there can also be original nonsense, its products must at the same time be models, i.e., **exemplary**, hence, while not themselves the result of originality, they must yet serve others in that way" (1790, §46, 5: 307–308). It is in the course of his discussion of genius that Kant introduces his account of aesthetic ideas, and then he clarifies the theory of genius by explaining that it must be considered a talent both for the invention of aesthetic ideas, which contain "rich material" for the work of art, but also for the "presentation" (*Darstellung*) of such ideas (1790, §49, 5: 317), or the invention of means to communicate them to others. In the case of presentation there is room for "something mechanical, which can be grasped and formed according to rules, and thus something **academically correct**"; thus with regard to "**form**" genius requires "a talent that has been academically trained, in order to make a use of it that can stand up to the power of judgment" (1790, §47, 5: 310). Many techniques for the effective communication of artistic ideas can be reduced to rules and taught by their means, although there is also room for invention of new means to present ideas. But it is particularly the invention of powerful ideas for the content and overall conception of beautiful works of art that cannot be reduced to rules, thus taught by rules, and that can instead be taught only by example, examples that, at least when successful, stimulate the originality of students rather than presenting them with a model they can mechanically follow. Thus,

> Since the gift of nature must give the rule to art (as beautiful art), what sort of rule is this? It cannot be couched in a formula to serve as a precept, for then the judgment about the beautiful would be determinable in accordance with concepts; rather, the rule must be abstracted from the deed, i.e., from the product, against which others may test their own talent, letting it serve them as a model not for copying [*Nachmachung*], but for imitation [*Nachahmung*]. (1790, §47, 5: 309)

We might even say that the function of a canonical work of artistic genius is to serve as a provocation for future artists: it shows them what can be achieved and challenges them to find their own way—for there must be a free play of their own cognitive powers—to accomplish something equally great. Of course, even the greatest works of genius cannot have this effect on every subsequent artist, for not everyone has received the gift of genius from nature: thus "The ideas of the artist arouse similar ideas in his apprentice [only] if nature has equipped him with a similar proportion of mental powers." And works of genius can have their challenging or provocational power on more than the original creator's immediate followers, but on subsequent generations of creators as well, because as models of originality that can seed further originality if they fall on fertile ground, their power is never exhausted. As models, though never through "mere descriptions," they "transmit" their stimulus to "posterity" (1790, §47, 5: 310).

Kant returns to the theme that works of artistic genius must manifest "exemplary originality" rather than being "original nonsense" in a further section that asks whether "imagination or the power of judgment counts for more" in matters of beautiful art, and answers that "since it is in regard to the first of these that an art deserves to be called **inspired**, but only in regard to the second that it deserves to be called a **beautiful** art," judgment "is thus the primary thing to which one must look in the judging of art as beautiful art." He dramatizes this point by saying that "Taste . . . is the discipline (or corrective) of genius, clipping its wings and making it well behaved," giving genius "guidance as to where and how far it should extend itself if it is to remain purposive," that is, "capable of an enduring and universal approval, of enjoying a posterity among others and in an ever progressing culture" (1790, §50, 5: 319). Here he seems to treat the capacity for invention and the capacity for effective communication as two separate talents and to identify genius with the former only. But in the preceding section he has included the capacity to discover effective means for the communication of aesthetic ideas as well as the capacity to invent them among the components of genius, even though he had previously acknowledged that techniques for the former can be formulated into rules and taught at least to some degree. In the present section he adds no new reason for thinking that taste can be taught by more than models, so it is not clear why he should now oppose taste to genius rather than including it as part of genius. When he concludes the present paragraph by stating that "For beautiful art, therefore, **imagination, understanding, spirit** and **taste** are requisite," adding that "The first three faculties achieve their **unification** through the fourth" (1790, §50, 5: 320 and note), he should still be explicating genius, not opposing genius to something external to it.[23]

But whether or not taste should be considered part of genius or a constraint upon it, it is clear that Kant wants the aesthetic experience of works of genius to be communicable. But since what must be communicated is their beauty, and the experience of beauty consists in the free play of our cognitive powers, what must be communicated to the audience for art is, paradoxical as it might sound, the free play of their own cognitive powers; that is, just as a work of artistic genius must be a model for originality rather than for mere copying by subsequent artists, so must it be a stimulus for the free play of the mental powers of its audience rather than something they passively perceive. And this means that even with regard to audiences as well as with regard to artists, the works of artistic genius that constitute a critical canon or models for posterity must be challenges or provocations to their own free play or originality. Perhaps this is a point at which a real difference between Hume's and Kant's underlying theories of aesthetic response emerges, because this means that for the Kantian audience the role of a critical canon must be more than merely to point out fine strokes they can relish; the canon must present to audiences as well as to artists models that stimulate their "imagination, understanding, spirit, and taste," setting the first three of these into a harmonious play unified by the fourth. Kant emphasizes that the works of genius that become models for posterity serve as exemplars of originality for artists, but because artistic genius is just the mirror image in artists of free play in audiences, the models for posterity must really be provocations to originality for both artists and audiences. Here perhaps Kant does take a clear step beyond Hume in the direction of Romanticism.

Abbreviations of Works Cited

ESY   *Essays: Moral, Political, and Literary.* Revised edition by E. F. Miller. Indianapolis: Liberty Classics, 1985.

T   *A Treatise of Human Nature.* Edited by D. F. Norton and M. J. Norton. Oxford: Clarendon, 2007.

Notes

1. As is customary, citations from Kant will be located by volume and page number from *Kant's gesammelte Schriften*, edited by the Royal Prussian (later German, then Berlin-Brandenburg) Academy of Sciences (Berlin: Georg Reimer, later Walter de Gruyter, 1900—). The *Kritik der Urteilskraft* in volume 5 was edited by Wilhelm Windelband.

2. I have attacked Kant's "deduction of judgments of taste," focusing on the first of these assumptions, in a series of works from Guyer (1979), chapter 9, to Guyer (2008a: 483–494). Among other recent interpreters, it is perhaps Hannah Ginsborg who has most vigorously defended Kant's assumption that the conditions of the possibility of aesthetic judgment are identical to the conditions for cognition in general; see for example Ginsborg (1997: 37–81).

3. For discussion of Nietzsche's charge against Kant (and Schopenhauer), see Guyer (2009: 22–23).

4. As is well known, in the eighteenth century the term "aesthetics" was used to designate this discourse only in Germany, having been introduced for that purpose by Alexander Gottlieb Baumgarten in his master's thesis (1735: §CXVI, 86–7), and was not adopted into English until the nineteenth century.

5. The other three essays in this volume were "Of the Passions" and "Of Tragedy" as well as a toned-down "Natural History of Religion." "Of the Standard of Taste" seems to have been "finished in the spring or summer of 1756" (Mossner 1954: 325).

6. See also EM App. 1.14/291–2.

7. I have outlined a general theory of beauty to be found in the *Treatise* in Guyer (1993: 37–66), reprinted in Guyer (2005: 37–74); see also Townsend (2001: 105–116). For a discussion of the "foundation" of Hume's "aesthetic critique" in the *Treatise* that deals with Hume's conceptions of imagination, enjoyment, and sentiment without finding an explicit theory of beauty in the work, see von der Lühe (1996: 15–101).

8. See Alison (1811: 296).

9. See Gerard (1759), part I, section II, note (i), pp. 21–22.

10. "*Utilitas*" and "*venustas*" were two of the three fundamental goals of architecture recognized by Vitruvius, with the third, "*firmitas*" or durability, clearly being an aspect of utility; see Pollio (1914: 17). For further discussion, see Guyer (2011a: 7–8).

11. In this example, Hume tacitly makes the same distinction that Kant would later make between the beautiful, the agreeable, and the good; see Kant (1790: §§2–5).

12. Although translated into English only in 1748, the *Critical Reflections* (Du Bos 1719) had by then already enjoyed five French editions and was widely known in Britain (as well as Germany). Hume was clearly familiar with the work long before it was translated into English, and indeed it could be argued that Hume's most fundamental assumption that

ideas are weaker copies of original impressions may have been suggested by Du Bos's observation that "the impression of [an] imitation differs from that of the object imitated only in being of an inferior force, [and] it ought therefore to raise in our souls a passion resembling that which the object imitated would have excited" (1719: 22). For a discussion of the influence of Du Bos on Hume, although one that does not mention this point about Hume's theory of impressions and ideas and which concentrates on Du Bos's influence on "Of the Standard of Taste" rather than "Of Tragedy," see Jones (1982: 93–106).

13. To borrow a phrase from the title of the first chapter of Henry Home, Lord Kames, *Essays on the Principles of Morality and Natural Religion* (Kames 1751: 11), which also refers directly to Du Bos.

14. Adam Smith would develop a version of Gerard's approach in his posthumous essay on "The Nature of that Imitation which takes place in what are called The Imitative Arts" (Smith 1790).

15. On this, see, of course, Kristeller (1951–2). Kristeller's thesis was that the inclusion under a single concept of "fine art" of literature, music, dance, painting and sculpture, sometimes joined by architecture and horticulture or landscape architecture, was an invention of the eighteenth century, not to be found in antiquity. This thesis has been contested; see Porter (2009a), and the ensuing discussing: Shiner (2009), Porter (2009b). But even if Kristeller's claim that the unified concept of fine art originated only in the eighteenth century is rejected, it can be agreed that it was accepted in the eighteenth century, and that Hume's inclusion of history and even eloquence on his own list of arts is non-standard for the period.

16. See Kant (1790: 338–339).

17. I am here taking one side in a long-standing debate about how Hume's conception of the qualified critics should be understood, as defining an ideal to which anyone can aspire or as identifying an historical body of critics whose judgments should be canonical for the rest of us. I originally defended the latter position (Guyer 1993) against Noël Carroll (1984), who had defended the former position. Subsequently, Shelley (1994) defended the first position, while Ross (2008) defended the second, and I supported Ross's position by means of the contrast between Hume on the one side and Gerard and Beattie on the other (Guyer 2008b).

18. For just a sample of relevant work, see Carroll (1996: 223–238), Jacobson (1997: 155–199), Gaut (1998: 182–203), Gaut (2007), and Schellekens (2007: part II).

19. The classical debate about whether Hume's criteria are circular was between Harold Osborne (1967: 50–56) and Peter Kivy (1967: 57–66).

20. In this passage Hume thus seems to be anticipating the famous account of "critical communication" by Arnold Isenberg, who however does not mention Hume in his paper. See Isenberg (1949/1973), especially pp. 162–164 of 1973 edition.

21. For this interpretation, see Guyer (1979) chapter 3, especially pp. 79–99, or pp. 70–88 (1997 edition), and Guyer (2005) chapter 3, pp. 77–109.

22. For this approach to Kant's conception of adherent beauty, see Guyer (2005) chapter 4, pp. 129–40, and chapter 5, pp. 141–162.

23. For further discussion of this issue, see Cannon (2011) and Guyer (2011b).

Bibliography

Alison, Archibald. (1811). "Of the Beauty of Colours," in *Essays on the Nature and Principles of Taste*, second edition, Edinburgh: Bell & Bradfute, vol. I, 295–313.

Aristotle. (1984). *Poetics*, in *The Rhetoric and Poetics of Aristotle*, edited by P.J. Corbett. New York: The Modern Library.

Batteux, Charles. (1746). *Les beaux arts réduit à un même principe*, Paris: Durand.

Baumgarten, Alexander Gottlieb. (1735). *Meditationes philosophicae de nonnullis ad poema pertinentibus*, edited by Heinz Pätzold, Hamburg: Felix Meiner Verlag, 1983.

Beattie, James. (2004). "Of Taste, and Its Improvement," in Beattie, *Selected Philosophical Writings*, edited by James A. Harris, Exeter: Imprint Academic, 161–182.

Cannon, Joseph. (2011). "The Moral Value of Artistic Beauty in Kant," in *Kantian Review* 16.1, 113–126.

Carroll, Noël. (1984). "Hume's Standard of Taste," *Journal of Aesthetics and Art Criticism* 43: 181–194.

Carroll, Nöel. (1996). "Moderate Moralism," in the *British Journal of Aesthetics* 36: 223–238.

Carroll, Nöel. (1996). *Beyond Aesthetics*, Cambridge: Cambridge University Press, 2001.

Du Bos, Abbé Jean-Baptiste. (1719). *Critical Reflections on Poetry, Painting, and Music*, translated by Thomas Nugent, 3 vols., London: John Nourse, 1748.

Gaut, Berys. (1998). "The Ethical Criticism of Art," in Jerrold Levinson, *Aesthetics and Ethics: Essays at the Intersection*, Cambridge: Cambridge University Press, 182–203.

Gaut, Berys. (2007). *Art, Emotion and Ethics*, Oxford: Oxford University Press.

Gerard, Alexander. (1759). *An Essay on Taste*, London: A. Millar, and Edinburgh: A. Kincaid and J. Bell.

Ginsborg, Hannah. (1997)."Lawfulness without a Law: Kant on the Free Play of Imagination and Understanding," *Philosophical Topics* 25: 37–81.

Guyer, Paul. (1979). *Kant and the Claims of Taste*, Cambridge, Mass.: Harvard University Press;—enlarged edition, Cambridge: Cambridge University Press, 1997.

Guyer, Paul. (1993). "The Standard of Taste and the 'Most Ardent Desire of Society," in Ted Cohen, Paul Guyer, and Hilary Putnam, editors, *Pursuits of Reason: Essays in Honor of Stanley Cavell*, Lubbock: Texas Tech University Press, 37–66.

Guyer, Paul. (2005). *Values of Beauty: Historical Essays in Aesthetics*, Cambridge: Cambridge University Press, 37–74.

Guyer, Paul. (2008*a*). "The Psychology of Kant's Aesthetics," *Studies in History and Philosophy of Science* 39: 483–494.

Guyer, Paul. (2008*b*). "Humean Critics, Imaginative Fluency, and Emotional Responsiveness: A Follow-Up to Stephanie Ross," *British Journal of Aesthetics* 48: 445–456.

Guyer, Paul. (2009). "Back to Truth: Knowledge and Pleasure in the Aesthetics of Schopenhauer," in Alex Neill and Christopher Janaway, editors, *Better Consciousness: Schopenhauer's Philosophy of Value*, Oxford: Wiley-Blackwell, 11–25.

Guyer, Paul. (2011*a*). "Kant and the Philosophy of Architecture," *Journal of Aesthetics and Art Criticism* 69: 7–19.

Guyer, Paul (2011*b*). "Genius and Taste: A Response to Joseph Cannon," *Kantian Review* 16.1: 127–134.

Hutcheson, Francis. (1725). *An Inquiry into the Original of Our Ideas of Beauty and Virtue*, edited by Wolfgang Leidhold, Indianapolis: Liberty Fund, 2004.

Isenberg, Arnold. (1949/1973). "Critical Communication," in *Philosophical Review* 58 (1949): 330–44; reprinted in *Aesthetics and the Theory of Criticism: Selected Essays of Arnold Isenberg*, edited by William Callaghan, Leigh Cauman, Carl Hempel, Sidney Morgenbesser, Mary Mothersill, Ernest Nagel, and Theodore Norman, Chicago: University of Chicago Press, 1973, 156–171.

Jacobson, Dan. (1997)."In Praise of Immoral Art," *Philosophical Topics* 25: 155–199.

Jones, Peter. (1982). *Hume's Sentiments: Their Ciceronian and French Context*, Edinburgh: Edinburh University Press.

Kames, Lord. [Henry Home]. (1751). *Essays on the Principles of Morality and Natural Religion*, edited by Mary Catherine Moran, Indianapolis: Liberty Fund, 2005.

Kant, Immanuel. (1790). *Critique of the Power of Judgment*, edited by Paul Guyer, translated by Paul Guyer and Eric Matthews, Cambridge: Cambridge University Press, 2000.

Kivy, Peter. (1967). "Hume's Standard of Taste: Breaking the Circle," in the *British Journal of Aesthetics* 7: 57–66.

Kristeller, Paul Oskar. (1951-2). "The Modern System of the Arts," *Journal of the History of Ideas* 12 (1951): 496–527 and 13 (1952): 17–46, reprinted in Kristeller, *Renaissance Thought and the Arts: Collected Essays*, Princeton: Princeton University Press, 1965: 163–227.

Mossner, Ernest Campbell. (1954). *The Life of David Hume*, Austin: University of Texas Press.

Neill, Alex. (1992). "Yanal and Others on Hume on Tragedy," *Journal of Aesthetics and Art Criticism* 50: 151–154.

Nietzsche, Friedrich. (1887). *On the Genealogy of Morals*, edited by Keith Ansell-Pearson, translated by Carol Diethe, revised edition, Cambridge: Cambridge University Press, 2007.

Osborne, Harold. (1967). "Hume's Standard and the Diversity of Taste," in the *British Journal of Aesthetics* 7: 50–56.

Pollio, Marcus Vitruvius (1914). *Ten Books of Architecture*, translated by Morris Hickey Morgan, edited by Herbert Langford Warren, Cambridge, Mass.: Harvard University Press.

Porter, James I. (2009*a*). "Is Art Modern? Kristeller's 'Modern System of the Arts' Reconsidered," *British Journal of Aesthetics* 49: 1–24.

Porter, James I. (2009*b*). "Reply to Shiner," *British Journal of Aesthetics* 49: 171–178.

Ross, Stephanie. (2008). "Humean Critics: Real or Ideal?," *British Journal of Aesthetics* 48: 20–28.

Schellekens, Elisabeth. (2007). *Aesthetics and Morality*, London: Continuum.

Shelley, James. (1994). "Hume's Double Standard of Taste," *Journal of Aesthetics and Art Criticism* 52: 437–445.

Shiner, Larry. (2009). "Continuity and Discontinuity in the Concept of Art," *British Journal of Aesthetics* 49: 159–169.

Smith, Adam. (1790). "The Nature of that Imitation which takes place in what are called The Imitative Arts," *Essays on Philosophical Subjects*, edited by W.P.D.Wightman and J.C. Bryce, Oxford: Oxford University Press, 1980: 176–213.

Townsend, Dabney. (2001). *Hume's Aesthetic Theory: Taste and Sentiment*, London: Routledge, 2001.

von der Lühe, Astrid. (1996). *David Hume's ästhetische Kritik*, Hamburg: Felix Meiner Verlag.

CHAPTER 26

HUME'S TASTE AND THE RATIONALIST CRITIQUE

PETER KIVY

THERE can be little doubt that real philosophical aesthetics, as we know it, was inaugurated, in 1725, by Francis Hutcheson, in his *Inquiry Concerning Beauty, Order, Harmony, Design*—the first of the two treatises that comprise his *Inquiry into the Original of Our Ideas of Beauty and Virtue*. Furthermore, it has been the judgment of contemporary philosophy that this first period in the history of the discipline produced two works of lasting value and enduring interest: Hutcheson's *Inquiry* and Hume's essay "Of the Standard of Taste." And it is these two works that have dominated contemporary discussion of eighteenth-century British aesthetic theory.

This judgment of posterity I believe to be, on the whole, a sound one. However, I believe as well that the rationalist critique of Hutcheson's aesthetic sentiment theory has received less attention than it deserves and that, in consequence, Hume's aesthetics of sentiment should be seen not only in the context of his own broader philosophical program, as is customary, but in the broader context of the rationalist critique of Hutcheson's theory that precedes it. The redressing of the balance between Hume's aesthetics of sentiment and the rationalist critique in this formative period in the history of the discipline is the task I have set for myself here.

The general plan and argument, then, will be as follows. In part one I begin, naturally enough, by outlining the theory of what Hutcheson calls *absolute beauty*, as opposed to relative beauty or the beauty of representation, for it is the theory of absolute beauty that exercised Hutcheson's contemporaries and later eighteenth-century figures.

In the second part, I present the rationalist critique of Hutcheson's theory of absolute beauty that developed in the years immediately following its first presentation, concentrating, for reasons that will become apparent as things develop, on John Balguy, a figure less known than I think he deserves to be.

And in the third part, I discuss Hume's account of the standard of taste and argue that one way to look at it is as a response to the rationalist critique of Hutcheson, in which the judgment of beauty remains a judgment of sentiment, as in Hutcheson, but alterations are made to accommodate the rationalists' insistence that judgments of beauty are judgments of *fact*.

First, then, to Hutcheson.

I Sensibility: Phase 1

In the "Preface" to the two treatises, Hutcheson apparently identifies his own doctrine of an inner sense of beauty and morality with that of the Third Earl of Shaftesbury. He writes there that: "This Moral Sense of Beauty in Actions and Affections, may appear strange at first View. Some of our Moralists themselves are offended at it in my Lord Shaftesbury" (1738, xiv-xv). But at least with regard to the sense of beauty, first appearances to the contrary notwithstanding, it becomes abundantly clear in reading beyond the "Preface" that it is Locke, not Shaftesbury, who provides the inspiration for Hutcheson, both in his remark in the *Essay Concerning Human Understanding* that "I have here followed the common Opinion of Man's having but five Senses; though, perhaps, there may be justly counted more" (1689/1975: 121), as well as in his theory of perception, *tout court*, which, without question, informs Hutcheson's account of beauty from start to finish. Indeed, even within the "Preface," we can discern a fairly clear echo of Locke's suggestion that there may be counted more senses than the five external ones, where Hutcheson writes that "Our Gentlemen of good Taste, can tell us of a great many Senses, Tastes, and Relishes for Beauty, Harmony, Imitation in Painting and Poetry" (1738: xv). And the *Inquiry Concerning Beauty* begins with a clearly Lockean account of perception on which Hutcheson's account of the perception of beauty is founded.

Hutcheson's initial statement of what he takes the beautiful to be is as follows: "Let it be observed, that in the following Papers, the Word *Beauty* is taken for *the Idea rais'd in us*, and a *Sense* of Beauty for *our Power of receiving this Idea*" (1738: 7).

The idea of beauty, Hutcheson then makes clear, is analogous to a Lockean idea of a secondary quality. So, just as (say) the idea of bitter or sweet, on the Lockean model as Hutcheson construed it, is caused to arise in the perceiver by the interaction of the external sense of the palate with its appropriate object, so the idea of beauty is caused to arise in the perceiver by the interaction of the internal sense of beauty with *its* appropriate object. And it is a reaction in *both* cases, Hutcheson emphasizes, that can be caused in the subject, in complete ignorance, on the subject's part, of what the structure of the object *is* that is causing the reaction. But with this crucial difference: in the case of secondary qualities, the specific configuration of atomic structure that caused the idea of a secondary quality to arise in the perceiver was not known and perhaps never could be. Whereas Hutcheson thought he did know the cause of the idea of beauty: "The Figures which excite in us the Ideas of Beauty seem to be those in which there is *Uniformity amidst Variety*" (1738: 17).

But the point is that, in the usual cases, neither the perceiver of secondary qualities nor the perceiver of beauty knows what it is that is causing the respective idea to arise.

So, here is how the analogy of the idea of beauty and the ideas of Lockean secondary qualities is stated by Hutcheson. To begin with, "by *Absolute* or *Original* Beauty, is not understood any Quality suppos'd to be in the Object which should of itself be beautiful, without relation to any Mind which perceives it: For Beauty, like other Names of sensible Ideas, properly denotes the *Perception* of some Mind; so *Cold, Hot, Sweet, Bitter*, denote the Sensations in our Minds. . . ." (1738: 14). And, furthermore: "But in all these instances of *Beauty* let it be observ'd, That the Pleasure is communicated to those who never reflected on this general Foundation; and that all here alleg'd is this, 'That the pleasant Sensation arises only from Objects, in which there is *Uniformity amidst Variety*.' We may have the Sensation without knowing what is the Occasion of it; as a Man's *Taste* may suggest Ideas of Sweets, Acids, Bitters tho' he be ignorant of the *Forms* of the small Bodys, or their Motions, which excite these Perceptions in him" (1738: 29).

Thus, on Hutcheson's view, the perception of absolute beauty is what I term, as I have in the past, "nonepistemic." Which is to say, we do not *perceive that* the object possesses *uniformity amidst variety* and then have the idea of beauty aroused in us by the "perceiving that" any more than *perceiving that* an object possesses some particular atomic or molecular structure causes a bitter or sweet sensation on the palate. Rather, whether or not we know that the object possesses *uniformity amidst variety*, and whether or not we know that *uniformity amidst variety* causes the idea of beauty to arise in us, the *uniformity amidst variety* causally interacts with the sense of beauty to cause the idea of beauty to arise in us. The knowledge is irrelevant to the effect. One of Hutcheson's early commentators, James Martineau, had this exactly right and expressed it with admirable clarity and elegance: "Though beauty may be predicated of single objects, it must be in virtue of a complexity comprised within them, and the proportion and disposition of their parts or attributes. When these conditions are fulfilled, we intuitively feel the charm of the effect, without knowing anything of its cause; the individual thing itself, as an unanylised unit, gets the credit of the perfection" (1898, vol. 1: 529–130).

Now this is not to be misunderstood as the view that all knowledge is irrelevant to the perception of beauty, that we needn't perceive *any* of the relations that the parts of a beautiful object bear to one another epistemically to perceive its beauty. On the contrary, the "object" of the sense of beauty is a complex Lockean idea, one "constructed," as it were, by the perceptions of the external senses and various operations of the mind, including the rational part. And the sense of beauty is an "internal" sense in virtue of its having ideas, rather than physical entities, as its objects. Hutcheson later called such senses "reflex" or "subsequent" senses, reserving "inner sense" for the Lockean sense or senses of reflection and introspection. They are, thus, "senses . . . by which certain new forms or perceptions are received, in consequence of others previously observed by our external or internal senses. . ." (1747: 12–13).[1]

The property of *uniformity amidst variety*, then, is an emergent property, supervening on the various relations of part to whole that the observer perceives epistemically and which, when thus perceived, constitute the complex Lockean idea that is the object of the sense of beauty. But although these various relations that make up *uniformity amidst variety* are perceived epistemically, *it* reacts nonepistemically with the sense of beauty to produce in the perceiver the idea of beauty, as do "the *Forms* of the small Bodys, or their Motions," with the senses of touch and taste, to produce in the perceiver the "Sensations" of "*Cold, Hot, Sweet, Bitter.*"

Now I am not trying to convince you that this is the right way to conceive of how *uniformity amidst variety*, or other properties like it, which we would call, after Frank Sibley, "aesthetic properties," function in our aesthetic experience of artworks and other aesthetic objects. To the contrary, I think it is wrong-headed: the opposite of the truth, which is that our enjoyment of *uniformity amidst variety*, when it does function in our aesthetic experience, results from our epistemically perceiving, our perceiving *that*, our coming to the realization *that* it is present in the relations of parts to whole (although Hutcheson was not, perhaps, *totally* wrong, in that there may be some cases in which *uniformity amidst variety* operates nonepistemically, as Thomas Reid later pointed out).

What I *am* here to convince you of is that wrong-headed though it may be, Hutcheson's account of our perception of beauty is an utterly brilliant philosophical move, given the situation he was in. Hutcheson was in the process, remember, of inventing the discipline of modern philosophical aesthetics. And he did it in just the right way: by making it part of the cutting-edge philosophy of his time and his place: Lockean empiricism and the scientific worldview that it expressed. In so doing, he put the discipline prominently on the philosophical map, as was made apparent immediately by what I call the rationalist response to his theory of beauty. And to that I now turn my attention.

II Sense

To my knowledge, three philosophers responded to Hutcheson's theory of aesthetic perception in his own lifetime from what might be called the rationalist perspective, two of them, Berkeley and John Balguy, within ten years of its first presentation; the third, Richard Price, in 1758. I do not have time here to canvass them all, so I am going to concentrate on Balguy, who got there first.

Balguy was a "liberal divine," as *Chambers Biographical Dictionary* describes him. He was "born at Sheffield in 1686 and died at Harrogate in 1748" (Chambers 1931: 64).[2] The text on which the following account of his views is based is his *Collection of Tracts Moral and Theological*, published in London in 1734. It comprises six works, all previously published, anonymously, between 1726 and 1733.

Balguy begins: "The ingenious Author of the *Enquiry into the Original of our Ideas of Beauty and Virtue*, tho' he professedly maintains the contrary Opinion, yet has nevertheless fixed Beauty on such a Foundation, as seems to me entirely inconsistent with his own Notion" (1734: 226–7). Wherein lies the inconsistency?

We can begin to answer this question with some questions of Balguy's own (rhetorical ones): "For are not *Uniformity* and *Variety* real *Relations* belonging to the *Objects* themselves? Are they not independent on us, and our Faculties; and would they not be what they are, whether we perceived them or no?" (1734: 227). The answers to these rhetorical questions Balguy, of course, takes to be "Yes." But so, indeed, would Hutcheson. How then can Balguy think that they can provide the basis for a criticism of Hutcheson's position? Only, it seems, by *misunderstanding* Hutcheson to be saying that beauty *is uniformity amidst variety*, whereas he was very clear in insisting that it is the *cause* of beauty in much the same way the atoms in motion are the cause of redness. In both cases, the property in question is a sensation or idea, the cause something else entirely, either atoms in the void or a complex idea operating upon an internal sense, which takes the name of the sensation or idea secondarily, as it were.

Once that misreading is in place, Hutcheson's project collapses. If the property of *uniformity amidst variety* just *is* the property of beauty, then it is not like the property of redness, the product of human sensibility, a "subjective" property, but a property "out there in the world," although it is a world, on Hutcheson's Lockean view, of relations between ideas already delivered to the perceiver by the external world through the senses and the reason. Furthermore, it then follows that the perception of beauty, since it is a relational property, cannot be perception by sense but rather by reason. "However Sense may convey to us the Ideas of external *Objects*," Balguy says, "yet the *Relations* between them no *Sense* can reach. These are perceived by Intelligence only" (1734: 227).

Thus, by an initial misreading of Hutcheson, Balguy has turned what was a nonepistemic, causal theory of the perception of beauty into an epistemic one. As he puts the view: "The Understanding is the sole Faculty by which we are capable of comparing one Idea with another, and discovering their real Agreements and Disagreements," as in the case of our perceiving *uniformity amidst variety*. "That in consequence of such Perceptions, our Minds are affected with pleasing *Sensations*, does by no means prove that such Perceptions [of *uniformity amidst variety*] themselves are sensible" (1734: 227).

This, then, is Balguy's misreading of Hutcheson and the subsequent critique of his position that it generates. It seems, in retrospect, a more plausible view than a correct reading of Hutcheson. And Balguy, quite understandably, interpreted Hutcheson in such a way as to make the view more plausible in his eyes. That it also made Hutcheson's view inconsistent with itself was a small price to pay for a rationalist because what had to go—the sentimentalist metaphysics and epistemology of beauty—was just the part that Balguy, the realist and rationalist, could gladly do without.

This brings us, then, to Balguy's realist metaphysics and rationalist epistemology of beauty, which we have seen lurking in the critique of Hutcheson. Balguy's aesthetics is expressed in distinctly theological terms, and those are the terms in which we must initially understand it. If, as Balguy believes, the existence of beauty in the world is not to be explained as the product of sense perception, in Lockean terms, what is its origin and ontological status? Obviously, it is a creation of God's. But what is His purpose in that creation? Balguy answers, to begin with, that "it does not appear to me, that the *Order, Beauty,* and *Harmony* of the Universe are merely intended in Subordination and Subservience to the Welfare of Creatures" (1734: 223). In other words, beauty in the world is not an instrumental good but an intrinsic one. As Balguy puts it, ". . .*Beauty* is of an *absolute* Nature, and a real, objective *Perfection*" (1734: 226). Furthermore, if the beauties of the world "have any real and intrinsick Worth, they must appear amiable in the Sight of the Creator Himself. And though," Balguy goes on, "before the Creation, he had a clear and full Prospect of all that *Order* and *Beauty* which were afterwards diffused through the whole Universe: yet I humbly conceive that, in creating the World, He was under a Moral Necessity of suiting it to his own perfect Ideas, and the exact Model in his own Mind" (1734: 222).

So far, Balguy's statement of his views concerning beauty is couched in rather abstract terms but with the beauty of the natural world obviously at the center of attention. However, Balguy extends these views to the beauty of the fine arts as well. "Without Order, Symmetry, and Proportion," he writes, "no Works of Art are, or can be, beautiful; and according to the Degree wherein these prevail, the Beauty of these is greater or less." And like the beauty of nature, the beauty of art is real, intrinsic beauty. Thus: "However Men may differ about the Circumstantials of [artistic] Beauty, they are generally agreed as to the Essentials. And the Reason of it is," Balguy concludes, "because they are of a fixed, unalterable Nature: that is, absolute, intrinsick, and necessary *Relations*; and by consequence, Objects of the *Understanding* only" (1734: 229–230).

Balguy, then, in his views on the fine arts, is steady to his rationalist realist text. Beauty in the fine arts, as in the natural world, is "of an *absolute* Nature, and a real, objective *Perfection*," an "intrinsick property" that "appear[s] amiable in the sight of the Creator Himself."

At this juncture, if not before, the Euthyphro question is likely to have come to mind; in the present context: Is "*Beauty* . . . a real objective *Perfection*" of "intrinsick Worth" because it "appear[s] amiable in the sight of the Creator Himself" or does beauty "appear amiable in the sight of the Creator Himself" because it is "a real, objective *Perfection*" of "intrinsick Worth"? Balguy's answer, I presume, if there is one, must lie in the assertion that God "was under a moral Necessity" to beautify the world in accordance with "his own perfect ideas." Whether this murky theology implies one answer or the other to the Euthyphro question I cannot make out. But perhaps it would be useful, at least, to put his claim in a more contemporary context.

In contemplating Balguy's use of the phrases "intrinsick property" and "real, objective *Perfection*," it might be useful to look to G. E. Moore's seminal essay, "The Conception of Intrinsic Value," first published in 1922, in that author's *Philosophical Studies*. And although there is more recent work on the subject,[3] I think this essay can provide some needed clarification of what Balguy might have been trying to say.

With regard to the foes of value "subjectivism," Moore writes: "In the case of goodness and beauty, what such people are really anxious to maintain is by no means that those conceptions are 'objective,' but that, besides being 'objective,' they are also, in a sense I will try to explain, 'intrinsic' kinds of value" (1959: 254–5).

As Moore analyses these two concepts, what is intrinsic is also objective, but what is objective is not necessarily intrinsic. "The truth is, I believe, that though, from the proposition that a particular kind of value is 'intrinsic' it does follow that it must be 'objective,' the converse implication by no means holds, but on the contrary it is perfectly easy to conceive theories of e.g. 'goodness,' according to which goodness would in the strictest sense by 'objective,' and yet would not be 'intrinsic'" (1959: 255).

To see this we can go straight to Moore's "definition" of intrinsic value: "*To say that a kind of value is 'intrinsic' means that the question of whether a thing possesses it, and in what degree it possesses it, depends solely on the intrinsic nature of the thing in question*" (1959: 260). In other words, if a thing has intrinsic value, it is due to the "internal" nature of the thing alone and not to any relation it may bear to anything else.

With these conceptual distinctions of Moore's in hand, let us suppose, for the nonce, Balguy's answer to the Euthyphro question is that beauty is "a real objective *Perfection*" of "intrinsick Worth" *because* "amiable in the sight of the Creator Himself." In that case, we would have to locate it on Moore's conceptual map either as subjective or as objective but not intrinsic.

In a weird sort of way, beauty would be subjective since it would be dependent on some particular individual's having a certain kind of mental attitude toward it; for that, on Moore's view, defines subjectivism (1959: 255). That it is a weird kind of subjectivism of course results from the fact that the individual in question is God. And perhaps, at least for eighteenth-century theology and metaphysics, that would be bending the concept of subjectivism out of all recognizable shape.

So, let us instead say that this answer to the Euthyphro question amounts to a form of aesthetic objectivity. Nevertheless, it could not possibly make beauty an *intrinsic* value because, on Moore's definition, to say that beauty is an intrinsic value means that "the question of whether a thing possesses it, and in what degree it possesses it, depends solely on the intrinsic [internal] nature of the thing in question." But if the Euthyphro question is answered as it was in the preceding statement, it would depend, rather, on the state of God's consciousness, which could have been other than it is, on pain of negating his freedom of will, omnipotence, or both. And if being beautiful depends on the circumstances—in this case, the will of God—then beauty cannot be an intrinsic value; that is, a value depending on the internal, intrinsic nature of the beautiful things themselves and nothing more. For they could have not been beautiful, even though their internal, intrinsic natures remained exactly the same, if something other than what is "amiable" in God's sight were also amiable in his sight.

If, then, we are to take Balguy at his word that beauty is an "intrinsic" property, an "intrinsic" good, which is to say an intrinsic value or "perfection," then we must say Balguy's answer to the Euthyphro question has to be that beauty is "amiable in the sight of the Creator Himself" *because* it is "a real [intrinsic] *Perfection*" of "intrinsick Worth." And that, indeed, is what I propose. That it raises the familiar problems about the attributes of God, notably, the problem of apparently negating his omnipotence since He cannot change the nature of beauty, I will leave to the theologians to worry about.

III Sensibility: Phase 2

It would be hard to think of two more diametrically opposed accounts of the nature of aesthetic value and how it enters the world than those of Balguy and Hume. The theological aspects of Balguy's worldview, to begin with, are in such glaring contrast to Hume's oft-expressed suspicions of the claims of religion as to hardly need mentioning. And where Hume's allegiance lay in value theory is equally obvious. "Morality according to your Opinion as well as mine," he wrote Hutcheson, on 16 March, 1740, "is determin'd merely by Sentiment, it regards only human Nature & human Life" (LET 1.40). Furthermore, that the argument extended to aesthetic value as well became abundantly clear, in 1742, with the publication of the essay "The Sceptic," where Hume drew sharply the distinction between aesthetic value judgments and judgments of fact. "In the operation of reasoning," Hume tells us there,

> the mind does nothing but run over its objects, as they are supposed to stand in reality, without adding any thing to them. . . . To this operation of the mind, therefore, there seems to be always a real, though often unknown standard, in the nature of things; nor is truth or falsehood variable by the various apprehensions of mankind.

But, Hume continues,

> the case is not the same with the quality of *beautiful and deformed, desirable and odious*, as with truth and falsehood. In the former case, the mind is not content with merely surveying its objects, as they stand in themselves: it also feels a sentiment of delight or uneasiness, approbation or blame, consequent to that survey; and this sentiment determines it to affix the epithet *beautiful or deformed, desirable or odious*. (ESY 1.170-1)

Nevertheless, appearances to the contrary notwithstanding, I want to claim that we can detect some positive influence on Hume's theory of aesthetic sentiment from Balguy's direction, which combines with some negative reaction to the theory of Hutcheson, with which Hume implicitly aligns himself in the passages from "The Sceptic" previously quoted. In other words, without reversing the sound judgment that Hume is in Hutcheson's camp, not Balguy's, as regards aesthetic perception and judgment, there is a little less Hutcheson in Hume and a little more Balguy than might at first be suspected. But in order to make that case, I must put before you the general outline of Hume's argument in the 1757 essay "Of the Standard of Taste," which, to some of you, will be very familiar.

Hume was trying, in the essay on taste, to negotiate between two opposing intuitions: the first, that because "Beauty is no quality in things themselves . . .," but "exists merely in the mind which contemplates them . . .," then "every individual ought to acquiesce in his own sentiment, without pretending to regulate those of others . . .," since "each mind perceives a different beauty"; and the second, that "Whoever would assert an equality of genius between Ogilby and Milton, or Bunyan and Addison, would be thought to defend no less an extravagance, than if he had maintained a mole-hill as high as Teneriffe, or a pond as extensive as the ocean" (ESY 1/239). Or, in other words, Hume was trying to negotiate between what he calls two "species of common sense": that there is no arguing about taste and that there seem to be clear cases in which someone's judgment of taste is right and someone else's wrong.

Hume's solution to this "antinomy of taste," as Kant would later call it, was to claim that although beauty is indeed in the eye of the beholder, there are beholders and beholders; and what is or is not beautiful is determined, in the last analysis, by those beholders who possess the requisite qualifications for the job. As Hume puts the position, in summary: "Strong sense, united to delicate sentiment, improved by practice, perfected by comparison, and cleared of all prejudice, can alone entitle critics to this valuable character [of true judge]; and the joint verdict of such, wherever they are to be found, is the true standard of taste and beauty" (ESY 1/252).

I do not have the time here to parse these five characteristics of what Hume calls the "true judge" in the depth and detail they require. But at least some further explanation is in order for me to make my point.

Of the five requirements for the true judge, practice and use of comparisons play the smallest role in Hume's thinking and are obvious enough, it would seem, to require little comment. Suffice it to say that Hume, quite reasonably, required of the true judge in matters of taste practice in his vocation and acquaintance with various examples of the objects of his judgment for the purpose of making comparisons between them.

Of the remaining three, all are what might be called necessary requirements of the true judge's character as judge; two innate, one acquired, and all of major importance to Hume's argument.

By *good sense* Hume means, quite simply, intelligence; sound understanding. And his point—an important one in the historical context—is that good sense so defined has just as important a role to play in our perception and appreciation of the beautiful as does sensibility; which is to say, the response of sentiment. And this is the view, it should be well noted, of a theorist outspokenly, affirmatively on the side of sensibility and not of sense: a self-proclaimed follower of Hutcheson against the rationalists. As Hume puts this important point, in the essay on taste, "the same excellence of faculties which contributes to the improvement of reason, the same clearness of conception, the same exactness of distinctions, the same vivacity of apprehension, are essential to the operation of true taste, and are its infallible concomitants" (ESY 1/251); and this because "Where good sense is wanting," the critic "is not qualified to discern the beauties of design and reasoning, which are the highest and most excellent" (ESY 1/252). For, Hume explains, "in all the nobler productions of genius, there is a mutual relation and correspondence of parts; nor can either the beauties or blemishes be perceived by him whose thought is not capacious enough to comprehend all those parts, and compare them with each other, in order to perceive the consistence and uniformity of the whole" (ESY 1/250). Out of context, these words might just as well have been written by Balguy as by Hume.

But we are brought abruptly back into context by considering the requirement of what Hume calls, most tellingly, "delicate sentiment," which, as I read him, is the rough equivalent of Hutcheson's sense of beauty minus the suggestion of a separate mental faculty. It is, in other words, through *good sense* that we come to understand the aesthetic or artistic object we are contemplating but through *delicate sentiment* that we come to feel the sentiment of beauty—to enjoy the object, as we would say, "aesthetically"—suggesting that someone with good sense and without delicate sentiment would understand an art work but receive no aesthetic satisfaction from it, and someone without good sense and with delicate sentiment might receive aesthetic satisfaction from very simple, decorative objects, and "rustic" art works requiring little or no understanding but, because unable to comprehend what Hume calls "the nobler productions of genius," could not receive aesthetic satisfaction from those more difficult works of art. And, surely, we have all known such people of both deficient varieties.

Finally, we come to the true judge's *acquired* character of freedom from prejudice. It is not as obvious or trivial as it sounds and is really three different things bearing the same name.

To begin with the obvious and trivial—personal prejudice—Ogilby's father would, quite justifiably, be disqualified as a judge of his son's poetic accomplishments. As Hume puts it, "though I should have a friendship or enmity with the author, I must depart from this situation" (ESY 1/249). Well that, of course, is a no-brainer.

But how do I, as Hume puts it, "depart from this situation"? His advice is expressed in highly suggestive terms: "considering myself as a man in general, [I must] forget, if possible, my individual being, and my peculiar circumstances" (ESY 1/249). This sounds very much as if Hume is adumbrating here Kant's notion, as expressed in the third *Critique*, of a common humanity that we are in touch with in true, untainted judgments of taste. "One solicits assent from everyone else," Kant says, "because one has a ground for it that is common to all" (1790/2000: 121–2).

The idea, then—a familiar one—is that great works of art, those that withstand the test of time, are those that, when we put aside our individual circumstances both personal and historical, tap into something we all have in common—our common humanity, whatever that is. Those works that appeal to our common humanity survive the test of time because of that: time cannot wither nor custom stale them. Those that appeal to time-bound circumstances and fashions do not survive the temporal test. But *we* must do the work of ridding ourselves of our time-bound quirks and tastes, or the core of humanity that great works of art tap into will not be in the requisite receptive state.

But what happens next is that this notion segues into a very different, indeed apparently incompatible one, suggesting not that we seek what is common in us that great works of art all appeal to, but seek, on the contrary, what is peculiar to the artist's contemporaries, to whom, Hume argues, they were originally addressed; for *they*, the artist's contemporaries, represent "that point of view the performance supposes" (ESY 1.250). Which is to say: "We may observe that every work of art, in order to produce its due effect on the mind, must be surveyed in a certain point of view, and cannot be fully relished by persons whose situation, real or imaginary, is not conformable to that which is required by the performance" (ESY 1.249). In other words, we are being confronted here with historicism in criticism, the very opposite of the common core of humanity thesis.

I suspect that this aspect of Hume's argument in the essay on taste, with its apparent tension, has never been noticed, let alone adequately dealt with; and, alas, taking notice is all I have time for here. But with Hume's general argument in the essay before us, we can, as I said at the beginning of the discussion, begin to see what positive effect Balguy may have had on it and in what way it is a retreat from Hutcheson while remaining in his spirit.

The point lying at the center of my claim that there is *some* Balguy in Hume is this. The prevalent themes in Balguy's theory of beauty are: first, that whether or not something is beautiful is a matter of *fact* about *it*, not, as in Hutcheson, a matter of fact about *the perceiver*; and second, consequently, the judgment that it *is* beautiful is a perception of the understanding, not a perception of sense. And these two themes are reflected in Hume's prevalent theses in "Of the Standard of Taste" that his goal is to "mingle some light of the understanding with the feelings of sentiment" and his conclusion that, in identifying correct judgments of sentiment as regards beauty with the sentiments of those "qualified" to judge, he has succeeded in his goal to "mingle some light of the understanding with the feelings of sentiment" (ESY 1.243-4) because questions concerning the qualified judges "are questions of fact, not of sentiment" and "are submitted to the understanding," not to sentiment, for adjudication (ESY 1.252-3).

Of course, Hume's aesthetic "fact" of the matter is a far cry from Balguy's. For the latter, it is a fact by way of a theology and a metaphysics countenancing intrinsic values that Hume could never accept. Whereas for Hume, it is a purely natural fact of human nature and human sensibility. As Hume sums it up: "It is sufficient for our present purpose, if we have proved, that the taste of all individuals is not upon an equal footing, and that some men in general, however difficult to be particularly pitched upon, will be acknowledged by universal sentiment to have a preference above others"—with *sentiment* being used here, in the ordinary sense we share with Hume, of opinion or belief, not feeling or emotion (ESY 1.242).

Thus, I want to urge, although Hume's worldview, if I may so put it, is poles apart from Balguy's, the latter's insistence that, with regard to beauty, there must be a fact of the matter and not merely an appeal to sentiment left its mark in Hume's argument in "Of the Standard of Taste": in particular, in Hume's very prominent, out-front insistence that there does lie at the core of our experience of beauty, a *fact* of the matter, determined by the *understanding*.

So much, then, for the Balguy in Hume. What now for the absence of Hutcheson from him?

Hutcheson and Hume agree that beauty enters the world, so to speak, when a human being has aroused in him a certain pleasurable "idea," in Hutcheson's terminology, a certain "sentiment," in Hume's. It is a passage from matters of fact to matters of value, as Hume would put it. And in the form just stated, without any qualifications, it is a passage to what I will call "subjective normativity": "subjective" because, so far, there is nothing intersubjective in the equation. If I get the idea or sentiment and you don't, in contemplating the same object, either you or I may be "abnormal," but there is no sense in which either of us can be "wrong" or "right," which is to say, "mistaken" or "correct."

Is there any room in Hutcheson's scheme for what I will call "intersubjective normativity"; that is, a sense in which a perceiver can be thought not merely abnormal but mistaken as well? Or, to put it another way: is there, in Hutcheson's scheme, any value beyond the merely subjective value of having pleasure if you experience the idea of beauty? The answer is in the affirmative. The pleasurable idea of beauty that arises from the perception of *uniformity amidst variety* possesses instrumental value beyond the merely subjective value of the pleasure felt, which it owes to the wisdom and goodness of God.

The sense of beauty, on Hutcheson's view, is, as we might say, "programmed" to deliver a pleasurable experience in the presence of mental objects possessing *uniformity amidst variety*. And this arrangement, Hutcheson avers, "is probably not the Effect of *Necessity*, but *Choice*, in the SUPREME AGENT, who constituted our *Senses*" (1738: 100).

But to what purpose this choice in the supreme agent? Apparently, it is twofold: as an instrumentality to knowledge and as an instrumentality, simply, to pleasure in the human race, which, assumedly, its creator wishes well. With regard to the former, Hutcheson writes: "how suitable it is to the *sagacious Bounty* which we suppose in the DEITY, to constitute our *internal Senses* in the manner in which they are; by which Pleasure is join'd to the Contemplation of *those Objects* which a finite *Mind* can best imprint and retain the Ideas of with the least Distraction" (1738: 101). And, with regard to the latter: "the same *Goodness* might have determined the Great ARCHITECHT to adorn this *Theatre* in a manner agreeable to the Spectators, and that Part which is expos'd to the Observation of Men, so as to be pleasant to them" (1738: 102).

With this explanation for the existence and functioning of the sense of beauty before us, we can see that it adds a kind of normative objectivity to Hutcheson's scheme, in the following sense. A person who experiences the idea of beauty abnormally—and Hutcheson has an explanation for why this might occur (which we do not have time to go into), based on the principle of the association of ideas—is *more* than just deviating from the normal. He is, to a degree, at least, epistemically *dysfunctional*. His reactions are not, strictly speaking, "incorrect"; but they are "wrong" in the sense of being against his interest as a knowledge seeker.

Balguy was unhappy with Hutcheson's instrumentalist explanation for the existence of beauty and our experience of it, averring that "it does not appear to me, that the *Order, Beauty* and *Harmony* of the Universe are merely intended [by God] in Subordination and Subservience to the Welfare of Creatures" (1734: 223).

For Hume, of course, a theological explanation for the sense of beauty and a normative objectivity based on it were unacceptable. But it is a nice question whether or not he would have favored an instrumental account of the sentiment of beauty if he had had available to him (say) a reasonable Darwinian explanation of the thing. No doubt, however, in 1757, the instrumentalism and theology came in one package, so you could not have the one without the other—a price Hume was surely unwilling to pay. In any case, Hume's thoughts on normative objectivity in the perception of beauty were obviously going in an entirely different direction from Hutcheson's. And I conclude with a brief consideration of that matter.

Recall that, in Hume's account, what is beautiful is what arouses the sentiment of beauty in the qualified or true judge, and what characterizes the true judges, who the true judges are, is a matter of fact, generally agreed upon. Is there room in this account for any form of objective normativity?

Notice: it is not enough that there is general agreement among "the right sort of people" as to what constitutes the true judge to give us normative objectivity. General agreement does not mean *complete* agreement. And what can we say to someone who appears to be one of the right sort of people, who appears to possess all of the qualifications of the true judge, but who regularly feels the sentiment of beauty in the presence of art works (say) that leave most other true judges unmoved? We can say: "You are abnormal." Can we say: "You are mistaken"? What justification would we have for saying this? Why should *vox populi* be valid here and not elsewhere? Something is missing here that we need to get from "abnormal" to "incorrect." And Hume, I think, knows what it is. Hume writes: "If, in the sound state of the organ, there be an entire or a considerable uniformity of sentiment of men, we may thence derive an idea of the perfect beauty; in like manner as the appearance of objects in daylight, to the eye of a man in health, is *denominated* their *true and real* colour, even while colour is allow'd to be merely a phantasm of the senses" (ESY 1/234; emphasis added).

The analogy, then, that Hume wants to draw is between the perception of beauty and color perception. And note well where objective normativity enters the latter, as Hume draws the analogy. The "true and real colour" is "denominated" the color an object appears "in daylight to the eye of a man in health." Who denominates this? Certainly not some philosopher in a treatise on sense perception. It is, presumably, an established institutional standard of correctness in color vision, and that is the source of objective normativity for our perception of colors, so that someone who does not perceive colors the way they are perceived in daylight is not merely judged as deviating from the norm, like someone with absolute pitch—she is judged to be perceiving *incorrectly*; her color perceptions are "wrong."

It is this kind of objective normativity, apparently, that Hume had in mind for the perception of beauty in drawing his analogy. Colors are "true and real" even though "colour is allowed to be merely a phantasm of the senses." Beauty, too, is "merely a phantasm of the senses." But because being "merely a phantasm of the senses" does not prevent colors from being "true and real," why should it prevent beauty from being "true and real" in the same way? This, I believe, is the argument Hume is running for "objective normativity" in the perception of beauty: obviously, a very different one from Hutcheson's argument to instrumentalism through theology.

It is, needless to say, highly questionable just how far the analogy between color perception and the perception of beauty can be taken in the direction of analogous objective normativity. One's initial reaction is likely to be "not very far," given the apparent absence, in the latter case, of the kind of science-based institutional apparatus present in the former, which denominates, as Hume says, "correct" and "incorrect": that, in other words, gives teeth to the objectivity. But perhaps the initial reaction is too hasty, and deeper reflection will yield more than meets the eye. However, I must leave the matter there, and press on to my conclusion.

IV Conclusion

I have been trying to follow, here, the progress of what we would call the theory of aesthetic perception and judgment from its beginnings, in the very beginnings of the discipline of aesthetics itself—from, that is, Hutcheson's nonepistemic account—to the rationalist critique of Balguy's to, finally, Hume's revision of Hutcheson's account, under the influence, I have suggested, of the rationalist critique. But Hume is not the logical end to this particular story. It is Thomas Reid, who, on my reading, brings the tradition Hutcheson initiated and Hume continued to its final synthesis, which I would be tempted to call his rational empiricism. That, however, is a story for another day.[4]

ABBREVIATIONS OF WORKS CITED

ESY   *Essays: Moral, Political, and Literary*. Revised edition by E. F. Miller. Indianapolis: Liberty Classics, 1985.

LET   *The Letters of David Hume*, 2 Vols. Edited by J. Y. T. Greig. Oxford: Clarendon Press, 1932.

NOTES

1. This is Hutcheson's translation from his original Latin treatise.
2. For a more comprehensive account of Balguy's aesthetics, see Kivy (2004–2007).
3. See Langton (2007).
4. The present essay is a revised version of the inaugural lecture delivered at the Fourth Annual NYU Conference on Issues in Modern Philosophy, Department of Philosophy, New York University, New York City, November, 9, 2007.

BIBLIOGRAPHY

Balguy, John. (1734). *A Collection of Tracts Moral and Theological*. London.

Chambers, W. and R. (1931). *Chambers Biographical Dictionary*, ed. William Geddie and J. Liddell Geddie. Edinburgh: W. and R. Chambers.

Hutcheson, Francis. (1738). *An Inquiry into the Original of our Ideas of Beauty and Virtue*, 4th ed. London.

Hutcheson, Francis. (1747). *A Short Introduction to Moral Philosophy*. Glasgow.

Kant, Immanuel. (1790/2000). *Critique of the Power of Judgment*, trans. Paul Guyer and Eric Matthews. Cambridge: Cambridge University Press.

Kivy, Peter. (2004–2007). "John Balguy and the Sense of Beauty: A Rational Realist in the Age of Sentiment," *Enlightenment and Dissent*, 23.

Langton, Rae. (2007). "Objective and Unconditioned Value," *Philosophical Review* 116, 157–186.

Locke, John. (1689/1975). *An Essay Concerning Human Understanding*, ed. Peter H. Nidditch. Oxford: Clarendon Press.

Martineau, James. (1898). *Types of Ethical Theory,* 3rd ed. Oxford: Clarendon Press.

Moore, G. E. (1959). "The Conception of Intrinsic Value," in *Philosophical Studies*, 253–275. Paterson, NJ: Littlefield, Adams and Co.

CHAPTER 27

HUME'S *HISTORY*
OF ENGLAND

DONALD T. SIEBERT

I The *History*'s Importance

UNTIL the twentieth century, David Hume's fame rested primarily on what long was regarded as his masterpiece, the originally six-quarto-volume *History of England, from the Invasion of Julius Caesar to the Revolution in 1688* (1754–1762). In his autobiography, Hume may have named the second *Enquiry* the best of all his works, but he surely regarded the *History* as a great and monumental achievement. Before he published the first volume, Hume observed that "no post of honour in the English Parnassus [is] more vacant than that of History. Style, judgement, impartiality, care—everything is wanting to our historians" (LET 1.170). Clearly, he hoped that he would be the first to occupy that post. After all, history was still enshrined as a great genre, like tragedy and epic, and Mt. Parnassus has no place for the author of an inquiry into the principles of morals. Hume says something similar himself in "Of the Standard of Taste."

The young Edward Gibbon, struck by the brilliance of William Robertson's *History of Scotland* (1759) and Hume's Stuart volumes, confirms both Hume's complaint and his hope, even if Gibbon (1794/1966: 98–99) has Hume sharing place in Parnassus with Robertson: "The old reproach that no British altars had been raised to the muse of history, was recently disproved by . . . Robertson and Hume. . . . The perfect composition, the nervous language, the well-turned periods of Dr Robertson inflamed me to the ambitious hope, that I might one day tread in his footsteps: the calm philosophy, the careless inimitable beauties of his friend and rival [Hume] often forced me to close the volume, with a mixed sensation of delight and despair." And soon after publication of the whole work, the great Voltaire reviewed Hume's *History* with boundless praise: "Nothing can be added to the fame of this *History*, perhaps the best ever written in any language. . . . Mr Hume . . . is neither parliamentarian, nor royalist, nor Anglican, nor Presbyterian—he is simply judicial. . . . [Here] we find a mind superior to his materials;

he speaks of weaknesses, blunders, cruelties as a physician speaks of epidemic diseases" (quoted in Mossner 1980: 318).

The *History* occupied Hume most of his adult life, and it is longer than his other writings put together. Even after publishing the final two volumes in 1762, he continued to revise the *History* throughout his life, leaving his final improvements in the posthumous edition of 1778. In his famous deathbed conversation with James Boswell, Hume expressed pride in his *History* and spoke of his efforts to leave it as perfect as he could (Weis and Pottle 1970: 14).

To be sure, Hume's *History of England* is no longer a standard reference on its subject. It has long been superseded in terms of historical thoroughness and methodology. It is deficient in primary, thorough research, and it looks back to the practices and aims of ancient history even while anticipating future aspects of historiography. But no matter, for it now enjoys another, and higher, stature. Like other great histories of the past, such as Gibbon's *Decline and Fall of the Roman Empire*, Hume's *History* now finds a place among the world's classics for its enduring literary and intellectual value—indeed, as a cultural artifact.

Moreover, this work demonstrates a great philosopher leaving his study, or "closet" as Hume would have said, to deal with that practical, sometimes intractable reality outside the study. How is a priori thinking tested, confirmed, or refuted by the a posteriori record of human experience? Hume seems to anticipate this shift of attention in the Conclusion to Part 1 of the *Treatise*, when, after the travails and anxieties of abstract speculation, the philosopher returns to the redeeming world of common life, a world perhaps more real, certainly more central to existence, than that of analytical inquiry. Making sense of human history is surely the proper business of an empiricist. Thus, Hume writes to the Abbé Le Blanc: "The philosophical Spirit, which I have so much indulg'd in all my Writings, finds here ample Materials to work upon" (LET 1.193).

II THE *HISTORY*'S COMPOSITION AND RECEPTION

The first quarto volume of the *History*, covering the years 1603–1649, appeared in 1754, and the second, continuing English history to the Revolution of 1688/89, in 1757. The first treats the reigns of the early Stuarts, James I and Charles I, and the second, the Commonwealth and the reigns of the succeeding Stuart kings, Charles II and James II. In 1759 appeared the next two volumes treating the Tudor period, and the final two, in 1762, which cover the medieval period.[1] Why did Hume write his history retrogressively? Originally, he had intended to cover English history only from the union of the two crowns of England and Scotland, in 1603, through perhaps the reign of the last Stuart, Queen Anne. He regarded the period of the Stuarts as the crucible in which the modern British constitution was forged, achieving the laudable balance between monarch and parliament that would characterize British government from then on. To Adam Smith he wrote: "[These years] form the most curious, interesting, & instructive Part of our History . . . I confess that the Subject appears to me very fine; & I enter upon it with great Ardour & Pleasure" [LET 1.168]. It was thus a period that had all the ingredients for great history, certainly compared to what seemed the least attractive period, the Middle Ages. This choice explains Hume's advice to Robertson—advice Robertson ignored—not to write a history of the emperor Charles V because the subject, on the whole, "is not very interesting" (LET 1.315)—"interesting" meaning both intellectually *and* emotionally engaging. That emphasis on the emotional is a hallmark of Hume's historiographical intentions and excellence.

The reception of Hume's *History* and the controversy surrounding it stem mainly from the reaction to those first two volumes featuring the Stuarts. In particular, the earlier volume of 1754 stirred up a hornet's nest, with the second of 1757 in some measure calming down the fury. Hume had predicted as much, especially in regard to the political reaction, remarking that the first volume would be more agreeable to the Tories and the second to the Whigs (LET 1.180). Indeed, the first volume was attacked not only for its supposed bias in favor of the Royalist over the Parliamentary position, but just as much for its unfavorable portrayal of organized religion, especially that of extreme Protestantism. Clearly, many British readers did not see the judicial objectivity praised by Voltaire.

Because of its subject matter, the second volume of 1757 was bound to be less controversial. Religious acrimony and antagonism in the second volume became largely Protestant against Roman Catholic, rather than nonconformist Protestant against Anglican Protestant, as in the first, and so there were fewer sympathies to offend in Protestant Britain. And, despite his criticism of the fractious, double-dealing Parliament during the Restoration period, Hume has much to praise in the final establishment of personal liberty and a balanced or mixed constitution, with Parliament superior to a limited monarchy, culminating in the revolutionary settlement of 1688/89.

Much of this difference in reception is also because Hume was much more sympathetic to the two earlier Stuart monarchs than to the latter two, and among the Whigs any favorable treatment of James I, and especially his son Charles I, was intolerable. What Hume says himself may explain why he has so often been mischaracterized as an extreme Tory: "My views of *things* are more conformable to Whig principles; my representation of *persons* to Tory prejudices. Nothing can so much prove that men commonly regard more persons than things, as to find that I am commonly numbered among the Tories" (LET 1.237). And he seemed to take pleasure in being difficult to label, a situation that, of course, would substantiate his often stated claim of total impartiality: "Whether am I Whig or Tory? Protestant or Papist? Scotch or English? I hope you do not all agree on this head, & that there [are] disputes among you about my principles" (LET 1.196).[2]

Until the end of his life, Hume affected an indifference to the hostile reception of the *History*, especially the first volume, and took pride in pretending to be above criticism and thus in refusing to recant his views or respond to his critics. Thus, in his farewell or funeral oration entitled *My Own Life*, he portrays himself as a man who stood firm against a united conspiracy of enemies of different stamps and never compromised his principles or beliefs. In a highly rhetorical sentence, Hume expresses bitter surprise that a historian who aimed at strict impartiality and accuracy could have been so abused: "But miserable was my Disappointment: I was assailed by one Cry of Reproach, Disapprobation, and even Detestation: English, Scotch, and Irish; Whig and Tory; Churchman and Sectary, Freethinker and Religionist; Patriot and Courtier united in their Rage against the Man, who had presumed to shed a generous Tear for the Fate of Charles I, and the Earl of Strafford" (MOL 613). Hume had been only too prescient in observing that readers respond more to the treatment of persons than they do to events and principles. Apparently his "generous Tear" for Charles I had overshadowed his balanced analysis of the complex political struggle between King and Parliament. He had dared to be a man of feeling and had paid a price for his compassion.[3]

Hume was vexed that some critics attributed the better reception of the second volume to his efforts to be less offensive and thereby to promote the sale of the *History*. As we have seen, he had predicted that the second would be less offensive because of its subject matter. But although in his continuing revisions he struck out or reworded passages that were saliently offensive to some political and religious sensibilities or admitted new evidence even when it ran counter to his earlier presentation, he never backed down on his basic beliefs. In fact, concerning his putative Tory prejudice, Hume maintained that he continuously made succeeding editions even less favorable to the Whigs (LET 1.379). In that light, he gradually toned down his praise of Parliament's achievements. For example, in the first edition of 1754 Hume wrote that the actions of Parliament "should render the English for ever grateful to the memory of their ancestors, who, after repeated contests, at last established [the] noble principle" of civil liberty. In the edition of 1773, Hume deleted "for ever" and after the adjective "noble" added the almost oxymoronic qualification "but dangerous." Such modifications are evidence of Hume's ever-growing political conservatism.[4]

III EVALUATING HUME'S *HISTORY*

In evaluating Hume's masterpiece, let us proceed by asking two directionally opposed questions. How does the *History* look back to earlier traditions and models of historiography? In what respects is it distinctive in its own right or part of a trend toward future kinds of historiography?

III.1 Hume in the Tradition of the Ancients

As noted earlier, Hume saw himself vying for a "post of Honour" on Parnassus, and his intention in writing history was to emulate the great historians of Greece and Rome (LET 1.170, 193). That is not to say that his history is simply an imitation of Herodotus,

Thucydides, Livy, or Tacitus—hardly, as we shall see—but it is helpful to be aware, as Hume certainly was, of historians who already had a place on Mt. Parnassus. His contemporaries saw him in that great tradition, with Gibbon and many in France calling him the Tacitus of Scotland.[5]

History, according to the ancients, is the inspiration of Clio, one of the nine Muses. This distinction brings with it certain expectations. The Greeks thought of history almost as an extension of epic poetry; indeed, as poetry in prose. Also, history came to be associated with tragic drama. Like both epic and tragedy, history is concerned with great events and elevated personages—not like comedy, whose province is trivial, quotidian happenings and low characters. Thus Hume pronounces: "History charges herself willingly with a relation of the great crimes, and still more with that of the great virtues of mankind, but she appears to fall from her dignity when necessitated to dwell on . . . frivolous events and ignoble personages" (HE 5.53). Like his fellow members of the British historical triumvirate—Robertson and Gibbon—Hume is ever conscious of the dignity of his undertaking. Dignity applies not only to subject matter but also to style, "the dress of thought," to use Alexander Pope's metaphor. Thus, from the ancients, Hume and the others inherited the notion that history uses the tools of rhetoric and oratory to achieve its goals.

Likewise, history unites with poetry's sister art of painting in aiming for the grand style. Hume's renderings of executions—such as those of Mary, Queen of Scots; Charles I; or the Earl of Strafford—become tragic spectacles. The execution of Mary is already a great painting or dramatic scene in the first edition of 1759, but Hume heightens the coloring in the first revision of 1762. He adds a passage that displays the emotional response of the witnesses and magnifies the scene's power. When the executioner holds up the queen's head, "the melancholy scene," at least according to Hume, has transformed both her enemies and attendants: "Zeal and flattery alike gave way to present pity and admiration for the expiring princess" (HE 4.251).[6] The word "scene" clearly confirms Hume's intentions. That word is used twice, for example, in his dramatic painting of the Marquis of Montrose's execution (HE 6.24–5).

Scenes like these are designed to inculcate moral lessons, or, indeed, by the power of sympathy, actuate the reader in a moral response. In the second *Enquiry,* Hume lays the theoretical groundwork of this process: "No passion, when well represented, can be entirely indifferent to us; because there is none, of which every man has not, within him, at least the seeds and first principles. It is the business of poetry to bring every affection near to us by lively imagery and representation." He goes on to contrast the "indifferent, uninteresting style of SUETONIUS" with the "masterly pencil [that is, paintbrush] of TACITUS." The former "coldly relates the facts," while "the latter sets before our eyes the venerable figures of a SORONUS and a THRASEA, intrepid in their fate, and only moved by the melting sorrows of their friends and kindred. What sympathy then touches every human heart!" (EM 5.40–1/222–3) This praise of Tacitus equally applies to Hume's own treatment, a few years later, of Mary, Queen of Scots and other historical "heroes of feeling." Thus, for him, history takes philosophy's clear but unaffecting description of virtue and brings it into our hearts.[7]

In the largest sense, Hume's *History*, like that of the ancients, becomes the *arbiter vitae*. Hume makes this function explicit: "History, the great mistress of wisdom, furnishes examples of all kinds; and every prudential, as well as moral precept, may be authorized by those events, which her enlarged mirror is able to present to us" (HE 5.545). As historian, then, Hume is overtly and insistently didactic. Since his own time until today, Hume has been called a philosophical historian. Although this label can apply to several different aspects of his historical writing, in his day, it identified him most as a moral philosopher. His understanding of the connection between history and moral philosophy is that of his contemporary, Lord Bolingbroke—whose sentence goes back to Dionysius of Halicarnassus: "history is philosophy teaching by example."[8] Hume's text is thus replete with moral and political maxims drawn from history's examples.

Although these lessons represent timeless wisdom, there are several that seem particularly apt at the present. Consider this one, for instance, concerning political partisanship: "It is no wonder, that faction is so productive of vices of all kinds: For, besides that it inflames all the passions, it tends much to remove those great restraints, honour and shame; when men find, that no iniquity can lose them the applause of their own party; and no innocence secure them against the calumnies of the opposite" (HE 6.438). Or this one, which Hume added in his final revision, when prompted by the rising national debt of Britain. In the first edition he had simply noted the first instance of "debt contracted upon public security" in Henry VI's reign; later, he seizes the opportunity to editorialize: "The commencement of this pernicious practice deserves to be noted; a practice, the more likely to become pernicious, the more a nation advances in opulence and credit. The ruinous effects of it are now become apparent, and threaten the very existence of the nation" (HE 2.454).[9] And when Hume points to the dangerous consequences of religious zeal—whether illustrated by the Crusaders' massacre of the innocent inhabitants of Jerusalem, the persecutions that bloodied the Reformation and Counter-Reformation, or the near-destruction of law and order (indeed, of common human morality) by the Puritan fanatics, these lessons would appear to foretell that plague of religiously inspired terrorism—pious zeal and puritanism in a new guise—now sweeping the world.[10]

Hume is indebted to ancient models for other notable features of his *History*; for instance, the set speeches in which he presents two opposing sides of an attitude or argument. A good example is his presentation of the disagreement between Bishop Gardiner and Cardinal Pole about how to suppress religious heresy—that is, whether persecution or toleration works best (HE 3.430–5). Although Hume clearly favors toleration—a policy recommended frequently in the *History*—he gives each side's arguments in a balanced, seemingly unbiased way. Of course, Hume's bias is obvious, as, for example, in his observation that Pole humanely and wisely favored toleration despite his genuine attachment to Catholicism, whereas Gardiner was indifferent in his attachment but was primarily moved by a sanguinary disposition. Another good example of Hume's two-sided analysis occurs when he ponders the implications of "the tragical death of Charles [I]." Hume presents the opposing arguments of whether the people have the right to rebel against their monarch, as if "such might have been [each side's] reasoning." Under some extreme circumstances, yes, he appears to concede. "But between resisting a prince and dethroning him, there is a wide interval" and an even wider interval between "dethroning a prince and punishing him," and he goes on to present the royalist position (HE 5.544–5). Thus, these debates prove quite useful to Hume's didactic agenda.

Another feature of ancient history and literature is the "character"—either a verbal caricature of a general type of individual, such as the bore or the miser, or a verbal portrait of an actual historical figure. The "character" became a minor but important form in what is often termed the Neoclassical Age, with fashionable wits like Lord Chesterfield writing them and Samuel Johnson employing them in his *Lives of the Poets*. Hume, we remember, wrote "A Character of Sir Robert Walpole." In his *History*, Hume sometimes used this kind of summary to identify the behavior and traits of a group, such as the seventeenth-century Cavaliers and Roundheads, and also to evaluate the achievement of a famous author or thinker, such as Shakespeare or Newton. In individual portraiture, this form lent itself to discovering the subject's "ruling passion," that favorite concept of eighteenth-century psychology. A concise psychobiography, the character analyzes and evaluates the subject's thinking, personality, and behavior. Hume's general practice is to end his historical account of an important figure with a formal character. Indeed, the brilliance of his character writing resulted in a number of separate collections of these short essays themselves.

Among many good examples, the "character" of Charles II deserves special note because it had already been "elaborately drawn by two great masters, perfectly well-acquainted with him, the duke of Buckingham and the marquis of Halifax; not to mention several elegant strokes given by Sir William Temple. Dr. Welwood, likewise, and Bishop Burnet have employed their pencil on the same subject" (HE 6.446–8). Thus, Hume has the advantage of eminent models but also the challenge of producing a distinctive portrait of his own. Hume sometimes echoes his rivals' phrasing, giving it his own touches, as he does here with the character drawn by Halifax, perhaps the best one of all: "[The king's] wit, to use the expression of one who knew him well [that is, Halifax], and who was himself a good judge, could not be said so much to be very refined or elevated, qualities apt to beget jealousy and apprehension in company, as to be a plain, gaining, well-bred, recommending kind of wit" (HE 6.446). Later, Hume quotes a squib by Lord Rochester, although not mentioning his lordship by name, to illustrate the king's ready and easy wit. When rallied "that he never said a foolish thing nor ever did a wise one," Charles replied that "the matter was easily accounted for: . . . his discourse was his own, his actions were the ministry's" (HE 6.447).

Except for some praise of the king's "private character," Hume otherwise has little favorable to say about Charles. He does, however, take strong exception to Burnet's comparison of Charles to the emperor Tiberius: "It would be more just to remark a full contrast and opposition. The emperor seems as much to have surpassed the king in abilities, as he falls short of him in virtue. . . . And the only circumstance, in which, it can justly be pretended, he was similar to Charles, is his love of women, a passion which is too general to form any striking resemblance, and which that detestable and detested monster [Tiberius] shared also with unnatural appetites" (HE 6.448). It is somewhat surprising that in his character of the hedonistic Charles, Hume would defend the king's "virtue" and downplay, if not excuse, his notorious marital infidelity. But perhaps it is not that surprising, if Hume did indeed write that suppositious essay defending adultery (Mossner 1980: 327–8).

III.2 Hume as Innovator

It would be misleading, however, to regard Hume's masterpiece as British history written by an imitator of the ancients. His historiography is, in fact, more distinguished for its innovation. The emphasis in ancient history tends to be on battles in the field and on the subtler battles for power among the great. Hume's *History* includes that kind of narrative, to be sure, but other concerns are more dominant. When he relates battles, as of course he must, Hume can be perfunctory, sometimes observing that battles are not of great interest to the philosophical historian. The introduction of artillery, on the other hand, is of interest because its use altered the nature of warfare, thus paradoxically, as Hume argues, reducing the prevalence of belligerency (HE 2.230). Of course, when something occurs on the battlefield offering matter for instruction or satirical commentary, he is quick to take advantage of the opportunity—for example, when he notes how the Scottish Covenanters brought themselves needless defeat at the battle of Dunbar by their ridiculous religious scruples (HE 6.29–31).[11]

Overall, Hume's *History* is new—or similar to historiographical innovations by Machiavelli, Voltaire, and Montesquieu, and by Hume's colleagues in the Scottish Enlightenment—in several respects: (1) in its close attention to political, theological, economic, legal, and cultural developments (i.e., civil history); (2) in its interest in seemingly small but revealing factual information; (3) in its attempt to be impartial and to weigh historical evidence with a skeptical, critical eye; (4) in its free use of highly emotional, even sentimental narrative, including domestic detail, making it resemble the emerging novel in some respects; and (5) in what might seem to conflict with the feature just noted, its detached, ironical point of view characteristic of much eighteenth-century literature.[12]

These innovative features have been apparent to readers since the *History*'s first appearance—such as to Voltaire, whose encomium appears earlier in this essay and whose own historical writing was associated with Hume's, especially in the new attention of both historians to manners. I review each in turn.

III.2.1 *Civil History*

Hume faced a problem in presenting everything he thought a philosophical history should contain. How should he combine the traditional diachronic narration of events with information that gets at the truth of history differently—indeed, some of its most important lessons? His answer is to pause in his narrative, sometimes with a digression—some of them later relegated to a footnote or endnote—sometimes with a closing overview of interesting facts concerning a particular reign, and, at the end of each historical period, with an extensive appendix of facts and commentary.

Some critics have objected to these breaks in the narrative flow, but Hume defends his method often in passing and more specifically three different times. In these passages, he emphasizes how analysis like this can be more revealing than a chronological description of events, however well done. It is an essential part of philosophical history:

> It may not be improper . . . to make a pause: and to take a survey of the state of the kingdom, with regard to government, manners, finances, arms, trade, learning. Where a just notion is not formed of these particulars, history can be little instructive, and often will not be intelligible. (1754; HE 5.124)
>
> The chief use of history is, that it affords materials for disquisitions of this nature; and it seems the duty of an historian to point out the proper inferences and conclusions. (1757; HE 6.140)
>
> The rise, progress, perfection, and decline of art and science, are curious objects of contemplation, and intimately connected with a narration of civil transactions. The events of no particular period can be fully accounted for, but by considering the degrees of advancement which men have reached in those particulars. (1762; HE 2.519)

Hume may seem defensive. Should the dignified historian be telling his reader the price of grain during the Tudor period or of Harvey's discovery of circulating blood? But these things matter because they daily affect human life more than action on the battlefield, great speeches, or intrigues at court, and they are clues, if read aright, to the condition of society. Thus, by looking closely at a petition of damages submitted to Parliament in the reign of Edward II, Hume notes the heavy dependence on salted meat, even in a warm season, and concludes how wretched "the state of ancient husbandry" was in those primitive times. Hume seems pleased to have blown the dust off this old manuscript: "From this circumstance, however trivial in appearance, may be drawn important inferences, with regard to the domestic economy and manner of life in those ages" (HE 2.178–80).

Of course, Hume's appendices include much more than the apparently trivial and quotidian. Thus, in each appendix, he assesses the legal system and traces the shift of power from feudal barons to the monarch, and then gradually to Parliament. This continuing discussion brings into focus the empirical evidence scattered through the narrative, and it is central to his definition of constitutional government and his overall appreciation of civil liberty. And his examination of learning and of the arts, or the paucity thereof in the Middle Ages, is a manifest part of intellectual and cultural history. When he ventures into literary criticism—as illustrated, for example, by his evaluations of Edmund Spenser (HE 4.386), John Milton (HE 6.150–2), and other notable authors—Hume proves an impressive judge. Likewise, his critique of the philosopher Thomas Hobbes stands out for its perspicacity and wit (HE 6.153).

III.2.2 *Minute and Trivial Detail*

We have noted Hume's claim that the dignity of history precludes minute or low detail, but we just noticed that he does include such facts in his digressions and appendices, along with information and commentary whose importance needs no defense. He also uses minute or low material in the narrative portion itself to reveal insights into greater matters. Thus, in his actual practice, Hume often breaks his vow to observe high decorum, and this inclusion of undignified detail adds to the effectiveness and delight of his *History*.

A good example is the description of James I's undignified behavior during a conversation with his advisor Sir Francis Cottington: "'Cottington, . . . here is baby Charles and Stenny,' (these ridiculous appellations he usually gave to the prince [Charles] and [Lord] Buckingham), 'who have a great mind to go post into Spain, and fetch the Infanta.'" When Cottington expressed his disapproval, "The king threw himself upon his bed, and cried, *I told you this before*; and fell into a new passion and new lamentation, complaining that he was undone, and should lose baby Charles." After further vacillation and histrionics, James lets Charles and Buckingham have their way. Here is Hume's closing comment: "These circumstances . . . though minute, are not undeserving a place in history" (HE 5.105). Indeed so. Hume may feel the need to apologize, but his comic interlude tells us something that would never emerge from an elegant "Character of King James I," although Hume writes that as well.

A similar example is the treatment of John Knox. Hume subtly uses sexual double-entendre in his characterization of this "rustic apostle": "John Knox . . . had imbibed, from his commerce with Calvin, the highest fanaticism of his sect" (HE 4.22). "The political principles of the man, which he communicated to his brethren, were as full of sedition as his theological were of rage and bigotry" (HE 4.41). Hume uses the language of Swiftian satire, whose tropes "commerce" and "communicated," probably reinforced by "imbibed," suggest something filthy in the holy intercourse of the brethren.[13] When the young French uncle of Mary, Queen of Scots, and his libertine friends break into a bawdy house, Knox calls for the vengeance of God to punish "this *enormity*" unless Mary takes action herself. "She probably thought," however, "that breaking the windows of a brothel merited not such severe reprehension," and Hume goes on to observe that Alison Craig, the prostitute sought by the young rakes, a "damsel" normally quite "liberal of her favours," was known "to entertain a *commerce* with the earl of Arran, who, on account of his great zeal for the reformation, was, without scruple, indulged in that *enormity*" (HE 4.42–3, emphasis added).

After narrating this whole affair, which by the way takes up the space of a long and witty paragraph, Hume writes: "We have related these incidents at greater length, than the necessity of our subject may require: But even trivial circumstances, which show the manners of the age, are often more instructive, as well as entertaining, than the great transactions of wars and negociations, which are nearly similar in all periods and in all countries of the world" (HE 4.44). Hume may state in theory that history should be dignified and general, but in practice he often writes history of a very different kind.

III.2.3 *Weighing Evidence and Impartiality*

A number of scholars have called attention to Hume's impartiality and to his highly logical weighing of evidence.[14] Hume certainly tried to be impartial and prided himself on his success in that regard. And his *History* provides ample proof of his painstaking examination into the reliability of various sources and evidence. Signal examples include his inquiry into Perkin Warbec's imposture and the possible guilt of Richard III in the murder of his nephews (HE 3.465–9) and his examination into the possible complicity of Mary, Queen of Scots, in the murder of her husband, Lord Darnley, and the associated authenticity of the so-called Casket Letters (HE 4.390–3). In my view, his conclusion regarding the whole Marian controversy, which is still debated, is persuasive, and his presentation remains a model of evidentiary analysis.

Thus, Hume is typically logical and skeptical in weighing evidence, but his total impartiality remains open to question. Modern epistemology often suggests that "truth" is never an absolute in human knowledge, and this assumption certainly applies to the philosophy of history. Indeed, it is generally accepted that history involves an imaginative reconstruction of the past. Thus, Hume's presentation of historical truth is "Hume's truth," just as the relation of any happening depends on who is telling the story. Although Hume did aim for objective presentation, a careful comparison of his narrative with his sources reveals that he may sometimes favor one account over another because it supports his didactic intention. He also often shapes his narrative to achieve that end. Moved "to shed a generous tear" for Charles I, Hume emphasizes details that make the king highly sympathetic—courageous and unflinching, pitying his own followers but never himself, and magnanimous in adversity.[15] Hume's Charles is "a kind husband, an indulgent father, a gentle master, a stedfast friend" (HE 5.220), and his last interview with his two youngest children brings tears to the eyes of Oliver Cromwell himself, otherwise the arch-villain of the drama (HE 5.504-05). Likewise, to mortify and torment the king, the regicides place him close enough to the construction of his scaffold to hear hammering during the night, but Hume's Charles sleeps undisturbed. Hume bases this tendentious detail on only one source, most other earlier accounts placing Charles farther away from the construction.[16]

We saw earlier that Hume painted the execution of Mary, Queen of Scots, as a great historical scene. Yet Hume was no admirer of Mary, and an amusing story has him slipping up behind Walter Goodall (a man said to have had "two loves, Mary Queen of Scots, and liquor"), who was snoring over a manuscript in the Advocates Library and shouting loudly that Queen Mary was a whore who murdered her husband.[17] However, wanting to present Mary as triumphing over the malicious Protestant bigots in charge of her beheading, Hume takes care to ensure that her final hours support his polemical intention. All sources record her reliance on her Catholic religious faith for comfort and strength, such as using prayer beads and holding a large ivory crucifix. Hume tends to omit or downplay those details, presenting Mary instead as a secular heroine, splendid in the dignity, courage, and magnanimity—that greatness of mind— celebrated by Aristotle in his *Ethics*. In that regard, it is instructive to set Hume's account alongside that of his historical colleague, William Robertson, a Presbyterian minister. The two versions superficially agree, but a closer reading reveals how disparate values and intentions lead each historian to perceive and construct a different narrative.[18]

III.2.4 *Sentimental, Novelistic Elements*

As we have seen, Hume's recognition that the historian should enlist emotion in the cause of virtue has its roots, first of all, in ancient practice and agrees with his extra-*History* praise of sympathy's power—a power to move humans to virtuous action rather than simply to admire virtue passively in the abstract. The words "interesting" and "interested" imply for Hume emotional and, thus, moral involvement. An oft-quoted remark, in a letter to his friend William Mure, underlines his historical goals: "The first Quality of an Historian is to be true and impartial; the next to be interesting. If you do not say, that I have done both Parties justice; and if Mrs Mure be not sorry for poor King Charles, I shall burn all my Papers, and return to philosophy" (LET 1.210). The discussion in III.2.3 may call into question whether the *History* is always strictly "true and impartial." There is no question, however, that Hume aspired to write "interesting" history—the kind that would make Mrs. Mure, or Mr. Mure for that matter, feel sorry for poor King Charles.

Thus, Hume's historiography differs from that of the ancients in its even greater use of emotion, including domestic emotion. This aspect of the *History* can make it resemble the sentimental literature popular in his time, such as in the drama or novel of feeling.[19] Good examples are legion throughout Hume's six volumes, with the two Stuart volumes containing the highest concentration. That fact should not be surprising because Hume chose to begin with those volumes for the very reason that the Stuart period was to him the most "interesting" of all in British history.

Two representative examples illustrate the point. Both showcase a historian of feeling whose sympathetic response either to misery or noble sentiment can make him pause and respond emotionally. In his portrayal of James II, Hume is largely unsympathetic and condemnatory until the very end, when the king finds himself deserted by all, even those closest to him, like his daughter Anne. A wave of compassion takes Hume to the weeping king's side: " 'God help me,' cried he, in the extremity of his agony, 'my own children have forsaken me!' " Then Hume deplores that James was being treated, because of "religious antipathy," worse than "even Nero, Domitian, or the most enormous tyrants, that have disgraced the records of history" (HE 6.513).

A similarly involved historian relates the Duke of Ormond's elevated sentiment at the loss of his son, the illustrious Earl of Ossory, and then interrupts his narration: "These particularities may appear a digression; but it is with pleasure, I own, that I can relax myself for a moment in the contemplation of these humane and virtuous characters, amidst that scene of fury and faction, fraud and violence, in which at present our narration has unfortunately engaged us" (HE 6.411). Hume may apologize, but in fact he takes pride in being stirred by the dignity of human nature. He apologizes more for having to deal at all with the ugly realities that are much more commonplace in history than noble behavior and sentiment. His position here might appear tenuous, for history can never abandon the surviving records of what happened in the past to become romance.[20] What this digression does show is a strong belief that history should inculcate virtue, and so, in this case Hume goes out of his way to make sure that the right lesson is being taught. Virtue is intrinsically beautiful, as Plato and others have argued, and the historian in the role of *vir bonus* cannot resist its attraction.

III.2.5 *Detachment and Emotion*

Much like Gibbon, Hume often assumes a superior, almost Olympian perspective—a point of view that is detached and often ironical. This kind of historian may seem the opposite of the emotionally involved one, but the two can work together on the same page. Thus, much unlike Gibbon, Hume becomes a kind of Janus-faced historian, readily combining the two stances or perspectives and moving from one to the other as the subject demands.[21] In the passages already cited in this essay, we have seen examples of each stance operating mainly alone, but sometimes in tandem, as in treatment of James II just examined. A historian engaged in moral instruction need not be—indeed, should not be—a cold-blooded reptile. The principle that the philosopher should never be divorced from the man informs all of Hume's writing.

IV For Further Consideration

What has been said thus far by no means represents the last word on Hume's *History*, and scholars do not agree on which aspect of the work is most important. We tend to ride our own hobbyhorses, as I have probably been doing. In what follows, I would like to consider the uniqueness of the *History* in Hume's canon and sketch out ways of approaching the work that might prove rewarding for further study.

IV.1 The Division of Hume's Canon

The History of England differs from Hume's other work in several respects. Certainly, I do not have in mind that neat separation between philosophy and history implied in the letter to Mure—namely, that Hume would return to philosophy if his efforts in history failed. The *History* is part of his philosophy, as almost everyone now agrees. It differs from the rest of his philosophy not so much in the *matter* as in the *manner* of its composition.

Hume wrote his other work to develop a specific thesis, and so that work has the organization and argumentative rhetoric of the essay—even if "writ large," or larger, in the *Treatise*, the *Enquiries*, or the *Dissertations*. Thus, the ideas expressed in these writings are the result of a discrete period of concentrated attention and logical development. Even those essays using historical material have a unity of purpose like the others in the "philosophical" category. These may be said to represent Hume's theoretical oeuvre or canon, and are, thus, a product of the study.

Hume was, of course, not just spinning metaphysical webs in his study. All his philosophy is based on observing human behavior, but there is a difference between observing the general or norm and the specific instance. *The History of England*, unlike the other work, was written over a period of ten or more years, and it deals with a large number of unique historical events. This fact dictates a kind of ad hoc presentation as a long and varied chronology, with its conflicting or inadequate evidence, and invites the historian to a series of evaluative responses. Accordingly, the thought informing the *History* is constantly developing—from the penning of the first words until the close of last volume, or indeed until the final revisions. In this light, the *History* may be said to represent the practical part of Hume's canon discovered in the laboratory of human experience. Hume himself recognized this evolutionary aspect of his *History*. On his deathbed, for example, he told Boswell that "he became a greater friend to the Stuart family *as he advanced in studying for his history*" (emphasis added; in Weis and Pottle, 1970: 14).

This division of Hume's work into that based largely on general human experience and that based on specific instances has significant implications. Not recognizing this division may lead one to assume a monolithic unity in Hume's thought—that what he argues in the earlier, more theoretical work will be borne out and confirmed in the later, more strictly empirical work; that it is valid to use the earlier to illuminate the later. Indeed, the two can be mutually reinforcing, but not as a matter of course and certainty. Of course, Hume's more strictly philosophical canon also underwent recasting and modification from the version in the *Treatise* to that of the *Enquiries* and other such work. (In this essay, I have sought to minimize extra-*History* quotation and to base my evaluation mainly on citations from the *History* itself.)[22]

It follows that conclusions developed earlier might be tested and occasionally revised or even disproved in the *History*. For instance, that characteristic Humean assumption—Ovid's contention that humane learning softens the manners and prevents cruelty (*emollit mores, nec sinit esse feros*)—appears frequently in Hume's other writing and is usually confirmed in the *History*. However, the rule is tested with an egregious exception in the Earl of Worcester's example: "Knowledge had not produced, on this nobleman himself, the effect which naturally attends it, of humanizing the temper, and softening the heart" (HE 2.477).[23] The practicing historian may in fact discover that the record of human experience does not always follow the script written by the closeted philosopher.

The essay "Of Superstition and Enthusiasm," first published in 1742, is another case in point. In the essay, Hume prefers the extreme Protestant form, denominated "enthusiasm," because it promotes freedom of thought and action, which in turn leads to civil rights and representative government. Superstitious models, like Romanism, on the other hand, encourage a tyrannical suppression of human liberty. And that least desirable characteristic of enthusiasm—its rages of wild solipsistic theogeny setting the Puritan apart from ordinary humans and ordinary life—gradually subsides because enthusiasm lacks the ritual and structure to prolong fanatical zeal.

So goes the theory. Writing the *History of England* made Hume aware at close range how enthusiasm could threaten government and order. He recognized that enthusiasm frequently either promotes licentious freedom or suppresses liberty entirely. Thus, he began to see the advantages of religious forms and ceremonies in restraining enthusiasm's dangerous excesses—those that sanctified its votaries and insulated them from traditional standards of right and wrong. The saint, like that "perfect enthusiast" Sir Henry Vane, was "*a man above ordinances*," and thus "unrestrained by any rules, which govern inferior mortals" (HE 6.128–9). This estrangement from moral norms could threaten the very fabric of human society. By contrast, mitigated superstition—like that of the Anglican *via media*—had the ameliorating influence of bringing believers back into contact with material reality and so into conformity with the customary values engendered by the human moral sense.[24]

Not only did Hume adjust his earlier thinking in the course of writing the *History*, but he also modified his views as the work proceeded. Thus, if Hume's whole canon is not monolithic, neither is the *History* itself. The work has a protean or chameleon quality, its conclusions undergoing continuing revision. The thought of David Hume never sprang, like Athena, fully formed from the head of Zeus.

Hume's attitude toward the Middle Ages illustrates this point. We can begin by reviewing four summary statements in the *History* about this period—the first, appearing in 1759; the second, in 1762 at the beginning of the medieval volumes; and the third and fourth, also in 1762, *but* at the end of those volumes. The first passage celebrates the Renaissance sun that would break through the clouds enveloping the world of the "Dark Ages," to use that favorite metaphor of the Enlightenment. "Here . . . commences the useful, as well as the more agreeable part of modern annals," Hume announces, while relegating knowledge of the Middle Ages to antiquarian, dry-as-dust curiosity: "Whoever carries his anxious researches into preceding periods is moved by a curiosity, liberal indeed and commendable; not by any necessity for acquiring knowledge of public affairs, or the arts of civil government" (HE 3.81–2). With this presupposition, it is no wonder that Hume put off writing the first two volumes of his *History* until the last.

The second statement marks the chronological beginning of the *History*, and we are hardly surprised that Hume seems not to relish the task of composing the final two volumes. Because the surviving records of the medieval period are either scanty or unreliable, it is almost impossible to write this history at all, he says, but no matter, for such inquiry "could afford little or no entertainment to men born in a more cultivated age . . .; and it is rather fortunate for letters that they are buried in silence and oblivion" (HE 1.3–4). A historian of the present day, particularly an academic one, might be appalled by such a selective dismissal of the past. The point is that Hume saw nothing of much value in medieval history *before* he had to write it, but he had committed himself to writing it, nonetheless.

The third and fourth passages appear at the very end of the medieval volumes. After a lengthy caveat about seeking the beginning of English constitutional government in distant ages—a parting shot at the Whigs—Hume continues:

> An acquaintance with the ancient periods . . . is chiefly *useful*, by instructing [the English] to cherish their present constitution, from a comparison or contrast with the condition of those distant times. And it is also *curious*, by shewing them the remote, and commonly faint and disfigured originals of the most finished and most

noble institutions, and by instructing them in the great mixture of accident, which commonly concurs with a small ingredient of wisdom and foresight, in erecting the complicated fabric of the most perfect government. (HE 2.525)

This final word by itself hardly represents a great change of mind about the overall value of studying medieval history. Hume could never view that period as anything other than "dark," especially in the abstract. But medieval history is at least *"useful"* and *"curious"*—his emphasis—if it makes the English appreciate their present constitution. It also has value in demonstrating that the direction of history may owe more to chance than to human "wisdom and foresight."

The preceding passage is mainly political in its intention. The most significant is the fourth passage, appearing a few pages earlier. Hume repeats the theme that we have "pursued the history of England through . . . many barbarous ages; till we have at last reached the dawn of civility and science," and so we are ready "to present to the reader a spectacle more worthy of his attention." The phrase "more worthy" does not make these "many barbarous ages" unworthy of attention, however: "Nor is the spectacle altogether unentertaining and uninstructive which the history of those times presents to us. The view of human manners, in all their variety of appearances, is both profitable and agreeable" (HE 2.518). One need only read Hume's thoughtful "history of those times" to see what he means—and to conclude that he has significantly modified the prejudice he entertained before he immersed himself in medieval history.

Hume's treatment of chivalry is a more particular illustration. In his juvenile "Historical Essay on Chivalry and Modern Honour" (ca. 1725–6), the precocious schoolboy has great fun ridiculing the tomfoolery of chivalric honor. In the published essays of the early 1740s, Hume moderates that view, associating that remnant of chivalry—gallantry—with the polished manners of modern times, especially in monarchies. Much later in the medieval volumes of the *History*, he is even compelled to credit chivalry and its mythopoeia in medieval romances for civilizing those who would otherwise be hopeless barbarians. In one passage, Hume seems almost beside himself in admiration of the "Black Prince" Edward's chivalric treatment of the conquered French King John II after the Battle of Poitiers in 1356 (HE 2.251–3). Commenting on the scene, Hume emphasizes the superiority of this generous behavior, conceived by the code of chivalry, over the vulgar glory of military prowess, itself another less desirable product of chivalric overreaching. The lesson is clear. No matter how merely psychological or imaginary the chivalric code was—or even absurd in its extremes—its effect on human action was considerable. Medieval knights did indeed become actors in a plot invented by romancers and troubadours. So it would seem that the heroes of the songs had ridden out of the score into real life. That is to say, life had come to imitate art.[25]

Or consider Hume's treatment of Alfred the Great, who turns out to be one of the most important and exemplary monarchs in English history. Alfred drove the Scandinavians back into the Danelaw; he established a government of law and justice, "the origin of . . . the COMMON LAW" (HE 1.78); he promoted learning and the arts, founding the university of Oxford, and was himself a scholar of distinction; he encouraged "the vulgar and mechanical arts," so closely connected "with the interests of society"; and he introduced "even the elegancies of life" to his subjects (HE 1.81). Indeed, in Hume's account, Alfred seems the very embodiment of the Warrior-Scholar-Philosopher King. Hume pronounces Alfred "the greatest prince, after Charlemagne" in that age, and "one of the wisest and best that ever adorned the annals of any nation" (HE 1.81). Obviously, the example of Alfred the Great has much to teach Hume and his reader, and yet this paragon reigned in the middle of the Dark Ages.

IV.2 Suggestions for Future Study

What we have considered thus far leads to some possible new approaches and directions in evaluating Hume's *History*. More can be done, for example, in examining Hume's sources and comparing them with Hume's own presentation of the "truth." It is worth noting that the first edition of the Stuart volumes lacks documentation entirely—a feature harking back to ancient practice—and only after being questioned by Horace Walpole did Hume agree to include his sources (LET 1.284–5). Nonetheless, unlike more recent practice—or even that of his contemporaries Robertson and Gibbon—Hume's documentation can be imprecise or wanting; thus sometimes there would seem indebtedness to a source not cited.[26] In any event, attention to how Hume used his sources can reveal his thinking and intentions, as I have already shown. The same is true concerning Hume's continuing revisions. Some are clearly for stylistic polish or to remove Scotticisms, but others, even involving a word or a phrase, demonstrate Hume's intention to make his history accurately represent his final word.[27]

Further work on Hume's indebtedness to, or his differences from, other historians—from ancient to modern—strikes me as needed. For example, both Hume and Robertson covered the Tudor period of British history and published their two versions in the same year, 1759. They corresponded about what they were doing or had done, and they continued to adjust their respective views in revised editions. How these rival historians influenced, borrowed, and differed from each other would prove quite interesting.

And larger questions remain concerning Hume's historiographical assumptions. Does human history reveal gradual progress? There are passages that would seem to answer the question both yes and no. Or is the course of history cyclical, as it might seem in one important observation (HE 2.519–20) that civilization oscillates between the extremes of great ages and periods of enervation or barbarity—a common view in Hume's day? To what degree does individual human purpose and agency affect the course of history, as seen in the remarkable influence of one ruler, Alfred the Great (HE 1.63–81)? Or is history largely the result of unforeseen, uncontrollable phenomena—indeed, accidental happenings, such as the momentous discovery of the Justinian Pandects (HE 2.520–2)? And does Hume anticipate the historicist or relativist goal set forth, for example, by R. G. Collingwood? That is, does the historian try to understand the past on its own terms and withhold judgments based on more recent political, social, and ethical standards? There has been disagreement among scholars on that question.[28] The most striking statement of the historicist principle is this: "it seems unreasonable to judge of the measures, embraced during one period, by the maxims, which prevail in another" (HE 5.240). But this caution may stem mainly from Hume's desire to excuse the early Stuarts' claims of royal prerogative. Certainly, there are many examples of Hume's judging the past from the vantage point of present values, indeed, his own values. Of course, these conflicting judgments may simply result from the ad hoc method of composition, discussed earlier, and so there is bound to be a certain inconsistency in the *History*'s "philosophy."

Hume's *History*, like his whole canon, is rich in promise for future study, and these are but a few possibilities. No doubt many others will occur to every careful reader of this inexhaustible treasure.

V CONCLUSION

Hume's masterpiece—after a period of declining interest from about the middle of the nineteenth to the middle of the twentieth century—is once again receiving the attention and appreciation that it deserves. It continues to be a rich mine of his thinking on politics and law, religion, morality, commerce and economics, manners, the arts and sciences, and, of course, the larger and perplexing question of progress in human civilization—indeed, on what defines civilization. And it is the final version of his philosophical thought. The *History* displays Hume at his rhetorical best, a writer whose style—urbane, confident, forceful, and clear—has, ever since its publication, won over even readers opposed to his views. It is an absorbing narrative, for Hume knows how to tell a good story. Overall, it is history written by a man of letters, by a philosopher, and as he demonstrated, by a human being like us. His is not the work of a cold rationalist and skeptic or a documentary social scientist, but rather by a historian whose intellectual engagement with his subject is enlivened by his emotional involvement: "Be a philosopher; but, amidst all your philosophy, be still a man" (EU 1.6/9).[29]

ABBREVIATIONS OF WORKS CITED

EM   *Enquiry Concerning the Principles of Morals*. Edited by Tom L. Beauchamp. Oxford: Clarendon, 1998.

ESY   *Essays: Moral, Political, and Literary*. Revised edition by E. F. Miller. Indianapolis: Liberty Classics, 1985.

EU   *An Enquiry Concerning Human Understanding*. Edited by T. L. Beauchamp. Oxford: Clarendon, 2000.

HE   *The History of England*, 6 Vols. Foreword by W. B. Todd. Indianapolis: Liberty Classics, 1983.

LET   *The Letters of David Hume.* 2 Vols. Edited by J. Y. T. Greig. Oxford: Clarendon Press, 1932.

MOL   *My Own Life.* Reprinted in *Essays: Moral, Political, and Literary.* Revised edition by E. F. Miller. Indianapolis: Liberty Classics, 1985.

Notes

1. These are dates of publication; the 1757 volume actually appeared a year earlier.
2. The epithets "whig" and "tory" were coined during the Restoration period as abusive labels, and, by Hume's day, there were noteworthy political variations within each party. So, in some respects, it is simplistic to identify Hume as either a Tory or Whig. There is a substantial literature on Hume's politics that is beyond the purview of this essay.
3. For an analysis of Hume's autobiography, see Siebert (1984*a*: 132–147); see also Baier (2008: 265–281).
4. See Slater (1992)—a very useful study.
5. See Hicks (1996: 203–209)—an important study of the History; see also Wootton (2009: 448–452)—another useful study.
6. Noted in Slater (1992: 137). For a full discussion, see Siebert (1990*a*: 45–51). Karen O'Brien (1997: 118) calls the scene "a blackly comic encounter between Protestant fervor and Catholic piety"—a misreading, I believe, in an otherwise revealing study of the *History*.
7. See, for example, Hume's early statement in "Of the Study of History" (ESY 567–568). For Hume's "heroes of feeling" see Siebert (1990*a*: chapter 1) and Siebert (1989: 350–372).
8. For both sources, see Kelly (1991: 7, 451). For an instructive discussion of moral judgment, see Wertz (2000: chapter 7). Moral judgment in historiography is still a subject of controversy.
9. Noted by Slater (1992: 134).
10. On the dangers to civilization posed by religious zeal, see Siebert (1990*a*: chapter 2). Phillipson (1989) develops a similar analysis. The two books were published almost simultaneously, and so neither reflects the views of the other. Another useful discussion of Hume's treatment of religion in the *History* is by Herdt (1997: 168–218).
11. This contemporary reviewer's criticism is amusing and accurate: "[Hume] could describe a theological disputation with abundantly more energy and spirit than any warlike actions. . . .. His descriptions of the battles of Cressy, Poitiers, or Agincourt are much inferior . . . to his account of king Henry the Eighth's disputation with John Lambert" (quoted in Hicks 1996: 253). Indeed, the Lambert passage is pure mock-heroic. When Henry, the Pope's "Defender of the Faith," seconded by his battalions of theologians and lawyers, deploying their quotations and syllogisms, takes the field against the unyielding heretic Lambert, the king must finally resort to the argumentum ad baculum, that ultima ratio regum—words engraved on Louis XIV's cannons—asking Lambert "whether he were resolved to live or to die." In this case, Henry's "final argument of kings" was not the cannon but the burning stake (HE 3.262–4).
12. A number of studies take note of these newer features. One of the best is Phillips (2000); also see Philips (2008) for his informative general essay. Of course, ancient history is not totally devoid of some of these features: Herodotus, in particular, sometimes digresses, occasionally including minute but revealing detail.

13. Slater (1992: 146) suggests that Hume uses similar satiric diction when slyly describing the righteous constipation of the Presbyterians, "reposing on their seats" and thus "strenuously" rejecting "the posture prescribed to them" of kneeling for communion—a passage Hume expurgated after the first edition. O'Brien (1997: 74–82) discusses Hume's use of satire and notes persuasively that Hume's emphasis on Cromwell's inarticulate speech recalls Swift's association of enthusiasm with "bizarre, formless energy." Also see Potkay (2001).

14. Among them, Mossner (1980: chapter 23), Popkin (1965: ix–xxxi), Wootton (2009: 453–458). Certainly that was Voltaire's assertion as well: see my second paragraph.

15. Slater (1992: 155) documents Hume's continuing revisions that render Charles even more sympathetic and Parliament much more blameworthy.

16. See Siebert (1990*a*: 52–57); see also Siebert (1990*b*: 7–27).

17. An anecdote related with amusing detail in Mossner (1980: 251).

18. See Siebert (1990*a*: 45–51). Many contemporary reviewers faulted Hume for playing fast and loose with sources—especially when his accounts offended their own views or values. Hume's letters (e.g., LET 1.285) reveal that he regarded first-hand sources as conflicting and unreliable—indeed, even eyewitnesses of an event often differ in their accounts—and thus may have envisioned the historian as sorting through them judiciously and producing his own imaginative reconstruction—a goal recognized by some later historical theorists. Wootton (2009: 285) calls this "a novel . . . conception of progress in historical knowledge." True enough, although Hume's reconstructions, as I have shown, can sometimes be didactically biased or shaped.

19. That history could strongly—and properly—resemble fiction and romance was recognized in Hume's day, as in a passage by novelist Henry Fielding quoted by Hicks (1996: 210). Indeed many contemporary novels had a title beginning with "The History of . . . ." More recently, Hilson (1978: 205–222) has pointed to that possibility, especially the sentimental dimension of Hume's *History*. Other studies have also considered aspects of fictional representation: for example, Braudy (1970), Damrosch (1989), O'Brien (1997: 60), Phillips (2000: chapter 1). For a more general study, see Gossman (1990: 3, 242–256). According to a recent critic, the *History* was ideally suited for a remake into a sentimental novel published in 1785; see Wall (2008: 21–40).

20. Sometimes, however, Hume seems to go that far, as in his near-fabulous account of William Wallace (HE 2.125–31) or the marquis of Montrose (HE 6.20–5). See Price (1991: 93–95); see also Siebert (1992*a*: 57–60). Slater (1992: 139) points out that Hume later somewhat reduced the superhuman dimensions of Montrose, but Montrose still remains much larger than life.

21. Concerning irony, see, for example, Price (1965). Phillips (2003: 436–449) argues that Hume employs a double perspective—one intimate and sympathetic, the other detached and ironical; this he terms a "tension between cognitive distantiation and affective proximity." See also his (2000: 60–78, 342–344). It is admittedly remarkable that Hume's *History* could be perceived as both ironical and emotional.

22. Norton bases his introduction to *Hume: Philosophical Historian* mainly on Hume's philosophical canon and ends up judging the *History* "a non sequitur of his philosophical work" (1965: xlix). Wootton (2009) bases his assessment of the *History* more on Hume's other writings than on the text of the work itself. Thus, I believe he overstates Hume's praise of civil liberty. He claims that Hume was generally sympathetic to Parliament until after 1641 (Wootton 2009: 471–472). But in the actual text of the *History*, covering the years before and including 1641, Hume repeatedly defends royal prerogative and tradition and

excoriates the actions of Parliament. See HE 5.291–300, covering the year 1640, for one of many instances. Baier (2008) recognizes "some revisions of his moral theory" (55) in the *History*, but later observes that "the historical writings wonderfully unite" the views expressed in Hume's other writing (174). Herdt agrees with my argument. She observes that writing the *History* "presses Hume to turn from theorizing . . . to put his ideas into practice. . . . The clean air of theory is left behind" (Herdt 1997: 188–189). She does not pursue the possibilities very far, however. The subtitle of Wertz's (2008) book, *From Theory to Practice*, is misleading, for his discussions are preponderantly based on Hume's theory.

23. Sir Thomas More is another exception to the rule. In his case, religious zeal had vitiated the humanizing effect of liberal studies. See HE 3.215–16.

24. For one of many expressions of this view, see HE 5.379–81 and n. [AA], HE 5.572. For a detailed exposition of this argument, see Siebert (1984*b*: 379–96); also Siebert (1984*a*: 77–113).

25. For a detailed discussion, including the eighteenth- and early nineteenth-century context of Hume's views, see Siebert (1997: 62–79). Thus, when Mossner (1980: 47) says that "Hume never altered his youthful opinion of the Dark Ages," his conclusion is both wrong and indicative of the problem of assuming that Hume's thought is monolithic.

26. One example is Hume's vivid sentence that, during the Crusades, medieval Europe appeared "loosened . . . from its foundations, and seemed to precipitate itself in one united body upon the east" (HE 1.237). The phrasing comes directly from the Byzantine historian Anna Comnena without attribution. Both Robertson and Gibbon use the sentence and quote her by name. See Siebert (1997: 78 n20). Thorough documentation is of course an innovation of modern history.

27. Thus, Slater (1992) is invaluable in casting light on Hume's intentions. His entire study, to my knowledge, is available only in his unpublished dissertation (Oxford, D. Phil, 1990).

28. See, for example, Livingston (1984: chapter 8); also, Phillips (2000: 75–76) and Phillips (2008: 407). See also Herdt (1997: 264 nn. 37, 38).

29. In 1964, the distinguished British historian Hugh Trevor-Roper could lament the eclipse of Hume's *History* and assert that it "deserves to reappear"—from a collection of Trevor-Roper's essays (2010: 120–8). He continues, "Besides, [Hume] could write. A writer whose faultless, ironic style struck despair into the heart of Gibbon should not be allowed to die" (128). Hume's masterpiece has certainly reappeared, and it is as readable today as it was when first published. See, for example Price's just praise (1991: 104–5). I must confess that in reviewing passages to prepare this essay I frequently could not stop reading onward, even though I have read the whole work several times before. Should any admirer of Hume not have had this pleasure, please deny yourself no longer.

BIBLIOGRAPHY

Baier, Annette C. (2008). *Death and Character: Further Reflections on Hume*. Cambridge: Harvard University Press.

Braudy, Leo. (1970). *Narrative Form in History and Fiction: Hume, Fielding, and Gibbon*. Princeton: Princeton University Press.

Damrosch, Leo. (1989). *Fictions of Reality in the Age of Hume and Johnson*. Madison: University of Wisconsin Press.

Gibbon, Edward. (1794/1966). *Memoirs of My Life*, ed. Georges A. Bonnard. London: Nelson.

Gossman, Lionel. (1990). *Between History and Literature*. Cambridge: Harvard University Press.

Herdt, Jennifer A. (1997). *Religion and Faction in Hume's Moral Philosophy*. Cambridge: Cambridge University Press.

Hicks, Philip. (1996). *Neoclassical History and English Culture: From Clarendon to Hume*. New York: St. Martin's.

Hilson, J. C. (1978). "Hume: The Historian as Man of Feeling," in J. C. Hilson, M. M. B. Jones, and J. R. Watson, eds., *Augustan Worlds*. Bristol: Leicester University Press, 205–222.

Kelly, Donald R. (1991). *Versions of History from Antiquity to the Enlightenment*. New Haven: Yale University Press.

Livingston, Donald. (1984). *Hume's Philosophy of Common Life*. Chicago: University of Chicago Press.

Mossner, Ernest C. (1980). *The Life of David Hume*, 2nd ed. Oxford: Clarendon Press.

Norton, David Fate. (1965). "Introduction," in D. F. Norton and R. H. Popkin, eds., *David Hume: Philosophical Historian*. Indianapolis: Bobbs-Merrill.

O'Brien, Karen. (1997). *Narratives of Enlightenment: Cosmopolitan History from Voltaire to Gibbon*. Cambridge: Cambridge University Press.

Phillips, Mark Salber. (2000). *Society and Sentiment: Genres of Historical Writing in Britain, 1740–1820*. Princeton: Princeton University Press.

Phillips, Mark Salber. (2003). "Relocating Inwardness: Historical Distance and the Transition from Enlightenment to Romantic Historiography," *PMLA* 118, 436–449.

Phillips, Mark Salber. (2008). "'The Most Illustrious Philosopher and Historian of the Age': Hume's *History of England*," in E. Radcliffe, ed., *A Companion to Hume*, ed. Oxford: Blackwell Publishing, 406–22.

Phillipson, Nicholas (1989). *Hume*. New York: St. Martin's.

Popkin, Richard H. (1965). "Skepticism and the Study of History," in D. F. Norton and R. H. Popkin, eds., *David Hume: Philosophical Historian*. Indianapolis: Bobbs-Merrill, ix–xxxi.

Potkay, Adam. (2001). "Hume's 'Supplement to Gulliver': The Medieval Volumes of *The History of England*," *Eighteenth-Century Life* 25, 32–43.

Price, John Valdimir. (1965). *The Ironic Hume*. Austin: University of Texas Press.

Price, John Valdimir. (1991). *David Hume*. Boston: Twayne.

Siebert, Donald T. (1984a). "David Hume's Last Words: The Importance of *My Own Life*," *Studies in Scottish Literature* 19, 132–147.

Siebert, Donald T. (1984b). "Hume on Idolatry and Incarnation," *Journal of the History of Ideas* 45, 379–396.

Siebert, Donald T. (1989). "The Sentimental Sublime in Hume's *History of England*," *Review of English Studies New Series* 40, 350–372.

Siebert, Donald T. (1990a). *The Moral Animus of David Hume*. Newark: University of Delaware Press.

Siebert, Donald T. (1990b). "The Aesthetic Execution of Charles I: Clarendon to Hume," in W. B. Thesing, ed., *Executions and the British Experience from the 17th to the 20th Century*. Jefferson, NC, and London: McFarland & Company, 7–27.

Siebert, Donald T. (1997). "Chivalry and Romance in the Age of Hume," *Eighteenth-Century Life* 21, 62–79.

Slater, Graeme. (1992). "Hume's Revisions of *The History of England*," *Studies in Bibliography* 45, 130–157.

Trevor-Roper, Hugh. (2010). *History and the Enlightenment*. New Haven: Yale University Press.

Wall, Cynthia. (2008). "'Chasms in the Story': Sophia Lee's *The Recess* and David Hume's *History of England*," in R. Swenson and E. Lauterbach, eds., *Imagining Selves: Essays in Honor of Patricia Meyers Spacks*. Newark: University of Delaware Press, 21–40.

Weis, Charles M. and Frederick A. Pottle, eds. (1970). *Boswell in Extremes*. New Haven: Yale University Press.

Wertz, Spencer K. (2000). *Between Hume's Philosophy and History: Historical Theory and Practice*. Lanham, MD: University Press of America.

Wootton, David. (2009). "David Hume: 'The Historian,'" in D. F. Norton and J. Taylor, eds., *The Cambridge Companion to Hume*, 2nd ed. Cambridge: Cambridge University Press.

FOR FURTHER READING

The secondary literature cited above does not include everything worth consulting, of course. My own emphases dictated my references. I did not cite, for example, the useful books by Victor G. Wexler, *David Hume and the History of England* (1979); Nicholas Capaldi and Donald W. Livingston (eds.), *Liberty in Hume's History of England* (1990); James Fieser, *Early Responses to Hume's History of England*, 2 vols. (2005); the work of J. G. A. Pocock; or more general studies like those of Duncan Forbes, *Hume's Philosophical Politics* (1975) and Claudia M. Schmidt, *David Hume: Reason in History* (2003). For additional references, both primary and secondary, one may consult Hicks, *Neoclassical History*; Mossner, *Life of David Hume*; Norton and Popkin, *David Hume: Philosophical Historian*; O'Brien, *Narratives of Enlightenment*; Phillips, both *Society and Sentiment* and "The Most Illustrious Philosopher and Historian"; Siebert, *Moral Animus*; and Wootton, "David Hume: 'The Historian.'" The important study *David Hume: Historical Thinker, Historical Writer*, ed. Mark G. Spencer (University Park: Pennsylvania State University Press, 2013) appeared after I finished this essay. This book has much to say about Hume the historian, especially the connection between Hume's "philosophical" and historical writing. Finally I wish to thank Professor Mark A. Box for reading this essay in manuscript and making valuable suggestions and comments; also to acknowledge his important study *The Suasive Art of David Hume* (Princeton: Princeton University Press, 1990), which is among those books treating the evolving nature of Hume's thought.

CHAPTER 28

HUME'S PHILOSOPHICAL ECONOMICS

TATSUYA SAKAMOTO

I THE PHILOSOPHICAL CHARACTER OF HUME'S SOCIAL SCIENCE

IN eighteenth-century Britain, "economics" as a specialized study of economic subjects had not yet gained currency. Although the term "political economy" was becoming increasingly common, it had not established what modern economics has achieved both intellectually and institutionally. In Hume's time, there were two leading strands of economic discourse in Britain. One grew out of the academic tradition of natural law or jurisprudence. Major works of the natural law tradition extending from Hugo Grotius (1583–1645) to Francis Hutcheson (1694–1746) were taught and seriously studied at Scottish universities. They discussed various economic subjects, such as the division of labor, value, price, money, and the nature of wealth. Adam Smith (1723–1790), Hume's life-long friend and Hutcheson's former student and successor at the University of Glasgow, was educated and trained in this strand and became the "father" of modern economics with his *Inquiry into the Nature and Causes of the Wealth of Nations* (1776).

The other strand of economic discourse arose from the broader crop of less academic and more journalistic and practically oriented writings steadily growing since the previous century. This has traditionally been called "mercantilism," whose representative works were written by various illustrious figures including merchants, politicians, clergymen, and others with various professional backgrounds. Among many others, Thomas Mun (1571–1641), Josiah Child (1630–1699), Charles Davenant (1656–1714), Daniel Defoe (1660–1731), and Josiah Tucker (1713–1799) published important works with extensive and enduring influence on their contemporary and succeeding generations. A work of towering importance in this tradition, although with a more systematic character, was written by Sir James Steuart (1713–1780), Hume's and Smith's close friend and a Jacobite exile. His seminal work, *An Inquiry into the Principles of Political Oeconomy* (1767), is now believed to be comparable in its historical and scientific significance to Smith's *Wealth of Nations*. Against this background, Hume's *Political Discourses* (1752), his major work on economics, occupied an indispensable place. For both Steuart and Smith, Hume's work provided a vital starting point to develop their own systems of economics. Without Hume's work, neither of the two could have written his own classic works, at least not in the way he actually did.[1]

Here, I will not delve into any general account of Hume's economics itself or into any historical assessment of the particular issues involved. For this purpose, there is a wealth of literature from various perspectives easily available to general readers.[2] Given this galaxy of splendid works, I would rather explore in the present essay a specific philosophical issue related to the nature and origin of Hume's economics. Indeed, Hume was not the only or first philosopher-economist in the history of economics. As typical examples, we can cite John Locke (1632–1704) and George Berkeley (1685–1753), who composed with Hume a British empirical trio. Although Locke's treatise on money, trade, and the rate of interest (1691) and Berkeley's social criticism on Irish economic questions of his times (1735–1737) still occupy particular places in history, neither of them expressed any methodological or systematic intention as manifestly as Hume did in his economic work. Locke and Berkeley wrote on economic subjects simply because they were required to do so, confronted with the serious social and economic issues of their times. Their professional positions (a future member of the Board of Trade and Bishop of Cloyne respectively), as well as their respectable status as philosophers, made it imperative for them to publish what they thought on these issues quite independently of their philosophical projects.

By contrast, Hume's writing of economic essays was driven, before anything else, by a purely philosophical purpose of realizing his earlier announced project of "politics" as one of the principal departments of the Science of Man (T Intro. 4–5/xv–xvi). The project was steadily realized by Hume's successive publications: first, by the "morals" expounded in Book 3 of the *Treatise*; second, by the "politics" and "criticism" in thematically related essays in *Essays Moral and Political* (1741–1742, 1748); and third, by economic and political essays in the *Political Discourses*. The *History of England* in six volumes (1754–1762) also made effective use of his economic theory throughout his historical narrative.[3] In Hume's case, unlike in Locke, Berkeley, and others, his economic works were written quite independently of his social obligation or profession and were driven by his consistent purpose and intention to realize what he had promised to readers in the introduction to the *Treatise*. J. A. Schumpeter's (1994/1954: 472n) remark that Hume's economics "has nothing whatever to do with either his psychology or his philosophy" is challenged by the fact that a number of significant attempts have been made over the years and will arguably continue to be made to discover the philosophical nature of Hume's economic theories as one of the forerunners of various, and sometimes mutually opposing, modern social and economic theories.

They cover such wide areas of issues as monetarist, inflationist, institutionalist, public choice, and game theories.[4]

In the opening paragraphs of the first essay, "Of Commerce," in the *Political Discourses* (1752), his major work on economics, Hume distinguished between "shallow" and "abstruse" thinkers and gives credence to the latter as "the most useful and valuable" sort of people. After remarking that "[a]n author is little to be valued, who tells us nothing but what we can learn from every coffee-house conversation," Hume continues to define a more philosophical way for scientific argument on politics and economics. The detailed methodological observation placed at the beginning of the entire twelve essays has a philosophical quality never to be expected from any work contemporary to that of Hume. He says,

> All people of *shallow thought* are apt to decry even those of solid understanding, as abstruse thinkers, and metaphysicians, and refiners; and never will allow any thing to be just which is beyond their own weak conceptions. . . .. Every judgment or conclusion, with them, is particular. *They cannot enlarge their view to those universal propositions, which comprehend under them an infinite number of individuals, and include a whole science in a single theorem*. . . .. But however intricate they may seem, it is certain, that *general principles, if just and sound, must always prevail in the general course of things*, though they may fail in particular cases; and it is the chief business of philosophers to *regard the general course of things*. I may add, that it is also the *chief business of politicians*; especially in the domestic government of the state, where the public good, which is, or ought to be their object, depends on *the concurrence of a multitude of causes*; not, as in foreign politics, on accidents and chances, and the caprices of a few persons. (ESY 253–4, emphasis added)

In short, Hume was trying to say to readers that they were reading a kind of philosophical work different from any other that they were accustomed to. The opening also echoes Hume's earlier essay "Of Essay-Writing" in the *Essays Moral and Political* (1741–1742). He had there defined himself as, "a kind of resident or ambassador from the dominions of learning to those of conversation" and used an economic rhetoric to say, "[t]he balance of trade we need not be jealous of, nor will there be any difficulty to preserve it on both sides. The materials of this commerce must chiefly be furnished by conversation and common life: The manufacturing of them alone belongs to learning" (ESY 535). The contrast between the dominions of "learning" and those of "conversation" certainly foretells the abstruse-shallow contrast in the later work, as well as suggesting the philosopher-vulgar contrast generally employed throughout his works.

Thus, we know that as early as 1741, economic issues were already in Hume's intellectual purview, set against the background of fierce political and economic antagonism between European countries. Hume's liberalist outlook was also clear by his critical reference to the balance of trade as the hallmark of mercantilist policy. Undoubtedly, the opening passage of the *Political Discourses* was a natural growth of this early position and outlook. At the same time, Hume in the later essay proudly characterized his own work as "uncommon" and "too refined and subtle for such vulgar subjects" (ESY 255). The contrast with the speculative character of the 1741 essay provides a sure sign of the intellectual maturation in the meantime. Thus, given Hume's "economics" as a gradual product of his intellectual development since the early essay, it becomes a matter of historical and theoretical interest to trace this development and clarify how Hume's philosophy in the *Treatise* came to be recast in the first *Enquiry* into the methodological foundation of his social science in the *Political Discourses*.

In the following arguments, I will not examine strictly what place Hume's philosophical or methodological position should occupy in the spectrum of modern social and economic theories. I would rather seek to shed a modest light on the way in which Hume's economic theory was developed in conjunction with, or more properly speaking, as an integral part of his grand philosophical project. I thereby expect to confirm the degree to which Hume, as one of the pioneers of any alleged type of modern theory—be it quantity theory of money, game theory, public choice theory, or some other—paved the way to establish economics as a science. The crux of the matter is the theory of causal reasoning that served Hume's social and economic theorizing at the deepest level and sustained the methodological foundation of Hume's social science in general and of his "economics" in particular.

II HUME'S THEORY OF CAUSATION AS METHODOLOGY OF SOCIAL SCIENCE

When attempting to address the question of methodology of science in Hume's philosophy, the theory of causation, on the one hand, and the theory of liberty and necessity, on the other, deserve special attention. In the *Treatise*, the two arguments are divided between Book 1, Part 3 and Book 2, Part 3, but in the *Enquiry*, they are combined into one better-organized argument in Sections 7 and 8. As I argue, this indicates Hume's intention to recast the two theories in the *Treatise*—to reorganize and combine them—so that they can effectively serve as the methodological foundation of the Science of Man. Notwithstanding Hume's general confidence of the final validity of his theory of causation as the uniform and consistent foundation of both the natural/physical and moral/social sciences, he felt a serious need to establish the ultimate unity of the two sciences in more convincing ways than had been done in the *Treatise*. In fact, Hume's treatment of the issue in the *Enquiry* was much revised and substantially improved. The space devoted to this particular issue significantly increased between the two works (compare T 2.3.1.1–18/399–407 and EU 8.1–20/80–91). Given the special importance of the section "Of Liberty and Necessity" as "not only the longest but one of the most philosophically important sections of the *Enquiry*" (Millican 2002: 59)[5] and also given T. L. Beauchamp's expert observation that, "virtually all parts of [the *Enquiry*] are the products of fresh writing" (2000: lxi), there is no doubt that Hume made great efforts in the *Enquiry* to refresh his argument to establish the ultimate unity of the natural/physical and moral/social sciences.

In Hume's view, the idea of necessary connection in natural and moral realms ultimately derives from the same set of objective and subjective conditions. One is the observation of "constant conjunction" between cause and effect and the other is the customary "inference" from cause and effect in the mind of the observer. The idea of *necessary connection* or *power*, traditionally sanctioned as the ultimate and sacred origin of causation by great philosophers before Hume, was demolished by him as unfounded in experience. Hume boldly replaced the traditional idea by the customary and subjective belief that ultimately arises from observing contiguity, succession, and constant conjunction between cause and effect.

In the section "Of Liberty and Necessity" in Book 2 of the *Treatise*, Hume recapitulates the theory of causation in Book 1 and tries to prove the unity of the two kinds of sciences as follows: "To this end *a very slight and general view of the common course of human affairs* will be sufficient. ... Whether we consider mankind according to *the difference of sexes, ages, governments, conditions, or methods of education*; the same uniformity and regular operation of natural principles are discernible" (T 2.3.1.5/401, emphasis added). Hume proceeds to give each of the five differences an interesting illustration and effectively argues first that, "[t]here is *a general course of nature in human actions*, as well as in the operations of the sun and the climate" and second, that, "[t]here are also *characters peculiar to different nations and particular persons*, as well as common to mankind" (T 2.3.1.10/402–03, emphasis added). Notwithstanding a possible conflict between the "general course of nature in human actions" and the apparent diversity and peculiarity of human affairs, Hume emphasizes the essential identity of the natural/physical and the moral/social phenomena as follows:

> The skin, pores, muscles, and nerves of a day-labourer are different from those of a man of quality: So are his sentiments, actions and manners. *The different stations of life influence the whole fabric, external and internal*; and *these different stations arise necessarily, because uniformly, from the necessary and uniform principles of human nature.* Men cannot live without society, and cannot be associated without government. *Government makes a distinction of property, and establishes the different ranks of men. This produces industry, traffic, manufactures, law-suits, war, leagues, alliances, voyages, travels, cities, fleets, ports*, and all those other actions and objects, which cause *such a diversity*, and at the same time maintain *such an uniformity* in human life. (T 2.3.1.9/402, emphasis added).

Although the logical sequence of cause and effect here illustrated seems highly deterministic and even mechanical, Hume's strong desire to prove the methodological similarity of the two sciences is clearly expressed.

However, Hume twists the argument at this point and responds to a critic who might suspect that "[n]ecessity is regular and certain. Human conduct is irregular and uncertain. The one, therefore, proceeds not from the other" (T 2.3.1.11/403). Hume introduces a new argument here, on "the operation of contrary and concealed causes," to show that "the chance or indifference lies only in our judgment on account of our imperfect knowledge, not in the things themselves, which are in every case equally necessary" (T 2.3.1.12/403–4). As Hume argues, seeming irregularity and inconstancy in the causal sequence of human actions can be resolved by the discovery of "contrary and concealed" causes. He uses a striking example of the "mad-men" who are commonly regarded as having "no liberty," but in practice whose actions have "less regularity and constancy." This is a direct counterexample against the doubt that human liberty and the variety of motives and inclinations of men should endanger the possibility of the moral/social science. On the contrary, in Hume's view, the greater liberty a man acquires, the more regular and constant his actions become, and the greater possibility of the moral/social science emerges (T 2.3.1.13/404).

With this in mind, Hume not only twists the argument but makes an important step forward because it transposes his analytical viewpoint from the *objective* difference between nature and human action to the *subjective* difference between the natural/physical and moral/social observations in the manner of the observer's reasoning. This involves different levels of issues related to subjective insight or analytical power that are caused by the observer's custom, education, profession, and social class. Hume then distinguishes between the "vulgar" and the "philosopher" in terms of their scientific and observational ability as a determining factor in the quality of their causal reasoning. The vulgar "take things according to their first appearance, and attribute the uncertainty of events to such an uncertainty in the causes," whereas philosophers observe that "almost in every part of nature there is contained *a vast variety of springs and principles, which are hid, by reason of their minuteness or remoteness,*" and find that "'tis at least possible *the contrariety of events may not proceed from any contingency in the cause, but from the secret operation of contrary causes*" (T 1.3.12.5/132, emphasis added).

Hume continues to prove the argument through the interesting example of three sorts of professions (peasant, artisan, and philosopher), giving different views on the cause of a broken "clock." Unlike the peasant and artisan, who only make a superficial observation of the cause, a philosopher can "form a maxim that the connexion betwixt all causes and effects is equally necessary, and that its seeming uncertainty in some instances proceeds from the secret opposition of contrary causes" (T 1.3.12.5/132). Hume will reproduce the whole paragraph almost verbatim in the *Enquiry* (EU 8.13/86–8).

The distinction between the vulgar and the philosopher certainly reminds us of the distinction between the "shallow" and "abstruse" thinkers in the essay "Of Commerce." In that essay, Hume described the "abstruse" thinkers as having acquired a sufficient ability to arrive at "those universal propositions" by discovering the "general course of things" and underlying "concurrence of a multitude of causes." This naturally resonates with the "secret opposition of contrary causes" in the *Treatise* and the *Enquiry* as shown earlier. All these circumstances lead to the conclusion that Hume's vulgar–philosopher contrast in the *Treatise* and the *Enquiry* was transformed into the shallow–abstruse distinction in the *Political Discourses*. This suggests that Hume tried to solve the problem that might have made it difficult for him to establish the identity of the two sciences by combining the two methods: the theory of contrary or concealed causes on the one hand and the philosopher–vulgar distinction on the other. In fact, the two methods of reconciliation are two sides of the same coin. The secret causes hidden in the objective world of nature and society are more easily discoverable by the philosopher (or the abstruse thinker), and the consistent explanation of those causes by a more "intricate" theory is unquestionably better achieved by the same group of people.

Hume introduced the two theoretical devices (the concealed causes and the vulgar–philosopher dichotomy) as equally valid in the natural/physical and moral/social sciences, and the whole argument on this issue rested on the application of the method of natural/physical science to that of moral/social science. Given the full and complete compatibility between the two sciences, Hume finds no reason to acknowledge any unique nature of either kind of science and concludes the section with a well-known passage vividly describing a prisoner's psychology before execution as a typical example of "a connected chain of natural causes and voluntary actions," a prisoner who, "when conducted to the scaffold, foresees his death as certainly from the constancy and fidelity of his guards as from the operation of the ax or wheel" (T 2.3.1.17/406). Hume probably liked the example and reproduced it almost verbatim in EU 8.19/90–1.

III Historicization and Socialization of Methodology in the First *Enquiry*

Hume's philosophical position concerning the ultimate methodological unity of the natural/physical and moral/social sciences was certainly maintained and unchanged throughout his life. At the same time, when we compare the corresponding arguments in the *Treatise* and the *Enquiry* in closer detail, a significant change of emphasis emerges to indicate his growing awareness in the *Enquiry* of the nature and complexity of the question. Indeed, in a well-known passage in the *Enquiry*, Hume emphasizes the essential identity of the two sciences exactly as he did in the *Treatise* by presenting a highly universalistic view of human nature. "It is universally acknowledged that there is a great uniformity among the actions of men, in all nations and ages, and that human nature remains still the same, in its principles and operations. . . . Mankind are so much the same, in all times and places, that history informs us of nothing new or strange in this particular" (EU 8.7/83). Apart from Collingwood's criticism of the passage as a typical West-centered view of history (1946/1994: 83), Hume's strong desire to achieve the methodological unity of the two sciences is beyond doubt.

Behind the apparent simplistic universalism in this quotation, however, there is no ignoring a newly emerging historical outlook in Hume's awareness of the variety of human actions and social institutions. Hume not only proceeds to twist his argument as he did in the *Treatise*, but he also more explicitly qualifies the theoretical validity of the universalistic view. In the *Treatise*, Hume was more optimistic and complacent about reducing the irregularity of human actions into a mere manifestation of hidden or concealed causes in the moral and social realm. In the *Enquiry*, by contrast, he sounds seriously cautious and even critical of simplistic reductionism and more prepared to accept the historical and social variability of what we tend to regard as the product of timeless and unchangeable principles of human nature. He asks, "Are the manners of men different in different ages and countries? We learn thence *the great force of custom and education, which mould the human mind from its infancy and form it into a fixed and established character*" (EU 8.11/85–6, emphasis added). In the *Treatise*, Hume had indeed acknowledged the irregular cases of human conduct, but he preferred to deal with those cases with a one-dimensional view of the springs and principles of human action. In the *Enquiry*, by contrast, considerable emphasis is placed on the historical and social nature of our causal reasoning, ultimately rooted in "the great force of custom and education" as the historical origin of such reasoning.

After reproducing almost verbatim the entire paragraph on the vulgar–philosopher argument from the *Treatise*, as indicated earlier, Hume introduces an entirely new, extensive (three-page) argument on the social nature of causal reasoning in the moral/social sciences and defines it as the result of what happens in practical life in the real world. Between the vulgar–philosopher paragraph and the concluding "prisoner" paragraph, Hume deleted the "mad-men" passage, together with the related largely deterministic and mechanical view of human action and character. Instead, in the *Enquiry* he substituted a carefully articulated argument that goes so far as to suggest that the principles of human nature could be regarded as historical products. Hume says that "even when an action, as sometimes happens, cannot be particularly accounted for, either by the person himself or by others; *we know, in general, that the characters of men are, to a certain degree, inconstant and irregular*. This is, in a manner, the constant character of human nature." Indeed, Hume continues to compare the irregularity and unpredictability of human action to "the winds, rain, clouds, and other variations of the weather" that are equally unpredictable, but he stresses the fact that even though we truly believe that human action and weather are commonly "governed by steady principles," we confess in reality that they are "not easily discoverable by *human sagacity and inquiry*" (EU 8.15/88, emphasis added).

Let me show one major example of the change. Hume says in the *Treatise* that "[t]he same kind of reasoning runs thro' politics, war, commerce, economy, and indeed mixes itself so entirely in human life, that 'tis impossible to act or subsist a moment without having recourse to it." He then gives examples of "a prince," "a general," and "a merchant" who each expects certain regular patterns of action and behavior from those whom they deal with in their daily work, and he summarizes that, "[i]n short, as nothing more nearly interests us than *our own actions and those of others*, the greatest part of our reasonings is employ'd in judgments concerning them" (T 2.3.1.15/405, emphasis added). In the *Enquiry*, Hume expands this argument into four paragraphs, and the just quoted passage is replaced by the following:

The mutual dependence of men is so great in all societies that scarce any human action is entirely complete in itself, or is performed without some reference to the actions of others, which are requisite to make it answer fully the intention of the agent. *The poorest artificer*, who labours alone, expects at least the protection of the magistrate, to ensure him the enjoyment of the fruits of his labour. He also expects that, *when he carries his goods to market, and offers them at a reasonable price, he shall find purchasers, and shall be able, by the money he acquires, to engage others to supply him with those commodities which are requisite for his subsistence. In proportion as men extend their dealings, and render their intercourse with others more complicated*, they always comprehend, in their schemes of life, a greater variety of voluntary actions, which they expect, from the proper motives, to co-operate with their own. . . . *A manufacturer reckons upon the labour of his servants for the execution of any work as much as upon the tools which he employs*, and would be equally surprised were his expectations disappointed. *In short, this experimental inference and reasoning concerning the actions of others enters so much into human life* that no man, while awake, is ever a moment without employing it. (EU 8.17/89, emphasis added)

This is an extensive elaboration of the argument from the *Treatise* but entirely refreshed by a new quality of social and historical consciousness and expanded by strikingly economic illustrations. The prince, the general, and the merchant are replaced in the *Enquiry* by the poorest artificer and the manufacturer, and the overall economic tone is singularly emphasized. The three examples in the *Treatise* appear somewhat loose and disorganized, whereas the two contrastive examples of the "artificer" and the "manufacturer" suggest the maturity of Hume's view of class structure in market relations. Although still a pre-Smithian view of class structure and market relations constituted by independent producers (the poorest artificer, who "labours alone" and brings his products to the market) and capitalists (a "manufacturer" who employs his "servants" and owns "tools" as the means of production), Hume's view of newly emerging market relations here described is strictly in line with what he was going to present in a more systematic fashion in the *Political Discourses*.

Hume uses the example to show that interpersonal expectation and transaction between members of a market society provides a historical and institutional framework in which their everyday practice of causal reasoning and judgment effectively supports the stable functioning of the market relations *from within*. Apart from the prominently economic content, a clearly broadened historical perspective in the quoted passage serves to prove that people's everyday causal reasoning for making successful commercial transactions between themselves provides the social and historical foundation on which to build the moral/social science and, in particular, economics. This further shows that the moral/social science itself is essentially a historical product of the modern civilized society as constituted by market relations. By disclosing the other-directed or intersubjective nature of scientific causal reasoning in general, Hume established the social and historical nature of the moral/social science itself.

Following the previous argument, Hume points out the fundamental connection or identity between the vulgar person's causal reasoning, practically employed in everyday economic life, and the philosopher's professional practice of scientific reasoning. No matter how significant the differences in observational and analytical ability between the vulgar person and the philosopher, or between the shallow and the abstruse thinkers, the difference itself originates from the fundamental unity of the two sciences, on the one hand, and from the practical interaction between the two sorts of people, on the other. Hume asks:

> [w]hat would become of *history*, had we not a dependence on the veracity of the historian according to the experience which we have had of mankind? How could *politics* be a science, if laws and forms of government had not a uniform influence upon society? Where would be the foundation of *morals*, if particular characters had no certain or determinate power to produce particular sentiments, and if these sentiments had no constant operation on actions? And with what pretence could we employ our *criticism* upon any poet or polite author, if we could not pronounce the conduct and sentiments of his actors either natural or unnatural to such characters, and in such circumstances? (EU 8.18/90, emphasis added)

The reference to history, politics, criticism, and morals in this quotation reflects his clear sense of continuity in the idea of the Science of Man in the *Treatise*, as well as his conviction of the philosophical solution in *the Enquiry*. It also indicates his strong wish to further prosecute not yet completed parts of the same Science of Man that include politics, history, and aesthetics. Hume was certainly going to carry out the aspiration steadily after the *Enquiry*, in the *Political Discourses* and the two brilliant essays on criticism ("Of Tragedy" and "Of the Standard of Taste," published first in 1757 in the *Four Dissertations*) and six volumes of the *History of England* (1754–1762). As a whole, the just quoted passage shows Hume's confidence in the possibility of a moral/social science based on the regularity and constancy of social relations that are reliable and constant enough to more than compensate for the inherent irregularity and unpredictability of human nature and affairs, as he had admitted in the earlier quotation (EU 8.15/88).

IV PRACTICING SOCIAL SCIENCE: FROM THE *ESSAYS* TO THE *POLITICAL DISCOURSES*

As I have confirmed, Hume's theory of causation remained fundamentally the same from the *Treatise* to the *Enquiry*. At the core of the theory lay his philosophical ambition to establish the unity and identity of the two kinds of sciences, as well as to address problems related to the unique nature of the moral/social science. The theory was certainly improved and expanded in the later work, as we have seen, but the ambition itself remained intact. As Alexander Rosenberg observed, "Hume held that the methods of the social sciences must be fundamentally the same as those of natural science" (1993: 84). Immediately after publishing the *Treatise*, Hume started to realize his ambition in the form of specific researches in the moral/social sciences. More precisely speaking, the philosophical improvement of the *Enquiry* itself was a result of those exercises. In the rest of this essay, I seek to verify the specific ways in which Hume made successive applications of the method of social science presented in the *Treatise* in the works after the *Treatise* that have representative significance in this respect.

I first turn to two political and historical essays in the *Essays Moral and Political* (1741–1742). They are "That Politics May Be Reduced to a Science" (the "Politics" hereafter) and "Of the Rise and Progress of Arts and Sciences" (the "Rise and Progress" hereafter). These essays amply demonstrate Hume's philosophical profundity and historical erudition, and notwithstanding the different subjects they treat, both essays are driven by the same methodological motivation that has been discussed so far, namely, the nature and possibility of social science and, in particular, the problem of the extent to which the role of individuals with exceptional talent and caliber in politics and the history of arts and sciences might adversely affect and even endanger the science of politics or the general history of arts and sciences. Common to these essays are Hume's concern to examine the widely prevalent view doubting the plausibility of the science of society and history that he wished to establish. He believed that the possibility of social science would only be established once these critical views had been properly dealt with and effectively repudiated.

As Hume believed, the science of politics has long been regarded as difficult to achieve because of the common-sense view that the world of politics is, in the final analysis, controlled and determined by inclinations of and decisions made by a handful of exceptional individuals: monarchs and political leaders. Hume rebuts this view by saying in the "Politics" that "though a friend to moderation, I cannot forbear condemning this sentiment, and should be sorry to think, that human affairs admit of no greater stability, than what they receive from the casual humours and characters of particular men" (ESY 15). The similar view that a small number of geniuses truly matter was equally influential in the history of arts and sciences. Representing the common view, Hume says in the "Rise and Progress" that "[t]hose who cultivate the sciences in any state, are always few in number: . . . Chance, therefore, or secret and unknown causes, must have a great influence on the rise and progress of all the refined arts" (ESY 114). However, if the exceptional few were truly the prime engine of the rise and progress of the arts and sciences, genuine scientific research and inquiry in those areas must become impossible because such *infrequent and rare* occurrences of such events or actions caused by those exceptional few should undermine Hume's primary condition of experimental causal reasoning, viz., the observation of *constant and regular* conjunctions between causes and effects. Accordingly, Hume says in the "Rise and Progress" that

> [t]o judge by this rule, the domestic and the gradual revolutions of a state must be a more proper subject of reasoning and observation, than the foreign and the violent, which are commonly produced by single persons, and are more influenced by whim, folly, or caprice, than by general passions and interests,

and exactly for the same reason and with even more important consequence for the present essay that

> it is more easy to account for the rise and progress of commerce in any kingdom, than for that of learning. (ESY 113–114)

Commerce develops by universal human motives of self-interest or "avarice," and this special circumstance must certainly guarantee the sufficient degree of constant conjunction and customary inference from cause to effect in the world of economic activities. As discussed earlier, Hume in the *Treatise* chiefly focused on the comparative analysis of relative irregularity and uncertainty between human actions in general on the one hand and natural/physical phenomena on the other. This naturally led him to endorse the common view of the relative irregularity and uncertainty of the laws of society in comparison with the highest certainty of laws of nature. In this sense, Hume's methodological contrast in the *Treatise* was made by the qualitative difference between nature and society. By contrast, the "Politics" and the "Rise and Progress" draw a methodological dividing line not between nature and society but between the two groups of society—the elite and the commoners—and between the two contrastive motivations of each group. However, Hume's strategy for solving each problem in the *Treatise* and the two essays involved the same conceptual device; that is, in the case of the two essays, to link in one way or another the apparent irregularity and uncertainty of the actions of the few to the greater certainty and regularity of everyday actions of the common people.

Hume attempts in the two essays to identify the most profound and universal historical causes for the seemingly irregular or abrupt appearance of a few distinguished statesmen and philosophers. In Hume's view, a long course of history of a particular nation or society was certainly determined by these universal, although apparently invisible, causes. Hume's specific solution was twofold. For the first solution, he says in the "Rise and Progress" that

> [t]hough the persons, who cultivate the sciences with such astonishing success, as to attract the admiration of posterity, be always few, in all nations and all ages; it is impossible but *a share of the same spirit and genius must be antecedently diffused throughout the people among whom they arise*, in order to produce, form, and cultivate, from their earliest infancy, the taste and judgment of those eminent writers. The mass cannot be altogether insipid, from which such refined spirits are extracted. (ESY 114, emphasis added)

The second solution is presented in "Politics." Hume says, "So great is *the force of laws, and of particular forms of government*, and so little dependence have they on the humours and tempers of men, that *consequences almost as general and certain may sometimes be deduced from them, as any which the mathematical sciences afford us*" (ESY 16, emphasis added).

Thus, Hume identifies two historical and institutional conditions for overcoming the difficulty on the way to establish the science of politics and the history of arts and sciences. The first is an established *national character* that makes it possible for the particular taste and inclinations for polite arts and learning to grow, and the second is *a political system or constitution* that enables the nation to enjoy the rule of law to guarantee their liberty and property. In other words, the more polished and polite a society or nation grows historically, the higher and stronger are the possibility of moral and social science. When Hume seeks for historical and institutional conditions of the rise of social/moral science, he virtually questions the philosophical and historical validity of the civilized manners of the nation. Hume also emphasizes the utility and significance of these sciences for political leaders of a nation: "Legislators, therefore, ought not to trust the future government of a state entirely to chance, but ought to provide a system of laws to regulate the administration of public affairs to the latest posterity. Effects will always correspond to causes; and wise regulations in any commonwealth are the most valuable legacy that can be left to future ages" (ESY 24).

Hume's philosophical endorsement of the validity of causal reasoning in the moral/social sciences was inevitably combined with his historical, political, and even ideological justification of the particular type of society that makes it possible that people act and behave in their social, economic, and political relations in highly regular and predictable ways. This was also the society under the rule of law that guarantees people's rights and liberties and ensures a resulting harmonious order of market relations. Hume's renowned remark in the essay "Of Luxury" ("Of Refinement in the Arts" after the 1760 edition) in the *Political Discourses* succinctly synthesizes the methodological framework as developed by these past arguments in an impressive manner.

> The same age, which produces great philosophers and politicians, renowned generals and poets, usually abounds with skilful weavers, and ship-carpenters. We cannot reasonably expect, that a piece of woollen cloth will be wrought to perfection in a nation, which is ignorant of astronomy, or where ethics are neglected. *The spirit of the age affects all the arts*; and the minds of men, being once roused from their lethargy, and put into a fermentation, turn themselves on all sides, and carry improvements into every art and science. (ESY 270–271)

The passage is more than a typical Enlightenment manifesto about the positive and constructive nature of modern civilized society and clearly presents a theoretical vision of that society historically developing on the principle of social division of labor, not only among different sectors of industry, but also between intellectual and industrial sectors of society. It definitely shows Hume's understanding that modern civilized society is in the historical stage in which the rule of law, free economic activity, and the rising standards of people's life and polite taste for the arts and sciences all go hand in hand with each other to produce a wealthy and peaceful social order in which specialized scientific activities of "philosophers" about nature and society emerge and vigorously develop in conjunction with the steady development of the new social order. Hume does not deny some determining roles of exceptional philosophers, scientists, and politicians at certain points and situations in history, but, as a generalized understanding, he never hesitates to attach predominant importance to the more general and universal causes and conditions that promote or restrict the appearance of those exceptional individuals. When he famously says in the same essay that "[t]hus *industry, knowledge, and human-ity*, are linked together by an indissoluble chain, and are found, from experience as well as reason, to be peculiar to the more polished, and, what are commonly denominated, the more luxurious ages" (ESY 271), he is alluding to the central role of philosophy or scientific reasoning in general as necessary and inevitable products of the stable and permanent working of modern civilized society.

As I attempted to argue elsewhere (Sakamoto 2011), Hume started compiling a set of memoranda on economic subjects in the quiet solitude of his home at Ninewells in Scotland around 1747. According to my thesis, the compiling work exactly coin-cided with his finishing of the draft for the *Philosophical Essays Concerning Human Understanding* (the *Enquiry* from 1758 edition), to be published the following year. As M. A. Stewart (2002: 83) pointed out, Hume started to prepare the *Enquiry* as early as 1745–1746, when serving as a tutor to the Marquise of Annandale in England, and the work was almost finished when he started preparation for writing on economic sub-jects. In other words, Hume's full-scale thinking and writing on economics was initiated on the basis of the accomplished methodology of the *Enquiry*. This naturally suggests a close interaction between Hume's philosophy and economics. The *Enquiry* was finished in Scotland when Hume departed for his diplomatic mission to European countries with General St. Claire. As I have argued (Sakamoto 2003), it was probably during this mission that Hume started to write the brilliant essay "Of National Characters," added to the third edition of the *Essays Moral and Political*, published in 1748. The essay was intended to develop a fully consistent refutation of the climatic theory of national char-acter, which had considerable influence through the works of Dubos and Montesquieu. When finishing the essay on national character, Hume had probably not seen the latter's masterpiece, *The Spirit of the Laws*, published in the same year. All these facts strongly endorse the possibility that Hume's economic writing not only coincided with his revis-ing work of the *Treatise* into the *Enquiry*, but also that the economic work was philo-sophically sustained and encouraged by the revising work.

V CONCLUSION: HUME'S PHILOSOPHICAL ECONOMICS

Throughout this essay, I have sought to indicate a profound connection between Hume's philosophy and economics, mainly from a methodological point of view, by shedding new light on his theory of causation. Needless to say, I have not intended to develop a fully systematic study of the subject but only wished to confirm the simple fact that

Hume's economics could not have developed as it actually did without his clear purpose and intention of giving a definite philosophical status to that particular department of inquiry within his grand project of the Science of Man. I also expect that it will clarify the reason why Hume's economics ought to be regarded as occupying a unique place, even in the narrower context of the "Scottish triangle." Hume's economics was distinct from both the mass of contemporary mercantilist literature as finally synthesized by Steuart and from Adam Smith's *Wealth of Nations* as a product of the academic jurisprudence. Hume was trying to steer between the two extremes of economic discourses and meet the challenge by making a bold philosophical attempt to bridge the gap between the normative rationalism of natural jurisprudence and the practical empiricism of mercantilist literature. Consequently, Hume's economics finally established itself as a distinctive system that is neither simply normative or rationalistic nor one-sidedly journalistic.

Hume attempted to realize a "reconciling project" for the science of society. Although the expression was used by Hume to mean a philosophical reconciliation between liberty and necessity,[6] it may safely be used to indicate his ambition as an "economist" to develop a science of economics that was built on an exact philosophical foundation, as well as one inspired by the spirit of serving the public good of civilized society. The striking message in the essay on luxury that *"industry, knowledge, and humanity, are linked together by an indissoluble chain"* had already appeared in different wordings in Section 1 of the *Enquiry*, entitled "Of the Different Species of Philosophy." There, Hume gives a comparative analysis of two types of philosophizing: the active and social on the one hand and the speculative and solitary on the other. Hume apparently sounds as if he is giving unconditional support and approval to the former type of philosopher as the only historically relevant social existence in a civilized society, but, in the final analysis, his ideal philosopher is described as enjoying a mixed kind of life of the two opposite philosophers. A renowned remark appears therein:

> It seems, then, that nature has pointed out *a mixed kind of life as most suitable to the human race*, and secretly admonished them to allow none of these biasses to *draw* too much, so as to incapacitate them for other occupations and entertainments. Indulge your passion for science, says she, but *let your science be human, and such as may have a direct reference to action and society. Abstruse thought and profound researches I prohibit*, and will severely punish, by the pensive melancholy which they introduce, by the endless uncertainty in which they involve you, and by the cold reception which your pretended discoveries shall meet with, when communicated. *Be a philosopher; but, amidst all your philosophy, be still a man.* (EU 1.6/8–9, emphasis added, except *"draw"*)

Hume's final message was not simple and one-sided, however. In the same passages, he goes on to warn against the tendency, which he perceived as spreading in his time, of "the absolute rejecting of all profound reasonings, or what is commonly called *metaphysics*." Hume then repeats the same anatomy–painter dichotomy that he had used in the final part of the *Treatise* (T 3.3.6.6/620) and foretells the abstruse–shallow dichotomy in the opening essay ("Of Commerce") in the *Political Discourses* by strongly endorsing the former type of philosophy or science. He concludes the argument with a strikingly similar wording to the passage quoted earlier from the essay "Of Luxury" (ESY 270):

> Besides, we may observe, *in every art or profession, even those which most concern life or action, that a spirit of accuracy, however acquired, carries all of them nearer their perfection, and renders them more subservient to the interests of society.* And though a philosopher may live remote from business, *the genius of philosophy, if carefully cultivated by several, must gradually diffuse itself throughout the whole society, and bestow a similar correctness on every art and calling.* The politician will acquire greater foresight and subtility, in the subdividing and balancing of power; the lawyer more method and finer principles in his reasonings; and the general more regularity in his discipline, and more caution in his plans and operations. *The stability of modern governments above the ancient, and the accuracy of modern philosophy, have improved, and probably will still improve, by similar gradations.* (EU 1.9/10, emphasis added)

Here, Hume leaves no doubt that what he conceptualizes as "philosophy" has acquired a new historical meaning as an indispensable and working part of the entire network of civilized society. That society also functions as a system of social division of labor, under which the social significance of the philosopher's work and contribution is realized as an essential part of the civilizing process. Philosophy is no longer a solitary work engaged in separation from the rest of the world. No matter how specialized and "abstruse" it might appear in the eyes of the general public, it indeed serves the public in ways that no other professions of society can possibly do. The activities of politicians and generals, let alone those of merchants and artificers, are not guaranteed their stable workings and developments without a vital contribution from philosophers, no matter how distant and hidden the relationship may be. The nature of "the spirit of the age that affects all the arts" (ESY 270) is now known to mean precisely "a spirit of accuracy." Economic activities of the common people greatly benefit from the spirit of accuracy constantly supplied by philosophers, and the spirit of industry and commerce furnishes the practical foundation for philosophers to discover the laws of nature and society. The spirit of accuracy, speculative philosophy, and the wider network of people in society and markets develop in close communication with each other, mutually encourage each other, and participate in strengthening the order of civilized society: thus, the true meaning of Hume's celebrated manifesto, "industry, knowledge and humanity are linked together by an indissoluble chain."[7]

ABBREVIATIONS OF WORKS CITED

ESY   *Essays: Moral, Political, and Literary.* Revised edition by E. F. Miller. Indianapolis: Liberty Classics, 1985.

EU   *An Enquiry Concerning Human Understanding.* Edited by T. L. Beauchamp. Oxford: Clarendon, 2000.

T   *A Treatise of Human Nature*. Edited by D. F. Norton and M. J. Norton. Oxford: Clarendon, 2007.

Notes

1. See Hutchison (1988), Skinner (2003).
2. For instance, Dow (2002), Rotwein (2007/1955), Sakamoto (2008), Schabas (2012), Skinner (1993). A collection of remarkable papers by various scholars was edited by Wennerlind and Schabas (2008) to serve expert readers. Chapters in various monographs on related subjects contain fine introductions to Hume's economics as a whole: Hont (2005), Murphy (2009), Redman (1997), Rostow (1990), Schabas (2005).
3. See a pioneering work by Stockton (1976).
4. For instance, Marc-Arthur and Lapidus (2005), Lucas (1996), Moss (1991), Nakano (2006), Sturn (2004), Sugden (2005), Wennerlind (2001).
5. See also Millican (2010).
6. See Russell (1995: 58–70).
7. For the social background, see Berry (2006), Emerson (2009), Macfarlane (2001).

Bibliography

Berry, Christopher J. (2006). "Hume and the Customary Causes of Industry, Knowledge and Humanity," *History of Political Economy* 38, 291–317.

Beauchamp, Tom L. (2000). "Introduction: A History of the *Enquiry Concerning Human Understanding*," in David Hume, *An Enquiry Concerning Human Understanding*. Edited by T. L. Beauchamp. Oxford: Clarendon, xi–civ.

Caffentzis, George C. (2001). "Hume, Money, and Civilization: Or, Why Was Hume a Metalist?" *Hume Studies* 27, 301–335.

Collingwood, R. G. (1946/1994). *The Idea of History*, revised edition. Oxford: Oxford University Press.

Dow, Sheila. (2002). "Interpretation: The Case of David Hume," *History of Political Economy* 34 (2), 399–420.

Emerson, Roger L. (2009). *Essays on David Hume, Medical Men and the Scottish Enlightenment*. Farnham: Ashgate.

Henderson, Willie. (2010). *The Origins of David Hume's Economics*. London: Routledge.

Hont, Istvan. (2005). *Jealousy of Trade: International Competition and the Nation-State in Historical Perspective*. Cambridge, MA: Harvard University Press.

Hutchison, Terence. (1988). *Before Adam Smith: The Emergence of Political Economy, 1661–1776*. Oxford: Basil Blackwell.

Lucas, Robert. (1996). "Nobel Lecture: Monetary Neutrality," *Journal of Political Economy* 104 (4), 89–101.

Macfarlane, Alan. (2001). "David Hume and the Political Economy of Agrarian Civilization," *History of European Ideas* 27, 79–91.

Marc-Arthur, Diaye, and André Lapidus. (2005). "A Humean Theory of Choice of Which Rationality May Be One Consequence," *European Journal of the History of Economic Thought* 12 (1), 89–111.

Millican, Peter. (ed.). (2002). *Reading Hume on Human Understanding: Essays on the First Enquiry*. Oxford: Clarendon Press.

Millican, Peter. (2002). "The Context, Aims, and Structure of Hume's First Enquiry," in P. Millican ed., *Reading Hume on Human Understanding: Essays on the First Enquiry*. Oxford: Clarendon Press, 27–65.

Millican, Peter. (2010). "Hume's Determinism," *Canadian Journal of Philosophy* 40 (4), 611–642.

Moss, Laurence S. (1991). "Thomas Hobbes's Influence on David Hume: The Emergence of a Public Choice Tradition," *History of Political Economy* 23 (4), 587–612.

Murphy, Antoin E. (2009). *The Genesis of Macroeconomics: New Ideas from Sir William to Henry Thornton*. Oxford: Clarendon Press.

Nakano, Takeshi. (2006). "'Let Your Science Be Human': Hume's Economic Methodology," *Cambridge Journal of Economics* 30 (5), 687–700.

Paganelli, Maria Pia. (2009). "David Hume on Monetary Policy: A Retrospective Approach," *Journal of Scottish Philosophy* 7 (1), 65–85.

Redman, Deborah A. (1997). *The Rise of Political Economy as a Science: Methodology and the Classical Economists*. Cambridge MA: MIT Press.

Rosenberg, Alexander. (1993). "Hume and the Philosophy of Science," in D. F. Norton (ed.), *The Cambridge Companion to Hume*. Cambridge: Cambridge University Press, 64–89.

Rostow, W. W. (1990). *Theorists of Economic Growth from David Hume to the Present*. Oxford: Oxford University Press.

Rotwein, Eugene. (2007/1955). *Introduction to David Hume: Writings on Economics*. New Brunswick, NJ: Transaction.

Russell, Paul. (1995). *Freedom and Moral Sentiment: Hume's Way of Naturalising Responsibility*. New York: Oxford University Press.

Sakamoto, Tatsuya. (2003). "Hume's Political Economy as a System of Manners," in T. Sakamoto and H. Tanaka, eds., *The Rise of Political Economy in the Scottish Enlightenment*. London: Routledge, 86–102.

Sakamoto, Tatsuya. (2008). "Hume's Economic Theory," in E. S. Radcliffe, ed., *A Companion to Hume*. Oxford: Wiley-Blackwell, 373–387.

Sakamoto, Tatsuya. (2011). "Hume's Early Memoranda and the Making of His Political Economy," *Hume Studies* 37 (2), 131–164.

Schabas, Margaret. (2001). "David Hume on Experimental Natural Philosophy, Money, and Fluids," *History of Political Economy* 33, 411–435.

Schabas, Margaret. (2005). *The Natural Origins of Economics*. Chicago and London: University of Chicago Press.

Schabas, Margaret. (2007). "Groups Versus Individuals in Hume's Political Economy," *The Monist* 90 (2), 200–212.

Schabas, Margaret. (2008). "Hume's Monetary Thought Experiments," *Studies for the History and Philosophy of Science Part A*, 39, 161–169.

Schabas, Margaret. (2012). "Hume on Economic Well-Being," in A. Bailey and D. O'Brien, eds., *The Continuum Companion to Hume*. London and New York: Continuum, 332–348.

Schumpeter, Joseph A. (1994/1954). *History of Economic Analysis*, edited by E. B. Schumpeter with a new introduction by Mark Perlman. New York: Oxford University Press.

Skinner, Andrew. (1993). "David Hume: Principles of Political Economy," in D. F. Norton, ed., *The Cambridge Companion to Hume*. Cambridge: Cambridge University Press, 222–254.

Skinner, Andrew. (2003). "Economic Theory," in A. Broadie ed., *The Cambridge Companion to the Scottish Enlightenment*. Cambridge: Cambridge University Press, 178–204.

Stewart, M. A. (2002). "Two Species of Philosophy," in P. Millican, ed., *Reading Hume on Human Understanding: Essays on the First Enquiry*. Oxford: Clarendon Press, 67–95.

Stockton, Constance N. (1976). "Economics and Mechanism of Historical Progress in Hume's History," in D. W. Livingston and J. T. King, eds., *Hume: A Revaluation*. New York: Fordham University Press, 296–320.

Sturn, Richard. (2004). "The Sceptic as an Economist's Philosopher? Humean Utility as a Positive Principle," *European Journal of the History of Economic Thought* 11 (3), 345–375.

Sugden, Robert. (2005). "Why Rationality Is Not a Consequence of Hume's Theory of Choice," *European Journal of the History of Economic Thought* 12 (1), 113–118.

Susato, Ryu. (2006). "Hume's Nuanced Defense of Luxury," *Hume Studies* 32 (1), 167–186.

Wennerlind, Carl. (2001). "The Link Between David Hume's Treatise of Human Nature and His Fiduciary Theory of Money," *History of Political Economy* 33, 139–160.

Wennerlind, Carl. (2005). "David Hume's Monetary Theory Revisited: Was He Really a Quantity Theorist and an Inflationist?" *Journal of Political Economy* 113 (1), 223–237.

Wennerlind, Carl, and Margaret Schabas (eds.). (2008). *David Hume's Political Economy*. London and New York: Routledge.

PART V

RELIGION

CHAPTER 29

HUME ON MIRACLES

It's Part 2 that Matters

MICHAEL LEVINE

HUME's essay "Of Miracles" (1748) is not only one of the most widely read essays in the philosophy of religion—appealing to beginners and professionals alike—it is also one of the most contested. Discussion of Hume's view on miracles has focused less (and far too little) on whether he was correct than on exegetical issues—just what was he arguing? Not only is the question of whether Hume concludes (in Part 1) that one could never be justified in believing in a miracle on the basis of testimony disputed. but so too is the question of whether or not he was even arguing that no one ever could be so justified (i.e., that justified belief in miracles on the basis of testimony was not merely improbable but impossible). No matter how one answers these questions (affirmatively or negatively), Hume's essay is then employed in various ways in arguments for and against the possibility of justified belief in miracles. More than the essay itself, debates about Hume's essay are not merely instructive in relation to miracles. They also suggest something of significance about the state of philosophy of religion in general—or so I argue.

Hume (EU 10.13/116) concludes Part 1 by saying "If the falsehood of his testimony would be more miraculous than the event which he relates; then, and not till then, can he pretend to command my belief or opinion." But the idea that this sentence supports the view that Hume is claiming that one can be justified in believing in a miracle indicates not only a humorless reading of the text, but also a misinterpretation. Mackie (1982: 29) describes Hume's last sentence in "Of Miracles" to be "only a joke"—one that Mackie reiterates in the title of his book *The Miracle of Theism*. Contrary to Flew, Swinburne, and Fogelin, I argue that Hume's argument in Part 1 is a priori, and contrary to J. C. A. Gaskin, that Hume's argument applies to firsthand experience of a miracle as well as to testimony (Levine 1989; 2008).

Robert Fogelin was one of the first in several recent commentaries on Hume and miracles to claim that a close reading of the text does not support the view that Hume's argument is an a priori one. Although one cannot quarrel with exhortations to read the text closely, the disputed issues cannot be decided on how closely one reads the text or on what Hume "actually says." The crucial issues are all interpretive and require, on my view, setting them in the context of Hume's *Treatise*. Evidence indicating that Hume thought his argument against miracles was intrinsically related to the *Treatise* is contained in a letter to George Campbell, author of a *Dissertation on Miracles*. Hume writes,

> It may perhaps amuse you to learn the first hint, which suggested to me that argument which you have so strenuously attacked. I was walking in the cloisters of the Jesuits College at La Fleche . . . engaged in conversation with a Jesuit of some parts and learning who was relating to me, and urging some nonsensical miracle performed in their convent, when I was tempted to dispute against him; and as my head was full of the topics of my *Treatise of Human Nature*, which I was at that time composing, this argument immediately occurred to me.
>
> (quoted in Burns 1981: 133)

Hume's essay does not have to be placed in any historical context, as some have claimed, but rather as Hume did, in the context of his own (peculiar) empiricism, his empiricist account of meaning, his account of causation, and his theory of a posteriori reasoning. If I am right, then reading "Of Miracles" without considering it in the context of Part 1 of Hume's *Treatise*, as I think Fogelin has done, cannot result in a correct interpretation of Hume's argument in the first part of his essay.

In any case, the contemporary claim that a close reading of the text supports their respective positions implies that previous (and current) generations of Hume scholars have not read the text with sufficient care. Unlikely. Generations of interpreters have shown it is possible to read the text closely and have different views on the nature of Hume's argument in Part 1. It is, however, marginally less likely that there will be such divergent views of Hume's position on miracles if Hume's argument is exposited, as it was meant to be, in the context of the *Treatise*. His theory of a posteriori reasoning, a theory based on his account of causation and empiricism, supports an a priori reading of Hume's Part 1 argument—and no other. Given his view that divine activity is impossible to know, Hume's argument in Part 1 is in a sense superfluous. His a priori argument is logically preempted by his view on divine activity. If it were possible to know (have an *impression* of) divine activity as such, then it would be possible, on Hume's account, to justifiably believe a miracle had occurred.

Before returning to a discussion of the contemporary literature, it would be useful to present an abbreviated interpretation of Hume's argument—my own. (See Levine 1989, part I, for the complete account.) It is an interpretation that places Hume's argument in the context of his empiricism, his accounts of causation, and his related theory of a posteriori reasoning. Like Fogelin's, it is based on closely reading "Of Miracles," but my reading places it alongside Part 1 of the *Treatise*.

I Hume's Argument Against Justified Belief in Miracles in Part 1 "Of Miracles"

What is the connection between Hume's analysis of causation and his views concerning the lack of credibility of testimony to the miraculous? Hume thinks that all reasoning about matters of fact, all a posteriori reasoning, is a species of reasoning founded on the relation of cause and effect. Our judgments concerning the reliability of any testimony should therefore be consonant with the principles of experiential reasoning based on the cause–effect relation (see EU 10.5–6/111–2).

Hume's analysis of the causal relation, as he sees it, has shown that "the foundation of our inference [from cause to effect and vice versa] is the transition [in the mind, from the idea of an object to the idea of its usual attendant] arising from the accustomed union [of cause and effect]" (T 1.3.14.21/165). The inference that A will be followed by B will be warranted to the extent that our experience of B's following A has been constant (and frequent). This is because the "force," so to speak, of the "transition, in the mind, to pass from an object to the idea of its usual attendant," and the "strength" of that idea is ideally a direct function of our past experience with events "resembling" those present. The force fails to be a function of past experience to the extent that the transition is affected by ulterior motives, desires, and the like. Hume says, "If you weaken either the union or resemblance, you weaken the principle of transition, and of consequence that belief, which arises from it" (T 1.3.12.25/142). According to Hume, we should not believe any more (i.e., with a greater "strength") than we can justifiably infer on the basis of the mind's natural propensity to believe as a result of experience. To do otherwise would be to act "unnaturally." To the extent to which we believe beyond our warrant for that belief, the belief is unjustified and will be rejected by the reasonable person. All of our a posteriori reasoning is, in essence, causal reasoning according to Hume. Let's apply this to belief in miracles.

Why did Hume think that one could justifiably believe that an *extraordinary* event had occurred, under certain circumstances, but that one could never justifiably believe a *miracle* had occurred? The proposed interpretation of Hume's analysis of miracles in relation to his analysis of causation and his wider empiricism yields the answer. It also shows why it makes no difference whether we interpret Hume's argument in Part 1 "Of Miracles" against the possibility of justified belief in testimony to the miraculous as an a priori or a posteriori argument.

Hume gives the example of an extraordinary event ("a total darkness over the whole earth for eight days") that he thinks could be rendered credible on the basis of testimony (EU 10.36/127). Not only is the testimony to the event assumed very extensive and uniform, but Hume also thinks it necessary that our past experience does not render the event completely unlikely. He argues that the eight-day darkness can be "rendered probable by so many analogies." In such a case, Hume assumes that the event is natural and that "we ought to search for the causes." Hume compares this with another imaginary case. He says, "suppose, that all historians who treat of England, should agree, that, on the first of January 1600, Queen Elizabeth died . . . and that, after being interred a month, she again appeared. . . .. I must confess that I should be surprised at the concurrence of so many odd circumstances, but should not have the least inclination to believe so miraculous event" (EU 10.37/128). Since both events are equally well testified to, the reason that Hume thinks the former can be judged credible but not the latter is that, in the former case, the "event is rendered probable by so many analogies." This may appear to be nothing more than a subjective judgment on the part of Hume. His experience suggests analogies for the former type of event but not the latter. More is involved, however, than Hume's judgment.

Fogelin (2003: 18) says that Hume acknowledges "that under certain conditions it *could* be possible to establish the occurrence of a miracle based on testimony. The miracle in question concerns a worldwide interlude of eight consecutive days of darkness." Hume, however, never calls this darkness a "miracle," and he deliberately does not do so. Indeed, it is being juxtaposed with an imaginary event he does call miraculous—Elizabeth's resurrection—but says he would "not have the least inclination to believe" it. Hume's point about the darkness is that, insofar as we can accept the report of its occurrence, we must also, in accordance with his principles of a posteriori reasoning, opt for a naturalistic explanation. And so Fogelin attributes to Hume a view that he did not hold; that the eight-day darkness should be regarded as miraculous.

In the case of extraordinary events that are well attested to and for which we have suitable experiential analogies, Hume thinks that the most we are justified in believing is that the event did occur—not that the event is a miracle. We are to "search for the [natural] causes whence it might be derived" (EU 10.36/128). Such cases may require us to reassess our estimation of what nature is capable of. Statements of laws of nature must sometimes be reassessed in light of new experience, as we know on the basis of experience. Also, we must be careful not to extend our judgments as to what to believe or expect of nature to situations in which the relevant circumstances are different. This requires an explanation.

Hume relates the case of the Indian who refused to believe that water turned to ice. According to Hume, the Indian "reasoned justly" on the basis of his past experience. He refused, at first, to believe that water turned to ice, despite the fact that it was well attested to, because the event not only had the Indian's constant and uniform experience to count against it, but also because the event "bore so little analogy" to that experience (EU 10.10/113). The Indian "reasoned justly," but he extended his judgments about the properties of water to cases in which all the circumstances were not the same (i.e., the relevant circumstance here being temperature). In certain situations in which we hear testimony to extraordinary events, we may be in situations similar to that of the Indian. Indeed, according to Hume, if we justifiably believe that an extraordinary event did occur, then we *should* assume that we are in a situation like that of the Indian. We should assume this because, as I shall show, there are logically compelling reasons why the consistent Humean, in accordance with the principles of a posteriori reasoning based on Hume's analysis of causation and his empiricism, can do nothing else. A naturalistic explanation must be opted for even if one has no idea what such an explanation might be. The extraordinary event should be judged "[not] contrary to uniform experience of the course of nature in cases where all the circumstances are the same" (EU 10 n22/114n).

When we are justified in believing in an extraordinary event, then *on the basis of experience*, we should liken ourselves to the Indian. That is why, in a case like the eight days of darkness, "we ought to search for the [*natural*] causes whence it might be derived." Experience demands it. When an extraordinary event is extraordinarily well attested to, we have two options according to Hume. One is to accept the testimony and look for the event's natural causes. The other is to reject the testimony on the grounds that the event testified to bears no *significant* analogy to events as experienced. Hume thinks that testimony, no matter how reliable, *can never* establish the occurrence of a miraculous event in accordance with the principles of a posteriori reasoning (EU 10.5/111–12). Why?

Contrary to Hume, some philosophers, those employing Bayes's theorem and others, have tried to argue as follows:

> It is true that in some situations a seemingly naturally inexplicable event was later learned to have natural causes, but it is conceivable that there may be other inexplicable events for which no natural causes can be found. Why, in other words, must we liken ourselves to the Indian? Why does experience demand that we either reject belief in the event's occurrence or believe it but posit natural causes for the event? Justified belief does not entail belief in a natural cause. Experientially, you have not shown that it does. Moreover, if we had independent reasons for thinking that no natural cause of some extraordinary event could be found (e g., on the basis of prophecy), then it is conceivable that we could be justified in believing that an extraordinary event occurred without thereby likening ourselves to the Indian. The option of positing a natural explanation remains, but experience does not necessarily demand that we avail ourselves of it.
>
> Why then does Hume think that the most that testimony can establish is that an extraordinary event occurred, but never a miracle? Could not a resurrection be found analogous to past experience in precisely the same way that an eight-day darkness could (i.e., experience of the "decay, corruption, and dissolution of nature")? If the darkness can be justifiably believed, then why not a resurrection? Furthermore, under the appropriate circumstances, why couldn't the eight-day darkness be judged not merely extraordinary but, like the resurrection, miraculous? What would determine whether or not the event was to be judged miraculous would be whether we had better reason to believe that divine agency caused the event than for thinking that the event was naturally caused.

Hume would reject this argument, and therein lies the tale of his argument against justified belief in miracles—*whether on the basis of testimony or first-hand experience*. Given his principles of reasoning about empirical matters and philosophical empiricism (i.e., his theory of "impressions" and "ideas"), supernatural explanation cannot be justified experientially. David Johnson (2002) argues that Hume begs the question by assuming that *uniform experience tells or must tell against miracles*. It may well seem that way unless one takes account of Hume's empiricism and account of a posteriori reasoning in the *Treatise*. Hume may be wrong, he is wrong, but it is not because he begs the question. It is because the views on which his claim that uniform experience tells or must tell against miracles are themselves mistaken. Hume in effect assumes naturalism, and his naturalism is a result of his empiricism. His naturalism and empiricism may be wrong, but they are not question-begging.

We need to ask "What is it about experience, in the sense of expectations about future events or judgments about past events, that could justify the positing of a supernatural cause?" Positing such a cause is necessary if one is to justifiably believe some event to be a miracle. Hume would say that positing such a cause is speculative. It can have no basis in experience. Even if some event really were a miracle, whether it is a resurrection or "the raising of a feather, when the wind wants ever so little of a force requisite for that purpose" (EU 10 n23/115n), we would not be justified in believing that it was anything more than an extraordinary event. Extraordinary events are at the limits of our experience, the supernatural is beyond it. For Hume, a "cause," insofar as it can be used as an item in reasoning from experience, can only be something that we can have an "impression" of. The cause of a miracle would have to be identified as something we could perceive, even if we were to posit some metaphysical "power" of this cause and attribute it speculatively to God. The "cause" of Lazarus's coming forth from the grave would have to be identified with Christ's beckoning—either his voice or some physical gesture—both of which we have "impressions" of and both of which are events "in the usual course of nature."

If a resurrection were well enough attested to that it warranted belief, then that event could still only be assigned status as an extraordinary event with a natural explanation. Hume is thus constrained by his empiricism in such a way that, had he been at the shore of the Red Sea with Moses, and had Moses raised his staff and the Red Sea split up the middle (no low tide but raging waters on both sides—as in the movie version), and had the Red Sea crashed to a close the moment the last Israelite was safe—killing those in pursuit, and had Hume lacked grounds for assuming he was hallucinating or perceiving events in any way other than as they were actually happening—Hume would still be constrained by his principles to deny that what he was witnessing was a miracle. Alas, this example suffices to show the unacceptability of Hume's argument. Assuming Hume had been there with Moses and events transpired in a manner similar to the way just described, we can suppose he would have (readily) agreed that he was justified in believing that a miracle occurred. If so, his argument against justified belief in miracles can be used as a *reductio ad absurdum*.

A resurrection could only be well enough attested to so as to be justifiably believed if it could be judged as somehow analogous with something in our past experience. If it is, then it must be considered a natural event because, for Hume, anything analogous to our experience is at least analogous in the sense of suggesting that it, too, has a natural cause. Thus, unless one accepts Hume's analysis of a posteriori reasoning as a type of causal reasoning and also accepts his analysis of causation, which ultimately rests on his theory of impressions and ideas—a theory that even staunch empiricists should reject as simplistic—then there is no reason to accept *his* argument in Part 1 against the *possibility* of justified belief in miracles.

Hume's a priori argument against justified belief in miracles coalesces with his a posteriori argument against such justified belief. On a posteriori grounds, we could never justifiably believe testimony to the miraculous because we could never judge the occurrence of such an event to be similar, in relevant respects, to anything we have experienced. However, that a miraculous occurrence could never be judged relevantly similar to anything in experience (i.e., that there must be "a firm and unalterable experience" counting against belief in it) is something that, on Hume's account, we can know a priori, since a priori we can know that we cannot have an "impression" of a supernatural cause. Impressions (sensations or their copies in ideas) are by their very nature empirical, and there is no ground for supposing them supernatural. The supernatural is beyond the limits of our experience. It follows from this that, given Hume's empiricism (in effect a commitment to naturalism), we can also rule out the possibility of justified belief in testimony to the miraculous on a priori grounds.

II Miracles and Laws of Nature

Hume says "A miracle may accurately be defined, a transgression of a law of nature by a particular volition of the deity, or by the interposition of some invisible agent" (EU 10 n23/115n). His slightly different definition of a miracle as "a violation of the laws of nature" appears to be central to his argument against justified belief in miracles. "A miracle is a violation of the laws of nature; and as a firm and unalterable experience has established these laws, the proof against a miracle, from the very nature of the fact, is as entire as any argument from experience can possibly be imagined" (EU 10.12/114).

Hume's argument against justified belief in miracles in Part 1, as well as much subsequent discussion, appears to depend heavily on the premise that "a miracle is a violation of the laws of nature." However, the actual role such a premise plays in Hume's argument is controversial. Whether Hume meant to define a miracle as a violation of a law of nature or merely to characterize a miracle as, in some epistemologically relevant sense, "contrary" to the ordinary course of nature is disputed. It is clear, however, that on philosophical or scientific accounts of what a law of nature is, technically speaking, miracles are not violations of such laws but instead are positive instances of those laws. This is because laws of nature do not, and are not meant to, account for or describe events with supernatural causes but only those with natural causes. Once some event is assumed to have a supernatural cause, it is, by that very fact, outside the scope of laws of nature altogether and so cannot violate them. This point has long been, yet for some reason still is, frequently argued in various ways in the literature. Pritchard (2011) finds it necessary to reiterate and never does get to the question—Hume's question—the right question—of whether one can justifiably believe in miracles on the basis of evidence.

Only if one disregards the possibility of supernatural causes can known exceptions to laws possibly be regarded as violations of laws. However, in such a case, there might, and generally would be according to Hume, better reason to suppose that the exception shows that what was taken to be a law is not a law, rather than that the exception is a violation of a genuine law of nature that otherwise universally holds.

The premise that "a miracle is a violation of a law of nature" plays no significant role in Hume's argument. It is a gloss for the underlying supposition that one cannot have an "impression" of a supernatural event. Because no such impression can be had, any allegedly miraculous event, simply because it is allegedly miraculous, cannot ex hypothesis be judged relevantly similar to any other event in experience. And, in accordance with Hume's principles of a posteriori reasoning, *any* event that cannot be judged relevantly similar to others in our collective experience cannot justifiably be believed to have occurred. Nor, can one justifiably believe, with any degree of probability whatsoever, that such an event will occur.[1]

To say that miracles are impossible *because* violations of laws of nature are impossible is to improperly assume either (1) that a miracle must involve a violation of a law, or (2) that nothing contrary to a law of nature can occur because laws of nature circumscribe the logically possible and not merely the naturally possible. But apart from arguments to the contrary, neither assumption appears to be warranted—at least not prima facie warranted. To say, "an event is naturally (or physically) impossible and a violation of laws of nature if a statement of its occurrence is logically incompatible with a statement of the laws of nature," and *then* to assume that laws of nature circumscribe that which is logically and not merely naturally impossible (impossible apart from supernatural interference) is to rule out the occurrence of the naturally impossible on ill-conceived logical grounds. It is to deal with the possibility of miracles in the most superficial of ways by defining them out of existence using either an indefensible concept of a law of nature or supposing a suppressed argument against the possibility of non-natural interference—against the possibility that naturalism is false.

If causal statements did require reference to laws of nature, then this would appear to rule out the possibility of miracles because a miracle refers to a type of causal statement whose nature rules out reference to laws of nature taken as generalized cases of which they are instances. John Locke (1706) denies that miracles are not instances of laws. They are not, however, instances of laws of nature according to Locke. He thinks that to say they are not instances of any laws whatsoever (e.g., not even of supernatural laws) is to say that they are random occurrences, and he thinks that this is absurd. Miracles are contrary to laws of nature, *not* "violations" of them and *not* instances of them. Miracles are *vacuous* instances of true laws of nature (Levine 1989: 65–74). Note that it is not simply a miracle's *uniqueness* that rules out such reference to laws of nature. It cannot be uniqueness because even miracles that are supposed to be repeatable, such as raising someone from the dead, cannot in principle refer to laws of nature for a complete explanation of their occurrence. Presumably, they must also refer to divine intervention.[2]

III Bayes's Theorem and Justified Belief in Miracles

Before turning to the question of whether "difficult and delicate empirical investigations" are needed or have turned up any evidence that a miracle has occurred, let's look at applications of Bayes's theorem to the problem of miracles. Bayesian approaches have recently been much in favor by those claiming, contrary to Hume, that one can be justified in believing in a miracle (an event whose occurrence had very low prior probability) on the basis of testimony.

There are various versions of Bayes's theorem. For example, John Earman (1993: 307 n4) employs the following:

$$Pr(H/E\&K) = \frac{Pr(H/K) \times Pr(E/H\&K)}{Pr(E/K)}$$

"The reader is invited to think of H as a hypothesis at issue; K as the background knowledge; and E as the additional evidence. Pr($H/E\&K$) is called the posterior probability of H. Pr(H/K) and Pr($E/H\&K$) are respectively called the prior probability of H and the (posterior) likelihood of E."

Bayesian analyses are prominent among recent interpretations of Hume's argument against justified belief in miracles. Broadly, they aim to show that one can be justified in believing in an event even if that event has a very low prior probability. However, since there is no consensus on just what Hume's argument is, or exactly what he is trying to establish, it is impossible that any Bayesian analysis or recasting of the argument in terms of some version of Bayes' theorem, will not beg crucial issues of interpretation. In so doing, such analyses will also beg pivotal epistemological issues concerning, for example, evidence. Furthermore, it is difficult to see how recasting Hume's argument in a Bayesian form can clarify the structure or substance of the argument without presupposing what the argument is.

Applying Bayes's theorem to the question of justified belief in alleged miracles, or Bayesian interpretations of justified belief of alleged miracles, is completely useless for two reasons. First, as in the case of Hume's argument in Part 1, it begs questions of interpretation. What counts as relevant evidence for a supernaturally caused "special" event? This is important in Hume's argument as I presented it. We can have no evidence—*none*—that something was supernaturally caused on his account. Because he misunderstands Hume's argument, Earman (1993) fails to see that it undermines any application whatsoever of the Bayesian theorem to that argument. Second, more importantly and altogether apart from Hume's argument in Part 1, we do not need Bayes's theorem to show that, given good reliable evidence in a single case, one could be justified in believing in some event with a very, very low antecedent probability (e.g., a miracle). After all, we can agree that the antecedent probability of the Red Sea parting is very,

very (very) low, and yet I can well imagine being justified in believing that it really did happen—were I there on the shore with Moses and it parted as in the movie *The Ten Commandments*—i.e., no low tide. Thus, Bayes's theorem is otiose as applied to the case of miracles. In those cases where one might be justified, one would certainly have no need of Bayes's theorem. (Fogelin's [1990; 2003] thesis and interpretation is relevant here as well. To suggest that Hume was claiming that standards for evaluating miracles need to be very high and that no testimony had yet met such standards is to say something *remarkably* uninteresting—albeit true. But this is not Hume's argument in Part 1. Fogelin plays right into the hands of those with Bayesian analyses because they can, by and large, agree with Fogelin on the issue of standards. Why not? All they need to do, or think they need do, is show that in some cases the standards can be met.) And in cases where one cannot be so justified, no application of Bayes's theorem will not be question-begging or render such a belief any more justified—not even slightly more justified.

Furthermore, and importantly, Bayes's theorem is of no use *whatsoever* in the cases of New Testament miracles. Applying Bayes's theorem in these cases will not make the belief that such miracles occurred one whit more justified simply because the evidence is not there. To suggest otherwise, as Swinburne (1970; 2002), Haldane (Smart and Haldane 1996), Wolterstorff (1995), and others explicitly have or have intimated, merely obfuscates the historical record.

To show that one could be justified in believing an event with low antecedent probability is, of course, not to show that one is so justified. Nor, given the kinds of things we know about those who proclaim miracles, does it indicate that "difficult and delicate empirical investigations" are in order. In Part 2 of his essay, Hume explains why such investigation is not needed, and the reasons he gives are the very reasons we do justifiably reject reports of miraculous occurrences. To claim that the convergence of probabilities indicates that in all likelihood the miracles (New Testament miracles—although presumably not those alleged in Islam, Buddhism, or Hinduism?) did occur reflects poor historical reasoning and wishful thinking. Even if it is true that the disease the nun had (Parkinson's) did disappear after she prayed for an intervention on her behalf by Pope John Paul II, after his death no less, no one is epistemologically justified on the basis of the historical record in believing that she was cured miraculously. This is a case where the Catholic Church affirms something where the evidence does not warrant it. This comes as no surprise. They also deny events for which there is good and ample evidence. They continue to deny that Pope Benedict XVI was complicit in and in no small way directly responsible for the worldwide reign of terror by Catholic clergy who sexually molested and otherwise abused children—orphaned and physically handicapped (deaf) children among them. The evidence shows that he personally and repeatedly refused to act in any meaningful way on information he had concerning the abuse.

The two cases are connected. The beatification of John Paul II is seen by many as "a major morale boost for a church reeling from the clerical sex abuse scandal,"[3] a scandal attributed by many to John Paul II and Benedict VXI, his principal adviser on these matters. Hume is often cited as a deist, and while his deism is questionable, it should be noted that a principal motivation and complaint of the deists was the level of corruption within the clergy (Levine 2007: 245). Hume's views about cases such as the nun's cure are expressed succinctly in a letter to Hugh Blair. "Does a man of sense run after every silly tale of witches or hobgoblins or fairies, and canvass particularly the evidence?" (quoted in Earman 2000: 59). We are now in a position to see why this same response is the one Hume would give to those who argue that Bayes's theorem shows what he wants it to show: that reports of miracles should be taken seriously and that "difficult and delicate empirical investigations" are in order.

One may believe in New Testament miracles on the basis of one's belief that the Bible is religiously authoritative. Or one may, even more problematically, believe in the authority of Church pronouncements on such matters as the "miraculous" cure of the nun. But this is not the same thing as being epistemologically justified on the basis of the historical record. It is important not to confuse what it means to believe something on religious grounds on the one hand, with sound epistemological grounds for justifiably believing something like a miracle, on the other.

IV   MIRACLES AND HISTORY AND HUME

Much recent and current literature on Hume's essay has distanced itself from Hume's fundamental purpose and concern. Hume's primary concern was with the question of whether people are in fact justified in believing in miracles such as the resurrection of Christ and other New Testament miracles. Minimally, it is clear that he intended to argue that they were not. Of course, if they *cannot* be justified (epistemologically rather than, say, psychologically, speaking) in such beliefs, then they *are not* in fact epistemologically justified. But even if they could be justified, it is clear that Hume (Part 2) thought they were not. This is particularly worth pointing out in view of literature which suggests that (1) if Hume's argument in Part 1 is mistaken and one can be justified in believing in a miracle on the basis of testimony, or (2) if Hume never thought (or argued) that one could never be justified in believing in a miracle on the basis of testimony; then this will have gone some way toward showing either that testimony has established the occurrence of such miracles or, more cautiously, that, in Earman's (2000: 61) words, "difficult and delicate empirical investigations" are needed in order to show whether such belief is or is not justified.

Flew (1967), Swinburne (1970), and Fogelin (2003) are among those who claim Hume's argument in Part 1 is not meant to show that one never could justifiably believe a miracle occurred on the basis of testimony.[4] But even if, contrary to the a priori reading of Hume's argument in Part 1, Hume never thought it impossible to justifiably believe in a miracle, or even if on the strong ("a priori") interpretation of Hume's argument in Part 1 the argument fails, this does nothing to support the view that anyone has ever been justified in believing in a miracle on the basis of testimony or that "difficult and delicate empirical investigations" are needed before one justifiably rejects such belief. (Finally, Fogelin is right.) That one never has been justified in believing in miracles, that such investigations are not needed, is what the arguments in Part 2 of his essay seek to establish.

I can easily conjure up cases—easily—in which someone can be justified in believing a miracle has occurred. But this does nothing whatsoever to show that any such cases have occurred or that "difficult and delicate empirical investigations" are necessary if one is to be justified in believing that they have not occurred (Levine 2011). History, it seems, is regarded as a relatively soft target (and indeed it is) as compared to science by those who argue that there is evidence that shows miracles have occurred—or that careful investigation is needed. Having somewhat given up on trying to undermine Darwin, some (e.g., Swinburne) turn to the historical record in efforts to support religious truth claims—for example, about miracles. In arguing that people cannot be (Part 1) or are not in fact (Part 2) epistemologically justified in believing in miracles, Hume was arguing that "difficult and delicate empirical investigations" are not necessary in order to justifiably reject a belief in a reported miraculous occurrence.

If Hume's primary concern was with the question of whether people are in fact justified in believing in miracles and in arguing that they are not, then whether or not one thinks Hume was arguing a priori that they could not be justified or a posteriori that they are not justified, although they might be, he was right in claiming that such belief was unjustified—for reasons given in Part 1—although not in Part 1. It is one thing to claim that there could be good epistemological grounds for believing in a miracle on the basis of testimony, and it is quite another to argue that there are in fact such grounds and that such belief is justified. Earman, Beckwith, Swinburne, Haldane, and others with a religious rather than a philosophical agenda (they are engaging in apologetics rather than philosophy) either elide the distinction between what could be the case epistemologically speaking (e.g., by employing Bayes's theorem) and what is the case, or else they claim or intimate that there are good epistemological grounds for believing in miracles (Beckwith 2003; Levine 2011). Apologetics superficially resembles philosophy in form but exercises its critical faculty in the service of inviolable assumptions, beliefs, and motivations. As such, it is virtually isolated from other academic disciplines—philosophy included. Virtually all of Plantinga's, Haldane's, Wolterstorff's, Swinburne's, Van Inwagen's, and others' "philosophy" of religion is apologetics, for underlying and prior to the arguments they give for some view is the belief that that view is correct (Levine 2009). Bayes's theorem, of course, does not and cannot support the factual claim that there are good epistemological grounds for believing in miracles. In short, in Part 2 at any rate, Hume was right.

The question of just how significant miracles are for religious belief is perhaps the most important question of all. It is also a question that is largely ignored by contemporary philosophers. Plantinga (2006) is one recent example among not just many but most. Unlike Hume, who took the question seriously, Plantinga (who like Swinburne and others "knows" miracles have occurred) favors the less interesting question as to whether miracles are consistent with contemporary science and views about laws of nature (also see Pritchard 2011). These are ultimately questions about the possibility of miracles. They are not, in the first instance, about religion or miracles at all but about laws of nature and how one understands science or nature and the supernatural. The answer to the question about whether miracles are possible will always be framed in terms of prior, and even more controversial, conceptions of laws of nature and science by such philosophers, even though it is religious allegiances that often give rise to their conceptions of science and laws of nature.

Nothing in my critique of Hume's argument in Part 1 suggests that miracles have ever occurred or that we are justified in believing they have. But it would be most surprising if some people, at some time and in certain circumstances, have not been, and will not again be, justified in believing in the occurrence of a miracle given other (objectively unjustifiable) and false beliefs that they have, along with what was or currently is commonly accepted and believed at the time. This is to say nothing more than that it was at one time perfectly justifiable to believe, for example, in witches or that the sun revolved around the earth. However, none of this suggests that the evidence available for the occurrence of any alleged miracle warrants justified belief in miracles for most people now—including those who really do believe in them. Ignoring large swaths of contemporary Biblical scholarship (what Wolterstorff [1995: 219] calls "excavative" biblical scholarship) and contemporary historical standards of evidence, Haldane (Smart and Haldane 1995: 205–207), for example, claims that the Bible is an accurate source of information about the alleged events as they actually happened—presumably including miracles. Wolterstorff's claims concerning scripture and divine discourse are even more excessive. Their beliefs, however, are not justified in any interesting or epistemologically robust sense, but only via other unjustified and some demonstrably false beliefs they hold. Objectively available evidence (historical inquiry and biblical scholarship) does not support them.

Nor, given what we know about reports of the miraculous (consider the recent case involving John Paul II's allegedly miraculous deed), is it necessary for us to embark on "difficult and delicate empirical investigations" to justifiably reject the veracity of such reports. There may well be an ethical duty to do. The report of this alleged miracle may, among other things, be seen as an opportunistic and manipulative insult (1) to those suffering from that terrible disease and (2) to the many thousands of those children terrorized and abused as a result of the Popes' *considered* refusal to act morally given what they knew. Will the sainthood be revoked if this exploited nun has a relapse?

Just as philosophical reasoning about things like consciousness, time, and bioethics should take account of, and not conflict with, the best scientifically relevant findings on these matters, so too should philosophers of religion pay attention to the best scientific, historical, and socioscientific findings relevant to the matters they investigate. Creationist views may have been justifiable for some before the facts of evolution were established, but they no longer are. (Haldane, Van Inwagen, and other Christian fundamentalists are, in varying degrees, creationists as well.)[5] Similarly, belief in biblical accounts of miracles may have been justified for some in the relevant epistemic sense before the advent of modern canons of historical evidence and biblical (textual) scholarship, but they no longer are.

So-called contemporary analytic philosophy of religion is not natural theology as Hume conceived it, but largely Christian apologetics. The agenda is wholly theirs. This can be seen in the literature on miracles, on evil, and elsewhere. The time to bring philosophy of religion up to speed—*if it can be brought up to speed*—is well and truly overdue. (The problem, if it is a problem, is that, with the exception of apologists, few philosophers are interested in apologetics.) Wasn't that Hume's view 250 years ago? Wasn't this the reason that Hume wrote the *Dialogues Concerning Natural Religion* (published posthumously) and *The Natural History of Religion* (1757)? Wasn't this also the reason he was discriminated against by the religious authorities and denied a professorship at Edinburgh? The truth is that Hume did not think that, philosophically speaking, the problem of miracles was very interesting.

ABBREVIATIONS OF WORKS CITED

EU   *An Enquiry Concerning Human Understanding.* Edited by T. L. Beauchamp. Oxford: Clarendon, 2000.

T   *A Treatise of Human Nature.* Edited by D. F. Norton and M. J. Norton. Oxford: Clarendon, 2007.

NOTES

1. See Levine (1989), part I.
2. See Clarke (2007) for a discussion that transmutes the problem about miracles being a violation of laws of nature (or attempts to push it aside) into one about what is meant by the term "supernatural." See Ward (2002) for an effort to make laws of nature central to the question of rational belief in miracles, a misinterpretation of Hume, and a failure to address Hume's arguments concerning justified belief in miracles.
3. http://www.cbsnews.com/stories/2011/01/14/world/main7245702.shtml (retrieved February 28, 2011).
4. The following quotation from Hume's essay is often cited in support of the a priori interpretation: "A miracle is a violation of the laws of nature; and as a firm and unalterable experience has established these laws, the proof against a miracle, from the very nature of the fact, is as entire as any argument from experience can possibly be imagined" (EU 10.12/114). Another reason for seeing the argument in Part 1 as a priori is Hume's likening his own argument to that of John Tillotson's (1820) against justified belief in transubstantiation. Hume appears to interpret Tillotson's argument as an a priori one ("by that very fact") and is likening his argument to Tillotson's on that basis. Whether or not Hume's argument resembles Tillotson's and, if so, in what other ways is not really important (Levine 1989: chapters 8–10).
5. Levine (2000; 1999). Swinburne accepts evolution (of a sort) but denies that laws of nature ("regularities of succession") can be reasonably accounted for apart from God. See Van Inwagen (1995a; 1995b).

Bibliography

Beckwith, Francis. (2003). "Theism, Miracles and the Modern Mind," in Paul Copan and Paul Moser, eds., *The Rationality of Theism*. London: Routledge, 221–236.

Burns, R. M. (1981). *The Great Debate on Miracles*. Lewisburg: Bucknell University Press.

Clarke, Steve. (2007). "The Supernatural and the Miraculous." *Sophia* 46, 277–285.

Campbell, George. (1762/1983). *A Dissertation on Miracles*. Edinburgh. Reprinted, New York: Garland.

Davis, Stephen T. (1984). "Is It Possible To Know that Jesus Was Raised from the Dead?" *Faith and Philosophy* 2: 147–59.

Earman, John. (1993). "Bayes, Hume, and Miracles." *Faith and Philosophy* 10, 293–310.

Earman, John. (2000). *Hume's Abject Failure: The Argument Against Miracles*. New York: Oxford University Press.

Earman, John. (2002). "Bayes, Hume, Price, and Miracles," in Richard Swinburne, ed., *Bayes's Theorem*. Oxford: Oxford University Press, 91–109.

Flew, Antony. (1961). *Hume's Philosophy of Belief*. London: RKP.

Flew, Antony. (1967). "Miracles," in *Encyclopedia of Philosophy*. New York: Macmillan and Free Press, vol. 5, 346–353.

Flew, Antony. (1984). *God: A Critical Enquiry*, 2nd edn. LaSalle, IL: Open Court.

Flew, Antony. (1990). "Fogelin on Hume on Miracles." *Hume Studies* 15, 141–144.

Fogelin, Robert, J. (1990). "What Hume Actually Said About Miracles," *Hume Studies* 16, 81–86.

Fogelin, Robert J. (2003). *A Defense of Hume on Miracles*. Princeton: Princeton University Press.

Gaskin, J. C. A. (1978). *Hume's Philosophy of Religion*. London: Macmillan.

Johnson, David. (2002). *Hume, Holism, and Miracles*. Ithaca, NY: Cornell University Press.

Levine, Michael. (1989). *Hume and the Problem of Miracles: A Solution*. Dordrecht: Kluwer Publishers.

Levine, Michael. (1999). "Critical Study of 'Atheism and Theism: J. J. C. Smart and J. J. Haldane.'" *Canadian Journal of Philosophy* 29, 157–170.

Levine, Michael. (2000). "Contemporary Christian Analytic Philosophy of Religion: Biblical Fundamentalism; Terrible Solutions to a Horrible Problem; and Hearing God." *International Journal of Philosophy of Religion* 48, 89–119.

Levine, Michael. (2007). "Non-Theistic Conceptions of God: When God Isn't God," in *Routledge Companion to Philosophy of Religion*, Paul Copan and Chad V. Meister, eds., London and New York: Routledge: 237–248.

Levine, Michael. (2008). "Hume on Miracles and Immortality," in Elizabeth Radcliffe, ed., *Blackwell Companion to Hume*. Oxford: Blackwell, 353–370.

Levine, Michael. (2009). "Philosophy of Religion's Political Character: Myths of Tolerance and the Re-Sanctification of Politics," in Philip Quadrio, ed., *Politics and Religion in the New Century: Philosophical Perspectives*. Sydney: University Sydney Press, 61–91.

Levine, Michael. (2011). "Philosophers on Miracles," in Graham H. Twelftree, ed., *The Companion to Miracle*. Cambridge: Cambridge University Press, 291–308.

Mackie, John L. (1982). *The Miracle of Theism*. Oxford: Clarendon Press.

Martin, Raymond. (2003). "Historians on Miracles," in Raymond Martin and Christopher Bernard, eds., *God Matters: Readings in the Philosophy of Religion*. New York: Longman, 412–427.

Plantinga, Alvin. (2006). "Divine Action in the World (Synopsis)." *Ratio* (new series) 19, 495–504.

Pritchard, Timothy. (2011). "Miracles and Violations." *Religious Studies* 47, 41–58.

Smart, J. J. C., and J. J. Haldane. (1996). *Atheism and Theism*. Oxford: Blackwell.

Swinburne, Richard. (1970). *The Concept of a Miracle*. London: Macmillan.

Swinburne, Richard. (ed.). (2002). *Bayes's Theorem*. Oxford: Oxford University Press.

Tillotson, John. (1820). "Discourse Against Transubstantiation," in T. Birch, ed., *Works, Vol. 2*. London.

Van Inwagen, Peter. (1995a). "The Problem of Evil, the Problem of Air, and the Problem of Silence," in *God, Knowledge and Mystery: Essays in Philosophical Theology*. Ithaca, NY: Cornell University Press, 66–95.

Van Inwagen, Peter. (1995b). "The Magnitude, Duration, and Distribution of Evil: A Theodicy," in *God, Knowledge and Mystery: Essays in Philosophical Theology*. Ithaca, NY: Cornell University Press, 96–122.

Ward, Keith. (2002). "Believing in Miracles." *Zygon* 37, 741–750.

Wolterstorff, Nicholas. (1995). *Divine Discourse: Philosophical Reflections on the Claim that God Speaks*. Cambridge: Cambridge University Press.

CHAPTER 30

HUME AND PROOFS FOR THE EXISTENCE OF GOD

MARTIN BELL

In "Of the Different Species of Philosophy," Hume comments that "the easy and obvious philosophy will always, with the generality of mankind, have the preference above the accurate and abstruse" (EU 1.3/6). He instances Cicero, La Bruyère, and Addison as writers in the easy and obvious style and Aristotle, Malebranche, and Locke as writers in the accurate and abstruse style. Hume later says he intends to unite the two species by writing accurate philosophy in an easy style, but he also gives justifications for writing accurate and abstruse philosophy "or what is commonly called metaphysics'" (EU 1.7/9). The third justification is one that is very important to him. This is to "cultivate true metaphysics with some care, in order to destroy the false and adulterate" (EU 1.12/12). He describes two ways in which metaphysics can be false and adulterate. One is through failing to recognize the limits of human understanding, misconceiving the powers and operations of the mind, especially of reason, and thinking that reason is able to transcend experience and "penetrate into subjects utterly inaccessible to the understanding." The other is "from the craft of popular superstitions" (EU 1.11/11), where philosophical investigations are subordinated to religious ends. Mixing theology and metaphysics results in "that abstruse philosophy and metaphysical jargon, which, being mixed up with popular superstition, renders it in a manner impenetrable to careless reasoners, and gives it an air of science and wisdom" (EU 1.12/12–13).

Two writers whom Hume thought used metaphysical jargon in the service of theology were John Locke (1632–1704) and Samuel Clarke (1675–1729). Locke and Clarke both published versions of the cosmological proof of the existence of God, drawing on rationalist principles concerning causation and the nature and powers of matter and created minds, and drawing also on Newtonian natural philosophy. Hume's critique of these arguments is directed at the obscurity of the ideas they use and the unsupported assumptions they employ. The critique is based on Hume's principle that it is necessary to clarify the nature of the ideas we have and of the operations of our minds. The theological impetus of which Hume complains is especially evident in the case of Clarke.

He not only argues a priori to prove the existence of a deity with many of the traditional divine attributes, but also, like many other Newtonian divines, assigns an important role in religious apologetics to versions of the a posteriori argument from design. In attacking this argument, Hume's critique is that the adulteration of metaphysics is due not only to obscurity of ideas and principles, but also to a failure to recognize the limits of human understanding.

Hume wrote "Of the Different Species of Philosophy" soon after he was rejected for the post of professor of moral philosophy at the University of Edinburgh in 1745 (Stewart 2002; Wright 2006). His candidacy was attacked in print, and Hume responded with an anonymous letter of his own (Mossner & Price 1967). The two pamphlets show that Hume's philosophy in the *Treatise* was understood by contemporary readers as a major critique of the project of natural religion, especially as developed by Newtonian philosophers such as Clarke.

Section I of this chapter gives a brief outline of the first three sections of Clarke's cosmological argument. I do not provide any summary of Locke's version of the argument for reasons of space and because Clarke's is more directly the target of Hume's criticisms. (For discussion of Locke's cosmological argument, see Bennett 2005). Section II concerns Hume's arguments against the a priori status of the causal maxim and the ways in which his positive theory of causation undermines all a priori constraints on causal relations. Section III looks at the debate in Part 9 of the *Dialogues Concerning Natural Religion* about Demea's version of Clarke's argument. Clarke held that the cosmological argument (in a form that incorporates the ontological argument) was essential in natural theology in order to prove the uniqueness, eternity, infinity, and omnipresence of God. But, in common with other Newtonian natural theologians, he also used the design argument to establish the intelligence of God. Section IV.1 concerns Hume's attack on the design argument in EU, and Section IV.2 moves on to the debate in D. The concluding section looks briefly at some wider questions about the place of Hume's attack on natural theology in his philosophical projects and mentions some recent scholarship that has raised questions for further research.

I Clarke's Cosmological Argument

This section gives no more than a brief outline of initial stages of Clarke's *A Demonstration of the Being and Attributes of God*, sufficient for an understanding of what it is that Hume attacks. In the first section (Clarke 1998: 8–10), there is an argument to prove that it is "absolutely and undeniably certain" that "something has existed from all eternity." One premise is that if there was ever a time at which nothing existed, then nothing would exist now. The argument for this is that if it is supposed that there exists something X whose beginning of existence is without a cause, then nothing causes X; but since nothing comes from nothing, X is itself nothing; that is, it does not exist, which contradicts the initial assumption. The supposition that something could exist whose beginning of existence has no cause has in this way been shown to be self-contradictory. A second premise is that something exists now. Therefore, something has existed from all eternity. (This proposition is to be understood *de dicto* not *de re*.)

In section II (Clarke 1998: 10–12), there is an argument to prove that it is absolutely certin that "there has existed from eternity some one unchangeable and independent being". The proof is a disjunctive syllogism: either there has existed from eternity (at least) "one unchangeable and independent being from which all other [dependent] beings that are or ever were in the universe have received their original," or there has been nothing in existence at all but an infinite succession of "changeable and dependent beings." But this second alternative is "impossible and contradictory to itself," so the first alternative is necessarily true. The second alternative can be shown to be self-contradictory as follows. If an infinite succession of dependent beings was all there is in the universe, and there is no being in the universe that is "self-existent or necessarily existing," then there could equally well have been nothing at all existing rather than the infinite succession. So, the question is what caused the infinite succession to exist rather than nothing? It cannot be that the infinite succession exists by necessity because, as just stated, there could have been nothing. "Chance is nothing but a mere word." And there is, by hypothesis, no other being that can cause the infinite succession to exist. Therefore, it is caused by nothing. As in the argument of the preceding section, Clarke argues that existing without a cause is a self-contradictory concept. Therefore, from eternity, there has existed (at least one) being that is unchangeable and independent. Such a being has no external cause of its existence.

Section III (Clarke 1998: 12–29) is devoted to showing that an unchangeable and independent being, the existence of which has just been proved, must be "self-existent, that is, necessarily existing." Clarke's account of self-existence is quite complex. He denies that a self-existent being causes itself because the idea of something causing itself is "an express contradiction." (At T 1.3.3.5/80–1, Hume claims that Clarke argued that everything X must have a cause because otherwise X would cause itself, which is self-contradictory. But that is not Clarke's argument in this section.) It cannot be caused by something else because it is independent. The remaining option, being self-existent, is to exist "by an absolute necessity originally in the nature of the thing itself." So, self-existence is founded on necessary existence, and this makes us expect a form of the ontological argument. Clarke, however, rejects the ontological argument from the idea of God as the most perfect being to God's existence, on the ground that any perfection of a being presupposes that being's existence (Clarke 1998: 113; in "Answer to a Sixth Letter"). Be that as it may, when he tries to explain the necessity by which a self-existent being exists, he says that it is the same kind of necessity as applies to mathematics, so that "the only true idea of a self-existent or necessarily existing being is the idea of a being the supposition of whose not-existing is an express contradiction." That is an obvious target of Hume's criticisms (Section III of this chapter). Another part of Clarke's argument in this section, drawing on Newtonian conceptions of matter, space, and time, is that infinite space and time are not attributes of matter, which might not have existed. Infinite space and time necessarily exist, but they are attributes not substances. Therefore, there is a necessarily existing nonmaterial and infinite substance of which they are attributes, and this is God.

II Hume's Critique: The Idea of Causation and the Causal Principle

Hume's critique of cosmological arguments is implicit in his whole argument about the idea of causation and about causal inference. That argument, which in the title page of the Abstract he calls the "chief argument" of the *Treatise*, gives a series of negative and positive arguments. In a negative vein it argues against theories that place a priori metaphysical constraints on causation or conflate causal inference with a priori inference. In a positive vein it argues that causal relations are matters of fact that could have been otherwise, that only experience can show what causal relations obtain between matters of fact, and that causal necessity is quite different from metaphysical necessity along with other important lessons. In neither the *Treatise* nor the first *Enquiry* does Hume explicitly state that cosmological arguments fail to achieve the aim of demonstrating the existence of God as a First Cause of the universe. But that verdict is not hard to discern.

It is clearly signaled in his attack on the "general maxim in philosophy, that whatever begins to exist, must have a cause of existence" (T 1.3.3.1/78). As described earlier, this principle is assumed as a necessarily true premise in versions of the cosmological argument that Hume refers to in the section, in footnotes to writings by Hobbes, Locke, and Clarke. These thinkers provided arguments to show that the maxim is true a priori in the course of offering proofs of the existence of God, and Hume's argument that the maxim is not a priori certain was consequently quite rightly seen by contemporaries to be a direct challenge to cosmological arguments. Hume does not argue that there are events that have no causes; he remarks, "And indeed there is nothing existent, either externally or internally, which is not to be consider'd either as a cause or an effect" (T 1.3.2.5/75). But the explanation he gives of why the causal maxim seems to us correct at the same time shows why it cannot be assumed a priori and therefore why it cannot be applied beyond the domain of human empirical experience. Hume argues that it is not self-evident, knowable by "intuition"; nor is it "demonstrable," validly deducible from premises that are true a priori. (For Hume's uses of "demonstrative," "demonstrable," "demonstration," etc., see Millican 2002: 132–136). The argument Hume gives is roughly as follows. Whatever is true a priori—that is, necessarily true in the broadly logical sense—is something whose contrary is impossible in that same sense. Hume holds as a general principle that if some proposition is conceivable, thinkable without self-contradiction, then it is metaphysically possible. So, he argues that to show something is not necessarily true it suffices to show that its contrary is conceivable and, hence, metaphysically possible. This is a pattern of argument he often uses, for example, when showing that causal relations are not discoverable a priori. In the Abstract, he says,

But no inference from cause to effect amounts to a demonstration. Of which there is this evident proof. The mind can always *conceive* any effect to follow from any cause, and indeed any event to follow upon another: Whatever we conceive is possible, at least in the metaphysical sense: But wherever a demonstration takes place, the contrary is impossible, and implies a contradiction. There is no demonstration, therefore, for any conjunction of cause and effect. And this is a principle, which is generally allowed by philosophers. (TA 11/650–1)

In this passage, Hume is talking about causal inferences and pointing out that they are not demonstrations of their conclusions. An inference from an observed cause to an unobserved effect is not a demonstrative proof that given the cause, the effect must occur. Causal connections between events are not and do not depend on conceptual connections between the ideas of these events. Rather, any relation of cause and effect is external to the items related. That the relation holds when it does is a matter of fact not a matter of logical relations between ideas. This is what Hume relies on in T 1.3.3 when arguing that we can conceive of the event of something coming into existence without a cause. This passage comes before Hume has investigated the nature of causal inference. Because Hume holds that the idea of cause and effect is genetically dependent on the mechanisms of causal inference, he cannot refer to his definitions of cause and of necessary connection at this point in the *Treatise*. The meanings of terms used in the argument such as "cause," "effect," "efficacy," "productive quality," and so on have not yet been clarified. Perhaps as a result, some criticisms of his argument seem to miss his point. For example, Anscombe (1974) complains that all Hume can conclude from the fact that the causal relation is external to its terms is that we can conceive of an event without conceiving of its cause. However, what he needs to show is that we can conceive of an event without a cause, and this she thinks he does not do. The Humean answer is that a cause of an "object" (such as the change Hume describes as "an object [being] non-existent this moment, and [being] existent the next") is another "object," another existent entity. The idea of each object is the idea of a possible existence. There is no conceptual connection between these distinct possible existences. Hence, by the conceivability principle, either may exist without the other existing. So, the existence of one entity is metaphysically possible without the existence of the other. This holds true even when the two entities are actual and are actually related as cause and effect.

The grounds on which Hume rejects the possibility of any a priori knowledge of causality, including any purported a priori causal maxims, are fully laid out in subsequent sections of the *Treatise* 1.3 and again in the first *Enquiry*. They are also summarized in the Abstract. Taken together, these many passages constitute a major revolution in philosophical accounts of causation, causal inference, and empirical belief and provide very strong arguments against the very possibility of a priori proofs of the existence of God. It is not intended to give here an adequate explanation or analysis of Hume's accounts of these topics. Interpretation and evaluation of such a major piece of philosophical reasoning is, of course, full of debate and dispute. But there are some passages that are directly relevant to the focus of this chapter and need to be considered. In T 1.3.14 and in

EU 7, he defines what it is for one object A to be a cause of B, in two ways corresponding to the difference (explained in T 1.1.5) between causation as a philosophical relation (a complex idea formed by the comparison of two or more ideas) and as a natural relation (an association of ideas that leads to a tendency for the mind to make a transition from one to the other). In regard to causation as a complex idea arising from comparison, it is worth looking back to T 1.3.1.1/69, where he distinguishes philosophical relations that "depend entirely on the ideas, which we compare together" and philosophical relations that "may be chang'd without any change in the ideas [i.e., of the two relata]." Where a comparison discovers a relation between two things simply from the ideas of them present to the mind in the process of comparison, then so long as the ideas are unchanged, so is the relation, and that relation is therefore discoverable a priori (in Hume's sense, which includes perceptions immediately present to the mind; see Millican 2002: 121–123) and is invariable. If, however, the discovery of a relation requires comparison of (the ideas of) objects other than the two relata, then the relation is not discoverable a priori from the ideas of the relata alone. This is the case with the philosophical relation of causation. To form the complex idea that a particular object A is a cause of another particular object B requires comparing them in terms of their relative locations in space and time, which cannot be discovered a priori, and in terms of the spatiotemporal locations of other objects that resemble them. That is why Hume comments that the definition of causation as a philosophical relation is "drawn from objects foreign to the cause"; that is, distinct from the particular object A. Causation as a natural relation is what genetically supports causal or probable inference from causes to effects and vice versa. Experience of constant conjunctions of similar pairs of objects produces a customary association of their ideas and a habitual transition of the imagination from the impression of one to the idea of the other. (At a basic level, causal inference does not employ the idea of causation, so Hume can refer to the genesis of causal inference in the second definition of the idea of causation without circularity.) The definition of causation as a natural relation therefore also requires reference to something other than the object that is the cause; namely, to the principles of human nature.

The two definitions (given at T 1.3.14.35/172 and, slightly differently, at EU 7.29/76–7) together emphasize that, for Hume, the idea of causation rests on experience of natural regularities and on the contribution of the mind. Neither experience nor the customs and habits of the imagination provide a priori insight into the behavior of empirical objects. But these two "principles" (T 1.4.7.3/265) do between them generate an idea of necessity that (unlike metaphysical necessity) does apply to causation. The idea of necessary connection between causes and effects is traced back to the elements Hume brings together in the two definitions: on the side of the objects, regularity; on the side of the mind, custom and habit. Hume is therefore able to return to his argument that the causal maxim is not metaphysically necessary now that the definitions (showing the legitimate provenance of the ideas) of causation and of necessary connection are in place:

> We may now be able fully to overcome all that repugnance, which 'tis so natural for us to entertain against the foregoing reasoning, by which we endeavour'd to prove,

that the necessity of a cause to every beginning of existence is not founded on any arguments either demonstrative or intuitive. Such an opinion will not appear strange after the foregoing definitions. If we define a cause to be, *An object precedent and contiguous to another, and where all objects resembling the former are plac'd in a like relation of priority and contiguity to those objects, that resemble the latter*; we may easily conceive, that there is no absolute nor metaphysical necessity, that every beginning of existence shou'd be attended with such an object. If we define a cause to be, *An object precedent and contiguous to another, and so united with it in the imagination, that the idea of the one determines the mind to form the idea of the other, and the impression of the one to form a more lively idea of the other*; we shall make still less difficulty of assenting to this opinion. Such an influence on the mind is in itself perfectly extraordinary and incomprehensible; nor can be certain of its reality, but from experience and observation. (T 1.3.14.35/172)

In giving these definitions, Hume not only completes his search for the origin of the idea of cause and effect and supplies legitimacy for the only conception of necessity that applies to matters of fact and existence, but he also provides the basis for throwing off metaphysical constraints on causal reasoning (Millican 2009). He can also answer the question of why we think it necessary that every beginning of existence has a cause. We think it necessary in much the same way as we think it necessary that the same causes will have the same effects; namely, on the basis of experience, custom, and habit.

III HUME'S CRITIQUE: THE IDEA OF NECESSARY EXISTENCE

In D Part 9, Demea gives an "argument a priori" for the existence of God based quite closely on Clarke's argument, which in fact explains why in some of the secondary literature there is disagreement about whether Demea's argument is cosmological or ontological (Stewart 1985). Demea begins with the causal maxim that whatever exists must have a cause or reason of its existence, and he moves swiftly to the dilemma that either there is an infinite succession of effects and causes "without any ultimate cause" or there is an ultimate cause, which is "*necessarily* existent." He argues that the first option is "absurd" in the style of Clarke: if the universe consisted only of an infinite sequence of effects, each of which resulted from a prior cause, there would be no reason for the existence of the sequence taken as a whole. If there is no explanation, then the causal maxim is violated, and this, Demea says, establishes the remaining option: that there is a "necessarily existent being" that is the reason why this succession exists rather than some other or nothing at all. This, however, is not the end of the argument, for Demea, again following Clarke, raises the question of what kind of being is a necessarily existent being. In other words, the final cause whose existence is here supposed to be demonstrated is not merely "necessary" in the sense of a necessary conclusion of the argument, but is necessary in the sense of being in itself logically necessary (Williford 2003). So, Demea argues that the final cause is a being whose nonexistence is logically impossible: "a necessarily existent being, who carries the REASON of his existence in himself; and who cannot be supposed not to exist without an express contradiction" (D 9.3).

Once this two-stage deployment of the idea of necessary existence in Demea's argument is clear, it is clear also why Cleanthes, first of all and without reference to the logical structure of the argument, presents the Humean criticism of the very idea of a being whose nonexistence implies a contradiction. There cannot be any such being because conceivability implies possibility, and "whatever we conceive as existent, we can also conceive as non-existent." This is very much a Humean thesis. At T 1.2.6.3/66, Hume says, "tho' every impression and idea we remember be consider'd as existent, the idea of existence is not deriv'd from any particular impression," which means that the idea of existence is, for Hume, quite like the ideas of space and time. As Garrett (1997: 53–54) explains, the idea of existence is simply an abstract idea in which the idea of any conceivable object serves as an instance. Whatever is conceivable is a possible existence, and whatever we conceive as possibly existing we can also conceive as possibly not existing:

> Whatever *is* may *not be*. No negation of a fact can involve a contradiction. The non-existence of any being, without exception, is as clear and distinct an idea as its existence. (EU 12.28/164)

Hume goes on to explain how, in this regard, matters of fact differ from a priori truths in mathematics.

As noted earlier, Clarke aims first to establish that it is logically necessary that there be an unchangeable and independent being and then, second, to show that such a being is one whose existence is itself logically necessary. Demea's argument has the same stages. Mounting attacks in the reverse order, Cleanthes next criticizes earlier parts of the argument. It is significant that, in one of these criticisms, Hume refers in a footnote directly to Clarke's Newtonian argument that the existence of matter is contingent, whereas space, time, and God are necessary beings. Cleanthes objects that Clarke uses the conceivability of the nonexistence of matter to prove its possibility, but (as Hume would say) the same argument can be applied to God. Another criticism concerns Demea's assumption that one can treat the infinite succession of contingent causes and effects as a single entity and then ask about its cause. Cleanthes implicitly follows Hume in arguing that this unity is only a fiction of the imagination, not a real entity capable of entering into causal relations. It is significant that the original of the argument (T 1.2.2.3/30–1) comes in the course of Hume's account of the ideas of space and time in which he criticizes Newtonian accounts.

III.1 The Design Argument in EU

The first of Hume's published examinations of the design argument is "Of a Particular Providence and of a Future State" (EU 11). It is written as a conversation between an author, "I," and a friend who is described as someone "who loves sceptical paradoxes" and who "advanced many principles of which I can by no means approve" but which "seem to be curious, and to bear some relation to the chain of reasoning carried on throughout this enquiry" (EU 11.1). At the start, the conversation is about the desirability that philosophical inquiry should be free of religious bigotry. The author asks whether political authorities might be justified in suppressing certain philosophical theories "such as those of Epicurus, which, denying a divine existence, and consequently a providence and a future state, seem to loosen, in a great measure, the ties of morality, and may be supposed, for that reason, pernicious to the peace of civil society" (EU 11.4/133–4). The friend offers to play the part of Epicurus in giving a defence before the Athenian people, represented by the author, against the charge that his skepticism about natural religion is a danger to morality and society.

The friend starts his defence by saying that he has no quarrel with traditional religious practices, but he does oppose combining philosophy with theology in the project of natural religion. Proponents of natural religion, says the friend, "have acknowledged, that the chief or sole argument for a divine existence (which I never questioned) is derived from the order of nature; where there appear such marks of intelligence and design, that you think it extravagant to assign for its cause, either chance, or the blind and unguided force of matter. You allow that this is an argument drawn from effects to causes" (EU 11.11/135–6). The friend says he does not challenge the claim that the order of nature displays "marks of intelligence and design," so he is content to infer that the gods possess these attributes. What he does deny, however, is that a further inference can be made from observation of the order of nature to divine providence and a future state (an afterlife in which God ensures that justice prevails by rewarding the virtuous and punishing the vicious). Furthermore, he argues that in rejecting such an inference he is not undermining morality.

Hume's purpose here is to show how his account of probable reasoning given earlier in EU supports the position of the friend in this section. Only from experience can it be discovered what effect results from a given cause or what cause produces a given effect. The friend has allowed that the order of nature displays effects of divine "power, intelligence and benevolence." But all the inference can show about the nature of divine power, intelligence, and benevolence is that these attributes are sufficient to produce the known effects from which they are inferred. The inference cannot justify ascribing any greater degrees of these qualities. Even if the design argument is allowed to have shown that there is a deity with intelligence and benevolent intentions, it cannot go further to establish that God is perfectly wise and good and has further intentions for his creation that are not yet realized: "When we infer any particular cause from an effect, we must proportion the one to the other, and can never be allowed to ascribe to the cause any qualities, but what are exactly sufficient to produce the effect" (EU 11.12/136). In short, it is human experience that the order of nature produces both human happiness and human misery. It is human experience that the virtuous sometimes suffer calamities, and the vicious sometimes prosper. If we follow the design argument so far as to ascribe the order of nature to divine intention and power, all we can say is that God intends and brings about just that distribution of happiness and misery that we actually find. The belief that God will eventually in the afterlife reward the virtuous with bliss and punish the vicious with torment has no basis whatever in the design argument. As a result, concludes the friend, inferring a divine origin for the order of nature (provided our basis for this inference conforms to the Humean principles of causal reasoning) provides no additional motive for virtue than we have already from our experience of the world. Our moral experiences, sentiments, and preferences are what they are whether we allow the inference from the order of nature to a divine designer or whether we do not. The question of whether that inference is justified is, the friend maintains, "entirely indifferent to the peace of society and security of government" and is therefore entirely "speculative" (EU 11.9/135).

The author raises an objection to the principle that an inference to a cause from an effect should be proportioned to the known effect. Suppose there is just one human footprint in the sand. Is it not legitimate to infer, first, that it was caused by a human being and, second, that it is probable there was a footprint of the other foot, which has been obliterated? The friend replies that the second inference depends on knowledge of the anatomy of human beings obtained by experience other than just the observation of the one print. But in the case of the inference from nature to a divine designer, there is no other relevant experience to draw on. "The Deity is known to us only by his productions, and is a single being in the universe, not comprehended under any species or genus, from whose experienced attributes or qualities, we can, by analogy, infer any attribute or quality in him" (EU 11.26/144). Philosophical reasoning cannot attribute to the deity any qualities, degree of qualities, or intentions other than those whose "marks" appear in nature; and if natural religion is strictly part of philosophy, it likewise cannot represent the nature of the deity in any other way and so "will never be able to carry us beyond the usual course of experience, or give us measures of conduct and behaviour different from those which are furnished by reflections on common life" (EU 11.27/146).

At the end of the section, the author raises a further problem. The friend has said that the deity is not analogous to any other kind of entity and that knowledge of his nature is strictly limited to what can be inferred from the nature of his creation. But if a cause really is not analogous to any other cause, then neither is the effect analogous to any other effect, so how can any inference at all be drawn? This objection also draws on Hume's positive account of causal inference. "It is only when two species of objects are found to be constantly conjoined, that we can infer the one from the other; and were an effect presented, which was entirely singular, and could not be comprehended under any known species, I do not see, that we could form any conjecture or inference at all concerning its cause" (EU 11.30/148). This raises a more general question about the nature, scope, and limits of the design argument and, at the same time, of Hume's theories of probable reasoning and beliefs based on such reasoning. This wider set of questions is examined in the *Dialogues*, with which the next section of this chapter is concerned.

III.2 The Design Argument in D

Dialogues Concerning Natural Religion (published posthumously in 1779) is a dialogue among three characters, Cleanthes, Demea, and Philo, whose conversation is reported by a young man, Pamphilus, to a friend, Hermippus. Pamphilus makes a few comments on the debate as it goes along and writes an introductory letter and supplies a closing comment, neither of which represents Hume's own opinions. There are twelve parts. Part 1 is important for a number of reasons. Clearly, it introduces a main theme: the relations between philosophical reasoning and theological speculation. It also provides the reader with early indications about the way each character is positioned in relation to that theme, and, what is not necessarily the same thing, how each character interprets the relations of the others to the theme. Demea asks Cleanthes, who is supervising the education of Pamphilus, whether he agrees that natural religion ought not to be studied by the young until they have learned logic, ethics, and natural philosophy. Philo suggests that there is a danger that the young may neglect or reject religious principles if they are not taught early in a program of education. Demea replies with a distinction between teaching "piety . . . by continual precept and instruction," which should be done from the earliest years, and natural religion, which is a matter of philosophical speculation and should be treated with some skepticism. He implies that religious belief rests on faith and tradition rather than on philosophical arguments. Philo seems to agree, although in fact his interest is not in traditional faith but in the scope of skepticism. He refers to a whole series of skeptical topics, such as those to do with sense perception and the ideas of matter, cause and effect, space and time, and mathematics, and he concludes that if reason cannot answer skeptical doubts in these areas, it is hardly likely to be able to reach any conclusions in natural theology, where philosophers try to "decide concerning the origin of worlds, or trace their history from eternity to eternity" (D 1.3).

There is now an important exchange between Cleanthes, who is the spokesman for the design argument, and Philo about the scope of skepticism. Cleanthes complains that Philo speaks like a Pyrrhonian, an extreme skeptic, and he suggests that perhaps Philo is a fideist, one who proposes "to erect religious faith on philosophical scepticism" (D 1.5). He queries Philo's sincerity, arguing that the Pyrrhonian aim of suspending all beliefs about reality cannot be achieved. Philo's reply makes clear (to the reader, if not to Cleanthes) that, in fact, his position is Humean "mitigated scepticism" rather than Pyrrhonian "excessive scepticism" (EU 12.24/161). However much a philosopher may be skeptical in metaphysical inquiries, "he must act, I own, and live, and converse like other men; and for this conduct he is not obliged to give any other reason than the absolute necessity he lies under of so doing." Furthermore, it is equally natural to us to form principles of both belief and conduct on the basis of experience, and "the larger experience we acquire, and the stronger reason we are endowed with, we always render our principles the more general and comprehensive" so that "what we call philosophy is nothing but a more regular and methodical operation of the same kind" as we employ when "reasoning on common life." But when we engage in speculations in natural religion about the origins of the universe and the possibility of an afterlife, and about the nature of God as traditionally understood, "omnipotent, omniscient, immutable, infinite, and incomprehensible: We must be far removed from the smallest tendency to scepticism not to be apprehensive, that we have here got quite beyond the reach of our faculties" (D 1.10). In a crucial passage, Cleanthes responds by questioning the distinction Philo makes between metaphysical speculations, which are beyond the scope of the kind of reasoning based on experience, custom, and instinct that mitigated skepticism accepts, and the domain of common life and those discoveries of natural philosophy made with a methodology likewise based on experience, custom, and instinct. "In vain would the sceptic make a distinction between science and common life, or between one science and another. The arguments, employed in all, if just, are of a similar nature, and contain the same force and evidence" (D 1.16).

In Part 2, Demea and Philo agree that the nature of God is beyond human comprehension. Their agreement is only verbal—although Demea fails to realize this. Nevertheless, the surface agreement Hume stages at this point provides the foil for a subsequent dialectic in which it becomes evident that the logic of Cleanthes's design argument pushes him more and more toward defending an unorthodox, anthropomorphic conception of God. The "just reasoning" he employs (the implication being that this is the kind of reasoning used in natural philosophy) shows, he thinks, that the author of nature is a being who possesses "design, thought, wisdom, and intelligence" that resemble the design, thought, wisdom, and intelligence of human beings. The world is a great machine, composed of parts that are themselves machines. The parts of these machines are "adjusted to each other" in such a way as to achieve the purposes of these machines, and so are all the machines that make up the world ordered and adjusted to each other. The whole world displays purposiveness and the adaptation of means to ends, wherever we look. There is therefore a resemblance between the world and its parts and machines and their parts made by human beings. In the latter cases, order and purposiveness is the effect of the design, thought, wisdom, and intelligence of human beings. The conclusion Cleanthes draws is:

> Since therefore the effects resemble each other, we are led to infer, by all the rules of analogy, that the causes also resemble; and that the author of nature is somewhat similar to the mind of man; though possessed of much larger faculties, proportioned to the grandeur of the work, which he has executed. By this argument a posteriori, and by this argument alone, do we prove at once the existence of a deity, and his similarity to human mind and intelligence. (D 2.5)

The criticisms Philo makes of the design argument are, of course, based on Hume's theory of causation, causal inference, and empirical belief. Cleanthes claims to be arguing according to the methodology of natural philosophy, but he never gives any general account of scientific method. Philo actually restates Cleanthes's argument (D 2.12–14) so that its logic is made more perspicuous, and, at the same time, so is its vulnerability. Repeating the point made at the end of EU 11, Philo points out (D 2.24) that there is no possibility of inferring a cause for the order and purposiveness of the universe other than by analogy with a part of it because no one has any experience of the conjunction of some kind of event, such as the action of a deity, with the coming into existence of universes. The strength of analogical inferences is proportioned to the degree of similarity. Philo remarks that the degree of similarity between the universe and man-made machines is slight, and so the inference from these effects to a similarity between the causes is no better than a guess or conjecture (D 2.8). Furthermore, Cleanthes is assuming that what experience shows to be the cause of order and purposiveness in one small part of the world—namely, machines made by humans—must be similar to the cause of order and purposiveness in the world as a whole. Yet there are many other parts of the world that display order and purposiveness, and there may be many other causes in nature of this; so why assume, with Cleanthes, that the only analogy that can be made is between the universe and machines made by humans? The analogy is weak, and no reason has been given why this analogy is to be preferred to any other.

In Part 3, Cleanthes's tries to evade objections based on Hume's theory of analogical reasoning. He gives two thought experiments of imagined instances in which the inference from certain phenomena to intelligence as their cause would be immediate and compelling, even though Philo's kinds of objections to the design argument could still be made. He is trying to show that there could be cases in which no one would "hesitate a moment" but would "instantly ascribe" intelligent design and intention as the cause of the phenomena (D 3.2). In fact, he thinks that there clearly are such cases in reality. Consider, he says, the anatomy and physiology of an organ like the human eye "and tell me, from your own feeling, if the idea of a contriver does not immediately flow in upon you with a force like that of sensation." In the style of many apologists for the design argument from the Boyle lecturers to today's proponents of intelligent design, Cleanthes claims that the persuasiveness of the design argument is a matter of "commonsense and the plain instincts of nature" and that Philo's objections are "perverse, obstinate metaphysics" (D 3.7). Abandoning his alleged adherence to the methods of the abstract sciences, Cleanthes is now trying to present himself as the thinker of common sense, borrowing Philo's Humean clothes.

One of the thought experiments Cleanthes uses is the idea of a world in which books are works of nature rather than of human production, things that reproduce themselves like animals and vegetables. They still, however, contain meaningful content in a universal language that everyone can read. No one would doubt that these natural books are produced by the action of a vast intelligence. Demea points out that Cleanthes appears to be assuming that the divine mind is of the same nature as the human minds of the authors of books, an analogy unacceptable to traditional theists. As before, there is a surface agreement between Demea's orthodox theology of the inconceivability of the divine nature and Humean themes. All human ideas, the elements of human thought, are derived either from impressions of the senses or from inner sentiments such as love, friendship, pity, envy, and so on, and all of these "have a plain reference to the state and situation of man, and are calculated for preserving the existence, and promoting the activity of such a being in such circumstances" (D 3.13). But God cannot be thought to have such human sentiments nor to derive ideas from sensation. Again, human thinking is "fluctuating, uncertain, fleeting, successive, and compounded" (idem), and these features, although essential to what we mean by "mind" and "thought" in the case of human beings cannot be applied to God. We have no idea what is the nature of the divine mind and the divine thought.

In Part 4, Cleanthes objects that Demea's insistence on the incomprehensibility of God is a kind of mysticism that is really no different from the position of "sceptics or atheists, who assert, that the first cause of all is unknown and unintelligible" (D 4.1). Demea (as discussed earlier in Section III) thinks that *a priori* metaphysical proofs can be given of the existence of a deity possessing the traditional divine attributes and so would reject Cleanthes's view that mysticism is much the same as skepticism or atheism. Philo, on the other hand, rejects both the a priori proofs and the design argument, pointing out that neither provides a philosophical basis for religious claims. He argues against Cleanthes that if God's thought is like human thought, a complex order of different ideas that change over time, then the question arises: what causes this thought? If the divine mind is like human minds, there is no ground for ascribing to God infinite or perfect attributes. Throughout Parts 4 and 5, Philo shows that the logic of Cleanthes's position takes him further and further away from traditional theology:

> In a word, Cleanthes, a man, who follows your hypothesis, is able, perhaps, to assert, or conjecture, that the universe, some time, arose from some thing like design: But beyond that position he cannot ascertain one single circumstance, and is left afterwards to fix every point of his theology, by the utmost licence of fancy and hypothesis. This world, for aught he knows, is very faulty and imperfect, compared to a superior standard; and was only the first rude essay of some infant deity, who afterwards abandoned it, ashamed of his lame performance: It is the work only of some dependent, inferior deity; and is the object of derision to his superiors: It is the production of old age and dotage in some superannuated deity; and ever since his death, has run on at adventures, from the first impulse and active force, which it received from him. (D 5.39)

Cleanthes dismisses all this as "rambling." The implication of this word is that Philo is following Pyrrhonian methods, simply arguing for or against positions in order to produce a total suspense of judgment on the questions under discussion. However, Hume uses Philo's barrage of objections to show something quite definite about the design argument: that it does not conform to the theory of causal reasoning that Hume presents as the basis of a proper scientific method and that it can provide no basis for religious practices nor any significant content for religious beliefs.

IV Conclusion: Some New Perspectives

Much of the material in this chapter is familiar to Hume scholars. However, my intention has been to take account of recent work by a number of Hume scholars that has made coherent the interconnections between Hume's theory of causation, his attack on natural religion, and his critique of Newtonian philosophers like Clarke by carefully exploring the historical contexts of Hume's philosophy.

Paul Russell's *The Riddle of Hume's Treatise* (2008) is essential for understanding these historical contexts. The riddle of the title is how to reconcile Hume's naturalism and his skepticism, and Russell amasses historical and textual evidence to show that the solution to the riddle is Hume's systematic destructive critique of natural religion and of metaphysical doctrines that support the project of natural religion. The scope and importance of Russell's work will make it a source of subsequent research on these topics for a long time.

One question that Russell's book raises is about the place of Hume's theory of causation in the development of his philosophy as a whole. When is it likely that Hume first examined and rejected Locke's and Clarke's cosmological arguments? Was this an early stimulus for the development of his theory? Millican (2009: 42) suggests this could be the case, and there is unpublished work by other scholars pointing in the same direction.

A third perspective that connects with these and that is becoming prominent in recent work is Hume's criticisms of Newtonian natural philosophy. Russell does indeed show that this informs his attacks on natural religion. But, in a number of recent publications, Eric Schliesser (2007; 2008; 2009) argues that Hume's anti-Newtonianism goes beyond that and concerns Hume's fundamental aim to construct a science of man that is a foundation for both moral *and* natural philosophy. On Hume and Newton, there is again so far unpublished work by other scholars.

Abbreviations of Works Cited

D   *Dialogues Concerning Natural Religion*. In D. Coleman, ed. *Dialogues Concerning Natural Religion and Other Writings*. Cambridge: Cambridge University Press, 2007.

EU   *An Enquiry Concerning Human Understanding*. Edited by T. L. Beauchamp. Oxford: Clarendon, 2000.

T   *A Treatise of Human Nature*. Edited by D. F. Norton and M. J. Norton. Oxford: Clarendon, 2007.

TA   *An Abstract of a Treatise of Human Nature*. Reprinted in T.

BIBLIOGRAPHY

Anscombe, G. E. M. (1974). "Whatever has a Beginning of Existence must have a Cause," *Analysis* 34 (5), 145–151.

Bennett, J. (2005). "God and Matter in Locke," in C. Mercer and E. O'Neill, eds., *Early Modern Philosophy—Mind, Matter and Metaphysics*. Oxford: Oxford University Press, 163–182.

Clarke, S. (1998). *A Demonstration of the Being and Attributes of God*. E. Vailati, ed., Cambridge: Cambridge University Press.

Garrett, D. (1997). *Cognition and Commitment in Hume's Philosophy*. Oxford: Oxford University Press.

Millican, P. (2002). "Hume's Sceptical Doubts Concerning Induction," in P. Millican, ed., *Reading Hume on Human Understanding*. Oxford: Clarendon Press, 107–173.

Millican, P. (2009). "Hume, Causal Realism, and Causal Science." *Mind* 118 (471), 647–712.

Mossner, E. C., and J. V. Price (eds.). (1967). *A Letter from a Gentleman to his friend in Edinburgh*. Edinburgh: Edinburgh University Press.

Russell, P. (2008). *The Riddle of Hume's Treatise: Skepticism, Naturalism, and Irreligion*. Oxford: Oxford University Press.

Schliesser, E. (2007). "Two Definitions of 'Cause,' Newton, and the Significance of the Humean Distinction Between Natural and Philosophical Relations," *Journal of Scottish Philosophy* 5 (1), 83–101.

Schliesser, E. (2008). "Hume's Newtonianism and Anti-Newtonianism," in E. N. Zalta, ed., *The Stanford Encyclopedia of Philosophy (Winter 2008 Edition)*. http://plato.stanford.edu/archives/win2008/entries/hume-newton/

Schliesser, E. (2009). "Hume's Attack on Newton's Philosophy," *Enlightenment and Dissent* 25, 167–203.

Stewart, M. A. (1985). "Hume and the Metaphysical Argument a priori," in A. J. Holland, ed., *Philosophy, Its History and Historiography*. Dordrecht: D. Reidel Publishing Company.

Stewart, M. A. (2002). "The Two Species of Philosophy: The Historical Significance of the First *Enquiry*," in P. Millican, ed., *Reading Hume on Human Understanding*. Oxford: Clarendon Press. 67–95.

Williford, K. (2003). "Demea's a priori Theistic Proof," *Hume Studies* 29(1), 99–123.

Wright, J. P. (2006). "The *Treatise*: Composition, Reception and Response," in S. Traiger, ed., *The Blackwell Guide to Hume's Treatise*. Oxford: Blackwell Publishing. 5–25.

CHAPTER 31

HUME ON EVIL

SAMUEL NEWLANDS

I HUME ON EVIL, THEN AND NOW

IN his posthumously published *Dialogues Concerning Natural Religion*, Hume offers powerful and influential criticisms of traditional arguments for God's existence. As part of this critical project in the *Dialogues*, Hume examines the relationship between the traditional concept of God as a morally good, providential agent and the evil we observe in our world, and he presents several versions of what is known as "the problem of evil." As with his critiques of arguments for God's existence, Hume's discussion of evil has transcended the dialogical and historical context in which it was imbedded, presenting ideas that philosophers continue to discuss today. In this essay, I examine Hume's claims about evil, both as Hume presented them in dialogue form in the eighteenth century and as contemporary philosophers might read them independently of that form and context.

Because the bulk of Hume's writing on evil occurs in the *Dialogues*, it is worth addressing a long-standing interpretative question up front. How closely do Hume's own views match those of his characters, Philo, Cleanthes, and Demea? In the early dialogues, Philo frequently voices claims that Hume himself endorses in other writings, but Hume rarely discusses the problem of evil in his own voice. Even where Hume says the most about the problem of evil in his published work (EU 11), he presents it as a recollection of a conversation he once had in which he and a friend constructed an imaginary dialogue and in which his friend (as best as Hume can recall) offered opinions similar to those Philo offers—a structure that thrice-distances Hume from the main critical claims.[1] So although it is surely the case that Hume was sympathetic with Philo's claims about evil, we should not assume that Hume's own position is exactly identical to Philo's. In what follows, I indicate those places where it is less clear whether Hume is committed to Philo's claims by ascribing the views to the character rather than to their author.

The immediate intellectual context of Hume's discussion of evil is Hume's own mid-eighteenth-century Scotland, an intellectual context dominated by feuds between moderate and conservative Calvinists. During the Scottish Enlightenment, the problem of evil received considerably less attention than it had in previous centuries. British philosophers and theologians continued to devote entire volumes to the topic in the eighteenth century; see, for example, William King's *De Malo* (1702) and Soame Jenyns's *A Free Inquiry into the Nature and Origin of Evil* (1756). But, on the whole, the topic had faded in importance and complexity among leading intellectuals of Hume's day, certainly by comparison to its treatment in the last half of the seventeenth century in continental Europe.

Hume's more thorough discussion of evil is something of an anomaly among his peers. Hume is most like a mid-eighteenth-century version of Pierre Bayle, the great gadfly to seventeenth-century theodicies—only without Bayle's interlocutors: Malebranche, Leibniz, Jacquelot. In Hume's *Dialogues*, Leibniz, the great seventeenth-century defender of God's goodness in the face of evil, has been reduced to a caricature, an eighteenth-century punch line (D X.6). Malebranche, from whom Hume borrowed much in other contexts, is given shallow and oblique treatment when it comes to the problem of evil. In fact, Hume's *Dialogues* contains no point of view from anything like a seventeenth-century rationalist: that perspective has been rejected from the outset. Hume, in effect, follows Bayle's strategy on evil, only having first dismissed Bayle's fiercest combatants from participating. I return to this point in the concluding section.

In what follows, I discuss Hume's claims about evil with an eye toward both contemporary discussions and Hume's early modern context. In Section II, I discuss the wide variety of problems of evil in Hume, which involves extracting Hume's claims from their original setting. In the third section, I return to the unfolding discussion of the *Dialogues* and present what Hume himself took to be the most important claims concerning evil. In the final section, I offer some evaluations of Hume's discussion from both contemporary and historical perspectives.

II THE PROBLEMS OF EVIL IN HUME

It is customary to refer to "*the* problem of evil," just as one might refer to "the problem of universals" or "the problem of skepticism." Although useful, this label obscures the fact that there are many different problems of evil, united mostly by the fact that they all have "God" and "evil" occurring somewhere in their formulations. In general, problems of evil concern whether the existence of a perfect, divine creator can be reconciled with the facts about evil in our world. The issue is commonly put in the form of a question: If God is all-good and all-powerful, whence evil? Philo provides an especially memorable version: "Is [God] willing to prevent evil, but not able? Then he is impotent. Is he able, but not willing? Then is he malevolent. Is he both able and willing? Whence then is evil?" (D X.11).

Hume was well aware that the relationship between God and evil raises a variety of philosophical problems. In fact, Hume's display of this variety in the *Dialogues* is one of his most important legacies for contemporary discussions on evil, even though the characters themselves sometimes blur versions together in the heat of discussion.

In this section, I present four major axes in Hume's discussions of evil: force, scope, kinds, and perspective. Hume offers multiple ways of filling out each dimension, which means that, strictly speaking, Hume provides us with hundreds of problems of evil. Although it is tempting to work through each of them one by one, I conclude this section by indicating the three versions on which Hume himself focuses.

II.1 Force

If we think of problems of evil as objections to the existence of God (as God is commonly conceived by the major monotheistic faiths), Hume recognizes that these objections can differ with respect to their strength. Evil might be *logically inconsistent* with God's existence, which means that facts about evil could be used to deductively prove that God does not exist. For 150 years after Hume, the objection from evil was most commonly presented in this very strong, deductive manner, known as the "logical problem of evil."

However, one could raise a less forceful objection. Facts about evil might make God's existence *unlikely,* without giving us reason to assign it a probability of zero. On this formulation, facts about evil provide some strong evidence against God's existence, even though they do not deductively prove that God doesn't exist. Versions of this problem are known as *evidential* or *probabilistic* problems of evil. Contemporary discussions of this family of problems have become highly sophisticated as theories of probability and evidence have become correspondingly more nuanced. But Hume's basic point still holds: even if evil doesn't outright disprove God's existence, it might still be the case that we shouldn't believe in God's existence due to facts about evil.

A third kind of force that Hume discusses is what we might call *defensive.* The logical and evidential versions attempt to use facts about evil to conclude something about God's nonexistence. By contrast, a defensive force uses facts about evil to *block* inferences from the character of our world to the existence of a perfectly good God. Evil, in other words, ought to prevent us from inferring that the world's original cause is good from what is empirically observable in the world. This might sound a little funny at first: who would have thought that facts about evil *do* provide a good basis from which to infer a morally good creator? Isn't the theist already committed to claiming that God exists *in spite of*—surely not *because of*—evil?

Hume employs this defensive force because it had become increasingly popular in his day to argue that the empirically observable facts about the world *by themselves* license us to infer the existence of a morally good, providential creator.[2] This brand of empirically minded theism was increasingly popular during the Scottish Enlightenment, and many took developments in the natural sciences to confirm the existence of an intelligent, powerful, benevolent creator (e.g., D 4.13). Hume's Philo argues against this inference from the observable world throughout the *Dialogues*, and in Parts X and XI, he argues that facts about evil provide an additional reason to block the inference:

> "But there is no view of human life or of the condition of mankind, from which, without the greatest violence, we can infer the moral attributes, or learn that infinite benevolence, conjoined with infinite power and infinite wisdom, which we must discover by the eyes of faith alone" (D X.36).

In other words, facts about evil prove that inferences to God's moral goodness from what we observe about the human condition are invalid. If so, facts about evil could also be used *defensively* to try to undermine arguments for God's existence.

II.2 Scope

Although Hume doesn't make this axis as explicit, he appeals to different *scopes* for problems of evil. Sometimes Hume appeals to the bare fact that there is some evil, any evil at all, in his arguments. "Why is there any misery at all in the world?" Philo asks (D X.34; see also D XI.17). According to this formulation, that any evil of any kind or amount exists is the relevant fact about evil. In contemporary discussions, this is sometimes called the *abstract* or *bare* problem of evil.

Hume discusses more than just the bare existence of evil, however. Philo sometimes uses the *amount* of evil in our world (D X.8) to raise a problem for theists. Sometimes he focuses on the *extent* of evil: that suffering is so widespread throughout the animal and human populations and present through most of the lifespans of individual organisms (D X.8–9; D XI.13). At other points, Hume suggests that especially intense forms of suffering occasion forceful problems of evil:

> "But pain often—good God how often!—rises to torture and agony, and the longer it continues, it becomes still more genuine agony and torture. Patience is exhausted; courage languishes; melancholy seizes us; and nothing terminates our misery but the removal of its cause" (D X.32; see also D X.11–14).

Hume has the most to say about another possible scope: the *distribution* of evil. This scope itself admits of variants. One kind of distribution problem that Hume mentions only in passing is the seemingly *haphazard* distribution of pain and suffering, one that resists clear correlation with other moral traits like virtue and vice. As he notes in his own voice, "Pains and pleasures seem to be scattered indifferently through life, as heat and cold, moist and dry are dispersed through the universe" (D 112; see also EU 11.20/140).

More often, Hume focuses on the *global* distribution of evil, the overall balance of good to evil (understood by Hume as the overall balance of pleasure to pain [e.g., D X.31–2]). In his "Fragment on Evil," Hume claims that facts about the global distribution of evil, if known, would allow us to determine whether or not the cause of the universe is morally good:

> Whether the author of nature be benevolent or not can only be proved by the effects, and by the predominancy either of good or evil, of happiness or misery, in the universe. If good prevail much above evil, we may, perhaps, presume that the author of the universe, if an intelligent, is also a benevolent principle. If evil prevail much above good, we may draw a contrary inference. (D 110)

However, Hume admits that this line of inquiry faces an insurmountable problem: we do not and probably will not ever know all the facts about the global distribution of happiness and misery in the universe:

> This is a standard by which we may decide such a question, with some appearance of certainty; but when the question is brought to that standard, and we would willingly determine the facts upon which we must proceed in our reasoning, we find that it is very difficult, if not absolutely impossible, ever to ascertain them. For who is able to form an exact computation of all the happiness and misery that are in the world, and to compare them exactly with each other? (D 110)[3]

Although the global distribution scope would decisively settle the issue, we cannot employ it, according to Hume. Of course, as Philo points out to Cleanthes at the end of Part X, this ignorance cuts both ways: it also prevents us from inferring the moral attributes of the cause of the universe from known facts about the global distribution of happiness and suffering (D X.34). This is an instance of Hume combining the *defensive* force with the *global distribution* scope to formulate a distinctive version of the problem of evil.

II.3 Kinds of Evil

I've been discussing evil in fairly general terms so far, but Hume distinguishes different kinds of evil, which means that one could combine different forces and scopes with different kinds of evil to formulate a huge range of conceptually distinct problems of evil. By the start of the eighteenth century, it had become standard to distinguish three kinds of evil: moral, physical (or "natural"), and metaphysical (or "evils of imperfection"). Here, for example, is Samuel Clarke's (1705: 78–79); version of the distinction: "All that we call evil is either an evil of imperfection, as the want of certain faculties and excellencies which other creatures have, or natural evil, as pain death and the like, or moral evil, as all kinds of vice."[4]

In Hume's *Dialogues*, the rich metaphysical backdrop of this taxonomy is either neglected or ignored. Instead, Hume distinguishes only moral evil from natural evil in passing. This is a rare instance in which Hume shrinks the range of interesting problems of evil rather than expands them. Hume even claims that, with respect to at least one family of arguments from evil, the difference between moral and natural evils is not terribly important: "What I have said concerning natural evil will apply to moral, with little or no variation" (D XI.16; see also EU 8.34–5/101–3), although he does allow that problems of evil focusing on the data of moral evil will be more compelling "since moral evil, in the opinion of many, is much more predominant above moral good than natural evil above natural good" (D XI.16). That is, the distinction between moral and natural evils is relevant mostly when we focus on the global distribution scope.

Although he doesn't say very much about the problem of moral evils, Hume indicates his dissatisfaction with the most common response from theists to this form of the problem, the so-called *freewill theodicy*. The basic idea of the freewill theodicy is that the exercise of creaturely freedom is incompatible with God's prevention of all moral evil, and such exercises of freedom are more valuable than God's prevention of all moral evil would be. In his early reading notes, Hume closely echoes Bayle in challenging this line of reasoning: "Liberty not a proper solution of moral ill: Because it might have been bound down, by motives like those of saints and angels" (D 107.23; see also D 107.24–5, 32).

Most of Hume's discussion in the *Dialogues* focuses on natural evils, which he equates with pain and suffering (D X.31–2; D XI.5–12). We might wonder whether this hedonistic framework for natural goods and evils, assumed throughout Hume's discussion of evil in the *Dialogues*, is an adequate theory of value. There appears to be a vast range of goods and evils whose value greatly outstrips their contributions to our feelings of pleasure and pain: friendship, courage, honor, humiliation, and shame, to name just a few. However, although Hume assumes a hedonistic framework in presenting the data of natural evils, there is no necessary connection here. One could present different forms of the problem of natural evils using very different axiological theories.

II.4 Perspectives

Philo and Demea illustrate the dismal state of the world by drawing on a variety of sources and perspectives. They refer to evils from the perspective of biology (D X.8–9), sociology and anthropology (D X.10–12), physiology and psychology (D X.13–14), history (D X.21–2), literature (D X.4–5, 13, 23), personal testimony (D X.7), and one's own feelings and experiences (D X.33). Hume doesn't intend these to be exhaustive catalogues of what these sources tell us about the scope of pain and suffering, but his presentation reminds us that the sources of information about evil are quite wide ranging. The natural sciences, the humanities, anecdotal testimony, and our own lived experience are distinct sources of data about evil that can occasion distinct forms of the problem of evil. More defensively, these sources might also provide counterexamples to theistic explanations of evil. For instance, facts from contemporary evolutionary biology about the extent of animal pain and death prior to the existence of human beings might defeat theistic attempts to explain all evil as the result of human freedom gone afoul.

Hume's *Dialogues* also brings to light a distinction among personal perspectives on evil that plays a prominent role in more recent discussions of evil.[5] Demea proclaims that everyone acknowledges the wretched misery of human life. "And who can doubt of what all men declare from their own immediate feeling and experience?" (D X.3)

Several paragraphs later, Cleanthes objects, "I can observe something like what you mention in some others . . . But I confess, I feel little or nothing of it in myself" (D X.20). Predictably, Demea immediately attacks Cleanthes and offers more testimony and anecdotal evidence to support his universal claim. Unfortunately, Hume never gives Cleanthes the chance to reflect on whether Cleanthes's own personal experience of natural *goods* might give him resources to respond to at least some problems of evil. Hume does, however, indicate that first-person perspectives on evil can provide indefeasible authority: "But this is contrary to everyone's feeling and experience: It is contrary to an authority so established as nothing can subvert: No decisive proofs can ever be produced against this authority" (D X.33).

More often, first-person perspectives on evil seem to make the problem of evil harder for traditional theists. Victims of some evils may have perspectives on their own suffering that elude adequate characterization and explanation by independent observers. Indeed, experiences of some truly horrific evils might be so transformative for the participants that projection from those who haven't experienced something similar is psychologically impossible. These sorts of considerations—evil from the first-person experience of the victim—provide novel versions of the problem of evil and might also be a defensive stumbling block to theodicies that focus solely on compensatory goods enjoyed by the perpetrators (such as the freedom to abuse another person) or by the world as a whole (such as the overall favorable balance of natural goods to natural evils).

II.5 Hume's Preferred Versions

Although one can mine Hume's *Dialogues* for these variations on the general problem of evil, Hume's own focus is mainly on a problem of evil that is (a) *defensive* in force, (b) *distributive* in scope, (c) *natural* in kind, (d) and *third-person* in perspective. His overarching claim is that observable facts about the distribution of pain and suffering block inferences to God's goodness from what we know about the world. This focus in the *Dialogues* mirrors Hume's own earlier ruminations on evil. His conclusion in "Fragment on Evil" is that what we know about the distribution of natural evils and natural goods (including the complex interworking of nature, the occasional delights of human life, beauty, joy, pleasure, love, and so on) can "never afford any proof" of the moral goodness of the source of those natural goods (D 112; see also EU 11.20–1, D X.35, D XI.2, D XI.8, D XI.12).

At several points in the *Dialogues*, Hume also discusses a problem of evil that is (a) *logical* in force and (b) *bare* or *abstract* in scope—the aforementioned logical problem of evil that rose to prominence in the first half of the twentieth century (D X.34; D XI.1). Hume's Philo concedes in several places that this version of the problem of evil is not wholly successful (D X.35, D XI.2; D XI.4, D XI.8, D XI.12), and it is not the main focus of the discussion.[6] Hume also presents a problem of evil with a *probabilistic* force. Philo asks, "Is the world, considered in general and as it appears to us in this life, different from what a man or such a limited being would, *beforehand*, expect from a very powerful, wise, and benevolent deity?" (D XI.4; see also D X.15 and D XI.2).[7] According to a more developed version of this argument, the prior probability of the existence (and/or distribution) of evil is much lower on the hypothesis of theism than on the hypothesis of a morally indifferent cause of the universe.[8]

III Hume's Discussion of Evil

III.1 Dialogue X: The Setup

Hume's discussion of evil in the *Dialogues* is as rich as it is compressed. Due to space limitations, I pass over many of the wonderful gems Hume sprinkles into the text, such as his suggestions that laziness is the root of most human evil (D XI.10), that fear of death alone prevents us all from committing mass suicide (D X.17[9]), and that what is now described as the "fine-tuning" of our universe for life may actually be evidence *against* the existence of a wise and benevolent creator (D XI.9). I focus instead on the most prominent philosophical claims Hume makes concerning evil, following the main thread of discussion in Parts X and XI to do so.

Leading up to Part X, the discussion has focused on whether the workings of the natural world provide sufficient evidence to justify the belief that the original cause of the world has the attributes traditionally ascribed to God, such as unity, intelligence, love, wisdom, and perfection. Philo has repeatedly argued that it does not. Philo instead advocates agnosticism about the nature of the original cause of the universe and uses the tools of Pyrrhonian skepticism to undermine Cleanthes's attempts to infer such properties from the empirically accessible properties of the natural world. In this critical project, Philo is often joined by Demea, who usually plays the role of an apophatic or "negative" theologian (i.e., someone who thinks that predications of attributes to God and created things are always equivocal). Part of Hume's point in linking Philo the agnostic and Demea the theologian is to show that these positions ultimately amount to affirming and denying (roughly) the same propositions (D IV.1; IV.12; VI.13; XII.7), in which case Philo's proposed agnosticism about the nature of the source of the universe is not as threatening as Hume's readers might have initially believed. By the conclusion of the *Dialogues*, Hume even argues that such epistemic modesty about the nature of the origin of the universe is compatible with central tenets of revealed religion and can actually pave the way for religious civility and toleration (D XII.7; see also D XII.33).[10]

In Part IX, the alliance between Philo and Demea shows signs of weakening. Having sided with Philo against Cleanthes's a posteriori arguments about the nature of the original cause, Demea suggests that a priori arguments might yield additional knowledge of God's nature. Cleanthes and Philo briefly join forces and raise objections to some of these arguments. Philo concludes the section by claiming that, even if these criticisms fail, this sort of a priori, abstract reasoning is not the true source of religious beliefs and practices; other sources must be sought (D IX.11).

As Part X opens, Demea proposes an alternative source of religion: every person "feels, in a manner, the truth of religion in his breast; and from a consciousness of his imbecility and misery, rather than from any reasoning, is led to seek protection from that being, on whom he and all nature is dependent" (D X.1). More fully, religious beliefs and practices spring not from careful reasoning but from a natural belief-forming mechanism that helps us cope with our feelings of threat, weakness, and misery.[11] Philo agrees with Demea and suggests that "the best and indeed the only method of bringing everyone to a due sense of religion is by just representations of the misery and wickedness of men" (D X.2). What follows is a tag-team effort by Demea and Philo to evoke such feelings.

From a literary perspective, the opening pages of Part X are the finest written passages in the *Dialogues* and come close to the best of Hume's entire corpus. It is unsurprising that these passages are regularly cited as a basis from which one might argue from evil against the existence of an omnipotent and omnibenevolent God. But the context of Philo and Demea's lament should not be forgotten: they are trying to stir up a particular sentiment via rhetoric. They are not offering straightforward premises in an argument, a point Philo explicitly notes at the outset:

> And for that purpose [of bringing everyone to a due sense of religion] a talent of eloquence and strong imagery is more requisite than that of reasoning and argument. For is it necessary to prove what everyone feels within himself? It is only necessary to make us feel it, if possible, more intimately and sensibly. (D X.2)

It is important to remember this goal of the opening passages. Otherwise, after reading several pages describing the utter and thorough misery of life, one might be tempted to object that Hume has surely exaggerated the data. Is it really the case that, for each of us, "The first entrance into life gives anguish to the newborn infant and its wretched parent: Weakness, impotence, and distress attend each stage of that life: And it is at last finished in agony and horror" (D X.8)? Similarly, it might otherwise be tempting to respond that citing a few juicy passages from ancient and modern Western literature is hardly the best method for determining the "united testimony of mankind" (D X.7) about the distribution of happiness and misery throughout the known universe. This method *would* be patently ridiculous if the goal was to establish facts for use in a premise in an argument, but it might be a wonderfully effective method to arouse the emotions of Western readers. Alternatively, one might worry, as Leibniz had objected to Bayle, that this rhetorical tour de force of pain and suffering tells us more about the dispositions of the observer than about the facts of the matter.[12] To his credit, Hume acknowledges the possibility of observational bias in his "Fragment on Evil":

> When I consider the subject with the utmost impartiality and take the most comprehensive view of it, I find myself more inclined to think that evil predominates in the world, and am apt to regard human life as a scene of misery. . . . I am sensible,

however, that there are many circumstances which are apt to pervert my judgment in this particular, and make me entertain melancholy views of things. (D 111)

But it would miss the point to chide Philo and Demea for getting some of the empirical facts about evil wrong in this part of the dialogue; their goal does not require perfect accuracy.

Hume's real goal in the first half of Part X is subtler and, in a way, more difficult. Speaking as a representative of eighteenth-century Scottish Calvinism, Demea claims that religious affection for God is best stirred up by an awareness of our own shortcomings and subsequent misery. Philo slyly agrees with Demea that stirring up feelings of misery can have a powerful effect on religious believers, but he doesn't think it always lead to greater piety. In the hands of Philo, the dramatic cataloguing of pain and suffering is supposed to help undermine our natural tendency to ascribe goodness and wisdom to the cause of the universe.

Philo has to be careful, however. He admits that, in the past, these sentiments of misery and weakness have naturally tended *toward* religious conviction, not agnosticism. Hence, Philo must stir up the reader's sense of misery while also redirecting it away from its natural belief-forming tendencies. In the second half of Part X and most of Part XI, Philo uses reasoning and arguments to help overpower, as it were, this natural tendency.[13]

Interestingly, in his earlier "Fragment on Evil," Hume admits that it would be underhanded to rely on the kinds of rhetorical ploys he uses in Part X of the *Dialogues* to win over his readers:

> Should I enumerate all the evils, incident to human life, and display them, with eloquence, in their proper colours, I should certainly gain the cause with most readers. . . . But I take no advantage of this circumstance, and shall not employ any rhetoric in a philosophical argument, where reason alone ought to be harkened to. (D 111)

Hume then offers the beginnings of an argument that is similar to one Philo offers in Part XI, which suggests that the discussion of evil in the *Dialogues* isn't entirely a matter of enflaming people's sentiments.

Around the midpoint of Part X, the discussion shifts away from presenting the horrors of existence to what look more like traditional philosophical arguments (D X.24). At first, Philo avoids using anything like the data of suffering he's just eloquently presented and instead offers variants on the abstract, logical problem of evil (see Section II). He concludes that "Epicurus' old questions are yet unanswered" (D X.25). These arguments are not made without rhetorical flourishes, of course. Philo claims that "through the whole compass of human knowledge, there are no inferences more certain and infallible than these" (D X.24) and that "nothing can shake the solidity of this reasoning, so short, so clear, so decisive" (D X.34), which harkens back to the sort of grand, sentiment-stirring claims with which Part X began. Perhaps the appearance of deductive reasoning isn't as entirely cool-headed and independent of the sentimentalist goal of the first half of Part X. In any case, Philo concedes for the sake of discussion that "I will allow that pain or misery in man is *compatible* with infinite power and goodness in the deity" (D X.35), and he does not rest his case on the stronger, logical problem of evil.

A central point of dispute between Philo (and sometimes Demea) and Cleanthes in the second half of Part X is whether the source of the universe—call it "God"—is morally good in the sense in which humans can be called morally good. Is goodness univocal to both God and humans? Cleanthes, the "anthropomorphite," claims that "if we abandon all human analogy [between God's nature and ours] . . . we abandon all religion" (D XI.1). This is a topic with a very long and rich theological and philosophical history that had become a flash point for disputes in continental Europe in the last half of the seventeenth century. Philo ultimately concludes that the evil in our world shows that if the original cause of the universe is good, it is not good in the way in which humans are good. Given the facts of evil, the deity is, at best, beyond good and evil—a conclusion with which both agnostics and mystics can agree.

More narrowly, the discussion focuses on whether God's univocal goodness can be inferred from the natural world, given the aforementioned facts about evil. This puts the *defensive* family of problems of evil front and center for Hume. Cleanthes purports to validly infer the goodness (and other attributes) of God from the empirically accessible world, but Philo objects, "How then does the divine benevolence display itself, in the sense of you anthropomorphites?" (D X.28). Cleanthes acknowledges that his religious convictions rest on this inference and that the goodness of God must be established if theism is to be tenable. "For to what purpose establish the natural attributes of the deity, which the moral are still doubtful and uncertain?" (D X.28)

Lest we be tempted to point to a different source of justification for the belief that God is morally good (as Demea pitifully tries to do), Cleanthes drives home the empiricist framework of the entire investigation: "Whence can any cause be known but from its known effects? Whence can any hypothesis be proved but from the apparent phenomena?" (D X.30). Philo then concludes by laying out the main challenge to be taken up in Part XI: "You [Cleanthes] must *prove* these pure, unmixed, uncontrollable attributes [i.e., infinite power and goodness] from the present mixed and confused phenomena, and from these alone" (D X.35). If Cleanthes cannot, then Philo thinks he will have succeeded in showing that the moral character of the deity cannot be validly inferred from observing the natural world. Furthermore, if Cleanthes's empirical framework is correct, Philo will also have shown that the moral character of the deity is entirely unknowable. Hence, the overarching use to which evil is put in the *Dialogues* is to restrict what we can know about the nature of the cause of the universe, not to outright deny the existence of a deity. Agnosticism, not atheism, is the desired conclusion of Hume's defensive argument from evil. (Admittedly, as we will see in the next section, Hume is not always consistent about pursuing this more modest goal.)

III.2 Dialogue XI: The Challenge

At the start of Part XI, Cleanthes suggests a way to wiggle out of the problem: perhaps God isn't infinitely powerful, just much more powerful than we are. This concession might explain evil, Cleanthes thinks: maybe God *is* trying to prevent all evil, and this world is just the best a limited God can do! This sounds like a significant departure from traditional theism, but when Cleanthes summarizes his alternative conception of God, it turns out to be a form of the most prominent concept of God in the seventeenth century, one advocated by the likes of Malebranche and Leibniz: "benevolence, regulated by wisdom, and limited by necessity, may produce just such a world as the present" (D XI.1).[14] Cleanthes imagines that there might be some outweighing goods that God cannot, as a matter of necessity, bring about without allowing some moral evil or causing some natural evil. He reasons that if there were such greater goods that even God can't realize without allowing evil, then perhaps God's pursuit of those goods explains the facts of evil in our world. Philo later challenges such "greater goods" appeals for natural evils. But, independent of that, notice that Cleanthes's opening concession is hardly a relief to most theists; if evil still poses a problem for theists using Cleanthes's "limited" God, it still poses a problem for the vast majority of theists who think God's power ranges over only what is possible.

Philo spends the bulk of Part XI arguing that a problem indeed remains, even for the theist whose God must act in conformity with wisdom and necessity. The discussion has three main sections. In the first, Philo argues that the facts of evil are antecedently unlikely, even given Cleanthes's proposed form of theism (D XI.2–4). In the second, Philo points to four circumstances that give rise to most evils in our world, and he argues that it is highly improbable that all (or even any) of them were unavoidable or necessary for God to bring about the goods that exist in our world (D XI.5–12). Or, at the very least, for all we know about the world, these circumstances were avoidable, in which case the resulting evils prevent us from inferring God's goodness from the known world (D XI.12). In the third part, Philo cranks the rhetoric back up and concludes that, given the known facts about evil, the origin of the universe is most likely to be amoral (D XI.13–15). In the end, the discussion breaks down completely and Demea hastily departs the scene.

I focus in this section on Philo's four circumstances. The four circumstances are really four greater goods that theists might point to in order to justify God's creation of a world as full of pain and suffering as ours seems to be. For each proposed justification, Philo points out that the relevant greater good could probably have been obtained by a deity without the corresponding evils.

First, perhaps the fact that pain contributes to our self-preservation justifies its institution by a benevolent creator. Pain very effectively prompts us to seek food, warns us not to touch hot objects, and so forth. Philo replies that it seems likely that God could have achieved the same good of self-preservation through lesser degrees of pleasure instead: "Pleasure alone, in its various degrees, seems to human understanding sufficient for this purpose" (D XI.6).

The second and fourth circumstances work in tandem. Perhaps pain and suffering is the result of simple, regular laws of nature, and the goodness of those laws outweighs the pain and suffering they sometimes occasion. (This appears to be a crude version of Malebranche's theodicy.) Philo offers three replies. First, it seems likely that God could, in fact, create a perfectly lawful world without occasioning suffering. Second, it seems likely that God could achieve the same goods associated with a perfectly lawful universe by creating a universe that *looked* perfectly lawful to creatures, even though it involved lots of hidden tinkering by God to prevent suffering. Third, it isn't at all clear that our world *is* regulated in a perfectly lawful fashion in the first place. "The irregularity is never, perhaps, so great as to destroy any species; but is often sufficient to involve the individuals in ruin and misery" (D XI.11).

The remaining circumstance mimics another popular greater good appeal: perhaps the great good of a plentiful and diverse cosmos can explain the existence of so much weakness and suffering (see also D 107.18). In such a plentiful world, someone has to play the role of the weak, the infirmed, the miserable wretch near the bottom of the great chain of being. Philo replies that such plenitude comes at an unreasonably high cost: animals generally have just enough ability to meet basic needs, that for only a short while, and even that is only for the lucky few. Instead of acting like a generous, "indulgent parent," nature appears to be "a rigid master" who gives her children the bare necessities to eek out a meager existence. Furthermore, there is no necessary connection between the good of diversity and the crowded, scarce conditions of our world: it seems likely that God could have settled for fewer individuals or could have endowed us all with just a few more powers (D XI.10). Variety by itself doesn't require that the happiness scale be populated *all the way down*, as it were.

Of course, the prior philosophers and theologians who had defended these greater goods appeals anticipated these sort of quick, off-the-cuff objections and offered preemptive replies. But demolishing traditional theodicies beyond the pale of reply isn't Hume's main goal here. Philo concedes that there are levelheaded, albeit speculative responses available to everything he's said in this section. Indeed, given Philo's own modestly skeptical position, it follows that his own speculative objections *cannot* be decisive:

> What then shall we pronounce on this occasion? Shall we say that these circumstances are not necessary and that they might easily have been altered in the contrivance of the universe? This decision seems too presumptuous for creatures, so blind and ignorant. Let us be more modest in our conclusions. (D XI.12)

Hume does, however, provide a much-needed reminder in this section that it is insufficient for theists to explain the justification of evil solely by pointing to a great good that accompanies the evils. One must also show that (a) the good could not have been brought about without bringing about those or worse evils, (b) the good is sufficiently great to outweigh the evils, and (c) that the constraints mentioned in (a) and (b) are consistent with God's other attributes, such as omnipotence.

Consider an obvious example. Peter decides to hike up a mountain where he becomes trapped, suffers alone in agony for days, and then dies in terrible pain as wild animals slowly devour him. We can imagine Philo asking, "If God exists and is all-powerful, all-good, and all-knowing, why did this happen to Peter?" Suppose someone replies, "Yes, it is terrible, but just before dying, Peter saw a truly beautiful sunset that he wouldn't have seen if he hadn't been trapped up on the mountain, and that good experience explains why God allowed Peter to suffer." This would be a terrible reply to Philo for reasons that Hume's discussion highlights. First, it fails condition (a): surely, God could have arranged for Peter to see the sunset without all the other horrific events. It also fails condition (b): however beautiful a sunset may be, the goodness of seeing it surely does not outweigh the pain and suffering Peter endured. And, depending on how one responds to these concerns, it may also violate (c): why couldn't God have simply given Peter a vision of the lovely sunset as Peter sits in paradise? Why couldn't God have created nonorganic matter for the wild animals to consume the instant they approached Peter? Why not give Peter the ability to climb mountains without getting trapped in the first place? Again, there may be answers to all these questions, but part of Hume's point is that it is incumbent upon the theist to provide them if she wants someone who isn't already convinced that God is good to find her account of evil compelling. Merely naming an attendant good isn't sufficient.

In summary, the main focus in the first two sections of Part XI, as it had been in Part X, is the defensive problem of evil. Philo repeatedly concedes that his arguments from evil establish that God is not morally good (in the sense in which humans are good) only if that property of God must be inferred exclusively from the observable world:

> Let us allow that if the goodness of the deity (I mean a goodness like the human) could be established on any tolerable reasons a priori, these phenomena [i.e., evils] however untoward, would not be sufficient to subvert that principle. . . . But let us still assert that as this goodness is not antecedently established, but must be inferred from the phenomena, there can be no grounds for such an inference". (D XI.12; see also D XI.2, D XI.4, D XI.8)[15]

However, Cleanthes has agreed that an empirical inference is needed to establish God's goodness, so Philo rests content with a hypothetical, agnostic conclusion: the benevolence of God cannot be inferred from what we know about the observable world. Although speculations about greater goods may "be sufficient to *save* the conclusion concerning the divine attributes, yet surely [they] can never be sufficient to *establish* that conclusion" (D XI.8).

III.3 Dialogue XI: The Breakdown

Just when everything seems to be going Philo's way, the dialogue breaks down. After discussing the four circumstances, Philo reiterates his modest, conditional conclusion that "the bad appearances . . . may be compatible with such attributes as you suppose," even though "they can never prove these attributes" (D XI.12). The discussion then takes an odd turn as Philo abruptly returns to his edgy, over-the-top rhetoric from Part X. As Philo's rhetoric builds, his epistemic modesty is shed: "Look round this universe . . . the whole presents nothing but the idea of a blind nature, impregnated by a great vivifying principle, and pouring forth from her lap, without discernment or parental care, her maimed and abortive children" (D XI.13). The switch from the conditional to the declarative continues in the next paragraph: "The true conclusion is that the original source of all things is entirely indifferent to all these principles and has no more regard to good above ill than to heat above cold, or to drought above moisture, or to light above heavy" (D XI.14). Philo then tosses out four possible views on the goodness of the "first causes of the universe" and quickly declares that the fourth option: "that they have neither goodness nor malice . . . therefore seems by far the most probable" (D XI.15).[16]

Philo's sudden shift has prompted a veritable field day of interpretative speculation. It is extremely difficult to see how Philo's claims here are consistent with his professed agnosticism throughout the rest of the dialogue. He is no longer playing defense. He's now claiming that not only do we have access to a view of "the whole" universe—a point he earlier denied (D VII.8)—but that we can also form a "true conclusion" about the moral character of its cause, namely that its amorality is "by far the most probable." Just a few paragraphs earlier, Philo himself had reminded Cleanthes that "we know so little beyond common life, or even of common life, that, with regard to the economy of the universe, there is no conjecture, however wild, which may not be just; nor any one, however plausible, which may not be erroneous" (D XI.5). So how does Philo suddenly know so much?

Some interpreters have bent over backward to save this portion of the dialogue from the charge of internal inconsistency, even going so far as to argue that Philo is actually offering a *parody* of Cleanthes's earlier arguments in these paragraphs and never intends to advocate any of these claims for himself.[17] Philo's seemingly straightforward inference to "the true conclusion" is tongue-in-cheek. Talk about the hermeneutics of charity! Suffice it to say that if parody was Hume's intended goal, the joke is on him, since not only do neither of the other characters pick up on the farce, but it also has eluded virtually every other reader of Hume's *Dialogues* for more than 200 years.

Another option, one I find more convincing even if less satisfying, is that the dialogue simply got away from Hume at this point. This could be a faint way of praising Hume's realism in dialogue writing: in actual philosophical conversation, discussion partners often contradict their earlier claims. But that doesn't apply here, as Hume's loss of control over his characters has been steadily building since the discussion turned to evil. Philo's speech in Part XI is the longest uninterrupted monologue in the entire *Dialogues*. Were Hume not such a good writer of a dialogue, we might excuse the harangue. But, independent of the content of what Philo says, it is deeply out of character for Philo to play this verbose, didactic role at all; he is the gadfly in the dialogues, the critic, the Pyrrhonian skeptic. He's the Socrates, not the Plato. Philo begins to lose his modesty in Part X when he claims his arguments are among the most certain and insurmountable in all of human history, but there he hesitates and backs off. His arguments appear to be based on certain and infallible inference unless "we assert that these subjects exceed all human capacity" (D X.34). However, by the end of Part XI, Hume's Philo has entirely forgotten the modesty "which I have all along insisted on" (D X.34).

Hume has also lost some of his grip on Cleanthes and Demea. In Part X, Cleanthes is made to assert that the only legitimate response to Philo is to "deny absolutely the misery and wickedness of man" (D X.31) and that "if you can make out the present point, and prove mankind to be unhappy or corrupted, there is an end at once of all religion" (D X.28)—claims that even Philo recognizes are unnecessarily strong (D X.33). Even more unevenly, Cleanthes uncharacteristically urges Philo to speak "at length, without interruption" (D XI.1) about Philo's views on evil, a rather heavy-handed way for an author to justify the lengthy, unbroken speech that follows. Although Demea's role in the *Dialogues* has always been a bit uneven and awkward, he is almost entirely absent in Part XI, piping up briefly at the very end just before leaving in a huff.

Even more tellingly, the point on which Philo heads off message is very similar to the unfinished conclusion of Hume's earlier "Fragment on Evil." There, Hume begins to compare the distribution of pain and suffering to the way "heat and cold, moist and dry are dispersed through the universe; and if the one prevails a little above the other, this is what will naturally happen in any mixture of principles . . . on every occasion, nature seems to employ either" (D 112), a comparison Philo echoes in this problematic section. One possible source of the derailment could be Hume's decision to insert his own opinion on what readers should conclude from the facts of evil, even though it isn't a view that naturally fits what any of his characters would say. Such speculation of authorial intrusion is impossible to confirm, of course, but I distinctly hear a new voice speaking in D XI.13–15, one that is far more convinced and dogmatic about the "true conclusion" of arguments from evil. Unfortunately, few if any arguments for this much stronger conclusion are offered in this section, and even Hume's own characters seem aware that none of the earlier ones they discussed entail such a strong conclusion. So, if it is an intrusion by an outsider, it is a philosophically disappointing one.

When at last someone breaks into Philo's rant at D XI.18, it is Demea. He seems deeply troubled by Philo's suggestion that if God is the "original principle" of all things, then God is the author of sin (D XI.17), despite the fact that this charge had been leveled at (and rebuffed by) Calvinists throughout the seventeenth and eighteenth centuries.[18] Once again, the absence of reference to the prior century's discussion is keenly felt, since no hint is given to readers that figures like Leibniz had devoted a good portion of their career to sorting through these matters with considerable care and ingenuity (even if not cogency). Instead, Cleanthes jumps on the anti-Demea bandwagon, implying that Demea's initial strategy in Part X of invoking the feeling of misery worked safely "in ages of stupidity and ignorance" (D XI.19)—but no longer. Frankly, I sympathize with Demea's decision to quit the discussion; it was no longer a genuine inquiry.

IV EVALUATING HUME ON EVIL

I conclude with some ways to think about what Hume has and hasn't achieved in his discussion of evil. Before evaluating Hume on evil, we need to decide which Hume is going to be evaluated: Hume for us or Hume in his own time and place? We might, for instance, try to extract, formalize, and evaluate arguments found in scattered passages, thereby mining Hume's texts for philosophical ideas relevant to contemporary interests. The danger of this approach is that we might easily misrepresent Hume's own views if we take some of his characters' claims about evil out of the context of the *Dialogues* itself, much less out of the historical context in which it was written. Nonetheless, contemporary interpreters and teachers often perform such extractions, and it is undoubtedly true that many of Hume's claims in the *Dialogues* have achieved a philosophical significance that far exceeds their immediate dialogical and historical context.

Alternatively, we might focus in on the historical context and/or genre of the *Dialogues* and evaluate Hume's discussion of evil in light of those contextualized goals. The danger of this more historicizing approach is that it can obscure how Hume's discussions may be relevant for our own time. I am not going to adjudicate this methodological issue here; both approaches can provide philosophical insights. Instead, I offer an example of how critical evaluations might go for each approach. I'll start with an extracted claim and then turn to a more historically sensitive point of evaluation. I'll conclude with a brief note on Hume's legacy for subsequent discussions of evil.

Although I've outlined the major foci of Hume's discussions of evil, the *Dialogues* are extremely rich. Alongside the main points of contention, Hume's Philo offers numerous quick arguments about evil in passing. In this, Hume wonderfully evokes the spirit of Bayle, Montaigne, and other self-styled Pyrrhonian skeptics who throw out lots of undeveloped arguments at a quick pace, perhaps hoping that the sheer multiplicity of arguments for the same conclusion will by itself offer a kind of meta-support for the conclusion.

For twenty-first-century readers of Hume, it is difficult to know what to do with this approach. On the one hand, Hume is sometimes thought to have presented one of the most decisive cases from evil against the existence of God. This reputation invites us to critically analyze and evaluate each argument carefully, laying out its assumptions, inferences, and conclusions far more fully than Hume himself ever does. At the same time, doing this for many of the arguments often reveals glaring holes or very contentious assumptions that greatly limit the scope of his conclusion. After running through a series of such analyses, it is hard to shake the feeling that Hume's intended point is somehow being missed.

For example, consider Philo's claim near the middle of Part X: "[God's] power we allow infinite: Whatever he wills is executed: But neither man nor any other animal is happy: Therefore, he does not will happiness . . . Through the whole compass of human knowledge, there are no inferences more certain and infallible than these" (D X.24; see also D X.34). Sticking with the human case, Philo's argument is as follows:

(1)   If God wills that people are happy, then people are happy.
(2)   People are not happy.
(3)   Therefore, God does not will that people are happy.

Philo claims that this is among the most certain and infallible inferences in human knowledge. Certainly it is, if by that he means only that it is an instance of *modus tollens*. He means more than this, of course, advocating it as an obviously and indisputably sound argument as well. As a general rule, I recommend becoming highly suspicious whenever philosophers invoke terms like "clearly" or "obviously" in stating their conclusions, much less when they claim that their argument is among the most certain and unassailable in the history of human thought. Hyperbole can easily blind us to questionable reasoning, and this argument is no exception. As a little reflection will show, there is an equivocation in the sense of "willing" between (1) and (3) that undermines the force of its conclusion.

According to the sense of willing in (1), God's willing a state of affairs suffices for the obtaining of that state of affairs. This is true when "God wills" is taken in a strong sense, akin to "God determines." For if God *determines* that state of affairs A obtains, then A obtains. However, if we apply that strong sense of willing to the conclusion of (3), the conclusion no longer appears worrisome for the traditional theist. The conclusion states that God doesn't fully *determine* that people are happy or that God's actions aren't sufficient for bringing about human happiness. However, a long-standing Christian tradition holds that people have the sort of freedom and characters that make it impossible or at least highly undesirable for God to wholly determine them to be happy. Although Hume himself rejects the underlying account of human freedom in this response, the necessary conditions on freedom is a controversial issue that surely falls short of his "certain and infallible" criteria.

The reason that (3) initially appears so worrisome for theism is that we naturally understand "will" in (3) in a much weaker sense, something like "prefers" or "wants it to be the case." Read in this weaker sense, (3) does seem like a troubling conclusion for theists: what sort of morally good deity doesn't want its rational creatures to be happy? However, if we apply this weaker, merely preferential sense of "will" to (1), (1) is no longer obviously true. If God prefers that state of affairs A obtain, does it follow that A obtains? Not necessarily. Perhaps there are bad consequences associated with A such that, necessarily, were A to obtain, those bad consequences would also occur. Suppose further that those bad consequences are so bad that they greatly outweigh the good involved in A. In that case, God might prefer A, but still refrain from bringing about A.

To use a silly example, suppose the only way in which I can stop the pain from the paper cut in Sally's pinky is by cutting off her hand. (Feel free to concoct the needed details: we're on a deserted island, we are medically ignorant, etc.) I might reasonably desire or prefer that Sally doesn't suffer from the paper cut without thereby desiring or preferring to bring it about that she doesn't suffer from the cut, on the grounds that I don't desire to bring about the associated suffering involved in cutting off of her hand. In this case, although I prefer that Sally doesn't suffer from the cut, considered in itself, I do not prefer Sally's nonsuffering, all things considered.[19]

This shows that, for some agents, willing in favor of a state of affairs, in the sense of preferring or desiring it, does not entail willing in favor of bringing about that state of affairs. If God were ever in a situation in which, necessarily, bringing about a good would thereby also bring about some vastly greater evil, God's preferring or desiring that good would not entail that God brings about that good. If so, then when "willing" is taken in the weaker sense that makes (3) troublesome for theists, (1) is false. Hume might respond (as Bayle did) that an omnipotent being could never be in such a situation, but, here again, his position would be in the small minority in the history of philosophical theology. At the very least, that God can do the impossible is surely not among the most certain and infallible of human beliefs.

In short, Philo's argument contains an equivocation on "willing": the sense of "wills" used in (1) renders (3) harmless, whereas the sense used in (3) renders (1) false. Although there are replies to be made on behalf of Hume, they will involve controversial premises about human freedom, human happiness, and divine power that move us well beyond the most "certain and infallible" deliverances.

Although it is not part of the inference itself, we might also wonder about the truth of premise (2), the empirical claim that people are not happy. Hume himself has already shown us that empirically determining overall human happiness is a difficult, if not impossible affair. If happiness is taken in a first-person, subjective way based on a report of perceived well-being, then it is outright false that no person is happy. If the generic statement in (2) isn't meant to be interpreted as a universally quantified statement (i.e., "No person is happy"), then what range of cases should we consider? People living in eighteenth-century Scotland? People throughout a broader range of history who have recorded their self-assessed happiness and passed it on to us? Or, more broadly, people across all human history and cultures? Although the scope of happiness has been studied recently by sociologists, psychologists, economists, historians, and neuroscientists, the sort of data gathering required is vastly trickier than Hume's breezy survey of Western literature can even begin to approximate, and (so far at least) the current research disconfirms Hume's claim in (2).[20]

This is just the tip of the iceberg. It is easy to find problems in many of Philo's arguments as Hume states them in the text, so much so that this way of evaluating Hume on evil becomes a glum homuncular exercise in refutation. At the very least, engaging Hume's arguments on evil fruitfully will require readers to develop his claims in ways that the texts do not supply. Numerous attempts to do just this have been made by later philosophers, and providing such inspiration is one important way that Hume's discussions have greatly influenced further work on the problem of evil.

As noted previously, one might complain that these nitpicky objections to Philo's arguments overlook the dialogical and historical framework of Hume's discussion of evil. Philo is a character in a philosophical dialogue, and, like many of us in oral philosophical discussions, he sometimes exaggerates the strength of his views or the firmness with which he holds them. We sometimes let our conversation partners pull us away from our claims before we have a chance to develop them fully, and so forth. Hume didn't write a treatise on evil, after all; he wrote a dialogue that discusses the problem of evil in the versions most relevant to his own context.

For those persuaded by such concerns, let me offer another avenue for critical reflection that takes the genre and historical context of the *Dialogues* more seriously. Hume has three characters in the dialogues: a moderate Pyrrhonian skeptic, an empirical theist, and an apophatic-style theologian. Missing from the discussion is a metaphysically savvy theist, the sort of philosopher one commonly finds among Scholastics and seventeenth-century rationalists. These philosophers and theologians set the framework for discussing evil in the Latin west for centuries, a framework that was imbedded in a host of metaphysical and axiological commitments. Indeed, many of the most animating questions in previous centuries about God's relation to evil were ineliminably metaphysical in character, such as the ontology of good and evil and the metaphysics of divine action. Theodician questions about God's moral justification for evil were raised only within this broader set of commitments.[21] However, Hume excludes those frameworks, theories, and perspectives at the outset of the discussion, a luxury that critics of religion in previous centuries didn't have.

That Hume leaves out historically important voices is not a devastating criticism. We all begin with particular philosophical assumptions, and, to Hume's credit, he defends his antimetaphysical, noncognitivist stance in other works. For the first half of the twentieth century in Anglo-American philosophy, the antecedent rejection of metaphysical speculation in addressing questions about God and evil seemed not only justified, but natural. However, more recent readers of Hume on evil need to be aware that Hume's discussion of evil presupposes a set of restrictions on possible questions and replies that have not always been accepted and are no longer widely accepted today. Even more, as the century before Hume and the last half of the twentieth century both demonstrated, a metaphysically loaded philosophical theism has much to contribute to discussions of evil. Its absence from the text invites readers to speculate on how Hume's dialogues on evil might have unfolded had he been willing to address such theists on their own terms.

Although Hume's discussion of evil is not without internal and external concerns, it cannot be denied that Hume has had a tremendous influence on nearly every subsequent discussion of the problem of evil. Hume's *Dialogues* elegantly articulates many of the main questions about evil taken up by later philosophers of religion. Even where contemporary discussions have moved beyond Hume, traces can be found in Hume's texts. The first half of Dialogue X also presents some of the most memorable and forceful presentations of the widespread distribution of evil. It is difficult to read it and not feel some of the sentiments Demea and Philo intended to stir up in us. Furthermore, although the sort of inferential claims to God's goodness made by Cleanthes and challenged by Philo are less common among philosophers today, undoubtedly some of that eclipse is due to Hume's probing challenges.

For quite some time, Hume's discussion of evil also helped shift the focus of discussions of evil in philosophy of religion from metaphysics to epistemology. The primary question about evil for theists became one of justification, rather than, say, ontology or causation. Hume's work also ushered in a greater focus on natural evils like pain and suffering, as opposed to sins and metaphysical evils, even though Hume imbedded his discussion within a hedonist value theory that is now widely rejected. And for many today, Hume's forceful presentations of various arguments from evil represent a progressive, eighteenth-century heralding of the winnowing of traditional theism and the rebirth of a more modest, empirically respectable naturalism.

ABBREVIATIONS OF WORKS CITED

D   *Dialogues Concerning Natural Religion*. In D. Coleman, ed. *Dialogues Concerning Natural Religion and Other Writings*. Cambridge: Cambridge University Press, 2007.

EU   *An Enquiry Concerning Human Understanding*. Edited by T. L. Beauchamp. Oxford: Clarendon, 2000.

NOTES

1. The two main exceptions are a few sentences in Hume's early reading notes on Bayle and King and in a recently discovered, unpublished fragment on evil, likely written during the 1740s.
2. Leading examples include Samuel Clarke and Joseph Butler, as well as Hume's own character, Cleanthes.
3. This marks a rare point of agreement between Hume and Leibniz. Bayle (1991: 144) had made claims about the vast scope of suffering in our world that were very similar to what Hume's Philo and Demea assert in the first half of Part X. Leibniz (1985: §13–19) replied, as Hume concedes in this passage, that we are too ignorant of the global distribution of happiness and suffering in the universe to use it in an argument against God's goodness.
4. See also King (1702: 37); and Leibniz (1985: §21). For Hume's awareness of this tri-fold distinction, see D 107.18. For a discussion of this classification and its historical development, see Newlands (forthcoming-*b*) and Newlands (forthcoming-*a*).
5. For recent work on distinctively first-person perspective on evil, see Adams (2000). For discussion of second-person perspectives as related to evil, see Stump (2010).
6. For this concession in Hume's own voice, see EU 11.21/141; Cleanthes suggests that this version of the problem may actually be successful (D XI.1).
7. Hume's formulation here blurs two distinct scopes: is it the evil of the world in general or as we have experienced it? Furthermore, Hume cannot mean by "in general" something like "on the whole" because he concedes that we do not have access to that kind of global data. His earlier formulation (D X.34) puts it in terms of "any misery at all," suggesting that he intends an abstract or bare scope.
8. I have only provided the most salient step; for a carefully developed version that takes its inspiration from this passage in Hume, see Draper (1996).

9. A striking contrast: Leibniz (1985: §13) suggests that only concerns of boredom would prevent everyone from willingly reliving their life over again.

10. This paragraph, which concludes with an exhortation to "consideration then where the real point of controversy lies, and if you cannot lay aside your disputes, endeavour at least to cure yourselves of your animosity" (D XII.7) was added to the manuscript in the final year of Hume's life. It echoes the call for a kind of civility and ecumenicalism among religious partisans that is repeated in the *Dialogues'* final paragraphs. The dangerous sort of religious person, for Hume, is not the pious but the enthusiast (D XII.16–30; EU 11.29/147). This overarching goal of Humean ecumenicalism—demonstrating that moderate skeptics, pious devotees, mystics, and even some dogmatists engage mostly in merely verbal disputes—helps us understand the otherwise puzzling concession of Philo at the end of Part XII: "to be a philosophical skeptic is, in a man of letters, the first and most essential step towards being a sound, believing Christian" (D XII.33; see also D X.36).

11. This account of the origin of religion echoes part of Hume's own account (see esp. NHR 3.1–6), although it is a bit surprising that Demea would voice it.

12. Leibniz (1985: §220) writes, "It is only people of a malicious disposition or those who have become somewhat misanthropic through misfortunes. . .who find wickedness everywhere."

13. Philo suggests that this shift is reflected in the rhetoric of religious leaders themselves who realized that "as men now have learned to form principles and to draw consequences," they need to employ arguments to achieve what fear-mongering once sufficed to accomplish (D XI.20). (It is unclear how well Philo's strategy of pitting reason and arguments against sentiments and natural mechanisms fits into Hume's larger theory about the impotence of reason in the face of the passions.)

14. Only the likes of Descartes and Arnauld would deny that God's goodness is regulated by God's wisdom and that God's power is "limited by" necessity.

15. On the basis of what Hume has and has not tried to demonstrate in the *Dialogues,* we should probably replace his "as" with an "if": "*if* this goodness is not antecedently established . . ."

16. As numerous commentators have pointed out, the four options Philo presents aren't actually mutually exhaustive, although I don't take Philo to be any more concerned with that than he is that the four circumstances are mutually exhaustive or that the cataloguing of the kinds of evils in Part X is exhaustive.

17. See Kraay (2003) and Holden (2010: 175–8).

18. Hume had claimed in his own voice that showing how God is not the author of sin, given other standard theistic commitments, "has been found hitherto to exceed all the power of philosophy" and involves a "boundless ocean of doubt, uncertainty, and contradiction" (EU 8.36/103).

19. A different way to reject the inference is to deny that willing is closed under known entailment and to argue that human misery is a known, but unintended entailment of the object of God's will (say, that humans have morally significant freedom). For a seventeenth-century version of this tactic, see Leibniz (2005: 63–5).

20. Two highly readable starting points are Laylard (2011) and Sharot (2011).

21. For an example from Leibniz, who was certainly very interested in questions of divine justification as well, see Newlands (2014).

Bibliography

Adams, Marilyn McCord. (2000). *Horrendous Evil and the Goodness of God*. Ithaca: Cornell University Press.

Bayle, Pierre. (1991). *Historical and Critical Dictionary, Selections*. Trans. Richard H. Popkin, Indianapolis: Hackett.

Clarke, Samuel. (1705/1998). *A Demonstration of the Being and Attributes of God and Other Writings*, Enzio Vailati, ed., Cambridge: Cambridge University Press.

Draper, Paul. (1996). "Pain and Pleasure: An Evidential Problem for Theists," in Daniel Howard-Snyder, ed., *The Evidential Argument from Evil*. Bloomington: Indiana University Press.

Holden, Thomas. (2010). *Spectres of False Divinity*. Oxford: Oxford University Press.

King, William. (1702). *De Origine Mali*. Dublin: Andreas Crook.

Kraay, Klaas J. (2003). "Philo's Argument for Divine Amorality Reconsidered," *Hume Studies* 29, 283–304.

Laylard, Richard. (2011). *Happiness: Lessons from a New Science*, 2nd revised ed. Penguin Books.

Leibniz, Gottfried Wilhelm. (1985). *Theodicy: Essays on the Goodness of God, the Freedom of Man, and the Origin of Evil*. La Salle: Open Court.

Leibniz, Gottfried Wilhelm. (2005). *Confessio Philosophi: Papers Concerning the Problem of Evil, 1671–1678*, trans. and ed. by Robert C. Sleigh, Jr. New Haven: Yale University Press.

Newlands, Samuel. (2014). "Leibniz on Privations, Limitations, and the Metaphysics of Evil," *Journal for the History of Philosophy*. 52(2): 281–308.

Newlands, Samuel. (forthcoming-*a*). "Evils, Privations, and the Early Moderns," in Scott MacDonald and Andrew Chignell, eds., *Evil: Philosophical Concepts*. Oxford: Oxford University Press.

Newlands, Samuel. (forthcoming-*b*). "The Problem of Evil," in Dan Kaufmann, ed., *Routledge Companion to 17th Century Philosophy*. Routledge.

Sharot, Tali. (2011). *The Optimism Bias*. Pantheon Press.

Stump, Eleanor. (2010). *Wandering in Darkness: Narrative and the Problem of Suffering*. New York: Oxford University Press.

CHAPTER 32

HUME'S *NATURAL HISTORY*
OF RELIGION

KEITH E. YANDELL

What those [religious-belief-producing] principles are, which give rise to the original belief, and what those accidents and causes are, which direct its operation, is the subject of our present enquiry. (NHR 33)

As every enquiry, which regards religion, is of the utmost importance, there are two questions in particular, which challenge our attention, to wit, that regarding its foundation in reason, and that concerning its origin in human nature. (NHR 33)

DAVID Hume's intention was to develop a systematic philosophy. (This claim is controversial, and defending it will require more quotation than usual.) Only part of this reading can be defended here—that concerning religion. His views concerning religion constitute an important part of his system. Here, I state and assess what I take to be Hume's overall program regarding religious belief, monotheistic and polytheistic (but no other). The program includes *A Treatise of Human Nature*, the *Dialogues Concerning Natural Religion*, and the *Natural History of Religion*. The first and last of these works develop a theory of human nature, with the *Treatise* account providing context for *Natural History of Religion*'s contribution. On the whole, the *Dialogues* treated the "foundation in reason" question. After an introduction, it discusses the argument(s) from design through the eighth dialogue; its ninth dialogue considers the cosmological and ontological arguments. Dialogues ten and eleven deal with the argument from evil. (It may be that the moral argument for God's existence is not presented on the grounds—correct or incorrect—that, where evil is concerned, the initial plausibility goes to atheism. It is noteworthy that, in the *Dialogues*, skepticism concerning external objects and causality makes no appearance, the strategy apparently being: "I grant you an external world in which nothing comes from nothing; even so your arguments fail.") The final dialogue, in which the critic Philo seems to offer a confession of faith, turns to the "origin in human nature" question. Save for the last dialogue, which changes the subject, the gist of the *Dialogues* is that theistic belief lacks support from argument or evidence.

The *Natural History of Religion* is devoted to the "origin in human nature" question. Much of the *Treatise*, Book 1, is devoted to the origin question regarding belief in an external world, causal connections, and enduring selves. The explanation there concerns what we would call "common sense," and Hume calls "natural" beliefs. A major goal of the *Treatise* is to explain why we have common-sense beliefs, given the lack of solid evidence or argument in their support. (The *Treatise* also gives Hume's reasons for thinking we have no such argument or evidence.) Thus, Book 1 of the *Treatise* provides explanation for natural beliefs, and *Natural History of Religion* provides it for religious beliefs. Thus, what follows comes in three sections: I. The *Treatise*'s Context; II. The *Natural History of Religion* Explanation; and III. Hume's Critique of Theism and Religion.

I THE *TREATISE*'S CONTEXT

> Nature, by an absolute and uncontroulable necessity has determin'd us to judge as well as to breathe and feel. (T 1.4.3.6/183)

Whether or not there is an external world of mind-independent objects, and if so how we know its contents, exercised the Modern philosophers. If you believed there are mind-independent extended objects, you could claim to be directly aware of them or directly aware of something else from which you inferred their existence. Or you could hold that there is just a mind-dependent something else, and no proper inference can be made from it to an external world. You could be a direct realist, an indirect realist, or an idealist. Hume's approach includes his holding that none of these positions can be justified, and, in spite of that, we will believe in an external world. He holds that every perception (impression or idea) exists independent of every other, and writes:

> Suppose an object perfectly simple and indivisible to be presented along with another object, whose *co-existent* parts are connected by a strong relation, 'tis evident the actions of the mind, in considering these two objects are not very different. The imagination conceives the simple object at once, with facility, by a single effort of thought, without change or variation. The connexion of parts in the compound object has almost the same effect, and so unites the object within itself, that the fancy feels not the transition in passing from one part to another . . . [the parts] are conceiv'd to form *one thing*; and that on account of their close relation, which makes them affect the thought in the same manner, as if perfectly uncompounded. But the mind rests not here. Whenever it views the object in another light, it finds that all these qualities are different, and indistinguishable, and separable from each other; which view of things being destructive of its primary and more natural notions, obliges the imagination to feign an unknown something, or *original* substance and matter, as a principle of union

or cohesion among these qualities, and as what may give the compound object a title to be call'd one thing, notwithstanding its diversity and composition. (T 1.4.3.5/221)

A similar process comes into play in cases of the right sort of successive perceptions, as in the explanation that follows.

Thus, there is a propensity to believe that there are:

External objects: Given a succession of closely resembling impressions of sensation, a mind automatically posits an object that exists independent of, and distinct from, those impressions, and given a succession of impressions of sensation describable as a process of change occurring to one thing, the mind automatically posits an object that exists independent of, and distinct from, those impressions.

Thus our "assurance of the continu'd assurance of the distinct existence of body must be entirely due to the imagination" (T 1.4.2.14/193).

The same holds for belief in causality and an enduing self. In none of these cases is there supporting evidence or argument. Thus, these beliefs lack a foundation in reason. Even learning this will not affect one's beliefs because their source lies in the imagination. Specifically, their origin is in propensities to form beliefs that are elicited by specifiable sorts of experiences. The other propensities can be described, and their eliciting experiences can be stated simply:

Causal connections: Given a background of impressions of one sort, each of which is followed by an impression of another sort, plus a new impression of the first sort, a mind expects a new impression of the second sort.

Enduring self: Given a succession of closely resembling impressions of reflection, a mind automatically posits a self that exists independent of, and distinct from those impressions, and, given a series of impressions of reflection that are describable as a process of change occurring to one thing, the mind automatically posits a subject that exists independent of, and distinct from those impressions.

The positing is not a conscious activity made in the search for the best explanation. It is a mental knee jerk.

Hume is an atypical skeptic. He denies that our common-sense belief in mind-independent extended objects, enduring selves, and mind-independent causal connections enjoys the support of evidence or argument. But he has no expectation that anyone who recognizes this will try to abandon these beliefs, nor that they could succeed if they made the effort. Beliefs that do not have their origin in reason are not extinguished by the discovery that they lack reason's support. Hume's view is that we are, by nature, believers. This is so because human nature is compromised by propensities to believe. Beliefs in external objects, selves, and causal connections have distinct sources—they come from different propensities activated by different sorts of experience. Two of the relevant propensities require the notion of "distinct existence"—an idea derived from the alleged fact that each perception exists distinct from and independent of all others. Thus, our having the idea of external existence does not require that there be external existents. One extrapolates to the notion of a nonperception that is related to all perceptions as each is related to all others. The idea is that, given this concept, the first two propensities can operate. Insofar as belief in an enduring self involves there being others than oneself, the third propensity needs it as well.

These perceptions operate in everyone; they are universal. Although no doubt the particular candidates for being external objects vary from place to place and time to time, the belief is that there are such things as mind-independent extended things, causes and effects, and enduring subjects of experience. (The scope of this chapter precludes a discussion of how to carry out the task of relating Hume's propensity account as universal and uniform, of his view of our lack of knowledge that there is an external world and the like, and whether this can be done in such a way as to render these views coherent and cogent.)

There is at least one more way in which the *Treatise* provides a context for the *Natural History of Religion*'s explanation. We need to give clear justification for this interpretation of the *Treatise* (and the *Natural History of Religion*). In various contexts, Hume expresses a concern for what we might call mental coherence—the continuing operation of those propensities that comprise human nature in such a fashion that the resulting web of belief and action, if not perfectly consistent, at least lets a person engage daily life in a manner that can be approved by one who takes (something like) the moral point of view. At various points in the *Treatise*, Hume speaks strongly of inconsistencies, contradictions, and conflicts in the world of the intellect. As regards belief in external objects:

> When we gradually follow an object in its successive changes, the smooth progress of the thought makes us ascribe an identity to the succession; because 'tis by a similar act of the mind we consider an unchangeable object. When we compare its situation after a considerable change the progress of the thought is broke; and consequently we are presented with the idea of diversity: *In order to reconcile which contradictions the imagination is apt to feign something unknown and invisible,* which it supposes to continue the same under all these variations; and this unintelligible something it calls a *substance,* or *original and first matter.* (T 1.4.3.3/ 220; emphasis added, except for second instance)

As regards custom versus judgments:

> *tho' custom be the foundation of all our judgements, yet sometimes it has an effect on the imagination in opposition to the judgement, and produces a contraiety in our sentiments concerning the same object.* (T 1.3.13.9/147; emphasis added)

In the matter of general rules:

> our general rules are in a manner set in opposition to each other. When an object appears, that resembles any cause in very considerable circumstances, the imagination naturally carries us to a lively conception of the usual effect, tho' the object be

different in the most material ... circumstances. ... Here is the influence of general rules. But *when we take a review of this act of the mind, and compare it with the general and authentic operations of the mind, we find it to be of an irregular nature, and destructive of all the most established principles of reasonings; which is the cause of our rejecting it. This is a second influence of general rules, and implies the condemnation of the former.* (T 1.3.13.12/149–50; emphasis added)

On causal propensity versus external object propensity:

'Tis this principle, which makes us reason from causes and effect, and 'tis the same principle which convinces us of the continued existence of external objects when absent from the senses. But *tho' these two operations be equally natural and necessary in the human mind, yet in some circumstances they are directly contrary ... This contradiction would be more excusable, were it compensated by any degree of solidity and satisfaction in the other parts of our reasoning. But the case is quite contrary.* (T 1.4.7.4/266; emphasis added)

And on the understanding when it acts alone:

if the consideration of these instances makes us take a resolution to reject all the trivial suggestions of the fancy, and adhere to the general and more established properties of the imagination ... even this resolution, if steadily executed, would be dangerous, and attended with the most fatal consequences ... *the understanding, when it acts alone, and according to its most general principles, entirely subverts itself* (T 1.4.7.7/267; emphasis added)

The examples range widely: coming to believe in external objects, custom versus judgment, use of general rules, the external object propensity versus the causal propensity, the understanding when it acts alone. For our purposes, this provides a context for a significant thesis in the *Natural History of Religion*.

II The *Natural History of Religion* Explanation

The first religious principles must be secondary; such as may be perverted by many accidents and causes, whose operation too, in some cases, may, by an extraordinary concurrence of circumstances, be altogether prevented. (NHR 33)

As we have noted, part of the overall project requires justification of the view that we lack solid evidence or argument for common-sense beliefs, as well as for religious beliefs. The *Treatise* purports to supply this for common sense and the *Dialogues* for religious belief. This leaves the field open for *Natural History of Religion* to explain the nonrational source of religious belief, sources in the imagination—propensities typically found accompanying the natural propensities

On one reading, Sections 10 and 11 of the *Dialogues* argue against the goodness of any God there might be, but Philo offers and conflates two escapes from this argument: retreat to mystery and granting that moral terms do not have the same meaning applied to God as they do applied to us. It is clear that he takes the presence of evil to thwart any inference to divine goodness. Natural theology endeavors to offer good evidence or argument for theism; natural atheology attempts the same regarding atheism. Essentially, the skepticism that blocks a successful Humean natural theology blocks a successful Humean natural atheology, although this is seldom recognized or admitted. Insofar as this is so, Hume is not in a position to argue that all (or any) religious belief is false other than on grounds of sheer inconsistency. Any fundamental criticism of such belief then must be on other grounds, as indeed it is for Hume.

Given the *Treatise*'s background, one would expect to find a specification of propensities that indicates the experiences that elicit beliefs and something of the propositional content of those beliefs. We are not disappointed. Hume describes various principles, tendencies, or propensities (different ways of referring to belief-forming functions activated by the relevant sort of experience) in *Natural History of Religion*. The first two appear in Section 3, the first being a propensity relevant to overall belief formation:

> Propensity 1: "a propensity in human nature, which leads into a system that gives them some satisfaction." (NHR 40)

We cannot rest content with the idea that the causes of our weal and woe are invisible and unknown:

> Propensity 2: "a universal tendency among mankind to conceive all things like themselves, and to transfer to every object, those qualities with which they are familiarly acquainted, and of which they are intimately conscious." (NHR 40)

We tend toward an inadequately constrained anthropomorphism:

> Propensity 3: "their [humanity's] propensity to flattery and exaggeration." (NHR 55)

We ascribe properties to the unknown causes that make them more likely to be accessible to being influenced by us:

> Propensity 4: "the propensity . . . to return back [from theism] to idolatry." (NHR 59)

The properties we ascribe to the unknown causes are unstable between an abstract and a concrete notion of deity or deities.

Humans are not rational animals. They are bundles of belief-producing propensities. Religious beliefs also find their source in propensities. These propensities, although nearly universal, can be prevented from becoming active. Furthermore, in contrast to the propensities that yield natural beliefs, the religion-relevant propensities produce beliefs that exhibit wide diversity because they arise under the influence of passions of various, typically melancholy, sorts. Fears of the unknown causes of our weal and woe, for example, push folk toward the ideas of nonhuman persons capable of being bribed, cajoled, persuaded, or the like to do as one wishes, or at least not to do as one does not wish.

> In contrast to religious beliefs, natural beliefs spring from an original instinct or primary impression of nature, such as gives rise to self-love . . . since every instinct of this kind has always a precise determinate object, which it inflexibly pursues. (NHR 33)

The primary propensities also are not typically accompanied by emotions, melancholy or not, and produce uniform products.

II.1 An Objection

It is time to face an apparent objection to my reading of Hume. It seems fair to suggest that Hume has considered the question of religion's foundation in human reason in the *Dialogues* and found it nonexistent. Yet, in *Natural History of Religion*'s introduction, we read that the foundation is in the reason question:

> which is the most important, admits of the most obvious, at least the clearest, solution. The whole frame of nature bespeaks an intelligent author; and no rational enquirer can, after serious reflection, suspend his belief a moment with regard to the primary principles of Theism and Religion. (NHR 33)

This *seems* to go very much against my interpretation of *Natural History of Religion*. It is possible to suggest that the propensity described in *Natural History of Religion*, and noted here—to seek an explanation that gives some satisfaction—is a propensity of reason and that the extremely thin Philonian belief is its proper result. If the passions would leave things at that and not fatten up the belief in various ways, all would be well regarding religion and theism. It would also be well regarding atheism and agnosticism. On this reading, there is at least one propensity of reason. So far as I am aware, this is an exegetically possible reading. But several points are worth noting. First, the "principles of Theism and Religion" are not specified in the passage from *Natural History of Religion*. Given the overall *Natural History of Religion* discussion of religious belief, I grant that it is possible—I think right—to suppose that nothing more is involved in Hume's positive remark, than Philo's "the cause or causes of order in nature bear some remote analogy to human intelligence." This makes a deism that holds that God created the universe and left us with the capacity to grasp the fundamental principles of morality seem theologically thick. Exactly what sort of religion can one base on the idea that the cause or causes of natural order bears some remote analogy to human intelligence? As Protagoras said, everything resembles everything else in some way or other. Second, according to *Natural History of Religion*, when this vague belief is given more content, there is no one way in which this may be done, no single set of properties that are ascribed to the cause or causes. When the cause or causes start to be identified as persons or significantly like persons, they are described in ways that more merit than not identification as superstition. Third, as noted, for Hume, we are not rational animals. "Reason is, and always ought to be, the slave of the passions":

> The victory is not gained by the men of arms, who manage the pipe and the sword, but by trumpeters, drummers, and musicians of the army. (T Intro. 10/xviii)

> 'Tis not solely in poetry and music we must follow our taste and sentiment, but likewise in philosophy. (T 1.3.7.11/103)

Thus asserting that a belief is inescapable for rational inquirers is not from Hume's pen what it would be from the pen of Aristotle or Descartes.

The overall context should be remembered. Religious principles (propensities) are an accompaniment to, rather than being part of, human nature. Furthermore, the phrases "invisible, intelligent power" and "cause or causes of order bearing remote analogy to human intelligence" are neither stated with precision nor placed in a conceptual context that further specifies their content, which is sullied by emotion. The additional elements further specifying that content of religious belief are not constrained by canons of truth or reasonability. I take it, then, that what might be called "Philo's confession of faith" expresses no distinctively religious faith. No personal commitment to a proposed person, no rites, rituals, practices, institutions, or specific doctrines follow or are even suggested. The actual operation of the religious propensities is neither universal nor are its products uniform. It follows that the operation of the religion-relevant propensities is not constitutive of human nature (nor, apparently, would their entire absence destroy it). Those in which they do not operate are not thereby rendered nonhuman. The relevant belief-contents, not being universal, do not penetrate every culture. Even given the passage in question from *Natural History of Religion*, there is no objective criterion for sorting out which religious beliefs are in better accord with discernible evidence or solid argument. Here, even were belief to track truth, one could not tell. The content of beliefs that result from their operation are saturated with, and shaped by, emotions—and most often by the less desirable among them. Given all of this, it may not matter much whether the propensity to seek explanation is a propensity of reason or not. If it is, it is sullied quickly when it mixes, as inevitably it will, with the passions. Even if the passions are not melancholy, the result is no more reliable regarding truth than are those produced when the propensity is joined by the darker emotions. In the end, then, I do not think that the passage in *Natural History of Religion* is evidence against my reading of

Natural History of Religion or, overall, of the *Treatise, Dialogues,* and *Natural History of Religion* in concert. This (for the present at any rate) being settled, we can turn to Hume's critique of Theism and Religion.

III HUME'S CRITIQUE OF THEISM AND RELIGION

> I must distinguish in the imagination betwixt the principles that are permanent, irresistible, and universal ... and the principles which are changeable, weak, and irregular ... the former are the foundation of all our thoughts and actions, so that upon their removal human nature must immediately perish and go to ruin. The latter are neither unavoidable to mankind, nor necessary, or so much as useful in the conduct of life. (T 1.4.4.1/225)

> The assistance is mutual betwixt the judgment and fancy, as well as betwixt the judgment and passion ... as a lively imagination very often degenerates into madness or folly, and bears it a great resemblance in its operations, so they influence the judgement after the same manner, and produce belief from the very same principles. (T 1.3.10.8/122–3)
> Generally speaking, the errors in religion are dangerous. (T 1.4.7.13/272)

We noted that, in Section 12 of the *Dialogues*, Philo, throughout the secular critic who critiques pro-theistic arguments and is the proponent of the argument from evil, seems to switch sides as he confesses his devotion to natural religion. (Demea's small but not unimportant role is that of a religious critic of natural theology.) But this natural religion involves only belief that "the cause or causes of order in nature bear some remote analogy to human intelligence"—a belief compatible with, among other things, Philo's suggestions that perhaps the universe is a large vegetable or animal, the product of a committee, or a system in which what occurs does so necessarily. From this sort of religion, nothing follows about morality or much of anything—something Hume finds entirely advantageous. To this "religion" Hume has no objection.

When "Theism and Religion" go beyond this, Hume seems to have four criticisms. The first plays little role in *Natural History of Religion*. Hume expresses his view in lively terms:

> If we take in our hand any volume, of divinity or school metaphysics for instance, let us ask: Does it contain any reasoning concerning quantity or number? No. Does it contain any experimental reasoning concerning matter of fact and existence? No. Commit it to the flames. For it can contain nothing but sophistry and illusion. (EU 12.34/165)

More precisely, Hume has a theory of meaning for words and for statements. The former has to do with a sound or mark naming—the most frequent Humean expression is "corresponding to"—some specifiable impression or idea. The latter concerns the possible assessment of truth by appeal only to impressions and ideas. Adding formal concepts to the story, we get a fuller expression of the relevant type of theory of word meaning. The constituents of sensory and introspective experience are observable qualities. The descriptive predicates of our language are names of these qualities. The terms that name such qualities, let us say, are *content terms*, and they are all the indefinable content terms of our language. There are also logical connectives, such as *and, or, therefore, entails,* plus quantifiers like *all, some,* and *none.* There is negation. Such logical terms, let us say, are *structure terms*, and they are all the indefinable structure terms that there are. These predicates, connectives, and quantifiers, plus negation, are the building blocks of language. One can then suggest *concept empiricism*: for any concept *C* that it is alleged that we have, either *C* is the concept of an observable quality or the concept of a structure term, or *C* is definable without remainder by the use of (indefinable) concepts of observable qualities and structure terms; if not, we lack the alleged concept. He concludes that the concept of God is meaningless, there being no corresponding impressions or idea.

The story regarding meaningful (actual) statements is that they are true or false only if they can be confirmed by reference to impressions and ideas. He infers that the alleged statements that express theism are meaningless. We can call this view *statement empiricism*. The idea is that one who accepts concept empiricism will have to admit that *God exists* cannot be expressed within its limits, and one who embraces statement empiricism will have to do the same. But then neither can a definition of concept empiricism be offered consistently with accepting the view, nor is the statement that expresses statement empiricism meaningful on its own terms.

There are other problems. Philo, in the *Dialogues*, suggests that at least one version of the problem of evil is "so short, so clear, so decisive" that its solidity cannot be shaken "except we assert, that the subject exceed all human capacity, *and* that our common measures of truth and falsehood are not applicable to them" (D 103, emphasis added). Two quite different responses are conflated, namely: (A) If God has a morally (or otherwise) sufficient reason for allowing the evils that occur, we do not know what it is; versus (B) a common measure of truth and falsehood regarding us and God is not available for ascriptions of good and evil. The former view is accepted by many contemporary theists. They add that if A is to be used in an antitheistic argument, it will require that it is a necessary truth that *if God exists then God has a morally (or otherwise) sufficient reason for allowing the evils that occur*. Given that, it will require some such premises as: (A1) if God exists, then if God has a morally (or otherwise) sufficient reason for allowing the evils that occur, we will know what that reason is; (A2) we do not know what that reason is; hence (A3) God does not exist. So, we have a proof of atheism, unless we claim equivocation on "good" and "evil" or admit that the matter exceeds our capacities. The theist can reject A1, taking it to be clearly false precisely because the subject does "exceed all human capacity." That is what puts the task of developing a satisfactory theodicy beyond us. But then we cannot reasonably be expected to offer one, and the fact that we cannot is no evidence against theism. Whether this line of reasoning is correct or not, it remains clear that B does not follow from A. Thus, we have here no reason to suppose that there is no common measure of truth and falsity (of cognitive meaning) in ascribing goodness to God and to humans. To admit that the subject—or much of it—exceeds all human capacity seems right, but no theist need say otherwise. This puts the weight on the other critiques.

The second is that the operation of religion-relevant propensities is typical but optional for human beings. This combines with the third critique that religion has a bad effect on morality. This objection has at least two aspects. One is that the gods and goddesses believed to exist are themselves hardly paragons of morality. The descriptions of fictional divine misbehavior are detailed and varied. We fear invisible causes that we do not, and cannot, control. Thus, we ascribe properties to invisible powers that make them possibly accessible to us—desiring praise, open to bribery, themselves possessed of weakness, envy, strife, and immorality. In contrast to those propensities that produce natural beliefs, passions play a crucial role in the production of religious beliefs. These emotions are responses to the fact that our happiness and sorrow, success and failure, health and sickness, and life and death, all depend on invisible, unknown factors. Even if it is risky, we need cosmic companions who may be within reach of our prayers and pleas.

Another aspect is that pleasing these gods and goddesses trumps being moral. Their power exceeds that of humans, and the deities rule what afterlife there may be, as well as the present. What the deities are typically said to desire is flattery and bribery, not love of neighbor. Human sacrifice is not too much if the deities want it. Focus on morally appropriate motivation and action is seldom essential to, and is often competitive with, religious rituals performed for religious reasons. These comments are controversial but clear.

The fourth critique is more complex. It concerns the fragility of human nature, a theme that Hume also picks up from the *Treatise*. Seeing its importance there, it is not surprising to see it reappear here in passages such as:

> where theism forms the fundamental principle of any popular religion, that tenet is so comfortable to sound reason, that philosophy is apt to incorporate itself with such a system of theology, and if the other dogmas of that religion be contained in a sacred book . . . *philosophy will soon find herself very unequally yoked with her new associate; and instead of regulating each principle, as they advance together, she is at every turn perverted to serve the purposes of superstition.* (NHR 66)

He adds that:

> Besides the unavoidable incoherencies, which must be reconciled and adjusted, one may safely affirm that all popular theology . . . has a kind of appetite for absurdity and contradiction. (NHR 66)

The idea seems to be that because "the mind of man appears of so loose and unsteady a texture" (NHR 72), even when only its constitutive propensities operate, it is still worse off if secondary propensities are also active. The secondary propensities not only pollute beliefs that result from the operation of their primary kin; they themselves conflict:

> Here therefore is a kind of contradiction between the different principles of human nature, which enter into religion. Our natural terrors present the notion of a devilish and malicious deity. Our propensity to adulation leads us to acknowledge an excellent and divine. And the influence of these opposite principles are various, according to the different situation of the human understanding. (NHR 77)

In another relevant passage, Hume writes of the effect of superstition on the mind:

> as superstition arises naturally and easily from the popular opinions of mankind, *it seizes more strongly on the mind, and is often able to disturb us in the conduct of our lives and actions.*

And again: "Whatever weakens or disorders the internal frame serves the interests of superstition" (NHR 84). It leads to "disastrous, melancholy accidents," and "while we abandon ourselves to the natural undisciplined suggestions of our timid and anxious hearts, every kind of barbarity is ascribed to the Supreme Being." The most significant comment for our purposes is that:

> the artifices of men aggravate our natural infirmities and follies of this kind, but never originally beget them. Their root strikes deeper into the mind, and springs from the essential and universal properties of human nature. (NHR 84)

The universal propensities themselves are a source of fragility.

The fourth Humean critique is, in a broad sense, psychological. It is detachable from Hume's skepticism about our knowledge of an external world. Waiving again the consistency and coherence of Hume's overall perspective, we can note that this is just the sort of criticism one might expect from someone who was, if I am correct, in no position to propound either a natural theology or a natural atheology. On its most natural reading, it is quite independent of his views on meaning, on the moral inelegance of religion's affect on morality, perhaps even of his view that the religion-relevant propensities are secondary (although this is less clear). The topic of psychology and religion, of course, is complex and controversial all on its own. How mental health and even sanity are construed varies from one overall worldview to another. These matters go far beyond anything we can discuss here. I will be satisfied if my reading of Hume is justified and my limited assessment of Hume's critique on target so far as it goes.

IV CONCLUSION

Even supposing that Hume's explanation of religious belief is correct, it does not follow that theism is false or that holding such belief is unreasonable. Nonetheless, various features of *Natural History of Religion* cast any "theism" that is stronger than that expressed in Philo's *Dialogues* profession in a negative light. Although not emphasized in *Natural History of Religion*, the question of cognitive meaning (propositional truth or falsehood) lies just under the surface of various *Natural History of Religion* passages. In Hume's view, when a theistic view becomes more specific than Philo's vague belief, there are various ways of adding to the concept of invisible power—none of which is more justified than another, even though the religious and moral significance of invisible power depends on the way in which the bare concept is expanded. The originating propensity does not by itself provide significant limits on what expansions are proper, and there is no other factor that dictates, in any objective manner, how the expansion of the basic concept should proceed. More basic than even these negative factors, in Hume's view, is the destructive potential of allowing the basic religious propensity to join its kin in ways dictated by passions alone. Human nature just is a bundle of propensities, and it functions properly only if the members of this bundle operate within certain limits. This requires that a fragile balance be maintained, and the elicitation of a profusion of arbitrary beliefs within any bundle can lead to a disorder that renders the human mind constituted thereby psychologically unstable. In Hume's mind, the basic danger is not that of unreasonable or irrational belief but of disorder.

David Hume's *Treatise of Human Nature, Dialogues Concerning Natural Religion*, and *Natural History of Religion* fit together in an explanation of religious belief. The first offers a theory of human nature for which certain propensities to form beliefs constitute that nature. The second argues that the teleological, cosmological, and ontological arguments fail, so natural theology should be rejected. The final section of the second book, and all of the third, deals with the propensities that produce religious belief. Because "reason is, and also ought to be, the slave of the passions," it is not by appeal to argument and evidence that beliefs are to be assessed. The proper grounds for their assessment comes in terms of how their presence affects the unity and functioning of human nature. Judged by this standard, the natural beliefs in an external world, real causal connections, and an enduring self, pass muster. Save for the highly abstract belief that "the cause or causes of order in nature bear some remote analogy to human intelligence"—a belief entirely lacking in moral implications—religious belief is competitive with, and often destructive of, the fragile structure of human nature. This is Hume's critique of "Theism and Religion."

ABBREVIATIONS OF WORKS CITED

D   *Dialogues Concerning Natural Religion.* In D. Coleman, ed. *Dialogues Concerning Natural Religion and Other Writings.* Cambridge: Cambridge University Press, 2007.

EU   *An Enquiry Concerning Human Understanding.* Edited by T. L. Beauchamp. Oxford: Clarendon, 2000.

NHR *The Natural History of Religion.* In T. Beauchamp, ed. *A Dissertation on the Passions; The Natural History of Religion.* Oxford: Clarendon Press, 2008.

T   *A Treatise of Human Nature.* Edited by D. F. Norton and M. J. Norton. Oxford: Clarendon, 2007.

BIBLIOGRAPHY

Fox, Marvin. (1964). "Religion and Human Nature in the Philosophy of David Hume," in William L. Reese and Eugene Freeman, eds., *Process and Divinity.* LaSalle, IL: Open Court, 561–577.

Gaskin, J. C. A. (1978). *Hume's Philosophy of Religion.* London: Macmillan Press.

Livingston, Donald, and James T. King. (1976). *Hume: A Reevaluation.* New York: Fordham University Press.

O'Connor, David. (2001). *Routledge Guidebook to Hume on Religion.* Routledge.

Penelhum, Terrance. (2000). *Themes in Hume: The Self, The Will, Religion.* Oxford: Oxford University Press.

Tweyman, Stanley. (1986). *Scepticism and Belief in David Hume's Dialogues Concerning Natural Religion,* Dordrecht: Martinus Nijhoff.

Yandell, Keith E. (1990). *Hume's "Inexplicable Mystery": His Views on Religion.* Philadelphia: Temple University Press.

CHAPTER 33

....

HUME ON SUICIDE

....

EUGENIO LECALDANO

I The History of the Text

HUME composed the essay "Of Suicide" in the mid-fifties of the eighteenth century, while he was engaged in revising the *History of England*.[1] In June 1755, he submitted four dissertations to Andrew Millar, which Millar accepted for publication. These were: "The Natural History of Religion," "Of the Passions," "Of Tragedy," and "Some Considerations Previous to Geometry and Natural Philosophy." Hume was, however, convinced by Lord Stanhope that there were certain defects in the pages of "Some Considerations," and he wrote to Millar withdrawing this dissertation. Millar protested that the three remaining dissertations "would not make a Volume," at which point Hume offered "Of Suicide" and "Of the Immortality of the Soul" in substitution of the text he had withdrawn. Millar then printed the set of essays as *Five Dissertations*, but it was never published, in part because Hume himself then withdrew both "Of Suicide" and "Of the Immortality of the Soul." In 1756, he composed and submitted a new essay on "The Standard of Taste," and Millar then published the resulting *Four Dissertations* in February 1757. It is known that a few copies of the proofs of the two withdrawn essays were circulated abroad, and one of these copies was the basis for the French translation. The two essays appeared in 1770, in the miscellaneous edition *Recueil Philosophique ou Mèlange de Pièces sur la Religion et la morale*, edited by Jacques Andrè Naigeon. In this volume, chapters X and XI were the "Dissertation sur l'immortalitè de l'àme" and the "Dissertation sur le suicide," and the translation was very probably by Baron Paul-Henry Dietrich d'Holbach.[2] After Hume's death in 1777, an unauthorized edition of the *Two Essays* appeared in London without the name of the author, and 1783 saw the publication of the *Essays on Suicide, and the Immortality of the Soul. Ascribed to the late David Hume, Esq. Never before published. With Remarks, intended as an Antidote to the Poison contained in these Performances. By the Editor*. It was not until 1875 that "Of Suicide" was inserted into the collection edited by T. H. Green and T. H. Grose of the *Philosophical Works of David Hume* as one of the *Unpublished Essays*.[3]

At present, there is discussion in progress on the motives for Hume's decision to suppress the two essays. Although "Of Suicide" had already been printed, Hume himself expressed a desire for its suppression. The received view is that put forward by E. C. Mossner[4], for whom some religious figures, and in particular William Warburton, made threats to Hume and Millar to prevent them from publishing. It is also thought probable that Adam Smith tried to convince Hume to suppress the essay. Mossner writes: "it was perhaps not too difficult for Millar to persuade Hume—despite his theoretical convictions on the freedom of the press—to suppress 'Of the immortality of the soul' as well as 'Of Suicide,' and to agree to the revision of certain passages in 'The Natural History of Religion.'"[5] Hume himself explained that he had suppressed the essays "from my abundant prudence" and following advice from a friend (LET 2.253). Tom L. Beauchamp rejects this explanation, largely on the grounds that, if prudence were the cause, then "The Natural History of Religion" would also have been suppressed. Beauchamp offers as an alternative explanation his own interpretation of the essay as deficient in its argumentation. On his view, Hume withdrew the essay "because of the internal inadequacies in the content" (1976: esp. 91–95).

❧

II THE SOURCES AND THE SOCIAL CONTEXT

To better understand the pages of the essay, an attempt at reconstruction of its historical background may be useful, particularly in the light of the earlier philosophical analyses on suicide with which Hume was probably familiar. Some indications of the contemporary discussion on suicide in England and Scotland up to the middle of the eighteenth century may also be useful. Last, the essay on suicide needs to be seen in the context of Hume's intellectual biography as a whole and of the works he had published in preceding years.

As regards the extant philosophical analyses of suicide, Hume was a confirmed adversary of theological views. Among these, of particular importance was the position of Thomas Aquinas on the immorality of suicide.[6] Aquinas's central argument was addressed by Hume in his essay, as well as nonreligious arguments. Hume writes: "If Suicide be criminal, it must be a transgression of our duty either to God, our neighbour, or ourselves" (ESY 580). Against the first, and most persistent, of these notions, the essay argues that suicide cannot be considered criminal aprioristically, as a transgression of our duty to God. Here, Hume was replying not only to Aquinas's thesis—and to subsequent reformulations by Anglican theologians—but also to John Locke (1988: 2.6/272) who had, in the preceding century, subscribed to the view that only God can make decisions about life and death.[7]

On the positive side, Hume reformulates certain arguments put forward in favor of suicide—in determined situations—by the Stoics and by other thinkers, both of ancient Rome[8] and of more recent eras. In the work of Michel de Montaigne, for example, there is some ambiguity on the question, but in certain pages he clearly takes the Stoics' view.[9] Of considerable importance in the seventeenth century was John Donne's *Biathanatos*, a theological discussion in favor of suicide, written in 1608 and published in 1648.[10] Francis Bacon (1857–74), too, was in favor of suicide, and there is also a discussion of suicide in Montesquieu (1897: *lettre* 76). Of particular relevance is the treatment of suicide in the second part of Bernard de Mandeville's *Fable of the Bees*. For Mandeville, in his project of finding an "anatomical" explanation of all human behavior in terms of egoism, the question of suicide is crucial. What, he asks, is the egoistic motivation for this conduct? Mandeville's reply is that this is only possible if one distinguishes two different egoistic levers: those of self-love and of self-liking. Mandeville's (1924: 2, 129–130) analysis purports to be neutral, but this neutrality is only apparent because, in maintaining that it may be a rational act for persons who—motivated from self-liking—consider their honor more decisive than their survival connected with self-love, he in effect justifies suicide. It is very probable that this analysis is the source of the many passages in Hume's essay opposing the notion of the existence of a natural law, willed by God, which dictates to human beings the moral necessity of their own survival. Hume was probably also drawing on Mandeville in those passages in which he identifies nonegoistical motivations for suicide.

The social context of eighteenth-century England and Scotland is also important. In these countries, severe punishments were determined by law not only for persons attempting suicide but also for their heirs, should their attempt prove successful. Attempting suicide was punished with terms in jail, and the heirs were liable to the confiscation of their property. And, of course, all the Christian churches denied both funerals and burial in consecrated land to persons committing suicide.[11]

With reference to the collocation of the essay in Hume's intellectual biography, there is controversy over whether "Of Suicide" is or is not discontinuous in relation to Hume's other published works, but we hold it to be in full continuity. Indeed, many specific arguments advanced in the essay are illuminated by theses already advanced elsewhere in his work. Hume himself saw the presentation of the arguments in this essay as specifically philosophical and as the only types of arguments capable of offering "remedies against" the "pestilent distemper" of "superstition and false religion" (ESY 577). Hume writes, from his habitual stance: "Love or anger, ambition or avarice, have their root in the temper and affections, which the soundest reason is scarce ever able fully to correct; but superstition being founded in false opinion, must immediately vanish when true philosophy has inspired juster sentiments of superior powers" (ESY 579). This amounts to a new formulation of conclusions already advanced in the *Treatise* and the two *Enquiries*. It is our contention, however, that in "Of Suicide" there is a new development of Hume's ideas. The essay on suicide, more than that on the immortality of the soul,[12] demonstrates a greater degree of integration of Hume's ideas. On our reading, two main extensions of Hume's ideas are realized in these pages. First, there is a coherent and comprehensive attack on the very notion of duty toward God, and, second, an explicit normative moral view on suicide is elaborated. As with other moral issues dealt with in his work—for example, his attack on the monastic virtues or on the hypocrisy of priests and the religious, or his refutation of polygamy and his acceptance of single motherhood—Hume eschews the anatomical and explicative approach in favor of elaborating explicit normative theses.[13] According to the ethical perspective that Hume was contesting (ubiquitous in his time and still widespread), which sees human life as not "disposable" by humans themselves under any circumstances, suicide is an action that is not "approvable." Conversely, in Hume's essay, he points to conditions that make suicide not only morally approvable but even, in determinate cases, a moral duty.

III First Reactions

The reactions to Hume's essay in the latter part of the eighteenth century were, in general, negative, as demonstrated by the events surrounding its publication. When "Of Suicide" and "The Immortality of the Soul" were first published under the author's name, they were to be found in a volume in which the editor added several pages of remarks as an "antidote to the poison contained in these performances." A further illustration of the cultural climate in Scotland at the time was the attitude of Adam Smith. He was probably the "friend" who, in 1756, advised Hume to abandon the idea of publication. In the same spirit of moderation, Smith, in 1776, said he would not give the requested help to Hume for the publication of the *Dialogues Concerning Natural Religion*. Smith's own ideas on suicide—ideas in marked contrast to Hume's conclusions—were expressed in *The Theory of Moral Sentiments* in its final revision of 1790 (Smith 1976: 278–93), by which time Hume's argument on suicide was well-known. Smith here discusses in detail the moral question of the propriety of suicide. He denies that suicidal acts were very frequent, and he rejects as ridiculous the "indulgence" of the Stoics toward such acts. On his view, suicide is always a reaction that is inappropriate, and the impartial spectator should not sympathize with it:

> The Principle of suicide, the principle which would teach us, upon some occasion, to conclude that violent action as an object of applause and approbation, seems to be altogether a refinement of philosophy. Nature in her sound and healthful state, seems never to prompt us to suicide. . . . Nature in her sound and healthful state, prompts us to avoid distress upon all occasions; upon many occasions to defend ourselves against it, though at the hazard, or even with the certainty of perishing in that defence. But when we have neither been able to defend ourselves from it, nor have perished in that defence, no natural principle, no regard to the approbation of the supposed impartial spectator, to the judgment of man within the breast seems to call upon us to escape from it by destroying ourselves. It is only the consciousness of our weakness, of our own incapacity to support this calamity with proper manhood and firmness, which can drive us to this resolution. (1976: 287)

Smith therefore considers suicide as never morally approvable, even though, in opposition to the legal system of his time, he declares that persons committing suicide "are the proper objects, not of censure, but of commiseration" and that "their surviving friends and relations, who are always perfectly innocent" have already been punished by nature (1976: 287).

In like vein, in almost all the early commentaries, Hume's thesis is generally condemned, with a typical judgment on the essay being that it is not a philosophical work but a confused congeries of fallacious argumentations.[14]

IV   The Interpretation of the Essay "Of Suicide" as a Text of Philosophy of Religion

Our reading of the essay must, of course, be compared with other interpretations. The history of the latter, however, is not centered on the acceptance or rejection of Hume's substantive position, that is, that suicide is, on some occasions, a legitimate moral act or even laudable. Rather, the prevailing discussion in the scholarship on Hume concerns the value of the essay and, more recently, its central argumentation. For much of this history of interpretation, a negative judgment of the essay has been prevalent, stressing the rhetorical significance of the essay and considering it to be a piece of occasional writing that Hume had composed in a hurry. These theses on the essay were presented in exemplary form in 1976 by T. L. Beauchamp.[15] And it is from this judgment of the value of the essay that Beauchamp derives his reinterpretation of the real motives of Hume's decision not publish it. That is, that Hume was motivated not by prudence but by awareness as an author that this work was not well accomplished.

Thomas Holden, in his article of 2005, initiates a very significant turn in the history of interpretation of this essay.[16] Holden re-evaluates the essay as a text that is engaged in a philosophical analysis with very particular and important results. On his view, the preceding interpreters of this essay had not recognized its specific contribution to Humean philosophy. For Holden, the task Hume took on here was not so much that of taking a position on the morality of suicide as that of making a concentric attack on the theological approach to ethics, which hinges on the existence of duties toward God. As such, this essay is seen as *the* decisive text for a definitive burial of the notion of "duty toward God." In fact, in these pages, there is a systematic collection of arguments against the doctrine that human beings can derive moral obligations from "God's" prohibitions of determinate actions. The case of suicide is, for Hume, an exemplification of a wider kind of moral obligation, founded on the apprehension of God's prohibition of certain behaviors.

In "Of Suicide," there are many lines of argument that render the idea of a duty toward God unacceptable, even to the believer in God and to those who accept the Christian revelation. As, for example, when Hume points out the incoherence of the theistic position: "Were the disposal of human life so much reserved as the peculiar province of the Almighty that it were an encroachment on his right, for men to dispose of their own lives; it would be equally criminal to act for the preservation of life as for its destruction. If I turn aside a stone which is falling upon my head, I disturb the course of nature, and I invade the peculiar province of the Almighty by lengthening out my life beyond the period which by the general laws of matter and motion he had assigned it" (ESY 583).

Hume shows the groundlessness of the different burdens that theists impose on the act of suicide, claiming that it is either "a disruption of the natural order," "the destruction of something of value to God," or else "an expression of ingratitude" (Holden 2005: 199–205). Hume offers arguments to believers on the impossibility of deriving a prohibition of suicide from laws of nature fixed at the Creation or formulated in sacred books. He shows that there is no possibility of justifying the notion that an act of suicide is a negation of a precise prohibition from God. Such a prohibition cannot be made to square either with reason or with revelation. With the help of reason, it would be possible to conclude that, in determinate circumstances, it is God who wills the act of suicide as an application of the laws of his creation. The natural laws that God fixed for the universe at the Creation are, it is to be supposed, valid for all living beings, and, as Hume says: "the life of a man is of no greater importance to the universe than that of an oyster" (ESY 583). In his criticism of the theists, Hume develops many arguments that are connected with the general, deterministic approach presented in the *Treatise*, which holds that the natural liberty of men is compatible with actions regulated by the causal laws of the universe. Hume also maintains that the believer must accept the act of suicide as a natural event that is willed—or at least permitted—by God, through these same causal laws, laid down at the Creation, that regulate all events. With reference to revealed religion, he writes: "It would be easy to prove that Suicide is as lawful under the Christian dispensations as it was to the Heathens. There is not a single text of Scripture with prohibits it. That great and infallible rule of faith and practices which must control all philosophy and human reasoning, has left us in this particular to our natural liberty. . ... *Thou shall not kill* is evidently meant to exclude only the killing of others over whose life we have no authority" (ESY 588).

Holden's interpretation is certainly very useful. It could be characterized as a proposal to insert "Of Suicide" in Hume's philosophy of religion rather that in his moral philosophy; a proposal that is accepted by other recent interpreters of Hume.[17] Nonetheless, we argue here that Hume's essay is also very important as an explicit defence of a particular solution in moral philosophy.

V THE CENTRAL ARGUMENTS OF THE ESSAY "OF SUICIDE" AS A TEXT OF MORAL PHILOSOPHY

Turning now to our interpretation of the essay as a text with positive moral objectives, here, Hume explains clearly his constructive moral direction thus: "Let us here endeavour to restore men to their native liberty by examining all the common arguments against Suicide, and shewing that that action may be free from every imputation of guilt or blame, according to the sentiments of all the ancient philosophers." The general purpose of the essay is to establish a "right, for men to dispose of their own lives" (ESY 580).

After his refutation of the Christian thesis "that the almighty has reserved to himself in any peculiar manner the disposal of the lives of men" (ESY 582), Hume puts forward the radically contrasting principle for which "every one [has] the free disposal of his own life" (ESY 582). This principle is the premise on which the solution to the question of the morality of suicide is grounded. Any intended action pertaining to the disposal of oneself is to be submitted to the judgment of "prudence" (ESY 582). At this point, Hume argues that the evaluation of acts of suicide must be undertaken case by case. On each occasion, we must check whether or not the individual has used her natural liberty and her right of disposal of her own life in a legitimate way. It is in the articulation of the criteria for the approval or disapproval of suicide, in coherence with his general approach to the morality,[18] that Hume sets out very innovative ideas in the history of reflection on suicide. This innovation does not, however, merely take the form of a general thesis claiming that suicide is not always prohibited as a negation of one's duties toward society or toward oneself. Rather, there are "cases [in which] my resignation of life must not only be innocent but laudable" (ESY 587). Again: "If it [suicide] be no crime, both prudence and courage should engage us to rid ourselves at once of existence, when it becomes a burthen. 'Tis the only way that we can then be useful to society, by setting an example, which if imitated, would preserve to every one his chance for happiness in life and would effectually free him from all danger or misery" (ESY 588).

What is so new in Hume's moral reflection on suicide is the overcoming of the requirement of rationality as a necessary constituent of any ethical analysis of the question. Hitherto, only cases in which human beings in full rationality have examined the possibility of ending their lives have been the object of moral evaluation. This had been the constant background of philosophical discussion on suicide. But, of course, Hume does not accept the division between rational and irrational as constitutive of the field of morality. The morally legitimate suicides are for him not only rational suicides. In Hume's ethics, an action is morally approvable if it derives from some motivation of the person that we can accept from a general point of view. Hume gives some indication of acceptable motives for suicide. First of all, he recalls prudence as a criterion for distinguishing what is morally legitimate from what is illegitimate. But we are not to confuse prudence with rationality, given that, for Hume, prudence is a natural ability, an instinctive and spontaneous character of persons (T 3.3.4.4–7/388–9).

In the essay, Hume also puts forward other acceptable motivations for suicide: we may choose to end our life because doing so may be useful to others or to ourselves, but also simply because it is too miserable, and "age, sickness or misfortune may render life a burthen, and make it worse even than annihilation" (ESY 588). With reference to our duties to others and to society Hume writes: "But suppose that it is no longer in my power to promote the interest of society; suppose that I am a burthen to it; suppose that my life hinders some person from being much more useful to society.[19] In such cases my resignation must not only be innocent but laudable" (ESY 587).

But Hume's most innovative conclusion remains his refutation of the notion that the distinction between rational and irrational suicide is morally decisive.[20] He writes: "I believe that no man threw away life, while it was worth keeping. For such is our natural horror of death, that small motives will never be able to reconcile us to it; and though perhaps the situation of a man's health or fortune did not seem to require this remedy, we may at least be assured that any one who, without apparent reason, has had recourse to it, was curst with such an incurable depravity or gloominess of temper as must poison all enjoyment, and render him equally miserable as if he had been loaded with the most grievous misfortunes" (ESY 588).

This essay thus serves as another important evidence of the partiality of the interpretations of Hume's position as a radical skeptical philosopher or, alternatively, as an anatomist of human nature who is fully neutral, without preconceived moral beliefs. As on other occasions, Hume shows that he is not at all skeptical with regard to certain moral conclusions. Hume's "science of man" suggests that, with regard to the end of life, we must abandon the traditional morality of the schools and churches and embark upon a new morality centered on the right of disposal of one's own life.

VI RECENT RECEPTION

It is through these interpretations of Hume's essay that we can understand its continuous presence in recent moral philosophy and in the bioethics of the end of life. It is necessary, therefore, to wait through the ethical reflections of the past fifty years before a change in the fortune of Hume's ideas on suicide will be witnessed. In all probability, the different conditions of human dying resulting from the inexorable advances in biomedicine since the mid-twentieth century will give new relevance to Hume's affirmation that death is a disposal process for human beings, and as such, an essential part of human natural liberty.

It is impossible to recall here all the recent works that make explicit reference to Hume's essay; we can therefore name just a few, and, in particular among these, R. B. Brandt's discussion of "Of Suicide."[21] Brandt adopts a utilitarian approach to the question of the morality of suicide and sees Hume's text as one that lists the motives that render suicide morally acceptable. In particular, Brandt discusses the point in which Hume "speaks of the propriety of suicide for one who leads a hated life," "loaded with pain and sickness, with shame and poverty" (ESY 584). Brandt (1992: 332) criticizes Hume for giving too much importance to shame and poverty, however: "a life that he would classify as one of shame and poverty might be a tolerable life, inferior to Hume's life style, but still preferable to nothing." This criticism of Brandt's clearly reflects the prevalence in philosophy of the preoccupation with rationality in the moral evaluation of suicide; in other words, it represents the approach to the morality of suicide that Hume wanted to supersede.

Many utilitarians, from Jonathan Glover to Peter Singer, consider Hume's essay to be a text with relevant proposals on the question of the morality of suicide.[22] Recently, Julian Savulescu (1999) has identified Hume's essay as the starting point for contemporary discussions on such themes as the "quality of life," the "living will," "advance directives," "respect for autonomy," "shared decision making," and "the right to die." Savulescu (1999: 533) thinks—subscribing to a utilitarian approach to ethics—that, in Hume, "there is a naïve optimism" in the belief "that no man ever threw away life, while it was worth keeping." For this reason, it is necessary to have some public rules for "the limitations of life-sustaining treatment for formerly competent and now incompetent patients."

James Rachels (1986), too, in his classic book, *The End of Life. Euthanasia and Morality*, recalls the discussion of suicide in Hume and his energetic claim that human beings have a right to end their own life; the life of man being—"for the universe," as he puts it—not more important than that of an oyster. Rachels interprets this affirmation as a way of making the connection between the value of life and the judgment of the person, in opposition to a religious or metaphysical interpretation of this value.

In conclusion, it can be said that the presence of Hume's essay in recent discussions in philosophical ethics helps us to read the text in a new way, as not only part of the history of the philosophy of religion, but also as part of the history of moral philosophy. "Of Suicide" is the first philosophical text that sets out a coherent approach to the ethical questions concerning the end of human life, not only in fully secular (and probably irreligious) terms, but also on the basis of the principle of autonomous choice of the person, taking into account both human suffering and a conception of the dignity of life.

Abbreviations of Works Cited

ESY   *Essays: Moral, Political, and Literary*. Revised edition by E. F. Miller. Indianapolis: Liberty Classics, 1985.

LET   *The Letters of David Hume*, 2 Vols. Edited by J. Y. T. Greig. Oxford: Clarendon Press, 1932.

T   *A Treatise of Human Nature*. Edited by D. F. Norton and M. J. Norton. Oxford: Clarendon, 2007.

Notes

1. There is a useful account of the genesis of the text "Of Suicide" in Mossner (1954: 322–3).
2. Mossner (1954: 330).
3. Hume (1874–5). Green and Grose published the text "Of Suicide"—on the basis of a copy of the prints of *Five Dissertations* in Advocate's Library of Edinburgh—in volume 4, pages 406–415. The quotations in this text from "Of Suicide" are followed by page references to *Essays: Moral, Political and Literary*, edited by E. F. Miller, Indianapolis, Liberty Fund, 1987.
4. Mossner (1950: 37–57); Mossner (1954: 322–330).

5. Mossner (1954), art. cit., page 42.

6. Beauchamp (1976) puts forward the thesis, perhaps too strong, that "the organization of the essay" on suicide "is that of a point by point reply" to the "three arguments against the morality of suicide" exposed in the *Summa Theologica* of Aquinas.

7. See also Samuel Clarke (1738/1978), vol. 2, page 263. The same ideas were expressed in a popular and literary form in Samuel Richardson's *Pamela, or Virtue Reconsidered* (1740–1).

8. Grisé (1982); Minois (1995); Barbagli (2009).

9. Montaigne (2007), book II, chapter III.

10. On this, see Sprott (1961).

11. For the social history of suicide, see Minois (1995).

12. In fact, many of the doctrines advanced in *The Immortality of the Soul* were already put forward by Hume in the *Treatise*. On this, see Russell (2008), especially chapter 14 on "Immateriality, Immortality and the Human Soul," pp. 187–203.

13. On the presence in Hume's works of explicit normative positions, see Siebert (1990). The relevant Hume texts are, respectively: *The Enquiry on the Principles of Morals, The History of Natural Religion, Of Polygamy and Divorce, Of Moral Prejudices.*

14. See the articles offered in Fieser (2001), especially pages 289–314, 319–325, and 360–370.

15. A similar judgment was offered in Merrill (1999: 395–411) and McLean (2001: 99–111).

16. For a useful reconstruction, see also Holden (2010), especially pages 183–189.

17. For example, Yandell (1990), especially pages 286–295. But see also McLean (2001), who offers a pretension of critical refutation of Hume's arguments.

18. For Hume's approach to morality, see the contributions of Annette Baier, Simon Blackburn, and Christine Swanton in this *Handbook.*

19. In the Miller edition, we read instead "useful to the public."

20. In this connection, Siebert (1990: 139) notes that this analysis of Hume has the implication that "clinical depression itself would appear a justification for suicide."

21. Brandt (1992), first published in 1976.

22. See Glover (1977: 170), in which the discussion of the subject of "suicide and gambling of life" starts with a quotation from Hume. Singer (1986) includes Hume's "Of Suicide" between the texts.

Bibliography

Bacon, Francis. (1857–74/1961–63). *De dignitate et augmentis scientiarum*, in J. Spedding, R. L. Ellis, and D. D. Heath, eds., *The Works of Francis Bacon*, 14 vols. London. (Reprinted in Stuttgart-Bad Cannstatt: Friedrich Frommann Verlag Gunther Holzboog.)

Barbagli, Marzio. (2009). *Congedarsi dal mondo. Il suicidio in Occidente e in Oriente.* Bologna: Il Mulino.

Beauchamp, Tom L. (1976). *An Analysis of Hume's Essay "On Suicide," Review of Metaphysics* 30, 73–95.

Brandt, Richard B. (1992). *Morality, Utilitarianism and Rights.* Cambridge: Cambridge University Press.

Clarke, Samuel. (1738/1978). *Concerning the Unchangeable Obligations of Natural Religion and Truth and Certainty of Christian Revelation, in The Works*, 4 vols. London. (Reprinted in New York: Garland.)

Donne, John. (1648). *Biathanatos*. Michael Rudick and Margaret Battin, eds. London: Humphrey Moseley.

Fieser, James (ed.). (2001). *Early Responses to Hume's Writings on Religion*, 2 vols. Bristol: Thoemmes Press.

Glover, Jonathan. (1997). *Causing Death and Saving Lives*. Harmondsworth: Penguin Books.

Grise, Y. (1982). *Le suicide dans la Rome antique*. Paris: Les Belles Lettres.

Holden, Thomas. (2005). "Religion and Moral Prohibition in Hume's 'Of Suicide,'" *Hume Studies* 31 (2), 189–210.

Holden, Thomas. (2010). *Spectres of False Divinity: Hume's Moral Atheism*. Oxford: Oxford University Press.

Hume, David. (1874–5/1964). *The Philosophical Works*, 4 vols. T. H. Green and T. H. Grose, eds. London. (Reprint *Scientia Verlag Aalen*.)

Locke, John. (1988). *Two Treatises of Government*. Peter Laslett, ed., Cambridge: Cambridge University Press.

Mandeville, Bernard de. (1924). *The Fable of the Bees*, 2 vols. F. B. Kaye, ed. Oxford: Clarendon Press.

McLean, G. R. (2001). "Hume and the Theistic Objection to Suicide," *American Philosophical Quarterly* 38, 99–111.

Merrill, Kenneth R. (1999). "Hume on Suicide," *History of Philosophy Quarterly* 16, 395–411.

Minois, G. (1995). *Histoire du Suicide: la societè occidentale face a la mort voluntaire*. Paris: Fayard.

Montaigne, Michel de. (2007). *Essais*. J. Balsamo, M. Magnien, C. Magnien-Simonin, eds., Paris: Gallimard (Pléiade).

Montesquieu, Charles, and Louis de Secondat. (1897). *Lettres Persanes*. H. Barckhausen, ed., Paris.

Mossner, Ernest Campbell. (1950). "Hume's Four Dissertations: An Essay in Biography and Bibliography," *Modern Philology* 48, 37–57.

Mossner, Ernest Campbell. (1954). *The Life of David Hume*. Oxford: Clarendon Press.

Rachels, James. (1986). *The End of Life: Euthanasia and Morality*. Oxford: Oxford University Press.

Richardson, Samuel. (1740–1). *Pamela, or Virtue Reconsidered*. London.

Russell, Paul. (2008). *The Riddle of Hume's Treatise: Scepticism, Naturalism and Irreligion*. Oxford: Oxford University Press.

Savulescu, Julian. (1999). "Rational Desires and the Limitations of Life: Sustaining Treatment," in H. Kuhse and P. Singer, eds., *Bioethics: An Anthology*. Oxford: Blackwell, 533–50.

Siebert, Donald T. (1990). *The Moral Animus of David Hume*. Newark: University of Delaware Press.

Singer, Peter (ed.). (1986). *Applied Ethics*. Oxford: Oxford University Press.

Smith, Adam. (1976). *The Theory of Moral Sentiments*. D. D. Raphael and A. L. Macfie, eds. Oxford: Clarendon Press.

Sprott, S. E. (1961). *The English Debate on Suicide from Donne to Hume*. La Salle, IL: Open Court.

Yandell, Keith E. (1990). *Hume's Inexplicable Mystery: His Views on Religion*. Philadelphia: Temple University Press.

PART VI

··

HUME AND THE ENLIGHTENMENT

··

CHAPTER 34

....

NEWTON AND HUME

....

YORAM HAZONY AND ERIC SCHLIESSER

In his *History of England* (1754–62), David Hume offered what was to be his final published assessment of Isaac Newton:

> In Newton this island may boast of having produced the greatest and rarest genius that ever arose for the ornament and instruction of the species. Cautious in admitting no principles but such as were founded on experiment; but resolute to adopt every such principle, however new or unusual: From modesty, ignorant of his superiority above the rest of mankind; and thence, less careful to accommodate his reasonings to common apprehensions: More anxious to merit than acquire fame: He was from these causes long unknown to the world; but his reputation at last broke out with a lustre, which scarcely any writer, during his own lifetime, had ever before attained. While Newton seemed to draw off the veil from some of the mysteries of nature, he shewed at the same time the imperfections of the mechanical philosophy; and *thereby* restored her ultimate secrets to that obscurity, in which they ever did and ever will remain. (HE VI 542; emphasis added)

This passage leaves no doubt as to Hume's admiration for Newton, whom he calls the "greatest and rarest genius that ever arose." But it is remarkable that as a historian Hume chooses to focus attention on two aspects of Newton's legacy that others might not have considered the most significant: first, Hume emphasizes that Newton decisively undermined the mechanical philosophy of Descartes and Boyle, in so doing ("thereby") ensuring that the ultimate workings of nature would remain unknowable. Thus, in Hume's hands, Newton's achievement in his *Mathematical Principles of Natural Philosophy* (1687, hereafter *Principia*) is turned into an argument for skepticism about fundamental ontology,[1] when it is by no means obvious that Newton and his followers understood his achievement as an argument for any such thing.

Second, Hume here presents Newton's so-called *analytic and synthetic method* in natural philosophy as a combination of cautious experimental foundationalism ("admitting no principles but such as were founded on experiment") and bold extrapolation ("resolute to adopt every such principle, however new or unusual") lacking in any real concern for the constraints of common sense ("thence, less careful to accommodate his reasonings to common apprehensions"). Hume, of course, was not usually one to praise a project for straying too far beyond common sense, and readers familiar with his philosophy would have noticed the backhanded nature of this compliment: as Hume writes in his *Enquiry Concerning Human Understanding* (1748), practitioners of a "mitigated scepticism" will not "be tempted to go beyond common life, so long as they consider the imperfection of those faculties which they employ, their narrow reach, and their inaccurate operations" (EU 12.3.25/162).

These two planks of Hume's assessment of Newton in his *History of England*—his backhanded treatment of Newton's disregard for common sense and his praise for Newton's contribution to the cause of ontological skepticism—serve to alert us to a not insignificant tension between Hume's views and those of the camp of mainstream Newtonians whose influence was by then felt everywhere in British philosophy and science. We can compare Hume's assessment, for example, with that of Samuel Clarke, the most influential early spokesperson for the Newtonian cause, who, in the context of using the authority of Newton's science to offer a detailed criticism of Spinoza, writes that "after all the discoveries of later ages," we are justified in agreeing with Ecclesiasticus that "There are yet hid greater things than these, and we have seen but a few of his works. For the Lord hath made all things; and to the godly hath he given wisdom" (1705: Part XI, 81–83).[2] Clarke thus inserts Newton as an important recent step in a godly and progressive unveiling of God's works, whereas Hume's philosopher can do without God's beneficence so long as he "proportions his belief to the evidence" (EU 10.1.4/110).[3]

This tension between Hume's assessment and that of more mainstream eighteenth-century British Newtonians raises significant questions regarding the true relationship between Hume's philosophy and Newton's. Hume has often been taken for a Newtonian, and for good reason: The subtitle of Hume's *Treatise of Human Nature*, "An attempt to introduce the experimental method of reasoning into moral subjects," makes it seem as though Hume's aim is to extend the methods of natural philosophy into the study of human nature. This conclusion is supported, as well, by Hume's comment in the *History* to the effect that Newton's experimental method is a decisive step on "the only road, which leads to true philosophy" (HE VI, 542). Moreover, there are passages in the *Treatise* and in Hume's later writings that strongly suggest that he wishes to be seen as the Newton of the human sciences.[4] But, in recent years, scholars have begun to suspect that Hume's relationship to Newton is in fact quite a bit more complicated—and more interesting—than this. On this view, Hume in fact has a dual agenda with respect to Newton: on the one hand, central aspects of Hume's proposed "system of the sciences" are in fact inspired and modeled on Newton's success in the *Principia*. On the other, Hume's *Treatise* is also bears a deeply subversive message with respect to Newtonian science.[5]

The aim of this chapter is to offer a revised overview of what Hume takes from Newton and what he rejects. Our discussion focuses on Hume's *Treatise* (1739), the work in which Hume's relationship with Newton is perhaps displayed most extensively and most fully. In the first part of the paper, we argue that, in the *Treatise*, Hume advocates a version of the analytic and synthetic method of philosophy as described in Newton's *Principia* and *Opticks*. This means that Hume places a form of explanatory reduction at the center of his own philosophical method. In the second part of the paper, we show that many of the most important aspects of Hume's argument in Book 1 of the *Treatise* can be understood as critical of core conceptual and ontological commitments of Newton's mechanics as developed in the *Principia*.

I   HUME AS NEWTONIAN

I.1 The Analytic and Synthetic Method

When Hume wrote his *Treatise of Human Nature* in the mid-1730s, Newton's *Principia* had already been in circulation for four decades, its first edition having appeared in 1687. And although the complete victory of Newtonian ideas and methods still lay in the future—with plenty of resistance still to be found in the great academies of France and Berlin[6]—they had already gathered sufficient momentum in Britain so that Berkeley could see reason to publish a pamphlet complaining of the loss of "free-thinking" in the field of mathematics.[7]

Although the young Hume was in many respects a dissenter from Newtonian orthodoxy, his *Treatise* was nonetheless consciously modeled on the explanatory-reductive method put to such extraordinary effect in Newton's *Principia*. This method is most clearly articulated in the "Queries" to Newton's *Opticks*. There, he explains that there exists a general method for the "investigation of difficult things," which he calls the "analytic and synthetic method." This is a two-step investigation that begins in (1) a movement from experiment and observation to general causes "by induction"; and then continues to (2) a second stage, which "consists in assuming the causes discover'd, and establish'd as principles, and by them explaining the phaenomena proceeding from them" (1730: 404–405).[8] In the case of the *Principia*, the general causes that have been discovered by induction are the "laws of motion" and the law of gravitation, all formulated in terms of a scheme of fundamental concepts such a *force* and *mass* presented in the definitions at the beginning of the work. Newton then "assumes the causes discover'd" and proceeds to explain the motions of celestial bodies, terrestrial projectile motion, the rise and fall of the tides, and the shape of the earth's surface—all of them by way of the basic terms he has assumed at the outset.[9] In the Introduction to his *Treatise*, Hume explicitly says that such explanatory reduction of the phenomena is the aim of his work:

> [W]e must endeavor to render all our principles as universal as possible, by [i] tracing up our experiments to the utmost, and [ii] explaining all effects from the simplest and fewest causes. (T Intro. 8/xvii)

In this passage, we see the same two-step method advocated by Newton in his *Principia*, which first seeks to "trace" upward from empirical data toward a small number of terms or causes and with these seeking to "explain all effects." Hume rehearses this view of the aim of scientific reasoning time and again in subsequent works.[10]

Examining the *Treatise* in light of this methodological declaration reveals that Hume's work is in fact consciously constructed in imitation of the *Principia*. Like the *Principia*, Hume's *Treatise* begins with the presentation of a scheme of fundamental "elements" that Hume has derived from his experiments and that are then to be used in explaining the rest of the phenomena. This presentation is to be found in the first thirteen pages of the body of the *Treatise* (Book 1, Part 1, Sections 1–4), whose subject, Hume informs us, "may be consider'd as the elements of this philosophy" (T 1.1.4.7/13).[11]

What, then, are the "elements" of Hume's philosophy? It would appear that Hume introduces six fundamental "elements," of which two are basic psychological entities or objects, and four are operations of the mind carried out with respect to them.[12] The basic psychological objects are *impressions* and *ideas*, which Hume describes as follows:

> *All* the perceptions of the human mind resolve themselves into two distinct kinds, which I shall call *impressions* and *ideas*. The difference betwixt these consists in the degrees of force and liveliness, with which they strike upon the mind . . .

> Those perceptions, which enter with most force and violence, we may name *impressions;* and under this name I comprehend all our sensations, passions and emotions, as they make their first appearance in the soul.

> By *ideas* I mean the faint images of these in thinking and reasoning; such as, for instance are all the perceptions excited by the present discourse, excepting only, those which arise from sight and touch. (T 1.1.1.1/1)[13]

In addition, Hume introduces us to four fundamental operations of the mind. The first of these is the operation of *copying* an impression, whose result is the production of an idea corresponding to this impression (T 1.1.2.1/8).[14] Second is the purposive *uniting* and *separation* of ideas by way of the imagination (T 1.1.4.1/10). Third is the operation of *association*, which is a force that works automatically on ideas and establishes relations among them without the assistance of any active effort on the part of the mind:

> ['T]is impossible the same simple ideas should fall regularly into complex ones (as they commonly do) without some bond or union among them, some associating quality, by which one idea naturally introduces another. . . . [This is] a gentle force, which commonly prevails, and is the cause why, among other things, languages so nearly correspond to each other. . . . The qualities, from which this association arises, and by which the mind is after this manner convey'd from one idea to another, are three, vis., *resemblance, continuity* of time and space, and *cause* and *effect*. (T 1.1.4.1/10–11)[15]

In addition to these three operations, it can be argued that Hume ends up relying on a fourth operation of the mind that is only touched on in Sections 1–4 of Book 1, Part 1.

This is the transfer of "force or liveliness" from an impression to an idea and, from there, possibly, to other ideas. Although the force and liveliness of impressions and ideas is discussed in the first lines of Book 1, the transfer of force and vivacity is discussed in an explicit fashion only later, where Hume writes that:

> [W]hen any impression becomes present to us, it not only transports the mind to such ideas as are related to it, but likewise communicates to them a share of its force and vivacity. (T 1.3.8.2/98)

This operation is discussed more thoroughly in the corrections to Book 1 that Hume published in 1740, leaving the impression that Hume's understanding of the importance of this operation grew as he progressed in writing the *Treatise* and thereafter.

In Newton's method of analysis and synthesis, the derivation of a scheme of fundamental terms by induction is followed by a second stage of investigation, in which the general causes discovered in this way are assumed as given and used to explain the phenomena. And, indeed, the body of Hume's *Treatise*, after the presentation of the elements of his system in Book 1 (the stage of "analysis"), consists of precisely such a second stage (the stage of "synthesis"), in which the elements of Hume's system are assumed, and the phenomena of human experience are given explanations in terms of these elements.[16]

Don Garrett has noted that the British philosophical tradition follows Locke in developing a pattern of reductive argument unknown in the writings of continental philosophers such as Descartes, Spinoza, or Leibniz. In such arguments, a given fundamental concept under investigation is said to "consist" of some other quality or qualities. Frequently, it is said that these other qualities are "what is meant" when we speak of the fundamental concept in question (Garrett 1997: 36). Hume's explanatory reductions in the *Treatise* follow this same pattern and are, in many cases, marked by an explicit statement to the effect that the concept or phenomenon being reduced is in fact "nothing but" some arrangement of Hume's psychological elements. Because Hume believes we have no access to anything other than the perceptions of things present in our own minds (T 1.2.6.7/67–8), he feels free to argue that if we want to understand the nature of some object of interest to us, we cannot dispense with an examination of how this same object is constituted in our understanding of it.[17] This move permits him repeatedly to reduce the objects of human experience to those operations of the human mind that constitute the entirety of what we can know of these objects, saying that, in fact, the object in question is "nothing but" a certain set of psychological entities and operations.

Given the way that the term *reduction* is often used in present-day philosophy, there is here a palpable danger that Hume's *nothing but* statements will end up being understood as though he means to say that the things he is reducing to psychological terms do not actually exist. But Hume's *nothing but* statements are not eliminativist. Indeed, even in contemporary philosophy, this interpretation of explanatory reduction in science is often mistaken. To say that water is "nothing but" atoms of hydrogen and oxygen arranged in a certain fashion is not to say that what is usually called *water* does not exist and that only atoms of hydrogen and oxygen exist.[18] In fact, quite the opposite is the case: such reductions often require us to make changes in the way we understand the world, but their aim is principally to permit us to understand how and why an object such as water comes to exist with the properties that we know it to have. This should be obvious from Newton's *Principia*. Newton does strive to show that, for example, the orbital motion of the planets is *nothing but* the force of gravity acting in accordance with the inverse-square law, together with the inertial motion of the moving body. But this does not mean that orbital motion does not exist! What Newton is doing when he reduces orbital motion to its components is showing us how and why the orbital motions of the planets come to exist with the properties we know them to have.

Hume's "nothing but" arguments should for the most part be read in the same way. It is true that, on occasion, Hume's explanatory reductions have an eliminationist edge to them (Loptson 1998). For example, Hume is quite clear that he thinks the Aristotelian philosophical category of *substance* should be discarded from our philosophical vocabulary, so that when he reduces the category of *substance* to psychological terms, it's easy to draw the conclusion that such reductions are part of an overall skeptical strategy of showing that the things he reduces in this way do not exist.[19] But in general Hume's *nothing but* statements do not arise as a result of a motive of this kind. They stem from the same aim as Newton's explanatory reductions, and they are concerned with things such as *time* and *space, causation, belief, reality,* the *self, sympathy,* and *morals* that Hume has no interest in saying do not exist. Indeed, all of these are things to which Hume refers time and again in the *Treatise* as though they do exist. His aim is rather to show us how and why these things exist with the various properties that we know them to have and, as a consequence, to show why we should discard properties that are wrongly attributed to them. In short, we should assume that Hume intends his "nothing but" statements to amount to explanations, rather than eliminations, unless he gives us good reason to think he has something else in mind.

Thus, for example, Hume rejects the medieval conception, adopted by Locke, according to which the mind has the power to "abstract" from the particulars of a series of similar objects, creating an abstract idea that consists of the essential and unifying aspects of an entire class. Instead, he wishes to show that what we call *abstract ideas* can, in fact, be reduced in their important properties to copies of particular impressions. He thus opens by informing his readers that abstract ideas are "nothing but" individual ideas responding in a certain fashion to the mention of a word that invokes all of them. As he writes:

> A great philosopher has disputed the receiv'd opinion . . . , and has asserted, that all general ideas are **nothing but** particular ones, annexed to a certain term, which . . . makes them recall upon occasion other individuals, which are similar to them. (T 1.1.7.1/17, emphasis added)[20]

Hume then explains how this reduction works. His first step is to argue that since ideas are nothing but copies of impressions, and impressions are always of a particular sight or sound, the ideas that are copies of these impressions must always be particular as well (T 1.1.7.6/19–20). We see, therefore, that given the nature of impressions and of the copying operation, all ideas must be particular ideas. What happens, then, when we deploy a general term, such as the word *triangle* or the word *bird,* which does not refer to any particular triangle or bird? Each such word, Hume tells us, triggers the activity of all the ideas that were ever associated with it (T 1.1.7.7/20). But because the mind can have only one idea fully before it at a time, the others remain on the sidelines of our consciousness, ready to be recalled if needed.[21] Hume goes on to discuss how general words can stand in for general ideas in conversation by invoking a particular simple idea as a stand-in, while at the same time activating other simple ideas in potential so that they are available to come to the fore as needed.[22] By this mechanism, we are able to think and speak in abstract terms without ever actually engaging in an operation of the mind that involves abstraction.

Hume's reduction of Scholastic terms such as *substance* and *abstraction* in *Treatise* 1.1.6–7 is in a sense preliminary. Hume's real interest is the reduction of the new natural philosophy to psychological entities and mechanisms. This project gets under way with Hume's reductions of the categories of *space* and *time* in Part 2; and reaches a climax in Part 3, in which not only *causation,* but also the very distinction between what is *real* and what is not are reduced to operations of human psychology. Thus, regarding space, Hume famously argues that the idea of space or extension is "nothing but" the idea of visible or tangible points distributed in a certain order (T 1.2.5.1/53; T 1.2.5.21/62):

> The table before me is alone sufficient by its view to give me the idea of extension. This idea, then, is borrow'd from, and represents some impression, which this moment appears to the senses. But my senses convey to me only the impressions of colour'd points, dispos'd in a certain manner. If the eye is sensible of any thing farther, I desire it may be pointed out to me. But if it be impossible to shew any thing farther, we may conclude with certainty, that the idea of extension is **nothing but** a copy of these colour'd points, and of the manner of their appearance. (T 1.2.3.4/34; emphasis added)

Regarding our concept of time, Hume argues that this, too, can be seen to be "nothing but" an abstract idea derived from primary distinct impressions succeeding one another:

> The ideas of some objects it [i.e., the mind] certainly must have, nor is it possible without these ideas ever to arrive at any conception of time; which since it appears not as any primary distinct impression, can plainly be **nothing but** different ideas, or impressions, or objects dispos'd in a certain manner, that is, succeeding each other. (T 1.2.3.10/37; emphasis added)

By the same token, Hume says that necessity is "nothing but" an internal impression reflecting the determination of the mind to pass from one object to the other in accordance with our previous experience:

These instances are in themselves totally distinct from each other, and have no union but in the mind, which observes them, and collects their ideas. Necessity, then, is the effect of this observation, and is **nothing but** an internal impression of the mind, or a determination to carry our thoughts from one object to another. . . . Upon the whole, necessity is something, that exists in the mind, not in objects; nor is it possible for us ever to form the most distant idea of it, consider'd as a quality in bodies. Either we have no idea of necessity, or necessity is **nothing but** that determination of the thought to pass from causes to effects and from effects to causes, according to their experienc'd union. (T 1.3.14.20–2/165–6)[23]

Similarly, when we speak of our *belief* in the reality of objects, what we mean is that "those ideas, to which we assent, are more strong, firm and vivid" (T 1.3.7.8/97). As Hume writes, *belief* and *assent* are nothing but this greater force or vivacity that accompanies certain ideas:

Thus it appears, that the *belief* or *assent*, which always attends the memory and senses, is **nothing but** the vivacity of those perceptions they present; and that this alone distinguishes them from the imagination. To believe is in this case to feel an immediate impression of the senses, or a repetition of that impression in memory. 'Tis merely the force and liveliness of the perception, which constitutes the first act of the judgment. (T 1.3.5.7/86; emphasis added to "nothing but.")

In the same way, we find that Hume's "nothing but" statements signal his reduction of numerous other phenomena to his basic vocabulary of terms, including the *continuous existence* of objects (T 1.4.3.2/219; T 1.4.6.7/255), the *self* (T 1.4.6.4/252–3),[24] *sympathy* (T 2.2.9.13/385–6; T 2.3.6.8/427), and *virtue* and *vice* (T 3.1.2.3/471; T 3.3.5.1/614). Together with Hume's presentation of the elements of his philosophy in *Treatise* 1.1.1–5, this systematic effort to show that the principal phenomena of our experience can be reduced to these same elements in the rest of the work constitutes the Newtonian template of analysis and synthesis around which the *Treatise* is built.[25] To explain the most widely recognized aspects of our experience in terms of a scheme of simplest and fewest terms was, for Hume, the method of the *Principia,* and he hoped that the science of the *Treatise* could win both scholarly and public acclaim in the same way that Newton's work had.[26]

I.2 Hume's Associative Laws and Newton's Law of Gravitation

In addition to embracing a version of Newton's method of analysis and synthesis, Hume's associative operation of the mind, mentioned earlier, is governed by three laws of "attraction" that are presented in self-consciously Newtonian terms. In the "Abstract" published anonymously after the appearance of the *Treatise,* Hume writes that if anything gives the author of this work "so glorious a name as that of an *inventor,* 'tis the use he makes of the principle of the association of ideas" (TA 35/661). Hume was not, of course, the first to describe the human mind in terms of the functioning of a fundamental associative mechanism.[27] But he was the first to have systematically reduced the associative action of mental operations (in what Hume calls the "imagination") to three natural relations: those of resemblance, contiguity, and causation. In particular, causation is shown to be that relation characteristic of the human imagination that governs any factual claim beyond what is immediately evident to the senses and memory. In the *Treatise*, Hume draws attention to the parallel between his laws of attraction and the effects of Newtonian gravitation in the natural world:

> These are therefore the principles of union or cohesion among our simple ideas, and in the imagination supply the place of that inseparable connexion, by which they are united in our memory. Here is a kind of *attraction*, which in the mental world will be found to have as extraordinary effects as in the natural, and to shew itself in as many and as various forms. Its effects are every where conspicuous; but as to its causes, they are mostly unknown, and must be resolved into original qualities of human nature, which I pretend not to explain. (T 1.1.4.6/12; emphasis in original)

Hume's associative principle is thus a kind of attraction governing the mental world in a way that is seen as parallel to the principle of gravitation in the physical world, and Hume suggests it is no less successful an explanation than Newtonian attraction. Indeed, in the Introduction to the *Treatise*, Hume had claimed that through judiciously collected experiments and cautious observations of human life "we may hope to establish . . . a science, which will not be inferior in certainty, and will be much superior in utility to any other of human comprehension" (T Intro. 10/xix). Here, Hume suggests that in providing the principles of cohesion among our simple ideas, he has delivered, at least in part, on the Introduction's promissory note.

Nevertheless, this passage from the *Treatise* also gives a skeptical slant to this achievement that already foreshadows Hume's summation of Newton's achievements in the *History of England* by emphasizing that the ultimate causes of the principle of association must be unaccountably located in the "original qualities of human nature, which I pretend not to explain." This passage closely parallels a famous passage from the General Scholium to the Second Edition of the *Principia* in which Newton had likewise declined to explain the causes of his law of universal gravitation. Newton's famous *hypotheses non fingo* ("I feign no hypotheses")[28] is the model for Hume's refusal here to speculate concerning the causes of the laws of attraction, as well as for Hume's other declarations against "hypothesis" in philosophy (e.g., T 1.4.7.14/272).

But although on the surface Hume's reticence to enter into ungrounded speculation is very much akin to Newton's, there is also a significant gap between their views. In the same passage just quoted, Hume continues as follows:

> Nothing is more requisite for a true philosopher, than to restrain the intemperate desire of searching into causes, and having established any doctrine upon a sufficient

number of experiments, rest contented with that, when he sees a farther examination would lead him into obscure and uncertain speculations. In that case his enquiry would be much better employed in examining the effects than the causes of his principle. (T 1.1.4.6/13)

Hume here identifies the "true philosopher" with the person who knows how to cease from further inquiry into his subject at the point where the effects susceptible to careful examination cannot responsibly sustain speculation into causes that are more deeply hidden. Putting an end to inquiry into causes avoids getting one involved in an obscure and uncertain enterprise—the sort that leads to useless speculations and invariably ends up encouraging the acceptance of false beliefs. Newton, despite his campaign against the fantastic "hypotheses" of his predecessors, was in practice quite far from the restraint that Hume advocates. In fact, the *Principia* contains Scholia dealing with subjects from God's nature to the character of the human nervous system—subjects that Hume would evidently have considered to be beyond self-imposed limits to inquiry that a "true philosopher" would have accepted on himself had the effects under examination been such as they were in the *Principia*. Further on, we will see further examples of Hume's hesitations concerning the *Principia* in this regard.

There is a second sense in which Hume's treatment of his laws of association is un-Newtonian. Recall that the associative mechanism is not an exceptionless law. It is "a gentle force, which commonly prevails." Of course, even the Newtonian force of gravitation only prevails *most* of the time—a wind blowing up a falling leaf will appear to neutralize the effect of gravitation, too. But, methodologically, Hume's stance on this point deprives him of a powerful Newtonian evidential strategy, which consists of showing how expected deviations from regularities follow from the same underlying mechanisms.[29]

II HUME AS ANTI-NEWTONIAN

As we have argued, Hume saw his philosophy as adopting the two-step procedure of the *Principia*, deriving a small vocabulary of simple terms or causes from observed data by induction and then explaining the rest of experience by means of these terms. But Hume's project was not only a Newtonian one. His ambitions were anti-Newtonian as well, being motivated by the sense that Newton and his followers were on the verge of interpreting the great physicist's triumphs as justification for the establishment of a rigid new scholasticism and natural religion. In the rest of this paper, we consider new arguments and evidence in support of the contention that Hume's *Treatise* should also be seen, in part, as advancing a systematic attack on Newton's science. In this regard, we here consider (1) Hume's rejection of Newton's introduction of absolute space and time into physics; (2) Hume's attack on Newton's claim that the exactness of geometry makes mathematical physics an exact science; (3) Rule 7 of Hume's "Rules by which to judge

of causes and effects," which seeks to limit Newton's claims to be able to extend empirically derived laws to the microworld and to the ends of the universe; and (4) Hume's
reduction of the category of *force* to psychological terms, amounting to the claim that
the Newtonian physics describes entities that are not mind-independent.

II.1 Absolute Space and Time

Almost everything in Hume's *Treatise* 1.2, which is devoted to a treatment *Of the ideas of
space and time,* can be seen as taking issue with Newton's *Principia.*[30] Hume's criticism
of the vacuum and of absolute space and time do not just takes sides on questions of
traditional philosophical interest; they challenge central claims of the *Principia.*[31] And
his argument against the infinite divisibility of space seems, in light of Berkeley's similar
arguments that are explicitly directed against Newton, to be an attack on the deployment of fluxions and reasoning with infinitisseminals in mechanics.[32] In this section, we
look more carefully at Hume's attack on the Newtonian treatment of absolute space and
time. Although previous scholarship has touched on this aspect of Hume's critique of
Newton,[33] we believe Hume's attack here is even more significant than has perhaps been
appreciated, representing a rejection of a Newtonian claim to be able to attain fundamental knowledge of physical reality beyond what is reported by the senses.

In the Scholium to the definitions at the front of the *Principia,* Newton distinguishes
the abstractions "true time" and "true space" from the time and space that are the subjects of common discourse. As he explains, space and time as normally considered are
relative terms, derived "solely with reference to the objects of sense perception."[34] In
the *Principia,* Newton also distinguishes between absolute space and true space, as well
as between absolute time and true time—using the concepts of "true space" and "true
time" for the derivation of true accelerations. Nevertheless, as the Scholium makes perfectly clear, it is not in this sense that the terms "true time" and "true space" are being
used here. Rather, Newton proposes that there exist an absolute space and time, each of
which is "in and of itself and of its own nature, without reference to anything external."[35]
Regarding such absolute space and time, Newton daringly argues that its existence can
be demonstrated experimentally.[36] Moreover, Newton introduces it into his system of
the world in a corollary to Prop. 12 of Book 3, where he writes that "the common center of the earth, sun, and all the planets is to be considered the center of the universe . . .
which is at rest";[37] and in the corollary to Prop. 14, he derives from this hypothesis the
conclusion that "The fixed stars also are at rest" (1687: 819).

Whether the *Principia* really provides readers with the tools necessary to follow
Newton to these conclusions was something that Hume doubted.[38] Hume, of course,
argues that what we know of space is "nothing but the idea of visible or tangible points
distributed in a certain order" (T 1.2.5.1/53; emphasis removed)[39] and that what we know
of time "can plainly be nothing but different ideas, or impressions, or objects dispos'd in
a certain manner, that is, succeeding each other" (T 1.2.3.10/37).[40] Like Newton, Hume
thus understands space and time in their conventional usage to be derived exclusively

from sense experience. But Hume breaks with Newton on the question of whether human beings can know anything beyond this. An abstract idea such as that of space or time is, for Hume, nothing more than a particular instance held before the mind as a kind of "short-cut" or placeholder while other concrete instances of our past experience crowd around.[41] When discussing space and time, what we have before us is therefore experienced extensions and durations, all of which are obviously relative. Indeed, Hume does not believe that we can so much as conceive of an absolute space or time independent of the objects of sense experience. As he writes concerning absolute time:

> [T]hat we really have no such idea, is certain. For whence shou'd it be deriv'd? Does it arise from an impression of sensation or of reflection? Point it out distinctly to us, that we may know its nature and qualities. But if you cannot point out *any such impression*, you may be certain you are mistaken, when you imagine you have *any such idea*. (T 1.2.5.28/65; emphasis in the original)[42]

At the end of Part 2, Section 5, Hume announces that, having explained what is in fact meant by space and time, he is "now prepar'd to answer all the objections that have been offer'd, whether deriv'd from *metaphysics* or *mechanics*" (T 1.2.5.22/62; emphasis in original)—the reference to *"mechanics"* in this context indicating that he is responding to Newton (whereas *"metaphysics"* apparently refers to the claims of Scholastic and Cartesian opponents).[43] Hume then proceeds to show how one may construct what is *called* an idea of absolute space or absolute time although the idea in question is in fact nothing more than a repetition of one's idea of relative space and time (T 1.2.5.22–9/62–5). Of course, Hume knows quite well that when Newton refers to absolute space and time, he isn't talking about our *ideas* at all. Newton writes explicitly of time and space, "in and of itself and of its own nature, without reference to anything external."[44] Hume addresses this claim in a crucial passage at the end of his discussion of time and space, in which he suggests that such knowledge is "beyond the reach of human understanding":

> 'Twill probably be said, that my reasoning makes nothing to the matter in hand, and that I explain only the manner in which objects affect the senses, without endeavouring to account for their real nature and operations. . . . I answer this objection, by pleading guilty, and by confessing that *my intention never was to penetrate into the nature of bodies,* or explain the secret causes of their operations. For . . . I am afraid, that such an enterprise is beyond the reach of human understanding, and that *we can never pretend to know body otherwise than by those external properties, which discover themselves to the senses.* (T 1.2.5.25/63–4; emphasis added)

Although this passage refers to the nature of bodies, the context is the climax of his discussion of the nature of time and space.[45] Indeed, Hume here criticizes the Newtonian conception of absolute time and space using the same language that Newton uses in the Scholium quoted earlier: whereas Newton writes that we can know time or space *as it is in its own nature, without reference to anything external*—Hume responds that the "external" properties by which things are known to our senses are all we have or can ever have in trying to know about anything.[46]

One might object that Hume is here conflating Newton's treatment of space and time with his treatment of bodies. But Hume's point is precisely that if one takes Newton as being committed to demonstrating all aspects of his science from the phenomena, there can be nothing that is said of time and space other than that which can be derived from the appearances of bodies. Indeed, in a late addition to this argument of the *Treatise* from 1740, Hume takes this line of argument to a clear point, emphasizing that "the Newtonian philosophy," if "rightly understood," in fact allows nothing to be said about the essential nature of space (i.e., whether it is a vacuum) except to the extent that space is known from the appearances of bodies in it:

> If we carry our enquiry [concerning the invisible and intangible distance, interpos'd betwixt two objects] beyond the appearances of objects to the senses, I am afraid, that most of our conclusions will be full of scepticism and uncertainty. Thus if it be ask'd, whether or not the invisible and intangible distance be always full of *body* . . . I must acknowledge, that I find no very decisive arguments on either side. . . . If *the Newtonian* philosophy be rightly understood, it will be found to mean no more. A vacuum is asserted: That is, bodies are said to be plac'd after such a manner as to receive bodies betwixt them, without impulsion or penetration. The real nature of this position of bodies is unknown. We are only acquainted with its effects on the senses, and its power of receiving body. (T 1.2.5 n12.2/639; emphasis in the original)

In the original text of the *Treatise* from 1739, Hume then proceeds to comment on the Newtonian project of attempting to gain knowledge of absolute time and space, saying that he "cannot approve of their ambition" until an example of success can be brought forward. He then rehearses his famous argument about resting contented with a given level of philosophical achievement:

> As to those who attempt any thing farther, I cannot approve of their ambition, till I see, in some one instance at least, that they have met with success. But at present *I content myself* with knowing perfectly the manner in which objects affect my senses, and their connections with each other, as far as experience informs me of them. *This suffices* for the conduct of life; and *this also suffices for my philosophy, which pretends only to explain* the nature and causes of our perceptions, or impressions and ideas. (T 1.2.5.26/64; emphasis added)

Usually unnoticed by scholars is that this passage, too, includes an oblique reference to Newton's *Principia* aimed at making it clear who Hume's target is. The reference is to one of the most famous passages in the *Principia*—the second to last paragraph of the General Scholium, already mentioned, in which Newton rejects criticism that he has not described the causes of his proposed force of gravitation, asserting that he will feign no hypotheses. This paragraph ends with the following sentence:

> *[I]t is enough* that gravity really exists and acts according to the laws we have set forth and *is sufficient to explain* all the motions of the heavenly bodies and of our sea. (1687: 493; emphasis added)

This Newtonian assertion that "it is enough" that gravity acts according to the laws proposed and is "sufficient to explain" the movements of the planets and the sea is parallel to Hume's assertion that he is "content" with the laws of perception and association, which achievement "suffices . . . to explain" the nature and causes of our perceptions. In other words, Hume commandeers Newton's famous "It is enough" argument (made in the context of a defense of an account of gravity that is based entirely on its "external properties"), turning it back against Newton himself. As Hume argues, if "It is enough" that we describe gravity by its "external properties," it should also be enough to describe time and space in such "external" terms as well. And this is precisely what Hume believes he has provided in his analysis of time and space.[47]

II.2   The Exactness of Geometry

If Hume's attack on absolute space and time in *Treatise* 1.2 is aimed at Newton's claim to have attained fundamental knowledge of physical reality beyond what is reported by the senses, his attack on geometry takes on another Newtonian commitment, the conceit to have brought a near-perfect exactness and certainty into physical science.

As Alan Shapiro and others have emphasized, one of the principal characteristics that recommended Newton's philosophy to its own time was its ability to introduce a very great degree of certainty into natural philosophy. Natural philosophy in seventeenth-century England had largely freed itself from the presumption that real science is demonstrative in character and was, in Boyle's day, inclined mostly to careful experimentation without insisting on better than probable results. In this context, Newton's aim was to show that probabilistic natural philosophy was not good enough. As he wrote in his first published paper, what he was after was "not an hypothesis but most rigid consequence . . . without any suspicion of doubt."[48]

It is therefore no accident that Newton's *Principia* and *Opticks* are, despite their differences, written as treatises in geometry—the very paradigm of what was considered to be an infallible science.[49] And, indeed, the first paragraphs of the *Principia* are devoted to a discussion of what Newton calls a "rational mechanics," which is the rendering of mechanics as a "science, expressed in exact propositions and demonstrations." According to Newton, the "exactness" of geometry, which is perfect, permits the mechanic who applies geometry to his discipline to become "the most perfect mechanic of all."[50] His point is that his method permits the infallibility of a demonstrative science to be applied, at least very nearly, to moving bodies.

As is well known, Hume had little sympathy for the Scholastic and Cartesian project of attaining knowledge "without any suspicion of doubt," and he had no more sympathy for these claims when they were made by Newton or his followers. And in Book 1, part 2 of the *Treatise*, he embarks on an examination of the "foundation of mathematics" (T 1.4.2.22/198)[51] in which he challenges the idea that geometric proofs possess the kind of perfection that can finally dispel imprecision and doubt. The only named target is Isaac Barrow, Newton's mentor (T 1.2.4.21/46).

Hume's argument in this section is straightforward: geometry is a science conducted by comparing constructions of points, lines, and surfaces, either on paper or in the mind of the geometer. Everyone admits that the truths of geometry are not to be judged by the "loose draughts" that mathematicians put to paper. No line we draw is really perfectly straight, and no surface is perfectly smooth (T 1.2.4.33/53). The question, then, is where the claim to absolutely certain and precise conclusions in geometry comes from. Hume believes it must derive from the supposition that the construction and comparison of geometric figures is absolutely certain and precise when conducted in the imagination. But Hume points out that this impression of absolute certainty and precision in our manipulation of imaginary geometric figures is illusory: "As the ultimate standard for these figures is deriv'd from nothing but the senses and imagination, 'tis absurd to talk of any perfection beyond what these faculties can judge of" (T 1.2.4.29/51). In fact, human imagination is capable only of constructing and manipulating *rough* geometric figures. Thus, anything we do with geometry is only roughly right:

> [Geometric proofs] are not properly demonstrations, because built on ideas, which are not exact, and maxims, which are not precisely true. When geometry decides any thing concerning proportions of quantity, we ought not to look for the utmost *precision* and exactness. None of its proofs extend so far. It takes the dimensions and proportions of figures justly; but roughly and with some liberty. (T 1.2.4.17/45; emphasis in the original)[52]

Hume concludes that geometry "can never afford us any security" if our claim is, by its means, to have attained a certain understanding of nature.[53]

The heart of Hume's attack on the infallibility of applied geometry is based on the absence of any real equality between geometric figures. Geometry proceeds entirely on the assertion that the extension of one line segment is equal to that of another. These equalities are judged of by the mind "without comparing the number of their minute parts" and often have to be corrected when we compare both segments "by use of some common and invariable measure, which being successively applied to each, informs us of their different proportions." Indeed, this process of correction toward ever-greater precision must continue indefinitely in accordance with the precision of the instrument we use in measuring. But because no instrument will ever measure the most minute differences, "we clearly perceive, that we are not possess'd of any instrument or art of measuring, which can secure us from all error and uncertainty" (T 1.2.4.24/47–8). Indeed, "'tis for want of such a[n absolute] standard of equality in extension, that geometry can scarce be esteem'd a perfect and infallible science" (T 1.3.1.5/71).[54]

Read in light of Newton's famous claim to have introduced exactness into mechanics, Hume's argument amounts to this: In the absence of any absolute standard against which to measure, Newton does not even have the ability to judge two lengths or velocities as equal to one another, except as an approximation—hardly an impressive achievement for one aspiring to be the "most perfect mechanic of all"! And, in fact, Hume makes sure we know this is what he has in mind with his oblique reference to "a mechanic" in the following passage, which appears at the end of his argument on the subject:

We are sensible, that the addition or removal of one of these minute [microscopic] parts, is not discernable either in the appearance or measuring. . . . [W]e therefore suppose some imaginary standard of equality, by which the appearances and measuring are exactly corrected. . . . [But] the notion of any correction beyond what we have instruments and art to make, is a mere fiction of the mind. . . . [Thus a] musician finding his ear become every day more delicate, and correcting himself by reflection and attention, proceeds with the same act of mind, even when the subject fails him, and entertains the notion of a compleat *tierce* or *octave*, without being able to tell whence he derives his standard. A painter forms the same fiction with regard to colours. A mechanic with regard to motion. To the one *light* and *shade*; to the other *swift* and *slow* are imagin'd to be capable of an exact comparison and equality beyond the judgments of the senses. (T 1.2.4.24/48–9; emphasis in the original)

The "mechanic" here is again almost certainly Newton, the application of geometry to mechanics being the signature achievement of Newton's *Principia*. And Newton's belief that he can judge two velocities equal to greater than a certain degree of precision is here called "a mere fiction of the mind." Indeed, Hume here mischievously compares Newton's supposedly exact science to the level of precision expected of an accomplished musician or painter.[55] Newtonian science is, like the geometry on which it is based, no better than an "art."[56]

II.3   The Universality of the Law of Gravitation

Earlier analyses of Hume's attack on Newton in *Treatise* 1.3 have focused on Hume's criticism of the Newtonian conception of causation, on Hume's rejection of Rule IV of Newton's "Rules for the Study of Natural Philosophy," and on Hume's treatment of the Newtonian category of *force*.[57] In this section, we discuss what we take to be another central aspect of Hume's criticism of Newton. This is Hume's attack on Rule III of Newton's rules for studying philosophy—which is the rule that underwrites Newton's claim that his Law of Gravitation is universal in character.[58]

Newton's Rule III stipulates that a quality observed to hold good for all bodies subject to experimental observation is to be ascribed to all bodies in the universe. As he writes:

Those qualities of bodies that cannot be intended and remitted [i.e., added and removed] and that belong to all bodies on which experiments can be made should be taken as qualities of all bodies universally. (1687: 795)

Thus, on Newton's view, we can tell that all objects in the universe, including microscopic objects and distant celestial bodies "beyond the range of our senses," are "extended, hard, impenetrable, movable, and endowed with force of inertia" because all objects that are within the reach of our experiments possess these properties.[59] This assumption of universality for properties that are always and everywhere observed is, for Newton, nothing less than "the foundation of all of natural philosophy," and, having established it in principle with regard to the essential qualities of matter,[60] Newton goes on to apply it to gravitation as well, concluding on the basis of the observations in the *Principia* that all bodies in the universe gravitate toward one another.[61] It is emblematic of what Hume, in the *History*, refers to as Newton's quality of being "resolute to adopt every . . . principle" derived from careful observation, "however new or unusual" (HE VI 542).

In the *Treatise*, Hume follows Newton's example by providing his own rules of philosophical reasoning, which he calls "Rules by which to judge of causes and effects." Indeed, Hume says that these rules are "all the *logic* I think proper to employ in my reasoning" (T 1.3.15.11/173–5).[62] But Hume's rules of reasoning depart from Newton's in a number of ways,[63] of which the most glaring is the absence in Hume's discussion of anything parallel to the *Principia*'s Rule III. Since it is Rule III that establishes a criterion for determining which observed properties can be said to apply universally, the absence of such a rule of reasoning immediately deprives Newtonian gravitation of its status as a genuinely "*Universal* Law of Gravitation."

But Hume does not stop at just editing out the Newtonian rule that permits gravity to be seen as a universal property of matter. His "Rules by which to judge of causes and effects" include an oblique treatment of Newtonian universal gravitation in the form of Hume's Rule VII, which reads as follows:

When any object encreases or diminishes with the encrease or diminution of its cause, 'tis to be regarded as a compounded effect, deriv'd from the union of the several different effects, which arise from the several different parts of the cause. The absence or presence of one part of the cause is here suppos'd to be always attended with the absence or presence of a proportionable part of the effect. . . . We must, however, beware not to draw such a conclusion from a few experiments. A certain degree of heat gives pleasure; if you diminish that heat, the pleasure diminishes; but it does not follow, that if you augment it beyond a certain degree, the pleasure will likewise augment; for we find that it degenerates into pain. (T 1.3.15.9/174)

The relationship between Hume's Rule VII and Newtonian gravitation, which is not explicit in his text, is established by Hume's wording, which closely follows Newton's phrasing in discussing gravity in the *Principia*:[64] In his Book 3, Proposition 7, Corollary 1, Newton describes gravitation as an action in which "every attraction toward a whole arises from the attractions toward the individual parts."[65] In Rule VII, Hume speaks in these same terms, arguing that a quality that "encreases or diminishes with the encrease or diminution of its cause," should be "regarded as a compounded effect, deriv'd from the union of the several different effects, which arise from the several different parts of the cause." And, elsewhere in the *Treatise*, Hume writes explicitly of the force of gravitation using just this language.[66] On the face of it, then, Hume's Rule VII seems to adopt Newtonian language in order to provide an alternative description of the kind of extrapolation involved in establishing Newtonian gravitation.

But only the first half of Rule VII is compatible with Newton's science. In the latter half, Hume turns against Newton, warning against the attempt to "draw such a conclusion from a few experiments." Indeed, we know quite well that effects can vary proportionately within a certain range of experience and yet behave completely differently outside of this range. Hume gives the example of our experience of fire. A "certain degree of heat gives pleasure; if you diminish that heat, the pleasure diminishes; but it does not follow, that if you augment it beyond a certain degree, the pleasure will likewise augment; for we find that it degenerates into pain." This argument, made with respect to heat, is no less applicable to the Newtonian force of gravitation: what appears to be a strictly proportional relation over a given range of experience can turn into something quite different when one strays from this range.

What we have, therefore, is as follows. Newton's Rule III, which is the basis for the claimed universality for his law of gravitation, is met and replaced by Hume's Rule VII, whose intent is in a certain sense precisely the opposite: The so-called universal law of gravitation must be regarded only as characterizing a certain range of human experience and no more.[67] Extension of this law beyond our experience, whether into the heavens or the microworld, cannot be admitted into science (except as "hypothesis"). And the same will have to be said for all other qualities that are attributed to bodies significantly outside of the bounds of our actual experience. What to Newton is nothing less than the "foundation of all natural philosophy"—his Rule III—is in Hume's philosophy shown to be unnecessary for scientific reasoning and of questionable validity.[68]

II.4 The Mind-Independence of Forces

To this point, we have discussed three aspects of Hume's attack on Newton that together challenge the *Principia*'s aspirations to attain fundamental, certain, and universal knowledge. These criticisms broadly fit within the view of Hume as seeking to use psychological science to establish the proper bounds for the sciences.[69] But at least one facet of Hume's attack on Newton in *Treatise* I, Book 3 seems to be much too far-reaching to be considered an exercise in bounds-setting for the sciences: Hume's analysis of the Newtonian category of *force*, the fundamental explanatory concept in the *Principia*.[70] In this section, we argue that what Hume wants to show is that forces are, like necessary connection, an aspect of reality that is *mind-dependent*.

No physical category is as significant to the Newtonian project as that of force: in the preface to the *Principia*, Newton extrapolates from his successful analysis of the mechanical movements of objects, proposing that perhaps *all* natural phenomena may be reducible to forces of attraction and repulsion. As he writes:

> [T]he basic problem of philosophy seems to be to discover the forces of nature from the phenomena of motions and then to demonstrate the other phenomena from these forces. . . . If only we could derive the other phenomena of nature from mechanical principles by the same kind of reasoning! For many things lead me to have a suspicion that all phenomena may depend on certain forces by which the

particles of bodies ... either are impelled toward one another ... or are repelled from one another. (1687: 382–383)

Thus, it is particularly important to notice that the Newtonian category of force is one of the principal targets of Hume's discussion in *Treatise* I, section 3.14, which is usually read only as a treatment of necessary connection.[71] That Hume's subject here is the physical category of force (and its twin, power) is easily missed because these terms are mixed together with references to necessary connection to such an extent that the two terms appear as though they are intended to be indistinguishable from one another.[72] Indeed, Hume says explicitly that these terms are "nearly synonimous":

> [T]he terms of *efficacy, agency, power, force, energy, necessity, connexion, and productive quality, are all nearly synonimous.* (T 1.3.14.4/157; emphasis in original)

It is not our intention to challenge the view that, for Hume, *force* and *necessity* are abstracted together in such a way that the two terms refer to more or less the same thing. Nevertheless, we do want to draw attention to the fact, often overlooked, that at certain junctures in his discussion, Hume carefully distinguishes force from necessity—not to establish them as distinct philosophical concepts, but because he wants to make sure he is understood as mounting a critique of the category of power or force no less than that of necessary connection. This occurs for the first time in the following passage:

> [W]hen we talk of any being, whether of a superior or inferior nature, as *endow'd with a power or force, proportion'd to any effect;* when we speak of a necessary connexion betwixt objects, and suppose, that this connexion depends upon an efficacy or energy, with which any of these objects are endow'd; in all these expressions, so apply'd, we have really no distinct meaning, and make use only of common words, without any clear and determinate ideas. (T 1.3.14.14/162; emphasis added; emphasis removed from "so apply'd.")

In this passage, Hume is making a single argument, but he carefully applies it to what he knows his readers might otherwise understand as two separate subjects: (1) "any being ... endow'd with a power or force, proportion'd to any effect"[73] and (2) "a necessary connexion betwixt objects." The first of these subjects is plainly intended to include Newton's use of the category of force in the *Principia*: Newton's Second Law of Motion stipulates that "*A change in motion is proportional to the motive force impressed*" (1687: 416), which is to say that, in Newtonian science, an object is paradigmatically endowed with a force proportioned to a given effect (i.e., its "change in motion")—which is precisely what Hume is here referring to.[74] This means that Hume here draws a clear parallel between Newtonian force and the second category he names, that of "a necessary connexion betwixt objects." Indeed, after this first passage, Hume's subsequent discussion refers to "power and necessity" in parallel time and again—by our count, ten times[75]—to signal that each of these categories is still being treated (and at the same time to encourage readers to bring them together in a single conception).

Because Hume conducts his discussion of power and force concurrently with his discussion of necessity, it is not surprising that what he says about forces is quite similar to what he says about necessity: The respective appearances of objects include qualities such as color, shape, and texture, but they possess no quality that could permit one object to exert an influence on another. As far as the reports of sensation are concerned, then, there is no such thing as a force.[76] The question is where our knowledge of things in the category of force or power comes from.

Hume's solution is to understand forces as added to objects by the mind of the human observer. What is perceived is pairs of objects appearing together repeatedly in accordance with a certain time order, and this repetition brings about the *imposition* of a force on the objects—an imposition whose source is not in the objects themselves but in our minds. As Hume writes:

> Tho' the several resembling instances, which give rise to the idea of power, have no influence on each other, and can never produce any new quality *in the object,* which can be the model of that idea, yet the *observation* of this resemblance produces a new impression *in the mind,* which is its real model. For after we have observ'd the resemblance in a sufficient number of instances, we immediately feel a determination of the mind to pass from one object to its usual attendant. . . . The several instances of resembling conjunctions leads us into the notion of *power and necessity.* These instances are in themselves totally distinct from each other, and have no union but in the mind, which observes them, and collects their ideas. (T 1.3.14.20/164–5; emphasis added to "power and necessity.")

With this in mind, consider, for example, the crucial "moon test" at Proposition 4 of Book III of the *Principia*, in which Newton identifies the centripetal force maintaining the moon in its orbit with terrestrial gravity. In this passage, Newton considers what the acceleration of the moon would be if it were brought to near the earth's surface, as calculated from orbital acceleration in conjunction with the inverse-square variation in the centripetal force. This turns out to be very nearly the acceleration of terrestrial bodies due to gravity, as measured by Huygens, permitting Newton to invoke his first and second "Rules for the Study of Natural Philosophy" to conclude that the two forces should be identified as a single force.[77] On Hume's view, however, no force of the earth acting on the moon is detected by the senses. If there had been anything there to be sensed, the gravitational pull of Earth on the moon would have been recognized millennia earlier. It was not until Newton "plac'd on the body"[78] of the earth such a power or force, by means of an operation of his own mind, that there was, strictly speaking, anything there to be detected. Hume's conclusion is that such a force is not part of the "operations of nature" if these are understood as being "independent of our thought and reasoning."[79] Power or force, like necessary connection, is drawn "from what we feel internally" in observing the objects of nature:

[W]e are led astray by a false philosophy ... when we transfer the determination of the thought to external objects, and suppose any real intelligible connexion betwixt them; that being a quality, which can only belong to the mind that considers them. ... [I]f we go any farther, and ascribe a *power or necessary connexion* to these objects; this is what we can never observe in them, but must draw the idea of it from what we feel internally in contemplating them. (T 1.3.14.27/168–9; emphasis added to "power or necessary connexion.")

With respect to Newtonian forces, then, Hume's view is unequivocal: The forces of attraction and repulsion, to which Newton proposes that we reduce all natural phenomena, are for Hume something that "can only belong to the mind that considers them."

III Conclusion

Hume was in important respects a Newtonian. His project in the *Treatise* was probably the most sophisticated attempt to apply the method of the *Principia*—Newton's method of analysis and synthesis—to the study of the human mind.[80] And although psychological science has moved in other directions, even today the attempt to understand the human mind in terms of general cognitive laws or mechanisms as proposed by Hume is occasionally recognized as a live possibility.

Yet Hume was also troubled by the growing influence of Newtonian ideas. Newton's thought was overtly religious and explicitly encouraged doctrines that Hume might have wished to see set aside.[81] But, more than this, Hume saw the science of the *Principia*, with its bold assertions of having attained fundamental, certain, and universal knowledge, as contributing to an ongoing willingness on the part of scholars and laymen to accept hypothesis as principle and principle as doctrine. What Hume regarded as a chronic lack of scientific caution on the part of Newton and his followers led, among other things, to Hume's attacks in the *Treatise* on Newton's advocacy of absolute space and time and claims regarding the infallibility of geometry, as well as on Newton's Rules for the Study of Philosophy, which underwrite the claim of universality for the law of gravitation. Most intriguing of all, Book 1 of Hume's *Treatise* insists that the central category introduced in the *Principia* as the proposed basis for all of natural science, that of force, refers to qualities of objects that are mind-dependent and thus ultimately rooted in human psychology.

That Hume's criticism of Newtonian science has been difficult for later readers to recognize is no surprise. Newtonian ways of thinking were so completely victorious in natural science for so long that Hume's critique may still seem to us to have been quixotic. But, in light of the considerations mustered here, it may be worth revisiting, for example, Einstein's own reports of Hume's influence on the theory of relativity—a development in physical science that becomes possible only after the abandonment of absolute space and time.[82] We are not accustomed to thinking that, on certain issues, Hume may have seen farther than Newton concerning the nature of science and reality. But Hume's critique of Newton was a powerful one. And, as the history of science unfolds, the validity of aspects of Hume's challenge to Newton may receive greater recognition.

ABBREVIATIONS OF WORKS CITED

D   *Dialogues Concerning Natural Religion.* In D. Coleman, ed. *Dialogues Concerning Natural Religion and Other Writings.* Cambridge: Cambridge University Press, 2007.

EM   *Enquiry Concerning the Principles of Morals.* Edited by Tom L. Beauchamp. Oxford: Clarendon, 1998.

ESY *Essays: Moral, Political, and Literary,* Revised edition by E. F. Miller. Indianapolis: Liberty Classics, 1985.

EU   *An Enquiry Concerning Human Understanding.* Edited by T. L. Beauchamp. Oxford: Clarendon, 2000.

HE   *The History of England,* 6 Vols. Foreword by W. B. Todd. Indianapolis: Liberty Classics, 1983.

T   *A Treatise of Human Nature.* Edited by D. F. Norton and M. J. Norton. Oxford: Clarendon, 2007.

TA   *An Abstract of a Treatise of Human Nature.* Reprinted in T.

NOTES

1. This implies that, on some level, Hume accepts the claim of the proponents of the mechanical philosophy that theirs is the only approach that could have made nature truly intelligible.
2. Clarke is quoting Ecclesiasticus 43: 32–33 from the King James edition.
3. For a discussion understanding Hume as responding to Clarke and focally concerned with an attack on religion and Christianity, see Russell (2008). For further background see Schliesser (2012).
4. The classic formulation of this view is in Kemp Smith (1941/2005). A similar approach is followed by Laird (1932/1967), Capaldi (1967), Stroud (1977), Pears (1990), Flage (1990: 6–18), Biro (1993), McDowell (1998), Loptson (1998: 317–8), Macarthur (2004), Millican (2007: x). A different but related view of Hume as an "arch-naturalist" is presented in Strawson (1985: 1–29). This phrase is on p. 3.
5. See Waxman (1996), Schliesser (2007; 2008; 2009; 2015), Boehm (2008; 2012), Hazony (2009; 2014).
6. See Shank (2008).
7. But even Berkeley had toned down his criticism of Newton between the first and second editions of his *Principles*.
8. Newtons' best-known discussion of analysis and synthesis is in Query 31, published at the end of the Second Edition of the *Opticks* in 1717. There, Newton describes the derivation of forces of nature from the phenomena "by induction" as follows: "By this way of analysis we may proceed from compounds to ingredients, and from motions to the forces producing

them; and in general from effects to their causes, and from particular causes to more general ones, till the argument end in the most general." (Newton 1740: 404). Newton already describes this method, although without using these terms, in the preface to the First Edition of the *Principia,* where he writes that "the basic problem of philosophy seems to be [i] to discover the forces of nature from the phenomena of motions and then [ii] to demonstrate the other phenomena from these forces" (Newton 1687: 382). For further discussion, see Cotes's introduction to the Second Edition of the *Principia* (1713: 386), Guicciardini (2009), Ducheyne (2012), and Hazony (2014). Note that while Newton's use of the term "induction" is distinctive from a modern perspective, Newtonian induction closely resembles Hume's description of the aim of philosophy in the *Treatise* and *Enquiries* (Hazony 2014).

9. The structure of the *Principia* is, in fact, more complex than this. The law of gravitation cannot be derived from the laws of motion alone, and Newton introduces a second induction from the phenomena at the beginning of Book III. See Guicciardini (2009: 322–323), Ducheyne (2005: 73–75).

10. See, for example, TA 1/646; EU 4.1.5/30. For further discussion, see Demeter (2012), Hazony (2014).

11. Scholars who do take notice of this expression include Norton (1993: 6–7), Norton (2000: I–16), Waxman (1994: 25f), Waxman (1996: 124, 152n), Allison (2008: 13f). Although David Owen doesn't comment on this expression, his treatment of the elements in this part of the *Treatise* as "fundamental explanatory principles" that are to be used "in an explanation of . . . more derivative phenomena" is similar to the view we are presenting here (Owen 1999: 150).

12. Our list is therefore somewhat more extensive than that of Owen (1999: 150) who counts Hume's "fundamental explanatory principles" as "the distinction between impressions and ideas in terms of force and vivacity, and the three principles of association." But we and Owen are in agreement that Hume's aim is simplicity and also roughly on the content of Hume's elements. A very different approach is that of Waxman (1994: 25), whose far more extensive list of items or "elements" includes close to two dozen of them. Waxman is right that Hume's philosophy cannot be understood without a thorough understanding of all of these terms from Book 1, Part 1. But he ignores Hume's claim that his aim is to discover "the simplest and fewest causes" of the phenomena he treats. Waxman therefore misses the fact that his list includes many items that can be reduced to other items, as well as items that are descriptions of other items, so that Hume's broader reductive purpose is lost.

13. Impressions are of two kinds, *impressions of sensation* and *impressions of reflection.* Impressions of this second kind "are the passions, and other emotions resembling them" (T 2.1.1.1/275; cf. T 1.1.6.1/16). But the second kind also turns out to serve as the subconscious basis for qualities of objects that are not reported by the senses, such as the property of being a *cause* or of being *real.* This means that, in Hume's theory, the mind brings its own contribution to the construction of the world. See Mounce (1999), Rocknak (2013).

14. Hume seems to admit that copies may be made of copies (T 1.1.2/8). The relatively strong original copies constitute *memory,* whose purpose is to "preserve the original form, in which its objects were presented," as well as "their order and position," whereas derivative copies are used in *imagination* and are even weaker (T 1.1.3.1/8–9). Compare: "Our imagination has a great authority over our ideas; and there are no ideas that are different from each other, which it cannot separate and join, and compose into all the varieties of fiction" (TA 35/662).

15. See further discussion in Section I.2 herein.

16. Hume's method obviously diverges from Newton's in that Newton seeks geometric proofs to demonstrate that the phenomena can be deduced from the causes he has discovered.

17. "Here therefore I must ask: *What is our idea of a simple and indivisible point?* No wonder if my answer appear somewhat new, since the question itself has scarce yet ever been thought of. We are wont to dispute concerning the nature of mathematical points, but seldom concerning the nature of their ideas" (T 1.2.3.14/38).

18. On this point, see Schaffer (2003: 498–517).

19. Even in the case of substance, Hume is ambigious. He allows that each perception may well be thought of as substance (T 1.4.5.5/233).

20. See also T 1.3.14.13/161.

21. These sidelined ideas are what Don Garrett (1997: 24) has called the "revival set" associated with the term in question.

22. Because actually bringing to mind "all the ideas, to which the name may be apply'd, is in most cases impossible, we abridge that work by a more partial consideration, and find but few inconveniences to arise in our reasoning from that abridgment" (T 1.1.7.7/21). Also: "All abstract ideas are *nothing but* particular ones, consider'd in a certain light; but being annexed to general terms, they are able to represent a vast variety, and to comprehend objects, which, as they are alike in some particulars, in other ways are vastly wide of each other" (T 1.2.3.5/34; emphasis added).

23. Emphasis added to *nothing but.* Compare T 1.4.7.5/266.

24. Although he does allow, sarcastically, that he is willing to exempt from this reductive description "some metaphysicians" who may be different from himself and the rest of mankind in this respect (T 1.4.6.4/252).

25. See Sturm (2014) for a broader overview of eighteenth-century uses of the method of analysis and synthesis.

26. Hume also insisted that in astronomy this explanatory reductionism is the achievement of Copernicus (T 2.1.3.7/282). For more on this issue, see Schliesser (2010).

27. See Kallich (1945).

28. See Newton (1726: 943).

29. See Schliesser (2004).

30. Space and time enjoy no comparably prominent treatment in Descartes or Locke, so Hume's placement of this subject at the very front of the *Treatise* (whereas Locke, for example, began with his attack on innate ideas) can be taken as a strong indication of the importance Hume ascribed to Newtonian philosophy.

31. On Hume's attack on the Newtonian idea of the vacuum, see Garrett (1997: 56–5), Boehm (2008: 91–100; 2012). On Newtonian absolute time, see Boehm (2008: 100–6) and Schliesser (2013).

32. For Berkeley's critique of Newton, see Berkeley (1721; 1734; 1735). See also, especially, Jesseph (2010), Guicciardini (1989).

33. See Boehm (2008: 100–106).

34. These "[r]elative qualities . . . are not the actual quantities whose names they bear but are those sensible measures of them . . . that are commonly used instead of the [absolute] quantities being measured" (Newton, 1687: 414). Compare: "[M]otion and rest, in the popular sense of these terms, are distinguished from each other only by point of view, and bodies commonly regarded as being at rest are not always truly at rest" (Newton, 1687: 405). This amounts to a defense of the possibility of absolute rest and motion, apparently as against Descartes's insistence that these were relative terms (Westfall 1971/1977: 126).

35. "Although time, space, place, and motion are very familiar to everyone, it must be noted that these quantities are properly conceived solely with reference to the objects of sense perception. And this is the source of certain preconceptions; to eliminate them it is useful to distinguish these quantities into absolute and relative, true and apparent. . . . 1. Absolute, true and mathematical time, *in and of itself and of its own nature, without reference to any-thing external,* flows uniformly. . . . Relative, apparent, and common time is any sensible and external measure . . . ; such a measure—for example, an hour, a day, a month, a year—is commonly used instead of true time. 2. Absolute space, *of its own nature without reference to anything external,* always remains homogenous and immovable. Relative space . . . is determined by our senses from the situation of the space with respect to bodies and is popularly used for immovable space. . . . [F]or primary places to move is absurd. . . . But since these [absolute] parts of space cannot be seen and cannot be distinguished from one another by our senses, we use sensible measures instead" (Newton 1687: 408–410; emphasis added). Newton is clear that our usual, nontechnical understanding of space and time is that which is derived from the experience of our senses, for "if the meanings of words are defined by usage, then it is these sensible measures which should properly be understood by the terms 'time,' 'space,' 'place,' and 'motion' " (1687: 413–414).

36. As Newton writes in the Scholium at the beginning of the *Principia,* detecting the effects of absolute space and time is "very difficult" but "not entirely hopeless": "[I]t is certainly very difficult to find out the true motions of individual bodies and actually to differenti-ate them from apparent motions, because the parts of that immovable space in which the bodies truly move make no impression on the senses. Nevertheless the case is not entirely hopeless. For it possible to draw evidence partly from apparent motions, and partly from the causes and effects of the true motions. . . . [I]n what follows, a fuller explanation will be given of how to determine true motions. . . . For this was the purpose for which I composed the following treatise" (1687: 414–415). This is an extraordinary claim—with Newton asserting that to teach his readers how to detect absolute space and time was nothing less than the "purpose" for which the whole *Principia* was written. See Stein (2002), di Salle (2002), Smeenk and Schliesser (2013). See also Schliesser (2013).

37. The "immobile point" that is the center of the universe in the *Principia* appears, as Newton is well aware, as an unsubstantiated hypothesis—although Newton unhelpfully writes that "No one doubts this" (1687: 816–817). Compare: "[I]t is possible that there is no body truly at rest to which places and motions may be referred" (1687: 411). To be clear, Corrolaries 5 and 6 to the Laws of Motion imply that Newton is treating the fixed stars as akin to an iner-tial frame.

38. In particular, it is crucial to Newton's enterprise that he can identify "absolute accelera-tions." But absolute velocities and positions are not required for this. See Corrolary 5. We thank Chris Smeenk for discussion.

39. Hume writes: "The table before me is alone sufficient by its view to give me the idea of extension. This idea, then, is borrow'd from . . . some impression, which this moment appears to the senses. But my senses convey to me only the impressions of colour'd points, dispos'd in a certain manner. If . . . it be impossible to shew any thing farther, we may conclude with certainty, that the idea of extension is nothing but a copy of these colour'd points, and of the manner of their appearance. . . . [A]fterwards having experience of the other colours . . . , we omit the peculiarities of colour, as far as possible, and found an abstract idea merely on that disposition of points, or manner of appearance, in which they agree" (T 1.2.3.4/34).

40. See, more generally, T 1.2.3.6–10/34–7: "The idea of time, being deriv'd from the succession of our perceptions of every kind, ideas as well as impressions . . . will afford us an instance of an abstract idea, which comprehends a still greater variety [of objects] than that of space, and yet is represented in the fancy by some particular individual idea. . . . Five notes played on the flute give us the impression and idea of time; tho' time be not a sixth impression, which presents itself to hearing or any other of the senses. . . . [S]ince [time] appears not as any primary distinct impression, [it] can plainly be nothing but different ideas, or impressions, or objects dispos'd in a certain manner, that is, succeeding each other."

41. See our discussion of Hume's reduction of the concept of an abstract idea in Section I.1.

42. This passage is particularly written about the possibility of conceiving of "time without changeable existence," which is to say, time as it is in itself in the absence of perceptible changes in the appearances, or absolute time. The argument is identical to Hume's argument against absolute space.

43. Such tacit attacks were commonplace in Hume's time. Thanks to Moti Feingold for discussion of this point. On Newton's complex embrace and reinterpretation of mechanical philosophy, see Kochiras (2013).

44. Interestingly, in a manuscript now the subject of considerable scholarly attention but unknown in Hume's time, *De Graviatione*, when Newton offers a probable account of the nature of "body," he insists that one of its essential qualities is to be able to "excite various perceptions of the senses and the imagination in created minds, and conversely be moved by them" (pre-1695: 28–29).

45. That is, Hume has been dealing with questions such as "the cause, which separates bodies [from one another], and gives them the capacity of receiving others betwixt them" (T 1.2.4.25/63–4). Thus, while referring to the qualities of bodies, he is in fact continuing his discussion of space and time. The Appendix to the *Treatise* also provides evidence for our strategy of treating Hume's argument on the vacuum, space, time, and body as intrinsically connected (T 1.2.5 n12.2/639).

46. Compare this with Newton's view as presented in the General Scholium to the second edition, in which he writes that "[W]e certainly do not know what is the substance of any thing. We see only the shapes and colors of bodies, we hear only their sounds, we touch only their external surfaces, we smell only their odors, and we taste their flavors. But there is no direct sense and there are no indirect reflected actions by which we know innermost substances" (1687: 942).

47. A second conclusion to Hume's argument concerning space and time is a brief section appended to the end of Book 1, part 2, entitled *Of the idea of existence, and of external existence*, in which Hume takes a parting shot at philosophers such as Newton who imagine that their reason can carry them beyond what is "present to the mind" and out "to the heavens, or to the utmost limits of the universe." To these, he writes: "[S]ince nothing is ever present to the mind but perceptions, and since all ideas are derived from something antecedently present to the mind; it follows, that 'tis impossible for us so much as to conceive or form an idea of any thing specifically different from ideas and impressions. Let us fix our attention out of ourselves as much as possible. Let us chace our imagination to the heavens, or to the utmost limits of the universe; we never really advance a step beyond ourselves; nor can conceive any kind of existence, but those perceptions, which have appear'd in that narrow compass" (T 1.2.6.8:67–8).

48. "A New Theory About Light and Colors" (1672), quoted in Shapiro (1993: 21). This aim of constructing a science of rigid consequences capable of eliminating any suspicion of doubt

sounds, to our ears, more Scholastic or Cartesian than something characteristic of empirical science. Yet Newton's interest in rebuilding natural philosophy on a mathematical basis is in fact aimed at attaining something very much akin to the Scholastic and Cartesian dream of *scientia*, knowledge free from doubt. Newton's concern is to "extend the bounds of mathematics," thus enabling the method of demonstrative proof to penetrate the realm of "physical things." From Newton's *Optical Papers*, quoted in Shapiro (1993: 25).

49. As Christopher Wren told his students in 1657: "Mathematical demonstrations being built on the impregnable foundations of geometry and arithmetick, are the only truths, that can sink into the mind of man, *void of all uncertainty*; and all other discourses participate more or less of truth, according as their subjects are more or less capable of mathematical demonstration. Therefore, this rather than logick is the . . . [basis for] all infallible science" (from Wren's inaugural lecture as professor of astronomy at Gresham College, as quoted in Shapiro [1993: 31]; emphasis added).

50. "[T]he whole subject of *mechanics* is distinguished from *geometry* by the attribution of exactness to geometry and of anything less than exactness to *mechanics*. Yet the errors do not come from the art, but from those who practice the art. Anyone who works with less exactness is a more imperfect mechanic, and if anyone could work with the greatest exactness, he would be the most perfect mechanic of all" (Newton 1687: 381–382).

51. Note that the claim that Hume's supposed inability to understand the mathematics of the *Principia* is apparently a myth. See Barfoot (1990).

52. He continues: "[N]or would it err at all, did it not aspire to such an absolute perfection."

53. "[G]eometry, or the art, by which we fix the proportions of figures; tho' it much excels both in universality and exactness, the loose judgments of the senses and imagination; yet never attains a perfect precision and exactness. Its first principles are still drawn from the general appearance of the objects; and that appearance can never afford us any security, when we examine, the prodigious minuteness of which nature is susceptible" (T 1.3.1.4/70-1).

54. For Hume's further use of this argument in his critique of matter, see Rocknak (2013: 119–20). Space constraints prevent us from exploring Hume's other more general argument(s) against the applicability of mathematics at *Treatise* 1.4.1–2. See Meeker (2007).

55. Hume speaks of the "art of measuring" at T 1.2.4.24/48, an expression that echoes Newton (1687: 382). But Newton speaks of "reducing the art of measuring to exact propositions and demonstrations." For Hume there is no such reduction to exactness, and measuring remains an art. Geometry itself, Hume affirms at T 1.3.1.4/70, is an "art."

56. Although Hume and Newton share an empiricism about geometry, it may be argued that Hume's argument is less compelling than he may have thought. First, Newton explicitly relies on *quam-proxime* reasoning. Second, what really matters for Newton is whether his conceptual apparatus is precise enough for the purposes of theory-mediated measurement. It is not clear that Hume appreciated either point fully (see Smith 2001). Third, Hume never offers an example of where the inferential uses of Newton's fluxional geometry is not up to its assigned task.

57. On Newton's Rule IV, see Schliesser (2009: 186–189); and on forces, see Schliesser (2009 195–198). On causation, see Schliesser (2009: 191–195), as well as Schliesser (2008).

58. The ability to determine the essential qualities of matter is what licenses Newton's ability to extrapolate from our experience to universal laws of physics such as gravitation. See McGuire (1968; 1970). In particular, Newton believes he can experimentally secure claims about the additive composition of matter with an empirical criterion for asserting what

is essential to systems of matter (Belkind 2012). Hume does not believe that any such criterion for distinguishing essential qualities of matter exists. Moreover, in Roger Cotes's influential presentation of these matters in his Editor's Preface to the Second Edition of the *Principia*, Newton is presented as applying a version of the distinction between primary and secondary qualities (Cotes 1713), which is the subject of Hume's attack on the "modern philosophy" in T 1.4.4. Hume's rejection of Rule III must therefore be seen as thoroughgoing and allowing no compromises. It is at the heart of Hume's attack on Newton.

59. As Newton writes: "[T]he qualities of bodies can be known only through experiments; and therefore qualities that square with experiments universally are to be regarded as universal qualities.... [N]ature is always simple and consonant with itself. The extension of bodies is known to us only through our senses, and yet there are bodies beyond the range of these senses; but because extension is found in all sensible bodies, it is ascribed to all bodies universally" (1687: 795).

60. "The extension, hardness, impenetrability, mobility, and force of intertia of the whole [sensible object] arise from the extension, hardness, impenetrability, mobility, and force of intertia *of each of the parts*; and thus we conclude that every one of the least parts of all bodies is extended, hard, impenetrable, movable, and endowed with force of intertia. And this is the foundation of all natural philosophy" (1687: 795–796; emphasis added). Compare this to the magnetic force, which "in one and the same body can be intended or remitted ..." (1687: 810; i.e., Book 3, Prop. 6, Corollary 5). Note that the compositionality claim is taken to be foundational. See Belkind (2012) for interesting discussion.

61. "Finally, if it is universally established by experiments and astronomical observations that all bodies on or near the earth gravitate toward the earth, and do so in proportion to the quantity of matter in each body, and that the moon gravitates toward the earth in proportion to the quantity of its matter, and that our sea in turn gravitates toward the moon, and that all planets gravitate toward one another, and that there is a similar gravity of comets toward the sun, it will have to be concluded by this third rule that all bodies gravitate toward one another" (1687: 796; translator's interpolation removed). In this way, Newton's rule functions as the engine for transforming what would otherwise be a science of systematized local observations into one that presents truths that are "by Rule III ... to be affirmed of all bodies universally" (1687: 809; i.e., Book 3, Prop. 6, Cor. 2).

62. Hume's "logic" is a logic of establishing the causes of things. This is the equivalent of Newton's "method of analysis." In this use of the term "logic," Hume follows the traditional definition of logic as "the art of thinking justly" (see Chambers, *Cyclopedia*).

63. See Schliesser (2007), sect. 4.5.

64. It is significant that Hume declines to follow Newton's concept of a quality that "cannot be intended and remitted," which he apparently rejects: Newton's Rule III is about a certain kind of quality. Newton has in mind qualities such as extension, solidity, inertia, and gravity, which, he believes, may be distinguished from other qualities of objects by the fact that they "cannot be intended and remitted." By this, Newton means that qualities of this type cannot be removed from objects that possess them: that is, there is nothing that can be done to an extended object such that it will cease to be extended or to a gravitating object such that it will cease to gravitate. (For discussion, see Ducheyne 2012: 115–8). Hume, on the other hand, declines to discuss qualities that "cannot be intended and remitted," and although he nowhere gives a reason for this omission, we suspect it is because Hume does not believe there is a way to know whether a given quality is such that it "cannot be

intended or remitted." Hume is fond of saying that "whatever we [can] conceive is possible" (T 1.4.5.10/236). Similarly: "Any thing may produce any thing. Creation, annihilation, motion, reason, volition; all these may arise from one another, or from any other object we can imagine" (T 1.3.15.1/173). And there is little that is more easily conceived than that something possessing hardness or gravity should cease to have these qualities.

65. This is because "the force of the whole will have to arise from the forces of the component parts" (1687: 811; i.e., Book 3, Prop. 7, Cor. 1). See Belkind, op cit.

66. "We may establish it as a certain maxim, that in all moral as well as natural phaenomena, wherever any cause consists of a number of parts, and the effect encreases or diminishes, according to the variation of that number, the effects properly speaking, is a compounded one, and arises from the union of the several effects, that proceed from each part of the cause. Thus, because the gravity of a body encreases or diminishes by the encrease or diminution of its parts, we conclude that each part contains this quality and contributes to the gravity of the whole. The absence or presence of a part of the cause is attended with that of a proportionable part of the effect. This connexion or constant conjunction sufficiently proves the one part to be the cause of the other" (T 1.3.2.16/136).

67. This anticipates Nancy Cartwright's criticism of physical law, for example in Cartwright (1983).

68. The view we have presented here is at odds with that of Graciela de Pierris, who builds her discussion of Hume's debt to Newton around Hume's putative embrace of Newton's Rule III as the cornerstone for his philosophical method (de Pierris 2006: 306–10, 312). De Pierris bases this conclusion on two controversial assumptions: (1) that Newton's Rule III provides a general instrument for extending inductive inferences from one observed phenomenon to another, and from locally observed phenomena to the entire universe of possible phenomena; and (2) that Hume follows Newton in accepting the possibility of extracting genuinely universal laws from the observation of local phenomena. Regarding (1), de Pierris ignores the fact that Newton's Rule III is explicitly written with reference *only to a very specific kind of quality*, namely, "[t]hose qualities of bodies that cannot be intended and remitted and that belong to all bodies on which experiments can be made." The universally observed presence of such essential qualities as extension and hardness, and of nonessential but nonremittable qualities such as gravitation (nonessential because, in principle, a body can be a body without the quality of gravity), is thus said to license the supposition that such qualities are present in all bodies in the universe. Nowhere does Newton hint, as de Pierris suggests, that this rule of universalization can be applied to anything other than such essential or quasi-essential qualities of physical bodies. Regarding (2), we have found no instance in Hume's writings in which he concedes to Newton the notion that we can know anything to be "either exactly or very nearly true" about the microworld or the ends of the universe on the basis of local experiments. Hume does constantly use the word "universal" to refer to things that always happen *in our experience*. But nowhere does Hume endorse the Newtonian idea that there are things that can be known concerning the qualities of "all bodies universally" on the basis of our local experience.

In arguing for Hume's endorsement of Rule III, de Pierris points to one passage in which she believes this endorsement is almost explicit. This is a comment of Hume's in *An Equiry Concerning the Principles of Morals*, Section 3, in which he argues that since "public interest and utility" is the cause of "esteem or moral approbation" in the case of justice, it should also be considered the cause of such esteem and approbation with respect to virtues such as "humanity, benevolence, friendship, public spirit," and others. Having proposed a like cause (public interest and utility) for like effects (esteem or moral approbation for virtues such as humanity, etc.), Hume then comments: "It is entirely agreeable to the rules of philosophy . . . , where any principle has been found to have great force and energy in one instance, to ascribe to it a like energy in all similar instances. This indeed is Newton's chief rule of philosophizing" (EM 3.48/204). Hume's footnote after this comment reads: "Principia, Lib. iii." (i.e., *Principia*, Bk. iii). De Pierris invokes this passage in de Pierris (2006: 306–308) and also in de Pierris (2002: 521–522, esp. n. 38). The trouble with this argument is that Hume does not *himself* tell us that "Newton's chief rule of philosophizing," which he has applied in the case at hand, is Newton's Rule III. And, in point of fact, Rule III does not have anything to do with the case Hume is talking about: the quality that Hume is writing about is "public interest and utility," which is neither a quality "that cannot be intended and remitted" nor one that "belong[s] to all bodies on which experiments can be made." Because Newton's Rule III is about qualities "that cannot be intended and remitted in all bodies on which experiments can be made," it is clear that Hume could not have been applying Newton's Rule III in this case. What, then, is Hume talking about when he says that he has applied "Newton's chief rule of philosophizing" to the case of "public interest and utility"? He is referring to Newton's Rule II, which says that *"causes assigned to natural effects of the same kind must be, so far as possible, the same"* (Newton, 1687: 795). Unlike Rule III, Newton's Rule II is directly applicable to the case Hume is describing in the passage in question in the *Enquiry*, Section 3: that is, it licenses the move from one natural effect (moral approbation in the case of justice) to another "of the same kind" (moral approbation in the case of benevolence) and assigns the cause of the one (public interest and utility) to the other. And unlike Rule III, Newton's Rule II, *is* included in Hume's own rules of reasoning—a version of it appears in Hume's Rule IV (and in its close relation, Rule V) (T 1.3.15.6–7/173–4).

This suggests that it is Newton's Rule II that Hume considers to be "Newton's chief rule of philosophizing"—an interpretation that fits well with what Hume writes about method in both the *Treatise* and in his later writings. It also reinforces the view that Hume rejects Rule III as being that part of Newton's philosophy that is worthy of being adopted and immitated. Indeed, Hume's point is precisely that it is Rule II, *chiefly,* that we should be interested in. Rule III, with its extravagant claims concerning the presence of supposedly essential qualities in every body in the universe far from common life is one we can afford to set aside.

69. A number of scholars have suggested that Hume's aim in *Treatise* Book 1 is something akin to a critique of the powers of the mind—by which is meant an inquiry whose purpose is to establish the limits of what may be known by means of the respective sciences. This has been emphasized in different ways in Laird (1932/1967: 22), Capaldi (1967: 69–70, 81) Garrett (1997: 10), Mounce (1999: 15–21), and Waxman (2008: 172–174).

70. Newton concludes the Scholium to his definitions, six out of the eight of which are concerned with defining what is meant by "force," with the statement that "in what follows, a fuller explanation will be given of how to determine true motions from their causes, effects, and apparent differences, and, conversely, of how to determine from motions, whether true or apparent, their causes and effects. For this was the purpose for which I composed the following treatise" (1687/1999: 413–414).

71. That this is a discussion of Newtonian forces has often escaped the attention of readers for a number of reasons, not least of which is the fact that in *Treatise* Book 1, Hume uses the word *force* almost exclusively to refer to mental forces such as the "force and vivacity" of ideas. The only section of Book 1 in which the term force is consistently used in something resembling its physical sense is Part 3, Section 14—and, in particular, T 1.3.14.4–29 /157–69.

72. His use of the term force as inseparable from necessity or causes leads to frequent Humean usages such as "the secret force and energy of causes" (T 1.3.14.7/158), which means that it isn't really possible to come up with a neat picture of the way Hume uses the word force even in T 1.3.14.

73. The conjunction of Hume's fourth and seventh rules produces a new rule: "An effect always holds proportion with its cause" ("Of Interest," ESY 297). We can call this "Hume's ninth rule;" Hume uses it to rule out alternative causal hypotheses in his criticism of mercantalism, as well as in the use of analogy in the Newtonian "argument from design" (see EU 11 and D 5–7).

74. For Newton's use of the term *effects* in this way, see Proposition 66 of *Principia*, Book I: "[T]hese forces . . . will always act in the same way and in the same proportion; thus it will necessarily be the case that all the effects will be similar and proportional and that the times for these effects will be proportional as well." (1687: 580); and Proposition 52 of Book II: "[S]ince the proportion of the causes remains the same, the proportion of the effects—that is, the proportion of the motions and the periodic times—will remain the same" (1687: 783).

75. Two such instances appear in the next two passages we have quoted from Hume: the one beginning "Tho' the several resembling instances;" and the one beginning "[W]e are led astray by a false philosophy." We have added emphasis to highlight this point.

76. Or, as Hume puts it: "[M]atter is confess'd by philosophers to operate by an unknown force" (T 1.3.14.12/App. 633).

77. This way of phrasing the example is taken from Smeenk and Schliesser (2013). For recent treatment of the moon test, see Harper (2011).

78. "To every operation there is a power proportioned; and this power must be plac'd on the body, that operates" (T 1.3.14.26/167–8).

79. "As to what may be said, that the operations of nature are independent of our thought and reasoning, I allow it. . . . But if we go any farther, and ascribe a power or necessary connexion to these objects; this is what we can never observe in them, but must draw the idea of it from what we feel internally in contemplating them" (T 1.3.14.28/168).

80. For other attempts, see Sturm (2014).

81. See Russell (2008).

82. See Norton (2010).

BIBLIOGRAPHY

Allison, Henry E. (2008). *Custom and Reason in Hume*. New York: Oxford University Press.

Barfoot, Michael. (1990). "Hume and the Culture of Science in the Early Eighteenth Century," in M. A. Stewart, ed., *Studies in the Philosophy of the Scottish Enlightenment*. New York: Oxford University Press, 151–190.

Belkind, Ori. (2012). "Newton's Scientific Method and the Universal Law of Gravitation," in A. Janiak and E. Schliesser, eds., *Interpreting Newton: Critical Essays*. Cambridge: Cambridge University Press, 138–168.

Berkeley George. (1721/2005). *Concerning Motion: Or the Origin and Nature of Motion, and the Cause of Communicating It*, in G. N. Wright, ed., *The Works of George Berkeley*. Lexington, Kent.: Elibron, 2005 [1843], vol. 2, 83–104.

Berkeley, George. (1734). *The Analyst: Or a Discourse Addressed to an Infidel Mathematician*, in G. N. Wright, ed., *The Works of George Berkeley*. Lexington, Kent.: Elibron, 2005 [1843], vol. 2, 105–142.

Berkeley, George. (1735). *A Defense of Free-Thinking in Mathematics*, in G. N. Wright, ed., *The Works of George Berkeley*. Lexington, Kent.: Elibron, 2005 [1843], vol. 2, 143–170.

Biro, John. (1993). "Hume's New Science of Mind," in D. F. Norton, ed., *The Cambridge Companion to Hume*. New York: Cambridge, 33–63.

Boehm, Miren Francisca. (2008). "Hume's Foundational Project in Book I of the Treatise," unpublished doctoral dissertation, University of California.

Boehm, Miren Francisca. (2012). "Filling the Gaps in Hume's Vacuums." *Hume Studies* 38 (1): 79–99.

Boehm, Miren Francisca (2013). "Hume's Foundational Project in the *Treatise*." *European Journal of Philosophy* 22 (1).

Capaldi, Nicholas. (1967). *David Hume: The Newtonian Philosopher*. Boston: Twayne.

Cartwright, Nancy. (1983). *How the Laws of Physics Lie*. Oxford: Oxford University Press.

Clarke, Samuel. (1705/1998). *A Demonstration of the Being an Attributes of God: And Other Writings*, Ezio Vailati, ed. Cambridge: Cambridge University Press.

Chambers, Ephraim. (1750, 5th ed.). *Cyclopdia, Or an Universal Dictionary of Arts and Sciences*, vol. 2. London: Midwinter.

Cotes, Rogers. (1713/1999). "Preface," in I. Bernard Cohen and Anne Whitman, eds., Isaac Newton, *Mathematical Principles of Natural Philosophy*, 2nd ed. California: University of California Press, 385–415.

Demeter, Tamas. (2012). "Hume's Experimental Method." *British Journal for the History of Philosophy* 20(3), 577–599.

Ducheyne, Steffen. (2012). *The Main Business of Natural Philosophy: Isaac Newton's Natural-Philosophical Methodology*. New York: Springer.

de Pierris, Graciela. (2002, May). "Causation as a Philosophical Relation in Hume." *Philosophy and Phenomenological Research* 64(3), 499–545.

de Pierris, Graciela. (2006, November). "Hume and Locke on Scientific Methodology: The Newtonian Legacy." *Hume Studies* 32(2), 277–329.

DiSalle, Robert. (2002). "Newton's Philosophical Analysis of Space and Time," in I. Bernard Cohen and George E. Smith, eds., *The Cambridge Companion to Newton*. Cambridge: Cambridge University Press, 33–56.

Flage, David. (1990). *David Hume's Theory of Mind*. New York: Routledge.

Garrett, Don. (1997). *Cognition and Commitment in Hume's Philosophy*. New York: Oxford University Press.

Guicciardini, Niccolò. (1989). *The Development of Newtonian Calculus in Britain, 1700–1800*. Cambridge: Cambridge University Press.

Guicciardini, Niccolò. (2009). *Isaac Newton: On Mathematical Certainty and Method*. Cambridge: Massachusetts Institute for Technology Press.

Harper, William L. (2011). *Isaac Newton's Scientific Method: Data into Evidence about Gravity and Cosmology*. Oxford: Oxford University Press.

Hazony, Yoram. (2009). "Hume's Program as an Alternative to Naturalism in Contemporary Epistemology and Philosophy of Mind," unpublished paper presented at the Hume Society in Halifax, Nova Scotia, August 5, 2009.

Hazony, Yoram. (2014). "Newtonian Explanatory Reduction and Hume's 'System of the Sciences,'" in Zvi Biener and Eric Shliesser, eds., *Newton and Empiricism*. Oxford: Oxford University Press, 138–170.

Jesseph, Douglas M. (2010). *Berkeley's Philosophy of Mathematics*. Chicago: University of Chicago Press.

Kallich, M. (1945). "The Association of Ideas and Critical Theory: Hobbes, Locke, and Addison." *ELH* 12(4), 290–315.

Kochiras, Hylarie. (2013). "The Mechanical Philosophy and Newton's Mechanical Force." *Philosophy of Science*, 80(4), 557–578.

Laird, John. (1932/1967). *Hume's Philosophy of Human Nature*. Archon.

Loptson, Peter. (1998). "Hume, Multiperspectival Pluralism, and Authorial Voice." *Hume Studies* 24 (2), 313–334.

Macarthur, David. (2008). "Naturalism and Skepticism," in Marion de Caro and David MacArthur, eds., *Naturalism in Question*. Cambridge: Harvard University Press, 106–124.

McDowell, John. (1998). "Two Sorts of Naturalism," in John McDowell, ed., *Mind, Value and Reality*. Cambridge: Harvard University Press, 167–197.

McGuire, J. E. (1968). "The Origin of Newton's Doctrine of Essential Qualities." *Centaurus* 12, 233–260.

McGuire, J. E. (1970). "Atoms and the 'Analogy of Nature': Newton's Third Rule of Philosophizing." *History and Philosophy of Science*, 1, 3–58.

McMullin, Ernan. (1985). "The Significance of Newton's 'Principia' for Empiricism," in Margaret J. Osler and Paul Lawrence Farber, eds., *Religion, Science, and Worldview: Essays in Honor of Richard S. Westfall*. New York: Cambridge University Press, 33–59.

Meeker, Kevin. (2007). "Hume on Knowledge, Certainty and Probability: Anticipating the Disintegration of the Analytic-Synthetic Divide?" *Pacific Philosophical Quarterly* 88(2), 226–242.

Millican, Peter. (2007). "Introduction" to David Hume's *Enquiry Concerning Human Understanding*. New York: Oxford University Press.

Mounce, H. O. (1999). *Hume's Naturalism*. New York: Routledge.

Newton, Isaac. (1687/1999). *Mathematical Principles of Natural Philosophy*, I. Bernard Cohen and Anne Whitman, eds. Berkeley, California: University of California Press.

Newton, Isaac. (1730/2003). *Opticks*. Amherst: Prometheus.

Newton, Isaac. (before 1685/2004). *De Gravitatione*. In Andrew Janiak, ed., *Philosophical Writings*. Cambridge: Cambridge University Press, 12–39.

Norton, David Fate. (1993). "An Introduction to Hume's Philosophy," in *The Cambridge Companion to Hume*. New York: Cambridge University Press, 1–32.

Norton, David Fate. (2000). "Editor's Introduction," in David Fate Norton and Mary J. Norton, eds., *David Hume, A Treatise of Human Nature*. New York: Oxford University Press, I9–I99.

Norton, John D. (2010). "How Hume and Mach Helped Einstein Find Special Relativity," in Mary Domski and Michael Dickson, eds., *Discourse on a New Method: Reinvigorating the Marriage of History and Philosophy of Science*. Chicago: Open Court Publishing, 359–386.

Owen, David. (1999). *Hume's Reason*. New York: Oxford University Press.

Pears, David. (1990). *Hume's System: An Examination of the First Book of His Treatise*. New York: Oxford University Press.

Rocknak, Stefanie. (2013). *Imagined Causes: Hume's Conception of Objects*. New York: Springer.

Russell, Paul. (2008). *The Riddle of Hume's Treatise: Skepticism, Naturalism, and Irreligion*. New York: Oxford University.

Schliesser, Eric. (2004). "Hume's Missing Shade of Blue Reconsidered from Newtonian Perspective." *Journal of Scottish Philosophy* 2(2), 164–175.

Schliesser, Eric. (2007). "Hume's Newtonianism and Anti-Newtonianism," in Edward N. Zalta, ed., *Stanford Encyclopedia of Philosophy*, available online at http://plato.stanford.edu/archives/win2008/entries/hume-newton/

Schliesser, Eric. (2008). "Two Definitions of Causation, Normativity, and Hume's Debate with Newton," in Steffen Ducheyne, ed., *Newton in Context*. Brussels: Royal Flemisch Academy of Sciences.

Schliesser, Eric. (2009). "Hume's Attack on Newton's Philosophy." *Enlightenment and Dissent*, 25, 167–203.

Schliesser, Eric. (2010). "Copernican Revolutions Revisited in Adam Smith by Way of David Hume." *Revista Empressa y Humanismo* 13 (1), 213–248.

Schliesser, Eric. (2012). "Newton and Spinoza: On Motion and Matter (and God of Course)." *The Southern Journal of Philosophy*, 50(3), 436–458.

Schliesser, Eric. (2013). "Newton's Philosophy of Time," in A. Bardon & H. Dyke, eds., *A Companion to the Philosophy of Time*. New York: Blackwells, 87–101.

Schliesser, Eric. (2015). "The Science of Man and the Invention of Usable Traditions," in T Demeter, K. Murphy, and C. Zittel, eds., *Conflicting Values of Inquiry: Ideologies of Epistemology in Early Modern Europe*, Leiden: Brill.

Schaffer, Jonathan. (2003). "Is There a Fundamental Level?" *Nous* 37, 498–517.

Shank, J. B. (2008). *The Newton Wars and the Beginning of the French Enlightenment*. Chicago: University of Chicago Press.

Shapiro, Alan. (1993). *Fits, Passions, and Paroxysms*, Cambridge: Cambridge University Press.

Smeenk, Chris, and Eric Schliesser. (2013). "Newton's *Principia*," in J. Buchwald and R. Fox, eds., *Oxford Handbook of the History of Physics*, Oxford: Oxford University Press, 109–165.

Smith, George E. (2001). "The Methodology of the *Principia*," in I. Bernard Cohen and George E. Smith, eds., *The Cambridge Companion to Newton*. Cambridge: Cambridge University Press, 138–173.

Smith, Norman Kemp. (1941/2005). *The Philosophy of David Hume*. New York: Palgrave.

Stein, Howard. (2002). "Newton's Metaphysics," in I. Bernard Cohen and George E. Smith, eds., *The Cambridge Companion to Newton*. Cambridge: Cambridge University Press, 256–307.

Strawson, P. F. (1985). *Skepticism and Naturalism: Some Varieties*. New York: Columbia.

Stroud, Barry. (1977). *Hume*. New York: Routledge.

Sturm, Thomas. (2014). "The Analytic and Synthetic Method in the Human Sciences: A Hope That Failed," in Tamas Demeter, Kathryn Murphy, and Claus Zittel, eds., *Conflicting Values of Inquiry: Ideologies of Epistemology in Early Modern Europe*. Leiden: Brill.

Waxman, Wayne. (1994). *Hume's Theory of Consciousness*. New York: Cambridge University Press.

Waxman, Wayne. (1996). "The Psychologistic Foundations of Hume's Critique of Mathematical Philosophy." *Hume Studies* 22 (1), 123–168.

Waxman, Wayne. (2008). "Kant's Humean Solution to Hume's Problem," in Daniel Garber and Beatrice Longueness, eds., *Kant and the Early Moderns*. Princeton: Princeton University Press, 172–192.

Westfall, Richard S. (1971/1977). *The Construction of Modern Science: Mechanisms and Mechanics*. New York: Cambridge University Press.

CHAPTER 35

HUME AND SMITH ON MORAL PHILOSOPHY

RYAN PATRICK HANLEY

ADAM Smith's debts to Hume's moral and political philosophy are profound and have long been appreciated. An earlier generation of scholars was even prone to regard Smith's moral philosophy as entirely derivative of Hume's; in this vein, it was once not uncommon to find even careful readers of Smith describing his moral theory as "a refinement on Hume's which differs from it in respects that, although very significant, are not decisive."[1] More recent scholarship has tended to endorse this judgment in part. Hume's influence is still considered profound; the important introduction to the Glasgow edition of *The Theory of Moral Sentiments* (TMS) argued that "among contemporary thinkers Hume had the greatest influence on the formation of Smith's ethical theory," and recent students of Smith's philosophy have similarly argued that in the TMS, Smith "above all engages in a running dialogue with Hume."[2] Yet today, unlike earlier, it is generally agreed that this dialogue was genuinely a two-way dialogue and that Smith was far from a mere cipher.

Herein lies the advance in recent scholarship. Even as Hume's influence on Smith is still seen as preeminent, today it is also commonly said "Smith rejects or transforms Hume's ideas far more often than he follows them."[3] In this vein, Smith is said to have followed Hume only "in relatively minor matters" and that the effect of his engagement was in fact to stimulate him "to criticism and to the production of alternative views that surmounted the faults he found in Hume."[4] Some of the most insightful students of the Hume–Smith relationship have similarly argued that, so far from merely replicating Hume's positions, Smith deserves to be numbered alongside Kant as "Hume's profoundest follower and critic."[5] And most recently three crucially important studies have independently argued that Smith's philosophy is "fundamentally shaped by the ideas of Hume, but seems to recognize the limitations of Hume's enlightenment project when it comes to ethics and religion," that even in appreciating the "distinctive and striking features of their shared view" it remains philosophically important "to get clear on the important differences," and that although "Smith's thought circles around Hume's," there is "almost no respect in which Smith agrees entirely with Hume."[6]

Taken collectively, these judgments attest to a general consensus that Smith, although deeply indebted to Hume, was also engaged in a comprehensive and creative transformation and extension of certain of Hume's fundamental concepts. But what exactly did Smith take from Hume, and precisely how did he seek to transform these concepts? In what follows, I trace Smith's appropriation and transformation along five fronts: sympathy and humanity, justice and utility, judgment and impartiality, virtue and commercial society, and epistemology and religion. In so doing, I aim to provide a synthetic account of previous scholarship on the Hume–Smith relationship and to supplement these accounts with an examination of several further points of contact that have yet to receive significant attention. At the same time, my aim is not merely to illuminate Smith's historical debts to Hume. Study of these debts is also of value for two philosophically significant reasons. One will be of interest primarily to Hume specialists: namely, that insofar as Smith's appropriation or transformation of Hume's concepts often points in a consciously practical direction, Smith's thought can offer a window on what a "practical Humeanism" may look like—that is, on how Hume's theoretical philosophy might "play out" in lived experience. A second reason will be of primary interest to Smith scholars. Smith is today often regarded through the lens of his contributions to the development of the eighteenth-century Scottish "science of man"; in this vein, his most recent biographer describes his philosophical project as an effort at "developing a science of man on Humean principles."[7] But this claim needs careful handling. If it is meant merely to suggest that Smith's project is grounded in a commitment to empiricism, then it is relatively unproblematic.[8] Yet if it is meant to suggest that Smith's exclusive or principal aim as a moral philosopher was to provide a scientific or descriptive account of the existence and operation of moral phenomena in the spirit of the sort of philosophical anatomist described by Hume, it would be incorrect. As one of the most careful recent students of Smith's "science of human nature" argues, Smith was, throughout his career, "engaged simultaneously in a descriptive and prescriptive enterprise."[9] So far from merely aiming to present a neutral or scientific account of the moral world, Smith was consistently concerned to intervene in and to shape that world for, as he thought, the better, and indeed the study of Smith's relationship to Hume may well be most valuable for its capacity to bring into relief Smith's normative commitments.

I SYMPATHY AND HUMANITY

No aspect of the Hume–Smith relationship has attracted more attention than their accounts of sympathy. The centrality of sympathy to each of their systems has long been recognized, and Smith's debts to and derivations from Hume's account are noted even by Hume himself, who observed to Smith in private correspondence that his innovations on sympathy are a "hinge" of his system (CAS 36).[10] Whether Smith's innovations represent genuine progress or regress has been a matter of debate; for every claim that Smith's theory is "more complex," one can find a counterclaim that he "does not develop a general theory of sympathy on the scale offered by Hume."[11] But leaving that aside for the moment, where exactly do Smith and Hume overlap on sympathy, and where do they differ?

The essential differences between Smith and Hume's theories of sympathy have been helpfully developed by Samuel Fleischacker and Geoffrey Sayre-McCord. Fleischacker reads the opening of TMS as a quite conscious engagement with Hume, dedicated to "setting up an alternative account of sympathy" in which Smith "uses technical terms borrowed from Hume to make an anti-Humean point."[12] The main difference, on this view, is that "Hume has a 'contagion' account of sympathy, while Smith has a 'projection' account" of sympathy."[13] Hume's sympathy, that is, is largely "non-cognitive"—"an automatic feature of our biological makeup."[14] On this account, others' feelings "communicate themselves directly" to us and "our imaginations only intensify those feelings so as to raise them to the level of an impression." In Smith's theory, however, "imagination is essential to the production of even the 'idea' that constitutes sympathy."[15] Smith's sympathy, we thus might say, is epistemically grounded in a way that Hume's isn't insofar as it utilizes the various resources of the projective imagination to effect the transference necessary to experience sympathy. But Smith's sympathy is also epistemically grounded in a second way. In addition to imagination, Smithean sympathy also requires a capacity for judgment; thus Smith's foundational account conspicuously emphasizes that we cannot fully sympathize with a feeling of another before we are "informed of its cause" and that any attempt to do so before we know this cause will be "entirely imperfect," on the grounds that our sympathy "does not arise so much from the view of the passion, as from that of the situation which excites it" (TMS 1.1.1.8–10). As Sayre-McCord has it, "Smith ends up holding that our conception of the circumstances matters significantly more than our idea of the passion itself," and appreciation of these circumstances is therefore indispensible to our decision of whether and how much to sympathize with others.[16]

Putting Smithean sympathy in terms of a decision reinforces its essential two differences from Hume's theory: first, for Smith, sympathy depends on imagination in a way Hume's does not; and second, for Smith, sympathy depends on judgments of fittingness and propriety in a way Hume's does not. Yet to this accepted view of Smith's departures from Hume on sympathy two further points can, I think, usefully be added. The first concerns the nature of the activity that makes possible the very projection of the Smithean sympathetic spectator into the condition and position of another. In brief: one of the most striking differences between Hume's and Smith's accounts concerns the relative degree of activity or passivity that each presumes in a sympathetic agent. Hume's sympathetic spectator is indeed not only strikingly noncognitive, but also strikingly passive; for Hume, sympathy leads us to "receive by communication" the feelings of others and experience them as if they have been "infus'd" on us (T 2.1.11.2–3). The experience of sympathy for Hume is furthermore a process that, as he explains from a first-personal perspective, "diffuses on me" and "draws along my judgment" and "operates on us"—all of which attest to the degree to which Hume conceives of sympathy as a principle of "so powerful and insinuating a nature" (T 3.3.2.2, T 3.3.2.5, T 3.3.2.3). Smith has almost an exact opposite account however. Contra Hume, Smith regards sympathy as something that spectators need to 'go out to get' as it were: something we cannot experience until we "form" an idea of the experiences of others, we take recourse to that which can "carry us beyond our own person," we "place ourselves" in their situation, and we "become" to some degree that person ourselves (TMS 1.1.1.2). Smith's heavy reliance on active verbs in his foundational account thus marks a striking difference from Hume. Of course, Smith admits—in a line that bears Hume's stamp—that sympathy "upon some occasions, may seem to be transfused from one man to another, instantaneously, and antecedent to any knowledge of what excited them in the person principally concerned" (TMS 1.1.1.6). Yet, in some sense, this is an exception that proves the general rule Smith means to establish: namely, that a genuine appreciation of the phenomenology of sympathy will reveal that even this seemingly instantaneous transmission is itself parasitic on a striking number of active and specifically cognitive exertions.

One particular active cognitive exertion that not only represents a departure from Hume but also a philosophically interesting move in its own right concerns the prominent emphasis that Smith places on "conception" in his foundational account of the sympathetic process. In this vein, Smith calls attention in a striking number of places to the need for sympathetic spectators not just to imagine but more precisely to "conceive" what others feel (TMS 1.1.1.1, TMS 1.1.1.2, TMS 1.1.1.3, TMS 1.1.1.7) and to generate thereby a "conception" of such (TMS 1.1.1.2–3). This is important for several reasons. First, in shifting from a readily available language of ideas and impressions (TMS 1.1.1.2) to this language of conception, Smith emphasizes a term and concept that, although hardly absent from Hume (e.g., EHU 2.2) is less prominent in Hume than in Smith. More importantly, Smith's embrace of the term suggests an important substantive departure from Hume. In the same letter quoted earlier, Hume revealingly says to Smith that "Sympathetic Passion is a reflex Image of the principal" that "must partake of its Qualities" (CAS 36). But Smith's own view is almost diametrically opposed, and his use of the language of "conception" suggests in a visceral and nontrivial sense the degree to which sympathetic spectators are not mere passive recipients of the phenomena of their world who simply mirror the sentiments of others but are actors in their own rights who form and give birth to new ideas by mixing their perceptions of external phenomena with their judgment. On Smith's account then, if not Hume's, the sympathetic spectator is an active agent engaged in a creative process that culminates in the generation of new entities.

Smith's sympathy is also active in a second sense. For Smith, sympathy not only presumes the spectator's active agency, but it also renders the agent capable of certain types of practical action. This side of Smithean sympathy has been helpfully emphasized in studies that call attention to the degree to which Smith conceived of sympathy as a principle of agent motivation.[17] Stephen Darwall also has helped to bring out this side of Smithean sympathy in comparison to Hume's. In describing the key difference between Smith and Hume on sympathy, Darwall emphasizes that, for Smith, sympathy involves caring "for" another in their being as a specific person with an individual standpoint of their own.[18] Sympathy thus "involves concern for him, and thus for his well-being, for his sake" and can thereby serve as the foundation for creation of "normative communities—like-minded groups who can agree on norms of feeling."[19] And this normative side also emerges in a second way. Not only does Smith think there are certain feelings that we ought to have for certain others, he also thinks there are certain feelings that we ought to feel in certain contexts; thus Fleischacker's observation that insofar as for Smith "certain feelings are appropriate to a situation, while others are not," it would seem that "for Smith but not for Hume there is a lot to learn about what sentiments we should have."[20]

One final point on this front deserves notice. As Hume specialists know well, in moving from the *Treatise* to the second *Enquiry* Hume seems to shift to his focus from sympathy to humanity—a shift that would culminate in his striking claim that humanity "can alone be the foundation of morals, or of any general system of blame or praise" (EM 9.6). This has, of course, given rise to a large literature dedicated to the question of the nature and significance of this shift.[21] Without entering into this debate here, we might only note that Smith is conspicuously less optimistic about the sufficiency of humanity left to itself; indeed, in a chapter that is itself dedicated largely to critique of Hume's concept of utility (and to which we turn to below), Smith insists that humanity is only an "exquisite fellow-feeling" that needs supplementation by "magnanimity" and "self-command" and the desire "to deserve applause" in order for it to be genuinely admirable (TMS 4.2.10). Smith's shift here introduces a host of other concepts that can only be dealt with in time, but for now we note only that here again Smith seems to insist on the difference between the quietism of Hume's system and the normative aims of his own system.

II Justice and Utility

Smith's and Hume's respective conceptions of justice and utility run a close second to sympathy in the amount of attention they have received from students of the Hume–Smith relationship. The essential core of their disagreement on this front is well known and easily enough stated: where Hume notoriously argues that justice is an "artificial" virtue that agents embrace only as a consequence of their rational reflection on its instrumental necessity to the preservation of social order, Smith argues that we are drawn to justice as a consequence of our natures and specifically our prerational sentimental predilections to a resentment felt when we when we see injuries inflicted on the undeserving innocent. What remains to be added to this now-familiar account are two points: first, that Smith not only drew the general contours of his anti-Humean argument from Hume but in fact took from Hume his specific claims on resentment; and, second, that Smith's development of his claims on resentment as the origin of justice provides a further window on the normative dimensions of his conception of sympathy.

To see this, we begin with Hume's basic argument. As readers of this volume know, Hume's theory of justice as an artificial virtue is founded on his claim that the purpose of justice is to mitigate two problems endemic to the human condition: a physical condition of scarce resources (EM 3.2–3) and a moral condition of limited benevolence and generosity (EM 3.6; T 3.2.2.18). Were we to discover remedies for either condition, Hume explains, justice would be unnecessary (EM 3.12). But stuck as we are in our middle state, justice is indispensible to the preservation of social order, and thus, Hume concludes, we are led to embrace justice and to create justice-preserving institutions as a result of having, "every moment, recourse to the principle of public utility" (EM 3.47; cf. T 3.2.1.11)— all of which leads Hume to his conclusion "that public utility is the *sole* origin of justice" (EM 3.1, EM 3.48; cf. T 3.2.6.9) and to insist that "the original motive to the *establishment* of justice" lies in considerations of utility and self-interest rather than in prereflective sentiments, even if "*sympathy* with *public* interest is the source of the *moral* approbation, which attends that virtue" (T 3.2.2.24). Hume indeed has little patience for those who propose to "discover" new sentiments in our nature that purport to explain this "original motive" to establishing justice (EM 3.40). On his account, there are only two essential options: "the sentiment of justice is either derived from our reflecting" on its capacity to promote public utility, or, like other passions, it necessarily "arises from a simple original instinct in the human breast" (EM 3.40), operating "without any reflection on farther consequences" (EM App 3.2–3).

How does Smith respond to this claim? As is well known, Smith targets it in several places (see, especially, TMS 4.2, TMS 7.2.3.21, TMS 7.3.3.17). His principal counterarguments to Hume's utility view of justice have been well explicated and consist in two principal claims. First, Smith questions Hume's seemingly uncharacteristic and pronounced optimism regarding the operations of reason in ordinary life; as he is at pains to argue in several places, the uncertainty and slowness of our reason, coupled with the undeniable necessity of justice to social order, makes it unlikely that nature would have entrusted so important a task to reason alone in the first instance (see, e.g., TMS 2.2.3.8–10 and TMS 4.2.3–5).[22] Second, Smith rejects Hume's suggestion that there is not in fact an original sense or instinct in the breast that renders justice attractive; as he insists, his own account of sympathy was in fact intended to provide an account of precisely this "natural and original" disposition and thereby obviate the need for recourse to the concept of utility (TMS 7.2.3.21; cf. TMS 7.3.3.17).

All of this is well known; what remains to be seen is the degree to which Smith was indebted to Hume himself for his anti-Humean arguments. These debts and agreements are in fact many; on a general level, as has been suggested, Smith's theory of justice is more consistent with Hume's general skepticism toward reason and his privileging of the passions than Hume's own theory of justice.[23] On a more particular level, Smith's account evidences a striking degree of reliance on certain specific elements of Hume's account, including Smith's utilization of Hume's own metaphors (see EM App 3.5 and TMS 2.2.3.4; EM 3.43 and TMS 1.3.2.3). But what can be added to these familiar points is that Smith drew not only the general contours and language of his anti-Humean argument from Hume, but indeed that he drew from Hume his own argument's central hinge: namely, his focus on resentment. As has been helpfully shown,[24] Smith grounds his account of the origins of justice in resentment—"a passion which is never properly called forth but by actions which tend to do real and positive hurt to some particular persons" (TMS 2.2.1.3). Resentment, he explains, has been "given us by nature" for the "safeguard of justice and the security of innocence" (TMS 2.2.1.4) and works on two levels—that of the "resentment of the sufferer" and that of what Smith alternately calls the "sympathetic resentment of the spectator" or the "sympathetic indignation of the spectator" (TMS 2.2.2.2, TMS 2.2.1.2). Each is crucial to the process of generating our attachment to justice because it is only by apprehension of the "natural resentment of the injured" that a spectator is led to experience that "just indignation for evil" necessary to generate our motivation to act justly and to support creation of just institutions (TMS 2.2.2.1; cf. TMS 2.1.3.3, TMS 2.1.5.6, TMS 2.2.2.3; LJB 181 and 201). What needs to be added to this though is the recognition that Smith likely drew these categories from Hume. In an important passage in EM 5—the significance of which for Smith has long been appreciated—Hume calls attention not merely to our "pleasing sympathy" with the fortunate and wealthy (EM 5.20), but also to the "immediate indignation" that we feel when we witness the unjust ravages of an "oppressive and powerful neighbor" (EM 5.21). Indeed, in his descriptions of this "liveliest resentment" (EM 5.27) and "strong resentment of injury done to men" (EM 5.39; cf. EHU 8.35), Hume attests to his familiarity with the central category Smith would use against him.[25]

The upshot of Smith's appropriation of Hume's resentment for his argument against Hume's utilitarian theory of justice is twofold. First, it illuminates a further side of Smith's complex engagement with Hume, which again uses central Humean categories to make not simply anti-Humean points, but in fact to argue for one side of Hume over another. In this sense, Smith's response to Hume on justice and utility represents less an argument against Hume than an effort to render Hume consistent with himself and thereby provide a rehabilitation of the Humean view (less obvious in EM than in the *Treatise*) that in fact "sympathy is the source of the esteem, which we pay to all the artificial virtues" (T 3.3.1.9). Indeed, it is precisely this that Smith himself claims in arguing that "the concern which is requisite" for resentment to be converted into a passion for justice is "no more than the general fellow-feeling which we have with every man merely because he is our fellow creature"; sympathy is sufficient for us to "enter into the resentment" and his "natural indignation" (TMS 2.2.3.10). In addition, Smith's investment in the concept of resentment lends further support to the view that his sympathy is action-motivating and thereby intended for normative ends. Students of Smith's theory of justice have traditionally made much of his striking claim that the duties of justice can often be fulfilled "by sitting still and doing nothing" (TMS 2.2.1.9)—an account that dovetails well with a liberal reading of Smith as privileging procedural justice over all other moral duties.[26] Yet Smith's seemingly quietist view of the duties of the just man demands to be set next to his account of resentment, which suggests that the just are obligated not only to resist a temptation to become agents of injustice (which can indeed be done passively), but are also charged with taking action to avenge injustices committed on the innocent—a task that demands action from us and, indeed, precisely the sort of action to which our natural resentment moves us. Hence, Smith's distinction between "the indolent and passive fellow-feeling" sufficient to restrain us from committing injustices and that "more vigorous and active sentiment" that enables us to avenge injustices (TMS 2.1.2.5), as well as "beat off the mischief which is attempted to be done to us" (TMS 2.2.1.4). This, Smith considers indispensible to security and public order, but yet insufficiently supported by Hume's cool and reasoned judgments of public utility. So far from promoting justice, reliance on such judgments would in fact be fatal to public order, Smith thinks. For although a "philosopher" might reason in generalities, it is only "particular examples" that lead us to feel "sympathetic resentment" (TMS 4.2.2)—a claim that may explain in part why theorists of procedural liberalism like Rawls have been drawn to Hume, whereas justice theorists such as Sen who seek to hasten a shift from "transcendental institutionalism" to "comparative solutions" concerned with "social realizations" have been drawn instead to Smith.[27]

III IMPARTIALITY AND JUDGMENT

A third focus of students of the Hume–Smith relationship has been their conceptions of impartiality and judgment. As many have seen, the device of the "impartial spectator" central to Smith's ethics is similar in both its intentions and its operations to Hume's "general point of view," and it has even been claimed that "the concept, though not the precise name, of an impartial spectator is there already in Hume."[28] But this seems too strong. Hume and Smith certainly share a common conception of the problem to which their mechanisms of impartial judgment are set forth as answers. Yet their proposed solutions differ in subtle but significant ways—ways that, in turn, point toward decidedly different normative horizons.

To begin with the problem: Hume and Smith each are well aware of a certain problem endemic to any sentimentalist theory of morals and especially those that are predicated on intersubjective sympathetic exchange as the foundation of moral norms. Put simply: if indeed, as has been argued, "peaceful intercourse with others requires a commonly accepted conception of morality," then, necessarily, our moral judgments must "suppose a common standard, one shareable (and often shared) with others we recognize as being of the same mind with us about virtue and vice, and such that it delivers the same verdict for us all."[29] Such standards are readily enough accounted for by deontologists or utilitarians, yet Smith's and Hume's treatments of sympathy seem to render the establishment of universally accepted standards difficult.[30] In addition, their sentimentalist theories, insofar as they are to some degree founded on recognition of the primacy of self-concern, also require a means by which moral agents can come to resist privileging self-concern over the well-being of others—another point to which we return later. For now, we need only see that Hume's general point of view and Smith's impartial spectator are each conceived, in the first instance, as mechanisms intended to assist us in overcoming the distortions endemic to our naturally partial perspectives, whether the product of sentimentalist predispositions to self-preference or the effect of the practical limits of sympathy. In Hume's formulation, what is needed is a means of "correcting our sentiments" via an effort to "correct the momentary appearances of things, and overlook our present situation" (T 3.3.1.16; EM 5.41); in Smith's terms, what is needed is a means of mitigating the potentially distorting effects of both our natural self-love and any "particular turn or habit of the imagination" that we have acquired (TMS 1.2.2.1).

Yet although Smith and Hume regard their respective impartiality mechanisms as answers to a common problem, their proposed remedies differ in certain specific ways. On Hume's account, spectators approach a general point of view by seeking to transcend their individual positional or sentimental biases and striving to occupy the only "common point of view" that can "appear the same to all": namely, "that of the person himself, whose character is examined; or that of persons, who have a connexion with him" (T 3.3.1.30; cf. T 3.3.1.17–8). On this view, the mark of a good spectator is not mere transcendence of particular biases, but also replication of the precise feelings experienced by the actual subject or subjects of her observation. Smith's view is different. Like Hume, he aims to overcome the idiosyncratic lenses endemic to particular positions. But in turning to the impartial spectator to achieve this end, Smith suggests that the proper end of impartiality is something other than a mere transcendence of self-preference culminating in replication of the sentiments of the person or persons principally concerned. He thinks this to be impossible in any case, insisting several times that feelings experienced by spectators can never match in pitch or intensity the feelings experienced by those principally concerned (e.g., TMS 1.3.1.3; TMS 1.3.1.8). But, more crucially, Smith thinks that attempts to replicate the actual feelings of others are not only futile, but also sterile insofar as the effort to do so would distract a spectator from a more ethically significant task: namely, the creation of an independent perspective that is new to and independent of the original positions of both spectator and actor.

Herein lies Smith's advance. For Smith, spectators and those being observed are constantly engaged in a process of mutual adjustment. As many have shown, the moral world described by Smith is one of continual dialectical engagement in which spectators and actors alike continually seek to adjust their sentiments in a manner that renders them reciprocally accessible and capable of being "entered into"; on this account, spectators, via deployment of their "amiable virtues" (the other-directed virtues of benevolence and humanity), heighten their feelings for others in order to approximate the actual feelings of others, at the same time that those observed, via deployment of their "awful virtues" (the self-directed virtues of self-command and propriety), lower their feelings for themselves to a level at which spectators are able to enter into them and approve them as fitting and admirable.[31] These mechanisms are well appreciated today, but setting them next to Hume can help to bring certain differences into relief. First, where Hume's common point of view aims to replicate an already extant position—that of the person being observed—Smith's impartial spectator occupies a new position that was known to neither the spectator nor the person principally concerned prior to their independent active exertions to achieve a commonly accessible disposition. Second, whereas for Hume the aim is to effect a transition from the spectator's to actor's position,

Smith conceives the end result of this motion as a newly created middle point and, indeed, a middle point on two axes. On the horizontal, the impartial spectator occupies a spatial midpoint between actor and spectator—a third space originally occupied by neither but reached and indeed defined through their independent efforts. Put slightly differently, and in the helpful terms of Michaël Biziou, Hume aims at an "exchange" where Smith strives rather for "convergence."[32] And, on the vertical axis, the impartial spectator occupies a midpoint in pitch or intensity, finding its balance in not only its fittingness to the circumstances, but also in "a certain mediocrity" between high and low (TMS 1.2.intro.1).

This difference ultimately matters for at least two reasons. First, in Smith's account, although not in Hume's, the actor and the spectator are engaged in a creative act as opposed to merely a mimetic act of replication. In some deep sense, Smith's account expects spectators and actors to collaborate together, in a spontaneous and unintended manner, in creating an independent and mutually accessible standard to a degree that Hume's agents are not. This in turn presumes, on Smith's part, a host of epistemic and moral virtues—flexibility, creativity, love of pluralism, desire for mutual accommodation— that may not be necessary (or at least not necessary in the same way) for Hume. Second, in suggesting that genuine impartiality is achieved only through the creation of a new independent perspective not previously occupied by any actual agent, Smith opens up a space for accommodation of certain types of ethical ideals. One of the most debated points in the recent Smith literature concerns the nature and the degree of work being done in his ethics by his frequent invocations of perfection.[33] Without aspiring to settle this debate here, it seems clear that Smith's conception of genuine impartiality as a newly created space opens up the possibility that this new standard can be informed by an appreciation of ideals in a manner in which Hume's concept, insofar as it is strictly limited to the replication of existing sentiments, cannot. And it is precisely this that opens up a space for Smith to defend his crucial distinction between what is praised and what is praiseworthy and that allows the impartial spectator, in a way Hume's general point of view cannot, to accommodate not only "the emotions and attitudes of people as they are" but also those of "people as they might be."[34]

IV VIRTUE AND COMMERCIAL SOCIETY

To this point our focus has been Smith's engagement with Hume's moral philosophy. Yet Smith's engagement, of course, also extended to Hume's political thought and is particularly evident in Smith's writings on economics, the field in which he would become most renowned. This influence has been known and appreciated for some time. Smith's first biographer, Dugald Stewart, reported that Hume's *Political Discourses* (which Smith commented on at a Glasgow Literary Society meeting in 1752 prior to their publication) "were evidently of greater use to Mr Smith, than any other book that had appeared prior to his lectures."[35] Smith's most recent biographer has concurred, insisting that Hume's

Essays introduced him to "an approach to the study of human nature" that enabled him to synthesize his disparate researches into a comprehensive vision of what enables us to flourish in civil society.[36] But what exactly did Smith take from Hume on this front, and where specifically did he disagree?

What follows particularly focuses on this second question concerning their disagreements. But their agreements should not be overlooked. Smith's technical economics relies a great deal on Hume's writings for its influential claims regarding the nature and function of money, the shortsightedness of then-fashionable balance of trade doctrines, and the proper function and limits of political intervention within a market society—all of which are well appreciated today and also extend beyond our focus on Hume's and Smith's moral philosophy. But where Smith's economics most directly treats properly moral questions is not in these technical discussions but in his striking comments on the relationship between morality and commercial progress—and it is here that we find the crucial departure of Smith from Hume.

The core of their disagreement concerns the effects of commercial progress on the evolution of morality. That both welcome commercial progress and, indeed, the liberalization of trade and the growth of the market economy is clear. Hume is at great pains to demonstrate across his corpus that the origin of government lies in the effort to guarantee security of property and that such security is precisely what makes possible the progress of civilization; indeed, in insisting that "from law arises security, from security curiosity, and from curiosity knowledge" (ESY 118), Hume lays out the core of the historical narrative that Smith would develop in his lectures and in the third book of the *Wealth of Nations*. Like Hume, Smith celebrates the social benefits this progress has made possible, emphasizing especially the degree to which it made possible the freedom of the lowest from the most destitute forms of poverty and dependence.[37] Smith even credits Hume with this discovery, insisting—in one of his very rare named references to a living philosopher—that the very fact that "commerce and manufactures gradually introduced order and good government, and with them, the liberty and security of individuals" is perhaps their "least observed" but "most important" effect and that "Mr. Hume is the only writer who, so far as I know, has hitherto taken notice of it" (WN 3.4.4). And, perhaps most importantly, Smith agrees that the engine that has driven this progress is precisely the seemingly universal psychological propensity to admire and esteem the wealthy that was Hume's focus in the chapter of the *Treatise* dedicated to sympathy. Indeed, however much they may have differed on the question of the relative influence of considerations of convenience and considerations of beauty (cf. T 2.2.5.16–7 and TMS 4.1.1–5), there can be no doubt that Smith found in Hume's account of the sympathy that gives rise to "an esteem for power and riches, and a contempt for meanness and poverty" (T 2.2.5.14; cf. T 2.2.5.21) his foundational claim that "it is chiefly from this regard to the sentiments of mankind, that we pursue riches and avoid poverty" (TMS 1.3.2.1; cf. TMS 1.3.2.2–3, TMS 1.3.2.8).[38]

Yet for all these crucial agreements on commercial society's ends and means, Smith departs sharply from Hume in his assessment of whether these gains ought to be regarded as unmitigated goods. Hume himself leaves no doubt where he stands on this front. Commercial progress and moral progress are necessarily connected: "industry, knowledge, and humanity, are linked together by an indissoluble chain, and are found, from experience as well as reason, to be peculiar to the more polished, and, what are commonly denominated, the more luxurious ages" (ESY 271). But Smith's own assessment is more qualified. He likewise welcomes the advances brought by commercial society, noting "opulence and commerce commonly precede the improvement of arts, and refinement of every sort." But Smith does not find the necessary connection between opulence and politeness that Hume does, qualifying his observation with the insistence that "I do not mean that the improvement of arts and refinement of manners are the necessary consequence of commerce. . . . but only that [it] is a necessary requisite" (LRBL 2.116). Smith also emphasizes a side of the story on which Hume is largely silent: namely, the 'negative externalities' that can accompany such otherwise welcome advances. In a series of observations that suggest a considerably more sober assessment of commercial society's moral future than any provided by Hume, Smith claims that the propensity to admire the rich that they each regard as an essential engine of commercial progress is at once "the great and most universal cause of the corruption of our moral sentiments" (TMS 1.3.3.1). So too Smith insists that the same division of labor that makes our collective progress possible (see, e.g., WN 1.1–2) is also the cause of the "mental mutilation, deformity and wretchedness" of the working class (WN 5.1.f.60). And so too the "commercial spirit" that enables individuals to progress and economies to grow has as its consequence that "the minds of men are contracted and rendered incapable of elevation, education is despised or at least neglected, and heroic spirit is almost utterly extinguished" (LJB 333). Smith, we can conclude, hardly endorses Hume's insistence on the "indissolubility" of the link between commercial growth and moral progress; so far from finding increased "humanity" among the emerging commercial class, he is prone to find in "the great body of the people" an "almost entire corruption and degeneracy" (WN 5.1.f.49) and is led as a result to fear that "all the nobler parts of the human character may be, in a great measure, obliterated and extinguished" (WN 5.1.f.51).

Such dire proclamations make Smith sound more like Rousseau than Hume—and perhaps for good reason, as recent scholars have emphasized.[39] Yet this, too, is a claim that demands careful treatment. Rousseau's pessimism and Hume's optimism on the question of the moral future of commercial society form two poles that define the middle point that Smith sought to occupy. To Rousseau, a decrease in humanity was an inexorable consequence of continued commercial progress, whereas for Hume its inexorable consequence was increase in humanity. Yet Smith doubts that either the pessimistic or the optimistic vision is quite so inevitable as his contemporaries would have us believe. For insofar as commercial progress has both its virtues and vices, as Smith clearly thinks, the crucial question is not whether we are somehow inexorably headed toward one future or another, but rather what we might do now to maximize the gains that Hume rightly finds in commercial society and to mitigate the evils to which Rousseau calls our attention. It is this project—itself a specifically normative project—that shapes Smith's conception of the nature and function of virtue and indeed helps to explain both its similarities and differences from Hume's conception.

In brief, Smith and Hume agree that the primary task of a theory of virtue is to discover a means of restraining our natural predilection to self-preference via an appreciation of our fundamental equality with others. But for Smith this project is informed by an appreciation of commercial society's exacerbation of the dangers of self-preference in a way that Hume's is not—and it is here that we find their basic difference. To some degree, we should take care not to overstate this difference. In several fundamental ways, Smith's virtue theory follows paths blazed by Hume. In particular, Smith follows Hume in arguing that an adequate theory of virtue requires the synthesis of several discrete elements traditionally seen as opposed; in this vein, both Smith's and Hume's virtue theories are distinguished, and indeed connected, by conscious efforts to harmonize ancient virtues and modern virtues, amiable virtues and awful virtues, self-directed virtues and other-directed virtues: balances evident in their respective portraits of individual perfection (cf. TMS 1.1.5.5 and EM 9.2). Hume and Smith furthermore inherited the same question regarding virtue; namely, that concerning the proper balance between self-love and benevolence. Neither, of course, found fully acceptable either the thoroughgoing egocentrism of Hobbes and Mandeville (e.g., TMS 7.2.4) or the thoroughgoing other-directedness of Hutcheson (e.g., TMS 7.2.3.3–13). But for Smith, the questions of how this balance was to be achieved and which virtues were necessary for its preservation were informed by his trepidations regarding commercial society's moral future in a way that Hume's were not.

To begin on the former front: Hume and Smith agree that a chief task of any theory of virtue is to provide a means whereby the propensity to self-preference can be mitigated without doing undue violence to our legitimate and natural sentiments of self-love. Indeed, the establishing of a proper balance between the priority our self-love legitimately demands and the respect for others that recognition of their humanity and essential equality with us demands might be said to be the key project at the heart of their virtue theory. This concern, although less prominent in Hume than Smith, is yet presented explicitly in the *Treatise*. Here, Hume calls attention to that "vicious and disagreeable" propensity to "over-weaning conceit of our own merit," insisting that indeed "nothing is more disagreeable" than this "impertinent, and almost universal propensity of men, to over-value themselves" (T 3.3.2.8–10). Smith likewise calls prominent attention to this propensity and goes on to explain that the problem here is twofold: first, the propensity of individuals to overvalue themselves relative to a standard of genuine worth (see, e.g., TMS 1.1.5.8–10), and, second, the propensity of individuals to overvalue themselves relative to others (see, e.g., TMS 2.2.2.1). On this front, the key problem lies in the predilection of the individual to develop a "sense of his own importance, which no other mortal can go along with" (TMS 1.3.2.5). Yet for Smith, this is not merely a moral failing but one fraught with practical and social dangers insofar as the propensity to prefer one's self and one's well-being to that of others threatens at all times to encourage a sort of egocentrism that subordinates the well-being of others to the pursuit of one's own interests. And it is this concern that, in turn, defines for Smith the chief task of any moral system and any theory of virtue in particular. Three times in TMS Smith explains in precisely the same words that the chief task of the virtuous agent is to "humble the arrogance of his self-love, and bring it down to something which other men can go along with"—a task that can be accomplished only by coming to the difficult appreciation encouraged by the full and conscious and sincere embrace of the truth that each of us is in fact "but one of the multitude in no respect better than any other in it" (TMS 2.2.2.1; TMS 3.3.4; TMS 6.2.2.2).

Smith is under no illusions about how difficult a task this is, calling it indeed the "hardest of all the lessons of morality" (TMS 3.3.8). Yet his insistence that virtue consists in the overcoming of self-preference binds him to an important eighteenth-century tradition that includes Rousseau and Kant as well as Hume (on the basis of the passages cited earlier). But what distinguishes Smith's effort on this front is his specific concern that the conditions of commercial modernity exacerbate self-love, which in turn renders all the more difficult this hardest of all moral challenges. It is for this reason, I think, that Smith dedicated himself to developing a comprehensive account of a virtuous character in the sixth and final edition of TMS. This theory of virtue is itself founded on a set of several virtues—including, most notably, prudence, magnanimity, and benevolence—intended to mitigate certain of the excessive or more pernicious forms of self-love encouraged by commercial modernity.[40] Hume, of course, admires these same virtues as well, but his reasons for doing so (namely, that they meet one of the four criteria of useful to self, useful to others, agreeable to self, agreeable to others) are not Smith's. For Smith, discrete virtues—like a theory of virtue itself—are valuable insofar as they not only command the approbation of an impartial spectator, but also because they help in some particular way to mitigate the challenges of commercial corruption that was such a prominent worry for him if not for Hume. Here, again, Smith's commitment to normativity is evident.

V Epistemology and Religion

A final area in which Smith reveals himself to be simultaneously indebted to and critical of Hume's positions lies in epistemology and religion. It is, of course, true that there are no obvious analogues in Smith's corpus to *Treatise* 1 and the first *Enquiry* or the *Dialogues* and the *Natural History*. Yet Smith's system depends throughout on a certain set of epistemological and theistic claims for which he was clearly indebted to Hume, even if, in his application of such claims, he ultimately reached positions at some remove from Hume's own. In particular, and as I hope to show, Smith's use of Hume's epistemological principles culminates in a skeptical realism true to the new Hume if not the old Hume and, in turn, leads Smith to a defense of theism as a natural belief that is both practically necessary and morally salutary.

We begin again with what Smith can be demonstrably shown to have taken from Hume. As several have noted, Smith's prominent reliance on the language of ideas and impressions early in TMS (TMS 1.1.1.2) and especially his conception of the role of the imagination in the process of the "association" of ideas as a "habit of the imagination" that leads to the establishment of a "customary conception" in the HA (HA 2.7–8) suggest an obvious engagement with Hume's central epistemological categories.[41] None of these ideas was, of course, exclusive to Hume; Smith's account of wonder, for example, bears more than a faint resemblance to Spinoza's,[42] and his account of the association of ideas could have easily been drawn from such Scottish sources as Hutcheson and Turnbull or French sources as Condillac and Helvétius, all of whom were well known to Smith. But, working on the assumption that Hume was in fact the most proximate and likely source for Smith's epistemology, how faithful is he in fact to Hume? This is a particularly difficult question insofar as its answer will depend both on how one reads Smith as well as what side one takes in the debate over the new Hume. But my own sense is that Smith's omnipresent concern with normativity shaped his views on epistemology and, ultimately, prevented him from subscribing to anything like a thoroughgoing or dogmatic skepticism. Instead, his commitments led him to focus less on the question of verifiability that animates true skepticism and to focus instead on the question of the practical implications of our holding certain types of beliefs.

On these grounds, Smith might be seen to emerge as subscribing to the sort of skeptical realism with which Hume has recently if somewhat controversially been associated. A version of the heart of this claim has recently been advanced through a comparison of Smith to Korsgaard's conception of Hume and Butler as "reflective endorsement theorists." On this view, Smith shares with the reflexive endorsement theorists a predilection to substitute for the question "are moral claims true" a more practical question of "are the claims of our moral nature good for human life."[43] A distinct advantage of this view is that it captures Smith's privileging of moral effects over epistemological tests of verifiability—which seems not only true to Smith, but also helps to reinforce his commitment to normativity. It also serves to capture his move away from skepticism and toward naturalism. As I've sought to argue elsewhere, there are good textual reasons to think that Smith, in composing TMS, was engaged with some of the central passages in EM 5 on necessary belief.[44] In employing such concepts in his own system, however, Smith was engaged less in an epistemological investigation per se than in "applying" this epistemology in his moral philosophy.[45] This is perhaps most evident in his ideas on the moral claims of religion.

Herein lies one of perhaps the most potentially interesting spheres of Smith's engagement with Hume. Previous students of their relationship have naturally been interested in the question of what Smith might have inherited from Hume's religious writings. But, in so doing, they have tended to focus on either (a) the degree to which Smith can be said to share Hume's atheism as a matter of personal conviction or (b) his explicit engagement with Hume's argument for state establishment of religion in the course of defending his counterclaim on behalf of religious freedom, culminating in a neutralizing multiplicity of sects (see WN 5.1.g.3–9).[46] The first claim has been a particular focus of Smith scholars and has led to a reading of Smith as having shared Hume's antipathy to revealed religion in particular; Raphael has, in this vein, insisted that Smith's notorious reworking of the passage on Atonement in the sixth edition of the TMS is "a sentence so Humean in tone that it might almost be called a libation to Hume's ghost."[47] Yet more recent scholars have given some reason to question the hard-line view of Smith's stance on revealed religion, in part on the grounds that Smith's emphasis on our creation in God's image does genuine heavy lifting in his theory of respect for the dignity of others.[48] Leaving this aside for now, what has received comparatively less attention is the degree to which he employed Hume's conception of natural and necessary belief to argue for religious belief as a natural belief. This question has been of interest to Hume scholars for some time and has manifested itself in a somewhat different form in recent treatments of the nature and status of "true religion" in Hume.[49] Smith himself, we should note, is keenly interested in the question of the "natural principles of religion," and his distinction between these morally salutary natural principles and their corruption by "factious and party zeal" bears more than a trace of Hume's influence (TMS 3.5.13). Yet, true religion aside, Smith is clearly invested in theism, and his arguments on its behalf eclipse anything to be found in Hume.

Smith's reliance on theistic conceptions of natural religion in a general sense has long been appreciated and has indeed witnessed a recent resurgence.[50] Much of this literature has focused on the degree to which Smith's cosmology depends on a certain view of teleology and final causes. But our present interest is different, given our focus on moral philosophy. It is specifically that Smith, unlike Hume, is invested in defending a certain type of theistic belief as not only natural and necessary, but in fact of practical benefit both to the promotion of the flourishing of the individual and to the promotion of social stability. On the former front, Smith often calls attention to the degree to which theistic belief can help promote the psychological tranquility that he continually suggests is indispensible to genuine happiness. And, on the latter front, Smith also frequently calls attention to the social utility of such belief. This is especially evident in Smith's discussions of belief in the afterlife—a place in which we conspicuously find Smith employing Hume's framework for moral ends far different from Hume's. Insisting that our belief in the afterlife is "deeply rooted in human nature" (TMS 3.2.33; cf. TMS 2.2.3.12)—itself the employment of a trope drawn from Hume's discussions of natural belief—Smith insists that this belief is beneficial as a means of supporting the commitment to justice necessary for social stability. In this sense, belief in an omnipotent and all-seeing deity who will reward the just and punish the unjust serves not only as an extension of Smith's spectator theory to the highest possible plane, but also shows how exactly natural religious belief of a sort can help to promote rather than hinder certain social purposes. Now, it should be said that Smith's conception of the afterlife is not merely instrumental; as has been helpfully demonstrated, Smith believes that our belief in the afterlife is as much the consequence of our "nobler sentiments" and our very love of justice as much as it is of our more instrumental concern for long-term collective stability.[51] But for our purposes vis-à-vis Hume, the crucial point is that religious belief of this sort, even if not justifiable in a strictly epistemic sense, is yet justifiable on moral grounds for Smith in a way it is not for Hume.

VI Conclusion

The foregoing has sought to demonstrate the extent and the sophistication of Smith's engagement with Hume's moral philosophy. In so doing, it has concentrated on the positions taken and arguments given in their published texts. But we would be remiss not to note that these were hardly two thinkers operating at a remove but rather close associates who have been admired by many for "a friendship on both sides founded on the admiration of genius, and the love of simplicity."[52] The history of this relationship is of historical and philosophical interest in its own right; among its significant episodes deserving further study are the story of Smith's supposed surreptitious reading of the *Treatise* as an Oxford student, credited with beginning the process of converting him into "a perfect Humean";[53] the possibility that Hume was the author of an anonymous abstract of TMS published in the *Critical Review* of 1759;[54] an important correspondence between Smith and Hume that includes not only their unvarnished thoughts on Rousseau but also Hume's attempts to "seduce" his friend to come live in Edinburgh;[55] Smith's notorious paean to Hume in the form of an open letter appended to the publication of Hume's autobiography, which Smith said "brought upon me ten times more abuse than the very violent attack I had made upon the whole commercial system of Great Britain" (CAS 208);[56] and Smith's reticence to bring Hume's *Dialogues* to the press in his capacity as Hume's literary executor.[57] This last episode particularly attests to the degree to which their personal relationship, for all its warmth, was not without its complexities. In this, it parallels their philosophical relationship, which, as this chapter has sought to demonstrate, was similarly animated by a simultaneously sympathetic and critical spirit. Smith was clearly sympathetic to Hume's questions, embraced Hume's terms, and thereby accepted the degree to which they staked out the conceptual field on which he would argue. Yet his own contribution to the development of this conceptual apparatus was to bring to its application a sensitivity to its normative applications—a sensitivity, moreover, that attests to Smith's fundamental concern to ameliorate the conditions of modern life as lived in a manner befitting a certain type of authentic Humean.

Acknowledgments

For comments and suggestions on earlier drafts of this essay, the author is extremely grateful to Remy Debes, Chad Flanders, Sam Fleischacker, and Eric Schliesser. For sharing their work in progress and permitting its citation here, the author is very grateful to the aforementioned, as well as to Andrew Corsa, Maria Carrasco, Wim Lemmens, and Geoff Sayre-McCord. The author is also grateful to the Earhart Foundation for a grant that supported work on this chapter.

Abbreviations of Works Cited

EM   *Enquiry Concerning the Principles of Morals.* Edited by Tom L. Beauchamp. Oxford: Clarendon, 1998.

ESY   *Essays: Moral, Political, and Literary.* Revised edition by E. F. Miller. Indianapolis: Liberty Classics, 1985.

T   *A Treatise of Human Nature.* Edited by D. F. Norton and M. J. Norton. Oxford: Clarendon, 2007.

Notes

1. Joseph Cropsey, *Polity and Economy* (South Bend, IN: St. Augustine's Press, 2001 [1st ed. 1957]), 120.
2. D. D. Raphael and A. L. Macfie, "Introduction," in *The Theory of Moral Sentiments* (Indianapolis: Liberty Fund, 1982), 10; Samuel Fleischacker and Vivienne Brown, "Introduction," in *The Philosophy of Adam Smith*, ed. Fleischacker and Brown (London: Routledge, 2010), 4.
3. Raphael and Macfie, "Introduction," 10.
4. Raphael, " 'The True Old Humean Philosophy' and Its Influence on Adam Smith," in *David Hume: Bicentenary Papers*, ed. G. P. Morice (Austin: University of Texas Press, 1977), 23–38, at 37.
5. Spencer J. Pack and Eric Schliesser, "Smith's Humean Criticism of Hume's Account of the Origin of Justice," *Journal of the History of Philosophy* 44 (2006): 47–63, at 53n21.
6. Chad Flanders, "Hume's Death and Smith's Philosophy," in *New Essays on Adam Smith's Moral Philosophy*, ed. Wade L. Robison and David B. Suits (Rochester: RIT Press, 2012), 195–209, at 196; Geoffrey Sayre-McCord, "Hume and Smith on Sympathy, Approbation, and Moral Judgment," *Social Philosophy & Policy* 30 (2013): 208–236, at 210; Fleischacker, "Adam Smith's Moral and Political Philosophy," *The Stanford Encyclopedia of Philosophy* (Spring 2013 edition; last accessed 6 June 2013), ed. Edward N. Zalta; available online at http://plato.stanford.edu/archives/spr2013/entries/smith-moral-political (quote at sec. 3).
7. Nicholas Phillipson, *Adam Smith: An Enlightened Life* (New Haven: Yale University Press, 2010), 2–4, 64–71, 279–281 (quote at 71).
8. Although this point itself demands careful handling. As Eric Schliesser insightfully argues, Smith's reliance on "proto-passions" would seem to commit him "to the existence of the very un-Humean notion of 'preconceptions' " in a way that necessarily renders problematic any simple association of Smith with empiricism; see Schliesser, *Adam Smith* (book ms in progress), Part 1, chapter 3b.
9. Christopher Berry, "Adam Smith's 'Science of Human Nature,' " *History of Political Economy* 44 (2012): 471–492 (quote at 489).
10. Citations to Smith's works are to the Glasgow Edition as published in hardcover by Oxford University Press and in paperback by the Liberty Fund and take the following abbreviations: CAS, *Correspondence of Adam Smith*, ed. E. C. Mossner and I. S. Ross (Indianapolis: Liberty Fund, 1987); EPS, *Essays on Philosophical Subjects*, ed. W. P. D. Wightman and J. C. Bryce (Indianapolis: Liberty Fund, 1982); LER, "Letter to the Edinburgh Review" in EPS; LJ, *Lectures on Jurisprudence*, ed. R. L. Meek, D. D. Raphael,

and P. G. Stein (Indianapolis: Liberty Fund, 1982); ED, "Early Draft" of the *Wealth of Nations*, in LJ; TMS, *Theory of Moral Sentiments*, ed. D. D. Raphael and A. L. Macfie (Indianapolis: Liberty Fund, 1982); WN, *Wealth of Nations*, ed. R. H. Campbell and A. S. Skinner (Indianapolis: Liberty Fund, 1981). Numerical references are in accord with the standard Glasgow system of part, chapter, section, and paragraph references, except in the case of CAS, which is referred to by page number.

11. Raphael and Macfie, "Introduction," 13; Sayre-McCord, "Hume and Smith on Sympathy, Approbation, and Judgment," 216.

12. Fleischacker, "Sympathy in Hume and Smith: A Contrast, Critique, and Reconstruction," in *Intersubjectivity and Objectivity in Adam Smith and Edmund Husserl*, ed. Christel Fricke and Dagfinn Føllesdal (Frankfurt: Ontos Verlag, 2012), 279.

13. Fleischacker, "Sympathy in Hume and Smith," 276; and "Smith's Moral and Political Philosophy," sec. 2.

14. Fleischacker, "Sympathy in Hume and Smith," 291; cf. Sayre-McCord, "Hume and Smith on Sympathy, Approbation, and Judgment," 211–214.

15. Fleischacker, "Smith's Moral and Political Philosophy," sec. 3; on how Smith's emphasis on imagination's role distinguishes his account from Hume's, see David M. Levy and Sandra J. Peart, "Sympathy and Approbation in Hume and Smith: A Solution to the Other Rational Species Problem," *Economics and Philosophy* 20 (2004): 331–349, at 335–337. Smith's own account of the imagination, of course, itself relies heavily on Hume's; see, e.g., Charles L. Griswold, Jr., "Imagination: Morals, Science, and Arts," in *The Cambridge Companion to Adam Smith*, ed. Knud Haakonssen (Cambridge: Cambridge University Press, 2006), 22–56, at 53–54, in addition to the several studies cited at n41 below.

16. Sayre-McCord, "Hume and Smith on Sympathy, Approbation, and Judgment," 215.

17. See, e.g., Levy and Peart's claim that "once sympathy takes the leap to affection we have a motivation for action" ("Sympathy and Approbation in Hume and Smith," 337). For fuller treatments in this vein, see Leonidas Montes, "Das Adam Smith Problem: Its Origins, The Stages of the Current Debate, and One Implication for Our Understanding of Sympathy," Journal of the History of Economic Thought 25 (2003): 63–90, especially 82–85; Montes, Adam Smith in Context (London: Palgrave Macmillan, 2004), 45–55; Schliesser's review of Montes and Raphael in Ethics 118 (2008): 569–575; and Sayre-McCord, "Hume and Smith on Sympathy, Approbation and Judgment," 209. I examine the wider eighteenth-century context of this side of sympathy in "The Eighteenth-Century Context of Sympathy from Spinoza to Kant," in Sympathy, ed. Schliesser (Oxford: Oxford University Press, 2015).

18. Darwall, "Empathy, Sympathy, Care," *Philosophical Studies* 89 (1998): 261–282, at 261 and 264.

19. Darwall, "Empathy, Sympathy, Care," 270, 273; cf. 278–279.

20. Fleischacker, "Smith's Moral and Political Philosophy," sec. 3.

21. See, e.g., Kate Abramson, "Sympathy and the Project of Hume's Second Enquiry," *Archiv für Geschichte der Philosophie* 83 (2000): 45–80; and Remy Debes, "Humanity, Sympathy, and the Puzzle of Hume's Second Enquiry," *British Journal of the History of Philosophy* 15 (2007): 27–57. I offer my take on this question in Hanley, "David Hume and the 'Politics of Humanity,'" *Political Theory* 39 (2011): 205–233.

22. For helpful accounts, see Cropsey, *Polity and Economy*, 122; Raphael, "Hume and Adam Smith on Justice and Utility," *Proceedings of the Aristotelian Society* 73 (1973): 87–103, at 90–5; Marie A. Martin, "Utility and Morality: Adam Smith's Critique of Hume," *Hume Studies* 16 (1990): 107–20, especially 111, 114–5; James Otteson, *Adam Smith's Marketplace of Life* (Cambridge: Cambridge University Press, 2002), 36; Pack and Schliesser, "Smith's Humean Criticism," 47, 53–54.

23. Otteson, *Smith's Marketplace of Life*, 51; Pack and Schliesser, "Smith's Humean Criticism," 53.

24. See especially Pack and Schliesser, "Smith's Humean Criticism," 60–61.

25. See also Pack and Schliesser, "Smith's Humean Criticism," 61–62, which rightly suggests that "Hume himself had opened to the door" to Smith's focus on resentment, calling helpful attention to Hume's references to resentment in EM 3.

26. For an important recent defense of this position, see Craig Smith, "Adam Smith: Left or Right?" *Political Studies* 61 (2013): 784–798.

27. See, e.g., Sen, *The Idea of Justice* (Cambridge, MA: Harvard University Press, 2009), 5–8 (quote at 7).

28. Raphael, *The Impartial Spectator: Adam Smith's Moral Philosophy* (Oxford: Oxford University Press, 2007), 30.

29. Otteson, *Smith's Marketplace of Life*, 187; Sayre-McCord, "Hume and Smith on Sympathy, Approbation, and Judgment," 228.

30. On this problem and its implications, see especially Fonna Forman-Barzilai, *Adam Smith and the Circles of Sympathy* (Cambridge: Cambridge University Press, 2010). For a creative account of Smith's solution to this problem, see especially Maria Alejandra Carrasco, "Adam Smith: Virtues and Universal Principles," *Revue internationale de philosophie* 68 (2014): 223–250.

31. On the mechanics of this process, see especially Otteson, *Smith's Marketplace of Life*, 101–133.

32. Biziou, "Kant et Smith, critiques de la philosophie morale de Hume," *Revue philosophique de la France et de l'étranger* 190 (2000): 449–64, at 459.

33. See, e.g., Forman-Barzilai, *Smith and the Circles of Sympathy*, 106–134.

34. Flanders, "Hume's Death and Smith's Philosophy," 200.

35. Stewart, "Account of the Life and Writings of Adam Smith, LL.D.," in EPS, 320–1; on the Glasgow society, see Phillipson, *Adam Smith*, 141.

36. Phillipson, *Adam Smith*, 66; see also 130–134, 249.

37. I aim to provide an explication of these arguments and references to the relevant literature in *Adam Smith and the Character of Virtue* (Cambridge: Cambridge University Press, 2009), 15–24.

38. Raphael and Macfie, "Introduction," 14; their related editorial note at 52n1 seems meant to refer to T 2.2.5.

39. On Smith's engagement with Rousseau, see most recently Pierre Force, *Self-Interest Before Adam Smith* (Cambridge: Cambridge University Press, 2003); Schliesser, "Adam Smith's Benevolent and Self-Interested Conception of Philosophy," in *New Voices on Adam Smith*, ed. Montes and Schliesser (London: Routledge, 2006), especially 341–51; Dennis Rasmussen, *The Problems and Promise of Commercial Society* (University Park, PA: Penn State University Press, 2008); Hanley, "Commerce and Corruption: Rousseau's Diagnosis and Adam Smith's Cure," *European Journal of Political Theory* 7 (2008): 137–58; Hanley, *Smith and the Character of Virtue*; and Griswold, "Smith and Rousseau in Dialogue: Sympathy, Pitié, Spectatorship and Narrative," in *The Philosophy of Adam Smith*, ed. Brown and Fleischacker, 59–84.

40. The explication of this claim is a principal aim of *Smith and the Character of Virtue*, especially chapters 4–6.

41. See, e.g., A. S. Skinner, "Adam Smith: Science and the Role of the Imagination," in *Hume and the Enlightenment*, ed. W. B. Todd (Edinburgh: Edinburgh University Press, 1974); Raphael, "'True Old Humean Philosophy,'" especially 27–31, 34–7; and Griswold, "Imagination," in *Cambridge Companion*, especially 23 and 26, as cited and discussed in

Hanley, "Scepticism and Naturalism in Adam Smith," in *The Philosophy of Adam Smith*, ed. Brown and Fleischacker, 198–211, at 209n3.

42. Compare, for example, HA 2.3 to Spinoza, *Ethics*, trans. Samuel Shirley (Indianapolis: Hackett, 1992), Pr 52, III.

43. Fleischacker, "Smith's Moral and Political Philosophy," sec. 4.

44. Hanley, "Scepticism and Naturalism in Adam Smith."

45. This is Martin's helpful perspective as well; see Hanley, "Scepticism and Naturalism," especially 210n13.

46. On the latter front, see, e.g., Cropsey, *Polity and Economy*, 96–97; and Fleischacker, "Adam Smith's Reception Among the American Founders, 1776–1790," *William and Mary Quarterly* 59 (2002): 907–910.

47. Raphael, "Adam Smith and 'The Infection of David Hume's Society,'" *Journal of the History of Ideas* 30 (1969): 225–248, at 246–247 (and as appended to the Glasgow edition of TMS at 400–401).

48. See Otteson, *Marketplace of Life*, 59–60, 255–6; Hanley, *Smith and the Character of Virtue*, 142n14, 201; cf. Debes, "Adam Smith on Dignity and Equality," *British Journal of the History of Philosophy* 20 (2012): 109–140.

49. See, e.g., Donald Garrett, "What's True About Hume's True Religion?" *Journal of Scottish Philosophy* 10 (2012): 199–220; and Willem Lemmens, "The Piety of the Sceptic: Hume on 'True Religion' and Atheism" (ms).

50. Recent studies of particular note include Lisa Hill, "The Hidden Theology of Adam Smith," *European Journal of the History of Economic Thought* 8 (2001): 1–29; A. M. C. Waterman, "Economics as Theology: Adam Smith's Wealth of Nations," *Southern Economic Journal* 68 (2002): 907–21; James Alvey, "The Secret, Natural Theological Foundation of Adam Smith's Work," *Journal of Markets and Morality* 7 (2004): 335–61; and several of the contributions in Paul Oslington, ed., *Adam Smith as Theologian* (London: Routledge, 2011).

51. Flanders, "Hume's Death and Smith's Philosophy," 204–205; see also Hanley, "Scepticism and Naturalism," 205–208.

52. Stewart, "Account of the Life," 273.

53. Phillipson, *Adam Smith*, 65–71 (quote at 71); Ian S. Ross, "Adam Smith's Smile: His Years at Balliol College, 1740-46, in Retrospect," in *Philosophy of Adam Smith*, ed. Brown and Fleischacker, 253–62, at 258–259.

54. For this abstract and a defense of Hume's authorship, see David Raynor, "Hume's Abstract of Adam Smith's Theory of Moral Sentiments," *Journal of the History of Philosophy* 22 (1984): 51–79; cf. Raphael and Tatsuya Sakamoto, "Anonymous Writings of David Hume," *Journal of the History of Philosophy* 28 (1990): 271–81; and Ross, *Life of Adam Smith*, 2nd ed. (Oxford: Oxford University Press, 2010), 190–192.

55. The quoted term is Stewart's; see his "Account of the Life," 307.

56. In addition to Flanders, "Hume's Death and Smith's Philosophy," see especially Schliesser, "The Obituary of a Vain Philosopher: Adam Smith's Reflections on Hume's Life," *Hume Studies* 23 (2009): 327–362; and Andrew Corsa, "Modern Greatness of Soul in Hume and Smith," *Ergo* 2 (2015): 27–58.

57. Phillipson says Smith's decision is "not easy to fathom" (*Adam Smith*, 244); I try to do so in my "Skepticism and Imagination," especially 173–174.

CHAPTER 36

···

HUME AND THE CONTEMPORARY "COMMON SENSE" CRITIQUE OF HUME

···

LORNE FALKENSTEIN

THE skepticism, the determinism, and the irreligion of Hume's philosophical works were deeply disturbing for his Scots contemporaries.[1] They read Hume as someone who had asserted that we cannot be assured of the existence of an external world, that we can have no idea of a necessitating power in causes, that we have no free will, that morality is independent of religious commitment, that testimony can give us no assurance of the occurrence of the miracles that support revealed religion, and that we cannot take the evidence of design in nature to prove the existence of an intelligent creator. They typically reacted to these conclusions by charging that they are too absurd to be taken seriously. And they backed up this charge both with ridicule[2] and with appeals to the dictates of common sense.

According to George Campbell (1762), "there are, and must be, in human nature, some original grounds of belief, beyond which our researches cannot proceed, and of which therefore 'tis vain to attempt a rational account." The testimony of good and honest witnesses is included among these grounds (1762: 16–18)[3] and cannot justly be balanced against the possibility of the events they relate (1762: 20–21, 28–30).

James Beattie (1774: 300–307) wrote that, "we cannot admit [Hume's] theory of power and causation, without admitting, at the same time, the grossest and most impious absurdities. Is this a sufficient confutation of it? I think it is."[4] In Beattie's contrary opinion, the existence of causal powers is so evident as not to stand in need of justification.

> [D]o you . . . really think it incumbent on me to prove by argument, that I, and all other men, have a notion of power; and that the efficacy of a cause . . . is in the cause, and not in my mind? Would you think it incumbent on me to refute you with arguments, if you were pleased to affirm, that all men have tails and cloven feet?[5]

Thomas Reid (1764: 61), treating of what he described as Hume's view that "ideas and impressions" are "the sole existences in the universe," charged that it was just as well that Hume had acknowledged that it is only possible for philosophers to sustain this skepticism in "their most speculative hours"[6] because "if they should carry their closet-belief into the world, the rest of mankind would consider them as diseased, and send them to an infirmary" (Reid 1764: 66). He added that,

> However this may be, it is certainly a most amazing discovery, that thought and ideas may be without any thinking being. A discovery big with consequences which cannot easily be traced by those deluded mortals who think and reason in the common track. We were always apt to imagine, that thought supposed a thinker, and love a lover, and treason a traitor: but this, it seems, was all a mistake; and it is found out, that there may be treason without a traitor, and love without a lover, laws without a legislator, and punishment without a sufferer, succession without time, and motion without any thing moved, or space in which it may move: or if, in these cases, ideas are the lover, the sufferer, the traitor, it were to be wished that the author of this discovery had farther condescended to acquaint us, whether ideas can converse together, and be under obligations of duty or gratitude to each other; whether they can make promises and enter into leagues and covenants, and fulfil or break them, and be punished for the breach. If one set of ideas makes a covenant, another breaks it, and a third is punished for it, there is reason to think that justice is no natural virtue in this system. (1764: 63–64)[7]

Were this the extent of Campbell's, Reid's, and Beattie's engagement with Hume, they would have deserved Kant's quip that Hume's critics had "appealed to common sense as an oracle when insight and research [failed them]" and had "[taken] for granted what [Hume] meant to call into doubt while emphatically, and often with great indignation, demonstrating what he had never thought to question" (1783: 259).[8]

Reid's reasons for accepting the existence of external objects were that it is not within our power to doubt their existence, that it would not be prudent to do so, and that we are better off doing so (1764: 412–415)—and this is no more than Hume himself said (EU 12.23/160). And, where Reid said that the belief in the existence of external objects of perception comes from "the mint of nature" (1764: 410), Hume said that we are "carried, by a natural instinct or prepossession, to repose faith in [our] senses; and . . . suppose an external universe, which depends not on our perception" (EU 12.7/151). Although Hume went on to say that this belief cannot stand up to philosophical scrutiny, Reid himself allowed that it cannot be justified by experience or reasoning.[9]

Beattie insisted that it is possible to distinguish between voluntary and involuntary action, which Hume never denied, while taking for granted that we have an idea of what necessarily connects will to action, which Hume had questioned (EU 7.10–20/64–9).

Campbell appealed to common sense like an oracle to justify instinctive belief in testimony.

But as apt as Kant's quip about Hume's critics may sometimes be, it does not do justice to everything they had to say. Their engagement with Hume also took the form of an inquiry into the reasons for Hume's doubts, an attempt to propose alternatives to those reasons, and an attempt to prove that those alternatives are preferable. Campbell attacked Hume's claim that testimony is founded on personal experience (1762: 37–61) and his "*arithmetic,* for the weighing and subtracting of evidence" (1762: 20, 26–30). Beattie did not simply propose to reject Hume's conclusions on account of their absurdity, but also attacked "the doctrine of impressions and ideas" on which they are based (1774: 307, 242–247). Reid's *Inquiry*, which will be a particular focus of the remainder of this paper, attacked Hume's account of testimony, his theory of belief, and his account of mental representation and argued for the superiority of a radically different account of belief and representation. His *Essays on the Intellectual Powers of Man* (IP) also attacked Hume's accounts of memory, abstraction, and geometry; his reasons for denying that we directly perceive external objects; and his reasons for rejecting the causal principle, the design argument, and the idea of power. In what follows, I concentrate on Reid's earlier concerns, both because they are more fundamental and because they were raised during Hume's lifetime—which invites comment on Hume's reception of those concerns.

I Testimony

By the time Reid wrote his *Inquiry*, a considerable body of work had appeared attacking the premises of Hume's essay on miracles, among them the claim that we only learn from experience to place trust in testimony. William Adams wrote in 1752 that each of us feels a "love and reverence for truth" within ourselves and likewise feels tempted to diverge from that natural inclination by certain circumstances. When we trust the testimony of others, it is not because we have learned from experience to trust it, but because we feel that the circumstances in which the testimony is given are those in which we ourselves would tell the truth. Adams further buttressed this claim with the remark that because most of our knowledge of matters of fact (including, presumably, the circumstances under which testimony has proven to be reliable or unreliable) is not obtained personally but drawn from the testimony of others, "It may with more propriety be said, that the evidence of experience is included in that of testimony" (1752: 8–9, 7n).

Campbell followed Adams in claiming that "testimony hath a natural and original influence on belief, antecedent to experience" (1762: 14). Campbell's reasons for this claim were both empirical and, as we might put it, transcendental. Empirically, he maintained that children give unlimited assent to testimony and that their trust in it is only narrowed with experience. "Youth, which is unexperienc'd, is credulous; age, on the contrary, is distrustful. Exactly the reverse would be the case were [Hume's] doctrine just" (1762: 15). Transcendentally, Campbell followed Adams in maintaining that it is only by relying on testimony that we can acquire the experience that proves that testimony is reliable. Distinguishing between personal and derived experience, over which he charged that Hume had equivocated, Campbell claimed that our own personal experience is too limited to put us in a position to place trust in the testimony of others. Were

Hume right, "No testimony ought to have any weight with us, that doth not relate an event, similar at least to some one observation, which we ourselves have had access to make" (1762: 39).

Reid's account of testimony followed in this same vein. Like Campbell, he claimed that it is empirically evident that youth are credulous and adults distrustful (1764: 479). He also embellished the transcendental argument. According to Reid, there are two kinds of language, a "natural language" of gesture, expression, and vocal modulation and an "artificial language" of words with conventionally established meanings. The natural language must be common to all peoples and understood and used instinctively, even by infants. This is because a prior understanding of the natural language is required to understand what people are doing when they teach us words in the artificial language (1764: 472). Another instinct is required to learn an artificial language as well. We instinctively rely on the supposition that people will continue to use words with the same signification as in the past. This supposition could not be justified by experience because experience can only inform us what people have done in the past (and we appreciate that they have it within their power to change their policy). Neither could it arise from any promise they have made to us because any such promise would have to be expressed in words that we already rely on to have the same meaning they had previously. Our trust must therefore be instinctive (1764: 473). It must be complemented by a further trust that people will not lie to us—a trust that is originally unbounded and only limited by subsequent discovery of circumstances in which people prove less than reliable. Otherwise, "no proposition that is uttered in discourse would be believed, until it was examined and tried by reason; and most men would be unable to find reasons for believing the thousandth part of what is told them" (1764: 478–9). Were this the case, children "would be absolutely incredulous; and therefore absolutely incapable of instruction" (1764: 479).

Hume was not impressed. Writing to Hugh Blair in 1761 about a prepublication draft of Campbell's dissertation, which almost certainly contained something like the thoughts just quoted—and in particular the charge that he had equivocated between personal experience and derived experience—he said simply, "No man can have any other experience but his own. The experience of others becomes his only by the credit he gives to their testimony; which proceeds from his own experience of human nature" (LET 1.349). In Hume's view, past experience that people have told us the truth about one thing establishes an association that leads us to believe what they, and others resembling them, say about other, different things. A parent tells a child not to touch a hot object. The child disobeys and gets hurt. The parent then suggests that maybe the next time the child should listen to what she is told. Campbell's and Reid's claims about the absolute incredulity of children notwithstanding, repeated experiences of this sort, gained very early in life, train children to take others' cautions seriously. Because people are instinctively kind to children, as well as concerned to teach them the language, the instances in which children are deliberately deceived by others, either with regard to facts or with regard to the established meanings of words, are rare, producing an early and strong association of people's words with their actual beliefs and sentiments and an early and strong belief that people will continue to use words with the same meaning. Once these associations have been learned, they do not need to be verified for each new reported fact or each new witness we come across.[10] Further experience is only required to mitigate a consequent unbounded credulity and teach us the circumstances in which the strength of belief in testimony ought to be lessened. (Compare Hume's discussion of the immature person's ascent from a "first species of probability," through a tendency to commit the post hoc fallacy, to a disposition to proportion belief to the evidence [T 1.3.12.2–6/130–3].)

As it turns out, one circumstance in which we discover testimony to be unreliable is the circumstance in which it reports an extraordinary event (EU 10.31, 38/126, 128–9). Adams, Campbell, and Reid seem to have taken Hume's recognition of our later learning of this contingent fact to commit him to the view that no one could accept testimony to anything they have not experienced for themselves on at least one occasion. But for Hume, when we come to learn that extraordinary testimony is not to be trusted, what we learn is specifically that testimony that runs counter to *widely reported* experiences (both of ourselves and others) is not to be trusted. Learning that testimony that runs counter only to my own personal experience is not to be trusted would be impossible because I find by personal experience that such testimony is more often reliable than not and were I to start off with that assumption, I would quickly be corrected for the same reason.[11]

II BELIEF

Reid quipped that Hume was unfairly charged with incredulity because it required more faith to accept his account of belief and the associated distinctions among perception, memory, and imagination than that displayed by Athanasius, the great codifier of orthodox Christianity (1764: 488). (Hume [NHR 11.4] had claimed that the orthodox resolution of theological disputes always rests on the side of absurdity.) Elsewhere, Reid declared Hume's account of perception, memory, belief, and imagination to be "as incredible as any thing that ever enthusiasm dreamed, or superstition swallowed" (1764: 50). (Hume used "enthusiasm" and "superstition" as technical terms to describe two "corruptions" of religious belief [in ESY 73–9 and elsewhere].) Reid also declared that "never any thing more absurd was maintained by any Philosopher, than this account of the nature of belief, and of the distinction of perception, memory, and imagination" (1785: 291).

Aside from this sarcasm and abuse, Reid had two serious objections to offer to Hume's account, both of which rest on Hume's claim that impressions, memories, beliefs, and fictions differ in degree of felt liveliness or vivacity. One is that the distinction cannot account for negative beliefs. If to believe in a life after death is to have a lively idea and to have no belief one way or the other is to have the same idea but with no vivacity, then there seems to be no accounting for strong disbelief in life after death (1764: 50–51).

Reid's second objection was that it is incongruous that a diminution in degree of vivacity should lead a thought to stir out of its place in time (as he put it), causing a present impression of an object to turn into a memory of the past existence of that same object. It is even more incongruous that, in losing vivacity, the idea should make leaps and sudden changes of course over the time line—as when the diminution in vivacity of a memory causes it to turn into a belief about the future existence of an object, or a loss of all the vivacity of a belief "carries it out of existence altogether" and turns it into a fiction (1764: 486–488).

In Reid's contrary estimation, belief is too simple to be defined (1764: 50; 1785: 227), but we can say that it is expressed in language by a proposition, whereby something is affirmed or denied (1785: 228), that propositions rather than ideas are the objects of belief (1785: 471), and that belief involves an act of assent to a proposition (1764: 51).

Reid's view of belief stands in stark contrast to Hume's early claim that acts of judging and reasoning do not "exceed" acts of conceiving one or more objects and that the belief that arises from judgment and reasoning is no different from the belief in the existence of a single object. All of these beliefs have only to do with the manner in which objects are conceived (T 1.3.7.5, n/96–97n). However, this claim, which occurs only once in a footnote to the *Treatise* and was never repeated, is something of an overstatement. EU 4.1/25 draws a sharp distinction between the "affirmation" of "propositions" asserting intuitively or demonstratively evident relations of ideas and the belief in matters of fact.

Hume's distinctions among perception, memory, belief, and imagination are also more complex than Reid made them out to be. Hume certainly did describe belief as a more forceful or vivid conception of an idea, and he certainly did rank impressions, memories, beliefs, and imaginings in terms of their degrees of force and vivacity. Occasionally, he supplemented the terms "force" and "vivacity" with others that are neither synonymous with them nor with one another (e.g., "solidity," "firmness," "steadiness"). But, as he made clear (EU 5.12/48-9), these are a variety of expressions that he employed while struggling to describe what he more generally identified as a particular "manner" of conceiving an object, distinct from the manner in which it is conceived when it is merely imagined. This manner of conception involves a number of distinct "dispositions," as Hume put it (T 1.3.8.2/98). In a passage that is often described as a retraction or set of afterthoughts (T 1.3.7.7/628-9), even though it was published in 1740 in the third volume of T[12] and reiterated without any substantive change in all of the eleven subsequent lifetime editions of EU, Hume described belief as something that draws and focuses attention ("renders more present," "weighs more in the thought," "has more force and influence," "appears of greater importance," "fixes the attention"); arouses passion ("elevates the spirits"); inspires deliberation ("has a superior influence on the imagination"); and serves as "the governing principles of all our actions" (EU 5.12/48-9).[13] It is these four dispositions, rather than the more commonly discussed (but vague) "force and vivacity" that accurately characterize Humean belief.[14] But because it feels a certain way to be in these dispositional states, Hume also described belief as a sentiment or feeling annexed to an idea (EU 5.12/48)—even though what it really is that we feel is not some weird, inexplicable thing called "vivacity" but an alteration in the strength of the mental dispositions involving the idea: a pull on the direction of our attention, an elevation of particular passions, a distraction to our other deliberations, and an impact on our inclinations to act.

It is uncontroversial that perception and memory have these same effects on our dispositions, although to a greater degree. The objects of perception do this more strongly than do those of memory. And those of memory generally do so more strongly than those that we only believe to exist on the basis of causal inference, whereas those we only imagine do so hardly at all or only in pathological cases. Hume was not expressing any unusual or exceptional insight in mentioning these facts or in ranking the strength of influence of perception, memory, causal or probabilistic inference, and bare imagination accordingly. Such originality as his account of belief has rests with its claim that causal inference is to be accounted for as a consequence of the transfer of some of the strength of the dispositions aroused by impressions and memories to ideas of objects that have been associated with them in the past.

In all other circumstances, Reid himself insisted that the proper method of investigation in the science of the mind is the method of induction, whereby general rules are derived from observation, and the temptation to form hypotheses that might explain why those rules are as they are is resisted (1764: 156–157, 287–288, 314–316). Given that it is introspectively obvious that imagination, belief, memory, and perception are increasingly more "vivacious," in the sense of having an increasingly greater influence on attention, passion, deliberation, and action, it is odd that Reid would not have rested content with allowing that this, too, is an "original principle of human nature" that is ultimately no more explicable than why an impact on the tongue should produce a sensation of taste whereas an impact on the eye should produce both a sensation of color and a belief that the cause of that sensation lies somewhere indeterminately far away in the direction pointed to by a line originating from the affected part of the retina and passing through the center of the eye (1764: 292–6, to cite one of his favorite examples). To lay down an a priori expectation that the relative degree to which perception, memory, belief, and imagination affect our dispositions ought to reflect where the objects of these faculties are placed in time is as arbitrary and unaccountable as anything Reid pretended to find in Hume's account of the faculties.

The complexities of Hume's account of belief in matters of fact and existence also put him in a position to address Reid's objection concerning negative beliefs. The key to Hume's approach to this problem is already supplied by a passing comment in T 1.1.5.6/15 to the effect that the idea of an object and the idea of the non-existence of that same object are resembling in that both involve the idea of the object, "tho' the latter excludes the object from all times and places, in which it is supposed not to exist." The way an idea excludes an object from a time and place is explained over the course of Hume's meditations on how "chances" and "inconstant causes" determine the mind to modify the strength of its beliefs when it reasons concerning probability of outcomes (T 1.3.11-12/124-42; EU 6/56-9). "[A]s contrary views are incompatible with each other, and 'tis impossible the object can at once exist comformable to both of them, their influence becomes mutually destructive, and the mind is determin'd to the superior only with that force, which remains after substracting the inferior." (T 1.3.12.19/138). To believe an object to be "excluded" from a place at a time is accordingly to believe some incompatible object to exist in that place at that time, and to recognize the incompatibility of the object believed to exist with the object denied to exist. This accords nicely with Hume's account of belief as a consequence of causal inference. On that account, the objects of belief do not just exist or fail to exist. Because belief arises from causal inference, and causes are prior to their effects in time and contiguous to them in space, the objects of belief are always conceived to exist at a place and time relative to the effects or causes from which they are inferred. This provides Hume with the ability to account for negative belief as the vivacious idea of an incompatible object at the given place and time and suspension of belief as the lack of a vivacious idea of any sort. If A testifies that fire was ignited by a touch from ice, and B believes this testimony, it is because B's ideas of liquid bursting into flame are enlivened by A's testimony.[15] If C disbelieves A's testimony, it is because A's testimony that an icicle touched some lamp oil does more to enliven C's incompatible ideas of the continued quiescence of the lamp oil in virtue of C's past experience of the effects of contact with icicles. If D neither believes nor disbelieves A's testimony, it is because D's sense of the strength of the testimony that the lamp oil was ignited by a spark passed through an icicle is counterbalanced by D's inclination to infer from past experience that such impure spirits could not be ignited by attempting to use an icicle to throw the kind of electric current that could be generated with the apparatus in use at that time, leaving D with no inclination to form lively ideas of either sort.[16]

III REPRESENTATION

Reid understood Hume to have maintained that the immediate objects of thought when we perceive, remember, believe, or imagine are not external objects but internal, mental "images and pictures," called sensations, impressions, and ideas, that exist only insofar as they are perceived (1764: v, vii–viii). Moreover, we can have no conception or thought of anything that does not resemble these immediate objects (1764: 165–166).

In his *Inquiry*, Reid maintained that this view, which he dubbed the "ideal theory" or "theory of ideas," is a "hypothesis" that had been accepted without proof by the entire philosophical tradition leading up to Hume (1764: vii, 149, 165–166). He attributed this surprising oversight to an inadequate study of mental phenomena (1764: 159–162). He further took the philosophical tradition culminating in T to have demonstrated that the hypothesis leads to absurd and unacceptable conclusions, notably skepticism about the existence of an external world and a persisting self. This is tantamount to a *reductio ad absurdum*, which justifies rejecting the ideal theory and looking for an alternative—one founded in our introspective experience of our own mental operations (1764: viii–ix, 32–34).

But the ideal theory was no mere hypothesis. Hume had offered two arguments for the claim that the immediate objects of perception are not external objects: that the objects of perception change as a consequence of the operation of causes that can only plausibly be supposed to have an effect on the perceiver, such as a decision to move to a different viewing position (EU 12.9/152), and that the qualities that are supposed to be primary and real qualities of external objects can only be conceived as modifications of other qualities that are universally acknowledged to have a merely subjective existence (EU 12.15/154).

To his credit, Reid eventually acknowledged that arguments had been given for the ideal theory. But his engagement with those arguments, among them Hume's argument from the relativity of perception at EU 12.9/152, only occurred in work published after Hume's death (1785: 203–13, esp. 206–123).[17] Fortuitously, however, the independent investigation into the nature of representation that Reid undertook in his earlier *Inquiry* led to results that challenged Hume's other argument for the ideal theory arising from the inseparability of primary and sensible qualities. These results did come to Hume's attention, and Hume responded to them privately.[18]

III.1 Reid's Alternative Account of Representation

According to Reid, immediate sensory experience is not one thing but two, sensation and perception. Although the two are radically distinct, their co-occurrence has caused them to be confused with one another, not only by philosophers, but even in common speech. It is only with care and pains that they can be introspectively distinguished (1764: 407–8).

In sensation, the mind feels a certain way. Tactile sensations of pain and pleasure are paradigmatic, but even in smelling, tasting, hearing, and seeing, the sensation is properly understood to be the experience of the way it feels to smell, taste, hear, and see. Sensations are, accordingly, mental states that exist only in the mind and only insofar as they are felt by the mind (1764: 408–409, 40–42).

Description of most sensations is rendered difficult because the words for smells, tastes, and sounds, as well as for heat and cold (although in Reid's estimation, not for colors [1764: 195]), are used ambiguously. Sometimes they refer to the state the mind is in when it smells, tastes, hears, or feels heat or cold. More often, however, they are used to name the thing that causes us to experience these feelings (1764: 73–75, 84–85). It takes some care to avoid false paradoxes that can arise from failing to distinguish the two. For instance, a mind that has a sensation of heat or sweetness does not become hot or sweet. That is, it does not take on the qualities that enable objects to cause minds to feel hot or smell sweet. But it does come to be in the sensory state we are in when we feel or smell an object that has these qualities (1764: 83–84).

In perception, by contrast, the mind does not feel anything but instead performs two acts. It performs the act of conceiving of an object and the act of believing in the present existence of this object. These acts are mental operations that likewise exist only in the mind and only insofar as the mind performs them. But both of them have the character of being about or directed toward an object. This object is distinct from and independent of the acts that refer to it. As Reid put it, when I perceive a tree, the object has roots, leaves, and branches, but the acts of conceiving of and believing in the present existence of this object do not have roots, leaves, and branches. Although the acts of conceiving and believing may exist only in the mind and only insofar as the mind performs them, it does not follow that the object of these acts only exists there or at that time (1764: 409–410).

Reid never explained how a mental act performs the trick of making reference to an object, but his sharp distinction between acts of conception and belief and their objects makes one thing clear: the acts do not refer to their objects by resembling them.

Reid was also explicit that the objects of perception are not sensations. Although we are conscious of our sensations, they are never the objects of perception.[19] Sensations each have their own unmistakable character. It feels a certain way to be in pain from a burn to the finger, and this is different from the way it feels to smell a rose. But the objects of perception can be characterless. It is possible to perceive nothing more than that they exist without perceiving their number, their location, or any of their other qualities, as when, upon hearing a strange noise, we perceive that there must be something that causes the noise without conceiving where it is or what it might be like (1764: 40–42, 111–113).

It is likewise possible, in misperception, illusion, and hallucination, to believe in the existence of an object or objects that have different characteristics from those possessed by the objects that actually surround us. But these are exceptional cases. Reid maintained that our sense organs were designed by God to perform reliably in normal circumstances. An aspect of this design is that we are innately so constituted that, on the occasion of feeling a sensation, we also perceive features of the external objects that normally cause that sensation (1764: 410–415).

In the case of some sensations (smell, taste, sound), all we perceive is that the object exists. In the case of others (vision), we perceive the direction in which each of its parts lies from our current position but not their distance. In yet others (touch), we perceive the distance and the direction of each of the parts from one another (1764: 292–296).

Regardless of whether perception is veridical or mistaken, the qualities that we perceive objects to have (other than existence at the current moment) are not qualities that could possibly be possessed by any sensation. The qualities we perceive objects to have are those arising from the primitive visual perception of position relative to the eye and the primitive tactile perception of position relative to other things: qualities like hardness, shape, size, extension, and motion. But sensations are feelings. It might feel a certain way to touch a hard object, but the feeling is a simple and unanalyzable mental state and, as such, can have no location (1764: 163, 204–205, 114–122, 129–132, 135–138, 538–539).

There is, accordingly, no systematic error in perception. We do not perceive only our own internal states, which we mistake for external things, and we are not confronted with a question of how we could know that there is any such thing as an external world. Instead, we directly perceive mind-independent objects,[20] and the mind-independent objects we perceive are generally the ones that actually do exist, and they have at least the qualities that we conceive them to have. In conceiving these objects, we do not perceive a "conception" or picture or impression or idea that exists only in our minds. Instead, an act of conceiving that exists only in our minds leads us to be directly aware of an object entirely distinct from us and anything we find within ourselves. In the case of veridical perception, we are directly aware of an object that actually exists in space outside of us; in the case of memory, of an object that no longer exists; and in the case of misperception or imagination, of an object that does not exist anywhere, not even in the mind.[21]

III.2 The "Experimentum Crucis"

In contrast to Reid, Hume maintained that the feelings we get on the occasion of touching or seeing objects are themselves disposed in space.[22] Minimally visible points of color (colors being sensations and not qualities of external objects) are disposed alongside one another on a visual field. Minimally tangible itches, pricks, pains, and the like are also disposed alongside one another.[23] The perception of position is the perception of the position of visual and tactile sensations relative to one another. The perception of hardness, shape, size, and motion reduces to the perception of compound visual and tangible sensations and how they behave over time.[24] Spatially disposed collections of visual and tactile sensations represent material objects by resembling them,[25] and ideas represent spatially disposed collections of visual and tactile sensations by copying them.[26] Conception does not involve the ultimately mysterious performance of an act that manages to make reference to an object despite being in no way like that object or associated with any other perception that is.[27] To conceive of something, and consequently to remember, believe, or imagine it, is simply for an image or copy of that thing to occur in the mind.[28] And nothing can be conceived or felt but spatially and temporally disposed sensations, copies of spatially and temporally disposed sensations, and the passions they arouse.[29]

At the basis of Hume's and Reid's opposed outlooks is a disagreement over the nature of the objects that we immediately perceive to be disposed in space. Are they tactile and visual sensations, like itches and colors? If not, then the immediate objects of perception are not our own sensations. But if the primary qualities are qualities of collections of spatially disposed sensations, then the argument for the ideal theory drawn from the inseparability of primary and sensible qualities (EU 12.15/154) succeeds.

Reid declared himself willing to take the outcome of the entire dispute over the validity of the ideal theory to be determined by the answer to this question.

> This I would therefore humbly propose as an *experimentum crucis*, by which the ideal system must stand or fall; and it brings the matter to a short issue: Extension, figure, motion, may, any one, or all of them, be taken for the subject of this experiment. Either they are ideas of sensation, or they are not. If any one of them can be shown to be an idea of sensation, or to have the least resemblance to any sensation, I lay my

hand upon my mouth, and give up all pretence to reconcile reason to common sense in this matter, and must suffer the ideal scepticism to triumph. (1764: 152)

Reid offered two reasons for maintaining that this *experimentum crucis* turns out in his favor. One was an appeal to a thought experiment (1764: 139–144). We are asked imagine a blind person[30] who, by "some strange distemper," has lost "all the experience and habits and notions he had got by touch; not to have the least conception of the existence, figure, dimensions, or extension, either of his own body or of any other; but to have all his knowledge of external things to acquire anew, by means of sensation, and the power of reason, which we suppose to remain entire." Reid's claim was that, placed in this position, there is no way the subject could acquire the idea of any primary quality, regardless of what sensation or sequence of sensations the person is supposed to experience. It is only when we grant that the person is innately so constituted as to acquire conceptions of objects distinct from any sensation, combination of sensations, or consequence that can be inferred from sensation by reasoning or association that we can account for the acquisition of these ideas.

However, Reid did not conduct his thought experiment very thoroughly. The experiences he allowed his blind person to have as a means of constructing concepts of position, extension, motion, and hardness are being pricked by a pin, being hit by a blunt object, being pressed by the surface of an extended object, being stroked with an object, attempting to move a limb without success, and successfully moving a limb. It is not surprising that these experiences should be too impoverished to do the job. If you are only ever allowed to feel one thing at a time, it is hardly surprising that you should not be able to form a concept of how multiple, simultaneously present tactile sensations are disposed in space.

Reid's second reason for maintaining that the *experimentum crucis* turns out his way was an appeal to the results of careful introspection. "[W]e need not surely consult Aristotle or Locke, to know whether pain be like the point of a sword," he wrote. "I have as clear a conception of extension, hardness, and motion, as I have of the point of a sword; and, with some pains and practice, I can form as clear a notion of the other sensations of touch, as I have of pain. When I do so, and compare them together, it appears to me clear as daylight, that the former are not of kin to the latter, nor resemble them in any one feature. They are as unlike, yea as certainly and manifestly unlike, as pain is to the point of a sword" (1764: 150).

But introspection is not as clearly and unambiguously on Reid's side as he claimed. The point of a sword is composed of a number of particles disposed in a certain configuration. Many pains are likewise disposed at locations relative to one another. When a mosquito bites me, I feel the bite disposed at a certain location relative to my feelings of my other body parts. Reid's claim that pains are states of feeling had by minds notwithstanding, I have never felt tempted to reach into my mind to slap at a mosquito bite that I felt to be located there. The sensation itself is felt to be at a particular location relative to others, and it is that location I aim at.

Reid tried to explain this appearance away by telling me that I do not, in fact, experience my tactile sensations to be disposed in space. Instead, I am innately so constituted that, on the occasion of being touched at a certain point, I both experience a certain sensation and perceive a "disorder" in a certain part of my body to be the cause of the sensation. Because the two go so constantly together, I confuse the one with the other (1764: 295–296).

Although this is certainly a way of explaining the appearances, it is not obvious to introspection, even very careful introspection, nor did Reid suggest any experiments that might be performed to prove his claim.[31] It is an ad hoc assertion tacked on to save the theory rather than a report on the phenomena of tactile experience.

The really hard case remains to be considered. Few things are as obvious to immediate perceptual experience as that the phenomenally evident qualities we experience in vision are extended and disposed at various locations on a visual field. To establish that the *experimentum crucis* turns out his way, Reid would have had to show that this is not in fact the case. Instead, it is introspectively obvious that colors are not extended or located relative to one another, do not move, and cannot be seen to be more or less resistant to deformation when they collide with one another. They are no more located in space than passions of joy or surprise or sensations of smell. The extended objects of visual perception, for their part, are colorless shapes that are at most believed to contain hidden qualities that cause our unextended, locationless color sensations. They are not "gilded or stained" over their surfaces with the perceptually evident qualities of our visual sensations.

When confronted with the challenge of justifying his law of visual positioning, Reid appealed to a series of introspective experiments conducted by Scheiner (1764: 296–308) that lead us to understand why the phenomena of vision dictate that the law must be stated in this way but no other. But when confronted with the challenge of justifying his claims that the objects of visual perception have no color and that colors have no location or extension, Reid's response was not to produce introspective evidence that might convince us that his view of the character of visual experience is correct. Instead, he pontificated on the ordinary meaning of color terminology in an attempt to put himself in a position to reinterpret the observation reports made by ordinary people as consistent with his theory. According to Reid, whereas our words for smells, tastes, sounds, and heat and cold are at least ambiguous, sometimes referring to what it feels like to experience the sensation, but more often referring to the quality in external objects that causes it, there is no ambiguity in our words for colors. No one, not even the vulgar, ever uses words for colors—such as "white" or "scarlet" or "colored"—to name the phenomenally evident qualities we experience in vision. Instead, these words are only ever used to name the invisible and (for the eighteenth century) entirely unknown features of the physical constitution of external objects that cause us to experience the phenomenally evident qualities (1764: 190–6).[32] Consequently, when ordinary people describe an extended and located patch as "red" or "colored," they do not mean to say that the phenomenally evident quality they feel in visual sensation is extended and located. They only ever mean to say that the invisible quality in external objects that causes their sensation is extended and located. Shocking though it may be to painters, gardeners, interior decorators, clothiers, and cosmeticians (and even more so to their customers whom they have convinced to spend considerable sums of money on such things), the phenomenally evident qualities we experience in vision are, in Reid's words, "so little interesting, that they are never attended to, but serve only as signs." They "have no names" nor are they even "made the objects of thought" (1764: 195). The "colors" we are concerned with and name are all invisible (1764: 196–197), and it is left to scientists to conjecture what they are like (1764: 199, cf. 111–113). Ordinary people think nothing more about them than that they are causes of nameless, uninteresting phenomenal qualities.

III.3 Hume's Reply to the Experimentum Crucis

Hume would have none of this. Writing to Hugh Blair about a prepublication draft of portions of Reid's *Inquiry* he observed, "The Author [Reid] supposes, that the Vulgar do not believe the sensible Qualities of Heat, Smell, Sound, & probably Colour to be really in the Bodies, but only their Causes or something capable of producing them in the Mind [cf. 1764: 111–113, 204–205]. But this is imagining the Vulgar to be Philosophers & Corpuscularians from their Infancy. You know what pains it cost Malebranche & Locke to establish that Principle.... And indeed Philosophy scarce ever advances a greater Paradox in the Eyes of the People, than when it affirms that Snow is neither cold nor white: Fire hot nor red" (Hume 1762).[33]

Hume did not believe that philosophers have come to occupy a different epistemological standpoint than ordinary people. Philosophers not only grew up as ordinary people but relapse back into the views of ordinary people as soon as they leave the study (EU 12.23/160). Each of us is therefore in a good position to say what the common folk think. In Hume's view, most of us would agree that we use color terminology to refer to qualities that are evident to us in visual perception. Moreover, we perceive the boundaries of objects only by perceiving contrasts in these evident qualities. "An extension, that is neither tangible nor visible, cannot possibly be conceived: And a tangible or visible extension, which is neither hard nor soft, black nor white, is equally beyond the reach of human conception" (EU 12.15/154). In arguing that we cannot so much as conceive the edges delimiting the objects of perception without conceiving them as defined by contrasting, spatially located, evident qualities, Hume was appealing to introspective evidence at least as strong and compelling as any Reid was able to invoke.

III.4 Beattie's Attack on the Ideal Theory

Beattie attempted to buttress Reid's appeal to introspection with a number of examples of his own, intended to exhibit the absurdity of supposing that "a thought of the mind should be endued with all, or any, of the qualities of matter" (1774: 244). He charged that if ideas are exact resemblances of impressions and hence of objects (supposing that the only objects we perceive are our impressions, and our ideas can only copy them), then ideas must have all the properties of material objects as we know them. Ideas of heat must be hot; ideas of eating must satisfy hunger and be nourishing; ideas of white must be white; ideas of a roaring lion must be roaring; ideas of an ass must be hairy, long-eared, sluggish, patient of labor and addicted to thistles; ideas of solidity must be solid; and ideas of extension must be extended. In particular, the idea of any particular extended object must have the same dimensions as that object. But if ideas are taken to be located in the mind, and the mind is taken to be located in "a body of no extraordinary dimensions," then we are compelled to accept that objects occupying millions of cubic feet, such as the idea of a mountain, must be contained in a space only a small fraction of that size (1774: 242–247). In Beattie's opinion, these consequences are all patently absurd.

This opinion does not stand up to scrutiny. As anyone who has suffered from an ear worm knows, ideas of sound can be loud or soft, high- or low-pitched, harmonious or discordant. Ideas of pain aroused by stories or images of torture and wounds can be painful. Ideas of the taste of cinnamon or the smell of diesel fuel have something of the quality of the original impressions.

Although ideas can be like sensations, they do not produce sensations. If we balk at the thought that an idea of cinnamon might itself be cinnamon-tasting, it is for the reason that Beattie's colleague, Reid, pointed out: that the way it feels to taste cinnamon is one thing, and the qualities that cause the impression of this taste are something else. We should not, on Hume's account any more than Reid's or Beattie's, expect that the idea of cinnamon would be cinnamon-tasting in the sense that it would be the sort of thing that suffices to produce sensations of the taste of cinnamon. If the ideas of food had by a starving or dieting person are not nourishing or satisfying, neither are the impressions. It is rather the ingestion of food that is the common cause both of impressions of taste and of the nourishment of the body and the consequent cessation of impressions of craving produced by hunger. To claim that mere ideas of ingesting food ought to produce impressions of taste and cause impressions of craving to cease is to claim that ideas ought to be able to produce sensations, which is not a consequence of Hume's account. Similarly, to suggest that an idea of heat must be hot, meaning thereby that it must cause impressions of shivering to cease and produce sensations of sweating, of an uncomfortable closeness and heaviness in the air, of difficulty breathing, and so on, is to similarly expect that ideas should produce sensations. On the other hand, to suggest that an idea of heat must be hot—meaning thereby that it is the sort of thing that, in virtue of past experience, is regularly followed by more or less vivid ideas of what it would feel like to sweat, have difficulty breathing, and the like—is not to suggest anything surprising or absurd.

Beattie further suggested that it is absurd that an idea of white must be white. But he did not say why. He likely held the view that ideas are mental states and that mental states are not the sort of things that could be white. But no eighteenth-century thinker accepted that the phenomenally evident quality of white is actually extended over the surfaces of external objects. It would then follow that the phenomenally evident quality of whiteness exists neither in the mind, as a quality of a mental state, nor in the external world, as a quality of an object. But few things are as obvious to "common sense" as that this phenomenal quality does exist somewhere—and exists there as extended over various locations. On Hume's account, whatever the phenomenally evident but also obviously extended quality of white is, that is what we call an impression or an idea. And wherever these extended, colored, felt, phenomenally evident qualities exist, be it in the external world, in the mind, or somewhere else, that is where impressions and ideas exist.

Beattie's charge that there is something absurd about taking white ideas to be not only white but also extended, perhaps for millions of miles, is no easier to make out. It neglects to appreciate that size is not an absolute quality but a relation between objects, determined by juxtaposition. In the case where the size of ideas is in question, the only juxtaposition that is possible is that with other ideas. For an idea to be an inch in length is for it to extend to the one inch mark on the *idea* of a tape measure. Where impressions of vision are concerned, the extended impression of an interval on a tape measure is no fixed quantity but can take up a greater or less angular distance on the visual field, depending on the distance from which it is viewed. (Given that the impressions being measured are proportionally smaller at greater distances, this variation does not change the results of measurement.) Something similar holds for ideas in imagination.

Beattie's further charge that there is something absurd about a perception that occupies a million cubic feet being contained in our heads makes the questionable assumptions that ideas are located in the mind and that the mind is located in the brain. But even if we grant these assumptions, the absurdity is still difficult to make out. It gains all its appeal from an elementary mistake. We have perceptions of our own heads. Rather than consider these perceptions of our heads to be among the many other perceptions that we have, Beattie made the mistake of considering all of our other perceptions to exist somewhere in our perceptions of our heads, and he further took the size of our perceptions of our heads relative to our perceptions of measuring tapes to mark off the maximum volume available to contain all of our perceptions. But if Hume was right, we have no perception of the thing that contains our perceptions (it is not our perception of our heads) and no means of measuring its size (T 1.4.6.4/253).

Granting that impressions and ideas can be colored and extended, Beattie's other attempts to reduce Hume's position to absurdity collapse. The idea of a roaring lion is not a roaring idea but a collection of ideas, some of which are colors disposed in the shape of a lion, others of which are the sound of a roar. To be hairy or long-eared is just to have a certain shape, and if visual and tangible impressions and ideas are disposed in space, they can certainly be disposed in the configuration of hairs or long ears. The idea of an animal addicted to thistles is likewise reducible to a description of how shapes move over time. The same can be said of the idea of solidity. Something that is solid is something that resists compression. That is, it is a shape that is such that continues to occupy the same volume when other shapes move toward it and impact it from all sides. Considered as such, solidity is something that can be seen as well as felt (as Hume, T 1.4.4.13/230, pointed out). Granting that ideas and impressions can be extended and moving, there can be no absurdity in considering them to be solid.

Hume never replied to Beattie's criticisms. However, in one piece of private correspondence that has come down to us, he referred to him as a "bigotted silly Fellow" (LET 2.301). Beattie was no bigot in our sense of the term.[34] But he was dogmatically committed to the dualist hypothesis that the mind is an immaterial substance, from which it follows that sensations, considered as mental states, cannot possibly be extended or located. Reid, for his part, never argued for this hypothesis and seldom even acknowledged his acceptance of it (but see 1764: 538–539). But it is hard not to conclude that it was a tacit reliance on this hypothesis, rather than any appeal to the evidence of introspection, that made him so convinced that no sensation could possibly be extended or located. The same criticism that Reid leveled against Berkeley and Hume (1764: 162, 165–6) could therefore be retorted against him: that he had argued from a hypothesis (dualism) against fact (the introspective evidence for the extension and location of visual and tactile sensations).

IV Conclusion

Between 1748 and 1757, Hume "cast anew"[35] his early *Treatise of Human Nature* in the form of four philosophical treatises, EU, DP, EM, and NHR, the first of which he revised no less than eleven times, both before and after Campbell, Reid, and Beattie published their attacks on his philosophy. The revisions that Hume made on these multiple occasions are almost uniformly inconsequential, with the most consequential being made early on, before Campbell, Reid, or Beattie had composed or published their work. Although Hume announced on numerous occasions that he had resolved never to reply to his critics,[36] and although the history of inconsequential emendations to his work shows that he was not much given to changing his mind, we know that he could be persuaded to shut up about things (even if quietly persisting in the same opinions). He persuaded himself to suppress his speculations about the self (TA 10–21/623, 633–636). Lord Stanhope persuaded him not to publish an essay recasting his thoughts on geometry (LET 2.253). Critical reactions to the first volumes of his *History of England* (likely those published by Daniel MacQueen) led him to make three substantial cuts to his discussions of the psychology of religious belief in that work.[37] But there are no cuts in later editions of EU to Hume's discussions of testimony, belief, the nature of impressions and ideas, or the inseparability of primary and sensible qualities. Campbell, Reid, and Beattie did not fail to engage Hume's tenets, as Kant thought. They understood what Hume meant to say, and they offered criticisms that went to the foundations of his views. But Hume seems to have remained confident that he had said everything he needed to say to make a compelling case before the public. In this essay, I have attempted to explain why he was justified in that confidence.

ABBREVIATIONS OF WORKS CITED

Ad   "Advertisement." An advertisement originally appearing in the front matter of the second volume of the 1777 edition of ESY, at the time entitled *Essays and Treatises on Several Subjects*. London: T. Cadell. Reprinted in EU front matter.

DP   *A Dissertation on the Passions*. In T. Beauchamp, ed. *A Dissertation on the Passions; The Natural History of Religion*. Oxford: Clarendon Press, 2008.

EM   *Enquiry Concerning the Principles of Morals*. Edited by Tom L. Beauchamp. Oxford: Clarendon, 1998.

ESY   *Essays: Moral, Political, and Literary*. Revised edition by E. F. Miller. Indianapolis: Liberty Classics, 1985.

EU   *An Enquiry Concerning Human Understanding*. Edited by T. L. Beauchamp. Oxford: Clarendon, 2000.

LET   *The Letters of David Hume*, 2 Vols. Edited by J. Y. T. Greig. Oxford: Clarendon Press, 1932.

NHR   *The Natural History of Religion*. In T. Beauchamp, ed. *A Dissertation on the Passions; The Natural History of Religion*. Oxford: Clarendon Press, 2008.

T   *A Treatise of Human Nature*. Edited by D. F. Norton and M. J. Norton. Oxford: Clarendon, 2007.

TA   *An Abstract of a Treatise of Human Nature*. Reprinted in **T**.

NOTES

1. See Fieser's (2000) collection of early responses to Hume, most of which are highly critical. In this paper, I focus on three critics who wrote in what has since been called the "common sense" tradition.
2. Thomas Reid's *Essays* (1785) contains an attempt to argue that ridicule is properly employed in response to those who would deny principles of common sense (567–569). For discussion, see Grandi (2008); for Hume's view, see LET 1.186 (to John Stewart, February 1754).
3. Campbell further supported this claim by observing that we place implicit faith in the reliability of our memories when drawing conclusions from past experience, even though memory is evidently not infallible and cannot be justified by experience of its reliability without falling into a vicious circle. Because Hume nonetheless relied on memory in drawing inferences from cause and effect, Campbell considered that he ought to have recognized testimony to have equal authority.
4. The "gross absurdity" Beattie had in mind is Hume's attempt to reduce causality to precedence, contiguity, and an impulse of the mind—something that he was content to dismiss with the claim that it would entail that one of two contiguous houses is the cause of the other and that night and day are causes of one another. A view of two contiguous houses does not satisfy the condition that a cause be precedent to its effect, but Beattie tried to get around this by claiming that one of the houses was built "last summer," whereas the other was built "two years ago." He did not explain how this would suffice to produce,

even now, the experience of a constant priority of impressions of the one house to those of the other. Similarly, taking "night" to consist of an experience of the darkness of the sky and "day" of light, Beattie offered no explanation of why, given that an experience of darkness is more often succeeded by continued experiences of darkness than by an experience of light, Hume would have been committed to considering night to be the cause of day.

5. Beattie was fond of making points by way of belligerent questioning.

6. At EU 12.23/160, Hume attributed this inconsistency to a "Pyrrhonian" skepticism distinct from the academic skepticism he meant to endorse. T 1.4.2.51/214 and 57/218, and T 1.4.7.9–10/269–70 are not so circumspect. In Ad, Hume denounced his critics for having "taken care to direct all their batteries against that juvenile work, which the Author never acknowledged" [the anonymously published T]. Although Reid was generally careful not to direct criticism of T at Hume by name (he instead referred to "the author of the *Treatise*"), in this particular case, it was harsh not to recognize the more nuanced statement of Hume's views expressed in the mature work.

7. As demonstrated by the sustained critique in his (1788: 409–444) Reid had no sympathy with the view that justice is an artificial virtue, which Hume had presented and defended in both T 3.2.1-6/477-534 and EM 3/183-204. The concluding sentence continues the sarcasm of the earlier ones, suggesting that only an absurd theory could make such an absurd consequence seem reasonable.

8. Page 259 in the standard pagination of the Prussian Academy edition of Kant's collected writings. My translation from Vorländer and Hinske (1976).

9. Had Hume returned to the belief in a persisting self in EU, he would likely have said the same thing about it: that though this belief is rationally unjustifiable, it nonetheless arises from a "natural instinct or prepossession" that cannot be resisted. The challenge for Reid would then have been to show why the mature Hume of EU would not have been entitled to offer such an account. Reid himself took the existence of a permanent subject of thought to be a "principle of common sense" that cannot be justified, and although he claimed that it can be proven that this subject must be an immaterial substance, his published works contain no such proof (1764: 538–539).

10. Hume also claimed, in the letter to Blair, that since children instinctively adopt all the opinions, principles, sentiments, and passions of their elders, it should not be surprising that they would also adopt their beliefs. But this extraordinary appeal to a special instinct is unnecessary.

11. Recent treatments of Hume's account of testimony have either criticized him for adopting the "reductionist" account defended here or attempted to defend him by denying that he adopted it. See Traiger (2010), Wilson (2010), Koenig and Harris (2007), and Pitson (2006).

12. In Hume's own estimation, it was at most a clarification. The passage was placed in the Appendix, along with a request to the reader to insert it as 1.3.7.7, but, like other corrections in the Appendix, it was described as "subjoin'd" to "guard against" what Hume claimed to have "found by experience" to be "mistakes in the readers" arising from "expressions" that were not "well chosen" (T App. 1/623). The view that the passage expresses a change of heart goes back to Reid himself (1764: 292–293).

13. Hume did change his mind on one significant point. In T App. 4/625, he attempted to prove that belief could not consist in some feeling, distinguishable from the conception although annexed to it. EU 5.11/48 asserts the opposite.

14. This remains controversial. For further discussion, see Bricke (1980: ch.3), Everson (1988), Loeb (2002: 60–100), Smalligan Marušić (2010).

15. "Can Mr. *Hume* experience that I have never seen fire kindled by a touch from ice," asked William Adams (1752: 18, cf. 29). See also Richard Price (1768: 419–420), who observed that "Testimony sometimes has convinced men of facts which they judged to be impossible; that is, it has convinced them that they were wrong in this opinion. Kindling spirits by a touch from ice would appear to a common person, impossible. The evidence of sense, however, would immediately convince him of the contrary; and from the preceding reasoning, I think, it appears, that there is nothing which sense is capable of proving that testimony may not also prove." After Adams, the example of kindling spirits with an icicle became commonplace in critical discussions of Hume's account of testimony.

16. For further discussion of this experiment, which became something of a parlor trick in mid-eighteenth century Europe, see Heilbron (1979: 272–273). As Heilbron notes, there were those at the time who asked what useful purpose was being achieved by devoting research dollars to figuring out how generate and play tricks with as trivial and unimportant a natural phenomenon as electrical sparks. Thanks to Brigitte Sassen for drawing my attention to this background to Adam's and Price's remarks.

17. For discussion of Reid's reply to this argument, see Falkenstein (2014).

18. The argument of the following three sub-sections is expounded and defended at greater length in Falkenstein (2000; 2002; 2005; forthcoming) and the appendix on Reid to (2011). For a more sympathetic take on Reid's position, see Somerville (1995) and Wolterstorff (2004; 2006). For a classic statement of an opposed view of Hume's account of representation, see Yolton (1984).

19. Reid allowed that we cannot have a sensation without conceiving of that sensation, conceiving of ourselves as things that have the sensation, conceiving a faculty for having that sort of sensation, and believing in the current existence of all of these things (1764: 43, 56, 67–69). Reid (1785: 16, 17–18) considers consciousness to be a distinct faculty from perception, the one directed toward internal mental states and operations, the other to external objects.

20. By "directly perceive mind-independent objects," I mean that the object we initially conceive of and believe in when performing an act of perception is the external object. It is not something else (e.g., a sensation) from which the external object is inferred by reasoning or association. Reid maintained that, in some cases, perceptions are "suggested" by sensations acting as "natural signs," whereas in others they are "suggested" by "material impressions" on the sense organs (1764: 122–129, 232). But the claim that the occurrence of a sensation is a cause or occasion on which we are instinctively led to directly perceive an external object is not the same thing as the claim that we directly perceive only our own sensations and arrive at beliefs in the existence of external objects only by inference or association. The etiology of perceptions is one thing; their immediate object is another.

21. The act of conceiving a nonexistent object exists in the mind (1764: 409–410), but the object does not (1764: 48), and the act is nothing like the object (1764: 409–410, cf. 1785: 357–395). So far as I know, Reid was the first philosopher to countenance the possibility of directly conceiving an object that does not exist (as opposed to perceiving an existing mental image of an object that has no external counterpart). For worries, see Van Cleve (2008) and (2015: 263–300).

22. The views attributed to Hume in this paragraph are not as explicitly stated in EU as they are in T. However, EU continues to maintain that ideas refer to impressions by copying them (EU 2.5/19) and to countenance only two positions on the external world: that our very perceptions are the external objects (not that they are *of* external objects) and that

our perceptions are internal, mental effects that resemble external objects (EU 12, Part 1). Consistently with this, the "physical points" or "images" discussed in EU 12.18n/156n, which are said to be indivisible to the eye or imagination but to compose an infinite extension in aggregate, must be spatially disposed perceptions. EU is otherwise consistent with the passages cited here from T.

23. See T 1.4.5.9/235; T 1.2.3.7/35; T 1.2.3.4/34; T 1.4.5.15/239–40.
24. See T 1.4.4.10–14/229–31; EU 12.15/154.
25. See T 1.4.5.3/232–3.
26. See T 1.1.1.7/4; EU 2.5/19.
27. See T 1.4.5.26–7/244–6.
28. See T 1.1.7.6/19–20.
29. See T 1.1.1/1; T 1.2.1/7–8; EU 2.3/18.
30. The limitation to a blind person is justified by the claim that the blind can form very complete ideas of extension and figure, but it retreats from the bravado expressed by the passage quoted here, which offers to concede the point as long as *any* sensation could be shown to be extended or shaped. Color is the really hard case for Reid.
31. He did assert that "If it were not so, a man who never before felt either the gout or the toothach, when he is first seized with the gout in his toe, might mistake it for the toothach" (1764: 295–296). But it is hard to see the pertinence of this observation. If the feelings of itches, pricks, and bites are disposed at specific locations, then there will be no mistaking where they are disposed relative to simultaneously occurring tactile sensations. If anything, the mistake would be more likely on Reid's view, according to which all pains are felt in the mind.
32. To support his position, Reid made the valid point that ordinary people distinguish between the color of an object, which they conceive to be a fixed and permanent quality of the object, and the appearance of that color, which varies with lighting conditions and disappears altogether in the dark. But he overreached himself when he went on to claim that it follows that ordinary people would agree that the fixed and permanent quality is invisible and unknown and conceived merely as a hidden cause of the appearances of color. Vulgar person that I am in my moments out of the study, I consider the fixed and permanent quality to be identical to the quality that is apparent under ideal viewing conditions. I also consider that apparent quality to be extended and located.
33. Hume, of course, took the people to be shocked by the assertion that the phenomenally evident qualities we experience in touch and vision are not in objects. Compare Reid's (1764: 197–203) inverted take on this. Far from failing to appreciate Reid's take, Hume was rejecting it outright.
34. See Beattie (1774: 463–468).
35. **Ad**, MOL, xxxv, xxxvi.
36. See MOL, xxxvi; LET 1.360 (to George Campbell, June 7, 1762).
37. Pages 7–9, 25–27 and 60–61 of the 1754 edition.

BIBLIOGRAPHY

Adams, William. (1752). *An Essay on Mr. Hume's Essay on Miracles*. London: E. Say.
Beattie, James. (1774). *An Essay on the Nature and Immutability of Truth in Opposition to Sophistry and Scepticism*, 5th ed. London: Edward and Charles Dilly.

Bricke, John. (1980). *Hume's Philosophy of Mind*. Princeton, NJ: Princeton University Press.

Brookes, Derek R. (ed.). (1997). Thomas Reid. *An Inquiry into the Human Mind on the Principles of Common Sense*. University Park: Pennsylvania State University Press.

Campbell, George. (1762). *A Dissertation on Miracles*. Edinburgh: A. Kincaid and J. Bell.

Everson, Stephen. (1988). "The Difference Between Feeling and Thinking," *Mind* 97, 401–413.

Falkenstein, Lorne. (2000). "Reid's Account of Localization," *Philosophy and Phenomenological Research* 61, 305–28.

Falkenstein, Lorne. (2002). "Hume and Reid on the Perception of Hardness," *Hume Studies* 28, 27–48.

Falkenstein, Lorne. (2005). "Condillac's Paradox," *Journal of the History of Philosophy* 43, 403–435.

Falkenstein, Lorne (ed.). (2011). David Hume. *An Enquiry Concerning Human Understanding*. Peterborough: Broadview.

Falkenstein, Lorne. (2014). "Reid's response to Hume's Perceptual Relativity Argument" *Canadian Journal of Philosophy* 41 Supplement 1: *New Essays on Reid* (2011/2014): 25–49. (Print edition dated 2014, but indexed online under the 2011 volume.) DOI:10.1080/004550 91.2014.897481.

Falkenstein, Lorne. (forthcoming). "Dualism and the *Experimentum Crucis*." *Philosophy and Phenomenological Research*. (Book symposium on James Van Cleve, *Problems from Reid*.)

Fieser, James. (2000). *Early Responses to Hume*, 2nd ed., 6 volumes. Bristol: Thoemmes.

Grandi, Giovanni. (2008). "Reid on Ridicule and Common Sense," *Journal of Scottish Philosophy* 6, 71–90.

Heilbron, J.L. (1979). *Electricity in the 17th and 18th centuries: a study of early Modern physics*. Berkeley: University of California Press.

Hume, David. (1762). Letter to Hugh Blair of 4 July 1762. Aberdeen University Library MS 2814/1/39. Transcribed in Wood (1986: 411–416) and Brookes (1997: 256–257).

Kant, Immanuel. (1783). *Prolegomena zu einer jeden künftigen Metaphysik, die als Wissenschaft wird afutreten können*. Riga: Johann Friedrich Hartknoch.

Koenig, Melissa A., and Paul L. Harris. (2007). "The Basis of Epistemic Trust: Reliable Testimony or Reliable Sources?" *Episteme* 4, 264–284.

Loeb, Louis. (2002). *Stability and Justification in Hume's Treatise*. Oxford: Oxford University Press.

[MacQueen, Daniel.] (1756). *Letters on Mr. Hume's History of Great Britain*. Edinburgh: A. Kincaid and A. Donaldson.

Pitson, Tony. (2006). "George Campbell's Critique of Hume on Testimony," *Journal of Scottish Philosophy* 4, 1–14.

Price, Richard. (1768). *Four Dissertations*. London: A. Millar and T. Cadell.

Reid, Thomas. (1764). *An Inquiry into the Human Mind on the Principles of Common Sense*. Edinburgh: A. Kincaid & J. Bell.

Reid, Thomas. (1785). *Essays on the Intellectual Powers of Man*. Edinburgh: John Bell.

Reid, Thomas. (1788). *Essays on the Active Powers of Man*. Edinburgh: John Bell.

Smalligan Marušić, Jennifer. (2010). "Does Hume Hold a Dispositional Account of Belief?" *Canadian Journal of Philosophy* 40, 155–183.

Somerville, James. (1995). *The Enigmatic Parting Shot*. Aldershot: Avebury.

Traiger, Saul. (2010). "Experience and Testimony in Hume's Philosophy," *Episteme* 7, 42–57.

Van Cleve, James. (2008). "Reid on Single and Double Vision: Mechanics and Morals," *Journal of Scottish Philosophy* 6, 1–20.

Van Cleve, James. (2015). *Problems from Reid*. Oxford: Oxford University Press.

Vorländer, Karl, and Norbert Hinske (eds.). (1976). Immanuel Kant. *Prolegomena zu einer jeden künftigen Metaphysik, die als Wissenschaft wird afutreten können*. Hamburg: Meiner.

Wilson, Fred. (2010). "Hume and the Role of Testimony in Knowledge," *Episteme 7*, 58–78.

Wolterstorff, Nicholas. (2004). *Thomas Reid and the Story of Epistemology*. Cambridge: Cambridge University Press.

Wolterstorff, Nicholas. (2006). "What Sort of Epistemological Realist was Thomas Reid?" *Journal of Scottish Philosophy 4*, 111–124.

Wood, Paul B. (1986). "David Hume on Thomas Reid's *An Inquiry into the Human Mind on the Principles of Common Sense*: A New Letter to Hugh Blair from July 1762," *Mind 95*, 411–16.

Yolton, John. (1984). *Perceptual Acquaintance from Descartes to Reid*. Minneapolis: University of Minnesota Press.

PART VII

AFTER HUME ...

CHAPTER 37

HUME AND NIETZSCHE

PETER KAIL

A comparative essay on Hume and Nietzsche might appear a strange exercise. Many readers probably view Nietzsche and Hume as poles apart in both style and content. Nietzsche's writings apparently replace reason with rhetoric, deny that there is any truth, are contemptuous of science, and are hostile to morality. Hume, by contrast, is a philosopher of great analytical rigor with a deep respect for science and a friendly, if complacent, attitude to morality. Even considering how Nietzsche engages with, and rejects, Hume's philosophy seems fruitless. Nietzsche had virtually no firsthand knowledge of Hume and references to the Scot by the German are both few and betoken no real engagement.[1] The exercise seems misconceived at the outset.

Whatever truth there may be in these cartoon sketches of Hume and Nietzsche completely obscures what others have noticed: namely, that there is a surprising degree of convergence in their philosophies.[2] Similarities between any given pair of philosophers are, of course, not hard to find, but what is interesting in this case is that these two thinkers share a particular form of *naturalism* that I shall call *explanatory* or *genealogical naturalism*, one that explains some of the substantive convergence between the two thinkers. This fact, although one not properly expanded on, explains why, in the recent rehabilitation of Nietzsche as a naturalistic philosopher, Hume is used as the main point of reference.[3] Both philosophers orient themselves around a general conception of human nature and seek to explain human thought and practice in its terms. This shared project stands in contrast to metaphysically oriented philosophy and to what they see as false, metaphysical-cum-religious interpretations of humanity. Roughly put, the project of explaining human thought and behavior naturalistically renders metaphysically loaded interpretations of it redundant and helps humanity properly orient itself to the world.

It is important not to confuse an emphasis on naturalism in both thinkers with a claim that naturalism exhausts the aims and character of their philosophies. Hume does foreground his naturalism, but that is not the only thing that concerns him. Nietzsche does not foreground his naturalism nor does he offer systematic treatise of the kind that Hume offers. He is concerned with, inter alia, the need for philosophers to create values and liberate the "higher types" from the threat of ascetic morality and the general problem of nihilism. But his naturalism stands behind, and is essential to, his therapeutic concerns. The therapy is appropriate only under the assumption that we *understand* human nature. So, he writes, we must "translate humanity back into nature" for only when we understand human nature are we able to "gain control of the many vain and fanciful interpretations that have been drawn and scribbled and that have drawn over that eternal basic text of *homo natura* so far" (BGE 230).

I Naturalism: Preliminaries

Both philosophies are naturalistic in the obvious sense that they reject of any role for God. One justly celebrated aspect of Hume's thought is his systematic critique of the purported rational grounds of religious belief, where reason at best suggests the extremely anemic conclusion that "the cause or causes of order in the universe probably bear some remote analogy to human intelligence" (DNR 12.33).[4] Nietzsche is not concerned with this issue (what "is now decisive against Christianity is our taste, no longer our reasons" [GS 123]) but, like Hume, he takes very seriously the complex nature of the cultural and psychological aspects of religion. His famous declaration of the "Death of God" expresses his concern about the deep and unrecognized ramifications of the gradual decline in Christian faith rather than an epistemic assessment of the belief.

We shall return to the issue of religion as a cultural and psychological phenomenon. More positively characterized, Nietzsche's and Hume's naturalism combines a particular subject matter—human nature itself—with a particular approach to it. Unlike the naturalism Spinoza expresses in his *Ethics*, Hume and Nietzsche approach their subject matter empirically and with a strong mistrust of the powers of a priori epistemology. This partly characterizes their *methodological* naturalism. The subtitle of Hume's *Treatise*—"being an attempt to introduce the experimental method of reasoning into moral subjects"—declares Hume's methodological naturalism. Hume follows Newton by approaching human nature with an observational methodology unconstrained by any a priori assumptions of what its nature and powers must be. This rejection of a priori approaches is shared by Nietzsche who holds that it is the "mark of a higher culture to value the little unpretentious truths which have been discovered by means of vigorous methods more highly than the errors handed down by metaphysical and artistic ages and men" (HAH 1, 3). He thinks philosophy is still too beholden to a priori metaphysics, and the "scientific spirit in men has to bring to maturity that virtue of *cautious reserve*, that wise moderation which is more familiar in the domain of the practical life than in the domain of the theoretical life" (HAH 1, 631). Such methods prevent dogmatism because their best practice is reflective and anti-dogmatic about those very methods. "On the whole," Nietzsche writes, "the procedures of science are at least as important a product of inquiry as any other outcome: for the scientific spirit rests upon an insight into the procedures, and if these were lost all the other products of science would not suffice to prevent a restoration of superstition and folly" (HAH 1, 635). This attitude is maintained in his later work where, for example, in *Antichrist* he writes that "scientific methods . . . are the essential thing, as well as the most difficult thing" (A 59) and of a certain "*factual sense*, the last and most valuable of all senses" (A 59).

Methodological naturalism expresses what Brian Leiter, in comparing Hume and Nietzsche, calls "methods continuity," which Leiter glosses as the claim that philosophy "take[s] over from the sciences the idea that natural phenomena have determinate causes" (2002: 5). However, the view here is a liberal one inasmuch as they both make use of a *speculative* account of nature to explain causally human thought and practice.[5] This is what is important to their shared naturalism, namely, their attempt to explain human thought and behavior causally, or, as Hume puts it, the attempt to "render all our principles as universal as possible, by tracing up our experiments to the utmost and *explaining* all effects from the simplest and fewest causes" (T Intro. 8/xvii).

Any explanatory practice needs to advert to some relatively basic set of materials, which then raises a question about the sense in which these materials are "natural." For both Hume and Nietzsche, this concern is answered by appeal to materials that are thought to be operative in the world of nonhuman animals. "Formally," Nietzsche writes at *Daybreak* 49, "one has sought the feeling of the grandeur of man by pointing to his divine origin; this has now become a forbidden way, for at its portal stands the ape, together with other gruesome beasts, grinning knowingly as if to say: no further in this direction!" Humans nevertheless become beguiled by the sound of "metaphysical bird catchers" who sing "You are more! You are higher! You are of a different origin!" (BGE 230). The ontology of drives that Nietzsche postulates as basic to human nature is deeply informed by German materialism[6] and more pertinently nineteenth-century biology,[7] and so he starts with the assumption that no fundamental metaphysical difference exists between humans and beasts. Hume, too, brings out the beast in the human. In Book 2 of the *Treatise* Hume explicitly tells us that in the "whole sensitive creation . . . [e]very thing is conducted by springs and principles, which are not peculiar to man, or any one species of animals" (T 2.2.12.1/397) and ends his respective discussions of the indirect passions with sections entitled "Of the Pride and Humility of Animals" and "Of the Love and Hatred of Animals." Both are placed at the end of Hume's long discussions of the topics of pride and love and declare that animals also have those emotions. However, the claim that human nature is continuous with animal nature is implicit in the opening pages of the *Treatise* because the materials he introduces there, such as impression, vivacity, association, and natural relations were already widely thought to govern the cognitive lives of the animal creation. So, although later Hume offers an argument from analogy to support the claim that "beasts are endow'd with thought and reason, as well as men" (T 1.3.16.1/176), he had already "animalized" human reason.

The appeal to the animal basis for human thought affords Hume and Nietzsche a way to give substance to the claim that human beings are "part of nature" without becoming embroiled in controversial views of how to demarcate the natural from the non-natural. They do not need to be committed to strong reductive naturalisms, such as physicalism, or to taking as the criterion of the natural only that which is recognized by the sciences. But it is not ontologically profligate either. For when they do seek to explain human thought and practice, their explanations dispense with appeals to distinctive ranges of facts that are (suspiciously) tailor-made to figure in our understanding of those thoughts and practices. Our talk about, say, freedom can encourage a metaphysic whereby humans have the capacity for contracausal action and agency, or our inferential practices the idea they reflect a sensitivity to a *sui generis* class of normative entities, or the apparent unity of consciousness the idea of a substantial self. Both thinkers deploy a battery of criticisms against such heavyweight metaphysics but, equally important, is the attempt to explain why human beings think and talk in the ways that they do without having to make such metaphysical appeals. In this respect, both anticipate what Huw Price calls "Subject Naturalism" rather than "Object Naturalism."[8] In brief, object naturalism starts with a particular naturalistic conception of the world that leads to certain "placement problems" with respect to distinct areas of commitment. So, for example, physicalism leaves modality, meaning, and morality as difficult features to "place" in a world in which there is only the physical. The placement solution is sought "in the objects," in the sense that ontological correlates are sought to answer the areas of commitment in terms of reductionism or implausible identity theories. Subject naturalism takes science seriously, too, and includes taking seriously what science tells us *about us*. It seeks to explain our thought and behavior. It also offers a different perspective on "placement problems." It does not seek to solve placement issues in the "material mode," namely, in the objects themselves. Instead, it concerns linguistic behavior, the use of certain problematic areas of discourse, and asks "how are we to understand the roles and functions of the behaviour in question in the lives of the creatures concerned? . . . Whence its genealogy?" (Price 2011: 232). Once we can explain just why creatures like us think and behave as we do, appeals to metaphysics seem ill motivated.

II INTERNAL THREATS TO NATURALISM?

Hume and Nietzsche offer speculative accounts of human nature continuous with the science with which they seek to explain human thought and behavior. But, interestingly, both their philosophies are susceptible to readings that threaten the very possibility of reading them as naturalists. Hume is thought to set the problem of induction, holding that inferences from past observations have no epistemic warrant. Yet the whole "science of mind" rests on such observational warrant. Nietzsche supposedly, and paradoxically, denies that any belief is true, writing that "truths are illusions we have forgotten are illusions" (TL 84). Both thinkers flirt dangerously with incoherence. However, not only does this exaggerate the character of these negative views of Hume and Nietzsche; the deeper irony is that their views are the *result* of naturalism rather than constituting a reason to think they are not naturalists. I cannot defend this adequately here but I can at least give a flavor of it.

Hume's conclusion about our inductive inferences is that they are not themselves *caused* by any grasp of a reason in favor of making that inference. But this is not the same as saying that they are epistemically worthless. It is a claim about the nature of our inferential practices, namely, that reason is "a kind of cause, of which truth is the natural effect" (T 1.4.1.1/180). This claim is a species of skepticism that is *consequent* to "science and enquiry" and that is initially supposed to show "either the absolute fallaciousness of [human] mental faculties, or their unfitness to reach any fixed determination in all those curious subjects of speculation, about which they are commonly employed" (EU 12.5/150). Hume does not accept that an a posteriori investigation into the mind's faculties issues in what he calls "excessive" or Pyrrhonian skepticism but instead a "mitigated scepticism"—a "small tincture of PYRRHONISM"—that is a welcome antidote to the "haughtiness," "obstinacy," and "pride" of the learned limiting "our enquiries to such subjects as are best adapted to the narrow capacity of human understanding" (EU 12.24–5/161).[9] Hume's investigation into our inferential faculties reveals that a non-naturalistic account of such inferences is incorrect.

Nietzsche's notorious views on truth flow from his naturalism combined with some other factors. His early unpublished essay "On Truth and Lies in a Non-moral Sense" endorses a robust correspondence theory of truth together with the assumption that true beliefs must correspond to the thing-in-itself. This, however, was combined with a Schopenhauer-inspired thought that our representations are inadequate to the thing-in-itself. Hence, our beliefs "falsify" reality. The published work gives a naturalistic turn to this argument. There, Nietzsche held that all our categorizing activity is the upshot of evolutionary pressures. The evolutionary nature of distinctive areas of human thought means that it is unlikely to carve a metaphysical reality at its joints and so is equally likely to be imbued with error (e.g., HAH I, 11, 16, 18). In the *Gay Science,* he offers conjectures on the "origin of knowledge" (GS 110) and the "origin of logic" (GS 111) that revolve around the general thought that central beliefs and inference patterns emerge from the need to survive, and he infers from this idea that they most likely engender error (GS 121). All creatures occupy a "perspective" on reality that falsifies and, like Hume, Nietzsche held that central categories like identity, substance, and the like are creative fictions that organize the chaos of experience. So, Nietzsche writes "What are man's truths ultimately? They are the irrefutable errors of man" (GS 265) and "Life is no argument" (GS 121).

This "falsification" thesis disappears from Nietzsche's later work because he came to reject the contrast between the world of the empirical and the thing-in-itself.[10] Nietzsche continues to talk of "perspective," but this is now linked to the conditions of representation and objectivity and not truth.[11] He then holds that certain metaphysical views are false (see TI), is also critical of the adequacy of some of the metaphysical assumptions of contemporary science, and, in his unpublished works, tries to articulate an alternative, albeit one motivated by his methodological naturalism.[12]

Nietzsche nevertheless maintains an interest in the *value* of truth and, more importantly, the overestimation of its value. Famously, he thinks that the ideals of science that instantiate this overestimation is the last expression of the ascetic ideal, and one task of Nietzsche's *Genealogy of Morality* is to show how his fellow naturalists ("we seekers after truth" [GM preface 1]) are unreflective about this ideal. Naturalism lacks awareness that the norm of truth is not self-justifying but instead is an expression of a certain devaluation of worldly existence. Now, the connection between the ascetic ideal and the ideals of science forged by Nietzsche is a complex and subtle one, but the relevant point for our purposes is the following: Nietzsche holds that naturalism is under an illusion and cannot constitute an ideal alternative to that which Christianity promulgates, but it does not follow that Nietzsche rejects naturalism. Nietzsche deploys naturalism because he thinks that it is the method most conducive to the truth, but he doesn't, unlike his naturalist contemporaries, take that aim to be a self-justifying one. Nietzsche wants to question that ideal, too. One can easily be a naturalist without taking truth to be an unconditional ideal, and, in this respect, Hume is no unreflective naturalist. The final section of *Treatise* Book 2 "Of the Passions" is entitled "Of Curiosity, or the Love of Truth," and Hume not only discusses why he is pursuing the project of the *Treatise*, but he also makes it clear that he does not take truth to be some self-justifying ideal. He considers the origin of our love of truth, which was "the first source of all our enquiries" (T 2.3.10.1/448), and locates it in a number of sources, including the pleasure derived from the exercise of genius and the utility of possessing certain "important truths." The interest in truth is relative to these ends, but Hume also notes that it is possible to become interested in truth per se because "where the mind pursues any end with passion; tho' that passion be not deriv'd originally from the end, but merely from the action and pursuit; yet by the natural course of the affections, we acquire a concern for the end itself" (T 2.3.10.7/451).

III Naturalism, Explanation, and Genealogy

Nietzsche and Hume are naturalists, although not ones who take the aim of naturalistic enquiry to be self-justifying. They are concerned with human nature and naturalize humanity by trying to understand humans as a certain kind of animal.

Human animals are self-conscious beings embedded in moral-religious cultures that are the products of historical forces. To understand them, Nietzsche counsels that we should move away from the "congenital defeat" of philosophy, namely, its tendency to treat humanity as essentially ahistorical, as some "*aeterna veritas*, as something that remains constant in the midst of flux" (HAH 1, 2). In naturalizing humanity, we need a "chemistry of the moral, religious and aesthetic conceptions, likewise all the agitations we experience within ourselves in cultural and social intercourse" (HAH 1, 1). This "chemistry of concepts" is subsumed under "historical philosophy," the goal of which is to explain "how something can originate in its opposite, for example, rationality in irrationality, the sentient in the dead, logic in unlogic, disinterested contemplation in covetous desire." This requirement that each and every phenomenon must emerge from its exact opposite is a Heraclitean hyperbole on Nietzsche's part. It is a rhetorical counterweight to what he calls the "faith in opposite values" (BGE 2), namely, the assumption that anything of value to humanity must have "another, separate origin *of their own*—they cannot be derived from the ephemeral, seductive, descriptive, lowly world, from this made chaos of confusion and desire."

Nietzsche's resists the siren song of the metaphysical bird-catchers that "You are more! You are higher! You are of a different origin!" (BGE 230) by offering explanations that typically involve situating creatures with a particular type-psychology—and importantly one that can be understood independently of the relevant *explanandum*—against a particular environment or stimulus and explaining the emergence of some new phenomenon (a belief, idea, practice) in its light. The stimulus and the psychology vary according to what is being explained, as we shall see in some examples below. The usual term for Nietzsche's explanatory chemistry is *genealogy* after *On the Genealogy of Morality*, a work containing a sustained attempt at offering a naturalistic explanation of a particular form of morality. The term "genealogy"[13] is also applied to Hume's thought, which should not be surprising given the emphasis on explanation in his philosophy—and it is in this respect that Nietzsche and Hume most overlap methodologically. As I noted, such explanations will differ considerably depending on what is trying to be explained, although we only have space to compare and contrast Hume and Nietzsche with regard to two important subject matters, religion and morality.[14]

Before we do so, we must forestall a potential misunderstanding. The notion of genealogy is most associated with Nietzsche and, because he uses his genealogy in the service of a critique of morality, it is now common to think that genealogy is essentially a critique. Understandable though this thought is, it is a mistaken one and Nietzsche is explicit that such accounts do *not* constitute a form of critique:

> The inquiry into the *origin* of our evaluations . . . is in no way identical with a critique of them . . . even though the insight into some *pudenda origo* certainly brings with it a *feeling* of a diminution in value of the thing that originated thus and prepares the way to a critical mood and attitude to it. (WP 254)

Instead, genealogies—construed as a naturalistic account of a distinct area of human thought or practice—*can*, depending on the character of the relevant explanation, either *vindicate* or *destabilize* what they explain. That is to say, the relevant explanations can reinforce or diminish our confidence in the belief our practice thus explained. We explore this in the following sections.

IV GENEALOGY AND RELIGION AS A NATURAL PHENOMENON

As remarked, one aspect of Nietzsche's and Hume's naturalism is that they dispense with appeals to God in articulating their accounts of human nature. Nevertheless, they are interested in explaining why creatures like us start to conceive of the world in religious terms. One aspect to this is explaining the presence of the core cognitive content of religious belief, and both seek to explain this by locating a generic psychology in a particular environment, and, indeed, offer very similar accounts.

Hume, in the *Natural History of Religion*, supposes that prereligious human beings are both highly dependent on the natural course of events and ignorant of their underlying causes. These unknown causes are the objects of hopes and fears, and our ignorance of them generates a deep anxiety. Religious belief emerges in early polytheism because this anxious state triggers a standing, and independently identifiable, disposition to anthropomorphize nature. The mechanism is so triggered because the belief generated palliates the anxiety by providing an intelligible model for the unknown causes, and, more importantly, gives the thinker the illusion that he can influence them in the way that other human beings can be influenced, giving us "recourse to every method of appeasing those secret intelligent powers, on whom our misfortune is supposed entirely to depend" (NHR 143). Once this belief is in circulation, it then becomes modified in certain ways, most significantly in its transmutation into monotheism. The essence of this account is recapitulated by Nietzsche at HAH 111 where the "origin of religious worship" is explained in terms of thinkers having no concept of "natural causality" and as disposed to interpret all events as the result of intentional action. Nature is the "sum of the actions of conscious and intelligent beings." This generalized view of causation in the world becomes focused into religious belief where "every individual in those times and conditions feels that his existence, his happiness . . . depends on those arbitrary acts of nature." Such a person then "asks himself anxiously" how some order can be imposed on these events. Nietzsche's answer, if translated, would fit seamlessly in the pages of Hume's NHR:

> entreaties and prayers, by submissiveness, by committing oneself to regular tributes and gifts, by flattering glorifications, it is also possible to exert pressure on the forces of nature, by making them favourably inclined: love binds and is bound.

Both philosophers have more to say on this score, but we will confine ourselves to one remark. Each thinks that such genealogies undermine confidence in the belief explained. Hume thinks that if we consider solely the natural causes of religious belief, one ought to suspend that belief. "Doubt, uncertainty, suspense of judgment appear the only result of our most accurate scrutiny, concerning this subject" (NHR 185). In outline, this conclusion follows because the causes of religious belief are revealed to be epistemically unreliable, a matter of forming belief in the service of calming the passions rather than constituting a sensitivity to epistemic considerations in its favor. Awareness that the belief's presence owes itself to an epistemically unreliable source provides a reason to suspend that belief unless and until some further grounds can be provided to justify it. Hume's response to such destabilization is the disingenuous suggestion that there are sound arguments in favor of theism,[15] but Nietzsche goes a step further:

Historical refutation as the definitive refutation. In former times, one sought to prove that there is no God—today one indicates how the belief that there is a God could arise and how this belief acquired its weight and importance: a counter-proof that there is no God thereby becomes superfluous. (DA 95)

Nietzsche, as I mentioned, does not concern himself with traditional arguments in favor of the existence God (or indeed against it) but here seems to run a redundancy argument. Presumably, the thought here is that once the belief has been explained in exhaustively naturalistic terms, arguments aimed to support it have no independent motivation. Here, Nietzsche thinks to explain is to explain away.

Religion is not, of course, exhausted by the existential claim that there is a God (or Gods) but is implicated in various deep and subtle articulations of the moral nature of humanity. We need to "de-deify nature" Nietzsche tells us before we can "naturalize humanity" (GS 109), and part of that is to try to understand naturalistically the religious interpretation of humanity. One particular concern for both is that Christianity is bound up with an asceticism that is inimical to human flourishing, and both offer genealogical explanations of how asceticism becomes valorized independently of the metaphysics of Christianity. Hume and Nietzsche seek to explain how such practices are the endpoints of natural psychological processes, showing how one can step back from practices that "from the inside" seem to be moral requirements rendered intelligible from within that evaluative system.

Hume is famously critical of the "monkish virtues" of celibacy, fasting, penance, mortification, self-denial, humility, silence, and solitude—but how does he explain just how they become valorized? Hume begins, in the NHR, with the Christian assumption that we are indebted to God, and a question then arises regarding how the debt is to be discharged. It cannot be a matter of the practice of daily life: in "restoring a loan, or paying a debt, [to another person] his divinity is nowise beholden to him; because these acts of justice are what he is bound to perform . . . were there no god in the universe" (NHR 181). So the believer "still looks for some immediate service of the supreme being" and seizes upon "any practice . . . which either serves no purpose in life, or offers the strongest violence to his natural inclinations." This make sense because we have a representation of God as "infinitely superior to mankind" that is such as to "sink the human mind into the lowest submission and abasement," and so the way to repay the debt is to acknowledge in a visceral way one's total inferiority and dependence. Hence, "mortification, penance, humility, and passive suffering [are conceived] as the only qualities which are acceptable to him" (NHR 163). Hume thinks asceticism is a natural concomitant of monotheism and is one reason why he prefers polytheism. The representations of ancient gods provided models for heroes to emulate (NHR section 10) and are more conducive to toleration (NHR section 9). Nietzsche and Hume here are on the same page. The Greeks saw their gods as the "reflection of the most successful specimens of their own caste," so that man "thinks himself noble . . . in a relationship similar to that of the lesser nobility to the higher" (HAH 114). Christianity, on the other hand, "crushed and shattered man completely, and submerged him as if in a deep mire." Nietzsche also shares Hume's assumption that asceticism emerges through the idea of an undischargeable debt to God, although his explanation is far more complicated and multifaceted than Hume's. Guilt emerges from ordinary relations of credit and debt, but when connected with a monotheistic religion like Christianity, our sense of indebtedness increases so that the guilty can "be tangibly certain of his absolutely unworthiness" (GM II, 22), which in turn becomes entangled with a sense of the agent being ultimately responsible for all their suffering. The gods of the ancient world did not encourage this sense of responsibility and self-punishment. The Greek gods viewed human failure as foolishness, not sin. Hume, in explaining the self-mortification associated with Christianity, makes a similar observation. The Romans do not conceive themselves as guilty before God but simply as victims of fate.

> When the old Romans were attacked with a pestilence, they never ascribed their suffering to their vices, or dreamed of repentance and amendment. They never thought, that they were general robbers of the world. . . . They only created a dictator, in order to drive a nail into a door, and by that means, they had sufficiently appeased their incensed deity. (NHR 14.1)[16]

V GENEALOGY AND MORALITY

The previous section displayed how both Hume and Nietzsche are concerned with the Christian religion's entanglement with ethics. To understand human nature properly helps to liberate humanity from false ethical views. Both instead look to the ancient world for their models of morality, although not with a naïve nostalgic eye. That is not the only place they meet. They also place feeling and passion, drive and affect, rather than reason, at the center of ethical life. For Hume "to have a sense of virtue, is nothing but to *feel* a satisfaction of a particular kind from the contemplation of character" (T 3.1.3.3/471) and for Nietzsche "moralities . . . are merely a sign language for the affects" (BGE 187). The particular ways in which the centrality of feeling are expressed in the philosophies of Hume and Nietzsche is subtle and complicated and beyond the scope of this essay. Instead, we shall concentrate on their explanatory genealogies.

Nietzsche acknowledges that it is the "English" psychologists whom we "have to thank for the only attempts so far to produce a history of the genesis of morality" (GM, I, 1), and yet it might seem that Nietzsche and the "English" radically different. First, Nietzsche's genealogy is in place because he thinks "we need a *critique* of moral values, *the value of these values should itself, for one be examined*" (GM, Preface 5). His genealogy is related to his "immoralism." Hume's genealogy seems *vindicatory* of morality. The moral "sense must certainly acquire new force, when reflecting on itself, it approves of those principles, from when it is deriv'd, and finds nothing but what is great and good in its rise and origin" (T 3.3.6.3/619). Second, Nietzsche is deeply critical of the methodology of his "English" predecessors, deeming them to be "no good" (GM II 4). However, these differences are either unreal or far less than they seem and actually obscure their common genealogical approach.[17]

The term "English" for Nietzsche refers not so much to a nationality but rather to a certain kind of *faulty* explanation.[18] The faults he identifies are that English genealogies (a) are speculative and ahistorical, (b) mistakenly infer originating causes from present functions, and (c) are insufficiently suspicious of morality. It is the first of these that is most important for our concerns.[19] Nietzsche holds that previous moral philosophies are insufficiently acquainted with many cultural and historical variations on the practice of appraising human beings (the "many different moralities" as he puts it in BGE), and this contributes to their being blind to the radical differences between the ancient and non-European moralities and modern "Christian morality." However, Hume is certainly not prone to such blindness. His writings amply attest to his sensitivity to cultural and historical variation and the influence of Christianity of the values of the modern world, even if he gives an explanation of those differences that is different from, and not as radical as, Nietzsche's. It is true: particular explanations he gives us in the *Treatise*, such as his account of the origin of justice (see Section VI), are speculative rather than historically grounded because he is here concerned with practices that emerge in prehistorical human groups and that marks no difference from accounts that Nietzsche offers of prehistorical phenomena. Thus, GM's account of the emergence of bad consciences is just as speculative as anything Hume offers. The account of the origin of justice given in HAH 92 is similar to Hume's, albeit in a compressed form, and *Daybreak* seeks to explain the morality of custom (*Sittlichkeit de Sitte*) whereby compliance to norms is explained by habituation reinforced by pain (see also GM II 1–3).

The complaint of ahistoricism is liable to a different understanding. It may seem that any similarity of genealogical project is only superficial because of a deep divide on the relation of human nature to history. Does not Hume hold that human nature is historically invariant, whereas Nietzsche insists that human nature is historically conditioned? Is not Hume exemplifying the "congenital defect" of treating the human as an "*aeterna veritas*, as something that remains constant in the midst of flux" (HAH 1, 2)? For Nietzsche, a genealogy is *essential* to understanding human beings because how we think—the distinctive character of our concepts—and how we feel—our responses—cannot be understood independently of our historical situation; whereas it seems that cannot be the case for Hume.

However, this is simply a mistaken view of Hume. It is true that Hume writes that humans "are so much the same, in all times and places, that history informs us of nothing new or strange in this particular. Its chief use is only to discover the constant and universal principles of human nature" (EU 8.7/83). But this claim functions more as a methodological heuristic rather than as a substantive claim.[20] Unless we assume some uniformity, historical knowledge would be impossible. From experience, we gain some knowledge of the "principles of human nature" and by

> means of this guide [the assumption of uniformity], we mount up to the knowledge of men's inclinations and motives, from their actions, expressions, and even gestures

and again, descend to the interpretation of their actions from our knowledge of their motives and inclinations. The general observations, treasured up by a course of experience, give us the clue of human nature, and teach us to unravel all its intricacies. (EU 8.9/84–84)

The assumption provides a framework against which particular historical events are to be interpreted. But this does not preclude the changeability of human nature. Indeed, as Hume claims in the *Treatise*, "human nature is inconstant" and "[c]hangeableness is essential to it" (T 2.1.4.3/283). Included within the objects of historical understanding are the "manners of men," which are "different in different ages and countries" and the circumstances which "mould the human mind from its infancy, and form it into a fixed and established character." Hume therefore recognizes the historical conditioning of human nature, and the assumption "affords room for many observations concerning the gradual change of our sentiments and inclinations, and the different maxims, which prevail in the different ages of human creatures" (EU 8.11/86). This last point will be relevant when we discuss Hume's genealogy of justice.

Turning now to different roles for genealogy—critical or vindicatory—the differences between the two thinkers are much less than it may seem, partly because the explanations concern different phenomena. Nietzsche's problematic morality involves a range of metaphysical presuppositions, namely, a certain conception of agency that involves a substantial self (a "doer behind the deed") and a conception of free will satisfying the principle of alternate possibilities. But, as we shall see in the next section, Hume will have no truck with any of this either, and, like Nietzsche, the rejection of this framework is simply an aspect of his naturalism. Second, Nietzsche's "immoralism" is not a flat rejection of all normative ideals (i.e., a radical nihilism) but a sustained criticism of "Christian" morality, involving two "negations." First, the "type of man that has so far been considered to be supreme: the good, the benevolent, the beneficent" (EH IV 4) and, second, the Christian "overestimation of goodness and benevolence" (EH IV 4). An aspect of Nietzsche's worry is that secular morality unwittingly and uncritically inherits this morality, leading to philosophers like Schopenhauer who, as he puts it, hate the Church but love its poison (GM I, 9). What is objectionable is a morality centered around an ideal of selflessness,[21] valorizing, although not necessarily in such religiously loaded language, the three "pomp words" of asceticism: "poverty, chastity and humility" (GM, III, 8). These function as placeholders for a range of values that embody negative attitudes toward natural goods. Thus, poverty stands against desires for material well-being; chastity against sensual pleasure, its gratification, and bodily conduct; and humility against self-interest and self-aggrandizement. Altruism[22] becomes the key moral virtue, and Nietzsche thinks it threatens to stifle human flourishing and drag creative types into the mire of pity and bad consciences (the wretched might succeed in "poisoning the conscience of the fortunate with their own misery" (GM III 14).

Nietzsche would no doubt see Hume as still too beholden to these norms—after all, Hume writes that the "benevolent or social affections . . . [are] the highest merit, which *human nature* is capable of" (EM 2.1/176). However, Hume's wider views on morality are far from the ideal of ascetic self-sacrifice and are silently radical in their own way. The first aspect to this is the obviously secular character of Humean morality. "Upon the whole," he writes in a letter, "I desire to take my catalogue of virtues from *Cicero's Offices*, not from the *Whole Duty of Man*."[23] But the secular character means not merely doing without God but also giving an account of moral judgment and its objects that is greatly at odds with other accounts. This is driven by his naturalism. His view of the actual mechanisms of human evaluation affords him a way to interpret competing accounts as "systems and hypotheses [that] have perverted our natural understanding" (EM 9.1/268). Thus, for example, he holds that the traditional distinction between virtues and talents is really only "verbal" and that this apparently weighty distinction rests on a false philosophical-cum-religious conception of morality. Philosophers "or rather divines under that disguise, treating all morals as on a like footing with civil laws, guarded by the sanctions of reward and punishment, were necessarily led to render this circumstance, of *voluntary* and *involuntary*, the foundation of the whole theory" (EM App. 4.21/322). This allows him to insinuate that, inter alia, sexual attractiveness should be classed as a virtue (T 3.3.5). His early critics were perplexed by Hume's liberalness here. A "strange morality, indeed!" said Balfour,[24] and authors like Leland criticized him for leaving out humility, as well as for including talents and attractiveness. His catalogue of virtues is not restricted to the altruistic and, indeed, classifies a person of excessive benevolence who "exceeds his part in society, and carries his attention for others beyond the proper bounds" as "too good" (EM 7.22/158). He recognizes the "great" or "shining" virtues such as courage, intrepidity, love of glory, and magnanimity—and further recognizes that we admire dangerous characters responsible for "the subversion of empires, the devastation of provinces, the sack of cities" (T 3.3.2.15/601). Viewed from the perspective of society, such a character is painful but "when we fix our view on the person himself, who is the author of all this mischief, there is something so dazzling in his character, there mere contemplation of it so elevates the mind, that we cannot refuse it our admiration." Pride, rather than humility, is given pride of place in his account of the virtues, a due pride being requisite for the conduct of life and for all "those great actions and sentiments, which have become the admiration of mankind," these being "founded on nothing but pride and self-esteem" (T 3.3.2.12/599).

Hume's view of ethics is, therefore, far from being driven by a monolithic concern with altruism. Let us now return to the issue of genealogy and Hume's apparent conclusion that his explanation of the emergence of morality vindicates it. The particular area where Hume is at his most genealogical is in the explanation of a range of practices he calls "artificial virtues." Artificial virtues contrast with *natural* virtues inasmuch as the latter require hardwired motivational dispositions of which we approve. So, for example, human beings can be naturally generous or kind, and our moral sense approves of those motives. The motivations are ones upon which we act quite independently of any distinct moral requirement to be so motivated. So, humans typically care for their children not because of an appreciation of its "being the right thing to do" but because of natural inclination. The lack of such an inclination can nevertheless be the object of moral disapproval. The artificial virtues comprise a set of practices—justice (construed as respect for property), fidelity to promises, allegiance to government, and female chastity—which govern interpersonal behavior and for which there is no natural motive *independent* of a sense of the moral rightness of the norms that circumscribe behavior.[25] So, Hume seeks to explain how such behavior could emerge and become the object of moral approval. Now, Hobbes and Mandeville had offered explanations of the emergence of cooperative behavior, but what marks those accounts out is that although they explain a pattern of cooperation, their accounts fall short of explaining that behavior as motivated by genuine *moral* concerns. Thus, for Mandeville, it is the "glory" of the public recognition of one's overcoming one's tendency to immediate gratification, reinforced by the rhetoric of politicians that underwrites seemingly cooperative behavior. "This was (or at least might have been) the manner after which savage man was broke," he writes in the *Fable of the Bees*. Explanations such as these explain but do not vindicate because the motivations are at odds with what the practice apparently aims at. It involves, at some level, a mismatch between what we think our motivations are (I am acting out of justice) and what those motivations actually are (I am acting from self-interest).

But Hume, unlike Hobbes and Mandeville, does not hold that what explains the presence of a convention is the same thing that now motivations compliance. The original self-interested motive to compliance with the relevant norms is replaced by a new motive, so that sentiments of justice take on such "firmness and solidity, that they may fall little short of those principles which are the most essential to our natures, and the most deeply radicated in our internal constitution"[26] (T 3.2.2.26/501). Hume does not therefore hold that the explanatory story is at odds with an endorsement of those practices just as they stand.

Nietzsche's genealogy serves to prepare "the way to a critical mood and attitude to it" (WP 254) by showing that, *pace* Hume it is false that there is "nothing but what is great and good in its rise and origin" (T 3.3.6.3/619). Among its *pudenda origo* is the *ressentiment* of the slave constituency, a reactive attitude elicited by the powerless and engendered by their miserable position, which in turn cooperates with a general propensity to falsification (*Fälschung*) (GM, I, 10), including the false belief (*Glauben*) in the neutral subject of free choice (GM, I, 13). This is aided and abetted by the mendaciousness of the priestly interpretation of human suffering as guilt before God. As Nietzsche makes clear, showing that (if he does show that) modern morality has such "shameful origins" does not constitute a critique of morality; it nevertheless destabilizes our confidence in it. If one acknowledges the correctness of the origin story, one stands in need of some further justification for those values, one that does not simply appeal to the values called into question. His predecessors "have taken the *value* of these 'values' as given, as factual, as beyond all question" and nobody "has had the remotest doubt or hesitation in placing higher value on the 'good man: than on the "evil' " (GM, Preface, 6). Instead, moral justification and reasoning has taken place within the framework of those values. Nietzsche's account of morality's origins "prepares the way to a critical mood and attitude to it."[27]

VI PERSONS AND AGENCY

The previous section tried to dispel what might seem to be a great difference between Nietzsche and Hume on morality. What they do share is a naturalistic explanatory project in the area of morality, coupled with a mistrust of Christian interpretations of human nature and its ethical dimension. Where there is substantive as well as methodological overlap is on their treatment the self.

Hume is justly famous for his denial of a substantial self. Minds are "nothing but a bundle or collection of different perceptions, which succeed each other with an inconceivable rapidity, and are in a perpetual flux and movement" (T 1.4.6.6/244); the self should be compared to "a republic or commonwealth, in which the several members are united by the reciprocal ties of government and subordination" (T.1.4.6.19/261). Nietzsche, too, rejected the self-as-substance, telling us, in an unconscious echo of Hume, that this "atomistic need" should be replaced with a view of the self as a "society constructed out of many 'souls'" standing in relations of "commanding and obeying" (BGE 19). The self is better considered as a "subject multiplicity," "a society constructed out of drives and affects" (BGE 12). The false view of a substantial self is a projection of our general need to believe in constancy through change,[28] further encouraged by the seductive grammar of "I" (e.g., BGE 17).[29] Hume explains the belief in such a fiction by associative error and insinuates that it is sustained by the wish for immortality.[30]

The rejection of a substantial self goes deeper than the rejection of a particular account of the unity of consciousness. It has profound and revisionary implications for our views of freedom, agency, and responsibility. The self as agent standing "behind" and in "control" of actions goes with it. As David Velleman puts it, a view of the self as simply the sum of various causal processes seems to leave it that "nobody—that is no person—*does* anything. Psychological and physiological events take place inside a person but the person serves only as an arena for these events" (1992: 462).[31] Anything approximating the phenomenon of agency is a matter of features of a bundle interacting with other features of a bundle. Nietzsche, in discussing how to gain "self-mastery" over vehement drives, tells us that the desire "to combat the vehemence of a drive . . . does not stand within our own power." Any intentional input into the process is not expressive of some locus of agency but rather "in this entire procedure our intellect is only the blind instrument of *another drive* which is a *rival* of the drive whose vehemence is tormenting us ... Whilst 'we' believe that we are complaining about the vehemence of a drive, at bottom it is one drive *which is complaining about another*" (DA 109). The analogue for Hume is "strength of mind," where what is commonly thought to be "reason" is a matter of the calm passions predominating over the violent (T 2.3.2–3).

Nietzsche takes agency to involve "self-creation," although this should not be confused with the idea that there is a self that *does* the creating. It is rather that a collection of drives might, as a matter of fortune, become sufficiently integrated so as to have a unity. "Persons" in one sense are a given collection of drives, so that when faced with the question of the identity of a person, "who he is . . . means, in what order of rank the innermost drives of his nature stand with respect to each other" (BGE 6).[32] A person who is an agent, as opposed simply to a mere collection of drives, is a collection that exhibits a hierarchy that integrates those drives. Nietzsche's cryptic and scattered remarks about self-creation (e.g., "we want to become those we are—human beings who are new, unique, incomparable, who give themselves laws, who create themselves" [GS 335]) can be understood as the extent to which such an integration can be achieved. "Becoming who you are" is aligning the drives in a single direction. In this way, then, we can understand the self as a "society constructed out of many 'souls'" which stand in relations of "commanding and obeying" (BGE 19). Tantalizingly, Hume, who wrote that we should compare the self to "a republic or commonwealth, in which the several members are united by the reciprocal ties of government and subordination" (T.1.4.6.19/261), also tells us that "everyone has a predominant inclination, to which his other affections and desires submit, and which governs him, though, perhaps, with some intervals, through the whole course of his life" (ESY 160). Perhaps the "ruling passion" plays a similar integrating function for the Humean bundle.

Nietzsche's persons—and such persons are rarely if ever actual—are "sovereign individuals" who have "the extraordinary privilege of *responsibility*" (GM II 2). "Responsibility" here can be understood as actions that issue from an integrated person rather than stemming from some self standing "behind" those drives.[33] Nietzsche rejects contracausal free will on a number of grounds,[34] but his view of the self as a collection of drives leads to a certain kind of *causal fatalism*.[35] The person is a collection of drives that circumscribe the trajectory of that person's life. The manifestations of the drives will also depend on the kind of environment in which he or she is placed, but what is operative here is simply the conspiracy of drive-collection and environment. The illusion of willing and intending that the shallows of consciousness intimate is just that: an illusion. Hume, too, thinks that the phenomenology associated with free will is misleading and offers a compatabilist view. Liberty is "a power of acting or not acting according to the determinations of the will" (EU 8.25/95) that contrasts with constraint. But Hume does not take free action as sufficient for responsibility. Instead, he controversially holds that persons are not responsible for actions that stem not from character (T 2.3.2.6/410–11). One way to read this controversial view is in light of the fact that Hume's conception of personhood in Book 2 of the *Treatise* includes *only* the enduring aspects of the bundle (see Aisnlie 1999), and so, if responsibility is tied to personhood, and only the enduring aspects of the bundle constitute an aspect of personhood, then it is no surprise that Hume locates responsibility where he does.[36]

VII · Conclusion

I have tried to give a flavor of the common naturalism of Hume and Nietzsche and how this sometimes leads to some substantial overlap in views. It should go without saying that there are many differences, but these should not obscure a common concern with the project of translating humanity back into nature. Much more remains to be said, but I hope that readers of Nietzsche might begin to see Hume in a new light and vice versa.

ACKNOWLEDGMENTS

I have benefited from discussions with a number of people in relation to this topic, and in particular, Brian Leiter, Ken Gemes, Jessica Berry, and Dario Perinetti, the last two of whom gave me extremely valuable comments on a related paper I presented at the American Philosophical Association in Seattle. I dedicate this paper to the memory of Paul McGoay, who died at the age of 42. It was from him that I first learned about Nietzsche and with him that I presented the earliest version of the ideas presented here.

ABBREVIATIONS OF WORKS CITED

EM   *Enquiry Concerning the Principles of Morals.* Edited by Tom L. Beauchamp. Oxford: Clarendon, 1998.

ESY   *Essays: Moral, Political, and Literary.* Revised edition by E. F. Miller. Indianapolis: Liberty Classics, 1985.

EU   *An Enquiry Concerning Human Understanding.* Edited by T. L. Beauchamp. Oxford: Clarendon, 2000.

LET   *The Letters of David Hume,* 2 Vols. Edited by J. Y. T. Greig. Oxford: Clarendon Press, 1932.

NHR   *The Natural History of Religion.* In T. Beauchamp, ed. *A Dissertation on the Passions; The Natural History of Religion.* Oxford: Clarendon Press, 2008.

T   *A Treatise of Human Nature.* Edited by D. F. Norton and M. J. Norton. Oxford: Clarendon, 2007.

NOTES

1. In "On the Use and Disadvantages of History for Life" (UM 1), Nietzsche ascribes a couplet to Hume ("And from the dregs of life hope to receive/What the first sprightly running could not give") that is in fact from Milton, although Hume quotes it in the *Dialogues Concerning Natural Religion*; GS 357 contains a brief remark on causality in connection with Hume and Kant; GS 370 in connection with the "sensualism" of the eighteenth century; BGE 252 classifies him as an "Englishman," one of the "unphilosophical race"; NCW 5 echoes GS 370's thought that eighteenth-century optimism gives way to nineteenth-century pessimism, and here Hume is put together with Kant and Hegel. WP 92 mentions Hume in the context of country and culture; WP 101 tells us that Locke and Hume's styles are "too bright, too

clear" for German tastes; WP 530 has Hume declaring "there are no synthetic a priori judgments." In WP 550, Nietzsche writes "We have no 'sense for the *causa efficiens*': here Hume was right." On Nietzsche's knowledge of Hume, and English-speaking philosophy more widely, see Brobjer (2008).

2. Two synoptic camparisons are Beam (1996) and (2001). Hoy (1994), Bernard Williams (2000; 2002), and Wiggins (2006) compare Hume and Nietzsche on genealogy. For Hume and Nietzsche on the self, see Davey (1987) and Poellner (1995: 33–38) for Hume and Nietzsche on causation. On asceticism in morality, see Christopher Williams (1999: 124). Swanton (2000) compares Humean sympathy with Nietzsche's views on pity. See Kail (2009) and (2011) for further discussion.

3. See, in particular, Leiter (2002: 3–11) and Leiter (forthcoming), to which I am deeply indebted, as well as Clark (1998: 55, 68–75), Schacht (2007: 115–116), and Bernard Williams (2002). Leiter and Williams, furthermore, articulate how naturalism is to be understood in this context. See also Kail (2009). For other naturalist readings of Nietzsche see Wilcox (1974) and Cox (1999).

4. The irreligion in Hume runs deeper than the surface. Craig (1987), chapter 2, orients Hume's philosophy and his naturalism as an assault on a version of the *imago dei* doctrine. Buckle (2001) reads Hume's *Enquiry Concerning Human Understanding* as an "enlightenment tract" and, more recently, Russell (2008) argues that the *Treatise* in its entirety is antireligious. It should be noted that Hume talks of a "true religion" but true religion is so anemic that it has no practical consequence and is indistinguishable from atheism.

5. Leiter takes Nietzsche's philosophy to exhibit what he calls "Results Continuity" with the sciences only in that Nietzsche takes nineteenth-century German materalism to be correct, although not immune from criticism. Leiter also does not hold that Nietzsche commits himself to determinism about causation.

6. See Leiter (2002).

7. See Moore (2002) and (2006).

8. See, e.g., Price (2011).

9. For further discussion, see Garrett (2004).

10. For a detailed account, see Clark (1990).

11. See also Leiter (1994) and Janaway (2006), chapters 10 and 11. For a different view, see Cox (1999), chapter 3.

12. This is the project expressed in the penultimate sentence of the pseudo-text *Will to Power*, namely "[t]his world is the will to power—and nothing besides!" (WP 1067) There are able reconstructions of it in Richardson (1996) and Poellner (1995), but it was a project that Nietzsche himself seems to have abandoned. As I mentioned, the whole project appears to be motivated on methodologically naturalistic grounds. At BGE 36, Nietzsche suggests that if the world of drives is the only thing "given," then we are allowed to "make the attempt and pose the question as to whether something like this 'given' isn't *enough* to render to the so-called mechanistic (and thus material) world comprehensible as well?" In fact, not only are we "allowed" but "the conscience of *method* demands it." Here, the methodological virtue is parsimony, expressed as the idea that "[m]ultiple varieties of causation should not be postulated until the attempt to make do with a single one has been taken as far as it will go."

13. See, e.g., Hoy (1994), Lottenbach (1996), Beam (1996), Williams (2000; 2002), and Wiggins (2006). William's account, however, appears problematic as an account of genealogy. For discussion, see Hartmann and Saar (2004), Owen (2007: 138–44), and Kail (2011).

14. For other areas of comparison, see Kail (2009). Evidently Book 1 of the *Treatise* is engaged in the project of locating the "origins" of the "higher" in the "lower," and some of the explanations offered destabilize what they explain, most notably the belief in body discussed in "Of Scepticism with Regard to the Senses." Hume also attempts to offer naturalistic explanations of philosophical theorizing, something of which Nietzsche is fond. Thus, Hume seeks to explain the emergence of the fictions of ancient philosophy by appeal to (a) their ignorance of genuine causal powers and (b) a propensity to anthropomorphize nature, so philosophy becomes dominated by models of causation that involve notions like sympathy and the abhorrence of a vacuum (T 1.4.3). The philosophical notion of a "double existence"—the indirect realist account of perception most associated with Locke—is given a psychological explanation that appeals to the dissonance felt between the realization that a compelling belief is false and the presence of the compulsion to believe it. The belief that our immediate objects of experience—perceptions—are continuous and distinct objects does not stand philosophical reflection and yet has such a natural tenacity that philosophers "arbitrarily invent" a new set of objects simply to satisfy the pull of the natural propensity.

15. See Kail (2007) for discussion.

16. This is a reference to Livy, *History* 7.3.3–9. The practice of driving a nail in the door is symbolic of the role of fate.

17. Of course, their psychologies are different, too, but the point here concerns their common naturalistic approach.

18. As Janaway shows, the person uppermost in Nietzsche's mind when characterizing English genealogies is his erstwile German friend Paul Rée, the author of the *The Origin of Moral Sensations.*

19. Hume does not infer originating causes from present function. The issue about Nietzsche's view that previous genealogies are insufficiently suspicious is a complex but fascinating one. For a brief discussion in connection with Hume, see Kail (2011) and, for a much fuller discussion, see Janaway (2007).

20. The following remarks are indebted to Wertz (1975). Cohen (2005) makes a similar argument.

21. On this, see Janaway (2006).

22. See Dixon (2008) for a fascinating account of the "invention of altruism" in the nineteenth century.

23. Letter to Francis Hutcheson, September 17, 1739 (LET i.32–4).

24. Quoted in Fieser (1998).

25. The artificial virtues also differ from the natural ones in that the good of the latter is determinable from particular acts, whereas the good of the former stems from the practice as a whole (see T.3.3.1.12/579).

26. There are different accounts of what these changes in human nature consist. See Cohon (2008), Garrett (2007), and Gill (2006). Notice also that Hume does not commit what Nietzsche takes to be an error in genealogical accounts, namely, inferring originating causes from present practice.

27. See Kail (2011) for discussion.

28. See, e.g., WLN 141.

29. He also argues that it is a fiction invented to provide a target for blame, a "doer" behind every deed who is capable of having acted otherwise. See GM I 13.

30. "Of the Immortality of the Soul" in ESY.

31. Compare Penelhum on Hume. Since "we all know that Hume maintains there is no such thing as the self . . . [selves] cannot be the *loci* of causation in their own right, for all the causes of actions are events *in* the agents" (2000: 171–172).
32. See Richardson (1996), 1.4 for discussion.
33. See, e.g., Gemes (2009). The issue of whether such an account affords conditions of responsibility and freedom is a controversial matter. For a critique, see Leiter (2011).
34. Including his rejection of the self as *causa sui* in BGE 15.
35. Here, I follow Leiter's (2002) characterization, although I depart a little from some of the implications he draws from it later on.
36. For a different view altogether, see Russell (1995).

BIBLIOGRAPHY

Ainslie, D. (1999). "Scepticism about Persons in Book II of Hume's Treatise." *Journal for the History of Philosophy* 37, 469–492.

Beam, C. (1996). "Hume and Nietzsche: Naturalists, Ethicists, Anti-Christians." *Hume Studies* 22, 299–324.

Beam, C. (2001). "Ethical Affinities: Nietzsche in the Tradition of Hume." *International Studies in Philosophy* 33, 87–98.

Brobjer, T. (2008). *Nietzsche and the "English": The Influence of British and American Thinking on his Philosophy.* Amherst: Prometheus Books.

Buckle, S. (2001). *Hume's Enlightenment Tract.* Oxford: Clarendon Press.

Clark, M. (1990). *Nietzsche on Truth and Perspective.* Cambridge: Cambridge University Press.

Cohen, A. (2005). "In Defence of Hume's Historical Method." *British Journal for the History of Philosophy* 13, 489–502.

Cohon, R. (2008). *Hume's Morality: Feeling and Fabrication.* New York: Oxford University Press.

Cox, Christoph. (1999). *Nietzsche: Naturalism and Interpretation.* Berkeley: University of California Press.

Craig, E. (1987). *The Mind of God and the Works of Man.* Oxford: Clarendon Press.

Davey, N. (1987). "Nietzsche and Hume on Self and Identity." *Journal of the British Society for Phenomenology* 18, 14–29.

Dixon, T. (2008). *The Invention of Altruism: The Making in Moral Meanings in Victorian Britain.* Oxford: Oxford University Press.

Fieser, J. (1998). "Hume's Wide View of the Virtues." *Hume Studies* 24, 295–331.

Garrett, D. (2004). "'A Small Tincture of Pyrrhonism' Skepticism and Naturalism in Hume's Science of Man," in Sinnot-Armstrong, ed., *Pyrrhonian Skepticism.* New York: Oxford University Press, 68–98.

Garrett, D. (2007). "The First Motive to Justice: Hume's Circle Argument Squared." *Hume Studies* 33, 257–288.

Gemes, K. (2009). "Nietzsche on Freewill, Autonomy and the Sovereign Individual," in Gemes and May, eds., *Nietzsche on Freedom and Autonomy.* Oxford: Oxford University Press, 33–49.

Gill, M. (2006). *The British Moralists on Human Nature and the Birth of Secular Ethics.* Cambridge: Cambridge University Press.

Hartmann, M., and M. Saar. (2004). "Bernard Williams on Truth and Genealogy." *European Journal of Philosophy* 12, 386–398.

Hoy, David. (1994). "Nietzsche, Hume and the Genealogical Method," in R. Schacht, ed. *Nietzsche, Genealogy, Morality: Essays on Nietzsche's On the Genealogy of Morals*. Berkeley: University of California Press, 251–268.

Janaway, C. (2007). *Beyond Selflessness*. Oxford: Oxford University Press.

Kail, P. J. E. (2009). "Nietzsche and Hume: Naturalism and Explanation." *Journal of Nietzsche Studies* 37, 5–22.

Kail, P. J. E. (2011). " 'Genealogy' and the *Genealogy*," in May, ed., *Nietzsche's On the Genealogy of Morality: A Critical Guide*. Cambridge: Cambridge University Press.

Leiter, B. (forthcoming). "Nietzsche's Naturalism Reconsidered" in Gemes and Richardson, eds., *The Oxford Handbook of Nietzsche*. Oxford: Oxford University Press.

Leiter, B. (2011). "Who Is the 'Sovereign Individual'? Nietzsche on Freedom," May, ed., in *Nietzsche's On the Genealogy of Morality: A Critical Guide*. Cambridge: Cambridge University Press.

Leiter, B. (2002). *Nietzsche on Morality*. London: Routledge.

Leiter, B. (1994). "Perspectivism in Nietzsche's Genealogy of Morals," in Schacht, ed., *Nietzsche, Genealogy, Morality*. Berkeley: University of California Press, 334–354.

Lottenbach, H. (1996). "Monkish Virtues, Artificial Lives: On Hume's Genealogy of Morality." *Canadian Journal of Philosophy* 26, 367–388.

Moore, G. (2002). *Nietzsche, Biology, Metaphor*. Cambridge: Cambridge University Press.

Moore, G. (2006). "Nietzsche and Evolutionary Theory," in Pearson, ed., *A Companion to Nietzsche*. Oxford: Blackwell.

Nietzsche, F. (1979). "On Truth and Lies in a Non-moral Sense" (TL), in Breazeale, ed., *Philosophy and Truth: Selections from Nietzsche's Notebooks of the Early 1870s*. Atlantic Highlands: Humanities Press International.

Nietzsche, F. (1878/1996). *Human, All too Human: A Book for Free Spirits* (HAH). Hollingdale and Schacht, eds. Cambridge: Cambridge University Press.

Nietzsche, F. (1876/1997a). *Untimely Meditations* (UM). Breazeale, ed. Cambridge: Cambridge University Press.

Nietzsche, F. (1881/1997b). *Daybreak: Thoughts on the Prejudices of Morality* (DA), Leiter and Clark, eds. Cambridge: Cambridge University Press.

Nietzsche, F. (1882/2001a). *The Gay Science* (GS), Williams, ed. Cambridge: Cambridge University Press.

Nietzsche, F. (1886/2001b). *Beyond Good and Evil* (BGE), Horstmann and Norman, eds. Cambridge: Cambridge University Press.

Nietzsche, F. (1887/1998). *On the Genealogy of Morality: A Polemic* (GM), Clark and Swensen, eds. Indianapolis: Hackett.

Nietzsche, F. (1888/2005). *The Anti-Christ, Ecce Homo, Twilight of the Idols* (A), (EH), (TI), Ridley, ed. Cambridge: Cambridge University Press.

Nietzsche, F. (1967). *The Will to Power* (WP), Kaufmann, ed. New York: Vintage.

Nietzsche, F. (1954/1994). *Nietzsche Contra Wagner* (NCW), in Kaufmann, ed., *The Portable Nietzsche*. Basingstoke: Penguin.

Nietzsche, F. (2003) *Writings from the Late Notebooks* (WLN), Bittner, ed. Cambridge: Cambridge University Press.

Owen, David. (2007). *Nietzsche's Genealogy of Morality*. Stocksfield: Acumen.

Penelhum, T. (2000). "Hume and the Freedom of the Will," in *Themes from Hume: the Self, the Will, Religion*. Oxford: Clarendon Press.

Poellner, P. (1995). *Nietzsche and Metaphysics*. Oxford: Clarendon Press.

Price, H. (2011). *Naturalism without Mirrors*. Oxford: Oxford University Press.

Richardson, J. (1996). *Nietzsche's System*. New York: Oxford University Press.

Russell, P. (1995). *Freedom and Moral Sentiment*. Oxford: Oxford University Press.

Russell, P. (2008). *The Riddle of Hume's Treatise: Skepticism, Naturalism and Irreligion*. New York: Oxford University Press.

Swanton, C. (2000). "Compassion as a Virtue in Hume," in Jacobson, ed., *Feminist Interpretations of David Hume*. Pennsylvania: Pennsylvania State Press.

Velleman, D. (1992). "What Happens When Someone Acts?" *Mind* 101, 461–481.

Wertz, S. (1975). "Hume, History and Human Nature." *Journal of the History of Ideas* 36, 481–496.

Wiggins, D. (2006). *Ethics: Twelve Lectures on the Philosophy of Morality*. Cambridge, MA: Harvard University Press.

Wilcox, J. (1974). *Truth and Value in Nietzsche: A Study in His Metaethics and Epistemology*. Ann Arbor: University of Michigan Press.

Williams, Bernard. (2000). "Naturalism and Genealogy," in Edward Harcourt, ed., *Morality, Reflection and Ideology*. Oxford: Oxford University Press, 148–161.

Williams, Bernard. (2002). *Truth and Truthfulness*. Princeton: Princeton University Press.

Williams, C. (1999). *A Cultivated Reason: An Essay on Hume and Humeanism*. Pennsylvania: Pennsylvania State Press.

CHAPTER 38

....

HUME AND COGNITIVE
SCIENCE

....

JESSE PRINZ

WITHIN philosophy, our continued interest in historical figures often reflects the conviction that they remain relevant to current philosophical debates. There is no one for whom this claim is more true than David Hume. Hume's philosophy is, both implicitly and explicitly, guiding cutting-edge research. In many domains, his theories are considered live options, and mounting evidence suggests that some of his core conjectures may have been correct. In this chapter, I focus on one particular dimension of contemporary Humean thought: his reception within empirically oriented philosophy and cognitive science.

Contemporary philosophy has taken an empirical turn. A growing number of philosophers have drawn on psychology, neuroscience, psycholinguistics, and other experimental sciences to assess philosophical theories. Some philosophers are also conducting their own experiments and surveys to see whether philosophical intuitions are shared and stable across contexts. This latter trend is known as *experimental philosophy*, and the broader trend of empirically assessing philosophical theories is sometimes called *empirical philosophy* or *naturalized philosophy*. All empirical approaches to philosophical questions place philosophy squarely within cognitive science—the interdisciplinary effort to understand how the mind works.

Hume did not draw on empirical methods in his work. Scientific psychology did not yet exist, and physiology had not advanced to a point where it could shed light on psychology or behavior. But Hume's work includes many speculations about psychological states and processes. These are not presented as conceptual claims, culled from analysis of the meaning of words, but seem rather to be based on observations of mental activities and behavior. Hume calls his magnum opus *A Treatise of Human Nature*, implying that he aims to understand how we function as entities that exist in the natural world. The choice of the word "nature" echoes the popular term "natural philosophy," which was a precursor to modern science. In the introduction to this work, he announces that he plans to undertake a "science of man," and this science "must be laid on experience and observation." Therefore, it is not outlandish to suppose that Hume would have welcomed the advent of cognitive science and seen its tools as valuable resources in investigating some of the theories that he advanced.

Here, I look at what cognitive scientists have to say about several Humean theses. The goal is not scholarly exegesis, but rather an exploration of influence. Although contemporary researchers have departed from the letter of Hume's philosophy, they have often retained its spirit. In presenting this survey, I follow the structure of Hume's *Treatise*, beginning with ideas, then moving on to passions, and, finally, to morals. I begin each section with a textbook statement of some of Hume's more famous views and then discuss relevant empirical work. We will see that there has not always been confirmation, but there is considerable support for a broadly Humean picture.

I IDEAS: CONCEPT EMPIRICISM

Hume's theory of ideas forms the foundation of his philosophical psychology; borrowing from Locke and the pioneers of British empiricism, Hume argues that ideas have their basis in experience. Whereas Locke uses the term "idea" to refer both to sensory states and to the elements of thoughts, Hume helpfully calls the sensory states "impressions" and argues that our simple ideas are copies of impressions.

Hume seems to have taken this Copy Principle seriously. Ideas for him seem to be stored records of sensory states, although they have less force and vivacity. Hume was also probably an imagist—he regarded visual impressions, and their corresponding ideas, as picture-like. This is reflected in his critique of Locke's notion of abstraction. Like Berkeley, he resists the idea that an idea of a triangle could be simultaneously scalene, isosceles, and equilateral or none of these. He favors a use-theory of abstract ideas, according to which ideas of particulars or collections thereof are used to think about more inclusive categories.

Hume's Copy Principle also implies that he was an opponent of nativism. Ideas are learned, and they are learned through experience. He places less emphasis on this than did Locke, who dedicated the first book of his *Essay* to an attack on nativism, but Hume does seem to follow Locke here. He does say that impressions are innate, however, by which he may mean that sensory systems have an innate stock of primitives.

Famously, Hume does acknowledge one exception to the Copy Principle: the missing shade of blue. When we imagine an array of contiguously arranged colors that we have seen before, we may notice that some shades in the array are missing. We can extrapolate what these shades are like. Strictly speaking, this violates the Copy Principle, but it fits with Hume's suggestion that impressions are innate. We ordinarily gain access to innate impressions through sensory stimulation, but the extrapolation of missing colors offers another method.

In contemporary cognitive science, the terms "impressions" and "ideas" are rarely used. Instead, impressions are called "percepts" or "perceptual representations," and ideas are called "concepts." The two central tenets of Hume's theory—the Copy Principle and the opposition to nativism—are jointly known as *concept empiricism*. Concept empiricism is contrasted with two theses familiar from figures in the rationalist tradition, such as Leibniz. First, there is the thesis the concepts are couched in a language-like code comprising amodal symbols (i.e., representations that are not borrowed from any sense modality), and, second, there is the thesis that many of our concepts are innate. For decades, this rationalist picture dominated in cognitive science. Cognitive science grew out of the computer revolution and out of Chomsky's critique of behaviorism in linguistics. Both sources of influence emphasized innate amodal symbols. In recent years, however, there has been an empiricist backlash that would make Hume smile.

Let's begin with the Copy Principle, the idea that concepts are stored copies of percepts. Hume argued for this principle by appeal to introspection. He could find no evidence for amodal symbols when he examined the contents of his own mind. Contemporary cognitive scientists believe that many mental processes go on outside of consciousness, so this method of confirmation is not decisive. But they have devised behavioral tests that lend some support to the Humean view. Unlike philosophical deductions, these tests are not demonstrative proofs, but they confirm predictions made by concept empiricism and not rationalism, suggesting that the former offers a better explanation.

Consider some examples. In one experiment, Pecher et al. (2003) asked people a series of questions about familiar categories: Are lemons yellow? Are cranberries tart? Do leaves rustle? Are blenders loud? And so on. They timed the responses and found that people were quicker at switching from a question involving one kind of sensory feature to a feature of the same kind (say, sound) as compared to when they moved from one sensory dimension to another (say, from sound to taste). Thus, being asked about whether blenders are loud can be answered more quickly after a question about rustling leaves as compared to a question about yellow lemons. This suggests that people answer these simple questions by forming sensory images of the objects involved, which is just what empiricism predicts.

The account has been confirmed by other experiments. For example, it has been found that people are slower to answer questions of this kind when they hold corresponding sensory images in their mind. Answering questions about rustling leaves is slower when people hold melodies in their minds than when they hold images of shapes in their minds (Vermeulen et al. 2008). Evidence from neuroscience has shown that when people reflect on such concepts, brain areas corresponding to the most salient sensory features are active. For example, reflecting on blenders activates both visual and auditory brain areas. Moreover, no one has identified any brain area that corresponds to a storehouse of amodal representations. Thinking reactivates sensory areas, along with executive centers that orchestrate activity in these sensory areas (Chao et al. 1999). Numerous other experiments show this pattern (Barsalou 2008).

Even very abstract concepts may be grasped using sensory imagery. To take one Humean example, there is evidence that we understand causal relations by tracking spatiotemporally contiguous events (Michotte 1963) or statistical regularities (Kushnir and Gopnik 2007). There is evidence that numerical concepts are understood either by attending to multiple concrete objects, by envisioning a number line, or by use of public language (Dehaene 1997). All these methods of representation may have a sensory basis. Logical concepts may be understood by operations on mental images. For example, when presented with the sentence, "There are no birds in the sky," people spontaneously imagine birds with outstretched wings, as opposes to birds standing with wings closed, which is how we visualize birds by default (Kaup et al. 2007). Why? One explanation is that we grasp negation by imagining the meaning of unnegated sentence and then we attempt to find a mismatch between that sentence and the world. Drawing on evidence of this kind, the psychologist Barsalou (1999) has concluded that people think using "perceptual symbols" rather than amodal symbols. In other words, Hume was right.

Some details of Hume's theory are harder to confirm. For example, are ideas less vivacious than impressions? This has not been empirically tested, but some confirmation comes from the fact that it is easier to introspect percepts that concepts. People are often surprised to learn that they use mental imagery in thought, but no one is surprised that, say, visual perception involves a representation of spatially arranged colors and shapes.

Hume's claim that we use particulars to represent abstract ideas enjoys some support. For example, "exemplar theorists" have provided evidence that people unwittingly store highly specific information garnered in perception and use this in subsequent classification. They propose that categories are represented using sets of particulars, and there is evidence that people call different particulars to mind in a context-sensitive way. For example, when asked to describe a dog in the Arctic tundra, people may mention thick fur, which is not a mentioned as a typical feature in other contexts (Barsalou 1987). On the other hand, Hume may have been wrong about triangles. There is some evidence that the visual system can abstract away from metric information and represent polygons without being specific about the size of their interior angles (Biederman 1987).

Cognitive scientists have not directly investigated Hume's claim about the missing shade of blue, but there is some evidence that he was right. For instance, Rosch (1972, 1973) investigated color and shape classification in a New Guinea tribe, the Dani, who lack pictorial imagery and a rich vocabulary for polygons and hues. They found that such individuals spontaneously abstract idealized instances of these categories even when presented with only imperfect ones in training sessions.

What about Hume's anti-nativism? Here, empiricists would meet with the most resistance. Most cognitive scientists think we have a stock of innate concepts, although some suggest that the range of innate concepts is relatively small (e.g., Carey 2009). On the other hand, there are some researchers who claim that the evidence for innate concepts is not decisive (e.g., Bogartz et al. 2000; Elman et al. 1996; Prinz 2002). And many arguments for specific innate concepts have been challenged. For example, Schilling (2000) challenges evidence for an innate concept of physical objects, Perner and Ruffman (2005) challenge evidence for innate concepts of psychological states, and Clearfield and Westfahl (2006) challenge evidence for innate concepts of number.

I cannot adequately review the debate between nativists and their opponents here, but I will give an example to illustrate. In a classic paper in developmental psychology,

Needham and Baillargeon (1993) argued that infants understand gravity because they expect unsupported objects to fall. On the other hand, infants have ample experience of seeing falling objects, including their own limp limbs, so this knowledge may derive from experience. And, strikingly, infants do not expect objects to fall when they are in contact with a surface, even if the amount of contact is so slight that any adult would expect the object to fall. This may be because infants are exposed to objects such as door-knobs, mobiles, and noses sewn on teddy bears, which appear to be suspended with scant support. They only learn through months of accumulated experience that such objects are exceptional. This simple example serves as an important reminder. In argu-ing for innate concepts, psychologists should establish that the conceptual knowledge evidence in infants could not be garnered from experience. All too often that burden is not met.

It would be prudent to conclude that the case for concept nativism remains unsettled, as does the case for amodal representations. Mounting evidence suggests that we use perceptual representations for cognitive tasks and that much of our conceptual knowl-edge emerges through learning. Thus, the Humean approach to ideas remains a live theoretical option, one that is actively researched and endorsed by numerous cognitive scientists.

II Passions: Noncognitivism

The second book of Hume's *Treatise* is perhaps the most neglected, both within Hume scholarship and beyond. There, he lays out a rich and inventive view of the passions. In that discussion, Hume advances several important claims. One is that passions are impressions of impressions. They do not follow immediately upon sensory stimulation, but are rather responses to such stimulation (or corresponding ideas). Hume also says that passions are not representations of anything, suggesting that they are feelings, but not, strictly speaking, intentional states. Thus, a passion cannot be mistaken, although it might result from a false impression.

Hume also offers a taxonomy of the passions. He says that they can be violent or calm, and he draws a distinction between passions that are direct and those that are indirect. The precise meaning of this distinction is a matter of debate within Hume studies, and the relevant passages are notoriously obscure. Here is one interpretation. A direct pas-sion is one that arises immediately from an impression or idea of an object, as when the sight of an attractive person excites lust; sometimes, the direct passions follow only after an object causes pleasure or pain in us. For example, if food strikes us as pleasurable, we will form a passion of desire. These are sometimes called primary and secondary pas-sions in the literature. An indirect passion is more complex. It occurs when the object that excites it is conceived as belonging to oneself (or to another). When the ownership is recognized, it causes a passion that differs from the direct passion, and that passion, in turn, further excites the direct passion and also triggers ideas of the self (or other). For example, if I cooked the food that causes gustatory pleasure and desire in me, I may feel pride because I know it comes from me, and this will cause me to think of myself. This account of secondary passions is consistent with what Hume says about them, but what he says is a little puzzling because, elsewhere in the *Treatise*, he claims we have no clear idea of the self. How, then, do indirect passions cause ideas of the self? I return to this question shortly.

The term "passion" has been replaced in contemporary English by "emotion," which used to refer to a strong affective state (what we might now call passions). Contemporary emotion research encompasses many theoretical perspectives, but the most central debate in the field concerns the question of whether emotions are cognitive or not. According to cognitive theories, emotions essentially involve cognitive states, such as concepts, beliefs, or judgments. The most popular class of cognitive theories in psychology identifies emotions with appraisal judgments. An *appraisal judgment* is a thought that represents a relationship between an organism and its environment that bears on well-being. For example, appraisal theorists identify anger with the thought that there has been an offense against me, and they identify fear with the thought that I am in danger, and sadness with the thought that there has been a loss. Some cognitive theories also say that emotions are accompanied by noncognitive states, such as sensations of feelings.

Opponents of cognitive theories argue that emotions are constituted by such noncognitive states. They admit that judgments can influence our emotions, but emotions themselves, such as sensations or feelings, are not cognitive states. Anger might be caused, on this view, by the thought that I have been insulted, but it is not identical to that thought, and it can last after the thought has ended. Noncognitivists say that emotions can even arise with no thoughts at all. An irritating sound may get someone mad even if she hasn't formed any judgments about it, much less the judgment that there has been an offense against her.

On this taxonomy, Hume is probably best described as a noncognitivist. First, he says that passions are impressions, which implies they are preconceptual (i.e., they are not ideas). Second, he says they do not represent anything, whereas cognitive states such as thoughts are representations. Third, he says that, although they can be caused by ideas, they are often caused by impressions, implying that we can have an emotion without cognitive precursors.

In assessing Hume's theory, then, we can begin by asking whether there is any empirical evidence for noncognitivism, and, indeed, there is. Noncognitivists point to several lines of evidence. For example, they show that emotions can be caused by simply changing one's facial expression, posture, or breathing rate (Duclos et al. 1989; Philippot et al. 2002; Strack et al. 1988). Emotions can also be induced via ancient subcortical pathways that bypass the neocortex, the presumed seat of higher cognition (LeDoux 1996). There are also many perceptual triggers for emotions: a loud sudden noise, a sudden loss of support, the sound of crying, the sight of a nude body, a noxious smell, a succulent food, a sunny day, nonvocal music, and so on. It is unlikely that judgments underlie such cases. Or, consider pain, which is widely believed to have an emotional component

(Melzack and Wall 1996). It seems unlikely that the aversive component of pain is cognitively mediated, even if it can be influenced by cognition.

The main empirical evidence for cognitive theories comes from the fact that judgments can cause emotions, but this is consistent with the view that emotions themselves are noncognitive. We should not equate emotions with judgments, according to noncognitivists, because judgments are neither necessary nor sufficient for emotions. We can judge that cigarettes are dangerous without fearing them, and we can judge that a roller coaster is safe while experiencing fear. Or, to take an example that philosophers have debated, there is empirical evidence that people experience fear during horror films, but presumably they know they are safe (Andrade and Cohen 2007). Such evidence does not prove that cognitive theories are wrong (perhaps people have inconsistent thoughts), but it is predicted by noncognitive theories such as Hume's.

If emotions are not cognitive, what are they? Hume does not present a clear answer, although he may think emotions are feelings. In contemporary cognitive science, the most popular feeling theory derives from William James (1884) who proposed that emotions are feelings of patterned changes in the body (Damasio 1994). Anger, for example, is the feeling of the body preparing for aggression. Hume says nothing of the kind, and, in fact, this link between emotion and body is closer to what we find in Descartes's *Passions of the Soul*. On the other hand, Hume does say that emotions are impressions, and that fits with the James view, since bodily feelings are perceptual states. Indeed, for James, emotions are felt bodily changes that follow up the perception of evocative stimuli, so they are impressions of impressions. To that extent, contemporary noncognitive theories are broadly Humean.

The Jamesian feeling theory is also like Hume's in another respect: bodily feelings are not usually regarded as representations of anything in the world. Thus, for James, like Hume, emotions are not said to be intentional states. Some contemporary Jamesians have tried to argue that bodily feelings can represent things. On contemporary theories of reference, a mental state is often said to represent that which it has the function of co-occurring with in the world (Dretske 1986). If the feeling of the body's preparation for fleeing has the function of occurring when we are in danger, that feeling can be said to represent danger (Prinz 2004). This may be a departure from Hume, but we can also interpret his claim that emotions don't represent more modestly as the claim that emotions do not resemble their objects. This is no doubt true. A visual image of a bear may resemble that of a bear, but the resulting fear does not.

Let us turn, now, to the emotion taxonomy presented in the *Treatise*. Hume tells us that some passions are calm and others are violent. If we consider physiological arousal a good surrogate for violence, then this is surely right; some emotions are more arousing than others. In fact, some researchers have found that all emotions can be plotted on two dimensions: valence and arousal. Anger is high in arousal, and sadness is generally low. That said, there are also researchers who claim that each emotion can vary in arousal: mild irritation and fury contrast this way, as do disappointment and despair. If so, the calm/violent distinction may arise within emotion categories rather than between them.

The next Humean distinction to consider is his distinction between what scholars call primary and secondary passions. Hume says that some passions derive from prior pleasure and pain, and others do not. In cognitive science, the pleasure and pain associated with emotions is referred to as valence, and there is no settled view about what valence consists. Some authors have suggested that valence is assessed before more specific emotions arise (Scherer 2001). Others suggest that valence is an aspect of each emotion, rather than a prior cause (Russell 1980). Such accounts do not distinguish primary and secondary cases. However, the empirical literature on animal learning, which came out of behaviorist psychology, clearly articulates a related distinction. Here, the term "primary reinforcers" refers to stimuli that can condition behavior (i.e., increase or decrease a response) without being paired with anything else. Food and sex, for instance, are primary positive reinforcers. Primary reinforcers are comparable to the objects that excite Hume's primary passions. Secondary reinforcers condition behavior in virtue of prior pairing with primary reinforcers. These do not align perfectly with Hume's secondary passions because Hume does not say that secondary passions are learned. On the other hand, Hume's examples of secondary passions, such as desire, can be interpreted in terms of secondary reinforcement. A particular kind of food is normally desirable only if it has brought about pleasure.

The most vexing aspect of Hume's taxonomy is his distinction between direct and indirect passions. Does this distinction have empirical validity? The short answer is that we don't know. There has been no study explicitly examining Hume's distinction. Still, there are findings that provide some support. We have already noted that perceptions can directly elicit emotions, which is consistent with Hume's definition of direct passions. The harder question concerns the empirical status of the indirect passions. Are there some emotions that depend in some way on ideas of self or other? The answer seems to be affirmative. Psychologists talk about "social emotions" and "self-conscious emotions," which are self-involving social emotions. Examples include guilt, shame, embarrassment, and—Hume's favorite case—pride. Some evidence suggests that these emotions involve an idea of the self, as Hume suggested. Developmental psychologists have observed that social emotions appear later than other emotions, and, in one striking study, Lewis et al. (1989) found that such emotions correlate in their developmental emergence with the capacity for mirror self-recognition. This implies that in order to feel embarrassment, for example, a child must have some idea of herself as someone distinct from and observable to others.

This empirical finding helps with a puzzle in Hume's account. He claims that self-directed indirect passions require an idea of the self, but elsewhere implies that we have no such idea. This looks like a tension in the *Treatise*. But there may be a way out. The notion of self that Hume deems problematic is the notion of a subject of experience—a Cartesian "I" that exists above and beyond the bundle of sensory impressions and ideas copied from those impressions. When we introspect, we find no subject. Now consider what notion of the self is implicated in recognizing one's reflection in a mirror. It is not self as subject, but rather self as object. It is a self as a physical entity in the world that can be seen by others. This kind of self is not problematic for an empiricist, and the research in developmental psychology suggests that this may be all we need for social emotions. Pride may involve the recognition that some pleasure-inducing thing was produced by these hands or is possessed by this body, where the demonstratives here refer to the body of the person having these thoughts.

In summary, empirical research on the emotions bears on Hume's account of the passions. Cognitive scientists rarely refer to Hume in this work, but various findings confirm and extend aspects of his account.

III Morals: Sentimentalism

Moral psychology is the area of empirical research that has drawn on Hume most explicitly. Some aspects of Hume's ethics find direct support in recent cognitive science, and other aspects remain controversial. Let's begin with a brief review of Hume's views.

The centerpiece of Humean moral psychology is sentimentalism: the view that moral judgments have an emotional basis. For Hume, moral judgments are emotional responses—feelings of approbation or disapprobation. Hume insists that reason and matters of fact are insufficient for morality. We cannot discover morals by observation and measurement but must, instead, look inward to our passions. The wrongness of murder is not discovered in the act itself, but in our reaction to it. Hume does not say much about what approbation and disapprobation consist in, but he calls these "peculiar sentiments," which may imply that they are not reducible to any other emotions.

Hume's sentimentalism was taken over from Hutcheson and other British moralists, but his version is distinctive in various ways. Hutcheson seems to endorse a kind of moral realism, according to which there are real moral truths, independent of our minds, and that God has given us passions that can detect these truths, in much the way that our senses can discover physical facts about the world. Hume seems to reject this moral sense view and favors what would now be called a projectivist theory. It is not clear from the text whether he would have endorsed expressivism (the view that moral judgments lack ordinary truth values and merely express attitudes) or rather a sensibility theory (the view that moral judgments refer to response-dependent properties, akin to Locke's secondary qualities). Such theoretical options had not been articulated in Hume's time. What is reasonably clear is that Hume sees morality as a product of human nature and history, rather than as an aspect of the mind-independent world. This does not mean that Hume was a relativist. He seems to think that our natural sentiments, together with the demands of social living, would lead to certain norms that are optimal from the perspective of self-interest. Justice, for instance, is a historically crafted norm for Hume, but it is an extension of natural benevolence for our near and dear that results in social structures that are stable and beneficial.

Another distinctive feature of Hume's moral theory is his focus on sympathy. For Hume, sympathy is a kind of emotional contagion. We see a person experience pleasure or pain, and this excites a similar feeling in us. Moral judgments depend on sympathy for Hume. We approve of actions that bring pleasure to someone, and we disapprove of actions that cause pain precisely because we experience sympathy when we contemplate these feelings in others.

The final Humean thesis that I mention is his commitment to an ethics of virtue. For Hume, moral judgments are principally judgments of character. We judge actions wrong if they stem from vicious character and right if they stem from virtue. Unlike virtue theorists in the Aristotelian tradition, Hume does not suggest that morality should focus on the cultivation of character rather than the rules of conduct, but he sees a link between the assessment of conduct and the assessment of character, and this link may be essential for him; we cannot assess an action without reflecting on the kind of motives that brought it about.

Empirical research in recent moral psychology has focused intensely on issues raised by Hume. For example, Hume's claim that we do not base morals on reasoning gains support from studies that show people are bad at providing justifications for their moral judgments. Haidt (2001) reports that people continue to think that consensual sibling incest is wrong but cannot justify this claim, and Hauser et al. (2007) found that people have strong moral convictions about trolley dilemmas but fail to come up with good explanations for these.

For Hume, the inadequacy of reasoning in the moral domain owes to the fact that moral judgments are based on emotions. Numerous studies support the sentimentalist hypothesis (Prinz 2007). Neuroimaging studies have consistently shown that emotions are active when people make moral judgments (Greene et al. 2001; Harenski and Hamann 2006; Heekeren et al. 2003), and behavioral studies have shown that emotions have a causal influence on moral assessments. For example, when disgust is induced, people make more stringent moral judgments. Wheatley and Haidt obtained this effect through hypnotic induction of disgust; Schnall et al. (2008) used disgusting film clips, dirty environments, and foul smells; and Eskine et al. (2011) used a bitter beverage. In all these studies, people misattribute externally induced disgust to moral vignettes that they read, which suggests that we make moral judgments by introspecting our emotional states. Anger induction makes people more morally stringent as well (Lerner et al. 1998; Seidel and Prinz, 2013), and induction of happiness can make people more helpful (Weyant 1978) and more likely to judge that helping is good or obligatory (Seidel and Prinz, 2013). People with reduced emotional capacities, such as psychopaths, have difficulty understanding the moral domain, failing to see a difference between moral rules and mere conventions (Blair 1995). And brain injuries that prevent people from adjusting goals in light of negative emotional feedback result in greater tolerance for harm in deliberating about moral dilemmas in which one person must be sacrificed to save others (Koenigs et al. 2007). There is also evidence that Huntington's disease, which impairs disgust, makes people less sensitive to sexual norms (Schmidt and Bonelli 2008). In summary, emotions arise when people make moral judgments, emotions are used to assess how good or bad something is, and, when emotions are impaired, such judgments may become impossible. Hume would be delighted by these findings.

Hume may have been wrong, however, in saying that approbation and disapprobation are peculiar emotions. Much of the research just cited suggests that moral emotions derive from emotions that have nonmoral applications, such as disgust and anger (see also Rozin et al. 1999). This may look like a significant departure from Hume, but it fits well with one aspect of his account. For Hume, much of morality is artificial. Our natural virtues tend to involve people with whom we have personal relationships. One can even think of natural virtues as pre-moral, since they do not govern actions between strangers. Full-fledged morality extends our natural sentiments, encompassing a wider group. The thesis that moral emotions are derived from emotions that govern one's personal interactions with the world accords nicely with this picture of moral artificiality. For instance, anger may begin as a kind of reactive aggression that protects the self against frustrations and threats but doesn't arise when contemplating the behavior of third parties. Then, this selfish sentiment is broadened, through moral education, and we come to condemn wrongdoers even when we are not directly affected. If moral emotions did not derive from such nonmoral or pre-moral sentiments, this developmental account would make less sense. So Hume's peculiarity thesis may have been wrong, but it may be inessential to his larger program.

Hume's claim that sympathy is crucial to morality has also met with mixed results. Hume's account of sympathy has empirical validity; people do have a propensity to catch the emotions that they observe in others (Hatfield et al. 1993). This is often called *empathy* in the empirical literature. Consistent with Hume, empathy promotes prosocial behavior in some circumstances (Batson and Shaw 1991), and people who lack sympathy—psychopaths again—have a limited capacity to make moral judgments (Blair 1995). Hume was also right when he observed that we have greater sympathy for those who are similar to us (Cialdini 1991), and this may help to explain why we show more moral concern for our near and dear. It is difficult, however, to find evidence that every moral judgment depends on sympathy. Although sympathy and moral judgment may often correlate, there are moral judgments that seem to arise without it. For example, evidence suggests that some people will condemn victimless crimes, such as consensual incest or necrophelic bestiality (Haidt et al. 1993). In these cases, the assessment of wrongness is unlikely to depend on a contemplation of someone's suffering. Sympathy may be primarily reserved for cases where harm is salient. That means sympathy may not be important for reasoning about rights (such as the right to free speech), economic distribution (such as the obligation to pay taxes), and general prohibitions against free riders. We could think about victims in all these cases, but it seems likely that we can access the relevant moral principles without recourse to that. Consistent with this, there is evidence that moral judgments about justice do not rely heavily on sympathy (Juujärvi 2005). Even more obviously, sympathy is poorly suited to explain moral judgments about some environmental causes (such as the conviction that we should protect insect species). This last case has not been tested to my knowledge, but it wouldn't even be surprising to discover that some environmentalists score low on sympathy, feeling contempt for people in their pursuit of planetary health.

Finally, let's turn to Hume's virtue theory. There hasn't been much research exploring the role of character judgments in the assignment of praise and blame, but there is some support for the linkage we find in Hume. For example, there is extensive research suggesting that acts are regarded as more wrong when they are done intentionally (e.g., Cushman 2008). There is, even more strikingly, some recent work that suggests that when people make moral judgments, they also draw inferences about the character of the person they judge (Pizarro and Tannenbaum, 2015). We tend to judge that the authors of bad acts are bad more generally. This is consistent with Hume's view. On the other hand, the capacity to make moral judgments seems to arise in children before they can reliably attribute intentions, and moral judgments are made by people with autism who are impaired in thinking about motives and other mental states (Arsenio and Lover 1995; Blair 1996). Additionally, Young and Saxe (2011) have shown that intentions do not matter much when making judgments about violations of sexual taboos and other purity norms. Thus, it is unlikely that all moral judgments are judgments of character.

Hume's moral psychology does not get a perfect scorecard in cognitive science, but the overall prognosis is good. Hume may have overestimated the role of sympathy and virtue, and he may have been wrong to think that moral sentiments are peculiar to morality. But there is strong evidence for the thesis that moral judgments are based on emotions. Thus, the heart of Hume's moral theory (so to speak) enjoys empirical support.

IV CONCLUSION

Writing in the eighteenth century, Hume had no access to empirical studies of the mind. He had to base his conclusions on introspection and careful observation. He couldn't measure brain activity, and experimental psychology, which manipulates psychological states, measures effects, and subjects the results to statistical analysis, had not been invented. Given those limitations, he did remarkably well. The theories he developed are broadly consistent with findings in contemporary cognitive science. Not every cognitive scientist endorses the Humean interpretation of the empirical findings surveyed here, but the tide seems to be moving in Hume's direction. Why, one might ask, was Hume so successful in predicting empirical results? One answer is that observation and introspection *are* empirical methods. They are prescientific in that they don't use experimental interventions, controlled variables, significance tests, or procedures that admit of easy replication. But they derive from careful examination of mental states and processes and are, consequently, answerable to the world. Hume's methodology is neither conceptual analysis, nor transcendental psychology, in Kant's sense. It is inductive, rather than deductive. In this sense, Hume is really a precursor to today's cognitive scientists, and his work shows that philosophy has always had an empirical dimension. We have more empirical tools at our disposal now, but there are few with Hume's skills for observation and theoretical integration.

BIBLIOGRAPHY

Andrade, E. B., and Cohen, J. B. (2007). "On the Consumption of Negative Feelings." *Journal of Consumer Research* 34, 283–300.

Arsenio, W. F., and Lover, A. (1995). "Children's Conceptions of Sociomoral Affect: Happy Victimizers, Mixed Emotions and Other Expectancies," in M. Killen and D. Hart, eds., *Morality in Everyday Life: Developmental Perspectives.* Cambridge: Cambridge University Press, 87–128.

Barsalou, L. W. (1987). "The Instability of Graded Structure in Concepts," in U. Neisser, ed., *Concepts and Conceptual Development: Ecological and Intellectual Factors in Categorization.* New York: Cambridge University Press, 101–140.

Barsalou, L. W. (1999). "Perceptual Symbol Systems." *Behavioral and Brain Sciences* 22, 577–660.

Barsalou, L. W. (2008). "Grounded Cognition." *Annual Review of Psychology* 59, 617–645.

Batson, C. D., and Shaw, L. L. (1991). "Evidence for Altruism: Toward a Pluralism of Prosocial Motives." *Psychological Inquiry* 2, 107–122.

Blair, R. J. (1995). "A Cognitive Developmental Approach to Morality: Investigating the Psychopath." *Cognition* 57, 1–29.

Blair, R. J. (1996). "Brief Report: Morality in the Autistic Child." *Journal of Autism and Developmental Disorders* 26, 571–579.

Biederman, I. (1987). "Recognition-by-Components: A Theory of Human Image Understanding." *Psychological Review* 94, 115–147.

Bogartz, R. S., Shinskey, J. L., and Schilling, T. H. (2000). "Object Permanence in 5.5-Month-Old Infants." *Infancy* 1, 403–428.

Carey, S. (2009). *The Origin of Concepts.* New York: Oxford University Press.

Chao, L. L., Haxby, J. V., and Martin, A. (1999). "Attribute-based Neural Substrates in Posterior Temporal Cortex for Perceiving and Knowing about Objects." *Nature Neuroscience* 2, 913–919.

Cialdini, R. B. (1991). "Altruism or Egoism? That is (Still) the Question." *Psychological Inquiry* 2, 124–126.

Clearfield, M. W., and Westfahl, S. M. C. (2006). "Familiarization in Infants' Perception of Addition Problems." *Journal of Cognition and Development* 7, 27–43.

Cushman, F. (2008). "Crime and Punishment: Distinguishing the Roles of Causal and Intentional Analysis in Moral Judgment." *Cognition* 108, 353–380.

Damasio, A. R. (1994). *Descartes' Error: Emotion, Reason and the Human Brain.* New York: Gossett/Putnam.

Dehaene, S. (1997). *The Number Sense.* New York: Oxford University Press.

Duclos, S. E., Laird, J. D., Schneider, E., Sexter, M., Stern, L., and Van Lighten, O. (1989). "Emotion-specific Effects of Facial Expressions and Postures on Emotional Experience." *Journal of Personality and Social Psychology* 57, 100–108.

Dretske, F. (1986). "Misrepresentation," in R. Bogdan, ed., *Belief: Form, Content and Function.*, 17–36. Oxford: Oxford University Press.

Elman, J., Bates, E., Johnson, M., Karmiloff-Smith, A., Parisi, D., and Plunkett, K. (1996). *Rethinking Innateness: A Connectionist Perspective on Development.* Cambridge, MA: MIT Press.

Eskine, K. J., Kacinik, N. A., and Prinz, J. J. (2011). "A Bad Taste in the Mouth: Gustatory Disgust Influences Moral Judgment." *Psychological Science* 22, 295–299.

Greene, J. D., Sommerville, R. B., Nystrom, L. E., Darley, J. M., and Cohen, J. D. (2001). "An fMRI Investigation of Emotional Engagement in Moral Judgment." *Science* 293, 2105–2108.

James, W. (1884). "What Is an Emotion?" *Mind* 9, 188–205.

Juujärvi, S. (2005). "Care and Justice in Real-life Moral Reasoning." *Journal of Adult Development* 12, 199–210.

Haidt, J. (2001). "The Emotional Dog and Its Rational Tail: A Social Intuitionist Approach to Moral Judgment." *Psychological Review* 108, 814–834.

Haidt, J., Koller, S., and Dias, M. (1993). "Affect, Culture, and Morality, or Is it Wrong to Eat Your Dog?" *Journal of Personality and Social Psychology* 65, 613–628.

Hauser, M., Cushman, F., Young, L., Jin, R., and Mikhail, J. (2007). "A Dissociation Between Moral Judgment and Justification." *Mind and Language* 22, 1–21.

Harenski, C. N., and Hamann, S. (2006). "Neural Correlates of Regulating Negative Emotions Related to Moral Violations." *Neuroimage*, 30, 313–324.

Hatfield, E., Cacioppo, J. T., and Rapson, R. L. (1993). "Emotional Contagion." *Current Directions in Psychological Science* 2, 96–99.

Heekeren, H. R., Wartenburger, I., Schmidt, H., Schwintowski, H. P., and Villringer, A. (2003). An fMRI Study of Simple Ethical Decision-making." *Neuroreport* 14, 1215–1219.

Hutcheson, F. (1738/1994). *An Inquiry into the Original of Our Ideas of Beauty and Virtue*, in *Philosophical Writings*, R. S. Downie, ed., London: J. M. Dent.

Kaup, B., Yaxley, R. H., Madden, C. J., Zwaan, R. A., and Lüdtke, J. (2007). "Experiential Simulations of Negated Text Information." *Quarterly Journal of Experimental Psychology* 60, 976–990.

Koenigs, M., Young, L., Adolphs, R., Tranel, D., Cushman, F., Hauser, M., and Damasio, A. (2007). "Damage to the Prefrontal Cortex Increases Utilitarian Moral Judgments." *Nature* 446, 908–911.

Kushnir, T., and Gopnik, A. (2007). "Conditional Probability versus Spatial Contiguity in Causal Learning: Preschoolers Use New Contingency Evidence to Overcome Prior Spatial Assumptions. *Developmental Psychology* 44, 186–196.

LeDoux J. E. (1996). *The Emotional Brain*. New York: Simon & Schuster.

Lerner, J., Goldberg, J., and Tetlock, P. (1998). "Sober Second Thought: the Effects of Accountability, Anger, and Authoritarianism on Attributions of Responsibility." *Personality and Social Psychology Bulletin* 24, 563–574.

Lewis, M., Sullivan, M. W., Stanger, C., and Weiss, M. (1989). "Self Development and Self-conscious Emotions." *Child Development* 60, 146–156.

Melzack, R., and Wall, P. D. (1996). *The Challenge of Pain*. New York: Penguin Books.

Michotte, A. (1963). *The Perception of Causality*. Andover: Methuen.

Needham, A., and Baillargeon, R. (1993). "Intuitions About Support in 4.5-Month-Old Infants." *Cognition* 47, 121–148.

Pecher, D., Zeelenberg, R., and Barsalou, L. W. (2003). "Verifying Properties from Different Modalities for Concepts Produces Switching Costs." *Psychological Science* 14, 119–124.

Perner, J., and Ruffman, T. (2005). "Infants' Insight into the Mind: How Deep?" *Science* 308, 214–216.

Philippot, P., Chapelle, C., and Blairy, S. (2002). "Respiratory Feedback in the Generation of Emotion." *Cognition & Emotion* 16, 605–627.

Pizarro, D. A., and Tannenbaum, D. (2015). "Bringing Character Back: How the Motivation to Evaluate Character Influences Judgments of Moral Blame," in M. Mikulincer and P.

Shaver, eds., *The Social Psychology of Morality: Exploring the Causes of Good and Evil*. New York: APA Press.

Prinz, J. J. (2002). *Furnishing the Mind: Concepts and their Perceptual Basis*. Cambridge, MA: MIT Press.

Prinz, J. J. (2004). *Gut Reactions: A Perceptual Theory of Emotion*. New York: Oxford University Press.

Prinz, J. J. (2007). *The Emotional Construction of Morals*. Oxford: Oxford University Press.

Rosch, E. H. (1972). "Universals in Color Naming and Memory." *Journal of Experimental Psychology* 93, 10–20.

Rosch, E. H. (1973). "Natural Categories." *Cognitive Psychology* 4, 328–350.

Rozin, P., Lowry, L., Imada, S., and Haidt, J. (1999). "The CAD Triad Hypothesis." *Journal of Personality and Social Psychology* 76, 574–586.

Russell, J. A. (1980). "A Circumplex Model of Affect." *Journal of Personality and Social Psychology* 39, 1161–1178.

Scherer, K. R. (2001). "Appraisal Considered as a Process of Multi-level Sequential Checking," in K. R. Scherer, A. Schorr, and T. Johnstone, eds., *Appraisal Processes in Emotion: Theory, Methods, Research*. New York and Oxford: Oxford University Press, 92–120.

Schmidt, E. Z., and Bonelli, R. M. (2008). "Sexuality in Huntington's Disease." *Wiener Medizinische Wochenschrift* 158, 78–83.

Schnall, S., Haidt, J., Clore, G. L., and Jordan, A. H. (2008). "Disgust as Embodied Moral Judgment." *Personality and Social Psychology Bulletin* 34, 1096–1109.

Schilling, T. H. (2000). "Infants' Looking at Possible and Impossible Screen Rotations: The Role of Familiarization." *Infancy* 1, 389–402.

Seidel, A, and Prinz, J. (2013). "Sound morality: irritating and icky noises amplify judgments in divergent moral domains," *Cognition*, 127, 1–5.

Strack, F., Martin, L. L., and Stepper, S. (1988). "Inhibiting and Facilitating Conditions of Facial Expressions: A Nonobtrusive Test of the Facial Feedback Hypothesis." *Journal of Personality and Social Psychology* 54, 768–777.

Vermeulen, N., Corneille, O., and Niedenthal, P. M. (2008). "Sensory Load Incurs Conceptual Processing Costs." *Cognition* 109, 287–294.

Weyant, J. M. (1978). "Effects of Mood States, Costs, and Benefits on Helping." *Journal of Personality and Social Psychology* 36, 1169–1176.

Wheatley, T., and Haidt, J. (2005). "Hypnotically Induced Disgust Makes Moral Judgments More Severe." *Psychological Science* 16, 780–784.

Young, L., Saxe, R. (2011). "When Ignorance Is No Excuse: Different Roles for Intent Across Moral Domains." *Cognition* 120, 202–214.

Bibliography and Further Reading

Each of the contributions in this volume contains a bibliography of the works and sources cited by the particular contributor. Readers may refer to these as a basis for further reading or sources. For those who are coming to Hume's thought with little background and are looking for a general introduction, any of the works cited below may be a good place to start. The works cited with an asterisk contain useful bibliographies that the reader may also refer to:

Ballie, James. 2000. *Hume on Morality*. London & New York: Routledge
Blackburn, Simon. 2008. *How to Read Hume*. London: Granta.
Coventry, Angela. 2007. *Hume: A Guide for the Perplexed*. New York: Continuum.
Dicker, Georges. 1998. *Hume's Epistemology and Metaphysics*. London: Routledge.
*Garrett, Don. 2015. *Hume*. London: Routledge.
Noonan, Harold W. 1999. *Hume on Knowledge*. London: Routledge.
O'Connor, David. 2001. *Hume on Religion*. London: Routledge.
    The following are useful collections relating to Hume's philosophy and thought:
Ainslie, Donald & Annemarie Butler, eds. 2015. *The Cambridge Companion to Hume's Treatise*. Cambridge: Cambridge University Press.
*Bailey, Alan & Dan O'Brien, eds. 2012. *The Continuum Companion to Hume*. London: Continuum.
Millican, Peter, ed. 2002. *Reading Hume on Human Understanding*. Oxford: Clarendon Press.
Norton, David & Jackie Taylor, eds. *The Cambridge Companion to Hume*. Cambridge: Cambridge University Press.
*Radcliffe, Elizabeth S., ed. 2011. *A Companion to Hume*. Chichester: Blackwell.
Traiger, Saul. 2006. *The Blackwell Guide to Hume's Treatise*. Oxford: Blackwell.

There are a variety of internet sources on Hume's philosophy, thought, and life but the best place to start is with the *Stanford Philosophy of Philosophy*. See, in particular, the following:

*Morris, William Edward and Brown, Charlotte R., "David Hume," *The Stanford Encyclopedia of Philosophy* (Summer 2014 Edition), Edward N. Zalta (ed.), URL = <http://plato.stanford.edu/archives/sum2014/entries/hume/>.
Cohon, Rachel, "Hume's Moral Philosophy," *The Stanford Encyclopedia of Philosophy* (Fall 2010 Edition), Edward N. Zalta (ed.), URL = <http://plato.stanford.edu/archives/fall2010/entries/hume-moral/>.
Russell, Paul, "Hume on Free Will," *The Stanford Encyclopedia of Philosophy* (Winter 2014 Edition), Edward N. Zalta (ed.), forthcoming URL = <http://plato.stanford.edu/archives/win2014/entries/hume-freewill/>.

Russell, Paul, "Hume on Religion," *The Stanford Encyclopedia of Philosophy* (Winter 2014 Edition), Edward N. Zalta (ed.), forthcoming URL = <http://plato.stanford.edu/archives/win2014/entries/hume-religion/>.

INDEX

CPSIA information can be obtained
at www.ICGtesting.com
Printed in the USA
BVHW070103121219
566147BV00006B/2/P

9 780190 095390